THE EDGE EVERY STUDENT NEEDS

⑨SAGE edge™   edge.sagepub.com/ritzeressentials2e

SAGE edge for Instructors supports teaching by making it easy to integrate quality content.

- **Course Management System**
- **Test banks**
- **Learning Objectives**
- **Lecture notes**
- **PowerPoint® slides**
- **Tables and figures from the book**
- **Sample course syllabi**
- **Discussion questions**
- **SAGE journal articles**
- **Chapter activities**
- **Video and multimedia content**

SAGE edge for Students provides a personalized approach to help students accomplish their coursework goals in an easy-to-use learning environment.

- **Action plan**
- **Learning Objectives**
- **eFlashcards**
- **Practice quizzes**
- **Video and multimedia content**
- **SAGE journal articles**

⑨SAGE datamaps

For a closer look at data presented in the text, interactive GIS data maps can be accessed through SAGE edge and the eBook.

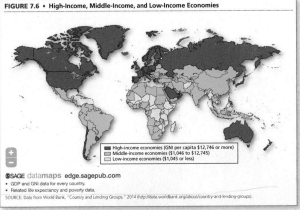

FIGURE 7.6 • High-Income, Middle-Income, and Low-Income Economies

High-income economies (GNI per capita $12,746 or more)
Middle-income economies ($1,046 to $12,745)
Low-income economies ($1,045 or less)

⑨SAGE datamaps edge.sagepub.com
- GDP and GNI data for every country.
- Related life expectancy and poverty data.

SOURCE: Data from World Bank, "Country and Lending Groups," 2014 (http://data.worldbank.org/about/country-and-lending-groups).

NEW TO THIS EDITION

- New and revised **chapter-opening vignettes** are drawn from issues and events of contemporary interest such as the Charlie Hebdo attacks and the ongoing debate over medical marijuana.

- **The chapter on Social Stratification** has expanded coverage of the causes and consequences of stratification on a global scale.

- **The Gender and Sexuality chapter** has undergone a major revision with the help of gender and sexuality expert Rebecca Plante. This edition also offers more thorough integration of issues pertaining to gender and sexuality throughout.

- Over 100 new and updated **maps, graphs, and tables** help students better visualize data and information.

FEATURE BOXES

▶ **PUBLIC SOCIOLOGY** boxes demonstrate that sociology is more than an academic discipline—it has tangible, real-world effects on our lives.

PUBLIC SOCIOLOGY

Naomi Klein: No Logo

Naomi Klein (1970–) is a journalist who is best known for books that have contributed to our understanding of consumption and globalization. While there is significant sociological analysis in her work, Klein's writing is most defined by her strong, perhaps sometimes overheated, criticism of many aspects of both of these phenomena.

In her book *No Logo* ([2000] 2010), Klein offers an unrelenting critique of the role of branding in the world of consumption. Among Klein's favorite targets are Nike, McDonald's, Microsoft, and Tommy Hilfiger, as well as celebrity brands such as Michael Jordan. In the context of an American society that has shifted from the dominance of production to the preeminence of consumption, corporations have discovered that the key to success is no longer what they manufacture but the creation and dissemination of a brand. While it concentrates on its brand, the modern corporation often [...] production to subcontractors [...] eloped parts of the world. [...] the work in such places

are paid a small percentage of what their counterparts in more developed nations would be paid. Klein is especially critical of the work done in free-enterprise zones in less developed countries, where corporations and subcontractors are able to do as they wish, free of local government control. In those settings, wages are particularly low and working conditions especially harsh.

Given these realities in less developed countries, it is clearly in the interest of corporations to produce little or nothing in high-wage, developed countries. With production costs minuscule in less developed countries, these corporations can spend lavishly on their brands and the associated logos, such as Nike's Swoosh and McDonald's Golden Arches. Low production costs also allow for great profits and make it possible for corporate leaders to be paid unconscionable sums of money. Especially egregious is the contrast between the wealth of Phil Knight, founder and chairman of Nike, and the economic situation experienced by those who work in

Naomi Klein

development zone factories to produce Nike products, including some trafficked workers who function as modern-day slaves and are forced to work in Nike factories against their will. Similarly egregious are the sums of money paid to celebrities like Michael Jordan to advertise products and, in the process, to become brands themselves.

Think About It

Would the conditions Naomi Klein criticizes be possible without the implied consent of consumers in Western countries? Do you look for logos when you shop? Why or why not?

GL🌐BALIZATION

The Self in the Global Age

The self is not fixed. It changes over the course of our lives and even on a day-to-day basis, depending on the nature of the impression we want to make on others (Goffman 1959). The self also changes with large-scale transformations in the social world, and no change has been more dramatic than globalization.

Globalization brings with it the increasingly easy movement of all kinds of objects, ideas, and knowledge, as well as of people. This mobility is of great importance in itself (Urry 2007), and also because "the globalization of mobility extends into the core of the self" (Elliott and Urry 2010: 3).

On the positive side, the self can become more open and flexible as a result of all the new experiences associated with the global age. The many brief interactions that happen, for example, online or through travel can lead to a different kind of self, perhaps more oriented to the short-term and the episodic than to that which is long-term or even lifelong.

Of great concern, however, are the negative effects of globalization on the self. At the extreme, Lemert and Elliott (2006) see globalization as "toxic" for the individual, including the self. Because people are increasingly mobile, they are likely to feel that their selves are dispersed and adrift in various places in the world or that they exist even more

Is it possible to be too involved with and dependent on digital technology? What do we gain from our use of digital devices, and what do we lose?

loosely in global cyberspace. While in the past the self was increasingly likely to be shaped by close personal relationships, it is now more likely to reflect the absence of such relationships and a sense of distance, even disconnection, from others. At the minimum, this can lead to a different kind of self than existed before the global age. At the maximum, it can lead to one that is weak because it is untethered to anything strong and long-lasting.

A more familiar pathology associated with the global age is being obsessed with digital mobile technologies. For one woman, the experience of being so

deeply enmeshed in these technologies "has left the self drained and lifeless" (Elliott and Urry 2010: 41). Globalization and its associated mobility have had a great effect on the self, and that impact is likely to grow exponentially in the future.

Think About It

Is the self today shaped more [by the] absence of close personal friendship [and] a sense of distance from others t[han by] close personal relationships? What [might] be some of the negative effects [of this] change, if it is real? How could [we] counteract them?

◀ **GLOBALIZATION** boxes expose students to cultures and communities outside the United States and provide insight into the increasingly interconnected world we inhabit.

▼ **DIGITAL LIVING** boxes help students recognize how their everyday lives are influenced by the Internet and mass media.

DIGITAL LIVING

The Family and the Internet

The Internet has radically altered family life. People now consume an average of 12 hours of media a day at home, compared with 5 hours a day in 1960. We can look at one family's experience with the Internet and its associated technologies as an example of what has come to be called "problematic Internet use" (Spada 2014). (While there are problems associated with excessive use of the Internet, we must not ignore the many advantages this technology offers, such as the ability to Skype with family members in different locations.)

The father is working on a software venture and is deeply enmeshed in, and dependent on, the Internet (Richtel 2010). Operating from home, he works with three computer screens simultaneously and sometimes adds an iPad (he is also reliant on his smartphone). One screen shows tweets, instant messages, and group chats. The second displays computer codes and is where Skyping takes place. The third has a calendar, his e-mail, a web browser, and his music. He is obsessed with computer technology (he falls asleep with either a laptop or a smartphone on his chest and goes online as soon as he opens his eyes in the morning), and that obsession has had a negative effect on his family.

When things are tough emotionally for the father, he deals with it by escaping into video games. When the family goes on vacation, he has a difficult time staying away from e-mail and the Internet.

With media consumption reaching an all-time high, how can families keep the Internet from taking over the time they would otherwise spend together? Should they be concerned about losing this time together?

Both mother and daughter complain that he prefers technology to interacting with the family. When the son's grades fall, blame is placed on the amount of time he devotes to his technologies (he has two computer screens in his bedroom as well as his own smartphone).

Although the wife (and mother) spends a lot of time on the Internet texting, browsing Facebook, and checking her own e-mail 25 times a day, she would love to see her husband spend less time with his technologies and more time with his family. However, she knows that he gets "crotchety" if he does not get his

technology "fix." The Internet contributes to innumerable stresses and conflicts in this family's life and in the lives of many other families.

Think About It

Do you know families like the one described here? If so, what effect does their engagement with the Internet and associated technologies have on their families? Do you know families in which these technologies play a less prominent role? What differentiates these families from others? Do you think there is really any such thing as problematic Internet use (PIU)?

> 66
> I liked the overall feel of the book, especially the opening vignettes, which help students immediately see in people's lives the concepts and theories they will cover in the chapter.
>
> —Regina Davis Sowers
> Santa Clara University
> 99

FEATURES FOR CRITICAL THINKING AND REVIEW

"Overall, I really like the book. It is well written, reviews key concepts in a complete but efficient manner, and will hold student interest.

—Eric P. Tranby
University of Delaware

"Excellent information, well organized, many relevant points that connect the information to the "real world."

—Cari Beecham-Bautista
Columbia College Chicago

▶ **LEARNING OBJECTIVES** preview key chapter topics and help students read with a purpose.

LEARNING OBJECTIVES

9.1 Discuss ways in which countries and individuals can be classified within global stratification.

9.2 Describe forms of global stratification, including the global digital divide, health inequalities, and gender stratification.

9.3 Identify ways in which countries' positions within the global stratification structure might be improved.

9.4 Discuss structural/functional and conflict/critical theories of global stratification.

9.5 Explain some of the relationships between consumption and global stratification.

ASK YOURSELF

What aspects of your life can you imagine as "liquids"? Which seem like "flows"? What do you imagine these elements looked like 20 years ago, before the advent of globalization?

▲ In-chapter **ASK YOURSELF** questions invite students to apply sociological concepts to everyday life.

◀ **END-OF-CHAPTER SUMMARIES** support retention of key ideas.

SUMMARY

The family is a crucial social institution that has changed in many ways over the last century. Marriage is a legal union of two people. It can involve monogamy, polygamy, or cenogamy. In an intimate relationship, partners have a close, personal, and domestic relationship with one another.

The traditional nuclear family now accounts for only about a fifth of all U.S. households. To explain the decline in such households, Cherlin focuses on the deinstitutionalization of marriage, while Giddens posits that the desire for pure relationships makes marriage more fragile. Simmel suggests that some degree of secrecy is necessary to a successful re

The structure of intimate re
Cohabitation, nonresident p
holds have increased in th
blended families are more co
are more visible.

Parsons believed that the
ally important to society be
behavior and socialize child
ily primarily as a place of i

between those of different ages and genders. Feminist theorists view the family as particularly problematic for women because they are oppressed by a system that adversely affects them. Symbolic interactionists focus on the meanings and identities associated with the family. Exchange theorists look at the rewards and costs associated with the choices individuals make within families.

Abuse and domestic violence severely affect many families, as does poverty. Gender inequality in marriages is visible in partners' decision making and power distribution, and in the dif-

REVIEW QUESTIONS

1. How has the structure of the family changed in the United States since 1900?
2. What about marriage makes it functionally important? Despite its importance, what are some problems that arise in marriage and the families formed through marriage?
3. According to structural-functionalists, why are families so important to society?
4. What criticisms do conflict and feminist theorists have of structural-functional theories of the family? In what ways are these criticisms related to ideas about social stratification?
5. What forms can intimate relationships take? Do you think that some forms of relationships are valued more highly than others in the United States? Do you think these values will change in the future? Why or why not?

6. Recent studies show that one out of every six relationships is started on an Internet dating site. In what ways are these dating sites reflective of the changes in the marriage market in the United States? How could one use exchange theories to explain the use of Internet dating sites to find partners?
7. What are the causes and consequences of divorce? What are the benefits and disadvantages of divorce?
8. What are some general conclusions sociologists have formed about domestic violence? Is there still debate concerning such violence? What are some other common problems that arise within families?
9. Many sociologists see a close relationship between family structure and poverty. What is this relationship? What role does gender play? What are some contrasting viewpoints?
10. In what ways has globalization affected the family?

◀ **REVIEW QUESTIONS** test student comprehension of core concepts.

APPLYING THE SOCIOLOGICAL IMAGINATION

The television program *Modern Family* depicts a diversity of intimate relationships and family structures. Nontraditional family structures have become increasingly prevalent in the United States. For this exercise, choose two other currently popular

the differences between the two shows in how they portray familial relationships? Despite the differences, what similarities do the familial relationships have? What structural factors related to the shows (e.g., network, time of day aired, target ferences

◀ **APPLYING THE SOCIOLOGICAL IMAGINATION** exercises encourage students to conduct their own research experiments to uncover the real-world application of sociological concepts.

KEY TERMS

blended family: A family that includes some combination of children from the partners' previous marriages or relationships, along with one or more children of the currently married or cohabiting couple. (p. 237)

cenogamy: Group marriage. (p. 229)

cohabitation: An arrangement in which a couple share a home and a bed without being legally married. (p. 235)

companionate love: A kind of love typified by gradual onset and not necessarily tied to sexual passion, but based on more rational assessments of the one who is loved. (p. 230)

companionate marriage: A marriage emphasizing a clear division of labor between a breadwinner and a home-maker and held together by sentiment,

friendship, and sexuality. Predominant model of marriage in the mid-twentieth century (see *companionate love*). (p. 232)

deinstitutionalization: Weakened social norms, especially with regard to the institution of marriage. (p. 231)

domestic violence: The exertion of power over a partner in an intimate relationship through behavior that is intimidating, threatening, harassing, or harmful. (p. 242)

endogamy: Marriage to someone with similar characteristics in terms of race, ethnicity, religion, education level, social class, and so on. (p. 229)

exogamy: Marriage to someone with characteristics that are dissimilar in terms of race, ethnicity, religion, education level, social class, and so on. (p. 229)

extended family: Two or more generations of a family living in the same household or in close proximity to one another. (p. 238)

family: A group of people related by descent, marriage, or adoption. (p. 228)

individualized marriage: A model of marriage emphasizing the satisfaction of the individuals involved. (p. 232)

institutional marriage: Predominant model of marriage in the early twentieth century; emphasizes maintenance of the institution of marriage itself. (p. 232)

intimate relationship: A close, personal, and domestic relationship between partners. (p. 230)

marriage: The socially acknowledged and approved and often legal union

◀ **KEY TERM** sections offer students easy access to definitions of important concepts.

ESSENTIALS OF SOCIOLOGY

EDITION 2

To Sue: With much love for enduring, mostly with her usual good humor intact,
all the years I was often unavailable while writing this book

ESSENTIALS OF
SOCIOLOGY

EDITION 2

GEORGE RITZER

University of Maryland

Los Angeles | London | New Delhi
Singapore | Washington DC

Los Angeles | London | New Delhi
Singapore | Washington DC

FOR INFORMATION:

SAGE Publications, Inc.
2455 Teller Road
Thousand Oaks, California 91320
E-mail: order@sagepub.com

SAGE Publications Ltd.
1 Oliver's Yard
55 City Road
London EC1Y 1SP
United Kingdom

SAGE Publications India Pvt. Ltd.
B 1/I 1 Mohan Cooperative Industrial Area
Mathura Road, New Delhi 110 044
India

SAGE Publications Asia-Pacific Pte. Ltd.
3 Church Street
#10-04 Samsung Hub
Singapore 049483

Copyright © 2016 by SAGE Publications, Inc.

All rights reserved. No part of this book may be reproduced or utilized in any form or by any means, electronic or mechanical, including photocopying, recording, or by any information storage and retrieval system, without permission in writing from the publisher.

Printed in Canada.

ISBN 978-1-4833-8089-6

Acquisitions Editor: Jeff Lasser
Development Editor: Nathan Davidson
Editorial Assistant: Alexandra Croell
eLearning Editor: Gabrielle Piccininni
Production Editor: Olivia Weber-Stenis
Copy Editor: Judy Selhorst
Typesetter: C&M Digitals (P) Ltd.
Proofreader: Laura Webb
Indexer: Judy Hunt
Cover Designer: Scott Van Atta
Marketing Manager: Johanna Swenson

This book is printed on acid-free paper.

MIX
Paper from
responsible sources
FSC® C011825

16 17 18 19 20 10 9 8 7 6 5 4 3 2 1

BRIEF CONTENTS

DETAILED CONTENTS

6 DEVIANCE AND CRIME   125

7 SOCIAL STRATIFICATION IN THE UNITED STATES AND GLOBALLY   149

8   RACE AND ETHNICITY   177

9   GENDER AND SEXUALITY   201

SOCIAL CHANGE, SOCIAL MOVEMENTS, AND COLLECTIVE ACTION 357

15

LETTER FROM THE AUTHOR

To me, the social world, as well as the field of sociology that studies that world, is always interesting, exciting, and ever-changing. My goal in this newly revised second edition of *Essentials of Sociology* is not only to introduce YOU, the student, to sociology, but also to discuss what has made sociology my lifelong passion. My hope is that readers of this text learn a good deal about the social world from the perspective of sociology, as well as get at least a sense of why I am so passionate about it. Please let me explain how this book is, in many ways, an expression of that passion as well as of my personal sociological journey.

My initial interests in the field were the sociology of work and of organizations, but I was quickly drawn to sociological theory and how even the most classical theories were relevant to, and at play in, my everyday life—and yours. This interest came to fruition in the publication of *The McDonaldization of Society* in 1993 (the eighth edition of that book was published in 2015, and a ninth edition is planned). In that book I apply and expand upon the famous classic theoretical ideas of Max Weber on rationality. I saw those ideas at work in my local fast-food restaurant, as well as in many other contemporary settings. The major themes addressed in *The McDonaldization of Society* are addressed in various places in this textbook.

Journalists often interview me on the ideas behind "McDonaldization," and these experiences have allowed me to better appreciate "public sociology," the impact of sociologists' work on the larger public. Public sociology is of increasing importance, and in this text I highlight not only the writings of sociologists whose work has had a significant public impact but also the work of journalists that is implicitly, and sometimes explicitly, sociological in nature.

After the publication of *The McDonaldization of Society*, my thinking and research moved in many related and interesting directions, and these interests are manifest throughout this text. I grew very interested in consumption and, more specifically, was drawn to the study of credit cards, which inspired *Expressing America: A Critique of the Global Credit Card Society*. I was surprised by the number of my undergraduate students who maintained one or more credit card accounts. I was also distressed by their fears of growing indebtedness (in hindsight perhaps a harbinger of the Great Recession). Also in the area of consumption, I authored *Enchanting a Disenchanted World: Continuity and Change in the Cathedrals of Consumption*. Shopping malls, theme parks such as Disney World, Las Vegas–style casinos, and cruise ships are all "cathedrals of consumption," which lure consumers and lead them to overspend and to go deeply into debt.

Later, as I reflected on my research on fast-food restaurants, credit cards, and cathedrals of consumption, I was drawn to a fascinating newly emerging area of sociology—globalization. This led me to write *The Globalization of Nothing* and *Globalization: A Basic Text*. I realized that all of the phenomena of interest to me had been pioneered in the United States but had spread rapidly throughout much of the world. Accordingly, this book includes a strong emphasis on globalization, with the hope that students will better understand that process and better appreciate their roles within our increasingly globalized world.

Most recently, my sociological journey has led me to the Internet, especially social networking sites such as Facebook, Twitter, and Pinterest. Internet sites are highly rationalized (or McDonaldized), are often places to consume (e.g., eBay, Amazon), and are all globalized (Facebook alone has more than one billion users throughout the world). Throughout this book—in boxes headed "Digital Living" and in the narrative—the sociological implications of the Internet are discussed and explained; there is much in this topic for students to contemplate.

The above describes much of my personal sociological journey. I hope that this book will provide YOU with a starting point to begin your own personal sociological journey, to examine your social world critically, and to develop your own sociological ideas and opinions. It is my hope that this book equips you to see the social world in a different way and, more important, to use the ideas discussed here to help to create a better world.

George Ritzer
University of Maryland

ACKNOWLEDGMENTS

I need to begin with my friends for decades, and coauthors of a previous introductory textbook, Kenneth C. W. Kammeyer and Norman R. Yetman. That book went through seven editions. It was most useful to me in this text in helping to define various sociological concepts that have changed little over the years. I have also been able to build on discussions of many issues covered in that text. However, because of the passage of time in sociology and in the social world, as well as the innumerable changes in them, this text has little in common with the earlier one. Nonetheless, my perspective on sociology was strongly shaped by that book and the many insights and ideas provided by my friends and coauthors before, during, and in the many years after the writing of that book.

Many thanks to Olivia Weber-Stenis, who amiably and capably managed the production of this book, as well as to Judy Selhorst, who handled the copyediting.

Professor Rebecca Plante played a key role in the second edition of this book. She offered useful comments and suggestions throughout, and she was especially central in the revision of Chapter 9, on gender and sexuality. These are her areas of expertise, and the chapter is much improved because of her contributions to it. Professor Wendy Wiedenhoft took on a critical role in the late stages of the writing of this edition and made innumerable contributions. I anticipate that she will play an even greater role in future editions. I would also like to thank Professor Paul Dean, coauthor of the second edition my book *Globalization: A Basic Text,* for his numerous and important contributions to Chapter 7, on social stratification.

I would also would like to thank Professors Jack Levin, Andrew Cherlin, and Robert J. Brulle for writing the material for boxes dealing with their own experiences in doing public sociology. Thanks also to P. J. Rey, William Yagatich, Jillet Sam, Zeynep Tufekci, and Margaret Austin Smith for their contributions. Also to be thanked for writing first drafts of parts of chapters are Professors William Carbonaro (Chapter 11, on education), Deric Shannon (Chapter 12, on politics), and Lester Kurtz (Chapter 11, on religion). Thanks to Professor Peter Kivisto, who made particularly important and numerous contributions to the first edition of this book. I'm especially thankful for his work on the religion and education chapter.

At SAGE Publications, I am especially grateful for Vice President Michele Sordi's confidence in, and support for, the project. She agreed from the beginning to do and spend whatever was necessary to make this a first-class introductory sociology text. As you can see from the finished product, she was true to her word. Michele also worked closely with me in an editorial capacity on the first edition to help get the project through some of its most difficult periods. Michele was a positive force and upbeat presence throughout the writing of this book, and I am deeply grateful for who she is and what she has done. Late in the process Brenda Carter took over Michele's role and performed it with the same level of expertise, good humor, and good sense (plus she got me prime seats to a game in New York involving my beloved Yankees). Jeff Lasser came on board at SAGE as Sociology Publisher during production of the first edition, in which he played a key role. Jeff has proven to be not only easy to work with but a sage (pun intended) adviser on many aspects of the book and its publication. Unfortunately, he is a Boston Red Sox fan, but nobody is perfect.

I also need to thank Nathan Davidson at SAGE. The production of the first edition of this book really took off when he took over its day-to-day management. We worked together closely for about a year on virtually every aspect of the final project. Before Nathan came on board I was in danger of being overwhelmed by the demands of finishing this book, but he provided the hard work, great organizational abilities, and good sense that helped me complete it—and on time. Nathan has continued to manage the second edition of this book and, if possible, he has done an even better job with it. While his imprint is found throughout this book, it is especially notable in the selection of an excellent set of photographs.

Also to be thanked for her work is Elisa Adams, who, first as a consultant and later as developmental editor, was instrumental in editing the entire book as well as helping to create various features of the book. Sheri Gilbert is to be thanked for her work on the many permissions needed for material included in this edition. Scott Van Atta did great work on the cover. Thanks to Gabrielle Piccininni, Associate Digital Content Editor, for her work on the ancillary materials and e-book resources.

I am particularly grateful to the following reviewers, who provided enormously helpful feedback for this edition: Paul Almeida, University of California, Merced; Cari Beecham-Bautista, Columbia College Chicago; Lynn G. Chin,

Washington and Lee University; Jessica L. Collett, University of Notre Dame; Linda S. Cook, Houston Community College; Denise N. Cook, University of Nevada, Las Vegas; Irene J. Dabrowski, St. John's University; Regina Davis-Sowers, Santa Clara University; Michaela DeSoucey, North Carolina State University; Colleen P. Eren, City University of New York; Kimberly E. Fox, Bridgewater State University; Paul S. Gray, Boston College; Geoff Harkness, Morningside College; Aimee E. Huard, Nashua Community College; Joy Inouye, College of DuPage; Gary Jones, University of Winchester; Joachim S. Kibirige, Missouri Western State University; Heather Mooney, Eastern Michigan University; Kaitlyne A. Motl, University of Kentucky; Jennifer J. Reed, University of Nevada, Las Vegas; Michael A. Robinson, East Carolina University; Eric Tranby, University of Delaware; Catherine Turcotte, Colby-Sawyer College; Okori Uneke, Winston Salem State University; Dennis L. Veleber, University of Great Falls; Heidi M. Williams, University of Louisville.

I'm also grateful to the following reviewers, advisory board members, and class testers who provided feedback for the previous edition: Sophia Krzys Acord, University of Florida; Kristian Alexander, University of Utah; Lori J. Anderson, Tarleton State University; Lester Andrist, University of Maryland; Augustine Aryee, Fitchburg State College; Meg Austin Smith, University of Maryland; Grace Auyang, University of Cincinnati, Raymond Walters College; Libby Barland, Lynn University; John Batsie, Parkland College; Cari Beecham, Columbia College, Chicago; Berch Berberoglu, University of Nevada, Reno; Denise Bielby, University of California, Santa Barbara; Donna Bird, University of Southern Maine; Miriam Boeri, Kennesaw State University; David Daniel Bogumil, California State University, Northridge; Craig Boylstein, Coastal Carolina University; Yvonne Braun, University of Oregon; Robert Brenneman, Saint Michael's College; Rebecca Brooks, Ohio Northern University; Ann Bullis, College of Southern Nevada; Paul Calarco, Hudson Valley Community College; Bradley Campbell, California State University, Los Angeles; Josh Carreiro, University of Massachusetts; Brenda Chaney, Ohio State University, Marion; Joyce Clapp, University of North Carolina, Greensboro; Susan Claxton, Georgia Highlands College; Langdon Clough, Community College of Rhode Island, Flan; Jessica Collett, University of Notre Dame; Evan Cooper, Farmingdale State College; Julie Cowgill, Oklahoma City University; William Danaher, College of Charleston; Keri Diggins, Scottsdale Community College; Scott Dolan, University at Albany—SUNY; Brenda Donelan, Northern State University; Gili Drori, Stanford University; Kathy Edwards, Ashland Community and Technical College; David Embrick, Loyola University, Chicago; Colleen Eren, Hunter College; Heather Feldhaus, Bloomsburg University; Rosalind Fisher, University of West Florida; Pam Folk, North Hennepin Community College; Tammie Foltz, Des Moines Area Community College; Douglas Forbes, University of Wisconsin–Stevens Point; Sarah Michele Ford, Buffalo State College; Karie Francis, University of Las Vegas, Nevada; S. Michael Gaddis, University of North Carolina, Chapel Hill; Deborah Gambs, Borough Manhattan, Community College–CUNY; Joshua Gamson, University of San Francisco; Robert Garot, John Jay College of Criminal Justice; Gilbert Geis, University of California, Irvine; Laura Gibson, Brescia University; Bethany Gizzi, Monroe Community College; Edward Glick, Des Moines Area Community College; Barry Goetz, Western Michigan University; Colin Goff, University of Winnipeg; Roberta Goldberg, Trinity Washington University; Tina Granger, Nicholls State University; Elizabeth Grant, Chabot College; Matthew Green, College of Dupage; Dan Gurash, Fairmont State University; Kristi Hagen, Chippewa Valley Technical College; Lee Hamilton, New Mexico State University; James Harris, Mountain View College; Gary Heidinger, Roane State Community College; Marta Henrikson, Central New Mexico Community College; Cedric Herring, University of Illinois, Chicago; Anthony Hickey, Western Carolina University; Joy Honea, Montana State University Billings; John C. Horgan, Concordia University–Wisconsin; Jeanne Humble, Bluegrass Community Technical College; Gabe Ignatow, University of North Texas; Mike Itashiki, Collin County Community College & University of North Texas; Dai Ito, Georgia State University; AJ Jacobs, East Carolina University; Wesley Jennings, University of South Florida; Mike F. Jessup, Taylor University; James R. Johnson, Southwest Indian Polytechnical Institute; Hanna Jokinen-Gordon, Florida State University; Ellis Jones, Holy Cross University; Faye Jones, Mississippi Community College; Carolyn Kapinus, Ball State University; Mary Karpos, Vanderbilt University; Barry Kass, Orange County Community College; Alan Kemp, Pierce College; Stacy Keogh, University of Montana; Zeynep Kilic, University of Alaska, Anchorage; Jeanne Kimpel, Fordham University; Lloyd Klein, York College; Chuck Kusselow, River Valley Community College; Richard Lachmann, University at Albany—SUNY; Steve Lang, Laguardia Community College; Barbara LaPilusa, Montgomery College; Erin Leahey, University of Arizona; Ke Liang, Baruch College; Maria Licuanan, Kent State University; John Lie, University of California, Berkeley; Cameron D. Lippard, Appalachian State University; Dongxiao Liu, Texas A&M University; David Lopez, California State University, Northridge; Jeanne M. Lorentzen, Northern Michigan University; Garvey Lundy, Montgomery County Community College; Crystal Lupo, Auburn University; Wade Luquet, Gwynedd-Mercy College; Kim MacInnis, Bridgewater State College; Mahgoub Mahmoud, Tennessee State University–Nashville; Aaron Major, University at Albany—SUNY; Vanessa Martinez, Holyoke Community College; Setsuko Matsuzawa, College of Wooster; Suzanne L. Maughan, University of Nebraska at

Kearney; Christine McClure, Cape Cod Community College; Patrick McGrady, Florida State University; Tara McKay, University of California, Los Angeles; Paul McLean, Rutgers University; Rohald Meneses, University of California, Pembroke; Eric Mielants, Fairfield University; Hosik Min, Norwich University; Ami Moore, University of Northern Texas; Amanda Moras, Sacred Heart University; Gail Mosby, West Virginia State University; Jeff Mullis, Emory University; Brigitte Neary, University of South Carolina, Spartanburg; Megan Nielsen, Midland University; Nirmal Niroula, Franklin University; Charles Norman, Indiana State University; Michael O'Connor, Hawkeye Community College; David O'Donnell, Vermilion Community College; Godpower Okereke, Texas A&M University–Texarkana; Aurea Osgood, Winona State; Johanna Pabst, Boston College; Tiffany Parsons, University of West Georgia; Donna Philips, Bluegrass Community and Technical College; Alex Piquero, University of Texas, Dallas; Dwaine Plaza, Oregon State University; Dan Poole, Salt Lake Community College; Winnie Poster, Washington University, Saint Louis; Malcolm Potter, Los Angeles Pierce College; Lindsey Prowell Myers, Ohio State University; Ekaterin Ralston, Concordia University, St. Paul; Rashawn Ray, University of California, Berkeley; P. J. Rey, University of Maryland; Adrienne Riegle, Iowa State University; Teresa Roach, Florida State University; Frank Roberts, Mount San Antonio College; Desireé Robertson, Mid South Community College; Lauren Ross, Temple University; Janet Ruane, Montclair State University; Amy Ruedisueli, Tidewater Community College; David N. Sanders, Angelo State University; Matthew Sargent, Madison Area Technical College; Mary Satian, Northern Virginia Community College; Dave Schall, Milwaukee Area Technical College; Elizabeth D. Scheel, St. Cloud State University; Lynn Schlesinger, SUNY College, Plattsburgh; Jerald Schrimsher, Southern Illinois University, Carbondale; Sandra Schroer, Muskingum University; Howard Schuman, University of Michigan; Frank Scruggs, National-Louis University; Sarah Scruggs, Oklahoma City University; Megan Seely, Sierra College; Vincent Serravallo, Rochester Institute of Technology; Meena Sharma, Henry Ford Community College; Mark Sherry, University of Toledo; Amber Shimel, Liberty University; Kristen Shorette, University of California, Irvine; Nicole Shortt, Florida Atlantic University, Boca Raton; Luceal Simon, Wayne State University; Nicolas Simon, Eastern Connecticut State University; Rhianan Smith, Carroll College; Chris Solario, Chemeketa Community College; Jennifer Solomon, Winthrop University; Julia Spence, Johnson County Community College; Steven Stack, Wayne State University; William Staudenmeier, Eureka College; Michael Steinhour, Purdue University; Paul Sturgis, Truman State University; Daniel Suh, Orange Coast College; Donna Sullivan, Marshall University; Kevin Sullivan, Bergen Community College; Richard Sweeney, Modesto Junior College; Sheryl Switaj, Schoolcraft College; Jaita Talukdar, Loyola University, New Orleans; Joyce Tang, CUNY Queens College; Rae Taylor, Loyola University New Orleans; Richard Tewksbury, University of Louisville; Mary Texeira, California State University-San Bernardino; Ha Thao, MiraCosta College; Miriam Thompson, Northwest Vista College; Ruth Thompson-Miller, University of Dayton; Santos Torres, California State University, Sacramento; Linda Treiber, Kennesaw State University; Deanna Trella, Northern Michigan University; Okori Uneke, Winston-Salem State University; Paul Van Auken, University of Wisconsin–Oshkosh; Jonathan Van Wieren, Grand Valley State University; Mark Vermillion, Wichita State University; PJ Verrecchia, York College; Kristie Vise, Northern Kentucky University; John Vlot, Lehigh Carbon Community College; Matthew Vox, Covenant College; Russell Ward, Maysville Community & Technical College; Debra Welkley, California State University, Sacramento; Beau Weston, Centre College; Bernadette White, Ohlone College; Wendy Wiedenhoft Murphy, John Carroll University; Jeff Wilhelms, Rutgers University; Matthew Wilkinson, Coastal Carolina University; George Wilson, University of Miami; Melisa Wingfield, Wichita Area Tech College; Elizabeth Wissinger, Borough of Manhattan Community College; Julie Withers, Butte College; Rowan Wolf, Portland Community College; Robert Wonser, College of the Canyons; Susan Wortmann, Nebraska Wesleyan University; Kassia Wosick, New Mexico State University; James Wright, Chattanooga Technical Community College; Jane Young, Luzerne County Community College; Yuping Zhang, Lehigh University.

ABOUT THE AUTHOR

George Ritzer is Distinguished University Professor at the University of Maryland. Among his awards are Honorary Doctorate from La Trobe University, Melbourne, Australia; Honorary Patron, University Philosophical Society, Trinity College, Dublin; American Sociological Association's Distinguished Contribution to Teaching Award; and 2013 Eastern Sociological Society's Robin Williams Lecturer. He has chaired four sections of the American Sociological Association: Theoretical Sociology, Organizations and Occupations, Global and Transnational Sociology, and the History of Sociology. In the application of social theory to the social world, his books include *The McDonaldization of Society* (8th ed., 2015), *Enchanting a Disenchanted World* (3rd ed., 2010), and *The Globalization of Nothing* (2nd ed., 2007). He is the author of *Globalization: A Basic Text* (Blackwell, 2010; 2nd ed. 2015, with Paul Dean). He edited the *Wiley-Blackwell Companion to Sociology* (2012), *The Blackwell Companion to Globalization* (2008) and co-edited (with Jeff Stepnisky) the *Wiley-Blackwell Companions to Classical and Contemporary Major Social Theorists* (2012) and the *Handbook of Social Theory* (2001). He was founding editor of the *Journal of Consumer Culture*. He also edited the eleven-volume *Encyclopedia of Sociology* (2007; 2nd ed. forthcoming), the two-volume *Encyclopedia of Social Theory* (2005), and the five-volume *Encyclopedia of Globalization* (2012). He co-edited a special double issue (2012) of the *American Behavioral Scientist* on prosumption and edited a symposium on prosumer capitalism in *Sociological Querterly* (2015). His books have been translated into over twenty languages, with more than a dozen translations of *The McDonaldization of Society* alone.

1

AN INTRODUCTION TO SOCIOLOGY IN THE GLOBAL AGE

A Sociology of Revolutions and Counterrevolutions

In December 2010, street demonstrations, labor strikes, and other acts of civil resistance swept through the small North African nation of Tunisia. The demonstrators met strong resistance from the Tunisian government. Nevertheless, their protests continued into 2011, eventually resulting in the overthrow of President Ben Ali after 23 years in power.

The immediate trigger for the Tunisian protests was the self-immolation of Mohamed Bouazizi, a 26-year-old street vendor who claimed he had long been harassed and humiliated by authorities. Bouazizi set himself on fire before the rural governor's office and died in a burn and trauma center 18 days later without regaining consciousness.

However powerful the public reaction to Bouazizi's death proved to be, the underlying causes of both the Tunisian revolution and the Arab Spring—the wave of social unrest and social revolution that Tunisia's uprising inspired throughout the Middle East—involved far more than a single act of protest. Unless we consider the social, polit-ical, and economic conditions of prerevolution Tunisia, it is impos-sible for us to understand why Bouazizi set himself alight, and why thousands of Tunisians and others throughout the Arab world saw his act as an appropriate—and necessary—call for change. Such events always lead to counterreactions by other individuals as well as by larger organizations. Those responses have since undermined the

LEARNING OBJECTIVES

1-1   Identify major social changes since the 1880s studied by sociologists.

1-2   Explain why sociologists today focus on trends in globalization and consumption.

1-3   Describe what we mean by the McDonaldization of society.

1-4   Explain sociology's approach to studying social life, including using the sociological imagination and examining the relationship between private troubles and public issues.

1-5   Differentiate between sociology's two possible purposes, science and social reform.

1-6   Evaluate the ways in which sociological knowledge differs from common sense.

Corbis

revolutions that occurred during the Arab Spring. In some cases, such as in Egypt, counterreaction by the military has led to a return to the kind of autocratic government that was a cause of the protests in the first place. In Libya a variety of heavily armed groups have reacted in various ways, leading to a vicious fight for power and, at least at the moment, the virtual dissolution of the country. In Syria and Iraq a radical Islamic group—Islamic State (IS; also known as Islamic State of Iraq and the Levant [ISIL], Islamic State of Iraq and Syria [ISIS], or Da'ish, from an acronym for a name of the group in Arabic)—has swept through large portions of those countries and succeeded in dismembering them in its effort to form an independent state that spans much of the area. The new state envisioned by IS is to be a caliphate, dominated by a leader—a caliph—devoted to a strict interpretation of Islam. The success of IS has, in turn, led to other counterreactions, both locally and globally, designed to limit the group's gains, if not to defeat it.

By drawing on modern sociology's 200-year history while looking to the future, sociologists today have the tools and resources to gain a better understanding of where we have been, where we are, and, perhaps most important, where we are going. Sociology has traditionally tried to understand the place of the individual—even a Tunisian street vendor—within society and society's effect on the individual. In today's global age, however, we need to look beyond a given society to global realities and processes. For example, IS has grown in strength through the influx of individual supporters and fighters from other parts of the world, including the United States and Great Britain. ●

One of the most important lessons you will learn in your study of sociology is that what you think and do as an individual is affected by what is happening in groups, organizations, cultures, societies, and the world. This is especially true of social changes, even those that are global in scope and seem at first glance to be remote from you. Take, for example, Mohamed Bouazizi's public suicide, which set in motion a revolution in Tunisia and throughout much of the Middle East. The roots of that dramatic act of protest lay in poverty, high unemployment, an authoritarian government, and political corruption that affected Bouazizi personally.

A second important lesson in sociology is that not only are you affected by larger events, but you are also capable to

some degree of having an impact on large-scale structures and processes. For example, the actions of Bouazizi helped lead to the Tunisian revolution, which, in turn, led to street demonstrations and civil war elsewhere in the Arab world, including Yemen, Egypt, Libya, and Syria (Kienle 2012; Noueihed and Warren 2012). Those events led, in turn, to counterreactions that continue to reverberate throughout the Middle East and many other parts of the world. It is very possible that actions you take in your lifetime will have wide-ranging, perhaps global, effects.

This example of the relationships between people and larger social realities and changes sets the stage for the definition of **sociology** as the systematic study of the ways in which people are affected by and affect the social structures and social processes associated with the groups, organizations, cultures, societies, and world in which they exist.

THE CHANGING NATURE OF THE SOCIAL WORLD—AND SOCIOLOGY

Sociology deals with very contemporary phenomena, but its deep historical roots have led to many longer-term interests. In the fourteenth century the Muslim scholar Abdel Rahman Ibn Khaldun studied various social relationships, including those between politics and economics. Of special importance to the founding of sociology was the eighteenth- and nineteenth-century Industrial Revolution. During this "industrial age," many early sociologists concentrated on factories, the production that took place in those settings, and those who worked there, especially blue-collar, manual workers. Sociologists also came to focus on the relationship between industry and the rest of society, including, for example, the state and the family.

By the middle of the twentieth century, manufacturing in the United States was in the early stages of a long decline that continues to this day. The United States had moved from the industrial age to the "postindustrial age" (Bell 1973; Leicht and Fitzgerald 2006). The center of the economy and the attention of many sociologists shifted from the factory to the office, from blue-collar manual work to white-collar office work (Mills 1951) as well as to the bureaucracies in which many people worked (Clegg and Lounsbury 2009; Weber [1921] 1968). Another change in the postindustrial age was the growth of the service sector of the economy, involving everyone from high-status service providers such as physicians and lawyers to lower-status workers behind the counters of fast-food restaurants.

The more recent rise of the "information age" (Castells 1996; David and Millwood 2012) can be seen as a part, or an extension, of the postindustrial age. Knowledge and

Prisma Archivo/Alamy

Nineteenth-century sociology was strongly shaped by the Industrial Revolution and its factory system.

information are critical in today's world. So, too, are the technologies—computers, smartphones—that have greatly increased the productivity of individual workers and altered the nature of their work. Rather than designers making drawings by hand, computer-assisted technologies are now used to create designs for everything from electric power grids to patterned fabrics. The widespread use of smartphones has enabled, among many other things, the rise of companies such as Uber and Lyft, the success of which is threatening the taxicab industry and the livelihoods of many taxi drivers. A passenger uses an app to indicate that he or she needs a ride, and one is provided by an independent car owner for a set fee, which is automatically charged to the passenger's credit card (no tipping allowed). Some drivers work a few hours a day for these services to make a little extra money, while others work full-time for the services. Their willingness to do this work has had the result of reducing the need for taxicabs and full-time taxi drivers.

However, it is not just work that has been affected by new technologies; virtually everyone and everything is being affected by them. Uber is part of the growing "sharing economy," in which people share (for a fee) many things; most notably, some share their homes through websites such as Airbnb.com (Pogue 2014). Thus, much sociological attention has shifted to computers and the Internet and to those who work with them (Baym 2010; DiMaggio et al. 2001; Scholz 2013).

The transition from the industrial to the postindustrial and now to the information age has important personal implications. Had you been a man who lived in the industrial age, you would have worked (if you could find as job) for money (pay). You would have done so to be able to buy what you needed and wanted. Women working in the private sphere were largely uncompensated or compensated at a lower rate, as is often still the case. However, in the postindustrial age, it is increasingly likely that men and women will be willing, or forced, to work for free (Anderson 2009; Ritzer and Jurgenson 2010; Terranova 2013), as in the case of interns, bloggers, and contributors to YouTube and Wikipedia.

You may be willing to perform free labor because you enjoy it and because much of what is important in your life is, in any case, available free on the Internet. There is no need for you to buy newspapers when blogs are free or to buy CDs or DVDs when music and movies can be streamed or downloaded at no cost or inexpensively from the Internet.

Sociologists as Bloggers and Public Sociologists

Philip N. Cohen, a leading sociologist, regularly posts on his blog Family Inequality (https://familyinequality.wordpress.com). I blog on many of the issues discussed in this chapter (globalization, consumption) and others of interest to introductory sociology students (https://georgeritzer.wordpress.com). A set of sociology blogs (a "blog ring") called the Society Pages (http://thesocietypages.org) includes blogs on topics such as race, ethnicity, and immigration (The Color Line), teaching sociology (Teaching TSP), visual sociology (Sociological Images), and technology and society (Cyborgology).

One blog on cyborgology discusses surveillance and the way those in power watch the rest of us and record their observations. With smartphones and low-cost portable cameras like those made by GoPro, however, virtually everyone can observe everyone else and record what they see. This gives rise to *sousveillance*, or the ability of the powerless to watch and document the behavior of those in power. One bicyclist recorded being given a $50 ticket by a police officer for not riding in the bike lane. Then, on his blog, the bicyclist showed how impediments in bike lanes make it impossible for cyclists to remain in those lanes.

Other blogs that address sociological issues include Feministing and Jezebel, which tackle the topics of sexuality and gender (see Chapter 9). One Feministing blog post urged readers not to access the nude photos of female movie stars

You may be interested in following one or two blogs written by sociologists or that deal with issues of concern to them.

(including Jennifer Lawrence) that had been hacked and published on the Internet.

Blogging is an alternate route to global influence and success for some sociologists. It is a kind of public sociology. In contrast to professional sociology, in which work is done mainly for other sociologists, **public sociology** addresses a wide range of local, national, and global groups, most of which are outside the academy. Public sociologists write for these groups, and they may engage in collaborative projects with them (Burawoy 2005; Clawson et al. 2007; Nyden, Hossfeld, and Nyden 2011).

Other types of public sociology include books and articles for a popular audience, op-ed pieces in newspapers, public lectures and TV appearances, and direct work with groups to help them achieve their goals. Sociology also often becomes public through the work of nonsociologists such as journalists whose thinking is shaped explicitly or implicitly by sociological knowledge and a sociological perspective. Such work often appears in the form of newspaper articles, books released by popular presses, and website postings and blogs capable of reaching a huge public audience. You will find a series of boxes headed "Public Sociology" throughout this book.

SOURCE: Printed with the permission of Nathan Jurgenson and P. J. Rey.

Think About It

What are some of the advantages for sociologists of the open and diverse dialogue made possible by blogs? What are some advantages for readers of such blogs? Can you think of any disadvantages for readers or for bloggers?

A whole range of software is also downloadable at no cost. However, while all of this, and much else, is available free of charge, the problem is that the essentials of life—food, shelter, clothing—still cost money, lots of money. Many hope that the labor they currently perform for free will eventually have an economic payoff, that their work as bloggers or on YouTube will lead to full-time jobs.

These are but a few of the many social changes to be discussed in this book. The essential point is that the social world (people, groups, organizations, and so on)—*your* social world—is continually changing. Sociology is a field that is, and must be, constantly attuned to and involved in studying those changes.

CENTRAL CONCERNS FOR A TWENTY-FIRST-CENTURY SOCIOLOGY

While sociology has adapted to these major changes, it has also continued to focus on many of its traditional concerns. We have already mentioned industry, production, and work as long-term sociological interests; others include deviance and crime (see Chapter 6), families (see Chapter 10), and the city (see Chapter 14). Of particular concern to many sociologists has been, and continues to be, the issue of inequality as it affects the poor, particular racial and ethnic groups, women, and gays and lesbians (see Chapter 7). The bulk of this book will be devoted to these basic sociological topics and concerns, but the discussion will also encompass the nontraditional and very contemporary issues of consumption, the digital world, and especially globalization.

GLOBALIZATION

No social change is more important today than globalization, which is continually affecting all aspects of the social world everywhere on the globe (Ritzer 2012b; Ritzer and Dean 2015). Today, globalization is a central issue in the social world as a whole as well as in sociology; globalization and talk about it are all around us. In fact, we can be said to be living in the "global age" (Albrow 1996).

Society, a complex pattern of social relationships that is bounded in space and persists over time, has traditionally been the largest unit of analysis in sociology. However, in the global age, societies are seen as declining in importance (Holton 2011; Meyer, Boli, and Ramirez 1997). This is the case, in part, because larger transnational and global social structures are growing in importance. These include the United Nations (UN), the European Union (EU), the Organization of the Petroleum Exporting Countries (OPEC), multinational corporations (MNCs) such as Google and ExxonMobil, and multinational nongovernmental organizations (NGOs) such as Amnesty International. In at least some cases, these transnational structures are becoming more important than individual societies. OPEC, for example, is more important to the rest of the world's well-being than are the organization's key member societies, such as Abu Dhabi or even Saudi Arabia.

Social processes, like social structures, exist not only at the societal level but also at the global level, and these global processes are increasing in importance. Consider migration (see Chapter 14). People move about, or migrate, within and between societies. For example, in the global age, people are increasingly moving between societies, some halfway around the world. The United States now has a higher percentage of immigrants than it has had in almost a century (see Figure 1.1). Many are migrating from and through Mexico to the United States (Massey 2003; Ortmeyer and Quinn 2012). More generally, large numbers of people are migrating from a number of predominantly Islamic societies in the Middle East and Africa to the West (Caldwell 2009; Voas and Fleischmann 2012). Recently, the movement of several thousand people from the West to join radical Islamist organizations (such as Islamic State), especially in Syria and Iraq, has been of increasing concern to Western governments. Some fear that those involved in radical Islamist activities there will migrate back to the West and engage in terrorist acts. Most jarring is the fact that at least 60 million people in the world have been forced to move because of war or persecution; almost a quarter of them fled their home countries in 2014 alone. Nearly half of Syria's population has been displaced by the war raging there (Peçanha and Wallace 2015). By the end of 2015, Western Europe was being flooded with refugees and forced, at least temporarily, to close some of its borders.

There have always been population movements. However, in the global age people generally move around the world far more freely and travel much greater distances than

FIGURE 1.1 • Number of Immigrants and Their Share of the Total U.S. Population, 1850–2012

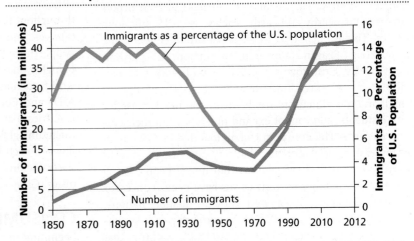

SOURCES: Migration Policy Institute tabulation of data from the U.S. Census Bureau's 2012, 2011, and 2010 American Community Surveys and 1970, 1990, and 2000 decennial census data. All other data are from Campbell J. Gibson and Emily Lennon, *Historical Census Statistics on the Foreign-Born Population of the United States: 1850 to 1990*, Working Paper 29, U.S. Census Bureau (Washington, DC: Government Printing Office, 1999)

ever before. Another way of saying this is that people—and much else—are more "fluid." That is, they move farther, more easily, and more quickly than ever before. Younger people, especially millennials (or Generation Y, those born from the early 1980s through the late 1990s), are particularly likely to be mobile, including globally.

The movement of products of all types is also more fluid as a result of the existence of massive container ships, cargo jets, and package delivery services such as FedEx and UPS. Even more fluid is the digital "stuff" you buy on the Internet when you download music, videos, movies, and so on. And in the realm of the family, tasks once confined to the home, such as caregiving and housework, have become increasingly fluid, as those who can afford to do so often outsource domestic labor (van der Lippe, Frey, and Tsvetkova 2012; Yeates 2009). More generally, the increase in fluidity is manifested in the information that flows throughout the world in the blink of an eye as a result of the Internet, texting, e-mail, and social networking sites such as Facebook, Instagram, and Twitter.

ASK YOURSELF

Have you ever thought of your posts on Facebook, Instagram, or Twitter as part of a global flow of information? In what ways do they actually fit this description? What does your position in this global flow of information reveal about you?

These flows can be expedited by structures of various types. For instance, air cargo delivery will increasingly be facilitated by the "aerotropolis" (Kasarda and Lindsay 2011), a preplanned city that is developed because of proximity and access to a large, modern airport. For example, New Songdo, South Korea, is being built because such an airport (Incheon) is nearby and easily reached via a 12-mile-long bridge. This is in contrast to the usual situation, where the airport (e.g., Reagan National in Washington, D.C.; LAX in Los Angeles; Heathrow in London) is built within or very close to a city center. Traditional airports are typically too small and too difficult to reach, create too much noise for city residents, and cannot expand much beyond their current confines. The European Union, founded in 1993, is an example of a social structure that serves to ease the flow of citizens among member nations (but not of people living outside the EU). Border restrictions have been reduced or eliminated completely among the 27 EU member nations. Similarly, the creation in 1975 of the euro has greatly simplified economic transactions among the 18 EU countries that accept it as their currency.

There are also structures that impede various kinds of global flows. National borders, passports and passport controls (Robertson 2010; Torpey 2000, 2012), security checks, and customs controls limit the movement of people throughout the world. Such restrictions were greatly increased in many parts of the world after the terrorist attacks on New York City and Washington, D.C., on September 11, 2001. This made global travel and border crossing more difficult and time-consuming. Then there are the even more obvious structures designed to limit the movement of people across borders, such as the fences between the United States and Mexico and between Israel and the West Bank, as well as one between Israel and Egypt, completed in 2013. In late 2015 Hungary finished building a fence on its border with Serbia to keep out unwanted migrants (Associated Press 2015a).

The fences at the U.S.–Mexico border, and increased border police and patrols, have led unauthorized migrants to take longer and more risky routes into the United States. One result is that more dead bodies are being discovered in the desert near the border (see Figure 1.2). The American Civil Liberties Union reports that border-crossing deterrence strategies have resulted in an increase in the annual death toll. Also increasing are human rights abuses in the detention centers where those caught crossing the border illegally are held (Androff and Tavassoli 2012; Jimenez 2009). A crisis arose at the Mexican border in mid-2014 when tens of thousands of children from Central America flooded the area and overwhelmed detention centers (Archibold 2014).

There are, of course, many other kinds of structural barriers in the world, most notably trade barriers and tariffs, that limit the free movement of goods and services of many kinds.

In sum, **globalization** is defined by increasingly fluid global flows and the structures that expedite and impede those flows. Globalization is certainly increasing, and it brings with it a variety of both positive and negative developments (Ritzer and Dean 2015). On one side, most people throughout the world now have far greater access to goods, services, and information from around the globe than did people during the industrial age. On the other side, a variety of highly undesirable things also flow more easily around the world, such as persons displaced by war, diseases like HIV/ AIDS and Ebola, and pollution released by industrialized countries that worsens the adverse effects of climate change (including global warming). Also on the negative side are the flows of such forms of "deviant globalization" as terrorism, sex trafficking, and the black markets for human organs and drugs (Gilman, Goldhammer, and Weber 2011).

CONSUMPTION

Beginning in the 1950s, another major social change took place in the United States and other developed countries. The central feature of many capitalist economies began to shift from production and work to **consumption**, or the

FIGURE 1.2 • Immigrant Deaths on the Southern U.S. Border, 2000–2010

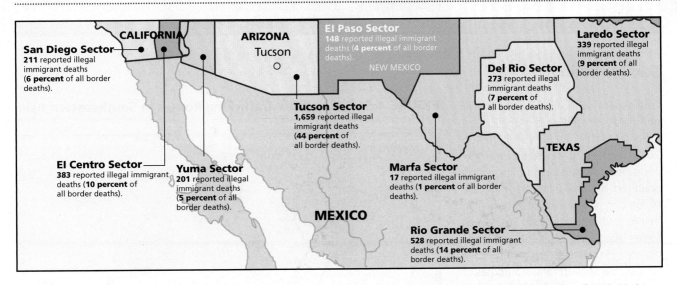

NOTE: Illegal immigrant deaths, by Border Patrol sector. Covering 262 miles, the Tucson Sector has recorded nearly half of all deaths along the U.S.–Mexico border in the last decade.

SOURCE: U.S. Border Patrol.

process by which people obtain and utilize goods and services. During that period, the center of the U.S. economy shifted from the factory and the office to the shopping mall (Baudrillard [1970] 1998; Lipovetsky 2005). For many people, work and production became less important than consumption.

ASK YOURSELF

Have your consumption habits changed over the last six months? The last three years? Do you anticipate that your habits will change in the next three years? If so, how and why? Will you consume more or less?

Consumption is certainly significant economically, but it is significant in other ways as well. For example, culture is very much shaped by consumption, and various aspects of consumption become cultural phenomena. A good example is the iPhone, which has revolutionized culture in innumerable ways. The iPhone and other smartphones have altered how and where people meet to socialize and the ways in which they socialize. In addition, the media and people in general spend so much time discussing the implications of the iPhone and similar products that these devices have become central to the larger culture in which we live.

Consumption and globalization are also deeply intertwined. Much of what we consume in the developed world comes from other countries. In 2013 alone, the United States imported $440 billion worth of goods from China; the comparable figure in 1985 was only $4 million in goods (U.S. Census Bureau 2013). Furthermore, the speed and convenience of Internet commerce tend to make global realities and distances irrelevant to consumers. Finally, travel to other parts of the world—a form of consumption itself—is increasingly affordable and common. A major objective of tourists is often the sampling of the foods of foreign lands, as well as the purchase of souvenirs (Chambers 2010; Gmelch 2010; Mak, Lumbers, and Eves 2012). Medical tourism is less common, but large numbers of Americans travel great distances for such services as cosmetic procedures and even open-heart surgery. They do so largely because the costs are much lower elsewhere in the world. Many U.S. women who have difficulty conceiving travel to developing countries such as India in order to hire surrogates, "rent" their uteruses and ovaries, and exploit their eggs (Pfeffer 2011).

Sociologists are understandably interested in these developments. Early sociologists completed many studies of work, production, factories, and factory workers. Today's sociologists continue to study work-related issues, but they are devoting increasing attention to consumption in general (Sassatelli 2007) and more specifically to such phenomena as online shopping, done increasingly through the use of smartphones (Horrigan 2008; Morris 2013), the behavior of shoppers in more material locales such as department stores (Miller 1998; Zukin 2004), and the development of more recent consumption sites, such as fast-food restaurants (Ritzer 2015) and shopping malls (Ritzer 2010b). All these have become increasingly global phenomena.

Sex Trafficking

One aspect of the increased flow of people associated with globalization is human trafficking (Rao and Presenti 2012; Weitzer 2014). Human trafficking is illegal worldwide, but it is widely practiced. It is characterized by the use of coercion or deception to force human beings into providing such services as forced labor, commercial sex, and organ donation. Sex trafficking involves victims who are transported for the purposes of commercial sex, including prostitution, stripping, and pornography (Hodge 2008). Not all commercial sex involves those who have been trafficked, so consumers of commercial sexual services and performances are not always aware that the sex workers have been trafficked.

One researcher estimates that 1.4 million women and girls are currently trafficked for sexual purposes each year (S. Lee 2012). Predictably, organized criminal networks have come to dominate transnational sex trafficking. Over the last few decades, many countries in the Global South (particularly in Southeast Asia), as well as countries of the former Soviet Union and Eastern Europe, have become major sources of sex workers, especially prostitutes.

The flow of people in the global sex industry involves both those who provide sexual services and those who consume those services. The providers of sexual services generally move within less developed countries, such as those in Southeast Asia, as well as to developed countries. Figure 1.3 shows the flow of providers of sexual services within Southeast Asia, especially in and around Thailand and Cambodia—major destinations for those in search of such services. Those interested in purchasing sexual services tend to flow from more to less developed areas of the world in order to avail themselves of the often cheaper

FIGURE 1.3 • Major Sex Trafficking Routes in Southeastern Asia

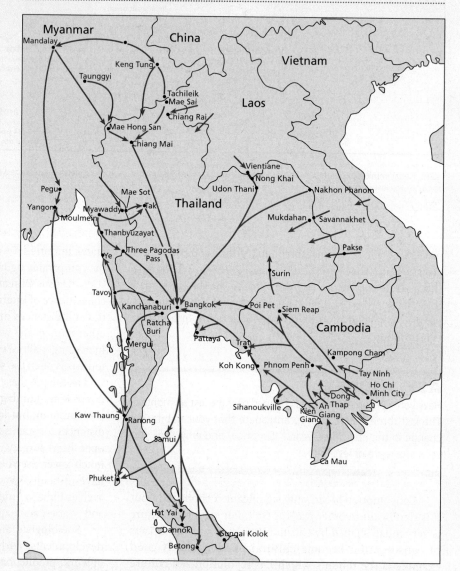

SOURCE: "Transnational Organized Crime in East Asia and the Pacific: A Threat Assessment," April 2013. Copyright © 2013, United Nations Office on Drugs and Crime (UNODC).

and more exotic sexual services available at their destinations (Flynn 2011). In the past the vast majority of buyers of sex have been men, but today women also travel the globe (for instance, from the United States to Costa Rica) in search of sexual services (Frohlick 2013).

Sex trafficking has far more negative consequences for the women who are trafficked than do other forms of human trafficking, such as for domestic work. Not only is sex work far more demeaning, but it also exposes victims to sexually transmitted diseases such as

HIV/AIDS, drug addiction, and a wide variety of other health risks. Trafficked individuals are frequently beaten, raped, stabbed, and strangled—sometimes to death—by traffickers, who are essentially their pimps. Pimps may threaten victims' family members and hold their children hostage to prevent the women from escaping.

Using the Internet, customers can find sex workers almost anywhere in the world instantly, read reviews about their services, exchange information about location and price, and so on. Websites offer package tours, quote prices, and advertise sex workers and their services to the men of the developed world. In Cambodia, a U.S. resident started a "rape camp" that offered "Asian sex slaves" who were gagged, bound, and forced against their will into performing a variety of sex acts (Hughes 2000). Internet viewers could request and pay for specific rape acts to watch online, while traffickers could avoid prosecution by using encryption technologies. This "rape camp" was ultimately shut down, but other creative methods of exploiting women and children continue to exist on the Internet.

Think About It

Do you think it was inevitable that the exploitation of women and children would migrate to the Global South? To the Internet? Why or why not? What effects have globalization and technology had on sex trafficking? Could they also be used to help prevent it?

McDonaldization

My study of fast-food restaurants led to the development of the concept of **McDonaldization**, or the process by which the rational principles of the fast-food restaurant are coming to dominate more and more sectors of society and more societies throughout the world (Ritzer 2015). This process leads to the creation of rational systems—like fast-food restaurants—that have four defining characteristics:

- *Efficiency.* The emphasis is on the use of the quickest and least costly means to whatever end is desired. Perhaps the best example of efficiency is the drive-through window, a highly organized means for employees to dole out meals in a matter of seconds (Horovitz 2002).

- *Calculability.* You hear a lot at McDonald's about quantities: how large the food portions are—the Big Mac—and how low the prices are—the dollar breakfast. You don't hear as much, however, about the quality of the restaurant's ingredients or its products.

- *Predictability.* McDonaldization ensures that the entire experience of patronizing a fast-food chain is nearly identical from one geographic setting to another—even globally— and from one time to another. For example, when customers enter a McDonald's restaurant, employees ask what they wish to order, following scripts created by the corporation.

- *Control.* In McDonaldized systems, technology exerts a good deal of control over people, processes, and products. French fry machines buzz when the fries are done and even automatically lift them out of the hot oil when they've reached just the right amount of crispiness. Workers must load fry baskets with uncooked fries and unload them when the baskets emerge from the oil.

Paradoxically, rationality often seems to lead to its exact opposite—the irrationalities of meaningless work, roadside litter due to drive-through services at fast-food restaurants, or the societal problems associated with childhood obesity, which has been blamed, in part, on the ubiquity of fast food. Another of the irrationalities of rationality is dehumanization. Fast-food employees are forced to work in dehumanizing jobs, which can lead to job dissatisfaction, alienation, and high turnover rates. Fast-food customers are forced to eat in dehumanizing settings, such as in the cold and impersonal atmosphere of the fast-food restaurant, in their cars, or on the move as they walk down the street.

Critiquing Consumption

The sociological study of consumption sites involves, among many other things, a critical look at the ways in which they are structured. (The above discussion of the irrationalities associated with McDonaldized settings is one example of such a critical perspective.) These sites may be set up to lead people to consume certain things and not others, to consume more than they might have intended, and to go into debt (Brubaker, Lawless, and Tabb 2012; Manning 2001; Marron 2009; Ritzer 1995). Take, for example, Rue La La (www .ruelala.com), an "invitation-only" website that was established to sell expensive clothing to members at what are supposed to be huge discounts. The rationale behind the site is that because of its seeming exclusivity, people will be lured into buying more items, and spending more money on each item, than they would elsewhere. In fact, however, the site is not as exclusive as it seems, since members are urged to recruit their friends, and they get a $10 credit after the first purchase of every new member they bring to the site.

Sociologists are also interested in how consumers use shopping malls and e-tailers in ways that were not anticipated by their designers. For example, people often wander through shopping malls and their many shops, which have been designed to spur consumption, without buying anything. Defunct malls are serving as impromptu skate parks.

George Ritzer and the McDonaldization of Society

I am considered a public sociologist (Ritzer 2006) or, as Rojek (2007) labels me, a "public intellectual." My public sociology has generally involved interviews with newspaper, radio, and TV reporters. While some of these have occurred in the United States, a disproportionate number of such interviews have taken place in other parts of the world, especially Great Britain. There is far greater interest in the work of academic sociologists in Great Britain (and in many other places) than there is in the United States. However, even elsewhere in the world there seems to be a decline in public interest in scholarly work by sociologists.

It is not easy for scholars to do public sociology. Interestingly, it is far easier for journalists to do "pop sociology." Thus, the journalist Eric Schlosser, who wrote the best-selling *Fast Food Nation* (2002), in part influenced by my earlier book *The McDonaldization of Society* (1993, 2015), has done much more public sociology than I have. A 2006 movie was even based (loosely) on his book. Sadly, Hollywood has yet to discover me or my work.

Beyond the challenge of getting the attention of the popular media, it is difficult for scholars to do interviews that are reported accurately by the media. Reporters are often ill prepared, having at best Googled a few of a scholar's writings prior to an interview. As a result, they often ask the "wrong" questions or fail to fully understand the answers. In any case, they are usually facing imminent deadlines and are forced to write up the interviews very quickly. I have often been disappointed by the way my thoughts have been translated by the media.

A bigger problem is the tendency for reporters to "McDonaldize" their stories. They seek to simplify what has been said

The four defining characteristics of McDonald's and of the fast-food industry in general—efficiency, calculability, predictability, and control—are coming to dominate many other sectors of society.

in an interview and to avoid anything they consider too complex for their readers. They want to produce what are, in effect, "News McNuggets" that in their simplicity resemble Chicken McNuggets. Neither is fully satisfying.

Reporters are often drawn to writing about the McDonaldization of society because it appears to be an idea that can be communicated simply. While I have tried to do that in my work, reporters usually go way too far in their efforts to McDonaldize the idea. As a result, much of the depth of the concept gets lost in translation.

This was particularly clear in an aborted interview with NBC TV a few years ago. The first part of the interview on McDonaldization went well, but then the reporter asked me about another of my books, *The Globalization of Nothing* (Ritzer 2007b). This involves a thesis

far more difficult to McDonaldize, but I plunged ahead. As I did, I sensed the reporter losing interest. At the end, she said, in effect, "Don't call us; we'll call you." I responded, "Well, I guess my ideas on the globalization of nothing are not McDonaldized enough." She laughed and said, "That's right."

The challenge for me and all public sociologists is to share our ideas with the larger public without McDonaldizing them or having them be McDonaldized. That is never easy!

Think About It

Why is it so difficult to be a public sociologist in the United States? Why is it easier in other parts of the world? Do you think it will be easier or harder to be a public sociologist in the United States in the future? How will blogging by sociologists affect this?

Students are using Amazon.com as a source for term-paper bibliographies rather than buying the books. Travelers are using Internet sites such as Expedia and KAYAK to compare prices but then buying airplane tickets from traditional travel agents or on airlines' own websites.

The Great Recession and its ongoing aftermath altered the degree to which society is dominated by consumption. Even today, long after the onset of the recession in 2008, many U.S. consumers remain reluctant to spend money, or at least as much as they did in the past, on consumption (Kurtz 2014). As a result, consumption sites have experienced great difficulties. Many outdoor strip malls and some indoor malls have emptied; they have become "dead malls" (as documented on the site http://deadmalls.com). Many of the malls that continue to exist have numerous vacant stores, including abandoned large department stores. Las Vegas, which has long been a capital for the consumption of entertainment and high-end goods and services, is hurting (Nagourney 2013). Casinos in Atlantic City, New Jersey, are being shuttered, and there are those who want to see the city become more like the simpler beach community it once was (Hurdle 2014). It seems possible, although highly unlikely, that we now may be on the verge of what could be called the "postconsumption age." While excessive consumption was a key factor in causing the Great Recession, a postconsumption age would bring with it problems of its own, such as fewer jobs and a declining standard of living for many.

ASK YOURSELF

What would your life be like in a postconsumption age? In what ways might it be better? Worse? Why?

THE DIGITAL WORLD

Sociology has always concerned itself with the social aspects and implications of **technology**, or the interplay of machines, tools, skills, and procedures for the accomplishment of tasks. One example is the assembly line, a defining feature of early twentieth-century factories. Later, sociologists became interested in the automated technologies that came to define factories. Sociologists are now devoting an increasing amount of attention to the digital world that has emerged as a result of new technologies already mentioned in this chapter, such as computers, smartphones,

the Internet, and social networking sites such as Facebook and Twitter (Clough 2013).

Living digitally is not separate from living in the social world. In fact, the two forms of living are increasingly intersecting and augmenting each other (Jurgenson 2012). For example, the wide-scale use of smartphones allows people to text many others to let them know they are going to be at a local club. This can lead to a spontaneous social gathering at the club that would not have occurred were it not for this new technology. However, the most dramatic examples of the effect of smartphones on the social world are seen in their use in mobilizing, especially through Twitter, large numbers of people to become involved, and stay involved, in social movements such as the revolutions in Egypt (2011) and Ukraine (2014).

The networking sites on the Internet that involve social interaction are the most obviously sociological in character (Aleman and Wartman 2008; Patchin and Hinduja 2010). These sites are especially important in North America, where the percentage of the population with access to the Internet is highest (see Figure 1.4). However, their importance is increasing elsewhere, especially in the Middle East and North Africa, as reflected in the role they played there in recent social revolutions. Protesters used cell phones and the Internet to inform each other, and the world, about the evolving scene.

While social networking sites can bring about greater interaction, they also come between people and affect the nature of interaction. For example, Twitter limits each message to 140 characters, but face-to-face communication has no such limits. On the other hand, face-to-face communication is limited to a shared physical space, whereas communication via Twitter travels anywhere there is a device

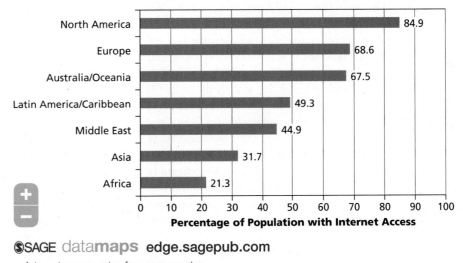

FIGURE 1.4 • Internet Access by Geographic Region, 2013

Region	Percentage
North America	84.9
Europe	68.6
Australia/Oceania	67.5
Latin America/Caribbean	49.3
Middle East	44.9
Asia	31.7
Africa	21.3

Percentage of Population with Internet Access

SAGE datamaps edge.sagepub.com

• Internet access rates for every country.

SOURCE: Data from Internet World Stats, Miniwatts Marketing Group.

Social changes brought about by the thorough integration of the Internet into most areas of our lives have been enormously influential—and the changes are far from over. Teenagers and even very young children take constant connectivity for granted, suggesting that most of the changes we are witnessing will become ever more pervasive.

connected to the Internet. Sociologists are interested in getting a better handle on the nature of the differences, as well as the similarities, between mediated and nonmediated (e.g., face-to-face) interaction. In technologically **mediated interaction**, technology such as the Internet and the smartphone comes between the people who are communicating, while there is no such interference in nonmediated interaction. People who are shy and insecure when it comes to dating or sex, for example, may be much more comfortable relating to others on mediated websites such as Match.com and OkCupid.

Another sociological issue related to the Internet is the impact on our lives of spending so much time interacting on social networking sites. Consider the effects of the 7.5 hours per day—up by a full hour in only five years—that young people between the ages of 8 and 18 spend on electronic devices of all types (Lewin 2010). In some cases, little time remains for other activities (schoolwork, face-to-face interaction). Increasing the ability of children to spend time on these devices is the growing availability of mobile devices such as smartphones, tablets, and iPods. In 2013, about 75 percent of children in the United States under 8 years of age lived in homes with mobile devices, compared to 52 percent just two years earlier. They were also more than twice as likely to use such devices in 2013 than they were in 2011 (Common Sense Media 2013). A recent study of parents and children in fast-food restaurants found that a significant majority of the parents were more absorbed in their mobile devices than they were in relating to their children (Radesky et al. 2014).

We may also multitask among several online and offline interactions simultaneously, such as in class or while doing homework. You may think you do a great job of multitasking,

but dividing focus in this way can actually reduce your ability to comprehend and remember and thus lower your performance on tests and other assignments (PBS 2010).

Internet technology also affects the nature of consumption. More of it is taking place on such sites as eBay and Amazon.com, and that trend is expected to continue to grow. In 2010, a Pew study found that during an average day 21 percent of Internet users in the United States look for information about a service or product they are thinking about buying (Jansen 2010). It is also easier for people to spend money on consumption on Internet sites than it is in the material world. It is worth noting that these sites, as well as the Internet in general, are global in their scope. The ease with which global interactions and transactions occur on the Internet is a powerful indicator of, and spur to, the process of globalization.

Smartphones are also having a variety of effects on consumption. For example, on the one hand, they are making it easier for people to find particular kinds of restaurants and to get to them quickly and efficiently. On the other hand, when people are eating in those restaurants, smartphones tend to slow down service because diners take time photographing the meal, taking selfies, and asking wait staff to take photos of them (Griswold 2014).

GLOBALIZATION, CONSUMPTION, THE DIGITAL WORLD, AND YOU

The three main issues discussed above are of great concern to you as a college student. You live a good part of your life in these three interrelated domains.

You live a truly global existence in a college or university. A significant number of your classmates come from elsewhere in the world. Your classes are increasingly being taught by teachers from other parts of the globe. The ideas you are learning are the most global of all, flowing freely from virtually everywhere in the world to become part of lectures and textbooks.

As consumers, you and your classmates are likely well acquainted with the college bookstore and the nearby shopping mall. In addition, on the Internet you are able to find a nearly infinite variety of goods (including this textbook) and services, the majority of which are likely to come from the far reaches of the world.

Finally, an increasing portion of your education is obtained through the inherently global Internet—for example, through e-learning on web-based courses and online degree programs. In 2013 the number of students taking at least one online course nearly doubled, to 45 percent from 23 percent five years before (Bolkan 2013). With the emergence of massive open online courses (MOOCs), you, and perhaps hundreds of thousands of students from around the globe, are increasingly likely to participate in global classes (including courses in sociology; Behbehanian and Burawoy 2014) and other programs available on the Internet (see Chapter 11 for more on MOOCs) (Heller 2013; Lewin 2012).

Globalization, consumption, and the Internet are of great importance on their own. However, perhaps more important are the ways in which they interact with one another and interpenetrate with your life as a college student—and the lives of virtually everyone else.

SOCIOLOGY: CONTINUITY AND CHANGE

This chapter has emphasized recent social changes and their impact on society and on sociology, but there is also much continuity in society, as well as in the field of sociology. This section deals with a number of traditional approaches and concerns in sociology that are of continuing relevance to even the most recent sociological issues.

THE SOCIOLOGICAL IMAGINATION

The systematic study of the social world has always required imagination on the part of sociologists. There are various ways to look at the social world. For example, instead of looking at the world from the point of view of an insider, one can, at least psychologically, place oneself outside that world. The U.S. "War on Terror" might look defensible from the perspective of an American, especially one who lived through 9/11, but it would look quite different if you imagined yourself in the place of an innocent Muslim caught in the middle of that war.

ASK YOURSELF

From what perspective do you view the 9/11 attacks on the United States? What might they look like from other perspectives? Could you ever consider them from a different angle? Why or why not?

C. Wright Mills (1959) argued that sociologists have a unique perspective—the **sociological imagination**—that gives them a distinctive sociological, rather than personal, way of looking at data or reflecting on the world around them. An example of the utility of the sociological imagination can be found in the ideas of one of the classic thinkers in the history of sociology, Georg Simmel ([1907] 1978). Among many other things, Simmel argued that money is crucial to a modern economy. For example, cash money allows people to be paid easily for their work and makes it just as easy for them to buy goods and services. However, money not only speeds up consumption but also allows people to consume more than they otherwise would. While a money economy creates problems, the sociological imagination

The U.S. sociologist C. Wright Mills achieved success early in life and died when he was only 46.

allows us to see that credit nearly wrecked the American, and much of the global, economy during the Great Recession. The availability of "money" had dramatically increased with the expansion of credit for individuals in the form of mortgage loans, auto loans, and credit cards. People not only tended to spend all of the cash (including savings) they had on hand, but they were also going into more and more debt because loans were easy to obtain. Simmel's imaginative thinking on money allows us to better understand the problems created by easy credit.

Private Troubles and Public Issues

The sociological imagination may be most useful in helping sociologists see the linkage between private troubles and public issues. For example, prior to the onset of the Great Recession, the sociological imagination would have been useful in alerting society to the fact that the increasing levels of individual consumption and debt, seen at the time as private issues, would soon morph into a public issue—the near collapse of the global economy. Credit cards can create both private troubles and public issues. A person going so deeply into debt that there is no way out other than declaring bankruptcy is experiencing a private trouble. However, private troubles become public issues when high levels of personal debt and bankruptcy lead to bank failures and even default on debts by various nations. A 2011 White House report detailing the fact that women are more likely than men to be concentrated in lower-paying jobs (see Figure 1.5; U.S. Department of Commerce, Executive Office of the President, and White House Council on Women and Girls 2011) provides another example: Women are much more likely to be comparatively poorly paid dental hygienists than they are to be dentists, or legal assistants rather than lawyers. For many women, being limited occupationally creates personal troubles, such as inadequate income and job dissatisfaction. But this is also a public issue, not only because the discrepancy between the sexes is unfair to women as a whole but also because society is not benefiting from the many contributions women could be making.

The decision to pursue one college major or career path over another could become a private trouble if a student makes a poor choice or has one forced upon him or her. Sociologists have also shown that such choices are very much related to larger public issues. If many people make poor choices, or are forced into them—as women and other minorities often are—this will lead to public issues such as wide-scale job dissatisfaction and poor performance on the job. Culturally based ideas about gender often shape personal preferences in choosing a college major (Charles and Bradley 2009), and gendered beliefs about career competence steer women and men toward different types of jobs and away from others (Correll 2001, 2004; Ridgeway and Correll 2004). Being in a poorly paid and unsatisfying job is a personal trouble for an individual woman, but it is a public issue when large numbers of women find themselves in this situation.

ASK YOURSELF
Do you agree that private choices sometimes lead to, or are part of, public issues? Can you think of an example from your own life or the life of a family member?

The Micro–Macro Relationship

The interest in personal troubles and public issues is a specific example of a larger and more basic sociological concern with the relationship between microscopic (**micro**, or small-scale) social phenomena, such as individuals and their thoughts and actions, and macroscopic (**macro**, or large-scale) social phenomena, such as groups, organizations, cultures, society, and the world, as well as the relationships among them (Turner 2005). For example, Karl Marx, often considered one of the earliest and most important sociologists, was interested in the relationship between what workers do and think (micro issues) and the capitalist economic system (a macro issue) in which the workers exist. To take a more contemporary example, Randall Collins (2009) has sought to develop a theory of violence that deals with everything from individuals skilled in violent interactions, such as attacking those who are weak, to the material resources needed by violent organizations to cause the destruction of other violent organizations. An example of the former type of violent organization is the well-equipped U.S. Navy SEALs team that killed Osama bin Laden in 2011 and through that act helped hasten the decline of al-Qaeda. A new violent organization, Islamic State, arose in 2014 and quickly routed the Iraqi army using, among other things, captured American weapons.

In fact, there is a continuum that runs from the most microscopic to the most macroscopic of social realities, with phenomena at roughly the midpoint of this continuum best thought of as meso (middle or intermediate) realities. The definition of sociology presented at the beginning of this chapter fits this continuum quite well. Individual actions and thoughts lie on the micro end of the continuum; groups, organizations, cultures, and societies fall more toward the macro end; and worldwide structures and processes are at the end point on the macro end of the continuum. Although in their own work the vast majority of individual sociologists focus on only very limited segments of this continuum, the field as a whole is concerned with

FIGURE 1.5 • Percentages of Women in Selected Occupations, 2010

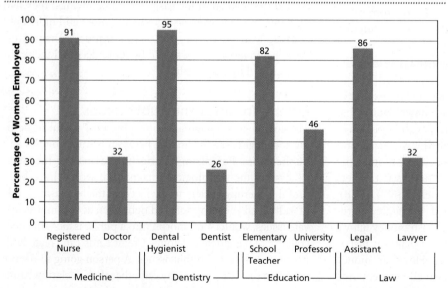

SOURCE: U.S. Census Bureau, 2012.

Granger

Workers and their unions is an example of the micro–macro relationship.

also constrained by it and the power it has over you. Agents (you as a student, in this case) have great power. Individual agents are **dangerous giants** (Goffman 1961b: 81). They have the potential to disrupt and destroy the structures in which they find themselves. Yet often agents do not realize the power they possess. As a result, social structures such as the university and the class you are currently taking function for long periods of time with little or no disruption by individual agents.

However, there are times, such as during the anti–Vietnam War protests of the late 1960s and early 1970s, when students come to realize that they are dangerous giants and act to change not only the university but also the larger society (Gitlin 1993). In one case, after a student protest that involved a six-day campout that completely trashed the office of Grayson Kirk, president of Columbia University, Kirk asked, "My god, how could human beings do a thing like this?"

There are far more minor, everyday actions that reflect the fact that people can be dangerous giants. Examples involving students include questioning a professor's argument or going to the dean to protest the excessive absences of an instructor. However, most people most of the time do not realize that they are dangerous giants.

THE SOCIAL CONSTRUCTION OF REALITY

The discussion of agency and structure leads to another basic concept in sociology: the **social construction of reality** (Berger and Luckmann 1967). People at the agency end of the continuum are seen as creating social reality, basically macro-level phenomena, through their thoughts and actions. That reality then comes to have a life of its own. That is, it becomes a structure that is partly or wholly separate from the people who created it and exist in it. Once macro phenomena have lives of their own, they constrain and even control what people do. Of course, people can refuse to accept these constraints and controls and create new social realities. This process of individual creation of structural realities, constraint, and coercion then begins anew, in a continuing loop. It is this continuous loop that is the heart of agency–structure and micro–macro relationships, the social world, and the field of sociology.

For example, in the realm of consumption, it is people—as designers, manufacturers, consumers, and bloggers—who create the world of fashion (Entwhistle 2009). However, once the fashion world comes into existence, that world has a great deal of influence over the social constructions, especially the tastes, of individuals who purchase the fashions it produces. Famous fashion houses such as Dior and Givenchy dominate the industry and perpetuate their existence through continual

the continuum in its entirety as well as with the interrelationships among its various components.

The Agency–Structure Relationship

American sociologists tend to think in terms of the micro–macro relationship. In other parts of the world, sociologists are more oriented to the agency–structure relationship. The agency–structure continuum is complex, but for our purposes we can think of agency as resembling the micro level and structure as resembling the macro level.

The utility of the agency–structure terminology is that it highlights several important social realities and aspects of the field of sociology. Of greatest significance is the fact that the term **agency** gives great importance to the individual—the "agent"—as having power and a capacity for creativity (Giddens 1984). In sociological work on agency, great emphasis is placed on the individual's mental abilities and the ways in which these abilities are used to create important, if not decisive, actions.

However, agents are seen as enmeshed in macro-level social and cultural structures that they create and by which they are constrained (King 2004). For example, as a student, you help create the university you attend, but you are style changes. These companies—and, more important, the "fast-fashion" companies that copy and mass-produce their products, like H&M, Forever 21, and Zara—control people's tastes in fashion and thereby the nature of the clothing they buy and wear. Changing fashions are highly profitable for the companies involved. Consumers are led to be eager to buy the latest fashions, although most often in the form of relatively inexpensive fast-fashion knockoffs.

Of course, many people do not accept such social constructions; they do not go along with the constraints of the fashion industry. They do not wear what the industry wants them to wear, and they do not change the way they dress because of changes in styles induced by the fashion industry. Many people have their own sense of fashion and create their own way of dressing. Others ignore fashion altogether. Of greatest importance from this perspective is the fact that the idea of what is in fashion often comes not from the fashion industry but rather from the ways of dressing that people put together themselves. These people, in a real sense, construct their own social reality. In fact, in a process known as "cool hunting" (Gloor and Cooper 2007), scouts for the fashion industry seek out new and interesting ways of dressing, often focusing on what young people in the suburbs and the inner cities are wearing. They bring those innovative ideas back to the fashion industry, and some of them are turned into the following year's fashions.

SOCIAL STRUCTURES AND PROCESSES

The nineteenth-century sociologist Auguste Comte was important not only for inventing the term *sociology* in 1839 but also for being the originator of sociology as a field. Crucial for our purposes here is his early distinction between what he called "social statics" and "social dynamics." In his social statics, Comte (1856) looked at the various "parts" (structures) of society, such as the manufacturers and retailers of clothing fashions, and the ways in which they relate to one another as well as to the whole of society. In examining such relationships, Comte investigated social processes among and between parts of society as well as in society as a whole. However, under the heading of social dynamics, his main focus was on a specific social process—social change—and how the various parts of society change.

It is important to emphasize here that **social structures** are enduring and regular social arrangements, such as the family and the state. When social structures change, they change very slowly. **Social processes** are the dynamic and ever-changing aspects of the social world.

The elements of globalization can be divided between structures (e.g., the United Nations) and a variety of more specific social processes (e.g., the migration of people across national borders). In terms of consumption, we can think of the shopping mall (or Amazon.com) as a structure and the shopping (or consumption) that takes place in it as a process. Finally,

The Granger Collection, NYC

Auguste Comte was an early sociological theorist who was interested both in discovering the laws of the social world and in solving social problems.

the Internet as a whole and social networking sites in particular are structures, while the communication and the social interaction that take place in them can be viewed as processes.

Needless to say, neither the shopping mall nor the Internet existed in Comte's day. Once again we see that the social world is constantly changing and that sociologists, as well as students of sociology, must be sensitive to those changes. However, some of sociology's earliest concepts continue to be applicable, and usefully applied, to the social world.

SOCIOLOGY'S PURPOSE: SCIENCE OR SOCIAL REFORM?

Comte was famous not only for examining the relationship between structure and process but also for arguing that such study ought to be scientific. He believed that the social world was dominated by laws and that sociology's task was to uncover those laws. As those laws were uncovered, the science of sociology would develop. But Comte was also concerned about the problems of his day and interested in solving them through social reform. In fact, to Comte, science and reform should not be separated from one another. A number of classical sociologists—Karl Marx, Émile Durkheim, Jane Addams, and others—shared this view. Marx and Engels's *Communist Manifesto* (1848) was not only a commentary on the social ills of the capitalist economy but also a rallying cry to workers to organize and abolish capitalism.

Many of today's sociologists study social problems of all sorts, such as poverty and crime. They use a variety of scientific methods to collect large amounts of data on these problems (see Chapter 2). They also seek to use what they learn about the problems to suggest ways of reforming society. They believe that these two activities—scientific research and social reform—can and should be mutually enriching. While many contemporary sociologists accept this position, some sociologists focus more on scientific research and others are more engaged in activities designed to reform society and address social problems.

The sociologists who engage in "pure science" operate with the conviction that we need to have a better understanding of how the social world operates before we can change it. For example, "ethnomethodologists" (see Chapter 2) argue that the task of the sociologist is to improve our understanding of common forms of social behavior (Rawls 2011). They research the details of everyday life, such as how we know when a laugh is expected in a conversation, or when to applaud or boo during a speech. For them, the goal is purely knowledge and understanding. Such sociologists argue that using that knowledge to reform society might adversely affect or distort social behaviors.

Other sociologists take the opposite position. C. Wright Mills was little interested in doing scientific research. He was mostly interested in such social reforms as limiting or eliminating the unwholesome and worrisome ties between the military and industry in the United States. He was also critical of many of the most prominent sociologists of his day for their orientation toward being pure scientists, their lack of concern for the pressing problems of the day, and their unwillingness to do anything about those problems.

Feminist sociologists have extended the argument, pointing out that the topics and methods of objective, scientific sociology themselves sometimes reflect, and ultimately reinforce, social inequality along the lines of race, gender, and class because they are based on the assumptions of society's elite. For example, feminist scholar Cynthia Fuchs Epstein (1988) has argued that supposedly scientific distinctions between males and females have often been based on social biases. These social biases can be explained by the "prejudices against women and cultural notions emphasizing differences between the sexes" (Epstein 1988: 17).

ASK YOURSELF

What do you believe should be the main purpose of sociology: pure science or social reform? Why? Make a note to ask yourself this question again at the end of your course. Did you answer it differently?

SOCIOLOGY, THE OTHER SOCIAL SCIENCES, AND COMMON SENSE

Sociology is one of the social sciences—that is, it is one of the fields that studies various aspects of the social world. Among the others are anthropology, communication studies, economics, geography, political science, and psychology. Generally speaking, sociology is the broadest of these fields; social scientists in other fields are more likely than sociologists to delve into specific aspects of the social world in great depth. Sociological study touches on the culture of concern to anthropologists, the nation-state of interest to political scientists, and the mental processes that are the focus of psychologists. However, that does not mean that sociology is in any sense "better" than—or, conversely, not as good as—the other social sciences.

This concluding section will focus on the different ways in which these fields approach one of this book's signature concerns—globalization.

- *Anthropology:* Focuses on cultural aspects of societies around the world, such as the foods people eat and how they eat them, as well as the differences among cultures around the globe (Inda and Rosaldo 2008).

- *Communication studies:* Examines communications across the globe, with the Internet obviously of focal concern in the contemporary world.

- *Economics:* Investigates the production, distribution, and consumption of resources through markets and other structures that span much of the globe, especially those based on and involving money.

- *Geography:* Studies spatial relationships on a global scale and maps those spaces (Herod 2009).

- *Political science:* Studies nation-states, especially the ways in which they relate to one another around the world as well as how they have grown increasingly unable to control global flows of migrants, viruses, recreational drugs, Internet scams, and the like.

- *Psychology:* Examines the ways in which individual identities are shaped by increased awareness of the rest of the world and tensions associated with globalization (e.g., job loss), which may lead to individual psychological problems such as depression (Lemert and Elliott 2006).

Sociology encompasses all these concerns, and many others, in its approach to globalization. It studies globe-straddling cultures (such as consumer culture or fast-food culture), relationships between political systems (the European Union and its member nations, for example), communication networks (such as CNN and Al Jazeera or Twitter and

Facebook), and markets (for labor or stocks and bonds, for example) that cover vast expanses of the globe. Sociology maps all of these, as well as their impacts, both good and bad, on individuals. You might want to study the other fields to get a sense of the depth of what they have to offer on specific aspects of globalization. However, if you are looking for the field that gives you the broadest possible view of all of these things as well as the ways in which they interrelate, that field is sociology.

While sociology and the other social sciences differ from one another in important ways, they are all quite different from commonsense understandings of the social world. Everyone participates in globalization in one way or another. However, few if any people research these phenomena in the same rigorous way and to the same degree that social scientists examine them. That research leads to, among other things, a greater understanding of the nature of globalization. For example, you probably have a sense that globalization has changed society—perhaps even an impression that it is changing your life. What you are unlikely to know are globalization's causes, effects, and linkages to other social phenomena, or its largely invisible effects on society and the world. Research on the topic is also likely to yield much more insight into the pros and cons of globalization on the personal, societal, and global levels. Such detailed knowledge and insight will help you, and others, more successfully navigate the accompanying changes in social processes and structures.

One example of the gap between common sense and social scientific knowledge relates to perceptions of the gap between the rich and the poor. A study of more than 5,000 Americans showed that people believe that the top fifth of the

FIGURE 1.6 • Wealth of the Top 20 Percent of U.S. Residents: Popular Views versus Reality

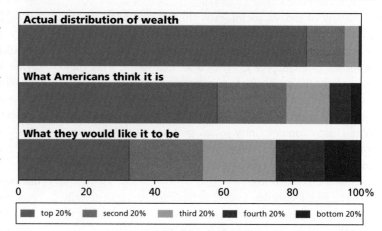

population in the United States possesses about 59 percent of the country's wealth. In fact, however, the top fifth actually holds almost 84 percent of the wealth (Norton and Ariely 2011). Figure 1.6 shows the results of this study. The commonsense view, then, is that wealth is far more evenly distributed than the scientific data reveal. This study also refuted the commonsense idea that the United States is a fair and equal society. When respondents were asked what the ideal wealth distribution would be, the average response was that the top fifth of the population should own only 32 percent of the wealth, not the 59 percent they guessed and certainly not the 84 percent that the upper fifth actually possesses.

While common sense is important, even to sociologists, there is no substitute for the systematic study of the social world in both its minutest detail and its broadest manifestations.

SUMMARY

Social changes in the last few centuries, including the Industrial Revolution, the growth of white-collar work, the increased participation of women in the labor force, and the arrival of the information age, have set the stage for sociology to come into its own. Sociology is the systematic examination of the ways in which people are affected by and affect the social structures and social processes associated with the groups, organizations, cultures, societies, and world in which they exist. This book deals with innumerable social issues, but it focuses especially on three powerful structural forces in the social world that have drawn the attention of contemporary sociologists: globalization, consumption, and digital technology.

As the world has become more globalized, individual societies have lost some of their significance, and larger, transnational organizations have become more prominent. Global society has also become more fluid. People move more quickly and easily across borders, as do goods, messages, and music, among many other things.

Consumption is the process by which people obtain and utilize various goods and services. While it may seem like a positive force, sociologists have also identified some of its negative aspects. Among these are overconsumption, excessive and rising debt, and the increasing likelihood of defining ourselves by what we own rather than by our actions or our social relationships.

Life in the digital world and its links to life in the real world have become major topics of study for sociologists. Technology also plays an important role in consumption, particularly with the shift from highly social shopping experiences, such as in a mall with other people, to the more isolated experience of shopping online.

The McDonaldization of society brings the rational principles of the fast-food industry into prominence in additional sectors of society and the world. These principles are efficiency, calculability, predictability, and control.

All these changes are easier to understand using C. Wright Mills's "sociological imagination," which calls on us to look at phenomena not just from a personal perspective but also from the outside, from a distinctively sociological perspective. It is also helpful to see the relationship between private troubles and larger public issues and to acknowledge that much of our reality is socially constructed.

Sociologists study many topics, sometimes to understand them through scientific research and sometimes to help generate change and reform. Many of the topics discussed in this book are familiar to you from your daily life. Try to take a more systematic sociological approach to understanding them. Keep in mind that sociological phenomena are all around you, and keep your own sociological imagination honed and ready as you explore the social world.

REVIEW QUESTIONS

1. Use your sociological imagination to think of ways that your individual choices and actions will be influenced by ongoing developments in the Muslim world.

2. Your social world is continually changing. What are some examples of new technologies that have been developed during your lifetime? How have they changed the way you interact with and relate to others?

3. How do shopping malls reflect increasing globalization? Do you think shopping malls lead to a sameness of culture around the world, or do they allow local areas to retain their differences?

4. What items are you most likely to buy using the Internet? How do social networking sites (Facebook, Twitter, Instagram) influence what you consume?

5. Beginning in 2010, WikiLeaks released thousands of confidential documents obtained from government, military, and corporate sources. What social structures have impeded the flow of this kind of information in the past? How have the Internet and social networking sites made it easier to get around these structural barriers?

6. According to C. Wright Mills, how are private troubles different from public issues? How can we use the micro/macro distinction to show how private troubles are related to public issues?

7. What is the difference between structure and agency? Within your classroom, could you be a "dangerous giant"? In what ways does your school prevent you from becoming a dangerous giant?

8. What do sociologists mean by the social construction of reality? How can you apply this perspective to better understand trends in the music industry?

9. How is *The McDonaldization of Society* an example of public sociology? Can you think of ways in which we can use "pure science" to better understand the process of McDonaldization? What do you believe should be the goal of research?

10. How is sociology's approach to globalization different from those of other social sciences? What are the advantages of using a sociological approach to understanding globalization?

APPLYING THE SOCIOLOGICAL IMAGINATION

Twitter has emerged as a way to share information instantaneously and to keep up-to-date with what is happening. But how can we use Twitter to make sense of the interrelated processes of globalization and consumption?

For this activity, go to Twitter.com and find the day's top trending topics worldwide. Explore these top trends by clicking on them and looking at the specific tweets. Do research online to get information on topics mentioned in the tweets that are unfamiliar to you.

In what ways are these topics and tweets reflective of a globalized world? How are these topics and tweets related to goods and services that you consume? In what ways does Twitter facilitate the flow of information and goods globally? How does this influence the decisions and choices that individuals make at the micro level? How do these trends affect your own choices?

KEY TERMS

agency: The potential to disrupt or destroy the structures in which one finds oneself. (p. 15)

consumption: The process by which people obtain and utilize goods and services. (p. 6)

dangerous giant: An agent who threatens social structures. (p. 15)

globalization: The increasing fluidity of global flows and the structures that expedite and impede those flows. (p. 6)

macro: Macroscopic; used to describe large-scale social phenomena such as groups, organizations, cultures, society, and the globe. (p. 14)

McDonaldization: The process by which the rational principles of the fast-food restaurant are coming to dominate more and more sectors of society and more societies throughout the world. (p. 9)

mediated interaction: Social interaction in which technological devices come between the participants, unlike in face-to-face interaction. (p. 12)

micro: Microscopic; used to describe small-scale social phenomena such as individuals and their thoughts and actions. (p. 14)

public sociology: Sociological work addressed to a wide range of audiences, most of which are outside the academy,

including a variety of local, national, and global groups. (p. 4)

social construction of reality: The continuous process of individual creation of structural realities and the constraint and coercion exercised by those structures. (p. 15)

social processes: The dynamic and ever-changing aspects of the social world. (p. 16)

social structures: Enduring and regular social arrangements, such as the family and the state. (p. 16)

society: A complex pattern of social relationships that is bounded in space and persists over time. (p. 5)

sociological imagination: A unique perspective that gives sociologists a distinctive way of looking at data and reflecting on the world around them. (p. 13)

sociology: The systematic study of the ways in which people are affected by and affect the social structures and social processes that are associated with the groups, organizations, cultures, societies, and world in which they exist. (p. 2)

technology: The interplay of machines, tools, skills, and procedures for the accomplishment of tasks. (p. 11)

$SAGE edge™ edge.sagepub.com/ritzeressentials2e

SAGE edge offers a robust online environment featuring an impressive array of free tools and resources for review, study, and further exploration, keeping both instructors and students on the cutting edge of teaching and learning.

LEARNING OBJECTIVES	FOR FURTHER EXPLORATION AND APPLICATION
LO 1-1: Identify major social changes since the 1880s studied by sociologists.	▶ How Social Networks Changed the World ◉ Should Internships Be Paid, Unpaid, or Illegal? ▣ The Origins and Effects of the Industrial Revolution
LO 1-2: Explain why sociologists today focus on trends in globalization and consumption.	▶ Blogging to Enhance Student Engagement in Social Problems ◉ How Globalization Impacts the Third World ▣ The Ultimate Media Consumption Device
LO 1-3: Describe what we mean by the McDonaldization of society.	▶ Understanding the McDonaldization Theory ◉ Saying Sayonara to "Super-Size Me" ▣ The Effects of Fast-Tracking Higher Education
LO 1-4: Explain sociology's approach to studying social life, including using the sociological imagination and examining the relationship between private troubles and public issues.	▶ The Sociological Imagination Explained ◉ Motivation behind Boston Marathon Bombing ▣ The International Center for Research on Women
LO 1-5: Differentiate between sociology's two possible purposes, science and social reform.	▶ "Data Science for Social Good" Summer Fellowship ◉ Defining the New "Social Animal" ▣ Using Social Media Outlets to Study Society
LO 1-6: Evaluate the ways in which sociological knowledge differs from common sense.	▶ Unravel the Myth of Common Sense ◉ Does Political Correctness Stifle Creativity? ▣ Sociology versus the Obvious

THINKING ABOUT AND RESEARCHING THE SOCIAL WORLD

Sociologists Theorize about and Study Climate Change

Humankind has made amazing advances during its existence on Earth, especially in the last few centuries. Developments from the Industrial Revolution to the current era of globalization have allowed many of us to enjoy longer lives, improved standards of living, instantaneous communication, and the ability to travel easily anywhere in the world. But our advancement as a species has come at a significant ecological price.

Climate change, marked by long-term fluctuations in Earth's intricate and interwoven weather patterns, has occurred since the formation of the planet. Although gradual climate change is a natural process, a growing body of careful research suggests that significant recent, potentially disastrous, changes are directly attributable to human actions, including the use of fossil fuels and deforestation.

Despite this scientific consensus, the human impact on climate change remains a hotly debated issue. If the available geological, atmospheric, and oceanographic evidence is solid enough to convince the scientific community, why do so many people remain fiercely unconvinced? Who is opposed to the notion that human actions are a major cause of climate change, and how have institutional forces influenced their personal beliefs over time?

Physical science can help us understand and explain climate change, but to understand the motivations, beliefs, and actions that affect our role in and response to it, we need sociologists

LEARNING OBJECTIVES

2-1 Define what theories are and explain why they are important in understanding social phenomena.

2-2 Identify the most important classical sociologists, particularly Marx, Weber, and Durkheim, and their major contributions to the field.

2-3 Compare and contrast the strengths and weaknesses of structural/functional, conflict/critical, and inter/actionist theories.

2-4 Describe the scientific method.

2-5 Describe the various methods of sociological research and the types of questions each one can help us answer.

2-6 Describe how sociologists engage in secondary data analysis.

2-7 Identify the key issues in social research, including reliability, validity, trust, legality, and objectivity.

Associated Press

and their theories and research methods. A sociologist's perspective is framed by the theories to which he or she subscribes. For example, a conflict theorist would frame the debate over climate change as a struggle between the strong and the weak. Powerful oil corporations might deny that climate change is a result of the burning of fossil fuels and therefore claim it is not their responsibility. Weaker groups suffering from the effects of climate change, such as the Tuvaluans, whose island is threatened by rising sea levels, might blame the oil companies and climate change for this catastrophe.

Sociologists not only have a number of theories to choose from, but they also have many different research methods at their disposal to study the debate about climate change. For example, they could use surveys to gather quantitative data on how many Tuvaluans believe human activities are causing climate change or conduct open-ended interviews with Tuvaluans to collect descriptive data on how they experience this debate in their everyday lives. With its many theories and methods, sociology is a science, like—and also unlike— any other. ●

THEORIZING THE SOCIAL WORLD

Sociological theories and methods are not, and should not be, clearly separated. However, to make it easier to understand them, this chapter is divided into two major sections. In this one we deal with theorizing, or thinking about, social issues, and in the next we discuss the use of sociological methods to research those issues.

Theories are sets of interrelated ideas that have a wide range of applications, deal with centrally important issues, and have stood the test of time (Ritzer and Stepnisky 2014). Theories can be said to have stood the test of time when they continue to be applicable to the changing social world and have withstood challenges from those who accept other theories. Sociological theories are necessary to make sense of both the innumerable social phenomena and the many highly detailed findings of sociological research. Without such theories, we would have little more than knowledge of isolated bits of the social world. However, once those theories have been created, they can be applied broadly to many areas, such as the economy, organizations, and religion, as well as to society as a whole and even the globe. The theories to be discussed in this chapter deal with very important social issues that have affected the social world for centuries and will likely continue to affect it.

CLASSICAL SOCIOLOGICAL THEORY

The emergence of sociological theory was closely related to intellectual and social developments throughout the nineteenth century in Europe, including the political revolutions that wracked European society (especially the French Revolution, 1789–1799), the rise of socialism, the women's rights movement, rapid urbanization, ferment in the religious realm, and the growth of science.

Among the most important early sociological theorists are Auguste Comte, Harriet Martineau, and Herbert Spencer:

- *Auguste Comte* invented the term *sociology* and developed a general, scientific theory of the social world (Pickering 2011).

- *Harriet Martineau,* like Comte, developed a scientific and general theory, although she is best known today for her feminist, women-centered sociology (Hoecker-Drysdale 2011).

- *Herbert Spencer* also developed a general, scientific theory of society, but his overriding theoretical interest was in evolutionary social change (Francis 2011).

Granger

Harriet Martineau was an unusual woman for her time, both in being well educated and in supporting her family with her published writing. What career might she pursue today?

Although Comte, Martineau, and Spencer were important predecessors, three other thinkers—Karl Marx, Max Weber, and Émile Durkheim—are the most significant of the classical era's social theorists and of the greatest continuing contemporary relevance to sociology (and other fields).

Karl Marx

Marx focused most of his attention on the structure of capitalist society. He defined **capitalism** as an economic system based on the fact that one group of people—the **capitalists**—owns what is needed for production, including factories, machines, and tools. A second group—the **proletariat**, or workers—owns little or nothing except their capacity for work and labor. In order to survive, the workers must sell their labor time to the capitalists in exchange for wages.

In Marx's view, the capitalist system is marked by **exploitation**. The proletariat produces virtually everything but gets only a small portion of the income derived from the sale of the products. The capitalists, who do little productive work, reap the vast majority of the rewards. Driven by the need to compete in the marketplace, the capitalists are forced to keep costs, including wages, as low as possible. Then, as competition with other capitalists intensifies, there is pressure to reduce wages further. As a result, the proletariat barely subsists, living a miserable, animal-like existence.

In addition, the workers experience **alienation** in the workplace (Mészáros 2006). They are alienated because

- the work they do—for example, repetitively and mechanically attaching hubcaps to cars—is not a natural expression of human skills, abilities, and creativity;
- they have little or no connection to the finished product; and
- instead of working harmoniously with their fellow workers, they may have little or no contact with them and compete with them to keep their jobs.

Thus, what defines people as human beings—their ability to think, to act on the basis of that thought, to be creative, to interact with other human beings—is denied to the workers in capitalism.

Over time the workers' situation grows much worse as the capitalists increase the level of exploitation and restructure the work so that the proletariat becomes even more alienated. Once workers understand how capitalism "really" works, especially the ways in which it works to their detriment, they will rise up and overthrow that system in a proletarian revolution and create a communist society.

Marx's theories about capitalism are relevant to contemporary society. For example, in the United States, a capitalist country, the disparity he predicted between those at the top of the economic system and the rest of the population is huge and growing. In 2013, the top 20 percent of the population

Karl Marx's work is often misunderstood, but his criticisms of capitalism, based on his humanism and idealism, are still influential today. What is your understanding of his theories?

in terms of household income had a greater average income than the rest of the population combined. Furthermore, as you can see in Figure 2.1, those at the top have greatly increased their average income since 1967; this is especially true of the top 5 percent of the population. In contrast, the lowest fifth has a lower average income than it had in 1967 (DeNavas-Walt, Proctor, and Smith 2012). However, history has failed to bear out much of Marx's thinking about the demise of capitalism. For example, there has been no proletarian revolution, and communism has failed. Although capitalism continues to exist, Marx's ways of thinking about it remain useful.

Max Weber

Weber's best-known work, *The Protestant Ethic and the Spirit of Capitalism* ([1904–1905] 1958), is part of his historical-comparative study of religion in various societies throughout the world (see "Historical-Comparative Method" later in this chapter). One of Weber's main objectives in this work was to analyze the relationship between the economy and religion. Like Marx, Weber accepted the central importance of the economy in general, and of capitalism in particular, but he wanted to demonstrate the importance of other sociological variables, especially the central role religion had played in the Western world's economic development.

Unlike Marx, Weber was not focally interested in capitalism per se. He was more interested in the broader phenomenon of **rationalization**, or the process by which social structures are increasingly characterized by the most direct and efficient means to their ends. In Weber's view, this process was becoming more and more common in many sectors of society, especially in bureaucracies and in the capitalist system. Capitalism is rational because of its continual efforts to find ways to produce more profitable products efficiently, with fewer inputs and simpler processes. An early example of rationalization in capitalism is the assembly line, in which raw materials enter the line and finished products emerge at the end. A more recent example is the fast-food restaurant's drive-through window.

Weber had a largely negative view of rationalization. He saw it as leading to an "iron cage," making it increasingly difficult for people to escape the process. In addition, as action comes to be guided more by efficiency than by ethics, magic, or even love, a gradual disenchantment with the world occurs (Shull 2005). This unfavorable attitude toward rationalization and its socially harmful effects has persisted and has frequently been portrayed in novels, such as George Orwell's *Nineteen Eighty-Four* (1949), and in movies, including *Brazil* (1985), *V for Vendetta* (2005), and the *Hunger Games* series (2012–2015).

Granger

Max Weber, who initially studied law, suffered a nervous breakdown triggered by a fight with his father shortly before his father's death and did not work for several years. Over the course of his lifetime, however, he was extremely productive.

FIGURE 2.1 • Mean Household Income Received by Each Fifth and Top 5 Percent, All Races: 1967 to 2013

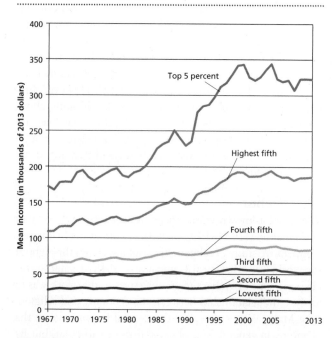

SOURCE: Data from U.S. Census Bureau, Current Population Survey, Annual Social and Economic Supplements.

Whereas Marx was optimistic and had great hope for communism, Weber was pessimistic about communism because it would not eliminate or prevent the iron cage from enveloping us. In fact, it would make the cage stronger because communism is a highly rationalized and bureaucratized system (Weber [1919] 1958: 128).

Émile Durkheim

For Durkheim, the major concern of the science of sociology was **social facts**. These are macro-level phenomena, such as social structures and cultural norms and values, that stand apart from people and, more important, impose themselves on people. Examples of social facts that impose themselves on you include the structures of your university and the U.S. government. Durkheim felt that such structures and their constraints were not only necessary but also highly desirable.

Both Marx and Weber had a generally positive sense of people as thoughtful, creative, and naturally social. They criticized social structures for stifling and distorting people's innate characteristics. In contrast, Durkheim saw people as being slaves to their passions. Left to their own devices, he believed, people would relentlessly seek to satisfy those

Émile Durkheim, from a family of rabbis, spent much of his life studying religion through a sociological lens, though not as a practicing Jew. Does studying sociology or any other science preclude an individual from holding deep religious beliefs?

passions. However, the satisfaction of one passion would simply lead to the need to satisfy others. In Durkheim's view, passions should be limited, but people are unable to exercise this control themselves. They need social facts that are capable of limiting their passions.

The most important of these social facts is the **collective conscience**, or the set of beliefs shared by people throughout society. In Durkheim's view, the collective conscience is a good thing. Without it, murderous passions would destroy individuals as well as society as a whole. The collective conscience is highly beneficial to society because it provides social integration and regulation.

Durkheim's understanding of the collective conscience informed his book *Suicide* ([1897] 1951), which demonstrates the power of sociology to explain one of the most private and personal of acts. Durkheim believed that if sociology could be shown to be applicable to suicide, it could deal with any and all social phenomena. He did not focus on why any given individual committed suicide. Rather, he dealt with the more collective issue of suicide rates and why one group of people had a higher rate of suicide than another. Using publicly available data, Durkheim found that suicide rates were not related to individual psychological and biological factors such as alcoholism, race, and heredity. Rather, suicide rates were related to social factors that exert negative pressure on the individual, including collective feelings of rootlessness and normlessness. Durkheim differentiated among four types of suicide. The most important of these for our purposes is *anomic suicide*. **Anomie** is defined as people's feeling that they do not know what is expected of them—the feeling of being adrift in society without any clear or secure moorings. According to Durkheim, the risk of anomie, and therefore of anomic suicide, increases when society's regulation over people is weak.

ASK YOURSELF

Does publicity associated with the suicide of a famous person, such as that of comedian Robin Williams in 2014, lead other people to commit suicide? Why? How do you think Durkheim would answer this question?

More generally, Durkheim believed that anomie is the defining problem of the modern world. This belief is central to another of his famous works, *The Division of Labor in Society* ([1893] 1964), which argued that an increasing division of labor took place over time. Instead of most workers doing the same sorts of things, people began to specialize. This resulted in people no longer necessarily sharing as strongly in the same set of ideas. This weakened the collective conscience, with the result that people were more likely to feel anomic and, among other things, were more likely to commit suicide.

OTHER IMPORTANT EARLY THEORISTS

Georg Simmel, W. E. B. Du Bois, and Thorstein Veblen also developed important social theories, and their ideas will be referred to throughout this book.

Georg Simmel

Simmel's major importance to sociology lies in his contributions to micro theory, especially the ways in which conscious individuals interact and associate with one another (Scaff 2011). Simmel was interested in the *forms* taken by social interaction. One such form involves the interaction between superiors and subordinates. He was also interested in the *types* of people who engage in interaction. For example, one type is the poor person and another is the rich person. For Simmel, it was the nature of the interaction between these two types of people and not the nature of the people themselves that was of greatest importance. Therefore, poverty is not about the nature of the poor person but about the kind of interaction that takes place between the poor and the rich.

Georg Simmel, W. E. B. Du Bois, and Thorstein Veblen were early sociological theorists who developed a number of ideas that are of continuing relevance to the contemporary world.

W. E. B. Du Bois

Du Bois is best known in sociology for his theoretical ideas, in particular concerning the "color line" existing between whites and blacks in the United States (Taylor 2011). This barrier was physical, but it was also political in that much of the white population did not see or accept African Americans as "true" Americans. One of Du Bois's ([1903] 1966) goals was to lift the veil of race and give whites a glimpse of "Negroes" in America. He also wanted to show blacks that they could see themselves in a different way, especially outside the view that white society had prescribed for them. Another of Du Bois's important ideas is **double consciousness**. By this he meant that black Americans have a sense of "two-ness," of being American and of being African American. Double consciousness produces great tension for black Americans, a tension much greater than that felt by white Americans in regard to their race. However, it also gives black Americans unusual insights into themselves, white Americans, and American society in general.

Thorstein Veblen

One of Veblen's ([1899] 1994) main concerns involved the ways in which the upper classes demonstrate their wealth. One way they do this is through *conspicuous leisure,* or doing things that demonstrate quite publicly that they do not need to do what most people consider to be work. However, the problem with conspicuous leisure is that it is often difficult for very many others to witness these displays. Thus, over time the focus of the wealthy shifts from publicly demonstrating a waste of time to publicly demonstrating a waste of money, or what Veblen called **conspicuous**

consumption. It is much easier for others to see forms of conspicuous consumption, such as driving a Porsche or wearing Dolce & Gabbana clothing, with its highly visible D&G logo. Veblen is important because he focused on consumption at a time when it was largely ignored by other social theorists.

CONTEMPORARY SOCIOLOGICAL THEORY

As sociology has grown as a discipline, the theories of earlier sociologists have evolved and branched out into at least a dozen newer theories. As Table 2.1 shows, these contemporary theories can be categorized under three broad headings: structural/functional, conflict/critical, and inter/actionist theories.

TABLE 2.1 • Major Sociological Theories

STRUCTURAL/ FUNCTIONAL THEORIES	CONFLICT/ CRITICAL THEORIES	INTER/ ACTIONIST THEORIES
Structural-functionalism	Conflict theory	Symbolic interactionism
Structuralism	Critical theory	Ethnomethodology
	Feminist theory	Exchange theory
	Queer theory	Rational choice theory
	Critical theories of race and racism	
	Postmodern theory	

Structural/Functional Theories

Structural/functional theories focus on large-scale social phenomena, including the state and culture, the latter encompassing the ideas and objects that allow people to carry out their collective lives (see Chapter 3 for more on culture). The two major theories under the broad heading of structural/functional theories are *structural-functionalism,* which looks at both social structures and their functions, and *structuralism,* which concerns itself solely with social structures, without concern for their functions. Note that while they sound the same, structural-functionalism is one theory under the broader heading of structural/functional theories.

Structural-Functionalism. Structural-functionalism focuses on social structures as well as the functions that such structures perform. Structural-functionalists are influenced by the work of, among others, Émile Durkheim. Like Durkheim, they have a positive view of social structures such as the military and the police, seeing them as desirable, necessary, and even impossible to do without. Structural-functionalism tends to be a "conservative" theory. The dominant view is that if certain structures exist and are functional, then they ought to be retained and conserved.

A series of well-known and useful concepts have been developed by structural-functionalists, especially Robert Merton ([1949] 1968; Crothers 2011). One central concept in Merton's version of structural-functionalism is that of **functions**. These are the observable, positive consequences of a structure that help it survive, adapt, and adjust. For example, national borders are functional in various ways. The passport controls at borders allow a country to monitor who is entering and to refuse entry to those it considers undesirable or dangerous (Torpey 2012). Merton differentiated between two types of functions. The first is **manifest functions**, or positive consequences brought about consciously and purposely. For example, the manifest function of tariffs imposed on goods imported into the United States is to make the prices of those goods higher compared with American-made goods and thereby protect U.S.-based producers. However, such actions often have **latent functions**, or unintended positive consequences. When foreign products become more expensive, U.S. manufacturers may produce more goods in the United States and create more jobs for Americans. In addition, functions can have either positive or negative **unanticipated consequences**. A negative unanticipated consequence of tariffs is a trade war. China, for example, might respond to an increase in U.S. tariffs by raising its own tariffs on U.S. imports.

Structural-functionalism is greatly enriched when we add the concept of **dysfunctions**, or observable consequences that negatively affect the ability of a given system to survive, adapt, or adjust. While border and passport controls clearly have functions, they also have dysfunctions. For example, after 9/11, Congress passed many immigration-related acts. As a result, it has become much more difficult to enter the

Increased U.S. border controls have various positive consequences (*functions*) such as making it more difficult for terrorists to enter the country, but there are also negative consequences (*dysfunctions*) such as making it more difficult for highly skilled workers to gain entry.

United States, not only for terrorists but also for students and highly educated workers (Kurzban 2006).

Structuralism. Structuralism focuses on structures but is not concerned with their functions. While structural-functionalism deals with quite visible structures such as border fences, structuralism is more interested in the social impacts of hidden or underlying structures, such as the global economic order or gender relations. It adopts the view that these hidden structures determine what transpires on the surface of the social world. Marx can be seen as a structuralist because he was interested in the hidden structures that determine how capitalism works. On the surface, capitalism seems to operate to the benefit of all. However, hidden below the surface is a structure that operates mostly for the benefit of the capitalists, who exploit workers.

Similarly, Marx's frequent collaborator Friedrich Engels ([1884] 1970) looked at relationships between women and men and theorized that the structures of capitalism and patriarchy kept women subordinated to men. Engels believed that female oppression was rooted in the hidden and underlying structure of private property rights in capitalism. When men gained control of agricultural production and wealth began to accumulate, men claimed more power over women. To guarantee the fidelity of wives and therefore the paternity of children, wives were subjugated to male power, and men sought to claim women as their own property.

A structuralist approach encourages sociologists to look beyond the surface for underlying structures and realities, which determine what transpires on the surface. For example, North Korea's military threats and test firing of missiles may not really be about military matters at all but instead about that country's failing economic system. North Korea may hope that the symbolic expression of military power will distract its citizens, strengthen its global prestige, frighten others, and perhaps coerce other countries, especially the United States, into providing economic aid.

Conflict/Critical Theories

Several theories are discussed under this heading: conflict theory, critical theory, feminist theory, queer theory, critical theories of race and racism, and postmodern theory. They all tend to emphasize stresses, strains, and conflicts in society. They are critical of society in a variety of ways, especially regarding the power that is exercised over less powerful members of society.

Conflict Theory. The best known of these theories is **conflict theory** (R. Collins 2012), which has roots in Marx's theory. While structural-functionalism emphasizes what is positive about society, conflict theory focuses on society's negative aspects. In contrast with structural-functionalists, who think that society is held together by consensus, conflict theorists argue that society is held together by coercion. Those who are adversely affected by society, especially economically, would rebel were it not for coercive forces like the police, the courts, and the military.

Ralf Dahrendorf (1959) was strongly influenced by Marx, but he was more strongly motivated by a desire to develop a viable alternative to structural-functionalism. For example, while structural-functionalists tend to see society as static, conflict theorists like Dahrendorf emphasize the ever-present possibility of change. Where structural-functionalists see the orderliness of society, conflict theorists see dissension and conflict everywhere. Finally, structural-functionalists focus on the sources of cohesion internal to society, while conflict theorists stress the coercion and power that holds together an otherwise fractious society.

Dahrendorf offered a sociological view of authority, arguing that it resides not in individuals (e.g., Barack Obama) but in positions (e.g., the presidency of the United States) and in various associations of people. In his view, those associations are controlled by a hierarchy of authority positions and the people who occupy them. However, there are many such associations in any society. Thus, a person may be in authority in one type of association but be subordinate in many others.

Dahrendorf was especially interested in the potential for conflict between those in positions of authority and those who are subordinate, because they usually hold different interests. For example, there is a potential for conflict to arise in a corporation between the top management, interested in higher profits, and low-level workers, interested in higher wages.

Critical Theory. While Marx's work was critical of the capitalist economy, **critical theory** shifts the focus to culture. Whereas Marx believed that culture is shaped by the economic system, the critical school argues that since the early twentieth century, and at an ever-accelerating rate to this day, culture has become important in its own right. Instead of being controlled by the capitalist economy, more of us are controlled, and controlled more often, by culture, specifically by the culture industry.

The **culture industry** consists of the rationalized and bureaucratized structures that dominate modern culture. In their early years, the 1920s and 1930s, critical theorists focused on radio, magazines, and movies. Today, movies remain important, but the focus has shifted to television and various aspects of the Internet. These are critiqued for producing, or serving as outlets for, **mass culture**, or cultural elements that are administered by organizations, lack spontaneity, and are phony. Two features of mass culture and its dissemination by the culture industry are of concern to critical theorists:

- *Falseness.* True culture should emanate from the people, but mass culture involves prepackaged sets of ideas that falsify reality. The so-called reality shows that dominate television today are a contemporary example of mass culture. They are presented as if they are authentic, but in fact they are scripted, highly controlled, and selectively edited.

- *Repressiveness.* The effect of mass culture is to pacify, stupefy, and repress the masses so that they are far less likely to demand social change. Those addicted to their favorite reality TV shows are unlikely to have much interest in, or time for, revolutionary activities, or even civic activities and reforms. Additionally, the culture industry has succeeded in creating a class of corporate brands that are globally recognized and sought after as cultural symbols (Arvidsson 2012; Lash and Lury 2007). Instead of engaging in revolutionary activities, many people strive to keep up with and acquire the latest and hottest brands.

Critical theory can be applied to some of the newest media forms, such as YouTube, Facebook, and eBay (Denegri-Knott and Zwick 2012). Despite there being plenty of false and stupefying content on these sites along with all the edifying material, the sites are not controlled by large rationalized bureaucracies—at least not yet.

Do you see evidence of critical theory's ideas of falseness and repressiveness in the elements of mass culture to which you are exposed? If so, what forms do the falseness and repressiveness take?

Feminist theory, including its critique of patriarchy, is a vibrant force in today's world.

Feminist Theory. A central aspect of **feminist theory** is the critique of patriarchy (male dominance) and the problems it poses not only for women but also for men. Feminist theory also offers ideas on how everyone's (women's *and* men's) situation can be bettered, if not revolutionized (Lengermann and Niebrugge-Brantley 2014; Tong, 2009). Despite the many global and individual changes that have taken place in women's lives, there is also a broad consensus among feminist theorists that women continue to face extraordinary problems related directly to gender inequality. As you will learn more about in Chapter 9, these problems include a persistent wage gap between men and women in the United States and systematic and widespread rape by invading forces in wartime. However, feminist theories vary in the degree to which they support dramatic, even revolutionary, changes in women's situation. Some suggest that the solution to gender inequality is to change social structures and institutions so they are more inclusive of women and allow more gender diversity. Other feminist theories argue that because those very structures and institutions create gender difference and inequality, we must first deconstruct and then rebuild them in a wholly different way.

Women of color have been dissatisfied with feminist theory for not representing their interests very well. Feminist theory generally reflects the perspective of white women while ignoring the unique experiences and viewpoints of women of color (Collins 2000; hooks 2000; Zinn 2012). Similarly, studies related to race tend to focus largely (or wholly) on the position of men. Many contemporary feminists have advocated scholarship that takes into account not just gender but also how it intersects with race and ethnicity, social class, and sexuality. The discussion of critical theories of race and racism in this chapter provides more detail on this view.

Queer Theory. Contemporary lesbians, bisexuals, and transgender and intersexed people have reclaimed the once negative label *queer* and given it a positive connotation. **Queer theory** challenges the traditional binary opposition between male and female; it argues instead that there are no fixed and stable identities determining who we are (Butler 1990; Plummer 2012). Some queer theorists posit that there are more than two genders, using the term **queergender** to connote a third gender. Others believe that it is possible to be **pangender**, or to identify as all genders. New pronouns such as *xe* and *ze* have been created to replace *he* and *she* (Scelfo 2015).

While queer theory does not focus exclusively on homosexuality, it does examine the dynamics of the relationship between heterosexuals and homosexuals. It is especially concerned with the historic, systematic exercise of power by heterosexuals over homosexuals. For example, homosexuals have often, at least in the past, governed their own behavior in public to avoid making heterosexuals feel uncomfortable, such as by forgoing mild displays of affection.

Critical Theories of Race and Racism. **Critical theories of race and racism** argue that racism continues to have adverse effects on people of color, especially in the United States (Outlaw 2010; Slatton and Feagin 2012). Critical theorists of race and racism argue that "color blindness," or the notion that race no longer matters in determining an individual's life chances and experiences, ignores the past and present realities facing racial minorities, including the social consequences of years of racial discrimination. Some suggest that color blindness is little more than a "new racism," a smoke screen that allows whites to practice and perpetuate racial discrimination (Bonilla-Silva 2009). Of particular importance to work in this area is the idea of **intersectionality** (Collins 1990), the concept that people are affected, often adversely, not only by their race but also by their gender, sexual orientation, class, age, and global location. The confluence, or intersection, of these various statuses and the inequality and oppression associated with the intersections are what matter most. For example, a poor black female lesbian faces a complex of problems different from, and perhaps more difficult than, the problems faced by a poor person or a black person or a woman or a lesbian.

Postmodern Theory. The term *postmodern* refers to a world that has moved beyond the modern era. **Postmodern theory** deals with this new epoch and is also a reaction against

The Voluntariat

A new term that builds on Karl Marx's concept of the proletariat (see page 25) is *the voluntariat* (Shullenberger 2014). While the proletariat works for low pay, the voluntariat works for *no pay*. The proletariat does work that requires little skill, but the voluntariat often does work that otherwise would be performed by highly paid skilled workers. Like the poorly paid labor of the proletariat, the free labor of the voluntariat contributes to a corporation's profitability. However, because skilled labor is more costly than labor requiring little skill, the voluntariat contributes much more to the profitability of capitalist firms, at least per person, than does the proletariat.

One example is those who perform free labor for massive open online courses, or MOOCs (Shullenberger 2014; see Chapter 11). Another is those who translate online courses taught in English into other languages at no charge, performing the work for its intrinsic reward. These workers are seen as "voluntarian scabs" because they threaten the livelihood of professional translators who do such work for a living. Free labor is often performed for corporations, including those developing MOOCs, that are aggressively seeking new ways to earn significant profits.

We are all voluntarians now on social media. When we post on Facebook or Twitter or buy products on Amazon.com, we are voluntarily providing invaluable and free information about ourselves that

The free labor of the voluntariat has replaced the paid labor of innumerable workers through, for example, self-check-in at airports and hotels. What are corporations giving you as a member of the voluntariat in return for your free labor?

these organizations could not otherwise obtain and that is the major source of their market value. Amazon's chairman and CEO Jeff Bezos believes Amazon.com can earn far more money exploiting the data provided by voluntarians than it can by selling products. It is increasingly clear that the free labor of voluntarians is preferable to even the poorly paid labor of the proletariat.

We are also increasingly voluntarians when we act as "working consumers" (Dujarier 2014) in using ATMs, scanning and bagging our own groceries in the supermarket, and putting our own IKEA furniture together. Voluntarianism increasingly pervades our lives on- and offline.

Think About It

Think about the various ways in which you meet the definition of voluntariat, on- and offline. Are people like Jeff Bezos (Amazon.com) and Mark Zuckerberg (Facebook) multibillionaires largely because of your free labor and that of millions of other voluntarians? How do you feel about that?

modern theory. Postmodern theorists are opposed to the broad depictions of history and society offered by modern theorists. An example of such a modern approach is Weber's theory of the increasing rationalization of the world and the rise of an "iron cage" constraining our thoughts and activities. Instead, postmodernists often deconstruct, or take apart, such modern grand narratives. Postmodernists are also opposed to the scientific pretensions of much modern social theory. Postmodern social theorists often look at familiar social phenomena in different ways or adopt very different focuses for their work. For example, in his study of the history of prisons, Michel Foucault ([1975] 1979) was critical of the modernist view that criminal justice had grown progressively liberal. He contended that prisons had, in fact, grown increasingly oppressive through the use of constant, enhanced surveillance of prisoners.

Jean Baudrillard described the postmodern world as characterized by **hyperconsumption**, which involves consuming more than we need, more than we really want, and more than we can afford. Baudrillard also saw the postmodern world as increasingly dominated by **simulations**—that is, inauthentic or fake versions of real things. For example, when we eat at McDonald's, we consume Chicken McNuggets, or simulated chicken. It is fake in the sense that it is often not meat from one chicken, but bits of meat that come from many different chickens and that contain many other ingredients.

Inter/Actionist Theories

The slash between *inter* and *actionist* in the heading to this section is meant to communicate the fact that we will deal with two closely related sets of theories here. The first consists of those theories that deal mainly with the interaction of two or more people (symbolic interactionism, ethnomethodology, and exchange theory). The second comprises those that focus more on the actions of individuals (rational choice theory). A common factor among these theories is that they focus on the micro level of individuals and groups. This is in contrast to the theories discussed above that focus on the macro structures of society.

Symbolic Interactionism. **Symbolic interactionism** is concerned with the interaction of two or more people through the use of symbols (Kotarba, Salvini, and Merrill 2012). We all engage in interaction on a daily basis, whether it be face-to-face or more indirectly via cell phone, e-mail, or social media. But this interaction could not take place without symbols: words, gestures, and even objects that stand for things. Symbols allow the communication of meaning among a group of people. Although we can interact with one another without words, such as through physical gestures like the shrug of a shoulder, in the vast majority of cases we need and use words to interact.

Symbolic interactionism has several basic principles:

- Human beings have a great innate capacity for thought, but it is shaped by social interaction. It is during social interaction that people acquire the symbolic meanings that allow them to exercise their distinctive ability to think.

- Symbolic meanings are not set in stone. People are able to modify them based on a given situation and their interpretation of it. The Christian cross, for example, is a symbol whose meaning can vary. Christians throughout the world define it in positive ways, but many in the Islamic world view it as a negative symbol associated with the medieval Crusades waged against their world by the Christian West.

- People are able to modify symbolic meanings because of their unique ability to think. Symbolic interactionists frame thinking as people's ability to interact with themselves. In that interaction with themselves, people are able to alter symbolic meanings. They are also able to examine various courses of action open to them in given situations, to assess the relative advantages and disadvantages of each, and then to choose among them.

- It is the pattern of those choices, of individual action and interaction, that is the basis of groups, larger structures such as bureaucracies, and society as a whole.

While symbolic interactionism deals primarily with people's interactions, it is also concerned with the thought processes that are deeply implicated in these interactions.

Ethnomethodology. **Ethnomethodology** focuses on what people *do* rather than on what they think (Liu 2012). Ethnomethodologists study the ways people organize everyday life, and their view of large-scale social structures differs from that of structural/functionalists, who tend to see those structures as highly constraining. Ethnomethodologists argue that this view tells us very little about what really goes on within structures such as courtrooms and hospitals. Rather than being constrained, people act within these structures and go about much of their business using common sense rather than official procedures.

The best-known ethnomethodological approach relates to gender (Stokoe 2006). Ethnomethodologists point out that people often erroneously think of gender as being biologically based. It is generally assumed that we do not have to do or say anything in order to be considered masculine or feminine; we are born that way. But, in fact, there are things we all do (e.g., the way we walk) and say (e.g., the tone of our voice) that allow us to accomplish being masculine or feminine. That is, being masculine or feminine is based on what people do on a regular basis. This is clearest in the case of those who are defined as being male or female at birth (based on biological characteristics) but then later do and say things that lead others to see them as belonging to the other gender (based on social characteristics).

Exchange Theory. Like ethnomethodologists, exchange theorists are not concerned with what goes on in people's minds. They are interested in the behavior itself and the associated rewards and costs (Molm, Whithama, and Melameda 2012). The key figure in **exchange theory**, George Homans (1910–1989), argued that instead of studying large-scale structures, sociologists should study the "elementary forms of social life" (Homans 1961: 13). Exchange theorists are particularly

Associated Press

The Christian cross is an uplifting symbol to many, but it is a negative symbol to others. How does the emotional impact of a symbol change within different cultural contexts?

interested in social behavior that involves two or more people and a variety of tangible and intangible exchanges. For example, you can reward someone who does you a favor with a tangible gift or with more intangible words of praise. Such exchanges are not always rewarding; they may also be punitive. You could, for example, punish someone who wrongs you by complaining about him to mutual acquaintances.

While exchange theory retains an interest in the elementary forms of social behavior, it has grown more concerned with how those forms lead to more complex social situations. That is, individual exchanges can develop into persistent **exchange relationships**. One particular type of exchange relationship is "hooking up," forming sexual relationships that are also sometimes called "friends with benefits." For example, because you and another person find your initial sexual interactions rewarding, you may develop a pattern of repeat interactions (also known as "hookups" or "booty calls"). Exchange relationships, including hookups, rarely develop in isolation from other exchange relationships. Sociologists study how hooking up happens within the context of college campuses, for example, where it has been normalized.

Rational Choice Theory. In **rational choice theory** people are regarded as rational, but the focus is not exchange, rewards,

and costs. Rather, the focus is on people having goals and intending to do certain things. To achieve their goals, people have a variety of means available to them and choose among the available means on a rational basis. They choose the means that are likely to best satisfy their needs and wants (Kroneberg and Kalter 2012). Important variables that constrain the ability to act rationally are access to scarce resources and the rules within social structures that restrict particular actions (Friedman and Hechter 1988). For example, if you do not have access to sufficient money, you cannot purchase a new car. If you are confined within a prison, you do not have the opportunity to drive a car, much less purchase one.

Rational choice theorists understand that people do not always act rationally. They argue, however, that their predictions about people's behavior generally hold despite occasional deviations (Coleman 1990; Zafirovski 2013).

RESEARCHING THE SOCIAL WORLD

Sociology is a science of the social world, and research is absolutely central to such a science. All sociologists study others' research and most do research of their own. Sociologists may theorize, speculate, and even rely on their imaginations for answers to questions about society. However, they almost always do so on the basis of data or information derived from research. Put another way, sociologists practice **empiricism**, which means that they gather information and evidence using their senses, especially their eyes and ears. In addition to using their senses, sociologists adopt the *systematic* scientific method in search of a thorough understanding of the social world. They have a variety of methods at their disposal in researching and analyzing society.

THE SCIENTIFIC METHOD

The **scientific method** is a structured way of finding answers to questions about the world (Carey 2011). The scientific method employed by sociologists is much the same as that used in other sciences. The following steps constitute the basic scientific method:

1. A sociologist uncovers *questions in need of answers*. These questions can be inspired by key issues in the larger society, personal experiences, or topics of concern specifically in sociology. The best and most durable research and findings often stem from issues that the researcher connects with personally. Karl Marx, for example, detested the exploitation of workers that characterized capitalism; Max Weber feared the depersonalizing impact of rationalized bureaucracies.

2. Sociologists review the *relevant literature* on the questions of interest to them. This is because others have likely done similar or related research in the past, and it would make no sense to start over from the beginning. For example, my work on McDonaldization (Ritzer 2015; see Chapter 1) is based on a review of work on rationalization by Max Weber ([1921] 1968), his successors (such as Kalberg 1980), and contemporary researchers (Ram 2007). Other scholars have since reviewed my work and that of other scholars on McDonaldization (for a collection of this work, see Ritzer 2010c) and extended it to religion (Drane 2008, 2012), higher education (Hayes and Wynyard 2002), social work (Dustin 2007), and Disney World (Bryman 2004).

3. Researchers often develop *hypotheses,* or educated guesses, about how social phenomena can be expected to relate to one another. For example, Uri Ram (2007) hypothesized that Israeli society would grow increasingly McDonaldized, and he found evidence to support that idea. As another example, Marx hypothesized that the conflict between capitalists and workers would ultimately lead to the collapse of capitalism; however, capitalism has not collapsed. This makes it clear that hypotheses may not be confirmed by research, but such speculation is important to the scientific method.

TABLE 2.2 • The Scientific Method

STEPS IN THE RESEARCH PROCESS	
1	Uncover a question in need of an answer.
2	Review the relevant literature.
3	Develop hypotheses about how phenomena relate to one another.
4	Identify an appropriate method for answering the research question.
5	Collect data.
6	Analyze the data.

4. Researchers must choose *research methods* that will help them to answer their research questions. Sociology offers diverse methodological tools, some of which are better than others for answering certain kinds of questions. For example, some sociologists are interested in how a person's social class shapes his or her opinions about social issues. Surveys and other quantitative tools may be most useful for evaluating the relationship between class and attitudes. Other sociologists may want to know how social class influences how people interpret and make sense of their social world, and how this shapes social action. Qualitative methods, such as observations and interviews, would be helpful for examining this issue.

5. Researchers use their chosen methods to *collect data* that can confirm—or fail to confirm—their hypotheses. Most sociologists venture into the field to collect data through observations, interviews, questionnaires, and other means.

6. Researchers *analyze the data* collected, assessing their meaning in light of the hypotheses guiding the research. For example, Émile Durkheim hypothesized that individuals who were involved with other people would be less likely to commit suicide than those who lived more isolated existences and experienced anomie. Analyzing data from several European countries in the nineteenth century, Durkheim ([1897] 1951) found that the suicide rates were, in fact, higher for widowed or divorced people than for those who were married and therefore presumably better integrated socially.

ASK YOURSELF

How would you use the scientific method to study attitudes toward climate change? What are the advantages and disadvantages of using this approach?

SOCIOLOGICAL RESEARCH

Sociological knowledge is derived from research using a variety of different methods. Typically, the method chosen is and should be driven by the nature of the research question. Imagine that you are a sociologist interested in studying differences in the behavior of people who visit Las Vegas. You might start by observing people gamble. You might look for variations: Are men and women equally represented at the slot machines? Are there age differences in who plays which games? In order to better understand such differences, you might participate, become a *participant observer*, gambling alongside those you are studying. Or you may realize that your research question is better answered through interviewing those who have come to Las Vegas to gamble, asking about their expectations for winning a lot of money. Or you might administer an anonymous questionnaire or survey.

You could also create an experiment. Using a social science lab at your university, you could set up a Las Vegas–style poker table and recruit students as participants. You could tell them that the typical player loses 90 percent of the time and that previous research has shown that *most* players lose *most of the time*. You could then ask whether, in spite of that information, they still want to gamble at your poker table. Those who agree to participate could be interviewed before they start gambling at your table, observed as they gamble, and interviewed again after they finish gambling. Did they start out believing, despite all the evidence to the contrary, that they would win? How likely are they to gamble again? Are there important differences between women and men in terms of their answers to these questions?

Observation, interviews, surveys, experiments, and other research methods are all useful and important to sociologists. All have strengths but also limitations. Before we examine these methods and their strengths and limitations in more detail, there is an important distinction between two broad types of research methods—qualitative and quantitative research—that should be clarified:

Qualitative and Quantitative Research

Qualitative research involves studies done in natural settings that produce in-depth, descriptive information about the social world (Denzin and Lincoln 2011). Such research does not necessarily require statistical methods for collecting and reporting data (Marshall and Rossman 2010). Observation—watching, listening, and taking detailed notes—and open-ended interviews are just two of the qualitative methods used by sociologists. Because qualitative methods usually rely on small sample sizes, the findings cannot be generalized to the broader population; for this, we use quantitative methods.

Quantitative research involves the analysis of numerical data, usually derived from surveys and experiments, to better understand important empirical social realities

Observation is a primary method in sociological research. Do you think people behave differently when they know they are being observed?

(Creswell 2008). The mathematical method used to analyze numerical data is **statistics**, which can aid researchers in two ways. When researchers want to see trends over time or compare differences between groups, they use **descriptive statistics**. The purpose of such statistics is to *describe* some particular body of data that is based on a phenomenon in the real world (Salkind 2004: 8–10). To test hypotheses, researchers use **inferential statistics**. Such statistics allow researchers to use data from a relatively small group to speculate with some level of certainty about a larger group. While such data allow researchers to make broad generalizations, they do not provide insight into people's lived experiences and interpretations of particular issues and events.

Each method has its own set of strengths and limitations in terms of what it can do to help a researcher answer a specific question. Sociologists often debate the relative merits of quantitative versus qualitative methods, but they generally recognize that both have value. There is a broad consensus that quantitative and qualitative research methods can complement one another (Ragin 2014; Riis 2012; Rueschemeyer, Stephens, and Stephens 1992). In practice, sociologists may combine both quantitative and qualitative research methods in a single study (*mixed-method research*).

Observational Research

Observation is one of the primary qualitative methods. It involves systematically watching, listening to, and recording what takes place in a natural social setting over some, usually extended, period of time (Hammersley 2007). There are several key dimensions to any type of observation in sociology:

- *Degree to which those being observed are aware that they are being observed.* This can vary from everyone being fully informed about the research to participants being observed from afar or through hidden cameras or one-way mirrors.

- *Degree to which the presence of the observer affects the actions of those being observed.* When they are aware that they are being observed, people often present themselves in the way they think the observer expects or will accept. For instance, gang members might not engage in illegal activities in the presence of a researcher.

- *Degree to which the research process is structured.* Highly structured observational research might use preset categories, codes, or checklists to guide observations, while less structured observation studies attempt to take note of as much as possible in the field setting with a totally open method.

Some of the most famous pieces of sociological research used the observational method. Examples include studies of the social and economic contexts of people's lives, such as *The Philadelphia Negro* (Du Bois [1899] 1996), *Street Corner Society* (Whyte 1943), *Tally's Corner: A Study of Negro Streetcorner Men* (Liebow 1967), *Floating City: A Rogue Sociologist Lost and Found in New York's Underground Economy* (Venkatesh 2013), and *On the Run: Fugitive Life in an American City* (Goffman 2014).

Participant and Nonparticipant Observation. There are two major types of observational methods. One is **participant observation**, in which the researcher actually plays a role in the group or setting being observed. A participant observer might become a hostess or bartender to study the sex industry in Ho Chi Minh City, Vietnam (Hoang 2010), sell books on the sidewalk to watch what happens on a busy city street (Duneier 1999), become a (quasi-)member of a gang to study its activities (Venkatesh 2008), or work in low-wage jobs (as a waitress, hotel maid, housecleaner, nursing home aide, and Walmart associate) to study the experiences of such workers (Ehrenreich 2001).

The CNN show *Somebody's Gotta Do It* is essentially an informal exercise in participant observation. The host, Mike Rowe, is *not* a trained sociologist, and he is *not* trying to uncover the sociological aspects of the jobs he is participating in, but he *is* a participant observer. In each episode, he actually does the job being examined—he is a participant—and he observes the workers doing their jobs. Anthony Bourdain does much the same in the places he visits on his CNN show, *Parts Unknown.*

In the second type of observational method, **nonparticipant observation**, the sociologist plays little or no role in what is being observed. Gary Fine has done nonparticipant observation research on Little League Baseball (Fine 1987), restaurant kitchens (Fine 2008), and meteorologists (Fine 2010). Clare L. Stacey and Lindsay L. Ayers (2012) spent six months observing (and interviewing) 16 people who provide home care for the elderly or the disabled. They found that although such workers are paid for their work, most of the care work that they do is normally provided free of charge by family members or friends of those in need of care.

There are no firm dividing lines between participant and nonparticipant observation, and at times the two blend imperceptibly into one another. The participant often becomes simply an observer. An example is the sociologist who begins with participant observation of a gang, hanging out with members in casual settings, but becomes a nonparticipant when illegal activities such as drug deals take place. And the nonparticipant observer sometimes becomes a participant. An example is the sociologist who is unable to avoid taking sides in squabbles among members of a Little League team or among their parents.

ASK YOURSELF

Do participant observers risk losing their objectivity when they grow too close to the subjects under study? Why or why not? What about nonparticipant observers? How can sociologists conducting observational research avoid becoming too involved with subjects?

Ethnography. **Ethnography** involves the creation of a detailed account of what a group of people do and the way they live (Adler and Adler 2012; Hammersley 2007), usually requiring intensive and lengthy periods of qualitative research. Researchers may live for years with the groups, tribes, or subcultures being studied. Such methods can reveal much about the experiences of traditionally understudied and marginalized groups, like women immigrant factory workers (Chin 2005), lap dancers (Colosi 2010), and ex-convicts (Opsal 2011). Some suggest that the personal relationships that develop between researchers and subjects in ethnographic studies make it less likely that the power researchers exert over subjects will distort the results (Bourdieu 1992).

Normally ethnographies are small in scale, micro, and local. Researchers observe people, talk to them, hang out with them, sometimes live with them, and conduct formal and informal interviews with them over an extended period of time. Nevertheless, the ethnographic method has now been extended to the global level. Michael Burawoy (2000; see also Tsuda, Tapias, and Escandell 2014) argues that a **global ethnography** is the best way to understand globalization. This type of ethnography is grounded in various parts of the world and seeks to understand globalization as it exists in people's social lives. For example, Kimberly Kay Hoang (2015) spent five years working at different hostess bars in Ho Chi Minh

Robert Park and "Scientific Reporting"

Robert Park (1864–1944), who coauthored the first real textbook on sociology, felt a strong need to work outside the academic world and thus started his career as a journalist. He said, "I made up my mind to go in for experience for its own sake, to gather into my soul . . . all the joys and sorrows of the world" (Park [1927] 1973: 253). He particularly liked to wander around and explore the social world. For example, he wrote of "hunting down gambling houses and opium dens" (Park [1927] 1973: 254).

In his reporting, Park wrote about city life in vivid detail. He would go into the field, observe carefully, and then write up his observations. He called his method *scientific reporting*, which was essentially the kind of social research that later came to be called *participant observation*.

In 1898, at age 34, Park left the newspaper business and returned to school, eventually completing his doctoral dissertation in 1904 at the University of Heidelberg in Germany. Instead of taking an academic position, Park went to work for the Congo Reform Association, which was dedicated to exposing the abuses and exploitation of the Congo by the Belgians. He then became secretary to Booker T. Washington at the Tuskegee Institute.

Park joined the Department of Sociology at the University of Chicago in 1914, playing a central role during its heyday. His use of the city as a laboratory for observational studies helped create and promote the "Chicago School" method of qualitative data collection. It also propelled the Chicago sociology department into a leadership position in what came to be known as urban sociology. Park's early experiences demonstrate the close association between the journalistic and at least some of the sociological ways of seeing the world. He retained a lifelong interest in, and passion for, the accurate description of social life. However, he grew dissatisfied with journalism because it did not fulfill his intellectual needs. In contrast, sociology draws on theory and uses more systematic methods of data collection and analysis to understand the social world. Park's ability to use sociological methods to pursue his deep interest in reforming society and overcoming its ills, especially with regard to race relations, is an important reason to consider him a public sociologist.

Associated Press

Robert Park

Think About It

How might journalists contribute to public sociology? What are the limitations of journalism's input into sociology? Do you think blogs and social networks can make the same kinds of contributions as traditional journalism? Why or why not?

City, Vietnam, to study global sex work. She found that domestic elite clients frequented such places to close business deals and, in the process, display their power and status. In contrast, Vietnamese living abroad and Western budget tourists were more interested in affirming their masculinity by purchasing the services of local sex workers.

Netnography. One of the newest forms of observational research is **netnography**, which involves accounts of what transpires online, particularly on social networking sites such as Facebook, Instagram, and Twitter (Kozinets 2009; Turkle 1995, 2011). Netnographers observe thousands of phenomena online. For example, they might join the online fan club of a rock star and interact directly with her and her fans to learn something about the relationship between them. Or they might study the political use of Facebook by activists such as those who overthrew longtime Egyptian dictator Hosni Mubarak in 2011 (Wolfsfeld, Segev, and Sheafer 2013). Netnographers have also studied the blogs of female Chinese tourists in Macau to examine, among other things, how such travel enhances the women's personal relationships (Zhang and Hitchcock 2014).

Interviews

While observers often interview those they are studying, they usually do so very informally and on the spur of the moment. Other sociologists rely mainly, or exclusively, on **interviews** in which they seek information from participants (respondents) by asking a series of questions that have been spelled out, at least to some degree, before the research is conducted (Gubrium et al. 2012). Interviews are usually conducted face-to-face, although they can be done by phone and are increasingly being done via the Internet (Farrell and Peterson 2010; Fontana 2007). In addition, large-scale national surveys increasingly include interviews.

The use of interviews has a long history in sociology. One very early example is W. E. B. Du Bois's ([1899] 1996) study of the "Philadelphia Negro." A watershed in the history of interviewing in sociology was reached during World War II when large-scale interview studies of members of the American military were conducted (Stouffer et al. 1949). More recently, Allison Pugh (2009) interviewed and observed children and their families over a three-year period. Among other things, she found that parents tend to buy things for their children to help them to be better integrated into groups at school and in their neighborhood, even when declining economic circumstances make it difficult for them to afford such purchases.

Types of Interviews. The questions asked in an interview may be preselected and prestructured so that respondents must choose from sets of answers such as *agree* and *disagree*. Or an interview may be more unstructured, with no preset questions or answers; respondents are free to say anything they want to say.

Prestructured interviews are attractive when the researcher wants to avoid any unanticipated reactions or responses from those being studied. The interviewer attempts to

- behave in the same way in each interview;

- ask the same questions using the same exact words and in the same sequence;

- ask closed-ended questions that the participant must answer by choosing from a set of preselected responses;

- offer the same explanations when they are requested by respondents; and

- not show any kind of reaction to the answers, no matter what they might be.

Interviews conducted in this way often yield information that, like data obtained from questionnaires, can be coded numerically and then analyzed statistically.

There are problems associated with prestructured interviews. First, interviewers often find it difficult to live up to the guidelines for such interviews because they are frequently unable to avoid reacting to answers. Furthermore, they may use different intonation from one interview to another or change the wording, and even the order, of the questions asked, which can affect respondents' answers. Another problem encountered with prestructured

Interviews can take many forms and may be more or less structured depending on the researcher's needs.

interviews is that respondents may not respond accurately or truthfully. For example, they may want to conceal things or give answers that they believe the interviewer wants to hear. A third problem is that closed-ended questions limit the responses, possibly cutting off useful unanticipated information.

The last problem is solved by the use of open-ended or *unstructured interviews*. The interviewer begins with only a general idea of the topics to be covered and the direction to be taken in the interview. The answers in unstructured interviews offer a good understanding of the respondents and what the issues under study mean to them. However, unstructured interviews create problems of their own, such as yielding so much information that it is hard to offer a coherent summary and interpretation of the results.

The Interview Process. Conducting interviews, especially those that are prestructured, usually involves several steps.

1. The interviewer must *gain access* to the setting being studied. This is relatively easy in some cases, such as when interviewing one's friends in the student union or at a local bar. However, access would likely be much more difficult if one wanted to interview one's friends in a sorority house or on the job. They might be less eager to talk to a researcher—to any outsider—in such settings.

2. The interviewer must often seek to *locate a key informant* (Brown, Bankston, and Forsyth 2013; Rieger 2007). This is a person who has intimate knowledge of the group being studied and is willing to talk openly to the researcher about the group. A key informant can help the researcher gain access to the larger group of respondents and verify information being provided by them.

3. The interviewer must seek to *understand the language and culture* of the people being interviewed. In some cases this is very easy. For example, it is not a great problem for

an academic interviewer to understand the language and culture of college students. However, it is more difficult if the academician interviews members of motorcycle gangs or prostitutes in a brothel. In these kinds of cases, it is all too easy for the researcher to misunderstand or to impose incorrect meanings on the words of respondents.

4. The researcher must *gain the trust of the respondents and develop a rapport* with them. Establishing trust and rapport can be easy or difficult, depending on the characteristics of the researcher. Well-educated and relatively powerful male researchers may intimidate less privileged female respondents. Older researchers may have trouble interviewing traditional-aged college students. Depending on the field site, a researcher's point of view and (perceived) similarities with the respondents may ease rapport.

Survey Research

Survey research involves the collection of information from a population, or more usually a representative portion of a population, through the use of interviews and, most important, questionnaires. While some sociologists do their own surveys, most rely on data derived from surveys done by others, such as the U.S. government (the U.S. census, for example) and the National Opinion Research Center, which conducts various opinion polls. Most survey research relies on **questionnaires**—self-administered, written sets of questions. While questionnaires can be presented to respondents on a face-to-face basis, they are more often delivered by mail or, increasingly, filled out on personal computers or over the phone (Snyder 2007).

Types of Surveys. There are two broad types of surveys. A **descriptive survey** is designed to gather accurate information about, for example, members of a certain group, people in a given geographic area, or people in a particular organization. The best-known descriptive surveys are those conducted by organizations such as Gallup to gather information on the preferences, beliefs, and attitudes of given samples of people.

For many years, the Institute for Social Research at the University of Michigan has conducted a descriptive survey of high school seniors in the United States. One of the subjects has been marijuana use. As you can see in Figure 2.2, the prevalence of marijuana use among high school seniors

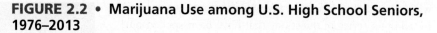

FIGURE 2.2 • Marijuana Use among U.S. High School Seniors, 1976–2013

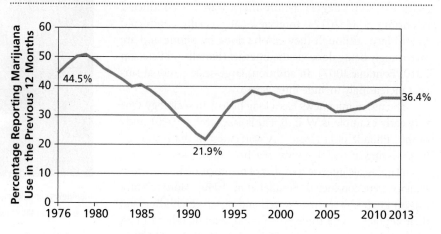

SOURCE: Data from Lloyd D. Johnston, Patrick O'Malley, Richard A. Miech, Jerald G. Bachman, and John E. Schulenberg. *Monitoring the Future: National Survey Results on Drug Use, 1975–2013: Overview, Key Findings on Adolescent Drug Use* (Ann Arbor: Institute for Social Research, University of Michigan, 2014).

has risen and fallen as if in waves. Marijuana use in this group peaked in 1979 (with over half of students admitting use of the drug), reached a low of 21.9 percent in 1992, and has generally been rising since then, although it has never again approached the 1979 level. In 2013, less than 40 percent of 12th graders reported having used marijuana in the previous 12 months.

The data in Figure 2.2 are derived from descriptive surveys, but what if we wanted to explain, and not just statistically describe, changes in marijuana use among high school seniors? To get at this, we would need to do an **explanatory survey**, which seeks to uncover potential causes of, in this case, changes in marijuana use. For example, having discovered variations in marijuana use by high school students over the years, we might hypothesize that the variation is linked to students' (and perhaps the general public's) changing perceptions about the riskiness of marijuana use. In this case, we would use the survey to learn more about respondents' attitudes toward and beliefs about the riskiness of marijuana use and not simply measure student use of marijuana.

Sampling. It is almost never possible to survey an entire population, such as all Americans, or even all sorority members at your college or university. Thus, survey researchers usually need to construct a **sample**, or a representative portion of the overall population. The more careful the researcher is in avoiding biases in selecting the sample, the more likely the findings are to be representative of the whole group.

The most common way to avoid bias is to create a **random sample**, in which every member of the group has an equal chance of being included. One way of obtaining a random sample is by using a list—for example, a list of the

FIGURE 2.3 • Random Samples and Stratified Samples

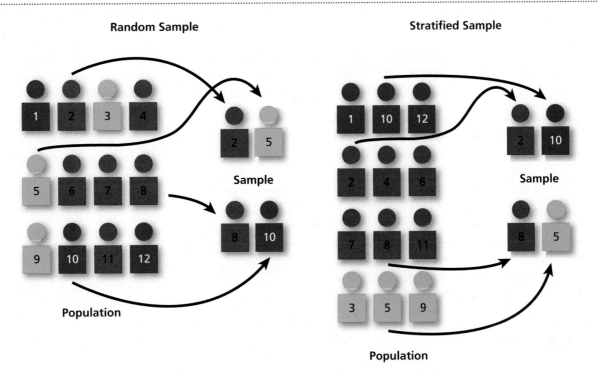

SOURCE: Reprinted with permission of Dan Kernler, Associate Professor of Mathematics, Elgin Community College, Elgin, IL.

names of all the professors at your university. A coin is tossed for each name on the list, and those professors for whom the toss results in heads are included in the sample. More typical and efficient is the use of random number tables, found in most statistics textbooks, to select those in the sample (Kirk 2007). In our example, each professor is assigned a number, and those whose numbers come up in the random number table are included in the sample. In recent years, researchers have also begun to use computer programs that generate random numbers. Additionally, a researcher might create a **stratified sample**, in which a larger group is divided into a series of subgroups (e.g., assistant, associate, and full professors) and then random samples are taken within each of these groups. This ensures representation from each group in the final sample, something that might not occur if one simply does a random sample of the larger group.

Random and stratified sampling are the safest ways of creating samples from which accurate conclusions can be drawn about a population as a whole. However, there is an element of chance in all sampling, with the result that findings can vary from one sample to another. Even though sampling is the most reliable way to reach conclusions about a population, errors are possible. Random and stratified sampling are depicted in Figure 2.3.

Sometimes researchers use **convenience samples**—that is, they eschew systematic sampling and simply include in a

research project those who are conveniently available to participate. An example of a convenience sample might involve researchers passing out surveys to the students in their classes (Lunneborg 2007). These nonrandom samples are rarely ever representative of the larger population whose opinions the researcher is interested in knowing. Nonrandom samples therefore may create a substantial bias in researchers' results, making it almost impossible to draw any definitive conclusions (Popham and Sirotnik 1973: 44).

Experiments

Some sociologists conduct **experiments**, which involve the manipulation of one or more characteristics in order to examine the effect of that manipulation (Kirk 2007; Schaefer 2012). The condition being manipulated is referred to as an **independent variable**, while the **dependent variable** is the measurement that results from the manipulation. Devah Pager (2009) conducted an experiment to examine how the background of a job applicant affects the likelihood of that individual's being called back for an interview. Pager randomly assigned fake criminal records to pairs of similar young men. In each pair, one person had a criminal record and one did not, and one was white and one was not. These young men then sent résumés to companies seeking entry-level jobs. One major finding of this experiment was that black men without criminal records received callbacks at about the same rate as white men with criminal records. In this experiment, we can clearly see the relationship between the independent variable, the job applicant's combination of race and criminal background, and the dependent variable, whether or not the applicant was called in for an interview.

There are several different types of experiments (Walker and Willer 2007):

- *Laboratory experiments.* **Laboratory experiments** take place in controlled settings. The "laboratory" may be, for example, a classroom or a simulated environment. The setting offers the researcher great control over the selection of the participants as well as the independent variables—the conditions to which the participants are exposed (Lucas, Graif, and Lovaglia 2008).

- *Natural experiments.* **Natural experiments** are those in which researchers take advantage of a naturally occurring event to study its effect on one or more dependent variables. Such experiments offer the experimenter little or no control over independent variables (De Silva et al. 2010). For example, Harvard University assigned first-year students from different races as roommates. Among the findings from the natural experiment that arose from this assignment of roommates was that breakups among roommates were more likely when an East Asian student lived with two white students (Chakravarti, Menon, and Winship 2014).

- *Field experiments.* In some natural situations, researchers are able to exert at least some control over who participates and what happens during experiments (Bertrand and Mullainathan 2004; Pager and Western 2012). These are called **field experiments**. In the famous "Robbers Cave" field experiment (Sherif et al. [1954] 1961), which took place in Robbers Cave State Park in Oklahoma, the researchers controlled important aspects of what took place at the site. For example, they were able to assign the 22 boys in the study to two groups, the "Rattlers" and the "Eagles." The researchers were also able to create various situations that led to rivalry, bickering, and hostility between the groups. At the end of the experiment, they had each group rate the other: 53 percent of ratings of the Eagles and nearly 77 percent of ratings of the Rattlers were unfavorable. Later, the researchers introduced conditions that they hoped would reduce bad feelings and friction between the groups. They created greater harmony between the groups by having them work together on tasks, such as securing needed water and paying collectively and equitably for a movie that everyone wanted to see. By the end of the latter part of the experiment, just 5 percent of the ratings of the Eagles were unfavorable, and unfavorable ratings of the Rattlers had dropped to 23 percent.

SECONDARY DATA ANALYSIS

All of the methods discussed thus far involve the collection of new and original data, but many sociologists engage in **secondary data analysis**, in which they reanalyze data collected by others. Secondary analysis can involve a wide variety of different types of data, from censuses and other surveys to historical records and old transcripts of interviews and focus groups. Obtaining and using some of these secondary data sets can be laborious and time-consuming, but many are becoming more accessible, with thousands of data sets now available online (Schutt 2007). Secondary data analysis very often involves statistical analysis of government surveys and census data. U.S. census data, collected every 10 years (last collected in 2010), are a gold mine for sociologists.

Historical-Comparative Method

The goal of **historical-comparative research** is to contrast how different historical events and conditions in various societies have led to different societal outcomes. The historical component involves the study of the history of societies as well as of the major components of society, such as the state, religious system, and economy. The addition of the comparative element, comparing the histories of two or more societies, or of components of societies, makes this method more distinctively sociological.

Historians go into much more detail, and collect far more original historical data, than do sociologists. In contrast, sociologists are much more interested in generalizing about society than are historians. Weber is the preeminent historical-comparative sociologist (Mahoney and Rueschemeyer 2003; Ragin 2014; Tyrell 2010; Varcoe 2007). He did comparative analyses of the histories of Protestantism in the West, Confucianism in China, and Hinduism in India. He sought to determine which religions fostered or impeded the development of capitalism. Weber knew that capitalism had developed in the West and not in China and India. The issue, then, was what about these religions did or did not lead to the emergence of capitalism. A key factor was that in contrast to Protestantism, Confucianism and Hinduism did not foster rationality and efficiency and a striving for material success.

More recent historical-comparative research has uncovered critical differences in the timing and character of modern pension systems developed in Britain, Canada, and the United States (Orloff 1993) and how the structure of local government and the timing of geopolitical competition played important roles in explaining different types of state formation in Europe (Kestnbaum 2012).

ISSUES IN SOCIAL RESEARCH

The research conducted by sociologists raises a number of issues of great importance. These include the reliability

World Values Survey

The World Values Survey (WVS) is a source of cross-cultural data on the impact of globalization on people's worldviews, values, and basic motivations. The WVS asks people in each surveyed country roughly 250 questions about personal values and beliefs. For example, respondents are asked to prioritize various aspects of their lives, including family, politics, work, religion, and service to others. They are also asked whether they would be comfortable having some of the following live near them: criminals, people of a different race, Muslims, Jews, immigrants or foreign workers, those with AIDS, homosexuals, and drug addicts.

In its first wave in 1981, the survey was limited to 20 highly developed European countries. Since then, it has expanded to 97 countries, covering nearly 90 percent of the population of the world. Since changes in values and preferences appear to be linked to level of economic and technological development, it was important for the survey to include the full range of less developed (or industrial) and highly developed societies. This led the WVS to hire native social scientists from many different countries. The result was more culturally conscious research design, analysis of data, and interpretation of results.

Sociologists have used data collected through the WVS for a wide variety of studies related to globalization. For instance, one study based on more than 20 years of WVS data found that people in almost all industrial societies have generally shifted from being religious and traditional toward being more secular and rational (at least in terms of the way being rational is defined in the developed Western world) (Inglehart and Baker 2000).

Another major dimension of global variation is the distinction between survival and self-expression values. Respondents in industrialized and developed countries have tended to have fewer worries about survival or about meeting their basic needs for food and shelter. As a result, their priorities have shifted from an emphasis on economic and physical security (survival) to an interest in well-being and personal happiness. With this greater self-expressiveness comes a greater tolerance of minorities—including foreigners, gays, and various ethnic groups—who might otherwise be found threatening. This increase in trust and tolerance creates the type of social environment that is most conducive to the development of democracy.

Think About It

What kinds of diversity among WVS social scientists would you recommend to the WVS, if any? Do you believe that there really are such things as "world values"?

---

and validity of findings and the ethics involved in the research process.

Reliability and Validity

A key issue with sociological data relates to one's ability to trust the findings. **Reliability** involves the degree to which a given question, or another kind of measure, produces the same results time after time. In other words, would the same question asked one day get the same response from the participants or the same measurement on the scale the following day, or week, or month? The other dimension of trustworthiness is **validity**, or the degree to which a question, or another kind of measure, gets an accurate response. In other words, does the question measure what it is supposed to measure?

Research Ethics

Ethics is concerned with issues of right and wrong, the choices that people make, and how they justify them (Zeni 2007). World War II and the behavior of the Nazis helped make ethics a central issue in research. The Nazis engaged in horrendous medical experiments on inmates in concentration camps. Unethical research was also conducted between 1932 and 1972 at Tuskegee Institute in Alabama on hundreds of poor black American men suffering from syphilis. The researchers, who were interested in studying the natural progression of the disease over time, never told the participants that they had syphilis. Despite regular visits to collect data from the participants, the researchers did not treat them for the disease and allowed them to suffer over long periods before they died painfully (Reverby 2009).

No research undertaken by sociologists has caused the kind of suffering and death experienced by the people studied in Nazi Germany or at Tuskegee Institute. Nonetheless, such research is the context and background for ethical concerns about the harmful or negative effects of research on participants in sociological research (the code of ethics of the American Sociological Association can be found at www .asanet.org/about/ethics.cfm). There are three main areas of

Depicted here is the interview method used in the Tuskegee study of syphilis and the experimental method employed in "Stanford County Prison" study.

concern: physical and psychological harm to participants, illegal acts by researchers, and deception and violation of participants' trust.

Physical and Psychological Harm. The first issue is concern over whether the research can actually cause participants physical harm. Most sociological research is not likely to cause such harm. However, physical harm may be an unintended consequence. In the Robbers Cave research, the hostility reached such a peak that the boys engaged in apple-throwing fights and in raids on one another's compounds.

A much greater issue in sociological research is the possibility of psychological harm to those being studied. Even questionnaire or interview studies can cause psychological harm merely by asking people about sensitive issues such as sexual orientation, drug use, and experience with abortion. This risk is greatly increased when, unbeknownst to the researcher, a participant is hypersensitive about a particular issue because of a difficult or traumatic personal experience.

Some of the more extreme risks of psychological harm have occurred in experiments. The most famous example is Stanley Milgram's (1974) laboratory study of how far people will go when they are given orders by those in authority. In the Milgram experiment, one group, the "learners," were secretly paid to pretend that painful shocks were being applied to them by the other group of participants, the "teachers," who were led to believe that the shocks they thought they were applying were very real (see Figure 2.4). The experimenter, dressed officially in a white coat and projecting an aura of scientific respectability, ordered the teachers to apply shocks that appeared to be potentially lethal. The teachers did so even though the learners, who were in another room and not visible, were screaming with increasing intensity. The research clearly showed that if they were ordered to do so by authority figures, people would violate the social norms against inflicting pain on, and even possibly endangering the lives of, others.

The results of the Milgram experiment are important in many senses, especially regarding what the study did to the psyches of the people involved. The "teachers" came to know that they were very responsive to the dictates of authority figures, even if they were ordered to commit immoral acts. Some of them certainly realized that their behavior indicated that they were perfectly capable in such circumstances of harming, if not killing, other human beings. Such realizations had the possibility of adversely affecting the way participants viewed, and felt about, themselves. But the research has had several benefits as well, for both participants and others who have read about the Milgram study. For example, those in powerful positions can better understand, and therefore limit, the potential impact of their orders to subordinates, and subordinates can more successfully limit

FIGURE 2.4 • The Teacher (T), Learner (L), and Experimenter (E) in the Milgram Experiment

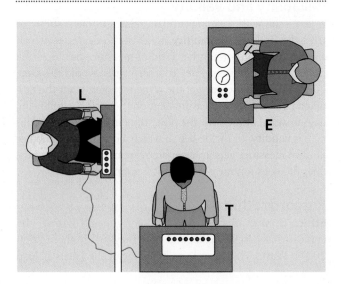

how far they are willing to go in carrying out the orders of their superiors.

Another famous study that raises similar ethical issues was conducted by Philip Zimbardo (1973). Zimbardo set up a prisonlike structure called "Stanford County Prison" as a setting in which to conduct his experiment. Participants were recruited to serve as either prisoners or guards. The "prison" was very realistic, with windowless cells, minimal toilet facilities, and strict regulations imposed on the inmates. The guards had uniforms, badges, keys, and clubs. They were also trained in the methods of managing prisoners.

The experiment was supposed to last six weeks, but it was ended after only six days when the researchers grew fearful about the health and sanity of the prisoners, whom some of the guards insulted, degraded, and dehumanized. Only a few guards were helpful and supportive. However, even the helpful guards refused to intervene when prisoners were being abused. The prisoners could have left, but they tended to go along with the situation, accepting both the authority of the guards and their own lowly and abused position. Some of the guards experienced psychological distress, but it was worse for the prisoners when they realized how much they had contributed to their own difficulties. Social researchers learned that a real or perceived imbalance of power between researcher and participant may lead the participant to comply with a researcher's demands even though they cause distress.

Illegal Acts. In the course of ethnographic fieldwork, a researcher might witness or even become entangled in illegal acts. This problem often confronted Venkatesh (2008) in his research on gangs in and around a Chicago housing project. He frequently witnessed illegal acts such as drug use, drug sales, and prostitution. Had he informed the police about these acts, he would likely have compromised his ability to continue his research. In not informing the police, he was forced to live with the fact that his silence was, at a minimum, not serving to reduce such illegal behavior.

Alice Goffman confronted similar issues while doing the research published in her book *On the Run* (2014). Goffman lived in a predominantly black neighborhood in Philadelphia for six years to examine firsthand the experiences of young black men with the criminal justice system. Many of the men in the neighborhood had outstanding warrants, so they literally ran to avoid being arrested whenever they saw the police or heard that the police were coming. On one such occasion Goffman ran with two of them to hide out in a neighbor's house. A more controversial decision Goffman made was to drive one of the men in her study around the neighborhood after his friend had been shot and killed, in order to help him find the shooter. The man in her car was armed, and though Goffman did not know if he would find and shoot the person who killed his friend, she could have been charged with

conspiracy to murder if he had. Furthermore, Goffman took the unusual, though not illegal, action of destroying all of her field notes so that they could not be subpoenaed and used in court against the people in her study.

Researchers must weigh sticky legal and ethical ramifications for participants and themselves. Publishing an account of dramatic illegal acts might help a researcher's career, but it might also send the perpetrators of those acts to jail. It is also possible that not informing the police of illegal acts, or refusing to turn over field notes, could lead to imprisonment for both participants and researchers (Emerson 2001; Van Maanen 1983).

ASK YOURSELF

Do you think that sociologists who witness illegal acts while collecting research data should be forced to testify in a court of law? Why or why not? Can you think of any instances where it would be acceptable for a researcher to participate in an illegal act?

Violation of Trust. Researchers can betray participants' trust in several ways. For instance, a researcher might inadvertently divulge the identity of participants even though they have been promised anonymity. There is also the possibility of exploitative relationships between researchers and participants, especially with key informants. Exploitation is of special concern in cases where there is a real or perceived imbalance of power—often related to race, class, or gender—between researcher and participant. In the Tuskegee case, for example, African American men suffered the adverse effects of the research even though syphilis is distributed throughout the larger population. Although this research should not have occurred under any circumstances, a more equitable research design would have meant that most of the participants were white males.

It is also a betrayal of trust for the researcher to develop inappropriate relationships with participants. One noteworthy example of this comes from a study conducted by Erich Goode (2002) to better understand the stigma of obesity. Goode has publicly acknowledged that he had sexual relations with some of his female informants. He argues that because of this he was able to obtain information that may not have been obtainable by any other means. However, one must ask about the cost to his participants of his obtaining the knowledge in this way. Because Goode's participants did not have full knowledge of his motives, they were unable to make informed choices about engaging in sexual relations with him. In this case, the power imbalance between researcher and participant led to exploitation.

The best-known example of sociological research involving deception and intrusion into people's lives is Laud

Humphreys's (1970) study of the homosexual activities of men in public restrooms ("tearooms"). Humphreys acted as a lookout outside tearooms and signaled men engaged in anonymous acts of fellatio when members of the public or the police were approaching. He interviewed some of the men with full disclosure. However, he also noted the license plate numbers of some of those he observed and tracked down their addresses. Humphreys appeared at their homes a year or so later, in disguise, to interview them under false pretenses. In this way he uncovered one of the most important findings of his study: More than half the men were married, with wives and families. They were active in the tearoom trade not because they were homosexual but because sexual relations in their marriages were problematic.

Humphreys deceived these men by not telling them from the outset that he was doing research on them and, with those he interviewed under false pretenses, by not revealing the true nature of the research. But the research itself is not without merit. It helped to distinguish between homosexual acts and homosexual identity. Humphreys's research, while ethically flawed and harmful to the unwitting participants, did have some benefit: It provided much-needed insight into the social construction of sexuality and the difficulties involved in understanding how people develop their sexual selves.

Objectivity, or "Value-Free" Sociology

Another issue relating to sociological research is whether or not researchers are, or can be, objective. That is, do they allow personal preferences and judgments to bias their research? Many argue that value-laden research jeopardizes the entire field of sociology. The publication of such research—and public revelations about researcher biases—erodes and could destroy the credibility of the field as a whole. In the history of sociology, this discussion, like many others, is traceable to the work of Max Weber. Taken to its extreme, *value-free sociology* means preventing all personal values from affecting any phase of the research process. However, this is not what Weber intended in his work on values. In fact, he saw at least two roles for values in social research. The first is in the selection of a question to be researched. In that case, it is perfectly appropriate for researchers to be guided by their personal values, or the values that predominate in the society of the day. The second is in the analysis of the results of a research study. In that analysis, sociologists can, and should, use personal and social values to help them make sense of their findings. These values are an aid in interpretation and understanding. However, they are not to be used purposely to distort the findings or mislead the reader of a report on the study.

SUMMARY

The most important early sociologists were Auguste Comte, inventor of the term *sociology*; Harriet Martineau; and Herbert Spencer. However, the main theorists of classical sociology are Karl Marx, Max Weber, and Émile Durkheim. Marx focused the majority of his attention on macro issues, particularly the structure of capitalist society. Weber did not focus exclusively on the economy but considered the importance of other social structures, particularly religion. Durkheim believed social structures and cultural norms and values exert control over individuals that is not only necessary but also desirable. Other early sociological theorists include Georg Simmel, who focused on interactions among individuals; W. E. B. Du Bois, who emphasized the importance of race; and Thorstein Veblen, who examined consumption.

Structural/functional, conflict/critical, and inter/actionist theories are the main types of contemporary sociological theories. Two influential structural/functional theories are structural-functionalism, which is concerned with both social structures and the functions and dysfunctions they perform, and structuralism, which uncovers the social impact of hidden or underlying structures. There are several conflict/critical theories: Conflict theory

stresses the ways in which society is held together by power and coercion, critical theory critically analyzes culture, feminist theory critiques patriarchy, queer theory suggests that there are no fixed and stable identities that determine who we are, critical theories of race and racism argue that race continues to matter and intersects with other social statuses, and postmodern theory is concerned that society is coming to be dominated by simulations. Inter/actionist theories deal with micro-level interactions among people and, to a degree, individual action. Symbolic interactionism studies the effect of symbols on the interaction between two or more people, ethnomethodology focuses on what people do rather than on what they think, exchange theory analyzes people's behavior based on rewards and costs, and rational choice theory considers how the rational evaluations of goals and the means to achieve them influence behavior.

Sociologists use the scientific method to study society systematically. First, the sociologist finds a question that needs to be answered and then reviews the literature to see what has already been found. Next, the sociologist develops a hypothesis, chooses a research method, and collects data that can confirm, or fail to confirm, the hypothesis. Finally, the researcher analyzes the data in relation to the initial hypothesis.

Sociologists use different research methods depending on the issues being studied. Quantitative methods yield data in the form of numbers, while qualitative methods yield verbal descriptions. Research methods used by sociologists to collect data include observations, ethnographies, interviews, surveys, and experiments. Sociologists also use historical-comparative methodology, in which they engage in secondary data analysis to reanalyze data collected by others.

When conducting research, sociologists strive for reliability, the degree to which a given measure produces the same results time after time, and validity, the degree to which a question gets an accurate response. They should also try to conduct their research ethically and to be objective even though it is impossible to avoid all bias.

REVIEW QUESTIONS

1. What are theories, and how do sociologists use theories to make sense of the social world? In what ways are theories developed by sociologists better than your own theorizing?

2. Max Weber said the world is becoming increasingly rationalized. What are the benefits and disadvantages of rationality?

3. Do your consumption habits reflect Veblen's theory of conspicuous consumption? Consider the brand names on your clothing, cell phone, and laptop. Are they expensive brands with visible logos and high status, or less expensive, no-name brands with little or no status?

4. What are the functions and dysfunctions of using the Internet to consume goods and services? On balance, do you think that consumption through the Internet is positive or negative? Why?

5. Is your life affected by intersectionality? Do the different statuses you hold intersect? How do those intersections adversely affect you?

6. What are the differences between participant and nonparticipant observational methods? In both approaches, how do sociologists ensure that their observations are systematic?

7. Have you ever conducted or participated in an interview, perhaps for a job or an internship? How closely did it adhere to the guidelines for prestructured interviews listed in this chapter?

8. Why do sociologists who conduct surveys rely on samples? What techniques do researchers use to avoid biases in their samples?

9. Some experiments allow researchers to take advantage of a naturally occurring event to study its effect on one or more dependent variables. Can you think of any recent events that might have been conducive to natural experiments? What would be the dependent variable or variables in your example?

10. What are some of the ethical concerns raised by sociological research? Use a specific example from research discussed in this chapter to describe these ethical concerns.

APPLYING THE SOCIOLOGICAL IMAGINATION

How can we use ethnomethodology to understand social interactions on the Internet? First, select a website that allows for people to interact with one another (e.g., Facebook, Twitter, your favorite interactive blog, an online discussion forum, the comments section of an article on your local newspaper's website).

Now apply an ethnomethodological approach by observing the actions and interactions on the site. In what ways do conversations and interactions on the site you've chosen have stable and orderly properties? What rules and conventions keep the interactions orderly and stable? How do people know what is expected of them? Do people violate the rules? How do others respond when the rules are broken? Are the rules that govern online interactions different from the rules that govern face-to-face interactions?

KEY TERMS

alienation: In a capitalist system, being unconnected to one's work, products, fellow workers, and human nature. (p. 25)

anomie: The feeling of not knowing what is expected of one in society or of being adrift in society without any clear, secure moorings. (p. 27)

capitalism: In Marx's view, an economic system based on one group of people (the capitalists or owners) owning what is needed for production and a second group (the proletariat or workers) owning little but their capacity for work. (p. 25)

capitalists: Those who own what is needed for production—factories, machines, tools—in a capitalist system. (p. 25)

collective conscience: The set of beliefs shared by people throughout society. (p. 27)

conflict theory: Theory that sees society as held together by coercion and focuses on its negative aspects. (p. 30)

conspicuous consumption: The public demonstration of wealth through consumption. (p. 28)

convenience sample: A readily available group of people who fit the criteria for participating in a research project. (p. 41)

critical theories of race and racism: A set of ideas arguing that race continues to matter and that racism continues to exist and adversely affect blacks. (p. 31)

critical theory: A set of critical ideas derived from Marxian theory but focusing on culture rather than the economy. (p. 30)

culture industry: The rationalized and bureaucratized structures that control modern culture. (p. 30)

dependent variable: A characteristic or measurement that is the result of manipulating an independent variable. (p. 41)

descriptive statistics: Numerical data that allow researchers to see trends over time or compare differences between groups in order to describe some findings based on a phenomenon in the real world. (p. 36)

descriptive survey: A questionnaire or interview used to gather accurate information about those in a group, people in a given geographic area, or members of organizations. (p. 40)

double consciousness: Among black Americans, the sense of "two-ness," that is, of being both black and American. (p. 28)

dysfunction: An observable consequence that negatively affects the ability of a given system to survive, adapt, or adjust. (p. 29)

empiricism: The gathering of information and evidence using one's senses, especially one's eyes and ears, to experience the social world. (p. 35)

ethics: A set of beliefs concerning right and wrong in the choices that people make and the ways those choices are justified. (p. 43)

ethnography: Observational, sometimes participatory research; usually intensive and conducted over lengthy periods, that leads to an account of what people do and how they live. (p. 37)

ethnomethodology: An inter/actionist theory focusing on what people do rather than on what they think. (p. 33)

exchange relationship: A stable and persistent bond between individuals who interact, generally formed because their interactions are rewarding. (p. 34)

exchange theory: A set of ideas related to the rewards and costs associated with human behavior. (p. 33)

experiment: The manipulation of a characteristic under study (an independent variable) to examine its effect on another characteristic (the dependent variable). (p. 41)

explanatory survey: A questionnaire or interview used to uncover potential causes for some observation. (p. 40)

exploitation: A feature of capitalism in which the workers (proletariat) produce virtually everything but get few rewards, while the capitalists, who do little, reap the vast majority of the rewards. (p. 25)

feminist theory: A set of ideas critical of the social situation confronting women and offering solutions for improving,

if not revolutionizing, their situation. (p. 31)

field experiment: Research that occurs in natural situations but allows researchers to exert at least some control over who participates and what happens during the experiment. (p. 42)

function: An observable, positive consequence that helps a system survive, adapt, or adjust. (p. 28)

global ethnography: A type of ethnography that is "grounded" in various parts of the world and that seeks to understand globalization as it exists in people's social lives. (p. 37)

historical-comparative research: A research methodology that contrasts how different historical events and conditions in various societies (or components of societies) lead to different societal outcomes. (p. 42)

hyperconsumption: Consumption of more than one needs, really wants, and can afford. (p. 33)

independent variable: In an experiment, a condition that can be independently manipulated by the researcher with the goal of producing a change in some other variable. (p. 41)

inferential statistics: Numerical data that allow researchers to use data from a small group to speculate with some level of certainty about a larger group. (p. 36)

intersectionality: The confluence, or intersection, of various social statuses and the inequality and oppression associated with each in combination with others; the idea that members of any given minority group are affected by the nature of their position in other systems or other forms of social inequality. (p. 31)

interview: A research method in which information is sought from participants (respondents) who are asked a series of questions that have been spelled out, at least to some degree, before the research is conducted. (p. 38)

laboratory experiment: Research that occurs in a laboratory, giving the researcher great control over both the selection of the participants to be studied and the conditions to which they are exposed. (p. 42)

latent functions: Unintended positive consequences. (p. 29)

manifest functions: Positive consequences that are brought about consciously and purposely. (p. 29)

mass culture: Cultural elements that are administered by large organizations, lack spontaneity, and are phony. (p. 30)

natural experiment: An experiment that occurs when researchers take advantage of a naturally occurring event to study its effect on one or more dependent variables. (p. 42)

netnography: An ethnographic method in which the Internet becomes the research site and what transpires there is the sociologist's research interest. (p. 38)

nonparticipant observation: A research method in which the sociologist plays little or no role in what is being observed. (p. 37)

observation: A research method that involves systematically watching, listening to, and recording what takes place in a natural social setting over some (extended) period of time. (p. 36)

pangender: Gender identity encompassing all genders. (p. 31)

participant observation: A research method in which the researcher actually plays a role, even a minor one, in the group or setting being observed. (p. 37)

postmodern theory: A set of ideas oriented in opposition to modern theory by, for example, rejecting or deconstructing the grand narratives of modern social theory. (p. 31)

proletariat: Workers as a group, or those in the capitalist system who own

little or nothing except for their capacity for work (labor), which they must sell to the capitalists in order to survive. (p. 25)

qualitative research: Research methods employed in natural settings that produce in-depth, descriptive information (e.g., in respondents' own words) about the social world. (p. 36)

quantitative research: Research methods that involve the analysis of numerical data usually derived from surveys and experiments. (p. 36)

queergender: Term used to connote a third gender. (p. 31)

queer theory: Theory based on the idea that there are no fixed and stable identities (such as "heterosexual" or "homosexual") that determine who we are; a diverse group of ideas about how cultures develop gender and sexuality norms, notions of conformity, and power relations. (p. 31)

questionnaire: A self-administered, written set of questions. (p. 40)

random sample: A subset of a population in which every member of the group has an equal chance of being included. (p. 40)

rational choice theory: A set of ideas that sees people as rational and as acting purposively to achieve their goals. (p. 34)

rationalization: The process by which social structures are increasingly characterized by the most direct and efficient means to their ends. (p. 26)

reliability: The degree to which a given question (or another kind of measure) produces the same results time after time. (p. 43)

sample: A representative portion of the overall population. (p. 40)

scientific method: A structured way to find answers to questions about the world. (p. 35)

secondary data analysis: Reanalysis of data, often survey data, collected by others, including other sociologists. (p. 42)

simulation: An inauthentic or fake version of something. (p. 33)

social facts: Macro-level phenomena—social structures and cultural norms and values—that stand apart from and impose themselves on people. (p. 26)

statistics: The mathematical method used to analyze numerical data. (p. 36)

stratified sample: A sample created when a larger group is divided into a series of subgroups and then random samples are taken within each of these groups. (p. 41)

structural-functionalism: A set of ideas focused on social structures as well as the functions and dysfunctions that such structures perform. (p. 29)

structuralism: Social theory interested in the social impact of hidden or underlying structures. (p. 29)

survey research: A research methodology that involves the collection of information from a population, or more usually a representative portion of a population, through the use of interviews and, more important, questionnaires. (p. 40)

symbolic interactionism: A sociological perspective focusing on the role of symbols and how their meanings are shared and understood by those involved in human interaction. (p. 33)

theory: A set of interrelated ideas that have a wide range of application, deal with centrally important issues, and have stood the test of time. (p. 24)

unanticipated consequence: An unexpected social effect, especially a negative effect. (p. 29)

validity: The degree to which a question (or another kind of measure) gets an accurate response, or measures what it is supposed to measure. (p. 43)

$SAGE edge™ edge.sagepub.com/ritzeressentials2e

SAGE edge offers a robust online environment featuring an impressive array of free tools and resources for review, study, and further exploration, keeping both instructors and students on the cutting edge of teaching and learning.

LEARNING OBJECTIVES	FOR FURTHER EXPLORATION AND APPLICATION
LO 2-1: Define what theories are and explain why they are important in understanding social phenomena.	▶ Breaking Down Sociology's Three Main Schools of Thought ◉ Exploring 21st-Century Sociology ▣ Durkheim and Weber's Contrasting Imagination
LO 2-2: Identify the most important classical sociologists, particularly Marx, Weber, and Durkheim, and their major contributions to the field.	▶ Four Major Figures in Sociology ◉ The Roots of Our Beliefs about the Value of Hard Work ▣ The 10 Most Influential Sociologists of the 20th Century
LO 2-3: Compare and contrast the strengths and weaknesses of structural/functional, conflict/critical, and inter/actionist theories.	▶ A Deeper Look into Sociology Theories ◉ Why a Sociologist Is Part of Building a Better Power Grid ▣ Analyzing Social and Behavior Theories
LO 2-4: Describe the scientific method.	▶ Sociology Speculating versus Scientific Method ◉ Big Data Is Not a Cure-All in Medicine ▣ Sociology/Sociological Methods
LO 2-5: Describe the various methods of sociological research and the types of questions each one can help us answer.	▶ How Sociology Methods Use Data to Think Deeper ◉ How Mad Cow Research Hints at Ways to Halt Major Diseases ▣ Tips for Writing Research Questions
LO 2-6: Describe how sociologists engage in secondary data analysis.	▶ How Sociologists Are Using Secondary Data Analysis ◉ Using Student Data to Spot At-Risk Students ▣ Recap on Secondary Data Analysis in Sociology
LO 2-7: Identify the key issues in social research, including reliability, validity, trust, legality, and objectivity.	▶ Clarifying Reliability versus Validity ◉ Scientists Urge Temporary Moratorium on Human Genome Edits ▣ Ethics Applied in Social Research

CULTURE

A Reflection of U.S. Culture

A jazz musician, Miles Davis, gave new life to the term *cool* in his 1957 album *Birth of the Cool*. Being cool—calm and steady as cool water—remains part of American culture, though that culture has many other characteristics. One influential cultural force today is HBO's *Girls* and its decidedly "uncool," even geeky, characters, especially its star, executive producer, writer, and director Lena Dunham, who was only 25 years old when the series premiered in 2012.

Girls and Lena Dunham have become cultural phenomena by portraying, and helping to define, the culture of urban millennials (those born between the early 1980s and the early 2000s). The show, which is somewhat autobiographical (like Dunham's recent book, *Not That Kind of Girl*), deals fearlessly with a wide range of topics, particularly the many varieties of human relationships, including between female friends and the sexual politics of male-female and homosexual and lesbian relationships. The characters are young, flawed, unstable, vulnerable, self-involved, and somewhat immature. Their relationships are fraught with difficulties, and their jobs and careers exist mainly at the bottom of the occupational hierarchy and are, if anything, more problematic than their social relationships.

Dunham's character, Hannah, is a paradigm of a millennial woman. A writer, she is a narcissistic, striving careerist who fails more often than not. She is irrepressible but anxious, self-loathing, often depressed, frequently badly treated by friends and lovers, and in need of prescription and nonprescription drugs and psychotherapy. She hates her overweight body and alternates between dieting and binge eating. When not clothed in some bizarre, unflattering outfit, she often unselfconsciously displays her nude, decidedly un-model-like, body. Sex for Hannah often seems unsatisfying, and many of the problems that she and her friends have appear to stem from the fact that they are women. *Girls* seems to get at the essence of millennial culture in the early twenty-first century.

LEARNING OBJECTIVES

3-1 Define culture.

3-2 Identify the basic elements of culture, including values and norms.

3-3 Discuss diversity within cultures, including the concepts of ideal and real culture, subcultures and countercultures, culture wars, and assimilation.

3-4 Describe emerging issues in culture, such as global and consumer culture.

Corbis

Millennials and their culture are not difficult to spot within U.S. borders. Around the world, however, the culture of the millennial generation may take on many other forms or be non-existent. But globalization and Americanization have spread U.S. millennial culture around a significant portion of the world.

Since you were likely born in the 1990s, you are considered part of the millennial generation. However, you also belong to many different cultures and subcultures. For example, you are likely to participate in consumer and digital culture, as well as the culture of university life. You are continually learning the dimensions and the rules of these and other cultures. Much of that learning happens almost effortlessly, as you live your daily life. But cultures that are new to you, such as university culture, or that are evolving rapidly, such as digital culture, are likely to require much, and continuing, effort, alertness, and flexibility on your part for you to learn how to behave in them. ●

A DEFINITION OF CULTURE

Culture encompasses the ideas, values, practices, and material objects that allow a group of people, even an entire society, to carry out their collective lives in relative order and harmony. There are innumerable ideas, values, practices, and material objects associated with most cultures. As a result, no one individual can possibly know them all or what they all mean. But people must know at least the most basic and important elements of their culture. Knowledge of a shared culture leads people to behave in similar ways and to adopt a similar way of looking at the world. However, it is important to remember that there are differences within, as well as between, cultures. This point was reflected in headlines in early 2015 concerning murderous attacks in Paris by Islamic radicals on such cultural symbols as a French humor magazine and a kosher supermarket. There are profound differences in France today among French, Muslim, and Jewish cultures.

Closer to home, consider the cultures of the Bloods and the Crips, two street gangs with origins in Los Angeles in the early 1970s but now existing nationwide (Deutsch 2014; Patton 1998; Simpson 2006). Members of the two gangs distinguish themselves from each other in a variety of ways, but most notably by their defining colors—red for Bloods and blue for Crips. These colors and other symbols are very meaningful to gang members, helping them to mark territories, easily identify friends and foes, and signify their values. The symbols—and their meanings—have been created by the group itself and passed down from one gang member to another. Symbols like these may also be passed along from a gang in one locale to those situated elsewhere. In contrast,

for those who are not members of the group, an idea, a value, a practice, or an object may have little meaning, may mean something completely different, or may even have no meaning at all. For example, to members of the general public, a person wearing a red shirt is simply wearing a red shirt.

The existence of a culture and common knowledge of it are so important that newcomers to any group, especially children, are taught its basic elements early. They then expand on that knowledge as they mature and become more integral members of the group.

At the same time, culture is constantly being affected by changes both internal and external to the group. Among the *internal changes* are the average age of the population within that group. Depending on whether the average age increases or decreases, a culture will need to reflect the needs and interests of either younger or older people. For example, in the United States and other aging societies, television programs and the advertisements associated with them are more oriented to older people than is the case in societies with increasing numbers of younger people (Carter and Vega 2011). A good example of this is the great popularity, especially among older viewers, of PBS's *Downton Abbey*. On the other hand, television certainly cannot and does not ignore its younger audience. The great popularity and cultural influence of HBO's *Girls* (see above) is indicative of that.

Similarly, cultures need to adapt to other changes, such as a group's gender composition. For example, today there are more female gang members in general, and this is also true of the membership of the Bloods and the Crips (Goldman, Giles, and Hogg 2014). As a result of this shift, a gang's culture needs to change to deal with things like the tasks to be allotted to female members (e.g., carrying concealed weapons) and, more specifically, to those who are pregnant or have young children.

Technological innovations are among the *external changes* likely to alter a group's culture significantly. For example, with the growth of smartphone use, texting has become wildly

The elite culture and lifestyle depicted in the series *Downton Abbey* is of interest primarily to older television viewers.

FIGURE 3.1 • Cell Phone Use and Texting-While-Driving Laws, 2014

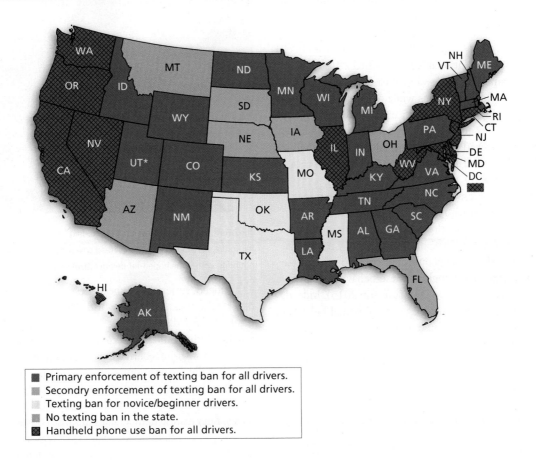

Legend:
- ■ Primary enforcement of texting ban for all drivers.
- ■ Secondry enforcement of texting ban for all drivers.
- □ Texting ban for novice/beginner drivers.
- ■ No texting ban in the state.
- ▦ Handheld phone use ban for all drivers.

NOTE: Under "secondary" laws, an officer must have some other reason to stop a vehicle before citing the driver for using a cell phone. Laws without this restriction are called "primary."

*Utah considers speaking on a cell phone without a hands-free device to be an offense only if driver also is committing some other moving violation (other than speeding).

SOURCE: "Distracted Drivers." Copyright © National Conference of State Legislatures. Reprinted with permission.

popular as a communication method (including among street gang members), and phone conversations have become proportionally less common. Thus, not only newcomers to the group but also those who have participated for years must constantly learn new aspects of culture (e.g., the need to use prepaid "burner" cell phones that are difficult or impossible to trace) and perhaps unlearn others (using traditional cell phones) that are no longer considered desirable.

The rise of the smartphone has created new realities for which clear and firm cultural rules are not yet in place. One such rule involves what should and should not be discussed on a cell phone in places where others, especially strangers, are close enough to overhear what is being said. Clearly, this is an issue for gang members who may be discussing criminal activities that must be concealed from nonmembers. For at least some in the larger public, there is concern over being forced to overhear very personal cell phone conversations on topics (e.g., illness or sexual relationships) that in the past were discussed only in private. Then there is the issue of loud cell phone conversations intruding on the consciousness of others. Long, loud, and frequent phone conversations are not a problem in the privacy of one's home, but they are a problem in public areas where there is an expectation of quietude, such as at a fine restaurant or in the "quiet car" of a train.

While people are generally only gently sanctioned for violating the rules surrounding smartphone use, such sanctions can sometimes be much more extreme. Violence is not the norm, but it is not unheard-of, as in the case of Curtis Reeves, who shot and killed a man in a movie theater for texting (his babysitter) during movie previews (the movie hadn't even started!) (Buie 2014).

A more formal set of rules is being developed to control drivers' use of cell phones for talking and texting. It has become apparent—both from insurance company statistics and from experimental research—that using a handheld cell phone while driving increases the risk of accidents (Horrey and Wickens 2006). In 2014, more than a quarter of automobile crashes in the United States involved the use of cell phones while driving (National Safety Council 2014). A very active media campaign has developed to discourage people from using handheld cell phones while driving. Many states have enacted laws against the practice (see Figure 3.1), and some safety advocates are pressing for a similar federal law. If both campaigns succeed, using a handheld cell phone while driving will no longer be culturally acceptable and will in fact become illegal across the nation.

Although we generally learn the various components of culture, we sometimes refuse to comply with, or even accept, them. For example, premarital and extramarital sexual relationships continue to be disapproved of by traditional American culture, but many people have come to reject these ideas and to engage increasingly in these behaviors (on premarital sex, see Elias, Fullerton, and Simpson 2015). Indeed, it could be argued that both these forms of sexual behavior have come to be widely tolerated and have, in fact, become accepted parts of the culture.

THE BASIC ELEMENTS OF CULTURE

As pointed out earlier, every group and society has a culture. Culture surrounds such diverse social phenomena as athletics, cooking, funeral ceremonies, courtship, medicine, marriage, sexual restrictions and taboos, bodily adornment, calendars, dancing, games, greetings, hairstyles, personal names, religion, and myths. However, the specific content of each of these domains, and many more, varies from culture to culture. Cultures differ from one another mainly because each represents a unique mix of values, norms, objects, and language inherited from the past, derived from other groups, and created anew by each group.

VALUES

The broadest element of culture is **values**, the general and abstract standards defining what a group or society as a whole considers good, desirable, right, or important. Values express the ideals of society, as well as of groups of every size.

In his classic work *Democracy in America* ([1835–1840] 1969), Alexis de Tocqueville detailed what he perceived to be America's values in the early nineteenth century. Among them were democracy, equality, individualism, "taste for physical comfort," spirituality, and economic prosperity. The vast majority of Americans today would accept most, if not all, of the values he described (Crothers 2010).

Associated Press

The overthrow of the dictatorship of Saddam Hussein (and the toppling of his statue, here depicted with his head covered by an American flag) did not bring with it the hoped-for democratization of Iraq.

Indeed, Americans expect these values to be accepted in other cultures around the world. However, this expectation has had some disappointing, even disastrous, consequences for the United States. For example, when the United States undertook invasions of Iraq and Afghanistan, one of the objectives was the creation of democratic regimes in those societies. The assumption was that Iraqis and Afghanis wanted the same kind of democracy as the one that exists in the United States. But creating democracies in those countries has proven to be extremely difficult for a variety of reasons, including the fact that their cultures lack a tradition of democratic government. It is extremely difficult, if not impossible, to impose a value, such as the value of democracy, on a society where it does not already exist, or where it exists in a very different form. As I write this in mid-2015, the dismemberment of Iraq (and Syria) by Islamic State and the continuing threat posed by the Taliban in Afghanistan make it seem even less likely that those countries will become functioning democracies.

The World Values Survey has found support for the idea that democracy is a hard, if not impossible, sell in many parts of the world (Welzel and Inglehart 2009). As you may recall from Chapter 2, the WVS has gathered data from a variety of countries around the world on such topics as individual views on democracy. Respondents in countries where personal freedom is not valued highly—such as Pakistan, Jordan, and Nigeria—tend to think of antidemocratic authoritarian regimes as being democratic. The data also show that citizens within these countries have little knowledge of the meaning of liberal democracy. There is little chance that American-style democracy will succeed in these countries.

Of course, there are many other reasons democracy has a difficult time succeeding in some countries. Among other things, before democracy can be established, people need to have enough to eat, to feel safe, to be able to get an education, and to trust the government. Unfortunately, many, if not all, of these needs are not being met in many parts of the world.

NORMS

Based on values, **norms** are the informal rules that guide what people do and how they live. Norms tell us what we should and should not do in a given situation (Dandaneau 2007). Many norms are informal. That is, they are not formally codified, not written down in any one place. **Laws** are norms that *have* been codified. They are written down and formally enforced through institutions such as the state. Rules prohibiting speaking and texting on handheld cell phones while driving are examples of how informal norms can come to be codified into laws.

You are expected to follow norms and obey laws, but the consequences of failing to do so are usually very different in the two cases. If you violate the law against homicide, you can expect to be arrested, incarcerated, and perhaps even executed. But if you fail to follow the norm of using utensils to eat your dinner and use your fingers instead, you can expect merely a few raised eyebrows and a "tsk tsk" or two from your dinner companions. However, reactions to violating norms are not always so gentle. For example, a gang member's violation of a norm against fleeing a fight with another gang may lead to physical violence, death, and other not-so-subtle outcomes.

Norms are reinforced through **sanctions**, which can take the form of punishments (negative sanctions) or rewards (positive sanctions). In general, when norms have been violated punishments are used, while rewards are employed when norms have been followed. For example, dinner companions might frown when you eat with your hands and grin approvingly when you use the right utensil. Gang members would be likely to disapprove of those who flee and approve of those who stay and fight. Children who bring home report cards with lots of As and Bs may be praised, while those whose report cards are dominated by lower grades may get stern lectures from their parents. In other words, sanctions may be applied when norms are observed as well as when they are violated. Sometimes either positive or negative sanctions are enough to enforce norms. However, enforcement is generally more effective when positive and negative sanctions are used in tandem—when *both* the "carrot" (reward) and the "stick" (punishment) are applied. Most people follow norms primarily because sanctions are associatedwith them.

ASK YOURSELF

What norms are operating in your classroom or your dorm or apartment? What negative sanctions have you observed when these norms have been violated?

TABLE 3.1 • 8 Norms of Air Travel

	NORM
1	Don't block the aisles when you are entering or leaving the airplane.
2	Limit your carry-ons to what realistically fits under your seat and in the overhead compartments.
3	Don't hog the armrests or encroach on people in seats on either side of you.
4	Don't talk to the people beside you if they are busily working on their laptops or trying to sleep.
5	Don't linger in the lavatory—others may be waiting—and don't leave behind a total mess.
6	Don't get angry at flight attendants. It's generally not their fault—whatever the problem is—and in any case they can make your life miserable for the remainder of the flight.
7	If traveling with a baby, use the restroom for diaper changes—not the seat next to you.
8	When it's time to deplane, wait your turn and allow people seated ahead of you to get off first.

Not all norms are the same, are equally important, or carry with them the same penalties if they are violated. On the one hand, there are **folkways**, or relatively unimportant norms. Whether they are observed or violated, they carry with them few if any sanctions (Sumner [1906] 1940). For example, many college classes have norms against texting during lectures, but those norms are frequently violated. When students' violations are detected by alert instructors, the negative sanctions, such as being asked to stop or to leave the room for the rest of class, are generally mild. In contrast, **mores** (pronounced MOR-ays) are more important norms whose violation is likely to be met with severe negative sanctions. Students who use their smartphones to cheat on college exams are violating mores (as well as campus rules). If their actions are witnessed or discovered, they may be subjected to severe negative sanctions, such as failing a class or even being expelled from school. While a clear distinction is often made between folkways and mores, in fact they exist along a continuum; it is often hard to distinguish where folkways end and mores begin.

MATERIAL CULTURE

Values and norms exist within the realm of ideas (see below for a related definition and discussion of symbolic, or nonmaterial, culture). However, culture also takes material—that is, tangible—forms. **Material culture** encompasses all the artifacts, the "stuff" (Molotch 2003; Steketee and Frost 2011), in which culture is reflected or manifested (Dant 2007). A wide range of things can be included under the heading of material culture, including the clothes we wear, the homes we live in, our computers and smartphones, our children's toys, and even the weapons used by our military.

Culture shapes such objects. For instance, the value Americans place on economic prosperity is reflected in such material objects as games like Monopoly. This game was first patented in the mid-1930s, and its icon is a well-dressed, economically successful tycoon. The goal of the game is to accumulate the most property and money. There are now also nonmaterial games (such as *Minecraft*) on websites such as Twitch that are not only enjoyed by millions of people online but are also played by thousands in quite material sports arenas for millions of dollars in very real and material prize money (Wingfield 2014b, 2014c).

Material culture also shapes the larger culture in various ways. For example, in playing Monopoly, children are learning about, helping to support, and furthering a culture that values wealth and material success. To take a different example, the centuries-old American value of individual freedom and individualism has been greatly enhanced by the widespread adoption of such material objects as the automobile, the single-family home, and the smartphone. The last, for example, gives us highly individualized and mobile access to the vast world available on the Internet.

SYMBOLIC CULTURE AND LANGUAGE

Symbolic culture includes the nonmaterial, intangible aspects of culture. We have already discussed two key forms of symbolic culture—values and norms. However, there is no clear line between material and nonmaterial culture. Most, if not all, material phenomena have symbolic aspects, and various aspects of symbolic culture are manifest in material objects. Our symbolic culture is manifest when we buy American-made rather than Japanese automobiles in a show of patriotism, purchase the latest iPhone as soon as it is released to denote our technological sophistication, or choose cloth diapers over disposables as a symbol of our commitment to "green" parenting.

One important aspect of symbolic culture is **language**, a set of meaningful symbols that enables communication. Language, especially in its written form, allows for the storage and development of culture. Cultures with largely oral traditions do manage to accumulate culture and transmit it from one generation or group to another, but written language is a far more effective way of retaining and expanding upon a culture.

Perhaps more important, language facilitates communication within a culture. Our words reflect the way we think and see the world. They also shape and influence culture. Suppose a time traveler from the 1950s arrived at a modern-day supermarket to buy something to eat for breakfast. Our time traveler would be bewildered by cereals with brand names like Bamm-Bamm Berry Pebbles and Bear Naked. The

exotic and varied cereals we have now would be considered a marvel by someone from the 1950s. The point, however, is that having names for many different kinds of cereals allows consumers to make much finer distinctions about breakfast and to communicate more precisely what it is they wish to eat.

The contemporary world has given us a wealth of new words. For example, in social networking, Twitter has given us the word *hashtag* to describe a label that helps us in searching *tweets*. The consumption-oriented nature of our society has also led to the creation of many new words, a large number of them brand names. The *iPhone* is the leading *smartphone* (another new word), and it has helped lead to a booming industry in *apps* (applications) of all sorts. Similarly, globalization has led to new words, including *globalization* itself, which was virtually unused prior to 1990 (Ritzer and Dean 2015). The explosion in companies sending work to be performed in other countries has given us the term *outsourcing* (Ritzer and Lair 2007).

Words like these are shared by people all over the world and allow them to communicate with one another. Communication among people of different cultures is also easier if they share a mother tongue. As you can see in the simplified map of world languages in Figure 3.2, African cultures use a variety of official and national languages. People in countries where French is the official language, such as Burkina Faso and Niger, can transact their business more easily with one another than they can with people in nations where Arabic or Portuguese is the primary language, such as Mauritania and Cape Verde.

In a world dominated by consumption, communication between cultures also takes place through the use of common brands. However, communication between cultures is never as easy or as clear as communication within a given culture. For example, brand names well known in some cultures may not translate well in other cultures. As a result, brands are often renamed to better reflect the cultures in which they are being sold. The following list shows the names of some well-known brands in the United States and elsewhere and the way they are translated into Chinese:

Brand	Chinese Translation
Nike	Enduring and Persevering
BMW	Precious Horse
Heineken	Happiness Power
Coca-Cola	Tasty Fun
Marriott	10,000 Wealthy Elites

While such name changes are common, some Chinese brand names are simply phonetic translations of the brands' names into Chinese. For example, Cadillac is translated "Ka di la ke." Although this name means little to the Chinese, the fact that it is foreign gives it an aura of status and respectability. However, if Microsoft had used a phonetic Chinese translation

FIGURE 3.2 • Distribution of Major Languages

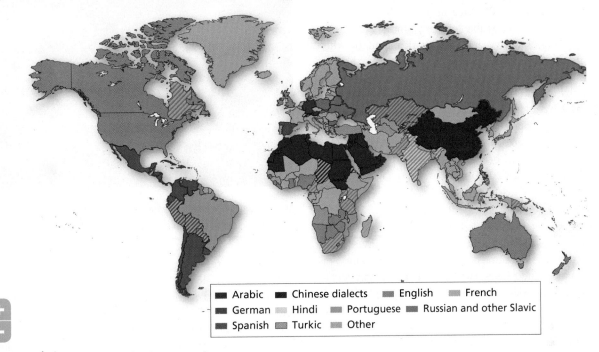

⑤SAGE datamaps **edge.sagepub.com**

- Official language for every country.
- Other languages spoken and percentage of English speakers.

SOURCES: Data from Languages of the World, One World, Nations Online Project.

of the name of its search engine Bing, it would have been in big trouble. In Chinese, the word *bing* translates into "disease" or "virus." To avoid being seen as disease-ridden or a carrier of a virus, Microsoft changed the search engine's Chinese name to Bi ying. This has the far more appealing meaning of "responding without fail." Peugeot did go ahead with the phonetically similar name Biao zhi, although it turned out that that sounds much like the Chinese slang word for prostitute. As a result, Peugeot has become the butt of a number of obscene jokes in China (Wines 2011).

ASK YOURSELF

Have you ever been in a situation, such as a trip abroad, in which understanding and communicating were difficult for you because you were unfamiliar with the language, symbols, and brands? How did you cope? Have you ever helped someone else who was in a similar situation? What did you do?

CULTURAL DIFFERENCES

As you have seen so far, we can think in terms of the culture of a society as a whole (for example, American culture), and later in this chapter we will even conceive of the possibility of a global culture. But you have also seen that there is great diversity within cultures, from gang culture to Internet culture and too many other variants of culture to enumerate. Studying and understanding culture becomes easier, however, with the aid of a few key ideas: ideal and real culture, ideology, subculture and counterculture, culture war, and multiculturalism.

IDEAL AND REAL CULTURE

There is often a large gap, if not a chasm, between **ideal culture**, or what the norms and values of society lead us to think people should believe and do, and **real culture**, or what people actually think and do in their everyday lives. For example, as we have seen, a major American value is democracy. However, barely a majority of Americans bother to vote in presidential elections—only 58.2 percent of eligible voters voted in the 2012 election, the same figure recorded four years earlier (McDonald 2013; see Chapter 12). A far smaller percentage of those who are eligible to vote in state and local elections. Worse, very few Americans are active in politics in other ways, such as canvassing on behalf of a political party or working to get people out to vote.

In another example, the cultural ideal that mothers should be completely devoted to their children (Blair-Loy 2003; Hays 1998) often comes into conflict with lived reality for many women who work outside the home and must balance their time between job and family. This contradiction is apparent in the incidence of breast-feeding, which, at least for some women, is once again a norm of motherhood (Avishai 2007; Stearns 2009, 2011). Breast-feeding is difficult or impossible for many mothers because it is labor- and time-intensive, and given work and all the other constraints they face in their lives, it is difficult for them to find the time and energy to do it. Despite its health benefits for baby and mother, under such circumstances breast-feeding can have adverse social and economic consequences for women (Rippeyoug and Noonan 2012). However, women who do not breast-feed can feel they have failed to live up to cultural standards of being a "good mom" (Blum 2000; Taylor, Funk, and Clark 2007).

IDEOLOGY

An *ideology* is a set of shared beliefs that explains the social world and guides people's actions. There are many ideologies in any society, and some of them become dominant. For example, in the United States, *meritocracy* is a dominant ideology involving the widely shared belief that all people have an equal chance of succeeding economically based on their hard work and skills. Many people act on the basis of that belief and, among other things, seek the education and training they think they need to succeed.

However, even with dedication and adequate education and training, not everyone succeeds. This reflects the key fact that not all ideologies are true. For one thing, they may come from, and be true for, some groups of people (such as those in the upper classes) and not for others (those in the lower classes) (Mannheim [1931] 1936). For another, they may be outright distortions used by one group to hide reality from another group (Marx [1857–1858] 1964). In this sense, it could be argued that meritocracy is an ideology created by the upper classes to hide the fact that those in the lower classes have little or no chance of succeeding. This fact is hidden from them to prevent them from becoming dissatisfied and rebellious. If the lower classes accept the ideology of meritocracy, they may be more likely to blame themselves for failing rather than blaming the upper classes or the American economic system as a whole.

SUBCULTURES

Within any culture there are **subcultures** or groups of people who accept much of the dominant culture but are set apart from it by one or more culturally significant characteristics. In the United States, major subcultures include the LGBT community (lesbians, gays, bisexuals, and transgender people), Hispanics, the Tea Party, Hasidic Jews, hip-hop fans, and youth. Muslims are becoming an increasingly important subculture in the United States (especially in some cities, such as Detroit). They already constitute a major subculture in many European countries, most notably France and Great Britain.

Corbis

Muslim women ride on an underground train in London. Muslims represent a growing subculture in Great Britain and other parts of Europe.

Subcultures arise in the realm of consumption as well. For example, "brand communities" develop around particular brand-name products (Meister, 2012; Muniz and O'Guinn 2001; Stratton and Northcote 2014). Harley-Davidson motorcycle riders are one such subculture (called HOGS, for Harley Owners Group), with distinctive clothing, events, and norms. Brand communities have formed around a number of Apple products, such as the Macintosh computer (the "Mac") and the iPad. The members of these communities share a number of cultural elements, including norms. In the case of the Mac, for example, some community members positively sanction "jailbreaking," a method for hacking into Apple's software in order to get around its restrictions and limitations.

Any society includes many subcultures, such as hackers, that develop around particular styles of life and share special vocabularies. A great deal of attention has been devoted to "deviant" subcultures, such as those of punks, goths, and the like (Berard 2007). In Great Britain, "football hooligans," those who often engage in violence at or in regard to soccer matches, constitute a deviant subculture largely specific to that society (Ayres and Treadwell 2012; Dunning, Murphy, and Williams 1988). However, there are also many "straight" youth subcultures, such as those who play online games such as *Minecraft* or "straight edge" music fans who eschew alcohol and drugs (see www.straightedge.com) (Wood 2006).

Another example of a subculture is the world of skateboarders. The majority of skateboarders accept most of the larger society's culture, norms, values, and language, but they also differ in some ways. For instance, many are more willing than most members of society to take physical risks, such as by participating in the sport known as parkour, which involves using the body to overcome urban obstacles such as walls and ledges (Kidder 2012). Skateboarders in general, as well as those who practice parkour, see such obstacles as enhancing the thrill of their activity.

COUNTERCULTURES

Countercultures are groups that not only differ from the dominant culture but also adhere to norms and values that may be incompatible with those of the dominant culture (Binkley 2007; Roszak ([1968] 1995; Zellner 1995). They may, in fact, consciously and overtly act in opposition to the dominant culture.

Computer hackers are a contemporary example of a counterculture (Corbett 2014; Levy 2010). Many hackers simply seek to show their technical mastery of computers through relatively benign actions such as writing free computer software, but a minority are devoted to subverting authority and disrupting the Internet, and some are involved in stealing personal identification data (identity theft) and money. They may write malicious code in order to interrupt or even shut down the normal operations of computers. Many attempted and successful break-ins have threatened government and corporate (e.g., Sony in 2014) computer systems; the hackers' goal has been to steal secret or personal information (e.g., gossip about movie stars in the e-mail of Sony personnel). In late 2014 the account information of 56 million Home Depot customers was compromised; information on 40 million Target accounts had been hacked the year before (Perlroth 2014). Personal accounts are also being hacked and locked until the account holders pay ransom demanded by the hackers (Simone 2015).

In the realm of consumption, an important contemporary counterculture is formed by those who are associated with or sympathetic to the "voluntary simplicity" movement (Elgin 2010; Grigsby 2004; Zammuel, Sasson-Levy, and Ben-Porat 2014). Sociologist Juliet Schor (1993, 1998) has critiqued the dominant American culture's emphasis on "work and spend." That is, we are willing to work long hours so that we can spend a great deal on consumption and live an ever more elaborate lifestyle. In addition, Schor (2005) points out the ways in which our consumer culture has led to the commercialization of childhood, with advertising pervading all aspects of children's lives. As a countercultural alternative, she suggests that we both work less and spend less and instead devote ourselves (and our children) to more meaningful activities. Living a simpler life means avoiding overconsumption, minimizing the work needed to pay for consumption, and doing less harm to the environment.

Globalization, especially economic globalization, has also spawned a number of very active countercultural groups. They are not necessarily antiglobalization, but they favor alternative forms of globalization (Kahn and Kellner 2007; Obara-Minnitt 2014; Pleyers 2010). The World Social Forum (WSF) was created in 2001 following a series of antiglobalization protests, particularly one in Seattle in 1999. The WSF's slogan is "Another world is possible." That other world would be less capitalistic. It would also allow for more democratic decision making on matters that affect large portions of the world's population. Those who accept this kind of perspective are clearly part of a counterculture. They oppose the global spread of the dominant capitalist culture that prioritizes maximizing profits over democratic decision making.

CULTURE WARS

In the 1960s, the hippies, student radicals, and anti–Vietnam War activists vocally, visibly, and sometimes violently rejected traditional American norms and values. Among other things, they rejected unthinking patriotism and taboos against recreational drugs and sexual freedom. The term *culture war* was used to describe the social upheaval that ensued. More generally, a **culture war** is a conflict pitting a subculture or counterculture against the dominant culture (e.g., anti-evolutionists versus evolutionists; Silva 2014), or a conflict between dominant groups within a society. Culture wars sometimes lead to the disruption of the social, economic, and political status quo (Hunter 1992; Luker 1984).

In the United States today, the major culture war is being fought between those who place themselves on the conservative and liberal ends of the sociopolitical spectrum. Conservatives generally favor less government spending, lower taxes for the wealthy, fewer entitlements for the poor, aggressive national defense, and minimal environmental regulations. Liberals usually support higher government spending on education, health care, and services for the poor; less spending on national defense; and stricter environmental regulations.

ASK YOURSELF

Do you think a culture war between political conservatives and liberals is inevitable? Why or why not?

There are also important differences in fundamental values between these groups. Consider, for example, the long-running political battle over legal limits to abortion and contraception. The values underlying this conflict have to do with differing definitions of life and attitudes toward women's role in society. Similarly, much heat is generated over "family values," with conservatives worrying about the decline in the traditional nuclear family, the increasing prevalence of cohabitation and single parenthood, homosexual marriage, and the adoption of children by same-sex couples. They place more emphasis on strict moral codes and self-discipline, whereas liberals accord more significance to empathy, openness, and fairness (McAdams et al. 2008). Liberals tend to see the developments in the family as signs of greater acceptance of people's differences and circumstances. The conservative–liberal culture war is fought endlessly in the popular media, which tends to be increasingly

Todd Gitlin and the Culture Wars

Todd Gitlin has been actively involved in the culture wars since his early days as a college student. In 1963 and 1964, he was president of Students for a Democratic Society (SDS), one of the most famous radical student movement organizations of the day. He helped organize both the first national protest against the Vietnam War and the first American demonstrations against corporate involvement in apartheid South Africa. Gitlin's view of his activist role is reflected in this statement: "I am a realist as well as an idealist, and I think that it is incumbent upon those of us in opposition to try to work within what are always arduous circumstances to stretch the limits of the possible" (Monbiot and Gitlin 2011).

Gitlin has written extensively on media and communications. His work has had an impact both on sociology and on the larger public. One of his most famous books is *The Whole World Is Watching* (1980), an analysis of major news coverage of the early days of the anti–Vietnam War movement. In this book, Gitlin draws on interviews with movement activists, news coverage, and his own experiences to analyze how the media reported on the antiwar movement and other movements. He shows that the media tend first to ignore movements, and when they finally do cover them, they selectively focus on only certain parts of the story. Despite their claims of neutrality and objectivity, they thereby distort reality and treat these movements as abnormal social phenomena. The media help to destabilize social movements by overemphasizing their revolutionary rhetoric and distorting what they do.

Todd Gitlin

In supporting "moderate" societal reforms, the media further undermine more radical social movements. Gitlin (2014) has most recently written about the culture war engaged in by the Occupy movement and that movement's decline.

Gitlin is professor of journalism and sociology at Columbia University. His former academic positions include professor of sociology and director of the mass communications program at the University of California, Berkeley, as well as professor of culture, journalism, and sociology at New York University. In line with his early activism, Gitlin has sought to reach wider audiences with his sociological analyses. His social commentary has appeared in a variety of newspapers (*New York Times, Los Angeles Times, Washington Post, San Francisco Chronicle*), magazines (*The Nation, Mother Jones*, poetry in

New York Review of Books), and other outlets (including National Public Radio). He also served as a member of the board of directors of Greenpeace USA from 2003 to 2006. Gitlin has sought to engage a variety of publics (including students, everyday citizens, and bystanders) by using sociological ideas to help them make better sense of the world and to imagine the range of human and social possibilities.

SOURCE: Printed with the permission of Paul Dean.

Think About It

What does Todd Gitlin mean by "stretching the limits of the possible"? Do you agree with his assessment of the media's coverage of movements? Why or why not? Can you think of other events the media first ignored and then distorted?

Reuters

Diverse street signs mark ethnic areas in and around Los Angeles, California. What do these markers of multiculturalism represent in terms of assimilation and integration?

divided along conservative (Fox News) and liberal (MSNBC) lines. The leading media pundits (e.g., Fox News's conservative Bill O'Reilly and MSNBC's liberal Rachel Maddow) are often at war with one another.

Examples of culture wars are also found in the digital world. For example, open-source advocates believe that the Internet, or at least large portions of it, should be protected from control by governments or corporations. They support free open-source software (Linux, Firefox, OpenOffice, GNU Image Manipulation Program) as well as free access to information. One of their models is Wikipedia, where anyone can create entries and modify them. They oppose the dominant players on the Internet, including Microsoft, Google, Apple, and Internet service providers, because they see these large corporations as carving up the digital world and controlling access in order to generate huge profits. There is a constant low-level conflict going on between members of these two cultures and the groups that support them. In 2015, a culture war broke out between those who want to give some corporations (such as Netflix) preferred status in the form of faster speeds on the Internet and those who favor "net neutrality," in which all Internet content is treated equally (Wyatt 2014).

MULTICULTURALISM AND ASSIMILATION

A great deal of attention has been paid in recent years to another aspect of cultural diversity—**multiculturalism**, or an environment in which cultural differences are accepted and appreciated both by the state and by the majority group (Modood 2007; Pakulski 2014). Cultural groups may be based on race, ethnicity, nationality, language, age, and other dimensions of difference. People in the United States, for example, generally accept that young and old have their own cultural preferences. Americans for the most part tolerate—sometimes even celebrate—the coexistence of different cultural groups within the larger culture.

When it comes to ethnicity and national origin, however, multiculturalism has not always been celebrated in this country. The dominant culture has been interested primarily in **assimilation**, or integrating minority groups into

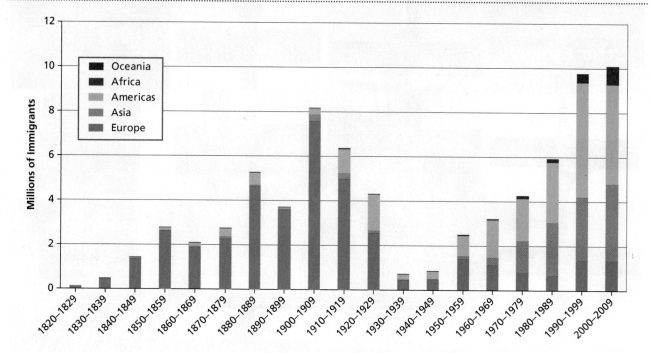

SOURCE: Data from Table 2, "Persons Obtaining Legal Permanent Resident Status by Region and Selected Country of Last Residence: Fiscal Years 1820 to 2012," in *Yearbook of Immigration Statistics: 2012 Legal Permanent Residents* (Washington, DC: U.S. Department of Homeland Security, 2012).

the mainstream. Until late in the twentieth century, most immigrants to the United States were from Europe, especially Eastern and Southern Europe (see Figure 3.3). Many of these groups did assimilate to a large degree, even if their assimilation occurred over a couple of generations. Today we do not think twice about whether or not Polish Americans or Italian Americans, for instance, are "regular" Americans.

But immigrants from the next large wave, in the 1990s and 2000s, have not assimilated so well. If you refer again to Figure 3.3, you can see that the largest flow of immigrants is now from the Americas, with another large—and growing—group from Asia. These immigrants, especially those from Mexico and China, often live in largely separate enclaves and speak their native languages (see Figure 3.4 for a map depicting the percentage of the U.S. population speaking a language other than English at home). They also often retain their basic cultures, such as their tastes in food. It remains to be seen whether, and to what degree, these groups will be assimilated into mainstream culture or their culture will be accepted as a valued element of American culture.

ASK YOURSELF

If you were born in the United States, imagine yourself as an immigrant to another country, one to which you have no cultural or genealogical ties and where you know no one. What would you do on your arrival in order to survive? Would you

seek out other Americans? Why or why not? Would you try to assimilate? How?

Multiculturalism is a relatively recent issue for many European societies, particularly the Scandinavian countries and the Netherlands. They have traditionally been almost monocultures and even now, during a period of widespread global migration, have a smaller proportion of foreign-born residents than the United States. However, beginning in the 1950s, many European countries began to experience labor shortages (Fassmann and Munz 1992; Fielding 1989). Large numbers of people from poorer Southern European countries such as Spain and Italy migrated to Northern European countries. Later, migration flowed from less developed countries outside Europe, such as Turkestan, other largely Islamic countries, and many African countries. The fall of the Soviet Union in 1991 brought additional Eastern Europeans from places like Albania. Many Northern European governments had intended for these immigrant workers to stay only a short time. However, the immigrants built lives for themselves, brought their families, and chose to remain. The result is that European countries today are far more multicultural than they were several decades ago.

More recent immigrants to largely Christian Europe bring with them very different cultures and very different religions (Islam, for example). They are also likely to be relatively poor.

FIGURE 3.4 • Percentage of U.S. Population Speaking a Language Other than English at Home, by County, 2007–2011

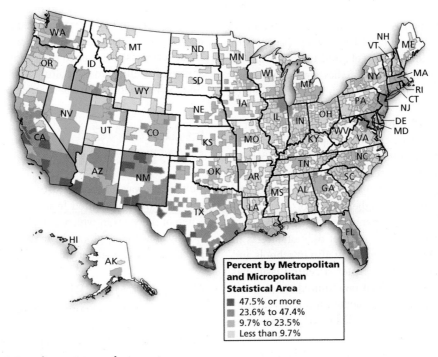

Percent by Metropolitan and Micropolitan Statistical Area
- 47.5% or more
- 23.6% to 47.4%
- 9.7% to 23.5%
- Less than 9.7%

SAGE datamaps **edge.sagepub.com**
- Percentage of non-English speakers in each county.
- Major languages spoken other than English.

SOURCE: Camille Ryan, "Language Use in the United States: 2011," American Community Survey Reports ACS-22, U.S. Census Bureau, August2013, p. 12.

In a 2011 protest against Muslim immigration to his country, a Norwegian right-wing extremist bombed government buildings in Oslo, killing 8 people. He later killed another 69 people during a shooting spree at a summer camp related to the country's ruling party. A relatively small, monocultural country like the Netherlands has had trouble digesting its roughly 1 million Muslim immigrants. Southern Europeans, especially in Italy, are increasingly having difficulty dealing with waves of immigrants from North Africa. In fact, many would-be immigrants are dying in accidents at sea before they even get to Italy as they seek to navigate the Mediterranean Sea in overcrowded and rickety boats. For years Italy and other countries sought to prevent migrants from leaving North Africa, especially the failed state of Libya. However, a 2012 ruling by the European Court of Human Rights stopped them from doing so. Now a more humane response is required, such as putting migrants, including many unaccompanied children, in holding centers until a decision can be made about what to do with them. Spain has an enclave in Morocco and has had great difficulties dealing with mass efforts of people from all over Africa to scale the enormous fence that separates the enclave from Morocco. Their goal is to gain entrée into Spain and thereby into Europe. Despite efforts to make the fence

more difficult to climb, thousands succeeded in 2014. The resistance of Italy, Spain, and other Southern European countries to such immigration, like that in Northern Europe, is motivated in part by economics and the fear that immigrants will cost natives their jobs. However, it is also cultural in the sense that the different cultures of these immigrants are seen as a threat to Italian, Spanish, and other European cultures.

In late 2015 the focus shifted to Eastern Europe, especially Hungary, which built a fence to prevent the entry of migrants moving through its neighbor Serbia and interested in going on to wealthier countries in Western Europe, especially Germany. While many Germans still see this as a cultural threat, Germany is more welcoming to migrants—and willing to put up with the cultural problems posed by them—than most other European countries for a variety of reasons, including the fact that its aging population needs an influx of young people.

Given these recent developments in Europe, the United States, and elsewhere in the world, some are declaring multiculturalism a failure. States, and especially majority groups, are growing less appreciative of, and less willing to accept, groups that represent different cultures (Gozdecka, Ercan, and Kmak 2014). However, there are other exceptions. Belgium, for instance, has sought to accommodate its burgeoning Muslim population by de-Christianizing its own holidays (for example, All Saints Day was renamed Autumn Holiday) (Kern 2014).

Identity Politics

While some majority groups have come to oppose multiculturalism, various minority groups have grown impatient with the dominant culture's limited view of multiculturalism and its unwillingness to accept them for who they are. Such minorities have asserted their right to retain their distinctive cultures and even their right *not* to assimilate, at least not totally. These groups have engaged in **identity politics** in using their power to strengthen the position of the cultural groups with which they identify (Nicholson 2008; Wasson 2007). Identity politics has a long history, in recent decades including the black power, feminist, and gay pride movements in many parts of the world. The goal of such movements has been the creation of a true multicultural society, one that accepts minorities for who they are.

Identity politics has played out not only on streets in public protests and demonstrations but also in schools and especially in universities. In the latter, a central issue has been whether all students should be required to learn the "canon"—a common set of texts, sometimes referred to as the "great books"—a body of knowledge long regarded as of central importance. For example, the works of Marx, Weber, and Durkheim are often thought to be the canonical texts in sociology. Minority cultures claim that the canon in sociology and many other fields reflects the interests and experiences of white middle- and upper-class males. They argue that alternative bodies of knowledge, such as those created by women, people of color, and the LGBT community, are at least as important. The result has been a proliferation of programs such as those devoted to black, Chicano, and feminist studies, where the focus is on those alternative texts and bodies of knowledge. However, such programs have been the subject of much controversy and political scrutiny (Lacey 2011).

Cultural Relativism and Ethnocentrism

Multiculturalism and identity politics are closely related to **cultural relativism**, which is the idea that aspects of a culture such as norms and values need to be understood within the context of that culture; there are no cultural universals, or universally accepted norms and values. In this view, different cultures simply have different norms and values. There is no basis for saying that one set of norms and values is better than another (Weiler 2007). Thus, for example, those in Western countries should not judge Islamic women's use of headscarves. Conversely, those in the Islamic world should not judge Western women's baring of their midriffs.

Cultural relativism runs counter to the tendency in many cultures toward **ethnocentrism**, or the belief that the norms, values, traditions, and material and symbolic aspects of one's own culture are better than those of other cultures (Brown 2007b; Machida 2012). The tendency toward ethnocentrism both among subcultures within the United States and in cultures throughout the world represents a huge barrier to greater cultural understanding. However, a belief in one's own culture can be of great value to a culture, giving people a sense of pride and identity. Problems arise when ethnocentrism serves as a barrier to understanding other cultures, a source of conflict among cultures, or an excuse for one culture to deny rights or privileges to another.

EMERGING ISSUES IN CULTURE

Culture is always changing, just as it is continually in the process of being transmitted from one generation to the next. Some of the ways in which today's cultures are changing are worthy of further exploration. In this section, we will focus on global culture, consumer culture, and cyberculture.

GLOBAL CULTURE

There are certainly major differences within American culture, such as those that exist among subcultures. Yet few would dispute the idea that it is possible to talk about American culture in general. However, discussing a global culture, a culture common to the world as a whole, is not as easy. Some elements of material culture, including hamburgers, sushi, cars, and communication technology, have spread widely around the world, but the global diffusion of nonmaterial culture—values, norms, and symbolic culture—has proven to be more difficult.

The Globalization of Values

We have already discussed how values differ, sometimes greatly, from one society to another. How, then, can we discuss global values—values that are shared throughout the world (Sekulic 2007c)? Some scholars argue that global values exist because all people share a biological structure that produces universal tendencies, including common values. Others contend that while particular values vary from country to country, the underlying structure of values is much the same across societies. However, the most persuasive argument for the existence of global values is traceable to the process of globalization. The global flow of all sorts of things—information, ideas, products, and people—produces realities in most parts of the world that are more similar than ever before in history (Lechner and Boli 2005). If these realities are increasingly similar, then it seems likely that what people value will come to be increasingly similar throughout the world.

Cultural Imperialism

Many observers believe that global culture is most affected by **cultural imperialism**, or the imposition of one dominant culture on other cultures (Tomlinson 1999, 2012). Cultural imperialism tends to have an adverse impact on, or even destroy, local cultures. For example, there is a long tradition in India of professional letter writers, men who place themselves in prominent locations (e.g., near train stations) and offer their services writing letters for poor, illiterate migrants. Many of these letter writers are able to survive on the pittance they are paid for each letter. However, the adoption of elements of Western culture—the cell phone, texting, and so on—is rendering the professional letter writers, and the cultural traditions associated with them, obsolete.

There is certainly a great deal of cultural imperialism in the world today, much of it associated with the United States (Crothers 2010; Kuisel 1993). The process of **Americanization** includes the importation by other countries of a variety of cultural elements—products, images, technologies, practices, norms, values, and behaviors—that are closely associated with the United States. One example is the American movie industry: The popularity of American movies around the world has decimated the film industries of many countries, including Great Britain and France. (India is one exception, with its thriving Bollywood productions, including the 2009 Academy Award winner for Best Picture, *Slumdog Millionaire*; Rizvi 2012.) Another successful U.S. cultural export is Americans' taste for food, especially fast food and the way in which it is eaten (quickly,

with one's hands, standing up or in the car). McDonald's is a prime example, but another of note is Starbucks (Simon 2009), which has been surprisingly successful in exporting its model of large, slowly consumed cups of coffee. There are now more than 21,000 Starbucks stores located around the world, in over 60 countries (see Figure 3.5).

While cultural imperialism certainly exists, it would be wrong to overestimate its power. Local cultures can be quite resilient. Not all cultures suffer the fate of French movie producers and Indian letter writers. For example:

- The powerful process of Americanization is often countered by **anti-Americanism**, which is an aversion to the United States in general, as well as to the influence of its culture abroad (Huntington 1996; O'Connor and Griffiths 2005).

- Many cultures—Chinese and Islamic cultures, for example—have long, even ancient, histories. These cultures have resisted, and are likely to continue to resist, at least some impositions from other cultures that threaten their basic values and beliefs.

- Local cultures modify inputs and impositions from other cultures by integrating them with local realities and in the process produce cultural hybrids that combine elements of both (Nederveen Pieterse 2009). McDonald's sells such

FIGURE 3.5 • Starbucks' Global Expansion: 1993–2014

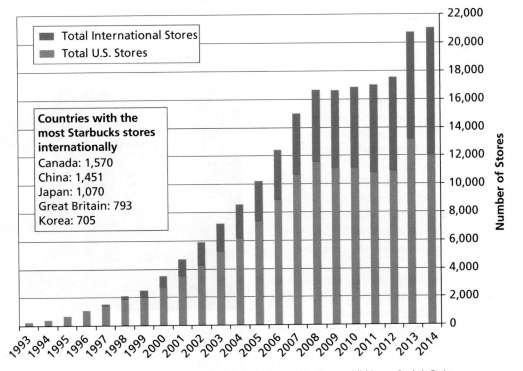

Countries with the most Starbucks stores internationally
Canada: 1,570
China: 1,451
Japan: 1,070
Great Britain: 793
Korea: 705

SOURCES: Data from Starbucks Company Statistics: Statistic Brain, Statistic Brain Research Institute, publishing as Statistic Brain.

hybrid foods as McChicken Korma Naan, which caters to those in Great Britain who have developed a taste for Indian food (including the many Indians who live there); McLaks, a grilled salmon sandwich served in Norway; and McHuevos, a hamburger with a poached egg served in Uruguay.

Thus, cultural imperialism needs to be examined in the context of the counterreactions to it, counterflows from elsewhere in the world, and the combination of global and local influences to produce unique cultural elements.

One of the counterreactions to cultural imperialism is *cultural cleansing,* or the process by which one culture seeks to eliminate elements of another culture that it sees as having been imposed on it. For example, anti-Americanism can lead to efforts to cleanse a culture of American influences. Much in the news these days are Islamic State's efforts to cleanse areas under its control of the symbols and material artifacts of other cultures and religions that it believes have been imposed on the Islamic world (Associated Press 2015d).

CONSUMER CULTURE

Consumption is clearly highly valued in the United States (and elsewhere; see Nwachukwu and Dant 2014). What makes American culture a **consumer culture** is the fact that many of its core ideas and material objects relate to consumption. Further, consumption is a primary source of meaning in American life (Belk 2007; Sassatelli 2007; Slater 1997). In a consumer culture, meaning may be found in the goods and services purchased, in the process of buying them (in shopping malls, cybermalls, and so on), in the social aspects of consumption (shopping with friends or family), and even in the settings in which consumption takes place (e.g., the Venetian or some other Las Vegas casino-hotel, eBay) (Ritzer, Goodman, and Wiedenhoft 2001). There are norms for the consumption process as well. For example, customers should wait patiently in the queue for the cashier, gamblers at a Las Vegas casino should not flaunt their winnings in front of other gamblers and should tip dealers, and so on.

Consumer culture is unique in the history of the world. In the past, culture has generally focused on some other aspect of social life, such as religion, warfare, citizenship, or work. In fact, in the not-too-distant past in the United States and other developed countries, the core ideas and material objects of culture related to work and production. People were thought to derive their greatest meaning from their work. This was true from the Industrial Revolution until approximately 1970, when observers began to realize that developed societies, especially the United States, were beginning to derive more meaning from consumption (Baudrillard [1970] 1998). Of course, work continues to be important, as do religion, warfare, and citizenship, but

many people in the developed world now live in a culture dominated by consumption.

While the roots of today's consumer culture can be traced further back in history (Williams [1982] 1991), the rise of consumer culture is linked to the rise of the modern world in the West (Campbell 1987). Today, of course, consumer culture has arguably become *the* culture of the modern West and indeed of modernity in general. But consumer culture has also globalized to a great degree. It has become firmly entrenched in such non-Western places as Singapore, Hong Kong, and Dubai. Japan has been called the premier consumer culture. Even in today's China, known for its production-oriented culture, a billion-plus citizens are becoming more and more consumption oriented.

Children in a Consumer Culture

The most controversial aspect of consumer culture may be the involvement of children. In a consumer culture, it is important that children be socialized into, and become actively involved in, consuming (Cook 2004, 2007; Pilcher 2013). Consumption by children has not always been valued, however. In fact, there were once strong norms against it. Children were not considered able to make informed choices about consumption and were therefore seen as even more susceptible than adults to exploitation by advertisers and marketers.

Today, norms and values have changed, and children are much more immersed in consumer culture than ever before. They learn at an early age to value consumption as well as the norms involved in participating in it. As adults, then, they will fit well into a culture with consumption at its core.

Marketing aimed at children is now pervasive. For example, the Disney Company has begun directly marketing

Some parents see buying and collecting certain toys, such as the American Girl dolls these girls are holding, as valuable activities. What cultural values are being promoted when young children are encouraged to participate actively in consumer culture?

Japanese Consumer Culture

We tend to think of the United States as having the ultimate consumer culture. However, Japan may be the world's premier consumption society. By the 1980s the Japanese were consuming with a vengeance, spurred on by an economic boom led by companies like Toyota and Sony. Rampant consumption soon helped lead Japan into an economic "bubble," which burst with the crash of the Tokyo stock market in 1989. More recently, the Japanese economy has suffered from the Great Recession in 2008, a massive recall of Toyota automobiles in 2010, and the effects of the devastating earthquake, tsunami, and Fukushima nuclear accident in 2011.

Nevertheless, the Japanese remain avid and sophisticated mass consumers (Clammer 1997), possibly even more rational and focused on convenience and efficiency than American consumers. Japan has the largest number of vending machines per capita in the world, providing everything from snacks and beverages to eggs, ice, beer, umbrellas, flowers, neckties, sneakers, fresh vegetables, batteries, hot French fries, board games, and pornographic magazines ("14 Cool Vending Machines" 2009).

Another example of the rationality of Japanese consumers is the eagerness with which they have embraced American fast-food chains. There are more than 3,000 McDonald's restaurants in Japan, a little less than 10 percent of the worldwide total (Ritzer 2015). Japan also has many fast-food chains of its own. The preference for a rationalized way of eating helped popularize the "beef

Associated Press

A conveyor belt brings sushi to restaurant customers in Japan. What are the downsides, if any, of this fast and efficient way of obtaining food?

bowl," an all-in-one meal including beef, rice, noodles, and other ingredients. There are three big chains of beef bowl restaurants in Japan—Sukiya, Yoshinoya, and Matsuya (Tabuchi 2010).

Kura is a Japanese chain of 262 sushi restaurants with conveyor belts instead of waiters carrying food to the diners (Tabuchi 2010). In these restaurants, the highly skilled and valued traditional sushi chef has been largely replaced by robots. Diners order from touch screens and put finished plates in table-side bays so their bills can be calculated automatically. Video cameras let supervisors in three control centers watch over each

restaurant. All this allows Kura to operate with relatively few workers, with a high degree of efficiency and much lower costs, and therefore greater profitability, than traditional sushi restaurants.

Think About It

What aspect of consumer culture accounts for Japan's apparent acceptance of sushi-making robots to replace chefs whose skills are highly valued? Can you think of any similar changes taking place in U.S. consumer culture, whether in the restaurant business or elsewhere? What about income tax software, for example, or virtual dressing rooms on websites selling clothing?

baby products, and thus the Disney brand, to new mothers in maternity wards. In schools, branded products are sold at book fairs, and corporate sponsorships adorn everything from sports stadiums to classroom supplies. Brands and logos are woven into textbook problems and examples. Market researchers observe the way children use and respond to products and advertising messages not just in focus groups and in the lab but also in natural settings such as school and

Associated Press

The Burning Man festival aims to celebrate self-expression and build community while simultaneously subverting money-based, commodified consumer culture.

the home. Marketers have also discovered the importance of the "pester power" of children—the ability of children to nag their parents into buying things. It is effective not only for selling children's products but also for getting children to influence their parents' purchases.

Nontraditional Settings for Consumption

An interesting aspect of consumer culture is the way in which it has spread beyond the economy to other aspects of society. For example, higher education is increasingly characterized by consumer culture. Students and their parents shop around for the best colleges and the most conspicuous degrees or for the best values in a college education. College rankings, such as those published by *Kiplinger* and *U.S. News & World Report,* are a big business. For-profit colleges have become a booming industry, with enterprises like the University of Phoenix and Kaplan University enrolling hundreds of thousands of students who pay for the opportunity to earn their degrees on a flexible schedule.

Not long ago students were largely passive recipients of what educational systems had to offer, but now they are more active consumers of education. College students shop for the best classes, or the best class times, and regularly rate their professors and choose classes on the basis of the professors' ratings. They are also much more likely to make demands for up-to-date "products" and attentive service from their professors and colleges, as they do from shopping malls and salespeople.

A key site of consumption is now the Internet (Miller and Slater 2000). A good portion of the time people spend online is related to consumption, either directly (purchasing items on sites like Etsy or Amazon) or indirectly (buying things on game sites like FarmVille2 with real dollars). In 2000, only 22 percent of Americans had purchased products online, including books, music, toys, and clothing. By 2013, that number had increased to 80 percent (Weinstein 2013). The growing importance of online consumption is reflected in the increasing amount spent each year on "Cyber Monday" (the Monday after Thanksgiving). In addition, in a process known as "contextual advertising," advertisements are often woven seamlessly into the content of Internet sites— even into games designed for children. Beyond that, many websites carry pop-up ads for goods and services targeting the interests of the individuals viewing the sites. More

DIGITAL LIVING

Commercialization and Web 2.0

In its early years, the Internet was dominated by a model called Web 1.0 (Ritzer and Jurgenson 2010). The early Yahoo and AOL sites were, and to a large extent the current versions still are, two examples of Web 1.0. Basically, those who owned and controlled these sites decided what was provided to those who accessed them. Few, if any, options were available to the user.

Web 1.0 sites continue to exist, but the Internet has come to be dominated by Web 2.0 sites featuring user-generated content. Those who access Web 2.0 sites are not simply consumers (as users of Web 1.0 sites were); rather, they are **prosumers** (Ritzer 2013; Ritzer, Dean, and Jurgenson 2012), both producing and consuming the content. While the concept of the prosumer is relatively new, it overlaps to a large extent with the older, more familiar idea of the "do-it-yourselfer" (Watson and Shove 2008). The prosumer is prominent on all the major sites as well as on blogs and many other areas of the Internet. Instead of passively reading news stories written by others on Huffington Post or the *New York Times* website, many of us are both creating and reading blogs. Instead of watching videos created for TV networks, we watch and produce the videos on YouTube. Rather than gazing at pictures produced by professional photographers, we upload and comment on photos on Facebook and Instagram.

Many investors believe free sites have huge potential for profit and will be the new media giants in the coming years. Take Facebook, for example. At the time of this writing, about 1.3 billion people worldwide are Facebook users, a number that continues to grow (Facebook 2014). It clearly costs a great deal of money to provide billions of users with the computer capacity to meet all their Facebook needs, and users pay nothing for those services. However, Facebook is already making a lot of money from paid and targeted advertisements, and it will continue to do so. Of Facebook's total revenue of $2.59 billion in the last quarter of 2013, $2.34 billion was from advertisements (Goel 2014). As the number of users, mobile and otherwise, continues to mushroom, Facebook will be able to attract many more advertisers and charge more for its ads.

Think About It

While users do not pay directly for accessing Facebook, their presence allows the website to sell on-site advertising directed at them. So the "price" of using this website, and many others, is the intrusion of advertising. How would the cultural experience of using the Internet be different if users paid for it directly? What if it were paid for by voluntary contributions, as public television and radio are? What if the government maintained the Internet as it does the roads and highways?

specifically, if you use Google to shop for shoes or Amazon for books, ads for shoes and books will pop up for days, or even months, afterward on many of the sites you visit.

YouTube offers several innovations in consumption, including "shopping haul" and "unboxing" videos. In shopping haul videos, consumers, often women, show viewers the results of their recent shopping trips. Haulers describe and display clothing, accessories, and cosmetics from popular chain stores (such as Superdry, Bebe, and Victoria's Secret) in malls and shopping strips around the world. Prices and bargains are mentioned frequently. Unboxing videos are a curious hybrid of unofficial marketing and product demonstration. Technology unboxers might demonstrate the features of new iPhones or computer games, while toy unboxers film children playing with various toys. Unboxers might assemble Lego kits, break open Disney *Frozen*-themed chocolate eggs, or open up McDonald's Happy Meals and then have children play with the toys.

It could be argued that people in general, and especially children and teens, are becoming more immersed in consumer culture as they become more deeply enmeshed with the Internet. This is even more the case now because we increasingly carry the Internet—and the ability to shop there—with us all the time on our smartphones. As a result, consumer culture has become an even more inescapable part of our daily lives. Furthermore, consumption on the Internet is increasingly wedded to the material world. You can now pay for parking and rental cars using smartphone apps. An iPhone app allows a driver to open the doors of her rented Zipcar with her phone and honk its horn to locate it. The Hunt is an app that brings into play a community of fashion-minded people to help us hunt down desired fashion items.

How much of the time you spend online is devoted to shopping or purchasing? Try keeping a log of your Internet use for a few days. Note how many times you went online and on how many of those occasions you bought something or browsed sites devoted to consumption. Are you a typical Internet consumer? Why or why not?

A Postconsumer Culture?

Many people are also doing something that would have been unthinkable only a few years ago—eschewing consumption and instead saving money. The personal savings rate in the United States has changed over the past few years. In late 2007 it dipped to close to 2.5 percent of disposable income. At the height of the Great Recession in 2008 and 2009, it spiked to more than 8 percent. By mid-2015, even though the economy had improved considerably, the personal savings rate still exceeded 5 percent. People who are saving more of their money are obviously using less of it to consume.

These changes in the behavior of consumers and their attitudes speak to a change in the larger value system. Consuming less is a sure indication of at least a temporary decline of consumer culture. It may even be the beginning of a postconsumer culture. Among the characteristics of such a culture, beyond buying less and saving more, are sharing more things in the "sharing economy" (Belk 2014), renting consumer items (such as dresses on sites like Rent the Runway, www.renttherunaway.com), taking pride in buying less expensive or even recycled items, buying less showy brands (a Kia rather than a BMW), dining at home more often than eating at restaurants, and showing a greater concern for the environment in terms of what we buy and, more important, do not buy. It is not clear that we are in a postconsumer culture, and if we are, it is uncertain how long it will last. However, just as we entered what is best described as a consumer culture in the last half of the twentieth century, it is at least possible that we are entering a postconsumer culture in the first half of the twenty-first century.

Culture Jamming

Another chink in consumer culture has been created by organized groups actively seeking to subvert aspects of both consumer culture and the larger culture. The success of Burning Man is one indication of such subversion. Begun in 1986, this annual weeklong event in Nevada's Black Rock Desert today attracts 50,000 participants, who commit themselves during their stay to self-expression, decommodification (for example, cash transactions between participants are banned), and community building (Chen 2009; Jones 2011). This is an example of **culture jamming**, which radically transforms mass media messages, often turning them on their heads completely (Lasn 2000). It is a form of social protest aimed at revealing underlying realities of which consumers may be unaware. The hope is that once people are made aware of these realities, they will change their behaviors or perhaps even band together to change the underlying realities.

The best examples of culture jamming are to be found in the magazine *Adbusters* and the media campaigns it sponsors. The magazine's main targets are in the realm of consumption, especially web and magazine advertisements and billboards. The idea is to transform a corporation's ads into anticorporate, anticonsumption advertisements (Handelman and Kozinets 2007).

The following are some examples of the ways in which culture jamming by *Adbusters* turns commercial messages inside out:

- "Joe Chemo"—rather than Joe Camel—shows an emaciated version of the Camel character (who, of course, smokes Camel cigarettes) in a hospital bed undergoing chemotherapy, presumably for lung cancer caused by smoking.

- "Tommy Sheep" is a spoof of a Tommy Hilfiger ad, with sheep (presumably representing the conformists who buy such clothing) pictured in front of a huge American flag.

- "Absolute on Ice," spoofing an Absolut vodka ad, depicts the foot of a corpse (presumably someone killed by excessive alcohol consumption) with a toe tag.

- "True Colors of Benetton" depicts a man wearing a Benetton shirt but with wads of money stuffed in his mouth. The ad is designed to underscore the true objective of Benetton, and of all corporations in capitalist society: money and profits.

All the above show the hidden realities (sickness, death, and other miseries) and goals (conformist consumers, obscene profits) of corporations. A broader objective is to reveal to viewers the folly of consumer culture, which encourages the consumption of numerous harmful (cigarettes, alcohol) and wasteful (expensive clothing) goods and services.

CYBERCULTURE

The Internet is, as mentioned before, one site for the proliferation of consumer culture and perhaps of postconsumer culture. It is also the site of an entirely new culture—**cyberculture** (F. Turner 2008). That is, the Internet as a whole (as well as the individual websites that it comprises) has the characteristics of all culture, including distinctive values and norms.

Some of the distinctive values within cyberculture are openness, knowledge sharing, and access. These values have their roots in the open-source software that emerged before computing became an attractive commercial opportunity. They are also rooted in the knowledge sharing and continuous improvement that were the practice when early computer professionals survived through reciprocity (Bergquist 2003). These roots have been maintained through the open-source movement, through actions against censorship, and through organizations such as the Free Software Foundation and the "copyleft" movement. In line with the values of a postconsumer society, these "cyberlibertarians" favor user control of information and applications and free products (Dahlberg 2010; Himanen 2001). They are in conflict with the more dominant values of profit maximization and control of the Internet by large corporations. This conflict of values, a culture war by the definition offered earlier in this chapter, goes a long way toward defining the Internet today.

Various norms have also come to be a part of cyberculture. Internet users are not supposed to hack into websites, create and disseminate spam, unleash destructive worms and viruses, maliciously and erroneously edit user-generated sites such as Wikipedia, and so on. Many norms relate to desirable behavior on the Internet. For example, creating and editing entries on Wikipedia is supposed to be taken seriously and done to the best of one's ability. Once an entry exists, the many people who offer additions and deletions are expected to do so in a similar spirit. Those who purposely add erroneous information on Wikipedia will suffer the stern disapproval of other contributors to, and users of, the site. They may even be banned from the site by those who manage it.

There is, of course, much more to the culture of the Internet. For example, in addition to a general cyberculture, there are a number of cybercultures that vary from nation to nation. But the point is that cyberculture, like all culture, is emerging and evolving as other changes take place within and around it. The biggest difference between cyberculture and other cultures is that, because the Internet is so new and the changes in it are so rapid, cyberculture is far more fluid than culture in general.

People need to be socialized in order to learn how to use the Internet, and they increasingly interact online rather than on a face-to-face basis. In Chapter 4 we turn to a broad discussion of the sociological perspective on socialization and interaction.

SUMMARY

Culture encompasses the ideas, values, norms, practices, and objects that allow a group of people, or even an entire society, to carry out their collective lives with a minimum of friction. Values are the general, abstract standards defining what a group or society as a whole considers good, desirable, right, or important. Norms are the rules that guide what people do and how they live. Culture also has material and symbolic elements. Material culture encompasses all the objects and technologies that are reflections or manifestations of a culture. Symbolic culture, the nonmaterial side of culture, is best represented by language.

We are immersed in a diversity of cultures. Subcultures include people who may accept much of the dominant culture but are set apart from it by one or more culturally significant characteristics. Countercultures are groups of people who differ in certain ways from the dominant culture and whose norms and values may be incompatible with it. Culture wars pit one subculture or counterculture against another or against the dominant culture.

Many cultures tend to be ethnocentric—that is, those enmeshed in them believe that their own culture's norms, values, traditions, and the like are better than those of other cultures. Many times newcomers are expected to assimilate, or to replace elements of their own culture with elements of the dominant culture. A society that values multiculturalism accepts and even embraces the cultures of many different groups and encourages the retention of cultural differences.

Some scholars argue that globalization has increasingly led to a global culture; others attribute the growing cultural similarity around the world to cultural imperialism. In consumer culture, core ideas and material objects relate to consumption. An increasingly important cyberculture thrives on the Internet.

REVIEW QUESTIONS

1. What do you and your peers think of the millennial culture depicted in HBO's *Girls*? Are you as "uncool" as the characters on that show? You are likely the right age to be considered a millennial, but do you feel you are part of that culture?

2. How and why might the American value of democracy have created tensions in Iraq and Afghanistan?

3. As part of our material culture, what values do smartphones reflect? In what ways have "brand communities" or other

subcultures formed around smartphones and the use of smartphones?

4. Consider the terminology that has developed around the Internet. How does this language reflect changes in the world around us? In what ways does it shape the world around us?

5. Skateboarders constitute a subculture because they have certain cultural differences (in language, dress, values) that set them apart from other groups in society. What is another example of a subculture in the United States, and what elements of this culture (both material and symbolic) make it unique?

6. How does a counterculture differ from a subculture? Is it reasonable to say that computer hackers are part of a counterculture? Can you think of other examples of countercultures?

7. What is the difference between assimilation and multiculturalism? Would you say that the United States is an assimilationist or a multiculturalist society? Would you say

that multiculturalism is more a part of the ideal culture or the real culture of the United States? Why?

8. What are some of today's important culture wars? In what ways and to what degree are you engaged in them? Even if you are not active in them, how is your life affected by them?

9. What do we mean by the term *global culture*? Do you think the evolution of popular social networking sites such as Facebook and Twitter is related more to the evolution of a global culture or to Americanization? In what ways are these sites reflective of cultural hybridization? Do you see yourself as a cyberlibertarian as far as the Internet is concerned?

10. To what extent are you and your friends embedded in a consumer culture? How has the development of technology (the Internet, smartphones, and so forth) helped create this consumer culture? Do you think that culture jamming and events such as Burning Man are significant threats to consumer culture?

APPLYING THE SOCIOLOGICAL IMAGINATION

Multinational chains (like McDonald's and Starbucks) are important cultural actors in an increasingly globalized world. These multinational corporations have made great efforts to promote images and cultures around their brands. For this exercise, spend some time at an outlet of one of your favorite global chains. Pay close attention to the ways in which informal and formal norms are created in the space through decor, language, layout, and so on.

How does the physical space govern behavior within the location? How does the physical space relate to the kind of image

the company is trying to create for its brand? In what ways are the norms that operate within the store reflective of the larger norms of society? Do any of the norms conflict with larger societal norms?

Do some research on the Internet to see the ways in which these chains operate differently in other countries. How do they compare and contrast? Given the similarities and differences across countries, would you say such global chains are signs of cultural imperialism or cultural hybridization?

KEY TERMS

Americanization: The importation by other countries of products, images, technologies, practices, norms, values, and behaviors that are closely associated with the United States. (p. 67)

anti-Americanism: An aversion to the United States in general, as well as to the influence of its culture abroad. (p. 67)

assimilation: The integration of minorities into the dominant culture. (p. 63)

consumer culture: A culture in which the core ideas and material objects

relate to consumption and in which consumption is a primary source of meaning in life. (p. 68)

counterculture: A group whose culture not only differs in certain ways from the dominant culture but also adheres to norms and values that may be incompatible with those of the dominant culture. (p. 61)

cultural imperialism: The imposition of one culture, more or less consciously, on other cultures. (p. 66)

cultural relativism: The idea that aspects of culture such as norms and values need to be understood within the context of a person's own culture and that there are no universally accepted norms and values. (p. 66)

culture: A collection of ideas, values, practices, and material objects that mean a great deal to a group of people, even an entire society, and that allow them to carry out their collective lives in relative order and harmony. (p. 54)

culture jamming: The radical transformation of an intended message in popular culture, especially one associated with the mass media, to protest underlying realities of which consumers may be unaware. (p. 72)

culture war: A conflict that pits subcultures and countercultures against the dominant culture or that pits dominant groups within society against each other. (p. 61)

cyberculture: An emerging online culture that has the characteristics of all culture, including distinctive values and norms. (p. 72)

ethnocentrism: The belief that one's own group or culture—including its norms, values, customs, and so on—is superior to, or better than, others. (p. 66)

folkways: Norms that are relatively unimportant and, if violated, carry few if any sanctions. (p. 57)

ideal culture: Norms and values indicating what members of a society should believe in and do. (p. 59)

identity politics: The use of a minority group's power to strengthen the position of the cultural group with which it identifies. (p. 66)

language: A set of meaningful symbols that makes possible the communication of culture as well as communication more generally within a given culture, and that calls out the same meaning in the person to whom an utterance is aimed as it does to the person making the utterance. (p. 58)

law: A norm that has been codified, or written down, and is formally enforced through institutions such as the state. (p. 57)

material culture: All of the material objects that are reflections or manifestations of a culture. (p. 57)

mores: Important norms whose violation is likely to be met with severe sanctions. (p. 57)

multiculturalism: The encouragement of cultural differences within a given environment, both by the state and by the majority group. (p. 63)

norms: Informal rules that guide what members of a culture do in given situations and how they live. (p. 57)

prosumer: One who combines the acts of consumption and production. (p. 71)

real culture: What people actually think and do in their everyday lives. (p. 59)

sanctions: The application of rewards (positive sanctions) or punishments (negative sanctions) when norms are accepted or violated. (p. 57)

subculture: A group of people who accept much of the dominant culture but are set apart from it by one or more culturally significant characteristics. (p. 60)

symbolic culture: Aspects of culture that exist in nonmaterial forms. (p. 58)

values: General and abstract standards defining what a group or society as a whole considers good, desirable, right, or important—in short, its ideals. (p. 56)

$SAGE edge™   edge.sagepub.com/ritzeressentials2e

SAGE edge offers a robust online environment featuring an impressive array of free tools and resources for review, study, and further exploration, keeping both instructors and students on the cutting edge of teaching and learning.

LEARNING OBJECTIVES	FOR FURTHER EXPLORATION AND APPLICATION
LO 3-1: Define culture.	▶ How Sociologists Define Culture ◉ Why Millennials Hate Voicemail ◉ What Is Culture?
LO 3-2: Identify the basic elements of culture, including values and norms.	▶ The Main Elements of Culture ◉ Are Culture Wars Over? ◉ Quick Guide to Culture
LO 3-3: Discuss diversity within cultures, including the concepts of ideal and real culture, subcultures and countercultures, culture wars, and assimilation.	▶ Subculture versus Counterculture ◉ The Red and Blue Language Dividing America ◉ The American Tradition of Multiculturalism
LO 3-4: Describe emerging issues in culture, such as global and consumer culture.	▶ Sudanese Immigrants React to American Culture ◉ How Internet Sales Threaten Shopping Mall Culture ◉ Instacart and Online Grocery Shopping

SOCIALIZATION AND INTERACTION

Socialization into Extremism

On January 7, 2015, two Islamist brothers—Saïd and Chérif Kouachi—burst into the Paris offices of the satirical magazine *Charlie Hebdo* and killed 12 people because the publication had repeatedly lampooned the Prophet Muhammad. The Kouachi brothers were later killed by French security forces.

Why would people commit such a heinous crime that they knew would cost them their own lives? Clearly, the Kouachis are only two of many who have accepted radical Islamic ideas and been offended at the way Muslims have been treated and depicted. They were not radical Islamists in their early years. They attended a boarding school for orphans in a small French town, played soccer, delivered pizza, and dreamed of moving to Paris. However, after the American invasion of Iraq in 2003, the brothers began attending a mosque and came under the influence of Farid Benyettou, who *socialized* the Kouachi brothers into the ideas and methods of radical Islam.

The Kouachi brothers are an extreme example, but you too are who you are because of the people, institutions, and social structures that have surrounded you since birth (and even before). You have been socialized to look, think, act, and interact in ways that allow you to live harmoniously, at least most of the time, with those around you. However, some of you come into contact with those who socialize you into ways that are at variance with the dominant culture. In the most extreme cases, such socialization can lead to actions like those taken by the Kouachi brothers.

Discovering how socialization and social interaction shape who we are and how we act, as we will do in this chapter, is the most basic level of sociological analysis. But in fact sociologists are concerned with everything along the micro-macro continuum (see Chapter 1). That

LEARNING OBJECTIVES

4-1 Describe the development of the self in the context of symbolic interaction.

4-2 Discuss the concept of the individual as performer, including the ideas of impression management and the front and back stages.

4-3 Explain the significance of socialization in childhood and adulthood.

4-4 Describe the key aspects of interaction with others as socialization.

4-5 Identify micro-level social structures, including social networks and groups.

77

Corbis 42-73701823

includes the individual's mind and self, interactions among individuals, and interactions within and between groups, formally structured organizations, and entire societies, as well as all the new global relationships of the "global age."

Sociology's micro-macro continuum means that rather than being clearly distinct, social phenomena tend to blend into one another, often without our noticing. For example, the interaction that takes place in a group is difficult to distinguish from the group itself. The relationships between countries are difficult to distinguish from their regional and even global connections. Everything in the social world, and on the micro-macro continuum, interpenetrates. ●

This chapter and the next will introduce you, at least briefly, to the full range of sociological concerns along the **micro-macro continuum**. We will start with the smallest-scale social phenomena and work our way to ever larger ones as these two chapters progress.

THE INDIVIDUAL AND THE SELF

What, if anything, distinguishes humans as individuals from other animals? Some would argue it is characteristics such as a larger brain or an opposable thumb. However, most sociologists believe the essential difference between humans and other animals is the distinctive interaction humans are capable of having with other humans.

An important source of this view lies in data about individuals who grew up in social isolation and did not experience normal human interaction during their development. For instance, we have information on cases in which children have been locked in closets or in single rooms for much or all of their childhoods (Curtiss 1977; Davis 1940, 1947). In a recent example, five children, ages 2–13, were discovered by authorities in York, Pennsylvania. They had lived their entire lives with their parents in a single room in a private home without any functioning utilities; their water source was rain dripping through the roof. The children had no birth certificates and had received no formal schooling, and there was no evidence that they had ever received any medical care, including vaccinations. They suffered from physical and mental health problems and were not where they should have been in terms of educational level ("Police Discover Five Children" 2010).

Of related interest is the existence of *feral,* or wild, *children*—that is, children who have been raised in the wilderness by animals (Benzaquen 2006; Dombrowski, Gischlar,

and Mrazik 2011; Newton 2002). A relatively recent example of a feral child is Oxana Malaya, from a small village in Ukraine (Grice 2006). In 1986, abandoned by her parents at age three, she crawled into a hovel housing dogs. The "Dog Girl" lived there for five years before a neighbor reported her existence. When she emerged, she could hardly speak. Like the dogs she lived with, she barked, ate by lapping up food with her tongue, and ran about on all fours. Years later, when she was living in a home for the mentally disabled, Oxana was found to have the mental capacity of a six-year-old. Among other things, she could not spell her name or read. She was able to communicate like other humans and talk because she had acquired some speech before she began living with dogs. She had also learned to eat with her hands and to walk upright (Lane 1975; Shattuck 1980).

Oxana has done better than other feral children (Lane 1975; Shattuck 1980). Long after another little feral girl was discovered, efforts to socialize her had been only minimally successful. For example, she persisted in spitting and blowing her nose on other people (Curtiss 1977). Feral children are generally unable to talk or to show much human emotion. Oxana, in contrast, has had boyfriends, although it is doubtful she has the emotional ability to develop long-term relationships. The overall conclusion from the literature on feral children and those raised in isolation is that people do not become human, or at least fully human, unless they are able to interact with other people, especially at an early age.

The concept of feral children relates to the fundamental question of the relationship between "nature" and "nurture." The nature argument is that we are born to be the kinds of human beings that we ultimately become; it is built into our "human nature" (Settle et al. 2010). The nurture argument is that we are human beings because of the way we are nurtured— that is, the way we are raised by other human beings, who teach us what it is to be human. Of course, both nature and nurture are important. However, the cases of feral children indicate that nurture is in many ways more important than nature in determining the human beings we become.

SYMBOLIC INTERACTION AND DEVELOPMENT OF THE SELF

As the example of feral and isolated children suggests, human development presupposes the existence of other humans and interaction with and among them. This is the domain of symbolic interactionism, which developed many ideas of great relevance to this view of humans. In general, the interaction that takes place between parents and children is loaded with symbols and symbolic meaning.

One early symbolic interactionist, Charles Horton Cooley (1864–1929), explained how parents help children develop the ability to interact with others with his famous concept of the **looking-glass self**. This is the idea that as humans we develop a self-image that reflects how others see and respond to us. We imagine how we appear to others and how they evaluate our appearance. Based on that, we develop some sort of self-feeling, such as pride or embarrassment. Since children's earliest interactions are typically with their parents, it is those interactions that are most important in the formation of a self-image. This helps explain why feral children and others who spend their formative years in prolonged social isolation are unlikely to form a fully developed self-image: There are no others to respond to them. It is as we interact with others, especially when we are young, that we develop a sense of our selves.

The major thinker associated with symbolic interactionism (see Chapter 2) is George Herbert Mead. Mead ([1934] 1962: 7) was very concerned with the micro level (the individual, mind, self). He prioritized the social, including interaction, and the importance of symbols in social interaction. In fact, it is this prioritization of the social that distinguishes sociologists from psychologists in their studies of individuals and interaction.

Humans and Nonhumans

Mead distinguished between humans and nonhumans. However, both are capable of making gestures (such as by raising a limb). By **gestures**, Mead meant the movements of one individual that elicit automatic and appropriate responses from another individual.

Both animals and humans are also capable of *conversations of gestures* whereby they use a series of gestures to relate to one another. Thus, the snarl of one dog may lead a second dog to snarl in return. That second snarl might lead the first dog to become physically ready to attack or be attacked. In terms of humans, Mead gave the example of a boxing match, where the cocking of one boxer's arm may cause the other boxer to raise an arm to block the anticipated blow. That raised arm might cause the first boxer to throw a different punch or even to hold back on the punch. A less aggressive example can be found in the realm of flirting (Delaney 2012; Henningsen 2004), where one person's prolonged eye contact (a subtle gesture) may cause another person to return the eye contact. The returned gaze might cause the first flirter to look away and then, perhaps, quickly glance again at the other person. As in the case of animals, the gestures of boxers and those who flirt are instantaneous and involve few, if any, conscious thought processes.

In addition to physical gestures, animals and humans are both capable of vocal gestures. The bark of a dog and the grunt of a human (boxer) are vocal gestures. In both cases, a conversation of vocal gestures is possible, as the bark of one dog (or the grunt of a boxer) elicits the bark (or grunt) of another. However, when humans (and animals) make facial gestures (such as originating eye contact in an effort to flirt), they cannot *see* their own facial gestures. In contrast, both animals and humans can *hear* their own vocal gestures. As a

The postures and gestures of this man and woman can tell us much about what they feel toward one another.

result, misunderstanding is more likely when people rely on facial rather than vocal gestures. For example, men may be more likely than women to interpret making eye contact as sexual in nature.

It is the vocal gesture that truly begins to separate humans from animals. In humans, but not other animals, the vocal gesture can affect the speaker as much and in the same way as the hearer. Thus, humans react to and interpret their own vocal gestures and, more important, their words. Furthermore, humans have a far greater ability to control their vocal gestures. We can stop ourselves from uttering sounds or saying various things, and we can alter what we say as we are saying it. Animals do not possess this capacity. In short, only humans are able to develop a language out of vocal gestures; animals remain restricted to isolated vocal gestures.

Many sociologists have come to reject the clear distinction between the abilities of animals and those of humans (Greenebaum and Sanders forthcoming). For example, some sociological work has examined symbolic interaction between humans and animals (Alger and Alger 1997; Irvine 2004).

ASK YOURSELF

In what ways do you interact with your pets in the same way you interact with humans? In what ways is the interaction different? Do you find it more satisfying to interact with people or with pets?

Symbolic Interaction

Of greatest importance in distinguishing humans from animals is a kind of gesture that can be made *only* by humans. Mead calls such a gesture a **significant symbol**, a gesture that arouses in the individual making it a response of the same kind as the one it is supposed to elicit from those to whom it is addressed. It is only with significant symbols, especially

In Mead's game stage of the development of the self, we learn how to work with others by understanding their roles as well as our own. Do you think this learning process is ever complete?

Associated Press

those that are vocal, that we can have communication in the full sense of the term. In Mead's view, ants, bees, and dogs are unable to communicate by means of such symbols, although more and more research on animals tends to contradict this view (Gerhardt and Huber 2002).

Over time, humans develop a set of vocal significant symbols, or language. According to Mead, language involves significant symbols that call out the same meaning in the person to whom an utterance is aimed as they do in the person making the utterance. The utterances have meaning to all parties involved. In a conversation of gestures, only the gestures are communicated. With language, both the (vocal) gestures and the meanings are communicated. One of the key functions of language is that it makes the mind and mental processes possible. To Mead, thinking (and the mind; see below) is nothing more than internalized conversations individual humans have with themselves. Thinking involves talking to oneself. It is little different from talking to other people.

ASK YOURSELF

What did George Herbert Mead mean by saying that thinking is so much like talking to yourself that it is little different from talking to other people? Do you agree with him? Why or why not? Think of some examples and counterexamples.

Symbols also make possible **symbolic interaction**, or interaction on the basis of significant symbols. Symbols allow for much more complex interaction patterns than those that occur where interaction is based only on gestures. Because people can think about and interpret significant symbols, they can interact with large numbers of people and make complex plans for some future undertaking. They can interpret the symbolic meaning of what others say and do and understand, for example, that some of them are acting in accord with their own plans. Animals lack the ability to make and understand complex plans.

Mind and Self

Central to Mead's ideas about the development of human beings and the differences between humans and nonhumans are the concepts of mind and self. As pointed out above, the **mind** is an internal conversation using words (and also images, especially, but certainly not only, for the autistic and the deaf; Fernyhough 2014; Grandin 2000). That internal conversation arises, is related to, and is continuous with interactions, especially conversations that one has with others in the social world. Thus, the social world and its relationships and interactions precede the mind and not vice versa. This perspective stands in contrast to the conventional view that prioritizes the brain and argues that we think first and then engage in social relationships. It also differs from the view that the mind and the brain are one and the same thing. The brain is a physiological organ that exists within us, but the mind is a social phenomenon. It is part of, and would not exist without, the social world. While the brain is an intracranial phenomenon, the mind is not.

The **self** is the ability to take oneself as an object. The self develops over time. Key to the development of self is the ability to imagine being in the place of others and looking at oneself as they do. In other words, people need to take the role of others in order to get a sense of their own selves. There are two key stages in Mead's theory of how the self develops over time, the **play stage** and the **game stage**:

1. *Play stage.* Babies are not born with the ability to think of themselves as having a self. However, as they develop, children learn to take on the attitudes of specific others toward themselves. Thus, young children play at being Mommy and Daddy, adopt their parents' attitudes toward the children, and evaluate themselves as do their parents. However, the result is a very fragmented sense of the self. It varies depending on the specific other (e.g., Mommy *or* Daddy) being taken into consideration. Young children lack a more general and organized sense of themselves.

2. *Game stage.* Children begin to develop a self in the full sense of the term when they take on the roles of a group of people simultaneously rather than the roles of discrete individuals. Each of those different roles comes to be seen as having a definite relationship to all the others. Children develop organized personalities because of their ability to take on multiple roles—indeed, the entirety of roles in a given group. The developed personality does not vary with the individual role (Mommy, Daddy) that a child happens to be taking. This development allows children to function in organized groups. Most important, it greatly affects what they will do within specific groups.

Mead offers the example of a baseball game to illustrate the game stage. It is not enough in a baseball game for you to know what you are supposed to do in your position on the field. In order to play your position, you must know what those who play all the other eight positions on the team are going to do. In other words, a player, every player, must take on the roles of all the other players. A player need not have all of those roles in mind all of the time; three or four of them will suffice on most occasions. For example, a shortstop must know that the center fielder is going to catch a particular fly ball; that he is going to be backed up by the left fielder; that because the runner on second is going to "tag up," the center fielder is going to throw the ball to third base; and that it is his job as shortstop to back up the third baseman. This ability

to take on multiple roles obviously applies in a baseball game, but it applies as well in a playgroup, a work setting, and every other social setting.

In a different example from the college classroom, students are often asked to work together on group class presentations. Each student will not only have to prepare his or her part of the project and presentation but will also need to know and coordinate with what each of the other presenters, as well as the group as a whole, will do. He or she might have to know the content of each presentation and the sequence of presentations, along with the time allotted to each. Such group work resembles that of Mead's baseball team, where all members have to be familiar with and know the roles of all the others involved to be successful as a group. This is what children learn in the game stage, and they continue to implement and practice this ability throughout their lives.

The Generalized Other

Mead also developed the concept of the **generalized other**, or the attitude of the entire group or community. The generalized other includes the roles, prescriptions, and proscriptions that individuals use to develop their own behaviors, attitudes, and so forth. Individuals take the role of the generalized other. That is, they look at themselves and what they do from the perspective of the group or community. "What would people think if I . . . " is a question that demonstrates the role of the generalized other.

The generalized other becomes central to the development of self during the game stage. In the classroom example, the generalized other is the attitude of the group working on the collaborative project. In the family, to take still another example, it is the attitude of all family members.

In taking on the perspectives of the generalized other, children begin developing more fully rounded and complete selves. They can view and evaluate themselves from the perspective of a group or community and not merely from the viewpoints of discrete others. To have a coherent self in the full sense of the term, as an adult one must become a member of a group or community. An adult must also be sensitive to the attitudes common to the community.

Having members who can take the role of the generalized other is also essential to the development of the group, especially in its organized activities. The group can function more effectively and efficiently because it is highly likely that individual members will understand and do what is expected of them. In turn, individuals can operate more efficiently within the group because they can better anticipate what others will do.

This discussion might lead you to think that the demands of the generalized other produce conformists. However, Mead argues that although selves within a group share some commonalities, each self is different because each has a unique biographical history and experience. Furthermore, there are many groups and communities in society and therefore many generalized others. Your generalized other in a baseball game is different from your generalized other in a classroom or in the family.

The "I" and the "Me"

Critical to understanding the difference between conformity and creative thinking and acting is Mead's distinction between two aspects, or phases, of the self—the "I" and the "me." Bear in mind that the "I" and the "me" are not things; they do not exist in a physical sense. We would not find the "I" or the "me" if we dissected the brain. Rather, the "I" and the "me" are subprocesses that are involved in the larger thinking process. An individual sometimes displays more of the "I" aspect of the self and sometimes more of the "me" aspect. In any given instance, the relative mix of "I" and "me" determines the degree to which an individual acts creatively (more "I") or more as a conformist (more "me").

The **"I"** is the immediate response of an individual to others. It is that part of the self that is unconscious, incalculable, unpredictable, and creative. Neither the person nor the members of the group know in advance what the response of the "I" is going to be. A daughter at a holiday dinner does not always know in advance what she is going to say or do, and the same is true of the other family members at the dinner table. That is what makes for frequent squabbles, if not outright battles, on such family occasions. As a result of the "I," people often surprise themselves, and certainly others, with the unexpected things they say and do.

Mead greatly values the "I" for various reasons, including the fact that it is the source of new and original responses. In addition, the "I" allows a person to realize the self fully and to develop a definite, unique personality. The "I" also gives us the capacity to have an impact on the groups and communities in which we live. Moreover, in Mead's view, some individuals, including the great figures in history, have a larger and more powerful "I." They are therefore able to have a greater impact on these entities, as well as on society and even on the globe.

The **"me"** is the organized set of others' attitudes and behaviors adopted by the individual. In other words, the "me" involves the acceptance and internalization by the individual of the generalized other. While your "I" might dispose you to find inventive ways of introducing yourself to an attractive student in this class, your "me" might counter that impulse by reminding you that such socializing in the classroom is considered inappropriate by your social group (the generalized other in this case). The "me" might lead you, then, to wait for someone to introduce you to that student or to find a way to run into that student outside of class. To Mead, the "me" involves a conscious understanding of what a person's responsibilities are to the larger group. The behaviors associated with the "me" also tend to be habitual and conventional. We all have a "me," but conformists have an overly powerful "me."

It is through the "me" that society is able to dominate the individual. In fact, Mead defines "social control" as the dominance of the "I" by the "me." Through the "me," individuals control themselves, with little or no need for control by outside influences. In the "me" phase, individuals analyze and critique their own thoughts and actions from the point of view of the social group and what its criticisms are likely to be. Thus, in most cases, the group need not criticize individuals; they do it themselves. In other words, self-criticism is often, in reality, criticism by the larger society.

Nevertheless, people and society as a whole need both "I" and "me." For the individual, the "me" allows for a comfortable existence within various social groupings. The "I" lends some spice to what might otherwise be a boring existence. For society, the "me" provides the conformity needed for stable and orderly interaction. The "I" is the source of changes in society as it develops and adapts to the shifting environment.

While the "me" generally provides the individual with some comfort and security, that is less the case in consumer society. The reason is that consumer society is all about change, and as a result the "me" is constantly changing. For example, one might be expected to adopt a given fashion at one time, but soon an entirely different fashion comes to be expected. Instead of attaining stability, "consumers must never be allowed to rest" (Bauman 1999: 38). Of course, the "I" always impels the individual in unpredictable directions, such as making unusual fashion statements. However, in consumer society *both* the "I" and the "me" are at least somewhat unpredictable. This serves to make many people uneasy because they lack, at least as far as fashion is concerned, the comfort of a strong and stable "me."

THE INDIVIDUAL AS PERFORMER

Erving Goffman is another important contributor to the symbolic interactionists' understanding of the self and how it develops. Goffman's work on the self was deeply influenced by Mead's thinking, especially the tension between the "I" and the "me." In Goffman's work, this distinction takes the form of the tension between what we want to do spontaneously and what people expect us to do (Goffman 1959).

Goffman's notion of **dramaturgy** views an individual's social life as a series of dramatic performances akin to those that take place on a theatrical stage. To Goffman, the self is not a thing possessed by the individual but the dramatic product of the interaction between people and their audiences (Manning 2007). While many performances of the self are successful, there is always the possibility that performances can be disrupted by the actions of audiences. For example, audiences can jeer at performances or even walk out on them. Goffman focuses on these possibilities and what people can do to prevent them by improving their dramatic performances or to deal with disruptions once they occur.

IMPRESSION MANAGEMENT

When people interact with others, they use a variety of techniques to control the images of themselves that they want to project during their social performances. Through **impression management** they seek to maintain these impressions even when they encounter problems in their performances (Goffman 1959; Manning 2005). For example, in your sociology class you might typically project an image of a serious, well-prepared student. Then one night you might stay up late partying and not get the required reading done before class. When the instructor asks a question in class, you might try to maintain your image by pretending to write busily in your notebook rather than raising your hand. Called on nonetheless, you struggle, in vain, to give a well-thought-out, serious answer to the question. The smiles and snickers of fellow students who know that you were out partying late the night before might well disrupt the performance you are endeavoring to put on. To deflect attention from you to them, you might suggest that they try to answer the question.

While the idea of impression management is generally associated with face-to-face social interaction, it also applies to interaction on social networking sites. For instance, many people constantly change the pictures on their Facebook pages to alter the images of themselves being conveyed to others (Cunningham 2013).

ASK YOURSELF

What impression management activities do you undertake? Have they generally been successful? Do you see yourself performing more of these activities as time goes on, or fewer? Why?

FRONT AND BACK STAGE

Continuing the theatrical analogy, Goffman (1959) argued that in every performance there is a **front stage**, where the social performance tends to be idealized and designed to define the situation for those who are observing it. When you are in class, you are typically performing on your front stage. Your audience is the teacher and perhaps other students. As a rule, people feel they must present an idealized sense of themselves when they are in the front stage (e.g., by giving a seemingly well-thought-out answer in class). Because it is idealized, things that do not fit the image must be hidden.

In the **back stage** people feel free to express themselves in ways that are suppressed in the front (Cahill et al. 1985). Thus, after class you might well confess to your friends in the cafeteria that you had been partying and faked your answer to a question asked in class. If somehow your front-stage audience—the instructor in this case—sees your back-stage performance, your ability to maintain the impression you are trying to project in the classroom, in the front stage, is likely to become difficult or impossible in the future.

The back stage plays a prominent role in our lives. For every one of our front-stage performances, there are one or more back stages where all sorts of things happen that we do not want to be seen in the front stage. For example, when summer camp is over, counselors are often "friended" by their former campers on Facebook. In order to allow the campers to stay in contact with them through Facebook, counselors might post limited, carefully edited profiles to special Facebook pages. These are, in effect, the counselors' front stages for former campers. However, the counselors might also retain back-stage versions of their Facebook profiles that the ex-campers are unable to see.

The existence of two stages, front and back, causes us all sorts of tensions and problems. We are always afraid that those in the front stage will find out about our back stage, or that elements of the back stage will intrude on the front stage.

These ideas are central to Leslie Picca and Joe Feagin's *Two-Faced Racism: Whites in the Backstage and Frontstage* (2007). This study of white college students shows that what they say and do differs depending on whether they are in their front stage or their back stage. When they are in their back stage with friends and family, as well as with other whites, they often feel free to talk and act in a blatantly racist manner. Examples include telling racist jokes and mocking minority group members. However, when they are in their front stage in a public setting, especially with African Americans present, what they say and do is very different. They may act as if they are blind to a person's color or even be gratuitously polite to African Americans. Thus, while overt racism may have declined in the front stage of public settings, it persists in the back stage (Cabrera 2014; Sallaz 2010).

While the distinction between front and back stage is important, bear in mind that these are not "real" places, nor are they rigidly separated from one another. That is, what is the front stage at one point in time can become the back stage at another. Nevertheless, in general, people are most likely to perform in an idealized manner on their front stage, where they are most concerned about making positive impressions. They are likely to perform more freely back stage, among those who are more accepting of less-than-ideal behavior and attitudes.

The Self in the Global Age

The self is not fixed. It changes over the course of our lives and even on a day-to-day basis, depending on the nature of the impression we want to make on others (Goffman 1959). The self also changes with large-scale transformations in the social world, and no change has been more dramatic than globalization.

Globalization brings with it the increasingly easy movement of all kinds of objects, ideas, and knowledge, as well as of people. This mobility is of great importance in itself (Urry 2007), and also because "the globalization of mobility extends into the core of the self" (Elliott and Urry 2010: 3).

On the positive side, the self can become more open and flexible as a result of all the new experiences associated with the global age. The many brief interactions that happen, for example, online or through travel can lead to a different kind of self, perhaps more oriented to the short-term and the episodic than to that which is long-term or even lifelong.

Of great concern, however, are the negative effects of globalization on the self. At the extreme, Lemert and Elliott (2006) see globalization as "toxic" for the individual, including the self. Because people are increasingly mobile, they are likely to feel that their selves are dispersed and adrift in various places in the world or that they exist even more

Associated Press

Is it possible to be too involved with and dependent on digital technology? What do we gain from our use of digital devices, and what do we lose?

loosely in global cyberspace. While in the past the self was increasingly likely to be shaped by close personal relationships, it is now more likely to reflect the absence of such relationships and a sense of distance, even disconnection, from others. At the minimum, this can lead to a different kind of self than existed before the global age. At the maximum, it can lead to one that is weak because it is untethered to anything strong and long-lasting.

A more familiar pathology associated with the global age is being obsessed with digital mobile technologies. For one woman, the experience of being so deeply enmeshed in these technologies "has left the self drained and lifeless" (Elliott and Urry 2010: 41). Globalization and its associated mobility have had a great effect on the self, and that impact is likely to grow exponentially in the future.

Think About It

Is the self today shaped more by the absence of close personal friendships and a sense of distance from others than by close personal relationships? What might be some of the negative effects of this change, if it is real? How could society counteract them?

SOCIALIZATION

Socialization is the process by which an individual learns and generally comes to accept the ways of a group or a society of which he or she is a part. It is during the socialization process that children develop a self as they learn the need, for example, to take on the role of the generalized other.

Socialization almost always involves a process of interaction as those with knowledge and experience teach those with a need to acquire that knowledge or to learn from others' experiences.

While socialization occurs throughout an individual's lifetime (Erikson, 1994), it can generally be divided into two parts. Socialization during childhood sets the course for a lifetime and has been a central focus for researchers. However, researchers have increasingly pointed up a variety of ways in which adults continue to learn how to function within their society.

CHILDHOOD SOCIALIZATION

A central concern in the study of socialization is those who do the socializing, or the **agents of socialization** (Wunder 2007). The first and often most effective agents of socialization are the child's parents as well as other family members and friends. These are defined as primary agents of socialization. In addition, broader, less personal influences, such as the educational system, the media, and consumer culture, are important in socialization. These are defined as secondary agents of socialization. All play a part in creating an individual who can effectively operate within and shape culture. Except for education, which will be discussed in Chapter 11, we will examine each of these various agents of socialization below.

Primary Socialization and the Family

In **primary socialization**, newborns, infants, and young children acquire language, identities, cultural routines, norms, and values as they interact with parents and other family members (Lubbers, Jaspers, and Ultee 2009). This socialization lays the foundation for later personality development (Rohlinger 2007). Early socialization performs various functions for society, such as equipping the young to fit into society and perpetuating the culture from one generation to the next.

In addition to a great deal of primary socialization, parents provide **anticipatory socialization**—that is, they teach children what will be expected of them in the future. Anticipatory socialization is how parents prepare children for the very important developmental changes (puberty, for example) that they will experience. Among the many other things that must be anticipated in family socialization are entrance into grade school, high school, college, the work world, and life as an independent adult. Anticipatory socialization is especially important in societies and in time periods undergoing a great deal of change. Many assumptions about primary and anticipatory socialization are changing dramatically as the nature of families and the way they are understood culturally undergo major transformations. The socialization process was thought to be rather straightforward when the ideal of the nuclear family, composed of a mother, a father, and two or more children all living in the same home, predominated, as it did throughout much of the twentieth century. The lesson children were required to learn, at least as far as the family was concerned, was that when they became adults they would go on to reproduce the same kind of nuclear family as the one in which they grew up. However, assumptions about the goodness and

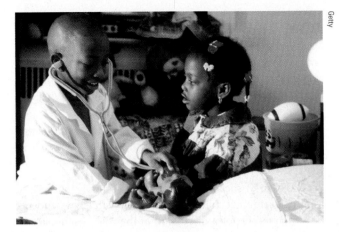

Playing doctor and nurse may be good anticipatory socialization for playing those roles as adults. Do children choose pretend occupations according to gender norms?

inevitability of the nuclear family and the ease of the socialization process now seem impossible to accept (McLanahan 1999). This is the case because of increasing public awareness of the many problems associated with the nuclear family, such as divorce, abuse, and unhappiness (see Chapter 10).

Then there is the expansion of what were at one time called "alternative family forms" (e.g., single-parent households, grandparents as primary caregivers) and the increasing centrality of day-care centers and their workers to the socialization process. The agencies doing the socializing today are much more complex and varied than they were in the era of the predominance of the nuclear family. As a result, socialization is not as straightforward as it once was thought to be. In addition, it is no longer possible to think of a seamless relationship between the agencies of socialization and the socialization process. For example, the family may be socializing its children one way, but the day-care center may be doing it very differently.

In addition, at one time socialization was seen as one-directional, for example, from parent to child. Current thinking sees such socialization among intimates as two-directional, with, for example, parents socializing children and children socializing parents, other adults, and families (Gentina and Muratore 2012). For example, children tend to be far more familiar than their elders with the latest advances in digital technology, and they teach their parents much about both the technology itself and the digital culture. Immigrant families provide another example. Children in these families are more likely than their parents to learn the language and culture of their new country (often in school). As a result, they are frequently the ones to teach that knowledge to their parents (Mather 2009). This is **reverse socialization**, in which those who are normally being socialized are instead doing the socializing.

ASK YOURSELF

Have you experienced any instances of reverse socialization? For instance, have you taught your parents how to use their smartphones or set up Facebook pages, or has a younger relative or friend introduced you to a new smartphone app? What was this experience like?

Peers

A good deal of socialization within the schools takes place informally, through children's interaction with fellow students (see Chapter 11 for a discussion of the role of schools and teachers in the process of socialization). This is a situation where primary agents of socialization (peers) compete with secondary agents of socialization (teachers and other employees of the school system). Such informal socialization grows increasingly important as students progress through the school years, especially the high school years (Steinberg and Monahan 2007). Peers are also important sources of socialization in contexts outside school, such as scouting groups and athletic teams of various kinds (Bennett and Fraser 2000; Fine 1987). As the child matures and spends an increasing amount of time in the company of friends, peer socialization is increasingly likely to conflict with what is being taught at home and in the schools. Peer involvement in risky and delinquent behavior exerts an influence that is often at odds with the goals set forth by parents and educators (Gardner and Steinberg 2005; Harding, 2010; Haynie 2001). Although peer socialization is especially important in, and associated with, childhood (Perez-Felkner 2013), it continues to be important throughout the life course (Preves and Mortimer 2013). For example, peers help us learn what we are expected to do at college (Brimeyer, Miller, and Perrucci 2006), at work

Peers are highly influential in the socialization process, especially during adolescence and early adulthood. What role do you think fellow students play in your socialization? Which ones will most influence you?

(Montoya 2005), in social settings (Friedkin 2001), and in civic arenas (Dey 1997), as well as how to be sports fans (Melnick and Wann 2011).

Gender

Sociologists devote a great deal of attention to gender socialization (McHale, Crouter, and Whiteman 2003; Rohlinger 2007), or the transmission of norms and values about what boys and girls can and should do. Even before babies are born, their parents (and many others) start to "gender" them. In the United States they do so by, for example, frequently buying blue clothing for boys and pink for girls. Parents often dress baby girls in frilly dresses and affix bows to their bald heads to signal to others that the babies are girls. These gender differences are reinforced by the toys children are often given by parents—trucks and soldiers for boys, dolls and dollhouses for girls. Boys may get toys and games organized around action, activity, and role-playing thought to be appropriate for boys. Girls may get toys and games focused on interactions, relationships, and less active play. Sociologist Emily Kane (2012) found that while parents often want to challenge gender assumptions about what are appropriate toys and clothing for children, they are constrained by traditionally gendered structures and social institutions.

As children grow up, they learn from their parents and other significant others (as well as the generalized other) what behaviors are considered appropriate and inappropriate for their gender. They also learn the consequences, or sanctions, for deviating from these expectations. For example, parents may give a girl a great deal of sympathy when she cries, whereas they may tell a boy to "be a man" and not cry after an injury. Boys may be expected to have an interest in sports, to play roughly with each other, and to be unable to sit still. Girls, in contrast, are expected to display more "ladylike" behaviors, such as sitting quietly and sharing. Many children come to see these traditional gender expectations as "natural" expressions of being male or female. Parents trying to raise boys are more likely to socialize them into narrow gender roles. They cite biology, or "nature," as the reason for doing so. Parents also do so because they fear social sanctions if they socialize the boys differently (Kane 2012).

The feminist movement of the 1970s challenged traditional notions about the socialization of boys and girls (Lorber 2000). Today, some parents pride themselves on their "gender-neutral" child rearing. They socialize their children without rigid adherence to traditional binary gender roles, rejecting the ideas that boys and girls are completely different (Martin 2005). Yet many parents continue to strongly discourage boys from expressing an interest in activities that are stereotyped as "for girls" (Kane 2006). Historically, traditional socialization for gender roles has been reinforced in schools, sports, and the mass media. In schools, teachers and curricula once tended to support traditional gender norms, and peer groups were likely to be segregated by gender (Thorne 1993). In sports, girls and boys were channeled into different sports; for example, girls tended to play softball while boys played baseball (Coakley 2007). When girls did play "male" sports, their efforts were often labeled differently; for instance, girls' football competitions might be called "powderpuff" football. The passage in 1972 of Title IX of the U.S. Education Amendments, which bars discrimination on the basis of gender in educationally based sporting activities receiving federal funding, has changed such views dramatically. Since the passage of Title IX, women's athletic activities in college and even in high school have become increasingly visible and, in some cases, more highly regarded as "real" sports. One of the best examples is women's basketball at the collegiate level. More generally, both men and women are now more likely to seek to build muscular and athletic bodies.

ASK YOURSELF

Why do you think traditional ideas about gender role socialization in childhood remain strong in U.S. culture today? Do you foresee that they will ever give way entirely to more egalitarian norms? Why or why not?

The media, especially movies, TV, and video games, have also tended to reinforce children's traditional gender role socialization. However, that, too, is changing. Television programs are increasingly featuring strong female characters (e.g., *The Good Wife*), and numerous shows have featured female cops and police chiefs (e.g., *CSI: Cyber*). Female action stars (e.g., Angelina Jolie in most of her films) are increasingly likely to play strong and aggressive characters. Young adult novels and the movies based on them often also have strong female leading characters, such as Katniss Everdeen in the *Hunger Games* series and Beatrice Prior in the *Divergent* series.

Change is less obvious in other settings. Malls tend to reinforce traditional gender roles by offering separate shops for boys and girls, men and women. Movies, television programming, and advertisements have been widely critiqued for their unrealistic portrayal of women's bodies (Bordo 1993; Cole and Daniel 2005; Milkie 1999; Neuendorf et al. 2009). Images of women have become increasingly sexualized over time (Hatton and Trautner 2011). Many action heroines (e.g., those in James Bond movies) continue to embody traditional male preferences for female bodies: young, attractive, and slender. Young women comparing themselves with these versions of adult Barbie dolls become anxious about their own bodies. Media images of women may also reaffirm racial stereotypes, with young women of color often being sexualized or portrayed as poor and irresponsible (Collins 2004).

Mass Media and New Media

Until recently, much of the emphasis on the role of the mass media in socialization has been on the effects of television and the enormous number of hours per week children spend in front of their TVs (Comstock and Scharrer 2007). TV remains an important socialization agent, especially for young children. However, it is clear that as children mature, especially in the middle and upper classes, more of their socialization is taking place via the computer, smartphones, video games, and other new and emerging technologies (Rideout, Foehr, and Roberts 2010). As the range of media devices has expanded, so has the portion of time spent using them. In 2009, children and young people between the ages of 8 and 18 spent almost 11 hours a day exposed to media of various sorts, reflecting an increase of more than 3 hours from 10 years prior. The percentage of young people who own their own media devices is high and, for the most part, increasing.

Of course, a world of wonderful information is available to children on the computer via Google and other forms of new media. However, there are also lots of worrying things online that children can easily find or stumble upon. In addition, access to computers has changed the viewing experience considerably. Watching TV programs or movies is a passive activity. Even when "adult themes" are presented, the child is an observer, not a participant. However, on computers and other new digital media, the child can play video games such as *Grand Theft Auto V* and *Call of Duty: Black Ops*. These games engage children in simulations of antisocial activities like stealing cars and evading police chases. Clearly, the nature of the socialization implicit in such games is at odds with the lessons that parents and teachers wish to impart.

Smartphones and social networking sites play a role in socialization as well, mostly through the influence of peers. A great deal of peer socialization takes place via sites such as Facebook, Twitter, and Snapchat (Buckingham 2008;

Associated Press

What do you think the impact will be of the increasing amount of time young children are spending with screen devices?

Watkins 2009). All of this is so new, and new forms of media are emerging so rapidly, that it is hard to know exactly what role the new media will play in socialization in the future, but their role is likely to be increasingly powerful and pervasive.

Consumer Culture

Children need to be socialized in order to become consumers, and especially in order to devote a significant portion of their lives to consumption (Atkinson, Nelson, and Rademacher 2015). Like many other types of socialization, much of this socialization takes place early on in the family, in schools, and in peer groups. Of course, we must not ignore the role of marketing, especially to children, in how people learn to consume (Schor 2005).

However, much socialization now takes place in consumption sites themselves rather than in the family, in schools, or through advertisements. For example, preteens and teens spend a large amount of time at shopping malls, either with their families or, as they mature, on their own and in the company of peers (Cook 2004; Rose 2010). Children readily learn the nuts and bolts of how to consume. They also learn various norms and values of consumption, and especially to value the processes of consumption and shopping as well as the goods and services acquired through those processes.

Online consumption and shopping sites (such as Amazon and eBay) are also socializing agents. Navigation and buying strategies are learned at digital retailers, and those have an effect on consumption in the brick-and-mortar world. For instance, many younger people who have grown up with online shopping are adept comparison shoppers. They are likely to compare products online and to search out the best possible deals before making purchases. Socialization into being a consumer also reinforces lessons about race, class, and gender (Otnes and Zayre 2012). Christine Williams (2006) shows that consumer choices contribute to the maintenance of social inequalities. Girls face pressure to consume beauty products that encourage them to live up to an idealized and usually unattainable level of female beauty (Wiklund et al. 2010). For example, the Barbie doll is often presented as an ideal form of the female body—a form that is physically impossible to attain in real life. Such toys socialize children not only into a consumer culture but also into one that reproduces and reinforces harmful gender expectations.

ADULT SOCIALIZATION

A great deal of adult socialization takes place at that point in life when people enter the work world and become independent of their families.

Workplaces

At one time socialization into a workplace was a fairly simple and straightforward process. Many workers were hired for jobs in large corporations (General Motors, U.S. Steel) and remained there until they reached retirement age. Especially for those who held jobs in the lower reaches of the corporate hierarchy, socialization occurred mainly in the early stages of a career. Today, however, relatively few workers can look forward to a career in a single position within a single company. Increasing numbers of workers are changing employers, jobs, and even careers with some frequency (Bernhardt et al. 2001; Legerski 2012). Each time workers change jobs, they need **resocialization** to unlearn old behaviors, norms, and values and to learn new ones. They can no longer rely (assuming it was ever possible) on what they learned as children, in school, or in their early years on the job.

ASK YOURSELF

In one or more of your jobs, have you ever been involved in an orientation or training period or program? What occurred during this time that you could now classify as part of a workplace socialization process? How successful was it, and, thinking back, are there ways you believe it could have been done better?

Total Institutions

At some point in their lives, many adults find themselves in some type of total institution (Gambino 2013; Goffman 1961a). A **total institution** is a closed, all-encompassing place of residence and work set off from the rest of society that meets all of the needs of those enclosed in it.

A major example of a total institution is the prison (another is the military). In 2011, 2.24 million Americans were housed in federal and state prisons and county jails (International Centre for Prison Studies 2011). On initial entry into prison, inmates undergo formal resocialization in

In what ways are branches of the military total institutions? Why are they set up as total institutions?

the form of being told the rules and procedures they must follow. However, of far greater importance is the informal socialization that occurs over time through their interactions with guards and especially with other inmates (Walters 2003). In fact, other inmates often socialize relatively inexperienced criminals into becoming more expert criminals; prisons are often "schools for crime" (Sykes [1958] 2007; Walters 2003).

Other Aspects of Adult Socialization

Adult socialization and resocialization also take place in many other ways and in many other settings. For example, medical schools, law schools, and graduate schools of various types socialize their students to be doctors, lawyers, and members of other professions (Becker and Geer 1958; Granfield 1992; Hafferty 2009). The students have to learn the norms that govern their appearance, conduct, and interactions with others in their professions, their patients or clients, and the public at large. Medical residents, for example, need to learn how to present their diagnoses to patients with sensitivity and confidence. They also learn to maintain and reinforce status differences between doctors and nurses.

Many consumption settings also offer formal socialization aimed mostly at adults, at least on initial visits. For a fee, Mall of America will give newcomers an orientation tour of the mall. Las Vegas casinos helpfully offer newcomers lessons on the various forms of gambling and implicitly on how to lose their money. Cruise lines offer first-time travelers tours of their sometimes vast ships, including their onboard casinos and shops.

There are a number of situations that lead to the need for adult socialization or resocialization (Brim 1968; Lutfey and Mortimer 2006; Wilson 1984):

- *Changes in societal values and norms.* Many aspects of American culture are experiencing rapid change, and people need to be socialized into the new cultural realities.

- *Family changes.* Separation, divorce, death of a spouse, and remarriage involve particularly important transitions for the adults who are involved, not just the children. They require considerable adult resocialization into new relationships, new household organization, and new public images.

- *Geographic mobility.* Job change, retirement, and migration are becoming increasingly likely. People undergoing any of these transitions must be resocialized into not only new physical environments but also new subcultures.

- *Changes associated with aging.* As people age, they gradually become disengaged from work, which has implications for relationships and financial well-being. A retired person must become resocialized into this new status.

INTERACTION

Socialization generally involves **interaction**, or social engagement involving two or more individuals who perceive and orient their actions to one another (vom Lehn 2007). Interaction has generally been seen as involving face-to-face relationships among people, but in the twenty-first century interaction is increasingly mediated by smartphones and social media.

Personal interaction occurs throughout our lifetimes. Examples include interactions between parents and children, between children and their siblings, between teachers and students, between coworkers, and between medical personnel and patients. Interactions early in the life cycle, especially in the family and in schools, tend to be long-term and intense. Later in life, many interactions tend to be more fleeting (a quick hello on the street or a brief conversation at a cocktail party), although interactions with family members tend to remain intense.

RECIPROCITY AND EXCHANGE

To sociologists who theorize about exchange, interaction is a rational process in which those involved seek to maximize rewards and minimize costs. Interaction is likely to persist as long as those involved find it rewarding, and it is likely to wind down or end when one or more of the parties no longer find it rewarding. An important idea in this context is the social norm of **reciprocity**, which means that those engaged in interaction expect to give and receive rewards of roughly equal value (Gouldner 1960; Molm 2010). When one party feels that the other is no longer adhering to this norm—that is, not giving about as much as he or she is receiving—the relationship is likely to end.

Studies of exchange relationships are now being challenged to find ways of dealing with new forms of virtual interaction: e-mail, social networking, and interaction on Skype. One researcher who has explored the effects of virtual reality on interaction in the "real" world, and vice versa, concludes that "the constantly evolving avatar [or digital representation of oneself] influences the 'real' self, who now also orients toward virtual, yet all-too-real others" (Gottschalk 2010: 522). In other words, interactions in the digital realm and those in the physical realm both influence the self. Additional research questions come to mind quite readily. For example, are people compelled to cooperate to the same extent in the digital realm (such as when using e-mail communication) as they are in the material world (such as during in-person communication) (Naquin, Kurtzberg, and Belkin 2008)? However, it is important to remember that the digital and material worlds are not separate from one another, but rather interpenetrate. An important issue, then, is the connection between, for example, collaborative relationships online and offline (Ritzer 2013).

"DOING" INTERACTION

Another interactionist theory of great relevance here is ethnomethodology, which focuses on people's everyday practices, especially those that involve interaction. The basic idea is that interaction is something that people actively "do," something that they accomplish on a day-to-day basis. For example, the simple act of two people walking together can be considered a form of interaction. Engaging in certain practices makes it clear that you are walking with a particular someone and not with someone else (Pantzar and Shove 2010; Ryave and Schenkein 1974). You are likely to walk close to, or perhaps lean toward, a close friend. When you find yourself walking in step with a total stranger, you probably behave differently. You might separate yourself, lean away, and say "Excuse me" to make it clear that you are not walking with that stranger and are not engaged in interaction with her. More complex forms of interaction require much more sophisticated practices. In the process of interacting, people create durable forms of interaction such as those that relate to gender (West and Zimmerman 1987) and the family.

Ethnomethodology also spawned **conversation analysis**, which is concerned with how people do, or accomplish, conversations (Heritage and Stivers 2012). For example, you must know and utilize certain practices in order to carry on a successful conversation: You must know when it is your turn to talk and when it is appropriate to laugh at a comment made by someone else (Jefferson 1979). Conversation analysts have taken the lead in studying conversations, and interaction more generally, in great depth. They typically record conversations using audio or video devices so they can study them in detail. Later, they transcribe the conversations to create written records of them.

INTERACTION ORDER

While every instance of interaction may seem isolated and independent of others, each is part of what Erving Goffman (2000) called the **interaction order**. This is a social domain that is organized and orderly. The order is created informally and governed by those involved in the interaction rather than by some formal structure such as a bureaucracy and its constraints (Fine 2012; Jacobs 2007). One example of an interaction order is a group of students who form a clique and develop their own norms to govern their interaction. The interaction order can be seen in many settings and contexts. One particularly good example is the way people spontaneously form queues and wait for the doors to open at a rock concert or at Walmart on "Black Friday" (the day after Thanksgiving). Some sociologists suggest that human interaction with animals is another place to observe the interaction order (Jerolmack 2009).

STATUS AND ROLE

Status and role are key elements in the interaction order, as well as in the larger structures in which such interactions often exist. A **status** is a position within a social system occupied by people. Within the university, for example, key statuses are professor and student. A **role** is what is generally expected of a person who occupies a given status (Hindin 2007). Thus, professors are expected to show up for class, to be well prepared, to teach in an engaging manner, and so on. Students are also expected to attend class, to listen and sometimes to participate, to avoid texting and checking their Facebook pages during class, to complete the required assignments, and to take and pass examinations.

The concept of status can be broken down further into ascribed and achieved status. An **ascribed status** is one that is not chosen; it is beyond the individual's control. It involves a position into which the individual is placed or to which he or she moves regardless of what that person does or the nature of his or her capacities or accomplishments. In some cases individuals are born into an ascribed status—for example, the status associated with race, ethnicity, social class, sex, or gender. In contrast, an **achieved status** is a position that a person acquires on the basis of accomplishment or the nature of the individual's capacities. It may be based on merit or earned, or the person may choose it—for example, by seeking out and finding someone who will be a mate for life. Spouse, parent, and "successful" entrepreneur are all achieved statuses. See Table 4.1 for the relative degrees of prestige, a measure of achieved status, commonly associated with some popular careers and occupations in the United States. In addition, adults can achieve improvement in their social class or socioeconomic status (children's social class is almost always ascribed).

Whether it is ascribed or achieved, a status can become a **master status**, or a position that is (or becomes) more important than any other status both for the person in the position and for all others involved. A master status becomes central to a person's identity, roles, behaviors, and interactions. Primary examples of master statuses are those associated with race, disability, gender, and even sexuality.

The social roles connected with any statuses can be congruent; that is, the expectations attached to a given status can be consistent. Student status (achieved) may have role expectations of attending class and doing homework outside of class. But roles can also come into conflict—for example, going to class and keeping up with your social life. **Role conflict** is defined as conflicting expectations associated with a given position or multiple positions (Merton 1957; Schmidt et al. 2014). A professor who is expected to excel at both teaching and research can be seen as having role conflict. Devoting a lot of time to research can mean that a professor is ill prepared to teach her classes. Or a professor may be torn between the expectations of being a teacher (preparing for class) and those of being a parent (playing with his children). A student may need to deal with the role conflict between being a student and studying and being a friend who spends the evening helping a close acquaintance deal with a personal problem.

TABLE 4.1 • Prestige of 23 Professions and Occupations (in percentages)

	VERY GREAT PRESTIGE	CONSIDERABLE PRESTIGE	SOME PRESTIGE	HARDLY ANY PRESTIGE AT ALL
Firefighter	62	21	13	5
Scientist	57	22	14	7
Doctor	56	28	13	3
Nurse	54	24	18	4
Military officer	51	24	17	7
Teacher	51	22	17	10
Police officer	44	24	24	7
Priest/minister/clergy	41	21	28	10
Engineer	39	27	28	5
Farmer	36	22	28	14
Architect	29	30	31	10
Member of Congress	28	21	27	22
Lawyer	26	22	33	19
Business executive	23	15	46	16
Athlete	21	18	42	19
Journalist	17	20	40	22
Union leader	17	17	34	30
Entertainer	17	17	40	25
Banker	16	21	43	18
Actor	15	19	33	33
Stockbroker	13	11	43	31
Accountant	11	23	46	19
Real estate agent/broker	5	14	50	50

SOURCE: Reprinted with permission from "Doctors, military officers, firefighters, and scientists seen as among America's most prestigious occupations yet engineering is what the highest percentage of adults would encourage a child to pursue." *The Harris Poll* #85, September 10, 2014.

Much research has been done on the role conflicts experienced by workers with domestic obligations. Each role interferes with the individuals' ability to satisfactorily meet the expectations associated with the other role (Moore 1995). For example, women who work outside the home, who still tend to be responsible for the care of children and the home, experience higher levels of stress and poorer physical health than do working men (Gove and Hughes 1979; Pearlin 1989; Roehling, Hernandez Jarvis, and Swope 2005). The heavy burden of the female caretaking role inhibits women's ability to fulfill their role as caretakers of themselves.

Another role-related problem is **role overload**, in which people are confronted with more expectations than they can possibly handle (Mathews, Winkel, and Wayne 2014). Students during final exams week are often confronted with role overload in trying to satisfy the expectations of several professors and courses.

There is a tendency to see roles as fixed, unchanging, and constraining. However, people do have the ability to engage in **role-making**. That is, they have the ability to modify their roles, at least to some degree (Turner 1978). Researchers have noted that parents adopt a variety of strategies to reduce work–family conflict (Becker and Moen 1999; Bianchi and Milkie 2010). Examples of such strategies include reducing work hours, turning down promotions, and negotiating trade-offs with one's partner.

MICRO-LEVEL SOCIAL STRUCTURES

Through an accumulation of persistent patterns of interaction and social relationships, individuals contribute to the creation of social structures, which are enduring and regular social

DIGITAL LIVING

Facebook Relationships

You're seeing someone. It's great! It's wonderful! You feel awkward and happy and nervous. But is it a "real" relationship? Is it "Facebook official"? Once you and your partner both confirm the relationship publicly via Facebook, the status change appears on your friends' (and friends of friends') Facebook pages, and they can publish comments on the relationship if they so choose. The status remains on your profile until you change it (recently, we have begun seeing more on Facebook about the endings of relationships; Seligson 2014). When that occurs, your friends will be alerted once again that your relationship status has changed.

Had he dealt with it, French sociologist Pierre Bourdieu might have described a Facebook relationship status as a kind of "symbolic capital," that is, a socially recognized symbol that offers status to individuals who hold it. For example, social titles like "Duke of Nottingham" and "president of the student body," as well as symbols like the Greek letters on the tote bag of a sorority member, confer prestige on their bearers. This symbolic capital legitimates these individuals' social activities. Symbolic capital alone is not enough to completely validate your activities or your social functions or to guarantee your competence. In other words, you will need more than just the symbolic capital of your degree and your teaching certification to be a good teacher. But symbolic capital can help individuals access resources associated with certain social positions.

Your Facebook relationship status is symbolic because the status alone

Is a relationship more real because it has been posted on Facebook? Was personal news more or less real before Facebook?

does not fully describe the complexity of your relationship even if you use the "it's complicated" status. It merely represents—symbolizes—that you and your significant other are involved in a mutually and publicly recognized relationship. As a symbol of that relationship, it is a simplification that makes the relationship easily and widely recognizable to others. Thus, knowledge of your relationship can "travel" easily—almost like cash, or capital. You can "exchange" that symbol for resources like attention, such as appearing on your friends' home pages. It can be exchanged for claims to legitimacy or exclusivity by marking that, for instance, you and your significant other are "taken." Or that symbol can be exchanged for claims about wrongs or grievances. For example, it becomes readily apparent to all

those who see that your significant other is leaving messages for someone else that you are entitled to some comfort, encouragement, advice, or even retribution. In short, your Facebook relationship status is itself a kind of "capital" that can quickly and easily be converted into meanings that may further advantage you and shape a number of your social relationships.

SOURCE: Printed with the permission of Margaret Austin Smith.

Think About It

Do you have any other types of symbolic capital online besides your Facebook status? What are they? Do your various online presences project a consistent image? In other words, how well are you managing your front stage online?

arrangements (Hunt 2007). Social structures include everything from the face-to-face interaction that is characteristic of the interaction order to networks, groups, organizations, societies, and the globe. This chapter focuses on micro-level social structures—interpersonal relationships, social networks, and groups. Chapter 5 covers larger-scale social structures.

INTERPERSONAL RELATIONSHIPS

Georg Simmel (1950) created a famous set of concepts to describe the structures common to interpersonal relationships. **Dyads,** or two-person groups, are the most basic of interpersonal relationships, but they often evolve into **triads**, or three-person groups, as when a couple welcomes a new child. The addition of one person to a dyad, creating a triad, would appear to be of minimal importance sociologically. After all, how important can the addition of one person be? However, Simmel demonstrated that no further addition of members to a group, no matter how many that might be, is as important as the addition of a single person to a dyad. A good example is the dramatic change in the husband–wife relationship caused by the arrival of a first child. Another is the powerful impact of a new lover on an intimate dyadic relationship. In cases like these, social possibilities exist in the triad that do not exist in a dyad. For example, in a triad, two of the parties can form a coalition against the third: A wife and child can form a coalition against the husband. Or one member of the triad—say, the child—can take on the role of mediator or arbitrator in disputes involving the other members.

The most important point to be made about Simmel's ideas on the triad is that it is the group structure that matters, *not* the people involved in the triad or the nature of their personalities. Different people with different personalities will make one triad different from another, but it is not the nature of the people or their personalities that make the triad itself possible (Webster and Sell 2012).

SOCIAL NETWORKS

Networks are broadly defined as interconnected nodes or positions. For example, individuals can be seen as nodes in a network of people. **Social networks** involve two or more individuals, but groups, organizations, and societies can also form such networks.

Network analysts are interested in how networks are organized and the implications of that organization for social life. They look at the nodes occupied by individuals (and other entities) in a network, the linkages among nodes, and the importance of central nodes to other nodes in the network. Figure 4.1 shows a network with low centrality and one with high centrality. In the low-centrality network, one node appears in the center, but it is actually linked to only two other nodes. The central node in the high-centrality example is far more influential. Every other node is connected to it, and there is only one link that is independent of the central node. Those who occupy positions that are central in any network have access to a great many resources and therefore have a considerable ability to gain and to exercise power in a network.

A key idea in network theory is the "strength of weak ties." We are all aware of the power of strong ties between, for example, family members, or among those who belong to close-knit social groups such as gangs. However, as Mark Granovetter (1973) has demonstrated, those who have only weak ties with others (that is, they are just acquaintances) can have great power. While those with strong ties tend to remain within given groups, those with weak ties can more easily move between groups and thus provide important linkages among and between group members (see Figure 4.2). Those with weak ties are the ones who hold together disparate groups that are themselves linked internally by strong ties.

Researchers generally find that at least half of all workers in the United States have obtained their jobs through informal means, meaning referrals, rather than formal job postings (Marsden and Gorman 2001; Pfeffer and Parra 2009). It makes sense, then, to understand the strength of weak ties. If you are looking for a job, you may want to seek out the help of friends and acquaintances who have weak ties to many groups. This is because they are likely to have many diverse and potentially useful contacts with people you *and* your strong ties do not know at a number of different employers.

Those who are responsible for hiring need to keep in mind that access to network resources is largely dependent on someone's social position. Social network research has shown that socioeconomically disadvantaged individuals suffer a huge deficit in both strong and weak network ties (Bian 1997; Granovetter 1973, 1974; Lin 1999; Lin and Bian 1991; Lin, Ensel, and Vaughn 1981; Wegener 1991). Thus, they are at a disadvantage in finding jobs. To overcome this barrier, an employer may want to seek ties to networks that include the socioeconomically disadvantaged.

One point worth underscoring in any discussion of social networks is the importance of Internet networks, including Facebook, Instagram, and Twitter. This is another domain where weak ties can be of great importance. On Facebook, for instance, you may have hundreds, even thousands, of "friends." However, it is clear that many of these "friendships" involve weak ties—in fact, far weaker ties than analysts such as Granovetter had in mind. It is also important to note that

FIGURE 4.1 • Social Network Centrality

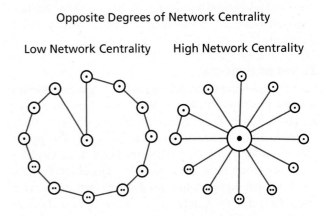

Opposite Degrees of Network Centrality

Low Network Centrality   High Network Centrality

SOURCE: Reprinted by permission of S. Joshua Mendelsohn.

FIGURE 4.2 • The Strength of Weak Ties

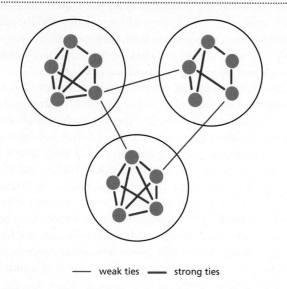

—— weak ties ——— strong ties

SOURCE: Adapted from "Weak Ties in Social Networks," Bokardo, a blog about interface and product design, Joshua Porter.

they leave objective traces, such as e-mail messages and writings on Facebook walls. As a result, such networks are much easier to study than, for example, those that exist in face-to-face interaction, which usually leave few material traces. The app Snapchat was developed to eliminate those traces; it forces you to arrange for traces—such as photos—to disappear within 1 to 10 seconds (Wortham 2013).

GROUPS

We have already encountered the key sociological concept of groups at several points in this chapter, especially in Simmel's ideas on the dyad and beyond. A **group** is a relatively small number of people who over time develop a patterned relationship based on interaction with one another. However, just because we see a small number of people who appear to be together—say, in a queue waiting to board a plane—that does not mean that they necessarily constitute a group. Most people in a queue are not likely to interact with one another, to have the time or inclination to develop patterned relationships with one another, or, if they interact, to do so beyond the time it takes to board the plane and find their seats.

Types of Groups

Several key concepts in sociology relate to groups. **Primary groups** are those that are small, are close-knit, and involve intimate face-to-face interaction (Cooley 1909). Relationships in primary groups are personal, and people identify strongly with the groups. The family is the model of a primary group, although as we will see in Chapter 10, the family is often riddled with many conflicts, and at least some members leave the family or are driven from it. Primary groups can also take unlikely forms. A study of people who

tend pigeons and fly them from rooftops documents the formation of primary group ties among members involved in this somewhat rare activity (Jerolmack 2009). Such group ties can be surprisingly strong.

Secondary groups are generally large and impersonal; ties are relatively weak, members do not know one another very well, and members' impacts on one another are typically not very powerful. A local parent–teacher association is a good example of a secondary group.

Reference groups are those groups that you take into consideration in evaluating yourself. Your reference group can be one to which you belong, or it can be another group to which you do not belong but nevertheless often relate (Ajrouch 2007; Merton and Kitt 1950). People often have many reference groups, and those groups can and do change over time. Knowing people's reference groups, and how they change, tells us a great deal about their behavior, attitudes, and values. We often think of reference groups in positive terms. An example would be a group of people whose success you would like to emulate. They also can be negative if they represent values or ways of life that you reject (say, neo-Nazis). The group to which one belongs is not necessarily the most powerful group in one's life.

Reference groups can be illustrated by the case of immigrants. Newly arrived immigrants are more likely to take those belonging to the immigrants' culture, or even those in the country from which they came, as their reference group. In contrast, their children, second-generation immigrants, are much more likely to take as their reference group those associated with the new culture in the country to which they have immigrated (Kosic et al. 2004).

Conformity to the Group

We have seen that group members generally conform to certain aspects of the group with which they prefer to identify. Some conformity is clearly necessary for a group to survive. If everyone "did his or her own thing," there would be no group. But too much conformity can have disastrous consequences. A central issue in the sociological study of groups has been the degree to which members conform to the expectations and demands of the group despite their own misgivings. The experiments by Stanley Milgram (1974) discussed in Chapter 2 demonstrate that people tend to conform to the demands of authority figures, even if they are ordered to inflict pain on others. Groups often develop informal authority structures that can induce the kind of conformity uncovered by Milgram. Research by Zimbardo (1973), also discussed in Chapter 2, showed similarly troubling tendencies toward conformity.

Another series of experiments, conducted by Solomon Asch (1952), showed that groups with no clear authority figure also promote conformity. The power of the group is so great that it may override an individual's own judgments and perceptions (see also Kinney 2007). In one of the experiments, groups of seven to nine students were assembled. All but one

FIGURE 4.3 • Solomon Asch's Conformity Experiment Cards

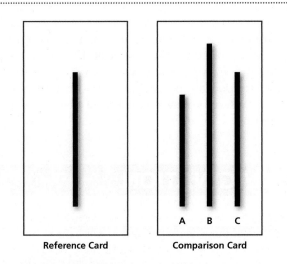

Reference Card   Comparison Card

SOURCE: Adapted from Solomon E. Asch, "Opinions and Social Pressure," *Scientific American* 193 (November 1955): 31–35.

(the subject) were confederates of the researcher. Only the subject believed that the experiment was investigating vision. Each group was shown two cards, one with one vertical line on it and a second with three such lines (see Figure 4.3). One of the lines on the second card was the same length as the line on the first card. The other two lines were clearly different. All the students were asked to choose the line on the comparison card that matched the single line on the reference card. As they had been instructed, each of the confederates chose, out loud, one of the wrong lines. The subjects were always positioned last in their groups. When the subjects' turns came, about a third of them conformed to their groups' erroneous choice and selected the same wrong line. They made the wrong choice even though they apparently knew it was the wrong choice.

There is no question that some people, like the subjects in the Asch experiment, conform to group demands at least some of the time. Conformity is especially likely when the demands come from someone in authority in the group. However, it is important to remember that about two-thirds of the choices made by subjects in the Asch conformity experiments indicated independence from the group. It is also important to note that these experiments are decades old, and many of them occurred in a period of American history more defined by conformity than the era we are in today.

This chapter has focused largely on such micro-level phenomena as individuals, interaction, and groups. In Chapter 5 we turn to the progressively more macro-level phenomena of organizations, societies, and the globe as a whole.

SUMMARY

The sociological perspective on the individual and the self focuses on how they affect a person's ability to take part in society. Symbolic interactionism is a key theory in the sociological study of how individuals develop a sense of self. The self is the ability to take oneself as an object and over time gain a sense of who one is.

In developing a self, children come to incorporate a sense of the generalized other, which allows them to take the role of the entire group or community in which they are embedded.

Erving Goffman argued that in every interaction, or performance, individuals maintain a front stage, where they operate in an idealized manner, and a back stage, where they are better able to freely express what is suppressed in the front stage.

Socialization is the process through which a person learns and generally comes to accept the ways of a group or of a society as a whole. Primary socialization begins with newborns and infants, and as they develop, children experience secondary socialization. Socialization does not end with childhood—adults continue to be socialized throughout their lives. Interaction is crucially important to socialization and many other aspects of the social world. Simmel believed that society is defined by interaction. Interaction is deeply involved in people's statuses within social systems and their related roles. Expectations associated with one status often conflict with those tied to others.

Patterns of interaction and social relationships that occur regularly and persist over time become social structures. The smallest social structure is the dyad, which may sometimes become a triad. A group is still a relatively small social structure, made up of a number of people who develop patterned relationships over time. Social networks involve two or more individuals, groups, organizations, or societies.

REVIEW QUESTIONS

1. How can we use the literature on feral children to explain the importance of interaction to human development? In what ways does this relate to the "nature versus nurture" debate?

2. According to Mead, what distinguishes humans from nonhumans?

3. How does the socialization process help individuals develop their sense of self? Why are games so important to the socialization process?

4. What is the difference between the "I" and the "me"? Why do people and society as a whole need both the "I" and the "me"?

5. According to Goffman, in what ways do we use impression management in our front-stage performances? Why would a sociologist say that racism has increasingly been relegated to the back stage? What is problematic about this development?

6. Why are families important agents of socialization? How do families in higher social classes differ from those in lower social classes in how they socialize their children? What effects might these differences in socialization have on children?

7. How are we socialized to be consumers? In what ways has the Internet resocialized us as consumers?

8. In what ways is being a fifth grader in the United States both an ascribed and an achieved status? What does this suggest about the differences between roles attached to ascribed statuses and those attached to achieved statuses?

9. In the realm of social networks, why are "weak ties" helpful to those who are looking for jobs? What effect has the Internet had on the development of weak ties and strong ties?

10. What images of groups are depicted in the mass media? In what ways do we use those images of groups as reference groups?

APPLYING THE SOCIOLOGICAL IMAGINATION

How can we understand gender socialization through consumption? This chapter argues that malls tend to reinforce gender roles by offering separate shops for female and male consumers.

For this activity, go to your local mall and identify stores for men (and boys) and stores for women (and girls). In what ways are the stores different? Pay attention to the differences in items sold, the nature of those items, the ways in which the stores are set up, and even differences in music and lighting. What do the differences in these stores suggest about the differences between men and women and what is expected of them?

KEY TERMS

achieved status: A position acquired by people on the basis of what they accomplish or the nature of their capacities. (p. 90)

agents of socialization: Those who socialize others. (p. 85)

anticipatory socialization: The teaching (and learning) of what will be expected of one in the future. (p. 85)

ascribed status: A position in which individuals are placed, or to which they move, that has nothing to do with what they have done or their capacities or accomplishments. (p. 90)

back stage: The part of the social world where people feel free to express themselves in ways that are suppressed in the front stage. (p. 83)

conversation analysis: Analysis of how people accomplish conversations. (p. 90)

dramaturgy: The view that social life is a series of dramatic performances akin to those that take place in a theater and on a stage. (p. 82)

dyad: A two-person group. (p. 93)

front stage: The part of the social world where the social performance is idealized and designed to define the situation for those who observe it. (p. 83)

game stage: Mead's second stage in the socialization process, in which a child develops a self in the full sense of the term, because it is then that the child begins to take on the role of a group of people simultaneously rather than the roles of discrete individuals. (p. 81)

generalized other: The attitude of the entire group or community taken by individuals in the process of developing their own behaviors and attitudes. (p. 81)

gesture: A movement of one animal or human that elicits a mindless, automatic, and appropriate response from another animal or human. (p. 79)

group: A relatively small number of people who over time develop a patterned relationship based on interaction with one another. (p. 94)

"I": The immediate response of an individual to others; the part of the self that is incalculable, unpredictable, and creative. (p. 82)

impression management: People's use of a variety of techniques to control the images of themselves that they want to project during their social performances. (p. 83)

interaction: A social engagement that involves two or more individuals who perceive, and orient their actions to, one another. (p. 89)

interaction order: An area of interaction that is organized and orderly, but in which the order is created informally by those involved in the interaction rather than by some formal structure. (p. 90)

looking-glass self: The self-image that reflects how others respond to a person, particularly as a child. (p. 78)

master status: A position that is more important than any others, both for the person in the position and for all others involved. (p. 90)

"me": The organized set of others' attitudes assumed by the individual; involves the adoption by the individual of the generalized other. (p. 82)

micro–macro continuum: The range of social entities from the individual, even the mind and self, to the interaction among individuals, the groups often formed by that interaction, formally structured organizations, societies, and increasingly the global domain. (p. 78)

mind: An internal conversation that arises in relation to, and is continuous with, interactions, especially conversations that one has with others in the social world. (p. 80)

networks: "Interconnected nodes" that are open, capable of unlimited expansion, dynamic, and able to innovate without disrupting the system in which they exist. (p. 93)

play stage: Mead's first stage in the socialization process, in which children learn to take on the attitudes of specific others toward themselves. (p. 81)

primary groups: Groups that are small, are close-knit, and have intimate face-to-face interaction. (p. 94)

primary socialization: The acquisition of language, identities, gender roles, cultural routines, norms, and values from parents and other family members at the earliest stages of an individual's life. (p. 85)

reciprocity: The expectation that those involved in an interaction will give and receive rewards of roughly equal value. (p. 89)

reference groups: Groups that people take into consideration in evaluating themselves. (p. 94)

resocialization: The unlearning of old behaviors, norms, and values and the learning of new ones. (p. 88)

reverse socialization: The socialization of those who normally do the socializing—for example, children socializing their parents. (p. 85)

role: What is generally expected of a person who occupies a given status. (p. 90)

role conflict: Conflicting expectations associated with a given position or multiple positions. (p. 90)

role overload: Confrontation with more expectations than a person can possibly handle. (p. 91)

role-making: The ability of people to modify their roles, at least to some degree. (p. 91)

secondary groups: Generally large, impersonal groups in which ties are relatively weak and members do not know one another very well, and whose impact on members is typically not very powerful. (p. 94)

self: The sense of oneself as an object. (p. 81)

significant symbol: A gesture that arouses in the individual the same kind of response, although it need not be identical, as it is supposed to elicit from those to whom the gesture is addressed. (p. 79)

socialization: The process through which a person learns and generally comes to accept the ways of a group or of society as a whole. (p. 84)

social networks: Networks that involve two or more individuals, groups, organizations, or societies. (p. 93)

status: A dimension of the social stratification system that relates to the prestige attached to people's positions within society. (p. 90)

symbolic interactionism: A sociological perspective focusing on the role of symbols and how their meanings are shared and understood by those involved in human interaction. (p. 80)

total institution: A closed, all-encompassing place of residence and work set off from the rest of society that meets all of the needs of those enclosed within it. (p. 88)

triad: A three-person group. (p. 93)

$SAGE edge™   edge.sagepub.com/ritzeressentials2e

SAGE edge offers a robust online environment featuring an impressive array of free tools and resources for review, study, and further exploration, keeping both instructors and students on the cutting edge of teaching and learning.

LEARNING OBJECTIVES	FOR FURTHER EXPLORATION AND APPLICATION
LO 4-1: Describe the development of the self in the context of symbolic interaction.	● Symbolic Interaction ● Can a Computer Change the Essence of Who You Are? ● Sociological Theory and Symbolic Interactionism
LO 4-2: Discuss the concept of the individual as performer, including the ideas of impression management and the front and back stages.	● The "I" and the "Me" ● Discover Why It Is So Hard to Say "No" ● Social Media's Effect on Real-World Interaction
LO 4-3: Explain the significance of socialization in childhood and adulthood.	● Genie Wiley: Overcoming 10 Years of Isolation ● Understanding the Sibling Effect ● How Children Are Socialized across Cultures
LO 4-4: Describe the key aspects of interaction with others as socialization.	● The Nature versus Nurture Debate ● Parenting Debate: Free Range or Neglect? ● Quick Guide on Agents of Socialization
LO 4-5: Identify micro-level social structures, including social networks and groups.	● The Dynamics of Ingroup and Outgroup Formation ● Micro-Level Groups in Politics ● Examining Group Behavior

ORGANIZATIONS, SOCIETIES, AND THE GLOBAL DOMAIN

Questioning Governmental Authority

Thirty-year-old U.S. Central Intelligence Agency contractor Edward Snowden caused an uproar in many parts of the world when he leaked thousands of classified documents. The clamor in the United States became especially loud in mid-2013 when Snowden told the world that the U.S. National Security Agency had attempted to prevent terrorist acts by spying on ordinary American citizens. This was being done through the systematic accumulation of bulk data (metadata) on routine phone calls. Public reaction was swift and divided, with some arguing that the government had gone to unwarranted lengths in breaching its citizens' privacy. This view was upheld in mid-2015 by a federal appeals court ruling that such data collection was illegal. Others continue to argue that any and all steps necessary to uncover terrorist plots are defensible. Snowden fled to Russia, where he received asylum and, in 2014, a three-year residency permit. Snowden's revelations continue to have an impact. Some terrorist groups have altered the way they communicate because documents Snowden released revealed information about U.S. surveillance techniques. The leaks also led to great changes in the way the government protects secret documents.

The events surrounding Snowden's leaks reveal the relationship between us as individuals and the different organizations and institutions that frame our lives, such as our local and national governments. These organizations cannot exist, at least for very long, without willing participants. When groups of individuals begin to

LEARNING OBJECTIVES

5-1 Describe the features of formal and informal organizations and bureaucracies.

5-2 Discuss new concepts in the study of organizations such as gendered and network organizations.

5-3 Contrast gemeinschaft and gesellschaft societies.

5-4 Describe global societies in terms of nations, states, and nation-states.

Corbis

question the authority and rationality of the bureaucracies that govern them, they may voice concern about, seek to change, or even rebel against those bureaucracies. The massive Hong Kong "umbrella" protests in late 2014 over the government's reneging on its commitments to create a more democratic society are another good example of such actions. Social order cannot be maintained if citizens refuse to adhere to society's shared laws and norms. How do governments react when this happens? Some believe they often overreact. Snowden is wanted by the U.S. government for violating the Espionage Act, and Hong Kong suppressed the umbrella protests.

We have seen how technology and globalization facilitate the global flow of information, fundamentally altering the way we communicate. But this nearly instantaneous dissemination of ideas has become a bonanza for everyone, including whistle-blowers, revolutionaries, rioters, potential terrorists, and even elected governments. For instance, revelations that swiftly followed Snowden's initial leak suggested that the United States had also been secretly conducting extensive monitoring of the communications of its European Union allies (including the prime minister of Germany). Some governments, such as that of the United Kingdom following a series of violent riots in London in 2011, have considered shutting down digital communication during public disturbances. Other countries, such as China, Syria, and Iran, routinely exert censorship power over their citizens' use of the Internet. China blocked the internal flow of information about the umbrella revolution. In late 2014 Russia indicated a desire to restrict Internet communication, perhaps creating something like China's powerful barriers to communication with the rest of the world. Such barriers to the flow of information, as well as efforts such as Snowden's to overcome them, are of profound interest to sociologists, public figures, and social activists alike. ●

Picking up where the previous chapter left off with groups, this chapter moves on to the more macroscopic levels of interest to sociologists: organizations, societies, and the globe as a whole. The individuals, interaction, and groups of focal concern in Chapter 4 all exist within, affect, and are affected by the various macroscopic phenomena of concern here.

ORGANIZATIONS

Organizations are collectives purposely constructed to achieve particular ends. Examples include your college or university, which has the objective of educating you as well as your fellow students; corporations, such as Apple, Google, and Walmart, whose objective is to earn profits; the International Monetary Fund (IMF), which seeks to stabilize currency exchanges throughout the world; and Greenpeace, which works to protect and conserve the global environment.

There is a particularly long and deep body of work in sociology that deals with organizations (Godwyn and Gittell 2011; Lammers and Hickson 2013), much of it traceable to the thinking of Max Weber on a particular kind of organization, the bureaucracy. A **bureaucracy** is a highly rational organization, especially one that is very efficient. However, as both Weber's own thinking and later sociological research (see below) make clear, bureaucracies are *not* always so rational and are even as irrational as you undoubtedly sometimes find them to be. Nevertheless, the bureaucracy is a key element of Weber's theory of the rationalization of the Western world. In fact, along with capitalism, the bureaucracy best exemplifies what Weber meant by rationalization. For decades the concept of bureaucracy dominated sociological thinking about organizations, and it led to many important insights about the social world.

BUREAUCRACIES

Weber created and used many "ideal types" as methodological tools with which to study the real world and conduct historical-comparative analysis (see Chapter 2). An **ideal type** greatly exaggerates the characteristics of a social phenomenon like a bureaucracy. It is a model of how the social phenomenon is supposed to operate in some optimal sense, but rarely does. Once the model has been created, we can compare it to the characteristics of any specific example of the social phenomenon anywhere in the world. It serves to identify the ways in which the ideal type differs from the way the social phenomenon actually operates.

The ideal type bureaucracy is primarily a methodological tool used to study real-life bureaucracies. However, it also gives us a good sense of the advantages of bureaucracies over other types of organizations. The ideal-typical bureaucracy is a model of what most large-scale organizations looked like or at least tried to resemble throughout much of the twentieth century. Figure 5.1 is the organization chart of a typical bureaucracy. A bureaucracy has the following characteristics:

- A continuous series of offices, or positions. Each office has official functions and is bound by a set of rules.

- Each office has a specified sphere of competence. Those who occupy the positions are responsible for specific tasks and have the authority to handle them. Those in related offices are obligated to help with those tasks.

FIGURE 5.1 • Organization Chart for a Typical Bureaucracy

U.S. DEPARTMENT OF TRANSPORTATION

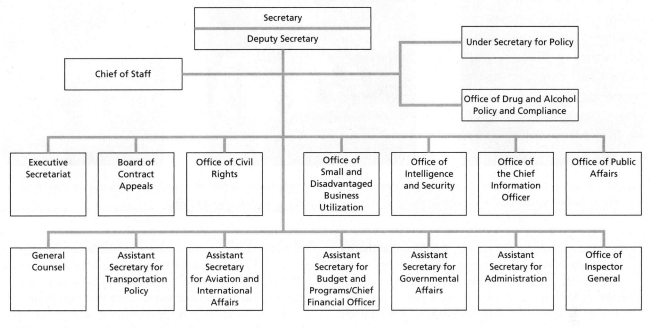

SOURCE: U.S. Department of Transportation.

- The offices exist in a vertical hierarchy.

- The positions have technical requirements, and those who hold those offices must undergo the needed training.

- Organizations, not those who occupy its positions, own the things (computers, desks) needed to do the job. Those who occupy particular offices—chief executive officers, for example—cannot take the offices as their own; these remain part of the organization.

- Everything of formal importance—administrative acts, decisions, rules—is documented in writing.

The development of the bureaucracy is one of the defining characteristics of Western society. In Weber's view, it was a key source of the superiority of the West over other civilizations in the operation of society as a whole as well as of its major components, such as the military. Weber felt that in meeting the needs of large societies for mass administration, there is no better organizational form than, and no alternative to, the bureaucracy.

ASK YOURSELF

Have you ever been a member of a bureaucracy? How many of Weber's characteristics did it have? How well or poorly did it meet the needs of the society it was designed to serve? Why?

Authority Structures and Bureaucracy

Weber's work on bureaucracy is related to his thinking on three types of authority structures. Before getting to those types, we need two preliminary definitions. **Domination** is the probability, or likelihood, that commands will be obeyed by subordinates (Weber [1921] 1968). There are degrees of domination. Strong domination involves a high probability that commands will be obeyed; domination is weak when the probability of obedience is low. **Authority** is legitimate domination. The key question, then, is what makes authority legitimate as far as subordinates are concerned.

Weber differentiates among three types of authority: rational-legal, traditional, and charismatic. **Rational-legal authority** is domination legitimated on the basis of legally enacted rules and the right of those with authority under those rules to issue commands. For example, the president of the United States has rational-legal authority to take a variety of actions, such as appointing federal officials, because the president is duly elected in accord with the country's election laws. It is also legitimate for the president, in the role of commander in chief, to issue various commands, such as to order the use of troops in the case of an attack on the United States. However, in some cases the scope of such authority is not clearly defined. For example, when President Barack Obama claimed the authority to order numerous drone strikes on enemies in places like Afghanistan, some argued that using drones in this way constitutes an act of war, and as such requires the approval of Congress, which alone has the

Elected officials such as President Barack Obama (left) wield rational-legal authority, while Queen Elizabeth of England (center) has traditional authority based on her inherited position. Charismatic authority characterizes such revered leaders as Mahatma Gandhi (right).

rational-legal authority to declare war. **Traditional authority** is based on the belief in long-running traditions. For example, although the pope is elected by the college of cardinals, his authority within Catholicism is based primarily on the long traditions associated with his position. **Charismatic authority** is based on the devotion of followers to what they define as the exceptional characteristics of a leader. Large numbers of people believed that Martin Luther King Jr. and Mahatma Gandhi had such exceptional characteristics and, as a result, became their devoted followers.

Each type of authority can spawn its own organizational form. However, it is rational-legal authority that is most associated with bureaucracy. In comparison to the bureaucracy, organizations based on traditional and charismatic authority are less rational. They are, for example, less efficient than the highly efficient bureaucracy.

Rationality and Irrationality

Much of the sociological research on organizations has taken Weber's highly rational model of a bureaucracy as a starting point for the study of the ways in which bureaucracies actually work. However, much of that research has found Weber's ideal-typical model to be unrealistic. For one thing, there is no single organizational model. The nature of the organization and its degree of rationality are contingent on such factors as the organization's size and the technologies that it employs (Orlikowski 2010; Pugh et al. 1968). For another, researchers have found Weber's ideal-typical bureaucracy to be overly rational. This is not surprising, since for Weber ([1903–1917] 1949: 47) it was "not a *description* of reality." Weber purposely exaggerated its degree of rationality. The ideal-typical bureaucracy is a fiction designed to serve as a reference point for the study of real-world bureaucracies. However, researchers have often overlooked the fact that this ideal type is a methodological tool and have mistaken it for an attempt to describe bureaucracies accurately. They have concluded that, at best,

real-world organizations exhibit a limited form of rationality, or what is called **bounded rationality** (Collet 2009; Simon [1945] 1976; Williamson 1975, 1985). That is, rationality is limited by the instabilities and conflicts that exist in most, if not all, organizations and the domains in which they operate (Scott 2008). It is also limited by inherent limitations on humans' capacities to think and act in a rational manner. Some members of any given organization are capable of acting more rationally than others. However, none are able to operate in anything approaching the fully rational manner associated with Weber's ideal-typical organization (Cyert and March 1963).

The military is an example of an organization with bounded rationality. One source of instability in the military is the cycling of personnel in and out of it, especially in combat zones. Newcomers to the battle zone rarely know exactly what to do. Their presence in, say, a platoon can reduce its ability to function. Another, larger source of instability lies in the conflicts that exist between branches of the armed forces, as well as between central command and those in the field. In addition, military actions are often so complex that military personnel cannot fully understand them or rationally decide what actions to take. This phenomenon is sometimes referred to as the "fog of war" (Blight and Lang 2005).

A good deal of sociological research on bureaucracies has dealt with how the rational (that is, what is efficient) often becomes irrational (or inefficient). This is often referred to as the "irrationality of rationality"—the irrationality that often accompanies the seemingly rational actions associated with the bureaucracy (Ritzer 2015). For example, Robert Merton ([1949] 1968) found that instead of operating efficiently, bureaucracies introduce great inefficiency due to, among other things, "red tape"—that is, the rigid rules that a bureaucracy's employees are required to follow, as well as the unnecessary online and offline questions to be answered and forms to be filled out by the clients of the bureaucracy.

Bureaucracies generally demand far more information than they need, often to protect themselves from complaints, bad publicity, and lawsuits. Red tape also includes the telephone time wasted by keeping clients on hold and forcing them to make their way through a maze of prerecorded "customer service" options. *Catch-22* is a term derived from the novel (and 1970 movie) of that name by Joseph Heller (1961). It refers to the fact that bureaucratic rules may be written in such a way that one rule makes it impossible to do what another rule demands or requires. Heller's story focuses on a burned-out World War II pilot who wants to be excused from flying further combat missions. One of the military's rules is that he can be excused from such missions if he has a doctor declare him crazy. However, there is another, contrary rule— Rule 22—stating that anyone rational enough to want to get out of combat cannot possibly be crazy. If the pilot follows the first rule and does what is required to avoid flying combat missions, Catch-22 will make it impossible for him to get out of those missions.

Lawrence J. Peter and Raymond Hull (1969) intended the *Peter Principle* to be a humorous characterization of a tendency in bureaucratic organizations for employees to rise to their "level of incompetence." According to the principle, if an employee does well in her position, she is rewarded by being promoted to a higher level in the organization. If she does well in that new position, she once again is offered a promotion. Promotions continue until the person ends up in a position of authority and responsibility for which she is not competent, because she does not possess the required skill set, and from which she will no longer be promoted. The result is an organization in which those in key leadership positions are not up to the task and thereby hamper the organization's ability to fulfill its mission.

Parkinson's Law was similarly conceived as a humorous attempt to point to another source of irrationality in bureaucratic organizations. Cyril Northcote Parkinson (1955) summarized the law, writing that "work expands so as to fill the time available for its completion." Thus, if a bureaucrat is assigned two reports to complete in a month, it will require a month to complete them. If that same employee is assigned one report during that time, it will still take a month to complete. Another source of irrationality is what Robert Merton ([1949] 1968) called the **bureaucratic personality**, someone who follows the rules of the organization to such a great extent that the organization's ability to achieve its goals is subverted. One example is a teacher who devotes so much time and attention to discussing and enforcing classroom rules that little real learning takes place. In these and in many other ways, the actual functioning of bureaucracies is at variance with Weber's ideal-typical characterization.

The Informal Organization

A great deal of research in the twentieth century focused on the **informal organization**, that is, how the organization actually works as opposed to the way it is supposed to work as depicted, for example, in Weber's ideal-typical formal bureaucracy (Blau 1963). For instance, those who occupy offices lower in the bureaucratic hierarchy often have greater knowledge of and competence in specific issues than those who rank above them. Thus, fellow employees may seek the advice of the lower-level bureaucrat rather than the one who ranks higher in the authority structure. While at variance from the ideal type, the informal organization can help to make up for inadequacies in the formal organization (Gulati and Puranam 2009).

ASK YOURSELF

What specific bureaucracy came to mind when you read about Weber's definition of this type of organization? Is there an informal organization at work there? How is it different from the formal organization? In what ways is it more effective or less effective than the formal one?

Employees sometimes do things that exceed what is expected of them by the organization. However, they more often do less, perhaps far less, than they are expected to do. For example, contrary to the dictates of the formal organization, the most important things that take place in an organization may never be put down in writing. Employees may find it simply too time-consuming to fill out every form or document they are supposed to use. Instead, and contrary to the organization's rules, they may handle many tasks orally. In addition, employees handle some tasks orally so that if anything goes wrong there is no damning evidence that could jeopardize careers and even the organization as a whole.

The problem for organizations (and individuals) is somewhat different in the digital age. Rather than too little information in writing, the danger is now that too much information is in written form, as e-mail messages, posts, tweets, and the like. Posts to the Internet in particular can exist forever and be widely and endlessly circulated. This was pointed up not only by Edward Snowden's leaks but also by the earlier release by WikiLeaks of unpublished official U.S. government documents, including documents revealing secret ties between Pakistan's security forces and the Taliban. The public release of this information jeopardized the lives of people in Afghanistan working undercover for the United States and disrupted already troubled Pakistan–U.S. relations. However, there are those who feel that secrets and secret agreements pose the greatest danger to human lives. For example, it is widely believed that Pakistan's security forces secretly helped the Taliban kill American soldiers.

Snapchat attempts to deal with the problem of information remaining on the Internet forever by automatically deleting posts and photos after a few seconds. However, as one of Snapchat's founders said, "Nothing ever goes away on the Internet" (Wortham 2013: A3).

While in some bureaucracies power is meant to be dispersed throughout the offices, an organization sometimes becomes an **oligarchy**. That is, a small group of people at the top illegitimately obtain and exercise far more power than they are supposed to have. This can occur in any organization. Robert Michels ([1915] 1962) first described such undemocratic processes in organizations—labor unions and socialist parties—that supposedly prized democracy. Michels called this phenomenon "the iron law of oligarchy" (Guillen 2010; Tolbert 2013). Those in power manipulate the organization (for example, by structuring elections to work to their advantage) so that they and their supporters can stay in power indefinitely. At the same time, they make it difficult for others to get or to keep power. However, the development of an oligarchy is neither "iron" nor a law; most organizations do not become oligarchical.

Weber's model also makes no provision for infighting within organizations. However, internal squabbles, and sometimes outright battles, are everyday occurrences within organizations. This is particularly evident in the government and other very large organizations, where one branch or office often engages in pitched turf battles with others. For example, in his book *Duty* (2014), published while he was U.S. secretary of defense, Robert Gates reveals conflicts between Barack Obama's advisers and others. Afghanistan commander General David Petraeus found it difficult to work with Obama adviser David Axelrod because he was "a complete spin doctor" (Baker 2010: A12).

CONTEMPORARY ORGANIZATIONAL REALITIES

As the social world has changed, so too has sociological thinking about many things, including organizations. New concepts such as gendered and network organizations are supplementing the concept of bureaucracy to enrich our understanding of these new realities.

GENDERED ORGANIZATIONS

Weber's model does not account for discrimination within organizations. In the ideal bureaucracy, any worker with the necessary training can fill any job. However, as "gendered organization" theorists such as Joan Acker (1990, 2009) have shown, bureaucracies do not treat all workers in the same way (Pager, Western, and Bonikowski 2009). Jobs are often designed for an idealized worker—one who has no obligations except to the organization. Women, who usually have the responsibility for child rearing, can have difficulty fitting this model (Williams 2001). Women often face the "competing devotions" of motherhood and work (Blair-Loy 2003; Wharton and Blair-Loy 2006). Organizations may also discriminate (consciously or unconsciously) in hiring and promotions, with white men (who tend to populate the higher levels of bureau-

Associated Press

Employing organizations increasingly seek to ease the burden for employees with young children by providing on-site daycare centers where the children can be visited by the employee during the work day.

cracies) being promoted over women and minorities (Alvesson and Due Billing 2009; Ortiz and Roscigno 2009). Some women in male-dominated business organizations find that they hit a "glass ceiling"—a certain level of authority beyond which they cannot rise (Acker 2009; Appelbaum, Asham, and Argheyd 2011; Gorman and Kmec 2009). This is also true in other contexts, such as medicine, as female surgeons have experienced (Zhuge et al. 2011). They can see the top—hence the "glass"—but cannot reach it. Within other organizations, particularly female-dominated ones, men can find themselves riding the "glass escalator" (Williams 1995). This is an invisible force that propels them past equally competent, or even more competent, women to positions of leadership and authority (Williams, Muller, and Kilanski 2012).

In a global context, American female executives face a "double-paned" glass ceiling. There is the pane associated with the employing company in the United States, and there is a second pane women executives encounter when they seek work experience in the corporation's foreign locales. This is a growing problem, since experience overseas is increasingly a requirement for top-level management positions in multinational corporations, but corporations have typically "masculinized" these expatriate positions and thereby disadvantaged women. Among the problems experienced by women who succeed in getting these positions are sexual harassment, a lack of availability of programs (such as career counseling) routinely available to men, inadequate mentoring, and male managers who are more likely to promote male than female expatriates. Much of the blame for this problem lies in the structure of the multinational corporations, and with the men who occupy high-level management positions within them. However, female managers' greater passivity and lesser willingness to promote themselves for such expatriate management positions can contribute to their difficulties (Insch, McIntyre, and Napier 2008).

FIGURE 5.2 • Glass-Ceiling Index

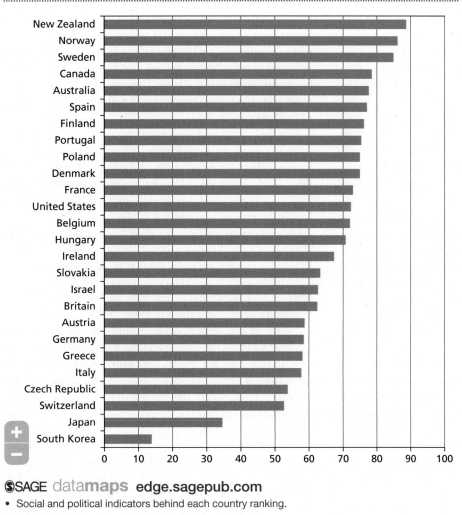

⑤SAGE datamaps edge.sagepub.com
• Social and political indicators behind each country ranking.

NOTE: 100 = best for working women.

SOURCE: Data from "The Glass-Ceiling Index," *The Economist*, March 7, 2013.© The Economist Newspaper Limited, London (2013).

While most of these ideas have been developed on the basis of studies of American organizations, they likely apply as well, or better, globally. For example, a recent study found that the glass ceiling exists in Durban, South Africa (Kiaye and Singh 2013). Figure 5.2 shows where women in industrialized nations have the best chance of circumventing the glass ceiling—that is, of being treated equally in the work world. New Zealand is best for working women; South Korea is the worst. The United States is in the middle of the pack.

The idea of a glass ceiling relates to vertical mobility—and its absence—for women in organizations. A related concept is the "glass cage," which deals with the horizontal segregation of women (and other minorities) (Kalev 2009). The idea is that men and women doing the same or similar jobs operate in separate and segregated parts of the organization. As in the case of the glass ceiling, women can see what is going on in other cages, but, compared with men, they find it more difficult to move between the cages. Although the cage is made

of glass, the skills and abilities of women tend to be less visible, and, as a result, stereotypes about them abound. In addition, women have less communication with those outside the cage, are less likely to learn about jobs available there, are not as likely to get high-profile assignments, and are less likely to get needed training. The situation confronting women would improve if there were more collaboration across the boundaries of the glass cage. Of course, the ultimate solution involves the elimination of the glass cage as well as the glass ceiling. However, men are unlikely to want to eliminate either, because they tend to benefit from the limitations placed on women. Many women may also accept both because they think their individual abilities will allow them to overcome those barriers.

The glass ceiling and the glass cage represent barriers to the mobility of women within organizations. The concept of the "glass cliff" describes what can happen to women who experience upward mobility when the organization is going through hard times (Ryan and Haslam 2005). In such a situation (and others) females are more likely than males to find themselves at the edge of that organizational cliff. A disproportionate number of those women (and minorities) are likely to be demoted or to fall off that cliff (lose their jobs) and be replaced by males (Cook and Glass 2014).

OTHER PROBLEMS IN ORGANIZATIONS

Beyond the specific problems in organizations to be discussed in this section, entire organizations can be seen as problematic (Friedrichs 2007). The most heinous example of a problematic (to put it mildly) organization is the Nazi bureaucracy responsible for the murder of 6 million Jews, and others, during the Holocaust (Bauman 1989). Islamic State, al-Qaeda, the Mafia, and Mexican drug cartels, among many others, would also be considered by most people to be problematic organizations. In addition, many less developed countries in the world regard global organizations like the International Monetary Fund and the World Bank as problematic organizations because of the damaging austerity programs they impose on recipient countries in exchange for monetary assistance and other help (Babb 2005).

Problems occur in organizations that in themselves are not seen as problematic. For example, a scandal broke out in the National Football League (NFL) in late 2014 when the website TMZ released a video of Baltimore Ravens star running back Ray Rice knocking out his then-fiancée (and later wife) in an elevator in an Atlantic City hotel-casino earlier in the year. The NFL claimed it did not know about the incident, although it turned out that it did. When the incident became public, Rice was at first suspended for two games, but when the public furor grew, he was released by the Ravens and suspended by the NFL. The NFL could increasingly come to be seen as a problematic organization as evidence of player spousal abuse mounts, along with alarming revelations about the disastrous long-term effects of brain-related injuries incurred by players during practices and games, including dementia and suicide, stemming from concussions. The NFL seems to have learned its lesson, as is clear in the case of another scandal known as "Deflategate." Various people associated with the New England Patriots deflated footballs before the 2015 Super Bowl game (won by the Patriots) in order to give the team an advantage over the Indianapolis Colts. A quick investigation was undertaken, and as a result the Patriots were penalized in various ways: They were fined $1 million and lost two future draft picks, and superstar quarterback Tom Brady was suspended without pay for the first four games of the next season (Pennington 2015). However, the suspension was nullified by a judge, and Brady was allowed to play football at the beginning of the 2015 season.

Sexual harassment, another organizational problem, involves unwanted sexual attention, such as sexually oriented remarks and jokes, advances, and requests that take place in the workplace or in other settings (Lopez, Hodson, and Roscigno 2009; Zippel 2007; see also Chapter 9). In the United States, the federal Equal Employment Opportunity Commission (2014) was informed of almost 6,900 charges of sexual harassment in the workplace in 2014. Such cases rarely get publicity, and many are never reported to management or find their way into the judicial or criminal justice system. One example of an exception is the suspected 2011 rape of a hotel worker by Dominique Strauss-Kahn, then head of the IMF and leading contender to become the next French head of state, which led to the revelation that this was far from the only case of such harassment in which he had been involved. While there is a tendency to ignore it, sexual harassment is widely practiced, and a great many women are harmed by it. The United Nations estimates that 40–50 percent of women in European Union countries experience some form of sexual harassment at work (Directorate-General for Employment, Industrial Relations and Social Affairs 1998: iii, cited in United Nations General Assembly 2006: 42; see also UN Women 2014).

To be illegal, sexual harassment must recur and/or be severe and result in a hostile workplace environment or even the firing of the harassed employment. The stereotype of the high-ranking man demanding sexual favors from subordinates (usually women) is generally accurate, although both men and women can perpetrate and be subject to all forms of sexual harassment. About 18 percent of 2012 charges reported to the Equal Opportunity Employment Commission were filed by men.

In the U.S. armed forces, however, sexual harassment does seem to follow the stereotypical pattern of males harassing females. There have been many allegations of sexual harassment (and sexual assault) of female service members, and criticism of the armed services for failing to react adequately has been mounting (Schemo 2003; Shear 2013; Verkaik 2006). According to the U.S. Department of Defense (2013), reported cases of sexual assault in the military increased almost 50 percent between fiscal year 2012 and fiscal year 2013 (see Figure 5.3). Military men and those at higher ranks perceived fewer barriers to reporting such assaults compared to military women and those at lower ranks.

One of the largest organizations in the world, the Catholic Church, has had to address a global organizational culture that enabled priests and other church officials to perpetuate a system of sexual assaults and abuses against children. This culture has been a huge problem not only because of the behavior of the priests and its impact on children, but also because church officials have not done nearly enough to dismiss those responsible and make it more difficult for such assaults to occur in the future (Doyle 2003; Spröber et al. 2014). The scandal was a factor in the abdication of Pope Benedict XVI in early 2013. His successor, Pope Francis, has taken a much stronger stance against sexual abuse of children.

FIGURE 5.3 • Total Reports of Sexual Assault Made to the Department of Defense, 2004–2013

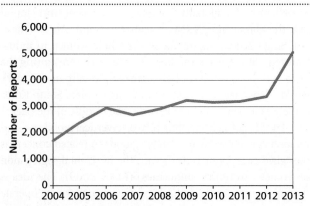

SOURCE: Data from U.S. Department of Defense, "Sexual Assault Prevention and Response," *Department of Defense Annual Report on Sexual Assault in the Military: Fiscal Year 2013* (Washington, DC: Author, 2014).

Disasters (and other unplanned outcomes) are deeply problematic for organizations. Such events often occur as the result of rational organizational processes (Vaughan 1996). For example, in the 1980s, the National Aeronautics and Space Administration (NASA) operated on the basis of what it considered a highly reliable and rational plan. As a result, it focused on, among many other things, a variety of quantifiable factors to keep the space shuttle *Challenger* on schedule for its launch. In doing so, the agency cut a number of corners and engaged in various economies. These actions made sense from the perspective of NASA as a rationalized organization. However, they contributed to the disaster on January 28, 1986, in which *Challenger*'s fuel tank broke apart, causing the in-flight destruction of the shuttle and the deaths of seven crew members.

CONTEMPORARY CHANGES IN ORGANIZATIONS

Bureaucratic organizations have undergone a number of important changes in the last several decades that do not fit well with Weber's view of organizations. For one thing, contrary to Weber's thinking on the likelihood of their growth and spread, many of the largest organizations, especially industrial organizations and labor unions, have been forced to downsize dramatically (Cooper, Pandey, and Campbell 2012). The idea that "bigger is better" is no longer the rule in most organizations. Instead of constantly adding new functions and more employees, organizations are now likely to focus on their "core competencies." For example, the Ford Motor Company is focusing on manufacturing automobiles and not, as it once did, on making (among many other things) the steel for the frames and the rubber for the tires. Ford also sold off the Volvo and Jaguar lines to focus on the Ford brand. In essence, organizations have come to concentrate on being "lean and mean" (Harrison 1994). Many newer organizations such as Facebook and even Google are likely to learn lessons from the problems experienced by organizational giants like Ford. They will seek to avoid ever losing their focus or becoming too large and diverse. As a result, it is unlikely that they will ever need to downsize or simplify to the degree that Ford has in order to accomplish these goals.

To adapt to a rapidly changing environment, contemporary organizations have also been forced to become more flexible and more agile than the ideal-typical bureaucracy suggests. For example, it appears that Ford has become flexible enough to compete with rising automobile manufacturers such as Hyundai and Kia. When today's organizations lack such flexibility, there is a strong likelihood that they will decline or disappear. For instance, the video store chain Blockbuster failed to adapt sufficiently and quickly enough to competition from Netflix and its movies by mail and later streaming of movies, as well as to Redbox and its video-dispensing kiosks. As a result, Blockbuster went bankrupt in 2010.

One form of offshore outsourcing that has become familiar to many U.S. consumers is customer service and product support provided by Indian call centers. Why are some employees in such centers encouraged to assume American identities?

Yet another important organizational development is the increasing trend toward **outsourcing**, or the transfer of activities once performed by one organization to another organization in exchange for money (Furneaux 2013; Ritzer and Lair 2007). Since the early 2000s, outsourcing has increased dramatically. Companies have become more likely to outsource functions such as those handled traditionally by human resource departments (Korkki 2012). Hospitals outsource the operation of their emergency rooms to businesses that employ people—including physicians—devoted to such work. Local, state, and federal governments also outsource work to other organizations, especially private businesses. An example that received a lot of negative publicity is the U.S. government's outsourcing of many military and paramilitary activities in Iraq to a company known as Blackwater (now Xe Services), which engaged in unwarranted killings and the use of unnecessary force.

Another recent trend in organizations involves turning over to clients some of the work formerly performed by

newscom krtphotos

officeholders. For example, we are increasingly filling out census forms on our own, thereby doing work that used to be done by census takers. We are scanning checks into our cell phones instead of handing them to tellers, reviewing restaurants and movies online rather than reading reviews by professional critics, and talking about our experiences with products or brands on social networking sites instead of leaving such work to those in marketing. More and more, we are scanning our own groceries; the first self-checkout machine was installed in the United States in 1992, and by 2014 it was estimated that 430,000 such machines were in operation across the country. In taking on these tasks, clients and consumers are turned into producers, at least for a time. In other words, consumers have been transformed into *prosumers,* combining the acts of consumption and production (Ritzer, Dean, and Jurgenson 2012; see also Chapter 3). The most recent changes are even eliminating the work performed by customers and clients and turning it over to "smart machines" (Ritzer 2014). For example, instead of requiring a person to unload a shopping cart and scan each product at checkout, a smart machine can now scan the products in the cart as the customer leaves the store and charge the total bill to the customer's credit card.

GLOBALIZATION AND ORGANIZATIONS

Most organizations of any significant size have become increasingly global. They are affected by numerous global realities and changes and in many cases have become global forces and players themselves. The global reach of McDonald's is well known. It has more than 35,000 restaurants in 119 countries throughout the world. However, in the fast-food industry, Yum! Brands (corporate parent of Pizza Hut, KFC, and others) is in slightly more countries—125—and has more than 5,000 more restaurants than McDonald's. Walmart is another American global powerhouse, with more than 11,000 stores in 27 countries. Other organizations with a presence in the United States have their roots elsewhere in the world. Examples include IKEA, based in Sweden, with 363 stores in 45 countries; H&M, an apparel retailer from Sweden; T-Mobile, a telecommunications company originating in Germany; HSBC, a financial services provider from Hong Kong and Shanghai; and Zara International, a fashion retailer whose home base is in Spain (Ritzer 2015).

Spanning much of the globe is a challenge to any organization and forces it to adapt to global realities in innumerable ways. Ford Motor Company, for example, recognized some years ago that producing a different model car for every country or global region was very inefficient, and so it focused on the manufacture and sale of a global car, the Ford Focus.

Globalization has also accelerated the transfer of work to organizations in other countries, known as **offshore outsourcing**. See Table 5.1 for a list of the world's top 20

TABLE 5.1 • Top 20 Outsourcing Destinations, 2014

RANK	COUNTRY	CITY
1	India	Bangalore
2	Philippines	Manila
3	India	Mumbai
4	India	Delhi
5	India	Chennai
6	India	Hyderabad
7	India	Pune
8	Philippines	Cebu City
9	Poland	Kraków
10	Ireland	Dublin
11	China	Shanghai
12	China	Beijing
13	Costa Rica	San José
14	China	Dalian
15	China	Shenzhen
16	Czech Republic	Prague
17	Vietnam	Ho Chi Minh City
18	Malaysia	Kuala Lumpur
19	Sri Lanka	Colombo
20	Brazil	São Paulo

SOURCE: Data from "Manila Ranks Top 2 Outsourcing Destination in the World," Outsourcing Insider, February 12, 2014 (http://www.blog.infinit-o.com/manila-ranks-top-2-outsourcing-destination-world).

outsourcing destinations. The top 8 destination cities are all in India and the Philippines, where a large proportion of the population is fluent in English. This is important because the United States is the world leader in offshore outsourcing. Offshore outsourcing takes many forms, but the one we are most familiar with is the offshore outsourcing of call center work. A call center is a centralized office that handles a large volume of telephone calls from people asking an organization for information and help.

McDonaldization and Bureaucratic Organizations

During the early twenty-first century, the fast-food restaurant can be seen as the best example of the ongoing process of rationalization first described by Weber (Ritzer 2015). While the fast-food restaurant is a relatively new and important organizational development, it is continuous with the bureaucracy and its basic principles: efficiency, predictability, calculability, control, and the seemingly inevitable irrationalities of rationality. What, then, distinguishes McDonaldized fast-food restaurants from bureaucracies?

McDonaldization is applicable to both large bureaucratic organizations and relatively small organizations. The principles of bureaucracy have tended to be applied only to state governments and giant corporations like Ford and Walmart. Such bureaucracies still exist, although in many cases they are much smaller than they once were. The principles of McDonaldization can be applied not only to large corporations such as Starbucks but also to small restaurants and all sorts of small enterprises. In short, the model of the McDonaldized fast-food restaurant has much wider applicability than the bureaucratic model. There are far more small enterprises throughout the United States and the world than there are state governments and large corporations.

McDonaldization is applicable to both consumption-oriented organizations and production-oriented organizations. The bureaucratic model is most applicable, outside of government, to large production-oriented corporations. However, the United States has moved away from a society dominated by work and production to one dominated by consumption. As a result, the large corporation involved in goods production has declined in importance, at least in the United States and other developed countries. In its place we have seen the rise of similarly large corporations, such as Subway, Walmart, and IKEA, devoted to consumption. While the corporate structures of these organizations remain highly bureaucratized, their real hearts lie in the numerous smaller outlets that constitute the sources of income and profit for the organizations. Thus, of greatest importance now is the McDonaldization of those outlets and not the bureaucratization of the larger organizations in which they exist.

Despite the spread of McDonaldization, some are speculating that it, like bureaucratization, has passed its peak. The "Digital Living" box on page 110 discusses an important online organization—eBay—as well as whether it is important and different enough to be a new model of organizational development in the contemporary world.

NETWORK ORGANIZATIONS

The bureaucracy and the fast-food restaurant both continue to be important in the early twenty-first century. However, organizations continue to change and evolve. Further, entirely new organizational forms are coming into existence. One such new form is the network organization. As discussed in more detail below, the **network organization** is defined by its networks, especially those based on and linked together by information (Blaschke, Schoeneborn, and Seidl 2012). The network organization came about in the wake of the revolution in informational technology in the United States in the 1970s. Developments included the penetration of television deep into American life and the introduction of home computers, personal data assistants (PDAs), and the Internet (Allan 2007; Van Dijk 2012). The network model is also inextricably entwined with globalization. Most of the important functions and processes in the information age are increasingly dominated by these networks, and many of them are global in scope. This revolution led, in turn, to a fundamental restructuring of the global capitalist system beginning in the 1980s. For example, multinational corporations grew in importance, in part because of great improvements in the ability to communicate globally. Those corporations that were narrowly nation-based experienced serious declines or were themselves transformed into multinationals.

Characteristics of the Network Organization

This new organizational form has several notable characteristics. Of greatest importance is the idea that an organization is composed of several networks, or "interconnected nodes" (see the discussion of social networks in Chapter 4). A network organization has the following characteristics:

- *Horizontal structure.* In contrast to the vertical and hierarchical structures that characterize classic bureaucracies, network organizations are flatter; there are fewer positions between the top of the organization and the bottom.

- *Fuzzy boundaries.* Unlike bureaucracies, network organizations are *not* seen as distinct entities with clear and definite boundaries. Rather, network organizations intertwine with one another in many ways. Most obviously, they form strategic alliances with other organizations that have similar or complementary goals.

- *Dispersed decision making.* Network organizations involve more collective decision making and the involvement of many more people in the decision-making process.

- *Flexible production.* Manufacturing organizations with a network model have moved away from mass production and toward more flexible production methods, such as variable and limited production runs.

An organization with these characteristics is, in comparison with a bureaucracy, more open, more capable of expansion, more dynamic, and better able to innovate without disrupting the system.

In the global information economy, at least in developed nations, the nature of work is being transformed. Workers, including manufacturing employees, are dealing more with information and less with material processes (Caprile and Serrano Pascual 2011). This has reduced the total number of employees needed, even as output increases. In addition, the network organization allows for new kinds of work arrangements because information can flow anywhere, especially

eBayization

Taking the eBay online auction site as a model, "eBayization" implies that the digitized world in which it exists is in the process of displacing in importance the material world that is the domain of McDonald's (Ahuvia and Izberk-Bilgin 2011). However, it is important to remember that the digital and material worlds are always interrelated. In the case of eBay, while a transaction may occur online, it usually ends with the very material transfer of some product from seller to buyer. In the current era of global, Internet-based, and information-based enterprises, the concept of McDonaldization may be of declining utility.

The basic dimensions of eBayization are very different from those of McDonaldization:

- *Variety.* Millions of products are available on eBay; McDonald's offers only a few dozen.
- *Unpredictability.* The predictable products of McDonald's are quite unlike the highly unpredictable products on eBay, such as a "Hero Chinese Symbol Engraved Stone Ocean Pebble Rock."
- *Highly specific and limited control.* Whereas eBay sellers interact directly with buyers of their products with little involvement from the eBay organization, McDonaldized systems exercise more widespread control.

Associated Press

Some suggest that a process named after eBay—eBayization—might become preeminent if the digital world becomes more important than the material world. What other factors are involved in an organization like eBay becoming so influential in the global culture?

McDonald's may be fast, but eBay is vast; McDonald's offers some things most of the time, eBay offers almost everything all of the time. As our world continues to move in the direction of digitization, eBayization may prove to be a more useful concept than McDonaldization. However, it is also possible to argue that eBay is a highly McDonaldized company. It is that high degree of McDonaldization that allows it to operate under the principles of eBayization. For example, it takes a highly rationalized company and system to offer millions of products for sale.

Think About It

Do you think the dimensions of eBayization described above are unique to eBay? Why or why not? Do you believe eBayization is a more useful concept than McDonaldization, or do you feel eBay is simply a highly McDonaldized organization? Why?

---

anywhere there is a computer. Thus, for example, more people can work from the comfort of their homes, in transit on airplanes, and in hotels anyplace in the world (Alexander, Ettema, and Dijst 2010; Kaufman-Scarbrough 2006).

Informationalism

The processing of knowledge, or what Manuel Castells (1996, 1997, 1998; Subramanian and Katz 2011; Williams 2012) calls **informationalism**, is a key feature of the network

organization. Forces of production and consumption, such as factories and shopping malls, are linked through knowledge and information. Thus, for example, the stocking of shelves at Walmart is done nearly automatically. Computerized technology at the local Walmart tracks stock on hand and transmits the information to centralized warehouses. As the stock is being depleted, new shipments are sent out automatically so that the shelves at the local Walmart will remain well stocked.

Informationalism has five basic characteristics:

- Technologies act on information, such as the depletion of stock at Walmart.

- These technologies have a pervasive effect, as information transmitted to personal computers, tablets, and smartphones increasingly becomes a part of all human activity.

- All organizations, and other systems, using information technologies are defined by a "networking logic" that allows them to affect a wide variety of processes and organizations to which they are linked. For example, Walmart has linkages to its many suppliers throughout the world.

- The new technologies are highly flexible, allowing them to adapt and change constantly.

- The specific technologies associated with information are already merging into a highly integrated system that cuts across many different organizations and areas of the world. Thus, for example, the Internet, e-mail, and text messaging link innumerable global organizations.

As a result of informationalism, a new, increasingly profitable global information economy has emerged. The productivity of firms and nations depends on their ability to generate, process, and apply knowledge-based information efficiently. Global communication systems allow those involved in this economy to operate as a unit on a worldwide scale.

The network organization, as well as the informationalism that defines it, is the latest organizational form to draw sociologists' attention, but it will certainly not be the last. New organizational forms are likely to emerge as society and the world continue to change.

SOCIETIES

Sociologists have traditionally defined society as a complex pattern of social relationships that is bounded in space and persists over time (Ray 2007). This definition has two key characteristics: First, it is very abstract; second, this abstractness allows it to encompass the gamut of social relationships. Thus, in these terms, a triad (a three-person group) and any larger group would be a kind of society, as would the United States and other countries, as well as global organizations such as the United Nations and the International Monetary Fund.

Ferdinand Toennies ([1887] 1957) differentiated between two broad types of societies—*gemeinschaft* and *gesellschaft*. He labeled traditional societies **gemeinschaft societies** and defined them as being characterized by face-to-face relations. Toennies considered families, rural villages, and small towns to be gemeinschaft societies. Such societies tend to be quite small because they are based on intimate interaction. Relationships between people are valued for their intrinsic qualities, such as familiarity and closeness, and not, or at least not merely, for their utility. Gemeinschaft societies continue to exist in many parts of the world, including the United States.

More modern societies are **gesellschaft societies**, characterized by impersonal, distant, and limited social

There is a stark contrast between a traditional gemeinschaft society and a modern gesellschaft society.

relationships. In such societies, people tend to enter relationships for what they can gain from them rather than for their intrinsic qualities. That is, relationships are often a means to an end. Gesellschaft societies are likely to be large-scale societies, or to exist within them.

Gemeinschaft and gesellschaft are ideal types. In the real world, including today's world, aspects of both exist in all societies. The definition of society mentioned above encompasses both gemeinschaft and gesellschaft societies, and everything in between. Furthermore, both concepts can be applied to every social relationship, from the smallest group, such as a dyad or triad, to the largest society, such as China.

ASK YOURSELF

Keeping in mind that gesellschaft and gemeinschaft societies are idealized abstractions of reality and that real societies can have characteristics of both, make a list of all the groups and communities to which you belong and decide which are more gesellschaft and which are more gemeinschaft. Why have you included each group or community in one category or the other? In which groups or communities do you prefer to spend time, and why?

Although the earlier general definition of society has its utility, society can be more narrowly and specifically—and usefully—defined as a relatively large population that lives in a given territory, has a social structure, and shares a culture. The United States, China, and Spain would be societies in this macro-level sense of the term; a triad or group or organization would not be such a society. This definition also fits the thrust of this chapter, which ends with a discussion of the most macroscopic level of social organization: the global society.

As a structural-functionalist, Talcott Parsons (1966) had a very positive view of macro-level societies. He was concerned with the major structures of societies, including the economy, the political system, systems responsible for transmitting culture and its norms and values (e.g., schools), and the legal system, which is responsible for the integration of society. Clearly, these are key components of society in the macro sense of the term.

Sociologists who study societies often ask big questions about them and their changing nature. One of the most notable recent efforts to think about the issues facing society as a whole is the work of Ulrich Beck (Anaïs and Hier 2012). Until recently, it was the norm to think of society as being dominated by industry. In "industrial society," the key issue was wealth and how to distribute it more evenly. This problem continues to concern many sociologists (see Chapter 7). However, Beck ([1986] 1992) argues that we have moved from an industrial society to a **risk society**, where the central issue is risk, and especially how to prevent, minimize, and channel

Associated Press

Has Japan become a risk society in the wake of the continuing leaks from its devastated Fukushima nuclear power plant? Here officials check children from the evacuation area around the plant for radiation.

it. In addition, while in an industrial society a central concern is equality, in a risk society the focus shifts to how to remain safe in the face of increasing risk. Most important, there is a big difference between the two types of societies in the ways in which solidarity is achieved. In an industrial society, solidarity is achieved by people joining together for the positive goal of creating a more equal society. In a risk society, solidarity is achieved through the largely negative and defensive goal of being spared from danger. The implication is that risk society is weaker, more individualized, and less laudable than industrial society and its humanitarian goal of increased equality.

What accounts for the emergence of risk society? The key is that the risks are far greater in scope today than ever before, and no society is safe from them; risks are increasingly global. Many societies produce various risks (climate change, the danger from nuclear plants and weapons, the global economic meltdown of 2008 that began in the United States, the Ebola epidemic that exploded in West Africa in 2014) that threaten not only those societies but others as well. Furthermore, even when risk is exported, consciously or unconsciously, to other societies, it tends to boomerang back on the society that is the source of the risk. For example, the United States has sought to cope with terrorism by combating it outside its own borders (e.g., in Pakistan and more recently in Yemen). However, those efforts have provoked attacks on the United States and its interests elsewhere in the world.

Globalization is the major reason there are far greater risks to society than ever before. Risks in one society easily flow to many other societies. For example, because of relatively easy and inexpensive air travel, a flu outbreak in one society can quickly engulf many other societies. Thus, modern risks are not easily restricted to one locale or society. A nuclear accident, such as the one that occurred at Chernobyl in Ukraine (then part of the Soviet Union) in 1986, can release radiation that affects surrounding societies and ultimately much of the world (see Figure 5.4). Modern risks are also not limited by time. The Chernobyl accident led to genetic defects in Ukrainians and those living in neighboring societies for decades afterward.

Globalization has led some sociologists to call into question the importance of society, arguing that in the contemporary world it is necessary to think globally. Debates about the possibility of global citizenship are one example of how the idea of globalization is reshaping how we think about the boundaries of what we call society (Kivisto and Faist 2007). Other sociologists have suggested that globalization requires a perspective on society that sees it as more fluid and unstable than would be implied by the work of earlier sociologists. Thus, Zygmunt Bauman (2007: 1) contends that we live in "liquid times," where structures and institutions—including societies— no longer "keep their shape for long."

It is clear from the preceding discussion that sociologists who analyze societies do not stop at their borders but also examine the relationships among and between societies. However, in recent years the focus of such scholarship has shifted beyond societies and their interrelationships to the even more macroscopic global level.

THE GLOBAL DOMAIN

Most work on the global level of social organization does not start with the concept of a society, but rather works with a different set of basic concepts. All of these concepts are consistent with the macroscopic sense of society:

- A **nation** is a large group of people linked through common descent, culture, language, or territory. Nations can exist in contiguous geographic areas regardless of country borders. For example, the Kurds (much in the news in 2015 as they battled Islamic State) live in Kurdistan, a region that overlaps parts of Iraq, Iran, Syria, and Turkey. Nations can also be spread throughout much of the world, such as the Roma people (so-called Gypsies), who live throughout Europe and increasingly in the United States.

- A **state** is a political organizational structure with relatively autonomous officeholders (for example, in the United States, the president functions largely independent

FIGURE 5.4 • Radiation from Chernobyl

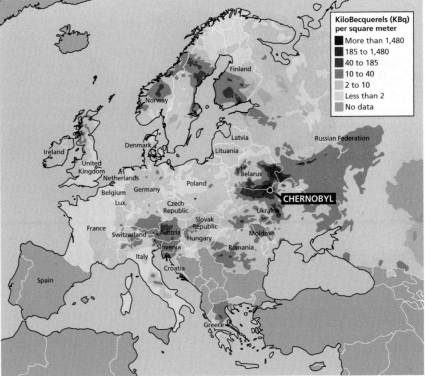

SOURCES: UNEP/GRID-Arendal, European Environment Agency; *AMAP Assessment Report: Arctic Pollution Issues*, Arctic Monitoring and Assessment Programme (AMAP), 1998, Oslo; European Monitoring and Evaluation Programme (MEP); Co-operative Programme for Monitoring and Evaluation of the Long-Range Transmission of Air Pollutants in Europe, 1999. Adapted from *Le Monde Diplomatique*, July 2000.

of Congress and the Supreme Court) that makes its own rules and receives its resources largely from taxes. The U.S. government would be an example of a state.

- A **nation-state** is an entity that encompasses both the populations that define themselves as a nation and the organizational structure of the state. Israel is a nation-state, since it has a state government and encompasses a nation of Jews (although there are large numbers of Muslims in Israel and its occupied territories as well).

Of greater importance in the global age is the idea that these entities, especially the nation-state, are losing influence because of globalization and broad global processes.

CONTROLLING GLOBAL FLOWS

The nation-state is under siege largely because it has lost or is losing control over a number of global flows (Cerny 2007; Ritzer and Dean 2015). In many ways, it is informationalism that threatens the nation-state. E-mail and tweets, to take two examples, flow around the world readily and quickly. There is little or nothing the nation-state can do to stop or limit those flows, although China, among others, keeps trying (see Figure 5.5 for a depiction of the levels of

FIGURE 5.5 • Freedom on the Internet, 2014

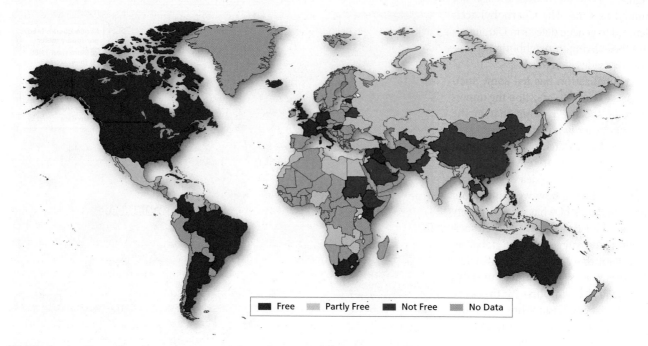

Free   Partly Free   Not Free   No Data

SOURCE: Freedom House, "Freedom on the Net," 2014 (https://freedomhouse.org/report/freedom-net/freedom-net-2014). Reprinted with permission from Freedom House.

Internet freedom in countries around the world). During the 2011 uprisings in Egypt, the government attempted to locate an "off switch" for the Internet to prevent the flow of news and images about the protests (Russia is currently searching for such a switch). However, Egypt was unable to block them completely (Richtel 2011). There are many economic, financial, and technological flows around the world that involve information of various kinds. Global information flows have the potential to subvert the authority of nation-states because they cover a much larger geographic area than the nation-state. This is especially true of information that would cast a negative light on the nation-state. One example would be the distribution of information throughout China about the great inequality that exists there and the Chinese government's human rights abuses.

A more specific example of the decreasing ability of nation-states to isolate themselves from global processes is the 2008 economic crisis that began in the United States and cascaded rapidly around the world. Dramatic drops in the U.S. stock market were followed by declines in many other stock markets. Similarly, bank failures in the United States were quickly followed by even more ruinous bank failures in other countries. This series of events illustrates the importance and power of global flows and demonstrates the inability of the nation-state to do much, if anything, to limit their impact within its borders on its economy and the lives of its citizens. "In a global financial system, national borders are porous" (Landler 2008: C1). Global economic flows move more quickly than ever, if not instantaneously, and are so fluid that they are difficult if not impossible to stop with the barriers available to nation-states.

The organization Islamic State has been very adept at using various types of media in a recruitment effort that reaches many parts of the world. Its communications are designed to transcend national boundaries in order to attract new supporters, who, the group hopes, will help force the creation of a new nation-state, a caliphate. Among other things, IS has released videos of threatened and actual beheadings, has been active on social media including Twitter, and has made imitations of popular video games and movies. Countries in which IS has been successful in finding recruits, such as France, England, and even the United States, would dearly love to stop its call to arms, but that is literally impossible given the nature of modern technology.

Information and economic flows are just two of the many global flows that nation-states cannot control. Among the others are flows of undocumented immigrants, new social movements, expertise in various domains, terrorists, criminals, drugs, money (including laundered money and other financial instruments), and human trafficking. Then there are global problems such as HIV/AIDS, flu, tuberculosis, and the effects of climate change that flow around the world readily and cannot be handled very well by a nation-state operating on its own.

The nation-state has become increasingly porous, but the fact is that no nation-state has ever been able to exercise complete control over its borders (Bauman 1992). For example, people's ability to travel from one European country to another was largely unimpeded until the World War I era, when passports were introduced on a large scale for the first time. It is not the porosity of the nation-state that is new, but rather the dramatic increase in that porosity.

Thus, the largest unit of analysis in sociology has now become the globe, and especially the global flows that best define globalization today. The concept of globalization appears throughout this book in an informal sense, but it is now time for a formal definition: **Globalization** is "a transplanetary *process* or set of *processes* involving increasing *liquidity* and the growing multidirectional *flows* of people, objects, places and information as well as the *structures* they encounter and create that are *barriers* to, or *expedite*, those flows" (Ritzer and Dean 2015: 2; see also Chapter 14). Clearly, this is a view that goes beyond the nation-state and sees it as enmeshed in and subordinated to a global set of flows and structures.

OTHER GLOBAL FLOWS

Globalization is increasingly characterized by great flows of not just information, ideas, and images but also objects and people. For example, food now flows more quickly and to more people around the world. Examples of foods sold in locales far from their sources include fresh fruit from Chile (Goldfrank 2005), fresh sushi from Japan, and live lobsters from Maine. Looking at a very different kind of flow, migration within countries and from one country to another has become more common as well.

In addition, other kinds of physical objects are becoming increasingly liquid and thus able to flow more easily. Not long ago, we might have been amazed by our ability to order a book from Amazon and receive it via an express package delivery system in as little as a day. That method, however, now seems sluggish compared with the speed of downloading that book in seconds on a wireless device such as Amazon's Kindle or Apple's iPad. That level of liquidity and flow is a major aspect of, as well as a major contributor to, globalization. Even places can be said to be flowing around the world. One example is the global spread of chains of nearly identical fast-food restaurants.

ASK YOURSELF

Beyond fast food restaurants, can you think of other places that have flowed around the world? What places find it difficult or impossible to flow around the world? Why?

Landscapes

Although global flows and globalization contribute to some degree of homogenization of the social experience around the world, they also contribute to greater global cultural diversity and heterogeneity. A very important contribution to thinking on the latter aspects of global flows is Arjun Appadurai's (1996) work on what he calls **landscapes**—*scapes* for short. These are fluid, irregular, and variable global flows that produce different results throughout the world. These scapes can involve the flow of many different things, including people and ideas. There are five types of landscapes that operate independent of one another to some degree, and may even conflict with one another:

- **Ethnoscapes** allow the movement, or fantasies about movement, of various individuals and groups, such as tourists and refugees. The ethnoscape of undocumented immigrants is of particular concern these days. They are often poor people who have in the main been forced to move because of poverty and poor job prospects in their home countries. They have also moved because of the belief, sometimes the fantasy, that economic conditions will be better for them elsewhere in the world, especially in the more developed countries of the United States and Western Europe.

- **Technoscapes** include mechanical technologies such as the containerized ships now used to transport freight, informational technologies such as the Internet, and the materials, such as refrigerators and e-mail, that move so quickly and freely throughout the world via those technologies.

- **Financescapes** use various financial instruments to allow huge sums of money and other items of economic value (like stocks, bonds, and precious metals, especially gold) to move through nations and around the world at great speed, almost instantaneously.

- **Mediascapes** include both the electronic capability to produce and transmit information around the world and the images of the world that these media create and disseminate. Those who write on Facebook walls, tweet, blog and download photos (e.g., on Flickr) and videos (e.g., on YouTube), global filmmakers and film distributors, and global TV networks (such as CNN and Al Jazeera) create a variety of mediascapes.

- **Ideoscapes**, like mediascapes, include images, although they are largely restricted to political images in line with the ideologies of nation-states. Also included here are images and counterideologies produced by social movements oriented toward supplanting those in power or at least gaining a portion of that power. Thus, for example, the United States has one ideoscape that disseminates

This fence erected on the border between Hungary and Serbia in late 2015 is one of many recent barriers designed to stop or limit the flow of migrants into the European Union.

negative images and information about Islamic State; in turn, IS has an ideoscape that responds with similarly negative images and information about the United States. News conferences by the U.S. president attacking IS's terrorism are met by videotapes by IS leaders critiquing American imperialism. Ideoscapes may be disseminated through mediascapes and technoscapes.

Further increasing the global heterogeneity that results from the interaction of these landscapes is the fact that the impact of one can be at variance, or even in conflict, with another. In addition, these landscapes are interpreted differently by people and groups in different parts of the world. Interpretations depend on both the cultures in which people exist and the people's own subjective perspectives on the scapes. Powerful forces create at least some of these scapes. Nonetheless, those who merely live in them or pass through them have the power not only to redefine them in idiosyncratic ways but also ultimately to subvert them in many different ways. For example, when tourists return home, they can portray a locale in a way that contradicts the image presented by tour creators and guides.

GLOBAL BARRIERS

The globe and the flows that increasingly pervade it are of central concern to sociology. However, there is another aspect of globalization that is of growing concern, and that is the various global barriers to these flows. The world is made up of not just a series of flows but also structures such as trade agreements, regulatory agencies, borders, customs barriers, and standards (Inda and Rosaldo 2008). Any thoroughgoing account of globalization needs to look at the ways in which structures alter and even block flows as well as produce and enhance them. In other words, there is interplay between flows and structures, especially between flows and the structures that are created in attempts to inhibit or stop them (Shamir 2005).

As mentioned above, the most important and most obvious barriers to global flows are those constructed by nation-states, in spite of nation-states' greater porosity. There are borders, gates, guards, passport controls, customs agents, health inspectors, trade regulations, and so on in most countries in the world. Although undocumented immigrants, contraband goods, and digitized messages do get through those barriers, some other phenomena (e.g., the sale of key companies to foreign entities) that nation-states

PUBLIC SOCIOLOGY

The "Flat World" of Thomas Friedman

Thomas Friedman (1953–), winner of several Pulitzer Prizes, is one of the most influential journalists in the world, a regular columnist for the *New York Times,* and the author of several books about globalization.

In *The Lexus and the Olive Tree* (1999), Friedman seeks to capture the tensions of globalization in his distinction between the modern automobile (the Lexus) and the ancient realities (the olive tree) that still dominate much of the world. Friedman (1999: 29) sees the Lexus as a threat to the olive tree; that is, "all the anonymous, transnational, homogenizing, standardizing market forces and technologies" constitute a threat to local culture and identity. He argues for a "healthy balance" between the Lexus model and the model of the olive tree.

Friedman has a highly positive view of globalization, seeing it as a democratizing force in technology, finance, and information as well as a triumph of free market capitalism. When a country recognizes the rules of the free market and agrees to abide by them, it dons what he calls the "Golden Straitjacket." It then experiences the advantages of globalization but also

the negative effects of this one-size-fits-all model. For example, many U.S. jobs have been lost to other areas of the world where wages are lower.

The central point of Friedman's even better-known *The World Is Flat: A Brief History of the Twenty-First Century* (2005) is that the barriers and hurdles to competing successfully on a global scale, such as tariffs, quotas, and regulations, have diminished if not completely disappeared. The global playing field has been increasingly leveled, making it possible for small companies and even individuals anywhere in the world to compete successfully on a global basis. Friedman (2005: 231) is not just describing a trend but praising it as well. In his view, everyone is benefiting from the flat world.

Many sociologists (e.g., Antonio 2007) disagree with Friedman about the desirability of all global flows, especially those associated with free trade. These sociologists believe that at least some barriers are worth retaining in order to protect some individuals and structures from the ravages of free-floating global flows. Further, most sociologists and other social scientists disagree with Friedman on the existence, or even the

Thomas Friedman

possibility, of a flat world. Much of sociology is premised on the idea that those with power will erect barriers of all sorts that enhance their interests and that, in the process, adversely affect others and create great inequalities.

Think About It

Do you agree with Thomas Friedman that the world is increasingly flat, or do you see barriers being erected that adversely affect some people and create inequality? Give specific examples to support your answer. Do you think the world *should* be flat? Why or why not?

---

deem counter to their national interests are successfully blocked or impeded.

Are Global Barriers Effective?

However, many of the barriers created by nation-states are not effective. For instance, it is highly doubtful that the very expensive fence that has been constructed between Mexico and the United States, combined with the use of cameras, lights, satellites, and drones, will be able to curtail the flow of undocumented immigrants to the United States. It has become more difficult, costly, and dangerous to enter the country illegally, but the fence has not stopped such entry.

Moreover, the fence has had the unintended consequence of making it harder for Mexican nationals who are already in the United States illegally to move back to Mexico. The fence between Spain's African enclave—Melilla—and Morocco has not stopped some migrants, who have scaled it to gain entry to Spain and thereby to the EU (Associated Press 2014). Similarly, it is not clear whether the wall between Israel and the West Bank (or the more recently erected wall between Israel and Egypt) will stop the flow of terrorists into Israel the next time hostilities in the Middle East flare up. On the positive side, the wall is not stopping Palestinians and Israelis from communicating person to person via digital media, as

A Virtual Bridge between Palestinians and Israelis

While globalization has made it easier for people and resources to move around the world, some borders remain rigorously defended (Naples 2009). One of these exists between Palestine and Israel. Leaders from the two sides have not met since 2009. Interaction between the populations is greatly limited by heavily guarded, walled borders (Zureik 2011), and concern in Israel about terrorism makes crossing those borders difficult.

However, Palestinians and Israelis can communicate virtually via the Internet. The Facebook page facebook.com/yalaYL (*yala* is Arabic for "let's go"; YL stands for Young Leaders) was created in 2011 by an Israeli, the president of the Peres Center for Peace, who said, "All communication today is on the Internet—sex, war, business—why not peace? . . . Today we have no brave leaders on either side, so I am turning to a new generation, the Tahrir Square [the main site of the Egyptian protests in 2011 that brought down the regime of Hosni Mubarak] and Facebook generation." Even though the site is Israeli in origin, it is supported by Palestinians, including a Palestinian National Authority official who said, "Believe me, they don't know each other at all. . . . Since Israelis and Palestinians don't meet face to face anymore, this is a virtual place to meet" (Bronner 2011: 9). More than half the active visitors to the site have been Arabs, and most of those have been Palestinians.

While many postings deal with common, everyday interests such as music and sports, of greatest importance are those about peace between Israelis and

While Palestinians and Israelis continue to conflict in the social world, the website facebook.com/yalaYL is able to unite them in an attempt to promote peace.

Palestinians. Said a Palestinian graduate student, "I joined immediately because right now, without a peace process and with Israelis and Palestinians physically separated, it is really important for us to be interacting without barriers" (Bronner 2011: 9). The site founder's hope is that joint projects between Israelis and Palestinians that develop on the site will influence their leaders to seek peace.

The site also enhances mutual understanding between Palestinians and Israelis. An 18-year-old Palestinian college student said, "This is my first contact with Israelis. . . . A friend of mine told me about it, and I think it's cool. I joined a few days ago. It helps me understand the differences between

Israel and the occupation" (Bronner 2011: 9). These Israelis and Palestinians are breaking through the physical borders and reconnecting in a more fluid, globally connected online world.

Inspired by the model of yalaYL, groups around the world (including the Italian government, a Barcelona soccer team, and MTV) have sought to engage in the processes of globalization.

Think About It

In which of Appadurai's "scapes" does the yalaYL Facebook page operate? Do you think this virtual meeting place can ever become as powerful as the physical barriers between the Palestinian and Israeli nations? Why or why not?

the "Digital Living" box (above) demonstrates. While there is no wall around the Gaza Strip, there is a closely watched and guarded wire fence. Nevertheless, in 2014 the Israelis discovered that Hamas fighters had dug numerous tunnels that they used to commit terrorist acts in Israel. In spite of all of the

problems with border fences, Bulgaria is currently building a fence in an effort to keep out refugees from Turkey (Lyman 2015).

In the European Union, barriers to movement between member countries have been greatly reduced, if not eliminated. The EU has created a structure that allows people (including, unfortunately, terrorists) and products (including, regrettably, illicit drugs and weapons) to move much more freely and quickly throughout Europe. However, in late 2015 the flood of refugees from Syria and elsewhere caused some EU countries, most notably Hungary, to reinstitute such barriers. It remains to be seen whether this is only a temporary development or whether these reconstituted barriers will become long-term realities in at least some EU countries.

Organizational Barriers

There are many different kinds of organizations that, though they may expedite flows for some, create all sorts of barriers for others. For example, nation-states create protectionist tariff systems (Reuveny and Thompson 2001) that help their own farms to send agricultural products (such as wheat) and their manufacturers to send goods (such as automobiles) across the borders of other nation-states while inhibiting the inflow of goods from their foreign competition. Another example is found in the two-tier system of passport control at international airports, where citizens usually pass through quickly and easily while foreigners wait in long lines.

Multinational corporations use market competition rather than trade policies to achieve similar results. Toyota, for instance, is devoted to optimizing the flow of its automobiles to all possible markets throughout the world. It also seeks to compete with and outperform other multinational corporations in the automobile business. If it is successful, the flow of automobiles from competing corporations is greatly reduced, further advantaging Toyota.

Labor unions are also organizations devoted to promoting the flow of some things while working against the flow of others (Bronfenbrenner 2007). Unions often oppose, for example, the flow of undocumented immigrants because they are likely to work for lower pay and fewer benefits (e.g., health insurance) than indigenous, unionized workers. Similarly, labor unions oppose the flow of goods produced in nonunion shops, in other countries as well as their own. They do so because the success of nonunion shops puts downward pressure on wages and benefits. This adversely affects unionized shops and, in turn, hurts the union and its members. On the other hand, many employers are willing to hire undocumented immigrant labor despite laws against their doing so. Because these laborers lack documentation, they are easy to exploit. Employers can threaten to deport them if they demand higher wages and better working conditions or attempt to organize.

ASK YOURSELF

What kinds of global flows does your college or university allow or promote? What kinds of global flows does it impede, and how?

More Open Organizations

Organizations of many types that seek to control global flows are facing increasing competition from organizations that are becoming more fluid and open. The best-known computer operating systems are produced by Microsoft (whose latest version is Windows 10). They cost a great deal and are closed. Only those who work for the company can, at least legally, work on and modify them. In contrast, IBM, a traditional closed organization, has embraced Linux, a free computer operating system that welcomes changes contributed by anyone in the world with the needed skills. IBM has also opened up more and more of its own operations to outside inputs. Another example is Apple, which has traditionally kept its Macintosh operating system closed but is now allowing outsiders to produce applications for its iPhone and iPad. Many other manufacturers of smartphones have followed suit. The free online encyclopedia Wikipedia and wikis more generally encourage virtually anyone, anywhere in the world, to contribute. In contrast, traditional and very costly dictionaries such as *Merriam-Webster's Collegiate Dictionary* and encyclopedias like *Encyclopedia Britannica* and the *Encyclopedia of Sociology* (Ritzer 2007a, forthcoming) are closed to contributions from anyone other than selected and invited experts.

Even with the new open systems, structural realities help some and hinder others. For example, to contribute to Linux or Wikipedia, one must have a computer, computer expertise, and access, preferably high-speed access, to the Internet. Clearly, those without economic advantages—people in the lower classes in developed countries and people who live in the less developed countries of the Global South—are on the other side of the "digital divide" and do not have access to the required tools. As a result, they are unable to contribute to, or to gain from, open systems to the same degree as those in more privileged positions. The fact that women are less likely than men to contribute to Wikipedia suggests that there are additional social factors to be considered here as well (Cohen 2011). This further suggests that women in the Global South are doubly disadvantaged when it comes to access to these open systems—and much else.

Thus, despite the new openness, most organizations and systems remain closed to various flows. These barriers usually benefit some (elites, males) and disadvantage others (the poor, females).

SUMMARY

Much sociological work on organizations is based on Max Weber's model of bureaucracy. However, one criticism of this model is that bureaucracies are not as highly rational as Weber believed. Their rationality is limited by the instabilities and conflicts that exist in organizations. McDonaldization has become an increasingly important model for organizations seeking to operate more rationally. This model is applicable both to large corporations and the relatively small outlets that are crucial parts of these organizations and to organizations increasingly devoted to consumption rather than just production.

Compared with classic bureaucracies, networks are less hierarchical, more open and flexible, and more capable of expansion and innovation.

The next level of social organization on the micro–macro continuum is the society, a large population that lives in a given territory, has a social structure, and shares a culture. Talcott Parsons identified several structures particularly important to modern societies, including the economy, the political system, the systems responsible for transmitting culture and its norms and values, and the legal system. A key recent change is the shift from industrial to risk societies.

A key structure in global analysis is the nation-state, which combines the organizational structure of the state and a population that defines itself as a nation of people with shared characteristics. However, the nation-state as a form of social organization is under siege because of global flows over which it has little control—for example, flows of information, economic phenomena, and new social movements.

Consequently, sociologists are coming to focus more attention on the global domain, the process of globalization, and in particular the global flows that best define globalization. Arjun Appadurai focuses on five different types of global landscapes, or scapes. There are also limits to global flows, mainly created by macro-level entities like nation-states and labor unions.

REVIEW QUESTIONS

1. What are the characteristics of the ideal-typical bureaucracy? What are some of the ways the ideal-typical bureaucracy is unrealistic?

2. It is often the case that those who occupy offices lower in the bureaucratic hierarchy have greater knowledge and competence than those who rank above them. What does this suggest about the ideal-typical bureaucracy? Can you think of examples from your own experiences where this has been the case?

3. According to Weber, what are the three types of legitimate authority? How is rational-legal authority related to Weber's concept of bureaucracy?

4. Over the last several decades, what changes have bureaucratic organizations undergone? How are these changes reflective of increasing globalization?

5. What is informationalism, and how has it affected the global economy? How is the emergence of informationalism related to the development of new communication technologies like the Internet, social networking sites, and smartphones?

6. How has the process of globalization threatened the nation-state? What sorts of barriers have nation-states developed to limit global flows? What sorts of flows have nation-states been unable to limit?

7. What sorts of things flow most easily around the world? What flows less easily or even not at all?

8. Discuss each of Appadurai's landscapes, with special focus on the disjunctures (with examples) among and between them. What are the implications of these disjunctures for the process of globalization?

9. How are network organizations different from classic bureaucracies? In what ways are network organizations reflective of what Thomas Friedman calls the "flat world"?

10. How are open-source technologies reflective of a more fluid and open world? What structural barriers have transnational corporations created to limit these open-source technologies? What do you think is going to be the direction of the future? Why?

APPLYING THE SOCIOLOGICAL IMAGINATION

You are at the center of two of the key issues discussed in this chapter—globalization and networks. Try to list the many ways in which your life on any given day is affected by globalization. Now enumerate the many networks in which you are involved.

How many of those networks are global in scope? Which ones? How has your involvement in each of them affected your sense and understanding of other parts of the world, as well as of the globe as a whole?

KEY TERMS ···

authority: A particular type of domination: legitimate domination. (p. 101)

bounded rationality: Rationality limited by, among other things, instabilities and conflicts within most, if not all, organizations, as well as by the limited human capacity to think and act in a rational manner. (p. 102)

bureaucracy: A highly rational organization, especially one that is highly efficient. (p. 100)

bureaucratic personality: A type of bureaucrat who slavishly follows the rules of the organization to such an extent that the ability to achieve organizational goals is subverted. (p. 103)

charismatic authority: Authority based on the devotion of the followers to what they define as the exceptional characteristics, such as heroism, of the leaders. (p. 102)

domination: The probability or likelihood that commands will be obeyed by subordinates. (p. 101)

ethnoscapes: Landscapes that allow the movement, or fantasies about movement, of various individuals and groups. (p. 115)

financescapes: Landscapes that use various financial instruments to allow huge sums of money and other things of economic value to move into and across nations and around the world at great speed, almost instantaneously. (p. 115)

gemeinschaft societies: Traditional societies characterized by face-to-face relations. (p. 111)

gesellschaft societies: Modern societies characterized by impersonal, distant, and limited social relationships (p. 111)

globalization: The increasing fluidity of global flows and the structures that expedite and impede those flows. (p. 115)

ideal type: An exaggeratedly rational model that is used to study real-world phenomena. (p. 100)

ideoscapes: Landscapes that include images, largely political images, often in line with the ideologies of nation-states. (p. 115)

informal organization: How an organization actually works as opposed to the way it is supposed to work. (p. 103)

informationalism: The processing of knowledge. (p. 110)

landscapes (scapes): Fluid, irregular, and variable global flows that produce different results throughout the world. (p. 115)

mediascapes: Landscapes that include the electronic capability to produce and transmit information and images around the world. (p. 115)

nation: A group of people who share similar cultural, religious, ethnic, linguistic, and territorial characteristics. (p. 113)

nation-state: The combination of a nation with a geographic and political structure; encompasses both the populations that define themselves as a nation with various shared characteristics and the organizational structure of the state. (p. 113)

network organization: A new organizational form that is flat and horizontal, is intertwined with other organizations, is run and managed in very different ways than traditional organizations, uses more flexible production methods, and is composed of a series of interconnected nodes. (p. 109)

offshore outsourcing: The transfer of work to organizations in other countries. (p. 108)

oligarchy: An organization with a small group of people at the top obtaining, and exercising, far more power than they are supposed to have. (p. 104)

organization: A collective purposely constructed to achieve particular ends. (p. 100)

outsourcing: The transfer of activities once performed by one organization to another organization in exchange for money. (p. 107)

rational-legal authority: Authority that is legitimated on the basis of legally enacted rules and the right of those with authority under those rules to issue commands. (p. 101)

risk society: A society in which central issues involve risks and ways to protect oneself from them. (p. 112)

sexual harassment: Unwanted sexual attention that takes place in the workplace or other settings. (p. 106)

state: A political body organized for government and civil rule. (p. 113)

technoscapes: Landscapes that use mechanical and informational technologies as well as the material that moves quickly and freely through them. (p. 115)

traditional authority: Authority based on a belief in long-running traditions. (p. 102)

$SAGE edge™ edge.sagepub.com/ritzeressentials2e

SAGE edge offers a robust online environment featuring an impressive array of free tools and resources for review, study, and further exploration, keeping both instructors and students on the cutting edge of teaching and learning.

LEARNING OBJECTIVES	FOR FURTHER EXPLORATION AND APPLICATION
LO 5-1: Describe the features of formal and informal organizations and bureaucracies.	▶ Max Weber's Theory of "Ideal Types" ◉ Slimming POW-MIA Bureaucracy ⊕ Formal versus Informal Organization
LO 5-2: Discuss new concepts in the study of organizations such as gendered and network organizations.	▶ How Gender Affects the Workplace ◉ Let's Talk about Our Teachers ⊕ The Digital Divide
LO 5-3: Contrast gemeinschaft and gesellschaft societies.	▶ Ferdinand Tönnies's Ideal Types of Social Organizations ◉ The "Bossless" Office, Where the Team Takes Charge ⊕ Gemeinschaft and Gesellschaft Societies
LO 5-4: Describe global societies in terms of nations, states, and nation-states.	▶ Nations, States, and Nation States ◉ Google's Attempt to Connect the Unconnected ⊕ The U.S. Agency for International Development (USAID)

DEVIANCE AND CRIME

Norms, Labels, and Judgment

In January 2011, Police Constable Michael Sanguinetti addressed a group of law students in Toronto, Ontario, Canada, on the topic of crime prevention. At one point the constable said, "I've been told I'm not supposed to say this; however, women should avoid dressing like sluts in order not to be victimized."

A few months later, more than 3,000 people responded by marching in Toronto in the first annual SlutWalk. The march was held to protest and to counter the misperception, articulated in Sanguinetti's remarks, that provocative clothing encourages—and even excuses—rape and other forms of sexual abuse. SlutWalkToronto brought greater awareness to the broader sociocultural issues of *sexual profiling* (a discriminatory practice of using appearance to attempt to predict behavior) and *slut shaming* (negative labeling of, or judgments against, a person based on presumptions about her sexual behavior). Similar marches, often accompanied by speeches and workshops, have since been held across the globe and in several U.S. cities. An all-volunteer SlutWalkToronto organization maintains a website and social media presence to encourage participation, and local groups are active in other cities as well.

Constable Sanguinetti's comments, for which he later apologized, reveal a great deal about Western perceptions of sexual deviance. The negative label "slut" is typically applied to a woman who deviates, or is believed to deviate, from expected norms and who engages in sexual activity outside a committed relationship. Any woman dressed in clothing defined as sexually provocative can be labeled a slut. Sanguinetti reasoned that because such women are, or present themselves as, sexually deviant, they should expect—and possibly deserve—to be punished by the application of negative labels. But what *are* the "expected norms" for women's dress and sexual behavior? And who has the power to apply such labels?

LEARNING OBJECTIVES

6-1 Define deviance.

6-2 Describe structural/functional, conflict/critical, and inter/actionist approaches to theorizing about deviance.

6-3 Discuss the relationship between deviance and crime.

6-4 Discuss the purpose and effects of the criminal justice system.

Associated Press

A 2003 study reached the somewhat surprising finding that victims' attire is *not* a significant factor in sexual assault by strangers. Instead, perpetrators look for indications of passivity and submissiveness. Like any disconnect between perception and reality, the kinds of ideas associated with being a "slut" may be slow to change. Inevitably, however, as a culture shifts, so too does its definition of deviance. And as global cultures change, groups everywhere are struggling with prevailing norms and laws. Norms defining sexual deviance are no different. The SlutWalks are a marker of that struggle. ●

This chapter deals with two closely related social phenomena: deviance and crime (Atkinson 2014; Downes and Rock 2011; Forsyth and Copes 2014; Goode and Thio 2007). Most forms of deviance—for example, having full-face tattoos—are not crimes. However, all crimes—theft, murder, rape—are forms of deviance. To become a crime, a form of deviance must be negatively sanctioned by the legal system, a process known as **criminalization** (Hillyard 2007; Jenness 2004; Muniz 2014). However, criminalization does not occur of its own accord. Some interest group must seek to have a type of deviance criminalized. This is a political decision, and it is linked to the desire on the part of one powerful group to exert social control over the actions of another group. As you will see, the determination that something is deviant is the result of a similar social process.

DEVIANCE

What exactly is deviance, and where is the line between deviance and nondeviance? Many people would likely express the absolutist view that certain things are deviant in all places, for all groups, and at all times (Little 2007). However, from a sociological perspective, no act, belief, or human characteristic is inherently deviant (Perrin 2007). Thus, even genocide, while morally reprehensible and indefensible, has not been defined as deviance in some societies and at certain points in time. Therefore, to the sociologist, deviance is socially defined. **Deviance** is any action, belief, or human characteristic that is considered a violation of group norms by a large number of members of a society or a social group and for which the violator is likely to be censured or punished (Ben-Yehuda 2012; Goode 2007a). **Crime** is deviance that is a violation of the criminal law (Whitehead 2007).

If a powerful group wants to have a form of behavior defined as deviant (or a crime), it is likely to be so defined. At the same time, a powerful group is likely to use its power to resist the efforts of others to define the powerful group's behaviors as deviant. For example, in the wake of the collapse of the home mortgage market in 2008, bankers fought, largely successfully, against being seen as deviant and even as criminal for their fraudulent predatory loan policies (Braithwaite 2010). However, borrowers who lied about their financial situation were less successful in avoiding being seen as deviant, and they suffered far greater negative consequences (Nguyen and Pontell 2011). They were likely to lose their homes, often their jobs, and sometimes even their health. Those who have social, political, legal, and/or financial power have a great deal of influence over who is (or is not) defined as deviant and suffers the negative consequences of such a definition.

SHIFTING DEFINITIONS OF DEVIANCE

In addition to being influenced by power relationships, what is thought to be deviant varies from one time period to another, from one geographic location to another, and from one group to another. Being tattooed used to be seen as a stigmatizing form of deviance, or it was assumed to signify membership

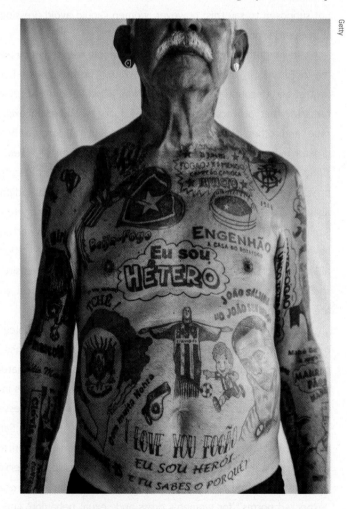

Getty

Tattoos, even as numerous as these, are no longer likely to be considered particularly deviant in most cultures.

in some deviant (or countercultural) group, such as a biker gang, but for many it now seems normal, or at least far less stigmatized (Dombrink and Hillyard 2007; Larsen, Patterson, and Markham 2014). Indeed, about 45 million Americans now have tattoos. We readily accept the sight of athletes—especially professional basketball players—covered with tattoos. Once restricted largely to men, tattoos are more popular today with women. Some women, such as Kat Von D, have even gained fame as tattoo artists, a historically male-dominated occupation (Maroto 2011). And tattoo parlors, once limited to the marginal areas of town, are now found on Main Street, as well as in the shopping mall. Tattoos have become just another product of our consumer society (Patterson and Schroeder 2010; Trebay 2008).

As another example of the movement from deviance to normality, consider U.S. attitudes toward premarital sex (Regnerus and Uecker 2011). Just a few decades ago, a leading textbook on the subject of deviance devoted a chapter to premarital sex (Bell 1971). Today, premarital sex is considered normal in most groups (Wellings et al. 2009). Furthermore, once-deviant "hooking up"—engaging in "something sexual" outside of committed romantic relationships—has become common among teens and twentysomethings (Bogle 2008; Lewis et al. 2012; Manning, Giordano, and Longmore 2006; Reay 2014). Cohabitation before marriage (see Chapter 10) once was defined as "living in sin," but today many people might consider couples who do *not* live together before marriage to be deviant. In other words, cohabitation has become normative and for some occurs instead of, or at least before, marriage (Popenoe 2009; Sassler and Miller 2011). Many no longer consider homosexuality a form of deviance (see Chapter 9). Its normalization is reflected in a host of social changes, such as the inclusion of same-sex partners in family benefits offered by employers, the repeal of the military's "Don't ask, don't tell" policy, and especially the 2015 Supreme Court decision legalizing same-sex marriage nationwide (see Figure 6.1 for a look at changing attitudes of U.S. adults toward same-sex marriage).

Of course, some cringe at the idea that homosexuality, premarital sex, and cohabitation before marriage are becoming normative. For example, religious fundamentalists believe that only married heterosexuals should live together and have sexual intercourse with one another (Hendershott 2002; Powell et al. 2010).

FIGURE 6.1 • Support of and Opposition to Same-Sex Marriage in the United States, 1996–2014

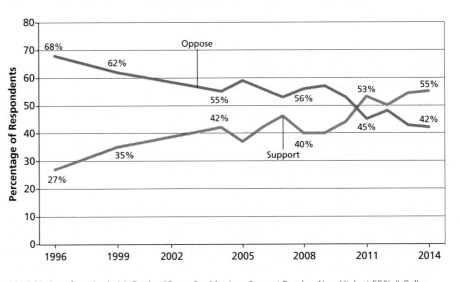

SOURCE: Data from Justin McCarthy, "Same-Sex Marriage Support Reaches New High at 55%." Gallup, May 21, 2014.

There are great differences from one geographic area to another in the ways some behaviors are defined. At one time, smoking cigarettes was an accepted, even admired, form of behavior in the United States, but now many Americans consider it deviant. Smoking is certainly not viewed as deviant in most parts of Europe, however, and it is considered quite normal in China (Kohrmann 2008), which consumes more tobacco than any other country in the world (Qin 2014). Smoking marijuana in public is considered deviant in most of the United States, but in the Netherlands (and now in some American states, such as Colorado and Washington) marijuana smoking is quite normal.

While there are great differences in what is considered to be deviant, it is important to remember that deviance has existed for all groups, in all parts of the world, and in all times. Virtually all groups define themselves by specifying the limits of acceptable behavior for their members. Such limits, and their violation, help a group sharpen its norms and values. Without limits and at least occasional violations, norms and values might become increasingly unclear and grow weaker over time.

ASK YOURSELF

Can you think of any behaviors other than those discussed above that were once considered deviant and are now accepted or even normative? What brought about the change in their status? Can you identify any behaviors that were once normative and are now considered deviant, such as using your cell phone while driving and failing to clean up after your dog?

GLOBAL FLOWS AND DEVIANCE

Deviance can be seen as a global flow. People defined as deviant can move around the world quickly and easily. In addition, definitions of deviance flow even more easily from society to society. For example, through its "war on drugs" the United States has made a strong effort to have the use of certain drugs defined as a form of deviance throughout the world and to make drug use illegal wherever possible. Global trends toward normalizing that which was defined at one time and in some places as deviant are even clearer and more pronounced. This is particularly the case with changes in the acceptability of various forms of sexuality. Ever greater portions of the world are accepting premarital sex, cohabitation before marriage, and, to a lesser degree, homosexuality. According to the International Lesbian, Gay, Bisexual, Trans and Intersex Association (ILGA), as of May 2014, "deviant" sexuality was protected by antidiscrimination laws in 70 countries, and same-sex unions were recognized in 32 countries (see Figure 6.2). However, the barriers to normalizing such forms of sexual behavior remain in place and are quite powerful in large parts of the world. As Figure 6.2 indicates, deviant sexual behavior is punishable by imprisonment in 78 countries and by death in 6. Such punishments are especially common in Islamic societies, which tend to be more absolutist on matters relating to sexual deviance and where deeply held religious beliefs serve as a barrier to normalization. In spite of the barriers, these behaviors exist, often covertly, in these societies and may well be expanding in the wake of increasing global acceptance.

THEORIES OF DEVIANCE

Deviance is a very good topic to study if you want to better understand the utility of, and contrasts between, the main types of sociological theories—structural/functional, conflict/critical, and inter/actionist.

STRUCTURAL/FUNCTIONAL THEORIES

Émile Durkheim argued that because deviance and crime have existed in all societies at all times (and in that sense are "normal"), they must have positive functions for the larger society and its structures. In other words, deviance would not have existed in the past and continue to exist were it not for the fact that it was and is functional; deviance served and continues to serve various purposes.

The most important function of deviance in Durkheim's view is that it allows societies, or groups, to define and clarify their collective beliefs—their norms and values. Were it not for

FIGURE 6.2 • Lesbian and Gay Rights around the World, 2014

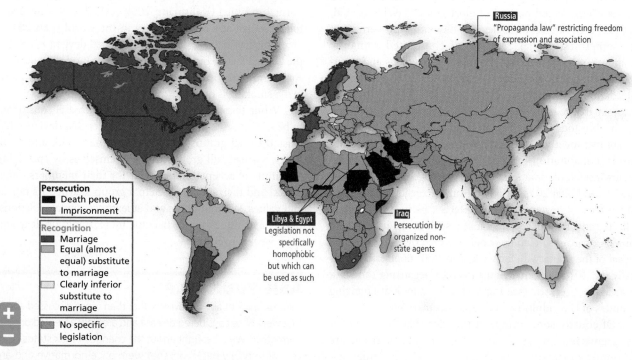

SAGE datamaps edge.sagepub.com

• Specific rights and legal protections in every country.

SOURCE: International Lesbian, Gay, Bisexual, Trans and Intersex Association, "Lesbian and Gay Rights in the World," May 2014. Reprinted by permission of the International Lesbian, Gay, Bisexual, Trans and Intersex Association.

Rethinking the Dutch Approach to Marijuana Use

The Netherlands was the first nation in the world to allow same-sex marriage and euthanasia. It is also one of the most secular nations in the world. However, globalization seems to be threatening its openness to the sale and use of marijuana and hashish. Although marijuana use is technically illegal in the Netherlands, smoking marijuana in public is not unusual, and there are "coffee shops" throughout the country where marijuana is sold openly. Many cafés have marquee-type menus, resembling those in fast-food restaurants, offering customers choices among many varieties of the drug.

Tourists have been drawn to these shops for decades. In recent years, however, Dutch citizens have begun to see "drug tourism" (Uriely and Belhassen 2005) as a social problem. This is especially the case in border cities like Maastricht, which lie just a few miles from Germany, France, or Belgium. Selling marijuana is illegal in these neighboring countries, but the European Union's open borders have made it easy for people to drive to the

Netherlands to get marijuana. As a result, Maastricht and other Dutch border cities are plagued with traffic jams, noise, and, more important, crime. The large numbers of visitors in search of marijuana have attracted criminals who want to sell them harder drugs. These criminals have been involved in shootouts and killings. The Dutch have been shocked by this development because they have long seen their openness to marijuana as a way of keeping their young people safer, not endangering them in new and unforeseen ways.

As a result, the Dutch passed a law prohibiting the sale of marijuana to nonresidents. Since the law took effect on January 1, 2013, there has been an increase in illegal sales of marijuana in Maastricht and other border areas (Corder 2014).

Think About It

Do the Dutch see marijuana use as normative or as deviant? Do you think they are likely to be successful in their attempts to manage marijuana use within their borders? Why or why not?

Corbis

Many "coffee shops" in Amsterdam, including this one, allow the purchase of marijuana even though it is technically illegal. How does the Dutch attitude toward marijuana compare to the American attitude? Will current changes in marijuana laws lead to such coffee shops in the United States?

---

deviance, norms and values would not come into existence. More important, the norms and values that limit or prohibit deviance would grow weak without the need to be exercised on a regular basis in response to deviant acts. The public as a whole, officials, and even potential deviants would grow progressively less aware of, and less sensitive to, the existence of these prohibitions. Thus, in a sense, society needs deviance. If periodic violations of standards of conduct did not occur, those standards would become less clear to all concerned, less strongly held, and less powerful (Dentler and Erikson 1959; Jensen 1988).

ASK YOURSELF

Do you agree with Durkheim that deviance is, in a sense, normal and therefore functional? To support this argument, can you think of an example of a deviant act or behavior that has helped society define its standards of conduct?

The most important structural-functional approach to deviance was developed in the mid-1900s by Robert K. Merton. The issue is the way people relate to the institutionalized means (e.g., getting a college degree and working hard) needed to achieve such cultural goals as economic success. Of greatest interest in this context is the relationship between means and ends. Merton identified five possible relationships between means and ends and associated them with five types of adaptation:

- **Conformists** are people who accept both cultural goals, such as making lots of money, and the traditional means of achieving those goals, including hard work. Conformists are the only ones among Merton's types who would not be considered deviant.

- **Innovators** accept the same cultural goals the conformists do, but they reject the conventional means of achieving them. Innovators are deviants in that they choose non-conventional routes to success. Bernie Madoff would be one example, though an extreme one. He was highly successful as a financier before he turned to illegal activities, through which he bilked his clients out of $65 billion. Other innovators choose legal routes to success. An example is Shaun White, who helped to create and competed in the new extreme and highly dangerous sport of snowboarding. It has become a lucrative and perfectly legal career for him and others.

- **Ritualists** realize that they will not be able to achieve cultural goals, but they nonetheless continue to engage in the conventional behavior associated with such success. Thus, a low-level employee might continue to work diligently even after realizing that such work is not going to lead to much economic success. Merton saw such diligent work with no realizable goal as a form of deviance.

- **Retreatists** reject both cultural goals and the traditional routes to their attainment. Retreatists have completely given up on attaining success within the system. One example is Theodore Kaczynski, who gained notoriety as the "Unabomber." At the time of his arrest in 1996, Kaczynski had been living for some 20 years in a cabin in a remote area of Montana without water or electricity, using a bicycle as his only means of transportation. To demonstrate his anger at modern society's "industrial-technological system," he had mailed off more than a dozen bombs, which killed 3 people and injured 23 others. He was sentenced to life in prison.

- **Rebels** are like retreatists in that they reject both traditional means and goals. However, they substitute non-traditional goals and means to those goals. In a sense, that makes them doubly deviant. Revolutionaries such as Ernesto "Che" Guevara can be seen as fitting into the rebel category. Guevara rejected success as it was defined in Cuba during the 1950s. Instead, he chose to assist Fidel Castro in his effort to overthrow the country's dictatorial system. Furthermore, he chose unconventional means—guerrilla warfare waged from the mountains of Cuba and, eventually, Bolivia—to attain his goals.

Adaptations of means to ends exemplify a structural-functionalist approach, because some of the adaptations are highly functional. Conformity certainly has positive consequences in the sense that it allows the social system to continue to exist without disturbance. Innovation is functional because society needs innovations in order to adapt to new external realities. No society can survive without innovation. Even rebellion can be seen as functional because there are times when society needs more than gradual innovation—it needs to change radically.

Structural-functionalism is concerned not only with functions but also with dysfunctions. For example, ritualists and retreatists can be seen as largely dysfunctional for society, or at least as having more dysfunctions than functions. The unchanging behavior of ritualists contributes little or nothing to the requirements of an ever-changing society, and retreatists contribute even less because they are uninvolved in, and have withdrawn from, the larger society.

CONFLICT/CRITICAL THEORIES

Proponents of structural/functional theories trace the source of deviance to the larger structures of society and the strains they produce. Conflict/critical theorists, especially conflict theorists, are also interested in those structures and their effects on people, but they adopt a different orientation toward them. A major focus is the inequality that exists in those structures and the impact that it has on individuals. In conflict theorists' view, inequality causes at least some of the less powerful individuals in society to engage in deviant—and criminal—acts because they have few, if any, other ways of succeeding in society (Goode 2007b). In this, they are similar to the innovators in Merton's taxonomy of adaptations to strain. Conversely, those in power commit crimes, especially corporate or white-collar crimes (Simpson 2002; Simpson and Weisburd 2009), because the nature of their high-level positions in various social structures (business, government) makes it not only possible but also relatively easy for them to do so. Further, conflict theorists argue, those in power in society create the laws and rules that define certain things as deviant, or illegal, while others are defined as normal. They do so in a self-serving way that advantages them and disadvantages those who lack power in society.

Deviance and the Poor

Conflict theories form the basis of research on vagrancy laws in medieval England (Chambliss 1964). In the feudal system, serfs were forced to provide labor for landowners, but with the end of feudalism, and therefore of serfdom, a new source of labor was needed. Not coincidentally, the former serfs now lacked permanent homes and sources of income and wandered about the countryside. Those in power saw them as a likely group to provide the needed labor at little cost, and so they created vagrancy laws. Under these laws it was illegal for those without work or a home to loiter in public places; some of the itinerants were arrested. As a result, many people who otherwise might not have worked for the landowners were forced to do so in order to avoid arrest and imprisonment.

Contemporary conflict theorists, heavily influenced by Marxian theory, have come to see deviance as something created by the capitalist economic system. Today's definitions of deviance serve the interests of the capitalists, especially by further enriching them. Conversely, these definitions adversely affect the proletariat, especially the poor, who grow even poorer. This view is well summed up by Jeffrey Reiman and Paul Leighton in *The Rich Get Richer and the Poor Get Prison* (2012). As the title of their book implies, the best examples of this process lie in the realm of crime rather than that of deviance, although to be seen as a crime an act must first be defined as deviant. For example, as we saw above, at the close of the Middle Ages it was in the interest of elite members of society to define vagrancy as deviance and as a crime. Such a definition seems fair and evenhanded until we realize that elite members of society are rarely if ever going to be without work and a home. They are therefore unlikely to be defined as vagrants. It is only the poor who are going to find themselves in that situation, with the result that they are just about the only ones who are going to be affected by the laws against vagrancy. As the great novelist Anatole France ([1894] 2011) once commented sarcastically, "The law, in all its majestic equality, forbids the rich as well as the poor to sleep under bridges on rainy nights, to beg on the streets, and to steal bread."

Conflict theorists do not argue that have-nots never commit crimes or deviant acts. Rather, they argue that it is because of the laws (e.g., those against sleeping under bridges) created by societal elites that the actions of the have-nots are singled out for notice and for sanctions. Furthermore, the costs to society of elite deviance are much higher than the costs associated with crime and deviance among society's have-nots. Compare, for example, the approximately $65 billion the disgraced and now imprisoned Bernie Madoff cost his clients by engaging in illegal activities to the few dollars a con artist or a mugger wrests from his victims.

Deviance and the Elite

Great efforts are made to legitimate elite crimes and acts of elite deviance (Simon 2012) and, failing that, to pay little or no attention to them. Those who rank high in such hierarchies as business, government, and the military have a much greater ability to commit deviant acts (such as sexually harassing subordinates), to have these acts be seen as legitimate, and to get away with them.

However, there are limits to the ability of elites to get away with deviant and criminal behavior. There are times when the acts are so extreme that they can no longer be hidden. They come to light and become great public issues. Once this happens, even the most elite members of society have a difficult time escaping negative judgment and perhaps even punishment and imprisonment.

Associated Press

As a result of one of the most famous and consequential examples of elite deviance—the Watergate break-in and its cover-up—Richard Nixon was forced to resign the presidency of the United States.

There is a long list of scandals involving elite public figures of various types who have been found to have committed deviant acts. In the main, their acts were so extreme, or the revelations about them became so public, that they could not be ignored. However, what has often caused difficulties for those involved has been their awkward efforts to lie about, or cover up, their offenses once they first became public. In many cases, especially in this era of the Internet, evidence is uncovered or witnesses provide testimony that makes it clear that the public figure has been deceiving the public and the authorities. The following are a few notable examples in the U.S. context (there are innumerable others everywhere in the world):

- In perhaps the most famous example of all, President Richard Nixon resigned in 1974 as he faced imminent impeachment for his role in the infamous Watergate break-in and for his efforts to conceal his and his associates' roles in it from the public.

- In 2008, the governor of New York State, Eliot Spitzer, was found to have been frequenting high-priced call girls and attempting to launder the money paid to them. The scandal forced him to resign.

- In 2013, New England Patriots football star Aaron Hernandez was charged with murder, and in 2014, after his release from the team, he was charged with a double murder that took place in 2012. In 2015, he was convicted of first-degree murder in the first case.

The view of conflict theorists is that, as lengthy as the list of elite deviants and criminals might be, it is merely the tip of the iceberg. Because elites have a wide variety of means at their disposal to conceal their actions, many, many more of their acts of deviance and criminality escape detection and punishment. Such acts by elites can persist for years, decades, or even the perpetrators' lifetimes.

INTER/ACTIONIST THEORIES

Inter/actionism can also be used to analyze deviance. For example, to the rational choice theorist, a person chooses deviance because it is a rational means to some desired goal. Gang members join gangs because of the camaraderie and perceived protection they offer (Melde, Taylor, and Esbensen 2009), as well as for access to a world in which members can obtain money and achieve recognition and high status (Bell 2009; Decker and Curry 2000). Ethnomethodologists are concerned with the ways in which people "do" deviance—that is, the everyday behaviors in which they engage that produce deviance. People need to adopt methods of speech and forms of behavior that make their deviance invisible to most others. In a classic ethnomethodological study, Harold Garfinkel (1967) describes the painstaking steps taken by Agnes, a transgender woman, to "pass" as a woman. She not only changed her manner of dress, posture, and demeanor but also underwent bodily changes. However, there are times when those who are deviant want to talk and act in ways that make it clear that they are deviant. For example, gang members may use certain phrases, dress in certain ways, and display certain tattoos to make their allegiance clear to other members of the same gang—and to members of opposing gangs (see Chapter 4). However, when they interact with the public or the police, gang members may speak and dress in ways that conceal, or at least attempt to hide, their membership in the gang.

ASK YOURSELF

Has engaging in any form of deviance ever seemed rational to you, in the sense that inter/actionist theories use the term? If so, was the deviance visible or invisible to others? Did it help you (or would it have helped you) achieve a goal?

Labeling

One variety of symbolic interactionism, labeling theory, is particularly useful in thinking about deviance. From this perspective, at least two things are needed for deviance to occur:

- A **symbol**, or in this case a "label." In the realm of deviance, a number of labels are particularly powerful negative symbols: *alcoholic, drug addict, pedophile, adulterer,* and so on.

- **Interaction** between the person or group doing the labeling (the labeler) and the person or group to whom the label is applied (the labelee). During this interaction, one or more of these labels is applied to the deviant.

Those who do the labeling are known as **social control agents**. Some of these agents (police, psychiatrists) are performing official functions, but far more often it is friends or family who label others as, for example, *drunks* or *womanizers*. When public figures are labeled as deviant, the media and their representatives are often the ones who do the labeling.

From the perspective of **labeling theory**, a deviant is someone to whom a deviant label has been successfully applied (Becker 1963; Goode 2014; Restivo and Lanier 2015). This stands in contrast to the view of the public and many sociologists, who focus on what an individual does in order to be labeled a deviant. Also of interest in labeling theory is the way the person labeled as deviant is affected by the label (Dotter and Roebuck 1988; Gove 1980; Walsh 1990). The person can accept the label to varying degrees or make efforts to resist, reject, or shed the label. People also vary greatly in how they react to, and feel about, being labeled as deviant. For example, some might be mortified by being labeled sex addicts, but others might take pride in it.

Labeling theory is also concerned about the actions and reactions of social control agents, as well as about their interactions with those being labeled (Pontell 2007). From the labeling perspective, "deviance is not a consequence of the act the person commits, but rather a consequence of the [creation and] application by others of rules and sanctions to an 'offender'" (Becker 1963: 9). A focus on social control agents, rather than deviants, leads to the view that deviant labels are not necessarily applied uniformly. Some people and some forms of behavior are more likely than others to be labeled as deviant. Thus, murderers and the act of murder are almost uniformly labeled as deviant (and criminal). However, in many other cases the process is more selective and less clear-cut: "Some men who drink too much are called alcoholics and others are not; some men who act oddly are committed to hospitals and others are not; some men who have no visible means of support are hauled into court and others are not" (Erikson 1964: 11–12). Overall, people are more likely to be socially defined as deviant when they are poor, work in low-status occupations, or are in similarly devalued circumstances (Goffman 1959). A person in a more advantageous social situation often escapes being defined or labeled as deviant, despite manifesting the same forms of behavior. Similarly, the poor are more likely to be labeled as criminals for their acts of deviance, while that is not the case for those in the middle and upper classes. For example, almost none of the leaders of financial institutions implicated as playing a large role in causing the Great Recession (such as Jamie Dimon of JPMorgan Chase) were ever charged with crimes, or even thought of as criminals, even though their investment houses have been fined billions of dollars by the government (Brinded 2014).

Primary and Secondary Deviance

An important distinction that flows from labeling theory is that between primary and secondary deviance:

- **Primary deviance** consists of early, random acts of deviance, such as an occasional bout of drinking to excess or an isolated act considered strange or out of the ordinary. Virtually all of us commit such acts; we all have engaged in various forms of primary deviance (Lemert [1951] 2012; Wallerstein and Wyle 1947). Isolated acts of primary deviance rarely, if ever, lead to the successful application of a deviant label. Primary deviance consists of acts and behavior, not identities or labels.

- Of far greater interest to labeling theorists is **secondary deviance**, or deviant acts that persist, become more common, and eventually cause people to organize their lives and personal identities around their deviant status (Liberman, Kirk, and Kim 2014). Secondary deviance usually occurs after an individual has been stigmatized and judged for deviant behavior and possibly labeled as "deviant." In response, the individual begins to see and define him- or herself as deviant. Thus, if a person moves from occasionally having short-term sexual encounters with strangers to being obsessed with such encounters and seeking them out whenever and wherever possible, that person may be labeled a sex addict. It is possible that the label of sex addict will become more important than all other definitions of the self. When that happens, sex addiction becomes a form of secondary deviance. In one recent study, body modifications such as tattoos and piercings were shown to be acts of primary deviance that were related to forms of secondary deviance such as drug abuse and juvenile delinquency (Dukes and Stein 2011).

While labeling theory tends to focus on others labeling an individual as deviant, it is possible, or even likely, that individuals will label themselves in this way (Thoits 1985, 2011), that they will do so before anyone else does (Norris 2011), and that they will act in accord with their self-imposed label (Lorber 1967). This is consistent with the view of the leading symbolic interactionist, George Herbert Mead (see Chapter 4), who saw the mind as an internal conversation with oneself. Such an internalized conversation may certainly lead to labeling oneself as deviant.

Key Ideas in the Labeling Process

Social control is the process by which a group or society enforces conformity to its demands and expectations. One way in which this is accomplished is through the creation and application of rules and labels. This leads to the distinction between rule creators and rule enforcers. **Rule creators** are usually elite members of society who devise its rules, norms, and laws (Ryan 1994). Without rule creators and their rules, there would be no deviance. Rule creators are usually (but not always) distinct from **rule enforcers**, who threaten to or actually do sanction the rule violators (Bryant and Higgins 2010). Another important idea here is that of **moral entrepreneurs**, or those individuals or groups of individuals who come to define an act as a moral outrage and who lead a campaign to have it defined as deviant and to have it made illegal and therefore subject to legal enforcement (Becker 1963; Lauderdale 2007; Nordgren 2013). Drugs provide a good example, especially globally, since moral entrepreneurs located primarily in the United States have taken it upon themselves to have particular drugs defined as illegal and their use as deviant. They have done so even though the use of many of these drugs (such as marijuana) is common and accepted not only in many societies throughout the world but also among a large portion of the American population.

Moral Panics

Moral entrepreneurs can stir up such a fuss that they can cause a **moral panic**, or a widespread and disproportionate reaction to the form of deviance in question (Goode and Ben-Yehuda 1994, 2009; Hier 2011; Krinsky 2013). It could be argued that today we are witnessing, in Europe and to a lesser degree in the United States, concern about Muslim immigrants that is quickly becoming a moral panic. This moral panic is related, at least in part, to the increasing threat of terrorism (e.g., the early 2015 murder by Islamist extremists of 12 people at the Paris satirical magazine *Charlie Hebdo* and 4 people at a Jewish supermarket) posed by radical Islamic groups, especially al-Qaeda and Islamic State. However, it is important to remember that very few Muslims are terrorists.

A good historical example of a moral panic is the witch craze that occurred in Europe between the fourteenth and sixteenth centuries (Ben-Yehuda 1980, 1985). The idea of witches had existed before this time, but it was seen as a more complex phenomenon involving both bad and good witches. In any case, no assumption had been made about a conspiracy between women and Satan to corrupt the world. However, in this era, Dominican friars took the lead in defining witchcraft as such a conspiracy and as a crime subject to corporal punishment, in this case burning at the stake. The friars were the moral entrepreneurs in this case. They played a key role in generating a moral panic that came to

Granger

Moral panics—such as the witch-hunting crazes of Renaissance Europe—rely in part on the use of labels to identify perceived threats. What might help to prevent the development of a moral panic?

involve large numbers of people. That panic, in turn, led to the painful deaths of hundreds of thousands of people, mostly women.

Moral panics are, by definition, exaggerated. Thus, the threats posed by witches in the fifteenth century, the communists in the 1950s, and immigrants and even terrorists today have been made out by many, especially moral entrepreneurs, to be greater than they really are. One of the ways to do this is to create a "folk devil" who stands for that which is feared. Terrorism made Osama bin Laden a folk devil.

Stigmas

A **stigma** is a person's characteristic that others find, define, and often label as unusual, unpleasant, or deviant (Goffman 1963). In his important book *Stigma* (1963), Goffman begins his analysis with physically stigmatized individuals, such as those missing a nose. He then introduces a wide array of other stigmas, such as being on welfare. In the end, readers come to the realization that they have been reading not only about people who are unlike them, with major physical deformities, but also about themselves: "The most fortunate of normals is likely to have his half-hidden failing, and for every little failing there is a social occasion when it will loom large, creating a shameful gap" (Goffman

1963: 127). Goffman's idea of stigma has attracted many scholars and has been applied to many forms of deviance, such as prostitution (Scambler and Paoli 2008; Wong, Holroyd, and Bingham 2011), mental illness (Payton and Thoits 2011), Asperger's syndrome (Hill and Liamputtong 2011), and tattooing (Dickson et al. 2014).

There are two types of stigmatized individuals. The individual with a **discredited stigma** "assumes his differentness is known about already or is evident on the spot." In contrast, those with a **discreditable stigma** assume that their stigma "is neither known about by those present nor immediately perceivable about them" (Goffman 1963: 4). An example of a discredited stigma might be the bodily symptoms of having advanced AIDS, a lost limb, or being a member of a minority group viewed negatively by others, while discreditable stigmas include having done poorly in school or having a prison record. Of great importance is the symbolic nature of the stigma and the individual's interaction with others, especially those thought to be normal. Because the physical nature of a discreditable stigma is not visible to others, neither are the stigma's symbolic qualities. Nevertheless, the people with such a stigma want to make sure it remains secret and thus try to conceal the stigmatizing information during most interactions. In contrast, in the case of a discredited stigma (such as being morbidly obese), those with the stigma must deal with the tension associated with interacting with people who view them negatively because of the stigma.

The idea of discreditable stigmas has wide applicability to the contemporary world. For example, the court records of juvenile offenders are often hidden from the public or expunged to avoid stigmatizing otherwise promising young people for a lifetime. People with mental illnesses or substance abuse problems often go to great lengths to hide the real reasons for unscheduled absences from work. Parents of mentally disabled children, especially the mildly impaired, "mainstream" their children in standard classrooms in part so the children's disability will be more likely to be discreditable than discredited. The theme of hiding stigmatizing conditions is common in popular entertainment as well: In the movie *Philadelphia* (1993), actor Tom Hanks plays a high-powered lawyer in a prestigious law firm who is diagnosed with HIV during the early years of the epidemic. As the disease progresses, he tries but ultimately fails to conceal the signs, such as skin blemishes associated with Kaposi's sarcoma. When it becomes clear to the leaders of his firm that he has AIDS, he is fired. This movie, unlike some, realistically portrays the painful, destructive effects of revealing a discredited stigma.

CRIME

As pointed out earlier, it is the fact that the law is violated that differentiates crime from deviance. **Criminology** is the field devoted to the study of crime (Brown 2007a; Maguire, Morgan, and Reiner 2012; Rosenfield 2011; Siegel 2014). Many, but certainly not all, criminologists are sociologists. There is a sociology of crime, but the field also includes those from many other disciplines, such as psychologists, economists, biologists, and anthropologists, as well as officials who once worked in the criminal justice system. In fact, the field today has become increasingly multidisciplinary, even interdisciplinary (Wellford 2012).

While there is growing interdisciplinarity in the study of crime, sociology plays an important role in it. Clearly, a variety of sociological factors (including social class and race; Chilton and Triplett 2007a, 2007b) are involved in who commits crimes and which crimes they commit. The same sociological factors are involved in who gets caught, prosecuted, and incarcerated, as well as how much of their sentences they actually serve. And such factors are involved in what happens to people after they serve their sentences and whether or not they end up back in prison.

The "father of criminology" is Cesare Lombroso, who published *The Criminal Man* in 1876 (McShane and Williams 2007). The title of the book reflects the fact that the focus of early criminologists was on criminals and their innate physical or psychological characteristics. In more recent years, criminology has shifted away from its focus on criminals and their defects and toward a concern with the social context of criminal actions and the effects of those actions on the larger society. A key figure in bringing a sociological perspective to criminology was Edwin Sutherland (1924). His work helped shift the focus in criminology from the criminal and his or her misdeeds to society, especially the societal reaction to those actions, including the labels placed on criminals.

Sutherland's most important contribution to the sociology of crime is **differential association** theory. The main point of the theory is that people learn criminal behavior. Therefore, whom a person associates with is crucial. One's family and friends—the primary group—are important sources of attitudes toward crime, knowledge about how to commit crimes, and rationalizations that help one live with being a criminal. Today, we would need to add the fact that criminal behavior can also be learned through the media, especially the Internet (a major site for learning how to be a terrorist). Many criticisms were leveled at differential association theory; even Sutherland later came to criticize it on various grounds. For example, it did not explain why some people became criminals while others exposed to the same situations and information did not. One of Sutherland's own criticisms was the fact that the theory did not give sufficient attention to the role of opportunity in committing crimes.

ASK YOURSELF

Can you think of any reasons some people become criminals while others exposed to the same situations do not? Consider the theories of deviance discussed above as you prepare your answer.

Associated Press

Prison education, counseling, and rehabilitation are designed to reduce recidivism among prisoners. Unfortunately, such programs are often poorly funded and inadequate.

FIGURE 6.3 • Prison Population around the World, 2012

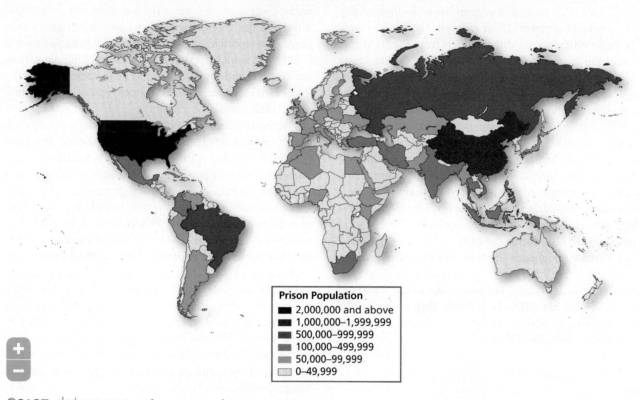

Prison Population
- 2,000,000 and above
- 1,000,000–1,999,999
- 500,000–999,999
- 100,000–499,999
- 50,000–99,999
- 0–49,999

$SAGE datamaps edge.sagepub.com
- Prison population and rate of incarceration for every country.
- Types of prisoners as a percentage of the total prison population.

SOURCE: International Centre for Prison Studies.

While the above discussion focuses on the causes of crime, especially those that are sociological in nature, criminology has long also had a focus on the criminal justice system (Wellford 2012). This interest is traceable to another early Italian scholar, Cesare Beccaria (1738–1794) (McShane and Williams 2007). He is best known for his 1764 book *On Crimes and Punishments,* and its concern with such issues as the origins of law and the criminal justice system. His work led to an interest not only in this system as a whole but also in whether its major components—law enforcement, courts, and corrections (Culver 2007)—are fair, effective, and just. In terms of the latter, much work has been done on the (un)fairness, especially as far as race is concerned, of arrest decisions by the police, the length of sentences, and the likelihood of receiving the death penalty.

THE CRIMINAL JUSTICE SYSTEM

The criminal justice system in the United States consists of various loosely connected government agencies and the individuals who work in those agencies. It is involved in the apprehension, prosecution, and punishment of those who violate the law. It also seeks to prevent such violations before they occur. Finally, the criminal justice system has much

more general responsibilities, such as ensuring public safety and maintaining social order (Culver 2007: 851). The major components of the criminal justice system are law enforcement, the courts, and the correctional system.

An enormous number of people are being held in the jail and prison systems (jails are locally controlled; prisons are controlled by the states or the federal government). In 2012, 2,228,424 adults were incarcerated in U.S. jails and federal and state prisons. The United States has the highest rate of incarceration (about 0.7 percent of the adult population) in the world. It has approximately 527,080 more prisoners than China and almost 1.6 million more than Russia (see Figure 6.3 for the prison population around the world). Although the United States has only 4.4 percent of the world's population, it has 22 percent of the world's prisoners (Cullen, Jonson, and Nagin 2011). This is a very costly system to operate (Bratton 2011). It is estimated that in 2008, local, state, and federal governments spent about $75 billion on corrections, much of it on incarceration (Schmidt, Warner, and Gupta 2010). Further complicating matters is the fact that the economic problems facing the United States in general, and state and local jurisdictions in particular, mean that fewer prisons and jails are being built while an increasing number of Americans are being

PUBLIC SOCIOLOGY

Jack Levin on Crime, in His Own Words

I have published the results of my research, mainly in the areas of murder and hate crimes, in scholarly books and journals accessible to fellow and future sociologists. However, I am also interested in reaching an audience of laypersons and opinion leaders.

I am certain that effective theory and research are essential for the development of important sociological ideas, but there is much more to the mission of the field than scholarship alone. Many sociologists share my conviction that we must apply sociological knowledge, not as some academic exercise, but toward improving the quality of social life generally.

My professional mission contains elements of both journalism and sociology. I seek to share sociological insights that might enhance the rationality of public discourse and the effectiveness of important policy decisions. I have written hundreds of opinion columns and have been interviewed for thousands of newspaper and magazine articles. On countless television programs I have been given the opportunity to apply a sociological perspective to some public controversy or breaking news event. For example:

- I suggested that our response to illegal immigration ought to be based on facts rather than stereotypes. Research has shown that immigrants have a much lower rate of violent crime and a lower rate of incarceration than native-born Americans.
- In popular thinking, mass killers suddenly snap, but I have pointed out that in reality they are almost always methodical and selective, planning their crimes for days, weeks, even months before they strike. In addition, most target family members, coworkers, or fellow students rather than random strangers.
- I suggested that the AMBER Alert program—the practice of going public with an urgent bulletin in the most serious child-abduction cases—is "not as good as people believe." By the time law enforcement alerts the public to a truly dangerous situation, the abducted child has already returned home or has been killed.

- I wrote a *Boston Globe* opinion column that was very critical of attempts to register sex offenders. Thanks to the severity of the stigma, many offenders are forced to relocate many times to different neighborhoods and shelters. Too often, they end up living under bridges or on the streets, where control over their activities is nonexistent (see Russell Banks's 2011 novel *Lost Memory of Skin*).

I seek to broaden the scope of the journalistic enterprise, to modify the thinking of reporters and commentators, so the sociological perspective is never left out of the public conversation.

SOURCE: Printed with the permission of Jack Levin.

Think About It

Do you think the "public conversation" about crime to which Jack Levin refers sometimes lacks the sociological perspective? Give an example to support your answer. Do you agree with Levin that sociological knowledge should be applied to improving the quality of social life? Why or why not?

---

sentenced to them. The growing number of prisoners creates other problems, including overcrowding of the prisons as well as increased violence among prisoners. Given the huge numbers involved, prisons have become little more than warehouses for prisoners. The ability of prisons to rehabilitate inmates has declined, and the focus on punishment has strengthened (Phelps 2011).

Beyond those in prisons and jails, as of 2011 more than 4.8 million people were under the control of the criminal justice system because they were either on parole (853,852) or on probation (3,971,319) (U.S. Department of Justice, Bureau of Justice Statistics 2011). **Parole** is the supervised early release of a prisoner for such efforts as good behavior while in prison. Parole officers work with those on parole to help them adjust to life outside prison and to be sure they are not violating the conditions of their release. If they do violate those conditions, they can have their parole revoked, and they can be sent back to prison. Those who are convicted of less serious crimes may be placed on **probation**, whereby they are released into the community with supervision. They are also released under certain conditions, such as that they must be enrolled in and complete a substance abuse program. If the offender does not adhere to these conditions, is arrested, or is convicted, probation can be revoked. In that case, a new, more restrictive probation can be imposed, or the offender can be sent to prison (Culver 2007). Both parole and probation require the participation of bureaucracies, and especially the parole and probation officers who are employed by them. These systems, like the prison and jail system, are very costly.

FIGURE 6.4 • The Death Penalty in the United States, 2014

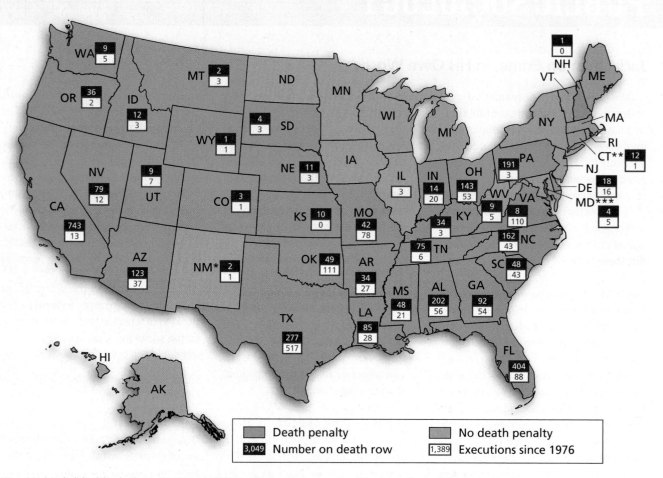

| Death penalty | No death penalty |
| 3,049 Number on death row | 1,389 Executions since 1976 |

*New Mexico abolished the death penalty in March 2009, but the law was not made retroactive, so 2 remain on death row.

**Connecticut abolished the death penalty in April 2012, but the law was not made retroactive, so 12 remain on death row.

***Maryland abolished the death penalty in May 2013, but the law was not made retroactive, so 4 remain on death row.

SOURCES: Data from NAACP Legal Defense and Educational Fund, "Death Row U.S.A.," July 1, 2014 (http://www.deathpenaltyinfo.org/documents/DRUSA_Summer_2014.pdf); and Death Penalty Information Center (http://www.deathpenaltyinfo.org).

It might be argued that the enormous cost of prisons—as well as the parole and probation systems—would be justifiable if incarceration taught people that "crime does not pay." In other words, a case might be made for mass imprisonment if it rehabilitated prisoners so that they were less likely to commit crimes after they were released. But does a prison term serve as deterrence to the commission of crimes after an inmate is released from prison? It is obvious that prisoners are deterred from further crime while imprisoned, although some seem to be able to engage in crimes while in prison. After a prisoner is released, those involved in the criminal justice system are interested in the issue of **specific deterrence**, or whether the experience of punishment in general, and incarceration in particular, makes it less likely that the ex-prisoner will commit crimes in the future. In other words, the issue is whether an individual will be "scared straight" by punishment, especially incarceration (Apel and Nagin 2011).

Most research in the field has shown that prisons do a poor job of rehabilitating prisoners, and as a result do not reduce **recidivism**, or the repetition of a criminal act by one who has been convicted of a prior offense (Smith 2007). Those who serve time in prison learn new and better criminal techniques during their incarceration. In other words, prisons have a "criminogenic" effect, leading to more rather than less crime (Cullen et al. 2011). Nonetheless, no expert would argue for the elimination of punishments, including imprisonment, for most crimes. However, there is a need for more focused forms of specific deterrence (Braga and Weisburd 2012). Furthermore, important individual and situational differences can have impacts on the effectiveness of such deterrence. What is needed is a focus on what forms of specific deterrence will be effective on what types of criminals and under what circumstances (Piquero et al. 2011).

General deterrence deals with the population as a whole and whether individuals will be less likely to commit crimes because of fear that they might be punished or imprisoned for their actions (Apel and Nagin 2011). Although it is not clear how many people do not commit crimes because of fear of punishment, it is clear that such fear constitutes some level of deterrence to some who might otherwise become criminals.

The ultimate example of both forms of deterrence is capital punishment, or the death penalty (Paternoster, Brame, and Bacon 2007). Someone who is executed clearly cannot commit another crime. However, there is evidence that even the threat of capital punishment is not a strong general deterrent to crime (Cohen-Cole et al. 2009).

Although a number of countries have abolished the death penalty, the United States is one of a handful that continue to employ it. Figure 6.4 shows the legality of the death penalty across U.S. states, as well as data on the number of people on death row per state and the number executed since 1976. The four leading countries in the world in terms of the number of people executed are China, Iran, North Korea, and Yemen. These are countries that the United States would not like to be associated with, especially on this issue. The United States ranks fifth, with 43 executions in 2011 (Amnesty International 2012). This is fewer than the 200 or so who were executed in each of two consecutive years in the 1930s. There have been nearly 1,400 executions in the United States since 1976. Overall, there have been more than 15,000 known executions in the United States (Paternoster 2007). There has also been a trend toward more "humane" execution (if such a thing is possible). Prior to 1930, most executions were done by hanging. Many of these were mishandled, resulting in those who were condemned gradually choking to death. From 1930 to 1967, the majority of executions in the United States were by electrocution. This did not seem to be much of an improvement, as the initial electrical charge, at least in some cases, did not cause death or even unconsciousness and in some cases caused the condemned to catch fire. Beginning

FIGURE 6.5 • Reported Violent Crime in the United States, 1994–2013

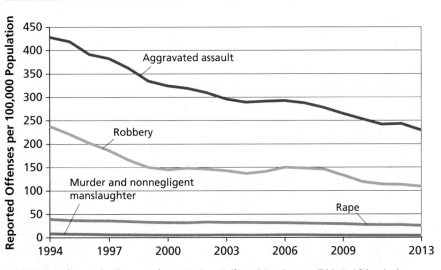

SOURCE: Data from Federal Bureau of Investigation, Uniform Crime Reports, Table 1: "Crime in the United States by Volume and Rate per 100,000 Inhabitants, 1994–2013," 2013.

FIGURE 6.6 • Reported Property Crime in the United States, 1994–2013

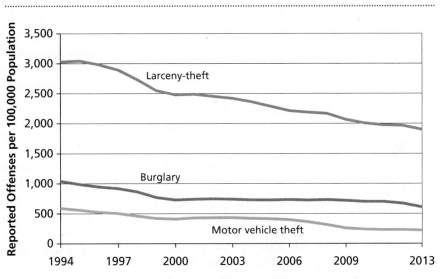

SOURCE: Data from Federal Bureau of Investigation, Uniform Crime Reports, Table 1: "Crime in the United States by Volume and Rate per 100,000 Inhabitants, 1994–2013," 2013.

in 1977, there was a movement toward the use of lethal injections, and about 80 percent of executions are now performed in that way. However, a number of recent botched executions by injection have caused long and painful deaths.

The application of capital punishment continues to be highly controversial. In fact, many death sentences are accompanied by active campaigns against them and vigils protesting executions both before and as they occur. There are many who feel that it is morally wrong for the government to kill anyone. Others are opposed to the death penalty because it is likely that at least some wrongly convicted people are killed in the process (Aronson and Cole 2009). Finally, there is strong evidence of bias, especially racial bias, in capital punishment. Many studies have shown that blacks, and nonwhites more generally, who are convicted of killing whites are more likely to get the death penalty than are whites who kill other whites (Paternoster 2007).

TYPES OF CRIMES

Data on crime across the United States are found in the Federal Bureau of Investigation's Uniform Crime Reports (UCR), which include data on crimes reported to police departments and police arrest statistics. Two broad types of crime are reported. **Violent crime** includes the threat of injury or the threat or actual use of force. The violent crimes tracked by the FBI are murder and nonnegligent manslaughter, forcible rape, robbery, and aggravated assault. Figure 6.5 shows the reported violent crime rates in the United States for 1994–2013. In recent years, increasing attention has been paid in the United States and elsewhere to violent crimes related to terrorism (although such crimes do not appear in the UCR), as well as globally to war crimes (Gartner 2007). **Property crimes** do not involve injury or force, but rather are offenses that involve gaining or destroying property. While there are others (such as shoplifting and forgery), the major property crimes are burglary, larceny-theft, motor vehicle theft, and arson; about three-fourths of all U.S. crime is property crime (Copes and Null 2007). Figure 6.6 shows the property crime rates in the United States for 1994–2013. Another important way of categorizing crimes is by separating **felonies**, or more serious crimes punishable by a year or more in prison, from **misdemeanors**, or minor offenses punishable by imprisonment of less than a year.

Beyond these broad types, a number of more specific types of crime are important to society and to criminologists:

- **White-collar crimes** are those committed "by a person of responsibility and high social status in the course of his occupation" (Geis 2007b: 850; Simpson 2013).

- **Corporate crime** involves legal organizations that violate the law. It includes such illegal acts as antitrust violations, stock market violations such as insider trading, and false advertisements (Geis 2007a).

- **Organized crime** can involve various types of organizations, but it is most often associated with criminal syndicates, especially the Mafia, which uses violence or the threat of violence and the corruption of public officials to profit from illegal activities (Griffin 2007). Other examples of criminal organizations are Mexican drug cartels and the Russian Mafia.

- **Political crimes** can be either offenses against the state to affect its policies, such as the assassination of one of its officials, especially its leader (John F. Kennedy, for example), or offenses by the state, either domestically (e.g., spying on citizens) or internationally (e.g., state-sponsored terrorism, bribery of a foreign official) (Tunnell 2007).

- **Hate crimes** are those that stem, in whole or in part, from the fact that those who are being victimized are in various ways different from the perpetrators. These differences include race, religion, sexual orientation, gender, national origin, and disability status. Victims are held in contempt by the perpetrators (Levin 2007).

- **Cybercrime** targets computers (for instance, by hacking) (see the "Digital Living" box on page 141). Cybercriminals use computers to commit traditional crimes, such as stealing from a bank account or theft of a credit card number. They also use computers to transmit illegal information and images to carry out such activities as insider trading, identity theft, child pornography, plans for terrorist acts, and "cyberterrorism" (Nunn 2007).

- **Consumer crimes**, or crimes related to consumption, include shoplifting and the use of stolen credit cards or credit card numbers.

Although all the offenses described above are classified as crimes, they are not all considered equally abhorrent. In line with the idea that deviance is defined by elites, so are crimes and criminal punishments. Thus, white-collar and corporate crimes are often downplayed, while the crimes usually associated with those in the lower social classes—for example, violent crimes, especially felonies, and property crimes—receive a great deal of attention from the police, the media, and the public.

ASK YOURSELF

Why are all crimes not considered equally serious? White-collar crime, for instance, can have far-reaching effects and untold numbers of victims. Consider the definitions of crime in your answer.

GLOBALIZATION AND CRIME

The amount of global, or cross-border (Andreas and Nadelmann 2006; Shelley, Picarelli, and Corpora 2011), crime has increased with globalization. Globalization makes cross-border crime increasingly possible and more likely. International crime has existed for centuries in such forms as piracy on the oceans and the African slave trade. However, today there seems to be far more of it. This may be due to the fact that, because of the increase in global criminal flows, much more public and government attention is devoted to these crimes. Action against crime flows almost as easily as the crimes themselves.

Cybercrime

The infinite reproducibility and easy distribution, including illegally, of online information lend themselves to new modes of increasingly globalized cybercrime, including cyberterrorism (Holt and Bossler 2014). One of the most common and widespread global Internet cybercrimes is hacking into accounts, or illegally accessing data. In the last few years a nearly endless list of major banks (such as JPMorgan Chase), businesses (including Sony Pictures and Target), and government agencies, including the military (for instance, the U.S. Central Command), have been hacked. Other Internet crimes include digital content piracy and government and industrial espionage. U.S. intelligence agencies have publicly condemned China, Korea, and Russia for using the Internet to steal valuable technology from the U.S. government and American corporations. The losses are so substantial it is impossible to estimate their value (Shanker 2011). In fact, China's digital espionage has been called a new "Cold War in cyberspace" (Sanger 2013).

Identity theft through phishing and hacking of databases is another common Internet crime (Holt and Turner 2012; Vieraitis et al. 2015). The most common form of identity theft is unauthorized use of a credit card account (Perlroth 2014). It has been estimated that over a two-year period 5 percent of U.S. adults were the targets of attempted or successful identity theft (U.S. Department of Justice, Bureau of Justice Statistics 2008).

Illegal content (such as child pornography) is also distributed through the Internet, and online sexual harassment is prevalent. Other frequent online

Are you surprised that new forms of crime have become possible with the development and worldwide use of the Internet? Is cybercrime inevitable?

activities, though they are not crimes, are cyberbullying through, for example, online social networks (Kowalski, Limber, and Agatston 2012; Rafferty and Vander Ven 2014) and sexting, or sending racy pictures to others over the Internet (via Snapchat, for example).

Music and video piracy is undoubtedly the most widespread form of criminal activity on the Internet. The Recording Industry Association of America (2012) has estimated that more than 40 billion illegal downloads occurred from 2004 through 2009 (roughly six songs for every person on Earth!). The International Federation of the Phonographic Industry reported in 2012 that 89 percent of all torrent files—the most popular protocol for peer-to-peer file sharing—linked to content that infringed on copyrights. The

same report estimated that digital sales would increase by 131 percent if piracy were eliminated. Although the recording industry and Hollywood saw profits plummet 32 percent from 2003 to 2010 (Sisario 2011), critics often argue that much of the damage was self-inflicted because the industries resisted modernization. For years, consumers who wanted to obtain digital content had few options other than piracy.

SOURCE: Printed with the permission of P. J. Rey.

Think About It

Do you believe file sharing is deviant? Should it be criminalized? What purpose does enforcing copyright laws serve? Who benefits and who is harmed?

Crime on the U.S.–Mexico Border

The international drug trade has a long and complex history that is rooted in, for example, the disparity in wealth between North America and South America, as well as the fact that the United States places stricter prohibitions on drug use than most other countries.

The United Nations Office on Drugs and Crime (2012) estimates that 203 million people globally (5 percent of the world's population ages 15 to 64) used illegal substances at least once in 2010, the largest markets being in North America and Europe. Because there is no way for affluent Americans who want these drugs to obtain them legally, a lucrative black market has emerged. Drug cartels, taking advantage of lax regulation and weak enforcement mechanisms in South and Central America, have developed a complex infrastructure to produce drugs and smuggle them into the United States (see Figure 6.7). Roughly 60 percent of all illicit drugs found in the United States enter through the border with Mexico (Archibold 2009). The illegal drugs most trafficked across that border include marijuana, methamphetamine, and cocaine. Efforts to stop the flow of drugs have not been notably successful. Furthermore, those involved in the drug trade are continually finding new ways to keep the drugs flowing across the border, including using catapults, digging a tunnel that went 600 yards beyond the border and ended in a San Diego warehouse (Dillon and Lovett 2013), and using drones to carry drug shipments ("Drug-Laden Drone" 2015).

FIGURE 6.7 • Mexican Cartel Territories and Drug Routes

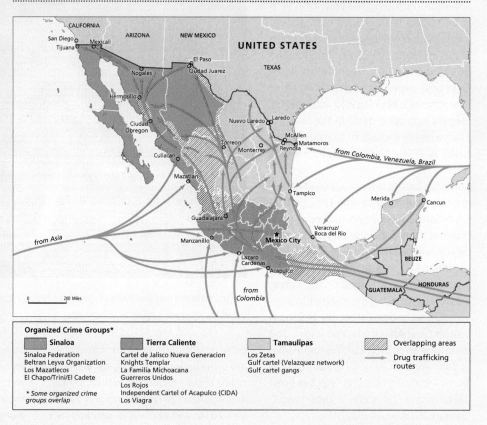

Organized Crime Groups*

▓ Sinaloa	▓ Tierra Caliente	▓ Tamaulipas	▨ Overlapping areas
Sinaloa Federation	Cartel de Jalisco Nueva Generacion	Los Zetas	→ Drug trafficking routes
Beltran Leyva Organization	Knights Templar	Gulf cartel (Velazquez network)	
Los Mazatlecos	La Familia Michoacana	Gulf cartel gangs	
El Chapo/Trini/El Cadete	Guerreros Unidos		
	Los Rojos		
*Some organized crime groups overlap	Independent Cartel of Acapulco (CIDA)		
	Los Viagra		

SOURCE: Republished with permission of Stratfor, www.stratfor.com.

The cartels, each competing for a larger share of the multibillion-dollar industry, have expanded into Honduras and Guatemala and ignited a series of turf wars there, as well as in Mexico ("Honduras, Guatemala" 2014). To secure or expand their hold on profitable drug routes, they are smuggling weapons from the United States, where guns are plentiful and laws regulating their purchase are comparatively lax. Possessing assault rifles, grenades, and bulletproof vests, gangs are now often better armed than local police forces. Moreover, because the drug trade is so much more profitable than other industries in Mexico (and throughout Latin America), cartels are often able to buy off poorly paid local police officials. Violent crime on the Mexican side of the border with the United States has become commonplace. In the peak year of 2009, about 3,400 people were killed in the border city of Ciudad Juárez alone, leading it to be defined as one of the most dangerous and deadly cities in the entire world (Thompson and Lacey 2010).

The murder rate in Mexico, especially in such border cities, has declined in recent years (Cave 2014), but it is still substantial. The violence is still so bad that thousands of Mexicans are fleeing their homes—some even seeking political asylum in the United States (McKinley 2010). Violence is also spilling over the American side of the border. For example, many home invasion robberies are directly linked to the drug trade (Archibold 2009). Police believe that in some cases, Americans have been murdered simply for crossing paths with drug traffickers who were in the process of sneaking across the border (Archibold 2010).

Violence stemming from the drug trade is now so significant that it dominates relations between the United States and Mexico.

Think About It

How would a conflict theorist explain the persistence of the violent drug trade occurring on the U.S.–Mexico border? How much do different definitions of deviance involving drugs and guns contribute to this ongoing problem?

The growth in global crime is largely traceable to increasing concern about illicit drug use in the United States in the late 1960s and early 1970s, as well as Western Europe's interest in terrorism during roughly the same period. Drugs and terrorism now top the list of global concerns as far as crime is concerned; others include "clandestine trade in sophisticated weaponry and technology, endangered species, pornographic materials, counterfeit products, guns, ivory, toxic waste, money, people [i.e., trafficking in human beings; Farr 2005], stolen property, and art and antiquities" (Andreas and Nadelmann 2006: 5). All of these involve flows of all sorts—drugs, money, human victims (for example, those to be used as prostitutes), and human perpetrators (such as terrorists). They also include various illegal things that flow through the Internet (e.g., child pornography, laundered funds, computer viruses).

These illegal flows have been aided by the decline of the nation-state and its increasing inability to reduce or halt them. Furthermore, global criminal cartels have come into existence to expedite illegal flows and to increase the profits that can be derived from them. In his book *McMafia* (2008), Misha Glenny attributes much of the cartels' success to increasingly sophisticated organizational methods (including economies of scale, global partnerships, and the opening of new markets) copied from leading legitimate businesses such as McDonald's. New technologies have also been employed to make at least some criminal flows more successful. The Internet has made a number of illegal flows (e.g., planning terrorist acts, disseminating child pornography, perpetrating scams) much easier and is largely impervious to efforts at control by individual nation-states.

Criminalization of Global Activities

As pointed out earlier, crime (and deviance) is always a matter of social definition or social construction. So, although the power of nation-states has generally declined in the global age, it continues to matter greatly in terms of what have come to be *defined* as global forms of deviance and crime. In the era of globalization, the nation-states of Western Europe and the United States have played the central role in criminalizing certain activities. It is *their* sense of morality and *their* norms of behavior that have come to be the rule in much of the world (Andreas and Nadelmann 2006). The global criminalization of drug use is a good case in point.

However, while there have been a number of efforts to define drug use as deviant and illegal, they have not always been successful. The global drug trade has in fact expanded in spite of great efforts by the United States and other nation-states to at least reduce it.

Much of the publicity about drugs and the ways in which they are implicated in globalization involves cocaine and heroin. Great attention is devoted to, for example, the growing of poppies in Afghanistan and drug production in Guatemala, and the ways in which drugs from those areas and many others make their way around the world. A relatively new global drug is methamphetamine (meth), made easily and cheaply in home-based "cooking facilities" from pseudoephedrine, the main ingredient in a number of cough, cold, and allergy medications. Once largely an American phenomenon, the production and use of methamphetamine is beginning to expand globally. For example, it is a growing problem in the Czech Republic and Slovakia, and the fear is that it will spread from there throughout the European Union and to many other parts of the world as well (Kulish 2007).

Several aspects of cross-border crime, especially as it relates to drugs, help to account for why global as well as national efforts to counter it have been largely unsuccessful. First, those who commit the crimes do not require a great many resources. Second, they do not need very much expertise to commit the crimes. Third, such crimes are easy to conceal. Fourth, in many cases the crimes are not apt to be reported to the police or other authorities. Finally, the crimes are those for which great consumer demand exists and for which there are no readily available alternative products (e.g., drugs) or activities (e.g., prostitution) (Andreas and Nadelmann 2006).

However, it would be wrong to judge global efforts to control drugs and other illegal substances and activities as complete failures. The fact is that while drugs continue to flow readily throughout the world for the reasons suggested above, the United States has had considerable success in internationalizing its views, laws, procedures, and efforts at enforcement. As mentioned earlier, powerful societies are often able to get weaker societies to adopt their ways of doing things. Foreign governments have

- altered their laws and methods of law enforcement to more closely match U.S. laws on drugs;

- acceded to demands by the United States to sign law enforcement treaties;

- adopted American investigative techniques;

- created specialized drug enforcement agencies;

- stationed law enforcement representatives in other countries;

- enacted various laws on conspiracy, asset forfeiture, and money laundering related to drugs; and

- provided greater assistance to the United States and changed their laws on financial secrecy.

In other words, we have seen an Americanization of law enforcement throughout much of the world.

Global Crime Control

The growth in global crime has been met, of course, by the expansion of international policing and of the role of the police in international relations (Andreas and Nadelmann 2006; Bowling and Sheptycki 2012). In addition to its role regarding drug trafficking, the United States has taken the lead in countering other forms of global crime and in influencing other nations to work against them. Since 9/11, there has been a dramatic increase in efforts to counter global terrorism. While there have been some successes, there have also been a growing number of failures in various parts of the world.

The world of criminal justice has seen an erosion of certain distinctions in its efforts to forestall further terrorist attacks and to catch or kill people defined as terrorists. For example, the distinction between law enforcement and intelligence operations has become less clear as law enforcement authorities have sought to gain intelligence on potential terrorists. The distinction between law enforcement and security has also eroded. The USA PATRIOT (Uniting and Strengthening America by Providing Appropriate Tools Required to Intercept and Obstruct Terrorism) Act, signed into law on October 26, 2001, has played a key role in this erosion by, for example, extending the concern of law enforcement agencies to domestic terrorism. (In mid-2015 Congress passed legislation limiting some of the excesses of the act, including the sweeping surveillance of Americans' phone records; Steinhauer and Weisman 2015.) In addition, surveillance of the border between the United States

and Mexico, and in immigrant communities in the United States, has increased. In the process, many immigrants have been defined as criminals, apprehended, and then returned to Mexico. Far less attention is devoted to surveillance on the much longer border with Canada, and those who do cross that border illegally are much less likely to be defined, or apprehended, as criminals.

Some European countries have instituted a similar, though not as extreme, toughening of border controls and surveillance. However, within the European Union, border controls and surveillance have relaxed. Border law enforcement within the EU has become more homogeneous as criminal justice norms and procedures have become more similar and law enforcement contacts and exchanges of information among member states have become more regular. Of great importance has been the formation of Europol, the EU's law enforcement agency, which enables better and increased communication and cooperation among national police agencies.

While these efforts have improved global crime control, they also have a variety of downsides. Democracy and civil rights may be threatened by these efforts. Crime control efforts are not always as transparent as they should be, and the officials involved often need to be more accountable. Tougher border and immigration controls have led to more daring and dangerous efforts to cross borders, leading to more deaths in the process. In addition, the global antidrug campaign has generated high levels of crime, violence, corruption, disease, and so on. Efforts by the United States to deal with trafficking in women and children have focused more on criminalizing that traffic than on protecting the human rights of the women and children being trafficked. The attention and money devoted to international crime and its control have tended to distract attention, and to take money away, from efforts to deal with a wide range of fundamental issues within nation-states, including the welfare of large portions of society.

Public efforts to control global crime have been far from totally successful. For example, in 2014, 43 Mexican college students were murdered by a drug gang. The murders were committed at the behest of the mayor of Iguala, who was later arrested, as were some members of the gang (Archibold 2015). Between 2007 and 2011, approximately 40,000 people were killed in the wars between drug gangs, and the wars continue to ravage Mexico (although, as noted above, to a declining degree), and they have spread across the border into the United States. The police in Mexico have failed to halt the carnage, and even the use of the Mexican military has not met with much success. The news media, often intimidated by the gangs, have often failed to provide needed and accurate information about criminal activities.

SUMMARY

For sociologists, a person or action is deviant when socially defined as such. Durkheim argued that since deviance and crime have always existed in all societies, they are, in essence, normal and have positive functions for society.

Merton's version of structural-functionalism argues that deviance is more likely to occur when a culture values something, such as material success, but the societal structure does not allow everyone the ability to achieve this value in a socially accepted way. Conflict/critical theorists see inequality, in particular economic inequality, as the cause of much deviance. In this view, those in the lowest classes engage in deviant or criminal behavior because they otherwise have few ways of achieving normative societal goals, whereas those in the upper classes commit crimes because the nature of their positions makes it relatively easy for them to do so.

From an inter/actionist perspective, deviance requires first a symbol or label, and second an interaction between a social control agent, the person or group doing the labeling, and the person or group to whom the label is applied. Another inter/actionist perspective comes from Goffman's writings on stigma, a characteristic in a person that others find, define, and often label as unusual or deviant.

Crime is a form of deviance that violates criminal law. The major components of the criminal justice system are law enforcement, the courts, and the correctional system. Increasing globalization has been associated with increases in global or cross-border crime, particularly the international drug trade. Illegal flows are aided by nation-states' declining ability to halt them. The United States and Western Europe have played a central role in defining global criminal acts and the most appropriate ways to deal with them.

REVIEW QUESTIONS

1. What do sociologists mean when they say that deviance is socially defined? Given a sociological approach, in what ways is tattooing deviant, and in what ways is it not?

2. How can we understand deviance as a global flow? How do countries differ in terms of their interpretations of what is deviant? In an increasingly globalized world, what are the consequences of these differing interpretations?

3. The Dutch seem to be limiting marijuana use to some extent just as some U.S. states are adopting a more liberal approach to the use of the drug. How do you explain these contradictory trends?

4. In what ways can the capitalist economic system be seen as creating deviance? Is this even more true of crime?

5. Why do those who rank high in such hierarchies as business, government, and the military have a much greater ability to commit deviant acts, to have them be seen as being legitimate, and to get away with them? What does this elite deviance suggest about the "fairness" of deviance?

6. What are the differences between a discredited stigma and a discreditable stigma? What is an example of each?

7. How is crime different from deviance? Why do some forms of deviance become criminalized whereas others do not?

8. How do you explain the fact that the United States has so many people in prison? Why is the U.S. incarceration rate the highest in the world?

9. Is the death penalty useful as a form of general deterrence? Are you in favor of the death penalty? If so, for what crimes?

10. What sorts of barriers have countries attempted to implement to limit the global flow of drugs? Why have these been relatively unsuccessful?

APPLYING THE SOCIOLOGICAL IMAGINATION

In this exercise, you will use an ethnomethodological approach (see Chapter 2) to understanding the stable and orderly properties of interactions on the Internet. You will need to pay specific attention to the ways in which rules are broken on the Internet.

First, select a website that allows people to interact with one another (such as Facebook, Twitter, your favorite interactive blog, an online discussion forum, or the comments section of an article on your local newspaper's website). In what ways does the Internet help facilitate behavior that would be deviant elsewhere? What norms are broken on the Internet that might not be broken in face-to-face interactions? What sorts of structural barriers exist on the Internet that might limit deviant behavior? Overall, do you think deviant behavior flows more easily because of the Internet? Given contemporary realities, a useful focus might be on efforts to encourage terrorism and to recruit terrorists.

conformists: People who accept both cultural goals and the traditional means of achieving those goals. (p. 129)

consumer crimes: Crimes related to consumption, including shoplifting and using stolen credit cards or credit card numbers. (p. 140)

corporate crime: Violation of the law by legal organizations, including antitrust violations and stock market violations. (p. 140)

crime: Deviance that is a violation of the criminal law. (p. 126)

criminalization: The process by which the legal system negatively sanctions some form of deviant behavior. (p. 126)

criminology: The study of all aspects of crime. (p. 135)

cybercrime: Crime that targets computers, uses computers to commit traditional crimes, or uses computers to transmit illegal information and images. (p. 140)

deviance: Any action, belief, or human characteristic that a large number of people who are members of a society or a social group consider a violation of group norms and for which the violator is likely to be censured or punished. (p. 126)

differential association: A theory that focuses on the fact that people learn criminal behavior and therefore that what is crucial is whom a person associates with. (p. 135)

discreditable stigma: A stigma that the affected individual assumes is neither known about nor immediately perceivable. (p. 134)

discredited stigma: A stigma that the affected individual assumes is already known about or readily apparent. (p. 134)

felonies: Serious crimes punishable by a year or more in prison. (p. 140)

general deterrence: The deterrence of the population as a whole from committing crimes for fear that they will be punished or imprisoned for their actions. (p. 139)

hate crimes: Crimes that stem from the fact that the victims are in various ways different from, and disesteemed by, the perpetrators. (p. 140)

innovators: Individuals who accept cultural goals but reject conventional means of achieving success. (p. 130)

interaction: A social engagement that involves two or more individuals who perceive, and orient their actions to, one another. (p. 132)

labeling theory: Theory contending that a deviant is someone to whom a deviant label has been successfully applied. (p. 132)

misdemeanors: Minor offenses punishable by imprisonment of less than a year (p. 140)

moral entrepreneurs: Individuals or groups who come to define an act as a moral outrage and who lead a campaign to have it defined as deviant and to have it made illegal and therefore subject to legal enforcement. (p. 133)

moral panic: A widespread and disproportionate reaction to a form of deviance. (p. 133)

organized crime: Crime that may involve various types of organizations but is most often associated with syndicated organized crime that uses violence (or its threat) and the corruption of public officials to profit from illegal activities. (p. 140)

parole: The supervised early release of a prisoner for such things as good behavior while in prison. (p. 137)

political crime: Crime involving either illegal offenses against the state to affect its policies or offenses by the state, whether domestically or internationally. (p. 140)

primary deviance: Early, nonpatterned acts of deviance, or an act here or there that is considered to be strange or out of the ordinary. (p. 133)

probation: A system by which those who are convicted of less serious crimes may be released into the community, but under supervision and under certain conditions, such as being involved in and completing a substance abuse program. (p. 137)

property crimes: Crimes that do not involve injury or force, but rather the theft or destruction of property. (p. 140)

rebels: Individuals who reject both traditional means and goals and instead substitute nontraditional goals and means to those goals. (p. 130)

recidivism: The repetition of a criminal act by one who has been convicted of a prior offense. (p. 138)

retreatists: Individuals who reject both cultural goals and the traditional routes to their attainment; they have completely given up on attaining success within the system. (p. 130)

ritualists: Individuals who realize that they will not be able to achieve cultural goals, but who nonetheless continue to engage in the conventional behavior associated with such success. (p. 130)

rule creators: Individuals who devise society's rules, norms, and laws. (p. 133)

rule enforcers: Individuals who threaten to or actually enforce the rules. (p. 133)

secondary deviance: Deviant acts that persist, become more common, and eventually cause people to organize their lives and personal identities around their deviant status. (p. 133)

social control agents: Those who label a person as deviant. (p. 132)

social control: The process by which a group or society enforces conformity to its demands and expectations. (p. 133)

specific deterrence: Deterrence from criminal behavior based on the concept that the experience of punishment in general, and incarceration in particular, makes it less likely that an individual will commit crimes in the future. (p. 138)

stigma: A person's characteristic that others find, define, and often label as unusual, unpleasant, or deviant. (p. 134)

symbol: A word, gesture, or object that stands in for something or someone (a "label"). (p. 132)

violent crime: Crime that involves the threat of injury or the threat or actual use of force, including murder, rape, robbery, and aggravated assault, as well as terrorism and, globally, war crimes. (p. 140)

white-collar crimes: Crimes committed by responsible and (usually) high-social-status people in the course of their work. (p. 140)

SAGE edge™ edge.sagepub.com/ritzeressentials2e

SAGE edge offers a robust online environment featuring an impressive array of free tools and resources for review, study, and further exploration, keeping both instructors and students on the cutting edge of teaching and learning.

LEARNING OBJECTIVES	FOR FURTHER EXPLORATION AND APPLICATION
LO 6-1: Define deviance.	▶ Perspectives on Deviance ◉ The Wild, Wild Web ▣ The Sociology of Deviant Behavior
LO 6-2: Describe structural/functional, conflict/critical, and inter/actionist approaches to theorizing about deviance.	▶ How Deviance Challenges Existing Norms ◉ Freddie Gray Rallies and Riots ▣ Delinquent, Dropout, At-Risk: When Words Become Labels
LO 6-3: Discuss the relationship between deviance and crime.	▶ How We Violate Social Norms ◉ Secular versus Nonsecular Views of Deviance ▣ Deviance and Crime
LO 6-4: Discuss the purpose and effects of the criminal justice system.	▶ A Closer Look at the American Criminal Justice System ◉ How Parole Requirements Contribute to Increased Crime Rates ▣ Quick Guide to the Criminal Justice System

SOCIAL STRATIFICATION IN THE UNITED STATES AND GLOBALLY

7

Something Is Right in Denmark: Life at the Bottom of the Stratification System Needn't Be So Bad

Hampus Elofsson has a low-skill service job at a Burger King in Copenhagen. At the end of his workweek, he makes sure his bills are paid, enjoys a night out with friends, and even sets aside some money for savings. He can afford to do this because he earns $20 per hour, which is the base salary for a fast-food worker in Denmark. As Elofsson notes, "You can make a decent living here working in fast food. You don't have to struggle to get by."

The benefits for fast-food workers in Denmark do not end there. They also enjoy five weeks of paid vacation each year, full health insurance (Denmark has universal health care), paid maternity and paternity leave, a pension plan, and overtime pay for working after 6:00 p.m. and on Sundays. These benefits contrast sharply with the wages and benefits of fast-food workers in the United States, who earn an average of $8.90 per hour. For example, Anthony Moore is a shift manager at a Burger King near Tampa, Florida, where he earns $9.00 per hour. He works 35 hours per week, and his weekly take-home pay is about $300. While his daughters, ages two and five, qualify for Medicaid, he has no health insurance. He says he sometimes asks himself, "Do I buy food or do I buy them clothes?" His earnings are often not enough to pay his electricity and water bills. Moore's situation is illustrative of other workers' experiences in low-wage work in the

LEARNING OBJECTIVES

 7-1 Describe the dimensions of social stratification in the United States.

7-2 Identify the factors involved in U.S. economic inequality.

7-3 Identify the types of social mobility in the United States.

7-4 Discuss structural/functional, conflict/critical, and inter/actionist theories of social stratification.

 7-5 Explain the relationship between consumption and social stratification in the United States.

7-6 Describe the positions in global stratification.

7-7 Discuss global economic inequalities.

7-8 Explain why and how positions change in global stratification.

7-9 Discuss structural/functional and conflict/critical theories of global stratification.

Getty

United States. One in five U.S. households with a family member working in fast food lives below the poverty line. Wages in the fast-food industry in the United States are so low that more than half of the industry's workers rely on some sort of public assistance.

The reasons for such vast differences across countries are complex. One of the most important factors is that, in contrast with workers in the United States, all fast-food workers in Denmark are represented by a union that bargains for their wages and benefits. Companies like Burger King, McDonald's, and other fast-food chains still earn a profit in Denmark, but their profits are not as high as they are in the United States. Other laws and regulations in Denmark, such as universal health care, further help workers. ●

We often hear that American society, as well as the world as a whole, is unfair. This is generally taken to mean that a relatively small number of people have way too much, while most of the rest have far too little. What is it that some people have, or are thought to have, and others lack? The most obvious answer is money and that which money buys. However, **social stratification** involves hierarchical differences not only in economic positions but also in other important areas, such as status, or social honor, and power. Social stratification has a profound effect on how monetary and nonmonetary resources are distributed in American society and around the globe.

DIMENSIONS OF SOCIAL STRATIFICATION

Any sociological discussion of stratification draws on an important set of dimensions derived from the work of the great German social theorist Max Weber ([1921] 1968; Bendix and Lipset 1966; Ultee 2007a, 2007b). These three dimensions are social class, status, and power.

SOCIAL CLASS

One's economic position in the stratification system, especially one's occupation, defines one's **social class**. A person's social class position strongly determines and reflects his or her income and wealth. Those who rank close to one another in wealth and income can be said to be members of the same social class. For example, multibillionaire entrepreneurs such as Bill Gates and Warren Buffett belong to one social class; the janitor in your university building and the

mechanic who fixes your car at the corner gas station belong to another. Terms often used to describe a person's social class are *upper class* (for example, large-scale entrepreneurs and many large investors, especially in hedge funds), *middle class* (nurses, teachers, veterinarians, air traffic controllers, travel agents, and firefighters), *working class* (manual, clerical, and full-time service workers in industries such as fast food), and *lower class* (part-time service and other workers and the unemployed). Figure 7.1 illustrates the relationships among occupation, income, and social class in the United States (Gilbert 2015). Its teardrop shape represents the percentage of Americans in each class; there are substantially more people in the working and lower classes than there are in the upper class. As we will soon see, the United States is even more stratified than this figure suggests.

STATUS

The second dimension of the stratification system, *status*, relates to the prestige attached to a person's positions within society. The existence and importance of this dimension

FIGURE 7.1 • Social Classes, Occupations, and Incomes in the United States

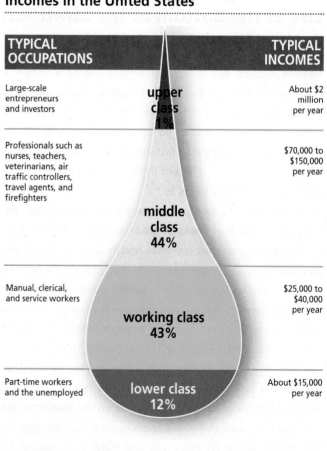

TYPICAL OCCUPATIONS		TYPICAL INCOMES
Large-scale entrepreneurs and investors	upper class 1%	About $2 million per year
Professionals such as nurses, teachers, veterinarians, air traffic controllers, travel agents, and firefighters	middle class 44%	$70,000 to $150,000 per year
Manual, clerical, and service workers	working class 43%	$25,000 to $40,000 per year
Part-time workers and the unemployed	lower class 12%	About $15,000 per year

SOURCE: Adapted from Dennis L. Gilbert, *The American Class Structure in an Age of Growing Inequality*, 9th ed. (Thousand Oaks, CA: Sage, 2015).

demonstrate that factors other than those associated with money are considered valuable in society. For example, in a 2014 Harris Poll of 2,537 U.S. adults, the well-paid doctor was ranked the most prestigious, followed by the far less well-paid military officer, and in third place the comparatively modestly paid firefighter. However, the often exorbitantly paid and rewarded corporate executive was not even in the top 10 occupations in terms of prestige (Harris Interactive 2014).

POWER

A third dimension of social stratification is **power**, the ability to get others to do what you want them to do, even if it is against their will. Those who have a great deal of power rank high in the stratification system, while those with little or no power are arrayed near the bottom. This is clearest in the case of politics, where, for example, the president of the United States ranks very high in power, while millions of ordinary voters have comparatively little political power.

Greater income is generally associated with more power, but there are exceptions to this rule. Recently, an increasing number of media stories focused on the phenomenon of "breadwinner wives," or "alpha wives"—women who earn more than their husbands (Mundy 2012; Roberts 2010). As shown in Figure 7.2, only 3.8 percent of wives in 1960 had income greater than that of their husbands, but by 2011, 22.5 percent of wives earned more than their husbands. In spite of their greater income, "breadwinner wives" may not have greater power in the marital relationship and in many cases are compelled to be content sharing power with their husbands (Cherlin 2010).

ECONOMIC INEQUALITY

A major concern in the sociological study of stratification is **inequality**, a condition whereby some positions in society yield a great deal of money, status, and power while others yield little, if any, of these. While other bases of stratification exist, the system of stratification in the United States, and in much of the contemporary world, is based largely on money. Money can take the form of income or wealth. **Income** is the amount of money a person earns from a job, a business, or returns on various types of assets (e.g., real estate rents) and investments (e.g., dividends on stocks and bonds). Income is generally measured year by year. For example, you might have an income of $25,000 per year. **Wealth**, on the other hand, is the total amount of a person's financial assets and other properties less the total of various

FIGURE 7.2 • **Percentage of Married Women Who Earn More than Their Husbands, 1960–2011**

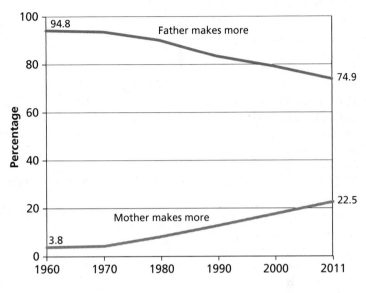

% based on married couples with children under age 18

NOTE: The category of father and mother having the same income not shown.

SOURCE: Data from Wendy Wang, Kim Parker, and Paul Taylor, "Breadwinner Moms," Pew Research Center, Pew Social and Demographic Trends, May 29, 2013.

kinds of debts, or liabilities. Assets include such things as savings, investments, homes, and automobiles, while debts include home mortgages, student loans, car loans, and amounts owed to credit card companies. If all your assets total $100,000 but you owe $25,000, your wealth (or net worth) amounts to $75,000.

Wealth can be inherited from others, so that a person can be very wealthy and yet have a modest income. Conversely, people can earn substantial incomes and not be very wealthy because, for example, they squander their money.

INCOME INEQUALITY

In many parts of the world, incomes became more equitable from the late 1920s until the 1970s. However, since the 1970s, there has been a substantial increase in income inequality in many countries, with a few individuals earning a great deal more and many earning little, if any, more. Even in the United States, which we erroneously (Massey 2008) regard as an egalitarian society, income inequality has been rising since the 1970s and now rivals levels that existed in the late 1920s (DeSilver 2013). That was at the peak of the end of the Roaring Twenties and just before the economic bubble burst that heralded the Great Depression. In 1928, the top 1 percent of families received almost 24 percent of all pretax income, while the bottom 90 percent of families earned only about 51 percent of that income. The Depression and World War II altered the economic landscape and led to greater equality. By 1944 those in the top 1 percent were receiving *only* about 11 percent of income, while those in the bottom 90 percent were earning more than 67 percent of that income. However, the situation began to change again in the 1970s, and by 2011, the top 1 percent of American families earned 19.82 percent of all income, up from 10.02 percent in 1960 (see Figure 7.3)—this was almost as much (in percentage terms) as in 1928. At the same time, the share of the bottom 90 percent was below 50 percent, even less than in 1928.

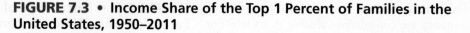

FIGURE 7.3 • Income Share of the Top 1 Percent of Families in the United States, 1950–2011

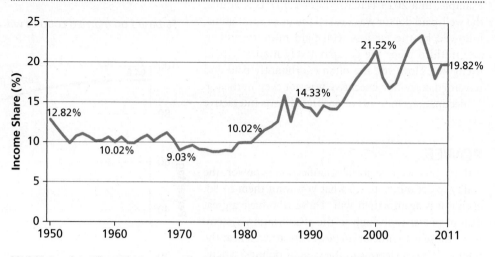

SOURCE: Dennis L. Gilbert, *The American Class Structure in an Age of Growing Inequality*, 9th ed. (Thousand Oaks, CA: Sage, 2015).

Income inequality today is even greater if we focus not on the top 1 percent but on the elite of the elite, the top 0.1 percent of households. In 2012, the average annual household income for the top 0.1 percent was a whopping $6,373,782. By comparison, the top 1 percent had to make do with an income of *only* $1,264,065. How about the bottom 90 percent? Their average household income was $30,997. In other terms, the top 0.1 percent earned 206 times as much as the bottom 90 percent, while the top 1 percent made 41 times the income of those at the bottom (Lowrey 2014).

Several broad reasons have been put forth to explain recent increases in income inequality:

- *Deindustrialization.* The decline of U.S. industry, as well as of industry in other developed countries, has led to the loss of many higher-paying industrial jobs (Bluestone and Harrison 1984; Kollmeyer and Pichler 2013). Deindustrialization is also related to the decline in the power of labor unions, which had helped many industrial workers obtain higher pay and generous benefits.

- *Technological advances.* The highest-paying new jobs in recent years have been created in high-tech, high-skill areas such as information technology (IT). Many Americans have not received the training necessary to shift from industrial to high-tech work.

- *Political climate.* A variety of political decisions help explain the increase in income inequality (Levy 1999; Sacchi and Salotti 2014). For example, there has been strong political opposition in the United States to raising the federal minimum wage, although there are signs that such opposition is abating (Ritzer 2015).

ASK YOURSELF

Which of the proposed reasons for the steady increase in income inequality do you think has had the greatest impact on those you know? What about in society at large? Why?

WEALTH INEQUALITY

As unfair as income inequality may seem, the greatest differences between the haves and the have-nots are found in the enormous disparities in wealth (that is, economic assets) in society. Wealth inequality tends to be much greater than income inequality. The two are linked, however, since wealth tends to produce various sources of income, such as dividends and interest. Those with significant amounts of income from such sources are far more likely to rank toward the top of the stratification system in terms of income than are those who rely mainly on wages and salaries.

Like income inequality, wealth inequality has tended to increase in recent years in the United States and other Western countries (Mishel and Bivens 2011; Wilterdink 2007). More than 80 percent of the wealth gain in the United States between 1983 and 2009 went to the wealthiest 5 percent of the population. Over the last three decades, the wealth of the top 0.1 percent of households has increased from 7 to 22 percent of the total. In contrast, the poorest 60 percent of the population saw a 7.5 percent *decline* in wealth. Their wealth has eroded because of such factors as the collapse of housing values and stagnant

DIGITAL LIVING

Stratification in the New Sharing Economy

In the sharing economy, instead of buying or renting in the usual ways, we share goods and services—at low cost or free of charge—with others (Gansky 2010; Stein 2015). Instead of renting a hotel room, we can get a room in a private home, or even an entire home, through the online site Airbnb. Instead of hailing a taxi, we can use Uber's smartphone app and get a prepaid ride in a private automobile.

The sharing economy is clearly the wave of the future. But while some sharing is free of profit making and the exchange of money (Atsushi 2014), big businesses have become deeply engaged, and the sharing economy is growing highly stratified.

At the top are the founders, executives, and financiers of the most successful companies. Uber is now valued at about $50 billion (Tam and de la Merced 2015), and its founders are likely to be millionaires or even billionaires. But for most of the drivers the job is part-time and the pay is low. Drivers use their own cars, pay their own expenses, and lack benefits and job security. Worse, their success is costing traditional taxi drivers their jobs.

Airbnb, valued at about $800 million, has created a similar stratification system, with founders and executives on top and many who list their apartments and homes nearer the bottom. However, not all of

In the sharing economy, Internet platforms allow people to find accommodations that others are willing to rent to them.

those participants are actually individuals sharing space with others. In New York City, commercial operators supply over a third of Airbnb rental units and earn over a third of the profits. Some critics argue that at least in this case, "the very term 'sharing economy' is ridiculous" (Streitfeld 2014: A1).

Belk (2014) argues that in all these cases and many others, sharing is being transformed into "pseudo-sharing" by, among others, profit-making organizations that have found in it a way to grow

rich. The sharing economy is creating a new stratification system, or at least new positions in the current system. Many will be at or near the bottom.

Think About It

Do you think the stratification taking place in the sharing economy is inevitable? Why or why not? Should consumers avoid participating in this economy, even if the services offered are desirable and affordable? Why or why not?

wages (Saez and Zucman 2014a), as well as the large number of people who have given up and left the labor force, thus earning no income and acquiring no wealth (Appelbaum 2014).

As with income inequality, the super-rich (the top 0.01 percent in terms of wealth) are growing dramatically better off in terms of wealth. The share of the wealth for the top 0.01 percent grew from about 3 percent in 1960 to about 11 percent in 2012.

Wealth brings with it a wide range of advantages:

- It can be invested to generate income and ultimately even greater wealth.
- It can be used to purchase material comforts of all sorts: large homes, vacation retreats, luxury cars, and custom-tailored clothes, as well as the services of housekeepers, gardeners, and personal trainers.

- It can afford a high level of financial security, allowing the wealthy, if they wish, to retire at an early age.

- It purchases far more freedom and autonomy than less wealthy individuals can acquire, such as the freedom to leave unsatisfactory employment without worrying about how the bills will be paid.

- It can be passed on to offspring, even generations away, guaranteeing that they live a similarly privileged lifestyle.

Wealth and the growing disparities in wealth received enormous academic and media attention in 2014 with the publication of economist Thomas Piketty's *Capital in the Twenty-First Century* (2014; see also Antonio 2014). Piketty sees wealth as being of greater importance than income. Rather than relying on pay or a salary (even though it might be high) for their labor, those with wealth rely much more on the income their wealth produces, such as earned interest, rental from properties, dividends on stocks and bonds, and royalties. Overall returns from such sources have historically outstripped increases in salaries and pay.

Status, Power, and Wealth

Perhaps of greatest importance is the fact that wealth not only accords a high-level position on one dimension of stratification, social class, but it is also an important factor in gaining similar positions on the other dimensions of stratification, status and power. In terms of status, the wealthy can afford more and better-quality education. They can, for example, send their children to very expensive and exclusive prep schools and Ivy League universities. In some elite universities, being a "legacy" applicant—the son or daughter of an elite who attended the same school—can increase the chances of gaining admission, perhaps by as much as 45 percent (Mandery 2014).The wealthy can purchase more of the trappings of high culture, such as subscriptions to the opera or multimillion-dollar paintings by famous artists. The wealthy can also achieve recognition as philanthropists by, for example, attending $1,000-a-ticket charity balls or even donating the money needed to build a new wing of a hospital.

Power over employees is a fact of life for wealthy individuals who own businesses or run other organizations. Their needs for financial, household, and personal services give the wealthy another source of power. They have the ability to direct the activities of many charities and civic groups. Furthermore, the wealthy can buy more power by making generous campaign contributions to favored politicians. In some cases, the wealthy choose to use their money to run for public office themselves; if successful, their families may come to occupy positions that give them great power. For example, Prescott Bush made his money on Wall Street and

became a U.S. senator. His son, George H. W. Bush, became president of the United States, as did his grandson, George W. Bush. Another grandson, Jeb Bush, former governor of Florida, is, as of this writing, a candidate for the Republican nomination for president in 2016.

The Perpetuation of Wealth

One of the great advantages of the wealthy is their ability to maintain their social class across generations. Their ability to keep their wealth, if not expand it, often allows the members of the upper class to pass their wealth, and the upper-class position that goes with it, to their children. The wealthy are able to perpetuate their wealth in large part because they have been able to use their money and influence to resist taxation systems designed to redistribute at least some of the wealth in society. For example, the wealthy have fought long and hard against the estate tax, which places a high tax on assets worth more than a certain amount that are left behind when an individual dies. Many of the wealthy prefer to refer to the estate tax in more negative terms, as a "death tax."

THE DECLINE OF THE AMERICAN MIDDLE CLASS

Much has been written in recent years about the decline of the American middle class (Frank 2013). While there is no clear economic dividing line that separates the middle class from the upper and lower classes, we can say that to be considered part of the middle class, a family of four must have earnings (adjusted for inflation) between $35,000 and $100,000 per year (Searcy and Gebeloff 2015). Between 1967 and 2013 the proportion of the U.S. population in the middle class *declined* from 53 percent to 43 percent (Parlapiano, Gebeloff, and Carter 2015). Some of those families have been able to rise into the upper class, which grew from 7 percent to 22 percent of the U.S. population between 1967 and 2013. However, many have dropped into the lower class (which, nonetheless, dropped from 40 percent to 34 percent of the population in that period).

The major reason for the decline of the middle class is the decline of middle-income jobs such as better-paid, often unionized, positions in manufacturing, usually owing to technological change (Ford 2015). In other cases, those jobs have been lost to successful companies elsewhere in the world. Some displaced workers have been able to get better-paying jobs and thereby move up the stratification hierarchy. However, many more have had to take lower-paying service jobs, such as in the fast-food industry. They have likely dropped into the lower class, as have those unable to find jobs or unwilling to accept poorly paid work.

Another major factor in the decline of the middle class is wage stagnation in the kinds of jobs that members of this

Sudhir Venkatesh's Floating City

Sudhir Venkatesh is a professor of sociology at Columbia University who operates as a public sociologist in a number of different ways. He has a blog, has written op-ed pieces for major newspapers, and has appeared in several television documentaries. Most important, he has written several very popular memoirs of his ethnographic work on gangs, poverty, and the underground economy. These books make his ideas accessible to a general audience; they deal with issues, including social stratification, of great interest to many in and out of sociology.

In these works Venkatesh is concerned with the ways in which the poor make ends meet by using the underground economy. This can range from engaging in explicitly illegal activities like dealing drugs and sex work to performing legal activities such as automotive repairs and babysitting "off the books." One of his key findings is that even though the poor may not be officially employed, they work hard. This is contrary to the stereotypical description of them as lazy. Another finding is that it is not only the poor who participate in the underground economy, but the wealthy as well.

Venkatesh turned his doctoral dissertation into the popular book *Gang Leader for a Day* (2008), in which he chronicled the daily experiences of those living in a Chicago public housing development. The residents were mostly impoverished African American women and children, and the housing development was spatially segregated from neighborhoods where people of other races and socioeconomic classes

lived. While his initial focus was on how a gang controls the underground economy through the drug trade, he found that the residents occupied other niches in the underground economy. For example, residents sold candy out of their apartments, engaged in sex work, took in boarders, and gathered scrap metal.

Sudhir Venkatesh

Furthermore, residents established social networks to help each other survive by, for example, sharing appliances and caring for each other's children.

In *Floating City* (2013), Venkatesh expanded his research to include how the wealthy are also involved in the underground economy. Unlike the segregated and insular community described in *Gang Leader for a Day*, the subjects of his investigation were the global, cosmopolitan inhabitants of New York City. He found that the underground economy brings together people from different races and socioeconomic classes. For example, a drug dealer from Harlem tried to expand his market to Wall Street bars and SoHo art galleries, while a Harvard-educated socialite operated an escort service. "New York forces multiple worlds upon you whether you like it or not, and even porn clerks and drug dealers need

to learn to cross social lines smoothly" (Venkatesh 2013: 201). Recent immigrants are especially reliant on the underground economy for income. Many work off the books for the wealthy as cleaners and nannies or in the service industry as cab drivers, store clerks, and busboys. Thus, much like the formal economy, the underground economy is highly stratified. Yet Venkatesh (2013: 146) found that, like the average American, the low-income underground economy worker believes in upward mobility and is "pursuing an American dream in the Big Apple just like anybody else."

Think About It

In what ways are you involved in the underground economy? Is your involvement legal, illegal, or both? Are you hoping to achieve a higher position in that stratified world?

class are likely to continue to hold (Wisman 2013). They may still have the same jobs they had a decade or two ago, but the wages associated with them have tended to increase little or to decline in real terms over that time. As a result, they may

no longer be able to afford the things usually associated with a middle-class lifestyle.

The Great Recession badly hurt the middle class. For example, many lost their homes because they could no longer afford their mortgage payments. Government efforts in the wake of the recession (such as bailing out banks and investment companies) greatly aided the upper class, but they did little or nothing for the middle class (the government bailed out few homeowners in danger of losing their homes) (Hacker and Pierson 2010).

The decline of the middle class is of great concern. From a large-scale perspective this decline creates a stratification system that splits into the upper and lower classes, with an increasingly massive hole in the middle. This leads to growing inequality and to increasingly less hope for those in the lower classes of finding middle-income positions that will allow them to rise in the stratification system.

POVERTY

While some in the middle class have become poor and dropped into the lower class, poverty is a problem mainly for the much more numerous and often long-term members of that class (Iceland 2007, 2012). Those suffering from poverty are likely to be in poor health and to have a lower life expectancy. More generally, poverty hurts the economy in various ways. Poverty adversely affects at least some employees and their ability to work. They may be less productive or lose more work time due to illness. Further, the level of consumption in society is reduced because of the inability of the poor to consume very much. Crime and social disorder are more likely where poverty is widespread.

The great disparity between the rich and the poor is considered by many to be a moral problem, if not a moral crisis, for society as a whole. The poor are often seen as not doing what they should, or could, to raise themselves out of poverty. They are seen as disreputable, which makes them objects of moral censure by those who have succeeded in society (Damer 1974; Matza 1966; Shildrick and MacDonald 2013). However, some see poverty as an entirely different kind of moral problem. They argue that the poor should be seen

How are poverty and social class related? Is poverty inevitable in a stratified society?

Associated Press

as the "victims" of a system that impoverishes them (Ryan 1976). The existence of large numbers of poor people in otherwise affluent societies is a "moral stain" on those societies (Harvey 2007). Something must be amiss about societies that perpetuate so much poverty.

ASK YOURSELF

Do you believe the poor are victims? If so, of whom? Or do you believe the poor have chosen not to raise themselves from poverty? If so, what sociological factors would explain this choice?

Analyzing Poverty

It may be tempting to blame the poor for the existence of poverty, but a sociological perspective notes the larger social forces that create and perpetuate poverty. To the sociologist, poverty persists for three basic reasons:

- Poverty is built into the capitalist system, and virtually all societies today—even China—have capitalist economies. Capitalist businesses seek to maximize profits. They do so by keeping wages as low as possible and by hiring as few workers as possible. When business slows, they are likely to lay people off, thrusting most of them into poverty. It is in the interest of the capitalist system to have a large number of unemployed, and therefore poor, people. This readily available pool of people can be drawn quickly into the labor force when business booms and more workers are needed.

- Competition among social classes encourages some elites to seek to enhance their economic position by limiting the ability of other groups even to maintain their economic positions. They do so by limiting the poor's access to opportunities and resources such as those afforded by various welfare systems.

- Government actions to reduce poverty, or ameliorate its negative effects on people and society, are generally limited by groups of people who believe that the poor should make it on their own and not be afforded the aid of the government. They also believe that government aid reduces people's incentive to do on their own what they need to do to rise above the poverty line.

Poverty in the United States

To measure poverty, the U.S. government employs a **poverty line**, or threshold, in terms of a set income. A household whose income falls below the threshold is considered poor. The formula used involves multiplying the cost of what is deemed to be a nutritionally adequate food plan by three. This is because a family is assumed to spend a third of its budget on food. It is worth noting that many people criticize this calculation for not considering other necessary

FIGURE 7.4 • Poverty in the United States, 1959–2013

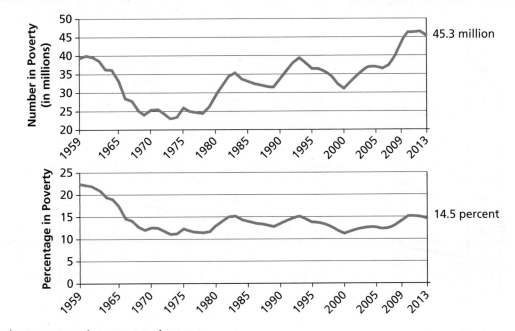

$SAGE datamaps edge.sagepub.com

- Poverty rates for individual counties.
- Changes in poverty rates over time.

SOURCES: Data from U.S. Census Bureau, Current Population Survey, 1960 to 2014 Annual Social and Economic Supplements; Carmen DeNavas-Walt and Bernadette D. Proctor, Figure 4: "Number in Poverty and Poverty Rate: 1959 to 2013," in *Income and Poverty in the United States*, 2013, Current Population Reports P60-249, U.S. Census Bureau, September 2014.

expenses, such as child care, housing, and transportation. The poverty line in 2014 for a family of four was a pre-tax income of $23,850; for a single adult, the figure was $11,670 (U.S. Department of Health and Human Services, Assistant Secretary for Planning and Evaluation 2014). In 2013, 14.5 percent of the U.S. population lived below the poverty line and was therefore officially categorized as poor (U.S. Census Bureau 2014b).

Of course, millions who exist at or slightly above that line would also be considered poor by many people in society. In the wake of the Great Recession's lingering effects there have been calls for a stronger focus on the "near poor" (DeParle, Gebeloff, and Tavernise 2011; Hokayem and Heggeness 2014). Those who have income that is less than 25 percent above the poverty line would be included in this category. Using this measure, it has been estimated that in 2014, almost 15 million people in the United States were considered near poor. If we combine that number with the number of the poor, we see that more than 60 million Americans are poor or very close to it.

Looking at the longer-term trends shown in Figure 7.4, we can see that there has been considerable variation in the numbers of people living in poverty from year to year since 1959. What is striking, however, is the sharp increase in poverty that coincided with the beginning of the Great Recession; 7 million more households were below the poverty line in 2013 as compared with 2009.

As you might expect, given their disadvantages in income and wealth, minorities suffer disproportionately from poverty. While the poverty rate in 2014 for non-Hispanic whites was 9.6 percent, it was 10.5 percent for Asians—down significantly from 16.1 percent in the mid-1980s, but still higher than for non-Hispanic whites. Even more telling, the poverty rate was over 20 percent for both blacks (27.2 percent) and Hispanics (23.5 percent) (U.S. Census Bureau 2014b).

The Feminization of Poverty

A central issue in the study of poverty is the degree to which women and children are overrepresented among the poor (Hamilton 2012; Hinze and Aliberti 2007; Morrow and Pells 2012). In 2013, 15.8 percent of U.S. women were below the poverty line, whereas only 13.1 percent of men lived in poverty (U.S. Census Bureau 2014b). Poverty levels vary by age: Women between the ages of 45 and 64 are less likely to be poor than those 18 and below and 65 and above. Female poverty levels also vary based on race and ethnicity: Both black and Latino women are more than twice as likely to be poor as are white women. Also, female-headed households with no husband present have far higher rates of poverty than families headed by married couples.

The **feminization of poverty**, first framed as a concept in 1978, means that those living in poverty are more likely to be women than men (Goldberg 2010; Pearce 1978). Although in recent years the improved position of women

FIGURE 7.5 • Female-to-Male Earnings Ratio and Median Earnings of Full-Time Workers in the United States by Gender, 1960–2013

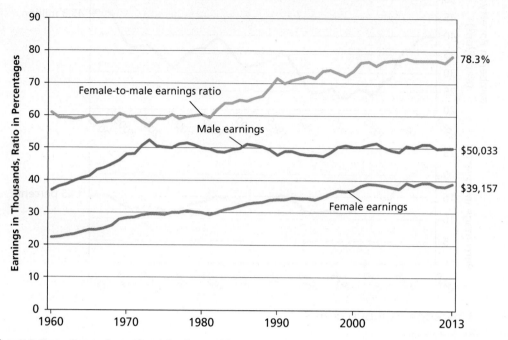

SOURCES: Data from U.S. Census Bureau, Current Population Survey, 1961 to 2014 Annual Social Economic Supplement, Figure 2; Carmen DeNavas-Walt and Bernadette D. Proctor, Table A-4: "Number and Real Median Earnings of Total Workers and Full-Time, Year-Round Workers by Sex and Female-to-Male Earnings Ratio: 1960 to 2013," in *Income and Poverty in the United States*, 2013, Current Population Reports P60-249, U.S. Census Bureau, September 2014.

in the work world, and increases in women's earnings, would seem to indicate that the poverty gap is narrowing, the gender gap persists (McLanahan and Kelly 1999). One of the reasons for that persistence is the fact that the trend toward gender wage equalization has been more than offset by the increasing tendency for a greater proportion of men to raise their earnings through "overwork"—that is, by working more than 50 hours per week (Cha and Weeden 2014).

A variety of demographic factors and changes help to explain the feminization of poverty:

- Women are more likely than men to live alone; single women marry later, divorced women are less likely to remarry than are divorced men, and women have longer life spans than men.

- Women have lower average earnings than men do.

- More children are being born to unmarried women, who tend to earn less than married women and who are more likely to be fully responsible for dependents.

Economically, women suffer from a variety of disadvantages. Historically, males were considered the main breadwinners, and women, if they worked, were thought of as secondary earners. Women today exist in a sex-segregated labor force in which the best and highest-paying positions go largely to men. They are routinely paid less than men, even for the same

work. Women are also adversely affected by the fact that they are more likely than men to work part-time, to hold temporary jobs, or to work at home (Presser 2005). Female workers have gained some ground in recent years: They earned about 61 percent of male earnings in 1960 but over 78 percent in 2013 (DeNavas-Walt and Proctor 2014), in part because of stagnation in male earnings. In spite of the improvement, the gender gap in earnings persists to this day (see Figure 7.5).

SOCIAL MOBILITY

Those who live in poverty are understandably eager to improve their lot. However, virtually everyone in a stratified system is concerned about **social mobility** (van Leeuwen and Maas 2010), or the ability or inability to change one's position in the hierarchy. *Upward mobility*, the ability to move higher (Kupfer 2012; Miles, Savage, and Bühlmann 2011), is obviously of great personal concern to many Americans. In addition, the possibility of such mobility for most is what lends legitimacy to the U.S. stratification system (Leventoğlu 2014). Recent research has shown that people throughout the stratification system greatly overestimate the amount of upward mobility in U.S. society, although such overestimation is greater among those who rank lower in that system (Kraus, Davidai, and Nussbaum 2015). The poor tend to end up in about the same place in the stratification system as where they started; they have little upward mobility (Alexander, Entwisle, and Olson 2014).

People in all social classes are also concerned about *downward mobility* (Wilson, Roscigno, and Huffman 2013). That is, people worry about descending to lower levels within their social class or to lower classes. Downward mobility causes people real hardships, and even its mere possibility is a great cause of concern. Immigrants and refugees who move to a new country almost always experience serious difficulties such as language differences (Guo 2013), and as a result they are likely to experience downward mobility during the first generation in their new locale. This is especially true of those who held high-level occupations in their countries of origin (Gans 2009). Given the current economic problems in the United States and Europe, it is likely that many people will experience downward mobility relative to their parents' status.

ASK YOURSELF

Why should the public be concerned about the prospect that young people today will be less well-off in the future than their elders? What negative effects could this future reality have on social institutions, such as schools, workplaces, and industries like banking and real estate? Would it be likely to have any positive effects, perhaps on consumerism or the natural environment? How might it affect the world standing of the United States as a society? Explain your answers.

TYPES OF SOCIAL MOBILITY

To this point, we have discussed upward and downward mobility, but there are a number of other types of social mobility as well. Upward and downward mobility are the key components of the general process of **vertical mobility**. Also of interest is **horizontal mobility**, or movement within one's social class. For example, the chief executive officer (CEO) of a given corporation may experience horizontal mobility by becoming the CEO of a different corporation. At the other end of the spectrum, the taxi driver who becomes a driver for Uber also exhibits horizontal mobility (Ultee 2007a).

Sociologists are also concerned about two other types of mobility. One is **intergenerational mobility**, or the difference between the parents' position in the stratification system and the positions achieved by their children (Corak 2013; Park and Myers 2010). Children who rise higher in the stratification system than their parents have experienced upward intergenerational mobility. Those who descend to a lower position on the ladder have experienced downward intergenerational mobility. **Intragenerational mobility** involves movement up or down the stratification system in one's lifetime. It is possible for some to start their adult lives in the lower class and to move up over the years to a higher

social class. However, it is also possible to start out in the upper class and to slide down the stratification ladder to a lower class in the course of one's lifetime (Corak, Lindquist, and Mazumder 2014; Ultee 2007b).

All the above types of mobility are concerned with individual mobility. **Structural mobility** describes the effects of changes in the larger society on the positions of individuals in the stratification system, especially the occupational structure (Gilbert and Kahl 1993; Miller 2001). For example, China under communism offered people little mobility of any type. Now that China has a booming capitalist economy, the country has experienced a vast increase in structural mobility, since many more higher-level positions (especially occupations) are now available (Lui 2014; Vogel 2011). Millions have moved out of the peasantry and into an expanding hierarchy of nonagricultural occupations and thus higher social positions.

ACHIEVEMENT AND ASCRIPTION

Thus far, we have been describing a system of social stratification defined by status, power, and class—especially economic class. This, however, is but one type of stratification system. A chief characteristic of this system is the idea that social positions are based on **achievement**, or the accomplishments, the merit, of the individual. For example, a person becomes a physician, and thereby attains a high-level position in the stratification system, only after many years of education, hard work, and practical experience. Conversely, some people believe that a person at or near the bottom of the stratification system is there because he or she lacks the necessary accomplishments. These people might suggest that a homeless person is homeless because that individual has not worked hard enough to earn a living wage. The idea that achievement determines social class is accurate to some

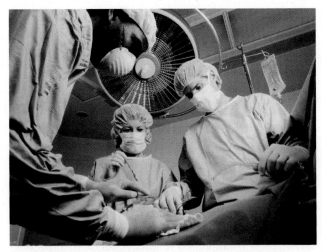

All of the positions on a surgical team are obtained on the basis of achievement, not ascription.

Corbis

While they do not rank high in the stratification system and they are not highly paid, sanitation workers are of great importance to society.

extent, but where a person ends up in the stratification system can be explained better by external factors over which the individual has little control.

A person's status usually has a great deal to do with **ascription**, being born with, or inheriting, certain characteristics such as race, gender, wealth, and status (Bond 2012). Thus, a person's position in the social hierarchy may be due to nothing more than the accident of being born a man or a woman, black or white. At the extremes, ascribed status has little or nothing to do with a person's accomplishments, skills, or abilities.

THEORIES OF SOCIAL STRATIFICATION

Within the sociology of social stratification, the dominant theoretical approaches are structural/functional theory and conflict/critical theory. Also to be discussed here are inter/actionist theories of stratification. Structural/functional and conflict/critical theories tell us much about the macro structures of stratification, while inter/actionist theories offer great detail about what goes on within those structures at the micro levels.

STRUCTURAL/FUNCTIONAL THEORIES

Within structural/functional theories, it is structural-functionalism that offers the most important—and controversial—theory of stratification. It argues that all societies are, and have been, stratified. Further, the theory contends that societies need a system of stratification in order to exist and to function properly (Davis and Moore 1945). Stratification is needed, first, to ensure that people are motivated to occupy the less pleasant, more difficult, and more important positions in society. Second, stratification is needed to ensure that people with the right abilities and talents find their way into the appropriate positions. In other words, society needs a good fit between people and the requirements of the positions they occupy.

The structural-functional theory of stratification assumes that higher-level occupations, such as physician and lawyer, are more important to society than such lower-level occupations as laborer and janitor. The higher-level positions are also seen as being harder to fill because of the difficulties and unpleasantness associated with them. For example, both physicians and lawyers require many years of rigorous and expensive education. Physicians are required to deal with blood, human organs, and death; lawyers have to defend those who have committed heinous

160   Essentials of Sociology

crimes. It is argued that in order to motivate enough people to occupy such positions, greater rewards, such as prestige and especially large amounts of money, need to be associated with them. The implication is that without these high rewards, high-level positions would remain understaffed or unfilled. As a result, structural-functionalists see the stratification system as functional for the larger society. In this case, it provides the physicians and lawyers needed by society.

CONFLICT/CRITICAL THEORIES

Conflict/critical theories tend to take a jaundiced view of stratified social structures because they involve and promote inequality. These theories are especially critical of the structural-functional perspective and its view that stratification is functional for society. Conflict/critical theories take a hard look at who benefits from the existing stratification system and how those benefits are perpetuated.

Social Rewards and Status

Conflict theorists ridicule the idea that higher-level positions in the social structure would go unfilled were it not for the greater rewards they offer (Huaco 1966; Tumin 1953). They ask, for example, whether higher-level positions in the stratification system are less pleasant than those at the lower end of the continuum. Is being a surgeon really less pleasant than being a garbage collector? Conflict theorists accept the idea that higher-level positions, such as being a lawyer, may be more difficult than lower-level positions, such as being a garbage collector. However, they wonder whether higher-level positions are always more important. Garbage collectors, after all, are important in society because they help prevent the spread of diseases that could develop if waste was left to accumulate.

Conflict theorists also criticize the idea that those at the upper levels of the stratification system require the large rewards offered to them. Many people would be motivated to occupy such positions as CEO of a multinational corporation or hedge fund manager without such extraordinary rewards. Conflict theorists argue that providing huge sums of money is not the only way to motivate people to pursue an advanced education or whatever else is necessary to occupy high-ranking positions. For example, the status or prestige associated with those positions would be a strong motivator, as would the power that comes with them.

Gender and Class

Operating from another variant of conflict/critical theory, feminist theorists tend to focus on the issue of stratification in the work world. Because men owned the means of production in the development of capitalism, they gained positions of great power and prestige that yielded major economic rewards (Hartmann 1979). Women, by contrast, were relegated to subordinate positions. Over the years, women's position in the U.S. stratification system has improved with the entrance of more women into the workforce and greater legal protections against workplace gender discrimination. There are now many more women in such high-ranking positions as executive, physician, and lawyer. Yet, compared with men overall, women still occupy a subordinate position in the stratification system. They can also find it harder to rise very high in that system. Further, while males have been advantaged by their ability to engage in overwork and earn extra income, females, especially in male-dominated occupations, are likely to be disadvantaged, and even forced to leave the labor force entirely, because of excessive work-related demands (Cha 2013).

While the occupational situation for women has improved in recent years, the occupational world remains segregated on the basis of gender (Gauchat, Kelly, and Wallace 2012). For example, women face a "motherhood penalty" (Budig, Misra, and Boeckman 2012; Correll, Benard, and Paik 2007) in the workplace that limits upward mobility among those with children. Mothers seeking jobs are less likely to be hired, are offered lower salaries, and are seen by others as less committed to the workplace. Indeed, the wage gap between women without children and mothers is greater than the wage gap between men and women (Boushey 2008; Hausmann, Ganguli, and Viarengo 2009). Recent research finds that women tend to boast less about their accomplishments and to give themselves lower self-ratings than do men. This internalized modesty about work performance contributes to lower upward mobility over and above external factors such as the glass ceiling (Hutson 2010; Smith and Huntoon 2014).

Critical theorists focus on the control that those in the upper levels of the stratification system exercise over culture (Kellner and Lewis 2007; Lash and Lury 2007). Elites are seen as controlling such important aspects of culture as television and movies, and as seeking to exert increasing control over the Internet and such major social networking sites as Facebook and Twitter. Elites use the media to send the kinds of messages that further their control. Furthermore, the amount of time that those lower in the stratification system are led to devote to TV, video games, movies, and the Internet is so great that they have little time to mobilize and oppose, let alone overthrow, those in power.

ASK YOURSELF

Do you agree with the structural-functional perspective that stratification provides an important function for society? Or do you believe, as conflict/critical theorists do, that stratification exists to perpetuate benefits for the elite and expand their control? Justify your choice.

INTER/ACTIONIST THEORIES

From an inter/actionist theory perspective, social stratification is not a function of macro-level structures but of micro-level, individual actions and interactions. While both structural/functional and conflict/critical theorists see stratification as a hierarchical structure, inter/actionists see it as much more of a process or a set of processes. As a process, stratification involves interactions among people in different positions. Those who occupy higher-level positions may try to exert power in their interactions with those below them, but the latter can, and usually do, contest such exertions of power.

To the symbolic interactionist, inequality ultimately depends on what happens in face-to-face interaction. One symbolic interactionist approach identifies four processes that produce and reproduce inequality (Schwalbe et al. 2000). First, the dominant group defines the subordinate group into existence. Second, once in existence, the subordinate group finds ways of adapting to its situation. Third, efforts are made to maintain the boundaries between the two groups. Finally, both groups must manage the emotions associated with their positions in the stratification system. For example, those at the top must not show too much sympathy for those below them, and those at the bottom must not display too much anger toward those above them.

Ethnomethodologists note that people may exist within a stratified structure, but what really matters is what they *do* within such a structure. As in other aspects of the social world, people use commonsense procedures to operate and make their way in such structures. Elites and the downtrodden alike use these procedures to "do" their positions in the system. For example, elite members of society are likely to carry themselves with authority and self-importance. In contrast, those at the bottom of the stratification system are more likely to appear overburdened and to slouch throughout the day. In other words, one of the ways in which people do stratification is in their body language.

CONSUMPTION AND SOCIAL STRATIFICATION

Much of this chapter relates to issues of production and work, but social stratification is also related to consumption in various ways. For one thing, different positions in the stratification system involve differences in consumption. Most obviously, those in the upper classes are able to afford to consume products and services that those in the middle and especially the lower classes cannot even contemplate. For another, the nature of consumption itself forms a stratification system. The consumption of certain sorts of things accords a higher position than does consumption of other kinds of things.

STRATIFIED CONSUMPTION

Fashion is a good example of a stratified form of consumption. Georg Simmel ([1904] 1971) argued that those in higher levels of the stratification system continually seek to distinguish their consumption from that of those below them. This is evident in the realm of fashion, where the elites adopt new fashions, thereby displaying that they can afford the latest styles. However, elites soon find that those below them have copied their fashions with cheaper, if not cheap, imitations. Thus fashion, as well as other choices by elites, has a tendency to "trickle down" the social stratification ladder to the middle and eventually the lower classes. To distinguish themselves from the masses, elites must continually move on to new and different fashions. This phenomenon most obviously applies to fashions in clothing, but there are fashions in many other things as well, such as cars, homes, vacations, and even ideas (Lipovetsky [1987] 2002, 2005).

Simmel's contemporary Thorstein Veblen ([1899] 1994) also theorized about stratification and consumption. In Veblen's view, the elite members of society want to be "conspicuous." In the past, they had been conspicuous about their accomplishments in the work world, but over time, these feats became less and less visible as they came to be concealed by the walls of factories and office buildings. As a result, elites shifted more toward *conspicuous consumption,* wanting others to see what they were able to consume, especially those things that served to differentiate them from those in lower social classes (see Chapter 2). Thus, their money came to be invested in mansions, fancy furnishings, and exquisite jewelry, because such things can easily be seen and admired by others.

ASK YOURSELF

Which do you think is a more accurate description of the relationship between consumption and social stratification, Simmel's trickle-down theory or Veblen's theory of conspicuous consumption? Why? Can you provide examples to support your answer?

SOCIAL CLASS AND TASTE

A person's taste in consumption also helps to indicate the social class to which that person belongs. For example, if you read the *New York Times,* you are likely to be classified as being in the middle or upper class. However, if you read *USA Today* or don't follow the news at all, you would be classified by most as standing lower in the stratification system. While taste can be demonstrated in the purchase and display of expensive consumer goods, it also can be shown more subtly in the way one talks, the kind of music one listens to, and the books one reads. Good taste in these and other areas demonstrates and enhances the position of elite members

This well-dressed man at Epsom Racecourse in the United Kingdom is demonstrating his "good taste" and that he wishes to be distinguished from most others viewing the races.

of society. It supposedly shows that they come from a good family, have a good education, and especially that they value things according to their quality and not simply because of how much they cost. Those without such refined taste are likely to be relegated to the lower reaches of the stratification system (Holt 2007; Prior 2011).

A more contemporary sociologist, Pierre Bourdieu (1984; Bennett et al. 2009), argued that the desire for **distinction**, or the need to distinguish oneself from others, motivates the consumption and leisure habits of elites. In particular, elites seek to distinguish themselves from others by their good taste (Gronow 2007; Marsh 2012). Distinction and taste are closely related to struggles for power and position within the stratification system. On the one hand, elites use culture to obtain and maintain their position. They might do this by focusing on high culture, such as opera or art (see Chapter 3). Such taste helps elites to gain high-level positions in the stratification system and to make those below them accept their lesser positions in that system. Even those from the lower classes who manage to acquire considerable wealth are often not likely to have or to develop the level of cultural sophistication needed to appreciate something like ballet.

GLOBAL STRATIFICATION[1]

So far this chapter has focused on social stratification in the United States. In this section we shift to the global level to understand how wealth, income, status, and power are distributed unevenly throughout the world. As is clear in the theories of Immanuel Wallerstein (1974), to be discussed later in this chapter, nations of the world form a stratified system. At the top are those that tend to be better off economically, to wield great power in many parts of the world, and to be looked up

---
[1]Paul Dean coauthored this part of the chapter.

to around the globe. Conversely, the nations at the bottom of the global stratification system are likely to be very poor and to have little power outside (and perhaps even inside) their borders. Global stratification is a macro-level phenomenon that has profound effects at the micro level of individuals and their relationships and opportunities.

ASK YOURSELF

How do you fit into the global stratification structure? How have the circumstances of your birth, not only within your own country but also within the world, shaped your life chances?

POSITIONS IN GLOBAL STRATIFICATION

The Global North and South

Stratification on the global level is often seen as a divide between those nation-states located in the Northern Hemisphere (more specifically, the north temperate climate zone), or the Global North, and those located in the tropics and Southern Hemisphere, or the Global South (Williams, Meth, and Willis 2014). For centuries, the North has dominated, controlled, exploited, and oppressed the South. Today the North encompasses the nations that are the wealthiest and most powerful, and that have the highest status in the world, such as the United States, China, Germany, France, Great Britain, and Japan. The South, on the other hand, has a disproportionate number of nations that rank at or near the bottom in terms of global wealth, power, and prestige. Most of the nations of Africa would be included here, as well as others, especially in Asia, such as Afghanistan and Yemen.

A society's position in the global stratification system greatly affects the stratification within that society. A nation that stands at or near the top of the global stratification system, such as the United States, has a large proportion of middle- and upper-class positions. In contrast, a low-ranking nation, like Somalia, is dominated by lower-class positions and the poverty associated with them.

While the terms *Global North* and *Global South* are widely used to describe positions within the global hierarchy, they do not always clearly relate to positions on the world map. For example, Australia is in the Southern Hemisphere but is clearly part of the Global North economically. Similarly, there are several very poor countries (e.g., Afghanistan) in the Northern Hemisphere that are economically part of the Global South.

High-, Middle-, and Low-Income Countries

The wide variation among and between countries is hidden when they are simply categorized as part of either the Global North or the Global South. For example, countries in the same category may have more or less inequality. The United States and France are generally placed in the same category

(Global North, high income), but the United States has a greater percentage of people at the bottom of the stratification system living in poverty. Argentina has a high standard of living compared with the immense poverty found in many African countries, such as Sudan. However, both countries are considered part of the Global South. The Global North–South dichotomy ignores many of the important economic (and political) differences between nations within each category.

A slightly more nuanced category system focuses on low-income, middle-income, and high-income economies (and their countries) (see Figure 7.6). As a general rule, low-income countries are concentrated in the Global South, while high-income countries are found in the Global North. Middle-income countries exist in both parts of the world, but a disproportionate number of them are in the Global South.

High-income economies exist in countries with the highest incomes in the world. Countries with gross national income (GNI) per capita of $12,746 are in this category (World Bank 2014a). Currently, 75 countries have GNI that high or higher. As a result, they occupy lofty positions in the global hierarchy. They include countries long considered part of the Global North (e.g., the United States, Canada, Japan, and those in Western Europe). However, they also include countries that are traditionally thought of as part of the Global South, including Chile and Uruguay (South America), Equatorial Guinea (Central Africa), and Oman (Middle East). Some of these countries have been considered to have high-income economies since the Industrial Revolution, while others (e.g., Japan) have industrialized—and grown wealthy—more recently. Still other high-income countries are not yet highly industrialized but derive their income from natural resources such as oil (e.g., Equatorial Guinea and Oman).

Middle-income economies are found in countries that have average levels of income on a global level. Countries are placed in this category if they have a GNI per capita between $1,046 and $12,745. This encompasses a significant range that begins at or near the bottom of per capita income, with the Kyrgyz Republic in central Asia (average GNI of $1,200 per capita), and includes Cabo (Cape) Verde and Sudan (Africa), Nicaragua (Central America), and Vietnam (Asia). Toward the top of this range are upper-middle-income countries including Argentina and Brazil (South America), Cuba (Central America), South Africa, and Thailand (Asia). The World Bank considers 105 countries to be in the middle-income category. Many countries in this range, such as China (and most of Asia), began industrializing relatively recently (the 1970s or later). Other middle-income countries were formerly communist countries. They were highly, albeit primitively, industrialized, but they declined industrially and economically after the collapse of the Soviet Union in the late 1980s.

Low-income economies are in countries that are home to many of the world's poorest people, have very little of

FIGURE 7.6 • High-Income, Middle-Income, and Low-Income Economies

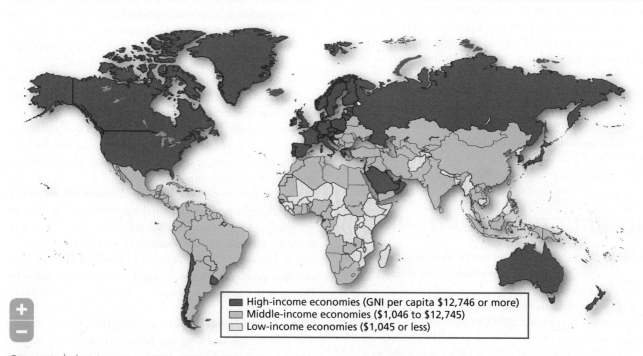

■ High-income economies (GNI per capita $12,746 or more)
□ Middle-income economies ($1,046 to $12,745)
□ Low-income economies ($1,045 or less)

$SAGE datamaps edge.sagepub.com
• GDP and GNI data for every country.
• Related life expectancy and poverty data.
SOURCE: Data from World Bank, "Country and Lending Groups," 2014 (http://data.worldbank.org/about/country-and-lending-groups).

the world's wealth, and are largely agrarian societies with low levels of industry. The World Bank counts 34 low-income countries with GNI per capita below $1,046. They include many of the countries in sub-Saharan Africa, Cambodia and North (Democratic Republic of) Korea (East Asia), Afghanistan and Nepal (Asia), and Haiti (Caribbean). Compared with their counterparts in higher-income countries, people in these countries are much more likely to experience disease, hunger, and malnutrition and have a lower life expectancy. Increasingly, they are moving into densely populated cities in search of economic opportunities, only to find themselves in very crowded and unsafe living conditions.

The Richest People in the World: The Global Concentration of Wealth

There is certainly great inequality between the North and the South, or between high-income and low-income countries, but a focus on such relationships tends to obscure the full extent of global inequality. A recent report by the global charity Oxfam offers a stunning picture of the concentration of wealth in the world (Hardoon 2015): As of 2014, the richest 1 percent of people in world owned 48 percent of the wealth. That left only slightly more—52 percent—for the other 99 percent of the world's population. Oxfam has projected that by 2016 the top 1 percent will have *more wealth* than everyone else in the world combined. The 80 richest people in the world (at the top are three U.S. men, Warren Buffett, Michael Bloomberg, and Carl Icahn) are worth $1.9 trillion, about the same as the poorest 3.5 billion people in the world combined. Further, no individual in the lowest 50 percent has more than $3,650 in assets (Wolfers 2015).

The Poorest People in the World: The Bottom Billion

Also worth considering is the broader category that includes the world's poorest people—the "bottom billion" of global residents (Collier 2007; Murphy and Walsh 2014). The vast majority (70 percent) of the people in the bottom billion are in Africa.

Wherever they live, the bottom billion have not only low incomes but also many other serious problems, such as

- a low life expectancy of about 50 years,

- a high infant mortality rate (14 percent of the bottom billion die before their fifth birthday), and

- a higher likelihood of malnourishment (36 percent of the bottom billion show symptoms of malnutrition) (Collier 2007).

GLOBAL ECONOMIC INEQUALITIES

The Global Digital Divide

By the end of 2014, there were about 3 billion Internet users worldwide (International Telecommunications Union 2014). At least theoretically, the Internet allows for participation by anyone, anywhere in the global, digital economy. However, in reality there is a daunting and persistent global digital divide (Drori 2006, 2012). The International Telecommunications Union found that the percentages of individuals using the Internet in 2012 remained very low in many low-income countries in the Global South, such as Ethiopia (1.5 percent), Cambodia (4.9 percent), and Nicaragua (13 percent). Compare these figures with the Global North, where Internet usage is usually above 80 percent, including in the United States (81 percent), Australia (82.4 percent), and Sweden (95 percent). Figure 7.7 shows the difference in Internet access between households in the developed world (Global North) and those in the developing world (Global South).

The main barrier to global equality in Internet access and use is the lack of infrastructure within the less developed countries of the Global South. Also important are the low incomes in those areas that make complex digital technologies prohibitively expensive (Wakefield 2013). Language represents another source of inequality on the Internet. Most websites are in English, and increasingly in Chinese; comparatively few sites are in the world's other languages (Bowen 2001; EnglishEnglish.com N.d.). Those who are illiterate are even worse off in a world increasingly dominated by the Internet.

However, there are signs that the digital divide is being reduced. This was clear in the wide-scale use of social media in the 2010–2011 Arab Spring revolutions in Tunisia, Libya,

FIGURE 7.7 • **Percentage of Households with Internet Access by Level of Development, 2002–2014**

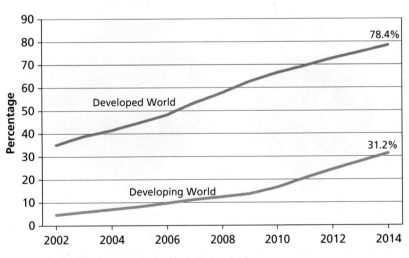

SOURCE: ITU World Telecommunication/ICT Indicators database.

and especially Egypt (see Chapter 15). More recently, the narrowing of the digital divide has been evidenced by the adept use of the Internet by the terrorist organization Islamic State to disseminate videos of people being beheaded and burned alive in cages. IS is also adept at using social media to recruit supporters throughout the world (Shane and Hubbard 2014). The digital divide is beginning to be bridged by the rising accessibility of relatively simple and inexpensive smartphones, laptops, and tablets that are essentially minicomputers.

An important reason for the rapid expansion of mobile access is that mobile devices are not only relatively inexpensive, but they also do not require the expensive, hardwired infrastructure needed by traditional computers and computer systems. Cellular signals provide Internet access at increasingly high speeds. Some nations have avoided having to build fixed phone line systems by moving straight to mobile phone technology (see Figure 7.8).

Global Health Inequality

While globalization has been associated with increased aggregate life expectancy throughout the world, it also has tended to widen global disparities in life span and in health (Hashemian and Yach 2007; Vogli et al. 2014; see also Chapter 13). For example, Johns, Cowling, and Gakidou (2013) found that the widening gap between the world's rich and poor is continuing to increase differences in life expectancy. Economic inequality drives many of these health disparities.

Those in poor nations tend to have poorer health as a result of limited access to health services, education, sanitation, adequate nutrition, and housing. In turn, the poor health of residents tends to limit economic growth in those nations mainly by adversely affecting productivity. The Global South has a disproportionate share of mortality and morbidity, much of which could be prevented inexpensively and treated effectively if the money were available. Of the total burden of disease in the world, 90 percent is concentrated in low- and middle-income countries, which account for only 10 percent of health care expenditures (Al-Tuwaijri et al. 2003). Furthermore, the Global South has lower levels of education, which lessens the likelihood of residents' knowing about preventive strategies and obtaining knowledge about how to control their own health (Rinaldo and Ferraro 2012).

Countries in the Global South also suffer disproportionately from hunger and malnutrition (Serra-Majem and Ngo 2012; von Grebmer et al. 2013). The causes include inadequate food supplies, a lack of continual access to food, and unbalanced diets. These problems especially effect children, who are likely to die young from malnutrition. Furthermore, those underweight children who survive are likely to be less physically and intellectually productive when they become adults, and to suffer more chronic illnesses and disabilities. This pattern carries on intergenerationally as the ability of such adults to provide adequate nutrition for their children is compromised.

An increase in obesity among other segments of the poor in the Global South is now being added to the problems associated with being underweight. Those in the Global South therefore now increasingly suffer from a "double nutritional burden"—that is, some do not have enough to eat, and others eat too much, especially food with little or no nutritional value.

FIGURE 7.8 • **Share of Active Mobile-Broadband Subscriptions, by Level of Development (2008, 2011, 2014)**

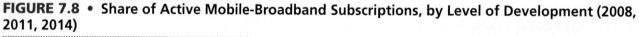

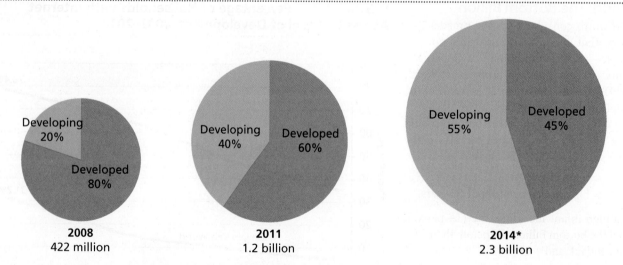

*Estimate.

SOURCE: ITU World Telecommunication/ICT Indicators database. Reprinted with permission.

Associated Press

The extent of inequality in access to health care around the world was made starkly apparent by the 2015 outbreak of the deadly and highly contagious Ebola virus in Africa. While stricken medical workers evacuated to the West were likely to survive, inadequate diagnostic and treatment facilities and even lack of information and transportation were blamed for the thousands of deaths that occurred in Africa before the epidemic subsided. Here a health worker sprays a dying man with disinfectant on a Liberian road while a crowd looks on.

Finally, poor countries are less likely to provide extensive health care for their populations. Low-income countries tend to have fewer hospitals, less capacity for research on health and disease, and fewer people covered by medical insurance programs.

Differences between countries in health care were especially apparent during the recent outbreak of Ebola. Ebola hemorrhagic fever is a deadly viral disease, killing between 50 percent and 90 percent of those who contract it. It is not spread by casual contact, but rather through direct contact with the blood, body fluids, and tissues of those infected with the disease. The most recent outbreak of Ebola, and the largest in history, began in several West African countries (mostly in Guinea, Liberia, and Sierra Leone) in 2014. By early 2015, more than 20,000 cases and nearly 8,000 deaths had been reported from the outbreak (Associated Press 2015e). The figures on Ebola cases and deaths included many medical workers treating Ebola patients, among them more than 300 medical workers who died in West Africa (Fink 2014).

The differences across countries in the experiences of people infected with Ebola reveal how global stratification shapes health inequalities. Guinea, Liberia, and Sierra Leone are all low-income countries with weak health care systems. Compared with high-income countries, they have fewer trained doctors, fewer resources to expend on fighting an outbreak, and far fewer people covered by health care systems. As such, these countries are more prone to outbreaks, and residents who contract the disease are more likely to die. To make matters worse for these members of the "bottom billion," these types of outbreaks involve a self-perpetuating

cycle. The economies of poor countries are adversely affected by outbreaks because money that could be used elsewhere is being spent fighting the disease. In addition, the labor force is negatively affected by deaths, illness, and fear of contracting the disease (Gettleman 2014; O'Grady 2014).

The severity of the 2014 Ebola outbreak was partially a result of the fact that high-income countries were slow to respond, and when they did respond, it was in an uncoordinated and fragmented manner (O'Grady 2014). A quicker response would have meant fewer deaths. Partially in reaction to the criticism, the U.S. military built a $10.4 million modular trauma hospital near Liberia's capital city, Monrovia (Fink 2014). It was equipped to serve 25 infectious patients and was staffed by 69 workers from the U.S. Public Health Service.

Gender Stratification

Inequality in Employment, Occupations, and Wealth.

While men's labor force participation rates worldwide have decreased slightly over the last several decades, a notable increase has occurred in women's labor force participation, particularly in the Americas and Western Europe. There are significant variations within and across regions, but women's labor force participation has also risen substantially in sub-Saharan Africa, North Africa, Eastern Europe, Southeast Asia, and East Asia over this period (Cagatay and Ozler 1995; Heintz 2006; Kivisto and Faist 2010; Moghadam 1999). While the progress in women's employment status is linked at least in part to gender equality movements, the key factor in this change is the better integration of an increasing number of areas into the world economy through trade and production. Nevertheless, in no part of the world are women as involved as men in the labor force (see Figure 7.9).

In much of the Global North, educated middle-class women have made inroads into salaried, professional employment. However, in the global wage-labor market, women are heavily employed in agriculture (Preibisch and Grez 2010) as well as in the labor-intensive manufacture of products such as garments and electronics. Women predominate in such office jobs as data entry, airline booking, word processing, and telecommunications (Freeman 2001; Gaio 1995; Pearson 2000). They are also likely to work as teachers and university professors, as nurses and doctors in public hospitals, and as workers and administrators in government offices (Moghadam 1999).

However, according to the World Bank, women earn less and participate in the labor force less than men. Globally, Gallup polling finds that men are twice as likely as women to have full-time jobs. The wage gap found in the United States is also a global phenomenon, and the gap is especially large in the Middle East and in North Africa. Mothers' wages are lower than fathers' in many countries (Misra and Strader 2013). The historical belief persists

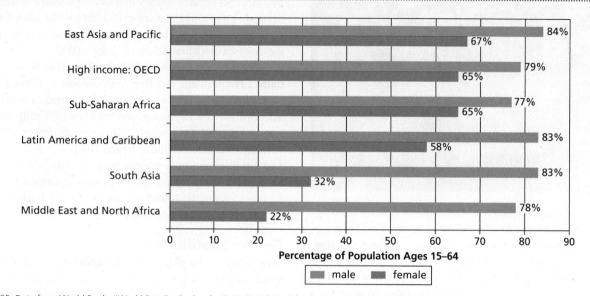

East Asia and Pacific — 84% / 67%
High income: OECD — 79% / 65%
Sub-Saharan Africa — 77% / 65%
Latin America and Caribbean — 83% / 58%
South Asia — 83% / 32%
Middle East and North Africa — 78% / 22%

Percentage of Population Ages 15–64

■ male ■ female

SOURCE: Data from World Bank, "World DataBank: Gender Statistics" (http://databank.worldbank.org/data/views/variableselection/selectvariables .aspx?source=gender-statistics#s_l).

that fathers are supporting entire families (and thus need a higher wage) and mothers are not. Despite the gains made by women, high-pay and high-status occupations continue to be dominated by men in both the Global North and the Global South.

The differences in wealth between men and women are much more extreme than the differences in labor force participation, occupations, or incomes. According to the United Nations Development Programme (2014), men own 99 percent of the world's wealth, while women hold only 1 percent. This provides men a huge advantage in economic power.

Women and Informal Employment. At the same time some women are finding success in the paid labor force, others are being limited by the nature of their arrangements with employers. Informal employment, which has increased in many countries, includes temporary work without fixed employers, paid employment from home, domestic work for households (de Regt 2009), and industrial work for subcontractors. Informal sectors are characterized by low pay and a lack of secure contracts, worker benefits, and social protections (Kabeer, Sudarshan, and Milward 2013). Informal sector workers often earn below legal minimum wage and may not be paid on time.

While greater informal employment characterizes the entire labor force globally, women and men are concentrated in different types of informal work (Vanek et al. 2014). Men are concentrated mainly in informal wage-based jobs and agricultural employment, while women are typically concentrated in nonagricultural employment, domestic work, and unpaid work in family enterprises. Compared with men's

informal employment, women's employment is much more likely to have lower hourly wages and less stability. Many women accept the lower wages and less formal working arrangements of home-based work in order to be able to continue to carry out household responsibilities.

Women in Global Care Chains. Another form of global gender inequality occurs within families through caregiving work. As men and women from low-income countries migrate to find better-paying jobs, women especially find employment in domestic work. Arlie Hochschild (2000) argues that the migration of domestic workers creates **global care chains** that involve a series of personal relationships

Child care is a critical part of the global care chain.

National Geographic

Domestic Workers in Kuwait

Because oil usually commands a high price on the global market, Kuwait, a small Persian Gulf nation-state with vast oil reserves, is exceptionally wealthy. Kuwait's wealth conveys many advantages to its citizens, who enjoy state-funded education, health care, and retirement income, as well as virtually guaranteed employment, usually in the oil industry or investment banking. Wealth allows Kuwaitis to hire domestic workers, mostly women, from many relatively poor countries, including the Philippines, Sri Lanka, Nepal, and Indonesia (Fahim 2010). Attracted to Kuwait by higher wages than they could earn elsewhere, these workers can send large sums home, but power relationships between them and their employers are starkly unequal (Fernandez 2010).

While some workers are treated well, a large number have complained of sexual and/or physical abuse, unpaid wages, and withholding of their passports. One maid said she was allowed to sleep only two hours a night and finally left when asked to wash windows at 3:00 a.m. A Sri Lankan maid escaped what she claimed had been 13 years of imprisonment, without pay, by her Kuwaiti employer. A Filipina maid was reported to have been tortured and killed by employers who tried to make her death appear an accident. When one Filipina domestic sought help because she was being abused by the family she worked for, her employers threw her out a third-floor window, breaking her back. Many domestics have fled to their home countries' embassies for protection, sleeping there on their luggage or on the floor in crowded rooms.

Globalization is drawing large numbers of poor people far from home in the hope of finding work; some are trafficked illegally. In many places, including the United States, such immigrants have few if any rights and are subject to a wide range of abuses. Existing at the bottom of often very highly stratified societies without rights, representation, or resources, they are often powerless.

A maid sweeps the front of her employers' house in Kuwait. Laws to protect such workers from abuse and exploitation have been slow in coming. Why?

Think About It

What accounts for the huge disparity in power between wealthy employers and the immigrants who work as their household help? Why do agencies that try to help these employees tend to focus on individual cases and not on the wider problem of power inequality? Would addressing power issues be more effective in the long run? Why or why not?

---

between people across the globe based on the paid or unpaid work of caring (Yeates 2012). Care includes social, health, and sexual care services, and usually involves menial tasks such as cooking, cleaning, and ironing. In global care chains, women supply their own care labor to their employers while consuming other women's care labor, both paid and unpaid. Migrant domestic workers often rely on female relatives, neighbors, and daughters as well as paid domestic workers for the care of their children back in their home countries.

The transfer of reproductive labor from women in high-income countries to those in low-income countries points to a paradoxical situation in women's empowerment through participation in the labor force. While women in the North are able to undertake careers, they tend to pass their caregiving work on to low-wage immigrant workers. As a result, the worth of reproductive labor (and of women) declines even further (Parreñas 2001). In this sense, women's labor force participation does not necessarily result in a change in traditional gender roles, but rather in the greater exploitation of immigrant women by middle- and upper-class women.

CHANGING POSITIONS IN GLOBAL STRATIFICATION

Despite the several forms of global inequality discussed above, it is possible for countries to develop economically and change their positions within the global stratification system. This section examines the risky strategy of a race to the bottom in offering cheap labor and the controversial use of foreign aid as a means of development.

Race to the Bottom

Those countries that rank low in the global stratification system often have to engage in a so-called economic race to the bottom in order to have a chance of eventually moving up the global hierarchy. The basic method is to offer lower prices than the competition—usually other low-ranking countries. Such nations may lower prices by reducing costs, which they do by offering their citizens lower wages, poorer working conditions, and longer hours. Figure 7.10 shows wage disparities among countries; pay special attention to the disparities between the Global North and South. An especially desperate nation will go further than the others to reduce wages and worsen working conditions in order to lower costs and attract the interest and investments of multinational corporations. However, the "winning" low-income nation remains a favorite

of the multinationals only until it is undercut by another low-ranking country eager for jobs.

ASK YOURSELF

What could the Global North do to reduce other countries' need to engage in the race to the bottom? Why have such efforts so far been few and generally ineffective? How would slowing or even ending the race to the bottom affect the trend toward consumerism in the countries of the Global North?

In actuality, winning the race to the bottom might mean that a country remains at or near the bottom. For example, some countries compete in the world economy by focusing on agricultural exports and employing cheap local labor to plant and harvest crops. As countries battle with one another by paying workers less money, they make their agricultural goods cheaper on the global market. But if these export sectors do not eventually transition to other types of goods and

FIGURE 7.10 • Minimum Wage Rates for Selected Countries, 2013

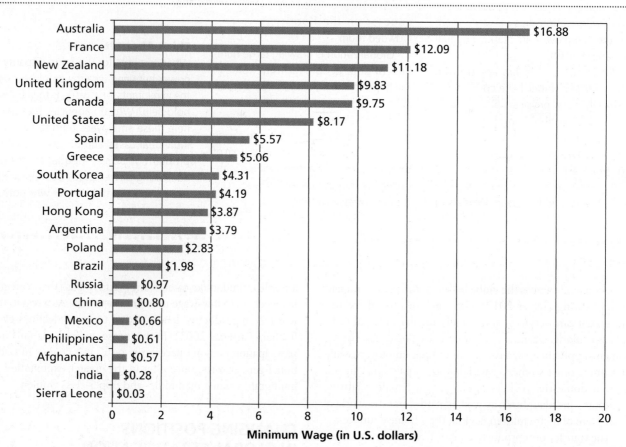

SOURCE: Data from Matthew Boesler, "Here's How America's Minimum Wage Stacks Up against Countries Like India, Russia, Greece, and France," *Business Insider*, August 19, 2013.

services, with higher wages, then the countries might never lift themselves off the bottom.

Foreign Aid and Development[2]

Another way in which global economic inequality can be addressed is through the use of foreign aid to improve a poor country's position within the world economy. **Foreign aid** is defined as economic assistance given by countries or global institutions to a foreign country in order to promote its development and social welfare. In the form that we now know it, foreign aid began following the economic devastation of World War II with the United States' Marshall Plan to help struggling European economies. Foreign aid has continued to expand since that time, totaling a record $134.7 billion in 2013, according to the Organisation for Economic Co-operation and Development (OECD 2014).

The OECD, which sets standards for official development assistance (ODA), states that aid may take the form of grants or subsidized loans and must promote development and welfare. This can include funding or other resources for education, health, debt relief, social or economic infrastructure, humanitarian assistance, or other development projects. Most aid is bilateral, or given directly from one country to another. Aid can also be multilateral, where resources of many donors are pooled through a third party like the World Bank, which then distributes the aid.

The 34 members of the OECD, which includes most of the Global North, provide the majority of foreign aid. Other providers of significant aid are Brazil, China, India, and Saudi Arabia (Williams 2014). The United States is by far the largest donor in terms of dollars, giving more than $31.5 billion in foreign aid in 2013 alone. However, this figure represents only 0.19 percent of gross national income for the United States, an amount considerably short of the target of 0.7 percent set by the United Nations. The countries that typically give the most in foreign aid as a percentage of GNI include several Nordic countries (Norway, Denmark, Finland, and Sweden), Luxembourg, the United Kingdom, and the Netherlands. They routinely meet or surpass the 0.7 percent target. However, in 2013, the United Arab Emirates gave 1.25 percent of GNI as foreign aid, the highest percentage of any country, with much of the aid going to Egypt (Provost 2014). The average percentage of GNI donated is about 0.3 percent (OECD 2014).

The aim of foreign aid is to generate economic growth and domestic savings in recipient countries, but efforts have achieved varying levels of success. Some of the top receivers of aid (in terms of both raw dollars and percentage of GNI), like Afghanistan, continue to experience significant economic and political turmoil despite long histories of receiving aid.

[2]Miranda Ames made significant contributions to this section.

Critics of foreign aid express concerns about its effectiveness and the political agendas of donors and recipients. Donors often seek to promote the economic growth of nations to enhance their own economic interests, preserve access to natural resources, and benefit their political positions. Foreign aid is also frequently tied to very specific stipulations about how countries may spend it. Donor countries often provide aid for specific purposes, such as education, transportation and communications infrastructure, and the development of government institutions. Issues can arise concerning such stipulations when the intentions of the donor country are not in line with those of the receiving country. Causes of this can be anything from miscommunication to blatant corruption, and the end result can be the misuse or misdirection of billions of dollars (Easterly and Pfutze 2008). In addition, countries receiving foreign aid may redirect their own funds toward the military.

Rather than really wanting people to buy more stuff, this demonstrator is critiquing mass consumption in a satirical way. Such a message would be acceptable to conflict/critical theory.

THEORIES OF GLOBAL STRATIFICATION

As noted above, the dominant theoretical approaches to social stratification are structural/functional theory and conflict/critical theory. These approaches are useful for examining social stratification not only in the United States but also globally.

Structural/Functional Theories

A dominant structural/functional theory of global stratification is **modernization theory**, which explains unequal economic distributions based on the structural (especially technological) and cultural differences between countries. According to this theory, the development of certain structures and cultural realities is essential for societies to modernize.

One of the thinkers best known for articulating and promoting modernization theory is Walt Rostow (1960, 1978), an economic theorist who served as an adviser to President John F. Kennedy. Rostow argued that low-income countries must abandon their traditional values and ways of life in order to improve their economic standards of living. He saw countries as progressing through four stages in a very linear path on their way to economic development:

1. *Traditional stage.* People in traditional societies have lived their lives the same way for many generations. Such societies are characterized by hardship and a lack of material comfort, conditions that they accept as inevitable features of life. With traditional values, people are encouraged to follow the paths of others in their families and communities. This acceptance of one's position in life, and a cultural focus on family and community, does not give people the incentive to work harder, save money, and acquire more material goods.

2. *Takeoff stage.* When people in poor countries begin to abandon their traditional values, they think more ambitiously about the future. They start to save and invest, trading with others to acquire profit, and new markets are developed for these exchanges. This stage is marked by greater individualism and a growing desire for material goods, with less emphasis placed on family and community.

3. *Drive to technological maturity.* A country in this stage continues to experience economic growth with the development of more advanced industries, high levels of investment, increasing urbanization, and higher standards of living. Institutions and societal values become more oriented toward production and consumption, with individualism trumping traditional values and norms. As people demand more material comforts and gain more education, they continue to promote economic advancement.

4. *High mass consumption.* For Rostow, a country is fully modernized when large numbers of its people are able to enjoy the high standard of living associated with mass consumption. In the mass consumption stage, people come to expect the everyday conveniences, and even luxuries, of consumer society. Absolute poverty falls significantly, but societal values have largely moved away from family and community.

Among the critics of modernization theory, some have argued that it focuses too narrowly on economic production. Putting forth a theory of **neomodernization**, Edward Tiryakian (1991) asserts that technological and cultural differences between countries are important for explaining both economic and social development. He notes that economic modernization can come at a high cost to forms of political and social life. A thriving civic culture, in which people can meaningfully participate in political processes, is also important for a country to be considered modern. The emphasis on cultural values is, therefore, extended beyond ideas such as individualism and competition to include democratization.

Conflict/Critical Theories

At the global level, world-systems theory is one of the most influential conflict/critical theories used to study global stratification. **World-systems theory** focuses on the current stratification system by viewing the world as a single economic entity (Wallerstein 1974). It envisions a world divided mainly between the *core* and the *periphery*. The core includes the wealthiest industrialized countries, such as Western European countries, the United States, Australia, and Japan. The nation-states associated with the periphery are dependent on, and exploited by, the core nation-states. The periphery includes most of Africa and parts of Asia (Indonesia, Vietnam, Afghanistan), the Middle East (Iran, Syria), and South America (Peru, Bolivia). There are also a number of states in the middle, the *semiperiphery,* including much of Eastern Europe, Thailand, India, China, South Africa, Brazil, and Argentina.

Core nation-states have helped keep the countries of the periphery focused on narrow export-oriented economies rather than on developing their industrial capacity. The "race to the bottom" discussed above benefits the core by providing the periphery's cheap labor and helps keep profits flowing back to the core. The core can also make loans to peripheral countries, but because of the power imbalance, the core is able to dictate the terms of the loans. Currently, poor countries owe the United States and other core countries more than $4 trillion, leaving them in a weak economic position relative to the core.

World-systems theory argues that we can understand a nation's position in the world system only by examining its current relationship to other countries. Of course, countries in the core, periphery, and semiperiphery can shift positions over time. At one time, Great Britain was the dominant core nation-state in the world, but by the time of World War II it had been replaced by the United States. Today, the United States is slipping, and China, at one time a peripheral country, shows every sign of moving to the core.

ASK YOURSELF

In the context of world-systems theory, could a time come when the United States is in the semiperiphery or even the periphery? What do you think would make such a shift more likely? What could perhaps prevent it?

SUMMARY

Social stratification involves hierarchical differences and inequalities. In the money-based stratification system in the United States, wealth and income are the main determinants of social class. Social stratification also involves status and power.

Since the 1970s, the United States has experienced increasing income inequality, but the greatest economic disparities are due to differences in wealth. People with great wealth often have high social class positions, status, and power and can usually pass these on to future generations. In contrast, those who are poor find it impossible to amass wealth and therefore have little or nothing to pass on to future generations. Members of minority groups, women, and children are overrepresented among the poor. The middle class in the United States has declined in recent decades. While many individuals in the United States desire upward mobility, it is difficult to achieve, and some even experience downward mobility.

Structural-functional theories of stratification argue that a system of stratification is needed in order for society to function properly. Conflict theorists challenge the idea that a high degree of stratification is necessary and that positions at the higher end of the stratification system are always more important than those at the lower end. Symbolic interactionists view stratification as a process or set of interactions among people in different positions.

In terms of consumption, those in the higher classes can afford expensive items that those in the lower classes cannot. Elites use their patterns of consumption to distinguish themselves, sometimes conspicuously, from those beneath them.

Global stratification involves hierarchical differences and inequalities between parts of the world, as well as between the individuals who live in them. Global stratification can be conceptualized in various ways—in terms of the oppression and domination of the Global South by the Global North; in terms of differences among upper-, middle-, and low-income countries; or in terms of differences between the richest and poorest areas of the world, the latter of which encompass the world's "bottom billion" individuals.

Global inequalities can take many forms. There is a large and persistent global digital divide, with widely varying levels of access to and use of the Internet. Differences in wealth also lead to global health inequalities, including vastly different life expectancies, levels of nutrition, and disease rates. Furthermore, gender stratification exists throughout the world because men have greater access to employment, income, and wealth than do women.

It is possible for countries and regions to develop economically and to improve their positions within the global stratification system. Poor countries can offer the lowest wages possible (the race to the bottom) in order to attract further development. Foreign aid can help a country develop and improve social welfare. However, problems are associated with both strategies.

The dominant structural/functional theory of global stratification is modernization theory, which argues that technological and cultural factors explain countries' varying levels of economic and social development. In contrast, conflict theories such as world-systems theory contend that rich countries oppress and exploit poor countries, thus keeping them poor.

REVIEW QUESTIONS

1. According to Max Weber, what are the various dimensions of social stratification? What are some examples of people who rank high on each of these dimensions? Other than the examples discussed in the chapter, can you identify individuals who are status-inconsistent?
2. What is the difference between income and wealth? Which is more important for explaining the differences between the haves and the have-nots? Why?
3. What has happened to the U.S. middle class in recent decades? What accounts for the change?
4. What do we mean when we refer to the feminization of poverty? What factors help to explain the position of women in the system of social stratification?
5. According to structural-functional theories, how is inequality beneficial to society? How can the income and

wealth of celebrities and sports stars be used as a criticism of this model?

6. Compare and contrast the different ways of classifying countries in the global stratification system. What does each classification system emphasize?

7. How does access to the Internet and new technologies relate to the global system of stratification? How can the Internet be used to alter this system?

8. How much health inequality exists in the world? Using the recent Ebola outbreak as an example, explain how differences in wealth affect health outcomes.

9. What are global care chains? In what ways do they constitute a stratified system?

10. If you lived in a country that ranked low in the global stratification system, would you like to see it engage in a race to the bottom? What would be the gains and losses from "winning" that race?

APPLYING THE SOCIOLOGICAL IMAGINATION

1. According to Pierre Bourdieu, elites create a distinction between themselves and the masses of people by defining "good taste." For this exercise, examine how taste works in the United States by taking a look at items in an industry of your choice (fashion, food, art, clothing, cars, homes) that supposedly reflect "good taste."

If necessary, use the Internet to research tasteful items in the industry you choose (search words like *luxury, designer, gourmet*). Go to different websites and pay attention to how the items are marketed and the language used to describe them. In what ways are differences created around these products? How do lower-cost versions mimic these items? Do you think that globalization and the Internet are changing how taste differentiates people? Why or why not?

2. By examining various forms of global inequality, this chapter provides a glimpse of how life is experienced in different parts of the world. For this exercise, imagine that you had been born in a different part of the world (Global South versus Global North, or as one of the bottom billion) and think about how life would have been different for you. Select a few different locations (e.g., West Africa, China, the United Kingdom, Peru, Haiti, the United States) and reflect on how global stratification would have shaped your life outcomes in those locations.

You might consider some of the following questions: How would your life expectancy differ across locations? How would the likelihood that you would be attending college change across locations? Would you have been more likely to experience hunger in some of these locations than in others? How would your possibilities of moving up in society differ across locations? What would it be like to be born a girl in Mexico, as compared with a boy in the United Kingdom? You might use the Internet to identify further differences in areas such as housing, poverty, schooling, and access to clean water and flushing toilets.

KEY TERMS

achievement: The accomplishments, or the merit, of the individual. (p. 159)

ascription: Being born with or inheriting certain characteristics (wealth, high status, and so on). (p. 160)

distinction: The need to distinguish oneself from others. (p. 163)

feminization of poverty: The rise in the number of women falling below the poverty line. (p. 157)

foreign aid: Economic assistance given by countries or global institutions to a foreign country in order to promote its development and social welfare. (p. 171)

global care chains: Series of personal relationships between people across the globe based on the paid or unpaid work of caring. (p. 168)

high-income economies: Economies in countries with the highest wealth and income in the world, defined by the World Bank in 2014 as having a gross national income per capita of at least $12,746. (p. 164)

horizontal mobility: Movement within one's social class. (p. 159)

income: The amount of money a person earns in a given year from a job, a business, or various types of assets and investments. (p. 151)

inequality: The condition whereby some positions in society yield a great deal

of money, status, and power while others yield little, if any, of these. (p. 151)

intergenerational mobility: The difference between the parents' social class position and the position achieved by their child(ren). (p. 159)

intragenerational mobility: Movement up or down the stratification system in one's lifetime. (p. 159)

low-income economies: Economies in countries with the lowest levels of income in the world, defined by the World Bank as a gross national income per capita below $1,046. (p. 164)

middle-income economies: Economies in countries with income that is average for the world, defined by the World

Bank in 2014 as having a gross national income per capita of between $1,046 and $12,745 (p. 164)

modernization theory: A structural-functionalist theory that explains unequal economic distributions based on the structural (especially technological) and cultural differences between countries. (p. 172)

neomodernization: A structural-functional theory that explains differences in the economic and social development of countries based on technological and cultural differences (p. 172)

poverty line: The threshold, in terms of income, below which a household is considered poor. (p. 156)

power: The ability to get others to do what you want them to do, even if it is against their will. (p. 151)

social class: One's economic position in the stratification system, especially one's occupation, which strongly determines and reflects one's income and wealth. (p. 150)

social mobility: The ability or inability to change one's position in the social hierarchy. (p. 158)

social stratification: Hierarchical differences and inequalities in economic positions, as well as in other important areas, especially political power and status or social honor. (p. 150)

structural mobility: The effect of changes in the larger society on the position of individuals in the stratification system, especially the occupational structure. (p. 159)

vertical mobility: Both upward and downward mobility. (p. 159)

wealth: The total amount of a person's assets less the total of various kinds of debts. (p. 151)

world-systems theory: A system of thought that focuses on the stratification of nation-states on a global scale. (p. 172)

$SAGE edge™ edge.sagepub.com/ritzeressentials2e

SAGE edge offers a robust online environment featuring an impressive array of free tools and resources for review, study, and further exploration, keeping both instructors and students on the cutting edge of teaching and learning.

LEARNING OBJECTIVES	FOR FURTHER EXPLORATION AND APPLICATION
LO 7-1: Describe the dimensions of social stratification in the United States.	▶ Social Stratification in the United States ● How Should We Distribute Our Wealth? ● Are You Important?
LO 7-2: Identify the factors involved in U.S. economic inequality.	▶ Land of the Free or Home of the Poor ● The Collapse of Minnesota's "Iron Range" ● Face the Facts on Economic Inequality
LO 7-3: Identify the types of social mobility in the United States.	▶ Obama on Social Mobility in America ● Challenges to Climbing the Ladder in the United States ● Social Class and Mobility Interactive Graph
LO 7-4: Discuss structural/functional, conflict/critical, and inter/actionist theories of social stratification.	▶ Functionalism versus Conflict Theory ● Working 3 Jobs in a Time of Recovery ● The U.S. Equal Employment Opportunity Commission
LO 7-5: Explain the relationship between consumption and social stratification in the United States.	▶ Bill Gates: Don't Tax My Income, Tax My Consumption ● How the Luxury Fashion Industry Became All Business ● 2014 Consumer Expenditures Report
LO 7-6: Describe the positions in global stratification.	▶ How and Why Global Fast Food Workers Unite ● When the World Bank Does More Harm Than Good ● Global Stratification: Quality of Life Across the Globe
LO 7-7: Discuss global economic inequalities.	▶ A Global View of the Digital Divide ● U.N. Reports that No Country Has Achieved Equality For Women ● Nurse Confessions: Don't Get Sick in July
LO 7-8: Explain why and how positions change in global stratification.	▶ Bill and Melinda Gates on the Top 3 Myths of Poverty ● Dr. Paul Farmer Joins West Africa's Fight against Ebola ● The World Bank's Broken Promise to Protect the Poor
LO 7-9: Discuss structural/functional and conflict/critical theories of global stratification.	▶ Examining Globalization Theories ● Lifting Families out of Poverty ● The Historical Development of Global Stratification

RACE AND ETHNICITY

Minorities Acquire Political Power

Evo Morales, a widely popular union leader and political activist, was elected and then reelected president of Bolivia on the basis of an unorthodox leadership style and a reformist agenda. Morales not only brought Bolivia a new socialist mandate and a reformed constitution, but as an Aymara, he also became the nation's first indigenous president.

The Aymara are a racially and ethnically distinct people who have lived in central South America for more than 2,000 years. Conquered first by the Incas and then by Spanish colonists, they lived as an indentured minority group until Bolivia won its independence in 1825. Despite achieving legal freedom, however, the Aymara continued to be stereotyped, discriminated against, and marginalized by the country's Spanish-descended majority.

After nearly two centuries of marginalization, the Aymara rose via a number of social movements, one led by Morales, to achieve social equality and political power for Bolivia's indigenous populations. Running on a string of successful movement actions (including the ousting of the previous president) and a populist platform of farmers' rights and antimilitarism, Morales transcended old stereotypes and expectations, rising to his country's highest office.

Like Nelson Mandela before him in South Africa and Barack Obama, his U.S. contemporary, Evo Morales is a symbol of a particular culture's ongoing struggle with prejudice, racism, and institutional discrimination. His presidency marks an important step in Bolivia's social evolution, but it by no means signifies that the Aymara have achieved social equality. Racism and ethnic discrimination have permeated Bolivia for hundreds—if not thousands—of years. During that time, the country's dominant groups have accumulated wealth, power, and prestige—assets they have been reluctant to share.

It took roughly eight generations for Bolivia to elect its first indigenous president and slightly longer for the United States to elect its

LEARNING OBJECTIVES

8-1 Contrast historical and recent views of racial categories and ethnic identities in the United States.

8-2 Describe the effects of stereotypes, prejudice, discrimination, and the social construction of difference on majority–minority relations.

8-3 Discuss the foundations of racism, including xenophobia, ethnocentrism, and social structures and institutions.

8-4 Describe how globalization is affecting ethnic identities, ethnic conflicts, and migrations.

Getty

first biracial one. These accomplishments have led some to suggest that we have achieved a postracial world. Racism is a sensitive topic for most people. However, denying that racism persists will only perpetuate it. ●

Associated Press

What is race, and what is ethnicity? This Ethiopian boy, newly arrived in Israel, is a member of an ancient Jewish community.

A discussion of race and ethnicity flows naturally from a discussion of social stratification. Racial and ethnic differences per se are not a problem. Problems arise when these differences are defined in such a way that people are ranked at or near the bottom of the stratification system *because* of their race or ethnicity. In addition, those in these groups confront prejudicial, often racist, attitudes and discriminatory conduct. **Racism** involves defining a minority group as a race, attributing negative characteristics to that group, and then creating the circumstances that keep that group at a disadvantage relative to the majority (Law 2012b).

While many scholars and citizens have come to believe that racism is on the wane and that the chances for racial integration and a postracial society have improved (Alba 2009; Khanna and Harris 2015; Wise 2010), others contend that racism not only continues to exist but also remains highly virulent (Feagin 2012; Jung, Vargas, and Bonilla-Silva 2011). To understand the conflicting claims, we need to put the issue of race into a broader context and define concepts basic to a sociological understanding of race, ethnicity, and majority–minority relations.

THE CONCEPTS OF RACE AND ETHNICITY

Globally, many groups of people have been singled out for differential treatment on the basis of "race." They include people whose complexions or skin colors are different— white, black, brown, red, and yellow—as well as those who share a lineage, such as Roma, Jewish, Arab, Navajo, Tibetan, Finnish, and Serbian. You may notice a difference between these two sets of groups. The reason is that **race** is a *socially constructed* definition based on some real or presumed physical, biological characteristic, such as skin color or hair texture, as well as on shared lineage (Law 2012a; Omi and Winant 1994). However, races are usually defined according to social and historical ideas about what has been deemed biologically important. While race is often based on real or presumed bodily characteristics, it is more about what people define it to be than about any meaningful physical differences. **Ethnicity** is also socially defined, but on the basis of some real or presumed cultural characteristic such as language, religion, traditions, or cultural practices.

Ethnic groups may define themselves on the basis of their ethnicity or they may be so defined by others. **Ethnic groups** have a sense of shared origins and relatively clear boundaries, and they tend to endure over time. These boundaries may be recognized by both insiders and outsiders (Carter and Fenton 2010).

While races and ethnic groups have been defined separately, the line between race and ethnicity is not always clear (Kivisto and Croll 2012). Races are often considered ethnic groups, and ethnic groups are often considered races. For instance, *white* is a racial category that is frequently subordinated to ethnic categories such as Italian American or White Russian. Similarly, *black* has become "ethnicized." For example, Davis (1991) argues that blacks in the United States are now a self-conscious social group with an "ethnic identity." The creation of Kwanzaa, soul food, and the development of hip-hop all speak to the significance of *African American* as a cultural identity—not just a racial one. On the other hand, Jews, most notoriously in Nazi Germany during the Holocaust, have frequently been thought of not simply as an ethnic group but, as mentioned above, also as a race. However, Jews do not all come from the same genetic stock; some have Semitic features, others have European features. They do tend to have some ethnic characteristics in common, most notably a religion and a shared cultural history. Thus, as you read this chapter, which at times discusses race and ethnic groups separately, bear in mind the strong overlap between race and ethnicity.

HISTORICAL THINKING ABOUT RACE

The concept of race has an ancient history. It has taken many different forms over the centuries, but it always serves as a way of differentiating among groups of people and creating hierarchies that empower some and disempower, or disadvantage, others (Song 2007). Race has also played a key role in most imperial conquests, often with whites imposing their will on, and then exploiting, other races. During the peak of the British Empire, for example, the British controlled India, the West Indies, and West Africa, all of whose dark-skinned populations were subordinated to the British. The rationalizations for this pattern of dominance included both "scientific" and cultural explanations.

"Scientific" Explanations

Following the Enlightenment, and especially in the nineteenth and early twentieth centuries, folk ideas about race were supplemented with "rational" (what today are seen as pseudoscientific) justifications for treating people of other races differently (Blatt 2007). While Enlightenment thinkers believed in the unity of humankind, they also believed in classifying people along a continuum from primitive to modern. One result was classification schemes based on race (Arthur and Lemonik 2007a).

A more ominous result was the use of allegedly fixed biological characteristics not simply to differentiate among groups of people but also to "scientifically" justify the unequal distribution of wealth, power, prestige, access to resources, and life chances to subordinate racial groups. In 1795, a German naturalist invented the idea of the Caucasian race as the first and most perfect race. In 1800, a French scientist argued that race was involved in social hierarchies and that whites stood on top of those hierarchies.

Evolutionary thinking spurred interest in racial categories. The idea of social Darwinism, associated with sociologist Herbert Spencer, was taken to mean that racial differences were the result of evolutionary differences among the races. One race was better off, and another was worse off, because of evolution. Further, society was not to try to tamper with, reduce, or eliminate these differences; it was not to interfere with a natural process that Spencer (1851: 151) defined as the "survival of the fittest."

Also during the nineteenth century, Gregor Mendel's work on genetics and heredity led to the idea that the races could be distinguished from one another on the basis of their genetic makeup. This idea played a role in the development of the eugenics movement, which notoriously argued that the human population could be improved genetically through scientific manipulation. Especially in the first half of the twentieth century and during the Nazi era, eugenicists defended racial segregation, opposed interracial marriage, and sought the restriction of immigration and the compulsory sterilization of those considered "unfit."

ASK YOURSELF

Do you think the ideas behind the eugenics movement would be widely accepted by many people today? Why or why not?

Others criticized these extreme ideas while still arguing the existence of genetically based racial differences in behavior. With the creation of the IQ test in the early 1900s, IQ was used not only to differentiate among races but also to attempt to demonstrate racial superiority and inferiority. Later scholars argued that it is possible to make predictions based on race about intelligence (Herrnstein and Murray 1994), the likelihood of inheriting certain diseases (Hatch 2009), and the propensity to engage in criminal activities (Duster 2003). In 2007, Nobel laureate James Watson (co-discoverer of the structure of DNA) controversially contended that races with darker skin have a stronger sex drive than those with lighter skin. He also stated that he was "gloomy about the prospect of Africa" because blacks scored lower on intelligence tests than whites. Watson later recanted, saying he did not believe that Africans were "genetically inferior" (Law 2012a).

The pseudoscientific focus on race as the source of significant social differences has gotten a recent boost because of the growing interest in genetics and the success of the international Human Genome Project, which seeks to create a map of human biological differences (Hauskeller, Sturdy, and Tutton 2013). However, the goal of this project is simply "to understand the genetic factors in human disease, paving the way for new strategies for their diagnosis, treatment and prevention" and to "accelerate the pace of medical discovery around the globe" (U.S. Department of Health and Human Services, National Institutes of Health 2011). Relative intelligence, personality types, and behaviors are not a focus of study.

Contemporary sociologists typically reject single-minded "scientific" explanations of race, including the view that genetic differences are responsible for socially significant differences among racial groups. Rather, most see the historical, structural, and institutional contexts of race as explanations for observable differences among racial groups. Sociological research focusing on genetics tends to take the stance that genes matter, but so does environment (Guo, Roettger, and Cai 2008). Conceptualizations by sociologists of race (and ethnicity) acknowledge that socially constructed racial categories overlap with some biological/genetic differences among racial groups. However, biological/genetic differences within racial groups are often as important as those between such groups.

Cultural Explanations

Even though "scientific" explanations of race continue to exist, explanations based on social and cultural factors such as religion, language, and national origin are more prevalent today. Ideas of cultural superiority and inferiority have increasingly replaced those associated with biological superiority and inferiority. For example, African Americans have been described as having a "culture of poverty," which suggests that they have a sense of learned helplessness and

Threats to the Roma

The Roma, often called Gypsies, have long been discriminated against for their dark skin, mysterious origins, and Romani language; their distinctive dress; and their itinerant lifestyle, which often leads them to refuse to integrate into any society in which they find themselves. They tend to form tight-knit groups, marry within the group, and form strong family ties.

A group of Roma may appear one day on the outskirts of a community and live there until eventually they are asked to leave. When they do, they may not go very far and may well return again in the future. Thus, they are an excellent example of what Georg Simmel ([1908] 1971) called the "stranger." They are never too close to or too far from the mainstream community.

The Roma live in many parts of the world today, including the United States and Brazil, but their population has long been concentrated in Europe (Vlase and Voicu 2014). In 2011, it was estimated that between 7 million and 8 million Roma were living in Europe (Lydaki 2012). Figure 8.1 indicates where they are concentrated.

During World War II, between 200,000 and 600,000 Roma died in Nazi concentration camps (Lydaki 2012). Recently, hostility against them has again increased throughout Europe, and while they tend to live in nomad camps under tight police controls and close surveillance, the Roma survive and continue to reinforce their distinct cultural identity.

Given the European Union's open borders, many more Roma than before have traveled from Eastern Europe to wealthy Western European countries, seeking relief from poverty and limited prospects. However, because of the Roma's numbers and other globalizing processes, many European countries

FIGURE 8.1 • Roma Population in Eastern Europe

Roma populations
Selected Western European countries

	Roma population in thousands	Percentage of total population
Spain	725	1.57
France	400	0.62
Britain	265	0.43
Italy	145	0.24
Germany	105	0.13

SOURCE: Council of Europe.

have violated the human rights guaranteed to the Roma by a 2009 European treaty (Phillips, Connolly, and Davies 2010). Some have expelled them, seeing them as a threat to national identity (Bancroft 2005). In 2010, the president of France, Nicolas Sarkozy, ordered recently arrived Roma ousted from the country and had their camps dismantled (Saltmarsh 2010). In late 2014, the mayor

of a town in France refused to provide burial space for a Roma child, although the furor that ensued led to the child's being buried after all, in early 2015 (Breeden 2015).

Sarkozy had offered the Roma several hundred dollars each to return to Romania or Bulgaria (Simons 2010a, 2010c), leading to a storm of protest over efforts to bribe a minority into leaving France (Erlanger 2010a, 2010b). Human rights groups threatened France with legal action for failing to protect the rights of the Roma, who are, after all, EU citizens (Castle 2010). Some critics said the Roma would take the money, leave, and then return, having received from France the equivalent of a paid vacation.

Ironically, Roma culture today is threatened by the Roma's own activities. Many are settling in cities, posing a threat to their itinerant way of life. Their traditional jobs (such as peddling) are undermined by social and technological change. A high rate of illiteracy persists among them, and children in the camps rarely attend school. Their lack of education will almost undoubtedly lock them into a marginal position in society for the foreseeable future, ensuring that relationships between the Roma and the dominant society remain problematic.

Think About It

Why have the Roma not assimilated into the majority culture in any areas in which they live? Do you think they are unlikely to do so in the future, despite the changes occurring in their way of life? Why or why not?

powerlessness (Cohen 2010). While this argument has been used against poor people more generally, it has often been racialized to explain the disproportionately high rates of black poverty (according to 2010 census data, about 27 percent of African Americans were poor, while about 15 percent of all people living in the United States were impoverished; National Poverty Center 2015).

As is the case with "scientific" explanations, there are often problems with cultural explanations. For instance, the concept of the culture of poverty has been used to legitimate racial differences in class position rather than to explain these differences in terms of the structural lack of economic opportunity that African Americans have faced throughout their history. Very recently, there has been a revival of interest in serious cultural explanations that avoid the excesses of the culture of poverty argument yet deal critically with aspects of black culture (e.g., the tendency to devalue traditional coparenting). However, such cultural explanations must not ignore the structural problems facing the black community (Patterson and Fosse 2015; Sanneh 2015). Racial differences, like poverty, are complicated and multivariate in cause, effect, and scope. Needless to say, biological, cultural, and structural explanations should not be used, on their own or collectively, to legitimate racial (or ethnic) differences in positions in the system of social stratification.

RACIAL CATEGORIES

Sociologists point to the fact that racial categories are often blurred and subject to change; race is a dynamic and fluid social concept. There are many examples of the fluidity and variability of the race concept in the United States. For example, President Barack Obama is the offspring of a white mother and a black African father, but he is referred to as black or African American, not "half black" or "half African American."

The fluidity and variability of the race concept are even clearer when we adopt a global perspective. In South Africa during apartheid (1948–1994), there were three racial categories: white, black, and colored. Whites were descended from Europeans and blacks from Africans. The colored category was more complex, including both those with mixed racial backgrounds (who might also have been labeled black) and those descended from Asians. In many Caribbean and Latin American countries, especially Brazil, race is a matter of gradations between black and white, with indigenous descent and social status factored in as well. In this case, it is especially clear that the color of an individual's skin does not determine whether that person is "black" or "white." It is also true that someone defined as black in the United States might be considered white in, say, Peru. Clearly, racial categories embrace far too much variation to claim a scientific basis. As pointed out above, variation within racial categories is often as great as, or greater than, variation between racial categories.

Race data have been collected by the United States since its first census in 1790. However, the categories have changed across time, reflecting the social, economic, and political climate of the era. It wasn't until 1970 that individuals were allowed to choose their own race in responding to census questionnaires. Prior to that time, census takers had filled in the race category, based at times on asking the individuals and at other times on their own assumptions (Passel 2010). Although many people have identified as "mixed race" for generations, it wasn't until the 2000 census that such individuals were allowed to identify officially with two or more races.

Table 8.1 shows the racial composition of the U.S. population based on data from the 2000 and 2010 censuses. Of great interest in this table is the strong increase between 2000 and 2010 in the Hispanic or Latino and Asian populations and the slow growth of the black or African American population.

RACIAL AND ETHNIC IDENTITIES

Because oppression and subordination are often based on race and ethnicity, many individuals from racial and ethnic minorities go to some lengths to identify with the dominant group. They might adopt the cultural values and practices of the dominant culture. For instance, linguistic assimilation—adopting English,

TABLE 8.1 • Racial Composition of the U.S. Population, 2000 and 2010

	2000		2010		CHANGE, 2000 TO 2010	
	NUMBER	PERCENTAGE OF TOTAL POPULATION	NUMBER	PERCENTAGE OF TOTAL POPULATION	NUMBER	PERCENTAGE
Hispanic or Latino	35,305,818	12.5	50,477,594	16.3	15,171,776	43.0
Not Hispanic or Latino	246,116,088	87.5	258,267,944	83.7	12,151,856	4.9
White Alone	194,552,774	69.1	196,817,552	63.7	2,264,778	1.2
One Race	274,595,678	97.6	299,736,465	97.1	25,140,787	9.2
White	211,460,626	75.1	223,553,265	72.4	12,092,639	5.7
Black or African American	34,658,190	12.3	38,929,319	12.6	4,271,129	12.3
American Indian and Alaska Native	2,475,956	0.9	2,932,248	0.9	456,292	18.4
Asian	10,242,998	3.6	14,674,252	4.8	4,431,254	43.3
Native Hawaiian and Other Pacific Islander	398,835	0.1	540,013	0.2	141,178	35.4
Some Other Race	15,359,073	5.5	19,107,368	6.2	3,748,295	24.4
Two or More Races	6,826,228	2.4	9,009,073	2.9	2,182,845	32.0

SOURCE: "Overview of Race and Hispanic Origin: 2010," Table 1, p. 4. *Census Briefs,* March 2011. U.S. Census Bureau, U.S. Department of Commerce.

perhaps leaving the old language behind—has almost been inevitable among nearly all ethnic minority groups in the United States. In the past it was common for individuals to change their names to have a more "Anglo" sound; some changed their names when they immigrated to the United States (Cannato 2009). Some individuals defined as part of a minority racial or ethnic group may physically resemble the dominant race or ethnic group, and they may go so far as to straighten, curl, or color their

hair or lighten their skin to increase that resemblance (Campbell 2010). They might even undergo cosmetic surgery (Luo 2013).

At the same time, many members of minority groups have strong and positive attachments to their racial or ethnic identities. They make this evident in various ways, including by supporting racial or ethnic organizations, participating in group-specific celebrations, taking pride in the achievements of highly successful members of their groups, and resisting dominant cultural expectations, such as those regarding beauty (Lloréns 2013).

MAJORITY–MINORITY RELATIONS

Race and ethnicity can be understood in the context of a wide range of relationships that can be subsumed under the heading of *majority–minority relations* (Chapman and Wertheimer 1990; Farley 2009; Yetman 1991). The focus in work on such relations is often on the difficulties experienced by minority groups, especially racial and ethnic minorities. Many of these problems are traceable to majority group prejudice and discrimination (Jackson 2007). Those in a dominant group are prone to exploiting and marginalizing members of subordinate groups.

However, the distinction between *majority* and *minority* raises a number of questions. How can the white race, to take

One of many ways of showing pride in one's race and ethnicity is in wearing traditional garb and in participating in events like this parade in the Little Tokyo area of the highly diverse city of Los Angeles.

FIGURE 8.2 • Majority-Minority Counties in the United States, 2012

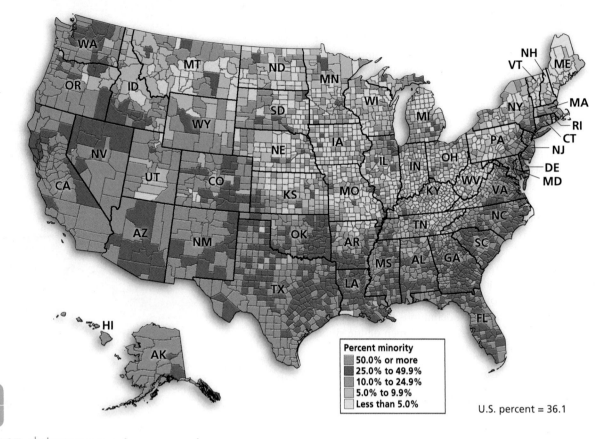

Percent minority
- 50.0% or more
- 25.0% to 49.9%
- 10.0% to 24.9%
- 5.0% to 9.9%
- Less than 5.0%

U.S. percent = 36.1

$SAGE datamaps edge.sagepub.com

• Percentage of population in each county for five major racial and ethnic groups.

SOURCE: U.S. Census Bureau, Population Division, Vintage 2012 Population Estimates.

one example, be considered a majority group when it is outnumbered by a wide margin in the world by those in other races? Whites are still numerically dominant in the United States, but the U.S. Census Bureau has projected that by 2043 the non-Hispanic white population in the country will be in the minority when compared with the combined nonwhite population groups, although whites will still outnumber any single racial/ethnic group (America.gov 2008). The 2010 census terms this demographic situation a **majority-minority population**, defined as a case "where more than 50 percent of the population is part of a minority group" (U.S. Census Bureau 2011c; see also Lichter 2013). Majority-minority populations already exist in California, Texas, Hawaii, New Mexico, and the District of Columbia. Figure 8.2 shows the percentage of minorities residing in each county in the United States in 2012.

Similarly, the U.S. Census Bureau (2012b) reports that there are 157 million women (51 percent) and 151.8 million men (49 percent) in the U.S. population. How can women be a minority when they outnumber men? The answer to this question lies in the sociological definitions of *majority* and *minority,* which do not rely on the numerical size of groups. Rather, these definitions are concerned with differences in levels of money, prestige, and power possessed by groups. As the classic social theorist Max Weber defined the terms, a **minority group** is in a subordinate position in terms of wealth, power, and prestige (status), while a **majority group** is in a dominant position on those dimensions. While these three factors often vary together, a higher ranking in only one or two can be enough to accord a group majority status and, by implication, define another as a minority group. Women are a minority group because, although they are in the numerical majority, as a group they have less wealth, power, and prestige than men.

The same principles apply at other times and in other places. The British colonialists in India were a distinct numerical minority. In fact, this was true of British (and other) colonials virtually anywhere they went. It is something of a marvel that the British were able to control the vast land area of India and its huge population with a comparative handful of soldiers and administrators. The British were the dominant group—with great wealth, power, and prestige in pre-independence India. In spite of their huge numbers, India's natives were the minority group.

THE SOCIAL CONSTRUCTION OF DIFFERENCE

Earlier in human history, quite incredibly, white people discussed whether black persons had souls and whether they were more beast than human. Their descriptions said less about the observable characteristics of black people than about the need of whites to construct a clear boundary between themselves and black people (Wimmer 2013). Today the white majority no longer denies that blacks and other racial and ethnic minorities are fully human. But the insistence on significant differences between the majority and minorities persists.

We tend to think of majority and minority statuses as being objective in the sense that they are based on such externally observable characteristics as skin color, sex, and age. However, the fact is that all majority and minority statuses are products of social definitions, including social definitions of seemingly objective traits. Since they involve social definitions, majority and minority statuses also differ—because those definitions vary, over time and from one locale to another. The emphasis on social definitions is based on one of the classic arguments in sociology: "If men define situations as real, they are real in their consequences" (Thomas and Thomas 1928: 572).

ASK YOURSELF

What does it mean to say that if we define a situation as real, it is real in its consequences? How does this sociological argument apply to majority and minority statuses? To what social constructions you have studied in other chapters might it also apply?

STEREOTYPES, PREJUDICE, AND DISCRIMINATION

A **stereotype** is a generalization about an entire category of people that is thought to apply to everyone in that category. Stereotypes are frequently manifested in daily social interaction. For example, people might assume that a clean-cut, young, white, middle-class man is highly trustworthy. In contrast, stereotypes about racial and ethnic minorities tend to work against them. In department stores, as a result of a stereotype linking black people and criminal behavior, security guards may follow black customers without apparent cause and salespeople may view black shoppers with suspicion (Staples 1986). In restaurants, servers may operate with a stereotype that black diners are "rude" or "demanding." Brewster and Rusche (2012) studied 200 mostly white servers in 18 restaurants in North Carolina and found that because of that stereotype, 38.5 percent of their subjects admitted to giving blacks poorer service. Nearly 53 percent reported seeing other servers treat black customers poorly.

Associated Press

Students at the University of Mississippi demonstrate against continuing racism in front of a monument to James Meredith. In 1962, Meredith was the first African American student admitted to the school.

Stereotypes are the basis for prejudice and discrimination. **Prejudice** consists of preconceived negative attitudes, beliefs, and feelings toward minorities, typically derived from unfounded opinions or stereotypes. **Discrimination** is the unfavorable, unjust treatment of minorities arising from the negative stereotypes associated with prejudice (Law 2007). Racial discrimination is unequal treatment based on race (Pager and Shepherd 2008). Discrimination occurs both formally (e.g., on the job) and informally (e.g., in interpersonal situations). It can occur in any social realm, including in schools, workplaces, health care institutions, housing, and the criminal justice system. Members of the majority group unfairly deny minority group members access to opportunities and rewards that are available to the majority. In the United States today, much overt discrimination has been outlawed.

Discrimination and prejudice do not necessarily occur in concert with one another. People can be prejudiced without discriminating; they need not act on their prejudices. However, stereotypes, prejudice, and discrimination often interact with one another. For example, black women often face stereotypes that identify them as overly sexual and financially irresponsible (Collins 2004). These stereotypes can have negative real-life consequences. Black women who receive welfare aid have at some points in U.S. history been subject to compulsory sterilization (Flavin 2008). The assumption in these cases was that black women would have too many children and be unable to support them financially. The stereotype of black men as dangerous criminals (Bolton and Feagin 2004; Ferguson 2001; Schilt 2010) has persisted and has created grave difficulties for black citizens. Demonstrations and riots occurred in Ferguson, Missouri, in late 2014 as a result of the killing of an unarmed young black man by a white police officer, who had assumed that the young man was dangerous. This was only one of a number of such incidents in 2014 and 2015.

While blacks and other racial minorities are legally entitled to receive fair treatment in jobs, housing, and education, prejudice has been harder to root out. Many minorities still face negative stereotypes. They are constantly reminded that their social group has been defined as "different" from the majority group. George Yancy (2008: 5) has described lingering prejudice as being reinforced on a daily basis through "the white imaginary," a "perspective that carries the weight of white racist history and everyday encounters of spoken and unspoken anti-Black racism." This white imaginary, or racist social construction of "difference," has a cumulative effect that can alienate, disempower, and psychologically oppress blacks (Trepagnier 2010).

Members of the majority group do not experience discrimination or prejudice on a regular and ongoing basis and thus may have trouble empathizing with members of minority groups (Croll 2013). Members of the majority do not have to consider repeatedly whether their daily experiences reflect or do not reflect discrimination and prejudice. Peggy McIntosh (2010) sees this freedom from daily consideration of such issues as "white privilege," which she defines as obliviousness to the sorts of challenges that minorities experience on a regular basis.

INTERSECTIONALITY

Many groups may be described as minority groups. Individuals may belong to more than one such group—for instance, gay Filipinos or disabled Native Americans. People's experiences as one type of minority may overlap and intersect with other experiences common to another type of minority. **Intersectionality** is the idea that members of any given minority group are affected by the nature of their position in other systems or other forms of social inequality (P. Collins 1990, 2012).

Minority group members are seen as being enmeshed in a "matrix of oppression" that involves not only race but also gender, ethnic group, sexual orientation, age, social class, religion, ability status, and the part of the globe, North or South, in which they live. The problems associated with being a member of multiple oppressed minority groups are not simply additive; rather, the disadvantages multiply, as do their effects (Kivisto and Croll 2012).

The converse is also true. That is, a person who holds a number of statuses that are highly valued by society is likely to be extremely advantaged. One of the most esteemed groups consists of people who are male, white, Anglo-Saxon, upper-class, heterosexual, and adult. This could be seen as a "matrix of power and advantage."

The allocation of Social Security benefits to the elderly yields a good illustration of the concept of intersectionality. Women over the age of 65 rely on Social Security benefits to a greater extent than do men in their age group, and racial minorities rely on such benefits more than do whites (Angel, Montez, and Angel 2010; Calasanti and Slevin 2001). In the calculation of Social Security and pensions, however, work and income history matters. People who earn more and work more during their lifetimes receive higher Social Security payments in retirement. Because women and minorities face labor force discrimination and thus lower lifetime wages, their retirement income is lower. Black women are particularly vulnerable, as they face both gender and racial discrimination (Calasanti and Slevin 2001). Since black women are less likely than white women to be married, they are also less likely to receive spousal benefits. Whites, especially men, whose work lives are not interrupted for childbearing, are more likely than blacks and Hispanics to receive pensions from employers. The disadvantages of being female and a member of a racial minority thus accumulate over time.

PATTERNS OF INTERACTION

When members of majority and minority groups interact, the outcomes tend to follow one of four patterns: pluralism, assimilation, segregation, or genocide.

Pluralism exists in societies where many groups are able to coexist without any of them losing their individual qualities. For example, in pluralistic societies, there may be multiple races, ethnic groups, and religions and many languages spoken.

Assimilation occurs when a minority group takes on the characteristics of the dominant group and leaves its old ways behind. In the United States, assimilation has occurred when immigrant groups have chosen to give up their native languages for English or when they have adopted mainstream American cultural values and customs. Sometimes, however, assimilation has been forced on certain groups. During the late nineteenth and early twentieth centuries, many Native American children were forced into boarding schools where they were given new names, forced to speak English (and punished for speaking their native languages), and taught Christianity.

The United States has at times leaned more toward pluralism and at other times toward assimilation. Even when minorities feel that their differences are respected, all majority–minority relations are fraught with at least the

Corbis

While segregation still exists informally in the United States, especially in schools, it is no longer supported by the law, as it was when this photo was taken in the American South.

potential for conflict. Members of the majority group act to maintain or enhance their positions, and minority group members struggle to improve theirs, or at least prevent them from declining any further. These conflicts, potential or real, are generally resolved in favor of the majority group because it has far greater resources (money, power) than the minority group.

ASK YOURSELF

If your parents or grandparents came to the United States from another country, did they arrive during a period when pluralism was the norm, or assimilation? How did this prevailing norm affect their experience as immigrants? Do you think it has had an effect on your life, or on the life of your family?

Segregation is the physical and social separation of majority and minority groups. Historically, segregation was mandated by law in the United States (and elsewhere). As a result, whites and minorities were not able to attend the same schools, live in the same neighborhoods, or share the same public facilities (such as restrooms, theater seating areas, swimming pools, or courtrooms). *Brown v. Board of Education* (1954) is seen as the beginning of the end of legally mandated segregation in the United States. While levels of segregation have declined, such history set into motion practices that continue to segregate majority and minority groups. For example, schools are generally still segregated, a reflection of the persistence of residential segregation (Logan, Minca, and Adar 2012).

Genocide—an active, systematic attempt to eliminate an entire group of people—is a fourth outcome of

majority–minority group relations. A genocidal campaign was conducted against Native Americans, even though an official governmental policy of extermination did not exist. In this regard, the tragedy of the Native Americans is not the same as the genocide experienced by Jews, the Roma, and homosexuals during the Nazi reign of terror known as the Holocaust (Berger 2012) or the Tutsi ethnic group during the genocide in Rwanda. In those cases genocide *was* official government policy.

RACISM

As noted at the beginning of this chapter, racism involves defining a group as a race and attributing negative characteristics to that group. It also involves creating the circumstances that keep that group at a disadvantage relative to the majority. Racism can be seen as a subtype of xenophobia, or "fear of strangers." **Xenophobia** involves the beliefs, attitudes, and prejudices that reject, exclude, and vilify groups that are not part of the dominant social group.

Note that the definition of racism used here allows us to discuss negative attitudes and treatment based on either race or ethnicity. Cultural characteristics that are different from the mainstream, the hallmark of ethnic identity, are almost always associated with racial groups, and so cultural discrimination is central to racial discrimination. In short, racism is based on **ethnocentrism**, or the belief that the norms, values, and customs of one's own group are superior to those of other groups (Brown 2007b; Sumner [1906] 1940).

If you were to ask any American on the street whether he or she is racist, you would be almost certain to be told that the person is not prejudiced and considers people of all races and ethnicities to be equal. Yet racist attitudes and behaviors persist. Minority members are likely to have experienced, or to know someone in their group who has experienced, discrimination at the hands of a white person or within the structure of an organization or society as a whole. A Pew Research Center poll of U.S. adults found that blacks are far more likely than whites to say there is "a lot of discrimination" against blacks (Doherty 2013): 46 percent of black respondents agreed with this statement, while only 16 percent of whites agreed (see Figure 8.3).

Erving Goffman's ideas on dramaturgy can be used to analyze this disparity (Slatton and Feagin 2012). Whites often quite unconsciously conceal or play down their racism in their *front stage*. However, when they are *back stage* with those they are confident hold similar views, they are quite comfortable making overtly racist comments or telling racist jokes (see Chapter 4 for a discussion of the concepts of front and back stage). If they happen to be in a place where outsiders, especially minority group members, might intrude, they may use code words or symbols instead of overt racial slurs.

FIGURE 8.3 • How Much Discrimination Is There against African Americans?

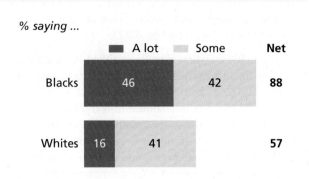

% saying ...

NOTE: Blacks and whites include only those who are not Hispanic.

SOURCE: Carroll Doherty, "For African Americans, Discrimination Is Not Dead," Pew Research Center, Fact Tank, June 28, 2013. Reprinted by permission of Pew Research Center, Washington, DC.

FOUNDATIONS OF RACISM

Social Structure and Racism

In the United States, whites disproportionately occupy higher-level positions, and blacks are more likely to be near or at the bottom of the racial hierarchy. However, this is an overly simplistic picture of U.S. racial stratification (Song 2007). There are blacks (and other minorities) scattered throughout every level in that hierarchy, even in its highest reaches, as exemplified, most notably, by Barack Obama. Undocumented immigrants to the United States are predominantly Latino, and they are much more likely than blacks

to exist at the lowest rungs in the racial hierarchy. About 33 percent of Hispanics in the United States are poor. Large numbers of whites also exist at or near the bottom rungs in that hierarchy: About 13 percent of whites in the United States are poor (Kaiser Family Foundation 2013).

As is clear in the preceding discussion, one of the main indicators of racial stratification is the extent to which poverty is linked to race. Figure 8.4 shows the relationship between race/ethnicity and poverty between 1959 and 2013. The fact that 27.2 percent of blacks and 23.5 percent of Hispanics were below the poverty line in 2013—compared with 12.3 percent of whites and 10.5 percent of Asians—is a strong indicator of economic disadvantage for the first two groups. Also worth noting is the strong increase beginning in 2008 in poverty among blacks and Hispanics right after the Great Recession. The historical influences of such social structural factors as segregation and legal discrimination, coupled with the economic benefits of white privilege, help link economic disadvantage and racism.

Culture and Racism

Some sociologists argue that a part of the larger culture of the United States involves a "white racial frame" through which whites, and to some degree blacks, view race (Feagin 2010, 2013; Slatton and Feagin 2012). The **white racial frame** includes an array of racist ideas, racial stereotypes, racialized stories and tales, racist images, powerful racial emotions, and various inclinations that discriminate against blacks. To a certain extent, blacks themselves have adopted elements of this frame. This is exemplified in "gangsta" style being identified as black culture. It is also found in measures of success—such

FIGURE 8.4 • Poverty Rates in the United States by Race and Ethnicity, 1959–2013

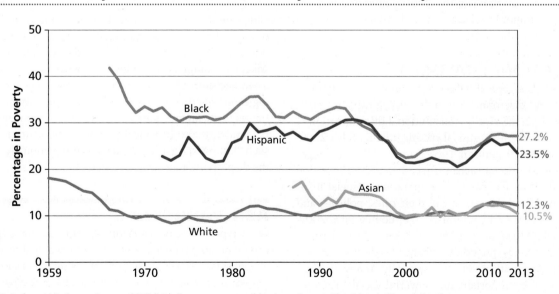

SOURCE: Data from U.S. Census Bureau, 2013 (http://www.census.gov/hhes/www/poverty/data/historical/people.html).

as graduating from college, gaining a professional job, or living in the suburbs—being seen by black culture as selling out or "acting white." This white racial frame is largely responsible for perpetuating racial stereotypes, as is seen throughout movies, music videos, and television shows.

This set of ideas is pervasive in American culture and is found in and affects many, if not all, of its structures and institutions. These ideas come to "operate as a taken-for-granted, almost unconscious common sense" (Winant 2001: 293) in the minds of the individuals who accept them.

Racism has often been, and can still be, a matter of physical domination of minorities by, for example, the state. However, racism is now more a matter of **hegemony**. That is, one race now subordinates another more on the basis of dominant ideas, especially about cultural differences, than through force.

Throughout this discussion, whiteness as a racial category has either been ignored or, especially in the case of the white racial frame, dealt with negatively as the source of prejudice and discrimination against blacks and other minorities. However, white is a "racial category," and whites can be considered a "racial group" (Hartigan 2014). Whiteness can be, and for some people is, a positive source of identity. It can also be seen as a source for good, not only for whites but also for minorities. Many whites are antiracist, and large numbers embrace other races. In any case, as we saw earlier in this chapter, in not too many decades whites will be a numerical minority in the majority-minority United States. As a group, whites will then need to be dealt with in very different ways in any discussion of race in the United States, more in line with the approach taken concerning minorities in this chapter. Nevertheless, the relationship of whites to minorities and the role of whiteness in prejudice and discrimination need to remain the focus of attention in work on majority–minority relations, as well as in efforts to create a more equitable society.

INSTITUTIONAL RACISM

While there is a general tendency to emphasize individual prejudice and discrimination in discussing racism, from a sociological perspective it is institutional discrimination—more specifically, institutional racism (Bonilla-Silva 2009; Carmichael and Hamilton 1967)—that is the far bigger problem. **Institutional racism** is race-based discrimination that results from the day-to-day operation of social institutions and social structures and their rules, policies, and practices (Arthur and Lemonik 2007b; Bonilla-Silva 2009; Carmichael and Hamilton 1967). In other words, racism is more than attitudes (prejudice) or behavior (discrimination); it is "systemic" within society, especially American society, and its most important and powerful social structures (Feagin 2006, 2010, 2013).

Institutional discrimination is found in many settings:

- Educational systems, where schools in which the student bodies are disproportionately black or Latino are often underfunded (Jaekyung Lee 2012).

- Labor markets, where equally qualified black candidates are less likely than their white counterparts to obtain interviews and jobs. Bertrand and Mullainathan (2004) sent out 5,000 résumés in response to real job ads. The only significant difference in the résumés was whether a name sounded very white (Emily or Greg) or very black (Lakisha or Jamal). The researchers found that people with white-sounding names received 50 percent more callbacks than people with black-sounding names. Labor market discrimination (indeed all forms of discrimination) affects others as well. A study of Muslim women who applied for jobs while wearing headscarves (hijab) revealed the effects of more formal discrimination (on the likelihood of callbacks) and more interpersonal discrimination (on the negativity felt from interviewers) (Ghumman and Ryan 2013).

- The courts and prison system, where drug laws and enforcement heavily penalize the selling and possession of the kinds of drugs, especially narcotics, that young black and Latino men are more likely to use or sell. In contrast, laws against use of the drugs of preference among affluent whites—especially cocaine—are less likely to be enforced by the system (Alexander 2012).

- The health care system, where blacks and Latinos are likely to receive no treatment at all or are more likely to receive poorer-quality treatment in, for example, emergency rooms rather than in the offices of physicians in private practice (Lara-Millán 2014).

Most social institutions and structures in the United States are not overtly designed to discriminate on the basis of race. Many policies and practices are designed to be fair but may nevertheless have unintended discriminatory effects. Take, for example, the employment policy that favors seniority in decisions regarding which employees are laid off during economic downturns. This is not an unreasonable idea, but minority members are overrepresented among less senior personnel due to historically limited opportunities. Thus, such "last hired, first fired" policies unintentionally result in the disproportionate firing of blacks and Latinos.

ASK YOURSELF

What type of workplace layoff policy might be less racially and ethnically discriminatory than "last hired, first fired" when minorities lack seniority? Do you think the setting of such policies should be up to employers or mandated by law? Why?

The Role of Individuals in Institutional Racism

Often, individual racism is rooted in, and supported by, racism in institutional structures. Thus, while much research indicates that prejudice and racism at the individual level are declining (Alba 2009), the larger structures in which those attitudes and behaviors are embedded continue to operate to the detriment of blacks and other racial minorities (Bonilla-Silva 1997; Slatton and Feagin 2012).

In fact, discriminatory policies may be carried out by persons who do not actually believe in them. For example, an employee may be expected to discriminate against minorities to please her superiors and to succeed on the job. Before laws against such practices were instituted, many real estate agents would not sell to black clients because they were afraid of alienating their white clients and thereby losing the income derived from selling homes to them. Selling to black clients would also anger white bosses, who might fire agents who sold homes to blacks and thereby jeopardized future sales to whites.

The "Invisibility" of Institutional Racism

Individual acts based on racism are often out in the open and easy for all to see, whereas institutional discrimination is far subtler—often even invisible. Individual acts that are reflective of prejudice (shouting a racial epithet) or discrimination (a taxi driver refusing to pick up a black passenger) are easy to discern. In contrast, discrimination within the mundane operations of a large organization is often difficult to see.

In addition, large numbers of whites benefit from the racism of larger structures by being awarded higher-paying jobs, better working conditions, and power over others, including over blacks and other minorities. These beneficiaries have a deep, if perhaps unacknowledged, interest in seeing institutions continue to operate to their benefit and to the detriment of blacks and other racial minorities.

Because their day-to-day operations are largely invisible, institutions that operate in a racist manner are much less likely to be seen as a problem than are individuals who carry out acts of prejudice or discrimination. This is the case in spite of the fact that institutional racism and discrimination represent a far greater problem for blacks and other minorities than individual discrimination and prejudice. In addition, the comparative invisibility of institutional racism makes combating it far more difficult than fighting individual racist acts.

SOCIAL MOVEMENTS AND RACE

Hate Groups

Most hate groups in the United States are white supremacist movements, with the Ku Klux Klan (KKK) being an archetype. It is best known for its antiblack positions and activities, but the KKK originated as a nativist, anti-Catholic,

Hate groups like the Ku Klux Klan continue to exist and to recruit young people. What is the source of their racial animosity and of their continuing attraction to some people?

and anti-Semitic group. KKK activity began at a time of high European immigration from places like Ireland, Italy, and other non-WASP (white Anglo-Saxon Protestant) nations. These new arrivals were seen as a threat to national identity. Other well-known racist hate groups include the neo-Nazis and skinheads.

In 2013, the Southern Poverty Law Center (SPLC) identified 939 active hate groups in the United States. The SPLC has cited a rise in ethnic-based hate crimes following 9/11. It reports that an increasing number of hate crimes are directed toward immigrant populations, thus reflecting continued xenophobia in American society. Activities of hate groups include rallies, speeches, marches, leafleting, publishing, the maintenance of websites, and criminal activities including vandalism, arson, sexual assaults against immigrant women, and other violence. Figure 8.5 reports the breakdown of hate crimes in 2013 and shows that almost half of them were motivated by race.

The Civil Rights Movement

While we have focused here on various forms of oppression of blacks and other minority groups, there also has been, and continues to be, resistance to this oppression by blacks and others. One major example is, of course, the modern civil rights movement (see Chapter 15), which arose, largely in the South, in the mid-1950s to deal with black oppression maintained by the Jim Crow system (Morris 1984, 2007). Under Jim Crow laws, instituted after the Civil War and Reconstruction, blacks were denied political and social rights and were exploited economically.

Blacks and progressive allies had long opposed and fought against this system. However, it was the civil rights movement that brought Jim Crow to an end. It did so by honing a variety of techniques, such as "boycotts, mass marches, mass arrests, sit-ins, freedom rides, attempts to register at all-white schools, lawsuits, and other unruly

FIGURE 8.5 • Breakdown of the 5,922 Single-Bias Hate Crime Incidents Reported in 2013

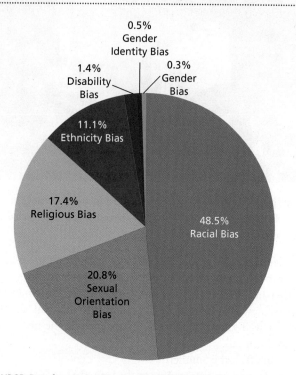

SOURCE: Data from Federal Bureau of Investigation, Uniform Crime Reports, "2013 Hate Crime Statistics: Incidents and Offenses" (http://www.fbi.gov/about-us/cjis/ucr/hate-crime/2013/topic-pages/incidentsand-offenses/incidentsandoffenses_final).

tactics" (Morris 2007: 510). For their part, racist whites and their representatives responded with "bombings, billy clubs, high-pressure water hoses, and attack dogs" (Morris 2007: 510). These responses often took place in front of TV news cameras, and the national coverage served to put pressure on the federal government and white public opinion to reform the system.

As a result, between 1955 and 1965, Jim Crow was dismantled. The civil rights movement of that era led to the passage of the Civil Rights Act of 1964 and the Voting Rights Act of 1965, formally striking down legal discrimination in various aspects of public life. While blacks today tend to suffer from many of the same problems they did before the civil rights movement, the problems are now caused more by institutional racism than by the law or racial hatred of individuals.

Collective Identity and "Power" Movements

After the successes of the civil rights movement in the mid-1960s, several social movements arose in the late 1960s and early 1970s that sought to energize racial minorities. Winning legal rights was one thing, but many individuals continued to feel belittled and oppressed. The Black Power movement was the best-known attempt to raise a racial minority out of its sense of inferiority. Its slogan was "Black is beautiful."

The visibility of the Black Power movement contributed to racialization among Hispanics. The Brown Berets saw themselves as analogous to the Black Panthers. The Brown Berets adopted the slogan "Brown Power" (and later "Viva la raza," or "Long live the race"). More recent politicized racial identities among American Latinos include the "indigena" movement, which elevates South American Indian ancestry to a matter of pride.

RACE AND ETHNICITY IN A GLOBAL CONTEXT

Historically, ethnic identities have been closely tied to nation-states. For instance, until the modern era, the population of Ireland embraced almost exclusively the Gaelic language and Irish culture. However, nation-based ethnic identity has declined over time. One major factor in this decline is **diaspora**, or the dispersal, typically involuntary, of a racial or ethnic population from its traditional homeland and over a wide geographic area. In recent years, mass migration in an age of globalization has had a powerful impact on ethnic identities and reduced their association with given nation-states.

Such population movement has led to the existence of multiple identities on the global stage. This, in turn, has increased the possibility of people having hybrid ethnic identities. That is, an increasing number of people identify not only with, say, the ethnic group into which they were born but also with other ethnic groups in geographic areas to which they may have migrated. Thus, migrants from India to China may see themselves as both Indian and Chinese.

ETHNIC IDENTITY AND GLOBALIZATION

Some see globalization as a threat to ethnic identity; they see globalization as leading toward a world of homogeneous identities. However, others disagree, citing the following reasons:

- Ethnic identities are not nearly as fragile as is often believed. Ethnicity is inculcated from birth, within the family, and then often in school and by the surrounding culture. Thus, it usually becomes part of a person's core identity.

- Globalization can be a force, maybe the most significant force, in the creation and proliferation of ethnic identity (Tomlinson 2000). Ethnic groups and many aspects of their cultures flow around the globe, creating new pockets

PUBLIC SOCIOLOGY

W. E. B. Du Bois and the "Negro Press"

W. E. B. Du Bois, the first African American to obtain a PhD from Harvard, held a variety of academic positions and published a number of important theoretical works and empirical studies. He also spent a good portion of his life as a journalist. He became a correspondent for a black newspaper, the *New York Globe,* in 1882 when he was only 15 years old. After he graduated from Harvard in 1905, he wrote for various black and white newspapers and magazines. He founded *The Crisis,* the official magazine of the National Association for the Advancement of Colored People (NAACP), which came into existence the same year.

Du Bois was the NAACP's director of publications and research. Through *The Crisis,* he was able to disseminate his ideas widely because he was solely responsible for the magazine's editorial content. Among his many targets was Booker T. Washington, whom he regarded as far too conservative. Du Bois felt that Washington was much too willing to subordinate blacks to whites. More specifically, he objected to Washington's well-known and influential view that blacks should be trained for, and be satisfied with, manual work. Du Bois was in charge of *The Crisis* until 1934, when a dispute with the director of the NAACP led him to resign because of the organization's position in favor of "voluntary segregation" in order to further black advancement.

Du Bois continued his journalistic career by writing for, among others, the *Amsterdam News* in New York City between 1939 and 1944. During World War II, some black journalists were attacked, primarily by white journalists,

W. E. B. Du Bois stands (top right) in the office of *The Crisis* magazine, which he founded and edited for many years, but which he eventually left over a policy disagreement with the NAACP. Would social movements be more effective or less effective if all members agreed all the time?

for disloyalty because they criticized fascism both abroad and in the United States (at least in relationship to the treatment of black Americans). Du Bois responded to the critics by writing that "apparently the white world has suddenly become conscious of the Negro press . . . . What white commentators think they have discovered is that the Negro press is exciting the mass of Negroes to discontent and even to violence. As a matter of fact what they are really seeing is the intensity of feeling and resentment which is sweeping over the Negro people" (quoted in Franklin 1987: 240–244).

Du Bois continued to function as a journalist for years, often writing for

relatively small black newspapers, which he felt made a contribution to publicizing the plight of black Americans and gave them an outlet to express both their grievances and their goals. Thus, in addition to being a first-rate sociologist, Du Bois was one of the great public sociologists of all time.

Think About It

Do you think that the press today expresses the real feelings of people, especially black Americans? Why or why not? Are those real feelings more likely to be expressed elsewhere today (e.g., on blogs or social networking sites)?

of ethnic identity and reinforcing that identity in particular locales. Global pressures toward a homogenized identity may also stiffen a person's resolve to maintain ties to an ethnic culture.

- Ethnic identity and globalization are part of the same modern process. For example, through the development of advanced forms of communication, globalization allows ethnic group members to stay in touch with one another for the express purpose of maintaining familiar traditions. This more powerful sense of ethnic identity can be exported back to the home country through the same global media. This is part of the broader process of transnationalism (Faist, Fauser, and Reisenauer 2013).

ASK YOURSELF

Do you believe globalization threatens ethnic identity by making the world more homogeneous through information and cultural flows? Or do you feel ethnicity is a strong enough identity factor to survive globalization, and that global communication flows can help preserve ethnic identities by keeping emigrants in touch with their home countries? Explain your answer.

GLOBAL PREJUDICE AND DISCRIMINATION

To this point, we have focused on majority–minority relations within specific nation-states, especially the United States. But we can also examine majority–minority relations in a global context. The North–South distinction is a key factor. Most of the "bottom billion," or the poorest billion people in the world (Collier 2007, 2012), are minority group members in the Global South. Few in the bottom billion live in the North. In fact, the richest billion people in the world are largely residents of the Global North and are mainly members of majority groups.

It has long been the case that the Global North and its majority groups have dominated, controlled, exploited, and oppressed the Global South and its minority groups. Historically, imperialism, colonialism, economic development, Westernization, and Americanization have worked in large part to Northerners' advantage and to Southerners' disadvantage. The system that dominates globalization today—neoliberal economics—helps those in the advantaged categories in the Global North and hurts, often badly, those in the disadvantaged categories in the Global South (Harvey 2005).

Majority groups from the Global North have often "invented" minority groups in the Global South. One example is the creation of "Indians" as an oppressed minority group after the British colonized India. Until that point, Indian society had had its own highly developed system of majority and minority castes. Another example derives from **Orientalism**, a set of ideas and texts produced by the Global North that

served as the basis of systems designed to dominate, control, and exploit the Orient (the East) and its many minority groups (Said [1979] 1994).

Racism is not exclusive to the West in general, or to the United States in particular, but exists in many societies throughout the world. For example, in Japan, differences in skin color, hair, and even body odor have been used to distinguish among races such as the Ainu and Buraku. Japanese citizens whose ancestry is partly Caucasian or African are also subject to prejudice within their own country. China has 56 officially recognized ethnic groups, totaling about 105 million people; nearly 92 percent (1.2 billion) of all Chinese are in the Han ethnic group. Figure 8.6 shows the geographic distribution of ethnolinguistic groups in China; note the concentration of Han in the heavily populated coastal areas. Uyghurs, a Muslim, Turkic-speaking minority in northwestern China, are discriminated against—job listings specify that applicants must be ethnic Han or be Mandarin Chinese speakers (Jacobs 2013). Uyghurs have held many protests against the Chinese government (Holdstock 2014).

GLOBAL FLOWS BASED ON RACE AND ETHNICITY

One way to think about globalized majority–minority relations is in terms of global flows. Both race and ethnicity can be said to flow around the world. One manifestation is the migration of people of various races and ethnic groups, who move around the world today with greater ease and rapidity than ever before. People from the North are more likely to be tourists or retirees who visit or take up residence in the nations of the South because of the good weather and low cost of living (Croucher 2009). In contrast, residents of the South typically migrate to wealthy nations in the North in search of employment, be it in low-skilled or high-skilled positions (Kivisto and Faist 2010: 49–54).

Another form of global flow involves the social and cultural aspects of race and ethnicity. As we have seen, neither race nor ethnicity is defined by objective characteristics such as "blood," genes, or skin color. Rather, both are defined socially and culturally. As social constructions—as ideas—race and ethnicity flow across borders and around the world effortlessly. A good example is the global spread of anti-Muslim prejudice today. Globalized mass communication helps to spread these ideas, but they are also carried by people who are taking advantage of inexpensive means of travel, especially by air.

Paul Gilroy's *The Black Atlantic: Modernity and Double Consciousness* (1993) is an important work on majority–minority relations that stresses global flows. As the title makes clear, Gilroy is particularly interested in the flows that relate to blacks in the Atlantic region (Figure 8.7 shows those flows, as well as another flow of slaves from Africa to Asia): "I have settled on an image of ships across the spaces between

FIGURE 8.6 • Chinese Ethnolinguistic Groups

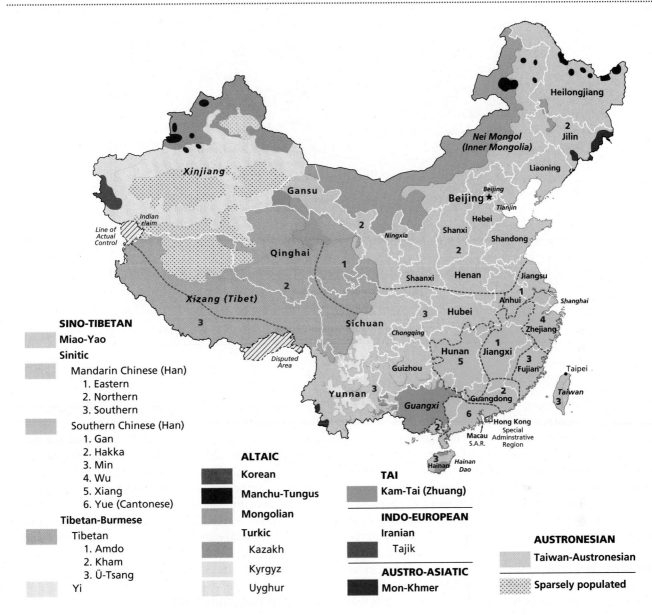

SINO-TIBETAN

Miao-Yao

Sinitic

  Mandarin Chinese (Han)
    1. Eastern
    2. Northern
    3. Southern

  Southern Chinese (Han)
    1. Gan
    2. Hakka
    3. Min
    4. Wu
    5. Xiang
    6. Yue (Cantonese)

Tibetan-Burmese

  Tibetan
    1. Amdo
    2. Kham
    3. Ü-Tsang

  Yi

ALTAIC

Korean

Manchu-Tungus

Mongolian

Turkic
  Kazakh
  Kyrgyz
  Uyghur

TAI

Kam-Tai (Zhuang)

INDO-EUROPEAN

Iranian
  Tajik

AUSTRO-ASIATIC

Mon-Khmer

AUSTRONESIAN

Taiwan-Austronesian

Sparsely populated

SOURCE: Courtesy of the University of Texas Libraries, The University of Texas at Austin.

Europe, America, Africa and the Caribbean as a central organizing symbol . . . . The image of a ship . . . in motion" (Gilroy 1993: 4). This image encompasses the flow of slaves from Africa to the eastern coast of the Americas and the later return of some blacks to Africa. It also encompasses the circulation of activists, ideas, books, works of art, and the like that relate to blacks and race relations. All are seen as involved in "displacements, migrations, and journeys" (Gilroy 1993: 111). Gilroy argues that in trying to understand global flows based on race, we should focus not on national boundaries but rather on the "Black Atlantic," which he portrays as a transnational space.

Positive and Negative Flows

Those in the Global North are able to create structures that greatly enhance positive or protective flows. For example, in the United States, the 911 phone system quickly summons help, and medical alert systems are available that allow elderly people and others who may not be able to get to a telephone to call for aid by pressing a button. Setting up the complex networks to handle these emergencies is expensive. In the Global South, minorities have little or no access to such networks and therefore to the positive flows expedited by them. Those in minority categories are far less likely to participate in the globe's positive flows of money, commodities, food,

FIGURE 8.7 • Slave Trade Routes, 1518–1850

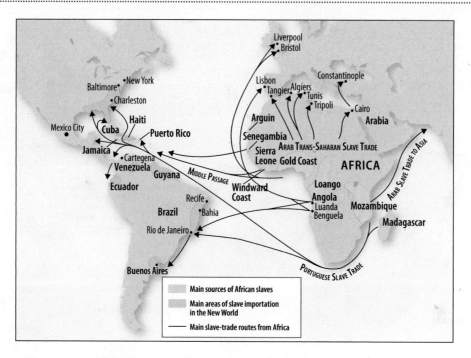

SOURCE: LatinAmericanStudies.org.

health care, technologies, and the like. Conversely, those in the majority categories are likely to be in the thick of these positive flows, both as creators and as beneficiaries.

On the other hand, the structures that expedite negative flows are more likely to dump into, and to be found in, areas dominated by minority groups. For example, illegal structures allow the relatively free flow of weapons into and through many poor areas of the world. Much stronger structures are in place to prevent their flow into the wealthier regions of the globe. Another example is the tendency for people in the Global South to live in close proximity to disease vectors, such as malaria-bearing mosquitoes and chickens carrying avian flu. The result is that they are at greater risk of contracting vector-borne diseases. In contrast, majority group members in the Global North are far more likely to live at some distance from, or to be heavily protected from, disease-carrying mosquitoes or live chickens, to say nothing of the vectors for many other diseases.

Those in minority groups throughout the world are more likely to be on the receiving end of such negative flows as borderless diseases, crime, corruption, war, and most environmental problems. Those in the majority groups certainly cannot completely avoid these negative flows, but they are far better able to insulate and protect themselves from them. Furthermore, those in majority groups often initiate negative flows (armaments, global warming) that have profoundly negative effects on minority groups.

Racism itself can be seen as having wide-ranging negative consequences for minority group members as the ideas and practices associated with it flow around the world (Goldberg 2009). This flow of racism around the world has been referred to as the "racialization of the globe" (Dikötter 2008). Nevertheless, racist ideas and practices are certainly not the same throughout the world, but rather are adapted and modified in each locale. They are affected by local ideas as well as by local economic, political, and military realities. As a result, racism as it involves blacks is not the same in Great Britain as it is in Ghana or the United States.

Racial and Ethnic Barriers

In all aspects of globalization, there are not only flows of various kinds but also barriers to flows. Thus, members of racial and ethnic minorities may be locked into particular racial or ethnic identities, or they may be physically unable to move from particular areas (such as ghettos) that define them in a certain way. They are also likely to reside in countries in the South from which it may difficult to move (because of poverty, for example).

Just as majority groups have the advantage when it comes to positive flows, they are better able than minority groups to create barriers between themselves and negative flows. These barriers can include border controls in the nation-states dominated by advantaged groups, local actions such as creating gated communities patrolled by guards, and even individual actions such as having alarm systems installed in homes. Minorities can afford few, if any, of these kinds of protective barriers.

Minority group statuses are likely, in and of themselves, to serve as "subtle" barriers that impede many positive flows. People in those categories are not likely to participate, or at least to participate equally, in such positive flows. For example, there are no physical barriers, no walls, between Muslims and Christians in Europe, or Hispanics and Anglos in the United States, but the mere fact of being a Muslim or a Hispanic, or being perceived as such, serves as a barrier to all sorts of positive flows (e.g., jobs, useful information) for members of these minority groups.

ETHNIC CONFLICT WITHIN NATION-STATES

Greater ethnic diversity has increased the possibility of ethnic conflict within many nation-states. Of course, such ethnic conflict is not new. Among the most notable examples in the twentieth and twenty-first centuries have been conflicts between Turks and Armenians in Turkey; between Germans, especially Nazis, and Jews in Germany; between Tamils and the Sinhalese in Sri Lanka; between the Tutsi and Hutu in Burundi and Rwanda; between Arabs and ethnic Africans in Darfur; and between various ethnic groups—Slovenes, Croatians, Serbs, Bosnians, Montenegrins, Macedonians, and Albanians—after the breakup of Yugoslavia in 1991. However, today, with more members of ethnic groups in more and more countries, there is the potential for a great increase in the number, if not the intensity, of ethnic conflicts. The most disturbing examples of ethnic conflict tend to involve the majority group's efforts to "deal" with ethnic minorities through expulsion, ethnic cleansing, or genocide.

Expulsion

Expulsion, or the removal of a group from a territory, may seem relatively benign because minorities are not purposely injured or killed in the majority's efforts to get rid of them. Expulsion can take two forms: direct or voluntary (Simpson and Yinger 1985). In *direct expulsion,* minority ethnic groups are ejected by the majority through military and other government action. In *voluntary expulsion,* a minority group leaves "of its own volition" because its members are being harassed, discriminated against, and persecuted. Of course, in the real world, these two forms of expulsion occur in concert with one another. And although physical harm may be relatively light, social and economic harm can be considerable. The people who are forced to leave typically lose much of their property, and their social networks are often irretrievably broken.

Many of the racial and ethnic groups involved in diasporas have experienced both forms of expulsion. This has been particularly true for Jews and the Roma, who have both often either been forcibly ejected (e.g., Jews from

U.S. citizens of Japanese descent were forced into internment camps during World War II in actions upheld by the Supreme Court at that time but now seen as discriminatory. Contrast these camps with steps the government is taking today to try to ensure national security.

Jerusalem by the Romans in the second century and from Spain and Portugal in the fifteenth century) or moved voluntarily (e.g., some Jews left the Stalinist Soviet Union because of harassment).

Ethnic Cleansing

Ethnic cleansing is the establishment by the dominant group of policies that allow or require the forcible removal, abuse, and even murder of people of another ethnic group (Oberschall 2012; Sekulic 2007a). Of course, Nazi actions against Jews and Roma fit the definition of ethnic cleansing.

Ethnic cleansing achieved more recent notoriety during the wars associated with the dissolution of Yugoslavia in 1991. The ethnic groups that dominated various regions sought to create areas that were ethnically homogeneous, and they did this by expelling and even killing members of other ethnic groups. For example, Croatians were expelled from parts of Croatia inhabited by Serbs. Bosnia, which declared independence in 1992, was composed of three major ethnic groups—Slavic Muslims (the largest single group), Serbs, and Croats. Serbian armed forces created ethnically homogeneous enclaves by forcibly removing and murdering members of the other ethnic groups, especially Muslims.

In situations of ethnic cleansing, women and girls often have been targeted for physical violence and murder, as well as, in many cases, sexual violence. In Bosnia in the 1990s, Serbian men systematically raped an estimated 50,000 Muslim and Croatian women as part of their campaign of terror. Since the Serbian police were in positions of power, it was difficult, if not impossible, for the women who were victims of rape to get help or to prosecute their attackers.

FIGURE 8.8 • Select Genocides around the World, 1914–Present

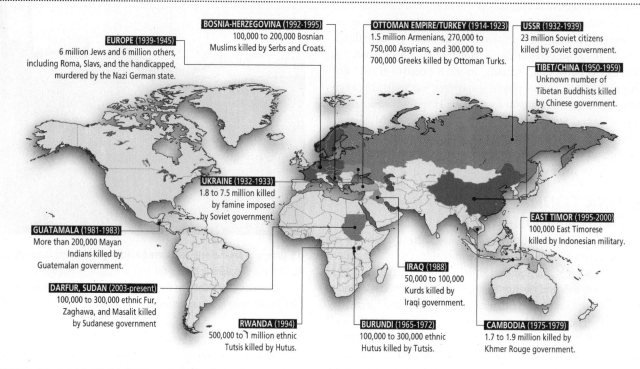

EUROPE (1939-1945)
6 million Jews and 6 million others, including Roma, Slavs, and the handicapped, murdered by the Nazi German state.

BOSNIA-HERZEGOVINA (1992-1995)
100,000 to 200,000 Bosnian Muslims killed by Serbs and Croats.

OTTOMAN EMPIRE/TURKEY (1914-1923)
1.5 million Armenians, 270,000 to 750,000 Assyrians, and 300,000 to 700,000 Greeks killed by Ottoman Turks.

USSR (1932-1939)
23 million Soviet citizens killed by Soviet government.

TIBET/CHINA (1950-1959)
Unknown number of Tibetan Buddhists killed by Chinese government.

UKRAINE (1932-1933)
1.8 to 7.5 million killed by famine imposed by Soviet government.

EAST TIMOR (1995-2000)
100,000 East Timorese killed by Indonesian military.

GUATAMALA (1981-1983)
More than 200,000 Mayan Indians killed by Guatemalan government.

IRAQ (1988)
50,000 to 100,000 Kurds killed by Iraqi government.

DARFUR, SUDAN (2003-present)
100,000 to 300,000 ethnic Fur, Zaghawa, and Masalit killed by Sudanese government

RWANDA (1994)
500,000 to 1 million ethnic Tutsis killed by Hutus.

BURUNDI (1965-1972)
100,000 to 300,000 ethnic Hutus killed by Tutsis.

CAMBODIA (1975-1979)
1.7 to 1.9 million killed by Khmer Rouge government.

SOURCE: Adapted from Online Resources from The Choices Program, Brown University.

As of 2010, only 12 of the potential 50,000 cases had been prosecuted (Cerkez 2010).

Mass rape as a weapon of war has also occurred in the region of Darfur within Sudan, with the government-supported Janjaweed militiamen raping Darfuri women and girls held in refugee camps. In 2008, Sudan's president, Omar Hassan Ahmed Bashir, was accused (and later indicted) by the prosecutor of the International Criminal Court (ICC) of the Hague of not only mass genocide but also propagating rape as a weapon of war and terror (Scheffer 2008). Bashir has yet to be tried by the ICC, but the accusations and the indictment did not prevent him from being reelected president of Sudan in 2015 with 94 percent of the vote (Kushkush 2015).

Genocide

The most extreme cases of ethnic conflict involve an active, systematic attempt to eliminate an entire group of people, or genocide. Genocide was defined in 1948 by the United Nations Convention on the Prevention and Punishment of the Crime of Genocide as "acts committed with the intent to destroy, in whole or in part, a national, ethnic, racial, or religious group" (cited in Karstedt 2007: 1909–1910). It is seen as the crime of the twentieth century, and it shows every sign of continuing to define the twenty-first century. Figure 8.8 shows select genocides of the twentieth and twenty-first centuries. The earliest genocide depicted here dates back to 1914, but there were many other instances of genocide long before that.

The 1948 UN convention on genocide was prompted by the Nazi Holocaust (Karstedt 2007: 1909–1910). At first, the Holocaust occurred within the confines of Germany, but it later spread to the European countries allied with, or conquered by, Germany. It was in that sense transnational, and it would have undoubtedly become far more of a global phenomenon had the Nazis achieved their goal of world conquest. For example, had the Nazis succeeded in conquering the United States, we would undoubtedly have seen the genocide of American Jews.

In the main, however, genocide continues to be practiced within nation-states. Examples include the murder of nearly 2 million people by the Khmer Rouge in Cambodia in the mid- to late 1970s, the killing in 1974 of as many as a million people (mostly minority Tutsis) by the majority Hutus in Rwanda, the murder of tens of thousands of Bosnians and Croats in the 1990s by Bosnian Serbs, and the killing of hundreds of thousands of ethnic Africans in Sudan since 2003 by ethnic Arabs.

The global age has brought with it the globalization of genocide, as instances of it have flowed around the world (Karstedt 2012). That is, genocide has become another negative flow making its way from one part of the world to another. Genocide may become more likely in the future because of proliferating and accelerating global flows of ideas, agitators, and arms. Added to this is the increased inability of nation-states to block many of these flows.

SUMMARY

Race has historically been defined on the basis of shared lineage and some real or presumed physical or biological characteristic. In the second half of the twentieth century, race began to be defined more as a cultural phenomenon, making it more akin to the concept of ethnicity. Ethnic groups are typically defined on the basis of some real or presumed cultural characteristic such as language, religion, traditions, or cultural practices.

Race and ethnicity have always served as a way of stratifying individuals into groups with more or less power. The majority group, even if it has fewer members, has more money, prestige, and power and is likely to exploit members of minority groups. Intersectionality, or belonging to more than one type of minority (for example, being black and female), often compounds disparities.

Majority–minority relations devolve into racism when the majority defines a group as a race and attributes negative characteristics to that group. It is the combination of xenophobia and ethnocentrism that makes racism so powerful. Current racism is often more a matter of hegemony, or the majority group foisting its culture on the minority, than of legal and material constraints on minority groups.

There is some evidence that individual-level prejudice and racism against African Americans and other minority groups in the United States are on the decline. However, institutional racism persists, and the white cultural frame is pervasive in American society and its structures and institutions.

Putting majority–minority relations in a global context, the North has more majority group members and dominates and oppresses those in the South. Majority groups are also better positioned than minority groups to create structures that enhance positive or protective global flows.

Greater ethnic diversity within nation-states has opened up more possibilities for internal ethnic conflicts. At the extreme, ethnic conflict leads to expulsion, ethnic cleansing, and genocide of minorities by the majority within a territory.

REVIEW QUESTIONS

1. What is the difference between race and ethnicity? What are the similarities? How have biological and cultural explanations helped to create racial and ethnic differences?
2. Barack Obama is the son of a white mother and a black African father, but more often than not he is referred to as black. What does this suggest about the nature of race in the United States? What are the consequences of this perception?
3. What criteria do sociologists use to define a majority group?
4. How do majority groups maintain their positions of privilege?
5. What are some mechanisms that minorities have used to resist racism?
6. What is institutional racism? What are some examples of institutional racism?
7. In what ways is institutional racism more problematic than individual racism?
8. How would you characterize majority–minority relations on a global level? What sorts of advantages do majority groups have on the global level?
9. How is globalization changing the nature of ethnicity on a global scale? In what ways have ethnic groups been able to use advances in communication and media to retain their ethnic identity?
10. Do you agree that globalization is creating a universal culture? Why or why not?

APPLYING THE SOCIOLOGICAL IMAGINATION

Some scholars and citizens have come to believe that racism is declining and that the chances for racial integration have improved, but we also know that corporations pay attention to racial and ethnic differences when marketing their products.

For this activity, conduct a qualitative content analysis of advertisements in two different magazines: a mainstream magazine that is part of the dominant culture (*Vanity Fair, Cosmopolitan,* *Businessweek*) and a traditionally black magazine (*Essence, Ebony, Jet, Black Enterprise*). Compare and contrast the ads in the magazines. Can you identify any differences between the magazines in terms of the products or the themes of the ads? What sorts of images are used in each of the magazines? In what ways are the advertisements reflective of larger majority–minority group relationships in the United States?

KEY TERMS ·····························

assimilation: The integration of minorities into the dominant culture. (p. 185)

diaspora: Dispersal, typically involuntary, of a racial or ethnic population from its traditional homeland and over a wide geographic area. (p. 190)

discrimination: The unfavorable treatment of black Americans and other minorities, either formally or informally, simply because of their race or some other such characteristic. (p. 184)

ethnocentrism: The belief that one's own group or culture—including its norms, values, customs, and so on—is superior to, or better than, others. (p. 186)

ethnic cleansing: The establishment by the dominant group of policies that allow or require the forcible removal of people of another ethnic group. (p. 195)

ethnic group: A group typically defined on the basis of some cultural characteristic such as language, religion, traditions, and cultural practices. (p. 178)

ethnicity: A sense, shared by members of the group, of belonging to and identifying with a given ethnic group. (p. 178)

expulsion: Removal of a minority group from a territory, either by forcible ejection through military and other government action or by "voluntary" emigration due to the majority's harassment, discrimination, and persecution. (p. 195)

genocide: An active, systematic attempt to eliminate an entire group of people. (p. 186)

hegemony: The subordination of one race (or other group) by another, more on the basis of dominant ideas, especially about cultural differences, than through material constraints. (p. 188)

institutional racism: Race-based discrimination that results from the day-to-day operation of social institutions and social structures and their rules, policies, and practices. (p. 188)

intersectionality: The confluence, or intersection, of various social statuses and the inequality and oppression associated with each in combination with others; the idea that members of any given minority group are affected by the nature of their position in other systems or other forms of social inequality. (p. 185)

majority group: A group in a dominant position along the dimensions of wealth, power, and prestige. (p. 183)

majority-minority population: A population in which more than 50 percent of the members are part of a minority group. (p. 183)

minority group: A group in a subordinate position in terms of wealth, power, and prestige. (p. 183)

Orientalism: A set of ideas and texts produced in the West that served as the basis for dominating, controlling, and exploiting the Orient (the East) and its many minority groups. (p. 192)

pluralism: The coexistence of many groups without any of them losing their individual qualities. (p. 185)

prejudice: Negative attitudes, beliefs, and feelings toward minorities. (p. 184)

race: A social definition based on some real or presumed physical, biological characteristic of a person, such as skin color or hair texture, as well as a shared lineage. (p. 178)

racism: The act of defining a group as a race and attributing negative characteristics to that group. (p. 178)

segregation: The physical and social separation of majority and minority groups. (p. 186)

stereotype: An exaggerated generalization about an entire category of people that is thought to apply to everyone in that category. (p. 184)

white racial frame: An array of racist ideas, racial stereotypes, racialized stories and tales, racist images, powerful racial emotions, and various inclinations to discriminate against blacks. (p. 187)

xenophobia: Prejudices that cause people to reject, exclude, and vilify groups that are outsiders or foreigners to the dominant social group. (p. 186)

$\circledS$SAGE edge™ edge.sagepub.com/ritzeressentials2e

SAGE edge offers a robust online environment featuring an impressive array of free tools and resources for review, study, and further exploration, keeping both instructors and students on the cutting edge of teaching and learning.

LEARNING OBJECTIVES	FOR FURTHER EXPLORATION AND APPLICATION
LO 8-1: Contrast historical and recent views of racial categories and ethnic identities in the United States.	▶ A Visual on Race and Ethnicity ⊕ What's in a Name? Jumping to Conclusions ▣ The Race Card Project
LO 8-2: Describe the effects of stereotypes, prejudice, discrimination, and the social construction of difference on majority–minority relations.	▶ How Minorities Become the Majority ⊕ Does Reading Harry Potter Affect Behavior? ▣ What is Race? Is Race for Real?
LO 8-3: Discuss the foundations of racism, including xenophobia, ethnocentrism, and social structures and institutions.	▶ The History of Racism in the United States ⊕ The Fight to Improve Race Relations ▣ Reply Rate on Applications with Race-Associated Names
LO 8-4: Describe how globalization is affecting ethnic identities, ethnic conflicts, and migrations.	▶ Global Migration and Its Problems ⊕ Napali Migrant Workers Issues ▣ Bilinguals in the United States

GENDER AND SEXUALITY

Challenging Gender Stereotypes

In a *favela* (slum) in Rio de Janeiro, Brazil, a thoughtful, handsome man named Marcio talks about his life (promundoglobal.org). "My dream was always to be a father. And to give my son something I never had." Marcio's childhood was marked by constant violence; his father beat his mother, and the community stood by and accepted it. "He had to show he was a man," he says of his father. Marcio learned from his father that manhood meant having many women, drinking, partying, and staying out all night.

Marcio managed to avoid becoming like his father by founding a group of men who had had similar experiences. As they met together, Marcio saw how traditional cultural gender stereotypes of masculinity and femininity had been harmful. He came to be willing to challenge his culture's sex and gender norms to create a better life for himself, his wife, and his son. With the help of a global organization called Promundo, he now works to challenge traditional gender expectations. Change in the lives of a few can lead to change in the lives of many and, indeed, even in an entire nation or culture.

As the founders of Promundo listened to accounts of men committing violence against women and children around the world, they saw an opportunity and a need for reform. Promundo now helps men and boys in 22 countries change themselves and their communities. ●

LEARNING OBJECTIVES

 9-1 Discuss the cultural influences on gender and the effects of gender inequalities.

 9-2 Describe the ways in which social forces and factors constrain sexuality.

 9-3 Describe the effects of globalization on gender and sexualities.

9-4 Discuss global flows related to gender.

Note: The author thanks Rebecca Plante for her help revising this chapter.

Associated Press

*S*ex and *gender* are terms that are often used interchangeably and confused with one another. However, it is important that they be distinguished clearly. **Sex** is principally a biological term, usually expressed as *female* or *male*. Sex is typically reflected in a person's chromosomes, gonads, genitalia, and hormones. **Gender** is a cultural term, connected to societal definitions of expected behaviors, attitudes, and personalities, and is usually reflected in terms like *woman* or *man*, *girl* or *boy*. Gender consists of the physical, behavioral, and personality characteristics that are defined as appropriate for one's sex. The key difference is that sex is based mainly on biology, whereas gender is based on social distinctions (Ryan 2007). Western conceptualizations of gender assume that there are strong, clear gender differences based on sex. Westerners often assume that genitalia are "not only the primary marker of gender identity, but indeed, the underlying *cause* of that identity" (Helliwell 2000: 797; emphasis added). But bodies and biology are socially constructed as the basis for gender. "Gender builds on biological sex, but it exaggerates biological difference, and it carries biological difference into domains in which it is completely irrelevant" (Eckert and McConnell-Ginet 2013: 2). There is nothing in human biology to explain why, for example, we think only women should wear high heels, or men should not paint their nails.

ASK YOURSELF

Why is gender so important in many cultures? Do you think we could make gender less important in the United States? Should we make gender less important? What would need to happen in order to minimize the importance of gender in our interactions with others?

Getty

These Lebanese men walked a mile in women's shoes during a 2015 event calling for an end to violence against women. Men have routinely worn high-heeled shoes in the past—for instance, during the time of King Louis XIV of France (1638–1715). Why don't they do so now?

GENDER AND SEX

Gender and sex are examples—another is race—of a master status, or a position that is more important than any others, both for the person in the position and for all others involved. Master statuses dominate all other statuses, including achieved (such as education) and ascribed (such as age) statuses, and are therefore of great consequence (see Chapter 4).

Biological sex has long been linked with gender as a social construct, but the two are not as neatly entwined as we have been taught. Furthermore, sex and gender, especially gender, are *not* simply natural, biological processes. They are both—again especially gender—strongly affected by social and cultural forces.

Although we tend to think in terms of only two biological sexes, in fact there is a continuum of sex (Fausto-Sterling 1999). **Intersex** is a "general term used for a variety of [medical] conditions in which a person is born with a reproductive or sexual anatomy that doesn't seem to fit the typical definitions of female or male" (Intersex Society of North America 2008). The majority of intersex conditions do not require medical interventions. Until quite recently, intersexed people were stigmatized with the label *hermaphrodite,* and doctors often surgically altered infants' and children's genitalia to attempt to match more typical male or female anatomy (Coventry 2006). Thanks to intersex advocacy and increased awareness among medical personnel, today intersexed people who may have been subject to surgery in the past have much more choice about whether, and how, to proceed (Zeiler and Wickstrom 2009).

Most aspects of maleness and femaleness are on a continuum as well. For example, both males and females have the hormones estrogen and testosterone. However, the amounts vary greatly from individual to individual within and between sexes, as well as over time (Liaw and Janssen 2014). Biologically, the differences between males and females are few, but much of U.S. culture is based on assumptions about sex (and gender) differences. Unfortunately, beliefs about differences are often translated into constructions of superiority and inferiority.

FEMININITIES AND MASCULINITIES

The terms *femininities* and *masculinities* refer to the cultural definitions of the traits associated with being a "woman" or a "man" acquired during the socialization process (Laurie et al. 1999; Lind 2007). They are plural because there are many forms of both, connected to other characteristics such as race, ethnicity, age, nationality, and social class (see Chapter 8 for a discussion of intersectionality). Cultural interpretations of femininities and masculinities are subject to change depending on place and historical era. There is a tendency to develop stereotypes about what it means to be a woman and to be feminine (mother, nurturant, emotional) and to be a man and masculine (father, tough, unemotional). However, in

DIGITAL LIVING

Gender Disappointment

Did you know that "gender disappointment" is a thing? . . . When the ultrasound technician found that white blob between the legs of my alien-looking unborn on the computer screen, I cried. I remember exactly what she [the technician] said, and it has stuck with me: "It's O.K. to be disappointed." (King 2014)

TABLE 9.1 • Gender Preference in the United States, 2011

SURVEY QUESTION: **SUPPOSE YOU COULD ONLY HAVE ONE CHILD. WOULD YOU PREFER THAT IT BE A BOY OR A GIRL?**

	BOY (%)	GIRL (%)	EITHER/DOESN'T MATTER (%)
Men	49	22	28
Women	31	33	36

SOURCE: Data from Frank Newport, "Americans Prefer Boys to Girls, Just as They Did in 1941," Gallup, June 23, 2011. Reprinted with permission from Gallup.

Women have taken to the Internet to share stories and ask questions about their feelings of gender disappointment, filling parenting and pregnancy sites around the world. A Google search for "gender disappointment" yields 1,650,000 results. What might explain why parents feel such disappointment, and why is there so much conversation about it online?

Historical preference for having male children is a possible answer. When Gallup first asked about gender preference in 1941, 38 percent said they preferred a boy and 24 percent a girl. A 2011 Gallup poll asked U.S. adults for their gender preference if they could have only one child (Newport 2011): 40 percent said they would prefer a boy, 28 percent a girl, and the rest had no preference. Men seem more strongly invested in gender preference, with 49 percent preferring a boy and only 22 percent preferring a girl. Women are more evenly split:

31 percent prefer a boy and 33 percent a girl (see Table 9.1). Having a girl is a source of feelings of disappointment, especially for men.

Beyond historical preference, the day-to-day social construction of gender may also explain why some parents are disappointed by the sex of their newborns. Parents themselves are socialized into cultural and social gender roles and rules and therefore have gendered expectations of their children and how to interact with them. Drawing on stereotypes of what boys are like, women who admit to gender disappointment talk about feeling they do not know how to be a good parent to a boy ("I don't know how to play baseball, so how can I teach a boy how to?") (Kane 2009). Some write about regretting missed opportunities to shop and do arts and crafts with the girls they aren't having. Women and men mention feeling like failures—not "man enough" (in the case

of a man not having a boy) or like a failed mother (for not being "happy and grateful" to have any child) (Booker 2012).

Why is there so much conversation about gender disappointment online? The Internet remains a mostly anonymous place, where people feel they can express their true emotions without direct judgment. Some online commentators are angry that any parent would ever express disappointment over having a child. Others anonymously thank parents for bringing the issue to light, saying it is worth sharing a topic that tends to be kept hidden.

Think About It

What do you think about "gender disappointment"? Would you ever seek online information and support for a feeling like this? Do you think the availability of online information has helped expectant parents admit to "gender disappointment"? Why or why not?

reality, these stereotypes are not natural or biological; rather, they are socially constructed. As Simone de Beauvoir ([1952] 1973: 301) famously put it, "One is not born, but rather becomes, a woman." The same is true, of course, for a man. Yet the distinction between masculine and feminine persists.

Sociologist Raewynn (née Robert W.) Connell (1987, 1997, 2009) coined the terms *hegemonic masculinity* and

emphasized femininity and analyzed the roles that these ideas have played in global gender inequalities. *Hegemonic* means dominant. Therefore, **hegemonic masculinity** refers to the dominant form or most idealized vision of masculinity. We take this form for granted as "natural." It is linked to patriarchy, a form of society that is dominated by men and focused on men and hegemonic masculinity (Johnson 2005). Hegemonic masculinity is the vision of masculinity that underlies patriarchal systems. **Emphasized femininity** is a set of socially constructed ideas about "model womanhood." These ideas are organized around accommodating the interests of men and patriarchy. Emphasized femininity focuses on social ability rather than intellect, ego stroking, and acceptance of the roles of mother and wife (Spade and Valentine 2011). Specific manifestations of femininity and masculinity are measured against these dominant forms.

Hegemonic masculinity and emphasized femininity adversely affect both men and women. Men who do not live up to the stereotype of hegemonic masculinity, including gay and working-class men, as well as men of color, are negatively affected. Generally, the rigid expectations of hegemonic masculinity mean that many men, even heterosexual, white, middle-class men, will be viewed, and will view themselves, as falling short of the ideal. Many women are adversely affected because they do not and cannot live up to the ideals associated with emphasized femininity (Butler 1990).

While some men benefit greatly from hegemonic masculinity, their advantages have, at least until recently, been largely invisible to them. Not having to think about masculinity, or what it means to "be a man," has been one of the dividends (or privileges) of gender inequality. In contrast, women often think a great deal about the disadvantages of masculinity and gender stereotypes, since they are oppressed by the system of gender inequalities in many different ways.

Masculinities and femininities can be detached from biological sex, the body, and gender. Men can act in socially defined "feminine" ways by nurturing others, and women can behave in a socially defined "masculine" manner by competing aggressively. As is true of the continuum of male and female sexes, we should not think in simple, either/or terms about gender. There is a continuum of masculinities *and* femininities, resulting in part from the variety of socialization patterns that we experience over the life course. People adapt throughout their lives, emphasizing different aspects of gender and interpreting the gender role expectations constructed by society. We merge gendered expectations with those of other intersectional statuses, including race, class, and sexual orientation. Moreover, individuals can be high in both masculinity and femininity or low in both. Gender performance is fluid, not static, and allows room for individuals to make some choices about how to perform gender within socially defined roles (Fields, Copp, and Kleinman 2007).

ASK YOURSELF

What did Simone de Beauvoir mean by saying, "One is not born, but rather becomes, a woman"? Do you agree with her view? Why or why not? Do you think she would say the same thing today?

TRANSGENDER AND NONBINARY GENDERS

As is the case with sex, we often think of gender in binary terms. We think of a *gender binary* involving only two genders, man and woman. But just as sex, most notably in the case of the intersexed, is not a simple binary, gender has multiple aspects, forms, and expressions; it is not a simple, neat binary. It is socially constructed and variable across cultures, times, and places. Individuals who might identify themselves as one of the two dominant genders—namely, as a man or a woman—enact a wide range of gender portrayals, roles, and identities, including being transgender.

Most basically, **transgender** is an umbrella term for people whose gender identity and/or gender presentation differs from the gender assigned to them at birth or in infancy. **Gender identity** is a person's internal sense of gender (Bornstein 1994). Trans individuals may have **gender roles**—the social presentation of gender that includes clothing, hairstyle, and attitudinal and behavioral traits—that differ from or correspond with their gender identities.

Trans individuals do not follow a single path. They may or may not locate themselves somewhere in the broad matrix of gender. They may or may not identify with either of the two culturally dominant genders. They may or may not wish to use hormones or obtain surgeries to change aspects of their physical sex. Trans individuals may choose identities and/or create self-applied labels—such as *genderqueer, agender,* or *gender fluid*—that do not fit neatly within the gender binary. People who are *agender* may not identify with any gender, while those who are *gender fluid* may feel that their identities change depending on the context. *Genderqueer* is a broad umbrella term that encompasses a range of gendered identities, feelings, and self-determined labels.

Although only about 8 percent of U.S. adults say they personally know someone who is trans (Pew Research Center 2013), general awareness of trans people has increased in recent years. *Time* magazine recently ran a cover story titled "The Transgender Tipping Point" (Steinmetz 2014). Perhaps the best-known transgender person is the Olympic gold medalist Bruce (now Caitlyn) Jenner, who announced publicly in 2015 that he was transitioning to being a woman and soon after appeared as a woman on the cover of *Vanity Fair.*

Trans history and context runs deeper than is suggested by a few years of increased public visibility. Sylvia Rivera (1951–2002), a "drag queen, bisexual transgender activist," was a "loud and persistent voice for the rights of people of color and low-income queers and trans people" (Sylvia Rivera Law Project 2015). She was among those who clashed with police in the 1969 New York Stonewall bar riot, in which gay, queer, and trans people resisted police harassment (see Chapter 15). The Transgender Day of Remembrance (TDOR) began in 1999, when trans woman of color Rita Hester was

Caitlyn Jenner (formerly Olympic star Bruce Jenner) posed provocatively on a mid-2015 cover of *Vanity Fair*.

the victim of a hate murder. Between 2008 and 2014, 1,612 trans people were murdered around the world (Transgender Europe 2014). Life is particularly hellish for trans individuals who find themselves in prison, where rape is an ever-present danger (Sontag 2015). Trans women of color in the United States—and elsewhere—are disproportionately targeted and beaten, abused, or murdered (National Coalition of Anti-Violence Programs 2014).

ASK YOURSELF

What might explain hate-based violence against trans people? Do you think there is a connection between this violence and the recent increase in the visibility of trans people? Why or why not?

GENDER DIVERSITY

Globally there are many cultures with various nonbinary genders. Some North American Native and First Nations tribes include roles for *two-spirit* individuals. They are socially defined as truly distinct, neither man nor woman nor a combination of the two, and are respected in their tribes (Roscoe 1998). Another kind of gender diversity can be found in some mountain villages in Afghanistan (Nordberg 2014), where a rigidly constructed culture dictates that sons are necessary for families hoping for prestige (Arbabzadah 2011). In order to gain such prestige, some families without male children present young girls as boys (called *bacha posh*), with the clothing, haircuts, and behavioral shifts common to boys. At puberty, they are "changed" into girls. In some rural areas of Albania, some women became men, adopting men's dress, habits, privileges, and responsibilities (Bilefsky 2008). They swore off marriage, sex, and children and were accepted by men and respected as if they were men.

GENDERED INEQUALITIES

As a master status and a primary basis for the persistence of structural, institutional inequalities, gender is a key variable in understanding life chances in the United States. Gender is structured into all our social institutions or systems—education, families, the economy, the law, and so on. Social institutions are powerful established sociocultural pathways that exist to meet our collective needs (Acker 1992). In the United States, we socialize people into the binary gender system through our social institutions and then channel them into differently valued activities, attributes, and pursuits.

Gender inequality is also a global problem (see the discussion of global social stratification in Chapter 7). The World Economic Forum (2014) measures gender inequality in terms of gender-related disparities in health care, education, economy, and politics. Statistics on men's and women's salaries, participation in paid labor, access to education, representation in political bodies, and life expectancy contribute to a country's score. No country in the world has a score of one, which would indicate full equality between men and women. The closer to one a country's score, the narrower the gap between men and women—that is, the better women are doing in relation to men. Iceland is the most equal country in the world in terms of gender with a score of 0.8594, while Yemen is the least with a score of 0.5145. The United States, with a score of 0.7463, ranks 20th (see Figure 9.1).

There are global differences in the ways societies deal with gender disparities and inequalities. Change.org petitioners in the United Kingdom and Ireland seek to send a message to toy retailers: Stop labeling some toys for boys (construction sets, cars, and the like) and others for girls (princess outfits, play kitchens). Some Swedes who strongly support the idea that traditional gender norms enhance inequalities have argued for the use of gender-neutral pronouns as a way of promoting equality. Swedish preschools and elementary schools have begun to use the gender-neutral pronoun *hen* (Braw 2014).

FIGURE 9.1 • Global Gender Gap Index, 2014

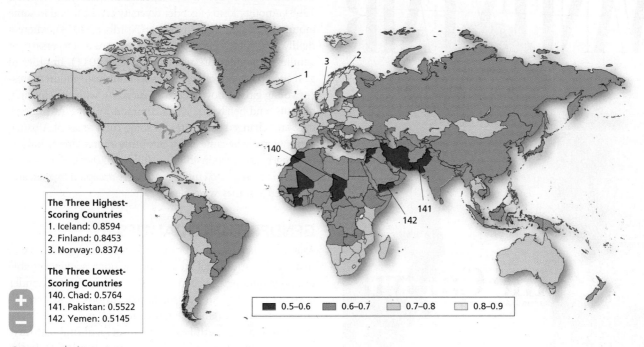

The Three Highest-Scoring Countries
1. Iceland: 0.8594
2. Finland: 0.8453
3. Norway: 0.8374

The Three Lowest-Scoring Countries
140. Chad: 0.5764
141. Pakistan: 0.5522
142. Yemen: 0.5145

0.5–0.6 0.6–0.7 0.7–0.8 0.8–0.9

⑤SAGE data**maps** edge.sagepub.com

• Gender equality indicators behind every country ranking.

SOURCE: Data from World Economic Forum, *The Global Gender Gap Report 2014* (Geneva: Author, 2014).

GENDER AND EDUCATION

Educational systems constitute an important site and source of gender inequality throughout American society and across the globe. Historically, families invested relatively little in the education of girls because they were expected to grow up to stay at home as wives and mothers. Thus, there has long been a gender gap in education in many countries, including the United States.

Clearly the formal educational system, especially at the primary and secondary levels, has been a major cause of that gap, and it continues to pose some persistent problems for women. One aspect of that system, and a root cause of the gender gap in education, is often the **hidden curriculum**, or a school's unofficial norms, routines, and structures that transmit dominant cultural norms and values (De Lissovoy and García 2013; Giroux and Purpel 1983). Schools reproduce unquestioned social norms such as obedience to authority, hard work, and the value of hierarchy. Most schools foster competitiveness, a push for achievement, and an understanding of the social hierarchy within the school (Scott and Schwartz 2008). Because boys are socialized from infancy to enact these preferred values, they are likely to get more attention in class from teachers, to be asked more questions, to get more constructive criticism, and, at least in the early years of school, to monopolize class discussions (Sadker and Sadker 1994; Sharp 2012).

There is a deeply hidden curriculum regarding gender conformity and norms (Surtees 2008). Analyses of elementary teacher training materials and in-depth studies of elementary school classrooms suggest that most teachers are not well trained to deal with gender (or sexuality) issues at school. A small, exploratory study found that elementary school teachers were afraid of the prospect of having a transgender student (Payne and Smith 2014). Lack of formal training, education, and institutional support combined with individual-level discomfort to create this fear. Institutional policies against discussing sexuality, and the mistaken perception that gender identity is linked to sexuality, hampered teachers' ability to deal with transgender students (Payne and Smith 2014; Surtees 2008).

ASK YOURSELF

Think back to your elementary and high school years. Did the schools you attended have a hidden curriculum? You were likely unaware of it at the time, but can you now identify any specific examples of the way it manifested itself?

Increasing awareness of the gender gap in education has led to significant efforts to overcome it and subsequently to great educational gains for women (Dorius and Firebaugh

2010). Nevertheless, a gender gap in education persists. In spite of this continuing gender gap, some girls, especially those who are white, experience success in primary and secondary schooling due, in part, to gendered socialization. They are more engaged in school and more likely to comply with school rules, such as doing homework and responding to teacher requests (Buchmann and DiPrete 2006). Such "noncognitive" skills are strong predictors of academic success. They partly explain why girls outperform boys on most academic indicators.

Another explanation for girls' success in primary and secondary school is structural, related to long-term job success. Many occupations continue to be segregated by sex. The most consistently male-segregated occupations (e.g., truck driver, auto mechanic, firefighter) do not require postsecondary schooling, whereas several of the most consistently female-segregated occupations (e.g., preschool teacher, registered nurse, dental hygienist) do require schooling beyond high school. Young women therefore must maintain some success in high school in order to get into the college programs needed for future job training. This occupational segregation is increasingly responsible for women's advantages in educational attainment (Jacobs 1996).

Changing societal attitudes about gender roles and declining sexism have had dramatic effects on women's educational attainment as they advance through the educational system. Women are significantly more likely than men to graduate from high school and to attend either a two- or four-year college (Carbonaro and Covay 2010). In 1960, women represented less than 40 percent of college undergraduates in the United States; today, roughly 57 percent of students at both two- and four-year colleges are women (Goldin, Katz, and Kuziemko 2006). Women are more likely than men to receive bachelor's or master's degrees (Alon and Gelbgiser 2011; Buchmann and DiPrete 2006). Figure 9.2 depicts the dramatic and increasing gap between men and women enrolled as undergraduates in the United States. By 2020 women are projected to be almost 59 percent of undergraduates, while men will be 41 percent. This constitutes an almost complete reversal of the situation in 1970, when almost 58 percent of undergraduates were men and only 42 percent were women. We can also see this trend in the dramatic increases in law and medical degrees earned by women. However, men continue to be more likely to be trained in the most prestigious colleges and universities and to obtain doctoral degrees. In part this is because elite institutions highly value (overvalue?) SAT scores, and men continue to perform better on the SAT (Bielby et al. 2014).

Even with women's gains in higher education, a significant pay gap exists between men and women once they leave school and begin their careers (Charles and Bradley 2009; Jacobs 1996). While in college, women are more likely to major in sex/gender-segregated academic fields such as education, English, and psychology, which tend to lead to jobs that do not pay as well as jobs dominated by men. While there are differences among the fields, women continue to be less likely to major in science, technology, engineering, and math (STEM fields) in college. Majoring in these fields tends to lead to higher-paying jobs. Figure 9.3 shows that women now earn a majority of degrees in biology, and they have shown strong gains in the physical sciences and mathematics-statistics. However, they continue to be less likely than men to earn degrees in STEM fields. Worse, women lag far behind men in bachelor's degrees in computer science and information sciences, as well as in engineering. Part of the reason for this underrepresentation is the fact that women continue to be likely to be stereotyped as being less capable scientifically and technically. Larry Summers, a noted economist and former president of Harvard University, once said that genetic differences explain why boys outperform girls in science and math (Goldenberg 2005). Female chemistry professor Donna Nelson responded, "I have heard men make comments like this my entire life and quite honestly if I had listened to them I would never have done anything." This kind of sex and gender stereotyping in education is frequent and continues to be not only an American problem but also a global one.

GENDER, FAMILY, AND WORK

The relationship between gender and work is one of the most studied issues in the field of gender (Thorn 2007). A primary concern has been documenting the intersections of gender, work, and family. As you can see in Figure 9.4, heterosexual families with men and women in the paid labor force earn more than all other family types. Even when their wives are not in the paid labor force, married men earn more than unmarried men (Ahituv and Lerman 2007; Ashwin and Isupova 2014). However, unmarried women's household income is far below that of all men and of married women. Many of these inequities are based on historical, traditional gender roles in families.

FIGURE 9.2 • Gender Differences in Undergraduate Enrollment in the United States, 1970–2020 (projected)

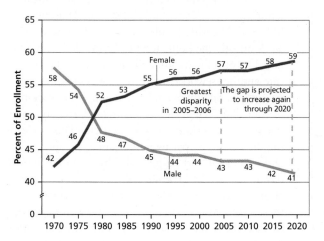

SOURCE: National Center for Education Statistics, "The Condition of Education 2011."

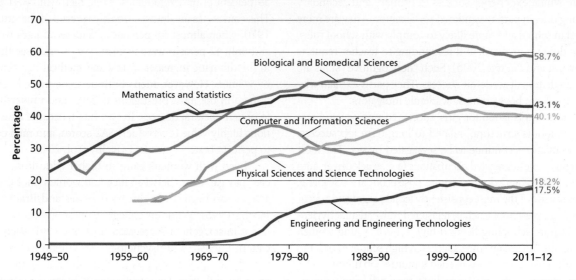

SOURCES: Data from U.S. Department of Education, National Center for Education Statistics, Higher Education General Information Survey (HEGIS), "Degrees and Other Formal Awards Conferred" surveys, 1970–71 through 1985–86; Integrated Postsecondary Education Data System (IPEDS), "Completions Survey" (IPEDS-C:87-99); and IPEDS fall 2000 through fall 2012, completions component.

The Decline of Separate Spheres

The once clear-cut, gender-based differentiation between the public and private spheres in the United States has been breaking down since the mid-twentieth century. Now women are more likely not only to be in the work world (England 2010) but also, increasingly, to be the principal—or even the only—wage earner in the family. The family characterized by a division between male/breadwinner and female/homemaker has increasingly given way to more blended roles, and even to role reversals, especially in dual-earner families (McClelland, Mok, and Pierce 2014). Figure 9.5 shows the steadily increasing percentage of mothers who earn most of the family income (breadwinners), along with those who are co-breadwinners.

FIGURE 9.4 • Median Income of Families in the United States, by Family Type, 1950–2010

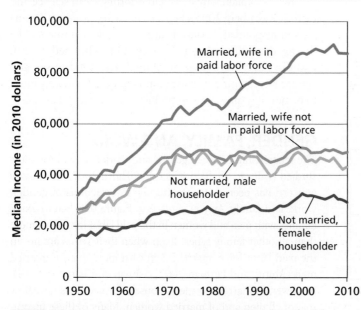

SOURCE: U.S. Census Bureau, Current Population Survey, 2011 (http://familyfacts.org/charts/340/married-couple-families-have-higher-incomes).

Dual-Earner Households and the Stalled Revolution

A key issue in the study of gender, work, and family is the difference between heterosexual men and women in the ways they use their time in the era of dual-earner families. Arlie Hochschild (1989, 2003) argues that in U.S. dual-earner families with children, wives who work outside the home tend to be saddled with additional labor—the traditionally gendered tasks of child care and housework—when they get home from their paid work. Such women can be said to be working a "second shift." Figure 9.6 presents 2013 data on gender differences in performing three household tasks: cleaning the house, preparing and cleaning up after meals, and caring for and helping children. On an average day, 68.1 percent of women did meal preparation or cleanup, while only 41.7 percent of men performed these tasks. More extremely, 48.5 percent of women cleaned the house on an average day, while only 19.4 percent of men did such work. In terms of caring for and helping household children, 25.3 percent of

FIGURE 9.5 • **Share of Mothers Who Are Breadwinners or Co-breadwinners in the United States, 1967–2011**

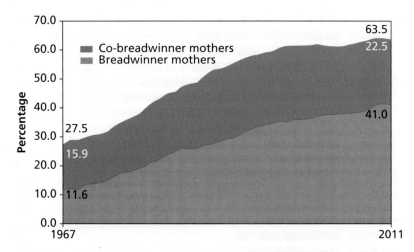

SOURCE: Family Matters: *The Economics of the Family and Human Capital in the United States*, June 20, 2013. Reprinted with permission from Heather Boushey, Center for American Progress, Washington, DC, & Institute for Public Policy Research, London.

women perform these tasks compared to only 16.2 percent of men.

However, other recent research indicates that the differences between heterosexual women and men in performing household tasks may be narrowing (Bianchi, Robinson, and Milkie 2006). While the second shift continues to exist for women, they are now spending more time at work and less at home. Thus, they have less time for, and are less involved in, the second shift. Between 1965 and 2011, the amount of time American women spent per week on housework decreased, on average, from 32 to 18 hours (Liss 2014). Men are spending less time at work and more time at home, participating more in the tasks associated with the second shift. Between 1965 and 2011 their average weekly time devoted to housework increased from 4 to 10 hours. However, according to the United Nations, women worldwide continue to shoulder vastly more household responsibilities than men.

ASK YOURSELF

Did your mother or grandmother work a "second shift"? How many women you know are doing so now? Do you know any men who could be said to be working a "second shift" to the same degree as women?

Men's tendency to do less domestic work than women (Lachance-Grzela and Bouchard 2010; Miller and Sassler 2010) has been attributed to a "stalled [gender equality] revolution," especially in the United States

(Coontz 2013; England 2010). Explanations for the stalled revolution are complex and extend beyond the bounds of individual families. Both men and women in the white-collar paid labor force in the United States are expected to work comparatively more hours than those in similar jobs in many other developed countries. The U.S. model of a two-week vacation each year also lags behind other developed countries, where four to eight weeks are standard. As a rule, the United States is not friendly to parents, whether heterosexual dual earners or single parents or those creating other family forms. The gender equality revolution has stalled, at least in part, because work-life policies lag behind domestic realities. For example, the United States has no federal maternity leave policies. The Family and Medical Leave Act grants 12 weeks of unpaid maternity leave, but only for full-time employees who work in companies with 50 or more employees. Thus, part-time employees and full-timers in workplaces that employ fewer than 50 people are not covered. Even full-timers may not be able to afford time off without pay for the responsibilities associated with childbirth and beyond. Papua New Guinea and the United States are the only countries that do not have federally supported paid time off for mothers. There is a similar situation with paternity leave. Unlike Sweden (a paternity leave of 480 paid days), Germany (365 days), and

FIGURE 9.6 • **Division of Household Labor in the United States, by Gender, 2013**

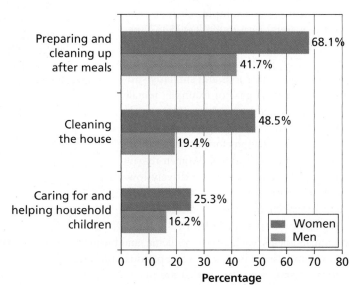

SOURCE: Data from U.S. Department of Labor, Bureau of Labor Statistics, "Daily Household Labor in the United States by Gender," in *American Time Use Survey Summary*, June 18, 2014 (http://www.bls.gov/news.release/atus.t01.htm).

Canada (245 days), the United States offers zero paid paternity leave days (see the Paid Family Leave website, paidfamilyleave.org). In fact, the United States ranks at the bottom globally in government-supported time off for new parents (see Figure 9.7).

In the past half century or so, there has certainly been a revolution in the United States (and elsewhere), with women participating in the paid labor force at much higher rates. Feminism and other movements for greater equality are having a wider effect on society as a whole, on men and women in the labor force, and on the family. However, it would be premature to argue that the revolution is now complete or that there is true equality in men's and women's work, either in the home or in the labor force.

Gender Inequality at Work

In nearly every kind of job and work setting, gender inequalities persist and begin to intersect with racial inequalities. Perhaps the most widely cited inequality is the wage gap, the difference between men's earnings and women's earnings, usually expressed as a percentage of men's earnings. In the United States in 2013, the wage gap was 80 percent. According to the U.S. Bureau of Labor Statistics, overall, women earn (on average) 80 cents to every dollar earned by white men. As is evident in Figure 9.8, a wage gap exists at all levels of the occupational ladder. Women in entry-level jobs or positions (for example, cashiers and food preparers) earn much less ($387) per week than similarly employed young men ($412). The gap between well-educated men in white-collar jobs and similarly situated women is large. For example, female financial managers earn $1,127 per week, while male financial managers earn $1,671.

Some explanations for the wage gap are structural and institutional. Women remain strongly clustered in some relatively low-paid occupations (for example, nursing, elementary school teaching), although they have made inroads into historically male-dominated fields, such as law, medicine, and business (Blau, Brummund, and Liu 2012). Occupations and specialties within certain occupations that are male-dominated tend to have higher salaries than occupations and specialties that are, or have been, female-dominated. The higher the percentage of women in an occupation, the lower the average

FIGURE 9.7 • Government-Supported Time Off for New Parents in Select Countries

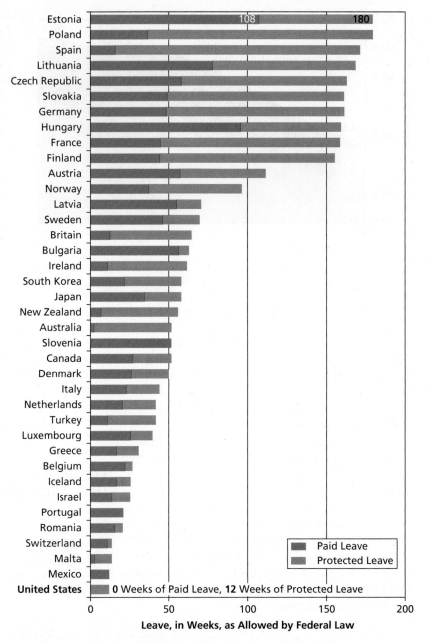

NOTE: The bars combine both maternity leave and parental leave (which is available to either a new mother or a new father). The data do not address paid leave or other accommodations that individual employers make available to employees or guarantees provided by a few individual states.

SOURCE: Gretchen Livingston, "Among 38 Nations, U.S. Is the Outlier When It Comes to Paid Parental Leave," Pew Research Center, Fact Tank, December 12, 2013. Data from OECD.

wages. Another explanation is more personal or family based. Historical gender roles and stereotyping, particularly in the middle class, have led to the expectation that women who have children will take time off from their paid employment to care for them. Such career disruptions certainly contribute to the wage gap. Women who take time away from the

FIGURE 9.8 • Median Weekly Earnings of Full-Time Wage and Salary Workers by Occupation in the United States, 2014

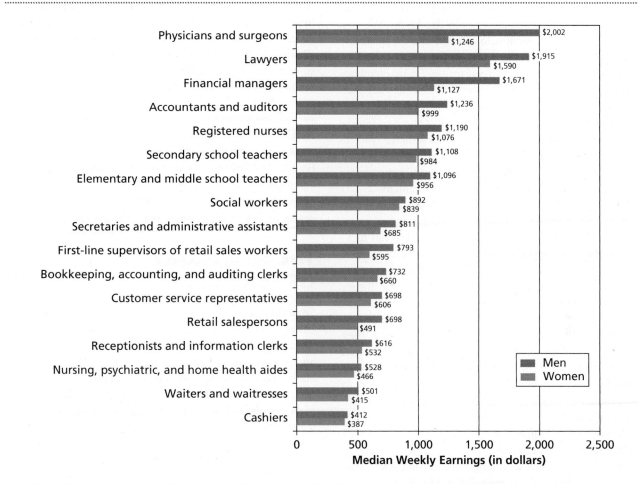

SOURCE: Data from U.S. Department of Labor, Bureau of Labor Statistics, Table 39: "Median Weekly Earning of Full-Time Wage and Salary Workers by Detailed Occupation and Sex," Labor Force Statistics from the Current Population Survey (http://www.bls.gov/cps/cpsaat39.htm).

paid labor force lose ground in terms of salaries and rate of advancement into higher-paying positions.

Many different consequences stem from the inequality of workplaces and work structures. Pudrovska and Karraker (2014) discovered that women with authority on the job—the ability to hire, fire, and influence—had more diminished mental health than women without job authority and men *with* authority. They argue that women in authority deal with a host of negative interpersonal stressors, stereotyping, and resistance from both subordinates and superiors. Mental health may be most adversely affected by contradictory social, gendered expectations (Cook and Glass 2014). On the one hand, women in leadership positions may be viewed as not assertive or confident enough. On the other hand, when they do display these characteristics, they are judged negatively for not being feminine enough. Snyder (2014) studied 248 performance reviews of 180 people (105 men and 75 women) from 28 companies. She found that "words like *bossy,*

abrasive, strident, and *aggressive* are used to describe women's behaviors when they lead; words like *emotional* and *irrational* describe their behaviors when they object. . . . *Abrasive* alone is used 17 times to describe 13 different women." The only word on this list that shows up in men's reviews is *aggressive.* Snyder saw it three times, but on two of those occasions the reviewer was encouraging the male employee *to be more aggressive.*

GENDER AND CONSUMER CULTURE

In consumption, as in many other aspects of the social world, gender matters. Since the Industrial Revolution, production has been centered outside the household and has primarily been the function of white men. White middle- and upper-class women, largely relegated to the home, were assigned the role of consumers (Williams and Sauceda 2007). This is both different and unequal, since historically production has been far more highly valued than consumption.

Consumption, Work, and Family

Women were not just defined as the prime consumers—their consumer practices were also closely tied to their domestic practices and their roles in the home. Women consumed goods and services to care for, and on behalf of, their families (DeVault 1991). Much of women's shopping was related to love, especially their love of family members (Miller 1998); it was an instrumental way of showing that they cared. In one way or another, women generally made purchases for their families and to fulfill their responsibilities in the home and to those who lived there. Women are still thought to constitute a "multiple market"—they purchase things for significant others, family members, and friends. As marketing expert Bridget Brennan (2013) observes: "If somebody, somewhere needs a gift, chances are there's a woman thinking about it; tracking it down; wrapping it; making sure it's accompanied by a personal message and then arriving to the person on the appointed day. I sometimes think entire industries would collapse overnight if women stopped being so thoughtful. Consider the impact to the greeting card industry alone."

As women have entered the paid work world in increasing numbers, their consumption patterns have changed. They are now more likely to consume an array of subcontracted services, such as cleaning and child care. Much of this work is done by other women—women are subcontracting work to other women (Bowman and Cole 2009). In addition, they are increasingly likely to consume more for themselves than for others. For example, greater involvement in the work world requires the use of a wider variety of clothing: business casual, conservative office work wear, uniforms, to name a few. This certainly contributes to the amount that U.S. women spend on clothing—$116 billion in 2013 (Madhok 2014).

Women and Girls as Consumers

As one sociologist put it, "For a large number of girls in modern America, participating in the consumer realm is the defining feature of life as a girl" (Best 2007: 724). As girls gain some freedom from gendered expectations and spend more of their own money, they are being courted more aggressively by advertisers and marketers (Deutsch and Theodorou 2010; Verde Group 2007). Now, of course, all children, including girls, are being targeted on their computers, their smartphones, and myriad other new and yet-to-be-created technologies that have a ready audience among teenagers and younger children (Kahlenberg and Hein 2010; Sheldon 2004).

This focus on consumption is particularly clear in the efforts made by the cosmetics and clothing industries to sell to young women by advertising in magazines aimed at them (*Seventeen, Teen Vogue*) and through pop-up advertisements on the Internet. "Women/girls . . . are expected to consume their way into attractiveness" (Deutsch and Theodorou 2010: 234).

One of the unfortunate consequences of this for young girls is increased rates of eating disorders and body dysmorphia—an obsession with perceived flaws in one's body—as well as the hypersexualization of their lives (Hesse-Biber 1996; Kimmel 2012). Hypersexualization has become such a concern globally that the Norwegian minister of family affairs urged chain stores to remove sexualizing clothing (for example, string bikini underwear) (Rysst 2008).

ASK YOURSELF

Think back to the discussion of sociological theory in Chapter 2. How might sociological theorists explain the link between gender and social inequalities? How can theory help us see why gender inequalities persist in most of the world?

THE SOCIOLOGY OF SEXUALITY

Sexuality is the ways in which people think about, and behave toward, themselves and others as sexual beings (Plummer 1975). Sexuality is, of course, related to both sex and gender, and includes sexual attitudes, behaviors, sensuality, values, anatomy, biochemistry, identities, and orientations. It is of central interest to sociologists, perhaps because of its complicated and seemingly opposed elements. Sexuality is both individual and personal *and* collective and public; it is biological and biochemical as well as cultural, social, and historical. There is variation in degrees of sexuality among individuals and across cultures and time periods.

There is now a large and growing body of literature on the sociology of sexuality (Plummer 2012). While bodies and biology are involved, the bulk of this work deals with the social, social psychological, and cultural aspects of sexuality. Sociologists have become increasingly interested in sexuality for a number of reasons:

- The growing number of sexually linked social problems, including the HIV/AIDS epidemic and sexual violence

- Social changes in attitudes and behaviors, including the increase in "hooking up" (see below) and casual sexual relationships

- The greater visibility of sexuality-related social movements, especially those associated with gays and lesbians

- Technological changes, such as the arrival of erectile dysfunction drugs like Viagra and Cialis

- The media's presentation of sex in its many forms

- The globalization of sexuality, for example, through sex tourism and sex trafficking (Frank 2012)

- The increase in overt expressions of sexuality in consumer culture—not only widespread commerce in sexual activity but also the use of sex to sell virtually everything

- The development of the Internet, where a vibrant commercial sex culture has developed

Sexuality is rarely simply a matter of sexual release or so-called reproductive imperatives. It is complex, contradictory, and confusing (Plante 2015). For example, we are told that "having sex"—meaning, engaging in heterosexual activities (Seidman 2003)—is "natural" and that reproduction is the key goal of these activities. Similarly, we are told that people "naturally" have hormones, sexual urges, and needs that must be fulfilled. However, we are also told that people should control themselves for religious, social, or cultural reasons (Plante 2014). Culture gives us patterns, rules, and codes to manage our sexualities and sexual identities. Laws and formal sanctions, along with informal sanctions, are intended to regulate cultural and individual sexualities. Contemporary and historical gender roles and power dynamics affect our sexualities, as do race and class (Scott and Schwartz 2008). Culture provides the big picture for our sexualities by communicating our shared attitudes, values, goals, and practices. Language and socialization convey these aspects of culture.

SEXUAL SELVES

Sexual Identities and Orientations

Sexual identity is an internal sense of one's sexual self (Manning 2015). The idea that people have sexual orientations and identities is fairly new in human history. Until as recently as 1923, one could still find *heterosexual* defined in the dictionary as a *medical* term (it was not an *identity* term) meaning "morbid sexual passion for one of the opposite sex" (Katz 2004: 44). In the past 125 years or so, we have begun to classify and label people according to culturally powerful decisions about what is "normal." One element of sexual identity is **sexual orientation**, which identifies whom you desire (fantasies), with whom you want to have sexual relations (behavior), and with whom you have a sense of connectedness (feelings) (Scott and Schwartz 2008). Sexual orientation is actually quite complicated. We have oversimplified it by assuming that there are only a few orientations—gay or lesbian, bisexual, and heterosexual.

Although there are cultural, social, and historical contexts for our sexualities, sexual expression varies among individuals. For example, someone may define herself as bisexual and may be sexual with men and women but may prefer romantic relationships with women. Another person may define himself as an asexual heteroromantic, someone with no sexual attractions but who is interested in a romantic relationship with a woman (DeLuzio Chasin 2011). Like sex and gender, sexualities and identities are also on continua. In fact, it may be most

Marchers celebrate their gender and sexual identities at a 2014 Trans Pride Parade in Istanbul, Turkey.

accurate to conceive of these aspects of ourselves as a matrix. And our interests, fantasies, tastes, and desires may change quite a bit through the life course (DeLamater 2012).

Our attitudes about sexual identities reflect changes in the larger society. Recently the changes have been profound, as have their effects. The best-known example today is the increasing openness many people feel about identifying as gay or lesbian. In many settings, it is no longer necessary to hide those identities. It is increasingly possible to be very public, and to feel very good, about having a gay or lesbian identity (Plummer 2007a). The Pew Research Center (2013) conducted a nationally representative survey of 1,197 lesbian, gay, bisexual, and transgender adults, and found that an almost unbelievable 92 percent of respondents said that, compared to 10 years ago, U.S. society is now more accepting of LGBT people. But the growing multiplicity of sexualities and sexual communities makes conflicts over the boundaries of sexualities increasingly likely (Köllen 2013).

Some of the conflicts *seem* individual and interpersonal, as you can see in Figure 9.9. For example, nearly 40 percent of the Pew survey respondents reported that they had been rejected by a close family member or friend, 30 percent had been physically threatened or attacked, and almost 60 percent had been verbally attacked. These statistics have social and historical roots in homophobia and heterosexism. **Homophobia** is defined as "the fear of being, appearing, or seeming gay; fear of anyone or 'anything' gay. . . . At its most virulent, homophobia inspires hate crimes, murders, assaults (sexual, physical, and emotional), rapes, batteries, and other forms of violence" (Plante 2015: 212). **Heterosexism** is the belief that heterosexuality is superior to other sexual orientations, along with individual and institutional discrimination against those with other orientations. Heterosexism and homophobia combine to drive some of the alienation and aggression experienced by lesbian, gay, bisexual, and trans people.

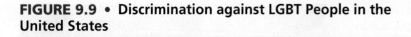

FIGURE 9.9 • Discrimination against LGBT People in the United States

% saying this . . . because of their sexual orientation or gender identity

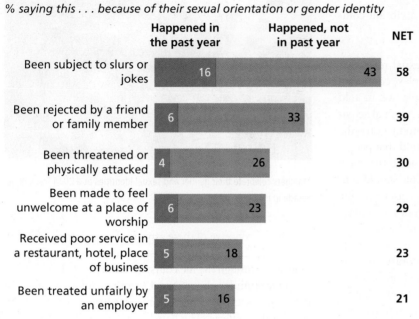

	Happened in the past year	Happened, not in past year	NET
Been subject to slurs or jokes	16	43	58
Been rejected by a friend or family member	6	33	39
Been threatened or physically attacked	4	26	30
Been made to feel unwelcome at a place of worship	6	23	29
Received poor service in a restaurant, hotel, place of business	5	18	23
Been treated unfairly by an employer	5	16	21

SOURCE: Pew Research Center, "A Survey of LGBT Americans: Attitudes, Experiences and Values in Changing Times," June 13, 2013. Reprinted by permission of Pew Research Center, Washington, DC.

Gendered Sexual Scripts

Gendered differences between men and women appear to be greater in sexuality than in any other aspect of our intimate lives (Naples and Gurr 2012). Although biology of course plays some role, the sociological view is that social and cultural factors are of far greater importance. Socialization plays a key role, as we learn sexual and gendered scripts by observing and learning from others. We are taught by socialization agents—parents, peers, mass media, teachers, and so on. Particularly important are gender-appropriate **sexual scripts**, the culturally produced, shared, and reinforced social norms that serve as blueprints, or maps, to guide sexual and gender behavior (Gagnon and Simon 1973). Scripts include the *who, what, where, when, how,* and *why* of socially constructed sexualities (Gagnon and Simon, 1973; Plante 2015).

ASK YOURSELF

Where and how do we learn sexual scripts? Do you think we can unlearn them, or learn new ones? Why or why not? How?

Spotlight on "Hooking Up"

What exactly is hooking up? It is *not* a clearly socially defined relationship such as dating, seeing someone, having a boyfriend or girlfriend, or being engaged to be married. It *can be* somewhat committed or somewhat casual, emotionally and physically intense or not, sporadic or fairly regular, sober or intoxicated; it can involve friends or strangers (Plante 2014). Hooking up involves the occurrence of some sort of sexual event—very broadly defined—usually between only two people, and sometimes including alcohol or other drugs. It may include only kissing and making out, or it may involve a range of behaviors from touching to oral sex, penile–vaginal sex, and/or anal sex. Hooking up is intended to be an ambiguous concept. Some of our most unquestioned cultural scripts argue that sex "should be" spontaneous, mysterious, even magical (Kleinplatz 1992). The ambiguity, spontaneity, and apparent lack of rules or expectations for hookups fit these expectations well.

Researchers have observed that hooking up maintains the heterosexual gendered double standard (Hamilton and Armstrong 2009). The **heterosexual double standard** describes a cultural belief system in which men are expected to desire and seek sex from whomever, whenever, while women are expected to be sexual only within committed, romantic relationships. Those who hold this double standard may also believe that women's sexual behavior is different from men's and should be judged differently (Allison and Risman 2013; Reid, Elliott, and Webber 2011). For instance, they may judge women negatively for seeking sex and pleasure outside relationships, while they judge men less harshly, if at all, for the same behavior (Armstrong, England, and Fogarty 2012).

Although there is some evidence that belief in the double standard is weakening, we still see it in heterosexual hooking up. For instance, it may lead to what Hamilton and Armstrong (2009: 594) call "sexual dilemmas," in which young women in particular find that social rules and expectations for gender and social class contradict each other. Heterosexual women are told they should be sexual only in romantic, committed relationships, but also that they should avoid the baggage (and feelings) of committed relationships in favor of self-development and the achievement of academic and career goals. Researchers have explored the sexual dilemmas of hooking up by examining the ways in which heterosexual young women are expected to look and act appropriately sexy—the "just right," or Goldilocks, amount (Plante 2015)—while also "distanc[ing] themselves from the troubling figure of the 'drunken slut'" (Griffin et al. 2012: 187).

SOCIAL CONSTRAINTS ON SEXUALITY

There is a growing sense, not without reason, that sexuality has become increasingly free of social constraints. Examples of changing consensus about sexualities and social constraints are abundant in modern culture. In 1969, only 21.4 percent of Americans said that sex between unmarried men and women was morally acceptable (Pennington 2003). By 1973, 43 percent were saying that it was acceptable morally. A majority of Americans (66 percent) now say that sex between unmarried men and women is morally acceptable (Riffkin 2014). Surprisingly, perhaps, American attitudes about heterosexual marital monogamy remain stable. For decades Gallup has found that 93 percent of Americans believe that "married men and women having an affair" is "morally unacceptable" (Riffkin 2014).

While there is much to support the idea of increasing sexual freedom, human sexuality is never totally free from social and cultural constraints and regulatory attempts. Social institutions such as schools, families, the law, the police, and formal religions, along with cultural customs and mores, constrain our sexualities. But generally speaking, culturally oppressed minorities' relationships and sexualities are more likely to be constrained than those of the hegemonic, or dominant, group. Sodomy laws, which loosely defined acts of sodomy as "crimes against nature" or "unnatural copulations," were intended to punish sexual activities and romantic relationships between homosexual men. People of color have been subject to numerous dehumanizing laws, customs, and discourses that constrain their sexualities (Garcia 2012; Rousseau 2011).

CULTURE AND CONSENT

Important to a discussion of social constraints on sexuality are the concepts of consensual sexual activities, sexual assault, and rape. All involve issues of the relative power of the individuals involved, along with complicated sociocultural histories and contexts regarding gender and sexualities. **Consensual sexual activities** are those agreed upon by the participants, any of whom have the right to decide to stop at any point and for any reason. **Informed, or "effective," sexual consent** has been in the news recently, as hundreds of college campuses have been investigated for poor enforcement of rape and sexual assault laws. Informed, effective consent can be defined as follows:

- "Informed: both parties demonstrate a clear and mutual understanding of exactly what they are consenting to.

- Freely and actively given: there is no coercion, force, threats, intimidation, or pressuring.

- Mutually understandable: expressed in words or actions that indicate a clear willingness to do the same thing, at the same time, in the same way, with each other. Silence does not equal consent.

- Consent is not indefinite; furthermore, consent may be withdrawn at any time, and at that time all sexual activity must cease unless and until additional effective consent is given" (Reed College 2015).

Under such informed consent, consenting to one behavior does not obligate an individual or imply consent to any other behaviors. Consenting to a person or an act on one occasion also does not obligate an individual or imply consent on any other occasion.

Sexual assault encompasses sexual acts of domination, usually enacted by men against women, other men, and children. Such assaults can occur between strangers, but they usually occur between acquaintances or intimates. **Rape**, also a form of domination, is defined as "penetration, no matter how slight, of the vagina or anus with any body part or object, or oral penetration by a sex organ of another person, without the consent of the victim" (Federal Bureau of Investigation 2014).

Communities vary in the probability of sexual violence and the effectiveness of legal, social, and moral constraints on the kinds of behaviors that often lead to such violence. In many religious communities, strong expectations for modesty and sexuality only within marriage keep sexual violence to a minimum. In contrast, the nature of residential colleges' sexual climates can promote a "rape culture" (Boswell and Spade 1996; Plante and Smiler 2014), an environment conducive to sexual assaults and rape. Rape cultures tend to be prevalent in and around college campuses due to several factors, including gender imbalances (more women than men enrolled), the routine presence of alcohol and other drugs at social events and parties, the age of the population, and the relatively unsupervised nature of life "at college." Structural aspects of college campuses that can reproduce gender

Associated Press

These Penn State students and supporters are protesting a campus fraternity's depiction on Facebook of sleeping or unconscious women in the nude. Why are women victimized in this way more often than men?

GL🌐BALIZATION

Group Sex in China

A reflection of global cultural differences in sexuality is the case of Ma Yaohai, a then 53-year-old Chinese professor of computer science whose online name was "Roaring Virile Fire." Ma was sentenced in 2010 for what was called "crowd licentiousness" (Wong 2010). His crime? He organized at least 18 orgies where swingers engaged in group sex and partner swapping. Ma was prosecuted under a law left over from an old Chinese law against "hooliganism"—sex outside marriage—that was abandoned in 1997. Before that old law was dropped, however, the leader of another swingers' club had been executed for his crimes under the "crowd licentiousness" law.

At his trial, Ma Yaohai exclaimed, "How can I disturb social order? What happens in my house is a private matter" (Wong 2010: A8). Nevertheless, he was sentenced to three and a half years in prison. Others in China protested this infringement on personal freedom, specifically the ability to engage in freely chosen sexual activity such as group sex.

China is changing dramatically due to its adoption of capitalism, consumer culture, the Internet, and globalization. The punishment of Ma Yaohai seems out of step in a rapidly changing country in which sexual content is readily available online, brothels are proliferating, and premarital sexual relations are common among young people. One survey found that more than 70 percent of 1,013 respondents ages 20 to 39 had engaged in premarital intercourse. Only 15.5 percent of same-aged respondents had done so in 1989 ("Over 70% of Chinese" 2012). A website, Happy Village, hosts a chat room devoted to swinging. Moreover, love and sex are being discussed more openly on radio and television (Scott and Schwartz 2008).

As in many other parts of the world, sexual culture in China has clearly been changing, but the country's laws have not kept pace. Ma's trial appears to be a case of "cultural lag" (Ogburn 1922) in which the sexual norms and values of the culture have not kept up with rapid social and

Associated Press

Ma Yaohai (center) is shown entering the courtroom for his trial in Nanjing. Do you consider orgies and group sex to be deviant sexual behaviors?

behavioral change. Since many Chinese are likely to resist efforts to make their lives less "sexy," it seems probable that the law will change or, at least, never be enforced again.

Think About It

What social function(s) do laws against certain types of sexual behavior serve? Do such laws benefit anyone? If so, whom? Do you agree that China's law against "crowd licentiousness" is unlikely to be enforced again? Why or why not?

---

imbalances include party systems controlled by fraternities and social life environments that actively or passively promote settings combining alcohol use with assumptions about sexuality (Corprew and Mitchell 2014; Flack et al. 2007).

Sexual assaults and rapes have very serious consequences. According to the World Health Organization (WHO) and the Rape, Abuse, and Incest National Network (RAINN), the largest anti–sexual violence network in the United States, survivors are 3 times more likely to suffer from depression, 4 times more likely to contemplate suicide, 6 times more likely to suffer from posttraumatic stress disorder (PTSD), 26 times more likely to abuse drugs, and 13 times more likely to abuse alcohol as a coping mechanism (RAINN 2014). Sexual violence

is endemic in the United States, where it has been estimated that 17.7 million women have been victims of completed or attempted rapes, along with 2.78 million men. Men and women of color appear disproportionately likely to be victimized, particularly Native American, First Nations (aboriginal people of Canada), and indigenous women. The mental and physical consequences of assaults combined with systematic racism are profound (McGuffey 2008).

SEX AND CONSUMPTION

Regardless of constraints on sexuality, everyday life has been sexualized to a high degree—the world has been "made sexy" (Rutherford 2007). In our consumer society, sex is used to encourage consumption of all sorts of things that are not inherently sexual. Advertisements use sexualized images to promote innumerable products, from cars to toothpaste and from clothing to soft drinks. The implication in many of these ads is that use of the products leads to sexual relationships. The well-known media adage that "sex sells" shows no signs of going out of fashion, and it is certainly applied to sexual products, such as Viagra. However, researchers have found that women usually have a strong negative reaction to explicit sexual content in advertising and are less likely to buy merchandise promoted with these types of ads, unless the sexual content is promoting an expensive item (Vohs, Sengupta, and Dahl 2014). In comparison, men tend to feel positively toward such ads.

More blatant than the use of sexual images to sell products and services is the way in which human sexualities have been increasingly turned into commodities and marketed (Sanders 2013; Y. Taylor 2007). Of course, the consumption of sex is nothing new—after all, prostitution is often referred to as the "oldest profession." What is new since the mid-twentieth century is the rise of a huge sex industry, one whose reach and influence spans the globe. This sexual marketplace may be described as being composed of five interlocking markets (Plummer 2007b):

- *Bodies and sexual acts.* This market includes sex work, such as transactional sexual acts, as well as stripping and table and lap dancing. "Real sex" involving "real bodies" is available for purchase by those who choose to pay.

- *Pornography and erotica.* The production, distribution, sale, and consumption of pornography and erotica are increasingly taking place on the Internet.

- *Sexualized objects.* These include sex toys (e.g., blow-up dolls, dildos, vibrators), drugs that are thought to enhance sexual sensations (e.g., "poppers," or nitrate inhalers), costumes for sadomasochistic sex, and lingerie (Comella 2013).

- *Sexualized technologies.* People around the world increasingly consume contraceptives as well as drugs like Viagra and Cialis (Katsulis 2010). Other sexualized technologies include surgeries for everything from making oneself more sexually attractive (breast enhancement surgery, rehymenization, vaginal rejuvenation, penile enlargement, genital reconstructive surgery) to building vaginas, vulvas, and phalluses as part of gender transitions. Digital technologies, such as smartphones and the Internet, have been similarly sexualized.

- *Sexualized relationships.* Bars and other consumption sites are often locales for beginning sexualized relationships. Help for improving sexualized relationships can be purchased from highly paid sex therapists, from self-help books, and increasingly from innumerable Internet websites.

SEXUALITY, GENDER, AND GLOBALIZATION

SOCIAL CHANGE AND THE GLOBALIZATION OF SEXUALITY

Globalization is one of a number of forces that are affecting and interacting with sexuality in the twenty-first century (Plummer 2012). The globalization of sexuality is linked to a variety of social changes that are altering not only sexuality but also much of what transpires in the social world:

- *Globalized media and technologies.* The global media have been sexualized; they can even be said to have undergone a process of "pornographication" (McNair 2002; Ogas and Gaddam 2012).

- *Increased urbanization.* Urbanization is a key trend across the globe, and it has contributed both to increased freedom of sexual expression and to the globalization of sexuality (Bell 2007). Sex trafficking and sex tourism take place primarily in the world's cities. Major cities such as London, Hong Kong, and Shanghai are the nodes in global "sexscapes" (Kong 2010; Maginn and Steinmetz 2015).

- *Globalized social movements and social change.* Women's movements and gay, lesbian, bisexual, and trans movements (see Chapter 15), as well as more specific social change efforts focused on repressive sex laws, are global. Activists, change agents, and ideas flow, spread, and adapt to their specific contexts (Parker, Garcia, and Buffington 2014).

- *Increased mobility.* Global travel for sex includes sex tourism and sex holidays (Altman 2001; Frank 2012).

Sex tourists are so numerous in places like Bangkok, Thailand, that the Atlanta Hotel found it necessary to post a sign indicating that they were not welcome there.

GLOBAL FLOWS RELATED TO SEX AND SEXUALITY

Sexuality "flows" globally in many other ways as members of various sexual subcultures travel and sexual goods and services move around the world (especially via the Internet). Globalization has had a real effect on sexual interactions, identities, and relationships (Wieringa and Sívori 2013). There are now a number of globally applied sexuality laws, such as those targeting the sexual exploitation of children. Organizations like UNICEF monitor these laws, which seek to protect the vulnerable from sexual abuse and violence. Laws in various countries dealing with sexual crimes, such as rape, have grown increasingly similar (DiMaggio and Powell 1983).

Some norms and values have also become increasingly similar in many parts of the world. For example, there has been a general movement away from trying to control sexuality and procreation while attempting to maintain the collective order. At the same time, there has been a movement toward viewing sexuality as a series of acts that are mainly about pleasure and self-expression. Premarital (or nonmarital) sex has become increasingly normative in many (but certainly not all) parts of the world.

Another example of global cultural change involves the diffusion of such sexual identities as straight, gay, and bisexual. The terms *gay* and *lesbian,* and the idea that they refer to identities, are exports from the Global North. Almost anywhere you go in the world, you may be able to find similar identities, norms, and values relating to sexuality.

Lesbian, Gay, Bisexual, and Queer Sexualities in a Global Context

A key issue for lesbian, gay, bisexual, and queer (LGBQ) people is the barriers that inhibit their movement around the world or encourage their movement from one place to another (Altman 2001; Carrillo and Fontdevila 2014; Lewis 2014). Such barriers may be erected within the home country as well as between countries. Barriers at home that might *push* LGBQ people to migrate include legal prohibitions of consensual sex acts and relationships with same-sex partners, lack of equal opportunity in the workplace, and bans on same-sex marriages. State-sanctioned physical assaults and even murders of LGBQ people can force them to seek better lives elsewhere in the world. They can also be *pulled* elsewhere by better conditions, such as more opportunities to work, marry, and live more freely with less fear. Urban environments are attractive, because large and visible groups of other LGBQ people often create communities and neighborhoods in cities around the globe (Nash and Gorman-Murray 2014).

Other aspects of globalization, such as inexpensive air travel, the Internet, and sex tourism, have made it easier for LGBQ people to communicate and be together anywhere in the world. Globalization has also contributed to the rise of

The Castro neighborhood of San Francisco has been a center of queer sexual expression since the 1960s.

gay and lesbian global social movements and to the increasing acceptance of same-sex sexual relationships in large parts of the world (Stone and Weinberg 2015).

Yet while globalization has aided sexual minorities, it has also facilitated the spread of homophobia and other forms of prejudice and discrimination (Binnie 2004; Kaoma 2014). Globalization clearly has not been an unmitigated good as far as LGBQ people are concerned.

The Global Sex Industry

Industries based on sex have become increasingly important to global capitalism. Bars, dance clubs, massage parlors, pornography, sex work establishments, international hotel chains, airline companies, and the tourist industry create, and help to meet, the demand for sexual labor around the globe.

Sex trafficking, a commercial sex act that includes force, fraud, or coercion and transporting and obtaining a person for sex acts, is truly a global issue. In 2007, the U.S. State Department's annual *Trafficking in Persons Report* estimated that perhaps 12.3 million people around the world had been trafficked, including those living as forced but nonsexual laborers. International governmental agencies estimate the figure to be as high as 27 million people (U.S. Department of State 2007). About 80 percent of transnationally trafficked victims are women and girls; up to 50 percent are children (U.S. Department of State 2011).

The UN Global Initiative to Fight Human Trafficking (2007) estimates that sex trafficking yields annual profits of $31.6 billion. Over the last few decades, most of the countries of the Global South and Eastern Europe have experienced unparalleled growth in at least one aspect of the global sex industry—prostitution, or sex work. Many of these sex workers find their way to the developed nations of the Global North.

The flow of people in the global sex industry moves not only from the South to the North but also in the other direction. Over the past 30 years, the global sex tourism industry has grown to be a multibillion-dollar enterprise (Weitzer 2012; Wortmann 2007). **Sex tourism** occurs when individuals travel to other countries specifically for the purpose of buying sex from men, women, and sometimes children; sex is the primary or sole purpose of these trips. These encounters can be complicated by the fact that locals and tourists usually do not have the same levels of economic privilege. Most sex tourism involves customers traveling from the North to the less developed countries of the South (Katsulis 2010). For example, Thailand receives millions of sex tourists every year from the United States, Western Europe, Australia, and Japan, bringing in billions of dollars (Hepburn and Simon 2013).

Several factors have contributed to the rise of sex tourism. The Internet expedites it, as information about destinations is readily available through websites, chat rooms, e-diaries, blogs, promotional videos, and guidebooks (Wortmann 2007). Websites offer advice on the best tourist sites to visit, the best sex workers at those sites, how to arrange visits, and even how to negotiate with sex workers to get the lowest prices (Katsulis 2010). Many popular destinations for sex tourists have histories of having been dominated by colonial empires (Dewey 2015). Tourists may see such destinations through a "conquering" lens. Social norms are seen as suspended on sex tourism trips, and participants may perceive host countries to be welcoming of such tourism (Padilla 2007). North American and Western European tourists may stereotype Global Southerners as hypersexualized, exotic, and exceptionally interested in sex with them (Kempadoo 1996–1997). Some gay male sex tourists argue that their presence improves the gay climate in the locales to which they travel and "liberates" the local men (Mitchell 2011). Many sex tourists—men and women—believe that their money, attention, and transactions are welcome to the local men, women, and children. That may be so, as poverty leads large numbers of people in sex tourism destinations to participate in the industry.

GLOBAL FLOWS RELATED TO GENDER

THE FEMINIZATION OF MIGRATION

The global economy has contributed to an unprecedented increase in women's migration: "Women are on the move as never before in history" (Ehrenreich and Hochschild 2002: 2). Some have referred to this trend as the "feminization of migration." Much of this flow involves women from the Global South moving, legally and illegally, to the Global North to handle work that was historically performed by Northern women (Runyon 2012). The migrants often become nannies (Eckenwiler 2014), maids (Ehrenreich 2002; Gündüz 2013), or sex workers (Brennan 2002). Most immigrant women are in service occupations (32.6 percent), but some are in professional (22.2 percent) and business/managerial positions (11.2 percent) (see Figure 9.10).

FIGURE 9.10 • Occupational Fields of Female Immigrants in the United States, 2009

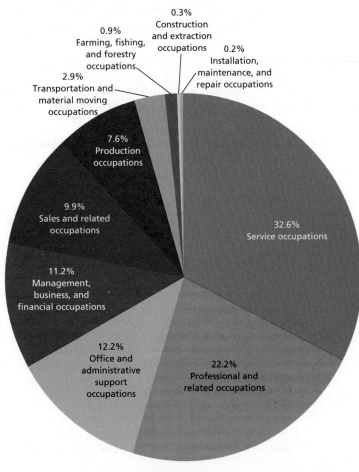

SOURCES: Data from U.S. Census Bureau, Basic Current Population Survey, October 2009; Ariel G. Ruiz, Jie Zong, and Jeanne Batalova, "Immigrant Women in the United States," Migration Policy Institute, March 20, 2015.

This migrant labor enriches the Global North and enhances its already elevated lifestyle. Domestic work is now considered the largest labor market for women worldwide. Many female immigrants clean the homes and care for the children of affluent families while trying to send money (remittances) to their own families in their home countries (Faist, Fauser, and Reisenauer 2013; Hondagneu-Sotelo 2000). They undertake this work because they believe it will bring them better pay and working conditions than they would have back home, improving the quality of life for both the immigrants and their families.

Undocumented and informal migration, which is common for women migrating to the North for domestic work, exposes women to the worst forms of discrimination, exploitation, and abuse (Adams and Campbell 2012; Jones 2008; United Nations 2006). They may be held as debt hostages by recruitment agencies until their transportation and placement fees are paid, imprisoned in the houses of their employers, treated inhumanely, and sometimes murdered. Increasing numbers of migrant women are victims of sexual abuse (including rape), sex trafficking, and prostitution, as discussed above.

THE FEMINIZATION OF LABOR

There has been a notable increase in women's labor force participation rates worldwide, particularly in the Americas and Western Europe. In the United States, 53 percent of women 16 years and older were employed in 2013, compared to 64 percent of men (see Figure 9.11). In 1948, only 31 percent of women were employed, in comparison to 84 percent of men. Even though there are significant variations within and across regions,

women's labor force participation has also risen substantially in sub-Saharan Africa, North Africa, Eastern Europe, Southeast Asia, and East Asia over this period (Cagatay and Ozler 1995; Heintz 2006; Kivisto and Faist 2010; Moghadam 1999). As noted in Chapter 7, while the progress in women's employment status is linked at least in part to gender equality movements, the key factor in this change has been the better integration of an increasing number of areas into the world economy.

The increasing participation of women in the labor force has been termed the **feminization of labor** (Standing 1989). This refers to the rise of female labor participation in all sectors and the movement of women into jobs traditionally held by men. This trend has occurred in both developing and developed countries (Hawkesworth 2006).

The Feminization of Poverty and Female Proletarianization

The feminization of labor, especially in the developing economies, is often accompanied by **female proletarianization** as an increasing number of women are channeled into low-status, poorly paid manual work. Globally, more women are being drawn into labor-intensive and low-paying industries, such as apparel, food processing, and electronics (Chen et al., 2013; Villareal and Yu 2007). Jobs in these industries are characterized by the flexible use of labor, high turnover rates, part-time and temporary employment, and a lack of security and benefits. Female employees are preferred in these industries because of the persistence of a number of stereotypes, including the idea that women will typically work for lower wages and that

FIGURE 9.11 • Employment in the United States, by Gender, 1948–2013

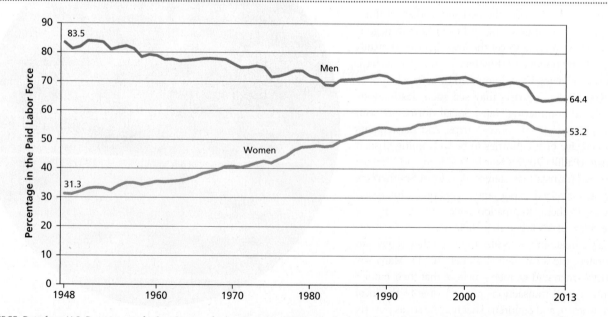

SOURCE: Data from U.S. Department of Labor, Bureau of Labor Statistics, "Women in the Labor Force: A Databook," *BLS Reports*, December 2014 (http://www.bls.gov/opub/reports/cps/women-in-the-labor-force-a-databook-2014.pdf).

Corbis

Women in the Global South, such as these workers at a silk factory in China, are much more likely than their counterparts in the more industrial Global North to be employed in assembly line work or other low-wage labor. Why does this situation persist?

they are easier for male employers and managers to supervise (English 2013). They are considered not only to be more docile but also to have greater patience and more dexterity than men in performing standardized and repetitive work. Female employment is also characterized by poorer and more dangerous working conditions and more compulsory overtime with no extra pay.

ASK YOURSELF

What is the relationship between the feminization of labor and the feminization of poverty? Is this relationship inevitable? What social, structural, and gender-related factors might account for it?

A great deal of attention has been focused on the place of women in what has been called the "global assembly line" (Collins 2003). While high-status research and management jobs are likely to be found in the North,

assembly line work is relegated to the less developed nations of the South (Ward 1990). Women are much more likely to be employed in the latter than in higher-level positions in developed countries.

In corporate economic centers, especially global cities, large amounts of low-wage labor are required, and again women often fill the bill. They help to maintain the offices and lifestyles of entrepreneurs, managers, and professionals through clerical, cleaning, and repair work and labor for companies, providing software, copying paper, office furniture, and even toilet paper (Sassen 2004). Furthermore, the vast majority of provisioning and cleaning of offices, child tending, and caring for the elderly and for homes is done by immigrants, primarily women (Acker 2004).

GENDER, WAR, AND VIOLENCE

Men are certainly more likely than women to be killed or wounded in warfare. However, a 2004 Amnesty International report describes the ways in which women bear the brunt of war, violence, and failed peace efforts. Specifically, women are more likely to be the noncombatant victims of organized

Rape as a Weapon of War

The use of rape as a weapon of war has been so virulent in the African nation of the Democratic Republic of Congo that the UN special representative on sexual violence in conflict called it the "rape capital" of the world (Mawathe 2010). Since 1996, Congo has been characterized by more or less constant warfare and ongoing rebellions. The warring groups often use women's bodies as a battleground, where rape is a sign of power of one group over another. Groups may also use rape in hopes of gaining concessions from those in power, or they may rape out of simple frustration or boredom with life in the forest (Hochschild 2011). Soldiers talk about feeling free and powerful after raping women and girls (Schlanger 2014).

The area is so dangerous that villagers are afraid to go to markets without a UN escort. When they do, they tend to walk behind trucks carrying a few peacekeepers. They constantly yell to the trucks to drive more slowly because they are afraid of a gap developing between the trucks and the line of villagers. Particularly vulnerable are women, who, in the current environment in Congo, are highly likely to be raped, perhaps repeatedly. Police and courts seem to do little about the situation. For example, in 2012, a group of soldiers committed mass rapes in Minova, a beautiful, agriculturally rich town in eastern Congo. As many as 97 women

A sign in the Democratic Republic of Congo ("Sexual violence? No!") is part of a campaign to change perceptions about the acceptability of rape and sexual assault against women. How else might nations try to stem the use of rape as a weapon of war, a problem that has been particularly widespread in Congo?

and 33 girls were raped, yet only 2 of 39 arrested soldiers were convicted of rape.

Many of the women who have been raped are rejected by their husbands and families, who call them "dirty" and cast them out (Mawathe 2010). Other survivors are severely physically injured. The psychological trauma leaves some women entirely emotionless and paralyzed. Rape survivors may find expert medical care and the support of other survivors at specially established medical centers, but their despair is likely to persist for years, if not for a lifetime.

Think About It

Why does rape as a tool of war persist? Is it an act of sex, or one of power and violence? Can its incidence be reduced? If so, how?

---

collective violence, including multinational wars that involve empire building; bilateral wars among nations, usually over territory; wars of liberation from colonialism and tyrannical governments; and civil wars (Gerami and Lehnerer 2007; Liebling-Kalifani et al. 2013). Women also deal with the effects of local and global terrorism and political violence (Gentry and Sjoberg 2015).

Several changes have made it more likely that women will be the victims of international violence. One is the change in the nature of warfare. For example, "asymmetric warfare," or warfare involving forces of unequal capabilities, often takes the form of shootouts in the streets. Generally, the line between combatants and civilians has blurred, with the result that more civilians, including women, have become the victims of warfare. Finally, more women are in the armed forces and in terrorist groups (e.g., Islamic State, Boko Haram; see below) in various countries, and this greatly increases their chances of being the victims of violence. In some cases, terrorist groups use women to carry concealed explosives and to detonate them in or near targets, killing themselves and those in the vicinity (Gentry and Sjoberg 2015).

A consequence of war that also affects women is the use of rape and sexual assault as weapons (see the "Globalization" box on page 222). Rape and sexual assault have long been used to weaken and demoralize the nation-states and ethnic enclaves in which victims live. Rape is also used as a tool of war to traumatize the victims and to humiliate the enemy by "taking" their women. As is true of rape in general (Kellezi and Reicher 2014; Rudrappa 2012), rape in warfare is not a sexual act, but rather an act of power (Brownmiller 1975).

THE GLOBAL WOMEN'S MOVEMENT

As you have seen, globalization and the rise of a global economy have created or exacerbated a variety of inequalities faced by women. One response has been expansion of the international women's movement (see Chapter 15). It has grown dramatically in recent years because of problems created for women by globalization. It has also expanded because of the increased ability of those working on behalf of the movement to travel globally and to communicate with one another. The international women's movement is traceable to the late 1800s (Rupp 1997). It has focused on issues such as sexual violence, reproductive rights, labor issues, and sexual harassment. Its greatest triumphs have related to women's right to vote in countries around the world (Ramirez, Soysal, and Shanahan 1997).

The larger global women's movement seeks to address a variety of issues: human rights (Yuval-Davis 2006), economic concerns, the environment, health care, and violence against women. The movement has also come to focus on the adverse effects of global capitalism (e.g., increased global trafficking in women), the lack of women's voices in global civil society, the growth of antifeminist fundamentalist movements (Taliban, Islamic State, Boko Haram), and the HIV/AIDS epidemic. More generally, the international women's movement has focused attention on issues of global justice for women and other minorities. Women throughout the world have also responded at local and regional levels to common problems caused by globalization. They also localize global political activities undertaken by the international women's movement and global human rights groups. In addition, they organize against global activities such as militarism and conflict and use global organizations (such as the UN and international nongovernmental organizations) to help in local and regional activities (Naples and Desai 2002). However, even the activities that have been primarily or exclusively local in nature have had profound effects globally. Even with all the local variations, feminism can be seen as "a truly global phenomenon" (Ferree and Tripp 2006: viii).

SUMMARY

Sex is principally a biological concept and is typically reflected in a person's chromosomes, gonads, genitalia, and hormones. *Gender* is a cultural term, connected to societal definitions of expected behaviors, attitudes, and personalities. It is the physical, behavioral, and personality characteristics that are defined as appropriate for someone's sex. While sex is based mainly on biology, gender is based on social distinctions and is subject to change.

Femininities and masculinities are socially constructed and also subject to change and variation. Transgender and intersexed individuals confront the difficulties of living in a society that is still based on binary gender and sex.

Gendered inequalities persist in numerous domains, including in education, at home and in families, and at work. Such inequalities affect people differently depending on race and class.

Humans enact a wide variation of expressions of both biological sex and sexuality—people are not simply female or male, homosexual or heterosexual. Learned, culturally specific sexual scripts account more for gender differences in sexuality than do biological differences. Global sexualities reveal similarities and differences in things like identities and homophobia.

Globalization reinforces but also destabilizes preexisting gender structures on a global scale. The greater flow of people also creates more opportunity for traffickers to transport women and children for sexual exploitation. Globalization is linked to the increasing number of women working in the Global South, although many are drawn into low-status, poorly paid, and sometimes dangerous manual work. Rape as a weapon of war and domination persists around the globe. The international women's movement has gained strength and has some goals in common with local and regional women's movements around the world.

1. What is the difference between sex and gender? How does sex affect gender? How does gender affect sexuality?
2. What do sociologists mean when they say that there are few clear-cut biological differences between men and women?
3. What are the differences in the ways that men and women experience "hegemonic masculinity" and "emphasized femininity"? How do these constructs help create and reinforce gender stratification?
4. How do men and women differ in terms of their educational experiences? In what ways does the hidden curriculum of educational systems reinforce gender stratification?
5. Why are women and men treated differently as consumers? What events in recent decades have changed the way women are thought of as consumers?
6. What are the differences in the ways that men and women approach sexuality? How are the differences related to the socialization process? Do you think increasing equality between men and women will affect sexualities?
7. In what ways has the sex industry become increasingly important to global capitalism? How is this sex industry reflective of gender stratification? How is it reflective of inequalities between the Global North and South?
8. In what positive and negative ways have lesbians, gays, bisexuals, and trans people been affected by globalization?
9. What do sociologists mean by the "feminization of poverty"? By "female proletarianization"? How are these related to one another and to the more general process of the "feminization of labor"?
10. What types of violence are women most likely to experience when they live in places experiencing war and other types of armed conflict?

APPLYING THE SOCIOLOGICAL IMAGINATION ·····················

The United Nations has been referred to as the "unlikely godmother" of the global women's movement because, while being led primarily by men, it has been a key ally of that movement. In fact, the United Nations is responsible for the most complete international agreement on the basic human rights of women, the Convention on the Elimination of All Forms of Discrimination against Women, known as CEDAW.

For this activity, do research on the history of CEDAW. How does CEDAW define discrimination against women? What are the basic principles of the articles of the convention? How do these relate to the issues discussed in this chapter? What countries have ratified CEDAW? What sort of success has CEDAW had in addressing issues of global gender stratification?

KEY TERMS ·····························

consensual sexual activities: Sexual activities agreed upon by the participants, any of whom have the right to decide to stop at any point and for any reason. (p. 215)

emphasized femininity: A set of socially constructed ideas about "model womanhood" organized around accommodating the interests of men and patriarchy. (p. 204)

female proletarianization: The channeling of an increasing number of women into low-status, poorly paid manual work. (p. 220)

feminization of labor: The rise of female labor participation in all sectors and the movement of women into jobs traditionally held by men. (p. 220)

gender: The physical, behavioral, and personality characteristics that are socially defined as appropriate for one's sex. (p. 202)

gender identity: A person's internal sense of gender. (p. 204)

gender role: The social presentation of gender that includes clothing, hairstyle, and attitudinal and behavioral traits. (p. 204)

hegemonic masculinity: The dominant form or most idealized vision of masculinity; taken for granted as natural and linked to patriarchy. (p. 203)

heterosexism: The belief that heterosexuality is superior to other sexual orientations; individual and institutional discrimination against those with other orientations. (p. 213)

heterosexual double standard: A cultural belief system in which men are expected to desire and seek sex from whomever, whenever, while women are expected to be sexual only within committed, romantic relationships. (p. 214)

hidden curriculum: A school's unofficial norms, routines, and structures that transmit dominant cultural norms and values. (p. 206)

homophobia: The fear of being, appearing, or seeming gay; fear of anyone or "anything" gay. (p. 213)

informed (effective) sexual consent: Participants' understanding of and free consent to specific sexual activities in a mutually understandable way. (p. 215)

intersex: A general term used for a variety of (medical) conditions in which a person is born with reproductive or sexual anatomy that does not seem to fit the typical definitions of male or female. (p. 202)

rape: Penetration, no matter how slight, of the vagina or anus with any body part or object, or oral penetration by a sex organ of another person, without the consent of the victim. (p. 215)

sex: A biological term, expressed as *female* or *male*; typically reflected in chromosomes, gonads, genitalia, and hormones. (p. 202)

sex tourism: Activity that occurs when individuals travel to other countries for the purpose of buying sex from men, women, and sometimes children there; sex is the primary or sole purpose of these trips. (p. 219)

sex trafficking: A commercial sex act that includes force, fraud, or coercion and transporting and obtaining a person for sex acts. (p. 218)

sexual assault: Sexual acts of domination, usually enacted by men against women, other men, and children. (p. 215)

sexual identity: An internal sense of one's sexual self. (p. 213)

sexual orientation: Involves whom one desires (fantasies), with whom one wants to have sexual relations (behavior), and with whom one has a sense of connectedness (feelings). (p. 213)

sexual scripts: The culturally produced, shared, and reinforced social norms that serve as blueprints, or maps, to guide sexual and gender behavior. (p. 214)

sexuality: The ways in which people think about, and behave toward, themselves and others as sexual beings. (p. 212)

transgender: An umbrella term for people whose gender identity and/or gender presentation differs from the gender assigned at birth or in infancy. (p. 204)

$SAGE edge™ edge.sagepub.com/ritzeressentials2e

SAGE edge offers a robust online environment featuring an impressive array of free tools and resources for review, study, and further exploration, keeping both instructors and students on the cutting edge of teaching and learning.

LEARNING OBJECTIVES	FOR FURTHER EXPLORATION AND APPLICATION
LO 9-1: Discuss the cultural influences on gender and the effects of gender inequalities.	▶ *Miss Representation*: How the Media Portrays Women ◔ Gay Masculinity: It's a Spectrum ▣ Myths, Stereotypes and Gender Differences
LO 9-2: Describe the ways in which social forces and factors constrain sexuality.	▶ The Sociology of Sexuality ◔ How To Be a 21st-Century "Gentleman" ▣ The Gender Identity Project
LO 9-3: Describe the effects of globalization on gender and sexualities.	▶ War, Work, and Sex: Human Trafficking and Globalization ◔ How Global Protests Challenged the Kenyan Court System ▣ An End to the Sex Trade
LO 9-4: Discuss global flows related to gender.	▶ Exposing Sexual Slavery and Enforced Prostitution in India ◔ Same-Sex Marriage in Ireland ▣ Protecting Children from Sexual Abuse and Violence

FAMILIES

10

Fictional Families Get Real

Fictional, very traditional, families were a staple in the early years of television, most notably on the shows *I Love Lucy* (1951-1957) and *Adventures of Ozzie and Harriet* (1952-1966). The best-known early series to deal with a real family, and TV's first reality show, was the groundbreaking *An American Family*, which aired on public television in the 1970s. It was intended simply to chronicle the happy, mundane lives of a husband and wife and their five children, but over the course of the series cracks in the family's calm and stable facade became apparent, exposing events never before seen on U.S. television. The public witnessed the husband and wife's real-life separation and subsequent divorce, for example, and the eldest son's coming out as television's first openly gay person.

Since then, family-based television shows, both fictional and nonfictional, have flourished and become increasingly "real," going far beyond the kinds of problems depicted in *An American Family*. The fictional *Transparent* (begun in 2014) portrays a family with an array of difficulties, most notably drug addiction and challenges traceable to the discovery that the father is transgender and frequently appears in public wearing dresses. The reality show *Keeping Up with the Kardashians* depicts a number of family members who deal with divorce, have numerous affairs, perform in a sex tape, are arrested for drunk driving, and so on. Compared to early TV shows about the family, those on the air today are not only more honest but also reflect the dramatically changing nature of the family.

It should come as no surprise that family-based TV shows are enormously popular. Family, after all, is a universal social institution. It constitutes a person's first group and primary socializer, and, for many, it is a lifelong source of companionship and security. Because the institution of family is such a central part of life, it is natural

LEARNING OBJECTIVES

 10-1 Explain basic sociological concepts of the family, marriage, and intimate relationships.

 10-2 Describe trends leading to the decline in marriage rates and changes in stepfamilies, blended families, and lesbian and gay families.

10-3 Apply structural/functional, conflict/critical, and inter/actionist theories to the family.

 10-4 Describe family conflict, forms of abuse and violence within the family, and the effects of poverty on family life.

10-5 Identify the effects of globalization and global flows on the family today.

Getty

Enoch Foster reads a bedtime story with his two wives and six of their their eight children. This family structure is known as polygamy or plural marriage.

that we are fascinated by—and even feel connected to—the intimate relationships, conflicts, and problems experienced by families.

As television shows indicate, the structure of a family can take a great number of forms. Extended and nuclear families have proven popular over the last 100 years, but recent social changes have opened a wide variety of other options. Some couples involve a man and woman, but homosexual and lesbian marriages are increasingly common (and, as of mid-2015, legal throughout the United States). Some couples, whatever their gender, marry for love, others for purely economic reasons, and an increasing number choose not to marry at all. Some have many children, while others have one child or none. Some maintain exclusive partnerships until death, others divorce and many of them remarry, and still others incorporate new members into existing relationships.

Family-based TV shows paint a picture of domestic dynamics and realities that is captivating and intriguing but by no means complete. They largely sidestep issues critical to sociology, such as poverty, gender inequality, and the prevalence of domestic abuse. Also unlike sociology, they have not adopted a global perspective, choosing instead to focus on American families. That leaves us with much to learn and study. ●

FAMILY, MARRIAGE, AND INTIMATE RELATIONSHIPS

The **family** is defined as a group of people who are related by descent, marriage, or adoption. However, because of the growth of families that include others, such as cohabiting adults with or without children, the U.S. Census Bureau simply defines the family as "two or more people residing in the same housing unit." Families are especially important in socializing children so that they are able to fit into the larger society. Although families often fail in this and many other things, sociologists continue to view the family as a universal social institution that is central to social life (Powell and Branden 2007). Sociologists are interested in such issues as the relationship between family and marriage, the different forms taken by families, and how families are formed and maintained, expand and contract, and even dissolve (Farrell, VandeVusse, and Ocobock 2012).

A Sociologist Teams with a Comedian to Analyze "Modern Romance"

Sociologist Eric Klinenberg recently teamed up with the popular comedian Aziz Ansari to write the best seller *Modern Romance* (2015). While it is not a scholarly book, it manages, in an accessible and appealing way, to bring important sociological ideas on this topic (such as companionate marriage; see page 232) to a large and youthful audience that would not normally be exposed to them. Ansari's comedic talents combine with Klinenberg's scholarship (and the work of other scholars, especially sociologists) to produce a humorous *and* sociologically informed analysis of (mainly) middle-class, heterosexual relationships in the modern era of smartphones, texting, online dating (now by far the most common way that people meet their future spouses), social media, and mobile dating swipe apps such as Tinder. The book is based not only on Ansari's stand-up comedy routines (as exemplified in his HBO and Netflix

specials) and his personal experiences but also on a variety of data sources, such as information derived from focus groups in the United States and elsewhere, large surveys and data sets, the tracking of information on subjects' smartphones, interviews with a number of experts in the field, and a Modern Romantics forum on the website Reddit.

Among the book's conclusions is that while in the past people were likely to be happy with a satisfactory choice for a spouse and a "good enough marriage," they are now more likely to seek a perfect spouse, a "soul mate." Because of new norms and technologies, as well as infinitely more options, people are able to meet, spend time with, and live with a number of people before deciding, if they ever do, on a long-term relationship, let alone marriage.

The key issue is whether these possibilities make for better choices and a

happier life than the more limited options open to people only a few decades ago. It turns out that negotiating the new romantic world in order to find one's soul mate is very time-consuming and stressful. The attempt to find a soul mate has the highest potential for *both* disappointment *and* happiness. While the book certainly does not argue for a return to the older and easier system of "settling" for someone who lives nearby or goes to the same school, it does make it clear that modern romance is not without its own difficulties.

Think About It

Do you think that a sociologist writing a best-selling, nonacademic book with a comedian helps or hurts the public image and status of sociology? Are you interested in getting married? If so, are you searching for a soul mate? Or would you settle for someone who is "good enough"?

SOME BASIC CONCEPTS

In this section, we will define such basic concepts and ideas as marriage, intimate relationships, and love and explore their roles in the family.

Marriage

Marriage is the socially acknowledged and approved and often legal union of two people, allowing them to live together and to have children by birth or adoption. Families govern various issues that relate to marriage, such as the "meanings of marriage" as well as "the number of marriage partners" (Shaw and Lee 2009: 378). **Monogamy** has traditionally been defined as marriage between one wife and one husband. However, given the changes in laws related to gay marriage, monogamy today might involve two wives or two husbands. There are also many other forms of marriage, such as **polygamy**, which allows multiple spouses. **Polygyny**, in which a single husband has multiple wives, is a more common form of polygamy than **polyandry**, in

which a single wife has multiple husbands. **Cenogamy** is group marriage.

Historically and around the world, rules, customs, and laws have been created to define and control marriage. Key to understanding marriage (and thus most families) is the concept of **endogamy**, or marriage to someone with similar characteristics in terms of race, ethnicity, religion, education level, social class, and so on (Penn forthcoming). In contrast, **exogamy** involves marriage to someone with characteristics that are dissimilar on these dimensions. Throughout history, families have been defined much more by endogamy than by exogamy. In recent years, endogamy has declined in importance, and there is more exogamy. For example, there has been an increasing tendency of Americans to marry persons of other races (Qian and Lichter 2011). However, as a general rule, families continue to be characterized more by endogamy than by exogamy.

In the last several decades, the nature of family and marriage has undergone a series of rapid and dizzying changes.

It is less and less clear exactly what constitutes marriage or a family. One thing is clear, however: The close linkage between marriage and the family has been greatly weakened, if not broken. Nevertheless, most people in the United States end up being married one or more times during their lifetimes. And those who marry often create families, although they may not stay together as long as families did in the past. Being married and in a family does not mean that the marriage or the family will remain the same for decades, or even years. Nevertheless, while marriage and the family will remain important intimate relationships, they will not be the only, or even the dominant, forms of intimacy in the future.

Intimate Relationships

An **intimate relationship** involves partners who have a close, personal, *and* domestic relationship with one another (Jamieson 2011). This relationship is usually a result of courtship rituals in which two people are attracted to each other, develop intimacy, enjoy each other's company, and identify as a couple after a period of dating.

The nature of intimacy is not static; rather, it changes over time. Fifty or a hundred years ago, couples could be intimate without necessarily sharing very much about themselves with each other, especially their most private thoughts. However, in Western culture today, intimacy increasingly involves disclosing much, if not everything, about oneself to one's partner (Jamieson 2007). Levels of disclosure tend to be gendered (Kimmel 2012). Women tend to function as emotional caretakers within heterosexual relationships. They do so because they are generally socialized to engage in communication in which they express their emotions, whereas men are socialized to suppress their emotions and communicate little about them. In other words, women tend to be the ones to share first and to help men to share by drawing them out. The assumption made by most women is that such self-disclosure will strengthen a relationship because there are no secrets and therefore there will be no surprises, or at least there will be fewer of them, as the relationship develops.

Love

Intimacy in domestic relationships is, of course, often associated with love (Ansari 2015; Frieze 2007). **Passionate love** has a sudden onset, inspires strong sexual feelings, and tends to include idealization of the one who is loved (Hatfield, Bensman, and Rapson 2012). Passionate love brings with it great intimacy, but it is an intimacy very likely to be short-lived. In contrast, **companionate love** develops more gradually, is not necessarily tied to sexual passion, and is based on more rational assessments of the one who is loved. Companionate love is more likely than passionate love to lead to long-lasting intimate relationships. However, these two types of love are not clearly distinguished from one another. This is clearest in the fact that long-term intimate relationships often start out with passionate love, but in those that succeed over time it tends to be combined with, or even supplanted by, companionate love.

Zygmunt Bauman has sought to get at the essence of love in the contemporary world in his book *Liquid Love* (2003). On the cover of the book is a heart drawn in the sand. However, the sea is nearby, and the implication is that love will soon be washed away by the waves. To Bauman, love, like everything else in today's liquid society, is fleeting. This clearly applies to passionate love, but Bauman sees even companionate love today as constantly at risk of erosion and disappearance. This represents a major challenge to all intimate relationships, especially marriage, and to all of those involved in them. However, liquid love can also be seen as offering people freedom from lifelong loveless relationships. It also offers the possibility of innumerable experiences with love and many different relationships built on love.

ASK YOURSELF

What do you think of Bauman's concept of "liquid love"? Do you agree that love is fleeting, and that this impermanence is a reflection of a society in which nothing lasts? Why or why not? Would you find the experience of liquid love troubling, or liberating? Why?

It can be argued that family and marriage are also becoming more liquid. Because they are now so liquid, the borders of marriage and the family are increasingly difficult to define. More important, many traditional forms of marriage and the family are confronting the possibility of being washed away. As a result, many sociologists have moved away from a focus on the family and marriage and prefer to discuss vaguer phenomena such as "relationships" and "personal life." Nevertheless, most people, including most sociologists, continue to think in terms of marriage and the family (Powell et al. 2010). We will do the same in this chapter, but with an understanding that both are changing dramatically and refer to phenomena that are far more liquid than they once were.

BROAD CHANGES IN MARRIAGE AND THE FAMILY

We will discuss two major changes in this section: the decline in marriage and changes in the family household, especially "going solo."

FIGURE 10.1 • U.S. Households by Type, 1970 to 2012

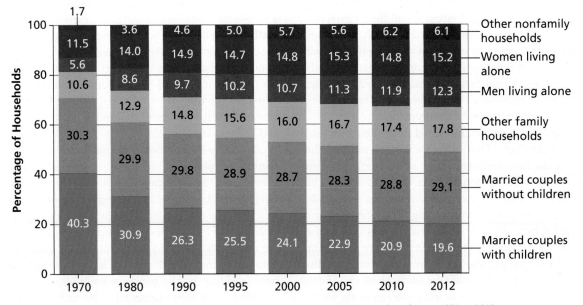

SOURCE: U.S. Census Bureau, Current Population Survey, Annual Social and Economic Supplement, selected years, 1970 to 2012.

DECLINE IN MARRIAGE

In 1970, married couples constituted 70.6 percent of all U.S. households (see Figure 10.1); by 2012, only 48.7 percent of all households were married couples. Similarly, the traditional **nuclear family** consisting of two adults and one or more children dropped from 40.3 percent of all households in 1970 to not quite 20 percent of all households in 2012.

Another way to get a sense of the dramatic change in marriage and the family is to look at the percentage of those who have never been married. Figure 10.2 shows that in 2012, 23 percent of men and 17 percent of women in the United States ages 25 and older had never been married, compared to 10 percent of men and 8 percent of women in 1960. It remains the case that as people age, they are more likely to marry. Figure 10.3 shows that in 2012, 32 percent of men and 25 percent of women had never been married by age 35. And by age 45, 19 percent of men and 14 percent of women had never married. In comparison, in 1960 only 7 percent of men and 6 percent of women had never married by the age of 45. Further declines are expected in most, if not all, age categories.

PERSPECTIVES ON THE DECLINE IN MARRIAGE

The decline in marriage (and the family) has led to some fascinating new perspectives on the status of marriage today.

The Deinstitutionalization of Marriage

Andrew Cherlin (2004; Treas, Lui, and Gubernskaya 2014) focuses on the "deinstitutionalization of American marriage." By **deinstitutionalization**, he means that the social norms relating to marriage have weakened. As a result, people increasingly question their actions, or those of others, as they relate to marriage. While Cherlin focuses on this

FIGURE 10.2 • Share of Never-Married Adults in the United States, by Gender, 1960–2012

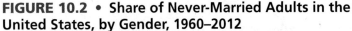

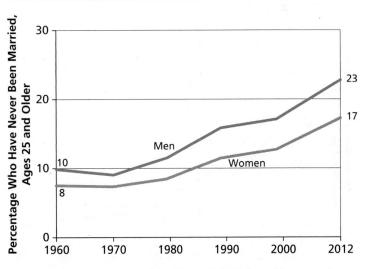

SOURCE: Pew Research Center analysis of the 1960–2000 decennial census and 2010–2012 American Community Survey, Integrated Public Use Microdata Series (IPUMS), September 24, 2014 (http://www.pewsocialtrends.org/files/2014/09/2014-09-24_Never-Married-Americans.pdf). Reprinted by permission of Pew Research Center, Washington, DC.

deinstitutionalization in the United States, he recognizes that a similar process is occurring in much of Europe as well as in Canada. In the mid-twentieth century, especially in the United States, few questioned marriage and the creation of a nuclear family. As a result, most plunged into both, sometimes successfully, but more often with dubious or even disastrous results. Now, with marriage and perhaps the nuclear family and the family household deinstitutionalized, it is much easier for people *not* to rush into such arrangements. They are freer to experiment with many other arrangements.

Five factors have been influential in the deinstitutionalization of marriage. First, as more women entered the labor force, the clear division of labor in the family between homemaker and breadwinner began to break down. The once-clear norms about what men and women were to do in a marital relationship were eroding. This contributed a more general lack of clarity about marriage as well as the family. Second, the norms about having children within the context of marriage and the family were also eroding. This was demonstrated in the dramatic increase in childbirth outside of marriage, which rose from one out of six births in the late 1970s to one out of three in the early twenty-first century. Third, the high and increasing divorce rate between 1960 and 1980 contributed to the deinstitutionalization of marriage. Although the divorce rate has declined in recent decades, the high rate between 1960 and the late 1970s and early 1980s had a seemingly irreversible impact on attitudes toward marriage. Fourth has been the growth in cohabitation, which began in the 1970s and accelerated as the twentieth century ended. Finally, same-sex marriage

flowered in the 1990s and has grown further in the twenty-first century.

These ideas on deinstitutionalization are embedded in a long-term model of change. In the early twentieth century, **institutional marriage** was the predominant form. The focus in such a marriage was on the maintenance of the institution of marriage itself. There was less concern that those involved would love or be good companions to one another. Today, many see the time of institutional marriage as past; others, however, see it as alive and well and as having a future (Lauer and Yodanis 2010).

By the middle of the twentieth century, a model of **companionate marriage** (see the discussion of companionate love above) had become predominant (Amato et al. 2007; Burgess and Locke 1945). Companionate marriage meshed well with the nuclear family. It involved a clear division of labor between the single-earner breadwinner—almost always the male—and the female homemaker. In spite, or perhaps because, of the strict division of labor, husbands and wives were held together by bonds of sentiment, friendship, and sexuality. They were supposed to be each other's companions, which included being each other's friends, confidants, and lovers. Romantic love was an essential component of companionate marriage.

In the 1960s, a dramatic shift began to take place in the direction of **individualized marriage** (Lauer and Yodanis 2011). The goal of companionate marriage was the satisfaction of the couple, the family as a whole, and the roles the couple played in the family. However, that focus began to shift in the direction of the satisfaction of each individual, as well as toward individuals' ability to develop and express their selves. In addition, in contrast to the rigidity of companionate marriage, individualized marriage became increasingly open and flexible. Furthermore, couples were becoming more open with each other in communicating about and dealing with problems. Many couples, as well as many observers, applauded the greater freedoms and sensitivities associated with individualized marriage.

A major factor in the rise of individualized marriage was the changing place of women, especially middle-class women, in society. For example, as more women went to work, they were no longer restricted to the homemaker role and reliance on the male breadwinner. As more women obtained higher education, their occupational prospects were enhanced. This put them in a context where ideas associated with companionate marriage were increasingly

FIGURE 10.3 • Share of Never-Married Adults in the United States, by Age, 2012

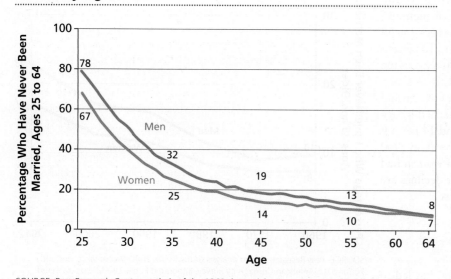

SOURCE: Pew Research Center analysis of the 1960 decennial census, Integrated Public Use Microdata Series (IPUMS), September 24, 2014 (http://www.pewsocialtrends.org/files/2014/09/2014-09-24_Never-Married-Americans.pdf). Reprinted by permission of Pew Research Center, Washington, DC.

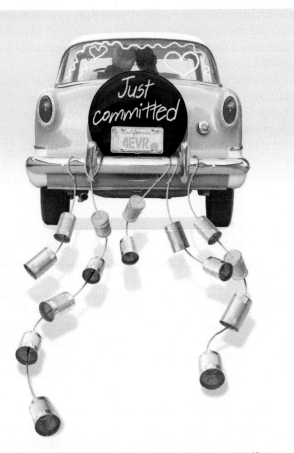

Given the deinstitutionalization of marriage, are "just committed" celebrations likely to supplant "just married" celebrations?

separation and divorce add to the merry-go-round and its increasingly dizzying speed. Then there may be a series of cohabitations into and out of which people move. Thus, many people have not given up on the idea and even the practice of marriage, but marriage exists side by side with the often conflicting notion of individualism. People want to be legally defined as couples and as families, but they also want to be free of constraints and to act as they wish as individuals. The findings of current sociological research underscore this paradox. On the one hand, researchers are told that most people, including young adults, want an "exclusive, lifelong intimate partnership, most commonly a marriage" (Hull, Meier, and Ortyl 2010: 37). Hoffnung and Williams (2013) surveyed about 200 female college seniors in 1993. A follow-up of those women in 2009 found, unsurprisingly, that 91 percent of them had married, nearly 75 percent were mothers, and 57 percent were combining motherhood and full-time work outside the home. The women contended that the most satisfying thing they had ever done was mothering. On the other hand, people often indicate by their behavior that they want to be free of such bonds. Americans remain committed to the ideal of marriage, but in reality they spend fewer of their adult years married than did those in previous generations.

Getty

ASK YOURSELF

Which do most of your peers seem to want, an exclusive lifelong partnership such as marriage or the freedom to live and act as an individual? What might account for their preference? Which is your preference?

---

open to question. Greater access to contraception and to abortion enabled more women to plan their reproductive lives, releasing them from some of the constraints of companionate marriage as they related to producing and socializing children.

As a result of all these changes, people today feel freer to never marry, to marry later, to end unhappy marriages, and especially to engage in many other types of intimate relationships. Yet, in spite of these changes, the vast majority of people—as many as 90 percent or more—will eventually marry, although many of their marriages will end long before they reach the "till death do us part" stage. Thus, marriage has not been deinstitutionalized to the degree anticipated by Cherlin, and it is likely to survive, although it will not be nearly as important as it once was (Lauer and Yodanis 2010).

Marriage as a Carousel

In *The Marriage-Go-Round* (2009), Cherlin adopts a somewhat different perspective involving a "carousel of intimate partners." Some intimate partners are to be found in marriages, but those marriages are more likely to end; people are likely to remarry, perhaps more than once. Rounds of

Self-Disclosing Intimacy and Pure Relationships

British sociologist Anthony Giddens (1992) offers an ambivalent view on the new individualized forms of marriage and of relationships more generally. The key to these new forms of relationships is "self-disclosing intimacy" (Duncan 2014). Couples are disclosing much more to each other. As a result, much more intimate relationships are likely to develop. This is contrasted with companionate marriages, which were more likely to be based on secrets and half-truths. Thus, companionate marriages may survive for decades or a lifetime even though they may be based on deceptions that leave one or both partners in the dark. The partners often remain in such marriages for reasons other than their openness and honesty. They may stay together because of social norms against divorce or "for the sake of the children."

Giddens recognizes the advantages of self-disclosing intimacy, but he also argues that intimate relationships based on full disclosure are made much more fragile by such disclosures, especially as the disclosures continue and proliferate over time. The more weaknesses someone reveals to a partner, the more likely that partner is to become disappointed with the relationship. Despite this, Giddens, as well as many others today, seems to prefer relationships based on mutual disclosure because he believes they are likely to be more mutually satisfying, equal, and democratic. Further, he contends that almost anything is preferable to being locked into the kind of dishonest and unsatisfying relationship often associated with companionate marriage.

Since marriage of any kind can be confining and limiting, Giddens (1992) has coined the term *pure relationships* to describe a new reality. A **pure relationship** is one that is entered into for its own sake, or for what each partner can get from it, and those in it remain only as long as each derives sufficient satisfaction from it. While pure relationships can exist within marriage, they are more likely to exist outside such legal relationships. As a result of the increasing predominance of this idea, at least among young people, a relationship is likely to be ended when the couple no longer finds it satisfying. It is also likely that another, different pure relationship (or several) will be formed in relatively short order, or perhaps even simultaneously with the existing one. This fits with the increasing individualization of contemporary society as well as the closely related phenomenon of individuals wanting more choices and greater freedom of choice. It represents a greater degree of individualization than even that found in individualized marriage. Less constrained by marriage, or more likely not married at all, couples are free to individualize their lives to a much greater degree. Marriage is seen as just one of a wide range of lifestyle choices open to couples. In whatever type of intimate relationship people find themselves today, the possibility that it will dissolve is never very far from their consciousness. This may be one of the reasons young adults are putting off developing intimate relationships. They are more likely to consider an intimate, committed relationship as the last stage of adult development, unlike in the 1950s, when such relationships were more likely to develop in early adulthood (Rauer et al. 2013).

The idea of the pure relationship has its origins in Western society, but, like many such ideas in the global age, it has flowed readily to many locales around the world.

Questioning the New Ideas on Marriage and Relationships

Some observers have challenged the range of new ideas about intimate relationships. For example, Lynn Jamieson (1998, 2012) questions the importance of self-disclosing intimacy. There are many forms of intimacy other than those based on self-disclosure, and

good relationships are based on more than such disclosures. For instance, negotiating an equitable division of labor in the home may do more for increasing intimacy than a wide range of self-disclosures.

Interestingly, a major critique of these new ideas on marriage and the family is implicit in the work of one of sociology's classic social theorists, Georg Simmel (see Chapters 1, 2, and 4). In his famous essay on secrecy, Simmel ([1906] 1950; Coll 2012) argues that while there is always a temptation to reveal all to a partner in an intimate relationship, especially marriage, making such revelations is a big mistake. In his view, all relationships require a certain proportion of both openness and secrecy, and marriage is no exception. Even if it were possible to disclose everything about oneself, and it almost certainly isn't, this would only serve to make marriage boring and matter-of-fact because all possibility of the unexpected would be eliminated. Finally, most of us have limited internal resources, and every revelation reduces the (secret) treasures that we have to offer our mates. Only those few with great storehouses of personal assets and accomplishments can afford numerous revelations to a marriage partner. All others are left denuded—and perhaps less interesting—by excessive self-revelation. The contrast is striking between Simmel's ideas, written more than a century ago, and the current thinking of many who emphasize the importance of revealing all to intimate partners.

NONFAMILY HOUSEHOLDS: "GOING SOLO"

A **nonfamily household** is one in which a person lives either alone or with nonrelatives. Of greatest interest is the

FIGURE 10.4 • Percentage of U.S. Households with One Person, 1960–2012

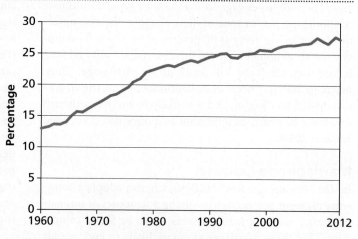

SOURCE: U.S. Census Bureau, Current Population Survey, 1960 to 2011, Annual Social and Economic Supplements (http://www.census.gov/newsroom/pdf/cah_slides.pdf).

growth of one-person households, or people living alone (Klinenberg 2012). As is clear in Figure 10.4, the United States has witnessed an increase in such households, from 13 percent in 1960 to more than 27 percent of all households in 2012.

Overall, 31 million Americans now live alone. The fastest-growing segment of the population going solo is young adults between ages 18 and 34. In 1950, only a half million of those in this age group lived alone, while today the total is 10 times that number. Among those who are middle-aged (35 to 64), 15 million live alone, while 10 million of the elderly are singletons. More women (17 million) than men (14 million) live alone. Going solo is mainly an urban phenomenon; more than half of dwellings in Manhattan are one-person residences.

There are several reasons for the increase in singletons. First, increasing economic affluence has made it possible for more people to afford the greater costs associated with living alone. Second, living alone is consistent with the growth of individualism in the United States and much of the developed world. Third, the rising status of women and their higher levels of education and higher-paying jobs (although their wages continue to be lower than men's and they are more likely than men to be poor) enable more to live alone. With greater independence, they are more likely to marry later, separate, or divorce. Fourth, the communications revolution has allowed people to communicate with other people, and to be entertained, while they are home alone. Fifth, mass urbanization has made the active social life of the city available to more people. Finally, the population is aging, and as people live longer, they are more likely to find themselves alone.

While living alone might well have been considered a problem in the past, Klinenberg (2012: 17–18) argues that increasing numbers of people are coming to prefer going solo. It allows people to pursue "individual freedom, personal control, and self-realization. . . . It allows us to do what we want, when we want, on our own terms." Interestingly, singletons may also be more socially active than those who live with others.

ALTERNATIVE FORMS OF FAMILIES

Recent social changes have made it possible for people to choose nontraditional family structures for themselves, such as cohabitation, single-parent families, families with nonresident parents, stepfamilies or blended families, or lesbian or gay families.

Cohabitation

Cohabitation is defined as an arrangement in which a couple shares a home and a bed without being legally married (Kroeger and Smock 2014; Manning and Cohen 2012; Sassler

2010; Thornton, Axinn, and Xie 2007). There are clearly more cohabiting couples today than there were previously, although they still compose only a small proportion (about 5.5 percent) of all U.S. households. The United States ranks in the middle among developed countries in terms of cohabitation. For example, cohabitation is much more common in France, Luxembourg, Finland, Denmark, and Norway (see Figure 10.5).

It is unclear exactly how many people are living in such relationships, but it is clear that more young men and women (especially those between 25 and 35) are living together outside marriage even if they are not considered, or do not consider themselves, cohabiting couples. Living together in this way has come to be considered a common tryout for, and pathway to, marriage, although few people plan to marry when they begin cohabiting. Then again, marriage may never occur or even be discussed, and cohabiting couples may break up and move on to other relationships. A declining number of cohabiting couples—less than 50 percent—end up getting married.

At one time, cohabitation was associated with being poor, less educated, or in the lower classes. More recently, cohabitation has become increasingly common among those with advanced education, even college degrees. In the past, black women were more likely to cohabit than white women, but in recent years the cohabitation rates for white women have increased dramatically, and they are now more likely to cohabit than black women (Manning 2013). There are differences between these groups in the function of cohabitation. For instance, for blacks, cohabitation is more likely to be an alternative to marriage; for whites, it is more likely a prelude to marriage (England and Edin 2009; Smock and Manning 2004). Whatever the differences, most of those who cohabit have a variety of reasons for making the decision to live together: support, friendship and companionship, sex and love, and commitment.

Huang and colleagues (2011) sought to better understand why young adults have cohabited or would cohabit. They found that the percentages of women who had ever cohabited ranged from 40 percent (Latinas) to 53.8 percent (both white and black women), consistent with previous studies of this phenomenon. The major findings of the study relate to people's rationales for cohabiting, as well as to gender differences in those rationales.

The first rationale was simply a desire to spend more time with one's partner. This was seen as a way of enhancing the relationship and desirable because it dealt with a variety of logistical problems, such as by eliminating lengthy trips to see one's partner. The second rationale was the belief that the partners would save money cohabiting because they were sharing expenses rather than paying for everything on their own. Third, cohabitation was seen as a kind of "test drive" of the relationship to assess the partners' compatibility.

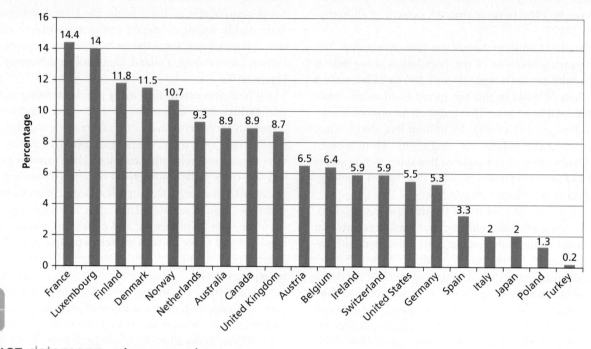

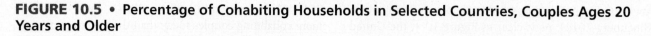

SAGE datamaps edge.sagepub.com

• Percentage of Cohabiting Households in Selected Countries, Couples Ages 20 Years and Older Marriage and cohabitation rates for every country.

SOURCE: Data from Organisation for Economic Co-operation and Development, 2009 (http://www.oecd.org/els/family/SF3_3_Cohabitation_rate_and_prevalence_of_other_forms_of_partnership_Jan2013.pdf).

Perhaps the most interesting results of the study related to gender difference in terms of the ways in which cohabiting enhanced the relationship: Women focused on love while men focused on sex. As one man put it, "Most girls want to have the connection with the guy and know it's a relationship. 'Cause women, their number one thing in life is to have good relationships with people. . . . Guys, the thing they strive for is sex, so it's kind of a tradeoff" (Huang et al. 2011: 887).

The biggest gender differences revolved around cohabitation's disadvantages. Women saw it as less legitimate and as entailing less commitment than marriage. Men were most concerned about the decline in freedom compared with being single. In terms of the latter, men focused on their loss of personal autonomy with regard to space, social activities, choice of friends, and sexual freedom. Overall, however, for both men and women the benefits of cohabitation outweighed the disadvantages.

Rates of cohabitation vary greatly around the globe. Sweden has a long history of cohabitation, and the process is well institutionalized there. In excess of 90 percent of first partnerships are cohabitations, and more than 40 percent of all first births are to cohabiting couples (Perelli-Harris and Gassen 2012). The legal status, or the rights and privileges, of those who cohabit is virtually the same as that of

married couples in terms of such things as social security and taxes (Wilk, Bernhardt, and Noack 2010). The high rate of cohabitation has led to a decline in the importance of marriage and of the customs, rituals, and ceremonies associated with it. Couples who cohabit and then marry might well give the date they met as their anniversary. Instead of making a decisive break, young people are likely to drift away from

Some nonresident parents are in the armed forces. How are the stresses on military families different from those faced by other families with nonresident parents?

their families of orientation, perhaps in stages, and then settle down and cohabit with someone (Popenoe 1987). However, since 1998 there has been evidence of a change in this pattern, as more Swedes are marrying. This reverses a long-term decline in marriage in Sweden between the 1960s and the 1990s (Ohlsson-Wijk 2011). Among European countries, those that are predominantly Catholic—Italy and Spain—have much lower rates of cohabitation. However, there is evidence of the spread of cohabitation throughout much of Europe, including Eastern Europe, and elsewhere.

Single-Parent Families

Among the developed countries, the United States has the highest rate of single-parent families (29.5 percent of all households with children), while Japan has the lowest (10.2 percent). In Europe, the northern countries—for example, the United Kingdom (25 percent), Ireland (22.6 percent), and Denmark and Germany (both 21.7 percent)—have the highest rates of single-parent families. It is mainly the southern European countries—Greece and Spain (5 percent), Portugal (6 percent), and Italy (7 percent)—that have the lowest rates of such families.

Nonresident Parents

Nonresident parents are fathers and mothers who live apart from their children (Smyth 2007). Most nonresident parents are fathers, although the number of mothers in this category is increasing. Historically, there have been many reasons for fathers to be absent from their families, including work, war, and incarceration. Today, although those reasons continue to exist, the major reasons are nonmarital childbearing with the parents never having lived together, the breakdown of cohabiting relationships, and marital dissolution.

Stepfamilies and Blended Families

A **stepfamily** consists of two adults who are married or cohabiting, at least one of whom has a child or children from a previous marriage or cohabitation living with him or her (Coleman, Ganong, and Russell 2013). A **blended family** includes some combination of children from the partners' previous marriages or relationships, along with one or more children of the currently married or cohabiting couple (Martin-Uzzi and Duval-Tsioles 2013). Stepfamilies and blended families have become very common in the United States, because about half of all marriages include a partner

The U.S. Supreme Court issued a historic decision in the summer of 2015 ruling that the Constitution allows gay and lesbian couples to marry.

who was previously married. It is estimated that about 30 percent of all American children will live in a stepfamily before they become adults.

Lesbian and Gay Families

Gay and lesbian couples have various similarities with, as well as differences from, straight families. One important difference is that gay and lesbian couples tend to be more reflexive and democratic in their family decisions and practices than straight couples. This is particularly the case concerning housework and other domestic duties, contentious issues for heterosexual couples who both work outside the home. Gay and lesbian couples are less constrained by social and institutional gender roles, with the result that they are freer in their negotiations over relational and family practices. Scripts for sexual relationships are less institutionalized among gay and lesbian couples as well, leading to some creative adaptations. Although monogamy is often assumed (but often violated) by straight couples, same-sex male couples are not as wedded to the idea or practice of sexual exclusivity. They negotiate over this issue and develop clear ground rules for nonmonogamous sexual relationships (Adam 2006; Barrett and Pollack 2011). Gay male relationships tend to be more fragile, while lesbian relationships tend to be far more stable. Some of the reasons for these gender differences are related to gender socialization patterns and sexual scripts (see Chapter 9) (Kimmel 2012).

The polar views on same-sex marriage are, on the one hand, that it is an expression of greater tolerance in the population as a whole and, on the other hand, that it is yet another threat to religion, morality, and heterosexual marriage. Whatever the perceived dangers, same-sex marriage has become increasingly common in the United States and in many other countries (Biblarz and Stacey 2010; Heaphy 2007). As recently as the 1990s, there was no legal recognition of such marriages *anywhere in the world,* and the prospect of same-sex marriage faced considerable hostility and intolerance. A key event occurred in September 2000, when the Netherlands extended the right to marry to same-sex couples. In the ensuing decade, a number of other countries throughout the world (Argentina, Canada, Belgium, Norway, Portugal, Sweden, Spain, South Africa, and Uruguay, as well as Mexico City) came to permit same-sex marriages. With the Supreme Court ruling of June 26, 2015, same-sex marriage became legal throughout the United States.

THEORIZING THE FAMILY

Whatever the family form, the main types of theories outlined in Chapter 2 and used throughout this book—structural/functional, conflict/critical, and inter/actionist theories—can be used to think about and shed light on the family (Cheal 2007; White 2013).

STRUCTURAL/FUNCTIONAL THEORIES

Writing in the mid-twentieth century, Talcott Parsons saw the family, especially the nuclear family, as a structure with very important functions for society as a whole. The structure of the nuclear family freed members from the obligations of an **extended family**—two or more generations of a family living in the same household or in close proximity to one another—and allowed them the mobility needed in industrial society. Of greatest concern to structural-functionalism is the need for order in society. A very important source of that order is the socialization of children into how they are supposed to act, as well as the process by which they learn the norms, values, and morality of society. The family, especially in the heyday of the nuclear family, played a crucial role in socialization. Furthermore, the nuclear family was more likely than any other family form to communicate a coherent sense of society's culture and morality.

This kind of thinking has been picked up by those sociologists who emphasize the functions of the family:

- First, society must at least replace those who die. This is accomplished through childbearing, which traditionally has been preferred to occur within the family.

- Second, the family fulfills the need to provide physical and emotional care to children.

- Third, the family fulfills the socialization function discussed above.

- Fourth, the family shares resources to meet its economic needs.

- Fifth, the family provides intergenerational support as parents continue to support their adult children economically, emotionally, and in many other ways.

- Sixth, the family has traditionally served to control sexual behavior. That control varies greatly from one society to another; in American society, whatever control the family had over sexuality seems to be in decline.

- Finally, the family is a mechanism for helping children find a place in society, especially in its stratification system.

There are many criticisms of the structural-functional theory of marriage and the family, not the least of which is that it is increasingly out of touch with today's realities. It simply "doesn't take into account the diversity of family structures and roles found in American marriages and families" (Scott and Schwartz 2008: 349). Moreover, structural-functional theory has a conservative bias that "tends to promote and rationalize the status quo," including that of marriage and the nuclear

Was structural/functional theory more relevant to nuclear families of the 1950s than it is to today's socially diverse families?

family. Furthermore, it tends to "understate disharmony and conflict" and, more generally, the array of family-related problems that will be discussed below (Scott and Schwartz 2008: 349).

CONFLICT/CRITICAL THEORIES

Unlike structural-functionalists, conflict theorists have never seen the family as a coherent unit or as contributing in an unambiguously positive way to the larger society. For one thing, the family itself is riddled with stresses, strains, and conflicts that lead to all sorts of problems for the family, its members, and society as a whole (Noller and Karantzas 2012). The family is an especially rich arena for conflicts based on gender and age (e.g., sibling rivalries, children versus parents). Such conflicts are closely related to the issue of power within the family—who has the most power, how it is used (and abused), and so forth. Above all, conflict can arise when one or more family members seek to wrest power from those who possess it.

ASK YOURSELF

If you have siblings, have you ever thought of any conflicts you may have had with them (or with your parents) as power struggles? If you didn't view them that way at the time, can you see them as power struggles now, in light of conflict theory? Does this perspective help you understand such disagreements better? Why or why not?

Randall Collins (1975) sees the family as an arena of gender conflict in which males have historically been the winners, leaving female family members in an inferior position. Similarly, when it comes to age-based conflict within the family, parents are generally victorious and children relatively powerless.

A key issue in looking at inequality and conflict within the family is the amount of resources possessed by the various parties involved. In terms of the conflict between adults and children, parents have a variety of resources, including greater size, strength, experience, and ability to satisfy the needs of the young, and as a result, the young are likely to be dominated by the adults. Among the few resources possessed by the young are their physical attractiveness and physical prowess. As a result, "girls are taught to capitalize on good looks, cuteness, and coyness [and] boys discover that athletic ability and performance are what count for males" (Kimmel 2012: 157). However, as children mature, they acquire other resources and are better able to resist adults. The result is more conflict between the generations as children mature.

Feminist Theory

Feminist theory tends to adopt a conflict view of the relationship between genders within the family. Feminist theorists see the family as being internally stratified on the basis of gender: Men and women possess different economic and social positions and interests, and they struggle over those differences. Males have been able to create and to impose a gendered division of labor within the family that benefits men and adversely affects women. The family is seen as a patriarchal structure in which males exercise power and oppress women. Male control is enhanced by an ideological mechanism whereby traditional family norms are upheld. For example, girls tend to learn to accept the idea that they should put family responsibilities ahead of everything else, including their personal development and satisfaction. This tends to engender and support masculine power and privilege. Some consequences of masculine privilege and power include men's "expecting or taking for granted personal and sexual services, making and/or vetoing important family decisions, controlling money and expenditures, and so forth" (Shaw and Lee 2009: 387). According to the staunch feminist Emma Goldman, "The institution of marriage makes a parasite of woman, an absolute dependent" (cited in Shaw and Lee 2009: 298). By buying into the ideology of masculine power and privilege, women are, in effect, supporting and enabling their own oppression. This ideology is seen as a major impediment to the liberation of women in

The Family and the Internet

The Internet has radically altered family life. People now consume an average of 12 hours of media a day at home, compared with 5 hours a day in 1960. We can look at one family's experience with the Internet and its associated technologies as an example of what has come to be called "problematic Internet use" (Spada 2014). (While there are problems associated with excessive use of the Internet, we must not ignore the many advantages this technology offers, such as the ability to Skype with family members in different locations.)

The father is working on a software venture and is deeply enmeshed in, and dependent on, the Internet (Richtel 2010). Operating from home, he works with three computer screens simultaneously and sometimes adds an iPad (he is also reliant on his smartphone). One screen shows tweets, instant messages, and group chats. The second displays computer codes and is where Skyping takes place. The third has a calendar, his e-mail, a web browser, and his music. He is obsessed with computer technology (he falls asleep with either a laptop or a smartphone on his chest and goes online as soon as he opens his eyes in the morning), and that obsession has had a negative effect on his family.

When things are tough emotionally for the father, he deals with it by escaping into video games. When the family goes on vacation, he has a difficult time staying away from e-mail and the Internet.

With media consumption reaching an all-time high, how can families keep the Internet from taking over the time they would otherwise spend together? Should they be concerned about losing this time together?

Both mother and daughter complain that he prefers technology to interacting with the family. When the son's grades fall, blame is placed on the amount of time he devotes to his technologies (he has two computer screens in his bedroom as well as his own smartphone).

Although the wife (and mother) spends a lot of time on the Internet texting, browsing Facebook, and checking her own e-mail 25 times a day, she would love to see her husband spend less time with his technologies and more time with his family. However, she knows that he gets "crotchety" if he does not get his technology "fix." The Internet contributes to innumerable stresses and conflicts in this family's life and in the lives of many other families.

Think About It

Do you know families like the one described here? If so, what effect does their engagement with the Internet and associated technologies have on their families? Do you know families in which these technologies play a less prominent role? What differentiates these families from others? Do you think there is really any such thing as problematic Internet use (PIU)?

the family and elsewhere in society. Overall, it could be argued that from a feminist perspective, the family is a concept and a structure created and disseminated by males in order to serve their own interests and not those of females. Yet it is important to note that "the balance of power in marriage (or any domestic partnership) depends in part on how couples negotiate paid labor and family work in their relationships" (Shaw and Lee 2009: 388).

INTER/ACTIONIST THEORIES

Inter/actionist theories look at the family from a more microscopic perspective than do either structural/functional or conflict/critical theories.

Symbolic Interactionism

Symbolic interactionism focuses on the meanings attached to identities, roles, and social relationships, treating meaning as socially constructed. This approach has long been used in family research (Stryker 1959). For example, men may attach different levels of significance to the role of father, and marital partners may redefine their relationship over time. Examples of research carried out from a symbolic interactionism perspective include Ball and Kivisto's (2006) study of couples considering divorce in marriage counseling settings and Aveline's (2006) study of the reframing of identities when parents learn that a child is gay.

Exchange Theory

Exchange theorists look at the family from the perspective of choices made on the basis of rewards and costs. People enter marital relationships because they think the rewards associated with marriage will outweigh the costs. They also tend to think marriage will be more rewarding than the alternatives to it: remaining single or becoming involved in other kinds of intimate relationships. Heterosexual marriage benefits men and women, although men generally benefit the most: "Married men are much happier than unmarried men. . . . Husbands report being more satisfied than wives with their marriages; husbands live longer and enjoy better health benefits than unmarried men" (Kimmel 2012: 153). However, both married men and married women live longer, have fewer health problems, have more sex, save more money, and have fewer psychological problems, such as depression, than unmarried men and women.

A marriage is likely to break down when the reward–cost calculation leads the partners involved to see the marriage as no longer profitable or to realize that other alternatives are more profitable. A marriage is likely to dissolve for two reasons. First, it will collapse if the individuals involved come to the conclusion that their marriage is not as profitable to one or both partners as other marriages with which they are familiar. In other words, they come to feel deprived relative to these other married couples. Second, the marriage is likely to break down if the spouses come to believe that greater rewards or lower costs are to be found in alternatives such as becoming single again, marrying someone else, or becoming involved in some other type of intimate relationship, such as cohabitation. In the last case, the rewards of a different partner might be offset by the costs, such as the effect such a change will have on any children involved.

PROBLEMS IN THE FAMILY

There are a wide variety of family troubles; we will focus on a few of the major ones in this section.

FAMILY CONFLICT

Conflict is endemic to family life, with numerous flash points between husband, wife, and children in a traditional nuclear family, and innumerable other possibilities for conflict in the wide array of other forms of intimate relationships (Kellerhals 2007). While divorce is usually seen as the major result of family conflict, conflict often exists long before a divorce, and it may not even lead to divorce. Much conflict simmers below the surface in many families, rising to visibility only now and then. Family conflicts may arise over such issues as the family's objectives, resources, and the need to protect the interests of various family members.

ABUSE AND VIOLENCE WITHIN THE FAMILY

Heightened conflict within the family can lead to abuse and violence. This can take various forms, but the most common are parental abuse of children and violence by husbands against their wives (who are considered "battered women"; Dunn 2005; LaViollete and Barnett 2014). Far less common is women abusing and behaving in a violent manner toward their children and even their husbands. Violence within the family can take emotional or psychological forms. It can also involve physical and sexual abuse (Carmody 2007). Although norms that relate to the acceptability of such behavior have changed in recent years, such abuse and violence are still common and accepted in some groups and parts of the world. In such cases, parents feel justified in abusing children, and husbands think it is acceptable to batter their wives. While there are exceptions, we should remember that the vast majority of those who engage in such behavior are not considered to be criminals (Straus 1980).

Child Abuse

Hundreds of millions of children throughout the world are abused, maltreated, and exploited (Bell 2011). According to the World Health Organization, "Child abuse or maltreatment constitutes all forms of physical and/or emotional ill-treatment, sexual abuse, neglect, or negligent treatment or commercial or other exploitation, resulting in actual or potential harm to the child's health, survival, development, or dignity in the context of a relationship of responsibility, trust, or power" (cited in Polonko 2007: 448). In the United States alone, reports indicate that several million children (15 percent) are severely maltreated, but this number reflects only official reports—the actual number is much higher. Furthermore, the official number includes only those who have been the victims of severe abuse and who clearly have been injured. The most common forms of child abuse are parents hitting their child with an object (20 percent), kicking or biting their child or hitting their child with their fists (10 percent), or physically beating up their child (5 percent) (Kimmel 2012). Fathers and father surrogates are most likely to commit these offenses.

The impact of child abuse is great, especially for the children involved, but also for the parents (or other adults) and the larger society. Physical and emotional abuse and violence experienced in childhood can lead to an increased likelihood of cognitive impairment (lower IQ and levels of educational attainment), impaired ability to reason morally (a weakly developed conscience), and a greater likelihood of engaging in violence and crime. Children who have been abused are themselves more likely to be violent toward other children, including siblings, and later in life to abuse their own children, their spouses, and even elderly parents.

There is often a cycle of violence and abuse toward children that stretches across several generations (Steinmetz 1987). Many of the parents who mistreat and abuse their children were themselves victims as children and, as a result, may have developed mental and substance abuse problems that can increase their own likelihood of mistreating others.

There is also a cost to society. The Centers for Disease Control and Prevention (2012) estimated that in the United States alone the economic cost of child abuse is more than $124 billion. This cost is traceable to such things as social services provided to families, the lesser contributions of victims to society, and related criminal justice and health care activities. While there are things that can be done to deal with the adults involved in terms of intervention and prevention, the structure of society as a whole needs to be addressed in various ways to reduce this problem. Of greatest importance is the need to change a culture where children are viewed as property that parents and other adults can treat, and abuse, in any way they want. Children also need to be seen as having human rights. In addition, children need to be better protected, helped, and treated by the various agencies involved. More generally, society and the government need to believe in and support a wide range of policies that are of benefit to children, such as more and better child care.

Domestic Violence

Domestic violence entails the exertion of power over a partner in an intimate relationship through behavior that is intimidating, threatening, harassing, or harmful (Carmody 2007). The partner can be harmed physically and/or sexually, emotionally, and psychologically; the violence can occur multiple times (Goodlin and Dunn 2011).

A great deal of research has been done on domestic violence, and several general conclusions can be drawn from this work:

- Women are about five times more likely than men to be victims.
- Women are about six times more likely to be assaulted by those they are intimate with (partners or former partners) than by strangers.
- One of the leading causes of injury to women is domestic violence.
- Among minority groups, blacks have the highest rate of such violence.
- Most likely to be victims are poor females between 16 and 24 years of age.
- It is difficult to leave a violent relationship, and the risk of serious, even fatal, injury is greatest when a victim tries to leave.
- Domestic violence is a major cause of homelessness.
- About a third of all female homicide victims are killed by those who are intimates.

Figure 10.6 shows that from 1994 to 2010, intimate partner violence dropped by more than 60 percent for both males and females. From 1994 to 2000, such violence was down 48 percent for females and 46 percent for males. From 2000 to 2005, the rate of intimate partner violence against females dropped an additional 31 percent, while male victimization rates remained nearly steady. The rate of intimate partner violence against females remained almost stable from 2005 to 2010, while males experienced a 39 percent decline, from 1.7 to 1.1 victimizations per 1,000 males age 12 or older.

Conflicts in families can sometimes turn violent. This woman points to a black eye as police respond to her call reporting an incident of domestic violence.

Associated Press

Andrew Cherlin on Public Sociology, in His Own Words

I have written for, and spoken to, the print and electronic media about family and demographic issues since I took a job as an assistant professor of sociology at Johns Hopkins University in the late 1970s. To write op-ed pieces for newspapers, I had to learn how to (1) engage the reader's interest, (2) make a single point, and (3) present my interpretation, all in about 700 words. I also had to be willing to accept failure. During my career, I have submitted more than 20 op-ed pieces to the *New York Times,* and the editors have accepted 9. That's actually a good batting average.

My early pieces led to telephone calls from reporters wanting a quote from an academic expert for a story they were writing. Then I had to learn how to say something that helps the reader understand the topic in 25 words or less. It's harder than you might think.

Many reporters cover family and demographic issues day after day, and they become quite knowledgeable. Interviewers on National Public Radio are quite good. Television, however, is another story. Typically, a harried producer who rarely covers the family will be given an assignment at 10:00 a.m., call me at 10:30, send a crew to film me by 2:00, and then splice five or ten seconds of my remarks, if anything, into a piece for the evening news at 6:30.

Overall, though, my work with the media has allowed me to place my ideas before a broad audience. It has also expanded the reach of my academic work because I have tried to apply the same principles of clear exposition and jargon-free prose to my scholarly books and articles.

If you would like to get your ideas to a general audience, how might you start? Submit short pieces to your local newspaper, where competition is less keen, or to the many websites that now post social commentary. These can get surprising visibility on the Internet and lead to opportunities to further expand your audience. And if you are serious, get a copy of a good guide to nonfiction writing, such as William Zinsser's *On Writing Well* or William Strunk and E. B. White's *The Elements of Style.* Good writing is essential to becoming a public sociologist.

SOURCE: Printed with the permission of Andrew Cherlin.

Think About It

Is there a need for sociologists who study the family, as Andrew Cherlin does, to share their ideas and findings directly with the public as well as with their peers? What do family members gain from such exposure to public sociology? What about legislators and policy makers who deal with issues affecting the family?

Because gender socialization often leads men to see violence as an appropriate means of communication, it follows that most abusers tend to be male. Heterosexual men and gay men can suffer intimate partner violence, however, as can lesbian, bisexual, and queer people (Dutton and White 2013; Messinger 2014). Men who experience such violence are often discouraged from reporting the crime or seeking social support. Societal assumptions that domestic violence cannot be perpetrated against men, combined with masculine socialization, can make male victims reluctant to report it.

In addition to being very costly to victims and their families, domestic violence is costly to society. Those abused are not likely to be able to function as well in the larger society as those who are not victimized. For example, the abused have higher levels of absenteeism from work. Furthermore, society often needs to pay the costs associated with medical treatment, police involvement, court expenses, and shelters for those who have been victimized.

Elder Abuse

The elderly do not escape abuse merely because of their advanced age. In a large national study, about 10 percent of elderly respondents reported some type of abuse (Acierno et al. 2010). The elderly are abused in various ways, including physically, psychologically, financially, sexually, and through neglect. Among other things, we know that elderly women are more likely to be abused than elderly men, the very elderly (over 80 years of age) are most likely to be victims, and adult children and spouses are most likely to perpetrate the abuse. Beyond the elder abuse committed by family members, such abuse also takes place in residential care facilities for the elderly.

ASK YOURSELF

Why is elder abuse most often committed by members of the victim's family? How do you explain this phenomenon?

FIGURE 10.6 • Intimate Partner Violence, by Sex, 1994–2010

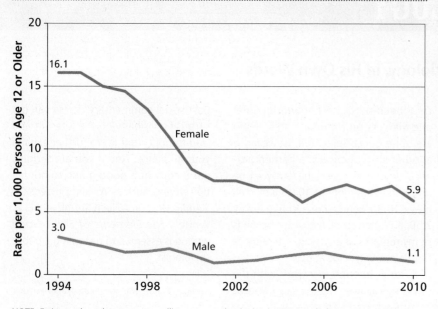

NOTE: Estimates based on two-year rolling averages beginning in 1994. Includes rape or sexual assault, robbery, aggravated assault, and simple assault committed by current or former spouses, boyfriends, or girlfriends.

SOURCE: Data from Bureau of Justice Statistics, National Crime Victimization Survey, 1993–2010 (http://www.bjs.gov/content/pub/pdf/ipv9310.pdf).

POVERTY AND THE FAMILY

There is a close relationship between family structure and poverty (Lichter 2007). For example, the poverty rate in 2013 in the United States for married-couple families was 5.8 percent, but for female-headed families it was 30.6 percent—almost five times as much. The likelihood of poverty for female-headed families is much less in many other developed countries, largely because of more generous social welfare programs. The concentration of poverty among female-headed households tends largely to reflect the consequences of gender inequality.

The big debate here is over whether the family structure causes poverty or poverty causes problems within the family. On the one hand, the argument is made that a weak family structure—one, for example, where women are left alone to raise children—causes poverty. Such women are apt to be poor because they are unlikely to be able to work, and the children are poor because they are not adequately supported by these women or their absent fathers. On the other hand, it is contended that poverty causes families to crumble. Women are left alone to raise children as the men leave because they cannot support them or because the mothers are more likely to qualify for welfare if the father is absent. The emotional and economic stresses associated with being poor are likely to put intolerable strains on the family.

Being unmarried is likely to be associated with poverty for women with children. Divorce is also likely to drive women, especially those who are already in a marginal economic situation, into poverty. More generally, divorce is likely to affect almost all women adversely. The only debate in this area concerns how badly women are affected and how much they are hurt economically, as well as in other ways.

GENDER INEQUALITIES

Intimate relationships, especially marriages, are unequal as far as the men and women involved are concerned. Marriages can be so different from the points of view of men and women that they seem like completely different systems. These inequalities take several forms (Shehan and Cody 2007).

The first is inequality in the amount of time devoted to household and childcare tasks (Patton and Choi 2014). Figure 10.7 shows the average number of hours per week mothers and fathers spent on paid work, housework, and child care in 1965 and 2011. In 2011, mothers on average spent almost twice as much time (18 hours a week) on housework as fathers (10 hours). Mothers also spent 7 hours more per week on child care than did fathers. Although the gap has been shrinking since 1965, gender inequalities are still clearly prevalent in the home, even as women's hours of paid work have increased dramatically. We know the intersection of race and class can affect the likelihood of men's greater participation in housework. In addition, men spend more time on tasks that are discretionary, at least to some degree, while women are more likely to perform regular, repetitive labor. Mothers are more likely to maintain the children, while fathers are more likely to engage in recreational activities with them. The disparity is even greater when it comes to the care of the ill and the elderly; this is almost always the near-total responsibility of females.

Then there are various gender inequalities in power and decision making. As in sociology in general, power here is defined as the ability to impose one's will on others despite their opposition. This can involve forcing a spouse to do something or to define a situation in a particular way. In heterosexual marriages, men are favored in terms of power within the marital relationship because of their greater size and strength. They are likely to earn more money, and they are likely to dominate conversations, thereby swinging decisions their way. In addition, male power tends to be institutionalized and

FIGURE 10.7 • Hours per Week Mothers and Fathers Spend on Paid Work, Housework, and Child Care, 1965 and 2011

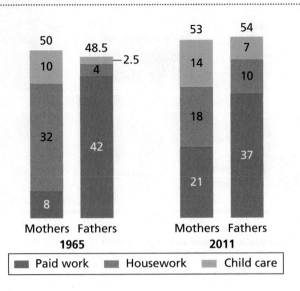

NOTE: Based on adults ages 18–64 with own child(ren) under age 18 living in the household. Total figures (at the top of each) may not add to component parts due to rounding.

SOURCE: Figure from *Modern Parenthood: Roles of Moms and Dads Converge as They Balance Work and Family*, March 13, 2013. Reprinted with permission of Pew Research Center, Washington, DC.

supported by religious groups and their customs (especially by Evangelical Christians, Hasidic Jews, Muslims, the Amish, and Mormons) as well as by governments and their policies. The latter often assume that husbands are the household heads and are responsible for the support of wives and children, and that wives are supposed to take care of the household and the children.

As we saw earlier, women are more likely than men to be the victims of intimate partner violence, even though men are more likely to be victimized by violence in general. In 1993, the United Nations adopted the Declaration on the Elimination of Violence against Women. Within the United Nations, UN Women (previously UNIFEM) is particularly concerned with the violence perpetrated globally against women and girls, especially in the family. There is a strong preference for male children throughout much of the world, with the result that female embryos are more likely to be aborted, female infants are more likely to be the victims of infanticide, and female children are more likely to be the victims of violence.

Globally, wife beating is the most common form of family violence. In some parts of the world this is taken to extreme lengths, with wives beaten to death. Brides may be burned to death because of (supposed) infidelity, or even because the bride's family was unable to pay the dowry in full to the husband. In some parts of the world women are

stoned to death for such offenses. The movie *The Stoning of Soraya M.* (2008), based on a 1994 novel of the same name, tells the true story of an Iranian woman who was stoned to death by members of the community, including her father and sons, on the basis of a false accusation by her husband—who wanted another woman—that she had been unfaithful to him. Some cultures support so-called honor killings, or killings of females because they have engaged in such "dishonorable" behaviors as infidelity, same-sex sexual relations, wanting out of arranged marriages, seeking marriage on their own, or even refusing to adhere to the dress code. There has been a good deal of publicity about, and public uproar over, honor killings in places like Pakistan, Egypt, Turkey, and Iran.

DIVORCE

Rates of divorce increased in Western nations during the twentieth century. The United States has one of the highest divorce rates in the world (Amato and James 2010); however, the often-repeated "statistic" that half of all U.S. marriages end in divorce is inaccurate.

The once-dramatic differences in divorce rates between the United States and Europe have declined, mostly because of increases in divorce across Europe. Europe has become more like the United States in terms of divorce (Amato and James 2010: 3).

Factors in Divorce

Regardless of how prevalent or rare it is, divorce is the best-known way of leaving a marriage. Divorce is a formal and legal mechanism that relates to legal marriages. Many marriages end with separations that become permanent without divorce. The dissolutions of other intimate relationships, even those that last a long time, do not require divorce; they end as informally as they began.

Divorce is often the result of a litany of family problems—for example, violence and abuse—that may have occurred over a long period of time before a divorce was ever contemplated, let alone takes place. Divorce itself can be seen as a problem, as well as one that creates many other problems, but it also can be seen as a solution to many problems. Divorce allows a spouse to get out of a bad, even disastrous, relationship. In fact, to some, it is the relationship, especially a "bad" marriage, that is the problem and not the divorce. Thus, we should not simply assume—as many do—that divorce is in itself a problem.

An important factor in divorce today in the United States, and in the Global North in general, is the increasing emphasis on the self and individualism. This is also linked to the idea of the pure relationship, discussed earlier. As we have seen, in such a relationship, including a marital relationship, the partners do not necessarily feel that they are locked into it for a lifetime, or even an extended period of time. Rather, they feel that they are in the relationship as long as it continues to work for *them*. Once individuals come to the conclusion that the relationship is no longer working for them, they are free to leave. Indeed, some take the view that they have an obligation to themselves to leave because they should not jeopardize their own need to have a satisfying life.

In the past, there was a tendency to value positively all marriages that remained intact. In many ways, however, a bad marriage can be a far greater problem than one that ends in divorce. For example, children in unhappily married families tend to feel highly neglected and humiliated (Kimmel 2012: 179). As acceptance of divorce has spread, the negative attitudes and social sanctions aimed at those who divorce have declined.

Although this storefront sign suggests otherwise, it is not true that half of all marriages in the United States end in divorce.

ASK YOURSELF

What are some of the reasons that divorce has become more socially acceptable? What specific norms and values about individuals, families, and the institution of marriage have changed to make this acceptance possible? Do you think the increase in the number of divorces has had an impact on society at large? If so, what sort of impact?

Not only have negative attitudes, norms, and values as they relate to divorce declined, but the material circumstances surrounding divorce have changed as well. Of prime importance is the fact that women today are likely to be better equipped materially to handle divorce than were women in the past. Among other things, they are better educated and more likely to be in the labor force. Thus, they may be more willing to seek divorce because they can better afford to be on their own. Furthermore, dissatisfied husbands are more likely to leave their marriages when they know that their wives can survive economically without them. Changes in the law are another important material factor that has followed from changes in the norms and values that relate to divorce. One important example is no-fault divorce, which not only has made it easier for people to divorce but also seems to be associated with an increase in the divorce rate. No-fault divorce laws have also acted on the larger culture, helping it to become even more accepting of divorce.

A long list of risk factors have been associated with the likelihood of divorce, including having relatively little education; marrying as a teenager, whether or not the couple cohabited before marriage; poverty; having divorced parents; infidelity; alcohol or drug abuse; mismanaged finances; and domestic violence. The reasons for divorce in Europe are very similar to those found in the United States. In terms of the nature of the relationship, marriages are more likely to be stable, and less likely to end in divorce, when couples handle their disagreements and anger well, such as by having a sense of humor about disagreements. Conversely, divorce is more likely when spouses are contemptuous of or belligerent toward each other or react defensively to disagreements (Gottman et al. 1998; Hetherington 2003).

GLOBAL FAMILIES

Just as the nation-state is eroding in the face of globalization, it could be argued that the traditional family, deeply embedded in a national context, is also declining. It is no longer necessary that family members live in the same country, have the same passport, be of the same ethnicity, or share a household in a given locale. Characteristics that used to separate people and made creating global families difficult or impossible are less important in the global age. National hostilities, religious differences, and even great geographic distances matter less to family formation today than they did in the past (Beck and Beck-Gernsheim 2012).

On the one hand, this clearly makes possible, and even highly likely, a wide range of new family types and configurations. For example, it is increasingly possible for family members, even spouses, to live in different countries, even on different continents, and to function quite well as a family (Nobles 2011).

On the other hand, these new realities also create many new possibilities for conflict within the family. That is, family members are now bringing to the family new and far broader stresses and strains of various types; clashes of different languages, cultures, religions, and races create new points of potential conflict and hostility. However, these differences

GL🌐BALIZATION

The Role of Families in Improving Relations between the United States and Cuba

In late 2014, the presidents of the United States and Cuba announced that they were beginning to normalize relations between their countries, including seeking to restore full diplomatic relations (Baker 2014). In mid-2015, embassies were reopened in the two countries. These developments need to be seen in the context of the recent history of relations between the United States and Cuba.

In 1962, after a communist regime headed by Fidel Castro had taken power in 1959, the United States placed an embargo on Cuba, and by 1963 all travel between the two countries was banned. A number of Cubans fled to the United States before the travel embargo; others left later, many illegally on rickety boats that cost many people their lives. Most settled in South Florida, especially in the Miami area (which has a "Little Havana" neighborhood). More than a million Cuban Americans live there today and represent a potent economic and political force. Many, especially the early immigrants, were middle-class and opposed to communism and the Castro regime, which seized their property and sought to redistribute their wealth more equitably among Cubans. For decades, they resisted U.S. efforts to improve relations with Cuba.

Many who fled Cuba left family members behind, and for decades it was difficult or impossible for them to visit. However, President Obama loosened restrictions on shipping and travel between the two countries in 2009, and since then there have been no restrictions on flights by Cuban Americans to visit family members in Cuba. For its part, Cuba began allowing its citizens

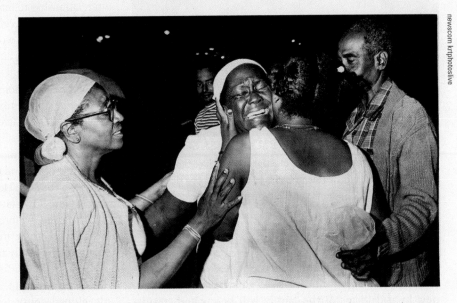

During the boatlift from Cuba in 1980, families like these were reunited after many years. Such scenes may soon be repeated as relations between Cuba and the United States continue to normalize. What challenges will reunited families face? Will they be the same as or different from those that confronted the family in this photo?

to own cell phones and computers, easing their ability to contact family members in the United States. Cuba also made it easier for Cubans to buy homes and businesses. As a result, Cuban Americans began sending all sorts of products to their families in Cuba, enabling them to open an array of small businesses. Furthermore, increasing amounts of money began flowing to Cuba from Cuban Americans seeking to help family members buy (and sell) property.

However, some in the United States (and in Cuba) would still like to limit or overturn the 2014 agreement. Some Americans, especially Cuban Americans in Congress, fear that the Cuban regime, which still regards itself as communist, will be strengthened by it.

Regardless of the future political direction, there is great desire and hope in Cuba (and in the United States) for more normal relations ("Return Visit to Communist Cuba" 2015). The drive to connect to family members is doing much, and will do much more, to reunite families and help overcome the lingering hostility between the two nations. As one expert on Cuba put it, "Cuban-Americans are normalizing relations one by one" (Alvarez 2011: A3).

Think About It

What flows between the United States and Cuba will change as a result of the 2014 agreement? Can the desire for family reunification overcome efforts by hardliners in the United States and Cuba to maintain the separation between the two countries?

Chris and Cori Schmaus of South Dakota have adopted three children from Africa. Couples in the United States lead the world in adopting children from abroad. What do such children gain from the adoption process? What do they lose?

are also likely to enrich the family, as well as the larger society, in various significant ways. As globalization increases, new hybrid forms of the family will be created, resulting in innovative and interesting differences within and between families. New combinations of, and interactions between, hybrid cultures will result in unforeseen sociological developments, such as wholly new customs and traditions. Another way of putting this is to say that global families are increasingly liquid (Bauman 2000). That is, they no longer—if they ever did—form solid and immutable structures that are impervious to outside, especially global, influences. Families are subject to global flows of all types, and they and their members are increasingly part of those global flows.

While there are great variations in family forms throughout the world, there are also great commonalities. Thus, many of the general ideas discussed throughout this chapter apply globally. It is well beyond the scope of this section to describe similarities and differences in the family throughout the world. There are sociologists who spend their entire careers doing just that—engaging in the comparative analysis of families in various societies (Goode 1963; Ingoldsby and Smith 2006). Globalization on the whole is more about global flows and how these flows relate to the family than it is about comparing families across the world (Ritzer and Dean 2015). In this section, then, we will examine at least some of the global flows that involve or affect the family. It is clear that many families are actively engaged in global flows of one kind or another, and that no family is totally unaffected by those global flows (Karraker 2008; Trask 2010).

GLOBAL FLOWS THAT INVOLVE THE FAMILY

Global flows that involve the family take four major forms. First, entire families, even extended families, can move from one part of the globe to another with relative ease (assuming they have the resources to do so). They can do so on vacation, in relationship to temporary job changes, or permanently.

Second, individual family members can move to a different part of the world and then bring the rest of the family along later. It is ordinarily the case that males are those doing the initial moving. Once they are secure enough economically in their new locations, they are then able to bring over the rest of their family members. Of course, it sometimes happens that males make new lives for themselves in the new locales and leave their families behind in their countries of origin. With increasing economic independence, women are now moving first more often, and then bringing the remainder of their families over (or not). However, many women move globally into low-paying, low-status jobs—for example, as care workers—or are moved, by force, into the global sex trade. Such women are unlikely to be in a strong enough economic position to enable other family members to join them.

Third, individuals can immigrate to create new families. For example, there are many marriage bureaus in developed countries that are in the business of bringing together men from those countries with women who are usually from less developed countries. Various differences between such men and women often create enormous problems for their relationships, however. For one, there is great economic disparity between the spouses. For another, the women often come from societies that are unstable politically and economically, and this makes it difficult for them to adapt to a more stable environment. Finally, marriage bureaus often portray the women as fitting traditional gender expectations, but when they arrive it may turn out that they do not really measure up to those expectations. Overall, these differences put females in a weak position vis-à-vis males, and they are therefore more vulnerable to abuse of various kinds.

Fourth, transnational adoptions generally involve the flow of children from less to more developed countries (Briggs 2012; Marre and Briggs 2009). The United States is the world leader in the adoption of children from other countries, while very few American children are adopted elsewhere. Adopting a child from another part of the world transforms the family in many ways. There are also various problems associated with such adoptions, such as the health risks that accompany being born in and having spent at least some time in less developed countries. There are also stresses involved in the differences between the culture from which a child comes and the culture of the country to which the child is sent. This is especially a problem if the adopted child is not an infant.

GLOBAL FLOWS THAT AFFECT THE FAMILY

As a liquid phenomenon in a liquid world, the global family is affected by, and affects, all of the other liquid phenomena that make up the global world. We will examine just a few of them in this section.

Global Migration

The global family is affected by population flows of various kinds. Of utmost importance is the high rate of global migration (Castles 2013), both legal and illegal (see Chapter 14). Among other things, this means that very different people from very different parts of the world are coming together in greater numbers than ever before. Some will settle and marry in diasporic communities composed of people like them; many others will not. Those who do not are likely to create families with mates who are very different from themselves in terms of place of origin, race, ethnicity, religion, and the like (Qian and Lichter 2011). Those entering such hybrid families are likely to encounter various difficulties and hostilities. These problems are likely to be greatest for undocumented immigrants, whose family problems are compounded by the fact that they are in the country illegally.

Global Trafficking

Human trafficking involves selling and buying humans as products. It is likely to affect the family in many ways (Jakobi 2012). Children are sometimes trafficked for the purpose of illegal adoption. As with legal transnational adoption, the children generally flow from poor, weak countries to those that are rich and powerful. Recall from Chapter 9 that women are trafficked for purposes of prostitution and forced marriage, both of which have the potential to disrupt family life. Then there is the illegal global traffic in human organs. People in developed countries who need organ transplants but cannot obtain the organs locally are better able to survive because of this traffic. Poor people in less developed countries sell organs not critical to their lives, which are then transported to developed countries and implanted into well-to-do recipients (Scheper-Hughes 2001). Although the poor in less developed countries do receive some money for their organs, this is but another form of exploitation of the global poor by the global rich. It is a particularly heinous form of exploitation, since the poor must sacrifice one or more of the things that make them human in order to survive.

The family today is an integral part of globalization, which it is both affecting and being affected by. There is no such thing as a typical global family; at best, there are many global families. More to the point, the people involved in today's families are at the intersection of innumerable global flows and as a result are enmeshed in constantly changing intimate relationships of all sorts. This may be as good a definition of the family as any in the global age.

SUMMARY

The family is a crucial social institution that has changed in many ways over the last century. Marriage is a legal union of two people. It can involve monogamy, polygamy, or cenogamy. In an intimate relationship, partners have a close, personal, and domestic relationship with one another.

The traditional nuclear family now accounts for only about a fifth of all U.S. households. To explain the decline in such households, Cherlin focuses on the deinstitutionalization of marriage, while Giddens posits that the desire for pure relationships makes marriage more fragile. Simmel suggests that some degree of secrecy is necessary to a successful marriage.

The structure of intimate relationships has changed over time. Cohabitation, nonresident parenting, and single-parent households have increased in the United States. Stepfamilies and blended families are more common, and gay and lesbian families are more visible.

Parsons believed that the family is functional and structurally important to society because of its ability to control adult behavior and socialize children. Conflict theorists see the family primarily as a place of inequality and conflict, particularly between those of different ages and genders. Feminist theorists view the family as particularly problematic for women because they are oppressed by a system that adversely affects them. Symbolic interactionists focus on the meanings and identities associated with the family. Exchange theorists look at the rewards and costs associated with the choices individuals make within families.

Abuse and domestic violence severely affect many families, as does poverty. Gender inequality in marriages is visible in partners' decision making and power distribution, and in the different amounts of time they devote to household tasks. Some people find their lives enhanced by divorce, whereas others experience many other problems.

Global flows that affect the family take four major forms: Entire families can move from one part of the globe to another; individual family members can move to a different part of the world and bring the rest of the family later; individuals can immigrate to create new families; and transnational adoptions can bring children from less developed to more developed countries. Global migration and human trafficking affect the global family.

REVIEW QUESTIONS

1. How has the structure of the family changed in the United States since 1900?
2. What about marriage makes it functionally important? Despite its importance, what are some problems that arise in marriage and the families formed through marriage?
3. According to structural-functionalists, why are families so important to society?
4. What criticisms do conflict and feminist theorists have of structural-functional theories of the family? In what ways are these criticisms related to ideas about social stratification?
5. What forms can intimate relationships take? Do you think that some forms of relationships are valued more highly than others in the United States? Do you think these values will change in the future? Why or why not?
6. Recent studies show that one out of every six relationships is started on an Internet dating site. In what ways are these dating sites reflective of the changes in the marriage market in the United States? How could one use exchange theories to explain the use of Internet dating sites to find partners?
7. What are the causes and consequences of divorce? What are the benefits and disadvantages of divorce?
8. What are some general conclusions sociologists have formed about domestic violence? Is there still debate concerning such violence? What are some other common problems that arise within families?
9. Many sociologists see a close relationship between family structure and poverty. What is this relationship? What role does gender play? What are some contrasting viewpoints?
10. In what ways has globalization affected the family?

APPLYING THE SOCIOLOGICAL IMAGINATION

The television program *Modern Family* depicts a diversity of intimate relationships and family structures. Nontraditional family structures have become increasingly prevalent in the United States. For this exercise, choose two other currently popular television (or Internet) shows and describe how they portray the types of relationships discussed in this chapter. What are the differences between the two shows in how they portray familial relationships? Despite the differences, what similarities do the familial relationships have? What structural factors related to the shows (e.g., network, time of day aired, target audience, television or Internet) could lead to the differences that you noted?

KEY TERMS

blended family: A family that includes some combination of children from the partners' previous marriages or relationships, along with one or more children of the currently married or cohabiting couple. (p. 237)

cenogamy: Group marriage. (p. 229)

cohabitation: An arrangement in which a couple share a home and a bed without being legally married. (p. 235)

companionate love: A kind of love typified by gradual onset and not necessarily tied to sexual passion, but based on more rational assessments of the one who is loved. (p. 230)

companionate marriage: A marriage emphasizing a clear division of labor between a breadwinner and a home-maker and held together by sentiment, friendship, and sexuality. Predominant model of marriage in the mid-twentieth century (see *companionate love*). (p. 232)

deinstitutionalization: Weakened social norms, especially with regard to the institution of marriage. (p. 231)

domestic violence: The exertion of power over a partner in an intimate relationship through behavior that is intimidating, threatening, harassing, or harmful. (p. 242)

endogamy: Marriage to someone with similar characteristics in terms of race, ethnicity, religion, education level, social class, and so on. (p. 229)

exogamy: Marriage to someone with characteristics that are dissimilar in terms of race, ethnicity, religion, education level, social class, and so on. (p. 229)

extended family: Two or more generations of a family living in the same household or in close proximity to one another. (p. 238)

family: A group of people related by descent, marriage, or adoption. (p. 228)

individualized marriage: A model of marriage emphasizing the satisfaction of the individuals involved. (p. 232)

institutional marriage: Predominant model of marriage in the early twentieth century; emphasizes maintenance of the institution of marriage itself. (p. 232)

intimate relationship: A close, personal, and domestic relationship between partners. (p. 230)

marriage: The socially acknowledged and approved and often legal union of two people, allowing them to live together and to have children by birth or adoption. (p. 229)

monogamy: Marriage between two individuals, whether one wife and one husband, two wives, or two husbands. (p. 229)

nonfamily household: A household consisting of a person who lives either alone or with nonrelatives. (p. 234)

nonresident parents: Fathers and mothers who live apart from their children. (p. 237)

nuclear family: A family with two married adults and one or more children. (p. 231)

passionate love: A kind of love typified by sudden onset, strong sexual feelings, and idealization of the one who is loved. (p. 230)

polyandry: Marriage (of a wife) to multiple husbands. (p. 229)

polygamy: Marriage to multiple spouses. (p. 229)

polygyny: Marriage (of a husband) to multiple wives. (p. 229)

pure relationship: A relationship that is entered into for what each partner can get from it, and in which those involved remain only as long as each derives enough satisfaction from it. (p. 234)

stepfamily: A family in which two adults are married or cohabiting and at least one of them has a child or children from a previous marriage or cohabitation living with him or her. (p. 237)

$SAGE edge™ edge.sagepub.com/ritzeressentials2e

SAGE edge offers a robust online environment featuring an impressive array of free tools and resources for review, study, and further exploration, keeping both instructors and students on the cutting edge of teaching and learning.

LEARNING OBJECTIVES	FOR FURTHER EXPLORATION AND APPLICATION
LO 10-1: Explain basic sociological concepts of the family, marriage, and intimate relationships.	▶ The Evolving Family System ⊕ Have Millennials Inherited the Black Marriage Gap? ▣ Are Marriages Better or Worse Than They Used to Be?
LO 10-2: Describe trends leading to the decline in marriage rates and changes in stepfamilies, blended families, and lesbian and gay families.	▶ What Is the "American" Family? ⊕ Emerging Issues for Same-Sex Divorce ▣ The Marriage Equality Revolution
LO 10-3: Apply structural/functional, conflict/critical, and inter/actionist theories to family.	▶ Functions of the Family ⊕ Bill Cosby's Legacy and Impact on Race Relations ▣ Five Major Theories of Family Crisis
LO 10-4: Describe family conflict, forms of abuse and violence within the family, and the effects of poverty on family life.	▶ Adoption Tracing Rights ⊕ A North Dakota Family Breaks the Silence on Gay Marriage ▣ Know the Signs of Domestic Abuse in Relationships
LO 10-5: Identify the effects of globalization and global flows on the family today.	▶ Global Family Trends ⊕ A Model of Manhood Drawn from Two Worlds ▣ Elian Gonzalez on His Desire to Return to the United States

11

EDUCATION AND RELIGION

Science versus Religion in the Public Schools

Proposed by Charles Darwin in 1859 and affirmed by countless twentieth-century biologists, the theory of evolution has achieved scientific consensus as an explanation of the natural origin of humankind over time. In contrast, proponents of the idea of intelligent design see the overwhelming complexity of the universe, including the creation of humankind, as the work of a rational, omnipotent designer, such as a god or other supernatural entity. In the United States, debate has arisen over whether these competing explanations for the origin of humans and the universe should be taught in public schools.

Since 1925, U.S. laws and court cases have challenged the teaching of evolution, creationism (the belief that the biblical God created the universe), and intelligent design in public schools. Advocates of evolution-only science programs cite the First Amendment's Establishment Clause, which supports the separation of church and state and the imperative to teach scientifically valid ideas in the classroom. Many advocates of the teaching of evolution contend that intelligent design has no place in educational courses dedicated to evidence-based knowledge. Intelligent design proponents argue that evolution and intelligent design should be taught equally and that students should be encouraged to decide for themselves which one is valid.

Some religious beliefs are at odds not only with scientific knowledge that is taught in public schools but also with social issues that might be discussed, such as same-sex marriage and abortion. Parents who feel strongly about not exposing their children to ideas and practices that contradict their religious beliefs often opt to send their children to religious schools or to homeschool them. In some U.S. states, parents can use government-issued vouchers, funded by

LEARNING OBJECTIVES

11-1 Explain how the educational process is related to socialization, employment, and income.

11-2 Describe inequality in education, its sources, and its effects.

11-3 Compare the educational system in the United States to the systems in other countries.

11-4 Define the major components of religion.

11-5 Explain and provide examples of secularization.

11-6 Identify different types of religious organizations.

11-7 Describe the relationship between globalization and the world's major religions.

Associated Press

public tax dollars, to pay for their children's tuition at private religious schools. Critics of voucher programs question the constitutionality of this practice, asserting that it violates the separation of church and state.

Teaching evolution and other controversial topics in schools is not a problem exclusive to the United States. The radical organization Islamic State recently banned the teaching of evolution in the schools it controls. Globally, however, religious schools play an important part in education, particularly in countries where there are few if any alternatives. The most recent World Values Survey found that, with the exception of Europe, higher levels of education are not significantly associated with a decline in the importance of religion in people's lives. ●

The fact that there are innumerable "teachable moments" is illustrated by this class lesson on earthquakes, held following a recent massive quake in Japan.

EDUCATION

Education is closely related to socialization (discussed in Chapter 4), since both involve the learning process. As a general rule, socialization tends to be a more informal process, while education takes place more formally in schools of various types (Zerelli 2007). Much socialization—for example, learning not to eat with one's hands—takes place largely within families in children's early years. By the time most U.S. children are five years old, the focus has shifted from the highly informal process of socialization in the family to the more formal educational process in schools. Formal educational settings, like preschools, elementary and high schools, colleges, and universities, build upon and expand the base of knowledge acquired through the early socialization process. In addition, classroom rules teach children about order, respect for authority, and the benefits of conformity. In adulthood, much socialization takes place when individuals start new jobs, but adults also increasingly participate in formal education programs.

While five years of age is the norm for starting school in the United States and other developed countries, much younger children are increasingly entering preschools. Of course, preschool is only the beginning of the educational process. In the United States, as in all other advanced industrial countries, education continues for many years, through grade school, high school, college, graduate school, and professional school, and even beyond in formal adult socialization programs (Kotarba 2007). Most people do not progress through all these stages, though the stage at which someone's formal education ends has profound implications for that person's future.

Clearly, educational attainment is closely related to employment and earnings. Figure 11.1 shows the correlation between educational attainment and employment

and income in 2013. Individuals age 25 and over with less than a high school diploma were almost three times more likely to be unemployed than those with a bachelor's degree; they were five times more likely to be unemployed than those with a doctorate. A person's likelihood of being unemployed decreases as he or she ascends the educational ladder.

Higher levels of education serve as a protection against unemployment, especially in hard economic times. During the recession that began in 2008, the hardest-hit segment of the population was people with less than a high school diploma. The recession's smallest negative effect was on those with doctoral and advanced professional degrees. According to the U.S. Department of Labor's Bureau of Labor Statistics (2013), the unemployment rate in 2013 for individuals with doctoral degrees was 2.2 percent, and for those with advanced professional degrees it was 2.3 percent. At the same time, the rate for individuals with less than a high school diploma was 11 percent, and it was 7.5 percent for people with no more than a high school diploma.

Individuals' median weekly earnings increase significantly with level of education, although there is a slight decrease for those with a doctoral degree compared to those who hold a professional degree. Those with a professional degree have the highest median weekly earnings at $1,714, nearly four times the earnings of those without a high school diploma and almost three times the earnings of individuals with a high school diploma. While there are many other measures of success in life, levels of education and earnings are obviously of great importance (Blau and Duncan 1967). Other individual benefits of having more education (Brennan, Durazzi, and Séné 2013) include being less likely to commit a crime and being better off in terms of overall health (Smith et al. 2015); those with more education are also more open politically (Bills 2007; Buchmann and Hannum 2001).

FIGURE 11.1 • Unemployment Rates and Earnings by Educational Attainment in the United States, 2013

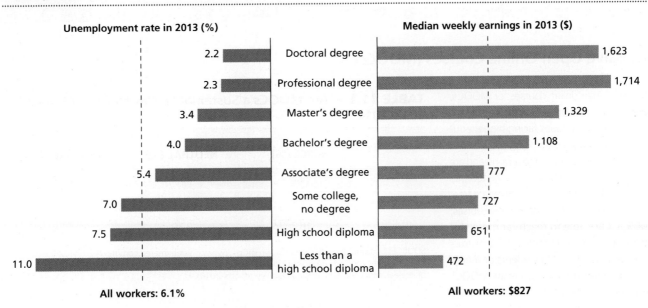

Unemployment rate in 2013 (%)		Median weekly earnings in 2013 ($)
2.2	Doctoral degree	1,623
2.3	Professional degree	1,714
3.4	Master's degree	1,329
4.0	Bachelor's degree	1,108
5.4	Associate's degree	777
7.0	Some college, no degree	727
7.5	High school diploma	651
11.0	Less than a high school diploma	472

All workers: 6.1%   All workers: $827

NOTE: Data are for persons age 25 and over. Earnings are for full-time wage and salary workers.

SOURCE: U.S. Department of Labor, Bureau of Labor Statistics, Current Population Survey (http://www.bls.gov/emp/ep_chart_001.htm).

ASK YOURSELF

How much did the prospects of future employment and income influence your decision to attend an institution of higher education? What other reasons might influence such a decision?

INEQUALITY IN EDUCATION

A **meritocracy** is a system based on a dominant ideology involving the widely shared belief that all people have an equal chance of succeeding economically based on their hard work and skills (see Chapter 3). A meritocratic social system also requires that people's social origins, such as class background, and ascribed characteristics, such as race and gender, be unrelated to their opportunities to move up in the social system. Education is a centrally important institution in a meritocracy because it has the potential to level the playing field and provide equal opportunities for students to learn, work hard, and compete to move up in the social hierarchy.

Who Succeeds in School?

In a meritocratic society, we would expect to find that social origin and ascribed status (see Chapter 4) have little effect on how much students learn and how far they go in school. However, there is a clear pattern of inequality in the United States that suggests that our educational system is not meritocratic. Students with the highest reading and math scores

at the end of high school are those whose parents have the most education. The same pattern is evident if we look at family income and parental occupational status. In terms of race/ethnicity, we see in Figure 11.2 that Asian and white students, both male and female, are more likely than black or Hispanic students to complete high school and attain either a bachelor's or master's degree, or higher. Looking at sex differences in the figure, we see that females across the board have better high school completion rates than their male counterparts and are more likely to obtain a bachelor's or master's degree (or higher). Clearly, social origins and ascribed (race, gender) characteristics are strongly related to educational outcomes. To many observers, this suggests that American society is decidedly unmeritocratic.

The Coleman Report: How Much Do Schools Matter?

The first large-scale study of American schools was conducted in the 1960s by James Coleman. Coleman's findings, published in what has become known as the Coleman Report, were a surprise, and they changed the way that sociologists understand educational inequality. They led to a rethinking of the assumption that educational institutions can create equal opportunities that will overcome existing class and racial inequalities in the larger society.

First, Coleman (1966) estimated how much schools differ in "quality." He collected data on teachers' salaries, teacher quality, the number of books in the library, the age of school

Massive Open Online Courses (MOOCs)

Massive open online courses, or MOOCs, are a recent development that some believe may solve many issues facing higher education today, especially rising costs (Heller 2013). MOOCs are open to anyone and are designed to enroll thousands of students per course. Most important, they are free. Compared with traditional college courses, MOOCs are able to reach far more students at much lower cost (a single instructor can teach 100,000 students or more). In 2011 three Stanford University MOOCs each enrolled more than 100,000 students from nearly every country in the world. By 2012 a corporation named Coursera had enrolled more than 2 million students in its MOOCs. Corporations like Udacity and edX joined it.

But MOOCs have not served to democratize education. The vast majority of students enrolled in MOOCs in two universities in the United States, as well as in universities in several other countries, were *not* those who lacked access to higher education, but rather those who already had college degrees (Selingo

TABLE 11.1 • Are MOOCs a Sustainable Way to Offer Courses? 2012–2014

	AGREE (%)	NEUTRAL (%)	DISAGREE (%)
2012	28.3	45.4	26.2
2013	23.2	38.3	38.5
2014	16.3	32.9	50.8

SOURCE: Babson Survey Research Group (https://www.insidehighered.com/news/2015/02/05/babson-survey-research-group-considers-changes-annual-report-distance-education) (http://onlinelearningconsortium.org/read/survey-reports-2014).

2014). Furthermore, MOOCs have low completion rates (Lewin 2014).

While MOOCs are currently free, this is not a sustainable business model. How to collect fees and what to charge remain unanswered questions (Lewin 2013). Table 11.1 shows the results of an annual survey of more than 2,800 academic leaders about whether MOOCs represent a sustainable way to offer courses. Among respondents to the 2014 survey, only 16.3 percent believed MOOCs were sustainable.

Given that free courses are not sustainable, it is likely that MOOCs will follow other institutions of higher education and become increasingly commercialized in order to persist.

Think About It

Do you think MOOCs have a future in higher education? Would you ever enroll in one? What do you think would be the strengths and weaknesses of a MOOC compared to a traditional college course?

---

buildings, the curriculum, and numerous other features of schools. On average, schools were much more similar in these respects than was commonly believed.

Second, Coleman found few school characteristics that were related to student learning. School resources, such as per-pupil spending or the books in a library, did not predict student achievement; rather, achievement was most strongly related to teacher quality and the family background and racial composition of the students attending the school. Students learned more in schools with better teachers and white, middle-class peers. Finally, Coleman found that the most important predictor of student learning was a student's family background.

Recent research on "school effects" has generally been supportive of Coleman's conclusion that school differences in resources contribute less to educational inequality than has often been assumed. There have been many studies of

the importance of school funding for student learning, and generally the results have been mixed. Numerous studies of public–private differences in student learning have indicated at best only a small advantage in learning for Catholic high school students (Elder and Jepsen 2014), mostly due to more rigorous coursework (see Bryk, Lee, and Holland 1993; Carbonaro and Covay 2010). In elementary and middle school, public school students actually outperform private school students in math, and they do equally well in reading (Lubienski 2006).

However, recent large-scale surveys indicate that socioeconomic and racial and ethnic differences in student ability are sizable when children *begin* kindergarten. Furthermore, these differences can be detected when children are as young as two years of age (Aud and Hannes 2011). Clearly, schools cannot be implicated in producing educational inequalities if the inequalities are present *before students even enter school!*

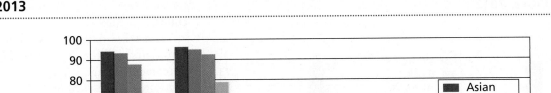

SOURCES: Data from U.S. Department of Commerce, Census Bureau, U.S. Census of Population: 1960, Vol. I, Part 1; J. K. Folger and C. B. Nam, *Education of the American Population* (1960 Census Monograph); Current Population Reports, Series P-20, various years; and Current Population Survey (CPS), March 1970 through March 2013.

In short, Coleman's study and subsequent research undermine the simplistic explanation that educational inequality merely reflects unequal opportunities available to students while they are in school.

This is not to argue, as some have, that family backgrounds are determinative and schools are irrelevant. They are not. Indeed, they play a significant role. Coleman conducted his study during the height of the civil rights movement, and one of his concerns was the impact of segregated schools. Using standardized test results, he observed that blacks did not do as well as whites. However, he found that black students did best when they were in integrated schools rather than in predominantly black ones. Integration, in other words, was a resource, just like teacher quality. The integration of public schools peaked in the 1980s, and since then the nation has witnessed the resegregation of schools (Orfield 2001). As Figure 11.3 shows, students of color attend public schools in some cities overwhelmingly more than white students. For example, in 2012 African Americans and Latina/o students were in schools that were almost as segregated as they were before the seminal Supreme Court case *Brown v. Board of Education* in 1954 (Decuir-Gunby and Taliaferro 2013). The educational achievement gap between blacks and whites (Condron et al. 2013) narrowed between the 1960s and 1990s, but since that time it has remained basically unchanged (Gamoran and Long 2006).

Intelligence and School Success

One possible explanation for Coleman's findings focuses on what are hypothesized as innate differences in intelligence.

Richard Herrnstein and Charles Murray offered the most detailed and widely cited argument in support of this thesis in their controversial book *The Bell Curve* (1994). They argued that educational inequalities are due mostly to "natural" differences in intelligence in human populations rather than systematic differences in educational opportunities. Far more troubling were their claims that whites had dis-

Students who learn more may have higher IQs, but even more important to their academic success are their solid work habits, self-discipline, and perseverance, as well as mastery of the "hidden curriculum." How do these conclusions reflect the propositions of structural/functional and conflict/critical theories?

FIGURE 11.3 • Racial Composition of U.S. Public Schools in Selected Cities, 2012

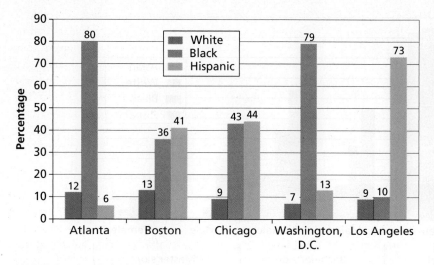

SOURCE: Data from Federal Education Budget Project, "Comparative Analysis of Funding, Student Demographics and Achievement Data," New America Foundation, 2012.

cernibly higher intelligence levels than blacks and Latinos. However, the consensus of the social scientific community is that there are no grounds for contending that there are innate intelligence differences along racial lines (Fischer et al. 1996). Indeed, students' self-discipline, including study habits and perseverance, has been found to have a greater impact on grades than intelligence (Duckworth and Carlson 2013; Duckworth and Seligman 2005).

Class Differences in Early Childhood

If both school-based and "natural" explanations of educational inequality fail, what remains? Many social scientists have turned their attention to inequalities in children's earliest experiences—the home environment. Betty Hart and Todd Risley (1995) performed an in-depth study of 42 families with children. Each child studied was seven to nine months old when the study began. The researchers visited each family once every month until the children were three years old. For each hour-long visit, Hart and Risley recorded every spoken word and took notes on what happened. They found that the three types of families in their study—professional, working-class, and welfare—differed markedly in how they spoke to and interacted with the children. By the time the children were three years of age, there were massive differences in the numbers of words that had been addressed to them among these different families: 35 million words in professional families, 20 million in working-class families, and fewer than 10 million in welfare families. Hart and Risley also found that children in professional families experienced the most encouragement by their parents. In terms of interaction styles, parents in professional families tended to use questions rather

than commands to direct children's behavior and were more responsive to their children's requests.

Did these differences in home environments matter for early learning outcomes? By age three, the children's exposure to differences in parenting practices and styles was highly correlated with vocabulary growth, vocabulary use, and intelligence. These effects persisted when intelligence was measured at ages nine and ten. In addition, class differences in early cognitive outcomes were explained almost entirely by differences in parenting. A recent study that reanalyzed Hart and Risley's data found that it was not the parents' socioeconomic status but the quality of education given by the parents that mattered most in the children's cognitive development (Rindermann and Baumeister 2015).

Preschool

Can we change children's educational outcomes by changing the cognitive culture that they experience when they are very young? Several intensive preschool programs have shown impressive results. From 1962 to 1967, 123 black children whose families were living in poverty in Ypsilanti, Michigan, participated in a policy experiment (Heckman et al. 2010; Schweinhart, Barnett, and Belfield 2005). Half of the children were assigned to an enriched preschool program (High/Scope Perry Preschool), while the other half—the control group—received no preschooling (Stoolmiller 1999). By the time the program ended, children who had attended the Perry Preschool program for two years were experiencing larger gains in intelligence than the control group. However, this IQ advantage faded only a few years after the program ended. The Perry students performed better in school because they were more motivated to learn. Researchers followed these two groups of students well into adulthood (age 40) and found that the Perry students did substantially better as adults than did members of the control group. The Perry students were more likely to finish high school and college and to hold steady jobs, and they had higher earnings than the control group. Those in the control group were more likely to be arrested, to use public assistance, and to have out-of-wedlock children. Since the differences in cognitive ability between the two groups were negligible, James Heckman (2006) attributes the success enjoyed by Perry students as adults to the better social skills they learned in preschool.

Inequality within Schools: Tracking and Student Outcomes

Many studies have examined whether students who attend the same school receive similar learning opportunities. It is common at all levels of schooling in the United States to group students by ability, which is typically measured by standardized test scores and/or grades. This is commonly known as *tracking*. Barr and Dreeben (1983) examined first-grade reading groups to which students were assigned based on their reading abilities at the beginning of the year. Students in higher-ability groups learned more new words and improved their reading skills more rapidly than did students in low-ability groups. Those in high-ability groups received more instructional time, were exposed to more new words, and experienced a faster pace of instruction than students placed in low-ability groups. In short, higher-performing students received more learning opportunities than did lower-performing students. Consequently, the gap between high- and low-achieving students grew larger during the year. This process is known as **cumulative advantage**—the most advantaged individuals are awarded the best opportunities, and this increases inequality over time (DiPrete et al. 2006).

As students progress through middle and secondary school, curricular differentiation takes the form of different classes with different content. Traditionally, these curricular tracks are aligned with students' future ambitions: The "high" track entails coursework that prepares students for four-year colleges and professional careers, and the "low" track focuses on basic and/or vocational skills for semiskilled occupations that do not require a college degree. Research consistently finds that high-track classes offer better learning opportunities to students because they are taught by more experienced, higher-quality teachers who have higher expectations of their students (Kelly 2004). Higher-track classes cover more material, and students receive higher-quality instruction (Gamoran et al. 1995). Students in high-track classes are more engaged and exert greater effort in school (Carbonaro 2005), which also helps them learn at a faster rate. Research consistently shows that otherwise similar students learn more when placed in a higher-track class because of higher expectations, greater effort, and better learning opportunities. Ultimately, high-track students are more likely to attend college than low-track students.

What determines how students are assigned to different ability groups, tracks, and classes? In a meritocracy, achieved characteristics—hard work and prior academic success—should determine which students have access to high-track classes. Most studies show that prior achievement and grades are indeed the most important predictors of track placement. Since students from families with high socioeconomic status (SES) are more likely to be high achievers, they are much more likely than low-SES students to take high-track classes. However, when students with the same test scores and grades are compared, students from higher-SES families are still more likely than their low-SES counterparts to be enrolled in high-track classes (Gamoran and Mare 1989). Thus, high-SES students are doubly advantaged in the track placement process.

What accounts for the SES advantage in track placement? Useem (1992) studied how families affect students' placement in middle school math classes. She found that college-educated parents had several key advantages in the placement process that ensured that their children would end up in the high-level classes. First, college-educated parents were much more knowledgeable about which classes were the most demanding and which were linked to high-level classes in high school. Indeed, some less educated parents seemed unaware that math classes were tracked. College-educated parents also better understood how the placement process worked, and they knew how to intervene successfully on their children's behalf. Second, college-educated parents were much more integrated into social networks in the school—through parent–teacher associations and volunteering, for example. They used these connections to gain information about classes and teachers in the school. Finally, college-educated parents influenced their children in selecting classes by encouraging them to challenge themselves and think about the long-term consequences of their choices.

Alternatives to Traditional Public School

Not everyone attends public schools. For one thing, elite families often send their children to private boarding schools where they can interact with members of their own upper-class stratum and remain apart from members of other classes (Khan 2011). For another, members of some religious groups opt to send their children to parochial schools to reinforce particular worldviews. In general, three alternatives to public school have emerged in the past few decades: vouchers, homeschooling, and charter schools. Proponents of the various alternatives are highly critical of existing public schools, either for what they claim are shortcomings in educational achievement or for promoting values at odds with their particular beliefs.

Vouchers. School **vouchers** are government-issued certificates that allow students to use public tax dollars to pay tuition at private schools. Parents seeking to remove their children from underperforming public schools find vouchers an attractive alternative. As of 2013, 17 U.S. states offered 33 programs relying on vouchers (Santos and Rich 2013). Many voucher schools are religious schools. This raises constitutional issues about the separation of church and state and the use of public money to support religious schools. Moreover, whereas public schools are required by law to accept all students, this does not apply to private schools.

Proponents of school vouchers argue that voucher programs provide parents—particularly poor parents—with options for their children's educations that they otherwise would not have. In addition, they contend that under voucher programs the increased competition the local public schools face from private schools stimulates them to enact changes to improve their educational programs (Figlio and Hart 2014). Opponents counter that vouchers encourage the creaming off of the best students from public schools. They also question the constitutionality of voucher programs on the basis of the First Amendment (Harris, Herrington, and Albee 2007) and express concern that vouchers will reduce funding levels for already underfunded public schools.

There has been limited research on whether students in voucher schools do better than their counterparts remaining in public schools. In a study in Florida, Rudolfo Abella (2006) found that over a two-year period, voucher students did about as well as students in public schools.

Homeschooling. The popularity of homeschooling has grown over the years (Rich 2015). About 3 percent of the U.S. school-age population was homeschooled in 2011–2012. The vast majority of these approximately 2 million children were white (68 percent). Among the minority children being homeschooled, 15 percent were Hispanic, 8 percent were black, and 4 percent were Asian or Pacific Islander (U.S. Department of Education, National Center for Education

Homeschooling is one of several increasingly popular alternatives to the traditional educational system. Would you homeschool your children?

TABLE 11.2 • School-Age Children Who Were Homeschooled, Ranked by Reasons Parents Gave as Important and Most Important for Homeschooling, 2011–2012

REASON	IMPORTANT[a]		MOST IMPORTANT	
	NUMBER	%	NUMBER	%
A desire to provide religious instruction	692,299	64	176,338	16
A desire to provide moral instruction	831,842	77	51,210	5
A concern about environment of other schools[b]	986,643	91	268,628	25
A dissatisfaction with academic instruction at other schools	799,336	74	204,312	19
A desire to provide a nontraditional approach to child's education	474,545	44	56,045	5
Child has a physical or mental health problem	166,878	15	50,652	5
Other reasons[c]	404,313	37	226,423	21

NOTE: Homeschooled students are school-age children (ages 5–17) in a grade equivalent to at least kindergarten and not higher than grade 12. Excludes students who were enrolled in public or private school more than 25 hours per week and students who were homeschooled only because of temporary illness.

a. Respondents could choose more than one reason.

b. Based on the response to the question, "Are you concerned about the school environment, such as safety, drugs, or negative peer pressure?"

c. Parents homeschool their children for many reasons that are often unique to their family situation. "Other reasons" parents gave for homeschooling included family time, finances, travel, and distance.

SOURCE: U.S. Department of Education, National Center for Education Statistics, Parent and Family Involvement in Education Survey of the National Household Education Surveys Program (NHES), 2012.

Statistics 2014). Homeschooling is also growing in many other countries (Lois 2013; Stevens 2001, 2007), but the United States has the largest percentage of school-age children currently being taught at home (Kunzman and Gaither 2013).

As shown in Table 11.2, many parents of children who are homeschooled (74 percent) are dissatisfied with the quality of the instruction offered in the public schools and believe that their children are not adequately challenged in those schools. Even more parents (91 percent) express concern about environmental factors in schools, such as safety, drugs, and negative peer pressure. However, a large number of parents homeschool their children to ensure they receive religious (64 percent) and moral (77 percent) instruction that the parents do not think can be found outside the home and in traditional schools. Many parents (44 percent) desire a nontraditional approach to their children's education. A smaller number (15 percent) opt for homeschooling because their children have physical or mental health problems.

As the numbers of homeschooled students have risen, universities have begun to address the need to assess such students as they apply for admission. Based on standardized tests, homeschooled children may on average perform slightly better than their public school counterparts, but this is not the case in all regions of the country. Critics point to limitations in much of the research in this area, but, more important, they identify two topics that standardized tests do not address. The first has to do with whether homeschooled students have the social skills to function in a diverse society. The second raises concerns about the critical abilities of homeschooled students and whether they look at the world unreflectively, embracing their parents' worldviews.

Charter Schools. Charter schools are a hybrid: They are alternatives to traditional public schools, but nevertheless they remain part of the public school system. They receive funding from public tax dollars, although they can also receive private funding. When charter schools were first created, they were intended to be schools of choice, alternatives for parents dissatisfied with the local public schools and interested in sending their children to schools over which they had greater control. Unlike private or parochial schools, charter schools do not charge tuition. In other words, they are publicly funded but privately operated. The ideal of charter schools was that they would be more responsive to the concerns of parents and more accountable in terms of ensuring solid student outcomes.

Charter schools are granted greater autonomy than traditional public schools. They define their own missions and establish criteria for determining whether or not they achieve their objectives. Charter schools have sponsors, and they are accountable to those sponsors and to the states in which they are located. One of the chief objectives of early proponents of charter schools was to reduce racial segregation in schools by bringing together people who shared a vision of what they wanted for their children's education. At the same time, since the traditional public schools would end up competing with charter schools, proponents argued that the traditional schools would be forced to improve in order to remain viable.

The results from a quarter century of experience with charter schools are mixed at best. For one thing, the schools have experienced managerial problems. Somewhere between 10 percent and 15 percent of charter schools have failed and closed. This has led some to propose larger-scale administrative organizations that would overcome some of the shortcomings of existing local charter management (Farrell, Wohlstetter, and Smith 2012). Second, the evidence does not support the idea that racial segregation is being reduced

TABLE 11.3 • Academic Performance of Charter Schools Compared to Local Noncharter Schools

	READING (%)	MATH (%)
Significantly better	25	29
No significant difference	56	40
Significantly worse	19	31

SOURCE: Center for Research on Education Outcomes, Stanford University, "National Charter School Study 2013" (http://credo.stanford.edu/documents/NCSS%202013%20Final%20Draft.pdf). © 2013 CREDO.

by charter schools. On the contrary, it appears that the self-selection process built into the idea of choice actually increases levels of racial segregation (Garcia 2008; Roda and Wells 2013). Third, there is no clear evidence supporting the idea that charter school competition results in improved performance of traditional public schools (Silvernail and Johnson 2014; Zimmer and Buddin 2009).

A 2013 study conducted by the Center for Research on Education Outcomes at Stanford University found that charter schools are improving, but the findings reveal wide differences across states. While in some states charter schools achieve better results than their traditional counterparts, in others their results are significantly worse. Table 11.3 shows the performance of charter schools relative to that of the traditional public schools in their markets. Students in 25 percent of charter schools demonstrated significantly stronger academic growth than their public school counterparts in reading, those in 56 percent of charter schools were not significantly different, and those in 19 percent of charter schools had significantly worse growth than students in public schools. In math, students in 29 percent of charter schools had stronger academic growth than their public school counterparts, those in 40 percent of charter schools had growth that was not significantly different, and those in 31 percent of charter schools had growth that was significantly worse. Overall, this is a decidedly mixed picture and does not represent a clear case for or against charter schools.

Who Goes to College?

Student learning is an important outcome of schooling, but successfully obtaining educational credentials is critically important for numerous life outcomes, such as income, occupational status, health, and well-being. Figure 11.4 shows that students with more advantaged family backgrounds are more likely to graduate from high school and to enroll in college. Although college enrollment for students from low-income households rose from 31.2 percent in 1975 to 53.5 percent in 2011, these students still lagged far behind middle-income students, who in 2011 were 12.7 percent

FIGURE 11.4 • College Enrollment in the United States, by Income Level, 1975–2011

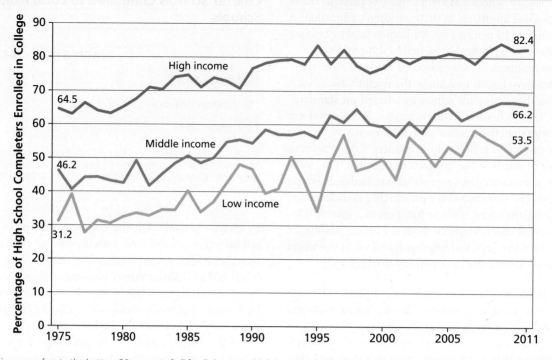

NOTE: Low income refers to the bottom 20 percent of all family incomes, *high income* refers to the top 20 percent of all family incomes, and *middle income* refers to the 60 percent in between.

SOURCE: Data from U.S. Department of Commerce, Census Bureau, Current Population Survey, October 1975 through 2011 (http://www.census.gov/compendia/statab/cats/education/educational_attainment.html).

more likely to enroll in college, and high-income students, who had college enrollment rates almost 30 percent higher than those of their low-income peers.

Students from high-income families are more likely to attend and to graduate from college because they encounter a "college-going habitus" at home and in school. A **habitus** is an internalized set of preferences and dispositions that are learned through experience and social interactions in specific social contexts (Bourdieu and Passeron 1977). For example, children raised in families with highly educated parents may constantly be exposed to justifications of the importance of education in adult life. They may also hear dismissive and derogatory comments that devalue people with less education. It may become clear that education is a critical part of being accepted as a member of the group. Ultimately, children in this situation may not see the pursuit of a college degree as a "choice"; rather, they may see it as an obligation. As students experience different social contexts that correspond with their family backgrounds, they form different ideas about the importance of college and the role it plays in their lives.

Globalization and Education

We have spent much time discussing educational inequality in learning outcomes in the United States. Is the American system typical? How do other school systems around the world differ, and with what consequences?

PISA Rankings. The Program for International Student Assessment, or PISA, is a worldwide study of student educational performance (Meyer and Benavot 2013). The Organisation for Economic Co-operation and Development (OECD) created the program in 1997. Since 2000, it has measured the proficiency of 15-year-olds in reading, math, and science every three years. Critics have pointed to shortcomings in the assessment, but it remains the best comparative portrait we have today. Figure 11.5 shows the top-performing nations in 2012, when the most recent test was carried out. Students in Asian countries consistently garnered the highest scores in math, reading, and science. Especially worrisome for the United States is the fact that American students ranked toward the bottom of the list of countries—36th in math, 24th in reading, and 28th in science (for more details, see Weisenthal 2013).

Educational experts have been especially fascinated by Finland's consistently high rankings over the years and have pondered whether it may be possible to translate the lessons of the Finnish case to other countries. What does the Finnish educational system look like? First, teachers are well trained. Gaining acceptance into teacher training

FIGURE 11.5 • PISA Scores for Math, Reading, and Science, Top Countries, 2012

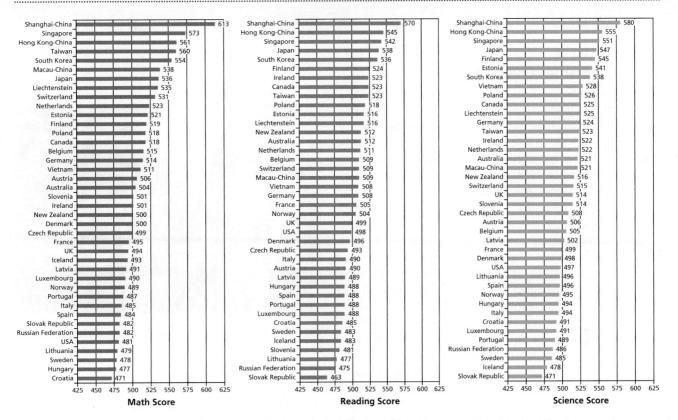

SOURCES: Organisation of Economic Co-operation and Development (OECD) (http://www.theguardian.com/news/datablog/2013/dec/03/pisa-resultscountry-best-reading-maths-science) and (http://www.businessinsider.com/pisa-rankings-2013-12).

programs in universities is competitive. Teachers are unionized and are paid well, and the teaching profession remains highly respected. Indeed, there is evidence that teachers in Finland exhibit a high level of accountability not because of imposed standards but because of their commitment to their profession.

Second, Finland has not embraced any of the policies pursued in recent decades in the United States, including charter schools, vouchers, merit pay for teachers, and evaluation of teachers and schools in terms of how well they perform on standardized tests (Ravitch 2012: 19).

Third, Finnish schools perform at remarkably similar levels. In other words, there is less variation in achievement across the educational system than there is in other countries (Sahlberg 2011). This has led educational reformer Diane Ravitch (2012: 19) to conclude that Finland comes "closest to achieving equality of educational opportunity." This commitment to equal opportunity means, among other things, that school funding is uniform and equitable. The school system reflects the larger national culture, which has been shaped for many decades by a social democratic commitment to equality and to a welfare system that promotes it.

ASK YOURSELF

Are you surprised by the poor showing of U.S. students in the PISA rankings? What do these low rankings mean for the future of the United States?

Education in Germany, Japan, and the United States.
Germany and Japan also differ from the United States in their approaches to education. In Germany, all elementary school students attend *Grundschule,* which does not practice ability grouping; all children are exposed to the same curriculum. At the end of fourth grade, teachers make a recommendation to each child's family regarding the type of secondary school the child should attend based on his or her test scores and the teachers' subjective assessments of the student's ability. There are three types of schools that represent academic and vocational tracks: lower-level *Gymnasium* (the college track), *Realschule* (the middle track), and *Hauptschule* (the lowest track). Each of these has its own curriculum, which is designed to correspond with the future occupational trajectories of its students. Only 30 percent of students are placed in the *Gymnasium* level. Transferring to a different

U.S. Universities Overseas

U.S. universities have long been active overseas, and many have recently constructed branch campuses in other countries (Clotfelter 2010; Lewin 2008a, 2008b, 2008c; Sutton 2014), including China, India, Singapore, and especially the nations of the Persian Gulf area. Why there? Nations in that region are awash in oil revenues and can afford to host such educational centers and to pay for many students to attend them. For example, the president of New York University was led to create a branch campus in Abu Dhabi by a $50 million gift from that country's government. Education City has developed in Doha, Qatar. Local students are able to study at branch campuses of leading institutions like Weill Medical College of Cornell University, Georgetown, Carnegie Mellon, Virginia Commonwealth, and Texas A&M. U.S. universities are becoming *global universities*, with faculty and students traveling to their various branches around the globe.

An obvious question is to what degree these international campuses reflect U.S. culture or the cultures of the host nations. Yale University has announced a joint venture, Yale–National University of Singapore College (Yale–NUS), with the National University of Singapore. It began accepting students in 2012.

Critics, including some Yale faculty, have questioned the institution's commitment to freedom and equality because this alliance was established in a city-state known for its excessive control over people and institutions. Like all students in Singapore, students at Yale–NUS are prohibited from engaging in any kind of protest movement (Gooch 2012). NYU's Abu Dhabi campus created a controversy when reports revealed that the immigrant laborers who built it were treated cruelly, underpaid, and forced into substandard housing (Kaminer and O'Driscoll 2014).

Then there is the issue of whether campuses like these are really exposing students to other cultures. The campuses are relatively self-contained and tend to reflect the hyperefficient, hyperrationalized culture of the United States in general, and of U.S. education in particular, rather than local culture. To the degree that students are exposed to the local culture, it is likely

Yale University and the National University of Singapore recently opened an independent liberal arts college in Singapore. The small first graduating class included students from more than 25 countries.

to be a simulated version (see Chapter 2) (Daley 2011).

Think About It

Do you think the extension of U.S. universities abroad is overall a positive or a negative development for the societies in which the campuses are located? Why? Is the cultural and informational flow these campus branches represent good or bad for the United States? Why? Would you welcome the arrival of an extension of, say, Oxford or Cambridge University or the Sorbonne in your state? What about Cairo University, or Qatar University? Why or why not?

---

track is possible, but it is difficult and rare. Between-school tracking continues at the next level of schooling, and only students who attend upper-level *Gymnasium* can proceed to the university system and attain the equivalent of a baccalaureate degree.

Japan has a very different system, with little or no ability grouping among students from school entry through ninth grade, either between or within schools. For the first nine years of school, Japanese students are exposed to a remarkably uniform curriculum. At the end of ninth grade, Japanese

students take a high-stakes test that determines which type of high school they will attend. About 75 percent of students attend *futsuuka*, which has a college preparatory curriculum. The remaining 25 percent of students attend a variety of technical and vocational schools. Family background plays an important role in educational success for Japanese students because of a "shadow education" system, in which informal schooling opportunities outside school give more advantaged students better preparation for both high school and college entrance exams.

National Geographic

The waters of the Ganges are considered sacred by the pilgrims who bathe there. What do you consider sacred?

The German and Japanese systems are much more centralized than education in the United States. The United States has 50 different educational systems (one run by each state) with different levels of funding and varying curricula. The United States also has more variability in school quality by geographic region. In the United States, more so than in Japan and Germany, the quality and character of a student's education is likely to be affected by where the student's family lives.

These differences have implications for achievement outcomes in each nation (Montt 2011). Germany has the highest levels of achievement inequality because of its highly stratified system. Japan has higher average achievement than Germany but much less inequality in outcomes because it does not practice curricular differentiation until very late. The United States actually has the lowest average achievement and the least variability of these three nations.

Two features of educational systems are significant for student outcomes. First, nations with highly differentiated school systems—with between-school tracking—have more unequal learning outcomes for students, and family background tends to matter more for student outcomes (Van de Werfhorst and Mij 2010). Second, standardization—the degree to which the curriculum and examinations are the same across schools—produces less inequality in student outcomes and a weaker correlation between family background and achievement. Thus, institutions do matter greatly, and the choices nations make have important consequences for how learning is distributed within society.

RELIGION

Religion is of great importance to billions of people throughout the world. Similar to education, religion is related to the process of socialization. Religious institutions and organizations teach their members particular beliefs and rituals that shape their identities and influence their behaviors. Some of this religious socialization occurs within educational institutions run by religious groups, such as madrassas (Muslim schools) and parochial schools. Furthermore, as the opening vignette to this chapter illustrates, religious beliefs can influence what is taught even in public schools.

The definition of religion employed here is largely derived from Durkheim's ([1912] 1965) classic statement: **Religion** is a social phenomenon that consists of beliefs about the sacred; the experiences, practices, and rituals that reinforce those beliefs; and the communities that share similar beliefs and practices (Kurtz 2012).

COMPONENTS OF RELIGION

Three of the major components of religion are beliefs, rituals, and experiences.

Belief

Every religion has a set of interrelated **beliefs**, or ideas that explain the world and identify what should be sacred or held in awe—that is, the religion's ultimate concerns. Religious beliefs have been shaped over thousands of years; they are embedded in religious traditions and also serve as the "raw material" for new religions.

Durkheim argued that all human experience could be divided into two categories. The **sacred** is that which is extraordinary, set aside, and of ultimate concern and that leads to awe and reverence. The **profane**, in contrast, is the ordinary and mundane. People can come to *believe* that virtually anything is sacred—a deity, a place (like Jerusalem or Mecca), a particular time or season (Ramadan, Diwali), an idea (freedom), or even a thing (an animal, a mountain, a tree, a canyon, a flag, or a rock). The sacred is treated with respect, and one's relation to it is often defined in rituals: You might genuflect when passing in front of an altar or take off your shoes when entering a temple. People believe that anything that is not considered sacred is profane.

Beliefs are often presented in sacred stories and scriptures. They address questions about the origin and meaning of life, theories about why the world was created, and explanations of suffering and death. They first express a *worldview,* that is, a culture's most comprehensive image of the ways in which life—nature, self, and society—is ordered (Geertz 1973). That worldview, in turn, shapes an *ethos,* which "expresses a culture's and a people's basic attitude about themselves and the world in general" (Geertz 1973: 173). Thus, beliefs are at the same time both models of and models for reality. They provide believers with information and a framework for interpreting the world around them.

One of the most difficult dilemmas for any religion is to explain why good people suffer and bad people sometimes flourish. While the suffering of the righteous is problematic, most religious explanations suggest that ethical behavior will eventually be rewarded. Most mainstream religions suggest that suffering is just part of the way the universe functions, so that everyone is subject to it at one time or another. It is how you deal with suffering that is most important.

Ritual

In most religious traditions, simply believing is never enough; one also has to act. The belief systems of religious traditions are loaded with rituals that reinforce those beliefs, serve as reminders, and help believers enact their beliefs

in the world. A **ritual** consists of regularly repeated, prescribed, and traditional behaviors symbolizing a value or belief. Rituals are enacted during ceremonies and festivals, such as funerals, weddings, and baptisms. Rituals are a central part of the **rites of passage** that accompany major transitions in life, such as birth, puberty, marriage, and death (van Gennep 1961). Also included under the heading of rituals are ongoing spiritual practices, such as personal prayer and attending worship services of faith communities, as well as elements of everyday language that serve as religious reminders for many people.

Rituals come in many forms. Some, such as prayer, chanting, singing, and dancing, help people communicate with or show devotion to the gods. Some, such as mantras and meditations, help believers organize their personal and social lives. Some frame daily life, like those relating to diet, hygiene, and sexual practices, while others celebrate cycles of nature and build community, like holidays, seasonal festivals, and processionals.

Rituals solve problems of personal and collective life by providing time-tested actions, words, and sentiments for every occasion. When addressing a serious problem, such as death, violence, natural disaster, or social crisis, people often use rituals to

1. identify the source of the problem,

2. characterize it as evil,

3. mark boundaries between "us" and "them," and

4. arrive at some means of working toward a solution, or at least the satisfaction that they are doing something about the problem.

In times of crisis, rituals can help people deal with tragedy and offer an opportunity to strengthen social bonds. Such rituals build a sense of solidarity that provides support for the suffering and reinforces the authority of the social order and the institutions that sponsor the rituals, especially when they are being threatened. Rituals can also provide a theory of evil and focus participants' attention on some abstract issue, a personified devil or mythical figure, or a human enemy who needs to be denounced or attacked.

ASK YOURSELF

Which religious rituals have you been involved in or witnessed in your life? Consider those of your own religion, if any, and those of other religions to which you have been exposed through friends or relatives. What was the stated purpose of these rituals? Were there other reasons for these rituals that were less obvious? If so, what were they?

Religious rituals are also crucial for social change and cultural innovation, especially when traditional rituals can

This ritual bathing is part of a voodoo pilgrimage. Do you participate in any religious rituals?

be transformed for revolutionary purposes. For example, in Egypt in 2011, the Muslim Friday prayers became occasions for large gatherings that moved from prayer to protest and to regime change.

Religious rituals often mark a **liminal period**, or a special time set apart from ordinary reality (Turner 1967). The sacred time during a religious ceremony may involve an inversion of apparent reality, giving hope for the oppressed that they will be liberated, for the sad that they will be comforted, and for the last that they shall be first. In the traditional Catholic Carnival ritual preceding Lent (a period of penitence), the

norms of appropriate behavior appear to be suspended as the celebrants sing, dance, and drink to excess.

Experience

The combination of beliefs, rituals, and other practices forms the variety of religious experiences for believers, regardless of which tradition they celebrate. Much of the human community views the world through a religious lens and constructs an identity around religious affiliation and experiences, such as prayer or attendance at religious services. In a survey of 57 countries, large numbers of people, especially in sub-Saharan Africa, the Middle East, and parts of Asia, reported that religion is very important in their lives (see Figure 11.6).

While religion remains important to most Americans, young people do not necessarily accept this view. They—and many others—are increasingly religiously unaffiliated. Almost a third of those between 18 and 29 years of age are unaffiliated (see Figure 11.7). However, this does not mean religion is completely unimportant to them; more than two-thirds say they believe in God. In comparison, only 9 percent of those over 65 report being unaffiliated.

SECULARIZATION

Secularization is defined as the declining significance of religion (013; Calhoun, Juergensmeyer, and VanAn Dobbelaere 2007; Perez-Agote t occurs at both the societal and

FIGURE 11.6 • **The Importance of Religion Worl**

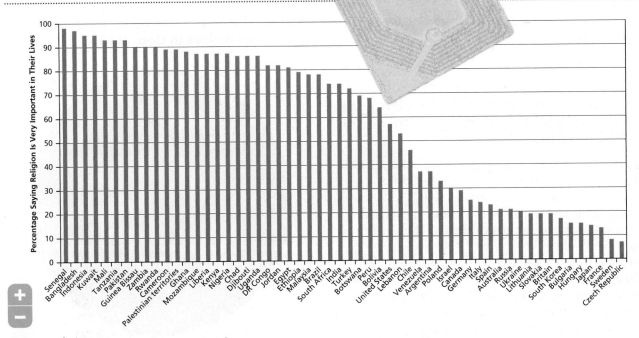

⑤SAGE datamaps edge.sagepub.com
- Religious observance data for every country.
- Majority religion in every country.

SOURCE: "Tolerance and Tension: Islam and Christianity in Sub-Saharan Africa," Pew Research Center, Washington, DC, April, 2010 (http://www.pewforum.org/2010/04/15/executive-summary-islam-and-christianity-in-sub-saharan-africa).

FIGURE 11.7 • Religious Affiliation by Age Group, 2011

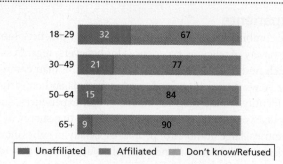

Age	Unaffiliated	Affiliated
18–29	32	67
30–49	21	77
50–64	15	84
65+	9	90

■ Unaffiliated ■ Affiliated ■ Don't know/Refused

SOURCE: "'Nones' on the Rise," Pew Research Center, Washington, DC, October, 2012 (http://www.pewforum.org/2012/10/09/nones-on-the-rise).

individual levels. At the societal level, it can involve the declining power of organized religion as well as the transfer of functions such as education from religion to the state. At the individual level, secularization means that individual experiences with religion are less intense and less important than other kinds of experiences.

Secularization includes historical developments in the modern world that undermine the authority of religion. Among the mechanisms that are seen as contributing to secularization are the following:

1. The rise of scientific thinking as an alternative way of interpreting the world

2. The development of industrial society, particularly when it encourages materialism and downplays otherworldly concerns

3. The rise of governments that do not mandate or promote an established religion

4. The encouragement of religious tolerance, which leads to a "watering down" of religion in general and religious differences in particular

5. The existence of competing secular moral ideologies, such as humanism (Smelser 1994: 305–306)

Given the combined impact of these developments, by the 1960s proponents of secularization theory (such as Berger 1969; Wilson 1966) assumed religion would continue to decline. It was thought that people would be less likely to believe in God, attend religious services, join religious institutions, or embrace religious beliefs. This was already happening in the wealthy industrial nations of Western Europe, the first to become "modern," and it was believed that it would inevitably happen elsewhere, too, at some point in the future. But religion continues to be vibrant in most of the world, and the United States remains a religious nation.

A 2013 poll found that 74 percent of Americans believed in God (see Figure 11.8). Given this reality, as well as the rise of Islam in much of the world, it is the more secularized Europe that increasingly looks like the exception.

Two examples of secularization are civil religion and how religion is becoming a form of consumption. While both challenge the authority of conventional religions, they do not necessarily reject the components of religion: beliefs, rituals, and experiences.

Civil Religion

Civil religion, or the beliefs, practices, and symbols that a nation holds sacred, is particularly important to Americans (Turner 2014; Yamane 2007). Robert Bellah (1967) argued that civil religion has existed in U.S. society since the nation's founding. Examples of civil religion include presidential addresses (Gorski 2011), the Constitution, revered geographic locations, and community rituals, like parades and fireworks on the Fourth of July. Civil religion becomes especially prominent and important in difficult times, such as after 9/11.

Civil religion provides a sense of a collective national identity by promoting and reaffirming shared ideas and ideals. It reinforces a sense of solidarity, defining who the "we" is in "we the people." While many Americans continue to believe in the country's civil religion, others contend that it is less important today. Divisions within American society, especially between liberals and conservatives, suggest that there may no longer be a consensus on the major

FIGURE 11.8 • Percentage in the United States Who Believe in God, 2013

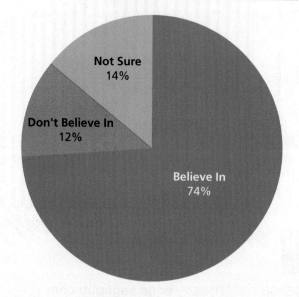

Not Sure 14%

Don't Believe In 12%

Believe In 74%

SOURCE: Harris Interactive (http://www.harrisinteractive.com/NewsRoom/HarrisPolls/tabid/447/ctl/ReadCustom%20Default/mid/1508/ArticleId/1353/Default.aspx).

components of America's civil religion. This lack of consensus is not surprising, given that the existence of competing worldviews is one mechanism that contributes to secularization.

Religion as a Form of Consumption

Oddly, secularization can be connected to the development of an extensive religious marketplace in societies that have a great deal of religious diversity and in which people are free to choose their religion. Roger Finke and Rodney Stark (2005) describe religious institutions in terms of a "religious economy" that operates like commercial economies. In this view, religious institutions are like business firms seeking to serve a market, and in so doing, they enter into competitive relationships with other "firms" in order to maintain or expand market share and attract more "consumers" (believers).

Religious consumers have different tastes, which can be influenced by class, race, gender, educational attainment, age, region, and similar factors. When consumers "purchase" religious institutions, they do so for different reasons. Some might seek a family-friendly place with quality child care on the premises, some might emphasize worship that is very traditional, others may value contemporary worship formats, and still others might place a premium on the religious leaders' stances on various social and moral issues.

Like all other aspects of consumer culture, religions need to respond to the demands of those who consume them and advertise what they have to offer (Roof 2001). Among the more obvious examples are efforts to sell all sorts of goods and services linked to religion (Moore 1997). All major holidays are associated with one form of consumption or another, but this is most clearly true of Christmas (Belk 1987, 2013). There are even religious theme parks devoted to consumption (O'Guinn and Belk 1989). For example, in Orlando, Florida, near Disney World, the Trinity Broadcasting Network runs the Holy Land Experience. At this theme park, customers can visit such places as the Garden of Eden, Bethlehem, and the Garden of Gethsemane.

Many churches, especially megachurches (churches having more than 2,000 members), are increasingly oriented to making themselves consumer-friendly (Sanders 2014). In these churches, the founders "have created sanctuaries that can only be intended to be entertainment spaces, complete with stages, lighting, and even theater-style seats" (Drane 2012: 105). The fanciest megachurches may have Christian rock music (Bowler and Reagan 2014), aerobics classes, food courts, and bowling alleys, as well as multimedia Bible classes presented in ways that resemble MTV videos (Niebuhr 1995). Ironically, secular forms of entertainment might help recruit and retain worshippers and increase attendance at religious services.

Associated Press

How do megachurches like this one exemplify the features of McDonaldization—efficiency, predictability, calculability, and control? What are the advantages for the church? For its congregation? Are there any disadvantages?

While religion has become increasingly like more secular forms of consumption, it can be argued that consumption has become our new religion. As a result, shopping malls and fast-food restaurants, among many other settings, have become places where people go to practice their consumer religion. A trip to Disney World has been described as the "middle class hajj, the compulsory visit to the sunbaked city" (Garfield 1991). Similarly, the shopping mall has religious qualities and can be considered a "cathedral of consumption" (Ritzer 2010a). It is in such cathedrals, and in the process of consumption, that many people have what can only be described as religious experiences.

TYPES OF RELIGIOUS INSTITUTIONS

Various typologies describe the most common religious institutions. Much of this work begins by distinguishing between *sects* and *churches*. These two terms are poles on a continuum, from the sect at one end to the church on the other.

Andrew M. Greeley: Sociologist, Priest, Novelist

Andrew Greeley was a unique public sociologist. He obtained degrees in theology and served as an assistant priest at a church in Chicago. However, he also studied sociology at the University of Chicago and received his PhD there in 1962. As a priest, Greeley gave homilies and wrote religious books and articles that dealt with sociological and religious issues confronting the Catholic Church and its members. He wrote a weekly column for the *Chicago Sun-Times* and was a frequent contributor to other newspapers, including the *New York Times*.

What most distinguished Greeley as a public sociologist was the fact that he published many best-selling novels, including *The Priestly Sins* (2005), which confronts the issue of priests who are pedophiles and the church bureaucracy that ignores and even protects them. Though Greeley wrote about important sociological issues, his major objective was to teach moral and religious lessons both to laypersons and to those who labored in the church hierarchy.

In 2008, Greeley suffered a devastating brain injury when his coat caught in the door of a taxicab as it pulled away. He was under 24-hour care for years, during which he had difficulty speaking and was no longer able to write. He died on May 29, 2013.

Think About It

Do you agree that fiction can serve a public sociological purpose? Why or why not?

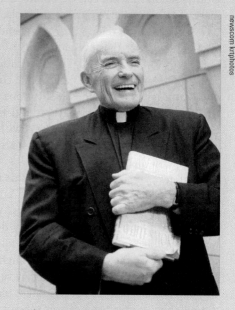

newscom krtphotos

Andrew M. Greeley

Sect

A **sect** is a small group of people who have joined that group consciously and voluntarily to have a personal religious experience. They see themselves as the "true believers" who have privileged access to religious truths. The members' religious experiences and general behavior tend to be spontaneous and unregimented. A sect's leadership is usually composed of laypersons rather than those with specialized training. As such, the organizational structure is nonbureaucratic and nonhierarchical. Leaders often arise because they are seen as possessing charisma and thus should be obeyed without question. Sects tend to be antiestablishment, and the members often feel alienated from, and as a result are prone to reject, society and the status quo. In fact, sects can be seen as breakaway, dissident groups that leave established religious institutions. They do so because they think such institutions have compromised too much with "the world" and therefore have polluted the religion's teachings.

Sects tend to set themselves apart from the larger society and admit only those who rigorously conform to the group's norms. There is a demand for high levels of commitment on the part of members. Likewise, doctrinal purity is emphasized, and diversity of opinions within the group is not permitted. Sect members frequently set themselves apart from society in terms of how they dress and what they eat. In addition, they might even segregate themselves physically and live in isolated areas.

Numerous sects within the Christian tradition have long histories in the United States, including the Amish, Hutterites, Seventh-day Adventists, and Jehovah's Witnesses. Within Judaism, Hasidic Jews are an example of a sect.

Church

A **church** is a large group of religiously oriented people into which members are usually born rather than joining consciously and voluntarily. The church's leadership is composed of professionals who have highly specialized training. The church as a whole tends to have a highly bureaucratic structure and a complex division of labor (Diotallevi 2007). While a sect tends to restrict membership to true believers, a church seeks to include as many people as possible. Churches often actively seek out new members, sometimes by employing missionaries. A church's belief systems tend to be highly codified, and rituals are often elaborate and performed in a highly prescribed manner. In comparison with members of sects, church members tend to have a lower level of commitment, and much less is expected of them. While sects tend to reject the status quo, churches accept it.

While *sect* and *church* are presented here as if they are totally distinct, in reality there is no clear dividing line between them. In fact, over time there is a tendency for a sect to become transformed into something that takes on the organizational features of a church. As sects become larger, they need, among other things, ever-larger bureaucratic structures with less charismatic leadership and more leadership based on expertise. The behavior of sect members becomes less spontaneous and more formal.

Cults and New Religious Movements

A cult resembles a sect in many ways, but it is important to distinguish between the two (Stark and Bainbridge 1979). While a sect is a religious group that breaks off from a more established religion as a result of a schism, a **cult** is a new, small, voluntary, and exclusive religion that was never associated with any religious organization. A cult is often at odds with established religions as well as the larger society. Those who found cults tend to be religious radicals, and because they are new, cults, even more than sects, tend to be led by charismatic figures. Like sects, cults demand high levels of commitment and involvement on the part of members. Among the better-known cults are Baha'i, the International Society for Krishna Consciousness (Hare Krishnas), Rastafari, and the Unification Church, founded in South Korea by the Reverend Sun Myung Moon.

The term *cult* has fallen out of favor in sociology because it is has come to be associated in the popular mind and press with such destructive groups as Charles Manson and his "family," who murdered a number of people, including actress Sharon Tate, in 1969. The Manson cult was not actually a religious organization, but a number of religiously based cults have proved to be very destructive. These include Jim Jones's People's Temple, David Koresh's Branch Davidians, and Heaven's Gate. All of these groups ended in tragedy. In the case of the People's Temple, the end involved the 1979 mass suicide and murder of 918 of Jones's followers in their jungle compound in Guyana. In the case of the Branch Davidians, the leader and members died in a controversial confrontation in Waco, Texas, with federal officials from the Bureau of Alcohol, Tobacco, and Firearms. And in the case of Heaven's Gate, a charismatic leader convinced his followers that Comet Hale-Bopp was hiding a mother ship that would take them to a better world. The result was that 39 members committed suicide.

Given the negative connotations associated with the term *cult*, some sociologists prefer to use the term *new religious movements* to encompass sects, cults, and a wide array of other innovative religious groups. **New religious movements** are typified by zealous religious converts, charismatic leaders, an appeal to an atypical portion of the population, a tendency to differentiate between "us" and "them," distrust of others, and proneness to rapid fundamental changes (Barker 2007). Use of the term *new religious movement* is intended to eliminate or reduce the negative connotations associated with cults. It also emphasizes the idea that each unconventional religious organization should be examined objectively based on its own characteristics.

ASK YOURSELF

What role can technology play in recruiting new members to sects, churches, or new religious movements? Are online religious communities new forms of religious institutions? Why or why not?

Denominations

Like a church, a **denomination** is an organized form of religious expression that is usually supportive of the social order and of other religious forms. Religious services of denominations, like those of churches, are formal and reserved, with an emphasis on teaching rather than on an emotional religious experience. Denominations are hierarchical and bureaucratic. Local organizations are not independent but part of larger regional or national institutional structures. They rely on specialized, professionally trained, full-time clergy who are trained in seminaries run by the denominations to ensure conformity to doctrines.

Among major Christian denominations today are a long list of Protestant groups, including American Baptist, Assemblies of God, Church of Christ, Episcopal, Evangelical Lutheran, Lutheran, Presbyterian, Southern Baptist, United Church of Christ, and United Methodist (Figure 11.9 shows the largest Protestant Christian groups in the United States at the county level). The Roman Catholic Church and the Eastern Orthodox Church are also Christian denominations.

RELIGION AND GLOBALIZATION

Religion globalized before anything else. We can focus on institutional religion and, under that heading, on two aspects of its relationship to globalization. Today, as Figure 11.10 shows, Christians make up over 33 percent of the world's population (Britannica 2012; Kurtz 2012: 46). More than 22 percent are Muslims, 14 percent are Hindus, and smaller proportions are followers of Buddhism (7 percent), Sikhism (0.36 percent), Judaism (0.21 percent), and the Baha'i faith (0.11 percent). Atheists (those without any religious belief) account for 2 percent of the world population.

Two issues are of particular importance in regard to the relationship between religion and globalization. First,

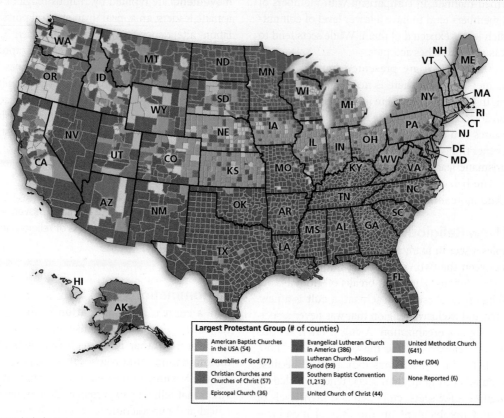

Largest Protestant Group (# of counties)

- American Baptist Churches in the USA (54)
- Assemblies of God (77)
- Christian Churches and Churches of Christ (57)
- Episcopal Church (36)
- Evangelical Lutheran Church in America (386)
- Lutheran Church–Missouri Synod (99)
- Southern Baptist Convention (1,213)
- United Church of Christ (44)
- United Methodist Church (641)
- Other (204)
- None Reported (6)

*The "Other" category includes 37 groups with less than 20 counties each. Six of these had at least 10 counties where each was the largest group: Lutheran Congregations in Mission for Christ (16 counties), Wisconsin Evangelical Lutheran Synod (16), Church of the Nazarene (15), Amish Groups, undifferentiated (13), National Baptist Convention, USA, Inc. (12), and African Methodist Episcopal Church (10).

SOURCE: Clifford Grammich, Kirk Hadaway, Richard Houseal, Dale E. Jones, Alexei Krindatch, Richie Stanley, & Richard H. Taylor. 2010 U.S. *Religion Census: Religious Congregations & Membership Study.* (Kansas City, MO: Nazarene Publishing House, 2012). © Association of Statisticians of American Religious Bodies (ASARB).

transnational migration brings institutional religion to new locales. Migrants transplant religions into new places, making those places more multireligious. They also generate in those locales new and different versions of the local religions, even as the migrants' versions are influenced and altered by local religions. This, in turn, can alter religion in the migrants' homeland. Thus, transnational migration globalizes religion spatially and contributes to the further pluralization of religion around the world. Migrants help to unify various parts of the world by, for example, making pilgrimages to religious sites like Mecca and the Wailing Wall, posting prayers in cyberspace, and sending money to religious centers in their homelands.

Second is the spread of religious organizations and movements through independent missions. Here the Christian churches, especially the Roman Catholic Church, have played a central role through their missionaries. In fact, Christianity became the first worldwide religion. However, messengers for Islam created the most global system prior to the modern era (see the discussion of Islam below).

ASK YOURSELF

Have any other social institutions spread as widely as religion? What do you think accounts for religion's staying power in the places to which it has been transported? Why are religions still expanding globally today?

The Most Significant Global Religions

In this section we will deal with several globally important religions—Judaism, Buddhism, Hinduism, Islam, and Christianity. Although Mormonism is not a large global religion, and debate continues about whether it should be defined as a Christian denomination or a new religion, we will also examine it here because of its very contemporary efforts to become a global religion. However, as is clear in Figure 11.11, many of the world's dominant religions, despite their spread, are still to a large extent concentrated in particular parts of the world.

FIGURE 11.10 • The World's Dominant Religions, by Percentage of Believers

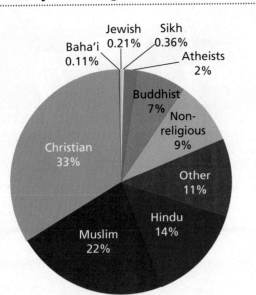

SOURCE: CIA World Factbook, "World," 2013 (https://www.cia.gov/library/publications/the-world-factbook/geos/xx.html).

Judaism. Founded more than 3,000 years ago, Judaism is today one of the smallest of the world's religions, with roughly 13.4 million people in the world defining themselves as Jews (Goldberg 2007; Goldscheider 2012). However, for a variety of reasons, Judaism's importance both historically and contemporarily has been far greater than one would think by simply looking at the numbers involved. By the late nineteenth century, there were 12 million Jews in the world, many of whom had migrated from the Middle East and were spread in mostly small enclaves across many countries. There was and continues to be a large concentration of Jews in Europe, but migrations to North America, as well as to Palestine (then under Ottoman control), began during this period. By the onset of World War II, the number of Jews in the world had grown to 16.6 million, but the atrocities of the Nazis led to a reduction in the population to about 10 million. The founding of Israel in 1948 marked an important turning point for Jews, and that nation's population is now approaching 6 million people. Another large concentration of Jews—approximately 6 million—is found in North America, mostly in the United States. The vast majority of the more than 13 million Jews alive today live in either North America or Israel, with fewer than 2 million living elsewhere, mostly in Europe. Just a few of the factors that give Judaism great global significance are the spread of Jews throughout the world, Zionism (which helped lead to the founding of Israel),

FIGURE 11.11 • The World's Dominant Religions

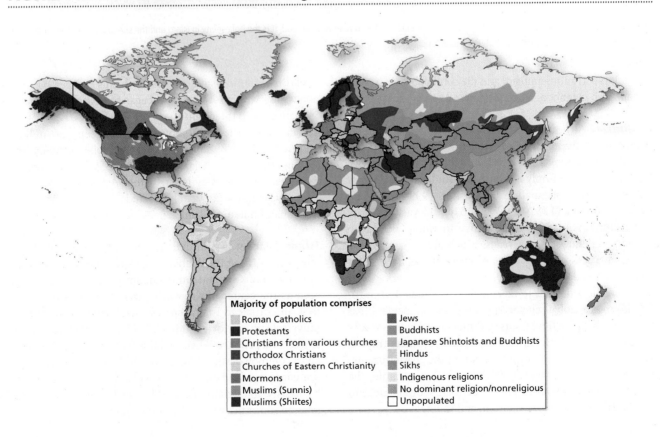

Majority of population comprises

Roman Catholics
Protestants
Christians from various churches
Orthodox Christians
Churches of Eastern Christianity
Mormons
Muslims (Sunnis)
Muslims (Shiites)

Jews
Buddhists
Japanese Shintoists and Buddhists
Hindus
Sikhs
Indigenous religions
No dominant religion/nonreligious
Unpopulated

The city of Mecca in Saudi Arabia is a sacred place. The birthplace of the Prophet Muhammad, it is the holiest city in Islam and the site of a mandatory pilgrimage for all who are able. Non-Muslims are forbidden to enter.

Associated Press

the Holocaust, anti-Semitism, and the conflict between Israel and its Arab neighbors over Palestine.

Hinduism. Although no precise starting date can be determined, Hinduism began sometime between 800 and 200 BCE (Abrutyn 2012). While it has ancient origins, Hinduism became firmly established in India as the country opposed foreign occupation by Muslims (999–1757) and later the British (1757–1947). Today, the vast majority of Hindus (about 800 million) live in India. Hinduism is strongly defined by the *Vedas*, which are both historical documents and enumerations of incantations needed for successful rituals.

While it continues to be heavily concentrated in India, Hinduism is a global religion spanning six continents. It has been spread by both migrants and itinerant religious teachers (Madan 2007). Despite its geographic concentration, Hinduism has been important as part of the "Easternization of the West" (Campbell 2007) through, for example, the spread of yoga (including now "he-man" yoga; Bluestein 2014), Transcendental Meditation, and so on.

Buddhism. Buddhism arose in the Indus Ganges basin in about the sixth century BCE and began to have a transnational influence about three centuries later (Nichols 2012; J. Taylor 2007). Today there are somewhere between 230 million and 500 million Buddhists across the globe, although the vast majority are in Asia. China has the largest number of Buddhists, followed by Japan. Other Asian countries with majority Buddhist populations include Thailand, Cambodia, Myanmar, Bhutan, Sri Lanka, Laos, and Vietnam.

Islam. Islam was founded by the Prophet Muhammad, who was born on the Arabian Peninsula and lived between 570 and 632 CE. The lands encompassed by Islam were seen as the center of the world, with all else subordinate to it. Important to Islam's spread (see Figure 11.11) was its universalistic worldview; Muslims did not view themselves as a chosen people but believed that they and all of humanity had a common destiny. Islam's universalistic ideas (God-given standards that lead everyone to search for goodness) had to be diffused throughout the world. Such beliefs led to a global mission to rid the world of competing idea systems, such as

DIGITAL LIVING

Wahhabism, Islamic State, and the Internet

Wahhabism, a variety of Salafism and ultimately of (Sunni) Islam, is particularly strong in Saudi Arabia (Husain 2014). This strength is traceable to an agreement hundreds of years ago between the country's ruling family and the founder of Wahhabism. The Saudi government continues to support Wahhabism in various ways, especially financially. Osama bin Laden (a Saudi) and his followers were Wahhabists, and Wahhabism is the religion that lies at the root of the self-proclaimed Islamic State (IS). Wahhabism and its radical ideas and practices are in tension with modernism and the political position of those who rule Saudi Arabia, including their pro-Western—especially American—orientation.

Wahhabism is a particularly radical and austere form of Islam, with a strict, rigid, and literal reading of sharia law. Wahhabists see themselves as practicing a purer form of Islam than other Islamists,

and they are hostile toward them, to say nothing of nonbelievers.

Not only is Wahhabism in tension with the practices of the Saudi government, but it is also in conflict with some of IS's activities. While Wahhabism is anti-modern, even medieval, IS has adopted various aspects of modernity, especially the highly effective use of the media, in particular the Internet, to publicize itself and to attract new adherents from many places, including Europe and the United States (Shane and Hubbard 2014).

IS has used online videos with very modern and sophisticated production values copied from contemporary American movies to garner attention worldwide. This is especially true of videos of its prisoners and the murders, most notably beheadings, of a number of them. These videos have shocked, even repulsed, most viewers, but they have certainly gotten the world's attention. And some of those angry at the West in general, and

the United States in particular, have been galvanized to travel to Syria to join Islamic State and, in some cases, to commit acts of violence, including the murders associated with the 2015 attacks in Paris on the satirical magazine *Charlie Hebdo* and a kosher supermarket.

Perhaps of greater importance than the videos has been IS's use of social media (Facebook, Twitter) to lure young people in the West to their cause (Knowlton 2014). Young people associated with IS communicate with their peers in the West, employing messages designed to induce them either to join IS or to commit acts of violence on its behalf.

Think About It
Given Islamic State's use of online sites such as Facebook, would you favor action to ban the group's supporters, if possible, from using that site and others like it? What kind of precedent would be set by such a ban?

---

idolatry and superstition. Islam saw itself as building on, but going beyond, Judaism and Christianity and "was the first of the world's great religious civilizations to understand itself as one religion among others" (Keane 2003: 42).

Believers in Islam, as well as their armies, traveled with the belief that they were the messengers and that everyone was eagerly awaiting their message. Thus, the belief emerged that "Islam would prevail among the world's peoples, either by willing acceptance, or by spiritual fervour, or (in the face of violent resistances) by conquest" (Keane 2003: 42). Because there was only one God and therefore only one law according to Islam, such a view—and mission—meant that followers of Islam took no notice of nation-states and their borders.

In the end, of course, the efforts of Islam's early missionaries were thwarted. One factor in this failure was the efforts of alternative religions, especially Christianity and its various militaristic campaigns against Islam. Another was that the principle of *jihad,* or the duty to struggle on behalf of God

against those who doubt him or are his enemies, was rarely pursued unconditionally. Furthermore, Muslims believed that contact, trade, and traffic with nonbelievers was acceptable, even encouraged. However, efforts to globalize Islam remain strong among many devotees and help inform the contemporary thinking of jihadists and Islamic fundamentalists (Sayyid 2012).

Christianity. Christianity and Islam are the two fastest-growing religions in the world today (Garrett 2007; Thomas 2012). Christianity spread in the Middle East following the death of Jesus of Nazareth. By 1000 CE, a schism had developed between Roman Catholicism in the West and Orthodoxy in the East, with more Christians living in the East than the West. A major series of events in the history of globalization was the Crusades, which began in 1095 CE and lasted for centuries. The Crusades were designed to liberate the Holy Land from Muslims and others who had gained control of Jerusalem in 638 CE. This is still a sensitive issue for Muslims, as reflected in protests that erupted when President George W. Bush used the word *crusade* in a speech shortly after the 9/11 terrorist attacks.

Christianity today is declining in Europe, but that is more than compensated for by strong growth in the Global South, including parts of Asia, Africa, and Latin America. Growth is so strong in the Global South that it is predicted that by 2050, 80 percent of the world's Christians will be Hispanic. Furthermore, Christianity is different in the Global South—"more . . . morally conservative, and evangelical" (Garrett 2007: 143).

Pentecostalism, a charismatic movement, offers another example of the spread of Christianity around the globe (Anderson 2013). This religion had its origins in revivals attended by poor blacks and whites in Los Angeles in 1906. It is now the second-largest and fastest-growing form of Christianity, with somewhere between 150 million and 400 million adherents, and has come to exceed in size all forms of Christianity except Catholicism. Its growth has been especially great in Asia, Africa, and Latin America (Lechner and Boli 2005). In fact, today only 69 percent of adults in Latin America say they are Catholic compared to 90 percent throughout much of the twentieth century. The growth of Pentecostalism is a major factor in this decline (Paulson 2014). Many variations and localized forms of Pentecostalism are linked through publications, conferences, electronic media, and travel.

Mormonism. Mormonism, or the Church of Jesus Christ of Latter-day Saints, has shown substantial growth in the last 60 years. Founded in the United States in the nineteenth century, Mormonism had fewer than 2 million members in 1960, but today the number has risen to approximately 15 million (McCombs 2013).

The Church of Jesus Christ of Latter-day Saints is centrally controlled from its headquarters in Salt Lake City, Utah. The organization exercises considerable oversight over its churches in the United States and around the world from these headquarters. It also transmits much content, such as conferences and leadership training, via satellite throughout the world and maintains websites for the use of its global members.

Once almost exclusively an American religion, today Mormonism has more members outside the United States and thousands of churches and meetinghouses in most of the world's countries and territories. Eighty thousand missionaries spread Mormonism across the globe. Although the church banned blacks from becoming priests until 1978, today it is growing rapidly in Africa and has about a quarter million members there (Jordan 2007).

The global acceptance and expansion of Mormonism is especially notable because of the church's sectlike character and practices. For example, the church has a history

Getty

While it is a very small religion by global standards, Mormonism has been growing rapidly. How do you account for its recent growth, especially outside of the United States?

of polygamy and the marriage of preteen girls to older men—practices that are not easily accepted by many cultures around the world. In contrast to other globally successful religions, Mormonism has not significantly adapted to local customs and realities. For example, unlike the far more rapidly expanding Pentecostalism, Mormonism has *not* incorporated a variety of indigenous customs (such as drumming and dancing) into its African Sunday services.

Fundamentalism

Religious **fundamentalism** is a strongly held belief in the fundamental or foundational precepts of any religion (Stolow 2004). It is also characterized by a rejection of the modern secular world (Kivisto 2012a). Fundamentalists see the world in stark terms, dividing it into true believers, who are saved, and the rest of the world's population, who are damned.

Fundamentalism can be seen as being involved in globalization in at least two major senses (Brouwer, Gifford, and Rose 2013; Lechner 1993). First, it is often expansionistic, seeking to extend its reach into more and more areas of the world and to extend its power in those areas. Second, it is profoundly affected by various globalizations. For example, the globalization of one fundamentalist religion, such as Islamic militants, is likely to lead to a counterreaction by another, such as Hasidic Jews. Another important reaction involves movements against various forces seen as emanating from the modern world, including secularism, popular culture, and the West in general. For example, IS is reacting against artificial borders in the Middle East drawn and imposed by the West largely after World War I, as well as the West's military involvement and cultural imperialism in that region.

Faith on the Move

The globalization of religion—and the growing diversity of religions around the globe—is also the result of the movement of people. The United Nations estimates that in 2010, there were 214 million immigrants globally. This figure represents just over 3 percent of the total population of the world. Recently, an attempt was made to determine what that movement of people meant in terms of the movement of religions across international borders. The Pew-Templeton Global Religious Futures Project provided a broad overview of the movement of major world religions in a study led by Phillip Connor (2012). It is perhaps not surprising that the world's two largest religions—Christianity and Islam—contribute the largest numbers of immigrants. Christians account for 2.3 billion adherents worldwide, and nearly a half of all immigrants. Islam has 1.6 million adherents, and Muslim immigrants amount to 27 percent of all immigrants. Hinduism is the third-largest religion, but only 5 percent of Hindus are migrants. Jews, though the smallest of the world's religious groups, contribute 2 percent of all immigrants. Because of the rise of anti-Semitism, especially in Europe, we are likely to see an increase in Jewish immigration, especially to Israel and the United States. In fact, in light of the *Charlie Hebdo* massacre in 2015 (and similar events elsewhere in Europe), the prime minister of Israel encouraged the mass immigration of Jews from Europe (Kershner 2015).

SUMMARY

Education is closely related to the process of socialization, although it most often takes place more formally in schools. Level of education is closely associated with employment and lifetime earnings.

Many people believe that educational success is a result of meritocracy or innate intelligence, but studies have found that teacher quality, family background, home environment, and the racial composition of the student body are important factors affecting student achievement. Differences in children's cognitive development are particularly influenced by parenting practices. Inequality in schools is often the result of tracking, which leads to cumulative advantage for students placed in higher tracks. Students with more advantaged family backgrounds are more likely to graduate from high school and to enroll in and graduate from college.

Three alternatives to public school have emerged in the past few decades: vouchers, homeschooling, and charter schools. Countries across the globe vary greatly in their ability to educate students and educate them well. Students in the United States fall near the bottom in PISA rankings on math, reading, and science.

Religion is also related to socialization, teaching individuals particular worldviews. The three components of religion are beliefs, rituals, and experiences. Some sociologists think that religion will decline in importance as the world becomes more secular. One example of secularization is civil religion, the beliefs and rituals that a nation holds sacred and that function to provide a sense of collective identity. Religion may also be seen as a form of consumption that must compete for consumers to remain viable.

Sociologists have identified different types of religious institutions: sects, churches, cults, and denominations. Some sociologists prefer to use the term *new religious movements* for innovative religious groups, rather than referring to them as sects or cults.

The spread of religion is not new, but it has accelerated with increased globalization. The most significant global religions are Christianity, Islam, Hinduism, Buddhism, and Judaism. Two factors that contribute to the globalization of religion are transnational migration and the spread of religious organizations and movements through independent missions.

REVIEW QUESTIONS

1. What is a meritocracy, and why is the educational system an important component of a meritocratic society? In what ways is the U.S. education system meritocratic, and in what ways is it not meritocratic?

2. According to the Coleman Report, how important is the quality of schools to student achievement? What other factors affect student achievement? What factors have not been found to affect student achievement to any great extent?

3. What is the relationship between income of parents and the ability of their children to enroll in and graduate from college? What role does one's habitus play in shaping the decision to go to college or not?

4. What kinds of alternatives do vouchers, homeschooling, and charter schools offer compared to the traditional public education system in the United States?

5. What are some of the differences between the U.S. education system and the education systems in Finland, Germany, and Japan? What do you think most accounts for why U.S. students score lower on the PISA rankings than students in these countries?

6. What is a ritual? Why is it an important component of religion? Offer an example of a ritual from one of the religions discussed in the chapter.

7. Define civil religion and describe its functions. Provide an example of civil religion that is most important to you and explain why.
8. Describe how religion can be understood as a form of consumption. Do you think that the commercialization of religious holidays, like Christmas, undermines the sacredness of religion? Why or why not?
9. Why has the term *cult* fallen out of favor with sociologists of religion?
10. What role does transnational migration play in the globalization of religion?

APPLYING THE SOCIOLOGICAL IMAGINATION

1. As this chapter indicates, an increasing number of people seeking alternatives to conventional public schools have opted to homeschool their children. As a result, a number of organizations have emerged that are designed to promote homeschooling and to ensure that the parents doing the homeschooling are provided with necessary training and instructional resources. Use the Internet to examine some of the websites of these organizations to get a better understanding of the messages they convey about the rationales for homeschooling and the audiences to which they are targeting these messages. Given that parents engaged in homeschooling are prosumers, consuming information about and producing education for their children, how do the messages attempt to convince them that they are capable of doing so? Do the messages criticize public schools explicitly or implicitly? Do you find the claims convincing? What would you want to know before making a sociologically informed assessment of the homeschooling alternative?

2. This chapter points out that a large and increasing number of people in the world today consider themselves nonreligious. For this activity, think of yourself as someone who is nonreligious seeking to become a member of one of the major world religions. Use the Internet (Google search, Twitter hashtags) to learn more about the major world religions and to determine the pros and cons of trying to adopt and participate in a specific religion. What would you do to facilitate your membership? How is choosing a religion different from choosing to buy a certain product or join a certain gym?

KEY TERMS

beliefs: Ideas that explain the world and identify what should be sacred or held in awe—that is, a religion's ultimate concerns. (p. 266)

church: A large group of religiously oriented people into which members are usually born rather than joining consciously and voluntarily. (p. 270)

civil religion: The beliefs, practices, and symbols that a nation holds sacred. (p. 268)

cult: A new, innovative, small, voluntary, and exclusive religious tradition that was never associated with any religious organization. (p. 271)

cumulative advantage: The process by which the most advantaged individuals are awarded the best opportunities, which increases inequality over time. (p. 259)

denomination: A religious group not linked to the state that exhibits a general spirit of tolerance and acceptance of other religious bodies. (p. 271)

fundamentalism: A strongly held belief in the fundamental or foundational precepts of any religion, or a rejection of the modern secular world. (p. 276)

habitus: An internalized set of preferences and dispositions that are learned through experience and social interactions in specific social contexts. (p. 262)

liminal period: A special time set apart from ordinary reality. (p. 267)

meritocracy: A system based on a dominant ideology involving the widely shared belief that all people have an equal chance of succeeding economically based on their hard work and skills. (p. 255)

new religious movements: Movements that attract zealous religious converts, follow charismatic leaders, appeal to an atypical portion of the population, have a tendency to differentiate between "us" and "them," are characterized by distrust of others, and are prone to rapid fundamental changes. (p. 271)

profane: To Durkheim, that which has not been defined as sacred, or that which is ordinary and mundane. (p. 266)

religion: A social phenomenon that consists of beliefs about the sacred; the experiences, practices, and rituals that reinforce those beliefs; and the communities that share similar beliefs and practices. (p. 265)

rites of passage: Events, usually rituals, that surround major transitions in life, such as birth, puberty, marriage, and death. (p. 266)

ritual: A set of regularly repeated, pre-scribed, and traditional behaviors that serve to symbolize some value or belief. (p. 266)

sacred: To Durkheim, that which is extraordinary, set aside, and of ultimate concern and that leads to awe and reverence. (p. 266)

sect: A small group of people who have joined the group consciously and voluntarily to have a personal religious experience. (p. 270)

secularization: The declining signifi-cance of religion. (p. 267)

vouchers: Government-issued certifi-cates that allow students to use public tax dollars to pay tuition at private schools. (p. 259)

$SAGE edge™ edge.sagepub.com/ritzeressentials2e

SAGE edge offers a robust online environment featuring an impressive array of free tools and resources for review, study, and further exploration, keeping both instructors and students on the cutting edge of teaching and learning.

LEARNING OBJECTIVES	FOR FURTHER EXPLORATION AND APPLICATION
LO 11-1: Explain how the educational process is related to socialization, employment, and income.	▶ The Functionalist View of Education in the United States ◉ How Small Government Can Help Fix Economic Inequality ▣ The Federal Education Law Makeover
LO 11-2: Describe inequality in education, its sources, and its effects.	▶ The Rising Costs and Financial Competition in Higher Education ◉ Reimagine Education for the 2030s ▣ Social Inequality and Educational Disadvantage
LO 11-3: Compare the educational system in the United States to the systems in other countries.	▶ The High School Experience around the World ◉ German Schools Beckon Americans Seeking Affordable Degrees ▣ Global Grade: How Do American Students Compare?
LO 11-4: Define the major components of religion.	▶ Five Major World Religions ◉ A Conflict between Religion and Science among Hawaiian Natives ▣ Religious Symbolism and Iconography
LO 11-5: Explain and provide examples of secularization.	▶ Religion and its Role in Society: A Secular Perspective ◉ The First Freedom Seder ▣ Broadening the Debate on Religion and Secularism
LO 11-6: Identify different types of religious organizations.	▶ Definitions and Approaches to Religion ◉ The Origins of the American Republic: Christian or Heretical? ▣ Did Corporate America Invent Christian America?
LO 11-7: Describe the relationship between globalization and the world's major religions.	▶ Religion and the Faithful: Seeking the Apocalypse ◉ German Protesters Express Their "Defensive Nationalism" ▣ The World's Most and Least Religious Places

POLITICS AND THE ECONOMY

12

The Interrelationship of Government and the Economy

The worldwide economic collapse of 2008 set off a chain reaction that devastated much of the international economy, triggering a global recession whose effects continue to be felt today, most noticeably in Greece. While the United States has largely recovered from the 2008 recession, some of its effects linger. Unable to find jobs, many Americans have left the labor force completely, and wages have stagnated, especially for the middle and lower classes. Because of these and other continuing economic problems, the U.S. government, specifically the Federal Reserve, continues, at least as of late 2015, to stimulate the economy by, for example, keeping interest rates artificially low in order to encourage investment.

Given that the U.S. government, like the EU governing body and the governments of many countries, intervenes in the economy, it is clear that the global financial crisis and its continuing effects are not just economic issues—they are political issues too. In fact, in many ways the two fundamental social institutions of the government and the economy are inseparable; thus, this chapter considers them together. The state of a nation's economy has enormous influence on the political system. For example, political incumbents are likely to be blamed for a recession or a depression and, as a result, may lose their offices in the next election. In addition, a nation's political system—and the policy makers who populate it—has a huge impact on the way money and resources are distributed, spent, and saved at every level of society. The basic economic questions of what goods and services a society will produce, how it will produce them, and who will consume them have yielded different answers in societies with very

LEARNING OBJECTIVES

 12-1 Contrast democracy and dictatorship.

 12-2 Explain how globalization affects war and terrorism, geopolitics, and the nation-state.

12-3 Describe the U.S. economy's transition from industrialization to deindustrialization.

 12-4 Discuss your relationship to employment, unemployment and underemployment, and consumption.

12-5 Describe the effects of globalization on the world economy.

Corbis

different political philosophies, such as communism, socialism, and capitalism.

Whatever a country's political and economic system, it is powerfully affected by global economic processes and changes. Sociology looks at how people make political and economic choices and how societies deal with the personal, national, and global consequences of those choices. ●

POLITICS: DEMOCRACY OR DICTATORSHIP

Society can be seen as a collection of groups that compete to determine whose members get what, as well as when and how they get it (Lasswell 2012). When groups operate through established governmental channels to do so, this competition is referred to as **politics**. The state is the political body organized for government and civil rule. By putting pressure on the state, a group can advance a given position or promote policies that benefit its members. Therefore, politics is one way of exercising power in society.

DEMOCRACY: CITIZENSHIP AS A RADICAL IDEA

Democracies are political systems in which people within a given state vote to choose their leaders and in some cases vote on legislation as well. In modern democracies, people vote to choose their legislators rather than actually managing their own political affairs and directly making decisions about the things that affect their lives. Nevertheless, contemporary theorists of democracy often suggest that the power to rule in democracies comes from the *consent* of the people.

Sometimes these systems are called **representative democracies**. The people, as a whole body, do not actually rule themselves but rather have some say in who will best represent them in the state. In **direct democracies**, by contrast, the people have a say in decisions that directly affect them.

Democratic states are organized into bureaucracies (see Chapter 5), with clear hierarchies as well as established and written codes, laws, and rules. The authority that legislators have under democracies is based on legal codes that confer this authority on them. Democracies tend to extend rights to **citizens**, the people represented by the state and most often born within its territories. **Citizenship** means that the people of a given state can vote for their representatives and that they have rights and responsibilities as citizens (Soysal 2012; Turner 2011). Under *universal*

Getty

A rally in Brooklyn, New York, is oriented toward achieving citizenship, or some form of permanent legal status, for the estimated 11 million undocumented immigrants in the United States. Do you think such efforts are likely to be successful in the near future? Why or why not?

citizenship, the rights of citizenship are generally conferred on most people residing in a given state's territory. At times, however, citizenship is still denied to groups of immigrants residing within that territory. In the United States, citizens have certain rights and can vote on who will be president and on who will represent them in Congress.

Most democratic states guarantee citizens the right to freely express dissent, the right to due process and equality before the law, the rights of freedom of speech and of the press, and the right to privacy. These rights and others are sometimes extended to noncitizens

Freedom House, an organization committed to monitoring democratic trends and human rights around the world, publishes an annual survey on 195 countries rating political rights and civil liberties (Figure 12.1). In 2015, of the 195 countries assessed, 89 (46 percent) were rated "free," 55 (28 percent) were rated "partly free," and 51 (26 percent) were rated "not free." Ratings for the Middle East and North Africa were the worst in the world, followed by Eurasia. Syria, a dictatorship mired in civil war, ethnic division, and uncontrolled terrorism, received the lowest score of any country in more than a decade. The

DIGITAL LIVING

The State and the Power of the Internet

A new threat to the power of the state arose early in the twenty-first century in the form of social revolutions facilitated by social media, the so-called Twitter and Facebook Revolutions (Wolfsfeld, Segev, and Sheafer 2013). While one of the state's abilities is to set the public agenda, ever-expanding access to the Internet and social media allows groups outside of power to define and publicize their own sense of the public agenda. Islamic State, for example, is free of state control and has used the Internet to relay its message. It has also aggressively used social media to attract supporters from all over the world (see the "Digital Living" box "Wahhabism, Islamic State, and the Internet" in Chapter 11).

If threatened with a revolution, including one fomented on the Internet, the state has four choices: repression and suppression, censorship, propaganda, or efforts to remain off the grid.

1. In Egypt in 2015, President Abdel Fattah el-Sisi struggled, increasingly unsuccessfully, to *suppress* rebels intent on overthrowing his regime. Repression, however, often heightens the opposition and fuels the revolution. It can radicalize those who are for the regime or harm society by, for example, shutting down needed public dialogue and debate.

2. Newspapers, radio programs, and television shows can be censored, but such *censorship* is easy compared to censoring the Internet. China continues to combat dissidents by censoring the Internet, most recently blocking information about the 2014 protests in Hong Kong. Such efforts seem futile, at least in the long run.

3. The state often resorts to *propaganda* delivered via the media, perhaps including the Internet, to counter the messages put forth by rebels.

4. Finally, it is possible, as in North Korea today, to stay *off the grid* almost completely and to deny Internet access to people who might even contemplate rebelling.

While many see social media as a revolutionary force, others see it as fostering "slacktivism" rather than activism (Gladwell 2010). That is, some potential activists might be more inclined to blog than to take to the streets. However, even if this is the case, social media are likely to increase solidarity among the disaffected (Valenzuela 2013; Woods 2011). Another view is that state officials will ultimately make better use of social media than the crowd can, and that the state's position will be strengthened, not jeopardized, by social media messages (Morozov 2011).

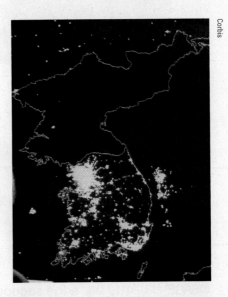

A stark demonstration of the differential access to technology across the world's countries is this satellite image of South Korea awash in light and North Korea nearly dark. Why would a government wish to restrict citizens' access to the Internet and social media?

Think About It

Do you feel social media inspire slacktivism rather than activism? Why or why not? Do you think states may eventually be able to use social media for their own agendas and purposes, appropriating the power of the crowd? What qualities or characteristics of the state as an organization might make this possible?

---

other "worst of the worst" countries are the Central African Republic, Equatorial Guinea, Eritrea, North Korea, Saudi Arabia, Somalia, Sudan, Turkmenistan, and Uzbekistan.

Democracies are not without their critics, even from within. For example, critics have argued that voters are typically ill informed about many political issues. Similarly, some argue that liberal democracies extend *too many* rights and tend to allow too much diversity of thought and interests, making them unstable.

DICTATORSHIP: THE SEIZURE OF POWER

Dictatorships are states that are usually totalitarian and ruled either by a single individual or by a small group of people.

FIGURE 12.1 • Freedom in the World, 2015

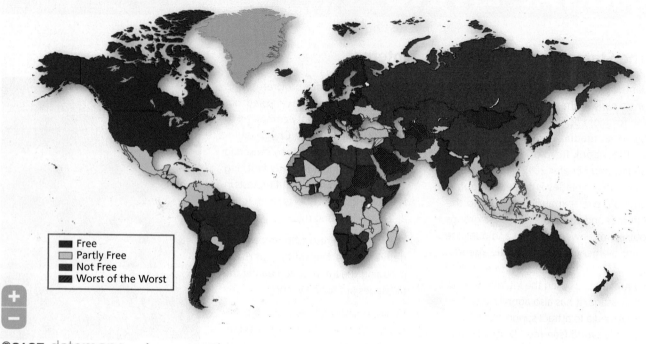

Legend:
- Free
- Partly Free
- Not Free
- Worst of the Worst

$SAGE datamaps edge.sagepub.com
- Political rights and civil liberties data for every country.

SOURCE: Data from Freedom House (2015). Freedom in the World. *Issues.*

Dictatorships are governments *without* the consent of the people being governed. In the modern period, dictatorships are often formed in formerly democratic states that have been seized by small groups of political fanatics.

In the years just before and during World War II, the world saw an alliance of dictatorships based on fascist principles. These dictatorships shared some very basic institutional arrangements and principles. They

- were totalitarian in that they attempted to control every facet of social life;

- saw conflict and war as natural states and methods for human betterment; and

- were viciously opposed to liberalism, anarchism, and any form of socialism or communism.

Dictatorships did not end with the defeat of the fascist powers in World War II. Indeed, in the postwar era, the Soviet Union and its satellites in the Eastern Bloc were often organized as dictatorships, with small groups of Communist Party officials controlling society. North Korea today is a dictatorship led by Kim Jong-un. The United States has often sponsored dictatorships and fought against democracy. This has occurred particularly where democratically elected leaders might turn toward political orientations (such as socialism or Islamism) that would make their governments problematic for American political and business interests (Chomsky 1985).

WHO RULES THE UNITED STATES?

Even though the United States is a democracy, the issue of who rules the nation is a source of continuing debate among sociologists (and political scientists).

THE STRUCTURAL/FUNCTIONAL PERSPECTIVE: PLURALISM

Within structural-functionalism, the typical position put forward regarding who rules America is pluralism (see Chapter 8). That is, the United States is characterized by a number of powerful competing interest groups, and no one of them is in control all of the time. There is a kind of balance of power among these interest groups. In addition, there is a **separation of powers** in the government. That is, the different branches of government are separate and counterbalance one another so that there is little danger that any one branch of government can wield too much power.

Among pluralists, there are two major strands of thought. **Group pluralism** focuses on society's many different interest groups and organizations and how they compete for access to political power to attempt to further their interests (Drache 2008; Fung 2004). For group pluralists, this jockeying for power by various organizations provides stability for society. They see a *balance of group power,* where no one group retains power indefinitely and any group can always be challenged by another group. Further, there are *crosscutting group memberships,* with group members belonging to a variety of organizations that see to their needs and interests. This allows people to be political actors in a variety of collective processes. Group pluralists also believe that there tends to be a general *consensus of values* in society. As a result, the state is expected and pressured to legislate according to the common good and according to the cultural values largely held in common by members of society. Group pluralists also see *potential groups* as a source of stability. Accordingly, if, for example, the state expects that particular legislation might mobilize people in opposition to it, that threat might hold political actors back from taking action. There might not yet be an oppositional interest group, but the expectation of *mobilization of latent interests* can serve to pressure politicians to legislate for the common good.

Elite pluralism focuses specifically on how political elites form similar interest groups and organizations that vie for power (Higley and Burton 2006; Lipset 1981; Rose 1967). While voters may decide which elites represent them, the ultimate decision-making power rests in the hands of those elites. Similar to group pluralists, elite pluralists look at political elites as a diverse social body that organizes into groups to compete with one another for votes. This competition for votes ensures that no one group retains political power indefinitely. Stability is achieved in the system because these political elites must forge agreements with one another in order to pass legislation. This allows for a diversity of interests to be satisfied through those agreements, which tend to represent the common values of the larger society.

THE CONFLICT/CRITICAL PERSPECTIVE: THE POWER ELITE

Pluralism is often juxtaposed to a theory produced by conflict/critical theorists: C. Wright Mills's (1956; Maclean, Harvey, and Chia 2010) **power elite theory**. This theory holds that power is not dispersed throughout a stable society. Rather, power is concentrated among a small number of people who control the major institutions of the state, the economy, and the military. The powerful people who make up these institutions may have minor disagreements about policy, but for the most part they are unified in their interests and in the business of owning and operating much of American society.

These elites develop a common worldview. First, they undergo a process of *co-optation* whereby they are taught the common ideology of the elite. Further, they forge a shared ideology through their common *class identity.* That is, members of the power elite tend to come from wealthy families, go to similar schools, and belong to similar clubs. These clubs count as their members many of the most powerful people in the world, including corporate leaders, politicians, and top military brass. The clubs provide private spaces where friendships and common policies are forged (Clogher 1981; Domhoff 1974, 2013).

In his college days George H. W. Bush (standing nearest the clock on the left) belonged to the elite and secret Yale University society called Skull and Bones. How does membership in such groups confer advantage on members later in life?

The power elite within the military, the state, and the corporate world are also often *interchangeable.* That is, the people who hold leadership positions within these three major institutions switch from one powerful institution to another.

There are strengths and weaknesses in both pluralism and power elite theory.

GLOBAL POLITICS

In this section we examine geopolitics in general (Steinmetz 2012) as well as the nation and the nation-state, war, and terrorism as specific aspects and forms of geopolitics.

GEOPOLITICS

Geopolitics entails political relationships that involve broad geographic areas, including the globe as a whole. Geopolitics is concerned with how politics affects geography, such as the ways in which national borders are redrawn after the end of a war. Geopolitics is also concerned with the ways in which geography affects politics. One example is the (usually) constant low-level warfare between Israel and its neighbors. This conflict occurs, at least to some degree, because Israel is a tiny nation surrounded by much larger hostile nations. After World War II, much of geopolitics focused on the relationship between the United States and the Soviet Union and their allies. There was great concern over the global expansion of communism. The United States and the Soviet Union clashed, usually indirectly, over their political influence in Germany, Korea, Cuba, Vietnam, and so on. While the Soviet Union sought to expand geopolitically, the United States followed a policy of containment of Soviet efforts to expand communism. For decades, the United States acted based on what was known as the *domino theory:* If one nation was allowed to fall to communism, many neighboring nations would also fall. For example, the United States feared that if

George Bush Presidential Library and Museum

Vietnam fell to the communists, neighboring countries like Laos and Cambodia would be next. The United States and its relationships with Russia, China, and the Islamic world are at the center of geopolitics today.

THE NATION AND THE NATION-STATE

As discussed in Chapter 5, geopolitics relates to core concerns in the global age: the future of the nation and the nation-state. A nation is a group of people who share, often over a long period of time, similar cultural, religious, ethnic, and linguistic characteristics (Chernilo 2012). Jews are a nation by this definition, and, ironically, so are their frequent geopolitical enemies, the Palestinians. While many Jews and Palestinians live in the Middle East, many others, especially Jews, are spread throughout the world. They are scattered or dispersed; as described in Chapter 8, they exist in a *diaspora* (Fiddian-Qasmiyeh 2012). All diasporas share certain characteristics. First, they involve people who have been dispersed from their homelands. Second, the people in the diaspora retain a collective and idealized memory of the homeland that they transmit to their offspring as well as to other members of the diaspora. Third, as a result of this idealization, they are often alienated from their host countries; the realities of the latter cannot measure up to the idealizations associated with the homeland. Fourth, those in the diaspora often take as a political goal the idea and the objective of returning to the homeland (Cohen 1997).

Many of those involved in a nation, especially those in the diaspora, may have no direct contact with the homeland or with those who live there. Their linkages to them may be largely or purely imaginary. In other words, they exist in **imagined communities** (Anderson 1991; Roudometof 2012), or communities that are socially constructed by those who see themselves as part of them. Thus, Jews who have never been to Israel, or who may never even want to visit there, may still be part of an imagined community rooted in Israel. The same is true of the relationship between Palestine and many Palestinians scattered throughout the world.

The nation-state combines the nation with a geographic and political structure. In other words, in addition to encompassing people with a shared identity and culture, a nation-state exists in a bounded physical location and encompasses a government to administer the locale.

Nation-states exist within a global context, but they are affected, even threatened, by globalization in various ways (Hershkovitz 2012). First, global flows of many kinds—undocumented immigrants, drugs, terrorists, and so on—easily pierce the borders of nation-states and serve to erode their national sovereignties. Second, even if it does not threaten national sovereignty, globalization serves to alter the nation-state's structure and functions. For example, corporations have become increasingly important on the global stage and have come to operate more autonomously from states. Third, the government itself has to change to adjust to global changes.

For example, the United States created the Department of Homeland Security in 2002 to deal with, among other things, the global threat of terrorism. Fourth, there is the possibility that global flows can strengthen the nation-state. For example, external threats can lead citizens to put their differences aside, at least for the time being, and rally around the government and the nation-state more broadly.

In spite of changes such as those described above, we continue to think of nation-states as being all-powerful. However, not only have states experienced the kinds of problems described here, but a number of them have failed, or are on the verge of failing, to fulfill the "basic conditions and responsibilities" of sovereign states (Boas 2012: 633). Among the characteristics of a failed state are a "lack of control over own territory, widespread corruption and criminality, huge economic recession and/or hyperinflation, failure to provide basic services, and large flows of refugees and internally displaced persons" (Boas 2012: 633). In addition, states that do not have economic and political institutions that include broad segments of society are more likely to fail. Failed states also tend to exploit one segment of society (the middle and lower classes, for example) for the benefit of another subset, especially the rich (Acemoglu and Robinson 2012). The Fragile States Index, an annual ranking of 178 nations, highlights weak and failing states around the world based on their levels of stability (Figure 12.2). In 2014, the countries that received the worst scores were South Sudan, Somalia, Central African Republic, Congo, and Sudan. The economic and political burdens caused by the Ebola outbreak in West Africa (see Chapter 13) threatened to reduce Liberia, Sierra Leone, and Guinea (and perhaps other countries in the future) to the status of fragile, if not failed, states.

Failed states cause many problems for themselves and their residents, but from a global perspective, it is the problems they cause for others that are the main concern. Pirates based in Somalia have, at least until recently, roamed the high seas and succeeded in carrying out a number of acts of high-stakes piracy, such as holding huge oil tankers for millions of dollars in ransom. The Somalian government, to the extent that it exists, has been unable to control the pirates or their activities. The inability of the governments in West Africa to cope with the Ebola epidemic gave rise to fears of a global epidemic.

WAR

War occurs when a nation uses its military in an attempt to impose its will on others outside the nation (Malesevic 2010). It also occurs when a nation uses its military to impose its political will within its borders—the case of civil war. War is one method of "doing politics," or dealing with political disagreements.

Why does war occur? First, there needs to be a cultural tradition of war. Second, a situation must exist in which two political actors have objectives that are incompatible. Finally,

FIGURE 12.2 • Fragile States Index, 2014

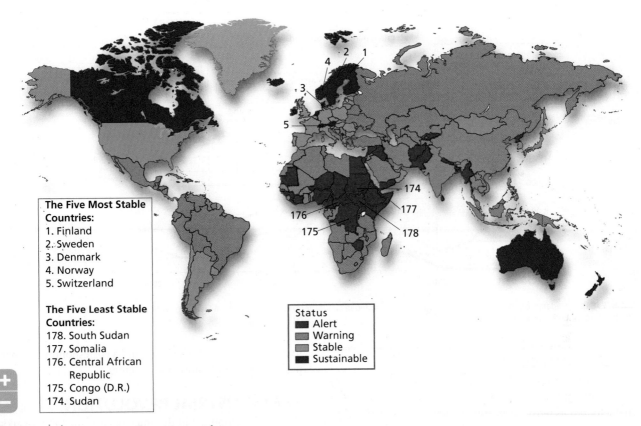

The Five Most Stable Countries:
1. Finland
2. Sweden
3. Denmark
4. Norway
5. Switzerland

The Five Least Stable Countries:
178. South Sudan
177. Somalia
176. Central African Republic
175. Congo (D.R.)
174. Sudan

Status
- Alert
- Warning
- Stable
- Sustainable

Ⓢ SAGE datamaps edge.sagepub.com
• Social, economic, political indicators for every country.
SOURCE: Data from The Fund for Peace, "Fragile States Index 2014."

a "fuel" must bring the situation from thinking about war to actually *making war* (Timasheff 1965).

In the United States, the cultural tradition of war is all around us. We are often taught in our history classes about U.S. involvement in foreign wars, in which we are depicted as saviors, the bringers of democracy, and so on. In our own history, we can see antagonistic situations that brought us into military conflict with other nations or peoples. Acts of aggression such as the Japanese attack on Pearl Harbor and the September 11 terrorist attacks served as the fuels that ignited war.

TERRORISM

Terrorism typically involves nongovernmental actors engaging in acts of violence targeting noncombatants, property, or even military personnel in order to influence politics (Vertigans 2011). The term *terrorism* is often controversial, because it is usually the powerful who define who is and who is not a terrorist. Consider, for example, that if property destruction as a way to express political grievances is terrorism, then the people who were part of the Boston Tea Party fit the description. And where is the line between terrorists and revolutionaries fighting against invading or occupying armies? Who gets to draw that line and why? Can states be terrorists?

Nevertheless, all over the world, people refer to acts such as suicide bombings and the targeting of civilians of enemy nations or groups as examples of terrorism. More specifically, in the West today, a group is likely to be labeled terrorist if it has a history of engaging in violence against the citizens of a government, is Islamic, and targets airplanes (Beck and Minor 2013). Terrorist attacks are quite common in the early twenty-first century and do not seem to be on the decline. This is particularly the case in settings where one nation occupies another and attempts to police its population. Figure 12.3 shows that the number of people who have died from terrorist activity each year has increased fivefold since 2000. In 2013, approximately 18,000 deaths resulted from terrorist attacks. The vast majority of these incidents occurred in Iraq, Afghanistan, Pakistan, Nigeria, and Syria. These countries experienced fatalities reaching 14,722 collectively. Excluding these five countries in 2013, the rest of the world lost 3,236 lives due to terrorism. From 2000 to 2013, more than 107,000 people died around the world from terrorist incidents. And these statistics do not even include the uncountable number of deaths caused by the rise of Islamic State and other radical Islamic groups such as Boko Haram.

FIGURE 12.3 • Deaths from Terrorism Worldwide, 2000–2013

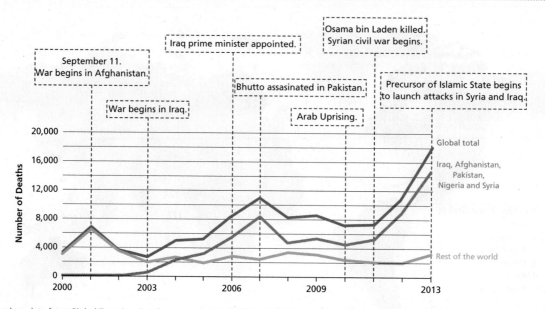

SOURCE: Based on data from Global Terrorism Database, as reprinted in *Global Terrorism Index, 2014: Measuring and Understanding the Impact of Terrorism,* The Institute for Economics and Peace.

ASK YOURSELF

It is often pointed out that those revered in U.S. history as the instigators of the American Revolution could be characterized as terrorists in another light. Do you agree with this characterization? What is the difference between a terrorist and a revolutionary hero?

THE U.S. ECONOMY: FROM INDUSTRIALIZATION TO DEINDUSTRIALIZATION

The **economy** is the social system involved in the production, consumption, and distribution of goods and services. The devastating effects of the Great Recession have reminded us that the economy is of overwhelming importance to everyone (Orr 2012; Smith et al. 2011). For those who had forgotten, or who might have grown complacent about the economy because of the economic boom throughout most of the first decade of the twenty-first century, the onset of the recession and its continuing effects have been a rude awakening. While the economy in the United States and elsewhere is currently strengthening, and stock markets are booming, there is always the danger of another recession or even a depression like the one that began in 1929.

Over the last 200 years, the U.S. economy has moved from reliance on industrial employment and mass production to the decline of manufacturing and a corresponding increase in the service and information sectors.

THE INDUSTRIAL REVOLUTION

The key development in the emergence of the modern economy was the nineteenth-century Industrial Revolution (see Figure 12.4), which introduced the factory system of production (Hobsbawm and Wrigley 1999). Instead of making products alone at home or in small groups in workshops, large numbers of workers were brought together in factories. Eventually, manual factory work with hand tools gave way to work in conjunction with machines. In addition, human and animal power were replaced by power supplied by steam and other energy sources. While there were skilled workers in these early factories, they tended over time to be replaced, because skills were increasingly likely to be built into the machinery. This meant that less skilled or even unskilled workers, less well-trained and lower-paid workers, and even children could be—and were—hired to do the work. They tended to work increasingly long hours in harsh conditions and at ever lower pay. Another defining characteristic of this factory system was an elaborate division of labor by which a single product was produced by a number of workers, each performing a small step in the overall process.

The factories of the early Industrial Revolution were quite primitive, but over time they grew much larger, more efficient, more technologically advanced, and more oriented toward the mass production of a wide variety of goods. **Mass production** has a number of defining characteristics, including large numbers of standardized products, highly specialized workers, interchangeable machine parts, precision tools, a high-volume mechanized production process, and the synchronization of the flow of materials used in production, with the entire process made as continuous as possible. The logical outcome of this was the assembly line, which came to fruition in the early twentieth century in the mass production of Ford automobiles. By the mid-twentieth century, these systems had reached their fullest application in the United States and had spread to many other parts of the world. After World War II, the Japanese—and later manufacturers in other nations, such as Korea—adopted these American innovations and came to outstrip the United States in many industries, most notably the production of electronics and automobiles. Today, it is China that leads the world in many forms of mass production.

FROM FORDISM TO POST-FORDISM

Fordism consists of the ideas, principles, and systems created by Henry Ford and his associates at the beginning of the twentieth century. Ford is generally credited with the development of the modern mass production system, primarily through the creation of the automobile assembly line. Among the characteristics associated with Fordism are the mass production of homogeneous products, reliance on inflexible technologies such as the assembly line, the use of standardized work routines, economies of scale, and the creation of a mass market for products, like automobiles, that flow from the assembly line (Beynon and Nichol 2006; Bonanno 2012).

Fordism dominated much of the twentieth-century American automobile industry and many others. It declined in the 1970s, especially with the 1973 oil crisis and the rise of the Japanese automobile industry. It was also done in by the fact that consumers were no longer content with homogeneous products. They demanded greater choice in their automobiles and their components. **Post-Fordism** is associated with smaller production runs of more specialized products, especially those high in style and quality; more flexible machinery, made possible by advances in technology largely traceable to the computer; more skilled workers with greater flexibility and autonomy; less reliance on economies of scale; and more differentiated markets for those more specialized products (Amin 1994; Janoski and Lepadatu 2013; Prechel 2007).

SOCIALISM, COMMUNISM, AND CAPITALISM

From its inception, the Industrial Revolution was capitalist in nature, but it eventually gave rise to the opposing and alternative systems of socialism and communism.

Socialism and Communism

The terms *socialism* and *communism* are often used more or less interchangeably. However, it is important to differentiate between them.

In Chapter 2, you learned that communism is closely associated with Karl Marx. Communism is an economic system oriented to the collective, rather than the private, ownership of the means of production (Lovell 2007). Recall from Chapter 7 that the means of production are the tools, machines, and factories that in capitalism are owned by the capitalists and are needed by the workers—the proletariat in Marx's terms—in order to produce. Marx hoped that the exploitation of the proletariat would lead them to revolt against the capitalist system. That, in turn, would lead to collective rather than private ownership of the means of production, resulting in a communist economy. Control of the economic base would lead to control of everything else of importance, including the political system.

From a Marxian perspective, **socialism** can be seen as a historical stage following communism. It involves the effort by society to plan and organize production consciously and rationally so that all members of society benefit from it (Cox 2007; Shevchenko 2012). The collective control of the means of production in communism is a first step, but in itself it is not enough to run a society. Once in control

Granger

This Russian poster of 1920 depicts Soviet leader Vladimir Lenin sweeping the exploiting classes off the Earth. Would a social change as radical as that depicted in the cartoon ever be likely?

FIGURE 12.4 • Timeline of the Industrial Revolution, 1712–1903

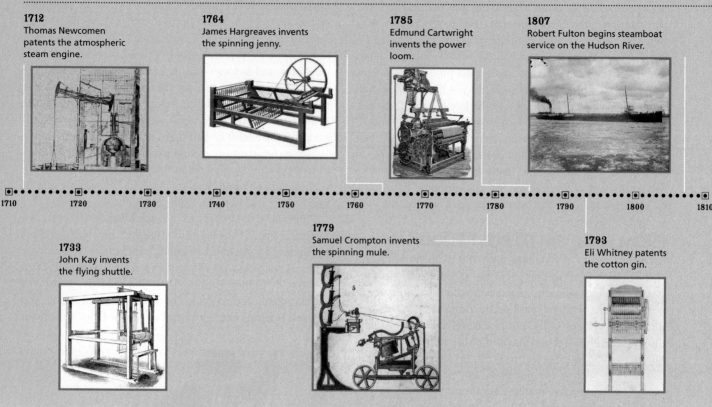

1712
Thomas Newcomen patents the atmospheric steam engine.

1764
James Hargreaves invents the spinning jenny.

1785
Edmund Cartwright invents the power loom.

1807
Robert Fulton begins steamboat service on the Hudson River.

1733
John Kay invents the flying shuttle.

1779
Samuel Crompton invents the spinning mule.

1793
Eli Whitney patents the cotton gin.

SOURCE: Adapted from Industrial Revolution: Timeline, Facts, and Resources, Research by B. Sobey, TheFreeResource.com.

of the means of production, the collectivity must set about the task of creating a rational centralized economy (and society) that operates for the good of all and creates social and economic equality.

The ideas associated with communism and socialism are less important today than they were only a few decades ago, before the fall of the Soviet empire in late 1991. There is little that passes for communism in the world today, except in North Korea ("North Korea Country Profile" 2015) and possibly Cuba. China continues to see itself as a communist society, even though it is on the cusp of becoming the most powerful capitalist country in the world. In China, a political commitment to communism exists uncomfortably side by side with a highly capitalistic economic system.

Welfare States

Socialism is more vibrant today than communism. However, even Israel, not long ago a strongly socialist economy, has moved decidedly in the direction of capitalism (Ram 2007; Zilberfarb 2005). Although there are no fully socialist societies in the world today, many societies have socialistic elements. Many Western European countries have become "welfare states" (Cousins 2005). They have powerful social welfare programs that are socialistic in nature in that they are run consciously and rationally by centralized authorities.

Welfare states seek both to operate their economic markets efficiently, as capitalism does, and to do so equitably, which capitalism does *not* do (Esping-Anderson 1990; Gangl 2007; Lessenich forthcoming). Their goal is to provide for the welfare—the well-being—of their citizens (Peoples 2012). There are many examples of social welfare programs, including national health plans, old-age plans, child-care and parental leave systems, and social safety nets of various kinds (e.g., unemployment insurance).

Even the United States has social welfare programs such as unemployment insurance, Social Security, and Medicare. However, the United States lags far behind leaders in Western Europe (and Canada) in these kinds of programs. And there are powerful forces in the United States aligned with capitalism that strongly resist efforts to expand social welfare programs. For example, President Barack Obama was criticized for being a socialist because of his efforts to reform the U.S. health care system (through the Affordable Care Act, which came into effect on January 1, 2014). Still, for all the criticism in the United States, socialism remains alive and well in many parts of the world today.

While the United States struggles to implement more social welfare programs, the most developed social welfare states in Europe are experiencing something of a crisis and finding it difficult to maintain existing programs (Kangas

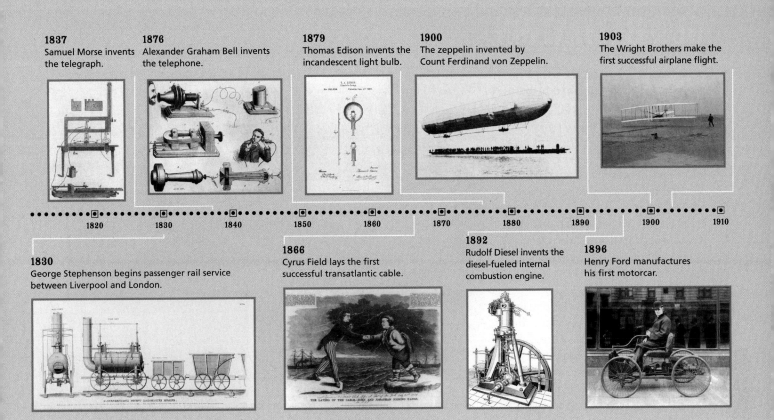

1837
Samuel Morse invents the telegraph.

1876
Alexander Graham Bell invents the telephone.

1879
Thomas Edison invents the incandescent light bulb.

1900
The zeppelin invented by Count Ferdinand von Zeppelin.

1903
The Wright Brothers make the first successful airplane flight.

1820   1830   1840   1850   1860   1870   1880   1890   1900   1910

1830
George Stephenson begins passenger rail service between Liverpool and London.

1866
Cyrus Field lays the first successful transatlantic cable.

1892
Rudolf Diesel invents the diesel-fueled internal combustion engine.

1896
Henry Ford manufactures his first motorcar.

2007). In fact, some, especially Great Britain, are retrenching in various ways, such as offering less generous benefits and programs, making it more difficult for people to qualify for them, and making people take greater responsibility for providing for their own welfare. Threats to, and declines in, social welfare programs have spread throughout Europe as a result of both the Great Recession and the euro crisis (see below) that has threatened the European economies. Those countries worst hit by the latter—Greece and Spain—have had to cut back on these programs. Programs are even in danger in countries such as Sweden, which has long been at the forefront in social welfare programs.

Welfare states have been threatened before. However, today they are more seriously threatened than ever by the realities of the global economy. With today's markets for virtually everything becoming increasingly global and highly competitive, the lion's share of global business is very likely to go to the countries, and the industries in them, where costs are lowest (see Chapter 7). This advantages countries like China, India, and Vietnam, where social welfare costs are minimal or nonexistent. By contrast, in Western European countries the costs of production are far higher, in part because of the extraordinary social welfare expenses that must be factored in. This has made Western Europe, and the United States to a lesser degree, less competitive or even uncompetitive in various global markets. Many observers see this situation as a profound threat to these economies and societies. Some argue that these countries must reduce social welfare expenditures to compete in the global marketplace. Others contend that the more generous welfare states lower costs of business in some sectors and help make the workforce more productive (Hall and Soskice 2001). They assert that greater spending on social welfare programs can contribute to a more educated, healthier, and more flexible workforce.

Capitalism

Karl Marx lived during the era of **competitive capitalism**, characterized by a large number of relatively small firms. No single firm or small subset of firms could completely dominate and control a given area of the economy. However, in the late nineteenth century and into much of the twentieth century, this situation changed. Huge corporations emerged and, alone or in combination with a few other similarly sized corporations, came to dominate, or monopolize, certain markets. This was **monopoly capitalism** (Baran and Sweezy 1966). Perhaps the best example is the American automobile industry, which for much of the twentieth century was dominated by three huge corporations—General Motors, Ford, and Chrysler.

Fordlandia in Brazil

Beginning in the late 1920s, Henry Ford decided he needed greater control over the supply of rubber required for the tires of the cars he was manufacturing. The best and closest source of rubber was a remote jungle area near the Amazon River in Brazil. This was a wild and untamed area inhabited by people unaccustomed to the modern, standardized, and rationalized world that Ford had played such a huge role in creating.

Ford sought to apply to his Brazilian rubber plantations the principles and methods that had made him successful in the production of automobiles. However, the wilds of the Amazon were far from the urban realities of Detroit, and they proved resistant to Ford's methods of operation.

Ford created a town—Fordlandia—as the hub of his rubber operations in Brazil (Grandin 2010). This was a version of small-town America with suburban-type houses built in perfect rows along neatly laid-out streets. It was out of place in the jungles of Brazil. For example, the houses that already existed there had thatched roofs. They functioned reasonably well in the extremely hot and humid climate because they allowed hot air to escape easily. Ford had his new houses built with modern metal roofs lined with asbestos. The new houses retained much more heat than did those with thatched roofs and were transformed into ovens.

In the wild, rubber trees tend to grow in a haphazard manner and at some distance from one another. This makes obtaining the rubber very time-consuming. However, it is also more difficult for diseases and insects to attack trees that are widely dispersed throughout the jungle. The Ford

This uniform row of cottages in Fordlandia symbolizes the failure in the 1920s to impose Henry Ford's ideas on the Amazon River jungle in Brazil. Was Ford ahead of his time? Has the recent acceptance of such ideas been good for Brazil? For the environment?

people had their rubber trees planted close to one another in neat rows. This made it much easier for workers to tap the trees for their rubber, but also for the trees to contract disease and to be assaulted by insects. Many of the trees died, and Ford's rubber plantation eventually failed.

Ford management also decided that it would be more efficient for Fordlandia employees to be fed cafeteria-style. However, the native workers were unfamiliar with this modern mode of food service. A resulting riot by the workers destroyed much of Fordlandia, although it was later rebuilt.

Fordlandia represented the battle to apply modern techniques to a wilderness and to a people who operated on the basis of their own, very different,

principles. In the short run, the wilderness and the natives and their ways won out. However, in more recent years, Brazil has become one of the world's rising economic powerhouses, a good portion of the Amazon basin has undergone deforestation, and major metropolises have burst forth out of the forest. It may be that Henry Ford was just way ahead of his time.

Think About It

Could Ford's management have prevented any of the problems that arose in Fordlandia? If so, how? Why did plans for the settlement fail to take account of the area's biological, environmental, and cultural realities? If they had done so, would the result have been different? Why or why not?

Of course, capitalism has changed once again, as is clear in the recent misfortunes of these automobile companies. In addition, a number of foreign companies (Toyota, Honda, Nissan, Hyundai, BMW, Mercedes) now compete successfully with the U.S. firms. We may have seen the end of monopoly capitalism in the United States, but it is likely that we will see the emergence of a global system of monopoly capitalism in which a small number of corporations come to dominate a global, not just a national, market.

Whether or not capitalism once again becomes monopolistic, in recent years it has certainly become increasingly global. This can be seen as **transnational capitalism**, where it is no longer national but transnational economic practices that predominate (Kauppinen 2013; Sklair 2002). Thus, the global flow of automobiles and even money has become far more important than their existence and movement within national boundaries.

It could also be argued that the center of capitalism no longer lies in production, but rather in consumption. That is, the focus is on inducing large numbers of people throughout the world to consume at high levels. While the capitalism of Marx's day was described as producer capitalism, we now live more in an era of consumer capitalism. Within the realm of consumption, some of the leading transnational corporations are Walmart, IKEA, H&M, and McDonald's.

DEINDUSTRIALIZATION IN THE UNITED STATES

Industry and industrial employment were clearly crucial to economic development in the United States and other developed nations. However, a number of developed nations, especially the United States, have been undergoing a process of deindustrialization. **Deindustrialization** involves the decline of manufacturing as well as a corresponding increase in various types of services (Bluestone and Harrison 1984; Dandaneau 2012; Flynn 2007; Koistinen 2013; Wren 2013).

We tend to think of deindustrialization in the United States as a process that has been going on for decades, is now far advanced, and may even be near completion. The focus tends to be on the Rust Belt in middle America and the demise, beginning in the 1960s, of such steel cities as Pittsburgh and Bethlehem, Pennsylvania, as well as Akron and Youngstown, Ohio, the heart of the rubber industry (see Figure 12.5). These industries are all but gone, and these cities have suffered greatly, although in a few cases, such as Pittsburgh, they have been able to reinvent themselves. The decline of the auto industry began a bit later, but it, too, has clearly undergone massive deindustrialization. This is reflected in the decline of many American cities, but in no city is it more evident than in Detroit, Michigan. In early 2013, conditions had gotten so bad in Detroit that the state of Michigan appointed an emergency manager to take control of the city's finances (Vlasic 2013). The city filed for bankruptcy in mid-2013, but a plan to eliminate billions of dollars of debt allowed it to begin exiting bankruptcy in late 2014. However, it is highly unlikely that Detroit's economic woes are over. Deindustrialization in the United States has not yet run its course, and other industries, such as the glass industry, are now experiencing this process (Uchitelle 2010).

FIGURE 12.5 • The U.S. Rust Belt

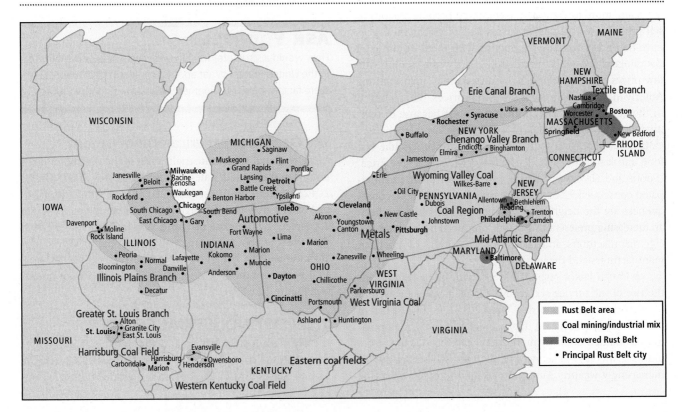

Factors in Deindustrialization

Several factors were responsible for deindustrialization in the United States. First was the aging technology in many American industries. This made them vulnerable to foreign competitors, which were often building new, state-of-the-art factories. Another technological factor was the rise of automation, which greatly reduced the need for many blue-collar workers (Noble 2011) and, more recently, many other types of workers (Ford 2015). Furthermore, the increased efficiency of automated technologies made it possible for corporations to close unnecessary factories, thus cutting many more jobs.

Second was globalization, which brought with it industrial competition from low-wage workers in less developed countries. This was especially true in the early years of the emergence of China as an industrial power. Now, of course, China is developing rapidly, but its low wages and seemingly endless stream of workers will make it nearly impossible for American industries to compete with Chinese industries. For example, most of the work that goes into manufacturing Apple's iPhone is done in China at Foxconn City (Duhigg and Bradsher 2012). About 230,000 people work there, often six days a week and for as many as 12 hours a day. Workers sleep in on-site barracks provided by the company, and many earn less than $17 a day. How many American workers would be willing to work in such enormous factories, work such long hours, and live in company barracks, all for $17 a day?

A third factor in deindustrialization was the rise of consumer society and the increasing demand for goods of all types. This should have helped American industries, but it led many more foreign manufacturers to become anxious to sell products to that consumer market. American industries have had great difficulty competing with them. In terms of the demand for goods, there arose, partly as a result of the low prices offered by foreign manufacturers, a mania among American consumers for ever lower prices. This worked to the advantage of foreign manufacturers because of their much lower cost structures, especially their lower labor costs. Consumer obsession with lower prices for things like fast food and fast fashion has led to the "high cost of low price" (Spotts and Greenwald 2005), or the unfortunate unanticipated consequences of such low prices. Among those consequences are the heightened exploitation of foreign workers, an increasing preference for goods produced by low-cost foreign manufacturers, and a decline in the number of American manufacturers and the jobs they offer.

A fourth factor responsible for deindustrialization was the rise of the service sector in the United States (as well as in other developed countries; Wren 2013). In the last half of the twentieth century, an increasingly affluent U.S. population demanded not only more and cheaper goods but also a dramatic increase in services of all types (Kollmeyer 2009). Increasingly wealthy Americans seemed to prefer spending their newfound money on services rather than on industrial products. Among other things, this led to the expansion of service industries, such as the health, education, and personal and social services industries. More recently, other service industries have come to the fore, such as the financial, real estate, tourism, and hospitality (hotels, cruise ships) industries.

Service jobs proliferated, and some proved to be not so desirable. Millions of such jobs have been created for U.S. workers of all age groups, even seniors, in the retail sector, most notably at Walmart and Target. Women are disproportionately represented in these service occupations. The best example of less-than-desirable jobs is provided by the fast-food industry (Leidner 1993; Ritzer 2015). Fast-food workers generally earn the minimum wage (although there is now a growing movement in the United States to raise that wage significantly; Associated Press 2015b) and often are not allowed to work a 40-hour week (Allegretto et al. 2013). As a result, they frequently do not earn enough to rise above the poverty line and are able to survive only with the help of government assistance in the form of SNAP (Supplemental Nutrition Assistance Program) benefits, Medicaid, the earned income tax credit (which is a refundable credit on taxes rather than an additional tax), and Children's Health Insurance Program (CHIP) benefits. It costs taxpayers almost $7 billion a year to pay for these programs for workers in the fast-food industry. McDonald's alone costs U.S. taxpayers $1.2 billion annually. This is the case even though McDonald's is hugely profitable; it had net income of $5.47 billion in 2012 (Sauter, Frohlich, and Hess 2013).

ASK YOURSELF

How would a structural/functionalist explain deindustrialization in the United States? What about a conflict/critical theorist? Are there factors in this development about which they would agree?

The Decline of American Labor Unions

Closely related to deindustrialization is the decline of labor unions in the United States (Fantasia and Voss 2007; Timms 2012; Western and Rosenfeld 2012). The American labor movement grew from 3 percent of the labor force in 1900 to 23 percent by the close of World War II. A decline began in the 1960s, at about the same time as the onset of deindustrialization and the rise of the service sector. As of 2014, only 11.1 percent of the U.S. labor force belonged to labor unions (see Figure 12.6).

THE POSTINDUSTRIAL SOCIETY

Clearly, deindustrialization and the decline of unions set the stage for the emergence of postindustrialism in the United States and in the developed world in general. An

FIGURE 12.6 • U.S. Union Membership among All Wage and Salary Workers, 1973–2014

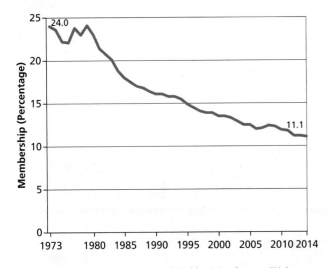

SOURCE: Data from Barry T. Hirsch and David A. Macpherson, "Union Membership and Coverage Database From the Current Population Survey: Note," *Industrial and Labor Relations Review* 56 (January 2003), 349–354. © 2002, 2015 by Barry T. Hirsch and David A. Macpherson.

increasing emphasis on consumption and the dramatic growth in service jobs, many of which exist to serve a consumer-oriented society, pushed the United States even further from industrialization and toward a truly postindustrial society (Bell 1973; Cohen 2008; Hage and Powers 1992; Smart 2011).

A **postindustrial society** is one that was at one time industrial, but the focus on the manufacture of goods has been replaced by an increase in service work. The latter is work in which people provide services for one another rather than producing goods. It encompasses a wide range of service-oriented occupations, including lawyer, physician, teacher, financial adviser, and computer geek as well as salesperson, clerk, and counter person at a fast-food restaurant. Employment in such occupations has increased dramatically in the United States in the last century, while there has been a similarly dramatic decline in work relating to goods production. Agricultural work declined earlier and even more steeply.

WORK AND CONSUMPTION

Much of the preceding has dealt with the economy in terms of general trends and developments. However, most people connect to the economy either through their work or through the process of consumption, to be discussed below. The relationship between people and their work is undergoing rapid change.

EMPLOYMENT, UNEMPLOYMENT, AND UNDEREMPLOYMENT

Not long ago, we tended to think of people as taking jobs, perhaps in large and stable organizations, and embarking on lifelong careers. Those careers entailed at least some upward mobility, sufficient earnings for workers and their families to live on, and retirement with ample pensions—perhaps in sunny Florida or Arizona—when workers reached their early 60s.

However, there are several problems with this romantic scenario. First, even in its heyday from about 1950 to 1990, it applied to only a very small proportion of the population. Employment has ebbed and flowed over time. It has always been the case that a number of people have been unable to get any jobs at all. In the United States, **unemployment** is defined as the state of being economically active and in the labor force (e.g., not retired), able and willing to work, and seeking employment but unable to find a job (Nordenmark 2007). The unemployment rate in the United States has generally run at about 5 percent of the labor force. However, in the midst of the recession in 2009, it reached 10 percent, although by May 2015 it had dropped to 5.5 percent (see Figure 12.8). Many observers believe that is an underestimate, since many people have given up searching for work and are therefore not included in the unemployment statistics (discouraged workers).

ASK YOURSELF

The government's reported rate of unemployment includes those who are actively seeking employment. Why do you suppose it does *not* include those who have given up looking for work, or who have settled for less employment than they need or would like, such as part-time instead of full-time work? What would happen to the unemployment picture if the reported unemployment rate did include these people, and how might that difference affect economic policy making about labor?

William Julius Wilson (1997) focuses on long-term unemployment and the problems it creates for black Americans. Many observers have traced these difficulties (such as children without involved fathers, drug abuse) to social structural problems (like institutional racism) that are difficult, if not impossible, to solve. However, Wilson links them directly to unemployment and thus sees them as solvable through a number of reforms, including the creation of more work for all black Americans. At the moment, black Americans experience not only greater unemployment but also a long list of additional difficulties associated with being unemployed, not the least of which is a higher incidence of poverty. In 2014, the unemployment rate for black Americans was more than double the rate for whites and Asians and four percentage points higher than that for Hispanics (Figure 12.9).

Barbara Ehrenreich and Being "Nickel and Dimed" at Work

In *Nickel and Dimed: On (Not) Getting By in America* (2001), Barbara Ehrenreich (1941–) is primarily interested in the low-paying jobs that millions of U.S. women (and men) are forced to take, their experiences on and off the job, and whether they can actually survive on what they are paid.

Ehrenreich adopted the time-honored sociological research method of becoming a participant observer and took a number of low-paying, entry-level jobs, including being a waitress, working for a cleaning service, and working for Walmart. The work, of course, did not provide a living wage. In fact, she made only about a quarter of the income needed to live. Figure 12.7 shows that in no U.S. state can a minimum-wage worker, working a standard 40-hour workweek, afford a two-bedroom unit at fair-market rent. In some states, one would need to work around 100 hours a week to afford to pay such rent. On one occasion Ehrenreich was forced, as many people (especially women) are, to take a second job in order to get by. Living conditions were dismal, eating well was problematic, and there was little left for savings or leisure activities. The work was often hard, even backbreaking.

Perhaps worst of all were the innumerable humiliations. Few potential employers bothered to respond to Ehrenreich's applications. Supervisors could be harsh, and they had the power to embarrass or even fire her at will. Customers at her waitressing job could be difficult and would often leave minimal tips or no tips at all. As a housecleaner, she found her employer closely monitored her work and

FIGURE 12.7 • Hours at Minimum Wage Needed to Afford Rent, 2014

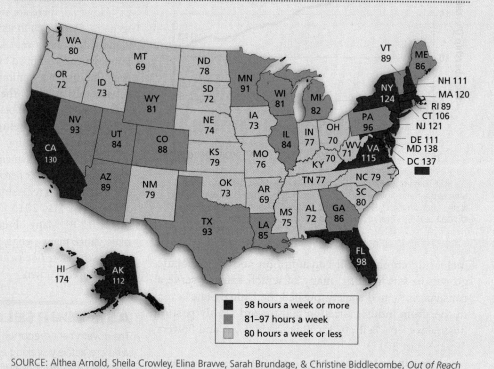

SOURCE: Althea Arnold, Sheila Crowley, Elina Bravve, Sarah Brundage, & Christine Biddlecombe, *Out of Reach 2014*. Copyright © 2014 by The National Low Income Housing Coalition. (www.nlihc.org/oor/2014); (http://nlihc.org/sites/default/files/oor/OOR2014_MW-Map.pdf).

required her to perform tasks in certain ways, like washing the floor on her hands and knees.

Some of Ehrenreich's fellow workers had to live with roommates or extended family members to survive. Those who lived alone might find themselves in trailers or fly-by-night motels, as Ehrenreich did. Those with children had trouble finding affordable and reliable day care. Normal medical care was beyond reach, and free care was difficult to obtain. Help from charitable agencies was often humiliating and insufficient. Living costs were high because, for example, humble living arrangements might lack a kitchen or provide only a hot plate. As a result, low-wage workers often had to rely on comparatively expensive (and unhealthy) junk food.

Ehrenreich found that the "nickels and dimes" millions of U.S. women and men are paid to work are grossly inadequate. Their pay forces them to the edge of poverty and into a wide variety of humiliating circumstances and experiences.

Think About It

Why, given the reporting of Ehrenreich and others, has there not been a revolutionary change in the working conditions and pay many U.S. workers must accept with their jobs? What function would a structural/functionalist say is served by the existence of such low-paying jobs, and why are women most often hired for them?

FIGURE 12.8 • U.S. Unemployment Rate, 2005–2015

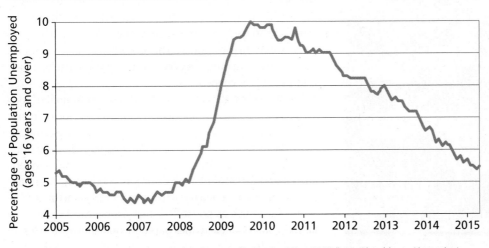

SOURCE: Data from U.S. Department of Labor, Bureau of Labor Statistics, 2015 (http://data.bls.gov/timeseries/LNS14000000).

A large number of Americans must also cope with the problem of **underemployment** (Dooley and Prause 2009). This involves (a) being in jobs that are not up to one's training and ability, such as a college professor driving a taxi at night; (b) being an involuntary part-time worker, that is, working part-time because one cannot find full-time work; or (c) working in jobs that are not fully occupying, such as in a seasonal industry like agriculture, where work slows down dramatically or disappears in the off-season.

Being without a job is a major problem. However, as pointed out above, most Americans who want jobs have them, although they might not always have the jobs that they want. An even bigger problem is that many jobs (especially service jobs) do not pay a *living wage,* an income that is high enough to meet the most basic family expenses.

CONSUMPTION AND THE POSTMODERN SOCIETY

Recall from Chapter 1 that consumption is the process by which people obtain and utilize goods and services (Cook and Ryan 2015; Sassatelli 2007). More specifically, it is a process involving the interrelationship among consumer objects and services, consumers, the consumption process, and consumption sites (Murphy forthcoming; Ritzer, Goodman, and Wiedenhoft 2001). First, consumption involves that which is to be consumed, largely consumer objects (clothes, cars, electronic gear) and services (help from computer experts, medical services). Second, consumption requires consumers, or people who do the consuming. Third, there must be a process of consumption. Fourth, this process often takes place at

consumption sites, such as farmers' markets, shopping malls, theme parks, cruise ships, and, increasingly, Amazon.com and other online sites.

These sites can all be seen as **cathedrals of consumption** (Ritzer 2010a; see also Ostergaard, Fitchett, and Jantzen 2013). These are the large, sometimes lavish, consumption sites created mostly in the United States in the last half of the twentieth century and into the early twenty-first century. The use of the term *cathedrals* is meant to indicate the fact that consumption has in many ways become today's religion. We go to the cathedrals of consumption to practice that religion. Thus, for example, many middle-class children make a pilgrimage to Disney World at least once in their lives.

Outdoor strip malls are traceable to the 1920s, and the first indoor malls were built in the 1950s, but it is the megamall, which arrived in the 1980s and 1990s (e.g., Mall of America in Minneapolis in 1992), that is the crucial innovation here. What defines the megamall is the combination under one roof of a number of cathedrals of consumption, especially a shopping mall and a theme park. The theme park itself is a second cathedral of consumption—the first landmark development for theme parks was the opening of Disneyland in Southern California in 1955. Third is the modern cruise ship, the first of which set sail in 1966 (Clancy

FIGURE 12.9 • U.S. Unemployment Rate by Race/Ethnicity, 2014

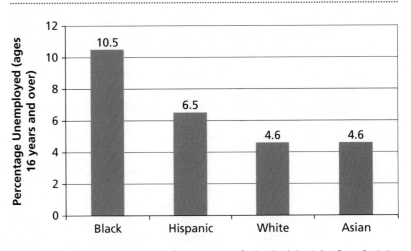

SOURCE: Data from U.S. Department of Labor, Bureau of Labor Statistics, Labor Force Statistics from the Current Population Survey (http://www.bls.gov/web/empsit/cpsee_e16.htm).

Is it possible not to consume in a society that values consumption so much that it offers innumerable theme parks, casino-hotels, cruise ships, and shopping malls like this one? What would happen to the economy if large numbers of people consciously limited their consumption?

2012). The final major cathedral of consumption is the casino-hotel, most notably of the type that defines Las Vegas. The first of these—the Flamingo—was built in 1946. It was the idea of the mobster Bugsy Siegel.

Of course, there are many other important cathedrals of consumption—superstores such as Bed Bath & Beyond and Best Buy, huge discounters such as Walmart and Costco, and online retailers and malls such as Amazon.com and eBay. These cathedrals, along with other consumption sites, especially chain stores such as McDonald's and Starbucks, have come to define not only the sites themselves but also much of consumption as a whole.

In the past we had to travel, sometimes long distances, to cathedrals of consumption, but now many of them are available via the Internet on our home computers or on the smartphones in our pockets or bags. As a result, brick-and-mortar cathedrals of consumption such as shopping malls and casinos are in decline. Nevertheless, consumption continues to grow even though much of it has shifted from offline to online cathedrals.

Consumption is generally considered to be the hallmark of postmodern society. That is, while modernity is defined by production and work, postmodernity is defined by

consumption. This change is best seen in the United States, which moved from being the preeminent industrial society in the world in the mid-twentieth century to being the world's most important consumer society in the late twentieth and early twenty-first centuries. This is reflected in, for example, the fact that consumption accounts for approximately 70 percent of the U.S. economy today.

Consumption is central to the idea of a postmodern society precisely because it represents a shift from the focus on production in modern society. However, in another sense, there is such a thing as postmodern consumption that is different from, and stands in contrast to, modern consumption (Hamouda and Gharbi 2013; Venkatesh 2007). In modernity, consumption is seen as a secondary activity, as well as something to be avoided as much as possible so that people can focus on the far more important activities of production and work. This, of course, is the view associated with Max Weber's ([1904–1905] 1958) famous conception of the Protestant ethic. According to this ethic, people are to concentrate on work because it is there, especially in being successful in one's work, that the signs of religious salvation can be found. People are expected to consume minimally, to be frugal, to save their money, and to reinvest what they earn from productive activities.

ASK YOURSELF

Why is a farmers' market not a cathedral of consumption? What other places in which you can engage in consumption are not cathedrals of consumption? Are Internet sites such as Amazon.com really cathedrals of consumption? Why or why not? If not, could they ever become cathedrals of consumption?

Postmodern consumption is best thought of as **consumerism**, an obsession with consumption (Barber 2007). We have become consumed by consumption. This reflects the view, outlined in Chapter 2, that postmodern theory can be seen as a new kind of critical theory. For example, Baudrillard ([1970] 1998) argues against the conventional view that consumption is about the satisfaction of needs. He contends that if that were the case, consumption would cease when one's needs were satisfied. However, in contemporary consumerism, as soon as one need is satisfied, a new and different need comes to the fore, requiring additional consumption. Baudrillard further argues that what consumption is really about is difference. That is, it is through consumption that people seek to demonstrate that they are different from others in, for example, their taste in clothes or in cars. In the postmodern world, where an endless and ever-expanding set of differences is created, consumption becomes a never-ending process of demonstrating those differences.

Postmodernists are prone to appending the prefix *hyper-* to many things (Lipovetsky 2005). Appending *hyper-* to any modern characteristic tends to turn it into something associated with, and critical of, the postmodern world. For example, the postmodern world is associated with hyper-consumption, or buying more than you want, need, and can afford (Ritzer 2001). Related to the idea of hyperconsumption, especially consuming more than you can afford, is the idea of **hyperdebt**, or borrowing more than you should, thereby owing more than you will be able to repay (Ritzer 2012a).

However, some postmodernists have a more complex view of consumption; a more positive perspective coexists with this critical orientation (Venkatesh 2007). For example, they tend to see consumption as an aesthetic undertaking, or as a form of art. Consumers are seen as artists in, say, buying and putting together, in highly creative ways, the various elements of different outfits. This is particularly related to the postmodern idea of *pastiche,* or the mixing together of various elements, especially those that most would not see as fitting together. While a modern consumer might purchase an outfit composed of matching elements (e.g., skirt and top) predesigned and preselected by the manufacturer, the post-modern consumer is seen as creatively and artistically putting together components from a wide range of manufacturers and styles. Furthermore, new and used clothing, or clothing from different time periods, is combined in unique ways to create outfits that can be seen as works of art.

GLOBALIZATION AND THE ECONOMY

Globalization is associated with many changes in the econ-omy. One of the most remarkable changes has been in **macrofinance**, or globalization as it relates to money and finance. Not long ago, money and finance were closely tied to the nation-state that issued the money and to the financial trans-actions that took place therein. Moving money and financial instruments—for example, stocks and bonds, as well new instruments such as derivatives—from one part of the world to another was difficult and cumbersome. Travelers needed to change their own country's currency into the currency of the country to which they were traveling. And if they were going to many different countries, they needed to repeat this transaction for each one. Now, however, all a traveler needs is a debit card, which can be used in most nations in the world to rapidly and efficiently pay for goods and services with the currency of each of the nations visited. As Dodd (2012: 1446) puts it, "We are witnessing the end of money's geography."

As a result, money is increasingly liquid, and it flows around the world quite readily. This is clearly true for tour-ists and businesspeople, but it is true in other ways as well: Substantial flows of money are associated with the infor-mal economy, criminal networks, the international drug trade, and money laundering. To take another example, much money flows in the form of remittances, largely from migrants in the Global North to family and friends back home in the Global South. In fact, in 2010, recorded remittances—much more probably went unreported—totaled $325 billion (Ratha and Mohapatra 2012). While this sounds like a great deal of money, it pales in compari-son with other types of global financial transactions. For example, in only one aspect of the global financial market, the market for the world's currencies, about $5.3 trillion changes hands *every day* (Knorr Cetina 2012).

The largest amounts of money by far flow easily and quickly through electronic transmissions associated with global financial markets (Knorr Cetina 2012). People and businesses are increasingly dependent on electronic transfers for the credit they need, or think they need, in today's world. Individuals usually need credit to purchase such things as homes and automobiles. Credit is also central to the growth and investments of corporations and governments.

Even more important is global trade in a series of obscure financial instruments. Banking practices tied to the U.S. housing market and such financial instruments set off a chain reaction that devastated international economic flows and triggered a global recession. Central to these problems was the fact that financial markets in both the United States and much of the rest of the world were deregulated to a great degree. Without governmental oversight, many of these mar-kets were allowed to run wild. For example, rampant specu-lation in exotic financial instruments produced an economic bubble that burst violently, causing the recession to develop and gather momentum.

The bursting of the bubble created a global liquidity cri-sis because nations and their banks were reluctant to lend to one another. They were afraid the economic crisis would render other nations and banks unable to repay their loans. Without these loans, many nations were plunged into deep recessions. This was especially true in the European countries that constitute the *eurozone,* the 19 of 27 European nations that use the euro as a common currency.

Over the years, this led to the *euro crisis,* which grew particularly intense in late 2011 and early 2012 (Riera-Crichton 2012). The wealthier European societies, especially Germany, were able to deal with the recession well. Other countries, especially Greece, Portugal, Ireland, Spain, and later Italy and Cyprus, were not (Stewart 2013). They suffered huge economic problems, such as the collapse of their housing markets and high unemployment. Several of these countries had their credit ratings diminished. In such a situation, the typical course of action for a country is to devalue its currency, thereby reducing its costs. This makes its products cheaper and more competitive in the global economy, allowing the economy to begin to grow again. However, because those troubled countries were part of the eurozone, they were unable to devalue their currency. Their economies were left without the traditional method of deal-ing with recessions and depression.

In spite of this mid-2015 protest, Greek voters accepted another economic reform package put forth by the country's creditors. Is more economic austerity in Greece's interest? Can the euro be saved in the long run?

Further worsening the situation for these countries was the fact that it became more difficult for them to borrow money to keep their economies functioning. Lenders increasingly believed that the troubled nations might not be able to repay those loans. The result was that the struggling eurozone countries had to pay ever-higher interest rates to get loans. Countries like Ireland, Cyprus, and Greece had to get bailouts (and Greece continues to need a bailout) from European sources. In exchange for those bailouts, they had to agree to practice greater austerity. For example, they fired government employees and cut back welfare programs. Paradoxically, this austerity further weakened their economies, at least in the short run, because many people had less money to spend.

There were many fears associated with the euro crisis. First, those living in the countries most affected by the crisis might face unavoidable economic hardships. Second, at least some of the affected countries might find it necessary to abandon the euro and return to the currencies they used before the creation of the euro, which began circulating in 2002. This could lead to huge internal economic problems for those countries in the short term and, in the long term, to the collapse of the eurozone (and more broadly the EU). This, in turn,

could lead to a return to the era in which European nations fought horrendous wars against one another. Third, there was a fear that affected countries would drag the rest of the euro-zone countries, and eventually much of the rest of the world, down economically. Fourth, there was the worry that people in the most affected countries would grow increasingly disaffected, leading to political revolutions. In fact, what did happen in Greece in 2015 was a dramatic political change with the victory of a left-wing party, Syriza, intent on reducing the economic burden placed on Greece by the harsh terms of the bailout. Finally, there was the fear of the possibility, in the face of looming insurrections, of the rise of right-wing governments and possibly the emergence of new dictatorships. This was what had happened as a result of economic disruption after World War I and the Great Depression, which, among other things, led to the rise of fascism in Europe and eventually to World War II (Thomas 2011).

As of late 2015 Greece seemed to have stabilized, at least for the time being, with additional economic aid from several sources. However, continuing economic problems in Greece and other EU countries, as well as basic problems with the euro itself, suggest that this is only a lull in a longer-term euro crisis.

SUMMARY

Politics is one way to advance a given position or policy through the use of, or by putting pressure on, the state. Democracy is a political system in which people within a given state vote to choose their leaders and, in some cases, to approve legislation. This is in contrast to dictatorships, which are usually totalitarian governments operating without the consent of the governed.

The question of who rules the United States is a source of continuing debate. In analyzing politics, structural-functionalists emphasize pluralism, while conflict theorists focus on power elite theory.

Global politics is dominated by geopolitics, the nation-state and threats to it, war, and terrorism. Terrorism involves nongovernmental actors engaging in violence targeting noncombatants, property, or military personnel.

Sociologists define the economy as the social system that ensures the production and distribution of goods and services. In the last 200 years, the capitalist U.S. economy has transitioned from the Industrial Revolution to industrialization to deindustrialization. Communism is an economic system oriented to the collective, and socialism, which followed it historically, is characterized by a society's efforts to plan and organize production consciously and rationally. The United States has some social welfare programs but still lags far behind more developed welfare states in what it provides.

In addition to general shifts in the U.S. economy, there have been dramatic changes in the nation's labor force. Deindustrialization and the decline of labor unions, as well as the growth of service jobs and an increasing focus on consumption, set the stage for a postindustrial society, in which the focus on the manufacture of goods has been replaced by an increase in service work.

Consumption is generally considered to be the hallmark of postmodern society. Consumerism is an obsession with consumption. Cathedrals of consumption show that consumption has in many ways become today's religion. The postmodern world is also associated with hyperconsumption and hyperdebt.

Capitalism has become increasingly global in that transnational, not national, economic practices predominate. The eurozone has faced, and may again confront, a euro crisis that threatens to destabilize the EU and possibly the world.

REVIEW QUESTIONS

1. What factors help to explain the emergence of democratic political systems? How is democracy related to bureaucracy and rational-legal concepts that you learned about in previous chapters?

2. In what ways is citizenship an important component of a democratic political system? Do you think low voter turnout in the United States is due to a failure of the nation's citizens? Or do nonvoters in the United States express their political interests in other ways? In what ways could new technologies facilitate political involvement?

3. The question of who rules the United States is still being debated. In what ways does a pluralist understanding of power and politics in the United States differ from the power elite perspective? Do you think globalization has an effect on who rules the United States? Why or why not?

4. How are socialism and communism alternatives to capitalism? What elements of welfare states are socialistic, and what forces in the United States are resistant to social welfare programs?

5. What factors help to explain deindustrialization in the United States? What effects has deindustrialization had on other countries?

6. How is deindustrialization related to the decline of labor unions? Is there any hope for the labor movement in the United States? Elsewhere in the world?

7. How is our society characterized by rampant and insatiable consumerism? How do we use consumption to satisfy our needs in the world today? Do you agree that we tend to consume beyond our needs?

8. In what ways might consumption today be described as the new religion?

9. What is the critical view of consumption offered by postmodernists? What is their positive view of consumption? Can these views be reconciled?

10. What was the euro crisis? In what ways was it an economic crisis? In what ways did it show the linkage between the economy and government? Were the great fears associated with the crisis well-founded? Is another euro crisis looming?

APPLYING THE SOCIOLOGICAL IMAGINATION

1. This chapter poses the question "Who rules the United States?" According to the power elite perspective, power is concentrated in the hands of a small number of people who control the major institutions of the state, the corporate

economy, and the military. The powerful people who make up these institutions might have minor disagreements about policy, but for the most part they are unified in their interests and in owning and operating much of American society.

For this activity, choose an organization from the top 10 of the Fortune 500. Use the Internet to find the most up-to-date data. After selecting the company, go to its website to find information on its board of directors. A good place to start is the company's annual report. For the most part, annual reports are made available on company websites, often on the "About Us" page. Finally, select two members from the company's board of directors and answer the following questions:

- What are their racial or ethnic backgrounds?
- What are their educational backgrounds? Where did they go to school?
- What are their primary occupations?
- Do they have military backgrounds?
- Have they held formal positions in government?
- Do they have affiliations with other organizations? If so, which ones?
- Are they outspoken members of particular political parties?

- Do they belong to any specific social clubs?
- Are they often mentioned in news reports? What types of mentions?

Do you think the answers to these questions provide evidence for or against the power elite perspective? How might a group pluralist or elite pluralist respond to the limited evidence you have compiled here?

2. How can you use the clothes on your back to understand the nature of globalization? As has been explored throughout this book, the things we consume say a lot about who we are and how we want others to perceive us. Rarely, however, do we pay attention to how these individual choices are situated within larger global processes. For this activity, choose five of your favorite articles of clothing and check their tags to see where they were made. Then do research on the companies and their production sites in these various countries. In what ways are the clothes you wear part of an increasingly globalized economy? What are the benefits of such an economy for you? What are the benefits and disadvantages for the workers producing the clothes? What are the consequences for each of the different countries?

KEY TERMS

cathedrals of consumption: Large and lavish consumption sites, created mostly in the United States in the last half of the twentieth century and into the early twenty-first century. (p. 297)

citizens: The people represented by a given state, most often born within its territories. (p. 282)

citizenship: The idea that people of a given state can vote for their representatives within the state, but also that they have access to rights and responsibilities as citizens. (p. 282)

competitive capitalism: A form of capitalism where there are a large number of relatively small firms, with the result that no one or small subset of them can completely dominate and control a given area of the economy. (p. 291)

consumerism: An obsession with consumption. (p. 298)

deindustrialization: The decline of manufacturing as well as a corresponding increase in various types of services. (p. 293)

democracy: A political system in which people within a given state vote to choose their leaders and in some cases vote on legislation. (p. 282)

dictatorships: States that are usually totalitarian and are ruled either by a single individual or by a small group of people. (p. 283)

direct democracy: A political system in which people directly affected by a given decision have a say in that decision. (p. 282)

economy: The social system involved in the production and distribution of a wide range of goods and services. (p. 288)

elite pluralism: The formation by political elites of similar interest groups and organizations that vie for power. (p. 285)

Fordism: The ideas, principles, and systems created by Henry Ford (who is credited with the development of the modern mass production system) and his associates at the beginning of the twentieth century. (p. 289)

geopolitics: Political relationships that involve large geographic areas or the globe as a whole. (p. 285)

group pluralism: The competition of society's various interest groups and organizations for access to political power in an attempt to further their interests. (p. 284)

hyperdebt: Borrowing more than one should, thereby owing more than one will be able to pay back. (p. 299)

imagined communities: Communities that are socially constructed by those who see themselves as part of them. (p. 286)

macrofinance: The globalization of money and finance. (p. 299)

mass production: Production characterized by large numbers of standardized products, highly specialized workers, interchangeable machine parts, precision tools, a high-volume mechanized production process, and the synchronization of the flow of materials used in production, with the entire process made as continuous as possible. (p. 288)

monopoly capitalism: A form of capitalism in which huge corporations monopolize the market. (p. 291)

politics: Societal competition through established governmental channels to determine which group's members get what, as well as when and how they get it. (p. 282)

post-Fordism: A production environment associated with smaller production runs of more specialized products, especially those high in style and quality; more flexible machinery made possible by advances in technology largely traceable to the computer; more skilled workers with greater flexibility and autonomy; less reliance on economies of scale; and more differentiated markets for those more specialized products. (p. 289)

postindustrial society: A society that was at one time industrial, but where the focus on the manufacture of goods has been replaced by an increase, at least initially, in service work—that is, work in which people are involved in providing services for one another rather than producing goods. (p. 295)

power elite theory: A theory holding that power is not dispersed throughout a stable society but is concentrated in a small number of people who control the major institutions of the state, the corporate economy, and the military. (p. 285)

representative democracy: A political system in which people, as a whole body, do not actually rule themselves but rather have some say in who will best represent them in the state. (p. 282)

separation of powers: The separation and counterbalancing of different branches of government so that no one branch of government can wield too much power. (p. 284)

socialism: A historical stage following communism involving the effort by society to plan and organize production consciously and rationally so that all members of society benefit from it. (p. 289)

terrorism: Acts of violence by nongovernmental actors that target noncombatants, property, or military personnel to influence politics. (p. 287)

transnational capitalism: An economic system in which transnational economic practices predominate. (p. 293)

underemployment: Employment in jobs that are not consonant with one's training and ability, as a part-time worker when one is capable and desirous of full-time work, or in jobs that are not fully occupying. (p. 297)

unemployment: The state of being economically active and in the labor force, being able and willing to work, and seeking employment, but being unable to find a job. (p. 295)

war: Armed conflict in which a nation uses its military to attempt to impose its will on others. (p. 286)

welfare states: States that seek both to run their economic markets efficiently, as capitalism does, and to do so equitably, which capitalism does not do. (p. 290)

$SAGE edge™ edge.sagepub.com/ritzeressentials2e

SAGE edge offers a robust online environment featuring an impressive array of free tools and resources for review, study, and further exploration, keeping both instructors and students on the cutting edge of teaching and learning.

LEARNING OBJECTIVES	FOR FURTHER EXPLORATION AND APPLICATION
LO 12-1: Contrast democracy and dictatorship.	▶ A 1940s Description of Democracy and Dictatorship ◉ China's Social Media Policy May Be Used to Target Political Speech ◉ Key Differences between Democracy and Dictatorship
LO 12-2: Explain how globalization affects war and terrorism, geopolitics, and the nation-state.	▶ How Governments Respond to Terrorism ◉ Will It Work? The House Considers Bill to Stop NSA Bulk Collection Program ◉ The Top 10 Geopolitical Risks of 2015
LO 12-3: Describe the U.S. economy's transition from industrialization to deindustrialization.	▶ The Deindustrialization of America ◉ Will Future Manufacturing Jobs in the United States Require More Brain Than Brawn? ◉ The Unintended Consequences of Outsourcing
LO 12-4: Discuss your relationship to employment, unemployment and underemployment, and consumption.	▶ Unemployment and Underemployment of College Graduates ◉ Why Carmakers Ditched Luxury Names for Something More Practical ◉ How Food and Consumption Patterns Shape Society
LO 12-5: Describe the effects of globalization on the world economy.	▶ The Effects of Globalization on Developing Nations ◉ Global Bankers Meet to Resolve a Two-Speed World Economy ◉ Explore World Bank Projects in Developing Nations

THE BODY, MEDICINE, HEALTH, AND HEALTH CARE

The Debate over Medical Marijuana

The use of marijuana is increasingly legal, or at least accepted, in many U.S. states. However, 23 states continue to ban the drug. In addition, marijuana is illegal under federal law (along with heroin and LSD). Yet marijuana is the most heavily used illegal substance in the United States.

Controversy remains about marijuana's use, including in the treatment of various medical conditions. Opponents fear that federal legalization allowing unlimited medical use of the drug would lead to the legalization of nonmedical marijuana use throughout the United States. Their opposition is motivated by a concern that recreational use of marijuana can be harmful, especially addictive, and that it is a portal to the use of other illegal and more dangerous drugs. This concern is complicated by the fact that we have insufficient knowledge of marijuana's effects. Research has been greatly limited because of the federal government's definition of it as an illegal substance.

These limitations have prevented research scientists from ascertaining whether marijuana is a useful medical treatment for a long list of diseases and medical problems, including cancer, HIV/AIDS, hepatitis C, multiple sclerosis, seizures, severe nausea, glaucoma, and chronic pain. Yet there is consensus among the medical community that the drug *is* beneficial for such problems. About a million people in the United States now use medical marijuana, but even in states where such use is legal, patients live in fear of prosecution by the U.S. government for violating federal narcotics law. In addition, across states where marijuana use is legal, there is wide variation in the

LEARNING OBJECTIVES

13-1 Discuss sociological concepts that relate to the body, including sexuality, health and beauty, body modifications, and risky behaviors.

13-2 Outline the issues studied in medical sociology, including the U.S. medical profession, the health care system and its weaknesses and inequities, and consumerism in health care.

13-3 Discuss the influence of globalization on health, illness and disease, and health care.

Corbis

diseases that qualify for treatment with the drug. The quality and potency of marijuana also goes largely unregulated by those states.

Some who smoke marijuana for medical reasons are concerned about the fact that doing so exposes them to carcinogens. Others are disturbed by the psychoactive effect—the high—that is the great attraction for most other users. Said one ophthalmologist, "None of my 60-year-old patients are interested in being stoned to treat their glaucoma." However, the cause of the high—tetrahydrocannabinol (THC)—can be removed.

Because of the great demand for marijuana and its apparent usefulness in the treatment of many medical problems, efforts to ease federal limitations on its medical use continue. In early 2015 a bill was introduced in Congress to reclassify marijuana as a Schedule II drug, which would acknowledge that it is medically useful but with high potential for abuse. ●

The central concerns of this chapter—the body, medicine, health (including mental health), and health care—are at the top of the social, as well as almost everyone's personal, agenda. Globally, there is much concern about epidemics such as AIDS, malaria, the flu, Ebola, and SARS-like viruses, as well as the great inequalities in health and health care that exist throughout the world. At the societal level, the United States has been—and may well continue to be—wracked by an acrimonious debate over reforming health care. Among other things, reformers have sought to address flagrant inequalities and increasing costs in health care. Some changes in health care have recently been instituted (to be discussed later in this chapter), although they have been far less significant than many hoped. Millions of Americans still do not have health care even though governmentally mandated reforms took effect in 2014. These global and societal issues affect the health and health care of individuals. Among those most concerned about such issues are those who are or will be patients—that is, virtually everyone—as well as the large and growing number of people who work in health care.

Ultimately, much of the interest in health comes down to a growing focus on, and concern about, the state of our bodies. However, interest in the body manifests itself in different ways for various social groups. If you are young, your main concerns are likely to be how to remain good-looking, healthy, and fit through diet, exercise, and perhaps even a nip or a tuck here or there (Anderson 1991; Roudometof 2012). As you age, your focus will shift to the increasing likelihood that you may develop various diseases—breast cancer for

women and prostate cancer for men, as well as heart disease for both men and women. You will also become increasingly concerned about how to avoid those diseases, if possible. If you are diagnosed with one, your focus will be on how to deal with it—*if* it can be dealt with. Gender affects the types of health-protective behaviors that you employ. Women tend to be more active participants in their health maintenance than men. Health-protective behaviors include screenings, self-examinations, and regular checkups.

Some of you will fall ill, be hospitalized, and perhaps die in middle age (or even earlier). However, most of you will face health-related issues with increasing frequency and intensity as you move into old age. New health-related concerns will then emerge, such as the possibility of developing Alzheimer's disease. It is estimated that the number of people age 65 and older with Alzheimer's disease will almost triple between 2010 and 2050 (see Figure 13.1). The number of people 85 years of age and over with the disease will quadruple. As you age, you may wonder whether you are going to have the funds, or the insurance, needed to pay the often astronomical health care costs associated with the inevitable illnesses of your last years. You may also worry about how you will die and whether you will be able to do so with dignity.

For these reasons as well as others, the body has emerged in recent years as a major concern in sociology (Garlick 2014; McLaughlin and Coleman-Fountain 2014; B. Turner 2008). However, it is important to remember that the mind and mental processes have long been of concern and of interest to many sociologists. (For example, see the discussion of Mead's work on these topics in Chapter 4.) Mental illnesses such as depression, schizophrenia, and attention-deficit/hyperactivity disorder (ADHD) are major concerns at the global, national, and individual levels (Clark 2014; Koivusalo and Ollila 2014). There is no clear line between the mind and the body. The brain, which houses the mind, is, after all, a body part. Mental processes affect

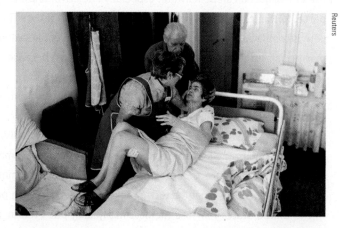

With populations aging in many places throughout the world, Alzheimer's disease is likely to become increasingly common. What are the personal, social, and economic costs associated with this disease?

FIGURE 13.1 • Number of People Age 65 and Over in the U.S. Population with Alzheimer's Disease, 2010–2050 (projected)

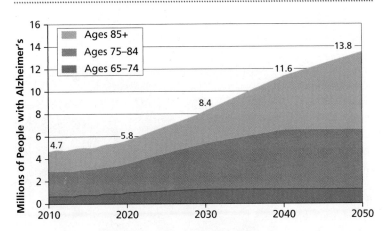

SOURCE: Figure 4, Projected Numbers of People Age 65 and Over in the U.S. Population with Alzheimer's Disease, 2000–2050, p. 20, from 2013 *Alzheimer's Disease Facts and Figures.* Reprinted with permission from the Alzheimer's Association (http://www.alz.org/downloads/Facts_Figures_2014.pdf).

the body (such as through psychosomatic illnesses), and the body affects the mind. One example of the latter is postpartum depression, which is caused, at least in part, by hormonal imbalances (Mollard 2014). Another is depression that develops following a diagnosis of breast or prostate cancer, as well as heart disease (Love, Thompson, and Knapp 2014). However, it is important to remember that mental processes can also have positive effects on the body and its well-being. A strong sense of self-efficacy can be helpful to an individual who is trying to lose weight or who is recovering from a heart attack.

THE BODY

While sociology has always had some interest in the body, the recent explosion of such interest is largely traceable to the work of French social theorist Michel Foucault.

THE THINKING OF MICHEL FOUCAULT

In *Discipline and Punish: The Birth of the Prison,* Foucault ([1975] 1979) is concerned, at least initially, with the punishment of the criminal's body. The book opens with a description of the punishment inflicted on a condemned murderer in 1757:

> [His flesh was] . . . torn from his breasts, arms, thighs and calves with red-hot pincers. . . . On those places where the flesh will be torn away, poured molten lead, boiling oil, burning resin, wax and sulphur melted together and then his

body drawn and quartered by four horses. . . . When that did not suffice, they were forced to cut off the wretch's thighs, to sever the sinews and hack at the joints. (Foucault [1975] 1979: 3)

Clearly, at this point in the history of punishment, the focus was on the body.

Between 1757 and the 1830s, the abysmal treatment of criminals and their bodies gave way to the rise of what seemed to be more humane treatment in prison. There, prisoners' bodies were contained and controlled rather than tortured. However, Foucault argues that in some ways, the prison system was far *less* humane than the earlier systems of physical torture. Imprisonment, as well as the continual surveillance associated with it, involved constant mental torture of the "soul" of the prisoner. Today, it can be argued that the souls of prisoners and nonprisoners alike are being tortured to an increasing degree because surveillance is so much more pervasive (Bauman and Lyon 2012). We are being watched by omnipresent video cameras, through scanners at airports, and on the computer, where Google and others keep tabs on the websites we visit (Andrejevic 2009). Most of us are not aware of much of this surveillance. Even when we are, we may not mind it, and we may even enjoy doing the things that allow us to be watched, such as writing on Facebook walls. However, all this surveillance, especially when taken together, has the potential to be used to gather information needed to exert great control over us.

In *The Birth of the Clinic* (1975), Foucault begins with an analysis of medicine prior to the nineteenth century. At this time, in order to diagnose a disease, doctors focused on lists of diseases and their associated symptoms. However, in the nineteenth century, the gaze of doctors shifted from such lists to human beings, especially their bodies and the diseases that afflicted them. Of great importance was the ability to see and touch diseased or dead bodies. The focus shifted to performing autopsies—cutting into bodies—to learn about diseases, their courses, and their effects on bodies and their organs.

In *The History of Sexuality,* Foucault (1978) emphasizes the importance of sexuality and the role of the body in obtaining sexual pleasure. He asserts that society uses sexuality, and restrictions on it, to gain access to the body in order to control, discipline, and govern it. He suggests that people should reject such constraints on the body as well as constricted forms of sexuality. Instead, Foucault (1978: 157) argues, people should focus on sexuality that is about "bodies and pleasures." One way to do that, Foucault writes, is to push one's body to the limit in sexual experiences. While most people do not come close to such limit

Theatrical Presentations

Most of the "Public Sociology" boxes in this book deal with sociologists who are in the public eye or with nonsociologists, especially journalists, who conduct sociological analyses. However, public sociology can take other forms, including dramatic presentations. One example is the 2014 movie *Still Alice,* which deals with a college professor experiencing early-onset Alzheimer's disease.

In another example, sociologists working in collaboration with a performing arts company used theatrical techniques to enhance public understanding of early-onset dementia (Jenkins, Keyes, and Strange 2015). Based on workshops with dementia victims and their families, they developed four realistic vignettes and employed professional actors to depict them. The sociologists engaged in several forms of public sociology, including making presentations to government officials, people with dementia and their families, and professionals and students engaged in caring for people with dementia. In addition, the vignettes were filmed and are available to a global public audience (including you) on YouTube (at https://www.youtube.com/watch?v=MFyDv9r2sQE). By making you aware of this work, this box serves as another example of public sociology.

Here are brief summaries of the issues addressed in the four vignettes:

- *Vignette 1.* Dementia patients often experience time differently than their family members. As a result, efforts to hurry them along can cause them to become confused and disoriented and ultimately lead to family conflict.
- *Vignette 2.* The everyday risks to dementia patients, such as when lighting a stove, can make them angry at family members for allowing them to be put in that situation. Families also worry about going too far in restricting dementia patients and not allowing them to handle everyday tasks on their own.
- *Vignette 3.* The telephone can be a source of danger to dementia patients when they are home alone and might be taken advantage of by callers such as telemarketers.
- *Vignette 4.* In a social setting such as a restaurant, a dementia patient can commit a faux pas by, for example, mistaking a stranger for an old friend and be forced to deal with the resulting embarrassment.

Julianne Moore won an Academy Award for her portrayal of a professor confronting Alzheimer's disease in the 2014 film *Still Alice.*

While presenting these brief descriptions is a form of public sociology, the videos that depict them offer much greater detail and have a more powerful impact on those who view them.

Think About It

Movies and plays are not often thought of as public sociology. Think about a movie or play you have seen recently that can be viewed, at least retrospectively, as public sociology. How does thinking of the movie or play in this way affect your sense of what you got out it and, more generally, your view of the social world?

---

experiences, there is today much more openness and freedom as far as sexuality is concerned.

With the work of Foucault and many others as a base, the study of the body has become increasingly important. It is defined by a general focus on the relationships among the body, society, and culture (Turner 2007a, 2007b). It also includes a wide range of more specific concerns, including the gendered body, sexuality, body modifications like tattooing, bodily pain, and abominations of the body (such as stigmas; see Chapter 6). Of course, the issue of the body is

also central to the main focus of this chapter, the sociology of health and medicine.

THE HEALTHY BODY: LIFESTYLE, BEAUTY, AND FITNESS

We live in an increasingly reflexive society, which creates a heightened awareness of the body and of ourselves more generally. Nevertheless, many of us engage in risky behaviors (for example, basking for hours in the summer sun) that endanger

Calvin Klein agreed to stop using an ad campaign in which emaciated teenagers were provocatively posed. In what ways does this billboard reveal the influence of the "appearance culture"?

Reuters

our health as well as the way we look and our physical fitness. However, reflexivity can lead us to be more likely to avoid risky situations, protect ourselves when we are in them (for example, by using sunblock), and seek out more beneficial ones. More generally, many of us focus on creating lifestyles that we hope will make us fit, attractive, and healthy. We may feel a responsibility to take care of ourselves, and especially to do everything possible to avoid becoming sick and dying. Our bodies, and our health, have become "projects" to be worked on continually. We are likely to mold, and perhaps even alter, our bodies throughout the course of our lives (Brumberg 1998; Strandbu and Kvalem 2014). In spite of this, there is no shortage of times—that trip to the fast-food restaurant, one too many beers on Saturday night—during which health and the body take a backseat.

ASK YOURSELF

Do you view your body and health as "projects" you work on? Do you know others who do? What beliefs and activities can you identify that characterize this outlook on the body and health?

Reflexivity often leads to dissatisfaction with the body, especially as a result of the influence of peers and the media.

We live in what might be called an "appearance culture," that is, one in which appearance is of central importance to peers and in the media. That culture includes ideas about what makes an appearance "attractive," and such ideas can negatively affect people's feelings about their own appearance. This is particularly true for adolescents, especially young women. Derogatory comments about their bodies and appearance-related teasing, among other influences, can have profoundly damaging effects on young people (Webb, Zimmer-Gembeck, and Donovan 2014).

More generally, both boys and girls have concerns about their bodies, although the nature of those concerns is often different. For example, boys tend to want strong bodies in order to engage in sports, while girls are apt to want bodies that "look good" (Tatangelo and Ricciardelli 2013). Boys who do not have strong bodies and girls who do not look good are likely to feel dissatisfied with their bodies. However, beliefs about the body are socially contextualized and socially constructed, and they vary by, among other things, race. For example, Latina college students report more dissatisfaction than their white and black counterparts with specific areas and features of their bodies (Warren 2014). Even desired skin tone and complexion have cultural and social determinants. In one study, adult British whites were found to want darker skin tones, while British South Asians and British

African people from the Caribbean wanted lighter skin tones (Swami et al. 2013).

Beauty: Cultural Contexts

The social construction of beauty made it onto more people's radar after the publication of Naomi Wolf's book *The Beauty Myth* ([1991] 2002). Wolf argues that the media present the vast majority of people with an unattainable standard of beauty. The "objectifying gaze," rooted in patriarchal and Eurocentric ideals of beauty and attractiveness and expressed through media, includes a narrow standard for beauty and desirability (Gervais, Holland, and Dodd 2013). Heterosexual men and women report feeling more positive toward women who meet that standard—for example, women who have a typical hourglass shape (small waist, curvy chest and hips).

Some argue that the elevation of the importance of beauty has its roots in evolution (Singh and Singh 2011). That is, beauty may be an indicator of health and fertility. As a result, beautiful heterosexual women are more likely to be selected for mating. They are also more likely to have children who are beautiful and who have a greater chance of survival and success. Regardless of the potential biological roots of beauty, we use beauty as a means of determining who is attractive and as a way of distributing socially valuable resources. Those deemed beautiful earn more and are more successful at work (Hamermesh 2011). We often are not even consciously aware of the ways in which stereotypical beauty matters in the decisions we—and others—make (Kwan and Trautner 2011).

Race, ethnicity, and class are implicated in stereotypical conceptualizations of beauty. Biracial women are most satisfied with their skin tone, while Afro-Caribbean and African women are more satisfied with their body shapes compared to African American women (Mucherah and Frazier 2013).

Efforts to attain a high standard of stereotypical beauty may include excessive dieting, bingeing, and purging. Women are particularly susceptible to these actions, which often lead to failure, negative self-image, and low self-esteem (Daniels 2009; Rosenberg 1979). Some gay men feel compelled to diet excessively in order to fit the "twink" body type, a very slender physique deemed particularly attractive by some within the gay male community (Kimmel 2012). Similarly, increased media attention to men's bodies may lead to a preoccupation with ideas about the ideal male form. Internalization of ideals about the superiority of muscular bodies influences some men's drive to develop muscular physiques (Pritchard and Cramblitt 2014). However, male desire for a muscular body is not universal. For example, college-age men in Hong Kong have less positive attitudes toward muscularity than do American college-age men (Jung, Forbes, and Chan 2010).

The Quest for the Ideal, the Consumption of Beauty, and the Fit Body

The rewards for being beautiful are so great that many try to at least approximate the mythic ideal. In consumer culture, beauty has become a commodity that can be bought (or at least we think it can) through great effort, often pain, and expenditures of large sums of money. This is clear, for example, in the hundreds of billions of dollars (Hamermesh 2011) spent in the United States on cosmetics, fitness, and clothing and, at the most extreme, on cosmetic surgeries of all sorts (Gimlin 2007). The global beauty product industry is, of course, much larger. Most of the American and global consumers of beauty products are women. Beauty is deemed so important in Brazil, for example, that cosmetic surgeries are offered to all who can pay for the anesthesia. Poor and rich Brazilians alike can thus buy procedures to create the culturally ideal physique. For women, that physique features small breasts, small waist with large derriere, and slim nose and lips (Edmonds 2010).

About 90 percent of cosmetic surgical procedures in the United States are undergone by women. As Table 13.1 shows, the most popular modifications are breast augmentation, nose reshaping, eyelid surgery, liposuction, and facelift. Some people have genital cosmetic surgeries intended to enhance sexual response (clitoral hood reduction, vaginal tightening) or to improve genital aesthetics (vulvaplasty) (Braun 2010).

Looks-related stress affects both men and women, although young women are particularly susceptible. The greater likelihood of such stress, including looks-related depression and low self-esteem, among young women has been found in Sweden, South Korea, and New Zealand (Jose, Kramar, and Hou 2014; Landstedt and Gådin 2012; Julie Lee 2012).

Consumption related to beauty and appearance pervades teen romance novels, which link young women's romantic and sexual desirability to their use of brand-name

TABLE 13.1 • The Five Most Popular Cosmetic Procedures in the United States, 2013

PROCEDURE	NUMBER
Breast augmentation	290,000
Nose reshaping	221,000
Eyelid surgery	216,000
Liposuction	200,000
Facelift	133,000

SOURCE: American Society of Plastic Surgeons, "2013 Top Five Cosmetic Surgical Procedures" (http://www.plasticsurgery.org/Documents/news-resources/statistics/2013-statistics/top-five-cosmetic-procedures-2013.pdf). Reprinted with the permission of the American Society for Aesthetic Plastic Surgery.

products and types of body modification (Johnson 2010). Like many movies, the books engage in *product placement* to earn money and sell advertisers' products. Products mentioned in such books include clothing (Valentino tank tops), lingerie (La Perla negligees), shoes (Jimmy Choo high heels), cosmetics (Chanel Vamp lip gloss), and body modifications (Brazilian body waxes).

Interest in the way we look, while not new, has grown dramatically in the current era of increasing reflexivity. We are more aware of how we (and others) look. We are more conscious not only of the steps we can take to improve our appearance but also of the many means available to us for doing so. The increase in pure relationships (see Chapter 10) may add greater importance to this focus on appearance, since others are more likely to leave relationships with us if they are dissatisfied with the way we look (and vice versa). Our good looks are seen as a resource, or a form of capital, that is socially constructed (Hakim 2011).

Fitness and the Healthy Body

Closely related to the emphasis on beauty is the focus on both female and male physical activity, physical fitness, sports, and bodybuilding (Klein 1993; Scott 2011). These are seen, at least in part, as ways of obtaining a body that is not only more beautiful but also healthier (Waddington 2007)—or at least that appears that way. However, we must distinguish among the methods employed to achieve a healthy body. The clearest link is between regular physical activity and health. Walking, cycling, and jogging typically do not include competition and are clearly good for most people. However, the increasingly competitive nature of many sports may actually have adverse effects on health and appearance. Such sports require great exertion and are often violent. They can be damaging, even dangerous, to the body. Consider the increasing alarm over concussions and other brain traumas in various sports, especially professional football (Belson 2014; "Head Injuries in Football" 2010).

Fitness is possible at any age. Does your fitness routine improve your body or adversely affect it?

Some contact sports, such as wrestling and boxing, require competitors to qualify for, and remain in, very restrictive weight classes. This can lead participants to engage in bouts of starvation and dehydration in order to "make the weight." Such practices, in turn, can evolve into "manorexia," a male analogue of the mainly female disorder of anorexia, by which women strive to attain slimmer bodies (Kershaw 2008). There is also a phenomenon known as "bigorexia" (Kimmel 2012; Mosley 2009), which may affect men who have grown up with G.I. Joe action figures or photos of bodybuilders and who aspire to have similar physiques. They might be led to lift weights obsessively and to consume mainly, or only, proteins. Such practices are especially rampant among competitive bodybuilders. Some sports, taken to extremes, can have a variety of deleterious effects on the body in both the short and the long term.

Exercise, sports, and physical activity often take as their goal the improvement of the body and of health more generally. They are increasingly oriented toward *outcomes,* such as losing weight and strengthening muscles. However, such a focus often overlooks the fun associated with exercise (Wellard 2012). As a result, people do not explore the full potential of various kinds of physical activities.

ASK YOURSELF

Consider any and all sports you have played in your life so far. What was your goal? Were you forced to play during gym or fitness class, or did you play for fun, or in an effort to earn a college scholarship? What effect did your motives have on your level of engagement and the outcomes for your health? Do you still play?

BODY MODIFICATIONS

Practices of body modification have been nearly universal across societies and throughout history (Ferreira 2014; Pitts 2003). However, in recent years, there has been something of a boom in such practices in the United States and elsewhere. There are several major forms of body modification, including tattooing (Atkinson 2003; Dukes and Stein 2011), scarification (scarring or cutting of the skin; see Dargent 2014), piercing (Vail 2007; Wessel and Kasten 2014), and even intentional self-injury (Adler and Adler 2011). At one time, body modification was mainly associated with deviants (see Chapter 6) of various types, including gang members, prisoners, and prostitutes. Today, some body modifications, especially tattoos, have become mainstream (Adams 2009). For example, tattooing occurs these days in tattoo parlors found in shopping malls. The media are full of images of movie stars and especially

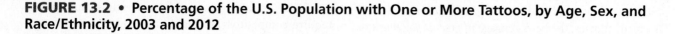

FIGURE 13.2 • Percentage of the U.S. Population with One or More Tattoos, by Age, Sex, and Race/Ethnicity, 2003 and 2012

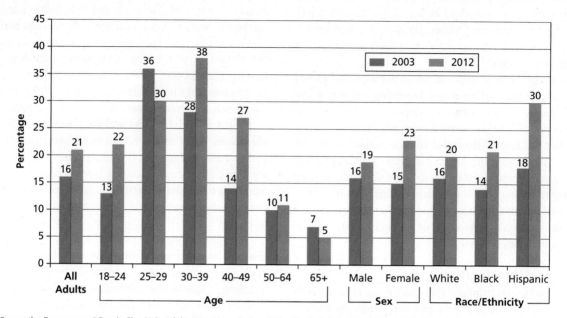

SOURCE: Samantha Braverman, "One in Five U.S. Adults Now Has a Tattoo." The Harris Poll ® #22, February 23, 2012. Harris Interactive (http://www .harrisinteractive.com/NewsRoom/HarrisPolls/tabid/447/mid/1508/articleId/970/ctl/ReadCustom%20Default/Default.aspx).

star athletes adorned, if not covered, with tattoos. Historically associated with men, body modifications now seem to be much more common among women (Botz-Bornstein 2013; Laumann and Derick 2006). Parents seem less likely to reject the idea of tattoos on their children. They may even have tattoos themselves, though perhaps concealed most of the time by clothing.

Body modification is now in fashion and is itself a fashion statement. Figure 13.2 shows the percentages of U.S. adults with one or more tattoos, grouped by age, sex, and race/ethnicity. In 2012, one in five adults had at least one tattoo (21 percent), an increase of 5 percentage points from 2003. Adults ages 30–39 are most likely to have a tattoo (38 percent), compared to those both younger (30 percent of those 25–29 and 22 percent of those 18–24) and older (27 percent of those 40–49, 11 percent of those 50–64, and just 5 percent of those 65 and older). Women are now more likely than men to have a tattoo (23 percent versus 19 percent). The proportion of Hispanics with at least one tattoo is at 30 percent, an increase of 12 percentage points since 2003. In comparison, 21 percent of blacks and 20 percent of whites report having a tattoo.

Body modification reflects the increase in reflexivity. Ever-greater reflexivity is required with each succeeding decision about which new form or style of body modification to have. Among the issues to be decided are whether the modification—say, a new tattoo—should be visible, where it should be placed, and how traditional or creative

and unique it should be. Furthermore, a variety of different tastes in tattooing have emerged, many of which are gendered (Anastasia 2010; Atkinson 2003), raced, and classed (Santos 2009).

A study of tattooed Mexican American women in Los Angeles revealed that some preferred symbolically feminine images, such as flowers, for their tattoos, while others preferred images that reflected their heritage, such as the Mexican flag (Santos 2009). Men tend to get tattoos that reinforce conventional ideas of masculinity, while women favor symbols that challenge or reinforce conventional ideas of femininity (Kang and Jones 2007). Gang members tend to prefer tattoos that identify them as such and that have autobiographical elements. Bikers often want tattoos that not only distinguish them from the general population but also tend to intimidate or frighten people. Collectors of tattoos are likely to prefer personalized and highly distinctive designs (Vail 1999). Various groups also gain status for different types of tattoos. For example, a full-back tattoo, a "back piece," is highly valued in artistic circles.

As tattoos have grown more mainstream and even common among some groups, those originally drawn to them have sought other ways of distinguishing their bodies from those of others. Many have been drawn to piercings of various types (Schorzman et al. 2007). Most popular are tongue and eyebrow piercings. However, as those, too, have become more common, more people are piercing other parts of the body, even the genitals, and are getting more body piercings in general.

Different kinds of work involve different levels of danger. More people are killed in construction in the United States than in any other kind of work. Could you envision taking such risks in your career?

Corbis

ASK YOURSELF

Thinking back on the definition of deviance, can you identify body modifications that you think are deviant, if any? What about modifications others might see as deviant that are normal to you? What makes the difference between these two categories?

RISKY BEHAVIOR

Ulrich Beck ([1986] 1992) argues that we live in a "risk society." Risk has become a central concern in sociology, including the way in which it relates to the body and to health. Interestingly, this meshes well with Foucault's ideas on limit experiences, since it is in such experiences that risks are greatest. Indeed, it is the risks that draw at least some people to these experiences (Lupton 2007).

People take a wide range of risks that have the potential to jeopardize their health. On the one hand, there are the things people do *not* do, such as see their physicians, have regular medical checkups, and take prescribed medicines. Another example is the failure, or refusal, to be vaccinated against various diseases. This was made clear in the recent outbreak of measles in the United States caused, at least in part, by the refusal of some parents to have their children vaccinated (Grady 2015).

On the other hand, people engage in many behaviors that they know pose health risks; cigarette smoking is at, or near, the top of the list. Other examples include the following:

- Taking illegal drugs, especially those that are addictive.

- Drinking alcohol to excess or driving (or boating) under the influence of alcohol.

- Consuming energy drinks such as Red Bull and 5-Hour Energy. Among the symptoms associated with these drinks are anxiety, irregular heartbeat, and even heart attacks (Meier 2013).

- Having unprotected sex, especially with multiple partners. Engaging in unprotected sex has been linked to other risky behaviors, such as drug and alcohol abuse.

- Overeating, allowing oneself to become obese, and staying that way. The overwhelming evidence linking obesity to various illnesses makes it clear that this is a risky behavior.

- Talking on cell phones and texting while driving. Engaging in these behaviors increases the risk of having an accident (see, e.g., Caird et al. 2014).

In some cases, the nature of work is risky. One example is the exposure to radiation risked by nuclear weapons workers, which can make them ill and perhaps kill them (Cable, Shriver, and Mix 2008). Of course, there are many occupations, such as coal mining (Chen and Zorigt 2013), that carry with them a variety of health risks. Figure 13.3 shows the total number of fatal work injuries and the fatal work injury rate by industry. In 2013, construction workers accounted for the most fatalities (796), with transportation and warehousing second with 687 fatalities. The agriculture, forestry, fishing, and hunting industries had the highest injury rate at 22.2 fatalities per 100,000 full-time workers. Mining, quarrying, and oil and gas extraction also had a high fatal work injury rate, with 12.3 deaths per 100,000.

There is, however, another side to engaging in risky behavior. It may well be that taking some risks makes some people happier and mentally, and perhaps even physically, healthier. This connection may help account for the growing interest in extreme sports such as surfing and snowboarding.

THE SOCIOLOGY OF HEALTH AND MEDICINE

Medical sociology is concerned with the "social causes and consequences of health and illness" (Cockerham 2007: 2932; 2012). Social factors are also deeply involved in the delivery of health care. Medical sociology addresses a wide variety of specific issues, including the following:

- Racial/ethnic differences in health care

- The basic causes of health inequalities by social class, gender, and race/ethnicity

- The linkage between stress and health

- The relationships between patients and health care providers

FIGURE 13.3 • Number and Rate of Fatal Occupational Injuries, by Industry Sector, 2013

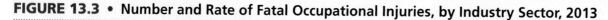

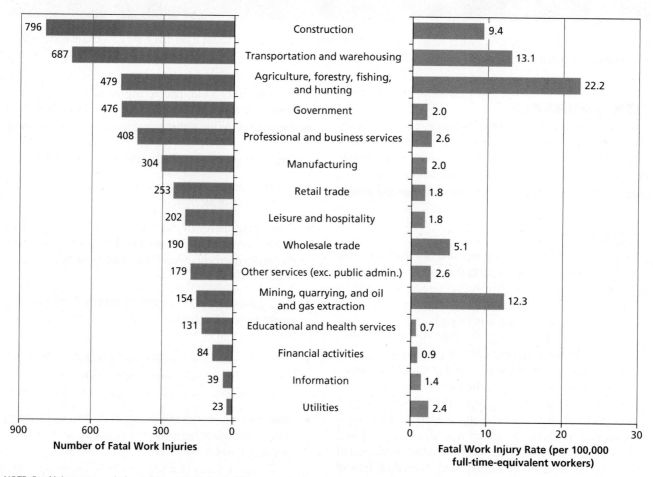

NOTE: Fatal injury rates exclude workers under the age of 16 years, volunteers, and resident military.

SOURCE: Data from U.S. Department of Labor, Bureau of Labor Statistics, 2014 (http://www.bls.gov/iif/oshwc/cfoi/cfch0012.pdf).

FIGURE 13.4 • Percentage of Women among Medical Student Graduates in the United States, 1966–2011

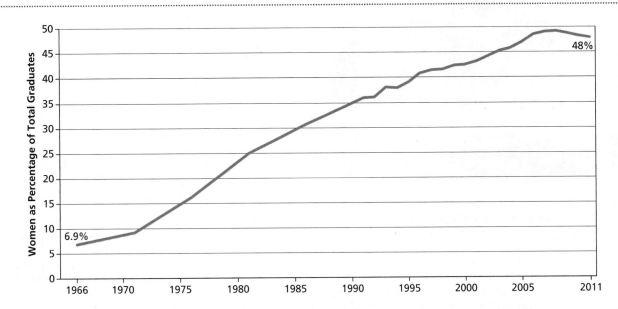

SOURCE: Data from the Association of American Medical Colleges (https://www.aamc.org/download/170248/data/2010_table1.pdf).

- The increasing use of advanced medical technology

- The astronomical and spiraling cost of medical care

- The changing nature of the medical profession (Hankin and Wright 2010)

THE MEDICAL PROFESSION

In the mid-twentieth century, a great deal of power was accorded to the health care system and especially to the medical profession, the key player in that system. Physicians exercised significant power over virtually everyone else involved in the health care system—nurses, hospital administrators, and so on (Hafferty and Castellani 2011). They also gained and retained great power over birth and death. This was an era in which the professions of medicine, law, and other fields not only exercised great power but also acquired great autonomy. In fact, a **profession** is distinguished from other occupations mainly by its high level of power and considerable autonomy. Other characteristics often associated with the professions are advanced education, mastery of knowledge and skills, the need to be licensed, and high prestige (Young and Muller 2014).

Historically, physicians in the United States have been disproportionately male (and white). However, that profile has changed dramatically. For example, women earned only 6.9 percent of medical degrees in 1966, but by 2011 they earned 48 percent of those degrees (Figure 13.4; Williams, Pecenco, and Blair-Loy 2013). However, white male physicians' starting salaries are consistently higher than those of

their female counterparts. In fact, female physicians' 2008 starting salaries were about the same as those of male physicians in 1999. And women earn less than men in every medical specialty, including those they dominate, such as pediatrics, where they earn only 66 percent of what male pediatricians earn.

The professions generally, and the medical profession in particular, continue to enjoy considerable power, autonomy, and high status. However, in the last several decades the professions have been characterized by a process of **deprofessionalization**. That is, their power and autonomy, as well as their high status and associated wealth, have declined, at least relative to the exalted position they once held (Brooks 2011; Epstein 2014). A variety of factors are involved in the declining power of the medical profession, especially the increasing power of patients, third-party payers such as the government through Medicare and Medicaid, and the pharmaceutical industry. However, while the medical profession is weaker than it once was, it remains a powerful force in the practice of medicine and in the larger society; the medical profession has proven quite resilient (Timmermans and Oh 2010).

How do we account for the deprofessionalization of physicians? First, they simply had acquired too much power a half century ago to be able to sustain it at that level for very long. Second, the public, which had granted (or at least ceded to) the medical profession that power and autonomy, came to question the medical profession. One basis of this increasing doubt was a growing awareness of the extraordinary wealth and power acquired by many physicians. Another was the

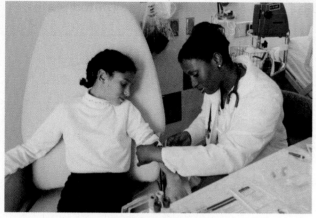

While many men have entered the nursing profession in recent years, nursing is still seen as a female occupation. Why?

revelation of medical malpractice, which demonstrated that physicians do not always adhere to their own code of ethics (Ocloo 2010). The growth in medical malpractice lawsuits was aided, if not instigated, by the other major profession, law, which reaped great economic rewards from these suits. Third, the government came to exert more power over the medical profession through, for example, Medicare and Medicaid. Fourth, patients became much more active and aggressive consumers of physician services as well as of other aspects of the medical system. Fifth, and perhaps most important, private health insurance companies like UnitedHealthcare became the most powerful players in the medical care system. Among other things, the insurance companies squeezed physicians' income by reimbursing them for office visits and medical services at much lower rates than the amounts billed.

Of course, there are many other kinds of workers in the health care system—most notably nurses (Riska 2007). Historically, nurses were unable to achieve full professional status. Nursing was often thought of as a semiprofession (Etzioni 1969). It lacked anything approaching the power, status, income, and autonomy of the medical profession. Much of this failure had to do with the enormous power wielded by physicians and their desire to keep occupations that had the potential to compete with theirs in a subordinate position (Ocloo 2010). However, a more important factor was the fact that the occupation of nursing was—and still is—dominated by females (Apesoa-Varano 2007: 250–253). Males in powerful positions were generally opposed to according professional status to occupations dominated by women. Nevertheless, doctors have come to rely heavily on nurses because nurses engage in, among many other things, "emotion work," or the emotional maintenance of patients (Lorber and Moore 2002; Rees 2013). This reliance on nurses is reinforced by the fact that, historically, "most people believed that caring came naturally to women, and this belief continues to be widely held to this day" (Weitz 2013: 363).

The result has been that while physicians have almost all of the formal power, nurses often have a great deal of informal power over the day-to-day decisions and operation of hospitals and doctors' offices.

WEAKNESSES IN THE U.S. HEALTH CARE SYSTEM

There has been a broad consensus that the U.S. system of health care is badly flawed, and it remains to be seen whether it will improve substantially as a result of the changes associated with the Affordable Care Act (Galston, Kull, and Ramsay 2009). One major problem is high costs. In 2013 health care spending in the United States reached $2.9 trillion, almost $9,255 per person (Centers for Medicare and Medicaid Services 2013).

The United States spent almost 17 percent of its gross domestic product on health care in 2012—the highest percentage among OECD (Organisation for Economic Co-operation and Development) countries by a considerable margin (see Figure 13.5). In percentage terms, the United States spends more on health care than any other country in the world (World Bank 2014c).

Costs of health insurance are rising rapidly. Among the reasons for the high cost of American medicine are

- the American love affair with expensive advanced medical technologies like magnetic resonance imaging (MRI);

- the profit motive at the base of decisions by for-profit hospitals, large medical equipment and pharmaceutical manufacturers, and physicians in private practice;

- these entities' use of lobbyists in Washington to resist efforts to cut costs and reduce profits;

- the cultural notion that Americans have a right to the best health care possible;

- an aging population that spends more proportionately on health care than other age groups; and

- the large numbers of well-off Americans who drive up costs for all because they are willing to spend almost anything to remain healthy or to recover from illness.

In spite of spending more than almost any other country absolutely and per capita, the U.S. health care system fares poorly in comparison to the health care systems in other countries. Life expectancy in the United States is among the lowest of the high-income nations in the world (Woolf and Aron 2013). More broadly, the United States ranks 42nd in the world in terms of life expectancy (Central Intelligence Agency 2014). Infant mortality is higher in the United States than in most other industrialized countries. Tens of thousands of Americans die each year because of a lack of medical care (Wilper et al. 2009).

FIGURE 13.5 • Total Expenditures on Health as a Percentage of Gross Domestic Product, OECD Countries, 2012

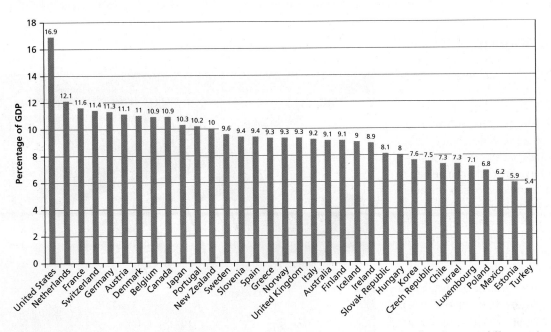

SOURCE: Data from OECD Health Statistics 2014, Health: Key tables from OECD, ISSN 2075-8480, © OECD 2014 (http://www.oecd-ilibrary.org/socialissues-migration-health/total-expenditure-on-health_20758480-table1); (http://www.oecd.org/unitedstates/Briefing-Note-UNITED-STATES-2014.pdf).

ASK YOURSELF

Why does the U.S. health care system achieve such comparatively low-quality outcomes, considering the huge financial costs it imposes on U.S. society? Why do Americans accept such poor-quality health care? What might be standing in the way of Americans' receiving the level of care experienced by citizens of other industrialized societies? What can be done to remedy this situation?

Inequalities in U.S. Health Care

There are great inequalities in the American health care system. The well-off in the United States can afford any medical care they wish and are even able to purchase expensive "Cadillac" health insurance policies that pay a large proportion of medical costs. In contrast, even with the Affordable Care Act, millions of Americans have no health insurance, and many others are underinsured.

The inequalities in health and health care that exist in the United States are unjust, artificial, undesirable, and likely avoidable (Lahelma 2007, forthcoming). Among the major inequalities are those based on social class, race, and gender.

Social Class and Health. There is a largely constant relationship between social class and health. That is, the lower one's social class, the poorer one's health is likely to be (Elo 2009; Warren and Hernandez 2007). This relationship holds across countries (although there are variations from country to country) and over time. In fact, inequalities based on social class have generally increased over the years.

There are a number of causes of social class differences in health (Lahelma 2007). First, early differences among children may have long-lasting health consequences. Living in poverty can contribute to ill health in childhood and therefore later in life (Duncan, Ziol-Guest, and Kalil 2010). Second, conditions in the adult years also affect health. Contributors to poor physical and mental health among adults include poor living conditions, especially those associated with living in unhealthy urban neighborhoods (Cockerham 2012); working lives that are unrewarding economically and psychologically; and high levels of stress. Third, a variety of health-related behaviors contribute to inequalities in health. These include the greater likelihood that those in the lower classes will use illegal drugs, smoke (see below), drink to excess, and be obese as a result of poor eating habits and lack of exercise. Finally, the presence or absence of health care in general, and high-quality health care in particular, can play a huge role in health inequalities.

A good example of the relationship between social class and health is seen in the adverse health consequences associated with smoking (Marmot 2005). In the 1950s, those in the upper social classes were more likely

Medical Tourism

Rapidly growing numbers of people, especially from the United States and other developed counties, are engaging in medical tourism. That is, they travel to other, usually less developed, countries for medical care, often nonemergency surgery. Such care can be had at a fraction of the cost of similar care in more developed countries. In addition, the quality of that care is deemed by many to be as good as or better than the quality obtainable at home (Turner 2007). Medical tourism is also attractive because such trips can be combined with vacations easily paid for with the savings associated with overseas medical care. Thailand, for example, is now a major tourist destination both because of its affordable, high-quality health care and because of its weather and sites of interest. For similar reasons, Mexico is another favorite destination for medical tourism (Medina 2012). With the opening of relations between the United States and Cuba, and the latter's reputation for high-quality, low-cost health services, we can expect a dramatic increase in American medical tourists heading to Cuba in the next few years (Neuman 2015).

Medical tourism is a good illustration of both globalization and the increasing degree to which medical treatment is seen as a form of consumption. From a global perspective, people increasingly flow around the world in search of medical treatment. In addition, medical knowledge, associated advanced technologies, and medical professionals flow around the world and are therefore available in an increasing number of locales. From the

This is a waiting room at a hospital in Chennai, India, that caters to medical tourists. To save money, would you travel to such a location to deal with a major health problem? Would you do so if you couldn't afford treatment in the United States?

point of view of consumption, medical treatment is increasingly seen as a service to be consumed as cheaply (assuming high quality) and in as pleasant a locale as possible. It is not unusual for less developed countries and the medical facilities associated with them to market themselves as destinations for medical tourists. For example, Argentina promotes itself as a destination for cosmetic surgery (Viladrich and Baron-Faust 2014).

It is primarily the well-to-do from developed countries who are able to avail themselves of these medical services and the associated vacation opportunities. And only the wealthy from less developed countries can afford to travel to developed countries for medical care

and pay the high costs associated with it. Medical tourism also underscores the stratification in the destination countries in that the quality of care, the technologies used, and the state-of-the-art facilities are likely to be out of reach of most of those native to those countries (Buzinde and Yarnal 2012).

Think About it

If being treated for a serious medical problem in the United States would leave you with debt that would take years to repay, would you consider leaving the country for treatment? Would you go to another country for treatment if you simply wanted to save some money?

than those in the lower classes to be smokers. This difference was due, in part, to the the movies, which glamorized smoking, associating it with travel and romance (Kimmel 2012). However, by the 1960s those in the lower social classes were more likely to smoke. It was during this

period that medical knowledge about the adverse health effects of smoking became better known and publicized. While that knowledge was disseminated quickly in the upper classes, it had a much harder time working its way to and through the lower classes (Phelan et al. 2004: 269;

Phelan, Link, and Tehranifar 2010). A key factor here was the lower educational level among members of the lower classes, who thus had less ability to access and understand the research and data available on the negative effects of smoking (Layte and Whelan 2009). In any case, to this day the lower classes suffer much more from the ill effects of smoking than do the upper classes.

Race and Health. The relationship between race and health is closely related to that between social class and health. In the United States, for example, whites are more likely to be in the middle and upper classes, while blacks and Hispanics are disproportionately in the lower classes. Overall, whites tend to have better health than blacks (and Hispanics). As a result, blacks have a life expectancy 4.8 years *shorter* than that of whites (Centers for Disease Control and Prevention 2011; Olshansky et al. 2012). Why do blacks have poorer health than whites? Racism, both today and as a legacy of the past, plays a major role. Given the history of experiments on black women's bodies during slavery, as well as notoriously unethical clinical trials such as the Tuskegee experiments (see Chapter 2), many black women and men have great distrust of the American medical system because of what they see as its practice of medical racism (Westergaard et al. 2014). Blacks continue to have great difficulty getting the education they need to gain higher-status occupations and the higher incomes associated with them (U.S. Census Bureau 2011a, 2011b). Even with such education, they may still be unable to obtain those jobs. As a result, they remain in the working class and are less likely to have the best health insurance, or they may have none at all. They are also less likely to have the money to visit health care professionals, at least on a regular basis. The health care they do get from hospital emergency rooms, public hospitals, or more marginal physicians is likely to be inferior.

Blacks are also more likely to be poorly treated, or even mistreated, by the health care system (Perloff et al. 2006; Quach et al. 2012; Wasserman, Flannery, and Clair 2007), even if they are suffering from life-threatening diseases such as cancer (Merluzzi et al. 2014). As a result, they are likely to underutilize that system, to not utilize it at all, or to use alternative medicines (such as folk and faith healers). They are also likely to be put off by the underrepresentation of blacks in high-status health care positions and occupations—only about 3.8 percent of physicians are black (Boukus, Cassil, and O'Malley 2009).

Working-class and lower-middle-class blacks are more likely to be relegated to neighborhoods and conditions that adversely affect their health. Examples include living near waste dumps where the land, air, and water are contaminated and in apartments or houses with lead-based paint that poses a health risk, especially to young children (Crowder and Downey 2010). And stress associated with racism throughout the life course increases the mortality rates of black adults and infants (David and Collins 2014; Nuru-Jeter et al. 2009).

It is possible, even likely, that health conditions began to improve for blacks and other racial minorities in 2014, when the Affordable Care Act went into effect—a topic that will be discussed in more detail later in the chapter. As a result of that act, the U.S. Department of Health and Human Services (2014) has a plan to reduce racial and ethnic health disparities. Also pointing in the direction of such improvement is the fact that unless researchers receive a special dispensation, research funded by the National Institutes of Health must now include proportionate numbers of racial minorities. In part, this is a result of outcries from sociologists, minority activists, and others (Epstein 2009). Knowing more about the health problems of blacks should lead to improved prevention and treatment.

ASK YOURSELF

What could social institutions like schools, employers, the insurance industry, the medical profession, and local governments do to reduce the racial disparities in health we observe in the United States? What costs would such efforts incur, and who is likely to bear them? Does anyone benefit from these health disparities? If so, who, and how?

Gender and Health. On the surface, inequality in health does not appear to be a problem that afflicts females, since their life expectancy throughout the Western world exceeds that of males by a significant margin. However, as we saw in Chapter 9, while women live longer, there is a widespread view that they have poorer health than men during their lifetimes (Shinberg 2007).

A good example of an area in which women *are* disadvantaged in comparison to men is coronary heart disease. Men are more likely than women to have this disease, but the gap is narrowing as more women are smoking—a major risk factor in heart disease. Heart disease is the leading killer of *both* men and women. Medical care helps in the prevention and treatment of coronary heart disease, but it has reduced the disease more for men than for women. Doctors are less likely to give women with coronary symptoms close attention and the needed diagnostic tests (Adams et al. 2008; Ayanian and Epstein 1991). Women are more likely not to get treatment until the disease is well advanced. They are also more likely to have emergency surgery for it. Less is known about heart disease in women because in the past epidemiological studies and clinical trials tended not to include female subjects. Even though the disease is somewhat different in women and men, the medical profession has simply treated women based on the findings from research on men.

Coronary heart disease is related to stress, and women appear to experience more stress. This is largely because they are less likely than men to be in control of the settings in which they find themselves. At work, they are more likely to be in lower-status jobs that give them less control over what they do as well as offer less security and fewer financial rewards. Many women who work outside the home have the additional stress of having to continue to handle household responsibilities, including child rearing (see Chapter 9).

Women have experienced the medicalization of aspects of their lives that are specific to them. **Medicalization** is the process of labeling and defining as medical problems aspects of life that were not previously so labeled and defined. It also involves a tendency to exaggerate the ability of medicine to deal with certain phenomena or syndromes (Conrad 1986; Conrad, Mackie, and Mehrota 2010; Conrad and Schneider 1980). Medicalization is particularly clear in the case of childbirth, a natural process now defined as a medical problem that can be dealt with only by physicians in hospital settings. Perhaps the most infamous example of an aspect of life that was once medicalized is the female orgasm. This was long seen not as a natural aspect of female sexuality but rather as an element of "hysterical" disease that required medical attention (Maines 2001). Many other aspects of women's health have been medicalized in recent years, including premenstrual syndrome (PMS), renamed premenstrual dysphoric disorder (PMDD) and argued to affect potentially as many as 85 million menstruating women (Gehlert et al. 2009). Infertility and menopause have also been medicalized. Overall, women receive too little medical attention in some crucial areas (such as coronary care) and too much medical attention in others (such as reproductive health).

Health Care Reform in the United States

In the wake of the kinds of problems discussed above, especially those that relate to social class differences, new health care legislation—the Patient Protection and Affordable Care Act of 2010 ("Obamacare")—was enacted into law. The law has been fully in effect since 2014, although it continues to be contested by Republicans. In early 2015 the Affordable Care Act was threatened by a legal challenge in the U.S. Supreme Court, but in mid-2015 the Court turned aside this challenge, and the law continues in force. Some key aspects of the law are as follows:

- Health insurance coverage was expected to be extended to an additional 32 million people by 2014, although the Congressional Budget Office later reduced the likely number of additions to 26 million people.

- It is estimated that by 2019, approximately 95 percent of Americans will have health insurance, although that estimate may be reduced as well.

- Medicaid coverage has been expanded for the poor, allowing them an income of up to 133 percent of the federal poverty line (se Chapter 7).

- Americans are required to have health insurance. If they do not, they must pay a tax penalty of up to 2.5 percent of their income.

- Employers with more than 50 employees are required to provide health insurance for them or be fined.

- Health insurance companies are not allowed to reject applicants because they have preexisting conditions, to charge excessive rates, or to cancel policies after policyholders become sick (Cockerham 2012).

CONSUMERISM AND HEALTH CARE

Historically, thinking about health care involved a tendency to focus on the "producers" of health care, especially physicians, nurses, other health care workers, hospitals, and government agencies. While much attention continues to be paid to all of those producers of health care, the focus began to shift several decades ago in the direction of the consumers of that care. Larger numbers of patients began to realize that they did not simply have to accept what was offered to them by physicians, hospitals, and others. They came to the recognition that they were consumers of those services in much the same way they were consumers of many other services (and goods).

This was due, in part, to the deprofessionalization of physicians. As physicians came to be seen as less powerful professionals, it was increasingly easy for patients to question them. At the same time, the questioning furthered physicians' decline in status and power. The entry of consumerism into medicine meant that more patients began to shop around for physicians and to question doctors' diagnoses and treatment recommendations.

The best example of increasing consumerism in contemporary medicine is associated with pharmaceutical companies' decision to improve sales of prescription drugs through direct appeals to consumers using catchy advertisements in newspapers and magazines, online, and on television. The avalanche started in 1997 when the U.S. Food and Drug Administration began to relax restrictions on direct-to-consumer prescription drug advertisements. Since that time, the pharmaceutical companies have increasingly used direct-to-consumer advertising to supplement their marketing to physicians through advertisements in medical journals, salespeople, and free samples. Direct marketing targets the ultimate consumer of pharmaceuticals—the patient (Morgan 2007). The irony is that, in general, patients cannot go out and obtain the advertised drugs on their own; they need prescriptions from their physicians. Thus, the idea is to motivate patients to ask their doctors for, and in some cases demand, the desired prescriptions. The evidence is that this works,

Reuters

What are some of the arguments for and against the Affordable Care Act? Which arguments are most persuasive for you?

and as a result the pharmaceutical companies have become increasingly ubiquitous presences in the media (e.g., Singer 2009). For example, the marketing of a vaccine for the human papilloma virus, a sexually transmitted infection, encouraged young women to be vaccinated (Manika, Ball, and Stout 2014).

We are all familiar with endless advertisements for the leading and most profitable prescription drugs, such as Lipitor (to treat high cholesterol), Plavix (a blood thinner), Nexium (for heartburn), and Advair (an asthma inhaler), and especially the seemingly ubiquitous advertisements for drugs that treat erectile dysfunction, especially Viagra and Cialis. All of these ads suggest, either directly or indirectly, that viewers ask their physicians to prescribe these medications for them.

ASK YOURSELF

Overall, do you think the shift to consumerism is a positive or a negative development for patients? Why? What about for the medical profession? Why? Would a structural-functionalist see medical consumerism as functional for society? Why or why not?

THE INTERNET AND THE CONSUMPTION OF HEALTH CARE

The Internet has become implicated in the consumption of health care (e-health) in various ways. For example, it is a vast resource for finding providers, by specialty, on the local, national, and even global levels. It is also a source of lots of information about them. One can get rankings of health care providers as well as information from previous patients about their experiences and recommendations. There is also a wealth of information and evaluation available online about pharmaceuticals, medical technologies, and alternative treatments.

The increasing amount of health care–related data of all sorts on the Internet allows people to become much more knowledgeable consumers of health care services and products. For example, there are sites such as Health in Reach (www.healthinreach.com) and Healthcare Bluebook (https://healthcarebluebook.com) where people can compare prices on everything from flu vaccines and annual physicals to mastectomies and bowel surgeries. Health insurance companies are also increasingly providing information online about benefits, stating, for example, what they pay out for office visits and various medical procedures. However, it is often difficult for consumer-patients to compare medical procedures because there are no standard terminological codes, available information is highly jargonistic, and the same procedure may have a dozen different prices at the same hospital because of separate negotiations with different health insurers.

The Internet has become a global source of medical information. One specific example is the Clearinghouse on Male Circumcision for HIV Prevention (www.malecircumcision.org), a website devoted to providing information about, and debunking the myths related to, circumcision and HIV/AIDS (McNeil 2009). The Internet also opens a global range of views, possibilities, and alternatives to the consumers of medical goods and services. Consumers are better able to make themselves aware of alternatives available elsewhere in the world, obtain information and advice about them, and find ways of obtaining them.

The net result of the above is that a patient who uses online resources can become a much more sophisticated, knowledgeable, and independent consumer of medical services and products. For example, consumers can obtain many products and services legally or illegally—and often more inexpensively—through the Internet without going through intermediaries associated with the health care system (Krauss 2004; Napoli 1999). Among the problems associated with using the Internet for health-related consumption is the possibility of getting counterfeit, and perhaps ineffective, medications, as well as bogus services and information of various types (Lavorgna 2015). While consumers may become more sophisticated by exploring medical information on the Internet, they are often not trained in medicine and therefore are likely to be unable to understand fully the advantages and disadvantages of what is available. As a result, they run the risk of being duped in various ways.

The Internet is also an increasingly important resource for health care providers, who can use it to access information on new research, pharmaceuticals, and technologies.

GLOBALIZATION AND HEALTH

A nearly endless array of issues could be discussed under the heading of globalization and health (Linn and Wilson 2012). We can do little more than touch on a few of them in this section.

GROWING GLOBAL INEQUALITY

While globalization has been associated with increased aggregate life expectancy, it also has tended to widen global disparities in health (Hashemian and Yach 2007; McMichael 2013). Women and children tend to be the most vulnerable populations globally, due to such things as economic inequality (Goli, Doshi, and Perianayagam 2013) and poor access to health care (Fillipi et al. 2006). As noted in Chapter 7, people in poor nations tend to have poorer health as a result of limited access to health care services, poor education, inadequate sanitation, and inadequate nutrition and housing. In turn, poor health tends to limit economic growth in those nations, mainly by adversely affecting productivity. Developing countries have a disproportionate share of mortality and morbidity, much of which could be prevented inexpensively and treated effectively if the money were available.

For the reasons mentioned above, and others, there is a significant gap in life expectancy between developed and less developed, high- and low-income, countries. Figure 13.6 shows life expectancy at birth for select countries

around the world. Note the 35-year difference in life expectancy between highly developed Japan at the top of the list and the far less developed Chad at the bottom. The greatest increases in life expectancy have occurred in developing countries such as Brazil, Egypt, and Malaysia, which have tended to be increasingly and successfully involved in economic globalization. However, for most of the rest, especially the least developed, low-income countries in the Global South (such as Chad, South Africa, and Afghanistan), globalization has been accompanied by a decline in economic growth, an increase in poverty, and, as a result, a decline in health.

Disease

The vast majority of not only acute but also chronic diseases occur at younger ages and in low- and middle-income countries. The rising cost of dealing with chronic diseases in developing countries adversely affects their ability to deal with acute infectious diseases. Of special importance from the point of view of globalization is the increasing global marketing of tobacco, alcohol, sugar, and fat—the latter two especially aimed at children—and the consequent global spread of the diseases associated with these products.

Malnutrition

As discussed in Chapter 7, countries in the Global South suffer disproportionately from hunger and malnutrition (Van de Poel et al. 2008). Roughly 850 million people there are affected by these problems, which are the result of inadequate, or totally unavailable, food supplies and poor and unbalanced diets. Dealing with hunger and malnutrition is especially important for children, because those who are underweight are likely, when they reach adulthood, to be less physically and intellectually productive and to experience more chronic illnesses and disabilities. This carries on across generations as the ability of such adults to provide adequate nutrition for their children is compromised.

Undernutrition is a form of malnutrition involving an inadequate intake of nutrients, including calories, vitamins, and minerals. The other form of malnutrition involves obesity, which is caused by an excessive intake of nutrients, especially calories. Developing countries now increasingly suffer from a "double nutritional burden," with some people not having enough to eat and others eating too much, especially of the wrong kinds of foods (e.g., foods that are high in fat and cholesterol) (Vogli et al. 2014). Although obesity is increasing in the less developed world, undernutrition remains the greatest problem there, particularly for mothers and children. Undernutrition creates difficulties that continue throughout the life cycle and is responsible for stunted growth, lower levels of schooling, lower productivity, and chronic diseases; undernourished women also give birth to low-weight infants. Undernutrition has also been linked to rapid weight gain and obesity among formerly underweight children (Serra-Majem and Ngo 2012).

FIGURE 13.6 • Life Expectancy at Birth among Select Countries, 2014

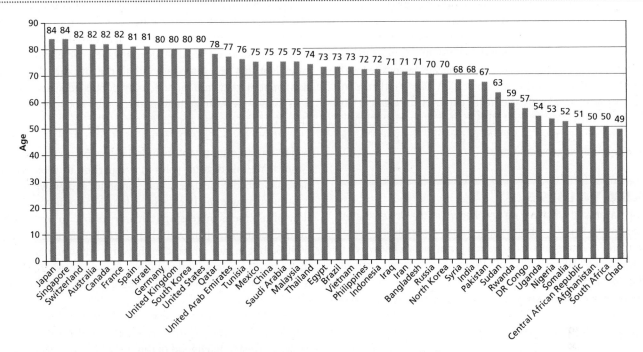

SOURCE: Data from (https://www.cia.gov/library/publications/the-world-factbook/rankorder/2102rank.html).

Undernutrition is a major problem in many parts of the world. Beyond the problems for those who are ill-fed, what are the negative effects for the societies in which they live?

Undernutrition is related to problems not only for individuals but also for societies as a whole. It leads to underdevelopment and tends to perpetuate poverty. Without adequate nutrition, the human capital needed for economic development cannot develop.

Food insecurity is an important cause of undernutrition. Such insecurity exists when people do not have sufficient access to safe and nutritious food—a condition necessary for leading a healthy and productive life. There are many causes of food insecurity, but one of the most important is a lack of adequate agricultural development. A number of global programs have been undertaken to help deal with this problem through the creation of community gardens, farmers' markets, agricultural diversification programs, and the like.

SMOKING

Smoking is an important cause of health problems around the world. In spite of those health problems, however, a highly profitable tobacco industry continues to be central to the global economy (Fulbrook 2007). According to a World Health Organization (2013) estimate, nearly 6 million people die each year from tobacco use, and unless there are dramatic changes, that number will rise to 8 million by 2030. It is also projected that 1 billion people will die in the twenty-first century from smoking-related diseases.

With the Western market for cigarettes shrinking because of growing awareness of the risks associated with smoking, the tobacco corporations have shifted their focus to Africa and Asia. India accounts for almost a third of the world's tobacco-related deaths. China is now the world's biggest market for cigarettes (Gu et al. 2009), with 1.7 trillion cigarettes smoked every year. The Chinese consume about 30 percent of the world's cigarettes, although China has about 20 percent of the world's population. Many Chinese appear to have little knowledge of the health hazards associated with smoking (World Health Organization 2010a). For their part, the Western powers are the major exporters of cigarettes to the rest of the world. The United States is the single largest exporter of cigarettes as well as of globally recognized cigarette advertisements and brands.

ASK YOURSELF

The hazards of smoking are well known in the United States. Should it be legal for tobacco companies to export their products to markets where such information is not widely known or is disregarded? Why or why not? What would a conflict/critical theorist say is happening here?

BORDERLESS DISEASES

Another negative aspect of globalization is the flow of borderless diseases (Ali 2012). While such diseases have become much more common in recent years, they are not a new phenomenon. Tuberculosis (TB) was known in ancient times. Today the World Health Organization estimates that more than a third of the world's population is infected with the cause of the disease—the TB bacillus (Linn and Wilson 2012). Sexually transmitted infections (STIs) of various types have long diffused globally. A specific example of the latter is syphilis, which has spread globally and continues to circulate, especially throughout a number of less developed countries. However, the roots of the disease were probably in Europe, from which it was spread by colonialism and military exploits.

Then there is the increasing prevalence of other borderless diseases, many of them relatively new. Examples include severe acute respiratory syndrome (SARS); bovine spongiform encephalopathy (BSE, or "mad cow disease"), which is often found in cattle and can cause a brain disease in humans (Ong 2007); avian flu; Ebola; and HIV/AIDS. The nature of these diseases and their spread, either in fact (HIV/AIDS, Ebola) or merely, at least so far, as a frightening possibility (avian flu), tells us a great deal about the nature and reality of globalization in the twenty-first century. The pathogens that cause these diseases flow, or have the potential to flow, readily throughout the globe.

Several factors help explain the great and increasing global mobility of borderless diseases. First, there is the increase in global travel and the increasing rapidity of that travel (Rosenthal 2007). Second, there is growing human migration and the ease with which people can cross national borders, often bringing with them diseases that are not

detected. Third, the expansion of massive urban areas such as Lagos, Nigeria, has created vast mixing bowls where large numbers of people in close and frequent proximity can easily infect one another. Until 2014, outbreaks of Ebola had been limited to relatively small African villages; the explosion of cases late that year was traceable to the fact that the virus had found its way into more densely populated areas. Figure 13.7 shows the African nations affected by Ebola. While the spread of the disease abated in early 2015, as of April 12, 2015, there had been 25,826 cases and 10,704 deaths worldwide, the vast majority of them in Liberia, Sierra Leone, and Guinea. Yet this disaster pales in comparison to what might have happened if the disease had spread to, and grown out of control in, a huge city like Lagos. A fourth factor in the global flow of disease is increasing human presence in previously untouched natural habitats. There, people can have contact with pathogens for which they have no immunity and that they can spread rapidly throughout the world (Ali 2012). It is believed that humans initially caught Ebola (and other diseases) from wild animals.

The flow of efforts to deal with these diseases must be equally global. That is, there is a need for global responses to the increasing likelihood of the spread of various diseases. However, some nations have proven unable or unwilling to respond adequately to this global need. For example, there has been widespread criticism of the slowness of the global response to Ebola and the relatively small amounts of money committed to fight the disease.

ASK YOURSELF

Could medical practitioners or governments have anticipated the possibility that germs and viruses might begin to flow more easily around the world, along with people, goods, and information? Communicable diseases have always existed, so why is their ability to travel globally of such concern? Does the Global North bear any particular responsibility for dealing with potential outbreaks? Why or why not?

HIV/AIDS

HIV/AIDS was first recognized in the United States in 1981 and has since been acknowledged as a scourge throughout not only the United States but also much of the world (Whiteside 2008, 2012). In 2013, it was estimated that 39 million people worldwide had died from AIDS since the first diagnosis. Another 35 million, many of whom will die from the disease, are living with AIDS. The numbers of people infected with HIV and living with AIDS vary widely around the globe. Table 13.2 shows that sub-Saharan Africa has been hit hardest, with 71 percent (24.7 million) of the world's HIV population living in that region. Of the 2.1 million people newly infected in 2013 around the world, 1.5 million live in sub-Saharan Africa.

FIGURE 13.7 • Ebola Outbreaks in Africa as of April 2015

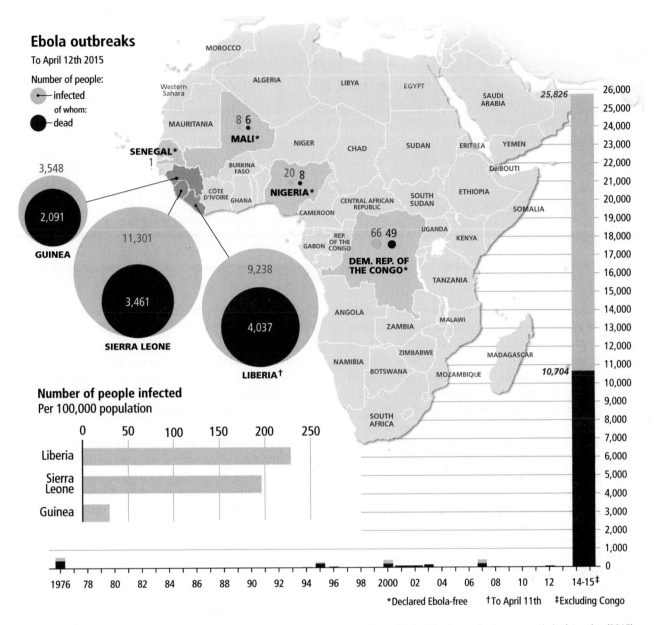

Ebola outbreaks

To April 12th 2015

Number of people:
- infected
- of whom:
- dead

Number of people infected
Per 100,000 population

SOURCES: The Economist (http://www.economist.com/blogs/graphicdetail/2015/02/ebola-graphics) © The Economist Newspaper Limited, London (2015); World Health Organization, United Nations (http://apps.who.int/ebola/en/ebola-situation-report/situation-reports/ebola-situation-report-18-february-2015).

About 1.9 million people live with HIV in Latin America and the Caribbean combined, including 106,000 newly infected in 2013. The Caribbean, with an adult HIV prevalence rate of 1.1 percent, is the second-hardest-hit region in the world, after sub-Saharan Africa. An estimated 4.8 million people are living with HIV in Asia and the Pacific. The huge population of this region means that even relatively low prevalence rates translate into large numbers of people infected with HIV.

HIV/AIDS cannot be contracted through casual contact with people who have the disease. The disease spreads only through intimate human contact with body fluids, especially through unprotected sex and intravenous drug use. Thus, in spite of the large numbers of people with AIDS, it is *not* an easy disease to contract. For instance, fellow passengers on an international flight will not contract AIDS simply because they sit next to, or talk with, a fellow passenger with the disease.

The spread of AIDS is linked to globalization, especially the increased global mobility associated with tourism (notably, sex tourism), the greater migration rates of workers, increased legal and illegal immigration, much higher rates of commercial and business travel, the movement (sometimes

TABLE 13.2 • HIV Prevalence and Incidence by Region, 2013

REGION	TOTAL NUMBER (% LIVING WITH HIV)	NEWLY INFECTED	ADULT PREVALENCE RATE (%)
Global total	35.0 million (100)	2.1 million	0.8
Sub-Saharan Africa	24.7 million (71)	1.5 million	4.7
Asia and the Pacific	4.8 million (14)	350,000	0.2
Western and Central Europe and North America	2.3 million (7)	88,000	0.3
Latin America	1.6 million (5)	94,000	0.4
Eastern Europe and Central Asia	1.1 million (3)	110,000	0.6
Caribbean	250,000 (<1)	12,000	1.1
Middle East and North Africa	230,000 (<1)	25,000	0.1

SOURCES: The Global HIV/AIDS Epidemic, December 1, 2014, Kaiser Family Foundation (http://kff.org/global-health-policy/fact-sheet/the-global-hivaids-epidemic/).

on a mass basis) of refugees, military interventions and the movement of military personnel, and so on. People who have the disease can travel great distances over a period of years without knowing they have been infected. They therefore have the ability to transmit the disease unknowingly to many others in widely scattered locales. When people with HIV/AIDS travel to other countries and have sexual contact with people there, they are likely to transmit the disease to at least some of them. Similarly, those without the disease can travel to nations where HIV/AIDS is prevalent, contract it, and then bring it back to their home country. In either case, the disease moves from region to region, country to country, and ultimately globally, carried by human vectors.

One well-known way in which HIV/AIDS has spread across the African continent is through truck drivers working their way from country to country. If they have the disease, they may infect those who live in areas that were previously free of the disease. The data on specific countries in the southern part of Africa are sobering. For example:

- As of 2008, about 19 percent of Swazis were HIV-positive. In the U.S. context, that would translate into 57 million infected Americans.

- Life expectancy in Swaziland was 54 years in 1980 and 58 in 1990, but fell to 40 in 2007. Most of the decline in life expectancy is traceable to HIV/AIDS and to the early age at which HIV/AIDS victims are likely to die.

- In South Africa, 180,000 people died from HIV/AIDS in 2000; by 2007, the number of deaths had risen to 350,000.

- It has been estimated that 6 million South Africans—about 13 percent of the population—will have perished from HIV/AIDS by 2015 (UNAIDS 2008; Whiteside 2012).

The disease, as well as the many burdens associated with it, is having an adverse effect on all aspects of social and economic life throughout Africa. Some observers predict the failure of African states and the complete economic collapse of some as a result of the spread of the disease. The economies of many African nations have already contracted as average life expectancy has declined and it has become harder to find healthy adults to perform basic tasks.

The prevalence of HIV/AIDS in sub-Saharan Africa is just one example of the greater vulnerability of the world's have-nots to this and many other borderless diseases. This is a question not just of economic marginality but also of social and political marginality. Compounding the problem is the fact that it is precisely this *most* vulnerable population that is *least* likely to have access to the high-quality health care and the very expensive drugs that can slow the disease for years, or even decades.

New Forms of Flu

In 2009 and 2010, the world witnessed an avian flu (H1N1) pandemic, but it proved to be a relatively mild form of the disease. Prior to that, there had been fear of a pandemic of a potentially far more deadly strain of avian flu. Because we live in a global age, the spread of the flu would be faster and more extensive than in earlier pandemics. However, it is also the case that the ability to deal with such a pandemic is enhanced as a result of globalization. For example, global monitoring has increased, and there is greater ability to get health workers and pharmaceuticals rapidly to the site of an outbreak.

Some flu subtypes can spread through casual human contact with an infected animal, but there is little evidence of human-to-human spread of the avian flu virus. The relatively small number of humans in the world who have gotten the disease, including the even smaller number who have died from it, contracted it through direct contact with infected birds. Those in less developed nations are more likely to have direct contact with birds—some literally live with their birds. In contrast, in the developed world relatively few people have direct contact with birds, and so contracting bird flu in this way is highly unlikely.

There is some fear, however, that the virus that causes bird flu might eventually transform itself into a strain that can be spread by casual human-to-human contact. This fear stems from the fact that viruses have taken this route before and caused global human pandemics such as the infamous "Spanish flu" of 1918–1920, which killed a half million people in the United States and tens of millions worldwide (Kolata 1999). Were this virus transformation to occur, the increased global mobility of people would lead to rapid spread of the disease.

GLOBALIZATION AND IMPROVEMENTS IN HEALTH AND HEALTH CARE

Globalization has also brought with it an array of developments that have improved, or at least should improve, the quality of health throughout the world. One example is the growth of global health-related organizations, such as the Red Cross and Médecins sans Frontières (Doctors without Borders) (Inoue and Drori 2006). Of course, as with much else about globalization, the effects have been uneven and affected by a variety of local circumstances.

Increasing interpersonal relations among and between various regions throughout the world means that positive developments in one part of the world are likely to find their way to most other parts of the world, and quite rapidly. In addition, there is a ready flow of new ideas associated with health and health care. In the era of the Internet and online medical journals, information about new medical developments flashes around the world virtually instantaneously. Of course, how those ideas are received and whether, and how quickly, they can be implemented vary enormously. There is great variability around the world in the number of professionals able to comprehend and utilize such information. Furthermore, the institutions in place in which such ideas can be implemented vary greatly. Thus, hospitals in developed countries would be able to implement changes to reduce the risks of hospital-based infections, but those in less developed countries would find such changes difficult or impossible because of the costs involved.

New medical products clearly flow around the world much more slowly than new ideas, but because of global improvements in transport, they are more mobile than ever before. Included under this heading would be pharmaceuticals of all types. Clearly, the superstars of the pharmaceutical industry are global phenomena. In fact, while North America (primarily the United States) accounted for about 41 percent of the $981 billion in pharmaceutical sales worldwide in 2013, sales in emerging markets are growing

A worker for Doctors without Borders helps children in South Sudan, where the World Health Organization hopes to carry out a massive vaccination campaign against cholera. What challenges does this effort face, given that unrest in that country has displaced almost a million people?

more rapidly than U.S. sales (Alazraki 2010; Herper and Kang 2006; Statista 2015). As new drugs are approved and come to be seen as effective, they are likely to flow around the world, especially to developed countries and to the elites in less developed countries.

Of course, the drugs that are most likely to be produced and distributed globally are those that are expected to be most profitable. Those are the drugs that address the health problems of the wealthier members of global society, such as hypertension, high cholesterol, arthritis, mental health problems, impotence, and hair loss. The well-to-do are most able to afford the diets that lead to high cholesterol, acid reflux, and heartburn, and they are therefore the likely consumers of Lipitor, Zocor, Nexium, and Prevacid. Because they produce the greatest earnings for pharmaceutical companies, these drugs are most likely to achieve global distribution.

Conversely, some kinds of drugs that might save many lives are not apt to be produced (Moran et al. 2009). Few, if any, pharmaceutical companies in the United States, Europe, and Japan devote significant research and development money to creating drugs that would help those in less developed countries who suffer from diseases such as sleeping sickness and malaria. Such drugs are unlikely to yield great profits because those who need them are mainly the poor in less developed countries. If the drugs are produced, their flow to those parts of the globe is likely to be minimal. Thus, as we have seen, Africa is a hotbed of many diseases, such as malaria, some of which kill millions of people each year. However, these are largely poor people in impoverished countries, and the major drug companies based primarily in the West and wealthy developed countries are little interested in doing the research and paying the start-up and production costs necessary to produce drugs that are not likely to be profitable and may even lose money. To be fair, we are beginning to see a glimmer of hope for drugs to treat sleeping sickness and malaria (Kennedy 2013; Willyard 2014). In the meantime, millions continue to die from these diseases.

There has been no vaccine for Ebola largely because, prior to 2014, there had been too few cases *and* because those infected were poor people from impoverished African countries. Now that we have seen tens of thousands of cases, and thousands have died, great progress seems to be taking place in the development of an Ebola vaccine. A cynic would also say that now that the developed countries have themselves had to deal with a few cases and have recognized at least the potential for some threat of an Ebola epidemic there, the drug companies have suddenly discovered the ability to test and create an Ebola vaccine at warp speed.

Similar points can be made about the flow of advanced medical technologies, including MRIs and CAT scans, throughout the world. These are extraordinarily expensive technologies found largely in the wealthy developed countries of the Global North. The machines are not only more likely to exist in these developed countries but also more likely to be used extensively there because patients, either on their own or because of health insurance, are able to afford the very expensive scans and tests associated with them. In contrast, relatively few of these technologies flow to less developed, Southern countries; they are used there less extensively; and there are relatively few trained people there capable of conducting the tests and interpreting the results (Debas 2010; World Health Organization 2010b).

In terms of networks of people, much the same picture emerges. Medical and health-related personnel in the North are tightly linked through an array of professional networks. As a result, personnel can move about within those networks. More important, the latest findings and developments in health and medicine are rapidly disseminated through those networks. The problem in the Global South is not only that fewer professionals are involved in these networks but also that the flow of new information to them is more limited (Godlee et al. 2004; Horton 2000). More important, even if they are able to get the information, they generally lack the resources and infrastructure to use it, or to use it adequately.

SUMMARY

In many ways, beauty has become a commodity that can be bought. The emphasis on beauty has also led to more attention to physical activity and its links to healthy bodies. Body modifications are an example of society's increase in reflexivity and have become more common. The explosion of sociological interest in the body can be traced to the work of Michel Foucault. This field is defined by a general focus on the relationship between the body and society and culture. It encompasses concerns such as the gendered body, sexuality, and bodily pain.

The medical profession has gone through a process of deprofessionalization, characterized by a decline in power and autonomy as well as of status and wealth among members. Unlike doctors, nurses have never been able to achieve full professional status.

Health inequalities in the United States are often linked with social class, race, and gender. The full impact of the Affordable Care Act remains unclear. Even with the law's full implementation, there is broad consensus that the U.S. health care system remains seriously flawed, with higher costs and lower outcomes than in the rest of the developed world.

Patients have become more active consumers in the health care system. For example, they use the Internet to locate doctors, shop for the lowest prices on procedures, read fellow patients' reviews, and become more knowledgeable about health and health care.

Global disparities in health and health care are tied to globalization. Individuals in the Global South suffer disproportionately from hunger and forms of malnutrition, including obesity and undernutrition. The spread of diseases such as HIV/AIDS and Ebola is linked to globalization and increased global mobility. The ability to implement new medical technologies and afford new treatments clearly varies by region, with the global South lagging far behind the global North.

REVIEW QUESTIONS

1. We live in an increasingly reflexive society with a heightened awareness of our bodies. According to Naomi Wolf, how does the beauty myth perpetuate such reflexivity?
2. How is risk-taking behavior related to Michel Foucault's idea of limit experiences? What satisfaction do people get from risk-taking behavior?
3. What are the pros and cons of our obsession with our appearance and the fitness of our bodies?
4. What are the characteristics of a profession? What factors can help explain why physicians have become increasingly deprofessionalized?
5. What are the weaknesses of the health care system in the United States? How are these weaknesses related to systems of stratification?
6. Explain the increasing medicalization of society. How has it affected women in particular?

7. How have the Internet and new social media technologies affected the consumption of health care? What are some of the disadvantages of having access to more information about health care?

8. In what ways are patients increasingly consumers of health care? How has this change affected the power of physicians?

9. How has globalization tended to widen global disparities in health care? What kinds of health problems are most likely to be found in the Global South? What could be done to avoid some of these problems?

10. What are the major borderless diseases? In what ways are they made worse by globalization? Can globalization also play a role in curing them, or at least in reducing their prevalence?

APPLYING THE SOCIOLOGICAL IMAGINATION

This chapter highlights the inequalities in U.S. health care and health care around the world. For this activity, compare the United States to two other countries—one from the Global North and one from the Global South—based on their health care spending and health outcomes (such as life expectancy and infant mortality). Use the Internet to locate data from the World Health Organization. What do the data suggest about health and health care in each of the countries? How is this reflective of global stratification? How could globalization be used to help change the outcomes in each of these countries?

KEY TERMS

deprofessionalization: The process whereby a profession's power and autonomy, as well as high status and great wealth, have declined, at least relative to the exalted position the profession once held. (p. 315)

food insecurity: Lack of sufficient access to safe and nutritious food. (p. 323)

medicalization: The process of labeling and defining as medical problems aspects of life that were not previously so labeled and defined. (p. 320)

medical sociology: A field concerned with the social causes and consequences of health and illness. (p. 314)

profession: An occupation distinguished from other occupations mainly by its power and considerable autonomy. (p. 315)

undernutrition: A form of malnutrition involving an inadequate intake of nutrients, including calories, vitamins, and minerals. (p. 322)

$SAGE edge™ edge.sagepub.com/ritzeressentials2e

SAGE edge offers a robust online environment featuring an impressive array of free tools and resources for review, study, and further exploration, keeping both instructors and students on the cutting edge of teaching and learning.

LEARNING OBJECTIVES	FOR FURTHER EXPLORATION AND APPLICATION
LO 13-1: Discuss sociological concepts that relate to the body, including sexuality, health and beauty, body modifications, and risky behaviors.	▶ Tattoos and Taboo ◉ The Teenage State of Mind: Stress and Appearance ⊜ South Korea: The Plastic Surgery Capital of the World
LO 13-2: Outline the issues studied in medical sociology, including the U.S. medical profession, the health care system and its weaknesses and inequities, and consumerism in health care.	▶ How Social Theories Relate to Medicine ◉ Controversial Fertility Treatment to Recharge Old Eggs ⊜ The Benefits of Hospice Care for Patients and Families
LO 13-3: Discuss the influence of globalization on health, illness and disease, and health care.	▶ Outsourcing Your Health Care ◉ The New Phenomenon of "Maternity Tourism" ⊜ The World Health Organization

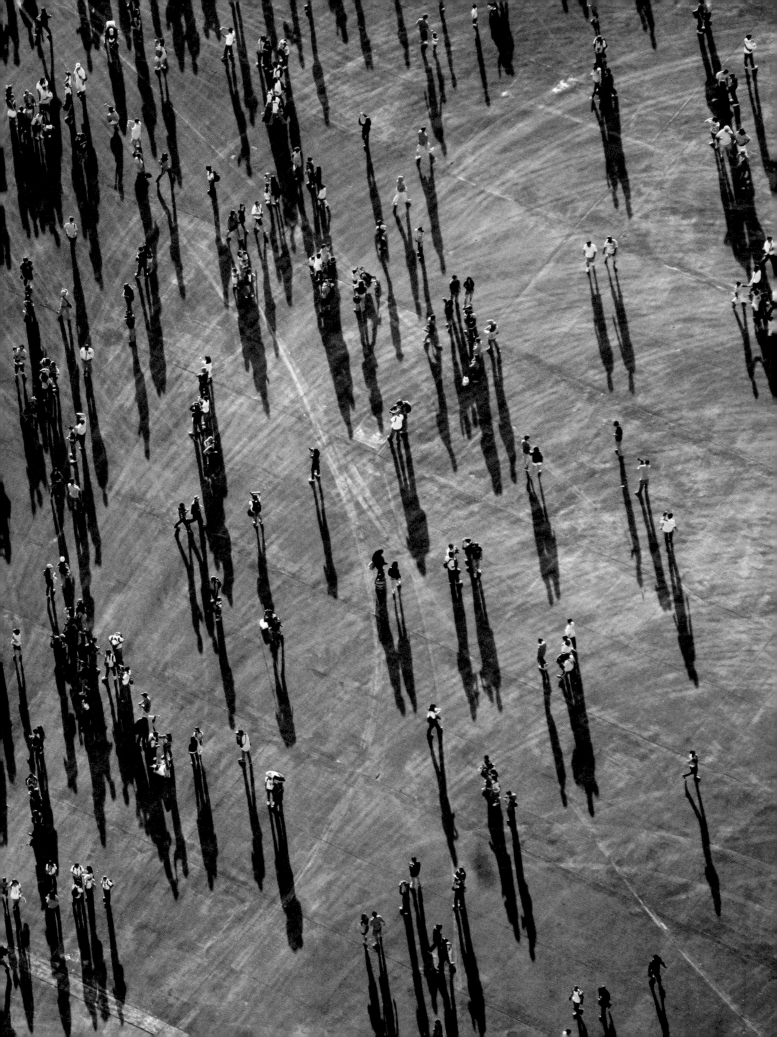

POPULATION, URBANIZATION, AND THE ENVIRONMENT

A New Global Milestone

At two minutes to midnight on October 30, 2011, the world's population reached 7 billion; by the middle of 2015 the number had grown to 7.3 billion. It would have been impossible to identify the actual 7-billionth human, but Danica May Camacho, born in Manila, Philippines, was the first baby chosen by the United Nations to represent this major milestone. A series of media events and press conferences were held throughout the following "Day of 7 Billion" to draw attention to the challenges posed by an ever-growing population.

For media outlets around the world, reaching the 7 billion mark proved a fascinating but passing diversion. For sociologists, demographers, environmentalists, and other scientists, however, the growing global population is a major and ongoing social phenomenon that will continue to have enormous consequences for the planet's finite and fragile resources.

Population growth and other demographic changes over the last 150 years, such as shifts in the proportions of young and old in many countries and the increasing concentration of people in urban environments, have helped give rise to new patterns of living. Urbanization, for instance, has brought with it the emergence of megacities, edge cities, and megalopolises. The rising global consumption that accompanies population growth has contributed to serious worldwide environmental problems, such as climate change, unchecked pollution, the rapid accumulation of human and manufactured waste, and the increasing scarcity of water. These effects will further challenge

LEARNING OBJECTIVES

 Discuss the causes and effects of population growth, population decline, and migration.

14-2 Describe the growing urbanization of the world's population and the effects of deindustrialization on U.S. cities.

 Discuss the major environmental problems and responses to them.

Reuters

the way we perceive and interact with our environments, both natural and social.

While Danica May Camacho's birth did not have a direct effect on urbanization or the environment, the rapid growth of the global population that her arrival represented certainly has. As long as new births outpace deaths and the population climbs, Earth's cities and the environment will be challenged, and we will need to adapt. ●

T his chapter covers three broad topics—population, urbanization, and the environment. They are covered together here because of the many ways in which they interrelate.

POPULATION

Demography is the scientific study of population (Bianchi and Wight 2012; Weeks 2011; Wight 2007), especially its growth, decline, and movement. **Demographers** study these population dynamics. Demography is both a distinct field of study and a subfield within sociology.

POPULATION GROWTH

A great deal of attention has been devoted to population growth and the idea of a population explosion (Ehrlich 1968). Some of the fears about such growth have dissipated in recent years, at least in part because of the ability of the world's most populous country, China, to slow its population growth through, among other things, its one-child policy, discontinued in late 2015. Nevertheless, China's population is huge and continues to grow, and China will soon be surpassed by India in population. Population increases are important and of interest not only in themselves but also because of the need for greater resources to support a growing population. Also of concern is the strain such increases place on national and city services, as well as on the environment.

While overall fertility rates are dropping globally, the world's population continues to increase, although at a declining rate. It was not until the early 1800s that the global population exceeded 1 billion; it reached 2 billion in just one century (1930), then 3 billion by 1960. In the next 14 years it reached 4 billion (1974); 13 years more and it was 5 billion (1987); and in another 12 years it reached 6 billion (1999) (Roberts 2009). As pointed out in the vignette that opens this chapter, in 12 more years the world's population exceeded 7 billion—with 37 percent living in China and India (Population Reference Bureau 2010). It will likely take only another decade—to the spring of 2025—to achieve the next milestone of 8 billion people (Worldometers 2015). By

China officially abandoned its one-child policy in late 2015. Among the reasons is a rapidly aging population; there is a growing need for more young people to bring greater dynamism to the country's economy and to help support older people who will be retiring in droves in the future.

2100 there will be as many as 12.3 billion people in the world (Gerland et al. 2014). In spite of the ravages of warfare and of diseases such as malaria, AIDS, and Ebola, the population of Africa as a whole is expected to double by 2050 (United Nations Department of Economic and Social Affairs 2015).

Rapid growth after World War II led to dire predictions about future overpopulation. At one time, projections were for a global population of about 16 billion by 2050. However, it is now estimated that *only* about 9.4 billion people will be in the world by that date (see Figure 14.1; Bianchi and Wight 2012). While this is a dramatic reduction in future estimates, it still represents a major increase in the world's population. This growth is occurring in spite of high death rates in many parts of the world due to high infant mortality, war, starvation, disease, and natural disasters. The death rate may increase dramatically in the twenty-first century if, as many expect, the disastrous effects of climate change accelerate, although that increase is unlikely to have much of an impact on overall population projections. Nevertheless, although there is less talk these days about a population explosion, there is little doubt that the world's population is increasing, perhaps at an unsustainable rate.

POPULATION DECLINE

Historically, population decline has not been considered as important as growth, but it has recently come to the fore in various parts of the world, especially in a number of European countries (Italy, Germany, Russia) and Japan (Coleman and Rowthorn 2011). By 2050, the population of Germany is projected to *drop* from 82.4 million to 71.5 million, while Japan's population is projected to decline from 127.7 million to 107.1 million (Coleman and Rowthorn 2011: 220; U.S. Census Bureau 2012a). Perhaps of greatest concern is the decline expected to occur in Russia, from 142.8 million to

FIGURE 14.1 • World Population, 1950–2050 (projected)

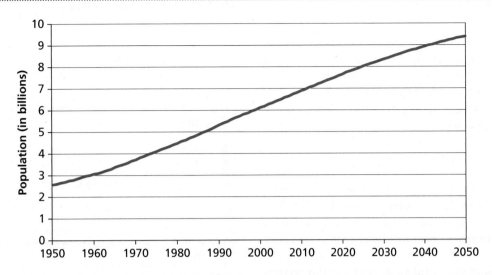

SOURCE: Data from U.S. Census Bureau, International Data Base, 2013 (http://www.census.gov/population/international/data/worldpop/table_population.php).

109.1 million in 2050. A variety of problems, such as high alcoholism rates and greatly unequal development across the country, have led to predictions of the "depopulation" of Russia. Even greater declines, and problems, are expected in a number of former Soviet Bloc countries, such as Ukraine, Bulgaria, and Latvia. Population decline can be caused by a low **birthrate**, the number of childbirths per 1,000 people per year. It can also be caused by a high death rate, more emigration than immigration, or some combination of the three. In countries with aging populations, birthrates are often below the level needed to maintain the population.

Of interest here are not only the various causes of such declines but also their impact on society as a whole. For one thing, population decline can weaken nations in various ways, including militarily (Yoshihara and Sylva 2011). The power of nations is often associated with having large populations; a smaller population generally translates into a smaller and weaker military (Israel is an exception). For another, population decline can weaken a nation's economy because of the reduction in the total number of productive workers. Third, the fact that population decline is generally accompanied by an aging population brings with it various problems, including a "financial time bomb" caused by the high costs associated with caring for the elderly—especially government pensions and health-related expenses. A parallel decline in the number of younger people in the labor force means that there are fewer people who are able to help pay those costs through taxes (Singer 2010). Among other things, this financial time bomb brings with it a great increase in national debt. However, there are actions that can be taken to mitigate this problem, such as raising the retirement

age so that older people can support themselves longer. Another possibility, although it is difficult politically, is for nations to reduce pensions and medical coverage.

ASK YOURSELF

What are some of the problems nations would face in reducing expensive government benefits in attempts to defuse the "financial time bomb" of an aging population? Who would benefit from such reductions? Who would be harmed, and how could governments protect them?

It would be wrong to conclude that population decline brings with it only a series of problems. Among the gains of such a decline is a reduction of the ecological problems caused by a growing population. For example, a smaller population produces fewer automobile emissions and creates less pollution. In addition, the pressure on the world's supplies of oil, water, and food are reduced when populations shrink.

While some nations will be hurt by an aging population, others, especially developing countries, will get a "demographic dividend" (Desai 2010; Lee 2007) because they have a favorable ratio between those who are able to work and those who are dependents, such as the aged and children. The dividend results, in part, from the presence of a large younger population able to work and earn money. At the same time, there are relatively few in need of their support. A significant part of the dividend is traceable to education and the greater productivity associated with a better-educated younger generation (Cuaresma, Lutz, and Sanderson 2014).

THE PROCESSES OF POPULATION CHANGE

Three basic processes are of concern to demographers. The first is **fertility**, or people's reproductive behavior, especially the number of births. Key to understanding fertility is the birthrate. Second is **mortality**, or deaths and death rates within a population. Finally, there is **migration**, or the movements of people, or *migrants,* and the impact of these movements on both the sending and the receiving locales (Bianchi and Wight 2012; Faist, Fauser, and Reisenauer 2013).

Fertility

On average, a woman could give birth as many as 16 times throughout her reproductive years. Few women reach that number, however. In 2012, fertility levels ranged from just over 1 birth per woman in Macau to 6 or more per woman in several African countries; Mali was the highest at 6.9 births per woman (World Bank 2015). In this section, we deal with the economic and social factors affecting fertility, regional differences in fertility, and fertility trends in the United States.

Economic Factors. Fertility is affected by a variety of economic factors. For example, we know that record low points in population growth were associated with the Great Depression. Low points were also recorded in the 1970s, when an oil crisis led to a dramatic jump in oil prices and rampant inflation.

Social Factors. Fertility is also affected by a variety of social factors. For instance, there is the obvious impact of age on fertility. Most childbearing involves women between the ages of 15 and 45. Especially important in the context of age is the fertility and childbearing of adolescents (less than 20 years old). Globally, adolescents give birth to an estimated 15 million

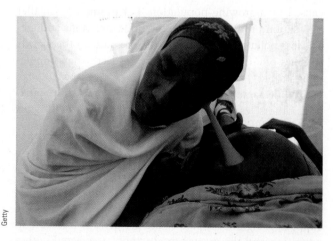

Getty

Fertility rates remain very high in several African countries, including in this camp for internally displaced people in Sudan where traditional obstetric care has resulted in poor maternal and fetal health outcomes.

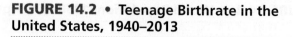

FIGURE 14.2 • Teenage Birthrate in the United States, 1940–2013

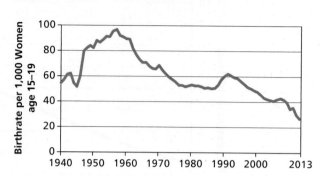

SOURCE: Data from CDC/NCHS, Division of Vital Statistics (http://health.usnews.com/health-news/articles/2015/01/15/us-birth-rate-continues-decline-cdc-reports); (http://www.cdc.gov/teenpregnancy/about/index.htm); (http://www.cdc.gov/teenpregnancy/prevent-teen-pregnancy/index.htm); (http://www.cdc.gov/nchs/data/databriefs/db58.htm); (http://www.cdc.gov/nchs/data/databriefs/db58_tables.pdf#1).

babies a year: The rate is as high as 200 per 1,000 births in some African countries, 24 per 1,000 in most developed countries, and only 5 or fewer per 1,000 in China, Japan, and Korea (Cooksey 2007). The United States has the highest rate of births to teenage mothers of all industrial nations; it is 5.5 times the rate in Western Europe (Centers for Disease Control and Prevention 2015). However, the teenage birthrate in the United States has been declining dramatically in recent years. The peak year was 1957, with a birthrate of 96.3 per 1,000 teenage women ages 15–19. By 2013, the birthrate for such women had reached a record low of 26.5 (see Figure 14.2).

A second, and related, issue involves the broader category of nonmarital fertility; not all of such fertility is accounted for by adolescents (Musick 2007). Nonmarital fertility has increased dramatically in the United States, rising from only 5 percent of all births in 1960 to a third in 2000, and it now accounts for about 40 percent of all births (Bianchi and Wight 2012). The United States is not unique among Western industrialized countries in this: Its rate of nonmarital fertility is higher than some, such as Germany's; on a par with others, such as Ireland's; and lower than others, such as Scandinavia and Iceland, where almost two-thirds of children are born outside marriage (Haub 2013).

Regional Factors. While countries in many less developed areas of the world still worry about high birthrates, officials in many developed countries have grown increasingly concerned about *low* birthrates. A birthrate of 2.1 is needed to replace an existing population. However, in the early twenty-first century, the average fertility in developed countries was 1.6 children for each woman; in some of those countries it approached "lowest low fertility" of less than 1.3 children (in Russia it was 1.1). In other words, the birthrates in these countries are inadequate to replace the current population.

FIGURE 14.3 • Number of Children per Woman in the United States, 1911–2012

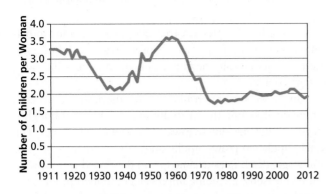

SOURCE: Data from CDC/NCHS, National Vital Statistics System (http://national.deseretnews.com/article/1522/the-potential-impact-of-falling-fertility-rates-on-the-economy-and-culture.html).

This is a particular concern throughout Western Europe and has led to worry over the issues discussed above in terms of an aging population. Another concern is the future of the historical cultures of various European countries where the birthrates of immigrants (especially Muslims) far exceed those of "natives" (Caldwell 2009). This fact has contributed to increasing animosity between natives and immigrants.

U.S. Fertility Trends. When the United States was founded, the average birthrate was slightly less than 8 per woman; that rate declined throughout the nineteenth century and most of the first half of the twentieth century. World War II led to an increase in the birthrate, and it remained high throughout the 1950s. In fact, the rise in the birthrate between 1946 and 1960 is referred to as the *baby boom*. The peak in fertility in the United States was reached in 1957, after which the birthrate declined for almost two decades, reaching a low of 1.7 in 1976. Today the birthrate is 1.9 (see Figure 14.3; World Bank 2014b). Fertility in the United States is just below "replacement level"—the number needed to replace the population.

Mortality

A population's death rate is the number of deaths per 1,000 people. Life expectancy is the number of years an individual can be expected to live.

Life Expectancy. In prehistoric times, life expectancy across the world ranged between 20 and 30 years; by 1900, that number had increased only slightly, but today it has reached an average of 69 years. Nearly half of the decline in mortality in developed countries took place in the twentieth century. Life expectancy is now 77 years in the more developed countries, 67 years in less developed countries, and 56 years in the least developed countries (Bianchi and Wight 2012). Life expectancy in Africa is only 50 years (Elo 2007).

As we saw in Chapter 13, the longest life expectancy is found in Japan, where women live an average of 87.3 years and men are apt to live 85 years. Life expectancy for women in the United States is about 82.2 years; for men it is 77.4 years (Bianchi and Wight 2012). By 2050, U.S. women are projected to live between 89.2 and 93.3 years, while men are expected to live between 83.2 and 85.9 years.

Macro-social Factors. Increased life expectancy and lower death rates can be affected by a variety of macro-social factors (Elo 2007):

- A general improvement in standards of living (better housing, improved nutrition)

- Better public health (improved sanitation, cleaner drinking water)

- Cultural and behavioral factors (stronger norms regarding healthy lifestyles)

- Advances in medicine and medical technologies (antibiotics and newer drugs, immunizations, improved surgical techniques), leading to both an aging population and reduced infant mortality rates

- Government actions (control of diseases such as malaria)

Of course, important factors that keep death rates high continue to exist (including infectious diseases such as malaria, Ebola, and AIDS), and other factors that could increase the death rate, including global flu epidemics, loom on the horizon.

Mortality is greatly affected by one's position in the system of social stratification (see Chapter 7). In the United States, those in the lower classes are likely to have shorter life spans than those who rank higher in the stratification system. As for race, blacks have a lower life expectancy than whites, but black males are more disadvantaged in comparison to white males than black females are compared to white females. Lower life expectancies among black men are the result of the fact that they are more likely to live in rural areas, where life expectancy in general is lower, are less likely to seek health care, are at higher risk of death by homicide, and are more likely to engage in substance abuse (Sabo 1998; Singh and Siahpush 2014).

In terms of gender, women have a longer life expectancy than men in spite of the various disadvantages they confront stemming from the system of gender stratification (see Chapter 9). This difference is due, in part, to the fact that women engage in more health-protective behaviors than men, such as visiting physicians more often. Gender roles also tend to protect women from fatal disease and injury (Rieker and Bird 2000). For example, women are less likely than men to engage in potentially disabling or deadly activities such as using illegal drugs, driving dangerously, and engaging in violent behavior. Higher death rates for male fetuses, as well

This 113 year-old man celebrates his birthday with his three great-great-granddaughters. The chances are that more and more of you will live to that age...or beyond. What problems could that create for you, your loved ones, and society as a whole?

as for male infants in the first four months of life, suggest that females may be more viable organisms than males. However, in general, "women now live longer than men not because their biology has changed, but because their social position and access to resources have changed" (Weitz 2010: 52). Nevertheless, in some parts of the world, such as India and Pakistan, females have a lower life expectancy than males. This is traceable, at least in part, to the fact that females in some regions are more likely to die in infancy, perhaps because of parental neglect or female infanticide, or when giving birth to their own children.

Micro-social Factors. Mortality is also affected by a number of micro-social factors, especially those associated with poor lifestyle choices, including smoking, failing to exercise, overeating, and eating unhealthy foods. Obesity has long been related to higher death rates from heart disease and stroke. A more recent discovery is the linkage between obesity and death from various forms of cancer, including breast and endometrial cancer. More than 100,000 new cases of cancer per year in the United States can be traced to obesity. Conversely, healthy lifestyle choices can lead to longer lives. For example, members of religious groups, such as the Mormons, that restrict the use of tobacco products, alcohol, coffee, and addictive drugs tend to have longer life expectancies. Globally, the lifestyle of the Japanese, which includes eating more fish and less red meat, is closely related to their greater longevity.

The Demographic Transition

The issues of fertility and mortality are central to demographic transition theory. According to this theory, population changes are related to the shift from an agricultural society to a more industrialized and urbanized society (Davis 1945; Weeks 2007). Four stages are associated with the *demographic transition* (see Figure 14.4).

In the first, or preindustrial, stage, there is a rough balance between high death rates (mortality) and high birthrates (fertility). As a result, the population growth rate, while high, is fairly stable.

In the second, or transitional, stage, the death rate declines dramatically while the birthrate remains high (although it begins to decline slowly toward the end of this stage). The total population grows rapidly under these circumstances. In this stage, death rates decline first in developed countries for various reasons, including improvement in food production, a higher standard of living, a better-informed population, improved hygiene, and better health care. This was the situation in most of the developed countries of Europe beginning in the eighteenth century.

In the industrial stage, the death rate drops more slowly over time to its lowest level, leading to more children in the family and the community. As a result, people begin thinking about limiting the number of children. Women begin to have greater access to, and are more likely to use, birth control. In addition, fewer children are required because not as many workers are needed on the family farms. Many family members move into the cities and take jobs in industries and other organizations. Thus, another main cause of the decline of the birthrate in the industrial age is the fact that women have increased work-related opportunities. For these and other reasons, it is to the family's advantage to limit family size. Eventually, the birthrate drops to a level roughly equal to the low level of the death rate.

FIGURE 14.4 • The Demographic Transition Model

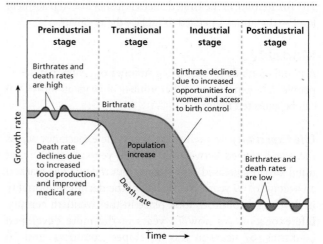

SOURCE: Adapted from *A Dictionary of Geography*, 2nd edition by Susan Mayhew (1997). Figure 20, p. 122. By permission of Oxford University Press.

In the postindustrial stage, while there is some variation over time, birthrates and death rates remain low. As a result, in this stage, as in the latter part of the industrial stage, population growth remains slow or stabilizes.

As a general rule, birthrates drop more slowly than death rates largely because it is difficult to overcome the positive value individuals and cultures place on children and on life more generally. In contrast, reducing the death rate is relatively easy, at least when the means to do so exist, because postponing death is consistent with valuing life. This contradicts the myth that a population grows because of a rise in the birthrate. Rather, such growth is better attributed to a decline in death rates with birthrates remaining largely unchanged.

In Western Europe, the entire demographic transition took about 200 years, from the mid-1800s until the mid-twentieth century. The process continues today in much of the rest of the world. However, in recent years, in less developed countries, the process has taken significantly less time. This is traceable to the much more rapid decline in the death rate because of the importation of advanced, especially medical, technologies from developed countries. Since birthrates have remained high while death rates have declined, population growth in less developed countries has been extraordinarily high.

Given this recent rapid population growth in less developed countries, the issue is what can be done about it, especially in the areas of the world where fertility remains high. How can the birthrate be reduced in those areas?

Reducing Fertility. One approach to reducing fertility is economic development. This follows from what has been learned from the demographic transition in Europe and the United States, where economic development did lead to lower fertility. A second approach is voluntary family planning. This includes providing people with information about reproductive physiology and the use of contraceptive techniques, actually providing such things as birth control pills and condoms, and developing societal or local informational programs to support the use of contraception and the ideal of small(er) families. A third approach involves a change in the society as a whole, especially where it has been considered both advantageous and desirable for families to have large numbers of children. In many societies, children are still needed to work to help their families survive and to provide for their parents in their old age. Changes such as compulsory childhood education and child labor laws can counter the fact that these realities lead families to have large numbers of children. Such changes serve to make children less valuable economically because they cannot work when they are in school and they are kept out of the labor force for years by child labor laws. As a result, at least some parents have fewer children. Another important step is to be sure women acquire public roles beyond the family realm. When women have greater educational and occupational opportunities, their fertility declines, and families have fewer children (Fillipi et al. 2006; Hwang and Lee 2014). However, solutions that require changing cultural ideas about women and reproduction can be difficult and slow to achieve.

ASK YOURSELF

What happens to families that depend on children's earnings for survival when those children are required to attend school instead of working? Should society help address the loss of income to such families, and, if so, how? Should companies that hired child workers in the past be responsible for these families' survival? Why or why not?

The practice of infanticide is an unfortunate reality in some parts of the world. The selection of females for infanticide is especially problematic for various reasons, including its impact on fertility. The selective killing of female fetuses ("female infanticide") subsequently affects fertility because males end up outnumbering females in a population and there are fewer potential mothers (Bhatnagar, Dube, and Dube 2006). Infanticide is most common in South and East Asia, although it is also found in other areas of the world, including North Africa and the Middle East (United Nations 2006).

A Second Demographic Transition. In the 1980s, some scholars began thinking in terms of a second demographic transition to describe the general decline in the fertility rate and of population growth, especially in developed countries (Lesthaeghe 2010; Lesthaeghe and van de Kaa 1986; Ochiai 2014). This decline is linked to parents coming to focus more on the quality of life of one child, or a few children, as well as on the quality of their own lives. Better occupational prospects, and therefore a more affluent lifestyle, have come to be associated with having fewer children.

The second demographic transition involves three stages. The first stage, between 1955 and 1970, is of greatest importance. The key factor during this period was the end of the baby boom, aided by the revolution in contraception that made it less likely that people would have unwanted children. Also beginning at this time was the gender revolution, which meant, among other things, that women began to marry later and to divorce more. They also entered the work world in greater numbers. This tended to reduce the birthrate, as did the fact that there were fewer women at home to care for children. These and other factors can be said to be associated with a second demographic transition involving subreplacement fertility, lower birthrates, and a declining rate of population growth (Lesthaeghe 2007). This transition has also been accompanied by the proliferation of a variety of living arrangements other than marriage and an increasing disconnect between marriage and procreation (Klinenberg 2012).

Migration

Although a great deal of migration takes place within national borders (Crowder and Hall 2007), our primary concern here is cross-border, international (Kritz 2007), or global migration (Faist 2012; Scherschel 2007). In the United States, migration drew a great deal of media and political attention in 2014 for various reasons, not least of which was the massive influx of unaccompanied minors from Central America through the border with Mexico. This led to questions about what to do with the children once they were in the country (Chishti, Hipsman, and Bui 2014). As shown in Figure 14.5, the children came mainly from El Salvador, Guatemala, and Honduras. Although the number of child migrants from Mexico remained high in 2014, it had declined slightly from 2013.

Globally, there is "more mobility at this moment than at any time in history" (DeParle 2015). Concern about migration reached a crescendo in 2015 as massive numbers of people fled their home countries because of warfare, failed states, and hostility to minority groups. Syria, Iraq, Libya, and Yemen were sites of catastrophic warfare and can be considered failed, or at least failing, states. Minority groups such as the Yazidi in Syria and Iraq fled as a result of persecution and even genocide at the hands of Islamic State (Cumming-Bruce 2015). In Myanmar (and Bangladesh), many Rohingya, a Muslim minority, fled to escape violence perpetrated by the Hindu majority (Fuller and Cochran 2015). In the seas around Europe and Southeast Asia, many rickety boats (some of which sank) carried people to what they thought would be safe havens in other countries. However, at least some countries did not welcome them or even rejected them—fearing, among other things, the cost of maintaining them until they could be integrated into those countries or sent home.

A great deal of population movement is associated with globalization (Kritz 2008; Kritz, Lim, and Zlotnik 1992). In the early twenty-first century, about 3.2 percent of the global population lived outside their countries of origin (United Nations Population Fund 2015). To some observers, this represents a large and growing number, and, in fact, it constitutes a substantial increase of 36 percent since 1990. However, to other observers, the sense that we live in a global era of unprecedented international migration is exaggerated; they note that the actual rate was higher in the late nineteenth and early twentieth centuries (Guhathakurta, Jacobson, and DelSordi 2007).

While it is true that the rate is lower than it was a century ago, migrants make up significant proportions of the populations of many countries (Kivisto and Faist 2010). If the migratory wave persists, the proportion of migrants in the United States will reach 15 percent between 2020 and 2025, exceeding the previous high of nearly 15 percent achieved in the late nineteenth century (Roberts 2008); it will rise to 19 percent by 2050.

ASK YOURSELF

What social functions does migration serve? What are the downsides of efforts to restrict migration?

Today, much attention is devoted to efforts to control global human migration, but these efforts face daunting problems. For one thing, the sheer numbers of migrants make control extremely difficult. According to one estimate, "tens of millions of people cross borders on a daily basis" (Hollifield and Jacobson 2012: 1390). The greatest pressure is on the United States and Europe, which are the most desirable destinations for migrants, both legal and illegal. For another thing, controls are very costly, and few nations can afford to engage in much more than token efforts. Then there is the fact that attempts to control migration inevitably lead to heightened and more sophisticated efforts to evade those controls. A lucrative market opens up for those, such as smugglers, who are in the business of transporting people across borders illegally. Finally, increased efforts at control lead to increasingly desperate efforts to evade them. This, in turn, leads to more deaths and injuries. For example, in 2012, there were 477 known deaths of people who sought to cross the U.S. border from Mexico illegally.

Explaining Migration. Migration is influenced by a combination of push and pull factors. Among the *push* factors are the desire of migrants for better or safer lives; problems in the home country, such as unemployment and low pay, making it difficult or impossible for migrants to achieve their goals; and major disruptions such as war, famine, political and religious persecution, and economic depression. *Pull* factors include features of the host country such as its being a nation at peace and having a favorable immigration policy, a prosperous economy, higher pay and lower unemployment, available food, formal and informal networks that cater to

FIGURE 14.5 • Unaccompanied Minors Caught at the U.S. Border, 2009–2014

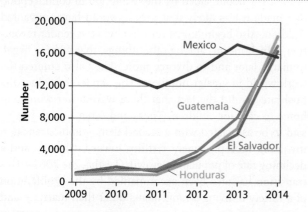

SOURCE: Data from U.S. Customs and Border Protection (http://www.cbp.gov/newsroom/stats/southwest-border-unaccompanied-children).

immigrants, labor shortages, and language and culture similar to those of the home country.

In addition to these traditional factors are factors specific to the global age. There is, for example, the global diffusion of information, which makes it easier for migrants to find out about, and become comfortable in, a host country. Then there is the interaction of global–local networks, either through formal networks mediated by modern technologies, like mobile phones and the Internet (especially e-mail and Skype), or through more informal family and social networks that might well employ the same technologies. All of this makes it much easier for migrants to relocate and to become comfortable in new settings, while it is simultaneously easier for them to send money (remittances) to family and friends back home.

Types of Migrants. **Refugees** are migrants who are forced to leave their homeland, or who leave involuntarily because they fear for their safety (Haddad 2003; Kivisto 2012b; Loyal 2007). In late 2015 Europe was swamped with refugees, especially from war-torn Syria.

Asylum seekers flee their home country, usually in an effort to escape political oppression or religious persecution. They seek to remain in the country to which they flee. They are in a state of limbo until a decision is made on their request for asylum (Schuster 2012). If and when that claim is accepted, the asylum seeker is considered a refugee. If the claim is rejected, it is likely that the asylum seeker will be returned to the home country.

Labor migrants move from their home country to another country because they are driven by push and pull factors (Kritz 2008). Examples of labor migrants are the Mexican and South American women who immigrate to the United States to find employment as domestics. Among the push factors for such women are "tenuous and scarce job

People fleeing violence, like these members of the minority Yazidi sect walking toward the Syrian border, are usually considered refugees rather than simply migrants. War and fighting in the Middle East and Africa have forced millions of people from their homelands in the last few years. What obligation toward them do the rest of the world's people have?

FIGURE 14.6 • Undocumented Immigration to the United States: Total Number versus Mexican Immigrants, 1990–2012

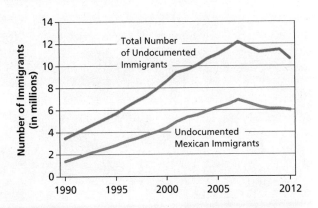

SOURCE: Data from Jeffrey Passel, D'Vera Cohn, and Ana Gonzalez-Barrera, "Population Decline of Unauthorized Immigrants Stalls, May Have Reversed," Pew Research Center, September 23, 2013.

opportunities," civil wars, and economic crises in their home countries (Hondagneu-Sotelo and Avila 2005: 308). The major pull factor is the existence of jobs paying higher wages.

Undocumented immigrants reside in a receiving country without valid authorization (Torpey 2012; Yamamoto 2012). This category overlaps with some of the above types of migrants; both asylum seekers and labor migrants may be undocumented immigrants. There are three broad types of undocumented immigrants. The first are those who manage to gain entry without passing through a checkpoint or without undergoing the required inspection. The second type comprises those who gain entry legally but then stay beyond the period of time permitted by their visas. Third are those who immigrate on the basis of false documents. As shown in Figure 14.6, the number of undocumented immigrants to the United States increased from about 3.5 million in 1990 to a high of 12.2 million in 2007, before declining to about 10.7 million in 2012. Immigrants from Mexico account for the majority of undocumented immigrants. Of the 10.7 million undocumented immigrants in 2012, just over 6 million were of Mexican descent.

It is estimated that more than 10 percent of Mexico's total population lives in the United States. As of 2009, about 6.7 million Mexicans, the majority of Mexican immigrants, were in the United States illegally (Hoefer, Rytina, and Baker 2010). They come because, although they may be paid poverty wages by U.S. standards, that may be as much as four times what they could earn in Mexico (Preston 2006). Furthermore, there are more jobs and better future job opportunities in the United States than there are in Mexico.

Another reason many immigrants enter the United States is for educational opportunities that are not available in their home countries. Many become undocumented students. Harmon and colleagues (2010: 69) estimate that

National Geographic

Breathtakingly tall skyscrapers distinguish Tokyo's commercial and administrative hub in the Shinjuku ward. Tokyo is one of the world's largest megacities.

"approximately 1.8 million undocumented immigrants are under 18 years of age with an estimated 65,000 students graduating from public high schools annually." Furthermore, because the U.S. Supreme Court holds that states cannot deny undocumented students access to primary and secondary education, "education plays a central role in social mobility" for these students (Harmon et al. 2010: 75).

URBANIZATION

Urban areas are the destinations for many migrants and the locales most affected by population changes of various types. Until very recently, the world was predominantly rural; even in 1800 there were only a handful of large urban areas in the world. As late as 1850, only about 2 percent of the world's population lived in cities of more than 100,000 residents. Urban areas have grown rapidly since then. In the first decade of the present century, a "watershed in human history" occurred as for "the first time the urban population of the Earth" outnumbered the rural population (Davis 2007: 1). However, there are great differences among the nations of the world in terms

of their degrees of urban development: Just over 80 percent of the population in the United States and the United Kingdom is urban, while only 27 percent of Rwanda's population is urban (World Bank 2014d). It is projected that by 2050, 66 percent of the world's population will live in urban areas (54 percent do today) (United Nations 2014). In the more developed areas of the world, 86 percent of the population will live in cities. The greatest growth will be in developing areas, where 67 percent of the population will be urban dwellers.

The importance of **cities**, or large, permanent, and spatially concentrated human settlements, has progressively increased. Even when there were not very many of them, cities were at the heart of many societies (Weber ([1921] 1968). The city has become increasingly central, especially in the context of today's "global cities" (discussed later in this chapter).

The term *urban* generally refers to city dwelling (Coward 2012), but it also has a more specific and technical meaning, although what is considered urban varies from society to society (Parrillo 2007). To be considered **urban** in the United States, an area must have more than 50,000 inhabitants. In comparison, to be classified as urban in Iceland, an area need have only 200 residents. The U.S. government labels a city of 50,000 residents or greater an "urbanized area," or a "metropolitan statistical area" (Farley 2007). **Urbanization** is the process by which an increasing percentage of a society's population comes to be located in relatively densely populated urban areas (Orum 2007). It is clear that urbanization occurred even in ancient times, when large numbers of people moved to Rome, Cairo, and Peking (now Beijing); however, it has accelerated greatly in the modern era. **Urbanism** is the way of life that emerges in, and is closely associated with, urban areas. That way of life includes distinctive lifestyles, attitudes, and social relationships. In terms of the last, one example would be the greater likelihood of relating to strangers (Elliott 2012).

EVER-LARGER URBAN AREAS

Cities have grown considerably larger in recent decades. (We will discuss the world's largest cities—megacities—below when we turn to the issue of globalization.) However, cities have become part of an even larger spatial form. After 1920 in the United States (and later elsewhere), there emerged a new urban form—the **metropolis**—a large, powerful, and culturally influential urban area that contains a central city and its surrounding communities, known as **suburbs**, that are economically and socially linked to the center but located outside the city's political boundaries (Friedman 2007). Suburbs often create band-like structures around cities. While suburbs in the United States have tended to be populated by the middle class, in other societies, such as France and South America, suburbs are more likely to be dominated by the lower class, including many recent immigrants. A **megalopolis** is a cluster of highly populated cities that can stretch over great distances (Gotham 2007; Gottman 1961). There are currently 11 megalopolises in the United States, with the area between and encompassing Boston and Washington, D.C., being the classic example. Another now stretches from San Diego to San Francisco and ultimately may extend as far as Seattle and even Vancouver. The cities that surround the Great Lakes constitute another megalopolis.

SUBURBANIZATION

The process of **suburbanization** occurs when large numbers of people move out of the city and into nearby, less densely populated, environs. They are often impelled by urban problems such as crime, pollution, poverty, homelessness, and poor schools. The "American dream" of the last half of the twentieth century of an affordable one-family home was more likely to be found in the suburbs than in the city.

Suburbanization was first associated with the United States, although it is now a global phenomenon. However, there is considerable variation around the world in this process and the nature of suburbs. It would be a mistake to assume that the American model fits suburbs elsewhere in the world (Clapson and Hutchison 2010).

Various criticisms have been directed at suburbanization. One is that it leads to the creation of vast areas characterized by the seemingly endless sprawl of tract houses and the businesses created to serve them (Duany, Plater-Zyberk, and Speck 2010). More recently, critics have noted the problem of suburban sprawl promoting high levels of traffic congestion and environmental degradation.

In the past few decades suburban development has seen the emergence of **gated communities**. Usually associated with the United States, gated communities have developed globally in many places, including Hungary (Kovacs and Hegedus 2014) and China (Wu, Wei, and Wang 2014). Gates, surveillance cameras, and guards are intended to provide residents of these communities with a feeling of security from the dangers they think they have left behind in the city (Atkinson and Blandy 2005; Blakely and Snyder 1997). There are, for example, fewer burglaries in such communities (Addington and Rennison 2015). Nevertheless, no matter the reality, there remains a heightened sense of fear and insecurity among residents of gated communities (Low 2003).

Detroit's return to prosperity may be a long and slow process. Vacant homes like this one have become a common sight after years of declining tax revenues and population flight. What are some possible effects of blight on those who remain behind?

The Flow of the Super-Rich to the World's Great Cities

The world has become increasingly stratified, with the super-rich ever more able to afford things 99 percent of the world would find unimaginable. Among these things are homes in the world's great cities, especially New York and London. The wealthy from various countries (Russia, for example) are paying astounding prices for these residences. The resulting flow of global money is driving up other housing prices in those cities, making it increasingly difficult for ordinary people to live in them. For instance, a residence in the Belgravia area of London can cost between $7.5 million and $75 million. A Ukrainian recently paid $204 million for two penthouse condominiums at One Hyde Park and then spent another $90 million for renovations (Lyall 2013). In New York City, $8 billion is spent each year on residences that cost more than $5 million each; in 2015 one New York condo sold for over $100 million (Story and Saul 2015).

Even more striking is that many who buy such ultraexpensive residences live in them for only a few days a year (say, the Christmas holidays), or not at all if they are buying them as long-term investments or rental properties. They move between several extremely costly residences throughout the world, spending very little time in any one of them. This means the prime areas of the world's great cities are largely devoid of people for much of the year.

Many of the actual purchasers of elite real estate—such as the owners of the condos at New York's Time Warner Center, which houses at least 17 billionaires—are not only rarely if ever seen but also difficult to identify (Story and Saul 2015). The reason is that the purchases are often made in the name of shell companies, trusts, or limited liability companies in order to conceal the identities of the actual owners, who want to keep a low profile. However, some buyers have also been found to have been arrested or fined for engaging in corrupt practices in their home countries. They might not be accepted by the condominium associations were their true identities known, although associations anxious to sell properties at greatly inflated prices might prefer *not* to know. Owners of condos and officials of the global cities in which they exist are often eager to have the super-rich as residents, no matter who they are and even if only for a few days a year.

Think About It

Is there anything that the world's great cities can or should do about the influx of the global super-rich and the fact that the resulting increases in real estate prices are driving out the middle class, to say nothing of the poor?

Exurbia

Cities and suburbs continue to push outward, to where land and housing costs are lower. Developments in these outlying areas, the crabgrass frontiers between the suburbs and rural areas, are called **exurbia** (Crump 2007).

Edge Cities

Associated with the rise of exurbia is the emergence of what have come to be called **edge cities** (Garreau 1991; Phelps and Wood 2011)—developments at the outermost rings surrounding large cities that in many ways function more like cities than suburbs. As part of exurbia, edge cities become indistinguishable from the hinterlands, giving rise to the idea of the "edgeless city." Like suburbanization, the phenomenon of edge cities originated in the United States, but there are signs that such cities are becoming increasingly global (Bontje and Burdack 2005).

The Postsuburban Era

In the United States, suburbanization peaked in the late twentieth century. Today, there is much talk about the idea that we live in a postsuburban era. In part, this is related to the growing realization that a way of life that includes large, energy-devouring private homes and vast thirsty lawns is ecologically unsustainable. High gasoline prices and home heating and air-conditioning costs further help to make the cost of a suburban home prohibitive for many. Renting an apartment in or close to the city is back in vogue.

ASK YOURSELF

What do you think of gated communities? What is their impact on those who live in them as well as those who are excluded from them? Could you ever see yourself living in such a community? Why or why not?

THE DECLINE OF MAJOR U.S. CITIES

Many major American cities that developed with the industrialization of the nation have undergone substantial deterioration as a result of deindustrialization (see Chapter 12). This decline was accompanied by *white flight*—the exodus of whites from cities—which led not only to highly segregated urban areas but also to areas that have declining tax bases and deteriorating infrastructure (roads, water and sewage systems, public transportation) and thus declining ability to provide basic services for residents (Williams 1999). While all this had a negative impact on those who remained in the cities, especially less well-off blacks, it had some positive effects. For example, the lower-priced homes left empty by the flight of white households allowed more blacks to afford home ownership (Boustan and Margo 2013).

In some cases, cities have rebuilt at least some of their infrastructure in a process of urban renewal (Crowley 2007). A related process is **gentrification,** in which real estate capital is reinvested in blighted inner-city areas to refurbish housing for the upwardly mobile middle class (Lees, Slater, and Wyly 2010; Patch and Brenner 2007). A prominent example is the borough of Brooklyn, New York, which in the 1940s and 1950s was largely shunned by New Yorkers because of its industrial-era slums. Today, much of Brooklyn, with its famous brownstones, has been transformed into a model postindustrial landscape. Town houses and condominiums have been renovated, and many are ultraexpensive. Brooklyn has become the least affordable home ownership market in the United States (Gopal 2014). Restaurants, bars, and other businesses catering to the new residents have sprung up all over the borough (Osman 2011). Pioneers in the process of gentrification are often young professionals, hipsters, younger gay men, and artists (Zukin 1982). Gentrification allows the wealthier residents (the "gentry") who grew up in the suburbs to return to the city. The expectation is that they will rebuild its depressed areas not only physically but also economically, socially, and culturally. In the process, working-class and poor residents are often forced out.

ASK YOURSELF

Does gentrification serve a social purpose? If so, what is it? Does conflict theory apply to the fate of the working class and the poor in this process? If so, how?

CITIES AND GLOBALIZATION

From the beginning, cities have been central to both scholarly and popular work on globalization (Sassen 2012; Timberlake and Ma 2007). Cities are seen as being **cosmopolitan**, or open to a variety of external and global influences (Beck 2007). In contrast, small towns and rural areas are more likely to be viewed as **local**, or inward rather than outward looking. Cities therefore came to be seen as inherently global, and they grew more so as they came to encompass a range of populations, cultures, ethnicities, languages, and consumer products from around the world. Cities also exerted a powerful influence over surrounding areas.

Cities today are part of global flows of people, products, information, and more. This has been described as "mobile urbanism" (McCann and Ward 2011). Urban policies and ideas on how to improve the city flow easily throughout the world's urban areas. The many city-based organizations are linked through elaborate networks to organizations in other cities throughout the home country and the world. Furthermore, the people in those cities are themselves involved in a wide range of global networks and are linked to people throughout the world.

Global Cities

At the top of the world's hierarchy of cities are the global cities. New York City, London, and Tokyo are generally included in this elite category. Saskia Sassen (1991) embeds her notion of global cities in the process of economic (capitalistic) globalization. In this context, she accords priority to the three cities mentioned above on the basis of their place in the world economy. Specifically, they are **global cities** because they are

- the key locations for leading industries and marketplaces and the high-level management and specialized services they require;

- the centers of the production and creation of innovative, cutting-edge financial services;

- the homes of new financial, legal, and accountancy products; and

- the settings from which businesses and organizations exercise global command and control.

Much of what global cities achieve is made possible by a wide range of new electronic technologies. In light of the recent history of the Great Recession, we also know that these cities, with their great financial centers, are likely to be at the epicenter of monumental collapses in the global economy and, presumably, of economic renaissances.

Global cities are central nodes in a new international division of labor. Of great importance are the linkages among and between these cities and the flows, both positive and negative, among and between them. In many ways, the global cities have more in common with one another than with the smaller cities and the hinterlands within their own countries. They are also more integrated into the global economy than those hinterlands. The direct linkages between global cities point to the fact that nation-states are less important in the global age than previously. They are unable to control the flows between global cities. As Sassen (2012: 189) puts it, the global city "engages the global directly, often bypassing the national." In addition, the nation-state is unable to stem such global flows as undocumented immigrants and illegal drugs.

Megacities (and Beyond)

Megacities are defined as cities with populations greater than 10 million. Of course, the global cities discussed above meet that criterion, but what is striking is the large and growing number of cities in the less developed world that can be defined as megacities (Krass 2012). In 2014, there were 28 urban areas qualifying as megacities (up from 10 in 1990), led by Tokyo with almost 38 million people (see Figure 14.7). China alone has six megacities, and India will likely have seven by 2030 ("Number of Megacities" 2014). Extant cities are expected to grow dramatically in the coming years.

Such population concentrations bring with them enormous problems associated with the large numbers of very poor people living in these cities, especially those in less developed countries. More generally, Mike Davis (2007: 19) envisions a planet of urban slums that are a far cry from what early urban visionaries had in mind:

> The cities of the future, rather than being made out of glass and steel as envisioned by earlier generations

of urbanists, are instead largely constructed out of crude brick, straw, recycled plastic, cement blocks and scrap wood. Instead of cities of light soaring toward heaven, much of the twenty-first-century urban world squats in squalor, surrounded by pollution, excrement, and decay.

Of course, these megacities, even the most blighted of them, have wealthy residents as well, and thus they are sites of some of the most profound inequalities in the world. A stunning example of this inequality is found in Mumbai, where Mukesh Ambani, the richest person in India, built a 27-story, single-family home that may be valued at as much as $1 billion. Among other things, it has nine elevators, a six-level garage, helipads, "airborne swimming pools," a spa, hanging gardens, a 50-person theater, and a grand ballroom. To function, the structure requires hundreds of servants and staff. All this is found in a city noted for its poverty, where about 60 percent of the population lives in slums (Yardley 2010).

Because of the riches associated with its oil industry, Luanda, Angola, is the world's most expensive city for expatriates. For example, a 10-mile taxi ride might cost $450; a modest trip to the grocery store can run $150, including $17 for a pint of Häagen-Dazs ice cream. In contrast, the natives live in grinding poverty; half the population survives on less than $2 a day (Specter 2015).

FIGURE 14.7 • The World's Megacities, 2014

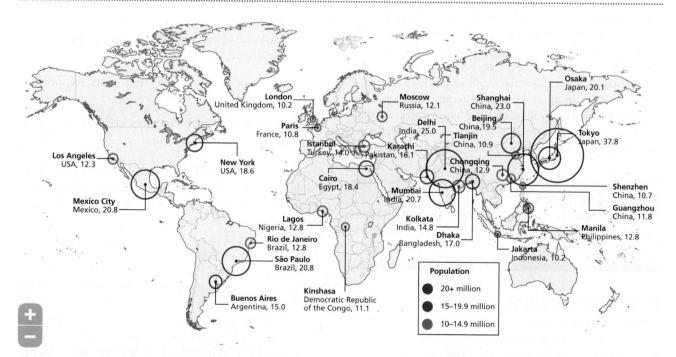

SAGE datamaps edge.sagepub.com
- All world cities with 5 million or more inhabitants.
- Projected growth by the year 2030.

SOURCE: Data from Jeffrey Passel, D'Vera Cohn, and Ana Gonzalez-Barrera, "Population Decline of Unauthorized Immigrants Stalls, May Have Reversed," Pew Research Center, September 23, 2013.

Uber

Uber is a company that offers call-ahead car service as an alternative, and a threat, to traditional taxicabs. (Lyft is another). Its rapid success represents another digital revolution.

Uber has been a hit in the United States since its founding in 2009; it has also become a global phenomenon. As of the end of 2014, it operated in 250 cities in 50 countries, and both numbers are growing rapidly (Isaac and de la Merced 2014). As a result, the company has attracted a huge amount of funding and may be valued at as much as $50 billion (Tam and de la Merced 2015). Yet it has run into opposition in the United States, as well as globally (a dramatic protest occurred in France in mid-2015), from taxi companies, taxi drivers, and government agencies. In several countries it has been challenged for, among other things, running an illegal taxi service. Global opposition increased when an Uber driver in India was accused of raping a passenger who had dozed off in the backseat of the car (Barry and Raj 2014). In late 2015 the driver was sentenced to life in prison for the rape. The incident raised serious questions about Uber's vetting of its drivers; the safety of it vehicles has also been questioned.

Instead of paid drivers, Uber relies on private drivers using their own cars, whose services are arranged as needed through smartphone apps. This convenience is highly attractive to passengers, especially younger ones. Uber relies on the smartphone's GPS

Taxi drivers in New York City, and in many other places around the world, have protested against the growth of Uber and the threat it poses to their livelihood. Do you think such protests will be successful? Or does the future belong to Uber, its apps, and its drivers?

capability to identify where a request is coming from. It notifies a nearby driver of the request and sends the passenger a text when the car has arrived. The fare (including tip) is automatically charged to the passenger's credit card account, which is on file with Uber. Uber charges its drivers a portion of every transaction (roughly 20 percent) for the use of the apps on its online platforms; the drivers keep the rest.

The wait time for an Uber car can be close to zero, in stark contrast to the amount of time a person might spend standing on a street corner in many cities in the world trying to hail a taxi during peak periods or in bad weather, in what

now seems a primitive system. Younger customers especially are likely to continue to shift to using such car services. As a result, the jobs of taxi drivers are being threatened, as is the taxi industry as a whole.

Think About It

Have you ever used Uber? If not, would you ever use it? Are you sympathetic to the loss of income and jobs that traditional taxi drivers have experienced with the advent of Uber and similar services? Or do you see such losses simply as unfortunate by-products of an otherwise beneficial technological change?

The Main Sites of Global Problems

Global cities are home to the rich and powerful, the main beneficiaries of globalization. However, it is also the case that cities, including the global cities, are especially hard-hit by a wide range of global problems. Among other things, some of the world's great cities—New York, London, Madrid, Paris—have been the targets of major terrorist attacks; the destinations for large numbers of immigrants, many of them undocumented; and the settings where large numbers of those affected by global health problems are likely to end up in search of medical help. This has led Zygmunt Bauman (2003: 101) to contend that "cities have become dumping grounds for globally begotten problems."

In spite of the global nature and source of these problems, dealing with them becomes a local political necessity, and city officials often lack the economic resources required to address them. For example, the mayor of London is limited in what he can do to deal with the forces that lead many to migrate to his city—the roots of Islamic State–inspired terrorism, the global HIV/AIDS epidemic, and climate change (see below) generated elsewhere. To quote Bauman (2003: 102) again: "Local politics—and particularly urban politics—has become hopelessly overloaded."

Centers of Culture and Consumption

In spite of their problems, cities have played a highly positive role in the development of societies throughout the world. Cities tend to have better-educated residents, are more tolerant, are more likely to generate new ideas, have the best hospitals, offer more jobs, and so on. Much of what we think of as culture, especially "high culture," has its origins, and has become centered, in the city. Thus, many of the world's great universities, museums, symphony orchestras, opera companies, theaters, and restaurants are found in the world's great cities. It is also the case that much of pop culture—such as hip-hop and rap—emanates from the cities.

Cities are also the sources of many developments in the world of consumption. For example, shopping arcades (Benjamin 1999), world's fairs, and department stores had their origins in nineteenth-century Paris and other European cities (Williams [1982] 1991). In the twentieth century, U.S. cities became the world leaders in such consumption sites, most notably New York City, with its world-famous department stores (Macy's and Gimbels) as well as the 1939 and 1964 World's Fairs. When those who lived outside the city could afford to travel and wanted to consume, they often made regular treks to the city to shop, go to the theater, and so on. Cities like Paris and New York also played other key roles in consumption, such as being national and global centers of fashion (Lipovetsky [1987] 2002; Simmel [1904] 1971). Furthermore, cities, especially New York and its famed Madison Avenue, became centers for the advertising industry, which functions to drive consumption (Schudson 1987). A number of cities have become more specialized centers of consumption, the most notable examples being gambling centers such as Las Vegas and Macau. Dubai has undergone a massive building boom in an effort to become the commercial

Reuters

Environmental problems such as air pollution are traceable to the excesses of capitalism's "treadmill of production." Are the economic gains produced by such a system worth the costs?

and consumption center for a good part of the world, stretching from Cairo to Tokyo.

Fantasy Cities. A **fantasy city** is one in which great emphasis is placed on creating a spectacle, especially in the areas of consumption, leisure, tourism, and real estate, dominated by impressive buildings and other developments. Hannigan (1998, 2007) sees only two cities as full-scale fantasy cities: Las Vegas, Nevada, and Orlando, Florida (home of Disney World and many other tourist attractions). However, many others, especially Dubai, have moved in that direction.

Fantasy cities are characterized by infrastructure dominated by such "cathedrals of consumption" (Ritzer 2010a) as "themed restaurants, nightclubs, shopping malls, multiplex cinemas, virtual reality arcades, casino-hotels . . . sports stadiums and arenas, and other urban entertainment centers" (Hannigan 2007: 1641). The whole idea is to draw people, especially tourists, to fantasy cities, and once they are there to lure them into the various cathedrals of consumption, where they will spend large sums of money. Like many developments in the realm of consumption, the fantasy city was largely a U.S. creation, but it has now become increasingly global.

In spite of the increasing importance of ever-larger cities throughout the world, there has been a decline in the central role of cities in consumption. Suburban shopping malls supplanted urban shopping centers and department stores as the prime destination for many shoppers. More recently, the shopping malls themselves have been being supplanted by online shopping (Amazon.com, eBay). Globally, such major players in the world of consumption as IKEA (from Sweden with Dutch ownership) and Carrefour (French) are most likely to be located outside cities. Entertainment giant Disney has placed its theme parks outside some of the world's great cities—Los Angeles, Orlando, Paris, Tokyo, Hong Kong, and Singapore (in 2014).

In many ways, roles have been reversed, and instead of cities being the sources of innovations in consumption, external developments are increasingly finding their way into the cities. They are making the distinctions among cities, suburbs, edge cities, and other geographic areas less clear and meaningful. For example, fast-food restaurants (especially McDonald's) were originally suburban and small-town phenomena, but they have increasingly become urban phenomena as well. In the process, they have tended to displace distinctive urban cafés and restaurants, driving many of the latter out of business and into oblivion. Similarly, discount retail chains (Target and Kohl's) have increasingly made their way into American cities. Even New York City, long known for its highly distinctive consumption sites, has come to look more and more like the rest of the United States (and much of the world) with its large numbers of McDonald's, KFC, and even Kohl's stores.

THE ENVIRONMENT

Because of the explosive growth of a wide range of environmental problems in recent years, as well as the growing attention to, concern over, and even fear of those problems, many sociologists have been drawn to the study of the environment, and especially to the analysis of environmental problems (Antonio and Brulle 2012; Dunlap 2007; Dunlap and Jorgenson 2012). There is now a large and growing group of environmental sociologists as well as a relatively new specialty, environmental sociology (Hannigan 2014; York and Dunlap 2012).

THEORIES OF THE ENVIRONMENT AND ITS PROBLEMS

Sociological approaches to the environment differ depending on the theoretical perspective employed (Preisendorfer and Diekmann 2007). Structural/functional theories tend to focus on large-scale structures and systems and their impact on environmental problems, as well as on the ability to deal with them. For example, one line of thinking is that because large-scale structures are differentiated functionally (politically, economically, legally), they have difficulty coming together to deal with environmental problems. The conflict/critical perspective focuses on capitalism and the need for corporations to grow and to show ever-increasing profits. In other words, capitalism creates a **treadmill of production** whereby everyone in the system depends on continuous productive growth (Gould, Pellow, and Schnaiberg 2008). Such capitalistic needs lead to the exploitation of nonrenewable natural resources and other negative effects on the environment. Among the inter/actionists, symbolic interactionists focus on the ways in which we come to define various environmental issues as problems. Rational choice theorists focus on the fact that there have been great rewards, such as high profits and pay, for those who adversely affect the environment. Conversely, there have been weak, or nonexistent, rewards and even high costs (lower profits, lower wages, higher prices for environmentally friendly products) for those who are interested in being more environmentally responsible. Clearly, from this perspective, the reward and cost structures need to be changed if we hope to induce people to change their behavior and to take actions that help, rather than hurt, the environment.

GLOBALIZATION AND THE ENVIRONMENT

The environment performs three general functions for humans and other species (Dunlap and Catton 2002; Dunlap and Jorgenson 2012). First, the environment is a kind of "supply depot" that provides the natural resources needed for life to exist. Among the renewable and nonrenewable resources provided are air, water, food, shelter, and the materials needed for industries to operate. However, overuse of such renewable resources as water and such nonrenewable resources as fossil fuels can deplete, if not empty, the supply depot.

Second, the environment serves as a "sink" to absorb or dispose of the waste that humans produce in consuming natural resources. However, it is possible to produce so much waste that the environment cannot absorb it all. For example, too much sewage can lead to water pollution. There are ongoing efforts to find various uses for the waste we produce. For instance, human excrement is being converted into fuel for everything from buses to rockets (Buck 2014; Sullivan 2014).

Third, the environment provides us with living space, or a "habitat—where we live, work, play, and travel" (Dunlap and Jorgenson 2012: 530). However, having too many people in a living space creates numerous problems associated with overcrowding and overpopulation.

In terms of all three functions, it could be argued that humans are beginning to exceed the "carrying capacity" of Earth.

There is great global inequality in these three functions. Basically, the developed nations adversely affect the ability of the environment in less developed nations to perform these functions. For example, they use less developed nations as supply depots for natural resources for which they have historically underpaid. In the process, they often adversely affect the ability of the less developed nations to continue to produce these resources. Developed nations also often ship e-waste—that is, discarded electronic equipment—to developing countries, polluting them and their people with the minerals and chemicals in this dangerous debris. This, in turn, despoils the living spaces and the ecosystems of those developing countries.

While environmental problems can and do affect specific countries, the vast majority of these problems are global in nature and scope. As a result, one of the most enduring and important issues in the study of the environment involves its relationship to globalization (Stevis 2005). The environment is inherently global. That is, we all share the atmosphere, are warmed by the Sun, and are connected by the oceans (Yearley 2007). Further, much that relates to the environment has an impact on and flows around the world, or at least large portions of it (such as through weather patterns).

Although the idea that environmental problems are global issues may seem indisputable, this view has been challenged in various ways:

- Not everyone or every part of the world is equally to blame for the most pressing global environmental problems; those from the most developed countries are disproportionately responsible for them (Olivier, Janssens-Maenhout, and Peters 2012).

- Such problems do not, and will not, affect everyone and all areas of the world in the same way. For example, the rise of the level of the seas as a result of climate change will mostly affect those who live in coastal areas or on islands. In addition, because of their greater wealth, those in the Global North will be better able than those in the Global South to find ways of avoiding or dealing with all but the most catastrophic of the problems caused by climate change.

- There are global differences in the importance accorded to, and the dangers associated with, these problems. For example, many in the developed North are highly concerned about climate change, while many in the Global South feel that they are faced with more pressing problems, such as health problems related to disease and malnutrition.

- The main sources of environmental problems change. For example, the center of manufacturing, with its associated pollutants, has been moving from the United States to China.

ASK YOURSELF

Do you think environmental problems are local, global, or both? Why? Do you think it matters who is responsible for creating them, if we are to solve them? Why or why not?

THE LEADING ENVIRONMENTAL PROBLEMS

There are many important environmental problems, and we have touched on several in the preceding sections. In this section we deal with a few in more depth: the destruction of natural habitats, adverse effects of human activity on marine life, the water crisis, and climate change, especially global warming.

Destruction of Natural Habitats

Natural habitats such as the "forests, wetlands, coral reefs, and the ocean bottom" are being destroyed across the globe, often as the result of population growth and the conversion of some of those natural habitats into human habitats (Diamond 2006: 487; Mackay 2014). The most notable deforestation in the world has been taking place in the Amazon rain forest (mostly in Brazil) ("Welcome to Our Shrinking Jungle" 2008), but other parts of the world (e.g., Indonesia) are also destroying their forests (Margono et al. 2014). The Amazon forest is being decimated to create farms and areas for livestock to graze and to prepare for the creation of more human settlements. Brazil's forests are so huge, and they play such a large role in the global ecology, that their destruction will have negative effects on the world as a whole. For example, the burning of all those felled trees releases huge amounts of carbon dioxide, which drifts into the atmosphere and flows around

"Tree huggers," such as these in Kathmandu, Nepal, have been derided and mocked. However, is it possible that we need more "tree hugging" and other forms of protest against a wide array of environmental problems?

the globe, contributing to climate change. The loss of other natural habitats, such as wetlands, coral reefs, and the ocean bottom, will also have a variety of negative consequences for life on Earth. For example, the decline of coral reefs due to runoff from agriculture adversely affects the sea life that exists in and around these reefs.

Adverse Effects on Marine Life

Marine life in the world's oceans has been greatly diminished by overfishing. According to the United Nations Food and Agricultural Organization, 69 percent of the world's most important fisheries can be considered either "fully exploited" or "overexploited." Industrial fishing has led to a 90 percent decline in swordfish, tuna, and marlin populations (Khatchadourian 2007).

A major culprit in the decimation of marine life is industrial fishing. As the amount of sea life declines, the fishing industry compensates by using much more industrialized and intensive techniques. Among these techniques is the use of huge nets that catch large numbers of fish, including many that are not wanted and are discarded. Modern industrial fishing is also characterized by the use of factory ships that process the fish on board rather than waiting until the ships return to port. These technologies contribute to overfishing and in the process destroy complex ecosystems.

The Water Crisis

Water is becoming an increasingly critical global issue (Conca 2006; Hoekstra 2012). Many observers have expressed concern about the "water crisis" in some parts of the world, including California and Nevada in the United States (Nagourney 2015; Subramaniam, Whitlock, and Williford 2012). However, it is the less developed countries in the world that are most likely to be negatively affected by a water crisis as water-dependent manufacturing industries locate themselves within their borders. In addition, they are the least likely to have environmental regulations to prevent problems or to be able to do very much about problems once they begin. Among the concerns about water are the following:

- *Water inequality.* The United States has a water footprint double that of the world average and four times that of China. While many in the world have little access to water, many Americans "water their gardens, fill their swimming pools, and . . . consume considerably more meat than the world average, which significantly enlarges their water footprint" (Hoekstra 2012: 2207).

- *Water pollution.* Humans contribute to the pollution of water through manufacturing processes, mining, agriculture, and inadequate treatment and management of waste (especially fecal matter). This pollution increases waterborne diseases, especially those that affect children (Jorgenson and Givens 2012).

- *Marine pollution.* This involves "a disruption to the natural ecology of water systems, particularly oceans, as a direct or indirect result of human activity" (Burns 2012: 1324). Among the most important causes of marine pollution is the dumping into the oceans of the herbicides, pesticides, and fertilizers used in modern industrial agriculture.

- *Increasing scarcity of water.* There is a possibility that the flow of water could slow or stop completely, at least in some locales (Veldkamp et al. 2014). Some nations are forced to choose between essential uses of water, such as drinking and irrigating crops (Martin 2008). There are tensions within nations and between nations—and even the possibility of war—over increasingly scarce water supplies (Dunn 2013).

ASK YOURSELF

What can individuals do to help alleviate potential problems in the world's freshwater supply? Is it realistic to think that individuals can make a difference in this environmental challenge? Why or why not?

Desertification is the decline in the water supply as a result of the degradation and deterioration of soil and vegetation (Glantz 1977). Water, once considered a public good, is increasingly becoming a valuable and privatized commodity as many places run low on drinkable water. Another preventable decline in water supply is caused by the wasting of water; for example, nearly two-thirds of all water used for irrigation, in addition to as much as half of city water supplies, is wasted due to leaky pipes.

Although we usually think of water as abundant and readily accessible, the fact is that over a billion people do not have reliable sources of safe drinking water, and more than

2.5 billion do not have adequate sanitation systems (Conca 2007; World Health Organization 2015). The poorest areas of the globe and the poorest people within those areas experience a disproportionate share of water-related problems. The situation is apt to grow worse in coming years; it is possible that half the world's population will be faced with water-related problems by the 2030s.

Climate Change and Global Warming

The major form of climate change is global warming, which will make some parts of the world wetter while other parts grow drier. As a general rule, already wet areas will grow wetter and already dry areas drier; both floods and droughts will intensify. It is in the latter that we are likely to see increasingly desperate and expensive efforts to find water by, for example, drilling ever deeper for underground water supplies (Struck 2007). Among the areas likely to grow drier are Southern Europe, the Middle East, South Australia, Patagonia, and the southwestern United States. There are predictions of Dust Bowl–like conditions in the American Southwest and the resulting possibility of mass migrations. In Mexico, similar conditions may lead to mass migrations to Mexican cities and to the United States. Such increases threaten to create even greater problems and animosities than those that already exist in the United States as a result of both legal and, especially, undocumented immigration from Mexico. In more general terms, we are increasingly likely to see the emergence of an entirely new group of people in the world—climate refugees (Gray and Mueller 2012).

Another problem traceable to global warming is the melting of mountaintop glaciers that are important sources of drinking water for many people in the world. As those glaciers melt and fail to re-form fully, they will produce less and less water for those who need the water to survive. The affected populations, too, are likely to become climate refugees, and they are apt to come into conflict with residents of the still water-rich areas to which they are likely to move.

Humans have produced greenhouse gases that have damaged the atmosphere and, in the view of most experts, are leading to a dramatic rise in the temperature of Earth. During the twentieth century, Earth's temperature rose by about 0.74 degrees centigrade; projections for the twenty-first century are for a rise of between 2 and 8 degrees centigrade. Because of the accumulation of greenhouse gases, heat generated by the Sun that would ordinarily be reflected back into the atmosphere is trapped and "radiated back to the Earth at a greater rate than before" (Beer 2012). Great concern is currently focused on the burning of fossil fuels (coal, gas, oil), the resulting emission of carbon dioxide, and the role that this plays in the accumulation of greenhouse gases and global warming. Rates of carbon dioxide emissions, mainly from industrialized countries, increased by 80 percent between 1970 and 2004 and have grown by 3 percent a year since

2000. Figure 14.8 shows the relationship between global temperature and carbon dioxide concentration.

There is little or no doubt, at least among scientists, that global warming and more generally climate change are real phenomena with human-made causes (Cook et al. 2013). Furthermore, the predominant view is that global warming is already well advanced and is progressing rapidly. Many scientists have further added that some negative effects of global warming will be irreversible once they start. Global warming is expected to affect humans adversely in a number of different ways (Brown 2007). It will bring with it more, and more intense, heat waves, and excessive heat can be deadly. A heat wave in Europe in 2003, the worst in almost 500 years, caused about 30,000 deaths from heat-related illnesses. A recent study concludes that heat waves such as the one in 2003 will be "commonplace" in Europe by 2040 (Jolly 2014). The aging of the population throughout much of the developed world makes more people vulnerable to being made ill and dying due to excessive heat. Urbanization also increases the likelihood of death, since cities can become heat islands. Other factors that make death from excessive heat more likely are being very young, ill, poor, or someone who lacks the ability to move away from superheated areas. There are things that can be done to mitigate the dangers of heat stress, such as greater use of air-conditioning, but many people in the world have no access to air-conditioning or cannot afford it. Further, the use of air-conditioning causes other problems, such as huge demand on energy resources.

Sea levels are projected to rise dramatically, especially as the glaciers melt. A conservative estimate is that sea levels will rise about 1 meter during the twenty-first century. Approximately 100 million people in the world, mostly in Asia and in island nations, live within a meter of sea level, and their homes would be washed away by such a rise. However,

FIGURE 14.8 • Global Temperature and Carbon Dioxide Concentration, 1880–2010

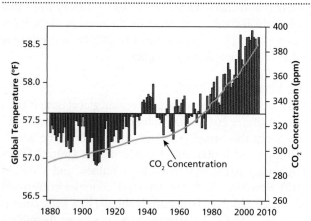

SOURCE: Global Climate Change Indicators, National Oceanic and Atmospheric Administration.

FIGURE 14.9 • Natural Catastrophes Worldwide, 2012

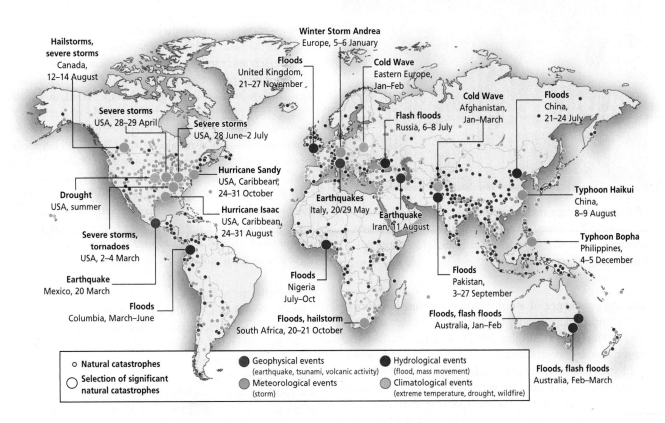

Hailstorms, severe storms
Canada, 12–14 August

Severe storms
USA, 28–29 April

Severe storms
USA, 28 June–2 July

Floods
United Kingdom, 21–27 November

Winter Storm Andrea
Europe, 5–6 January

Cold Wave
Eastern Europe, Jan–Feb

Cold Wave
Afghanistan, Jan–March

Floods
China, 21–24 July

Flash floods
Russia, 6–8 July

Hurricane Sandy
USA, Caribbean, 24–31 October

Drought
USA, summer

Hurricane Isaac
USA, Caribbean, 24–31 August

Earthquakes
Italy, 20/29 May

Earthquake
Iran, 11 August

Typhoon Haikui
China, 8–9 August

Severe storms, tornadoes
USA, 2–4 March

Typhoon Bopha
Philippines, 4–5 December

Earthquake
Mexico, 20 March

Floods
Nigeria
July–Oct

Floods
Pakistan, 3–27 September

Floods
Columbia, March–June

Floods, hailstorm
South Africa, 20–21 October

Floods, flash floods
Australia, Jan–Feb

○ Natural catastrophes
○ Selection of significant natural catastrophes

● Geophysical events
(earthquake, tsunami, volcanic activity)
● Meteorological events
(storm)

● Hydrological events
(flood, mass movement)
● Climatological events
(extreme temperature, drought, wildfire)

Floods, flash floods
Australia, Feb–March

SOURCE: Natural Catastrophes, 2012 World Map. © 2013 Münchener Rückversicherungs-Gesellschaft, Geo Risks Research, NatCatService.

this estimate does not take into account the melting of the Greenland and West Antarctic ice sheets, which could add 10 or more meters to the rising seas. In such a case, much larger areas of both the less developed and developed worlds would be inundated.

More severe storms will lead to more deaths, especially from increased flooding. The residents of coastal areas are in particular danger due to storm surges. Extreme variations in weather may lead to more droughts and shortages of water. Food production may not increase as rapidly as expected, with the result that the number of the world's hungry will increase. Figure 14.9 shows all the natural catastrophes around the world in 2012, including extreme weather events.

Rising temperatures will speed up chemical reactions and worsen pollution from ozone and soot. Deaths from ozone pollution (mostly among those with lung or heart problems) could increase by 5 percent by 2050. Pollen production could increase, adversely affecting those with allergies, asthma, and other respiratory conditions.

Waterborne diseases (e.g., cholera) will increase with higher temperatures and more torrential rains. Food-borne infections (e.g., salmonella) will also increase with hotter weather.

The incidence of diseases caused by animals and insects may increase. For example, it is expected that malaria and dengue borne by mosquitoes will become more widespread. Exposure to malaria is expected to increase by 25 percent in Africa by 2100. Other diseases of this type that are likely to become more prevalent are yellow fever, also carried by mosquitoes, and Lyme disease, carried by ticks (Brown 2007). Ebola is now well established in the human populations in West Africa and will be difficult, if not impossible, to eradicate completely. In any case, increasing numbers of people will come into contact with the wild animals that carry the disease.

GLOBAL RESPONSES

Many global environmental problems, including climate change, are traceable to capitalist economic development (Antonio and Brulle 2012). That is, as economies grow and generate greater wealth, they are likely to do increasing damage to the environment. As concerned as nation-states are becoming about damage to the environment, they are not about to either give up the fruits of economic development or cease seeking to become more developed.

As a result, a variety of efforts have arisen to at least reduce the magnitude of environmental problems. We have

Wind turbines like these in Africa hold the promise of supplying cleaner and more affordable energy, but this technology is not without problems. What intergenerational concerns arise in the process of attempting to reduce human reliance on fossil fuels?

There are a number of dimensions to the relationship between globalization and sustainability. First, there is the *economic* dimension and the issue of whether economic development irretrievably destroys the environment or whether it gives countries the desire and the ability to better control factors that are adversely affecting the environment. Second, *technology* can be seen as both producing environmental degradation and creating the possibility of limiting the damage. Third, there is the dimension of *awareness* and whether the global media create greater awareness of environmental problems and their causes or whether consumerism, also pushed by the global media, increases people's blindness to these issues. Finally, there is the *politics* of environmentalism, with some global organizations, such as the World Trade Organization (WTO), pushing for more economic growth while many others, like Greenpeace, are seeking to reduce it or to limit its negative impact on the environment. Overall, many aspects of globalization adversely affect efforts at sustainable development.

seen the emergence of a number of environmental movements and organizations, such as Greenpeace, oriented toward this goal (Caniglia 2012). In addition to these movements and organizations, but more general in nature, is an increase in environmental activism (Fisher 2012). Environmental activists are generally interested either in protecting some aspect of the environment, such as a coral reef or a virgin forest, or in protesting environmental hazards, such as toxic waste or the use of a particular site as a garbage dump. In terms of globalization, activists might oppose the global exportation of environmental problems or support international efforts and treaties to mitigate these problems. While some environmental movements and activists may want to slow or stop economic development, many favor sustainable development.

Sustainable Development

Sustainable development involves economic and environmental changes that meet the needs of the present, especially of the world's poor, without jeopardizing the ability to meet the needs of the future (Blewitt 2014). While the focus of sustainable development is primarily physical sustainability, it is also concerned with promoting equity within the current generation and for future generations.

Globalization can be seen as either a threat or a boon to sustainability. Globalization can threaten sustainable development by reducing the regulatory capacities of governments over environmental threats. On the other hand, globalization can aid sustainable development through the spread of modern, less environmentally destructive technologies and the creation of standards for more efficient resource utilization. Globalization can also lead to a greater demand for cleaner environments.

Technological Fixes

There is growing interest these days in finding technological fixes for at least some global environmental problems, especially those related to climate change. There is a long-standing attraction to finding technological solutions to all social problems. To many, creating new technologies seems far easier and less painful than the much harder task of getting large numbers of people to change their behavior. That is, people tend to be reluctant to change their consumption patterns and thus prefer the hope of technological fixes for any resultant ecological problems. Furthermore, many industries have a vested interest in the continuation of high levels of consumption. Thus, even though the burning of fossil fuels is a major cause of global warming, innumerable industries and people are wedded to it. Automobile culture, which exists in both the developed and developing worlds, is one consequential example.

Enter "geoengineering" and a series of relatively new and controversial proposals for dealing with global ecological problems, especially global warming, while leaving untouched and unaddressed the underlying and growing causes of climate change (Asayama 2015). Among the ideas that have been discussed are cooling the Earth's poles by injecting chemicals into the upper atmosphere and putting mirrors in space (Dean 2007). More recently the focus has been on capturing and storing harmful carbon dioxide emissions, which would permit the Earth's atmosphere to retain less heat, or on reflecting sunlight and its heat away from the Earth (Fountain 2015).

Undertaking such projects would require truly global efforts and a massively funded global governance structure. In any event, it seems unlikely that geoengineering, or any other technological fix, will solve a set of problems that are at their base caused by human actions (Huesemann and Huesemann 2011). While technology can help, the only real solution lies in dramatically changing those behaviors.

SUMMARY

While overall fertility rates are dropping globally, the world's population continues to increase, although at a declining rate. Population decline can weaken nations in various ways, but it can also have benefits. Demographers focus on three main processes: fertility, or people's reproductive behavior; mortality, or death and death rates within a population; and migration, the movements of people and the impact of these movements on both sending and receiving societies.

Urbanization is the process by which an increasing percentage of a society's population comes to be located in relatively densely populated urban areas. Cities are large, permanent settlements that are cosmopolitan in that they are open to a variety of external, including global, influences. Despite some problems, they play a positive role in the development of societies around the world. The most important of the world's cities are global cities. Megacities have populations greater than 10 million.

Suburbs are communities adjacent to but outside the political boundaries of central cities. Edge cities are on or near major highways, house large corporate offices, and have important commercial and consumption centers such as shopping malls. Looking for cheaper land and housing, people have pushed even farther out into areas between the suburbs and rural areas,

known as exurbia. Major American cities have seen significant declines as they have lost the industries they once relied on. Gentrification has lured some white, middle-class residents back to cities' urban centers.

Increasing environmental problems have led sociologists to examine the environment more closely. Structural/functional theorists examine the ability of large-scale structures to deal with these problems. Conflict/critical theorists focus on capitalism and the impact on the environment of corporate expansion and the increasing use of natural resources. Inter/actionists focus more on the ways in which we come to define various environmental issues as problems. Most environmental problems are global in nature and scope.

Global environmental problems include the destruction of natural habitats, adverse effects of human activity on marine life, the water crisis, and climate change, especially global warming, and its many negative effects. The relationship between globalization and sustainability has a number of dimensions, including economic, technological, and political, as well as media awareness. While geoengineering provides some hope that technological advances might be able to deal with some environmental problems, it does not address their human causes.

REVIEW QUESTIONS

1. How does the "demographic dividend" differ from the "financial time bomb"? Overall, is the United States in a period of a demographic dividend or a financial time bomb? Why?

2. According to demographic transition theory, what role do technological advances play in changing demographics? What role does development play in reducing fertility and the death rate?

3. How have the "push" and "pull" factors associated with migration changed in the global age?

4. Distinguish among refugees, asylum seekers, labor migrants, and undocumented immigrants.

5. What are the arguments against international migration? How might you counter those arguments? What are some arguments *for* international migration?

6. Discuss the contradiction between the two roles played by the world's cities—as the sites of some of the world's

worst problems and as the sites of some of its greatest achievements.

7. What makes cities cultural and consumption centers? How is a "fantasy city" different from a traditional urban area? In what ways are fantasy cities related to processes of Americanization?

8. How can sustainable development create a more ecologically friendly city? How would this development differ from that of the last 200 years?

9. What are the world's major environmental problems? Are there technological fixes that can deal with our environmental problems? If so, what are they?

10. Do you think that globalization is ultimately a threat or a boon to sustainability? What current evidence would you cite to support your position?

APPLYING THE SOCIOLOGICAL IMAGINATION

This chapter examines global differences in environmental issues. For this activity, choose one highly developed and

one less developed country, and compare and contrast their environmental policies with those of the United States. How does each country approach climate change, especially global warming? Based on the chapter, why do you suppose these countries have similar or different approaches to environmental policy? How does this reflect their positions in a global system of stratification? What are the potential consequences of their positions?

KEY TERMS

asylum seekers: People who flee their home country, usually in an effort to escape political oppression or religious persecution. (p. 339)

birthrate: The number of births per 1,000 people per year. (p. 333)

cities: Large, permanent, and spatially concentrated human settlements. (p. 340)

cosmopolitan: Open to a variety of external and global influences. (p. 343)

demographers: Those who study population dynamics. (p. 332)

demography: The scientific study of population, especially its growth and decline, as well as the movement of people. (p. 332)

desertification: A decline in the water supply as a result of the degradation and deterioration of soil and vegetation. (p. 349)

edge cities: Cities that are on or near major highways, have corporate offices that offer employment to many, and have important commercial and consumption centers, in particular shopping malls. (p. 342)

exurbia: Outlying areas between the suburbs and rural areas. (p. 342)

fantasy city: A city in which great emphasis is placed on creating a spectacle, especially in the areas of consumption, leisure, tourism, and impressive buildings and other real estate developments. (p. 347)

fertility: People's reproductive behavior, especially the number of births. (p. 334)

gated communities: Communities in which gates, surveillance cameras, and guards provide the residents with a feeling of security from the problems (crime, panhandling) that they think they left behind in the city. (p. 341)

gentrification: The reinvestment of real estate capital in blighted inner-city areas in order to rebuild residences and create a new infrastructure for the well-to-do. (p. 343)

global cities: The cities, especially New York City, London, and Tokyo, with the world's leading industries and marketplaces. (p. 343)

labor migrants: Those who migrate because they are driven by either "push" factors (a lack of work, low pay) in their homeland or "pull" factors (jobs and higher pay available elsewhere). (p.339)

local: Inward looking rather than outward looking. (p. 343)

megacities: Cities with populations greater than 10 million. (p. 344)

megalopolis: A cluster of highly populated cities that can stretch over great distances. (p. 341)

metropolis: A large, powerful, and culturally influential urban area that contains a central city and surrounding communities that are economically and socially linked to the center. (p. 341)

migration: The movements of people and their impact on the sending and receiving locales. (p. 334)

mortality: Deaths and death rates within a population. (p. 334)

refugees: Migrants who are forced to leave their homeland, or who leave involuntarily because they fear for their safety. (p. 339)

suburbanization: The process whereby large numbers of people move out of the city and into nearby, less densely populated, environs. (p. 341)

suburbs: Communities that are adjacent to, but outside the political boundaries of, large central cities. (p. 341)

sustainable development: Economic and environmental changes that meet the needs of the present, especially of the world's poor, without jeopardizing the ability to meet the needs of the future. (p. 352)

treadmill of production: The dependence of everyone in the capitalist system on continuous growth in production and in the economy. (p. 347)

undocumented immigrants: Immigrants residing in a receiving country without valid authorization. (p. 339)

urban: City dwelling; in the United States, to be considered urban, an area must have more than 50,000 inhabitants. (p. 340)

urbanism: The distinctive way of life (lifestyles, attitudes, social relationships) that emerges in, and is closely associated with, urban areas. (p. 341)

urbanization: The process by which an increasing percentage of a society's population comes to be located in relatively densely populated urban areas. (p. 341)

$SAGE edge™ edge.sagepub.com/ritzeressentials2e

SAGE edge offers a robust online environment featuring an impressive array of free tools and resources for review, study, and further exploration, keeping both instructors and students on the cutting edge of teaching and learning.

LEARNING OBJECTIVES	FOR FURTHER EXPLORATION AND APPLICATION
LO 14-1: Discuss the causes and effects of population growth, population decline, and migration.	▶ Why Birth Rates Are at an All-Time Low ◉ "School for Husbands" Promotes Family Planning ◉ Reproductive Health and Teen Pregnancy
LO 14-2: Describe the growing urbanization of the world's population and the effects of deindustrialization on U.S. cities.	▶ The World's Poorest Megacities ◉ The Fastest Growing Cities in the Unites States ◉ When an American City Goes Bankrupt
LO 14-3: Discuss the major environmental problems and responses to them.	▶ Environmental Sociology: What Is It and Where Did It Come From? ◉ How the Santa Barbara Oil Spill Reopened a Fierce Environmental Debate ◉ What Is Environmental Racism?

SOCIAL CHANGE, SOCIAL MOVEMENTS, AND COLLECTIVE ACTION

From Occupy to Blockupy

On September 17, 2011, social and political activists took to New York City's Zuccotti Park to bring attention to problems produced by capitalism, such as the struggles of the lower classes and governmental partiality toward corporate and upper-class interests. Calling their budding social movement Occupy Wall Street, the group established an encampment that served as home base for a series of demonstrations, marches, and speeches in the city's bustling financial district. Media attention and support from large labor unions bolstered the movement's legitimacy—and its numbers. Large crowds gave rise to a unique culture with distinct roles, norms, values, and social institutions.

Occupy movements modeled on the original began to appear across the United States and, soon after, around the world. More than 1,000 were documented globally, including several dozen large encampments across the Americas, Europe, Australia, and Asia. The nearly instantaneous dissemination of news and videos across social media networks, combined with the sheer number of these interconnected protests, marked Occupy as a truly global social movement, at least for a short time. By late 2012, the Occupy movement seemed to have become a historical footnote.

However, its impact and influence live on, especially in the German-based Blockupy movement, which had its beginnings in 2012 just as Occupy was beginning to fade. That Blockupy is alive and well is demonstrated by its largest and most heated demonstration

LEARNING OBJECTIVES

 15-1 Use sociological concepts to explain the rise and impact of social movements such as the women's movement, the gay and lesbian movement, the civil rights movement, and the Tea Party.

15-2 Contrast social movements and other types of collective action, such as crowds, riots, and disasters.

15-3 Describe the process of social change, particularly the interactions of globalization, consumption, and the rise of the Internet.

Corbis

in March 2015 in Frankfurt, Germany. Like Occupy, Blockupy is animated, most generally, by its opposition to the abuses of the capitalist system. Its specific focus, at least at the moment, is the European Union's austerity policies, in particular toward Greece, and the negative effect of those policies on the Greek economy and especially its workers.

The growing inequality in the United States and elsewhere is, in large part, a product of the capitalist system. That inequality and other economic problems are likely to continue to spawn social movements, some of them likely inspired by Occupy and Blockupy. ●

Social change involves variations over time in every aspect of the social world, ranging from changes affecting individuals to global transformations (Sekulic 2007b; Sztompka 1993; Weinstein 2010). Sociologists are concerned with the effects of social changes on the self-concepts of individuals, the structures of the United States, global economic and political systems (McMichael 2011), and much more. Social change has been at the heart of sociology since its inception. This interest continues to this day, and it will be at least as strong, if not stronger, in the future.

A good recent example of social change is the ongoing dramatic transformation of much of the Arab world that began in late 2010. Aspects of this change, usually referred to as the Arab Spring, have been discussed several times throughout this text. However, the "Arab Spring" label no longer seems appropriate, since many of the changes wrought by these movements have not turned out as hoped: "Springtime" does not seem to have arrived in many of the countries involved. Among other things, we have seen a return to authoritarianism in Egypt, anarchy in Libya, terrorism in Tunisia, and continuing civil war in Syria and Iraq, both of which seem to be in the process of being permanently dismembered.

The most important transformation wrought by the Arab Spring was the 2011 overthrow of longtime Egyptian dictator Hosni Mubarak and the coming to power of a former leader of the Islamic Brotherhood, Mohamed Morsi. However, Morsi's rule was uneasy and marked by much protest and disorder. In fact, Morsi was overthrown in a military coup in July 2013, and the general who led the coup—Abdel Fattah el-Sisi—became the new Egyptian president with dictatorial powers. The dictator of Tunisia, Zine El Abidine Ben Ali, was also overthrown in 2011, but his successor was forced from office in early 2013 as a result of a continuing conflict between Islamists and secularists. An election in December 2014 resulted in the first freely elected president in that country's history. In Libya, another dictator, Muammar Gaddafi, was killed in 2011. Libya now has a weak and highly

Reuters

Antigovernment protesters demanded the ouster of Yemen's president. What happens to a society when a revolution fails?

unstable political system, with local tribes, militias, and warlords battling for control of parts of the country. President Ali Abdullah Saleh of Yemen was badly injured in a bomb attack and was forced out of office in late 2011. The government of Yemen disintegrated, and the country is now being ravaged by Houthi rebels. An extremely bloody rebellion in Syria is well into its fifth year in late 2015, with President Bashar al-Assad clinging to control over an ever-smaller part of the country (Lynch, Freelon, and Aday 2014; Ma'oz 2014). The rest of Syria is largely under the control of the Sunni-based terrorist organization Islamic State, which has extended its control into much of Iraq and poses a threat to stability there as well as in Lebanon and other parts of the region. Syria abuts Israel, which could be drawn into the conflict in various ways, especially if Islamic State fighters draw close to its borders and engage in direct conflict with the Israeli military. That could lead Arabs in Gaza and Israel's Occupied Territories to grow more restive. The social changes associated with, and set in motion by, the Arab Spring continue, and the effects of the Arab Spring reverberate throughout world, especially the Middle East (Lynch 2013; Moss 2013). Other North African countries such as Mali and Algeria have also been drawn into the turmoil.

What is most important for our purposes is that even though it now seems misnamed, the Arab Spring is an excellent illustration of the major sociological ideas to be discussed in this chapter. It brought about *social change,* and it exemplifies both *collective action* and *social movements.*

SOCIAL MOVEMENTS

A **social movement** is a sustained and intentional collective effort, usually operating outside established institutional channels, either to bring about or to retard social change (Cross and Snow 2012; Snow 2013b; Snow et al. 2013). The social movements associated with the Arab Spring sought to bring about social change, while the Tea Party (see below) seeks to retard, or even reverse, changes in the United States associated with liberalism, such as President Obama's Patient Protection and Affordable Care Act. Having already touched on the Arab Spring movements, we will discuss other examples of social movements later in this chapter. Beyond the Tea Party, the chapter addresses the feminist movement, the gay and lesbian movement, and the civil rights movement. Following brief overviews, various sociological concepts and ideas that help us to better understand these social movements will be discussed.

THE TEA PARTY

The Tea Party (www.teaparty.org) is a national movement named for the Boston Tea Party of 1773. The word *Tea* in Tea Party is an acronym for "taxed enough already." The Tea Party is *not* a political party, but it wields great power over and within the Republican Party. It emerged in the United States in 2009 as a protest against high taxes and other government actions (Pullum 2013; van Dyke and Meyer 2014). It especially targeted the Obama administration's efforts to address the Great Recession and the associated housing crisis, as well as efforts to stimulate the economy through the American Recovery and Reinvestment Act of 2009. The Tea Party also opposed passage of the Affordable Care Act, or "Obamacare" (Barstow 2010; see Chapter 13). It has more recently been enraged by President Obama's late 2014 executive order shielding as many as 5 million undocumented immigrants from deportation (Peters 2014). The Tea Party will undoubtedly seek to overturn that executive order, as well as some or all of Obamacare, should the Republicans win the White House in 2016 and retain control of both houses of Congress. As Figure 15.1 shows, 94 percent of Tea Party members disapprove of Obamacare. Among those who disapprove, 64 percent say they think elected officials should try to make the law fail.

The initial impetus for the Tea Party movement was a February 19, 2009, on-air rant by commentator Rick Santelli on the conservative and pro-business cable TV network CNBC. Among other things, Santelli said: "The government is promoting bad behavior. . . . How many of you people want to pay your neighbor's mortgage, that has an extra bathroom,

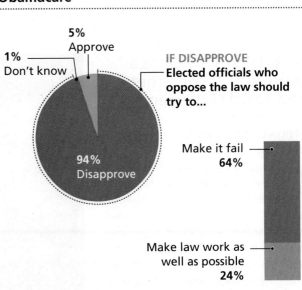

FIGURE 15.1 • Tea Party's Views of Obamacare

SOURCE: Data from Pew Research Center, "As Health Care Law Proceeds, Opposition and Uncertainty Persist," September 16, 2013 (http://www.people-press.org/2013/09/16/as-health-care-law-proceeds-opposition-and-uncertainty-persist).

and can't pay their bills? Raise their hand! . . . We're thinking of having a Chicago Tea Party in July. . . . I'm going to start organizing" (quoted in Williamson, Skocpol, and Coggin 2011: 37). Interest in the Tea Party boomed in 2009 and beyond. However, it remains a loosely organized group of local and national conservative organizations. According to one estimate, there are only a few hundred active Tea Party groups in the United States, and only a fraction of them have more than 500 members (Williamson et al. 2011). The movement's impact has been greatly magnified by the media, especially the "advocacy journalism" of cable television news networks—the conservative and pro–Tea Party Fox News and the liberal and anti–Tea Party MSNBC (Boykoff and Laschever 2011). Whatever else the overheated media coverage managed to accomplish, it brought a degree of attention and influence to the Tea Party far out of proportion to the number of active participants in the movement.

The Tea Party had almost immediate success when on April 15, 2010, there were hundreds of Tax Day protests throughout the United States, with between 5,000 and 10,000 people participating in the main protest in Washington, D.C. The Tea Party's greatest success occurred in the November 2010 congressional elections, when candidates linked to the movement won 39 of 129 races for the House of Representatives and 5 of 9 races for the Senate (Karpowitz et al. 2011).

The Tea Party is also a force in presidential politics. For example, Jeb Bush's ability to win the 2016 Republican presidential nomination is threatened by the fact that his stands

A Sociologist Debates a Journalist: The Internet and Social Movements

Malcolm Gladwell is a journalist who draws on many different fields in his work, especially a number of social sciences, including sociology. His work ranges across not only a number of different academic disciplines but also an incredibly wide variety of social phenomena. In 2010, before the height of the Arab Spring and the rise of Islamic State, he wrote an essay for the *New Yorker* titled "Small Change: Why the Revolution Will Not Be Tweeted." He argued *against* the notion that social activism had been radically transformed by the new social media. More generally, he contested the idea that "Facebook and Twitter and the like upended the traditional relationship between political authority and popular will, consequently making it easier for the less powerful to engage in collective action."

Gladwell based this view on the sociological argument that social media are built on the basis of people who have only "weak ties" with one another (Granovetter 1973) (see Chapter 4). People who are not strongly related to one another are unlikely to come together to engage in high-risk behaviors such as a social revolution. Since part of my research (Tufekci 2010) deals with how Internet use interacts with the composition of people's social networks, I knew that the assertion that social media relationships involve only people with weak ties was wrong. In fact, extensive research shows that people use social media to relate to those with whom they have *both* strong and weak ties. Most people use Facebook to interact with close friends and family as well as with acquaintances with whom they do not have close ties.

Would the Arab Spring have been possible without social media? Thousands of Egyptians used cell phones to record the celebrations in Cairo after the overthrow of President Hosni Mubarak in 2011.

Seeking to correct such errors, I penned a reply to Gladwell on my blog, www.technosociology.org. I argued that social media could well be a major contributor to social change by facilitating connections and collective action among ordinary people, which would otherwise be very hard to coordinate. Also, the Internet allows citizens to circumvent censorship and to express their preferences. Unlike with television, which is primarily a one-way medium, ordinary citizens can have a voice via the Internet.

Just a few months after I wrote this blog entry, revolutions in Tunisia and Egypt burst onto the world scene. It was clear that the activists involved in these revolutions were using Facebook, Twitter, YouTube, and other platforms to disseminate information that would otherwise be censored. They were communicating with people with whom they were weakly *and* strongly connected to

mobilize the masses in order ultimately to overthrow the existing regimes. Contrary to Gladwell's argument, it was clear in these instances, and in many others (e.g., Islamic State's use of Facebook to recruit followers), that social media can enable social movements and facilitate social change.

SOURCE: Printed with the permission of Zeynep Tufekci.

Think About It

Do people who have strong links to leaders of a social movement react differently to social media messages about the movement than people with weak links? Why or why not? Consider your close friends and your distant acquaintances. Do they react differently to your Facebook messages? Why or why not?

Associated Press

Is the Tea Party a social movement, a political party in the making, or a flash in the pan?

- It is a *collective effort,* since it includes *a significant number of people* from throughout the United States.

- It has been *sustained* for several years.

- It was certainly brought into being *intentionally.*

- It is *outside established institutional channels,* since it is not formally affiliated with either political party.

- It is an *effort to retard some political changes,* such as tax increases and President Obama's health care reform act.

- It is an *attempt to bring about substantial political change* in the Republican Party and the government as a whole. The Tea Party seeks to change the Republican Party by moving it further to the right and to change the American government by forcing it to reduce taxes, better control government spending and debt, and reduce its size and power.

FEMINIST MOVEMENTS

The movements of concern in this section are based on **feminism**, or the belief that women are equal to men, especially socially, politically, and economically (see Chapter 9). These movements have all of the characteristics of a social movement outlined above (Crossley and Hurwitz 2013). The large number of people involved certainly intended to bring the movements into being and to maintain them. Feminist movements—often called women's movements—have, at least until recently, had to work outside established institutional channels. Historically, women were likely to be denied access to these channels by the men in control of the institutions. For example, U.S. women did not gain the right to vote until 1920. The movements have certainly demonstrated durability, as you will soon learn, both in the United States and around the world (Basu 2010). And they are oriented toward dramatically improving the position of women throughout the world.

The Women's Movement in the United States

The women's movement can be traced back to England and Mary Wollstonecraft's 1792 book *A Vindication of the Rights of Woman,* which made the case for women's equality (Reid 2014; Tetrault 2014). The first wave of the women's movement in the United States began in the 1840s (Reger 2007). It was focused largely on the issue of suffrage, or gaining the right to vote for women. It had its roots in the early involvement of women in the antialcohol (temperance) and antislavery movements. However, women were largely subordinated and ignored in these movements. Anger about such treatment led a group of women to organize the 1848 Seneca Falls Convention, which focused on such issues as restrictions on women's roles within the family, women's rights in terms of education and property, and, especially, women's suffrage (Wellman 2004). Decades of meetings, protests, marches, and social activism

on various issues are at variance with Tea Party positions (for instance, he is pro-immigration). Bush is generally not seen as being sufficiently conservative by Tea Party standards (Edsall 2015).

The Tea Party is unlikely to become a new political party, in part because the United States has long been dominated by a two-party system. However, if it were to become a full-fledged political party and became institutionalized, it would no longer be a social movement. It would also no longer be a social movement if it were to peter out and die. It is possible that the Tea Party will remain what it is, a social movement, for some time to come.

Like the other examples to be discussed later, the Tea Party has *the basic characteristics of a social movement*:

FIGURE 15.2 • When Women Won the Right to Vote in Selected Countries, Twentieth Century

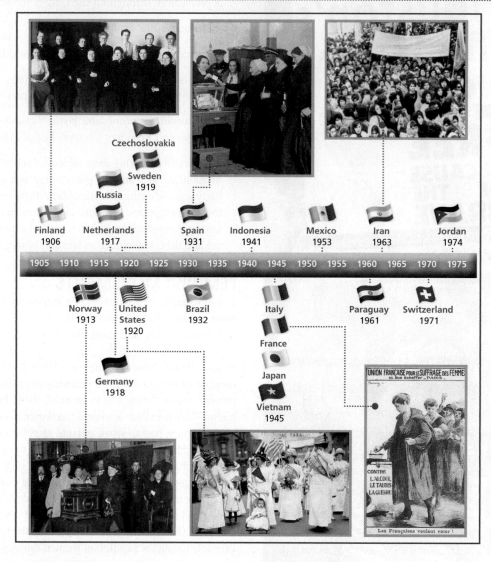

SAGE data**maps** edge.sagepub.com
• Year when women's suffrage was established in every country.

SOURCE: Data from "Women's Suffrage: When Did Women Vote?" Interactive Map. Scholastic.com.

followed, including the arrest of prominent suffragist leaders (for attempting to vote). Several national organizations were formed to push forward women's right to vote. The movement included battles between black and white women, with prominent white suffragist Susan B. Anthony saying, "I will cut off this right arm of mine before I will ever work or demand the ballot for the Negro and not the [white] woman" (quoted in Wilson and Russell 1996: 30). Black suffragists were routinely excluded from the white women's marches and protests. Although the Nineteenth Amendment gave women voting rights as early as 1848, it did not become law until August 26, 1920. (Figure 15.2 shows when women won the right to vote in select countries in the twentieth century.) By the 1930s, black women's voting rights had become severely

circumscribed; their political disenfranchisement lasted until the civil rights movement of the 1960s.

The second wave of the women's movement began in the 1960s. It drew from the first wave but went beyond it in various ways. Several key books, including Simone de Beauvoir's *The Second Sex* ([1952] 1973) and Betty Friedan's *The Feminine Mystique* (1963), had a strong effect on the movement and articulated a number of its key ideas. More practically, the second wave, like the first, grew out of the dissatisfaction of activists with their involvement in other social movements, especially the New Left and civil rights movements (Houck and Dixon 2011), and those movements' failure to deal with gender issues. Activists were also angered by the fact that the movements themselves were patriarchal.

An important event in the midst of the second wave was the founding of the National Organization for Women (NOW) on October 29, 1966. The founders were women in government dissatisfied with its failure to deal with sex discrimination against women in the workplace. NOW eventually came to focus on a much wider range of issues, including discrimination against women in education, the rights of women within the family, and the problems of poor women.

The second wave reached its peak between 1972 and 1982. A number of developments occurred during this period, including the founding of *Ms.* magazine; the appearance of women's studies programs on college campuses; the passage of Title IX of the U.S. Education Amendments, ending discrimination on the basis of sex in publicly funded education; and the 1973 Supreme Court decision in the case of *Roe v. Wade,* legalizing abortion. However, the second wave was soon wracked by internal conflicts. Some women—women of color, lesbians, working-class women—protested that their interests were not being adequately reflected in or addressed by the more publicly visible women's movement (Boris 2012; Roth 2004). These internal conflicts resulted in a polarization of feminism. More conservative feminists, the reformists, were primarily concerned about gender equality in the workplace (hooks 2000). Revolutionary feminists criticized the limited goals of the reformists, who focused primarily on the concerns of white middle-class women. They also emphasized the ways in which conservative feminists often acted in a patriarchal and sexist manner toward other women.

In addition, feminism lost its edge because of a decline among women engaging in feminist dialogue in "consciousness-raising" groups (hooks 2000). College campuses had served as one of the few arenas in which feminist politics were discussed. Consequently, feminist politics grew stunted, and some dissatisfied radical feminists left the movement. The rise of opposition groups and the emergence of a powerful conservative movement in the United States in the 1980s contributed to the development of a sense, at least among some observers and participants, that the country had entered a postfeminist era (Hall and Rodriguez 2003).

By the early 1990s, it was clear that feminism was once again alive and well as a third wave of the women's movement emerged. This wave, which is ongoing, has been marked by a reaction against the problems confronted by the movement in the 1980s. The defining characteristics of the third wave are greater racial and ethnic inclusivity and more focus on problems such as racism, classism, transphobia, and homophobia. The movement also addresses the place of women in the larger culture and a variety of specific issues such as the wage gap between men and women, sexual harassment, violence against women, and sexual assault and rape. Cyberfeminism and activism on the Internet can be seen as part of the third wave (Carty 2013; Haraway 1991; Wajcman 2010), although there are those who see these developments as marking the dawning of a fourth wave

(Munro 2013). Feminists discuss, debate, and mobilize on a variety of websites, including the Crunk Feminist Collective (www.crunkfeministcollective.com), The F-Word (www.thefword.org.uk), and Feministing (http://feministing.com). Although the third wave uses the latest technologies and is far more internally differentiated, it continues to draw on the first two waves (Snyder 2008). It is fusing the old and the new in an effort to adapt feminism to the rapidly changing realities of the twenty-first century.

Among the very contemporary issues being faced by the women's movement is the fact that many online video games (such as *Grand Theft Auto V*), among many other aspects of contemporary society, are sexist and misogynistic, to say nothing of being racist and classist (Fox and Tang 2014). Men who play these games are more likely than those who do not to develop sexist attitudes (Stermer and Burkley 2015). Given the Internet's booming importance, online abuses and other negative effects of Internet use take on special importance for many interest groups, including the women's movement. "Gamergate" is a new label for the problems posed by the Internet, especially concerning video games, for women (in particular those who have the audacity to criticize the sexism of the video game industry) (Wingfield 2014a). Since sexism remains a problem on the Internet—and in many other contexts—new and future developments will continue to reflect negative feelings toward women and become new targets for a continually evolving women's movement.

The Global Women's Movement

The organization of women on a transnational basis began between the 1830s and the 1860s (Berkovitch 1999, 2012). At first, this was highly informal, but formal groups did emerge, such as the World Women's Christian Temperance Union (WWCTU), founded in 1874. While the WWCTU focused on the problem of alcohol consumption, it was concerned about other issues as well, such as political equality for women. By the time of its first international convention in 1891, the WWCTU had branches in 26 countries. Members adopted the view that "universal sisterhood" existed and that women throughout the world experienced a common fate. Suffrage became an increasingly important issue globally, and that led to the founding of the International Woman Suffrage Alliance (IWSA) in 1904 (Rupp and Taylor 1999).

One of the most striking events in the early twentieth century was the gathering of more than a thousand women in 1915 at the International Congress of Women. The main goal of the meeting was to find ways to resolve conflicts and prevent future wars. After World War I, the founding of the League of Nations and the International Labour Organization (ILO) created new opportunities for global action by women (and others). However, women's activities in and through these organizations achieved few tangible results, in part because leaders within the organizations tended to be "elite, White, Christian women from Northern and Western Europe" (Freedman 2009: 48). Many women within these groups

These members of the World Women's Christian Temperance Union seem to have had little effect on the customers in the bar they entered, but the WWCTU later had more success fighting for women's suffrage. What is the role for a women's movement today, and what should be its goals?

supported colonialism despite the presence of fellow members who suffered under colonial rule. Moreover, the reproduction of colonial relationships within the movement was yet another facet of the contentious beginnings of an international women's movement. In reaction to this, black women from Africa and the United States formed the International Council of Women of the Darker Races in 1920. They called for support in their struggle not only for personal independence but also for national independence from colonial domination (Alexander and Mohanty 2013; Freedman 2009).

Much greater strides were made as a result of the founding of the United Nations after World War II. Instrumental in this progress was the UN Commission on the Status of Women. Its initiative led to a world conference on women in 1975 and to the declaration of the UN International Women's Year. Yet men dominated the speeches and leadership positions at the 1975 conference; they tended to represent the interests of their respective governments rather than those of women's organizations. Women continued to press for equality, however, and eventually acquired more leadership roles, which they used to foster discussions about the gaps between male and female opportunities. This was followed by the UN Decade for Women (1976–1985), conferences during that decade, and follow-up conferences held in 1995 (30,000 people attended the UN Fourth World Conference on Women in Beijing) and 2005. Because of such meetings, women from all over the world were able to interact on a face-to-face basis and to develop various transnational interpersonal ties (Davis [1991] 1999). As a result of these associations, many local and transnational women's organizations emerged (Fernandes 2013).

In addition to these formal organizations, many transnational feminist networks have developed in recent years (Ferree and Tripp 2006). These are more fluid organizational forms, lacking formal membership and bureaucratic structures. They have been aided in their formation and interaction by new communication technologies, especially the Internet. However, rather than these developments leading to a single global sisterhood, some fractures and divisions have grown deeper in the global women's movement. For example, women of the Global South often resist initiatives supported by women of the Global North. This resistance is due in part to Southern women's need to prevent the imposition of Northern notions of superiority and to recognize that injustice and emancipation can take various forms (Freedman 2009). In spite of these divisions, the women's movement today is far more global than ever. It is not only having an impact on the position of women throughout the world but also shaping, and being shaped by, globalization (Basu 2010; Crossley and Hurwitz 2013). This can be seen, for example, in arguments over the meaning(s) of feminism and women's rights during the war in Afghanistan and U.S. participation in other international conflicts (Ali 2010).

ASK YOURSELF

Does it surprise you to learn that the women's movement and its global arm are characterized by fractures? What might heal these divisions? Do men need to play a role in women's movements? Why or why not?

THE GAY AND LESBIAN MOVEMENTS[1]

The origins of U.S.-based gay and lesbian movements can be traced back to the 1890s (Shroedel and Fiber 2000). There were earlier gay and lesbian movements in other places, such as Germany (Newton 2009), and there are, of course, gay and lesbian movements throughout the world today (Tremblay, Paternotte, and Johnson 2013). These movements still have much work to do—same-sex acts remain illegal in at least 77 countries (Hildebrandt 2014). The focus here, however, is mainly on gay and lesbian movements in the United States (Valocchi 2013).

World War II and the Lavender Scare

Some problems for gays and lesbians (such as mobilization against them in the military) developed during the World War II era (Bérubé 2010). However, in general, that period was something of a golden age for gays and lesbians in the United States. Men and women engaged in new experiences as they left home, settled in new living situations, and found themselves in same-sex milieus in the military or in civilian workplaces. This period has been described as "somewhat of

---

[1]This section is printed with the permission of Tracy Royce and Danielle Antoinette Hidalgo.

a nationwide coming out experience" (Allan Bérubé, quoted in Johnson 2004: 51). The war years allowed for increased possibilities and opportunities for sexual encounters, as well as an "anything goes" mentality. However, beginning in 1948, the United States entered a period of mounting public criticism of the "moral decay" of homosexuality, as well as of communism.

What came to be known as the "Lavender Scare" signaled a turning point for the history of gay and lesbian movements in the United States. Starting in 1950, the Lavender Scare was a government-sponsored attack on sexual minorities, those who engaged in, or were suspected of, same-sex sexual behaviors (Johnson 2004). As in the better-known Red Scare (a response to fears of communism), agents attempted to ferret out government employees who were considered security risks. In this case, those suspected of engaging in "sexual perversions" or homosexuality were vulnerable because it was feared they might reveal government secrets to foreign agents under pressure to prevent their sexual activities from being made public. Thousands were discharged from government service; some committed suicide. This institutionalized attack on homosexuality also sparked political organization among gays and lesbians. The Mattachine Society (see below), founded by a government worker, marked the start of 25 years of efforts to dismantle federal job discrimination laws. In 1975 it became illegal to discriminate against gays and lesbian in hiring and firing decisions. Thus, the "crackdown" on homosexuals, "perverts," and those engaged in "immoral" sexual relations fostered a long-lasting collective movement to fight for the rights of gays and lesbians.

The U.S.-Based Homophile Movement

Early efforts to organize "homophile" (i.e., gay rights) movements crystallized in 1950–1951 in the formation of the Mattachine Society, originally based in Los Angeles. Other cities started chapters, and by 1966 there were 15 gay and lesbian rights organizations in the United States; by 1969 there were 50 (D'Emilio 1983; Hay 2012). The Daughters of Bilitis (DOB), an offshoot of the Mattachine Society focusing on the rights of gay women, was founded in 1955 (Rutledge 1992; Valocchi 2007). These organizations emphasized education and largely embraced assimilationist strategies in order to gain mainstream acceptance. Although gay and lesbian activists worked alongside each other, gender privilege (particularly male) remained and was a source of dissatisfaction for lesbians active in the homophile movement. As one lesbian activist stated, "There wasn't a Women's Movement yet. . . . We knew our place—we were always the coffee makers. . . . There was a clear set of chores for women" (Shroedel and Fiber 2000: 99).

Stonewall

The 1969 uprisings at Greenwich Village's Mafia-owned gay bar the Stonewall Inn are regarded by many as pivotal in the twentieth-century struggle for gay rights and as denoting the beginning of the modern gay rights movement (Armstrong

Patrons of the Stonewall Inn in Greenwich Village fought back when police raided the gay enclave in 1969, in what proved to be a watershed moment. Do you agree with those who feel the civil rights, antiwar, and feminist movements had an impact on the struggle for gay rights? If so, what was that impact?

and Crage 2006, 2013; Duberman 1994). On June 27, 1969, the patrons of the Stonewall Inn—"Puerto Rican drag queens, lesbians, effeminate men, and young street people" (Nardi, Sanders, and Marmot 1994: 14)—reacted violently to a police raid. Law enforcement officials and members of the gay community alike credited this event with inspiring gays and lesbians to more aggressively demand equality and freedom from abuse. Within a few years there were more than 800 gay and lesbian groups all over the United States. Today, gay pride days and marches continue to commemorate the assertion of collective queer identity and entitlement to rights that emerged as a result of Stonewall. However, some question gay history's emphasis on the Stonewall uprisings. They argue that new forms of the gay and lesbian movement owe much to the foundational work of homophile groups, as well as to twentieth-century civil rights, antiwar, and feminist organizations (Jay 1999).

Lesbian Herstory

Given the underlying male privilege that was embodied in groups such as the Mattachine Society, many lesbians were dissatisfied with their organizing experiences alongside gay men. And although lesbians found a respite from sexism in the mainstream second-wave women's movement, the heterosexism and sometimes overt hostility encountered by lesbians in feminist groups made these organizing spaces less than hospitable. Consequently, many lesbians split off from the mainstream gay and feminist movements. Numerous lesbian separatist groups emerged, such as the Furies, who framed lesbianism as a political choice in opposition to male supremacy.

Not all lesbians politicized their sexual identities in this way. For women who desired other women in butch/femme (traditionally male/traditionally female) space, a masculine–feminine relationship continued. But lesbian separatists argued that in order to truly be feminists, women had to remove themselves completely from the male sphere. In practice, this resulted in the formation of women-only communities or "womyn's lands" and lesbian-driven, woman-centered activism. These women "wanted to create entirely new institutions and to shape a women's culture that would embody all of the best values that were not male" (Faderman 1991: 216).

ASK YOURSELF

Do all gays and lesbians have the same goals or try to achieve equality by the same means? Do their philosophical and practical divisions help or hinder their efforts? Why?

HIV/AIDS, ACT UP, and Queer Nation

The recognition of HIV/AIDS in 1981 by the Centers for Disease Control and Prevention had a tremendous impact on gay and lesbian politics and communities. The activism that emerged from this period was embodied in the early efforts of the AIDS Coalition to Unleash Power (ACT UP) (Stockdill 2013). In 1989, ACT UP pressured pharmaceutical company Burroughs Wellcome to make its new antiretroviral drug, AZT, more affordable for HIV-positive patients. ACT UP embodied a new kind of activism that included civil disobedience, activist art, and other forms of creative activities and representations. ACT UP chapters opened throughout the nation. In 1990, some ACT UP activists formed a new group, Queer Nation, which, although short-lived, served as the beginning of a public and direct representation of LGBTQ (lesbian, gay, bisexual, transgender, and queer) issues. Out of HIV/AIDS activism and via the efforts of Queer Nation, the gay and lesbian movement shifted into a politics of queer spaces and identities.

The Fight for Marriage Equality

Gays and lesbians in the United States legally challenged the 1996 Defense of Marriage Act, which barred federal recognition of same-sex marriages. Their efforts met with considerable success, and in 2011 President Obama determined that the act was unconstitutional and directed the Justice Department to stop defending the law in court. In 2013 the U.S. Supreme Court struck down the section of the act that defined marriage as involving one man and one woman. It also declared unconstitutional the barring of federal recognition of same-sex marriages. As a result of this Supreme Court decision, gays and lesbians gained many federal and state benefits that were formerly denied to them and that are automatically conferred on heterosexual couples. Gays and lesbians continue to fight for other benefits that are still denied to them. In June 2015,

What arguments do opponents of gay and lesbian rights make to support their views?

another Supreme Court decision made same-sex marriage legal across the United States. Globally, same-sex couples enjoy the legal right to marry in a number of other countries.

Gay and lesbian movements have had mixed success globally. While at least some forms of homosexuality are legal in some parts of the world, in a much larger part of the world homosexuality is illegal or same-sex couples are not recognized. There are even parts of the world, mostly Islamic, where homosexuality is subject to severe penalties, life in prison, or even death.

THE CIVIL RIGHTS MOVEMENT

Arguably, the most notable social movement in the United States was, and may still be, the civil rights movement (Andrews 2013; Morris 1984, 2007). Perhaps the key event in the history of the civil rights movement was the successful 1955 boycott of segregated city buses in Montgomery, Alabama. While the boycott was organized locally, it was led nationally by the Reverend Martin Luther King Jr. ([1958] 2010). His success there catapulted him into the position of leader of the national civil rights movement. The Montgomery boycott served as a model for future civil rights action and all other subsequent social movements. It emphasized non-violent action, made it clear that the black community could overcome internal divisions to become an effective force for change, showed the central role that the black church could play in such a social movement, and demonstrated that the black community was able to finance these actions with little or no outside help.

The success of the Montgomery bus boycott led black organizations to become more involved in civil rights activities. These included the National Association for the Advancement of Colored People (NAACP), formed in 1910, and the Congress of Racial Equality (CORE), organized in 1942. It also led to the formation of new organizations, especially the Southern Christian Leadership Conference (SCLC), and to the creation and active involvement of innumerable local groups. The actions spurred on by these groups and organizations encountered significant opposition from whites, sometimes leading to violence. A key development in 1960 was the large-scale involvement of black, and some white, college students in sit-ins at segregated lunch counters throughout the South. These students were crucial to the formation of another new organization, the Student Nonviolent Coordinating Committee (SNCC), in 1960. SNCC, in turn, drew many white students into the movement.

In the 1960s the civil rights movement became a significant force through boycotts, sit-ins, freedom rides, mass marches, and mass arrests. In some cases, media coverage of vicious attacks against black activists gave the movement great visibility and elicited much sympathy from those not initially inclined to support it.

Many of the "invisible leaders" of the civil rights movement were black women such as Fannie Lou Hamer, Septima Poinsette Clark, and Ella Baker. Their invisibility was an unfortunate by-product of the gender hierarchy as it existed in the 1950s. When women spearheaded successful civil rights campaigns, more "visible" men in the movement took the credit and usurped women's leadership positions (Olson 2002). The many women who participated in the movement served as volunteers, and their numbers far surpassed those of their male counterparts.

ASK YOURSELF

Why are the black women who served as "invisible leaders" of the civil rights movement not more widely known today? Do you think women who are fighting racism today, whatever their color, are sufficiently recognized by the public? Why or why not?

The movement had great success, manifest especially in the Civil Rights Act of 1964, which banned discrimination on the basis not only of race but also of sex, religion, and national identity. Of course, the larger goal of eliminating racism in America eluded the civil rights movement and continues to elude achievement today (Pager, Western, and Bonikowski 2009).

The global nature of the civil rights movement is especially clear in the antiapartheid movement led by Nelson Mandela in South Africa (Van Kessel 2013). Apartheid was a system of racial separation that had been made legal in 1948. Soon thereafter a social movement against it emerged, led by the African National Congress. It garnered great international support and succeeded in achieving its goals in less than a half century (Waldmeir [1997] 2001). By 1994, both apartheid and white hegemony in South Africa had ended.

EMERGENCE, MOBILIZATION, AND IMPACT OF SOCIAL MOVEMENTS

A variety of conditions determine whether or not a social movement will emerge. To start with, there must be grievances, or matters that large numbers of people find troublesome (Snow 2013a). In the case of the Tea Party, for example, grievances included those against high taxes, the economic stimulus, and health care reform. Grievances about the unfair treatment of women, gays and lesbians, and blacks animated the other social movements discussed above. However, grievances alone are not sufficient for a social movement to arise. Individuals and organizations must be mobilized in order to do something about them. All of the movements discussed above were successful in mobilizing people to act.

Factors in the Emergence of a Social Movement

Assuming a set of grievances and efforts at mobilization, certain other conditions must exist for a social movement to

Perhaps no one symbolizes the civil rights movement so well as Martin Luther King Jr. Here King waves to supporters from the steps of the Lincoln Memorial during the 1963 March on Washington.

emerge. First, there must be openings or opportunities within the political system. For example, a deep and stubborn recession, high unemployment rates, a massive bailout of banks and large corporations, and a dramatic escalation in the national debt provided an opening for the rise of the Tea Party (Macdonald 2010; Pace 2010). That opening was widened as these and related problems, as well as public concern about them, increased (Crutsinger 2010).

A second factor involves various spatial arrangements, such as the physical proximity of those involved. Clearly, social movements develop more easily when those who at least have the potential to become involved come into contact with one another fairly easily or on a regular basis. Another spatial factor is whether or not there are "free spaces" where those involved can meet. It is in such spaces that a movement can develop, out of the limelight and free of external surveillance and control. Women on college campuses existed in close proximity to one another, and this helped in the formation of the women's movement, while free spaces such as churches were especially important to the development of the civil rights movement.

A third factor is the availability of resources. This is the concern of **resource mobilization theory**, one of the most popular approaches to understanding social movements today (Edwards and Gillham 2013; Jenkins 1983; Walder 2009). The focus is on what groups of people need to do in order to mobilize effectively to bring about social change. This theory assumes that there is some strain within the larger society and that there are groups of people who have grievances that result from those strains. One of the most important works in this tradition is that of Jack Goldstone (1991; Rojas and Goodwin 2013) on *revolutions*. These are social movements in which the strains produced by state breakdown (e.g., failure of the government to function properly, fiscal distress) play a key role, leading to the development of revolutionary movements. Major examples of revolutions include the French, American, and Russian Revolutions. Once a strain exists, the issue is what resources are needed for these groups to become social movements, perhaps even successful social movements.

Resources and Mobilization of Social Movements

Five types of resources have been identified as important to the mobilization of social movements. First are *material resources* such as money, property, and equipment. It is costly to mount a successful social movement, and money and other material resources are mandatory (Snow, Soule, and Cress 2005). Notable in this regard is the backing of the Tea Party by conservative billionaires. Second are *social-organizational resources,* which include infrastructure (Internet access is especially important today), social networks (insiders with access to important groups and organizations), and the

organizations that are formed by the social movement (Tea Party, NAACP, ACT UP) (Stepan-Norris and Southworth 2007). Third are *human resources* such as the leadership, expertise, skills, and day-to-day labor of those in the organization (Tsutsui and Wotipka 2004). More specific resources might be dynamic public speakers (such as Martin Luther King Jr.) and spokespersons, skilled web designers, and people skilled in organizational dynamics. Fourth are *moral resources* such as the degree to which the larger public regards the movement as legitimate. Other moral resources include a sense that there is a high level of integrity among the leaders as well as in the membership as a whole (Lowe 2002). Finally, *cultural resources* are important—such as bodies of knowledge or skills that are tacitly shared by at least some members of the movement. These might include knowledge of how to organize a protest, hold a news conference, or run a meeting. Overall, the keys to the success or failure of a social movement are the available resources and the ability to use some or all of them in order to mobilize effectively to pursue desired social change.

Another important issue is the source of such resources. One source is simply having members who are themselves able to produce the resources by, for example, raising money, developing networks, or socializing their children to become part of the movement as adults. Another is aggregating external resources, such as soliciting donations from a wide range of donors. Also of importance is the need to locate patrons who can be relied on to support the group monetarily and in many other ways (e.g., by providing staff members). Finally, a social movement can co-opt the resources of other organizations. For example, social movements in the United States have often co-opted the resources of churches by, for example, using their buildings, their staff, and their moral authority.

Participation. Once a social movement is under way, methods must be found to ensure member participation. First, people need to be asked to participate. For that to occur, they need to be embedded in social networks involving other movement members. Second, a variety of social psychological factors are involved. These include personally identifying with the movement and its causes, being aroused emotionally by the issues involved and becoming committed to dealing with them, and being at a point in life—retired, unemployed, in college—where one is available to participate in the movement. Third, incentives need to be offered so that the gains to members for their involvement outweigh the risks and costs. For example, for participants in the civil rights movement, the achievement of greater rights for blacks outweighed the risk of being beaten or murdered and the cost of lost time and income. While material incentives are important, of far greater importance are the social incentives associated with joining with others as part of the movement,

An environmental effort called 350.org staged this rally outside a coal plant to raise awareness of global warming on what it called an "international day of action." What other strategies and tactics relating to climate change are you aware of? Which do you think will be successful?

as well as the moral incentive of being involved in something one believes in strongly (Quadagno and Rohlinger 2009).

Goals, Strategy, and Tactics. Once formed, a social movement needs to have goals, a strategy, and a variety of tactics in order to succeed. Goals relate to what the movement seeks to do, such as cut taxes or make society more equal. Strategy involves the movement's long-term plan for achieving its goals. Once a strategy is in place, tactics become important. Tactics are more short-term in nature. They need to be quite fluid and able to adapt quickly in light of changes taking place in the immediate or larger environment. In the case of the civil rights movement, the strategy was to create situations that brought the plight of black Americans, especially those who lived in the South, to the attention of the media, the public, and political leaders. Tactics in this case involved engaging in *civil disobedience,* or nonviolent public acts that are against the law and aimed at changing the law or government policies (Tescione 2013). For example, blacks attempted to order food at segregated lunch counters. The acts of civil disobedience produced reactions (e.g., white protests, police action) that attracted

media and public attention and eventually public outrage. Of particular importance are the actions of countermovements and government officials. For example, the civil rights movement had to adapt to the hostile actions of both white supremacists and many local government officials.

Factors in Success. A variety of factors help to determine whether or not a social movement will succeed (Cross and Snow 2012; Rochon 1990). One is its sheer *size.* All social movements start small, but those that succeed are likely to have recruited large numbers of activists and supporters. Another is *novelty,* or the uniqueness of the movement and its goals. Uniqueness and size are important because they lead to a great deal of media attention, which, in turn, is likely to generate additional supporters and funds. The latter are two of the many *resources* social movements need to succeed (see above). *Violence,* as in the case of the Stonewall riots, can be useful in achieving results. However, it also can be counterproductive by turning off potential supporters and members. Perhaps more important, it can lead to violent reactions that can end in the suppression of the movement. *Militancy* can also be double-edged, since a highly militant social movement might be able to achieve its goals quickly, but militancy, like violence, can lead to counterreactions and suppression. *Nonviolence* has been a successful method for social movements because it avoids the powerful counterreactions engendered by violent and militant social movements. The nonviolent approach is traceable largely to Mahatma Gandhi and his use of such means as noncooperation with the British-controlled government to gain Indian independence in 1947. Today, a large number of social movements, including the Tea Party and the women's, civil rights, and gay and lesbian movements, have adopted a nonviolent approach. Globally, many organizations associated with the environmental movement, as well as those associated with the World Social Forum and operating in opposition to at least some aspects of globalization, rely almost exclusively on nonviolent methods.

Although various aspects of social movements themselves strongly affect whether or not they will be successful, many other factors are in play. Of great importance is the ability of individuals, groups, or the state (especially the police and the military) to suppress a social movement (Earl 2007). Efforts at suppressing social movements can be covert, such as the FBI's wiretapping of the phones of members of dissident groups, especially suspected communist and civil rights groups, in the United States in the mid-1950s through the early 1970s. They can also be overt, a major example being the violent suppression in 1989 of antigovernment protests in Tiananmen Square by the Chinese government and the military. Another example is the violence committed by local law enforcement officers and white supremacists against civil rights activists in the United States in the 1960s. Yet another is the police raid of the Stonewall Inn in 1969.

The Impact of Social Movements

Whether or not they are successful, social movements often leave their mark, which is sometimes a quite powerful imprint. A government may be able to suppress a social movement, but it is likely that aspects of the government and the way it operates will be affected by the movement as well as by the efforts to suppress it. For example, in the 1940s and 1950s, the U.S. government was able to suppress efforts to increase the influence of communism throughout the country. However, while it was successful in those efforts, it engaged in a variety of highly questionable actions. Major examples include the activities of the House Un-American Activities Committee (HUAC) and especially those of the infamous Senator Joseph McCarthy. Since that time, government actions that even hint at the kind taken during the 1940s and 1950s are labeled "McCarthyism" and, as a result, are unlikely to succeed.

Nevertheless, the government retains the ability to suppress social movements, and in many ways that ability and its extent have increased. This is a result, in part, of the fact that distinctions among activism, terrorism, and extremism are being eroded by government agencies, especially those concerned with law enforcement (Monaghan and Walby 2012). The danger here is that many activist social movements with positive goals and legal methods may end up being suppressed along with terroristic and extremist movements that pose a genuine threat to the United States.

Social movements, especially those that achieve some success, often leave strong legacies for, and have powerful impacts on, later movements. For example, the civil rights movement was an inspiration and a model for many later movements in the United States, such as the student, antiwar, environmental, gay and lesbian, and disability movements. Social movements outside the United States—for example, South Africa's antiapartheid movement, the Solidarity movement in Poland, and the democracy movement in China—have also been strongly affected by the civil rights movement.

While social movements are oriented toward changing society, they also have strong impacts on the individuals involved, both members of the movements and those who oppose them. The greatest impact is usually on the large numbers of people who actively participate in movements (Roth 2007). Their attitudes, and perhaps the entire courses of their lives, are often altered greatly by their involvement. Much the same is true of those who take an active role in opposing social movements.

THE INTERNET, GLOBALIZATION, AND SOCIAL MOVEMENTS

Two of the most important recent developments as far as social movements are concerned relate to globalization (Agrikoliansky 2013; Maiba 2005) and the Internet (Carty 2013), as well as other new media technologies such as smartphones (Castells 2008).

The Internet has proven to be an important means of involving and organizing large numbers of people, perhaps millions of them, who are widely separated from one another, perhaps even in different parts of the world. In other words, people no longer need to be in close physical proximity to be involved in social movements. People can also now communicate more easily through the use of smartphones, even from the sites of events. This communication offers new possibilities for mobilizing those engaged in social movements. It is possible for participants in a movement not only to communicate verbally with others in the movement but also to snap pictures or shoot videos with their smartphones and send them instantaneously via YouTube or Facebook to large numbers of interested parties. This allows them to see for themselves what is transpiring in the social movement. As noted previously, Islamic State has been effective in using the Internet to recruit supporters, many of whom have trekked to Syria to participate in conflict there and in the region. IS has been particularly successful at using Facebook to attract female adherents from the West (Erlanger 2014). There are also now online activists (e-activists) who are creating electronic social movements (e-movements). At least some e-movements have the possibility of becoming social movements in the material world.

The Internet and other technologies enable social movements to cover wide geographic areas and even to become global. Like much else in the world today, social movements are less constrained than ever before by national borders. It seems likely that the future will bring an increasing number of global social movements. We will discuss the Internet and globalization further later in this chapter.

COLLECTIVE ACTION

Collective action is generated, or engaged in, by a group of people to encourage or retard social change (Oliver 2013: 210). Social movements are one kind of collective action; others include crowds, riots, and disasters. Like all other forms of collective action, social movements usually occur outside established institutional channels. However, social movements are different from all other forms of collective action in at least two ways. First, most forms of collective action are short-lived compared to social movements. Thus, a crowd, for example, can come together and disperse within hours, but a social movement can be sustained for years or decades. Second, a social movement is intentional; other forms of collective action are not. For instance, a community that comes together immediately after a disaster such as an earthquake or a flood does not do so intentionally. It has been brought together and springs into action because of some unanticipated external event. After the 2011 earthquake and tsunami in northern Japan, newspapers reported that a strong sense of community emerged and helped people survive the aftermath (Fackler 2011). In 2014 and 2015, several killings of black males by white police officers across the United States—in Ferguson, Missouri; Cleveland, Ohio; Staten Island, New York; and Baltimore, Maryland—brought together blacks in those communities, as well as multiracial groups throughout the country, in an effort to deal with the problem and its roots.

While social movements have been theorized separately and somewhat differently (resource mobilization theory), the dominant approach to thinking about other forms of collective action is **emergent norm theory** (Arthur and Lemonik 2013; Turner and Killian 1987). This theory is based on the idea that new norms emerge in light of some precipitating event. These norms guide the often nontraditional behaviors that characterize collective action. Implicit in this theory is the idea that in collective action, conventional norms cease to be as effective or as important, at least to some degree. Contrary to popular opinion, however, collective action is not irrational, random, or out of control

A rash of widely publicized violence by white police officers against black males in several states led to many instances of collective action, including this rally in Washington, D.C., to protest the deaths of Michael Brown, Eric Garner, and others. Have you ever taken part in collective action? If not, what would it take to motivate you to do so?

(Aguirre et al. 2011). It is rational and guided by the new norms that develop in the situation.

CROWDS

The clearest application of emergent norm theory to collective action involves the case of a **crowd**, a temporary gathering of a relatively large number of people in a common geographic location at a given time (McPhail 2007; Snow and Owens 2013). We are all familiar with all sorts of crowds, such as those that gather at the sites of celebrations or catastrophes, but a relatively new type is the flash crowd (Massaro and Mullaney 2011). Flash crowds have become easier to generate as a result of the Internet, e-mail, and social networking sites.

One concern in the literature on crowds is the degree to which individuals behave differently in crowds than they do in other social contexts. Emergent norm theory suggests that they do behave differently, but that is because they are conforming to a different set of norms than exist elsewhere in the social world. That is more comforting than the alternative view, which sees people in crowds as losing control of their cognitive processes, complying blindly with the suggestions of crowd leaders, copying mindlessly what is done by those around them in the crowd, and acting selfishly. A large body of research has failed to find any support for the latter view (Postmes and Spears 1998; von Sivers et al. 2014).

However, it is possible that flash crowds brought together by messages on Twitter do operate differently and may be more in line with the alternative, discomforting view of crowds. It might be that because such crowds have been brought together so impersonally, and members might well not know one another when they do come together, they do not have time to develop norms.

ASK YOURSELF

Do you behave differently when in a crowd than you do when alone? How, and why? Have you ever been in a flash crowd? What was the experience like?

RIOTS

A **riot** is temporary unruly collective action that causes damage to persons or property (Myers 2007, 2013). There have been a number of major riots in the last half century in the United States, including race riots in the 1960s in Los Angeles, Detroit, and Washington, D.C. One notable race riot occurred in Los Angeles in 1992 following the acquittal of four police officers charged with the beating of motorist Rodney King. More recent, if less violent, race riots occurred in 2014 in Ferguson, Missouri, as well as in Baltimore, Maryland, in early 2015. Riots, of course, have happened elsewhere in the world; they are a global phenomenon.

Negative Views of Riots

We are likely to have negative views of riots and rioters. However, riots may not be irrational outbursts. Rather, they may be motivated by frustrations over various kinds of abuses and the inability to do much about them under normal circumstances (Auyero and Moran 2007). It is hard to generalize about rioters, but there is little support in the research for the idea that rioters are more likely to be criminals, unemployed, or uneducated. A few things seem clear about those who participate in riots. They are more likely to be men, to be young, to have been physically close to where the riots occur, and to feel that their actions can make a difference. The literature on police involvement in riots is also ambiguous, with police being seen as having the ability both to quell riots and to incite them further with repressive actions.

It is also worth noting that the mass media can contribute to rioting through the ways in which they treat riots. For one thing, live coverage of riots can inflame them by drawing in additional participants. Live, immediate media reports on rioting are also more likely to be inaccurate and to involve inflammatory reporting. For another thing, media reports of riots can suggest that this is a form of action to be emulated at other places and times. Social media can also quickly draw large numbers of people to riot sites.

Positive Effects of Riots

Riots can have positive effects. The Los Angeles Rodney King riot undoubtedly led to changes and improvements in the way the police deal with suspects and the general public, although similar incidents continue to be reported. More generally, riots have at times led to various programs designed to deal with the conditions that were seen to be at their source, such as poverty and unemployment. However, the lasting power of these changes is unclear, and, in any case, people are injured and die, and communities are ruined, in riots. In some cases, it takes decades for riot sites to recover (Cannon 1997; Schoch and Lin 2007; Spencer 2004).

DISASTERS

Disasters are often dealt with in sociology in the same context as social change and social movements. The reason is that disasters can result from social change (such as the "reign of terror" in the aftermath of the French Revolution) and social movements (such as the millions of deaths as a result of the rise of Nazism). Disasters can also cause various social changes (such as the building of earthquake-resistant buildings after a devastating earthquake) and lead to social movements (such as for democracy in Germany at the end of World War II in the wake of the disaster caused by the Nazis).

Disasters are events that suddenly, unexpectedly, and severely disrupt and harm the environment, the social structure, people, and their property (Silver 2007). They are distinguished from accidents (e.g., automobile and airplane crashes) by their far greater impact. Many U.S. disasters have resulted in billions of dollars' worth of damage, and the numbers of such huge disasters have increased in recent years (see Figure 15.3). One 2010 disaster was an earthquake in Haiti that decimated a significant portion of that Caribbean nation. No one knows the exact numbers, but it is estimated that more than 200,000 people were killed and another 300,000 were injured. Innumerable poorly constructed homes, schools, and other buildings were destroyed. The government virtually ceased functioning as its offices collapsed, literally and figuratively, and many officials were killed or injured (Bhatty 2010). By 2014, little progress had been made in rebuilding homes and the infrastructure in Haiti ("Haiti, Unfinished" 2014; Sontag 2012). While it is a stark example, this earthquake represents just one of many natural disasters that have occurred in recent years. Most notable in 2015 was a devastating earthquake in Nepal that killed more than 8,000 people and destroyed much infrastructure, including many poorly constructed homes and buildings (Associated Press 2015c).

Human Involvement in Disasters

Disasters such as earthquakes are natural phenomena, but humans often play a role in bringing disasters about and in exacerbating the consequences of natural disasters. People frequently build in areas—for example, on geological fault lines or on floodplains—where there should be no significant building. Furthermore, what they build is often quite flimsy and likely to be destroyed in a natural disaster. Building stronger structures can be very costly, and impoverished nations such as Haiti and Nepal simply cannot afford to do so (Interlandi 2010).

FIGURE 15.3 • Billion-Dollar Weather and Climate Disasters in the United States, 1980–2014

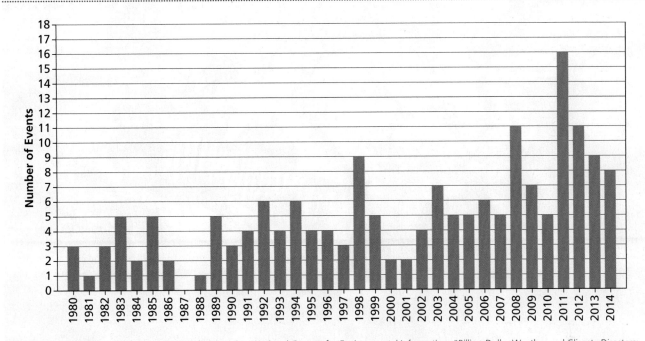

SOURCE: National Oceanic and Atmospheric Administration, National Centers for Environmental Information, "Billion-Dollar Weather and Climate Disasters: Time Series," 1980–2014 (http://www.ncdc.noaa.gov/billions/time-series).

There are, of course, disasters that are the result of human error or corruption. On April 20, 2010, a huge explosion on the BP *Deepwater Horizon* oil rig in the Gulf of Mexico killed 11 workers and left oil gushing into the gulf for three months ("Louisiana Oil Rig" 2010). During that period, 206 million U.S. gallons of oil flowed into the water, affecting nearly 1,000 miles of coastline (Morris et al. 2013). There had been warnings for decades about the dangers associated with deep-sea drilling and oil wells. However, such drilling was pushed forward by the desire for ever-escalating profits on the part of corporations like BP and the voracious need for oil in the United States and other developed nations. Once the *Deepwater Horizon* oil gusher occurred, it became clear that no one quite knew how to go about stopping it; the well was not finally capped until July 15. The spilled oil caused great damage to the gulf's marine life, its beaches, and the businesses that depend on tourists drawn to the area.

Recall from Chapter 5 that the space shuttle *Challenger* disintegrated a little over a minute into its flight on January 28, 1986, killing all seven crew members (Altabbakh et al. 2013; Vaughan 1996). To get needed funds and to launch space shuttles in a timely manner, NASA had ignored warnings, taken risks, and tolerated mistakes and deception. While Vaughan (1996) views this disaster as a unique occurrence, Charles Perrow (1999) sees such accidents as "normal." That is, highly complex systems such as those associated with NASA and the space shuttle will inevitably have such disasters, although they happen only rarely.

Human-made disasters also can be political in nature, and they are associated with revolutions, riots, and acts of terrorism. For example, in mid-2010, the center of Bangkok, Thailand, was ravaged by riots aimed at overthrowing the government. And then, of course, there was the 9/11 disaster caused by hijackers crashing planes into the World Trade Center towers and the Pentagon, as well as the downing of one plane before it reached its target. These terrorist attacks resulted in the deaths of nearly 3,000 people.

The Effects of Disasters

Disasters have enormous negative long-term consequences for the people and areas involved. Individuals and collectivities are traumatized for long periods after disasters (Erikson 1976). People's lives are disrupted for years, if not decades, as are the social networks in which they are enmeshed. Disasters also worsen existing inequalities. For example, females in Haiti suffered disproportionately from the effects of the 2010 earthquake. Furthermore, they were less likely than males to receive humanitarian aid in the aftermath of the quake. Haitian women were more likely than their male counterparts to live in tents, which, among other things, provided them little protection and security. They were especially vulnerable to "unwanted sexual advances and assault" (Jean-Charles 2010).

However, some people and groups are in a better position than others to handle disasters. Disasters can also bring people and communities together in unprecedented ways

newscom rrlhree

Parts of Haiti have still not recovered from the disastrous 2010 earthquake. What are the major short- and long-term problems associated with such disasters?

to deal with the aftereffects. The heroism of many of those involved in helping after the 9/11 disaster—firefighters, police officers, and citizens—is one example of this (Fritsch 2001; Rozdeba 2011; Saxon 2003). Within Haiti, a number of aid agencies are working to continue to provide aid to women and girls, including the UN Population Fund, the World Food Programme, and World Vision. In addition, "cash for work" programs, instituted by the Haitian Ministry of Women's Affairs, helped 100,000 women displaced by the earthquake to survive (Jean-Charles 2010). Moreover, in response to the increased vulnerability of women and girls, Femmes Citoyennes Haiti Solidaire, or Women Citizens Haiti United, formed an alliance of activists to continue addressing gender inequality and injustices within Haiti.

GLOBALIZATION AND CYBERACTIVISM

The existence of the Internet has given those opposed to globalization in general, or to some specific aspect of it, a powerful tool with which to mount their opposition on a regional and even a global basis. Indeed, the origins of the antiglobalization social movement at the World Trade Organization meetings in Seattle in late November 1999 were based on cyberactivism, as were the ensuing protests in Washington, D.C. (April 2000), Prague (September 2000), Genoa (July 2001), and other cities (Pleyers 2010). Further, the World Social Forum was also made possible by such activism (Kohler 2012; Sen et al. 2004; Smith et al. 2011).

World Social Forum

The World Social Forum (WSF), which was formed in 2001, has its roots in the 1999 protests against the World Trade Organization in Seattle. A key concern of the protesters was the lack of democracy in global economic and political affairs. The WSF was born of the idea that protests about this problem are insufficient. That is, there is a need for more positive and concrete proposals to deal with such issues, as well as for a forum in which these proposals can be generated. The WSF's slogan has been "Another world is possible" (Teivainen 2007). That is, there must be, and there is, an alternative to the free market capitalism that has dominated the world economically and politically (Smith 2008). Although the slogan is powerful and has facilitated the coordination of large and diverse groups, the WSF has not yet produced concrete actions and policies to make "another world" a reality.

What would it take to make an alternative to free market capitalism a reality? What would such a system be like? Would it be viable for the long term? Why or why not?

The initial 2001 meeting of the WSF in Porto Alegre, Brazil (Byrd 2005), drew about 5,000 participants, and the number of participants grew to 100,000 at the meetings in 2004 in Mumbai, India, and in 2005 in Porto Alegre. In 2006, the meeting was decentralized and held on three continents, and many local, national, and regional meetings have developed. In 2011, a centralized meeting in Dakar, Senegal, drew 75,000 participants. The 2013 meeting of the World Social Forum took place in Tunis, Tunisia.

The WSF is, by design, not a social movement; rather, it is an arena in which like-minded people can exchange ideas on specific social movements and global issues. The very diversity of the movements and people involved in the WSF makes the development of concrete political proposals, not to mention actions, difficult. The WSF continues to struggle with this issue and its identity and role in globalization.

The WSF is a huge social network, and it is based on the "cultural logic of networking" (see Chapter 5 for a discussion of network organizations). Such networking includes the creation of horizontal ties and connections among diverse and autonomous elements, the free and open communication of information among and between those elements, decentralized coordination among the elements that involves democratic decision making, and networking that is self-directed (Juris 2005).

SOCIAL CHANGE: GLOBALIZATION, CONSUMPTION, AND THE INTERNET

Social change is intimately connected to the topics discussed in the first part of this chapter. Social movements, especially those that are successful, often lead to major social changes. For example, the women's, gay and lesbian, and civil rights movements have all led, and continue to lead, to such social changes. Collective action is less likely to lead to social change, but there have certainly been many examples of crowd action, riots, and disasters that have led to change. For example, the Los Angeles race riots of 1992 and the more recent demonstrations in Ferguson, Missouri, and Baltimore, Maryland, led to changes not only in police behavior but also in efforts to deal with the underlying causes of the riots.

Although social change occurs throughout the social world, it is particularly characteristic of the three areas that are the signature concerns of this book—globalization, consumption, and the Internet. Globalization is, of course, a social process of relatively recent origin; it is changing the world in which we live and is likely to lead to a variety of even more dramatic changes in the future. For example, the changing nature of the global economy, especially the shift of its center away from the United States and in the direction of China and Asia more generally, means that the job prospects of Americans are changing and apt to change even more in the future. Some economic prospects have declined, especially those that relate to the production of goods and the jobs associated with it. However, others have improved. New jobs have arisen—especially those that involve computers and the Internet. Clearly, the Internet is important not only in this sense but also because it is an arena in which great and extremely rapid change has taken place in recent years. It is an arena that will certainly continue to change and to affect our lives in innumerable ways. The changes discussed here—globalization, the economy, and the Internet—are related to the changing nature of our other core concern—consumption. Consumption has itself become increasingly global as, for example, more of the things we buy come from outside the United States. The American economy has shifted away from one dominated by production to one dominated by consumption. It is clear that more consumption is taking place through the Internet, and that trend can only accelerate in the future.

GLOBALIZATION AS THE ULTIMATE SOCIAL CHANGE

Prior to the current epoch of globalization, one of the things that characterized people, things, information, places, and much else was their greater solidity. That is, all of them tended to (figuratively) harden over time, and therefore, among other things, to remain largely in place. As a result, people did not venture very far from where they were born and raised. Their social relationships were limited to those who were nearby. Much the same could be said of most objects (tools, food), which tended to be used where they were produced. The solidity of most material manifestations of information (stone tablets, books) also made them at least somewhat difficult to move very far. Furthermore, since people didn't move very far, neither did information. Places, too, were not only quite solid and immovable but also tended to be surrounded by solid barriers (mountains, oceans, walls, borders) that made it difficult for people and things to exit or enter.

Global "Liquids"

At an increasing rate over the last few centuries, and especially in the last several decades, that which once seemed solid has tended to "melt." Instead of thinking of people, objects, information, and places as being like solid blocks of ice, we need to see them as tending to melt and as becoming increasingly liquid (Beilharz 2012). Needless to say, it is far more difficult to move blocks of ice than it is to move the water that is produced when those blocks melt. Of course, to extend the metaphor, there continue to exist blocks of ice, even glaciers, in the contemporary world that have not melted, at least not completely. Solid material realities, such as people, cargo, and newspapers, continue to exist, but because of a wide range of technological developments in transportation, communication, and the Internet, they can move across the globe far more readily.

Thus, following the work of Zygmunt Bauman (2000, 2003, 2005, 2006), the perspective on globalization presented here involves increasing liquidity (Lakoff 2008; Ritzer and Dean 2015). However, there is a constant interplay between liquidity and solidity, with increases in that which is liquid (e.g., terrorist attacks launched against Israel from the West Bank) leading to counterreactions and the erection of new solid forms (a fence between Israel and the West Bank). However, at the moment and for the foreseeable future, the momentum lies with increasing and proliferating global liquidity.

Global "Flows"

Closely related to the idea of liquidity, and integral to it, is another key concept in thinking about globalization, the idea of "flows" (Appadurai 1996; Inda 2012). After all, liquids flow easily, far more easily than solids. Because so much of the world has "melted," or is in the process of "melting," globalization is increasingly characterized by great flows of increasingly liquid phenomena of all types, including people, objects, information, decisions, and places. In many cases, the flows have turned into raging floods that are becoming less and less likely to be impeded by place-based barriers of any kind, including the oceans, mountains, and especially the borders of nation-states. This was demonstrated once again in late 2008 in the spread of the American credit and financial crisis to Europe and elsewhere: "In a global financial system, national borders are porous" (Landler 2008: C1).

Looking at a very different kind of flow, as we saw in Chapter 14, many people in many parts of the world believe that their countries are being swamped by migrants, specifically poor undocumented migrants (Moses 2006). This is especially true of concerns in the United States about migrants from Latin America and in Europe about Muslim immigrants (Ahmed 2013). Whether or not these are actually floods, they have come to be seen as such by many people, often aided by politicians and media personalities who have established their reputations by portraying migrants in that way. Places, too, can be said to be flowing around the world, as immigrants re-create the places (and cultures) from which they come in new locales (Logan, Alba, and Zhang 2002; Sarwal 2012).

Ideas, images, and information, both legal (blogs) and illegal (child pornography), flow everywhere,

undoubtedly because of their immateriality. They do so through interpersonal contact and the media, especially now via the Internet. Much of what would have been considered the height of global liquidity only a few years ago now seems increasingly sludgelike. This is especially the case when we focus on the impact of the Internet on the global flow of all sorts of things. For example, instead of scouring an import VHS catalog and waiting weeks for an anime movie to ship from Japan, a person can simply open the Netflix app on her Xbox 360 and stream any number of anime movies instantly.

ASK YOURSELF

What aspects of your life can you imagine as "liquids"? Which seem like "flows"? What do you imagine these elements looked like 20 years ago, before the advent of globalization?

GLOBALIZATION AND THE INTERNET

Since its birth in the 1990s, the Internet has profoundly affected almost every aspect of life, especially in the developed world. The Internet has expedited the globalization of many different things and is itself a profound form and aspect of globalization (Powell 2012). The Internet is global in several senses, but the most important is that while its users are not equally divided between North and South, rich and poor, and so on, they *do* exist virtually everywhere in the world (Drori 2006, 2012). It is also global in the sense that it was produced and is maintained by a number of global and transnational corporations and organizations, including multinational corporations (such as Intel), intergovernmental organizations, and international nongovernmental organizations. For instance, the World Intellectual Property Organization regulates intellectual property rights, the Internet Corporation for Assigned Names and Numbers coordinates domain names, and the UN Educational, Scientific, and Cultural Organization promotes computer and Internet use in schools throughout the world.

Computer Viruses

In the 1980s a graduate student wrote the first computer program that was able to replicate and propagate itself. His professor, seeing its similarity to a biological phenomenon, suggested it be called a "computer virus." The first global computer virus was likely created in Pakistan in 1986. Since then, of course, many different viruses—some benign, some malicious (malware)—have been created, circled the globe, and in some cases caused great damage to computer systems. For example, some of these viruses (Win32/Fareit, Mariposa) "infect" personal computers and access users' information, such as credit card numbers, which the cyberthieves then use to purchase all sorts of goods and services illegally. At the same

PUBLIC SOCIOLOGY

Naomi Klein: No Logo

Naomi Klein (1970–) is a journalist who is best known for books that have contributed to our understanding of consumption and globalization. While there is significant sociological analysis in her work, Klein's writing is most defined by her strong, perhaps sometimes over-heated, criticism of many aspects of both of these phenomena.

In her book *No Logo* ([2000] 2010), Klein offers an unrelenting critique of the role of branding in the world of consumption. Among Klein's favorite targets are Nike, McDonald's, Microsoft, and Tommy Hilfiger, as well as celebrity brands such as Michael Jordan. In the context of an American society that has shifted from the dominance of production to the preeminence of consumption, corporations have discovered that the key to success is no longer what they manufacture but the creation and dissemination of a brand. While it concentrates on its brand, the modern corporation often outsources production to subcontractors in less developed parts of the world. Those who do the work in such places

are paid a small percentage of what their counterparts in more developed nations would be paid. Klein is especially critical of the work done in free-enterprise zones in less developed countries, where corporations and subcontractors are able to do as they wish, free of local government control. In those settings, wages are particularly low and working conditions especially harsh.

Given these realities in less developed countries, it is clearly in the interest of corporations to produce little or nothing in high-wage, developed countries. With production costs minuscule in less developed countries, these corporations can spend lavishly on their brands and the associated logos, such as Nike's Swoosh and McDonald's Golden Arches. Low production costs also allow for great profits and make it possible for corporate leaders to be paid unconscionable sums of money. Especially egregious is the contrast between the wealth of Phil Knight, founder and chairman of Nike, and the economic situation experienced by those who work in

Naomi Klein

development zone factories to produce Nike products, including some trafficked workers who function as modern-day slaves and are forced to work in Nike factories against their will. Similarly egregious are the sums of money paid to celebrities like Michael Jordan to advertise products and, in the process, to become brands themselves.

Think About It

Would the conditions Naomi Klein criticizes be possible without the implied consent of consumers in Western countries? Do you look for logos when you shop? Why or why not?

---

time, global organizations, including law enforcement agencies, have emerged to try to warn people about new viruses and malware—so-called *Trojans* and *worms*—and to develop countermeasures to protect against them (Chanda 2007). To the degree that they are successful, the latter are barriers to the largely free flow of computer viruses around the globe.

It is clear that no change has done more to further the process of globalization than the advent of the Internet (Subramanian 2012). It occupies pride of place in many analyses of globalization. Perhaps the most famous of these is Thomas Friedman's (2005) analysis of globalization as involving a "flat world" (see the "Public Sociology" box in Chapter 5); the major example of such a world is the Internet. The Internet is flat in the sense that virtually anyone, anywhere can, at least theoretically, become involved in

it. However, it is important to remember that many poor and undeveloped communities still lack Internet access.

CONSUMPTION AND GLOBALIZATION

The emphasis in the global economy is on greatly increasing flows of everything related to consumption and greatly decreasing any barriers to those flows (Brandle and Ryan 2012). Especially important is expediting global flows of consumer goods and services of all types and of the financial processes and instruments that facilitate those flows. Thus, for example, the relatively small number of credit card brands with origins in the United States, especially Visa and MasterCard, are increasingly accepted and used throughout the world (Ritzer 1995). This serves to expedite not only global consumption but also the flow of global consumers, including tourists.

Local and Regional Differences

Local areas have not always, or perhaps ever, been overwhelmed by globalized imports; rather, they have integrated such imports into local cultural and economic realities. Furthermore, much of consumption remains largely, if not totally, local in character. One example is the growing consumption of a mild stimulant, khat, or *qat,* in Kenya, where it is defined in a highly positive way locally. In addition, there is active resistance to external definitions of it, especially the U.S. definition of khat as a dangerous drug (Anderson and Carrier 2006).

Consumption also plays itself out differently in different parts of the world. For example, both the United States and Japan can be seen as consumer societies, but Japanese consumers differ from their U.S. counterparts in many ways. The Japanese have never fully embraced the idea of a consumer society. More specifically, unlike Americans, the Japanese continue to manage to save significant amounts of money (Garon 2006).

While many consumer objects and services remain highly local (e.g., the khat mentioned above, the services of street-based letter writers for illiterate Indians), an increasing number have been globalized. On the one hand are the global objects, such as automobiles from the United States, Germany, and Japan. On the other hand are global services, such as those offered by accounting firms like KPMG International, as well as package delivery services like DHL.

Global Brands

A **brand** is a symbol that serves to identify and differentiate one product or service from the others. A brand can be contrasted with, and seeks to contrast itself to, generic commodities such as flour and soap (Arvidsson 2012; Holt 2004; Muniz 2007). The process of branding a product or service is undertaken because, if successful, not only is the brand distinguished from the basic commodity but also more of it can be sold and at a higher price. We are all familiar with the most successful brands in the world (Apple, Coca-Cola, McDonald's, Walmart, Mercedes, and so on), and much consumption is oriented toward the purchase of brand-name products and services.

Nike is one of those brands that has made itself so important that it can be said to have created a culture, and, to some degree, we live in Nike culture (Goldman and Papson 1998; Hollister 2008). However, that culture is but a part of the larger *brand culture* in which we live. That is, brands are a key part of the larger culture: They infuse it with meaning, and contemporary society as a whole is profoundly affected by brands (Schroeder 2007).

Brands are of great importance not only within the United States and many other nations but also globally. Indeed, much money and effort are invested in creating brand names that are recognized and trusted throughout the world. Klein ([2000] 2010) details the importance of brands in the contemporary world and the degree to which they are globalized—corporate logos are virtually an international language—and have global impacts.

SUMMARY

Social change creates variations over time in every aspect of the social world. Social movements are sustained and intentional collective efforts, usually operating outside established institutional channels, either to bring about social change or to retard it. Prominent social movements include the Tea Party, feminist movements, gay and lesbian movements, and the civil rights movement.

The emergence of a social movement requires a set of grievances, efforts at mobilization, opportunities within the political system, the proximity of people, the availability of free space to meet, and the availability of resources. Factors that affect the success of a social movement include its size and uniqueness as well as other groups' ability to suppress the movement. When successful, a social movement can leave a lasting legacy.

Social movements constitute one type of collective action. Collective action is action generated, or engaged in, by a group of people. Emergent norm theory, based on the idea that new norms emerge in light of some precipitating event and guide the often nontraditional behaviors that characterize collective action, is the dominant theoretical approach to examining types of collective action. Other types of collective action include crowds, riots, and responses to disasters.

Social change is particularly characteristic of globalization, consumption, and the Internet. Globalization is arguably the most important change in human history and is characterized by great flows of liquid phenomena across the globe. The Internet is both a form and an aspect of globalization and has expedited globalization. The global economy focuses on increasing the flows of everything related to consumption and reducing the barriers to these flows.

REVIEW QUESTIONS

1. What about the Tea Party makes it a social movement? What were the conditions that brought about the emergence of the Tea Party movement?

2. What have been the three different waves of the women's movement? How did the goals and strategies of the women's movement change during each of these three waves?

3. How have new communication technologies like the Internet and social networking sites (Facebook and Twitter) aided global social movements? What types of resources move more easily because of these new technologies?

4. According to resource mobilization theory, what do groups of people need in order to mobilize effectively? How can we apply this theory to the discussion of the civil rights movement in this chapter?

5. What mechanisms do social movements use to ensure member participation? How are these mechanisms related to the gay and lesbian movements discussed in this chapter?

6. What factors are used to determine whether a social movement is successful? How has the Tea Party movement been successful to date? Has there been any resistance to the movement? How might this affect the movement's future success?

7. According to emergent norm theory, why are individuals likely to behave differently when they are in crowds? How can we explain some deviant behavior in bars (such as fighting or public displays of affection) using emergent norm theory?

8. The 2011 earthquake and tsunami in Japan and the 2015 earthquake in Nepal are examples of disasters. In what ways did humans exacerbate the consequences of these natural disasters? What sorts of negative long-term consequences can be expected from disasters like these?

9. In what ways is globalization the "ultimate social change"? How has the world become more liquid because of globalization? What role have new communication technologies played in making the world more liquid?

10. Why is branding an important process for transnational corporations? In what ways is branding reflective of the process of Americanization?

APPLYING THE SOCIOLOGICAL IMAGINATION

Using what you have learned about social movements in this chapter, do some research on one of the social movements in the Arab world today. What are some of the reasons that the social movement emerged? What resources has the movement been able to mobilize? What mechanisms has the movement used to encourage member participation? How have the processes of globalization affected the movement? How has the movement been affected by new communication technologies like the Internet and social networking sites? As it stands now, has the social movement been successful? Is it likely to be successful in the long run?

KEY TERMS

brand: A symbol that serves to identify and differentiate one product or service from the others. (p.378)

collective action: Action generated, or engaged in, by a group of people to encourage or retard social change. (p.371)

crowd: A temporary gathering of a relatively large number of people in a common geographic location at a given time. (p.371)

disasters: Events that suddenly, unexpectedly, and severely disrupt and harm the environment, the social structure, people, and their property. (p.372)

emergent norm theory: A theory arguing that, in light of some precipitating event, new norms emerge that guide the often nontraditional actions that characterize collective behavior. (p.371)

feminism: The belief that women are equal to men, especially socially, politically, and economically. (p.361)

resource mobilization theory: An approach to understanding social movements that focuses on what groups of people need to do to mobilize to bring about social change. (p.368)

riot: Temporary unruly collective behavior that causes damage to persons or property. (p.372)

social change: Variations over time in every aspect of the social world, ranging from changes affecting individuals to transformations having an impact on the globe as a whole. (p.358)

social movements: Sustained and intentional collective efforts, usually operating outside established institutional channels, either to bring about or to retard social change. (p.359)

⑤SAGE edge™ edge.sagepub.com/ritzeressentials2e

SAGE edge offers a robust online environment featuring an impressive array of free tools and resources for review, study, and further exploration, keeping both instructors and students on the cutting edge of teaching and learning.

LEARNING OBJECTIVES	FOR FURTHER EXPLORATION AND APPLICATION
LO 15-1: Use sociological concepts to explain the rise and impact of social movements such as the women's movement, the gay and lesbian movement, the civil rights movement, and the Tea Party.	▶ How Civil Rights Launched the Fight for LGBT Rights ◉ Is the Tea Party Here to Stay? ◉ Collective Behavior and Social Movements
LO 15-2: Contrast social movements and other types of collective action, such as crowds, riots, and disasters.	▶ How Social Movements Changed the World ◉ Distinguishing between an "Uprising" and a "Riot" ◉ The Mob Mentality
LO 15-3: Describe the process of social change, particularly the interactions of globalization, consumption, and the rise of the Internet.	▶ How Social Media Contributed to Unrest in the Middle East and North Africa ◉ Police Rethink Tactics amid New Technologies and Social Pressure ◉ Consumerism and Our Changing Culture

GLOSSARY

achieved status: A position acquired by people on the basis of what they accomplish or the nature of their capacities.

achievement: The accomplishments, or the merit, of the individual.

agency: The potential to disrupt or destroy the structures in which one finds oneself.

agents of socialization: Those who socialize others.

alienation: In a capitalist system, being unconnected to one's work, products, fellow workers, and human nature.

Americanization: The importation by other countries of products, images, technologies, practices, norms, values, and behaviors that are closely associated with the United States.

anomie: The feeling of not knowing what is expected of one in society or of being adrift in society without any clear, secure moorings.

anti-Americanism: An aversion to the United States in general, as well as to the influence of its culture abroad.

anticipatory socialization: The teaching (and learning) of what will be expected of one in the future.

ascribed status: A position in which individuals are placed, or to which they move, that has nothing to do with what they have done or their capacities or accomplishments.

ascription: Being born with or inheriting certain characteristics (wealth, high status, and so on).

assimilation: The integration of minorities into the dominant culture.

asylum seekers: People who flee their home country, usually in an effort to escape political oppression or religious persecution.

authority: A particular type of domination: legitimate domination.

back stage: The part of the social world where people feel free to express themselves in ways that are suppressed in the front stage.

beliefs: Ideas that explain the world and identify what should be sacred or held in awe—that is, a religion's ultimate concerns.

birthrate: The number of births per 1,000 people per year.

blended family: A family that includes some combination of children from the partners' previous marriages or relationships, along with one or more children of the currently married or cohabiting couple.

bounded rationality: Rationality limited by, among other things, instabilities and conflicts within most, if not all, organizations, as well as by the limited human capacity to think and act in a rational manner.

brand: A symbol that serves to identify and differentiate one product or service from the others.

bureaucracy: A highly rational organization, especially one that is highly efficient.

bureaucratic personality: A type of bureaucrat who slavishly follows the rules of the organization to such an extent that the ability to achieve organizational goals is subverted.

capitalism: In Marx's view, an economic system based on one group of people (the capitalists or owners) owning what is needed for production and a second group (the proletariat or workers) owning little but their capacity for work.

capitalists: Those who own what is needed for production—factories, machines, tools—in a capitalist system.

cathedrals of consumption: Large and lavish consumption sites, created mostly in the United States in the last half of the twentieth century and into the early twenty-first century.

cenogamy: Group marriage.

charismatic authority: Authority based on the devotion of the followers to what they define as the exceptional characteristics, such as heroism, of the leaders.

church: A large group of religiously oriented people into which members are usually born rather than joining consciously and voluntarily.

cities: Large, permanent, and spatially concentrated human settlements.

citizens: The people represented by a given state, most often born within its territories.

citizenship: The idea that people of a given state can vote for their representatives within the state, but also that they have access to rights and responsibilities as citizens.

civil religion: The beliefs, practices, and symbols that a nation holds sacred.

cohabitation: An arrangement in which a couple share a home and a bed without being legally married.

collective action: Action generated, or engaged in, by a group of people to encourage or retard social change.

collective conscience: The set of beliefs shared by people throughout society.

companionate love: A kind of love typified by gradual onset and not necessarily tied to sexual passion, but based on more rational assessments of the one who is loved.

companionate marriage: A marriage emphasizing a clear division of labor between a breadwinner and a homemaker and held together by sentiment, friendship, and sexuality. Predominant model of marriage in the mid-twentieth century (see *companionate love*).

competitive capitalism: A form of capitalism where there are a large number of relatively small firms, with the result that no one or small subset of them can completely dominate and control a given area of the economy.

conflict theory: Theory that sees society as held together by coercion and focuses on its negative aspects.

conformists: People who accept both cultural goals and the traditional means of achieving those goals.

consensual sexual activities: Sexual activities agreed upon by the participants, any of whom have the right to decide to stop at any point and for any reason.

conspicuous consumption: The public demonstration of wealth through consumption.

consumer crimes: Crimes related to consumption, including shoplifting and using stolen credit cards or credit card numbers.

consumer culture: A culture in which the core ideas and material objects relate to consumption and in which consumption is a primary source of meaning in life.

consumerism: An obsession with consumption.

consumption: The process by which people obtain and utilize goods and services.

convenience sample: A readily available group of people who fit the criteria for participating in a research project.

conversation analysis: Analysis of how people accomplish conversations.

corporate crime: Violation of the law by legal organizations, including antitrust violations and stock market violations.

cosmopolitan: Open to a variety of external and global influences.

counterculture: A group whose culture not only differs in certain ways from the dominant culture but also adheres to norms and values that may be incompatible with those of the dominant culture.

crime: Deviance that is a violation of the criminal law.

criminalization: The process by which the legal system negatively sanctions some form of deviant behavior.

criminology: The study of all aspects of crime.

critical theories of race and racism: A set of ideas arguing that race continues to matter and that racism continues to exist and adversely affect blacks.

critical theory: A set of critical ideas derived from Marxian theory but focusing on culture rather than the economy.

crowd: A temporary gathering of a relatively large number of people in a common geographic location at a given time.

cult: A new, innovative, small, voluntary, and exclusive religious tradition that was never associated with any religious organization.

cultural imperialism: The imposition of one culture, more or less consciously, on other cultures.

cultural relativism: The idea that aspects of culture such as norms and values need to be understood within the context of a person's own culture and that there are no universally accepted norms and values.

culture: A collection of ideas, values, practices, and material objects that mean a great deal to a group of people, even an entire society, and that allow them to carry out their collective lives in relative order and harmony.

culture industry: The rationalized and bureaucratized structures that control modern culture.

culture jamming: The radical transformation of an intended message in popular culture, especially one associated with the mass media, to protest underlying realities of which consumers may be unaware.

culture war: A conflict that pits subcultures and countercultures against the dominant culture or that pits dominant groups within society against each other.

cumulative advantage: The process by which the most advantaged individuals are awarded the best opportunities, which increases inequality over time.

cybercrime: Crime that targets computers, uses computers to commit traditional crimes, or uses computers to transmit illegal information and images.

cyberculture: An emerging online culture that has the characteristics of all culture, including distinctive values and norms.

dangerous giant: An agent who threatens social structures.

deindustrialization: The decline of manufacturing as well as a corresponding increase in various types of services.

deinstitutionalization: Weakened social norms, especially with regard to the institution of marriage.

democracy: A political system in which people within a given state vote to choose their leaders and in some cases vote on legislation.

demographers: Those who study population dynamics.

demography: The scientific study of population, especially its growth and decline, as well as the movement of people.

denomination: A religious group not linked to the state that exhibits a general spirit of tolerance and acceptance of other religious bodies.

dependent variable: A characteristic or measurement that is the result of manipulating an independent variable.

deprofessionalization: The process whereby a profession's power and autonomy, as well as high status and great wealth, have declined, at least relative to the exalted position the profession once held.

descriptive statistics: Numerical data that allow researchers to see trends over time or compare differences between groups in order to describe some findings based on a phenomenon in the real world.

descriptive survey: A questionnaire or interview used to gather accurate information about those in a group, people in a given geographic area, or members of organizations.

desertification: A decline in the water supply as a result of the degradation and deterioration of soil and vegetation.

deviance: Any action, belief, or human characteristic that a large number of people who are members of a society or a social group consider a violation of group norms and for which the violator is likely to be censured or punished.

diaspora: Dispersal, typically involuntary, of a racial or ethnic population from its traditional homeland and over a wide geographic area.

dictatorships: States that are usually totalitarian and are ruled either by a single individual or by a small group of people.

differential association: A theory that focuses on the fact that people learn criminal behavior and therefore that what is crucial is whom a person associates with.

direct democracy: A political system in which people directly affected by a given decision have a say in that decision.

disasters: Events that suddenly, unexpectedly, and severely disrupt and harm the environment, the social structure, people, and their property.

discreditable stigma: A stigma that the affected individual assumes is neither known about nor immediately perceivable.

discredited stigma: A stigma that the affected individual assumes is already known about or readily apparent.

discrimination: The unfavorable treatment of black Americans and other minorities, either formally or informally, simply because of their race or some other such characteristic.

distinction: The need to distinguish oneself from others.

domestic violence: The exertion of power over a partner in an intimate relationship through behavior that is intimidating, threatening, harassing, or harmful.

domination: The probability or likelihood that commands will be obeyed by subordinates.

double consciousness: Among black Americans, the sense of "two-ness," that is, of being both black and American.

dramaturgy: The view that social life is a series of dramatic performances akin to those that take place in a theater and on a stage.

dyad: A two-person group.

dysfunction: An observable consequence that negatively affects the ability of a given system to survive, adapt, or adjust.

economy: The social system involved in the production and distribution of a wide range of goods and services.

edge cities: Cities that are on or near major highways, have corporate offices that offer employment to many, and have important commercial and consumption centers, in particular shopping malls.

elite pluralism: The formation by political elites of similar interest groups and organizations that vie for power.

emergent norm theory: A theory arguing that, in light of some precipitating event, new norms emerge that guide the often nontraditional actions that characterize collective behavior.

emphasized femininity: A set of socially constructed ideas about "model womanhood" organized around accommodating the interests of men and patriarchy.

empiricism: The gathering of information and evidence using one's senses, especially one's eyes and ears, to experience the social world.

endogamy: Marriage to someone with similar characteristics in terms of race, ethnicity, religion, education level, social class, and so on.

ethics: A set of beliefs concerning right and wrong in the choices that people make and the ways those choices are justified.

ethnic cleansing: The establishment by the dominant group of policies that allow or require the forcible removal of people of another ethnic group.

ethnic group: A group typically defined on the basis of some cultural characteristic such as language, religion, traditions, and cultural practices.

ethnicity: A sense, shared by members of the group, of belonging to and identifying with a given ethnic group.

ethnocentrism: The belief that one's own group or culture—including its norms, values, customs, and so on—is superior to, or better than, others.

ethnography: Observational, sometimes participatory research; usually intensive and conducted over lengthy periods, that leads to an account of what people do and how they live.

ethnomethodology: An inter/actionist theory focusing on what people do rather than on what they think.

ethnoscapes: Landscapes that allow the movement, or fantasies about movement, of various individuals and groups.

exchange relationship: A stable and persistent bond between individuals who interact, generally formed because their interactions are rewarding.

exchange theory: A set of ideas related to the rewards and costs associated with human behavior.

exogamy: Marriage to someone with characteristics that are dissimilar in terms of race, ethnicity, religion, education level, social class, and so on.

experiment: The manipulation of a characteristic under study (an independent variable) to examine its effect on another characteristic (the dependent variable).

explanatory survey: A questionnaire or interview used to uncover potential causes for some observation.

exploitation: A feature of capitalism in which the workers (proletariat) produce virtually everything but get few rewards, while the capitalists, who do little, reap the vast majority of the rewards.

expulsion: Removal of a minority group from a territory, either by forcible ejection through military and other government action or by "voluntary" emigration due to

the majority's harassment, discrimination, and persecution.

extended family: Two or more generations of a family living in the same household or in close proximity to one another.

exurbia: Outlying areas between the suburbs and rural areas.

family: A group of people related by descent, marriage, or adoption.

fantasy city: A city in which great emphasis is placed on creating a spectacle, especially in the areas of consumption, leisure, tourism, and impressive buildings and other real estate developments.

felonies: Serious crimes punishable by a year or more in prison.

female proletarianization: The channeling of an increasing number of women into low-status, poorly paid manual work.

feminism: The belief that women are equal to men, especially socially, politically, and economically.

feminist theory: A set of ideas critical of the social situation confronting women and offering solutions for improving, if not revolutionizing, their situation.

feminization of labor: The rise of female labor participation in all sectors and the movement of women into jobs traditionally held by men.

feminization of poverty: The rise in the number of women falling below the poverty line.

fertility: People's reproductive behavior, especially the number of births.

field experiment: Research that occurs in natural situations but allows researchers to exert at least some control over who participates and what happens during the experiment.

financescapes: Landscapes that use various financial instruments to allow huge sums of money and other things of economic value to move into and across nations and around the world at great speed, almost instantaneously.

folkways: Norms that are relatively unimportant and, if violated, carry few if any sanctions.

food insecurity: Lack of sufficient access to safe and nutritious food.

Fordism: The ideas, principles, and systems created by Henry Ford (who is credited with the development of the modern mass production system) and his associates at the beginning of the twentieth century.

foreign aid: Economic assistance given by countries or global institutions to a foreign country in order to promote its development and social welfare.

front stage: The part of the social world where the social performance is idealized and designed to define the situation for those who observe it.

function: An observable, positive consequence that helps a system survive, adapt, or adjust.

fundamentalism: A strongly held belief in the fundamental or foundational precepts of any religion, or a rejection of the modern secular world.

game stage: Mead's second stage in the socialization process, in which a child develops a self in the full sense of the term, because it is then that the child begins to take on the role of a group of people simultaneously rather than the roles of discrete individuals.

gated communities: Communities in which gates, surveillance cameras, and guards provide the residents with a feeling of security from the problems (crime, panhandling) that they think they left behind in the city.

gemeinschaft societies: Traditional societies characterized by face-to-face relations.

gender: The physical, behavioral, and personality characteristics that are socially defined as appropriate for one's sex.

gender identity: A person's internal sense of gender.

gender role: The social presentation of gender that includes clothing, hairstyle, and attitudinal and behavioral traits.

general deterrence: The deterrence of the population as a whole from committing crimes for fear that they will be punished or imprisoned for their actions.

generalized other: The attitude of the entire group or community taken by individuals in the process of developing their own behaviors and attitudes.

genocide: An active, systematic attempt to eliminate an entire group of people.

gentrification: The reinvestment of real estate capital in blighted inner-city areas in order to rebuild residences and create a new infrastructure for the well-to-do.

geopolitics: Political relationships that involve large geographic areas or the globe as a whole.

gesellschaft societies: Modern societies characterized by impersonal, distant, and limited social relationships.

gesture: A movement of one animal or human that elicits a mindless, automatic, and appropriate response from another animal or human.

global care chains: Series of personal relationships between people across the globe based on the paid or unpaid work of caring.

global cities: The cities, especially New York City, London, and Tokyo, with the world's leading industries and marketplaces.

global ethnography: A type of ethnography that is "grounded" in various parts of the world and that seeks to understand globalization as it exists in people's social lives.

globalization: The increasing fluidity of global flows and the structures that expedite and impede those flows.

group: A relatively small number of people who over time develop a patterned relationship based on interaction with one another.

group pluralism: The competition of society's various interest groups and organizations for access to political power in an attempt to further their interests.

habitus: An internalized set of preferences and dispositions that are learned through experience and social interactions in specific social contexts.

hate crimes: Crimes that stem from the fact that the victims are in various ways different from, and disesteemed by, the perpetrators.

hegemonic masculinity: The dominant form or most idealized vision of masculinity; taken for granted as natural and linked to patriarchy.

hegemony: The subordination of one race (or other group) by another, more on the basis of dominant ideas, especially about cultural differences, than through material constraints.

heterosexism: The belief that heterosexuality is superior to other sexual orientations; individual and institutional discrimination against those with other orientations.

heterosexual double standard: A cultural belief system in which men are expected to desire and seek sex from whomever, whenever, while women are expected to be sexual only within committed, romantic relationships.

hidden curriculum: A school's unofficial norms, routines, and structures that transmit dominant cultural norms and values.

high-income economies: Economies in countries with the highest wealth and income in the world, defined by the World Bank in 2014 as having a gross national income per capita of at least $12,746.

historical-comparative research: A research methodology that contrasts how different historical events and conditions in various societies (or components of societies) lead to different societal outcomes.

homophobia: The fear of being, appearing, or seeming gay; fear of anyone or "anything" gay.

horizontal mobility: Movement within one's social class.

hyperconsumption: Consumption of more than one needs, really wants, and can afford.

hyperdebt: Borrowing more than one should, thereby owing more than one will be able to pay back.

"I": The immediate response of an individual to others; the part of the self that is incalculable, unpredictable, and creative.

ideal culture: Norms and values indicating what members of a society should believe in and do.

ideal type: An exaggeratedly rational model that is used to study real-world phenomena.

identity politics: The use of a minority group's power to strengthen the position of the cultural group with which it identifies.

ideoscapes: Landscapes that include images, largely political images, often in line with the ideologies of nation-states.

imagined communities: Communities that are socially constructed by those who see themselves as part of them.

impression management: People's use of a variety of techniques to control the images of themselves that they want to project during their social performances.

income: The amount of money a person earns in a given year from a job, a business, or various types of assets and investments.

independent variable: In an experiment, a condition that can be independently manipulated by the researcher with the goal of producing a change in some other variable.

individualized marriage: A model of marriage emphasizing the satisfaction of the individuals involved.

inequality: The condition whereby some positions in society yield a great deal of money, status, and power while others yield little, if any, of these.

inferential statistics: Numerical data that allow researchers to use data from a small group to speculate with some level of certainty about a larger group.

informal organization: How an organization actually works as opposed to the way it is supposed to work.

informationalism: The processing of knowledge.

informed (effective) sexual consent: Participants' understanding of and free consent to specific sexual activities in a mutually understandable way.

innovators: Individuals who accept cultural goals but reject conventional means of achieving success.

institutional marriage: Predominant model of marriage in the early twentieth century; emphasizes maintenance of the institution of marriage itself.

institutional racism: Race-based discrimination that results from the day-to-day operation of social institutions and social structures and their rules, policies, and practices.

interaction: A social engagement that involves two or more individuals who perceive, and orient their actions to, one another.

interaction order: An area of interaction that is organized and orderly, but in which the order is created informally by those involved in the interaction rather than by some formal structure.

intergenerational mobility: The difference between the parents' social class position and the position achieved by their child(ren).

intersectionality: The confluence, or intersection, of various social statuses and the inequality and oppression associated with each in combination with others; the

idea that members of any given minority group are affected by the nature of their position in other systems or other forms of social inequality.

intersex: A general term used for a variety of (medical) conditions in which a person is born with reproductive or sexual anatomy that does not seem to fit the typical definitions of male or female.

interview: A research method in which information is sought from participants (respondents) who are asked a series of questions that have been spelled out, at least to some degree, before the research is conducted.

intimate relationship: A close, personal, and domestic relationship between partners.

intragenerational mobility: Movement up or down the stratification system in one's lifetime.

labeling theory: Theory contending that a deviant is someone to whom a deviant label has been successfully applied.

laboratory experiment: Research that occurs in a laboratory, giving the researcher great control over both the selection of the participants to be studied and the conditions to which they are exposed.

labor migrants: Those who migrate because they are driven by either "push" factors (a lack of work, low pay) in their homeland or "pull" factors (jobs and higher pay available elsewhere).

landscapes (scapes): Fluid, irregular, and variable global flows that produce different results throughout the world.

language: A set of meaningful symbols that makes possible the communication of culture as well as communication more generally within a given culture, and that calls out the same meaning in the person to whom an utterance is aimed as it does to the person making the utterance.

latent functions: Unintended positive consequences.

law: A norm that has been codified, or written down, and is formally enforced through institutions such as the state.

liminal period: A special time set apart from ordinary reality.

local: Inward looking rather than outward looking.

looking-glass self: The self-image that reflects how others respond to a person, particularly as a child.

low-income economies: Economies in countries with the lowest levels of income in the world, defined by the World Bank as a gross national income per capita below $1,046.

macro: Macroscopic; used to describe large-scale social phenomena such as groups, organizations, cultures, society, and the globe.

macrofinance: The globalization of money and finance.

majority group: A group in a dominant position along the dimensions of wealth, power, and prestige.

majority-minority population: A population in which more than 50 percent of the members are part of a minority group.

manifest functions: Positive consequences that are brought about consciously and purposely.

marriage: The socially acknowledged and approved and often legal union of two people, allowing them to live together and to have children by birth or adoption.

mass culture: Cultural elements that are administered by large organizations, lack spontaneity, and are phony.

mass production: Production characterized by large numbers of standardized products, highly specialized workers, interchangeable machine parts, precision tools, a high-volume mechanized production process, and the synchronization of the flow of materials used in production, with the entire process made as continuous as possible.

master status: A position that is more important than any others, both for the person in the position and for all others involved.

material culture: All of the material objects that are reflections or manifestations of a culture.

McDonaldization: The process by which the rational principles of the fast-food restaurant are coming to dominate more and more sectors of society and more societies throughout the world.

"me": The organized set of others' attitudes assumed by the individual; involves the adoption by the individual of the generalized other.

mediascapes: Landscapes that include the electronic capability to produce and transmit information and images around the world.

mediated interaction: Social interaction in which technological devices come between the participants, unlike in face-to-face interaction.

medicalization: The process of labeling and defining as medical problems aspects of life that were not previously so labeled and defined.

medical sociology: A field concerned with the social causes and consequences of health and illness.

megacities: Cities with populations greater than 10 million.

megalopolis: A cluster of highly populated cities that can stretch over great distances.

meritocracy: A system based on a dominant ideology involving the widely shared belief that all people have an equal chance of succeeding economically based on their hard work and skills.

metropolis: A large, powerful, and culturally influential urban area that contains a central city and surrounding communities that are economically and socially linked to the center.

micro: Microscopic; used to describe small-scale social phenomena such as individuals and their thoughts and actions.

micro-macro continuum: The range of social entities from the individual, even the mind and self, to the interaction among individuals, the groups often formed by that interaction, formally structured organizations, societies, and increasingly the global domain.

middle-income economies: Economies in countries with income that is average for the world, defined by the World Bank in 2014 as having a gross national income per capita of between $1,046 and $12,745.

migration: The movements of people and their impact on the sending and receiving locales.

mind: An internal conversation that arises in relation to, and is continuous with, interactions, especially conversations that one has with others in the social world.

minority group: A group in a subordinate position in terms of wealth, power, and prestige.

misdemeanors: Minor offenses punishable by imprisonment of less than a year.

modernization theory: A structural-functionalist theory that explains unequal economic distributions based on the structural (especially technological) and cultural differences between countries.

monogamy: Marriage between two individuals, whether one wife and one husband, two wives, or two husbands.

monopoly capitalism: A form of capitalism in which huge corporations monopolize the market.

moral entrepreneurs: Individuals or groups who come to define an act as a moral outrage and who lead a campaign to have it defined as deviant and to have it made illegal and therefore subject to legal enforcement.

moral panic: A widespread and disproportionate reaction to a form of deviance.

mores: Important norms whose violation is likely to be met with severe sanctions.

mortality: Deaths and death rates within a population.

multiculturalism: The encouragement of cultural differences within a given environment, both by the state and by the majority group.

nation: A group of people who share similar cultural, religious, ethnic, linguistic, and territorial characteristics.

nation-state: The combination of a nation with a geographic and political structure; encompasses both the populations that define themselves as a nation with various shared characteristics and the organizational structure of the state.

natural experiment: An experiment that occurs when researchers take advantage of a naturally occurring event to study its effect on one or more dependent variables.

neomodernization: A structural-functional theory that explains differences in the economic and social development of countries based on technological and cultural differences.

netnography: An ethnographic method in which the Internet becomes the research site and what transpires there is the sociologist's research interest.

network organization: A new organizational form that is flat and horizontal, is intertwined with other organizations, is run and managed in very different ways than traditional organizations, uses more flexible production methods, and is composed of a series of interconnected nodes.

networks: "Interconnected nodes" that are open, capable of unlimited expansion, dynamic, and able to innovate without disrupting the system in which they exist.

new religious movements: Movements that attract zealous religious converts, follow charismatic leaders, appeal to an atypical portion of the population, have a tendency to differentiate between "us" and "them," are characterized by distrust of others, and are prone to rapid fundamental changes.

nonfamily household: A household consisting of a person who lives either alone or with nonrelatives.

nonparticipant observation: A research method in which the sociologist plays little or no role in what is being observed.

nonresident parents: Fathers and mothers who live apart from their children.

norms: Informal rules that guide what members of a culture do in given situations and how they live.

nuclear family: A family with two married adults and one or more children.

observation: A research method that involves systematically watching, listening to, and recording what takes place in a natural social setting over some (extended) period of time.

offshore outsourcing: The transfer of work to organizations in other countries.

oligarchy: An organization with a small group of people at the top obtaining, and exercising, far more power than they are supposed to have.

organization: A collective purposely constructed to achieve particular ends.

organized crime: Crime that may involve various types of organizations but is most often associated with syndicated organized crime that uses violence (or its threat) and the corruption of public officials to profit from illegal activities.

Orientalism: A set of ideas and texts produced in the West that served as the basis for dominating, controlling, and exploiting the Orient (the East) and its many minority groups.

outsourcing: The transfer of activities once performed by one organization to another organization in exchange for money.

pangender: Gender identity encompassing all genders.

parole: The supervised early release of a prisoner for such things as good behavior while in prison.

participant observation: A research method in which the researcher actually plays a role, even a minor one, in the group or setting being observed.

passionate love: A kind of love typified by sudden onset, strong sexual feelings, and idealization of the one who is loved.

play stage: Mead's first stage in the socialization process, in which children learn to take on the attitudes of specific others toward themselves.

pluralism: The coexistence of many groups without any of them losing their individual qualities.

political crime: Crime involving either illegal offenses against the state to affect its policies or offenses by the state, whether domestically or internationally.

politics: Societal competition through established governmental channels to determine which group's members get what, as well as when and how they get it.

polyandry: Marriage (of a wife) to multiple husbands.

polygamy: Marriage to multiple spouses.

polygyny: Marriage (of a husband) to multiple wives.

post-Fordism: A production environment associated with smaller production runs of more specialized products, especially those high in style and quality; more flexible machinery made possible by advances in technology largely traceable to the computer; more skilled workers with greater flexibility and autonomy; less reliance on economies of scale; and more differentiated markets for those more specialized products.

postindustrial society: A society that was at one time industrial, but where the focus on the manufacture of goods has been replaced by an increase, at least initially, in service work—that is, work in which people are involved in providing services for one another rather than producing goods.

postmodern theory: A set of ideas oriented in opposition to modern theory by, for example, rejecting or deconstructing the grand narratives of modern social theory.

poverty line: The threshold, in terms of income, below which a household is considered poor.

power: The ability to get others to do what you want them to do, even if it is against their will.

power elite theory: A theory holding that power is not dispersed throughout a stable society but is concentrated in a small number of people who control the major institutions of the state, the corporate economy, and the military.

prejudice: Negative attitudes, beliefs, and feelings toward minorities.

primary deviance: Early, nonpatterned acts of deviance, or an act here or there that is considered to be strange or out of the ordinary.

primary groups: Groups that are small, are close-knit, and have intimate face-to-face interaction.

primary socialization: The acquisition of language, identities, gender roles, cultural routines, norms, and values from parents and other family members at the earliest stages of an individual's life.

probation: A system by which those who are convicted of less serious crimes may be released into the community, but under supervision and under certain conditions, such as being involved in and completing a substance abuse program.

profane: To Durkheim, that which has not been defined as sacred, or that which is ordinary and mundane.

profession: An occupation distinguished from other occupations mainly by its power and considerable autonomy.

proletariat: Workers as a group, or those in the capitalist system who own little or nothing except for their capacity for work (labor), which they must sell to the capitalists in order to survive.

property crimes: Crimes that do not involve injury or force, but rather the theft or destruction of property.

prosumer: One who combines the acts of consumption and production.

public sociology: Sociological work addressed to a wide range of audiences, most of which are outside the academy, including a variety of local, national, and global groups.

pure relationship: A relationship that is entered into for what each partner can get from it, and in which those involved remain only as long as each derives enough satisfaction from it.

qualitative research: Research methods employed in natural settings that produce in-depth, descriptive information (e.g., in respondents' own words) about the social world.

quantitative research: Research methods that involve the analysis of numerical data usually derived from surveys and experiments.

queergender: Term used to connote a third gender.

queer theory: Theory based on the idea that there are no fixed and stable identities (such as "heterosexual" or "homosexual") that determine who we are; a diverse group of ideas about how cultures develop gender and sexuality norms, notions of conformity, and power relations.

questionnaire: A self-administered, written set of questions.

race: A social definition based on some real or presumed physical, biological characteristic of a person, such as skin color or hair texture, as well as a shared lineage.

racism: The act of defining a group as a race and attributing negative characteristics to that group.

random sample: A subset of a population in which every member of the group has an equal chance of being included.

rape: Penetration, no matter how slight, of the vagina or anus with any body part or object, or oral penetration by a sex organ of another person, without the consent of the victim.

rational choice theory: A set of ideas that sees people as rational and as acting purposively to achieve their goals.

rationalization: The process by which social structures are increasingly characterized by the most direct and efficient means to their ends.

rational-legal authority: Authority that is legitimated on the basis of legally enacted rules and the right of those with authority under those rules to issue commands.

real culture: What people actually think and do in their everyday lives.

rebels: Individuals who reject both traditional means and goals and instead substitute nontraditional goals and means to those goals.

recidivism: The repetition of a criminal act by one who has been convicted of a prior offense.

reciprocity: The expectation that those involved in an interaction will give and receive rewards of roughly equal value.

reference groups: Groups that people take into consideration in evaluating themselves.

refugees: Migrants who are forced to leave their homeland, or who leave involuntarily because they fear for their safety.

reliability: The degree to which a given question (or another kind of measure) produces the same results time after time.

religion: A social phenomenon that consists of beliefs about the sacred; the experiences, practices, and rituals that reinforce those beliefs; and the communities that share similar beliefs and practices.

representative democracy: A political system in which people, as a whole body, do not actually rule themselves but rather have some say in who will best represent them in the state.

resocialization: The unlearning of old behaviors, norms, and values and the learning of new ones.

resource mobilization theory: An approach to understanding social movements that focuses on what groups of people need to do to mobilize to bring about social change.

retreatists: Individuals who reject both cultural goals and the traditional routes to their attainment; they have completely given up on attaining success within the system.

reverse socialization: The socialization of those who normally do the socializing—for example, children socializing their parents.

riot: Temporary unruly collective behavior that causes damage to persons or property.

risk society: A society in which central issues involve risks and ways to protect oneself from them.

rites of passage: Events, usually rituals, that surround major transitions in life, such as birth, puberty, marriage, and death.

ritual: A set of regularly repeated, prescribed, and traditional behaviors that serve to symbolize some value or belief.

ritualists: Individuals who realize that they will not be able to achieve cultural goals, but who nonetheless continue to engage in the conventional behavior associated with such success.

role: What is generally expected of a person who occupies a given status.

role conflict: Conflicting expectations associated with a given position or multiple positions.

role-making: The ability of people to modify their roles, at least to some degree.

role overload: Confrontation with more expectations than a person can possibly handle.

rule creators: Individuals who devise society's rules, norms, and laws.

rule enforcers: Individuals who threaten to or actually enforce the rules.

sacred: To Durkheim, that which is extraordinary, set aside, and of ultimate concern and that leads to awe and reverence.

sample: A representative portion of the overall population.

sanctions: The application of rewards (positive sanctions) or punishments (negative sanctions) when norms are accepted or violated.

scientific method: A structured way to find answers to questions about the world.

secondary data analysis: Reanalysis of data, often survey data, collected by others, including other sociologists.

secondary deviance: Deviant acts that persist, become more common, and eventually cause people to organize their lives and personal identities around their deviant status.

secondary groups: Generally large, impersonal groups in which ties are relatively weak and members do not know one another very well, and whose impact on members is typically not very powerful.

sect: A small group of people who have joined the group consciously and voluntarily to have a personal religious experience.

secularization: The declining significance of religion.

segregation: The physical and social separation of majority and minority groups.

self: The sense of oneself as an object.

separation of powers: The separation and counterbalancing of different branches of government so that no one branch of government can wield too much power.

sex: A biological term, expressed as *female* or *male*; typically reflected in chromosomes, gonads, genitalia, and hormones.

sex tourism: Activity that occurs when individuals travel to other countries for the purpose of buying sex from men, women, and sometimes children there; sex is the primary or sole purpose of these trips.

sex trafficking: A commercial sex act that includes force, fraud, or coercion and transporting and obtaining a person for sex acts.

sexual assault: Sexual acts of domination, usually enacted by men against women, other men, and children.

sexual harassment: Unwanted sexual attention that takes place in the workplace or other settings.

sexual identity: An internal sense of one's sexual self.

sexuality: The ways in which people think about, and behave toward, themselves and others as sexual beings.

sexual orientation: Involves whom one desires (fantasies), with whom one wants to have sexual relations (behavior), and with whom one has a sense of connectedness (feelings).

sexual scripts: The culturally produced, shared, and reinforced social norms that serve as blueprints, or maps, to guide sexual and gender behavior.

significant symbol: A gesture that arouses in the individual the same kind of response, although it need not be identical, as it is supposed to elicit from those to whom the gesture is addressed.

simulation: An inauthentic or fake version of something.

social change: Variations over time in every aspect of the social world, ranging from changes affecting individuals to transformations having an impact on the globe as a whole.

social class: One's economic position in the stratification system, especially one's occupation, which strongly determines and reflects one's income and wealth.

social construction of reality: The continuous process of individual creation of structural realities and the constraint and coercion exercised by those structures.

social control: The process by which a group or society enforces conformity to its demands and expectations.

social control agents: Those who label a person as deviant.

social facts: Macro-level phenomena—social structures and cultural norms and values—that stand apart from and impose themselves on people.

socialism: A historical stage following communism involving the effort by society to plan and organize production consciously and rationally so that all members of society benefit from it.

socialization: The process through which a person learns and generally comes to accept the ways of a group or of society as a whole.

social mobility: The ability or inability to change one's position in the social hierarchy.

social movements: Sustained and intentional collective efforts, usually operating outside established institutional channels, either to bring about or to retard social change.

social networks: Networks that involve two or more individuals, groups, organizations, or societies.

social processes: The dynamic and ever-changing aspects of the social world.

social stratification: Hierarchical differences and inequalities in economic positions, as well as in other important areas, especially political power and status or social honor.

social structures: Enduring and regular social arrangements, such as the family and the state.

society: A complex pattern of social relationships that is bounded in space and persists over time.

sociological imagination: A unique perspective that gives sociologists a distinctive way of looking at data and reflecting on the world around them.

sociology: The systematic study of the ways in which people are affected by and affect the social structures and social processes that are associated with the groups, organizations, cultures, societies, and world in which they exist.

specific deterrence: Deterrence from criminal behavior based on the concept that the experience of punishment in general, and incarceration in particular, makes it less likely that an individual will commit crimes in the future.

state: A political body organized for government and civil rule.

statistics: The mathematical method used to analyze numerical data.

status: A dimension of the social stratification system that relates to the prestige attached to people's positions within society.

stepfamily: A family in which two adults are married or cohabiting and at least one of them has a child or children from a previous marriage or cohabitation living with him or her.

stereotype: An exaggerated generalization about an entire category of people that is thought to apply to everyone in that category.

stigma: A person's characteristic that others find, define, and often label as unusual, unpleasant, or deviant.

stratified sample: A sample created when a larger group is divided into a series of subgroups and then random samples are taken within each of these groups.

structural-functionalism: A set of ideas focused on social structures as well as the functions and dysfunctions that such structures perform.

structuralism: Social theory interested in the social impact of hidden or underlying structures.

structural mobility: The effect of changes in the larger society on the position of individuals in the stratification system, especially the occupational structure.

subculture: A group of people who accept much of the dominant culture but are set apart from it by one or more culturally significant characteristics.

suburbanization: The process whereby large numbers of people move out of the city and into nearby, less densely populated, environs.

suburbs: Communities that are adjacent to, but outside the political boundaries of, large central cities.

survey research: A research methodology that involves the collection of information from a population, or more usually a representative portion of a population, through the use of interviews and, more important, questionnaires.

sustainable development: Economic and environmental changes that meet the needs of the present, especially of the world's poor, without jeopardizing the ability to meet the needs of the future.

symbol: A word, gesture, or object that stands in for something or someone (a "label").

symbolic culture: Aspects of culture that exist in nonmaterial forms.

symbolic interaction: Interaction on the basis of not only gestures but also significant symbols.

symbolic interactionism: A sociological perspective focusing on the role of symbols and how their meanings are shared and understood by those involved in human interaction.

technology: The interplay of machines, tools, skills, and procedures for the accomplishment of tasks.

technoscapes: Landscapes that use mechanical and informational technologies as well as the material that moves quickly and freely through them.

terrorism: Acts of violence by nongovernmental actors that target noncombatants, property, or military personnel to influence politics.

theory: A set of interrelated ideas that have a wide range of application, deal with centrally important issues, and have stood the test of time.

total institution: A closed, all-encompassing place of residence and work set off from the rest of society that meets all of the needs of those enclosed within it.

traditional authority: Authority based on a belief in long-running traditions.

transgender: An umbrella term for people whose gender identity and/or gender presentation differs from the gender assigned at birth or in infancy.

transnational capitalism: An economic system in which transnational economic practices predominate.

treadmill of production: The dependence of everyone in the capitalist system on continuous growth in production and in the economy.

triad: A three-person group.

unanticipated consequence: An unexpected social effect, especially a negative effect.

underemployment: Employment in jobs that are not consonant with one's training and ability, as a part-time worker when one is capable and desirous of full-time work, or in jobs that are not fully occupying.

undernutrition: A form of malnutrition involving an inadequate intake of nutrients, including calories, vitamins, and minerals.

undocumented immigrants: Immigrants residing in a receiving country without valid authorization.

unemployment: The state of being economically active and in the labor force, being able and willing to work, and seeking employment, but being unable to find a job.

urban: City dwelling; in the United States, to be considered urban, an area must have more than 50,000 inhabitants.

urbanism: The distinctive way of life (lifestyles, attitudes, social relationships) that emerges in, and is closely associated with, urban areas.

urbanization: The process by which an increasing percentage of a society's population comes to be located in relatively densely populated urban areas.

validity: The degree to which a question (or another kind of measure) gets an accurate response, or measures what it is supposed to measure.

values: General and abstract standards defining what a group or society as a whole considers good, desirable, right, or important—in short, its ideals.

vertical mobility: Both upward and downward mobility.

violent crime: Crime that involves the threat of injury or the threat or actual use of force, including murder, rape, robbery, and aggravated assault, as well as terrorism and, globally, war crimes.

vouchers: Government-issued certificates that allow students to use public tax dollars to pay tuition at private schools.

war: Armed conflict in which a nation uses its military to attempt to impose its will on others.

wealth: The total amount of a person's assets less the total of various kinds of debts.

welfare states: States that seek both to run their economic markets efficiently, as capitalism does, and to do so equitably, which capitalism does not do.

white-collar crimes: Crimes committed by responsible and (usually) high-social-status people in the course of their work.

white racial frame: An array of racist ideas, racial stereotypes, racialized stories and tales, racist images, powerful racial emotions, and various inclinations to discriminate against blacks.

world-systems theory: A system of thought that focuses on the stratification of nation-states on a global scale.

xenophobia: Prejudices that cause people to reject, exclude, and vilify groups that are outsiders or foreigners to the dominant social group.

REFERENCES
Chapter-Opening Vignettes

CHAPTER 1

Ryan, Yasmine. 2011. "How Tunisia's Revolution Began." Al Jazeera English, January 26. Retrieved May 5, 2011 (http://english.aljazeera.net/indepth/features/2011/01/2011126121815985483.html).

"Tunisia Protests against Ben Ali Left 200 Dead, Says UN." 2011. BBC News, February 1. Retrieved May 5, 2011 (http://www.bbc.co.uk/news/world-africa-12335692).

CHAPTER 2

Freedman, Andrew. 2011. "Public Remains Confused about Global Warming, but Less So." *Washington Post,* June 14. Retrieved June 15, 2011 (http://www.washingtonpost.com/blogs/capital-weather-gang/post/public-remains-confused-about-global-warming-but-less-so/2011/06/13/AG04TaUH_blog.html).

Oreskes, Naomi. 2004. "Beyond the Ivory Tower: The Scientific Consensus on Climate Change." *Science* 306(5702): 1686. Retrieved June 15, 2011 (http://www.sciencemag.org/content/306/5702/1686.full).

CHAPTER 3

Carr, Ian. 1998. *Miles Davis: The Definitive Biography.* New York: Thunder Mouth Press.

Smith, Jeff and Jean Wylie. 2004. "China's Youth Define 'Cool.'" *China Business Review,* July/August. Retrieved June 17, 2011 (http://www.chinabusinessreview.com/public/0407/smith.html).

Thompson, Robert Farris. 1973. "An Aesthetic of the Cool." *African Arts* 7(1). Retrieved June 16, 2011 (http://www.jstor.org/pss/3334749).

CHAPTER 4

Callimachi, Rukmini and Jim Yardley. 2015. "From Amateur to Ruthless Jihadist in France." *New York Times,* January 17.

CHAPTER 5

Castle, Stephen. 2013. "Report of U.S. Spying Angers European Allies." *New York Times,* June 30. Retrieved November 3, 2013 (http://www.nytimes.com/2013/07/01/world/europe/europeans-angered-by-report-of-us-spying.html?pagewanted=all).

Neuman, William and Randal C. Archibold. 2013. "U.S. Is Pressuring Latin Americans to Reject Snowden." *New York Times,* July 12. Retrieved November 3, 2013 (http://www.nytimes.com/2013/07/12/world/americas/us-is-pressing-latin-americans-to-reject-snowden.html?pagewanted=1&ref=todayspaper).

Sanger, David E. 2014. "New N.S.A. Chief Calls Damage from Snowden Leaks Manageable." *New York Times,* June 29.

Savage, Charlie and Jonathan Weisman. 2015. "N.S.A. Collection of Bulk Call Data Is Ruled Illegal." *New York Times,* May 11.

CHAPTER 6

Beiner, Theresa M. 2007. "Sexy Dressing Revisited: Does Target Dress Play a Part in Sexual Harassment Cases?" *Duke Journal of Gender Law and Policy* 14(1). Retrieved August 24, 2011 (http://www.law.duke.edu/shell/cite.pl?14+Duke+J.+Gender+L.+&+Pol%27y+125).

"'SlutWalk' Marches Sparked by Toronto Officer's Remarks." 2011. BBC News, May 8. Retrieved August 24, 2011 (http://www.bbc.co.uk/news/world-us-canada-13320785).

CHAPTER 7

Alderman, Liz and Steven Greenhouse. 2014. "Living Wages, Rarity for U.S. Fast-Food Workers, Served Up in Denmark." *New York Times,* October 27.

Allegretto, Sylvia, Marc Doussard, Dave Graham-Squire, Ken Jacobs, Dan Thomson, and Jeremy Thompson. 2013. *Fast Food, Poverty Wages: The Public Cost of Low-Wage Jobs in the Fast Food Industry.* Berkeley: University of California, Center for Labor Research and Education.

Ehrenreich, Barbara. 2001. *Nickel and Dimed: On (Not) Getting By in America.* New York: Henry Holt.

CHAPTER 8

"Profile: Bolivia's President Evo Morales." 2011. BBC News, January 12. Retrieved October 21, 2011 (http://www.bbc.co.uk/news/world-latin-america-12166905).

Romero, Simon. 2009. "In Bolivia, a Force for Change Endures." *New York Times,* December 5. Retrieved October 21, 2011 (http://www.nytimes.com/2009/12/06/world/americas/06bolivia.html?ref=evomorales).

Webber, Jeffery R. 2011. *From Rebellion to Reform in Bolivia: Class Struggle, Indigenous Liberation, and the Politics of Evo Morales.* Chicago: Haymarket Books.

CHAPTER 9

Eckert, Penelope and Sally McConnell-Ginet. 2013. *Language and Gender.* 2nd ed. New York: Cambridge University Press.

Helliwell, Christine. 2000. "'It's Only a Penis': Rape, Feminism, and Difference." *Signs* 25(3): 789–816.

"MenCare Brazil." N.d. Video. Promundo Global. Retrieved April 22, 2015 (http://promundoglobal.org/resources/mencare-brazil-film).

CHAPTER 10

"Lance Loud! A Death in an American Family." 2011. PBS. Retrieved November 18, 2011 (http://www.pbs.org/lanceloud/american).

Winer, Laurie. 2011. "Reality Replay." *New Yorker,* April 25. Retrieved November 18, 2011 (http://www.newyorker.com/talk/2011/04/25/110425ta_talk_winer).

CHAPTER 11

Associated Press. 2005. "Judge Rules against 'Intelligent Design.'" MSNBC, December 20. Retrieved December 1, 2011 (http://www.msnbc.msn.com/id/10545387/ns/technology_and_science-science/t/judge-rules-against-intelligent-design).

Kenny, Charles. 2014. "Does More Education Lead to Less Religion?" *Bloomberg Businessweek,* October 27. Retrieved September 4, 2015 (http://www.bloomberg.com/bw/articles/2014-10-27/does-more-education-lead-to-less-religion).

"Muslim Medical Students Boycotting Lectures on Evolution . . . Because It 'Clashes with the Koran.'" 2011. *Daily Mail,* November 28. Retrieved December 1, 2011 (http://www.dailymail.co.uk/news/article-2066795/

Muslim-students-walking-lectures-Darwinism-clashes-Koran.html).

Timpane, John. 2011. "The Politics of Science: Evolution and Climate Change Are Shortcuts Conveying Broader Messages." *Philadelphia Enquirer,* August 23. Retrieved December 1, 2011 (http://articles.philly.com/2011-08-23/news/29917822_1_climate-change-evolution-presidential-candidate-jon-huntsman).

Webley, Kayla. 2010. "Brief History: The Textbook Wars." *Time,* March 29. Retrieved December 1, 2011 (http://www.time.com/time/magazine/article/0,9171,1973276,00.html).

CHAPTER 12

Appelbaum, Binyamin. 2015. "Fed Minutes Show Policy Makers Lean toward a Rate Rise after June." *New York Times,* May 20.

Chan, Sewell. 2011. "Financial Crisis Was Avoidable, Inquiry Finds." *New York Times,* January 25. Retrieved November 30, 2011 (http://www.nytimes.com/2011/01/26/business/economy/26inquiry.html).

Unmack, Neil. 2015. "New Greek Debt Deal Will Require More Brinksmanship." *New York Times,* January 27.

CHAPTER 13

Bostwick, J. Michael. 2012. "Blurred Boundaries: The Therapeutics and Politics of Medical Marijuana." *Mayo Clinic Proceedings* 87: 172–186.

Hoffmann, Diane E. and Ellen Weber. 2010. "Medical Marijuana and the Law." *New England Journal of Medicine* 362: 1453–1457.

Kramer, Joan L. 2015. "Medical Marijuana for Cancer." *CA: A Cancer Journal for Clinicians* 65(2): 109–122.

Saint Louis, Catherine. 2014. "Politicians' Prescriptions for Marijuana Defy Doctors and Data." *New York Times,* June 26.

"A Sensible Bill on Medical Marijuana." 2015. *New York Times,* March 11.

CHAPTER 14

Coleman, Jasmine. 2011. "World's 'Seven Billionth Baby' Is Born." *The Guardian,* October 31. Retrieved November 17, 2011 (http://www.guardian.co.uk/world/2011/oct/31/seven-billionth-baby-born-philippines).

"Don't Panic: A UN Study Sparks Fears of a Population Explosion. The Alarm Is Misplaced." 2014. *Economist,* September 24. Retrieved April 22, 2015 (http://www.economist.com/news/international/21619986-un-study-sparks-fears-population-explosion-alarm-misplaced-dont-panic).

McQueeney, Kerry. 2011. "Welcome to a Very Full World, Danica: Was This the World's Seven Billionth Baby?" *Daily Mail,* October 30. Retrieved November 17, 2011 (http://www.dailymail.co.uk/news/article-2055419/Danica-Camacho-Seven-billionth-baby-born-Philippines.html).

Newcomb, Alyssa. 2011. "7 Billion People: What Number Are You?" ABC News, October 30. Retrieved November 17, 2011 (http://abcnews.go.com/blogs/headlines/2011/10/7-billion-people-what-number-are-you).

World Bank Development Data Group. 2011. "World Development Indicators." Retrieved November 17, 2011 (http://data.worldbank.org/data-catalog/world-development-indicators?cid=GPD_WDI).

CHAPTER 15

Adam, Karla. 2011. "Occupy Wall Street Protests Go Global." *Washington Post,* October 15. Retrieved November 23, 2011 (http://www.washingtonpost.com/world/europe/occupy-wall-street-protests-go-global/2011/10/15/gIQAp7kimL_story.html).

Nir, Sarah Maslin. 2012. "Helping Hands Also Expose a New York Divide." *New York Times,* November 16.

"'Occupy Wall Street' UC Davis Protests Escalate after Pepper Spray Use Sparks Anger." 2011. *Washington Post,* November 21. Retrieved November 23, 2011 (http://www.washingtonpost.com/national/occupy-wall-street-uc-davis-protests-escalate-after-pepper-spray-use-sparks-anger/2011/11/21/gIQANOr2iN_story.html).

Pepitone, Julianne. 2011. "How Occupy Wall Street Has Evolved." CNN Money, October 6. Retrieved November 23, 2011 (http://money.cnn.com/2011/10/06/technology/occupy_wall_street/index.htm).

Sorkin, Andrew Ross. 2012. "Occupy Wall Street: A Frenzy That Fizzled." *New York Times,* September 18.

Wessel, Ruth and Jack Ewing. 2015. "Germans Protest European Austerity Measures." *New York Times,* March 19.

REFERENCES
Comprehensive List

Abella, Rudolfo. 2006. "An Analysis of the Academic Performance of Voucher Students in the Opportunity Scholarship Program." *Education and Urban Society* 38(40): 406–418.

Abrutyn, Seth. 2012. "Hinduism." Pp. 932–937 in *The Wiley-Blackwell Encyclopedia of Globalization*, edited by G. Ritzer. Malden, MA: Wiley-Blackwell.

Acemoglu, Daron and James A. Robinson. 2012. *Why Nations Fail: The Origins of Power, Prosperity, and Poverty.* New York: Crown Business.

Acierno, Ron, Melba A. Hernandez, Ananda B. Amstadter, Heidi S. Resnick, Kenneth Steve, Wendy Muzzy, and Dean G. Kilpatrick. 2010. "Prevalence and Correlates of Emotional, Physical, Sexual, and Financial Abuse and Potential Neglect in the United States: The National Elder Mistreatment Study." *American Journal of Public Health* 100: 292–297.

Acker, Joan. 1990. "Hierarchies, Jobs, and Bodies: A Theory of Gendered Organizations." *Gender & Society* 4(2): 139–158.

Acker, Joan. 1992. "Gendered Institutions: From Sex Roles to Gendered Institutions." *Contemporary Sociology* 21: 565–569.

Acker, Joan. 2004. "Gender, Capitalism and Globalization." *Critical Sociology* 30(1): 17–41.

Acker, Joan. 2009. "From Glass Ceiling to Inequality Regimes." *Sociologie du Travail* 51(2): 199–217.

Adam, Barry D. 2006. "Relationship Innovation in Male Couples." *Sexualities* 9: 15–26.

Adams, Ann, Christopher D. Buckingham, Antje Lindenmeyer, John B. McKinlay, Carol Link, Lisa Marceau, and Sara Arber. 2008. "The Influence of Patient and Doctor Gender on Diagnosing Coronary Heart Disease." *Sociology of Health and Illness* 30(1): 1–18.

Adams, Josh. 2009. "Bodies of Change: A Comparative Analysis of Media Representations of Body Modification Practices." *Sociological Perspectives* 52: 103–129.

Adams, Margaret E. and Jacquelyn Campbell. 2012. "Being Undocumented and Intimate Partner Violence (IPV): Multiple Vulnerabilities through the Lens of Feminist Intersectionality." *Women's Health and Urban Life* 11(1): 15–34.

Addington, Lynn A. and Callie Marie Rennison. 2015. "Keeping the Barbarians Outside the Gate? Comparing Burglary Victimization in Gated and Non-gated Communities." *Justice Quarterly* 32(1): 168–192.

Adler, Patricia A. and Peter Adler. 2011. *The Tender Cut: Inside the Hidden World of Self-Injury.* New York: New York University Press.

Adler, Patricia A. and Peter Adler. 2012. "Tales from the Field: Reflections on Four Decades of Ethnography." *Qualitative Sociology* 8: 10–32.

Agrikoliansky, Eric. 2013. "Globalization and Movements." Pp. 528–531 in *The Wiley-Blackwell Encyclopedia of Social and Political Movements*, 3 vols., edited by D. A. Snow, D. Della Porta, B. Klandermans, and D. McAdam. Malden, MA: Wiley-Blackwell.

Aguirre, B. E., Manuel R. Torres, Kimberly B. Gill, and H. Lawrence Hotchkiss. 2011. "Normative Collective Behavior in the Station Building Fire." *Social Science Quarterly* 92: 100–118.

Ahituv, Avner and Robert I. Lerman. 2007. "How Do Marital Status, Work Effort, and Wage Rates Interact?" *Demography* 44(3): 623–647.

Ahmed, Ishtiaq. 2013. "Muslim Immigrants in Europe: The Changing Realities." *India Quarterly* 69: 265–282.

Ahuvia, Aaron and Elif Izberk-Bilgin. 2011. "Limits of the McDonaldization Thesis: EBayization and Ascendant Trends in Post-industrial Consumer Culture." *Consumption, Markets and Culture* 14: 361–364.

Ajrouch, Kristine A. 2007. "Reference Groups." Pp. 3828–3829 in *The Blackwell Encyclopedia of Sociology*, edited by G. Ritzer. Malden, MA: Blackwell.

Alazraki, Melly. 2010. "Global Pharmaceutical Sales Expected to Rise to $880 Billion in 2011." DailyFinance, October 7. Retrieved January 25, 2012 (http://www.dailyfinance.com/2010/10/07/global-pharmaceutical-sales-expected-to-rise-to-880-billion-in).

Alba, Richard. 2009. *Blurring the Color Line: The New Chance for a More Integrated America.* Cambridge, MA: Harvard University Press.

Albrow, Martin. 1996. *The Global Age.* Cambridge: Polity Press.

Aleman, Ana M. and Katherine Link Wartman. 2008. *Online Social Networking on Campus: Understanding What Matters in Student Culture.* New York: Routledge.

Alexander, Bayarma, Dick Ettema, and Martin Dijst. 2010. "Fragmentation of Work Activity as a Multi-dimensional Construct and Its Association with ICT, Employment and Sociodemographic Characteristics." *Journal of Transport Geography* 18(1): 55–64.

Alexander, Karl, Doris Entwisle, and Linda Olson. 2014. *The Long Shadow: Family Background, Disadvantaged Urban Youth, and the Transition to Adulthood.* New York: Russell Sage Foundation.

Alexander, M. Jacqui and Chandra Talpade Mohanty, eds. 2013. *Feminist Genealogies, Colonial Legacies, Democratic Futures.* New York: Routledge.

Alexander, Michelle. 2012. *The New Jim Crow: Mass Incarceration in the Age of Colorblindness.* New York: New Press.

Alger, Janet M. and Steven F. Alger. 1997. "Beyond Mead: Symbolic Interaction between Humans and Felines." *Society and Animals* 5(1): 65–81.

Ali, Ayann Hirsi. 2010. "Not the Child My Grandmother Wanted." *New York Times*, December 2. Retrieved May 28, 2012 (http://www.nytimes.com/2010/12/02/opinion/global/02iht-GA13ali.html?_r=2).

Ali, S. Harris. 2012. "Diseases, Borderless." Pp. 446–449 in *The Wiley-Blackwell Encyclopedia of Globalization*, edited by G. Ritzer. Malden, MA: Wiley-Blackwell.

Allan, Stuart. 2007. "Network Society." Pp. 3180–3182 in *The Blackwell Encyclopedia of Sociology*, edited by G. Ritzer. Malden, MA: Blackwell.

Allegretto, Sylvia, Marc Doussard, Dave Graham-Squire, Ken Jacobs, Dan Thomson, and Jeremy Thompson. 2013. *Fast Food, Poverty Wages: The Public Cost of Low-Wage Jobs in the Fast Food Industry.* Berkeley: University of California, Center for Labor Research and Education.

Allison, Rachel and Barbara J. Risman. 2013. "A Double Standard for 'Hooking Up': How Far Have We Come toward Gender Equality?" *Social Science Research* 42(5): 1191–1206.

Alon, Sigal and Dafna Gelbgiser. 2011. "The Female Advantage in College Academic Achievements and Horizontal Sex Segregation." *Social Science Research* 40(1): 107–119.

Altabbakh, Hanan, Susan Murray, Katie Grantham, and Siddharth Damle. 2013. "Variations in Risk Management Models: A Comparative Study of the Space Shuttle Challenger Disaster." *Engineering Management Journal* 25(2): 13–14.

Altman, Dennis. 2001. *Global Sex.* Chicago: University of Chicago Press.

Al-Tuwaijri, Sameera, Louis J. Currat, Sheila Davey, Andrés de Francisco, Abdul Ghaffar, Susan Jupp, and Christine Mauroux. 2003. *The 10/90 Report on Health Research 2003–2004.* Geneva: Global Forum for Health Research.

Alvarez, Lizette. 2011. "Pull of Family Reshapes U.S.–Cuban Relations." *New York Times*, November 22.

Alvesson, Mats and Yvonne Due Billing. 2009. *Understanding Gender and Organizations.* 2nd ed. London: Sage.

Amato, Paul R. 2012. "Institutional, Companionate and Individualized Marriages: Change over Time and Implications for Marital Quality." Pp. 107–124 in *Marriage at the Crossroads: Law, Policy, and the Brave New World of Twenty-First-Century Families*, edited by M. Garrison and E. Scott. Cambridge: Cambridge University Press.

Amato, Paul R., Alan Booth, David A. Johnson, and Stacy J. Rogers. 2007. *Alone Together: How Marriage in America Is Changing.* Cambridge, MA: Harvard University Press.

Amato, Paul R. and Spencer James. 2010. "Divorce in Europe and the United States: Commonalities and Differences across Nations." *Family Science* 1: 2–13.

393

America.gov. 2008. "U.S. Minorities Will Be the Majority by 2042, Census Bureau Says." Archive, August 15. Retrieved April 14, 2011 (http://www.america.gov/st/peopleplace-english/2008/August/20080815140005xlrennef0.1078106.html).

Amin, Ash, ed. 1994. *Post-Fordism*. Oxford: Blackwell.

Amnesty International. 2004. "Lives Blown Apart: Crimes against Women in Times of Conflict: Stop Violence against Women." Retrieved March 28, 2012 (http://www.amnesty.org/en/library/info/ACT77/075/2004/en).

Amnesty International. 2012. *Death Sentences and Executions 2011*. London: Author.

Anaïs, Seantel and Sean P. Hier. 2012. "Risk Society and *Current Sociology*." *Current Sociology* 60(4): 1–3.

Anastasia, Désiré. 2010. "Living Marked: Tattooed Women and Perceptions of Beauty and Femininity." *Advances in Gender Research* 14: 11–33.

Anderson, Allan Heaton. 2013. *An Introduction to Pentecostalism: Global Charismatic Christianity*. Cambridge: Cambridge University Press.

Anderson, Benedict. 1991. *Imagined Communities: Reflections on the Origin and Spread of Nationalism*. 2nd ed. London: Verso Books.

Anderson, Chris. 2009. *Free: The Future of a Radical Price*. New York: Hyperion.

Anderson, David M. and Neil Carrier. 2006. "'Flower of Paradise' or 'Polluting the Nation': Contested Narratives of Khat Consumption." Pp. 145–166 in *Consuming Cultures, Global Perspectives: Historical Trajectories, Transnational Exchanges*, edited by J. Brewer and F. Trentmann. Oxford: Berg.

Andreas, Peter and Ethan Nadelmann. 2006. *Policing the Globe: Criminalization and Crime Control in International Relations*. New York: Oxford University Press.

Andrejevic, Mark. 2009. *Spy: Surveillance and Power in the Interactive Era*. Lawrence: University of Kansas Press.

Andrews, Kenneth T. 2013. "Civil Rights Movement." Pp. 193–199 in *The Wiley-Blackwell Encyclopedia of Social and Political Movements*, 3 vols., edited by D. A. Snow, D. Della Porta, B. Klandermans, and D. McAdam. Malden, MA: Wiley-Blackwell.

Androff, David K. and Kyoko Y. Tavassoli. 2012. "Deaths in the Desert: The Human Rights Crisis on the U.S.–Mexico Border." *Social Work* 57: 165–173.

Angel, Jacqueline, Jennifer Montez, and Ronald Angel. 2010. "Work, Marriage, and Women's Retirement Security: The Significance of Race and Mexican Origin." Paper presented at the annual meeting of the American Sociological Association, Atlanta , GA.

Ansari, Aziz with Eric Klinenberg. 2015. *Modern Romance*. New York: Penguin.

Antonio, Robert J. 2007. "The Cultural Construction of Neoliberal Globalization." Pp. 67–83 in *The Blackwell Companion to Globalization*, edited by G. Ritzer. Malden, MA: Blackwell.

Antonio, Robert J. 2014. "Piketty's Nightmare Capitalism: The Return of Rentier Society and De-democratization." *Contemporary Sociology* 43: 783–790.

Antonio, Robert J. and Robert J. Brulle. 2012. "Ecological Problems." Pp. 476–484 in *The Wiley-Blackwell Companion to Sociology*, edited by G. Ritzer. Malden, MA: Wiley-Blackwell.

Apel, Robert S. and Daniel Nagin. 2011. "General Deterrence: A Review of Recent Literature." Pp. 411–436 in *Crime and Public Policy*, edited by J. Q. Wilson and J. Petersilia. Oxford: Oxford University Press.

Apesoa-Varano, Ester Carolina. 2007. "Educated Caring: The Emergence of Professional Identity among Nurses." *Qualitative Sociology* 30: 249–274.

Appadurai, Arjun. 1996. *Modernity at Large: Cultural Dimensions of Globalization*. Minneapolis: University of Minnesota Press.

Appelbaum, Binyamin. 2014. "The Vanishing Male Worker, Waiting It Out." *New York Times*, December 12.

Appelbaum, Steven H., Neveen Asham, and Kamal Argheyd. 2011. "Is the Glass Ceiling Cracked in Information Technology? A Quantitative Analysis," parts 1–2. *Industrial and Commercial Training* 43(6): 354–361, 43(7): 451–459.

Arbabzadah, Nushin. 2011. "Girls Will Be Boys in Afghanistan." *The Guardian*, November 30. Retrieved April 18, 2015 (http://www.theguardian.com/global/2011/nov/30/afghanistan-girls-dressing-as-boys).

Archibold, Randal C. 2009. "Mexican Drug Cartel Violence Spills Over, Alarming U.S." *New York Times*, March 22. Retrieved September 10, 2013 (http://www.nytimes.com/2009/03/23/us/23border.html?pagewanted=all).

Archibold, Randal C. 2010. "Ranchers Alarmed by Killing Near Border." *New York Times*, April 4.

Archibold, Randal C. 2014. "As Child Migrants Flood to the Border, U.S. Presses Latin America to Act." *New York Times*, June 20.

Archibold, Randal C. 2015. "Mexico Officially Declares Missing Students Dead." *New York Times*, January 28.

Armstrong, Elizabeth A. and Suzanna M. Crage. 2006. "Movements and Memory: The Making of the Stonewall Myth." *American Sociological Review* 71(5): 724–751.

Armstrong, Elizabeth A. and Suzanna M. Crage. 2013. "Stonewall Riots." Pp. 1251–1253 in *The Wiley-Blackwell Encyclopedia of Social and Political Movements*, 3 vols., edited by D. A. Snow, D. Della Porta, B. Klandermans, and D. McAdam. Malden, MA: Wiley-Blackwell.

Armstrong, Elizabeth A., Paula England, and Alison C. K. Fogarty. 2012. "Accounting for Women's Orgasm and Sexual Enjoyment in College Hookups and Relationships." *American Sociological Review* 77(3): 435–462.

Aronson, Jay D. and Simon A. Cole. 2009. "Science and the Death Penalty: DNA, Innocence, and the Debate over Capital Punishment in the United States." *Law and Social Inquiry* 34: 603–633.

Arthur, Mikaila and Mariel Lemonik. 2007a. "Race." Pp. 3731–3734 in *The Blackwell Encyclopedia of Sociology*, edited by G. Ritzer. Malden, MA: Blackwell.

Arthur, Mikaila and Mariel Lemonik. 2007b. "Racism, Structural and Institutional." Pp. 3765–3767 in *The Blackwell Encyclopedia of Sociology*, edited by G. Ritzer. Malden, MA: Blackwell.

Arthur, Mikaila and Mariel Lemonik. 2013. "Emergent Norm Theory." Pp. 397–399 in *The Wiley-Blackwell Encyclopedia of Social and Political Movements*, 3 vols., edited by D. A. Snow, D. Della Porta, B. Klandermans, and D. McAdam. Malden, MA: Wiley-Blackwell.

Arvidsson, Adam. 2012. "Brands." Pp. 135–138 in *The Wiley-Blackwell Encyclopedia of Globalization*, edited by G. Ritzer. Malden, MA: Wiley-Blackwell.

Asayama, Shinichiro. 2015. "Catastrophism toward 'Opening Up' or 'Closing Down'? Going beyond the Apocalyptic Future and Geoengineering." *Current Sociology* 63(1): 89–93.

Asch, Solomon E. 1952. *Social Psychology*. New York: Prentice Hall.

Asch, Solomon E. 1955. "Opinions and Social Pressure." *Scientific American*, November, 31–35.

Ashwin, Sarah and Olga Isupova. 2014. "'Behind Every Great Man . . .': The Male Marriage Wage Premium Examined Qualitatively." *Journal of Marriage and Family* 76(1): 37–55.

Associated Press. 2014. "10 Injured as Migrants Storm Spanish Border Fence." *New York Times*, October 15.

Associated Press. 2015a. "Hungary: Anti-Migrant Fence Proposed." *New York Times*, June 17.

Associated Press. 2015b. "Los Angeles Becomes Latest US City to Favor $15 Minimum Wage." *New York Times*, May 20.

Associated Press. 2015c. "Thousands Spend Night Outdoors as Death Toll Rises in Nepal." *New York Times*, May 12.

Associated Press. 2015d. "UNESCO Chief Decries 'Cultural Cleansing' in ISIS Video." *New York Times*, February 27.

Associated Press. 2015e. "World Health Organization Reports 7,905 Ebola Deaths." *New York Times*, January 1. Retrieved May 7, 2015 (http://www.nytimes.com/aponline/2015/01/01/world/africa/ap-ebola.html?_r=0).

Atkinson, Lucy, Michelle R. Nelson, and Mark A. Rademacher. 2015. "A Humanistic Approach to Understanding Child Consumer Socialization in US Homes." *Journal of Children and Media* 9(1): 95–112.

Atkinson, Michael. 2003. *Tattooed: The Sociogenesis of a Body Art*. Toronto: University of Toronto Press.

Atkinson, Rowland. 2014. *Shades of Deviance: A Primer on Crime, Deviance, and Social Harm*. New York: Routledge.

Atkinson, Rowland and Sarah Blandy. 2005. "Introduction: International Perspectives on the New Enclavism and the Rise of Gated Communities." *Housing Studies* 20: 177–186.

Atsushi, Miura. 2014. *The Rise of Sharing: Fourth-Stage Consumer Society in Japan*. Tokyo: International House of Japan.

Aud, Susan and Gretchen Hannes, eds. 2011. *The Condition of Education 2011 in Brief* (NCES 2011-034). Washington, DC: U.S. Department of Education, National Center for Education Statistics.

Auyero, Javier and Timothy Patrick Moran. 2007. "The Dynamics of Collective Violence: Dissecting Food Riots in Contemporary Argentina." *Social Forces* 85(3): 1341–1367.

Aveline, David. 2006. "'Did I Have Blinders On or What?' Retrospective Sense Making by Parents of Gay Sons Recalling Their Sons' Earlier Years." *Journal of Family Issues*, 27(6): 777–802.

Avishai, Orit. 2007. "Managing the Lactating Body: The Breast-Feeding Project and the Privileged Mother." *Qualitative Sociology* 30: 135–142.

Ayanian, John Z. and Arnold M. Epstein. 1991. "Differences in the Use of Procedures between Men and Women Hospitalized for Coronary Heart Disease." *New England Journal of Medicine* 325(1): 221–225.

Ayres, Tammy C. and James Treadwell. 2012. "Bars, Drugs and Football Thugs: Alcohol, Cocaine Use and Violence in the Night Time Economy among English Football Firms." *Criminology and Criminal Justice* 12: 83–100.

Babb, Sarah. 2005. "The Social Consequences of Structural Adjustment: Recent Evidence and Current Debates." *Annual Review of Sociology* 31: 199–222.

Baker, Peter. 2010. "Book Says Afghanistan Divided White House." *New York Times,* September 22.

Baker, Peter. 2014. "U.S. to Restore Full Relations with Cuba, Erasing a Last Trace of Cold War Hostility." *New York Times,* December 17.

Ball, Derek and Peter Kivisto. 2006. "Couples Facing Divorce." Pp. 145–161 in *Couples, Kids, and Family Life,* edited by J. F. Gubrium and J. A. Holstein. New York: Oxford University Press.

Bancroft, Angus. 2005. *Roma and Gypsy—Travellers in Europe: Modernity, Race, Space, and Exclusion.* Burlington, VT: Ashgate.

Banks, Russell. 2011. *Lost Memory of Skin.* New York: HarperCollins.

Baran, Paul A. and Paul M. Sweezy. 1966. *Monopoly Capital: An Essay on American Economic and Social Order.* New York: Modern Reader.

Barber, Benjamin R. 2007. *Consumed: How Markets Corrupt Children, Infantilize Adults, and Swallow Citizens Whole.* New York: MTM.

Barker, Eileen. 2007. "New Religious Movements." Pp. 3201–3206 in *The Blackwell Encyclopedia of Sociology,* edited by G. Ritzer. Malden, MA: Blackwell.

Barr, Rebecca and Robert Dreeben. 1983. *How Schools Work.* Chicago: University of Chicago Press.

Barrett, Donald C. and Lance M. Pollack. 2011. "Testing a Typology of Adaptations to Same-Sex Sexual Orientation among Men." *Sociological Perspectives* 54: 619–640.

Barry, Ellen and Suhasini Raj. 2014. "Uber Banned in India's Capital after Rape Accusation." *New York Times,* December 8.

Barstow, David. 2010. "Tea Party Lights Fuse for Rebellion on the Right." *New York Times,* February 16.

Basu, Amrita, ed. 2010. *Women's Movements in the Global Era: The Power of Local Feminisms.* Boulder, CO: Westview Press.

Baudrillard, Jean. [1970] 1998. *The Consumer Society.* London: Sage.

Bauman, Zygmunt. 1989. *Modernity and the Holocaust.* Ithaca, NY: Cornell University Press.

Bauman, Zygmunt. 1992. *Intimations of Postmodernity.* London: Routledge.

Bauman, Zygmunt. 1999. "The Self in Consumer Society." *Hedgehog Review* 1(1): 35–40.

Bauman, Zygmunt. 2000. *Liquid Modernity.* Cambridge: Polity Press.

Bauman, Zygmunt. 2003. *Liquid Love.* Cambridge: Polity Press.

Bauman, Zygmunt. 2005. *Liquid Life.* Cambridge: Polity Press.

Bauman, Zygmunt. 2006. *Liquid Fear.* Cambridge: Polity Press.

Bauman, Zygmunt. 2007. *Liquid Times: Living in an Age of Uncertainty.* Cambridge: Polity Press.

Bauman, Zygmunt and David Lyon. 2012. *Liquid Surveillance: A Conversation.* London: Polity Press.

Baym, Nancy. 2010. *Personal Connections in the Digital Age.* Cambridge: Polity Press.

Beauvoir, Simone de. [1952] 1973. *The Second Sex,* translated by H. M. Parshley. New York: Vintage Books.

Beccaria, Cesare. [1764] 1986. *On Crimes and Punishments.* Indianapolis: Hackett.

Beck, Colin and Emily Minor. 2013. "Who Gets Designated a Terrorist and Why?" *Social Forces* 91: 837–872.

Beck, Ulrich. [1986] 1992. *Risk Society: Towards a New Modernity.* London: Sage.

Beck, Ulrich. 2007. "Cosmopolitanism: A Critical Theory for the Twenty-First Century." Pp. 162–176 in *The Blackwell Companion to Globalization,* edited by G. Ritzer. Malden, MA: Blackwell.

Beck, Ulrich and Elisabeth Beck-Gernsheim. 2012. "Families." Pp. 637–639 in *The Wiley-Blackwell Encyclopedia of Globalization,* edited by G. Ritzer. Malden, MA: Wiley-Blackwell.

Becker, Howard S. 1963. *Outsiders: Studies in the Sociology of Deviance.* New York: Free Press.

Becker, Howard S. and Blanche Geer. 1958. "The Fate of Idealism in Medical School." *American Sociological Review* 23: 50–56.

Becker, Penny Edgell and Phyllis Moen. 1999. "Scaling Back: Dual Earner Couples' Work-Family Strategies." *Journal of Marriage and the Family* 61: 995–1007.

Beer, Todd. 2012. "Global Warming." Pp. 841–844 in *The Wiley-Blackwell Companion to Sociology,* edited by G. Ritzer. Malden, MA: Wiley-Blackwell.

Behbehanian, Laleh and Michael Burawoy. 2014. "Appendix: Global Pedagogy in a Digital Age." *Current Sociology* 62(2): 285–291.

Beilharz, Peter. 2012. "Liquidity." Pp. 1299–1230 in *The Wiley-Blackwell Encyclopedia of Globalization,* edited by G. Ritzer. Malden, MA: Wiley-Blackwell.

Belk, Russell W. 1987. "A Child's Christmas in America: Santa Claus as Deity, Consumption as Religion." *Journal of American Culture* 10(1): 87–100.

Belk, Russell W. 2007. "Consumption, Mass Consumption, and Consumer Culture." Pp. 737–746 in *The Blackwell Encyclopedia of Sociology,* edited by G. Ritzer. Malden, MA: Blackwell.

Belk, Russell. 2013. "The Sacred in Consumer Culture." Pp. 69–80 in *Consumption and Spirituality,* edited by D. Rinallo, L. Scott, and P. Maclaren. New York: Routledge.

Belk, Russell. 2014. "Sharing vs. Pseudo-Sharing in Web 2.0." *Anthropologist* 18: 7–23.

Bell, Daniel. 1973. *The Coming of Post-industrial Society: A Venture in Social Forecasting.* New York: Basic Books.

Bell, David. 2007. "Sexualities, Cities and." Pp. 4254–4256 in *The Blackwell Encyclopedia of Sociology,* edited by G. Ritzer. Malden, MA: Blackwell.

Bell, Kerryn. 2009. "Gender and Gangs: A Quantitative Comparison." *Crime and Delinquency* 55: 363–387.

Bell, Robert R. 1971. *Social Deviance: A Substantive Analysis.* Homewood, IL: Dorsey.

Bell, Sheri. 2011. "Through a Foucauldian Lens: A Genealogy of Child Abuse." *Journal of Family Violence* 26: 101–108.

Bellah, Robert N. 1967. "Civil Religion in America." *Daedalus,* Winter.

Belson, Ken. 2014. "Brain Trauma to Affect One in Three Players, NFL Agrees." *New York Times,* September 12.

Bendix, Reinhard and Seymour Martin Lipset, eds. 1966. *Class, Status, and Power: Social Stratification in Comparative Perspective,* 2nd rev. ed. New York: Free Press.

Benjamin, Walter. 1999. *The Arcades Project.* Cambridge, MA: Belknap.

Bennett, M. D. and M. W. Fraser. 2000. "Urban Violence among African American Males: Integrating Family, Neighborhood, and Peer Perspectives." *Journal of Sociology and Social Welfare* 27: 93–117.

Bennett, Tony, Mike Savage, Elizabeth Silva, Alan Warde, Modesto Gayo-Cal, and David Wright. 2009. *Culture, Class, Distinction.* London: Routledge.

Ben-Yehuda, Nachman. 1980. "The European Witch Craze of the 14th to 17th Centuries: A Sociologist's Perspective." *American Journal of Sociology* 86(1): 1–31.

Ben-Yehuda, Nachman. 1985. *Deviance and Moral Boundaries.* Chicago: University of Chicago Press.

Ben-Yehuda, Nachman. 2012. "Deviance: A Sociology of Unconventionalities." Pp. 197–211 in *The Wiley-Blackwell Companion to Sociology,* edited by G. Ritzer. Malden, MA: Wiley-Blackwell.

Benzaquen, Adriana. 2006. *Encounters with Wild Children: Temptation and Disappointment in the Study of Human Nature.* Montreal: McGill-Queen's University Press.

Berard, T. J. 2007. "Deviant Subcultures." Pp. 4872–4877 in *The Blackwell Encyclopedia of Sociology,* edited by G. Ritzer. Malden, MA: Blackwell.

Berger, Peter L. 1969. *The Sacred Canopy: Elements of a Sociological Theory of Religion.* New York: Doubleday.

Berger, Peter L. and Thomas Luckmann. 1967. *The Social Construction of Reality: A Treatise in the Sociology of Knowledge.* New York: Anchor Books.

Berger, Ronald. 2012. *The Holocaust, Religion, and the Politics of Collective Memory: Beyond Sociology.* New Brunswick, NJ: Transaction.

Bergquist, Magnus. 2003. "Open-Source Software Development as Gift Culture: Work and Identity Formation in an Internet Community." In *New Technologies at Work: People, Screens, and Social Virtuality,* edited by C. Garsten and H. Wulff. New York: Berg.

Berkovitch, Nitza. 1999. *From Motherhood to Citizenship: Women's Rights and International Organizations.* Baltimore: Johns Hopkins University Press.

Berkovitch, Nitza. 2012. "Women's Movement(s), Transnational." Pp. 2233–2242 in *The Wiley-Blackwell Encyclopedia of Globalization,* edited by G. Ritzer. Malden, MA: Wiley-Blackwell.

Bernhardt, Annette, Martina Morris, Mark S. Handcock, and Marc A. Scott. 2001. *Divergent Paths: Economic Mobility in the New American Labor Market.* New York: Russell Sage Foundation.

Bertrand, Marianne and Sendhil Mullainathan. 2004. "Are Emily and Greg More Employable than Lakisha and Jamal? A Field Experiment on Labor Market Discrimination." *American Economic Review* 94(4): 991–1013.

Bérubé, Allan. 2010. *Coming Out under Fire: The History of Gay Men and Women in World War II.* Chapel Hill: University of North Carolina Press.

Best, Amy L. 2007. "Consumption, Girls' Culture and." Pp. 724–727 in *The Blackwell Encyclopedia of Sociology,* edited by G. Ritzer. Malden, MA: Blackwell.

Beynon, Huw and Theo Nichol, eds. 2006. *The Fordism of Ford and Modern Management: Fordism and Post-Fordism.* Cheltenham, England: Elgar.

Bhatnagar, Rashmi, Renu Dube, and Reena Dube. 2006. *Female Infanticide in India: A Feminist Cultural History.* Albany: State University of New York Press.

Bhatty, Ayesha. 2010. "Haiti Devastation Exposes Shoddy Construction." BBC News, January 15. Retrieved March 31, 2012 (http://news.bbc.co.uk/2/hi/8460042.stm).

Bian, Y. J. 1997. "Bringing Strong Ties Back In: Indirect Ties, Network Bridges, and Job Searches in China." *American Sociological Review* 62: 366–385.

Bianchi, Suzanne M. and Melissa A. Milkie. 2010. "Work and Family Research in the First Decade of the 21st Century." *Journal of Marriage and Family* 72: 705–725.

Bianchi, Suzanne M., John R. Robinson, and Melissa A. Milkie. 2006. *Changing Rhythms of American Family Life.* New York: Russell Sage Foundation.

Bianchi, Suzanne M. and Vanessa Wight. 2012. "Population." Pp. 470–487 in *The Wiley-Blackwell Companion to Sociology,* edited by G. Ritzer. Malden, MA: Wiley-Blackwell.

Biblarz, Timothy J. and Judith Stacey. 2010. "How Does the Gender of Parents Matter?" *Journal of Marriage and Family* 72(1): 3–22.

Bielby, Rob, Julie Renee Posselt, Ozan Jaquette, and Michael N. Bastedo. 2014. "Why Are Women Underrepresented in Elite Colleges and Universities? A Non-linear Decomposition Analysis." *Research in Higher Education* 55: 735–760.

Bilefsky, Dan. 2008. "Albanian Custom Fades: Woman as Family Man." *New York Times,* June 25. Retrieved April 18, 2015 (http://www.nytimes.com/2008/06/25/world/europe/25virgins.html).

Bills, David. 2007. "Educational Attainment." Pp. 1333–1336 in *The Blackwell Encyclopedia of Sociology,* edited by G. Ritzer. Malden, MA: Blackwell.

Binkley, Sam. 2007. "Counterculture." Pp. 809–810 in *The Blackwell Encyclopedia of Sociology,* edited by G. Ritzer. Malden, MA: Blackwell.

Binnie, Jon. 2004. *The Globalization of Sexuality.* London: Sage.

Blair-Loy, Mary. 2003. *Competing Devotions.* Cambridge, MA: Harvard University Press.

Blakely, Edward J. and M. G. Snyder. 1997. *Fortress America: Gated Communities in the United States.* Washington, DC: Brookings Institution Press.

Blaschke, Steffen, Dennis Schoeneborn, and David Seidl. 2012. "Organizations as Networks of Communication Episodes: Turning the Network Perspective Inside Out." *Organization Studies* 33: 879–906.

Blatt, Jessica. 2007. "Scientific Racism." Pp. 4113–4115 in *The Blackwell Encyclopedia of Sociology,* edited by G. Ritzer. Malden, MA: Blackwell.

Blau, Francine D., Peter Brummund, and Albert Yung-Hsu Liu. 2012. "Trends in Occupational Segregation by Gender 1970–2009: Adjusting for the Impact of Changes in the Occupational Coding System." Discussion Paper 6490, Institute for the Study of Labor (Bonn, Germany). Retrieved April 18, 2015 (http://ftp.iza.org/dp6490.pdf).

Blau, Peter. 1963. *The Dynamics of Bureaucracy.* Chicago: University of Chicago Press.

Blau, Peter and Otis Dudley Duncan. 1967. *The American Occupational Structure.* New York: Wiley.

Blewitt, John. 2014. *Understanding Sustainable Development.* New York: Routledge.

Blight, James G. and Janet M. Lang. 2005. *The Fog of War: Lessons from the Life of Robert S. McNamara.* Lanham, MD: Rowman & Littlefield.

Bluestein, Adam. 2014. "DDP Yoga Is Everywhere, but Does It Deliver?" *Men's Journal,* June. Retrieved April 18, 2015 (http://www.mensjournal.com/health-fitness/exercise/ddp-yoga-is-everywhere-but-does-it-deliver-20140609).

Bluestone, Barry and Bennett Harrison. 1984. *The Deindustrialization of America: Plant Closings, Community Abandonment, and the Dismantling of Basic Industry.* New York: Basic Books.

Blum, Linda. 2000. *At the Breast: Ideologies of Breastfeeding and Motherhood in the Contemporary United States.* Boston: Beacon Press.

Boas, Morten. 2012. "Failed States." Pp. 633–635 in *The Wiley-Blackwell Encyclopedia of Globalization,* edited by G. Ritzer. Malden, MA: Wiley-Blackwell.

Boesler, Matthew. 2013. "Here's How America's Minimum Wage Stacks Up against Countries Like India, Russia, Greece, and France," Business Insider, August 19. Retrieved May 7, 2015 (http://www.businessinsider.com/a-look-at-minimum-wages-around-the-world-2013-8).

Bogle, Kathleen. 2008. *Hooking Up: Sex, Dating, and Relationships on Campus.* New York: New York University Press.

Bolkan, Joshua. 2013. "Report: Students Taking Online Courses Jumps 96 Percent over 5 Years." Campus Technology, June 24. Retrieved April 22, 2015 (http://campustechnology.com/articles/2013/06/24/report-students-taking-online-courses-jumps-96-percent-over-5-years.aspx).

Bolton, Kenneth and Joe R. Feagin. 2004. *Black in Blue: African American Police Officers and Racism.* New York: Routledge.

Bonanno, Alessandro. 2012. "Fordism Post Fordism." Pp. 680–682 in *The Wiley-Blackwell Encyclopedia of Globalization,* edited by G. Ritzer. Malden, MA: Wiley-Blackwell.

Bond, Matthew. 2012. "The Bases of Elite Social Behaviour: Patterns of Club Affiliation among Members of the House of Lords." *Sociology* 46: 613–632.

Bonilla-Silva, Eduardo. 1997. "Rethinking Racism: Toward a Structural Interpretation." *American Sociological Review* 62: 465–480.

Bonilla-Silva, Eduardo. 2009. *Racism without Racists: Color-Blind Racism and the Persistence of Racial Inequality in the United States.* Lanham, MD: Rowman & Littlefield.

Bontje, Marco and Joachim Burdack. 2005. "Edge Cities, European-Style: Examples from Paris and the Randstad." *Cities* 22(4): 317–330.

Booker, Adriel. 2012. "Dealing with Gender Disappointment in Pregnancy." Adriel Booker.com. Retrieved April 18, 2015 (http://adriel-booker.com/dealing-with-gender-disappointment-in-pregnancy).

Bordo, Susan. 1993. *Unbearable Weight: Feminism, Western Culture, and the Body.* Berkeley: University of California Press.

Bornstein, Kate. 1994. *Gender Outlaw: On Men, Women, and the Rest of Us.* New York: Routledge.

Boris, Eileen. 2012. "Feminist Currents." *Frontiers: A Journal of Women Studies* 33: 101–105.

Boswell, A. Ayres and Joan Z. Spade. 1996. "Fraternities and Collegiate Rape Culture: Why Are Some Fraternities More Dangerous Places for Women?" *Gender & Society* 10(2): 133–147.

Botz-Bornstein, Thorsten. 2013. "From the Stigmatized Tattoo to the Graffitied Body: Femininity in the Tattoo Renaissance." *Gender, Place and Culture* 20(2): 236–252.

Boukus, Ellyn R., Alwyn Cassil, and Ann S. O'Malley. 2009. "A Snapshot of U.S. Physicians: Key Findings from the 2008 Health Tracking Physician Survey." Data Bulletin 35, Center for Studying Health System Change. Retrieved April 18, 2015 (http://www.hschange.com/CONTENT/1078/).

Bourdieu, Pierre. 1984. *Distinction: A Social Critique of the Judgment of Taste.* Cambridge, MA: Harvard University Press.

Bourdieu, Pierre. 1992. *The Logic of Practice.* Palo Alto, CA: Stanford University Press.

Bourdieu, Pierre and Jean-Claude Passeron. 1977. *Reproduction in Education, Society, and Culture.* Beverly Hills, CA: Sage.

Boushey, Heather. 2008. "Motherhood Penalty and Women's Earnings, Opting Out? The Effect of Children on Women's Employment in the United States." *Feminist Economics* 14(1): 1–36.

Boustan, Leah P. and Robert A. Margo. 2013. "A Silver Lining to White Flight? White Suburbanization and African-American Homeownership, 1940–1980." *Journal of Urban Economics* 78: 71–80.

Bowen, Ted Smalley. 2001. "English Could Snowball on Net." *Technology Research News,* November 21. Retrieved January 3, 2012 (http://www.trn-mag.com/Stories/2001/112101/English_could_snowball_on_Net_112101.html).

Bowler, Kate and Wen Reagan. 2014. "Bigger, Better, Louder: The Prosperity Gospel's Impact on Contemporary Christian Worship." *Religion & American Culture* 24: 186–230.

Bowling, Ben and James W. E. Sheptycki. 2012. *Global Policing.* London: Sage.

Bowman, John R. and Alyson Cole. 2009. "Do Working Mothers Oppress Other Women? The Swedish 'Maid Debate' and the Welfare State Politics of Gender Equality." *Signs* 35(1): 157–184.

Boykoff, Jules and Eulalie Laschever. 2011. "The Tea Party Movement, Framing, and the U.S. Media." *Social Movement Studies* 10: 341–366.

Braga, Anthony A. and David L. Weisburd. 2012. "The Effects of Focused Deterrence Strategies on Crime: A Systematic Review and Meta-analysis of the Empirical Evidence." *Journal of Research in Crime and Delinquency* 49(3): 323–358.

Braithwaite, John. 2010. "Diagnostics of White-Collar Crime Prevention." *Criminology and Public Policy* 9: 621–626.

Brandle, Gaspar and J. Michael Ryan. 2012. "Consumption." Pp. 289–295 in *The Wiley-Blackwell Encyclopedia of Globalization*, edited by G. Ritzer. Malden, MA: Wiley-Blackwell.

Bratton, William J. 2011. "Reducing Crime through Prevention Not Incarceration." *Criminology and Public Policy* 10: 63–68.

Braun, Virginia. 2010. "Female Genital Cosmetic Surgery: A Critical Review of Current Knowledge and Contemporary Debates." *Journal of Women's Health* 19: 1393–1407.

Braw, Elisabeth. 2014. "The Three Letter Word Driving a Gender Revolution." *Newsweek,* September 29. Retrieved April 17, 2015 (http://www.newsweek.com/2014/10/03/three-letter-word-driving-gender-revolution-272654.html).

Breeden, Aurelien. 2015. "A Furor in France over Resting Place for a Roma Child." *New York Times,* January 6.

Brennan, Bridget. 2013. "The Real Reason Women Shop More than Men." *Forbes,* March 6. Retrieved April 17, 2015 (http://www.forbes.com/sites/bridgetbrennan/2013/03/06/the-real-reason-women-shop-more-than-men).

Brennan, Denise. 2002. "Selling Sex for Visas: Sex Tourism as a Stepping-Stone to International Migration." In *Global Woman: Nannies, Maids, and Sex Workers in the New Economy,* edited by B. Ehrenreich and A. R. Hochschild. New York: Henry Holt.

Brennan, John, Niccolo Durazzi, and Tanguy Séné. 2013. "Things We Know and Don't Know about the Wider Benefits of Higher Education: A Review of the Recent Literature." BIS Research Paper, URN BIS/13/1244. Department for Business, Innovation and Skills, London.

Brewster, Zachary W. and Sarah Nell Rusche. 2012. "Quantitative Evidence of the Continuing Significance of Race: Tableside Racism in Full-Service Restaurants." *Journal of Black Studies* 43: 359–384.

Briggs, Laura. 2012. *Somebody's Children: The Politics of Transracial and Transnational Adoption.* Durham, NC: Duke University Press.

Brim, Orville. 1968. "Adult Socialization." Pp. 182–226 in *Socialization and Society,* edited by J. A. Clausen. Boston: Little, Brown.

Brimeyer, T. M., J. Miller, and R. Perrucci. 2006. "Social Class Sentiments in Formation: Influence of Class Socialization, College Socialization, and Class Aspirations." *Sociological Quarterly* 47: 471–495.

Brinded, Lianna. 2014. "JPMorgan CEO Jamie Dimon Cries That $13bn Mortgage Scandal Fines Were 'Unfair.'" *International Business Times,* January 23. Retrieved April 28, 2015 (http://www.ibtimes.co.uk/jpmorgan-ceo-jamie-dimon-cries-that-13bn-mortgage-scandal-fines-were-unfair-1433525).

Britannica. 2012. "Religion: Year in Review 2010." In *Britannica Book of the Year.* Retrieved May 29, 2012 (http://www.britannica.com/EBchecked/topic/1731588/religion-Year-In-Review-2010).

Bronfenbrenner, Kate, ed. 2007. *Global Unions: Challenging Transnational Capital through Cross-Border Campaigns.* Ithaca, NY: Cornell University Press.

Bronner, Ethan. 2011. "Virtual Bridge Allows Strangers in Mideast to Seem Less Strange." *New York Times,* July 10. Retrieved March 29, 2012 (http://www.nytimes.com/2011/07/10/world/middleeast/10mideast.html).

Brooks, Robert A. 2011. *Cheaper by the Hour: Temporary Lawyers and the Deprofessionalization of the Law.* Philadelphia: Temple University Press.

Brouwer, Steve, Paul Gifford, and Susan D. Rose. 2013. *Exporting the American Gospel: Global Christian Fundamentalism.* New York: Routledge.

Brown, David. 2007. "As Temperature Rise, Health Could Decline." *Washington Post,* December 17.

Brown, Stephen E. 2007a. "Criminology." Pp. 856–860 in *The Blackwell Encyclopedia of Sociology,* edited by G. Ritzer. Malden, MA: Blackwell.

Brown, Stephen E. 2007b. "Ethnocentrism." Pp. 1478–1479 in *The Blackwell Encyclopedia of Sociology,* edited by G. Ritzer. Malden, MA: Blackwell.

Brown, Timothy C., William B. Bankston, and Craig Forsyth. 2013. "'A Service Town': An Examination of the Offshore Oil Industry, Local Entrepreneurs, and the Civic Community Thesis." *Sociological Spectrum* 33: 1–15.

Brownmiller, Susan. 1975. *Against Our Will: Men, Women, and Rape.* New York: Simon & Schuster.

Brubaker, Ralph, Robert W. Lawless, and Charles J. Tabb. 2012. *A Debtor World: Interdisciplinary Perspectives on Debt.* Oxford: Oxford University Press.

Bruce, Steve. 2013. *Secularization: In Defense of an Unfashionable Theory.* New York: Oxford University Press.

Brumberg, Joan Jacobs. 1998. *The Body Project: An Intimate History of American Girls.* New York: Vintage.

Bryant, Melanie and Vaughan Higgins. 2010. "Self-Confessed Troublemakers: An Interactionist View of Deviance during Organizational Change." *Human Relations* 63: 249–277.

Bryk, Anthony, Valerie Lee, and Peter Holland. 1993. *Catholic Schools and the Common Good.* Cambridge, MA: Harvard University Press.

Bryman, A. 2004. *The Disneyization of Society.* London: Sage.

Buchmann, Claudia and Thomas DiPrete. 2006. "The Growing Female Advantage in College Completion: The Role of Family Background and Academic Achievement." *American Sociological Review* 71(4): 515–541.

Buchmann, Claudia and Emily Hannum. 2001. "Education and Stratification in Developing Countries: A Review of Theories and Research." *Annual Review of Sociology* 27: 77–102.

Buck, Brad. 2014. "Process Converts Human Waste into Rocket Fuel." University of Florida News Center, November 25. Retrieved May 22, 2015 (http://news.ufl.edu/archive/2014/11/process-converts-human-waste-into-rocket-fuel.html).

Buckingham, David, ed. 2008. *Youth, Identity and Digital Media.* Cambridge, MA: MIT Press.

Budig, Michelle J., Joya Misra, and Irene Boeckman. 2012. "The Motherhood Penalty in Cross-National Perspective: The Importance of Work–Family Policies and Cultural Attitudes." *Social Politics* 19: 163–193.

Buie, Lisa. 2014. "Judge Sets March 2 as Tentative Trial Date in Movie Theater Shooting Case." *Tampa Bay Times,* September 10. Retrieved April 27, 2015 (http://www.tampabay.com/news/courts/civil/judge-sets-march-2-as-tentative-trial-date-in-movie-theater-shooting-case/2197007).

Burawoy, Michael. 2000. "Introduction: Reaching for the Global." Pp. 1–40 in *Global Ethnography: Forces, Connections, and Imaginations in a Postmodern World,* edited by M. Burawoy, J. A. Blum, S. George, Z. Gille, T. Gowan, L. Haney, M. Klawiter, S. H. Lopez, S. Ó Riain, and M. Thayer. Berkeley: University of California Press.

Burawoy. Michael. 2005. "For Public Sociology." *American Sociological Review* 70(1): 4–28.

Burgess, Ernest W. and Harvey J. Locke. 1945. *The Family: From Institution to Companionship.* New York: American Book.

Burns, Thomas J. 2012. "Marine Pollution." Pp. 1324–1325 in *The Wiley-Blackwell Companion to Sociology,* edited by G. Ritzer. Malden, MA: Wiley-Blackwell.

Butler, Judith. 1990. *Gender Trouble: Feminism and the Subversion of Identity.* New York: Routledge.

Buzinde, Christine N. and Careen Yarnal. 2012. "Therapeutic Landscapes and Postcolonial Theory: A Theoretical Approach to Medical Tourism." *Social Science & Medicine* 74: 783–787.

Byrd, Scott. 2005. "The Porto Alegre Consensus: Theorizing the Forum Movement." *Globalizations* 2(1): 151–163.

Cable, Sherry, Thomas E. Shriver, and Tamara L. Mix. 2008. "Risk Society and Contested Illness: The Case of Nuclear Weapons Workers." *American Sociological Review* 73: 380–401.

Cabrera, Nolan L. 2014. "Beyond Black and White: How White, Male, College Students See Their Asian Peers." *Equity and Excellence in Education* 47: 133–151.

Cagatay, Nilufer and Sule Ozler. 1995. "Feminization of the Labor Force: The Effect of Long Term Development and Structural Adjustment." *World Development* 23(11): 1827–1836.

Cahill, Spencer E., William Distler, Cynthia Lachowetz, Andrea Meaney, Robyn Tarallo, and Teena Willard. 1985. "Meanwhile Backstage: Public Bathrooms and the Interaction Order." *Journal of Contemporary Ethnography* 14: 33–58.

Caird, Jeff K., Kate A. Johnston, Chelsea R. Willness, Mark Asbridge, and Piers Steel. 2014. "A Meta-analysis of the Effects of Texting on Driving." *Accident Analysis & Prevention* 71: 311–318.

Calasanti, Toni and Kathleen Slevin. 2001. *Gender, Social Inequality, and Aging.* Walnut Creek, CA: AltaMira Press.

Caldwell, Christopher. 2009. *Reflections on the Revolution in Europe: Immigration, Islam, and the West.* New York: Doubleday.

Calhoun, Craig, Mark Juergensmeyer, and Jonathan VanAntwerpen, eds. 2011. *Rethinking Secularism.* New York: Oxford University Press.

Campbell, Colin. 1987. *The Romantic Ethic and the Spirit of Modern Consumerism.* Oxford: Blackwell.

Campbell, Colin. 2007. *The Easternization of the West: A Thematic Account of Cultural Change in the Modern Era.* Boulder, CO: Paradigm Press.

Campbell, Nnenia M. 2010. "Coil Conscious: African American Women's Development of Internet-Based Alternative Hair Communities." Paper presented at the annual meeting of the American Sociological Association, Atlanta, GA.

Caniglia, Beth. 2012. "Environmental Protection Movement." Pp. 536–541 in *The Wiley-Blackwell Encyclopedia of Globalization,* edited by G. Ritzer. Malden, MA: Wiley-Blackwell.

Cannato, Vincent J. 2009. *American Passage: The History of Ellis Island.* New York: Harper.

Cannon, Lou. 1997. "Scars Remain Five Years after Los Angeles Riots." *Washington Post,* April 28. Retrieved March 28, 2012 (http://www.washingtonpost.com/wp-srv/national/longterm/lariots/lariots.htm).

Caprile, Maria and Amparo Serrano Pascual. 2011. "The Move Towards the Knowledge-Based Society: A Gender Approach." *Work and Organization* 18: 48–72.

Carbonaro, William. 2005. "Tracking, Student Effort, and Academic Achievement." *Sociology of Education* 78: 27–49.

Carbonaro, William and Elizabeth Covay. 2010. "School Sector and Student Achievement in the Era of Standards Based Reforms." *Sociology of Education* 83: 160–182.

Carey, Stephen. 2011. *A Beginner's Guide to Scientific Method.* Boston: Wadsworth.

Carmichael, Stokely and Charles V. Hamilton. 1967. *Black Power: The Politics of Liberation.* New York: Vintage Books.

Carmody, Dianne Cyr. 2007. "Domestic Violence." Pp. 1219–1220 in *The Blackwell Encyclopedia of Sociology,* edited by G. Ritzer. Malden, MA: Blackwell.

Carrillo, Héctor and Jorge Fontdevila. 2014. "Border Crossings and Shifting Sexualities among Mexican Gay Immigrant Men: Beyond Monolithic Conceptions." *Sexualities* 17(8): 919–938.

Carter, Bill and Tanzia Vega. 2011. "In Shift, Ads Try to Entice Over-55 Set." *New York Times,* May 13.

Carter, Bob and Steve Fenton. 2010. "Not Thinking Ethnicity: A Critique of the Ethnicity Paradigm in an Over-ethnicised Sociology." *Journal for the Theory of Social Behaviour* 40: 1–18.

Carty, Victoria. 2013. "Internet and Social Movements." Pp. 620–623 in *The Wiley-Blackwell Encyclopedia of Social and Political Movements,* 3 vols., edited by D. A. Snow, D. Della Porta, B. Klandermans, and D. McAdam. Malden, MA: Wiley-Blackwell.

Castells, Manuel. 1996. *The Information Age: Economy, Society and Culture,* Vol. 1, *The Rise of the Network Society.* Oxford: Blackwell.

Castells, Manuel. 1997. *The Information Age: Economy, Society and Culture,* Vol. 2, *The Power of Identity.* Oxford: Blackwell.

Castells, Manuel. 1998. *The Information Age: Economy, Society and Culture,* Vol. 3, *End of Millennium.* Oxford: Blackwell.

Castells, Manuel. 2008. *The New Public Sphere: Global Civil Society, Communication Networks, and Global Governance.* Los Angeles: University of Southern California.

Castle, Stephen. 2010. "France Faces European Action after Expulsions." *New York Times,* September 29.

Castles, Stephen. 2013. "The Forces Driving Global Migration." *Journal of Intercultural Studies* 34: 122–140.

Cave, Damien. 2014. "Mexico: Homicides Decline Near Border, Report Says." *New York Times,* April 14.

Center for Research on Education Outcomes, Stanford University. 2013. "National Charter School Study 2013." Retrieved May 18, 2015 (http://credo.stanford.edu/documents/NCSS%202013%20Final%20Draft.pdf).

Centers for Disease Control and Prevention. 2011. "Life Expectancy at Birth, by Race and Sex—United States, 2000–2009." *Morbidity and Mortality Weekly Report* 60(18): 588.

Centers for Disease Control and Prevention. 2012. "Child Abuse and Neglect Cost the United States $124 Billion." Press release, February 1. Retrieved May 13, 2015 (www.cdc.gov/media/releases/2012/p0201_child_abuse.html).

Centers for Disease Control and Prevention. 2015. "Teen Births." Retrieved March 19, 2015 (http://www.cdc.gov/nchs/fastats/teen-births.htm).

Centers for Medicare and Medicaid Services. 2013. "NHE Fact Sheet: Historical NHE, 2013." Retrieved May 19, 2015 (http://www.cms.gov/Research-Statistics-Data-and-Systems/Statistics-Trends-and-Reports/NationalHealthExpendData/NHE-Fact-Sheet.html).

Central Intelligence Agency. 2014. "Country Comparison: Life Expectancy at Birth." World Factbook. Retrieved May 20, 2015 (https://www.cia.gov/library/publications/the-world-factbook/rankorder/2102rank.html).

Cerkez, Aida. 2010. "UN Official: Bosnia War Rapes Must Be Prosecuted." *Washington Post,* November 26.

Cerny, Phillip G. 2007. "Nation-State." In *Encyclopedia of Globalization,* edited by J. A. Scholte and R. Robertson. New York: MTM.

Cha, Youngjoo. 2013. "Overwork and the Persistence of Gender Segregation in Occupations." *Gender & Society* 27: 158–184.

Cha, Youngjoo and Kim A. Weeden. 2014. "Overwork and the Slow Convergence in the Gender Gap in Wages." *American Sociological Review* 79: 457–484.

Chakravarti, Arjun, Tanya Menon, and Christopher Winship. 2014. "Contact and Group Structure: A Natural Experiment of Interracial College Roommate Groups." *Organization Science* 25(4): 1216–1233.

Chambers, Erve. 2010. *Native Tours: The Anthropology of Travel and Tourism.* Prospect Heights, IL: Waveland Press.

Chambliss, William J. 1964. "A Sociological Analysis of the Law of Vagrancy." *Social Problems* 12: 67–77.

Chanda, Nayan. 2007. *Bound Together: How Traders, Preachers, Adventurers, and Warriors Shaped Globalization.* New Haven, CT: Yale University Press.

Chapman, John and Alan Wertheimer, eds. 1990. *Majorities and Minorities: Nomos XXXII.* New York: New York University Press.

Charles, Maria and Karen Bradley. 2009. "Indulging Our Gendered Selves: Sex Segregation by Field of Study in 44 Countries." *American Journal of Sociology* 114: 924–976.

Cheal, David. 2007. "Family Theory." Pp. 1630–1634 in *The Blackwell Encyclopedia of Sociology,* edited by G. Ritzer. Malden, MA: Blackwell.

Chen, James K. C. and Dulamjav Zorigt. 2013. "Managing Occupational Health and Safety in the Mining Industry." *Journal of Business Research* 66: 2321–2331.

Chen, Katherine. 2009. *Enabling Creative Chaos: The Organization behind the Burning Man Event.* Chicago: University of Chicago Press.

Chen, Zihong, Ying Ge, Huiwen Lai, and Chi Wan. 2013. "Globalization and Gender Wage Inequality in China." *World Development* 44: 256–266.

Cherlin, Andrew J. 2004. "The Deinstitutionalization of American Marriage." *Journal of Marriage and Family* 66: 848–861.

Cherlin, Andrew J. 2009. *The Marriage-Go-Round: The State of Marriage and the Family in America Today.* New York: Knopf.

Cherlin, Andrew J. 2010. "The Housewife Anomaly." *New York Times,* January 24.

Chernilo, Daniel. 2012. "Nation." Pp. 1485–1492 in *The Wiley-Blackwell Encyclopedia of Globalization,* edited by G. Ritzer. Malden, MA: Wiley-Blackwell.

Chilton, Roland and Ruth Triplett. 2007a. "Class and Crime." Pp. 542–545 in *The Blackwell Encyclopedia of Sociology,* edited by G. Ritzer. Malden, MA: Blackwell.

Chilton, Roland and Ruth Triplett. 2007b. "Race and Crime." Pp. 3734–3737 in *The Blackwell Encyclopedia of Sociology,* edited by G. Ritzer. Malden, MA: Blackwell.

Chin, Margaret. 2005. *Sewing Women: Immigrants and the New York City Garment Industry.* New York: Columbia University Press.

Chishti, Muzaffar, Faye Hipsman, and Bonnie Bui. 2014. "The Stalemate over Unaccompanied Minors Holds Far-Reaching Implications for Broader U.S. Immigration Debates." Migration Policy Institute, August 15. Retrieved April 18, 2015 (http://www.migrationpolicy.org/article/stalemate-over-unaccompanied-minors-holds-far-reaching-implications-broader-us-immigration).

Chomsky, Noam. 1985. *Turning the Tide: U.S. Intervention in Central America and the Struggle for Peace.* Boston: South End Press.

Clammer, John. 1997. *Contemporary Urban Japan: A Sociology of Consumption.* Oxford: Blackwell.

Clancy, Michael. 2012. "Cruise Tourism." Pp. 360–362 in *The Wiley-Blackwell Encyclopedia of Globalization,* edited by G. Ritzer. Malden, MA: Wiley-Blackwell.

Clapson, Mark and Ray Hutchison, eds. 2010. *Suburbanization in Global Society.* Bingley, England: Emerald.

Clark, Jocalyn. 2014. "Medicalization of Global Health 2: The Medicalization of Global Mental Health." *Global Health Action* 7: 24000. Retrieved April 18, 2015 (http://dx.doi.org/10.3402/gha.v7.24000).

Clawson, Dan, Robert Zussman, Joya Misra, Naomi Gerstel, and Randall Stokes. 2007. *Public Sociology: Fifteen Eminent Sociologists Debate Politics and the Profession in the Twenty-First Century.* Berkeley: University of California Press.

Clegg, Stewart and Michael Lounsbury. 2009. "Sintering the Iron Cage: Translation, Domination and Rationalization." Pp. 118–145 in *The Oxford Handbook of Sociology and Organization Studies: Classical Foundations,* edited by P. S. Adler. Oxford: Oxford University Press.

Clogher, R. 1981. "Weaving Spiders Come Not Here: Bohemian Grove: Inside the Secret Retreat of the Power Elite." *Mother Jones,* August, 28–35.

Clotfelter, Charles T. 2010. *American Universities in a Global Market*. Chicago: University of Chicago Press.

Clough, Patricia Ticineto. 2013. "The Digital, Labor, and Measure beyond Biopolitics." Pp. 112–126 in *Digital Labor: The Internet as Playground and Factory*, edited by T. Scholz. New York: Routledge.

Coakley, Jay. 2007. "Socialization and Sport." Pp. 4576–4579 in *The Blackwell Encyclopedia of Sociology*, edited by G. Ritzer. Malden, MA: Blackwell.

Cockerham, William C. 2007. "Medical Sociology." Pp. 2932–2936 in *The Blackwell Encyclopedia of Sociology*, edited by G. Ritzer. Malden, MA: Blackwell.

Cockerham, William. 2012. "Current Directions in Medical Sociology." Pp. 385–401 in *The Wiley-Blackwell Companion to Sociology*, edited by G. Ritzer. Malden, MA: Wiley-Blackwell.

Cohen, Daniel. 2008. *Three Lectures on Post-industrial Society*. Cambridge, MA: MIT Press.

Cohen, Noam. 2011. "Define Gender Gap? Look Up Wikipedia's Contributor List." *New York Times*, January 30. Retrieved December 3, 2011 (http://www.nytimes.com/2011/01/31/business/media/31link.html).

Cohen, Patricia. 2010. "'Culture of Poverty' Makes a Comeback." *New York Times*, October 17. Retrieved March 29, 2012 (http://www.nytimes.com/2010/10/18/us/18poverty.html).

Cohen, Robin. 1997. *Global Diasporas: An Introduction*. London: Routledge.

Cohen-Cole, Ethan, Steven Durlauf, Jeffrey Fagan, and Daniel Nagin. 2009. "Model Uncertainty and the Deterrent Effect of Capital Punishment." *American Law and Economics Review* 11: 335–369.

Cole, Ellen and Jessica Henderson Daniel. 2005. *Featuring Females: Feminist Analyses of Media*. Washington, DC: American Psychological Association.

Coleman, David and Robert Rowthorn. 2011. "Who's Afraid of Population Decline? A Critical Examination of Its Consequences." *Population and Development Review* 37: 217–248.

Coleman, James. 1966. *Equality of Educational Opportunity*. Washington, DC: U.S. Department of Health, Education, and Welfare.

Coleman, James. 1990. *Foundations of Social Theory*. Cambridge MA: Belknap Press.

Coleman, Marilyn, Lawrence H. Ganong, and Luke T. Russell. 2013. "Resilience in Stepfamilies." Pp. 85–103 in *Handbook of Family Resilience*, edited by D. S. Becvar. New York: Springer.

Coll, Sami. 2012. "The Social Dynamics of Secrecy: Rethinking Information and Privacy through Georg Simmel." *International Review of Information Ethics* 17: 15–20.

Collet, Francois. 2009. "Does Habitus Matter? A Comparative Review of Bourdieu's Habitus and Simon's Bounded Rationality with Some Implications for Economic Sociology." *Sociological Theory* 27: 419–434.

Collier, Paul. 2007. *The Bottom Billion: Why the Poorest Countries Are Failing and What Can Be Done about It*. New York: Oxford University Press.

Collier, Paul. 2012. "The Bottom Billion." Pp. 126–130 in *The Wiley-Blackwell Encyclopedia of Globalization*, edited by G. Ritzer. Malden, MA: Wiley-Blackwell.

Collins, Jane L. 2003. *Threads: Gender, Labor, and Power in the Global Apparel Industry*. Chicago: University of Chicago Press.

Collins, Patricia Hill. 1990. *Black Feminist Thought: Knowledge, Consciousness, and the Politics of Empowerment*. Boston: Unwin Hyman.

Collins, Patricia Hill. 2000. *Black Feminist Thought: Knowledge, Consciousness, and the Politics of Empowerment*. 2nd ed. New York: Routledge.

Collins, Patricia Hill. 2004. *Black Sexual Politics: African Americans, Gender and the New Racism*. New York: Routledge.

Collins, Patricia Hill. 2012. "Looking Back, Moving Ahead: Scholarship in Service to Social Justice." *Gender & Society* 26: 14–22.

Collins, Randall. 1975. *Conflict Society: Toward an Explanatory Science*. New York: Academic Press.

Collins, Randall. 2009. "Micro and Macro Causes of Violence." *International Journal of Conflict and Violence* 3: 9–22.

Collins, Randall. 2012. "C-Escalation and D-Escalation: A Theory of the Time-Dynamics of Conflict." *American Sociological Review* 77: 1–20.

Colosi, Rachel. 2010. *Dirty Dancing? An Ethnography of Lap-Dancing*. Abingdon, England: William.

Comella, Lynn. 2013. "Fifty Shades of Erotic Stimulus." *Feminist Media Studies* 13(3): 563–566.

Common Sense Media. 2013. "Zero to Eight: Children's Media Use in America 2013." Fall. Retrieved April 22, 2015 (https://www.commonsensemedia.org/research/zero-to-eight-childrens-media-use-in-america-2013).

Comstock, George and Erica Scharrer. 2007. *Media and the American Child*. Burlington, MA: Academic Press.

Comte, Auguste. 1856. *A General View of Positivism*. New York: R. Speller.

Conca, Ken. 2006. *Governing Water: Contentious Transnational Political and Global Institution Building*. Cambridge, MA: MIT Press.

Conca, Ken. 2007. "Water." In *Encyclopedia of Globalization*, edited by J. A. Scholte and R. Robertson. New York: MTM.

Condron, Dennis J., Daniel Tope, Christina R. Steidl, and Kendralin J. Freeman. 2013. "Racial Segregation and the Black/White Achievement Gap, 1992 to 2009." *Sociological Quarterly* 54(1): 130–157.

Connell, R. W. 1987. *Gender and Power: Society, the Person, and Sexual Politics*. Palo Alto, CA: Stanford University Press.

Connell, Raewyn. 2009. *Gender*. 2nd ed. Cambridge: Polity Press.

Connell, Robert W. 1997. "Hegemonic Masculinity and Emphasized Femininity." Pp. 22–25 in *Feminist Frontiers IV*, edited by L. Richardson, V. Taylor, and N. Whittier. New York: McGraw-Hill.

Connor, Phillip. 2012. *Faith on the Move: The Religious Affiliation of International Migrants*. Washington, DC: Pew Research Center.

Conrad, Peter. 1986. "Problems in Health Care." Pp. 415–450 in *Social Problems*, 2nd ed., edited by G. Ritzer. New York: Random House.

Conrad, Peter, Thomas Mackie, and Ateev Mehrota. 2010. "Estimating the Costs of Medicalization." *Social Science & Medicine* 70: 1943–1947.

Conrad, Peter and Joseph W. Schneider. 1980. *Deviance and Medicalization: From Badness to Sickness*. St. Louis, MO: Mosby.

Cook, Alison and Christy Glass. 2014. "Women and Top Leadership Positions: Towards an Institutional Analysis." *Gender, Work & Organization* 21(1): 91–103.

Cook, Daniel Thomas 2004. *The Commodification of Childhood: The Children's Clothing Industry and the Rise of the Child Consumer*. Durham, NC: Duke University Press.

Cook, Daniel Thomas. 2007. "Consumer Culture, Children's." Pp. 693–697 in *The Blackwell Encyclopedia of Sociology*, edited by G. Ritzer. Malden, MA: Blackwell.

Cook, Daniel Thomas and J. Michael Ryan, eds. 2015. *The Wiley-Blackwell Encyclopedia of Consumption and Consumer Studies*. Malden, MA: Wiley-Blackwell.

Cook, John, Dana Nuccitelli, Sarah A. Green, Mark Richardson, Bärbel Winkler, Rob Painting, Robert Way, Peter Jacobs, and Andrew Skuce. 2013. "Quantifying the Consensus on Anthropogenic Global Warming in the Scientific Literature." *Environmental Research Letters* 8(2): 024024. Retrieved April 18, 2015 (http://iopscience.iop.org/1748-9326/8/2/024024).

Cooksey, Elizabeth. 2007. "Fertility: Adolescent." Pp. 1725–1729 in *The Blackwell Encyclopedia of Sociology*, edited by G. Ritzer. Malden, MA: Blackwell.

Cooley, Charles Horton. 1909. *Social Organization: A Study of the Larger Mind*. New York: Scribner.

Coontz, Stephanie. 2013. "Why Gender Equality Stalled." *New York Times Sunday Review*, February 17, SR1.

Cooper, Cary L., Alankrita Pandey, and James Quick Campbell, eds. 2012. *Downsizing: Is Less Still More?* Cambridge: Cambridge University Press.

Copes, Heith and Crystal Null. 2007. "Property Crime." Pp. 3675–3676 in *The Blackwell Encyclopedia of Sociology*, edited by G. Ritzer. Malden, MA: Blackwell.

Corak, Miles. 2013. "Income Inequality, Equality of Opportunity, and Intergenerational Mobility." *Journal of Economic Perspectives* 27: 79–102.

Corak, Miles, Matthew J. Lindquist, and Bhashkar Mazumder. 2014. "A Comparison of Upward and Downward Intergenerational Mobility in Canada, Sweden and the United States." *Labour Economics* 30: 185–200.

Corbett, Steven. 2014. "Challenging the Commodification of Public Spheres: The Hacker Work Ethic in a Free Media Lab." *First Monday* 19(12). Retrieved April 18, 2015 (http://firstmonday.org/ojs/index.php/fm/article/view/3555).

Corder, Mike. 2014. "Dutch Marijuana Laws Rollback Provides Lessons for Legalization in U.S. States." *World Post*, March 7. Retrieved April 18, 2015 (http://www.huffingtonpost.com/2014/03/07/dutch-marijuana-laws-us-states_n_4918305.html).

Corprew, Charles S., III and Avery D. Mitchell. 2014. "Keeping It Frat: Exploring the Interaction among Fraternity Membership, Disinhibition, and Hypermasculinity on Sexually Aggressive Attitudes in College-Aged Males." *Journal of College Student Development* 55(6): 548–562.

Correll, Shelley J. 2001. "Gender and the Career Choice Process: The Role of Biased Self-Assessments." *American Journal of Sociology* 106(6): 1691–1730.

Correll, Shelley J. 2004. "Constraints into Preferences: Gender, Status, and Emerging Career Aspirations." *American Sociological Review* 69(1): 93–113.

Correll, Shelley J., Stephen Benard, and In Paik. 2007. "Getting a Job: Is There a Motherhood Penalty?" *American Journal of Sociology* 112(5): 1297–1338.

Cousins, Mel. 2005. *European Welfare States: Comparative Perspectives.* London: Sage.

Coventry, Martha. 2006. "Tyranny of the Esthetic: Surgery's Most Intimate Violation." Pp. 203–211 in *Reconstructing Gender: A Multicultural Anthology,* edited by E. Disch. New York: McGraw-Hill.

Coward, Martin. 2012. "Urban." Pp. 2130–2134 in *The Wiley-Blackwell Encyclopedia of Globalization,* edited by G. Ritzer. Malden, MA: Wiley-Blackwell.

Cox, Lloyd. 2007. "Socialism." Pp. 4549–4554 in *The Blackwell Encyclopedia of Sociology,* edited by G. Ritzer. Malden, MA: Blackwell.

Creswell, John. 2008. *Research Design: Qualitative, Quantitative, and Mixed Methods Approaches.* Thousand Oaks, CA: Sage.

Croll, Paul R. 2013. "Explanations for Racial Disadvantage: Beliefs about Both Sides of Inequality in America." *Ethnic and Racial Studies* 36(1): 47–74.

Cross, Remy and David Snow. 2012. "Social Movements." Pp. 522–544 in *The Wiley-Blackwell Companion to Sociology,* edited by G. Ritzer. Malden, MA: Wiley-Blackwell.

Crossley, Alison Dahl and Heather McKee Hurwitz. 2013. "Women's Movements." Pp. 1402–1408 in *The Wiley-Blackwell Encyclopedia of Social and Political Movements,* 3 vols., edited by D. A. Snow, D. Della Porta, B. Klandermans, and D. McAdam. Malden, MA: Wiley-Blackwell.

Crothers, Charles. 2011. "Robert K. Merton." Pp. 65–88 in *Wiley-Blackwell Companion to Major Social Theorists,* Vol. 2, *Contemporary Social Theorists,* edited by G. Ritzer and J. Stepnisky. West Sussex, England: Wiley-Blackwell.

Crothers, Lane. 2010. *Globalization and American Popular Culture.* 2nd ed. Lanham, MD: Rowman & Littlefield.

Croucher, Sheila. 2009. *The Other Side of the Fence: American Migrants in Mexico.* Austin: University of Texas Press.

Crowder, Kyle and Liam Downey. 2010. "Interneighborhood Migration, Race, and Environmental Hazards: Modeling Microlevel Processes of Environmental Inequality." *American Journal of Sociology* 115(4): 1110–1149.

Crowder, Kyle and Matthew Hall. 2007. "Migration, Internal." Pp. 3014–3019 in *The Blackwell Encyclopedia of Sociology,* edited by G. Ritzer. Malden, MA: Blackwell.

Crowley, Gregory J. 2007. "Urban Renewal and Development." Pp. 5128–5132 in *The Blackwell Encyclopedia of Sociology,* edited by G. Ritzer. Malden, MA: Blackwell.

Crump, Jeff. 2007. "Exurbia." Pp. 1549–1551 in *The Blackwell Encyclopedia of Sociology,* edited by G. Ritzer. Malden, MA: Blackwell.

Crutsinger, Martin. 2010. "G20 Leaders Facing Worries about Rising Deficits." *Bloomberg Businessweek,* June 24. Retrieved March 29, 2012 (http://www.businessweek.com/ap/financialnews/D9GHNNI81.htm).

Cuaresma, Jesus Crespo, Wolfgang Lutz, and Warren Sanderson. 2014. "Is the Demographic Dividend an Education Dividend?" *Demography* 51: 299–315.

Cullen, Francis T., Cheryl Lero Jonson, and Daniel S. Nagin. 2011. "Prisons Do Not Reduce Recidivism: The High Cost of Ignoring Science." *Prison Journal* 91: 48S–65S.

Culver, Leigh. 2007. "Criminal Justice System." Pp. 851–856 in *The Blackwell Encyclopedia of Sociology,* edited by G. Ritzer. Malden, MA: Blackwell.

Cumming-Bruce, Nick. 2015. "United Nations Investigators Accuse ISIS of Genocide over Attacks on Yazidis." *New York Times,* March 19.

Cunningham, Carolyn, ed. 2013. *Social Networking and Impression Management: Self-Presentation in the Digital Age.* Lanham, MD: Lexington Books.

Curtiss, Susan. 1977. *Genie: A Psycholinguistic Study of a Modern-Day "Wild Child."* New York: Academic Press.

Cyert, Richard Michael and James G. March. 1963. *A Behavioral Theory of the Firm.* Englewood Cliffs, NJ: Prentice Hall.

Dahlberg, Lincoln. 2010. "Cyber-Libertarianism 2.0: A Discourse Theory/Critical Political Economy Examination." *Cultural Politics* 6: 331–356.

Dahrendorf, Ralf. 1959. *Class and Class Conflict in Industrial Society.* Stanford, CA: Stanford University Press.

Daley, Suzanne. 2011. "N.Y.U., in the U.A.E." *New York Times,* April 15.

Damer, Sean. 1974. "Wine Alley: The Sociology of a Dreadful Enclosure." *Sociological Review* 22: 221–248.

Dandaneau, Steven P. 2007. "Norms." Pp. 3229–3232 in *The Blackwell Encyclopedia of Sociology,* edited by G. Ritzer. Malden, MA: Blackwell.

Dandaneau, Steven P. 2012. "Deindustrialization." Pp. 385–387 in *The Wiley-Blackwell Encyclopedia of Globalization,* edited by G. Ritzer. Malden, MA: Wiley-Blackwell.

Daniels, Jessie. 2009. *Cyber Racism: White Supremacy Online and the New Attack on Civil Rights.* Lanham, MD: Rowman & Littlefield.

Dant, Tim. 2007. "Material Culture." P. 2835 in *The Blackwell Encyclopedia of Sociology,* edited by G. Ritzer. Malden, MA: Blackwell.

Dargent, Fanny. 2014. "Scarifications Rituelles = Ritual Scarifications." *Revue Adolescence* 32: 47–56.

David, Matthew and Peter Millwood. 2012. "Football's Coming Home? Digital Reterritorialization, Contradictions in the Transnational Coverage of Sport and the Sociology of Alternative Football Broadcasts." *British Journal of Sociology* 63: 349–369.

David, Richard J. and James W. Collins. 2014. "Layers of Inequality: Power, Policy, and Health." *American Journal of Public Health,* suppl. 104(S1): S8–S10.

Davis, F. James. 1991. *Who Is Black? One Nation's Definition.* Philadelphia: Penn State University Press. Retrieved January 27, 2012 (http://www.pbs.org/wgbh/pages/frontline/shows/jefferson/mixed/onedrop.html).

Davis, Kingsley. 1940. "Extreme Social Isolation of a Child." *American Journal of Sociology* 45(4): 554–565.

Davis, Kingsley. 1945. "The World Demographic Transition." *Annals of the American Academy of Political and Social Science* 237: 1–110.

Davis, Kingsley. 1947. "Final Note on a Case of Extreme Isolation." *American Journal of Sociology* 50: 432–437.

Davis, Kingsley and Wilbert E. Moore. 1945. "Some Principles of Stratification." *American Sociological Review* 10(2): 242–249.

Davis, Mike. 2007. *Planet of Slums.* London: Verso Books.

Dean, Cornelia. 2007. "Experts Discuss Engineering Feats, Like Space Mirror, to Slow Climate Change." *New York Times,* November 10.

Debas, Haile T. 2010. "Global Health: Priority Agenda for the 21st Century." *UN Chronicle* 47(2). Retrieved March 29, 2012 (http://www.un.org/wcm/content/site/chronicle/cache/bypass/home/archive/issues2010/achieving_global_health/globalhealth_priorityagendaforthe21stcentury?ctnscroll_articleContainerList=1_0&ctnlistpagination_articleContainerList=true).

Decker, Scott H. and G. David Curry. 2000. "Addressing Key Features of Gang Membership: Measuring the Involvement of Young Members." *Journal of Criminal Justice* 28: 473–482.

Decuir-Gunby, Jessica T. and Jocelyn D. Taliaferro. 2013. "The Impact of School Resegregation on the Racial Identity Development of African American Students: The Example of Wake County." Pp 139–163 in *The Resegregation of Schools: Education and Race in the Twenty-First Century,* edited by J. K. Donnor and A. D. Dixson. New York: Routledge.

DeLamater, John. 2012. "Sexual Expression in Later Life: A Review and Synthesis." *Journal of Sex Research* 49(2–3): 125–141.

Delaney, Tim. 2012. "Georg Simmel's Flirting and Secrecy and Its Application to the Facebook Relationship Status—'It's Complicated.'" *Journalism and Mass Communication* 2: 637–647.

De Lissovoy, Noah and José García. 2013. "Doing School Time: The Hidden Curriculum Goes to Prison." *Journal of Critical Education Policy Studies* 11(4): 49–68.

DeLuzio Chasin, C. J. 2011. "Theoretical Issues in the Study of Asexuality." *Archives of Sexual Behavior* 40(4): 713–723.

D'Emilio, John. 1983. *Sexual Politics, Sexual Communities.* Chicago: University of Chicago Press.

DeNavas-Walt, Carmen and Bernadette D. Proctor. 2014. *Income and Poverty in the United States, 2013.* Current Population Reports P60-249. Washington, DC: U.S. Census Bureau, September. Retrieved April 29, 2015 (http://www.census.gov/content/dam/Census/library/publications/2014/demo/p60-249.pdf).

DeNavas-Walt, Carmen, Bernadette D. Proctor, and Jessica C. Smith. 2012. *Income, Poverty, and Health Insurance Coverage in the United States: 2011.* Current Population Reports P60-243. Washington, DC: U.S. Census Bureau, September. Retrieved March 29, 2012 (https://www.census.gov/prod/2012pubs/p60-243.pdf).

Denegri-Knott, Janice and Detlev Zwick. 2012. "Tracking Presumption Work on eBay: Reproduction of Desire and the Challenge of Slow Re-McDonaldization." *American Behavioral Scientist* 56: 439–458.

Dentler, Robert A. and Kai T. Erikson. 1959. "The Function of Deviance in Small Groups." *Social Problems* 7: 98–107.

Denzin, Norman K. and Yvonna S. Lincoln. 2011. "Introduction: The Discipline and Practice of Qualitative Research." Pp. 1–20 in *The SAGE Handbook of Qualitative Research*, 4th ed., edited by N. K. Denzin and Y. S. Lincoln. Thousand Oaks, CA: Sage.

DeParle, Jason. 2015. "Global Migration: A World Ever More on the Move." *New York Times*, June 26.

DeParle, Jason, Robert Gebeloff, and Sabrina Tavernise. 2011. "Older, Suburban and Struggling." *New York Times*, November 19.

de Regt, Marina. 2009. "Preferences and Prejudices: Employers' Views on Domestic Workers in the Republic of Yemen." *Signs* 34(3): 559–581.

Desai, Sonalde. 2010. "The Other Half of the Demographic Dividend." *Economic and Political Weekly* 45(40): 12–14.

De Silva, Dakshina G., Robert P. McComb, Young-Kyu Moh, Anita R. Schiller, and Andres J. Vargas. 2010. "The Effect of Migration on Wages: Evidence from a Natural Experiment." *American Economic Review: Papers and Proceedings* 100(May): 321–326.

DeSilver, Drew. 2013. "U.S. Income Inequality, on Rise for Decades, Is Now Highest since 1928." Pew Research Center, December 5. Retrieved April 29, 2015 (http://www.pewresearch.org/fact-tank/2013/12/05/u-s-income-inequality-on-rise-for-decades-is-now-highest-since-1928).

Deutsch, Kevin. 2014. *The Triangle: A Year on the Ground with New York's Bloods and Crips*. Guilford, CT: Lyons Press.

Deutsch, Nancy L. and Eleni Theodorou. 2010. "Aspiring, Consuming, Becoming: Youth Identity in a Culture of Consumption." *Youth & Society* 42(2): 229–254.

DeVault, Marjorie. 1991. *Feeding the Family: The Social Organization of Caring as Gendered Work*. Chicago: University of Chicago Press.

Dewey, Susan. 2015. "Sex Work." In *Handbook of the Sociology of Sexualities*, edited by J. DeLamater and R. F. Plante. Dordrecht, Netherlands: Springer.

Dey, Eric L. 1997. "Undergraduate Political Attitudes: Peer Influence in Changing Social Contexts." *Journal of Higher Education* 68: 398–416.

Diamond, Jared. 2006. *Collapse: How Societies Choose to Fail or Succeed*. New York: Penguin.

Dickson, Lynda, Richard Dukes, Hilary Smith, and Noel Strapko. 2014. "Stigma of Ink: Tattoo Attitudes among College Students." *Social Science Journal* 51(2): 268–276.

Dikötter, Frank. 2008. "The Racialization of the Globe: An Interactive Interpretation." *Ethnic and Racial Studies* 31(8): 1478–1496.

Dillon, Liam and Ian Lovett. 2013. "Tunnel for Smuggling Found under U.S.-Mexico Border; Tons of Drugs Seized." *New York Times*, October 31.

DiMaggio, Paul J., Eszter Hargittai, W. Russell Neuman, and John P. Robinson. 2001. "Social Implications of the Internet." *Annual Review of Sociology* 27: 307–336.

DiMaggio, Paul J. and Walter W. Powell. 1983. "The Iron Cage Revisited: Institutional Isomorphism and Collective Rationality in Organizational Fields." *American Sociological Review* 48: 147–160.

Diotallevi, Luca. 2007. "Church." Pp. 483–489 in *The Blackwell Encyclopedia of Sociology*, edited by G. Ritzer. Malden, MA: Blackwell.

DiPrete, Thomas A., Gregory M. Eirich, Karen S. Cook, and Douglas S. Massey. 2006. "Cumulative Advantage as a Mechanism for Inequality: A Review of Theoretical and Empirical Developments." *Annual Review of Sociology* 32: 271–297.

Directorate-General for Employment, Industrial Relations and Social Affairs. 1998. "Sexual Harassment at the Workplace in the European Union." Brussels, European Commission.

Dobbelaere, Karel. 2007. "Secularization." Pp. 4140–4148 in *The Blackwell Encyclopedia of Sociology*, edited by G. Ritzer. Malden, MA: Blackwell.

Dodd, Nigel. 2012. "Money." Pp. 1444–1448 in *The Wiley-Blackwell Encyclopedia of Globalization*, edited by G. Ritzer. Malden, MA: Wiley-Blackwell.

Doherty, Carroll. 2013. "For African Americans, Discrimination Is Not Dead." Pew Research Center, Fact Tank, June 28. Retrieved May 7, 2015 (http://www.pewresearch.org/fact-tank/2013/06/28/for-african-americans-dis-crimination-is-not-dead).

Dombrink, John and Daniel Hillyard. 2007. *Sin No More: From Abortion to Stem Cells, Understanding Crime, Law, and Morality in America*. New York: New York University Press.

Dombrowski, Stefan C., Karen L. Gischlar, and Martin Mrazik. 2011. "Feral Children." Pp. 81–93 in *Assessing and Treating Low Incidence/High Severity Psychological Disorders of Childhood*. New York: Springer.

Domhoff, G. William. 1974. *The Bohemian Grove and Other Retreats: A Study in Ruling-Class Cohesiveness*. New York: Harper & Row.

Domhoff, G. William. 2013. *Who Rules America? The Triumph of Corporate Rich*. New York: McGraw-Hill.

Dooley, David and JoAnn Prause. 2009. *The Social Costs of Underemployment: Inadequate Employment as Disguised Unemployment*. Cambridge: Cambridge University Press.

Dorius, Shawn and Glenn Firebaugh. 2010. "Trends in Global Gender Inequality." *Social Forces* 88(5): 1941–1968.

Dotter, Daniel L. and Julian B. Roebuck. 1988. "The Labeling Approach Re-examined: Interactionism and the Components of Deviance." *Deviant Behavior* 9(1): 19–32.

Downes, David and Paul Rock. 2011. *Understanding Deviance: A Guide to the Sociology of Crime and Rule-Breaking*. Oxford: Oxford University Press.

Doyle, Thomas P. 2003. "Roman Catholic Clericalism, Religious Duress, and Clergy Sexual Abuse." *Pastoral Psychology* 51(3): 189–231.

Drache, D. (with M. D. Froese). 2008. *Defiant Publics: The Unprecedented Reach of the Global Citizen*. Cambridge: Polity Press.

Drane, John. 2008. *After McDonaldization: Mission, Ministry, and Christian Discipleship in an Age of Uncertainty*. Grand Rapids, MI: Baker.

Drane, John. 2012. *The McDonaldization of the Church: Consumer Culture and the Church's Future*. Macon, GA: Smith and Helwys.

Drori, Gili S. 2006. *Global E-litism: Digital Technology, Social Inequality, and Transnationality*. New York: Worth.

Drori, Gili S. 2012. "Digital Divide." Pp. 435–438 in *The Wiley-Blackwell Encyclopedia of Globalization*, edited by G. Ritzer. Malden, MA: Wiley-Blackwell.

"Drug-Laden Drone Crashes Near U.S.–Mexico Border." 2015. *New York Times*, January 21.

Duany, Andrés, Elizabeth Plater-Zyberk, and Jeff Speck. 2010. *Suburban Nation: The Rise of Sprawl and the Decline of the American Dream*. 10th anniversary ed. New York: North Point Press.

Duberman, Martin B. 1994. *Stonewall*. New York: Plume.

Du Bois, W. E. B. [1899] 1996. *The Philadelphia Negro: A Social Study*. Philadelphia: University of Pennsylvania Press.

Du Bois, W. E. B. [1903] 1966. *The Souls of Black Folk*. New York: Modern Library.

Duckworth, Angela L. and Stephanie M. Carlson. 2013. "Self-Regulation and School Success." Pp. 208–230 in *Self-Regulation and Autonomy: Social and Developmental Dimensions of Human Conduct*, edited by B. W. Sokol, F. M. E. Grouzet, and U. Müller. New York: Cambridge University Press.

Duckworth, Angela L. and Martin E. P. Seligman. 2005. "Self-Discipline Outdoes IQ in Predicting Academic Performance of Adolescents." *Psychological Science* 16: 939–944.

Duhigg, Charles and Keith Bradsher. 2012. "How the U.S. Lost Out on iPhone Work." *New York Times*, January 22.

Dujarier, Marie-Anne. 2014. "The Three Sociological Types of Consumer Work." *Journal of Consumer Culture*, published online April 9. doi: 10.1177/1469540514528198.

Dukes, Richard L. and Judith A. Stein. 2011. "Ink and Holes: Correlates and Predictive Associations of Body Modification among Adolescents." *Youth & Society* 43: 1547–1569.

Duncan, Greg J., Kathleen M. Ziol-Guest, and Ariel Kalil. 2010. "Early-Childhood Poverty and Adult Attainment, Behavior, and Health." *Child Development* 81: 306–325.

Duncan, Simon. 2014. "Women's Agency in Living Apart Together: Constraint, Strategy, and Vulnerability." *Sociological Review*, published online September 5. doi: 10.1111/1467-954X.12184.

Duneier, Mitchell. 1999. *Sidewalk*. New York: Farrar, Straus and Giroux.

Dunham, Lena. 2014. *Not That Kind of Girl: A Young Woman Tells You What She's Learned*. New York: Random House.

Dunlap, Riley E. 2007. "Environment, Sociology of the." Pp. 1417–1422 in *The Blackwell Encyclopedia of Sociology*, edited by G. Ritzer. Malden, MA: Blackwell.

Dunlap, Riley E. and William R. Catton Jr. 2002. "Which Functions of the Environment Do We Study? A Comparison of Environmental and Natural Resource Sociology." *Society and Natural Resources* 15: 239–249.

Dunlap, Riley E. and Andrew K. Jorgenson. 2012. "Environmental Problems." Pp. 529–536 in *The Wiley-Blackwell Companion to Sociology*, edited by G. Ritzer. Malden, MA: Wiley-Blackwell.

Dunn, Gregory. 2013. "Water Wars." *Harvard International Review* 35: 46–49.

Dunn, Jennifer L. 2005. "'Victims' and 'Survivors': Emerging Vocabularies of Motive for 'Battered Women Who Stay.'" *Sociological Inquiry* 75: 1–30.

Dunning, Eric, Patrick Murphy, and John Williams. 1988. *The Roots of Football Hooliganism.* London: Routledge & Kegan Paul.

Durkheim, Émile. [1893] 1964. *The Division of Labor in Society.* New York: Free Press.

Durkheim, Émile. [1897] 1951. *Suicide.* New York: Free Press.

Durkheim, Émile. [1912] 1965. *The Elementary Forms of the Religious Life.* New York: Free Press.

Duster, Troy. 2003. *Backdoor to Eugenics.* New York: Routledge.

Dustin, Donna. 2007. *The McDonaldization of Social Work.* Burlington, VT: Ashgate.

Dutton, Donald G. and Katherine R. White. 2013. "Male Victims of Domestic Violence." *New Male Studies* 2: 5–17.

Earl, Jennifer. 2007. "Social Movements, Repression of." Pp. 4475–4479 in *The Blackwell Encyclopedia of Sociology,* edited by G. Ritzer. Malden, MA: Blackwell.

Easterly, William and Tobias Pfutze. 2008. "Where Does the Money Go? Best and Worst Practices in Foreign Aid." *Journal of Economic Perspectives* 22: 1–35.

Eckenwiler, Lisa. 2014. "Care Worker Migration, Global Health Equity, and Ethical Place-Making." *Women's Studies International Forum* 47: 213–222.

Eckert, Penelope and Sally McConnell-Ginet. 2013. *Language and Gender.* 2nd ed. New York: Cambridge University Press.

Eder, Steve. 2014. "Points for Product Placement: N.C.A.A. Cashes In, but Not the Players." *New York Times,* April 5.

Edmonds, Alex. 2010. *Pretty Modern: Beauty, Sex, and Plastic Surgery in Brazil.* Durham, NC: Duke University Press.

Edsall, Thomas. 2015. "Can Jeb Bush Defy the Tea Party and Win?" *New York Times,* January 13.

Edwards, Bob and Patrick F. Gillham. 2013. "Resource Mobilization Theory." Pp. 1096–1101 in *The Wiley-Blackwell Encyclopedia of Social and Political Movements,* 3 vols., edited by D. A. Snow, D. Della Porta, B. Klandermans, and D. McAdam. Malden, MA: Wiley-Blackwell.

Ehrenreich, Barbara. 2001. *Nickel and Dimed: On (Not) Getting By in America.* New York: Henry Holt.

Ehrenreich, Barbara. 2002. "Maid to Order." In *Global Woman: Nannies, Maids, and Sex Workers in the New Economy,* edited by B. Ehrenreich and A. R. Hochschild. New York: Henry Holt.

Ehrenreich, Barbara and Arlie Russell Hochschild. 2002. "Introduction." Pp. 1–14 in *Global Woman: Nannies, Maids, and Sex Workers in the New Economy,* edited by B. Ehrenreich and A. R. Hochschild. New York: Henry Holt.

Ehrlich, Paul. 1968. *The Population Bomb.* New York: Ballantine.

Elder, Todd and Christopher Jepsen. 2014. "Are Catholic Primary Schools More Effective than Public Primary Schools?" *Journal of Urban Economics* 80: 28–38.

Elgin, Duane. 2010. *Voluntary Simplicity: Toward a Way of Life That Is Outwardly Simple, Inwardly Rich.* 2nd ed. New York: Quill.

Elias, Vicky L., Andrew S. Fullerton, and Joseph M. Simpson. 2015. "Long-Term Changes in Attitudes toward Premarital Sex in the United States: Reexamining the Role of Cohort Replacement." *Journal of Sex Research* 52(2): 129–139.

Elliott, Anthony and John Urry. 2010. *Mobile Lives.* London: Routledge.

Elliott, David L. 2012. "Urbanism." Pp. 2134–2136 in *The Wiley-Blackwell Encyclopedia of Globalization,* edited by G. Ritzer. Malden, MA: Wiley-Blackwell.

Elo, Irma T. 2007. "Mortality: Transitions and Measures." Pp. 3096–3102 in *The Blackwell Encyclopedia of Sociology,* edited by G. Ritzer. Malden, MA: Blackwell.

Elo, Irma T. 2009. "Social Class Differentials in Health and Mortality: Patterns and Explanations in Comparative Perspective." *Annual Review of Sociology* 35: 553–572.

Emerson, Robert M., ed. 2001. *Contemporary Field Research: Perspectives and Formulations.* 2nd ed. Long Grove, IL: Waveland Press.

Engels, Friedrich. [1884] 1970. *The Origins of the Family, Private Property and the State.* New York: International Publishers.

England, Paula. 2010. "The Gender Revolution: Uneven and Stalled." *Gender & Society* 24(2): 149–166.

England, Paula and Kathryn Edin. 2009. "Briefing Paper: Unmarried Couples with Children: Why Don't They Marry? How Can Policy-Makers Promote More Stable Relationships?" Pp. 307–312 in *Families as They Really Are,* edited by B. J. Risman. New York: Norton.

English, Beth. 2013. "Global Women's Work: Historical Perspectives on the Textile and Garment Industries." *Journal of International Affairs* 67(1): 67–82.

EnglishEnglish.com. N.d. "The English Language: Facts and Figures." Retrieved January 3, 2012 (http://www.englishenglish.com/english_facts_8.htm).

Entwhistle, Joanne. 2009. *The Aesthetic Economy of Fashion: Markets and Value in Clothing and Modelling.* New York: Berg.

Epstein, Cynthia Fuchs. 1988. *Deceptive Distinctions: Sex, Gender, and the Social Order.* New Haven, CT: Yale University Press.

Epstein, Richard A. 2014. "Big Law and Big Med: The Deprofessionalization of Legal and Medical Services." *International Review of Law and Economics* 38: 64–76.

Epstein, Steve. 2009. *Inclusion: The Politics of Difference in Medical Research.* Chicago: University of Chicago Press.

Equal Employment Opportunity Commission. 2014. "Charges Alleging Sexual Harassment: FY 2010–FY 2014." Retrieved May 6, 2015 (http://www.eeoc.gov/eeoc/statistics/enforcement/sexual_harassment_new.cfm).

Erikson, Erik H. 1994. *Identity and the Life Cycle.* New York: Norton.

Erikson, Kai T. 1964. "Notes on the Sociology of Deviance." In *The Other Side: Perspectives on Deviance,* edited by H. S. Becker. New York: Free Press.

Erikson, Kai T. 1976. *Everything in Its Path: Destruction of Community in the Buffalo Creek Flood.* New York: Simon & Schuster.

Erlanger, Steven. 2010a. "Expulsion of Roma Raises Questions in France." *New York Times,* August 19.

Erlanger, Steven. 2010b. "A French Castle Built of Stone and Dreams." *New York Times,* August 1.

Erlanger, Steven. 2014. "In West ISIS Finds Women Eager to Enlist." *New York Times,* October 23.

Esping-Anderson, Gosta. 1990. *The Three Worlds of Welfare Capitalism.* Princeton, NJ: Princeton University Press.

Etzioni, Amitai, ed. 1969. *The Semi-professions and Their Organization: Teachers, Nurses, and Social Workers.* New York: Free Press.

Facebook. 2014. "Quarterly Earnings Slides: Q2 2014." Retrieved April 27, 2015 (http://files.shareholder.com/downloads/AMDA-NJ5DZ/3349478089x0x770377/abc6b6d4-df03-44e1-bb4d-7877f01c41e0/FB%20Q2).

Fackler, Martin. 2011. "Severed from the World, Villagers Survive on Tight Bonds and To-Do Lists." *New York Times,* March 23. Retrieved March 29, 2012 (http://www.nytimes.com/2011/03/23/world/asia/24isolated.html?adxnnl=1&adxnnlx=1332612166-pPLwIe5hgFAW4cQM2m4bWQ).

Faderman, Lillian. 1991. *Odd Girls and Twilight Lovers: A History of Lesbian Life in Twentieth-Century America.* New York: Penguin.

Fahim, Kareem. 2010. "Away from Home, Fleeing Domestic Life: Immigrant Maids Suffer Abuse in Kuwait." *New York Times,* August 2.

Faist, Thomas. 2012. "Migration." Pp. 1384–1388 in *The Wiley-Blackwell Encyclopedia of Globalization,* edited by G. Ritzer. Malden, MA: Wiley-Blackwell.

Faist, Thomas, Margit Fauser, and Eveline Reisenauer. 2013. *Transnational Migration.* Cambridge: Polity Press.

Fantasia, Rick and Kim Voss. 2007. "Labor Movement." Pp. 2518–2521 in *The Blackwell Encyclopedia of Sociology,* edited by G. Ritzer. Malden, MA: Blackwell.

Farber, Henry. 2011. "Job Loss in the Great Recession: Historical Perspective from Displaced Workers Survey, 1984–2010." Paper presented at a Federal Reserve Conference, San Francisco, May.

Farley, John E. 2007. "Metropolitan Statistical Area." Pp. 2993–2996 in *The Blackwell Encyclopedia of Sociology,* edited by G. Ritzer. Malden, MA: Blackwell.

Farley, John E. 2009. *Majority–Minority Relations.* 6th ed. Upper Saddle River, NJ: Prentice Hall.

Farr, Kathryn. 2005. *Sex Trafficking: The Global Market in Women and Children.* New York: Worth.

Farrell, Betty, Alicia VandeVusse, and Abigail Ocobock. 2012. "Family Change and the State of Family Sociology." *Current Sociology* 60(3): 283–301.

Farrell, Caitlin, Priscilla Wohlstetter, and Joanna Smith. 2012. "Charter Management Organizations: An Emerging Approach to Scaling Up What Works." *Educational Policy* 26(4): 499–532.

Farrell, Dan and James C. Peterson. 2010. "The Growth of Internet Research Methods and the Reluctant Sociologist." *Sociological Inquiry* 80: 114–125.

Fassmann, Heinz and Rainer Munz. 1992. "Patterns and Trends of International Migration in Western Europe." *Population and Development Review* 18: 457–480.

Fausto-Sterling, A. 1999. "The Five Sexes: Why Female and Male Are Not Enough." *The Sciences,* March/April, 20–24.

Feagin, Joe R. 2006. *Systemic Racism: A Theory of Oppression*. New York: Routledge.

Feagin, Joe R. 2010. *The White Racial Frame: Centuries of Racial Framing and Counter-framing*. New York: Routledge.

Feagin, Joe R. 2012. *White Party, White Government: Race, Class, and U.S. Politics*. New York: Routledge.

Feagin, Joe R. 2013. *The White Racial Frame: Centuries of Racial Framing and Counter-framing*. 2nd ed. New York: Routledge.

Federal Bureau of Investigation. 2014. "Frequently Asked Questions about the Change in the UCR Definition of Rape." December 11. Retrieved April 19, 2015 (http://www.fbi.gov/about-us/cjis/ucr/recent-program-updates/new-rape-definition-frequently-asked-questions).

Ferguson, Ann Arnett. 2001. *Bad Boys: Public Schools in the Making of Black Masculinity*. Ann Arbor: University of Michigan Press.

Fernandes, Leela. 2013. *Transnational Feminism in the United States: Knowledge, Ethics, Power*. New York: New York University Press.

Fernandez, Bina. 2010. "Cheap and Disposable? The Impact of the Global Economic Crisis on the Migration of Ethiopian Women Domestic Workers to the Gulf." *Gender and Development* 8(2): 249–262.

Fernyhough, Charles. 2014. "Do Deaf People Hear an Inner Voice?" *Psychology Today*, Voices Within blog, January 24. Retrieved April 27, 2015 (https://:www.psychologytoday.com/blog/the-voices-within/201401/do-deaf-people-hear-inner-voice).

Ferree, Myra Marx and Aili Mari Tripp. 2006. "Preface." Pp. vii–ix in *Global Feminism: Transnational Women's Activism, Organizing, and Human Rights*, edited by M. M. Ferree and A. M. Tripp. New York: New York University Press.

Ferreira, Vitor Sérgio. 2014. "Becoming a Heavily Tattooed Young Body: From a Bodily Experience to a Body Project." *Youth & Society* 46(3): 303–337.

Fiddian-Qasmiyeh, Elena. 2012. "Diaspora." Pp. 430–433 in *The Wiley-Blackwell Encyclopedia of Globalization*, edited by G. Ritzer. Malden, MA: Wiley-Blackwell.

Fielding, A. J. 1989. "Migration and Urbanization in Western Europe since 1950." *Geographical Journal* 155: 60–69.

Fields, Jessica, Martha Copp, and Sherryl Kleinman. 2007. "Symbolic Interactionism, Inequality, and Emotions." Pp. 155–178 in *Handbook of the Sociology of Emotions*, edited by J. E. Stets and J. H. Turner. New York: Springer.

Figlio, David and Cassandra M. Hart. 2014. "Competitive Effects of Means-Tested of School Vouchers." *American Economic Journal: Applied Economics* 6: 133–156.

Fillipi, Veronique, Carine Ronsman, Oona M. R. Campbell, Wendy J. Graham, Anne Mills, Jo Borghi, Marjorie Koblinsky, and David Osrin. 2006. "Maternal Health in Poor Countries: The Broader Context and a Call for Action." *The Lancet* 368: 1525–1541.

Fine, Gary Alan. 1987. *With the Boys: Little League Baseball and Preadolescent Culture*. Chicago: University of Chicago.

Fine, Gary Alan. 2008. *Kitchens: The Culture of Restaurant Work*. Berkeley: University of California Press.

Fine, Gary Alan. 2010. *Authors of the Storm: Meteorologists and the Culture of Prediction*. Chicago: University of Chicago Press.

Fine, Gary Alan. 2012. "Group Culture and the Interaction Order: Local Sociology on the Meso-Level." *Annual Review of Sociology* 38: 159–179.

Fink, Sheri. 2014. "Treating Those Treating Ebola in Liberia." *New York Times*, November 5.

Finke, Roger and Rodney Stark. 2005. *The Churching of America, 1776–2005: Winners and Losers in Our Religious Economy*. New Brunswick, NJ: Rutgers University Press.

Fischer, Claude S., Michael Hout, Martin Sanchez Jankowski, and Samuel R. Lucas, eds. 1996. *Inequality by Design: Cracking the Bell Curve Myth*. Princeton, NJ: Princeton University Press.

Fisher, Dana. 2012. "Environmental Activism." Pp. 517–519 in *The Wiley-Blackwell Encyclopedia of Globalization*, edited by G. Ritzer. Malden, MA: Wiley-Blackwell.

Flack, William F., Jr., Kimberly A. Daubman, Marcia L. Caron, Jenica A. Asadorian, Nicole R. D'Aureli, Shannon N. Gigliotti, et al. 2007. "Risk Factors and Consequences of Unwanted Sex among University Students: Hooking Up, Alcohol, and Stress Response." *Journal of Interpersonal Violence* 22(2): 139–157.

Flavin, Jeanne. 2008. *Our Bodies, Our Crimes*. New York: New York University Press.

Flynn, Nicole. 2007. "Deindustrialization." Pp. 992–994 in *The Blackwell Encyclopedia of Sociology*, edited by G. Ritzer. Malden, MA: Blackwell.

Flynn, Sean. 2011. "The Sex Trade." Pp. 41–66 in *Deviant Globalization: Black Market Economy in the 21st Century*, edited by N. Gilman, J. Goldhammer, and S. Weber. London: Continuum.

Fontana, Andrea. 2007. "Interviewing, Structured, Unstructured, and Postmodern." Pp. 2407–2411 in *The Blackwell Encyclopedia of Sociology*, edited by G. Ritzer. Malden, MA: Blackwell.

Ford, Martin. 2015. *Rise of the Robots: Technology and the Threat of a Jobless Future*. New York: Basic Books.

Forsyth, Craig J. and Heath Copes, eds. 2014. *Encyclopedia of Social Deviance*. Thousand Oaks, CA: Sage.

Foucault, Michel. 1975. *The Birth of the Clinic: An Archaeology of Medical Perception*. New York: Vintage Books.

Foucault, Michel. [1975] 1979. *Discipline and Punish: The Birth of the Prison*. New York: Vintage Books.

Foucault, Michel. 1978. *The History of Sexuality*, Vol. 1, *An Introduction*. New York: Vintage Books.

Fountain, Henry. 2015. "Panel Urges Research on Geoengineering as a Tool against Climate Change." *New York Times*, February 10.

"14 Cool Vending Machines from Japan." 2009. Toxel.com, June 8. Retrieved August 25, 2011 (http://www.toxel.com/tech/2009/06/08/14-cool-vending-machines-from-Japan).

Fox, Jesse and Wai Yen Tang. 2014. "Sexism in Online Video Games: The Role of Conformity to Masculine Norms and Social Dominance Orientation." *Computers in Human Behavior* 33: 314–320.

France, Anatole. [1894] 2011. *The Red Lily*. Kindle ed.

Francis, Mark. 2011. "Herbert Spencer." Pp. 165–184 in *The Wiley-Blackwell Companion to Major Social Theorists*, Vol. 1, *Classical Theorists*, edited by G. Ritzer and J. Stepnisky. Malden, MA: Wiley-Blackwell.

Frank, David John. 2012. "Global Sex." In *The Wiley-Blackwell Encyclopedia of Globalization*, edited by G. Ritzer. Malden, MA: Wiley-Blackwell.

Frank, Robert H. 2013. *Falling Behind: How Rising Inequality Harms the Middle Class*. Berkeley: University of California Press.

Franklin, V. P. 1987. "W. E. B. Du Bois as Journalist." *Journal of Negro Education* 56(2): 240–244.

Freedman, Russell. 2009. *Freedom Walkers: The Story of the Montgomery Bus Boycott*. New York: Holiday House.

Freeman, Carla. 2001. "Is Local:Global as Feminine:Masculine? Rethinking the Gender of Globalization." *Signs* 26(4): 1007–1037.

Friedan, Betty. 1963. *The Feminine Mystique*. New York: Dell.

Friedkin, N. E. 2001. "Norm Formation in Social Influence Networks." *Social Networks* 23(3): 167–189.

Friedman, Debra and Michael Hechter. 1988. "The Contribution of Rational Choice Theory to Macrosociological Research." *Sociological Theory* 6: 201–218.

Friedman, Judith J. 2007. "Suburbs." Pp. 4878–4881 in *The Blackwell Encyclopedia of Sociology*, edited by G. Ritzer. Malden, MA: Blackwell.

Friedman, Thomas. 1999. *The Lexus and the Olive Tree*. New York: Farrar, Straus and Giroux.

Friedman, Thomas. 2005. *The World Is Flat: A Brief History of the Twenty-First Century*. New York: Farrar, Straus and Giroux.

Friedrichs, David O. 2007. "Organizational Deviance." Pp. 3303–3306 in *The Blackwell Encyclopedia of Sociology*, edited by G. Ritzer. Malden, MA: Blackwell.

Frieze, Irene Hanson. 2007. "Love and Commitment." Pp. 2671–2674 in *The Blackwell Encyclopedia of Sociology*, edited by G. Ritzer. Malden, MA: Blackwell.

Fritsch, Jane. 2001. "A Day of Terror: The Response; Rescue Workers Rush In, and Many Do Not Return." *New York Times*, September 12. Retrieved March 29, 2012 (http://www.nytimes.com/2001/09/12/us/a-day-of-terror-the-response-rescue-workers-rush-in-and-many-do-not-return.html?ref=sept112001).

Frohlick, Susan. 2013. *Sexuality, Women, and Tourism: Cross-Border Desires through Contemporary Travel*. New York: Routledge.

Fulbrook, Julian. 2007. "Tobacco." Pp. 1146–1149 in *Encyclopedia of Globalization*, edited by J. A. Scholte and R. Robertson. New York: MTM.

Fuller, Thomas and Joe Cochran. 2015. "Rohingya Migrants from Myanmar, Shunned by Malaysia, Are Spotted Adrift in Andaman Sea." *New York Times*, May 14.

Fung, Archon. 2004. *Empowered Participation: Reinventing Urban Democracy*. Princeton, NJ: Princeton University Press.

Furneaux, Craig. 2013. "Outsourcing and Subcontracting." Pp. 669–673 in *Sociology of Work: An Encyclopedia*, edited by V. Smith. Thousand Oaks, CA: Sage.

Gagnon, John and William H. Simon. 1973. *Sexual Conduct: The Social Sources of Human Sexuality*. Chicago: Aldine.

Gaio, Fatima Janine. 1995. "Women in Software Programming: The Experience in Brazil." In

Women Encounter Technology, edited by S. Mitter and S. Rowbotham. London: Routledge.

Galston, William A., Steven Kull, and Clay Ramsay. 2009. Battleground or Common Ground? American Public Opinion on Health Care Reform. Washington, DC: Brookings Institution.

Gambino, Matthew. 2013. "Erving Goffman's Asylums and Institutional Culture in the Mid-Twentieth-Century United States." Harvard Review of Psychiatry 21: 52–57.

Gamoran, Adam and Daniel A. Long. 2006. "Equality of Educational Opportunity: A 40-Year Retrospective." WCER Working Paper 2006-9, Wisconsin Center for Education Research, Madison. Retrieved July 13, 2013 (http://www.wcer.wisc.edu).

Gamoran, Adam and Robert D. Maré. 1989. "Secondary School Tracking and Educational Inequality: Compensation, Reinforcement, or Neutrality?" American Journal of Sociology 94: 1146–1183.

Gamoran, Adam, Martin Nystrand, Mark Berends, and Paul C. LePore. 1995. "An Organizational Analysis of the Effects of Ability Grouping." American Educational Research Journal 32: 687–715.

Gangl, Markus. 2007. "Welfare State." Pp. 5242–5246 in The Blackwell Encyclopedia of Sociology, edited by G. Ritzer. Malden, MA: Blackwell.

Gans, Herbert J. 2009. "First Generation Decline: Downward Mobility among Refugees and Immigrants." Ethnic and Racial Studies 32: 1658–1670.

Gansky, Lisa. 2010. The Mesh: Why the Future of Business Is Sharing. New York: Penguin.

Garcia, David. 2008. "The Impact of School Choice on Racial Segregation in Charter Schools." Educational Policy 22(6): 805–829.

Garcia, Lorena. 2012. Respect Yourself, Protect Yourself: Latina Girls and Sexual Identity. New York: New York University Press.

Gardner, Margo and Laurence Steinberg. 2005. "Peer Influence on Risk Taking, Risk Preference, and Risky Decision Making in Adolescence and Adulthood: An Experimental Study." Developmental Psychology 41: 625–635.

Garfield, Bob. 1991. "How I Spent (and Spent and Spent) My Disney Vacation." Washington Post, July 7.

Garfinkel, Harold. 1967. Studies in Ethnomethodology. Malden, MA: Blackwell.

Garlick, Steve. 2014. "The Biopolitics of Masturbation: Masculinity, Complexity, and Security." Body & Society 20: 44–67.

Garon, Sheldon. 2006. "Japan's Post-war 'Consumer Revolution,' or Striking a 'Balance' between Consumption and Saving." In Consuming Cultures, Global Perspectives: Historical Trajectories, Transnational Exchanges, edited by J. Brewer and F. Trentmann. Oxford: Berg.

Garreau, Joel. 1991. Edge City: Life on the New Frontier. New York: Doubleday.

Garrett, William R. 2007. "Christianity." Pp. 139–144 in Encyclopedia of Globalization, edited by J. A. Scholte and R. Robertson. New York: MTM.

Gartner, Rosemary. 2007. "Violent Crime." Pp. 5206–5208 in The Blackwell Encyclopedia of Sociology, edited by G. Ritzer. Malden, MA: Blackwell.

Gates, Robert M. 2014. Duty: Memoirs of a Secretary at War. New York: Knopf.

Gauchat, Gordon, Maura Kelly, and Michael Wallace. 2012. "Occupational Gender Segregation, Globalization, and Gender Earnings Inequality in U.S. Metropolitan Areas." Gender & Society 26: 718–747.

Ghumman, Sonia and Ann Maries Ryan. 2013. "Not Welcome Here: Discrimination towards Women Who Wear the Muslim Headscarf." Human Relations 66: 671–698.

Gibson, Campbell J. and Emily Lennon. 1999. Historical Census Statistics on the Foreign-Born Population of the United States: 1850 to 1990. Working Paper 29, U.S. Census Bureau. Washington, DC: Government Printing Office.

Geertz, Clifford. 1973. The Interpretation of Cultures. New York: Basic Books.

Gehlert, S., I. H. Song, C. H. Chang, and S. A. Hartlage. 2009. "The Prevalence of Premenstrual Dysphoric Disorder in a Randomly Selected Group of Urban and Rural Women." Psychological Medicine 39: 129–136.

Geis, Gilbert. 2007a. "Crime, Corporate." Pp. 826–828 in The Blackwell Encyclopedia of Sociology, edited by G. Ritzer. Malden, MA: Blackwell.

Geis, Gilbert. 2007b. "Crime, White-Collar." Pp. 850–851 in The Blackwell Encyclopedia of Sociology, edited by G. Ritzer. Malden, MA: Blackwell.

Gentina, Elodie and Isabelle Muratore. 2012. "Environmentalism at Home: The Process of Ecological Resocialization by Teenagers." Journal of Consumer Behaviour 11: 162–169.

Gentry, Caron and Laura Sjoberg. 2015. "Terrorism and Political Violence." Pp. 120–130 in Gender Matters in Global Politics: A Feminist Introduction to International Relations, 2nd ed., edited by L. J. Shepherd. New York: Routledge.

Gerami, Shahin and Melodye Lehnerer. 2007. "Gendered Aspects of War and International Violence." Pp. 1885–1888 in The Blackwell Encyclopedia of Sociology, edited by G. Ritzer. Malden, MA: Blackwell.

Gerhardt, H. Carl and Franz Huber. 2002. Acoustic Communication in Insects and Anurans: Common Problems and Diverse Solutions. Chicago: University of Chicago Press.

Gerland, Patrick et al. 2014. "World Population Stabilization Unlikely This Century." Science 346(6206): 234–237.

Gervais, Sarah J., Arianne M. Holland, and Michael D. Dodd. 2013. "My Eyes Are Up Here: The Nature of the Objectifying Gaze toward Women." Sex Roles 69: 557–570.

Gettleman, Jeffrey. 2014. "Ebola Ravages Economies in West Africa." New York Times, December 20.

Giddens, Anthony 1984. The Constitution of Society: Outline of the Theory of Structuration. Berkeley: University of California Press.

Giddens, Anthony. 1992. The Transformation of Intimacy: Sexuality, Love and Eroticism in Modern Societies. Stanford, CA: Stanford University Press.

Gilbert, Dennis L. 2015. The American Class Structure in an Age of Growing Inequality. 9th ed. Thousand Oaks, CA: Sage.

Gilbert, Dennis L. and Joseph A. Kahl. 1993. The American Class Structure: A New Synthesis. Belmont, CA: Wadsworth.

Gilman, Nils, Jesse Goldhammer, and Steven Weber, eds. 2011. Deviant Globalization: Black Market Economy in the 21st Century. London: Continuum.

Gilroy, Paul. 1993. The Black Atlantic: Modernity and Double Consciousness. London: Verso Books.

Gimlin, Debra. 2007. "Accounting for Cosmetic Surgery in the USA and Great Britain: A Cross-Cultural Analysis of Women's Narratives." Body and Society 13: 41–60.

Giroux, Henry A. and David E. Purpel, eds. 1983. The Hidden Curriculum and Moral Education. Berkeley, CA: McCutchan.

Gitlin, Todd. 1980. The Whole World Is Watching. Berkeley: University of California Press.

Gitlin, Todd. 1993. The Sixties: Years of Hope, Days of Rage. New York: Bantam.

Gitlin, Todd. 2014. "Occupy's Predicament: The Moment and the Prospects for the Movement." British Journal of Sociology 64: 3–25.

Gladwell, Malcolm. 2010. "Small Change: Why the Revolution Will Not Be Tweeted." New Yorker, October 4.

Glantz, Michael H., ed. 1977. Desertification: Environmental Degradation in and around Arid Lands. Boulder, CO: Westview Press.

Glenny, Misha. 2008. McMafia: A Journey through the Global Criminal Underworld. New York: Knopf.

Gloor, Peter and Scott Cooper. 2007. Coolhunting: Chasing Down the Next Big Thing. New York: AMACOM.

Gmelch, Sharon Bohn, ed. 2010. Tourists and Tourism: A Reader. Prospect Heights, IL: Waveland Press.

Godlee, Fiona, Neil Pakenham-Walsh, Dan Ncayiyana, Barbara Cohen, and Abel Packer. 2004. "Can We Achieve Health Information for All by 2015?" The Lancet 364: 295–300.

Godwyn, Mary and Jody Hoffer Gittell, eds. 2011. Sociology of Organizations: Structures and Relationships. Thousand Oaks, CA: Pine Forge Press.

Goel, Vindu. 2014. "Big Profit at Facebook as It Tilts to Mobile." New York Times, January 29. Retrieved May 5, 2015 (http://www.nytimes.com/2014/01/30/technology/rise-in-mobile-ads-pushes-up-revenue-and-profit-at-facebook.html).

Goffman, Alice. 2014. On the Run: Fugitive Life in an American City. Chicago: University of Chicago Press.

Goffman, Erving. 1959. The Presentation of Self in Everyday Life. Garden City, NY: Anchor Books.

Goffman, Erving. 1961a. Asylums: Essays on the Social Situation of Mental Patients and Other Inmates. Garden City, NY: Anchor Books.

Goffman, Erving. 1961b. Encounters. Indianapolis: Bobbs-Merrill.

Goffman, Erving. 1963. Stigma: Notes on the Management of Spoiled Identity. Englewood Cliffs, NJ: Prentice Hall/Spectrum.

Goffman, Erving. 2000. Exploring the Interaction Order. Cambridge: Polity Press.

Goldberg, David Theo. 2009. "Racial Comparisons, Relational Racisms: Some Thoughts on Method." Ethnic and Racial Studies 32: 1271–1282.

Goldberg, Gertrude Schaffner, ed. 2010. Poor Women in Rich Countries: The Feminization of Poverty over the Life Course. New York: Oxford University Press.

Goldberg, Harvey E. 2007. "Judaism." Pp. 690–693 in Encyclopedia of Globalization, edited by J. A. Scholte and R. Robertson. New York: MTM.

Goldenberg, Suzanne. 2005. "Why Women Are Poor at Science, by Harvard President." *The Guardian,* January 18. Retrieved April 19, 2015 (http://www.theguardian.com/science/2005/jan/18/educationsgendergap.genderissues).

Goldfrank, Walter. 2005. "Fresh Demand: The Consumption of Chilean Produce in the United States." Pp. 42–53 in *The Cultural Politics of Food and Eating: A Reader,* edited by J. L. Watson & M. L. Caldwell. Malden, MA: Blackwell.

Goldin, Claudia, Lawrence F. Katz, and Ilyana Kuziemko. 2006. "The Homecoming of American College Women: The Reversal of the College Gender Gap." *Journal of Economic Perspectives* 20: 133–156.

Goldman, Liran, Howard Giles, and Michael A. Hogg. 2014. "Going to Extremes: Social Identity and Communication Processes Associated with Gang Membership." *Group Processes & Intergroup Relations* 17: 813–832.

Goldman, Robert and Stephen Papson. 1998. *Nike Culture.* London: Sage.

Goldscheider, Calvin. 2012. "Judaism." Pp. 1225–1234 in *The Wiley-Blackwell Encyclopedia of Globalization,* edited by G. Ritzer. Malden, MA: Wiley-Blackwell.

Goldstone, Jack. 1991. *Revolution and Rebellion in the Early Modern World.* Berkeley: University of California Press.

Goli, Srinivas, Riddhi Doshi, and Arokiasamy Perianayagam. 2013. "Pathways of Economic Inequalities in Maternal and Child Health in Urban India: A Decomposition Analysis." *PLOS ONE* 8(3): e58573. Retrieved April 19, 2015 (http://www.plosone.org/article/info%3Adoi%2F10.1371%2Fjournal.pone.0058573#pone-0058573-g001).

Gooch, Liz. 2012. "With Opening Near, Yale Defends Singapore Venture." *New York Times,* August 27. Retrieved July 5, 2013 (http://www.nytimes.com/2012/08/27/world/asia).

Goode, Erich. 2002. "Sexual Involvement and Social Research in a Fat Civil Rights Organization." *Qualitative Sociology* 25(4): 501–534.

Goode, Erich. 2007a. "Deviance." Pp. 1075–1082 in *The Blackwell Encyclopedia of Sociology,* edited by G. Ritzer. Malden, MA: Blackwell.

Goode, Erich. 2007b. "Deviance: Explanatory Theories of." Pp. 1100–1107 in *The Blackwell Encyclopedia of Sociology,* edited by G. Ritzer. Malden, MA: Blackwell.

Goode, Erich. 2014. "Labeling Theory." Pp. 2807–2814 in *Encyclopedia of Criminology and Criminal Justice,* edited by G. Bruinsma and D. Weisburd. New York: Springer.

Goode, Erich and Nachman Ben-Yehuda. 1994. *Moral Panics: The Social Construction of Deviance.* Oxford: Blackwell.

Goode, Erich and Nachman Ben-Yehuda. 2009. *Moral Panics: The Social Construction of Deviance.* 2nd ed. Malden, MA: Blackwell.

Goode, Erich and Alex Thio. 2007. "Deviance, Crime and." Pp. 1092–1095 in *The Blackwell Encyclopedia of Sociology,* edited by G. Ritzer. Malden, MA: Blackwell.

Goode, William J. 1963. *World Revolution and Family Patterns.* New York: Free Press.

Goodlin, Wendi E. and Christopher S. Dunn. 2011. "Three Patterns of Domestic Violence in Households: Single Victimization, Repeat Victimization, and Co-occurring Victimization." *Journal of Family Violence* 26: 101–108.

Gopal, Prashant. 2014. "Brooklyn Worst in U.S. for Home Affordability." *Bloomberg Business,* December 3. Retrieved April 19, 2015 (http://www.bloomberg.com/news/articles/2014-12-04/brooklyn-worst-in-u-s-for-home-affordability).

Gorman, Elizabeth H. and Julie A. Kmec. 2009. "Hierarchical Rank and Women's Organizational Mobility: Glass Ceilings in Corporate Law Firms." *American Journal of Sociology* 114: 1428–1474.

Gorski, Philip S. 2011. "Barack Obama and Civil Religion." Pp. 179–214 in *Rethinking Obama,* edited by J. Go. Bingley, England: Emerald.

Gotham, Kevin Fox. 2007. "Megalopolis." Pp. 2942–2944 in *The Blackwell Encyclopedia of Sociology,* edited by G. Ritzer. Malden, MA: Blackwell.

Gottman, Jean. 1961. *Megalopolis: The Urbanized Northeastern Seaboard of the United States.* New York: Twentieth Century Fund.

Gottman, John M., Tames Coan, Sybil Carrere, and Catherine Swanson. 1998. "Predicting Marital Happiness and Stability from Newlywed Interactions." *Journal of Marriage and the Family* 60: 5–22.

Gottschalk, Simon. 2010. "The Presentation of Avatars in Second Life: Self and Interaction in Social Virtual Spaces." *Symbolic Interaction* 33(4): 501–525.

Gould, Kenneth, David N. Pellow, and Allan Schnaiberg. 2008. *The Treadmill of Production: Injustice and Unsustainability in the Global Economy.* Boulder, CO: Paradigm.

Gouldner, Alvin W. 1960. "The Norm of Reciprocity: A Preliminary Statement." *American Sociological Review* 25(2): 161–178.

Gove, Walter R. 1980. *The Labelling of Deviance.* Beverly Hills, CA: Sage.

Gove, Walter R. and Michael Hughes. 1979. "Possible Causes of the Apparent Sex Differences in Physical Health: An Empirical Investigation." *American Sociological Review* 44: 126–146.

Gozdecka, Dorota A., Slen A. Ercan, and Magdalena Kmak. 2014. "From Multiculturalism to Post-multiculturalism: Trends and Paradoxes." *Journal of Sociology* 50: 51–64.

Grady, Denise. 2015. "Measles: Perilous but Preventable." *New York Times,* February 2.

Grandin, Greg. 2010. *Fordlandia: The Rise and Fall of Henry Ford's Forgotten Jungle City.* New York: Picador.

Grandin, Temple. 2000. "My Experiences with Visual Thinking Sensory Problems and Communication Difficulties." Autism Research Institute. Retrieved April 27, 2015 (http://www.autism.com/advocacy_grandin_visual%20thinking).

Granfield, Robert. 1992. *Making Elite Lawyers: Visions of Law at Harvard and Beyond.* New York: Routledge, Chapman and Hall.

Granovetter, Mark. 1973. "The Strength of Weak Ties." *American Journal of Sociology* 78(6): 1360–1380.

Granovetter, Mark. 1974. *Getting a Job: A Study of Contacts and Careers.* Cambridge, MA: Harvard University Press.

Gray, Clark and Valerie Mueller. 2012. "Drought and Population Mobility in Rural Ethiopia." *World Development* 40(1): 134–145.

Greeley, Andrew. 2005. *The Priestly Sins.* New York: Forge Books.

Greenebaum, Jessica and Clinton R. Sanders. Forthcoming. "Human-Animal Interaction." In *The Wiley-Blackwell Encyclopedia of Sociology,* 2nd ed., edited by G. Ritzer. Malden, MA: Wiley-Blackwell.

Grice, Elizabeth. 2006. "Cry of an Enfant Sauvage." *Daily Telegraph,* July 17.

Griffin, Christine, Isabelle Szmigin, Andrew Bengry-Howell, Chris Hackley, and Willm Mistral. 2012. "Inhabiting the Contradictions: Hypersexual Femininity and the Culture of Intoxication among Young Women in the UK." *Feminism & Psychology* 23(2): 184–206.

Griffin, Sean Patrick. 2007. "Crime, Organized." Pp. 833–834 in *The Blackwell Encyclopedia of Sociology,* edited by G. Ritzer. Malden, MA: Blackwell.

Grigsby, Mary. 2004. *Buying Time and Getting By: The Voluntary Simplicity Movement.* Albany: State University of New York Press.

Griswold, Alison. 2014. "Are Smartphones Ruining the Restaurant Experience?" *Slate,* July 16. Retrieved April 22, 2015 (http://www.slate.com/articles/business/moneybox/2014/07/viral_craigslist_post_on_smartphones_in_restaurants_is_tech_ruining_the.html).

Gronow, Jukka. 2007. "Taste, Sociology of." Pp. 4930–4935 in *The Blackwell Encyclopedia of Sociology,* edited by G. Ritzer. Malden, MA: Blackwell.

Gu, Dongfeng, Tanika N. Kelly, Xigui Wu, Jing Chen, Jonathan M. Samet, Jian-feng Huang, Manlu Zhu, Ji-chun Chen, Chung-shiuan Chen, Xiufang Duan, Michael J. Klag, and Jiang He. 2009. "Mortality Attributable to Smoking in China." *New England Journal of Medicine* 360: 150–159.

Gubrium, Jaber F., James A. Holstein, Amir B. Marvasti, and Karyn D. McKinney, eds. 2012. *The SAGE Handbook of Interview Research: The Complexity of the Craft.* 2nd ed. Thousand Oaks, CA: Sage.

Guhathakurta, Subhrajit, David Jacobson, and Nicholas C. DelSordi. 2007. "The End of Globalization? The Implications of Migration for State, Society and Economy." Pp. 201–215 in *The Blackwell Companion to Globalization,* edited by G. Ritzer. Malden, MA: Blackwell.

Guillen, Mario F. 2010. "Classical Sociological Approaches to the Study of Leadership." Pp. 223–238 in *Handbook of Leadership Theory and Practice,* edited by N. Nohria and R. Khurana. Cambridge, MA: Harvard University Press.

Gulati, Ranjay and Phanish Puranam. 2009. "Renewal through Reorganization: The Value of Inconsistencies between Formal and Informal Organization." *Organization Science* 20: 422–440.

Gündüz, Zuhal Yesilyurt. 2013. "The Feminization of Migration: Care and the New Emotional Imperialism." *Monthly Review* 65(7): 32–43.

Guo, Guang, Michael E. Roettger, and Tianji Cai. 2008. "The Integration of Genetic Propensities into Social-Control Models of Delinquency and Violence among Male Youths." *American Sociological Review* 73(4): 543–568.

Guo, Shibao. 2013. "Economic Integration of Recent Chinese Immigrants in Canada's Second-Tier Cities: The Triple Glass Effect and Immigrants'

Downward Social Mobility." *Canadian Ethnic Studies* 45: 95–115.

Hacker, Jacob S. and Paul Pierson. 2010. *Winner-Take-All Politics: How Washington Made the Rich Richer—and Turned Its Back on the Middle Class*. New York: Simon & Schuster.

Haddad, Emma. 2003. "The Refugee: The Individual between Sovereigns." *Global Society* 17(3): 297–322.

Hafferty, Frederic W. 2009. "Professionalism and the Socialization of Medical Students." Pp. 53–69 in *Teaching Medical Professionalism*, edited by R. L. Cruess, S. R. Cruess, and Y. Steinert. New York: Cambridge University Press.

Hafferty, Frederic W. and Brian Castellani. 2011. "Two Cultures: Two Ships: The Rise of a Professionalism Movement within Modern Medicine and Medical Sociology's Disappearance from the Professionalism Debate." Pp. 201–220 in *Handbook of the Sociology of Health, Illness, and Healing: A Blueprint for the 21st Century*, edited by B. A. Pescosolido, J. K. Martin, J. D. McLeod, and A. Rogers. Dordrecht, Netherlands: Springer.

Hage, Jerald and Charles H. Powers. 1992. *Postindustrial Lives: Roles and Relationships in the 21st Century*. Newbury Park, CA: Sage.

"Haiti, Unfinished and Forsaken." 2014. *New York Times*, January 10.

Hakim, Catherine. 2011. *Erotic Capital: The Power of Attraction in the Boardroom and the Bedroom*. New York: Basic Books.

Hall, Elaine J. and Marnie Salupo Rodriguez. 2003. "The Myth of Postfeminism." *Gender & Society* 17(6): 878–902.

Hall, Peter and David Soskice, eds. 2001. *Varieties of Capitalism: The Institutional Foundations of Comparative Advantage*. New York: Oxford University Press.

Hamilton, Kathy. 2012. "Low-Income Families and Coping through Brands: Inclusion or Stigma?" *Sociology* 46: 74–90.

Hamilton, Laura and Elizabeth A. Armstrong. 2009. "Gendered Sexuality in Young Adulthood: Double Binds and Flawed Options." *Gender & Society* 23(5): 589–616.

Hamermesh, Daniel S. 2011. *Beauty Pays: Why Attractive People Are More Successful*. Princeton, NJ: Princeton University Press.

Hammersley, Martyn. 2007. "Ethnography." Pp. 1479–1483 in *The Blackwell Encyclopedia of Sociology*, edited by G. Ritzer. Malden, MA: Blackwell.

Hamouda, Manel and Abderrazak Gharbi. 2013. "The Postmodern Consumer: An Identity Constructor?" *International Journal of Marketing Studies* 5(2): 41–49.

Handelman, Jay M. and Robert V. Kozinets. 2007. "Culture Jamming." Pp. 945–946 in *The Blackwell Encyclopedia of Sociology*, edited by G. Ritzer. Malden, MA: Blackwell.

Hankin, Janet R. and Eric R. Wright. 2010. "Reflections on Fifty Years of Medical Sociology." *Journal of Health and Social Behavior* 51: S10–S14.

Hannigan, John. 1998. *Fantasy City: Pleasure and Profit in the Postmodern Metropolis*. London: Routledge.

Hannigan, John. 2007. "Fantasy City." Pp. 1641–1644 in *The Blackwell Encyclopedia of Sociology*, edited by G. Ritzer. Malden, MA: Blackwell.

Hannigan, John. 2014. *Environmental Sociology*. 3rd ed. New York: Routledge.

Haraway, Donna. 1991. "A Cyborg Manifesto: Science, Technology, and Socialist-Feminism in the Late Twentieth Century." Pp. 149–181 in *Simians, Cyborgs and Women: The Reinvention of Nature*. New York: Routledge.

Harding, David. 2010. *Living the Drama: Community, Conflict, and Culture among Inner-City Boys*. Chicago: University of Chicago Press.

Hardoon, Deborah. 2015. "Wealth: Having It All and Wanting More." Oxfam International, January. Retrieved April 17, 2015 (https://www.oxfam.org/sites/www.oxfam.org/files/file_attachments/ib-wealth-having-all-wanting-more-190115-en.pdf).

Harmon, Corinne, Glenda Carne, Kristina Lizardy-Hajbi, and Eugene Wilkerson. 2010. "Access to Higher Education for Undocumented Students: 'Outlaws' of Social Justice, Equity, and Equality." *Journal of Praxis in Multicultural Education* 5(1): 67–82.

Harris, Douglas N., Carolyn D. Herrington, and Amy Albee. 2007. "The Future of Vouchers: Lessons from the Adoption, Design, and Court Challenges of Florida's Three Voucher Programs." *Educational Policy* 21(1): 215–244.

Harris Interactive. 2009. "Firefighters, Scientists and Doctors Seen as Most Prestigious Occupations." Press release, August 4. Retrieved April 27, 2015 (http://www.harrisinteractive.com/vault/Harris-Interactive-Poll-Research-Pres-Occupations-2009-08.pdf).

Harris Interactive. 2014. "Doctors, Military Officers, Firefighters, and Scientists Seen as among America's Most Prestigious Occupations." Press release, September 10. Retrieved April 29, 2015 (http://www.harrisinteractive.com/NewsRoom/HarrisPolls/tabid/447/mid/1508/articleId/1490/ctl/ReadCustom%20Default/Default.aspx).

Harrison, Bennett. 1994. *Lean and Mean: The Changing Landscape of Corporate Power in the Age of Flexibility*. New York: Basic Books.

Hart, Betty and Todd Risley. 1995. *Meaningful Differences in the Everyday Experience of Young American Children*. Baltimore: Paul H. Brookes.

Hartigan, John. 2014. "Whiteness, Class and the Legacies of Empire: On Home Ground." *Ethnic and Racial Studies* 37(10): 1941–1944.

Hartmann, Heidi. 1979. "Capitalism, Patriarchy and Job Segregation by Sex." Pp. 206–247 in *Capitalist Patriarchy and the Case for Socialist Feminism*, edited by Z. Eisenstein. New York: Monthly Review Press.

Harvey, David. 2005. *A Brief History of Neoliberalism*. Oxford: Oxford University Press.

Harvey, David. 2007. "Poverty and Disrepute." Pp. 3589–3594 in *The Blackwell Encyclopedia of Sociology*, edited by G. Ritzer. Malden, MA: Blackwell.

Hashemian, Farnoosh and Derek Yach. 2007. "Public Health in a Globalizing World: Challenges and Opportunities." Pp. 516–538 in *The Blackwell Companion to Globalization*, edited by G. Ritzer. Malden, MA: Blackwell.

Hatch, Anthony. 2009. *The Politics of Metabolism: The Metabolic Syndrome and the Reproduction of Race and Racism in the United States*. PhD dissertation, University of Maryland.

Hatfield, Elaine, Lisamarie Bensman, and Richard L. Rapson. 2012. "A Brief History of Social Scientists' Attempts to Measure Passionate Love." *Journal of Social and Personal Relationships* 29: 143–164.

Hatton, Erin and Mary Nell Trautner. 2011. "Equal Opportunity Objectification? The Sexualization of Men and Women on the Cover of *Rolling Stone*." *Sexuality & Culture* 15: 256–278.

Haub, Carl. 2013. "Rising Trend of Births Outside Marriage." Population Reference Bureau, April. Retrieved April 20, 2015 (http://www.prb.org/Publications/Articles/2013/nonmarital-births.aspx).

Hauskeller, Christine, Steve Sturdy, and Richard Tutton. 2013. "Genetics and the Sociology of Identity." *Sociology* 47: 875–886.

Hausmann, Ricardo, Ina Ganguli, and Martina Viarengo. 2009. "The Dynamics of the Gender Gap: How Do Countries Rank in Terms of Making Marriage and Motherhood Compatible with Work?" Pp. 27–29 in *Global Gender Gap Report*, edited by R. Hausmann, L. D. Tyson, and S. Zahidi. Geneva: World Economic Forum.

Hawkesworth, Mary. 2006. *Globalization and Feminist Activism*. Lanham, MD: Rowman & Littlefield.

Hay, Harry. 2012. "Birth of a Consciousness." *Gay & Lesbian Review Worldwide* 19: 15–18.

Hayes, Dennis and Robin Wynyard, eds. 2002. *The McDonaldization of Higher Education*. Westport, CT: Bergin and Garvey.

Haynie, L. 2001. "Delinquent Peers Revisited: Does Network Structure Matter?" *American Journal of Sociology* 106: 1013–1057.

Hays, Sharon. 1998. *The Cultural Contradictions of Motherhood*. New Haven, CT: Yale University Press.

"Head Injuries in Football." 2010. *New York Times*, October 21. Retrieved March 30, 2012 (topics.nytimes.com/top/reference/timestopics/subjects/f/football/head_injuries/index.html).

Heaphy, Brian. 2007. "Same-Sex Marriage/Civil Unions." Pp. 3995–3998 in *The Blackwell Encyclopedia of Sociology*, edited by G. Ritzer. Malden, MA: Blackwell.

Heckman, James. 2006. "Skill Formation and the Economics of Investing in Disadvantaged Children." *Science* 312: 1900–1902.

Heckman, James J., Seong Hyeok Moon, Rodrigo Pinto, Peter A. Savelyev, and Adam Yavitz. 2010. "The Rate of Return to the HighScope Perry Preschool Program." *Journal of Public Economics* 94: 114–128.

Heintz, James. 2006. "Globalization, Economic Policy and Employment: Poverty and Gender Implications." Employment Strategy Unit, International Labour Organization. Retrieved November 4, 2013 (http://www.ilo.org/wcmsp5/groups/public/@ed_emp/@emp_elm/documents/publication/wcms_114024.pdf).

Heller, Joseph. 1961. *Catch-22*. New York: Simon & Schuster.

Heller, Nathan. 2013. "Laptop U." *New Yorker*, May 20, 80ff.

Helliwell, Christine. 2000. "'It's Only a Penis': Rape, Feminism, and Difference." *Signs* 25(3): 789–816.

Hendershott, Anne. 2002. *The Politics of Deviance*. San Francisco: Encounter Books.

Henningsen, David Dryden. 2004. "Flirting with Meaning: An Examination of Miscommunication in Flirting Interactions." *Sex Roles* 50: 481–489.

Hepburn, Stephanie and Rita J. Simon. 2013. *Human Trafficking around the World: Hidden in Plain Sight*. New York: Columbia University Press.

Heritage, John and Tanya Stivers. 2012. "Conversation Analysis and Sociology." Pp. 659–673 in *The Handbook of Conversation Analysis*, edited by J. Sidnell and T. Stivers. Malden, MA: Wiley Blackwell.

Herod, Andrew. 2009. *Geographies of Globalization: A Critical Introduction*. Malden, MA: Wiley-Blackwell.

Herper, Matthew and Peter Kang. 2006. "The World's Ten Best-Selling Drugs." *Forbes*, March 22. Retrieved January 25, 2012 (http://www.forbes.com/2006/03/21/pfizer-merck-amgen-cx_mh_pk_0321topdrugs.html).

Herrnstein, Richard J. and Charles Murray. 1994. *The Bell Curve: Intelligence and Class Structure in American Life*. New York: Free Press.

Hershkovitz, Shay. 2012. "Nation-State." Pp. 1492–1496 in *The Wiley-Blackwell Encyclopedia of Globalization*, edited by G. Ritzer. Malden, MA: Wiley-Blackwell.

Hesse-Biber, Sharlene. 1996. *Am I Thin Enough Yet? The Cult of Thinness and Commercialization of Identity*. London: Oxford University Press.

Hetherington, E. M. 2003. "Intimate Pathways: Changing Patterns in Close Personal Relationships across Time." *Family Relations* 52: 183–206.

Hier, Sean P. 2011. "Tightening the Focus: Moral Panic, Moral Regulation and Liberal Government." *British Journal of Sociology* 62: 523–541.

Higley, John and Michael Burton. 2006. *Elite Foundations of Liberal Democracy*. Lanham, MD: Rowman & Littlefield.

Hildebrandt, Achim. 2014. "Routes to Decriminalization: A Comparative Analysis of the Legalization of Same-Sex Sexual Acts." *Sexualities* 17: 230–253.

Hill, Jessica and Pranee Liamputtong. 2011. "Being the Mother of a Child with Asperger's Syndrome: Women's Experiences of Stigma." *Health Care for Women International* 32: 708–722.

Hillyard, Daniel. 2007. "Deviance, Criminalization of." Pp. 1095–1100 in *The Blackwell Encyclopedia of Sociology*, edited by G. Ritzer. Malden, MA: Blackwell.

Himanen, Pekka. 2001. *The Hacker Ethic, and the Spirit of the Information Age*. New York: Random House.

Hindin, Michelle J. 2007. "Role Theory." Pp. 3951–3954 in *The Blackwell Encyclopedia of Sociology*, edited by G. Ritzer. Malden, MA: Blackwell.

Hinze, Susan W. and Dawn Aliberti. 2007. "Feminization of Poverty." Pp. 1718–1725 in *The Blackwell Encyclopedia of Sociology*, edited by G. Ritzer. Malden, MA: Blackwell.

Hoang, Kimberly Kay. 2010. "Economies of Emotion, Familiarity, Fantasy, and Desire: Emotional Labor in Ho Chi Minh City's Sex Industry." *Sexualities* 13(2): 255–272.

Hoang, Kimberly Kay. 2015. *Dealing in Desire: Asian Ascendancy, Western Decline, and the Hidden Currencies of Global Sex Work*. Berkeley: University of California Press.

Hobsbawm, E. J. and Chris Wrigley. 1999. *Industry and Empire: The Birth of the Industrial Revolution*. New York: New Press.

Hochschild, Adam. 2011. "Explaining Congo's Endless Civil War." *New York Times Book Review*, April 1. Retrieved January 29, 2012 (http://www.nytimes.com/2011/04/03/books/review/book-review-dancing-in-the-glory-of-monsters-the-collapse-of-the-congo-and-the-great-war-of-africa-by-jason-k-stearns.html?pagewanted=all).

Hochschild, Arlie Russell (with Anne Machung). 1989. *The Second Shift*. New York: Viking.

Hochschild, Arlie Russell. 2000. "Global Care Chains and Emotional Surplus Value." In *On the Edge: Living with Global Capitalism*, edited by W. Hutton and A. Giddens. London: Jonathan Cape.

Hochschild, Arlie Russell (with Anne Machung). 2003. *The Second Shift*. Updated ed. New York: Penguin.

Hodge, David. 2008. "Sexual Trafficking in the US: A Domestic Problem with Transnational Dimensions." *Social Work* 53(2): 143–152.

Hoecker-Drysdale, Susan. 2011. "Harriet Martineau." Pp. 61–95 in *The Wiley-Blackwell Companion to Major Social Theorists*, Vol. 1, *Classical Theorists*, edited by G. Ritzer and J. Stepnisky. Malden, MA: Wiley-Blackwell.

Hoefer, Michael, Nancy Rytina, and Bryan C. Baker. 2010. "Estimates of the Unauthorized Immigrant Population Residing in the United States: January 2009." U.S. Department of Homeland Security. Retrieved February 28, 2012 (http://www.dhs.gov/xlibrary/assets/statistics/publications/ois_ill_pe_2009.pdf).

Hoekstra, Arjen J. 2012. "Water." Pp. 2202–2210 in *The Wiley-Blackwell Companion to Sociology*, edited by G. Ritzer. Malden, MA: Wiley-Blackwell.

Hoffnung, Michele and Michelle A. Williams. 2013. "Balancing Act: Career and Family during College-Educated Women's 30s." *Sex Roles* 68(5–6): 321–334.

Hokayem, Charles and Misty L. Heggeness. 2014. *Living in Near Poverty in the United States: 1966–2012*. Current Population Reports P60-248. Washington, DC: U.S. Census Bureau, May. Retrieved April 19, 2015 (https://www.census.gov/prod/2014pubs/p60-248.pdf).

Holdstock, Nick. 2014. What We Talk about When We Talk about 'the Uyghurs.'" *Dissent* 61: 65–69.

Hollifield, James E. and David Jacobson. 2012. "Migration and the State." Pp. 1390–1400 in *The Wiley-Blackwell Encyclopedia of Globalization*, edited by G. Ritzer. Malden, MA: Wiley-Blackwell.

Hollister, Geoff. 2008. *Out of Nowhere: The Inside Story of How Nike Marketed the Culture of Running*. Maidenhead, England: Meyer and Meyer Sport.

Holt, Douglas B. 2004. *How Brands Become Icons: Principles of Cultural Branding*. Cambridge, MA: Harvard Business School Press.

Holt, Douglas B. 2007. "Distinction." Pp. 1189–1191 in *The Blackwell Encyclopedia of Sociology*, edited by G. Ritzer. Malden, MA: Blackwell.

Holt, Thomas J. and Adam M. Bossler. 2014. "An Assessment of the Current State of Cybercrime Scholarship." *Deviant Behavior* 35: 20–40.

Holt, Thomas J. and Michael G. Turner. 2012. "Examining Risks and Protective Factors of On-Line Identity Theft." *Deviant Behavior* 33: 308–323.

Holton, Robert J. 2011. *Globalization and the Nation State*. 2nd ed. New York: Palgrave Macmillan.

Homans, George. 1961. *Social Behavior: Its Elementary Forms*. New York: Harcourt, Brace, and World.

Hondagneu-Sotelo, Pierette. 2000. *Doméstica: Immigrant Workers Cleaning and Caring in the Shadows of Affluence*. Berkeley: University of California Press.

Hondagneu-Sotelo, Pierette and Ernestine Avila. 2005. "'I'm Here, but I'm There': The Meanings of Latina Transnational Motherhood." In *Gender through a Prism of Difference*, edited by M. B. Zinn, P. Hondagneu-Sotelo, and M. Messner. New York: Oxford University Press.

"Honduras, Guatemala Establish Joint Anti-drug Force." 2014. *New York Times*, December 3.

hooks, bell. 2000. *Feminist Thought: From Margin to Center*. Cambridge, MA: South End Press.

Horovitz, Bruce. 2002. "Fast-Food World Says Drive-Thru Is the Way to Go." *USA Today*, April 3. Retrieved May 26, 2011 (http://www.usatoday.com/money/covers/2002-04-03-drive-thru.htm).

Horrey, William J. and Christopher D. Wickens. 2006. "Examining the Impact of Cell Phone Conversations on Driving Using Meta-analytic Techniques." *Human Factors* 48: 196–205.

Horrigan, John. 2008. "Online Shopping." Pew Internet and American Life Project, February 13. Retrieved April 19, 2015 (http://www.pewinternet.org/2008/02/13/online-shopping).

Horton, Richard. 2000. "North and South: Bridging the Information Gap." *The Lancet* 355: 2231–2236.

Houck, Davis W. and David E. Dixon, eds. 2011. *Women and the Civil Rights Movement, 1954–1965*. Jackson: University of Mississippi Press.

Huaco, George. 1966. "The Functionalist Theory of Stratification: Two Decades of Controversy." *Inquiry* 9: 215–240.

Huang, Penelope M., Pamela J. Smock, Wendy D. Manning, and Cara A. Bergstrom-Lynch. 2011. "He Says, She Says: Gender and Cohabitation." *Journal of Family Issues* 32: 876–905.

Huesemann, Michael and Joyce Huesemann. 2011. *Techno-fix: Why Technology Won't Save Us or the Environment*. Gabriola Island, BC: New Society.

Hughes, Donna M. 2000. "Welcome to the Rape Camp: Sexual Exploitation and the Internet in Cambodia." *Journal of Sexual Aggression* 6: 1–23.

Hull, Kathleen E., Ann Meier, and Timothy Ortyl. 2010. "The Changing Landscape of Love and Marriage." *Contexts* 9: 32–37.

Humphreys, Laud. 1970. *Tearoom Trade: A Study of Homosexual Encounters in Public Places*. Chicago: Aldine.

Hunt, Stephen. 2007. "Social Structure." Pp. 4524–4526 in *The Blackwell Encyclopedia of Sociology*, edited by G. Ritzer. Malden, MA: Blackwell.

Hunter, James Davison. 1992. *Culture Wars: The Struggle to Control the Family, Art, Education, Law, and Politics in America*. New York: Basic Books.

Huntington, Samuel P. 1996. *The Clash of Civilizations and the Remaking of the World Order*. New York: Simon & Schuster.

Hurdle, Jon. 2014. "A Casino Shuts Down amid Tears and Questions about a City's Direction." *New York Times*, September 1.

Husain, Ed. 2014. "Saudis Must Stop Exporting Extremism." *New York Times*, August 22.

Hutson, Brittany. 2010. "Overcoming Gender Differences." *Black Enterprise* 40(8): 56–57.

Hwang, Jinyoung and Jong Ha Lee. 2014. "Women's Education and the Timing and Level of Fertility." *International Journal of Social Economics* 41: 862–874.

Iceland, John. 2007. "Poverty." Pp. 3587–3588 in *The Blackwell Encyclopedia of Sociology,* edited by G. Ritzer. Malden, MA: Blackwell.

Iceland, John. 2012. *Poverty in America: A Handbook.* Updated ed. Berkeley: University of California Press.

Imtiaz, Saba and Declan Walsh. 2015. "Pakistan Raids Offices of Fake Diploma Company." *New York Times,* May 20.

Inda, Jonathan Xavier. 2012. "Flows." Pp. 668–670 in *The Wiley-Blackwell Encyclopedia of Globalization,* edited by G. Ritzer. Malden, MA: Wiley-Blackwell.

Inda, Jonathan Xavier and Renato Rosaldo, eds. 2008. *The Anthropology of Globalization: A Reader.* 2nd ed. Malden, MA: Blackwell.

Inglehart, Ronald and Wayne E. Baker. 2000. "Modernization, Cultural Change, and the Persistence of Traditional Values." *American Sociological Review* 65: 19–51.

Ingoldsby, Bron B. and Suzanna D. Smith, eds. 2006. *Families in Global and Multicultural Perspective.* 2nd ed. Thousand Oaks, CA: Sage.

Inoue, Keiko and Gili S. Drori. 2006. "The Global Institutionalization of Health as a Social Concern." *International Sociology* 21(1): 199–219.

Insch, Gary S., Nancy McIntyre, and Nancy C. Napier. 2008. "The Expatriate Glass Ceiling: The Second Layer of Glass." *Journal of Business Ethics* 83: 19–28.

Interlandi, Jeneen. 2010. "Why the Palace Fell: Lessons Learned from the Destruction of Haiti's Presidential Home." *Newsweek,* January 20. Retrieved March 31, 2012 (http://www.thedaily beast.com/newsweek/2010/01/20/why-the-palace-fell.html).

International Centre for Prison Studies. 2011. "World Prison Brief." Retrieved April 27, 2015 (http://www.prisonstudies.org/world-prison-brief).

International Centre for Prison Studies. 2012. "Highest to Lowest—Prison Population Total." Retrieved April 28, 2015 (http://www.prison-studies.org/highest-to-lowest/prison-popula-tion-total?field_region_taxonomy_tid=All).

International Federation of the Phonographic Industry. 2012. "Music Market Statistics." Retrieved March 30, 2012 (http://www.ifpi.org/content/section_statistics/index.html).

International Telecommunications Union. 2014. "ITU Releases 2014 ICT Figures: Mobile-Broadband Penetration Approaching 32 Per Cent, Three Billion Internet Users by End of This Year." Press release, May 5. Retrieved November 12, 2014 (http://www.itu.int/net/pressoffice/press_releases/2014/23.aspx#.VGNpycnDVFR).

Intersex Society of North America. 2008. "FAQ: What Is Intersex?" Retrieved May 15, 2015 (http://www.isna.org/faq/what_is_intersex).

Irvine, Leslie. 2004. "A Model of Animal Selfhood: Expanding Interactionist Possibilities." *Symbolic Interaction* 27: 3–21.

Isaac, Mike and Michael J. de la Merced. 2014. "Uber Adds a Billion Dollars More to Its Coffers." *New York Times,* December 24.

Jackson, Shirley A. 2007. "Majorities." Pp. 2701–2702 in *The Blackwell Encyclopedia of Sociology,* edited by G. Ritzer. Malden, MA: Blackwell.

Jacobs, Andrew. 2013. "Uighurs in China Say Bias is Growing." *New York Times,* October 8.

Jacobs, Jerry. 1996. "Gender Inequality and Higher Education." *Annual Review of Sociology* 22: 153–185.

Jacobs, Mark D. 2007. "Interaction Order." Pp. 2365–2366 in *The Blackwell Encyclopedia of Sociology,* edited by G. Ritzer. Malden, MA: Blackwell.

Jakobi, Anja P. 2012. "Human Trafficking." Pp. 953–956 in *The Wiley-Blackwell Encyclopedia of Globalization,* edited by G. Ritzer. Malden, MA: Wiley-Blackwell.

Jamieson, Lynn. 1998. *Intimacy: Personal Relationships in Modern Societies.* Cambridge: Polity Press.

Jamieson, Lynn. 2007. "Intimacy." Pp. 2411–2414 in *The Blackwell Encyclopedia of Sociology,* edited by G. Ritzer. Malden, MA: Blackwell.

Jamieson, Lynn. 2011. "Intimacy as a Concept: Explaining Social Change in the Context of Globalisation of Another Form of Ethnocentrism?" *Sociological Research Online* 16(4). Retrieved April 19, 2015 (http://www.socresonline.org.uk/16/4/15.html).

Janoski, Thomas and Darina Lepadatu. 2013. *Dominant Divisions of Labor: Models of Production That Have Transformed the World of Work.* New York: Palgrave Pivot.

Jansen, Jim. 2010. "Online Product Research." Pew Research Center, September 29. Retrieved May 27, 2011 (http://www.pewinternet.org/~/media//Files/Reports/2010/PIP%20Online%20Product%20Research%20final.pdf).

Jay, Karla. 1999. *Tales of the Lavender Menace: A Memoir of Liberation.* New York: Basic Books.

Jean-Charles, Régine Michelle. 2010. "Cracks of Gender Inequality: Haitian Women after the Earthquake." Social Science Research Council. Retrieved March 30, 2012 (http://www.ssrc.org/features/pages/haiti-now-and-next/1338/1428).

Jefferson, Gail. 1979. "A Technique for Inviting Laughter and Its Subsequent Acceptance Declination." Pp. 79–96 in *Everyday Language: Studies in Ethnomethodology,* edited by G. Psathas. New York: Irvington.

Jenkins, J. C. 1983. "Resource Mobilization Theory and the Study of Social Movements." *Annual Review of Sociology* 9: 248–267.

Jenkins, Nicholas, Sarah Keyes, and Liz Strange. 2015. "Creating Vignettes of Early Onset Dementia: An Exercise in Public Sociology." *Sociology,* published online January 29. doi: 10.1177/0038038514560262.

Jenness, Valerie. 2004. "Explaining Criminalization: From Demography and Status Politics to Globalization and Modernization." *Annual Review of Sociology* 30: 141–171.

Jensen, Gary F. 1988. "Functional Perspectives on Deviance: A Critical Assessment and Guide for the Future." *Deviant Behavior* 9: 1–17.

Jerolmack, C. 2009. "Humans, Animals, and Play: Theorizing Interaction When Intersubjectivity Is Problematic." *Sociological Theory* 27(4): 371–389.

Jimenez, Maria. 2009. "Humanitarian Crisis: Migrant Deaths at the U.S.–Mexican Border." American Civil Liberties Union of San Diego and Imperial Counties, October 1. Retrieved March 30, 2012 (http://www.aclu.org/files/pdfs/immigrants/humanitariancrisisreport.pdf).

Johns, Nicole, Krycia Cowling, and Emmanuela Gakidou. 2013. "The Wealth (and Health) of Nations: A Cross-Country Analysis of the Relation between Wealth and Inequality in Disease Burden Estimation." *The Lancet* 381: S66.

Johnson, Allan. 2005. *The Gender Knot: Unraveling Our Patriarchal Legacy.* Philadelphia: Temple University Press.

Johnson, David K. 2004. *The Lavender Scare: The Cold War Persecution of Gays and Lesbians in the Federal Government.* Chicago: University of Chicago Press.

Johnson, Naomi. 2010. "Consuming Desires: Consumption, Romance, and Sexuality in Best-Selling Teen Romance Novels." *Women's Studies in Communication* 33: 54–73.

Johnston, Lloyd D., Patrick M. O'Malley, Jerald G. Bachman, John E. Schulenberg, and Richard A. Miech. 2014. *Monitoring the Future National Survey Results on Drug Use, 1975–2013, Vol. 2, College Students and Adults Ages 19–55.* Ann Arbor: Institute for Social Research, University of Michigan. Retrieved April 24, 2015 (http://monitoringthefuture.org/pubs/monographs/mtf-vol2_2013.pdf).

Jolly, David. 2014. "Heat Waves in Europe Will Increase Study Finds. *New York Times,* December 9.

Jones, Adele. 2008. "A Silent but Mighty River: The Costs of Women's Economic Migration." *Signs* 33(4): 761–769.

Jones, Steven T. 2011. *The Tribes of Burning Man: How an Experiment in the Desert Is Shaping the New American Counterculture.* San Francisco: Consortium of Collective Consciousness.

Jordan, Mary. 2007. "The New Face of Global Mormonism: Tech-Savvy Missionary Church Thrives as Far Afield as Africa." *Washington Post,* November 19.

Jorgenson, Andrew and Jennifer Givens. 2012. "Pollution, Water." P. 1674 in *The Wiley-Blackwell Companion to Sociology,* edited by G. Ritzer. Malden, MA: Wiley-Blackwell.

Jose, Paul E., Kerstin Kramar, and Yubo Hou. 2014. "Does Brooding Rumination Moderate the Stress to Depression Relationship Similarly for Chinese and New Zealand Adolescents?" *Journal of Educational and Developmental Psychology* 4(1): 114–127.

Jung, Jaehee, Gordon Forbes, and Priscilla Chan. 2010. "Global Body and Muscle Satisfaction among College Men in the United States and Hong Kong–China." *Sex Roles* 63(1/2): 104–117.

Jung, Moon-Kie, João H. Costa Vargas, and Eduardo Bonilla-Silva, eds. 2011. *State of White Supremacy: Racism, Governance, and the United States.* Stanford CA: Stanford University Press.

Jurgenson, Nathan. 2012. "When Atoms Meet Bits: Social Media, the Mobile Web and Augmented Revolution." *Future Internet* 4: 83–91.

Juris, Jeffrey S. 2005. "The New Digital Media and Activist Networking within Anti-corporate Globalization Movements." *Annals of the American Academy of Political and Social Science* 597(January): 189–208.

Kabeer, Naila, Ratna Sudarshan, and Kristi Milward. 2013. *Organizing Women Workers in the Informal Economy: Beyond the Weapons of the Weak.* London: Zed Books.

Kahlenberg, Susan G. and Michelle M. Hein. 2010. "Progression on Nickelodeon? Gender-Role Stereotypes in Toy Commercials." *Sex Roles* 62(11–12): 830–847.

Kahn, Richard and Douglas Kellner. 2007. "Resisting Globalization." Pp. 662–674 in *The Blackwell Companion to Globalization*, edited by G. Ritzer. Malden, MA: Blackwell.

Kaiser Family Foundation. 2013. "Poverty Rate by Race/Ethnicity." Retrieved May 8, 2015 (http://kff.org/other/state-indicator/poverty-rate-by-raceethnicity).

Kalberg, Stephen. 1980. "Max Weber's Types of Rationality: Cornerstones for the Analysis of Rationalization Processes in History." *American Journal of Sociology* 85(5): 1145–1179.

Kalev, Alexandra. 2009. "Cracking the Glass Cages? Restructuring and Ascriptive Inequality at Work." *American Journal of Sociology* 114: 1591–1643.

Kaminer, Ariel and Sean O'Driscoll. 2014. "Workers at N.Y.U.'s Abu Dhabi Site Faced Harsh Conditions." *New York Times*, May 18.

Kane, Emily W. 2006. "'No Way My Boys Are Going to Be Like That!' Parents' Responses to Children's Gender Nonconformity." *Gender & Society* 20(2): 149–176.

Kane, Emily W. 2009. "'I Wanted a Soul Mate': Gendered Anticipation and Frameworks of Accountability in Parents' Preferences for Sons and Daughters." *Symbolic Interaction* 32(4): 372–389.

Kane, Emily W. 2012. *The Gender Trap: Parents and the Pitfalls of Raising Boys and Girls*. New York: New York University Press.

Kang, Miliann and Katherine Jones. 2007. "Why Do People Get Tattoos?" *Contexts* 6(1): 42–47.

Kangas, Olli E. 2007. "Welfare State, Retrenchment of." Pp. 5247–5249 in *The Blackwell Encyclopedia of Sociology*, edited by G. Ritzer. Malden, MA: Blackwell.

Kaoma, Kapya. 2014. "The Paradox and Tension of Moral Claims: Evangelical Christianity, the Politicization and Globalization of Sexual Politics in Sub-Saharan Africa." *Critical Research on Religion* 2(3): 227–245.

Karpowitz, Christopher F., Quin J. Monson, Kelly D. Patterson, and Jeremy C. Pope. 2011. "Tea Time in America? The Impact of the Tea Party Movement on the 2010 Midterm Elections." *PS: Political Science and Politics* 44: 303–309.

Karraker, Meg Wilkes. 2008. *Global Families*. Boston: Pearson.

Karstedt, Susanne. 2007. "Genocide." Pp. 1909–1913 in *The Blackwell Encyclopedia of Sociology*, edited by G. Ritzer. Malden, MA: Blackwell.

Karstedt, Suzanne. 2012. "Genocide." Pp. 793–797 in *The Wiley-Blackwell Encyclopedia of Globalization*, edited by G. Ritzer. Malden, MA: Wiley-Blackwell.

Kasarda, John D. and Greg Lindsay. 2011. *Aerotropolis: The Way We'll Live Next*. New York: Farrar, Straus and Giroux.

Katsulis, Yasmina. 2010. "'Living Like a King': Conspicuous Consumption, Virtual Communities, and the Social Construction of Paid Sexual Encounters by U.S. Sex Tourists." *Men and Masculinities* 27: 1–18.

Katz, Jonathan Ned. 2004. "'Homosexual' and 'Heterosexual': Questioning the Terms." Pp. 44–46 in *Sexualities: Identities, Behaviors, and Society*, edited by M. S. Kimmel and R. F. Plante. New York: Oxford University Press.

Kaufman-Scarbrough, Carol. 2006. "Time Use and the Impact of Technology: Examining Workspaces in the Home." *Time and Society* 15(1): 57–80.

Kauppinen, Ilkka. 2013. "Academic Capitalism and the Informational Fraction of the Transnational Capitalist Class." *Globalisation, Societies and Education* 11: 1–22.

Keane, John. 2003. *Global Civil Society*. Cambridge: Cambridge University Press.

Kellerhals, Jean. 2007. "Family Conflict." Pp. 1580–1583 in *The Blackwell Encyclopedia of Sociology*, edited by G. Ritzer. Malden, MA: Blackwell.

Kellezi, Blerina and Stephen Reicher. 2014. "The Double Insult: Explaining Gender Differences in the Psychological Consequences of War." *Peace & Conflict* 20(4): 491–504.

Kellner, Douglas and Tyson E. Lewis. 2007. "Cultural Critique." Pp. 896–898 in *The Blackwell Encyclopedia of Sociology*, edited by G. Ritzer. Malden, MA: Blackwell.

Kelly, Sean. 2004. "Are Teachers Tracked? On What Basis and with What Consequences?" *Social Psychology of Education* 7: 55–72.

Kempadoo, Kamala. 1996–1997. "'Sandoms' and Other Exotic Women: Prostitution and Race in the Caribbean." *Race and Reason* 1(3): 48–53.

Kennedy, Peter Ge. 2013. "Clinical Features, Diagnosis, and Treatment of Human African Trypanosomiasis (Sleeping Sickness)." *The Lancet Neurology* 12(2): 186–194.

Kern, Soeren. 2014. "The Islamization of Belgium and the Netherlands in 2013." Gatestone Institute, International Policy Council, January 13. Retrieved April 27, 2015 (http://www.gatestoneinstitute.org/4129/islamization-belgium-netherlands).

Kershaw, Sarah. 2008. "Starving Themselves, Cocktail in Hand." *New York Times*, March 2. Retrieved January 1, 2012 (http://www.nytimes.com/2008/03/02/fashion/02drunk.html).

Kershner, Isabel. 2015. "Netanyahu Urges 'Mass Immigration' of Jews from Europe." *New York Times*, April 15.

Kestnbaum, Meyer. 2012. "Organized Coercion and Political Authority: Armed Conflict in a World of States." Pp. 588–608 in *The Wiley-Blackwell Companion to Sociology*, edited by G. Ritzer. Malden, MA: Wiley-Blackwell.

Khan, Shamus Rahman. 2011. *Privilege: The Making of an Adolescent Elite at St. Paul's School*. Princeton, NJ: Princeton University Press.

Khanna, Nikki and Cherise A. Harris. 2015. "Discovering Race in a 'Post-racial' World: Teaching Race through Primetime Television." *Teaching Sociology* 43: 39–45.

Khatchadourian, Raffi. 2007. "Neptune's Navy." *New Yorker*, November 5.

Kiaye, Risper Enid and Anesh Maniraj Singh. 2013. "The Glass Ceiling: A Perspective of Women Working in Durban." *Gender in Management* 28: 28–42.

Kidder, Jeffrey L. 2012. "Parkour, the Affective Appropriation of Urban Space, and the Real/Virtual Dialectic." *City and Community* 11: 229–253.

Kienle, Eberhard. 2012. "Egypt without Mubarak, Tunisia after Bin Ali: Theory, History and the 'Arab Spring.'" *Economy and Society* 41: 532–557.

Kimmel, Michael S. 2012. *The Gendered Society*. 5th ed. New York: Oxford University Press.

King, Anthony. 2004. *The Structure of Social Theory*. London: Routledge.

King, Emily B. 2014. "It's a Boy, and It's Okay to Be Disappointed." *New York Times*, Motherlode blog, November 19. Retrieved April 19, 2015 (http://parenting.blogs.nytimes.com/2014/11/19/its-a-boy-and-its-okay-to-be-disappointed/?emc=edit_tnt_20141121&nlid=59159935&tntemail0=y&_r=2).

King, Martin Luther, Jr. [1958] 2010. *Stride toward Freedom: The Montgomery Story*. Boston: Beacon Press.

Kinney, William J. 2007. "Asch Experiments." Pp. 189–191 in *The Blackwell Encyclopedia of Sociology*, edited by G. Ritzer. Malden, MA: Blackwell.

Kirk, Roger E. 2007. "Experimental Design." Pp. 1533–1537 in *The Blackwell Encyclopedia of Sociology*, edited by G. Ritzer. Malden, MA: Blackwell.

Kivisto, Peter. 2012a. "Fundamentalism." Pp. 709–713 in *The Wiley-Blackwell Encyclopedia of Globalization*, edited by G. Ritzer. Malden, MA: Wiley-Blackwell.

Kivisto, Peter. 2012b. "Refugees." Pp. 1761–1765 in *The Wiley-Blackwell Encyclopedia of Globalization*, edited by G. Ritzer. Malden, MA: Wiley-Blackwell.

Kivisto, Peter and Paul R. Croll. 2012. *Race and Ethnicity: The Basics*. New York: Routledge.

Kivisto, Peter and Thomas Faist. 2007. *Citizenship: Discourse, Theory, and Transnational Prospects*. Malden, MA: Blackwell.

Kivisto, Peter and Thomas Faist. 2010. *Beyond a Border: The Causes and Consequences of Contemporary Immigration*. Thousand Oaks, CA: Pine Forge Press.

Klein, Alan. 1993. *Little Big Men: Bodybuilding Subculture and Gender Construction*. Albany: State University of New York Press.

Klein, Naomi. [2000] 2010. *No Logo: Taking Aim at the Brand Bullies*. Toronto: Vintage.

Kleinplatz, Peggy. 1992. "The Erotic Experience and the Intent to Arouse." *Canadian Journal of Sexuality* 1(3): 133–139.

Klinenberg, Eric. 2012. *Going Solo: The Extraordinary Rise and Surprising Appeal of Living Alone*. New York: Penguin.

Knorr Cetina, Karin. 2012. "Financial Markets." Pp. 653–664 in *The Encyclopedia of Globalization*, edited by G. Ritzer. Malden, MA: Wiley-Blackwell.

Knowlton, Brian. 2014. "Digital War Takes Shape on Websites over ISIS." *New York Times*, September 26.

Kohler, Kristopher. 2012. "World Social Forum." Pp. 2325–2327 in *The Wiley-Blackwell Encyclopedia of Globalization*, edited by G. Ritzer. Malden, MA: Wiley-Blackwell.

Kohrmann, M. 2008. "Smoking among Doctors: Governmentality, Embodiment, and the Diversion of Blame in Contemporary China." *Medical Anthropology* 27(1): 9–42.

Koistinen, David. 2013. *Confronting Decline: The Political Economy of Deindustrialization in Twentieth-Century New England*. Gainesville: University Press of Florida.

Koivusalo, Meri and Eeva Ollila. 2014. "Global Health Policies." Pp. 159–186 in *Understanding Global Social Policy*, edited by N. Yeates. Cambridge: Polity Press.

Kolata, Gina. 1999. *The Flu: The Story of the Great Influenza Pandemic of 1918 and the Search for the Virus That Caused It*. New York: Touchstone.

Köllen, Thomas. 2013. "Bisexuality and Diversity Management: Addressing the *B* in LGBT as a Relevant 'Sexual Orientation' in the Workplace." *Journal of Bisexuality* 13(1): 122–137.

Kollmeyer, Christopher. 2009. "Explaining Deindustrialization: How Affluence, Productivity Growth, and Globalization Diminish Manufacturing Employment." *American Journal of Sociology* 114: 1644–1674.

Kollmeyer, Christopher and Florian Pichler. 2013. "Is Deindustrialization Causing High Unemployment in Affluent Countries? Evidence from 16 OECD Countries, 1970–2003." *Social Forces* 91: 785–812.

Kong, Travis. 2010. *Chinese Male Homosexualities.* London: Routledge.

Korkki, Phyllis. 2012. "When the H.R. Office Leaves the Building." *New York Times,* December 12.

Kosic, Ankica, Arie W. Kruglanski, Antonio Pierro, and Lucia Mannetti. 2004. "The Social Cognition of Immigrants' Acculturation: Effects of the Need for Closure and the Reference Group at Entry." *Journal of Personality and Social Psychology* 86: 796–813.

Kotarba, Joseph A. 2007. "Socialization, Adult." Pp. 4563–4566 in *The Blackwell Encyclopedia of Sociology,* edited by G. Ritzer. Malden, MA: Blackwell.

Kotarba, Joseph A., Andrea Salvini, and Bryce Merrill, eds. 2012. *The Present and Future of Symbolic Interactionism: Proceedings of the International Symposium, Pisa 2010.* Pisa: Franco Angeli.

Kovacs, Zoltan and Gábor Hegedus. 2014. "Gated Communities as New Forms of Segregation in Post-socialist Budapest." *Cities* 36: 200–209.

Kowalski, Robin M., Susan P. Limber, and Patricia W. Agatston. 2012. *Cyberbullying: Bullying in the Digital Age.* 2nd ed. Malden, MA: Wiley-Blackwell.

Kozinets, Robert V. 2009. *Netnography: Doing Ethnographic Research Online.* Thousand Oaks, CA: Sage.

Krass, Frauke, ed. 2012. *Megacities: Our Global Urban Future.* New York: Springer.

Kraus, Michael W., Shai Davidai, and A. David Nussbaum. 2015. "American Dream? Or Mirage?" *New York Times,* May 3.

Krauss, Clifford. 2004. "Internet Drug Exporters Feel Pressure in Canada." *New York Times,* December 11. Retrieved March 30, 2012 (http://query.nytimes.com/gst/fullpage.html?res=9F04EED8 1131F932A25751C1A9629C8B63&&scp=4& sq=pharmaceutical%20purchase%20over%20 internet&st=cse).

Krinsky, Charles, ed. 2013. *The Ashgate Research Companion to Moral Panics.* Burlington, VT: Ashgate.

Kritz, Mary M. 2007. "Migration, International." Pp. 3019–3025 in *The Blackwell Encyclopedia of Sociology,* edited by G. Ritzer. Malden, MA: Blackwell.

Kritz, Mary M. 2008. "International Migration." In *The Blackwell Encyclopedia of Sociology Online,* edited by G. Ritzer. Malden, MA: Blackwell.

Kritz, Mary M., Lin Lean Lim, and Hania Zlotnik, eds. 1992. *International Migration Systems: A Global Approach.* Oxford: Oxford University Press.

Kroeger, Rhiannon A. and Pamela J. Smock. 2014. "Cohabitation." In *The Wiley-Blackwell Companion to Sociology of Families,* edited by J. Treas, J. Scott, and M. Richards. Malden, MA: Wiley-Blackwell.

Kroneberg, Clemens and Frank Kalter. 2012. "Rational Choice Theory and Empirical Research: Methodological and Theoretical Contributions in Europe." *Annual Review of Sociology* 38: 73–92.

Kuisel, Richard. 1993. *Seducing the French: The Dilemma of Americanization.* Berkeley: University of California Press.

Kulish, Nicholas. 2007. "Europe Fears That Meth Foothold Is Expanding." *New York Times,* November 23.

Kunzman, Robert and Milton Gaither. 2013. "Homeschooling: A Comprehensive Survey of the Research." *Other Education* 2: 4–59.

Kupfer, Antonia. 2012. "A Theoretical Concept of Educational Upward Mobility." *International Studies in Sociology of Education* 22: 57–72.

Kurtz, Annalyn. 2014. "Americans Still Hesitant to Spend More." *CNN Money,* June 26. Retrieved April 22, 2015 (http://money.cnn.com/2014/06/26/news/economy/americans-not-spend).

Kurtz, Lester R. 2012. *Gods in the Global Village.* Thousand Oaks, CA: Sage.

Kurzban. 2006. "Post-Sept. 11, 2001." Pp. xxi–xxiii in *Immigration Law Sourcebook.* 10th ed. Washington, DC: American Immigration Law Foundation.

Kushkush, Isma'il. 2015. "President of Sudan Is Re-elected with 94 Percent of Vote." *New York Times,* April 27.

Kwan, Samantha and Mary Nell Trautner. 2011. "Judging Books by Their Covers: Teaching about Physical Attractiveness Biases." *Teaching Sociology* 39: 16–26.

Lacey, Marc. 2011. "Rift in Arizona as Latino Class Is Found Illegal." *New York Times,* January 7. Retrieved March 30, 2012 (http://www.nytimes.com/2011/01/08/us/08ethnic.html).

Lachance-Grzela, Mylene and Genevieve Bouchard. 2010. "Why Do Women Do the Lion's Share of Housework? A Decade of Research." *Sex Roles* 63(11–12): 767–780.

Lahelma, Eero. 2007. "Health and Social Class." Pp. 2086–2091 in *The Blackwell Encyclopedia of Sociology,* edited by G. Ritzer. Malden, MA: Blackwell.

Lahelma, Eero. Forthcoming. "Health and Social Class." In *The Wiley-Blackwell Encyclopedia of Sociology,* 2nd ed., edited by G. Ritzer. Malden, MA: Wiley-Blackwell.

Lakoff, Andrew. 2008. "Diagnostic Liquidity: Mental Illness and the Global Trade in DNA." Pp. 277–300 in *The Anthropology of Globalization: A Reader,* 2nd ed., edited by J. X. Inda and R. Rosaldo. Malden, MA: Blackwell.

Lammers, Cornelis J. and David J. Hickson, eds. 2013. *Organizations Alike and Unlike.* New York: Routledge.

Landler, Mark. 2008. "Credit Cards Tighten Grip Outside US." *New York Times,* August 30.

Landstedt, Evelina and Katja Gillander Gådin. 2012. "Seventeen and Stressed: Do Gender and Class Matter?" *Health Sociology Review* 21: 82–98.

Lane, Harlan. 1975. *The Wild Boy of Aveyron.* Cambridge, MA: Harvard University Press.

Lara-Millán, Armando. 2014. "Public Emergency Room Overcrowding in the Era of Mass Imprisonment." *American Sociological Review* 79: 866–887.

Larsen, Gretchen, Maurice Patterson, and Lucy Markham. 2014. "A Deviant Art: Tattoo-Related Stigma in an Era of Commodification." *Psychology & Marketing* 31: 670–681.

Lash, Scott and Celia Lury. 2007. *Global Culture Industry.* Cambridge: Polity Press.

Lasn, Kalle. 2000. *Culture Jam: How to Reverse America's Suicidal Consumer Binge—and Why We Must.* New York: Quill.

Lasswell, Harold D. 2012. *Politics: Who Gets What, When, How.* Whitefish, MT: Literary Licensing.

Lauderdale, Pat. 2007. "Deviance, Moral Boundaries and." Pp. 1114–1116 in *The Blackwell Encyclopedia of Sociology,* edited by G. Ritzer. Malden, MA: Blackwell.

Lauer, Sean and Carrie Yodanis. 2010. "The Deinstitutionalization of Marriage Revisited: A New Institutional Approach to Marriage." *Journal of Family Theory and Review* 2: 58–72.

Lauer, Sean and Carrie Yodanis. 2011. "Individualized Marriage and the Integration of Resources." *Journal of Marriage and Family* 73: 669–683.

Laumann, Anne E. and Amy J. Derick. 2006. "Tattoos and Body Piercings in the United States: A National Data Set." *Journal of the American Academy of Dermatology* 55: 413–421.

Laurie, Nina, Claire Dwyer, Sarah Holloway, and Fiona Smith. 1999. *Geographies of New Femininities.* London: Longman.

LaViollete, Alyce D. and Ola W. Barnett. 2014. *Why Battered Women Stay: It Could Happen to Anyone.* Thousand Oaks, CA: Sage.

Lavorgna, Anita. 2015. "The Online Trade in Counterfeit Pharmaceuticals: New Criminal Opportunities, Trends and Challenges." *European Journal of Criminology* 12(2): 226–241.

Law, Ian. 2007. "Discrimination." Pp. 1182–1184 in *The Blackwell Encyclopedia of Sociology,* edited by G. Ritzer. Malden, MA: Blackwell.

Law, Ian. 2012a. "Race." Pp. 1737–1743 in *The Wiley-Blackwell Encyclopedia of Globalization,* edited by G. Ritzer. Malden, MA: Wiley-Blackwell.

Law, Ian. 2012b. "Racism." Pp. 1743–1746 in *The Wiley-Blackwell Encyclopedia of Globalization,* edited by G. Ritzer. Malden, MA: Wiley-Blackwell.

Layte, Richard and Christopher T. Whelan. 2009. "Explaining Social Class Inequalities in Smoking: The Role of Education, Self-Efficacy, and Deprivation." *European Sociological Review* 25: 399–410.

Lechner, Frank J. 1993. "Global Fundamentalism." In *A Future for Religion?,* edited by W. H. Swatos. Thousand Oaks, CA: Sage.

Lechner, Frank J. and John Boli. 2005. *World Culture: Origins and Consequences.* Oxford: Blackwell.

Lee, Jaekyung. 2012. "Educational Equity and Adequacy for Disadvantaged Minority Students: School and Teacher Resource Gaps toward National Mathematics Proficiency Standard." *Journal of Educational Research* 105: 64–75.

Lee, Julie. 2012. "The Relationship between Appearance-Related Stress and Internalizing Problems in South Korean Adolescent Girls." *Women's Studies International Journal* 40: 903–918.

Lee, Ronald D. 2007. *Global Population Aging and Its Economic Consequences.* Washington, DC: American Enterprise Institute Press.

Lee, Susan Hagood. 2012. "Sex Trafficking." In *The Wiley-Blackwell Encyclopedia of Globalization,* edited by G. Ritzer. Malden, MA: Wiley-Blackwell.

Lees, Loretta, Tom Slater, and Elvin Wyly, eds. 2010. *The Gentrification Reader.* New York: Routledge.

Legerski, Elizabeth Miklya. 2012. "The Cost of Instability: The Effects of Family, Work, and Welfare Change on Low-Income Women's Health Insurance Status." *Sociological Forum* 27: 641–657.

Leicht, Kevin and Scott Fitzgerald. 2006. *Postindustrial Peasants: The Illusion of Middle-Class Prosperity.* New York: Worth.

Leidner, Robin. 1993. *Fast Food, Fast Talk.* Berkeley: University of California Press.

Lemert, Charles and Anthony Elliott. 2006. *Deadly Worlds: The Emotional Costs of Globalization.* Lanham, MD: Rowman & Littlefield.

Lemert, Edwin. [1951] 2012. *Social Pathology: A Systematic Approach to the Theory of Sociopathic Behavior.* Whitefish, MT: Literary Licensing.

Lengermann, Patricia Madoo and Gillian Niebrugge-Brantley. 2014. "Feminist Theory." Pp. 440–485 in *Sociological Theory,* 9th ed., edited by G. Ritzer and J. Stepnisky. New York: McGraw-Hill.

Lessenich, Stephan. Forthcoming. "Welfare Regimes." In *The Wiley-Blackwell Encyclopedia of Sociology,* 2nd ed., edited by G. Ritzer. Malden, MA: Wiley-Blackwell.

Lesthaeghe, Ron J. 2007. "Second Demographic." Pp. 4123–4127 in *The Blackwell Encyclopedia of Sociology,* edited by G. Ritzer. Malden, MA: Blackwell.

Lesthaeghe, Ron J. 2010. "The Unfolding Story of the Second Demographic Transition." *Population and Development Review* 36: 211–251.

Lesthaeghe, Ron J. and D. J. van de Kaa. 1986. "Twee Demografische Transities?" Pp. 9–24 in *Bevolking: Groei en Krimp, Mens en Maatschappij* (book supplement), edited by R. Lesthaeghe and D. J. van de Kaa. Deventer, Netherlands: Van Loghum, Slaterus.

Leventoğlu, Bahar. 2014. "Social Mobility, Middle Class, and Political Transitions." *Journal of Conflict Resolution* 58: 825–864.

Levin, Jack. 2007. "Hate Crimes." Pp. 2048–2050 in *The Blackwell Encyclopedia of Sociology,* edited by G. Ritzer. Malden, MA: Blackwell.

Levy, Frank. 1999. *The New Dollars and Dreams: American Incomes and Economic Change.* New York: Russell Sage Foundation.

Levy, Steven. 2010. *Hackers: Heroes of the Computer Revolution.* 25th anniversary ed. Sebastopol, CA: O'Reilly Media.

Lewin, Tamar. 2008a. "Oil Money Cultivates a Mideast Ivy League." *New York Times,* February 11.

Lewin, Tamar. 2008b. "Universities Rush to Set Up Outposts Abroad." *New York Times,* February 10.

Lewin, Tamar. 2008c. "U.S. Universities Join Saudis in Partnerships." *New York Times,* March 6.

Lewin, Tamar. 2010. "Children Awake? Then They're Probably Online." *New York Times,* January 20.

Lewin, Tamar. 2012. "College of Future Could Be Come One, Come All." *New York Times,* November 19.

Lewin, Tamar. 2013. "Students Rush to Web Classes, but Profits May Be Much Later." *New York Times,* January 7.

Lewin, Tamar. 2014. "After Setbacks, Online Courses Are Rethought." *New York Times,* December 10.

Lewis, Melissa A., Hollie Granato, Jessica A. Blayney, Ty W. Lostutter, and Jason R. Kilmer. 2012. "Predictors of Hooking Up Sexual Behaviors and Emotional Reactions among U.S. College Students." *Archives of Sexual Behavior* 41(5): 1219–1229.

Lewis, Nathaniel. 2014. "Moving 'Out,' Moving On: Gay Men's Migrations through the Life Course." *Annals of the Association of American Geographers* 104(2): 225–233.

Liaw, Karen Ron-Li and Aron Janssen. 2014. "Not by Convention: Working with People on the Sexual and Gender Continuum." Pp. 89–117 in *Massachusetts General Hospital Textbook on Diversity and Cultural Sensitivity in Mental Health,* edited by R. Parekh. New York: Springer.

Liberman, Akiva M., David S. Kirk, and Kideuk Kim. 2014. "Labeling Effects of First Juvenile Arrest: Secondary Deviance and Secondary Sanctioning." *Criminology* 52: 345–370.

Lichtblau, Eric. 2011. "With Lobbying Blitz, Profit-Making Colleges Diluted New Rules." *New York Times,* December 10.

Lichter, Daniel T. 2007. "Family Structure and Poverty." Pp. 1463–1465 in *The Blackwell Encyclopedia of Sociology,* edited by G. Ritzer. Malden, MA: Blackwell.

Lichter, Daniel T. 2013. "Integration or Fragmentation: Racial Diversity and the American Future." *Demography* 50: 359–391.

Liebling-Kalifani, Helen, Ruth Ojiambo-Ochieng, Angela Marshall, Juliet Were-Oguttu, Seggane Musisi, and Eugene Kinyanda. 2013. "Violence against Women in Northern Uganda: The Neglected Health Consequences of War." *Journal of International Women's Studies* 9(3): 174–192.

Liebow, Elliot. 1967. *Tally's Corner: A Study of Negro Streetcorner Men.* New York: Little, Brown.

Lin, Nan. 1999. "Social Networks and Status Attainment." *Annual Review of Sociology* 25: 467–487.

Lin, Nan and Yanjie Bian. 1991. "Getting Ahead in Urban China." *American Journal of Sociology* 97: 657–688.

Lin, Nan, Walter M. Ensel, and John C. Vaughn. 1981. "Social Resources and Strength of Ties: Structural Factors in Occupational Status Attainment." *American Sociological Review* 46: 393–403.

Lind, Amy. 2007. "Femininities/Masculinities." Pp. 1662–1666 in *The Blackwell Encyclopedia of Sociology,* edited by G. Ritzer. Malden, MA: Blackwell.

Linn, James G. and Debra Rose Wilson. 2012. "Health." Pp. 910–923 in *The Wiley-Blackwell Encyclopedia of Globalization,* edited by G. Ritzer. Malden, MA: Wiley-Blackwell.

Lipovetsky, Gilles. [1987] 2002. *The Empire of Fashion: Dressing Modern Democracy.* Princeton, NJ: Princeton University Press.

Lipovetsky, Gilles. 2005. *Hypermodern Times.* Cambridge: Polity Press.

Lipset, Seymour M. 1981. *Political Man.* Expanded ed. Baltimore: Johns Hopkins University Press.

Liss, Miriam. 2014. "Inequality in the Division of Household Labor and Childcare." Pp. 23–40 in *Women, Work, and Family: How Companies Thrive with a 21st-Century Multicultural Workforce,* edited by M. A. Paludi. Santa Barbara, CA: ABC-CLIO.

Little, Craig B. 2007. "Deviance, Absolutist Definitions of." Pp. 1082–1084 in *The Blackwell Encyclopedia of Sociology,* edited by G. Ritzer. Malden, MA: Blackwell.

Liu, Yu Cheng. 2012. "Ethnomethodology Reconsidered: The Practical Logic of Social Systems Theory." *Current Sociology* 60: 581–598.

Livingston, Gretchen. 2013. "Among 38 nations, U.S. Is the Outlier When It Comes to Paid Parental Leave." Pew Research Center, Fact Tank, December 12. Retrieved May 10, 2015 (http://www.pewresearch.org/fact-tank/2013/12/12/among-38-nations-u-s-is-the-holdout-when-it-comes-to-offering-paid-parental-leave).

Lloréns, Hilda. 2013. "Latina Bodies in the Era of Elective Aesthetic Surgery." *Latino Studies* 11(4): 547–569.

Logan, John, Richard Alba, and Wenquan Zhang. 2002. "Immigrant Enclaves and Ethnic Communities in New York and Los Angeles." *American Sociological Review* 67(2): 299–322.

Logan, John R., Elisabeta Minca, and Sinem Adar. 2012. "The Geography of Inequality: Why Separate Means Unequal in American Public Schools." *Sociology of Education* 85(3): 287–301.

Lois, Jennifer. 2013. *Home Is Where the School Is: The Logic of Homeschooling and the Emotional Labor of Mothering.* New York: New York University Press.

Lopez, Steven H., Randy Hodson, and Vincent J. Roscigno. 2009. "Power, Status, and Abuse at Work: General and Sexual Harassment Compared." *Sociological Quarterly* 50: 3–27.

Lorber, Judith. 1967. "Deviance as Performance: The Case of Illness." *Social Problems* 14: 302–310.

Lorber, Judith. 2000. "Using Gender to Undo Gender: A Feminist Degendering Movement." *Feminist Theory* 1(1): 79–95.

Lorber, Judith and Lisa Jean Moore. 2002. *Gender and the Social Construction of Illness.* 2nd ed. Walnut Creek, CA: AltaMira Press.

"Louisiana Oil Rig Explosion: Underwater Machines Attempt to Plug Leak." 2010. *Telegraph,* April 26. Retrieved March 31, 2015 (http://www.telegraph.co.uk/finance/newsbysector/energy/oilandgas/7633286/Louisiana-oil-rig-explosion-Underwater-machines-attempt-to-plug-leak.html).

Love, Brad, Charee M. Thompson, and Jessica Knapp. 2014. "The Need to Be Superman: The Psychosocial Support Challenges of Young Men Affected by Cancer." *Oncology Nursing Forum* 41(1): E21–E27.

Lovell, David W. 2007. "Communism." Pp. 612–617 in *The Blackwell Encyclopedia of Sociology,* edited by G. Ritzer. Malden, MA: Blackwell.

Low, Setha. 2003. *Behind the Gates: Life, Security, and the Pursuit of Happiness in Fortress America.* New York: Routledge.

Lowe, Brian. 2002. "Hearts and Minds and Morality: Analyzing Moral Vocabularies in Qualitative Studies." *Qualitative Sociology* 25(1): 105–112.

Lowrey, Annie. 2014. "Even among the Richest of the Rich, Fortunes Diverge." *New York Times,* February 10.

Loyal, Steve. 2007. "Refugees." Pp. 3837–3838 in *The Blackwell Encyclopedia of Sociology,* edited by G. Ritzer. Malden, MA: Blackwell.

Lubbers, Marcel, Eva Jaspers, and Wout Ultee. 2009. "Primary and Secondary Socialization

Impacts on Support for Same-Sex Marriage after Legalization in the Netherlands." *Journal of Family Issues* 30: 1714–1745.

Lubienski, Christopher. 2006. "School Sector and Academic Achievement: A Multilevel Analysis of NAEP Mathematics Data." *American Educational Research Journal* 43: 651–698.

Lucas, Jeffrey W., Corina Graif, and Michael J. Lovaglia. 2008. "Prosecutorial Misconduct in Serious Cases: Theory and Design of a Laboratory Experiment: Can You Study a Legal System in a Laboratory?" Pp. 119–136 in *Experiments in Criminology and Law: A Research Revolution*, edited by C. Horne and M. J. Lovaglia. Lanham, MD: Rowman & Littlefield.

Lui, Li. 2014. "A Comparative Study of Intergenerational Mobility." *Russian Social Science Review* 55(4): 4–15.

Luker, Kristin. 1984. *Abortion and the Politics of Motherhood*. Berkeley: University of California Press.

Lunneborg, Clifford E. 2007. "Convenience Sample." Pp. 788–790 in *The Blackwell Encyclopedia of Sociology*, edited by G. Ritzer. Malden, MA: Blackwell.

Luo, Wei. 2013. "Aching for the Altered Body: Beauty Economy and Chinese Women's Consumption of Cosmetic Surgery." *Women's Studies International Forum* 38: 1–10.

Lupton, Deborah. 2007. "Health Risk Behavior." Pp. 2083–2085 in *The Blackwell Encyclopedia of Sociology*, edited by G. Ritzer. Malden, MA: Blackwell.

Lutfey, K. and J. Mortimer. 2006. "Development and Socialization through the Adult Life Course." In *Handbook of Social Psychology*, edited by J. DeLamater. New York: Kluwer Academic/Plenum.

Lyall, Sarah. 2013. "A Slice of London So Exclusive Even the Owners Are Visitors." *New York Times*, April 1.

Lydaki, Anna. 2012. "Gypsies." In *The Wiley-Blackwell Encyclopedia of Sociology Online*, edited by G. Ritzer. Malden, MA: Wiley-Blackwell.

Lyman, Rick. 2015. "Bulgaria Puts Up a New Wall, but This One Keeps People Out." *New York Times*, April 5.

Lynch, Marc. 2013. *The Arab Uprising: The Unfinished Revolutions of the New Middle East*. New York: PublicAffairs.

Lynch, Marc, Deen Freelon, and Sean Aday. 2014. "Syria in the Arab Spring: The Integration of Syria's Conflict with the Arab Uprisings, 2011–2013." *Research & Politics* 1(3), published online. doi: 10.1177/2053168014549091.

Macdonald, Neil. 2010. "The Tea Party's Freak Show." CBC News, September 27. Retrieved March 31, 2012 (http://www.cbc.ca/news/world/story/2010/09/24/f-rfa-macdonald.html).

Machida, Satoshi. 2012. "Does Globalization Render People More Ethnocentric? Globalization and People's Views on Cultures." *American Journal of Economics and Sociology* 71: 436–469.

Mackay, Richard. 2014. *The Atlas of Endangered Species*. New York: Routledge.

Maclean, Mairi, Charles Harvey, and Robert Chia. 2010. "Dominant Corporate Agents and the Power Elite in France and Britain." *Organization Studies* 31: 327–348.

Madan, T. N. 2007. "Hinduism." Pp. 571–573 in *Encyclopedia of Globalization*, edited by J. A. Scholte and R. Robertson. New York: MTM.

Madhok, Diksha. 2014. "For All Those Jibes about Shopping, Indian Men Buy More Clothes than Women." Quartz, September 4. Retrieved April 20, 2015 (http://qz.com/259305/for-all-those-jibes-about-shopping-indian-men-buy-more-clothes-than-women).

Maginn, Paul J. and Christine Steinmetz. 2015. "Spatial and Regulatory Contours of the (Sub) Urban Sexscape." Pp. 1–17 in *(Sub)Urban Sexscapes: Geographies and Regulation of the Sex Industry*, edited by P. J. Maginn and C. Steinmetz. London: Routledge.

Maguire, Mike, Rob Morgan, and Robert Reiner, eds. 2012. *The Oxford Handbook of Criminology*. 5th ed. New York: Oxford University Press.

Mahoney, James and Dietrich Rueschemeyer. 2003. *Comparative Historical Analysis in the Social Sciences*. Cambridge: Cambridge University Press.

Maiba, Herman. 2005. "Grassroots Transnational Social Movement Activism: The Case of People's Global Action." *Sociological Focus* 38(1): 41–63.

Maines, Rachel. 2001. *The Technology of Orgasm: "Hysteria," the Vibrator, and Women's Sexual Satisfaction*. Baltimore: Johns Hopkins University Press.

Mak, Athena H. N., Margaret Lumbers, and Anita Eves. 2012. "Globalisation and Food Consumption in Tourism." *Annals of Tourism Research* 39: 171–196.

Malesevic, Sinisa. 2010. *The Sociology of War and Violence*. Cambridge: Cambridge University Press.

Mandery, Evan. 2014. "End College Legacy Preferences." *New York Times*, April 24.

Manika, Danae, Jennifer G. Ball, and Patricia A. Stout. 2014. "Factors Associated with the Persuasiveness of Direct-to-Consumer Advertising on HPV Vaccination among Young Women." *Journal of Health Communication* 19: 1232–1247.

Mannheim, Karl. [1931] 1936. *Ideology and Utopia*. New York: Harcourt, Brace, and World.

Manning, Jimmie. 2015. "Communicating Sexual Identities: A Typology of Coming Out." *Sexuality & Culture* 19(1): 122–138.

Manning, Peter. 2005. "Impression Management." Pp. 397–399 in *The Encyclopedia of Social Theory*, edited by G. Ritzer. Thousand Oaks, CA: Sage.

Manning, Peter. 2007. "Dramaturgy." Pp. 1226–1229 in *The Blackwell Encyclopedia of Sociology*, edited by G. Ritzer. Malden, MA: Blackwell.

Manning, Robert D. 2001. *Credit Card Nation: The Consequences of America's Addiction to Debt*. New York: Basic Books.

Manning, Wendy D. 2013. "Trends in Cohabitation: Over Twenty Years of Change, 1987–2010." In *National Family Profiles*. Bowling Green, OH: National Center for Family and Marriage Research.

Manning, Wendy D. and Jessica A. Cohen. 2012. "Premarital Cohabitation and Marital Dissolution: An Examination of Recent Marriages." *Journal of Marriage and Family* 74: 377–387.

Manning, Wendy D., Peggy Giordano, and Monica Longmore. 2006. "Hooking Up: The Relationship Contexts of 'Non-relationship' Sex." *Journal of Adolescent Research* 21: 459–483.

Ma'oz, Moshe. 2014. "The Arab Spring in Syria: Domestic and Regional Developments." *Dynamics of Asymmetric Conflict* 7(1): 49–57.

Margono, Belinda Arunarwati, Peter V. Potapov, Svetlana Turubanova, Fred Stolle, and Matthew C. Hansen. 2014. "Primary Forest Cover Loss in Indonesia over 2000–2012." *Nature Climate Change* 4: 730–735.

Marmor, Michael. 2005. *The Status Syndrome: How Social Standing Affects Our Health and Longevity*. New York: Holt.

Maroto, Michelle Lee. 2011. "Professionalizing Body Art: A Marginalized Occupational Group's Use of Informal and Formal Strategies of Control." *Work and Occupations* 38: 101–138.

Marre, Diana and Laura Briggs. 2009. *International Adoption: Global Inequalities and the Circulation of Children*. New York: New York University Press.

Marron, Donncha. 2009. *Consumer Credit in the United States: A Sociological Perspective from the 19th Century to the Present*. New York: Palgrave Macmillan.

Marsden, Peter V. and Elizabeth H. Gorman. 2001. "Social Networks, Job Changes, and Recruitment." Pp. 467–502 in *Sourcebook on Labor Markets: Evolving Structures and Processes*, edited by I. Berg and A. L. Kalleberg. New York: Kluwer Academic/Plenum.

Marsh, Robert M. 2012. "Musical Taste and Social Structure in Taiwan." *Comparative Sociology* 11: 493–525.

Marshall, Catherine and Gretchen Rossman. 2010. *Designing Qualitative Research*. Thousand Oaks, CA: Sage.

Martin, Andrew. 2008. "Mideast Facing Difficult Choice, Crops or Water." *New York Times*, July 21.

Martin, Karin A. 2005. "William Wants a Doll. Can He Have One? Feminists, Child Care Advisors, and Gender-Neutral Child Rearing." *Gender & Society* 19: 456–479.

Martin-Uzzi, Michelle and Denise Duval-Tsioles. 2013. "The Experience of Remarried Couples in Blended Families." *Journal of Divorce and Remarriage* 54: 43–57.

Marx, Karl. [1857–1858] 1964. *Pre-capitalist Economic Formations*. New York: International Publishers.

Marx, Karl and Friedrich Engels. 1848. *The Communist Manifesto*. London: Communist League.

Massaro, Vanessa A. and Emma Gaalaas Mullaney. 2011. "The War on Teenage Terrorists: Philly's 'Flash Mob Riots' and the Banality of Post-9/11 Securitization." *City* 15: 591–604.

Massey, Douglas. 2003. *Beyond Smoke and Mirrors: Mexican Immigration in an Era of Economic Integration*. New York: Russell Sage Foundation.

Massey, Douglas. 2008. *Categorically Unequal: The American Stratification System*. New York: Russell Sage Foundation.

Mather, Mark. 2009. *Reports on America: Children in Immigrant Families Chart New Path*. Washington, DC: Population Reference Bureau.

Mathews, Russell A., Doan E. Winkel, and Julie Holiday Wayne. 2014. "A Longitudinal Examination of Role Overload and Work-Family Conflict: The Mediating Role of Interdomain Transfers." *Journal of Organizational Behavior* 35: 72–91.

Matza, David. 1966. "The Disreputable Poor." Pp. 289–302 in *Class, Status, and Power: Social*

Stratification in Comparative Perspective, 2nd rev. ed., edited by R. Bendix and S. M. Lipset. New York: Free Press.

Mawathe, Anne. 2010. "Haunted by Congo Rape Dilemma." BBC News, May 15. Retrieved January 29, 2012 (http://news.bbc.co.uk/2/hi/africa/8677637.stm).

McAdams, Dan P., Michelle Albaugh, Emily Farber, Jennifer Daniels, Regina L. Logan, and Brad Olson. 2008. "Family Metaphors and Moral Intuitions: How Conservatives and Liberals Narrate Their Lives." *Journal of Personality and Social Psychology* 95: 978–990.

McCann, Eugene and Kevin Ward, eds. 2011. *Mobile Urbanism: Cities and Policymaking in the Global Age*. Minneapolis: University of Minnesota Press.

McCarthy, Justin. 2014. "Same-Sex Marriage Support Reaches New High at 55%." Gallup, May 21. Retrieved April 28, 2015 (http://www.gallup.com/poll/169640/sex-marriage-support-reaches-new-high.aspx).

McClelland, Robert, Shannon Mok, and Kevin Pierce. 2014. "Labor Force Participation Elasticities of Women and Secondary Earners within Married Couples." Working Paper 2014-06, Congressional Budget Office, September. Retrieved April 20, 2015 (https://www.cbo.gov/sites/default/files/cbofiles/attachments/49433-LaborForce.pdf).

McCombs, Brady. 2013. "LDS Church Membership Hits 15 Million as Mormon Women Question Gender Inequality." Huffington Post, October 5. Retrieved April 20, 2015 (http://www.huffingtonpost.com/2013/10/05/lds-membership-numbers_n_4051539.html).

McDonald, Michael. 2013. "2012 General Election Turnout Rates." U.S. Elections Project, July 22. Retrieved September 16, 2013 (http://elections.gmu.edu/Turnout_2012g.html).

McGuffey, Shawn. 2008. "'Saving Masculinity': Gender Reaffirmation, Sexuality, Race, and Parental Responses to Male Child Sexual Abuse." *Social Problems* 55(2): 216–237.

McHale, Susan, Ann C. Crouter, and Shawn D. Whiteman. 2003. "The Family Contexts of Gender Development in Childhood and Adolescence Social Development." *Social Development* 12: 125–148.

McIntosh, Peggy. 2010. "White Privilege: Unpacking the Invisible Knapsack." Pp. 172–177 in *Race, Class and Gender in the United States*, 8th ed., edited by P. S. Rothenberg. New York: Worth.

McKinley, James C., Jr. 2010. "Fleeing Drug Violence, Mexicans Pour into U.S." *New York Times*, April 17.

McLanahan, Sara S. 1999. "Father Absence and the Welfare of Children." In *Coping with Divorce, Single Parenting, and Remarriage: A Risk and Resiliency Perspective*, edited by E. M. Hetherington. Mahwah, NJ: Lawrence Erlbaum.

McLanahan, Sara S. and Erin L. Kelly. 1999. "The Feminization of Poverty: Past and Future." Pp. 127–145 in *Handbook of the Sociology of Gender*, edited by J. S. Chafetz. New York: Kluwer Academic/Plenum.

McLaughlin, Janice, and Edmund Coleman-Fountain. 2014. "The Unfinished Body: The Medical and Social Reshaping of Disabled Young Bodies." *Social Science & Medicine* 120: 76–84.

McMichael, Anthony J. 2013. "Globalization, Climate Change, and Human Health." *New England Journal of Medicine* 368: 1335–1343.

McMichael, Philip. 2011. *Development and Social Change: A Global Perspective*. 5th ed. Thousand Oaks, CA: Sage.

McNair, Brian. 2002. *Striptease Culture: Sex, Media and the Democratization of Desire*. London: Routledge.

McNeil, Donald G., Jr. 2009. "New Web Site Seeks to Fight Myths about Circumcision and H.I.V." *New York Times*, March 3.

McPhail, Clark. 2007. "Crowd Behavior." Pp. 880–883 in *The Blackwell Encyclopedia of Sociology*, edited by G. Ritzer. Malden, MA: Blackwell.

McShane, Marilyn D. and Frank P. Williams. 2007. "Beccaria, Cesare (1738–94)." Pp. 255–256 in *The Blackwell Encyclopedia of Sociology*, Vol. 1, edited by G. Ritzer. Malden, MA: Blackwell.

Mead, George Herbert. [1934] 1962. *Mind, Self, and Society: From the Standpoint of a Social Behaviorist*. Chicago: University of Chicago Press.

Medina, Jennifer. 2012. "Mexicali Tour, from Tummy Tuck to Root Canal." *New York Times*, June 27. Retrieved November 5, 2013 (http://www.nytimes.com/2012/06/28/health/mexicali-lures-american-tourists-with-medical-care.html?pagewanted%253Dall&_r=0).

Meier, Barry. 2013. "More Emergency Visits Linked to Energy Drinks." *New York Times*, January 11.

Meister, Sandra. 2012. *Brand Communities for Fast-Moving Consumer Goods*. Wiesbaden, Germany: Gabler.

Melde, Chris, Terrance J. Taylor, and Finn Aage Esbensen. 2009. "'I Got Your Back': An Examination of the Protective Function of Gang Membership in Adolescence." *Criminology* 47(2): 565–594.

Melnick, Merrill L. and Daniel L. Wann. 2011. "An Examination of Sport Fandom in Australia: Socialization, Team Identification, and Fan Behavior." *International Review for the Sociology of Sport* 46: 456–470.

Merluzzi, Thomas V., Errol J. Philip, Zhiyong Zhang, and Courtney Sullivan. 2014. "Perceived Discrimination, Coping, and Quality of Life for African-American and Caucasian Persons with Cancer." *Cultural Diversity and Ethnic Minority Psychology*, published online August 4. doi: 10.1037/a0037543.

Merton, Robert K. [1949] 1968. *Social Theory and Social Structure*. 3rd ed. New York: Free Press.

Merton, Robert K. 1957. *Social Theory and Social Structure*. Rev. ed. Glencoe, IL: Free Press.

Merton, Robert and Alice S. Kitt. 1950. "Contributions to the Theory of Reference Group Behavior." In *Continuities in Social Research*, edited by R. K. Merton and P. F. Lazarsfeld. Glencoe, IL: Free Press.

Messinger, Adam M. 2014. "Marking 35 Years of Research on Same-Sex Intimate Partner Violence: Lessons and New Directions." Pp. 65–85 in *Handbook of LGBT Communities, Crime, and Justice*, edited by D. Peterson and V. R. Panfil. New York: Springer.

Mészáros, István. 2006. *Marx's Theory of Alienation*. 5th ed. London: Merlin Press.

Mettler, Suzanne. 2014. *Degrees of Inequality: How the Politics of Education Sabotaged the American Dream*. New York: Basic Books.

Meyer, Hans-Dieter and Aaron Benavot, eds. 2013. *PISA, Power and Policy: The Emergence of Global Educational Governance*. Oxford: Symposium Books.

Meyer, John, J. Boli, and F. Ramirez. 1997. "World Society and the Nation State." *American Journal of Sociology* 103: 144–181.

Michels, Robert. [1915] 1962. *Political Parties*. New York: Collier Books.

Miles, Andrew, Mike Savage, and Felix Bühlmann. 2011. "Telling a Modest Story: Accounts of Men's Upward Mobility from the National Child Development Study." *British Journal of Sociology* 62: 418–441.

Milgram, Stanley. 1974. *Obedience to Authority: An Experimental View*. New York: Harper & Row.

Milkie, Melissa A. 1999. "Social Comparisons, Reflected Appraisals, and Mass Media: The Impact of Pervasive Beauty Images on Black and White Girls' Self-Concepts." *Social Psychology Quarterly* 62: 190–210.

Miller, Amanda and Sharon Sassler. 2010. "Stability and Change in the Division of Labor among Cohabiting Couples." *Sociological Forum* 25(4): 677–702.

Miller, Daniel. 1998. *A Theory of Shopping*. Ithaca, NY: Cornell University Press.

Miller, Daniel and Donald Slater. 2000. *The Internet: An Ethnographic Approach*. London: Berg.

Miller, Robert. 2001. "The Industrial Context of Occupational Mobility: Change in Structure." *Research in Social Stratification and Mobility* 18: 313–353.

Mills, C. Wright. 1951. *White Collar*. New York: Oxford University Press.

Mills, C. Wright. 1956. *The Power Elite*. New York: Oxford University Press.

Mills, C. Wright. 1959. *The Sociological Imagination*. New York: Oxford University Press.

Mishel, Lawrence and Josh Bivens. 2011. "Occupy Wall Streeters Are Right about Skewed Economic Rewards in the United States." Briefing Paper 331. Economic Policy Institute, October 26. Retrieved March 31, 2012 (http://www.epi.org/files/2011/BriefingPaper331.pdf).

Misra, Joya and Eiko Strader. 2013. "Gender Pay Equity in Advanced Countries: The Role of Parenthood and Policies." *Journal of International Affairs* 67(1): 27–41.

Mitchell, Gregory. 2011. "TurboConsumers in Paradise: Tourism, Civil Rights, and Brazil's Gay Sex Industry." *American Ethnologist* 38: 666–682.

Modood, Tariq. 2007. "Multiculturalism." Pp. 3105–3108 in *The Blackwell Encyclopedia of Sociology*, edited by G. Ritzer. Malden, MA: Blackwell.

Moghadam, Valentine M. 1999. "Gender and Globalization: Female Labor and Women's Mobilization." *Journal of World-Systems Research* 5: 301–314.

Mollard, Elizabeth K. 2014. "A Qualitative Meta-synthesis and Theory of Postpartum Depression." *Issues in Mental Health Nursing* 35(9): 656–663.

Molm, Linda D. 2010. "The Structure of Reciprocity." *Social Psychology Quarterly* 73: 119–131.

Molm, Linda D., Monica M. Whithama, and David Melameda. 2012. "Forms of Exchange and Integrative Bonds: Effects of History and

Embeddedness." *American Sociological Review* 77: 141–165.

Molotch, Harvey. 2003. *Where Stuff Comes From.* New York: Routledge.

Monaghan, Jeffrey and Kevin Walby. 2012. "Making Up 'Terror Identities': Security Intelligence, Canada's Integrated Threat Assessment Centre and Social Movement Suppression." *Policing & Society* 22: 133–151.

Monbiot, George and Todd Gitlin. 2011. "How to Be Radical? An Interview with Todd Gitlin and George Monbiot." OpenDemocracy, April 5. Retrieved November 9, 2011 (http://www.opendemocracy.net/democracy-vision_reflections/article_1462.jsp).

Montoya, I. D. 2005. "Effect of Peers on Employment and Implications for Drug Treatment." *American Journal of Drug and Alcohol Abuse* 31: 657–668.

Montt, Guillermo. 2011. "Cross-National Differences in Educational Inequality." *Sociology of Education* 84: 49–68.

Moore, Dahlia. 1995. "Role Conflict: Not Only for Women? A Comparative Analysis of 5 Nations." *International Journal of Comparative Sociology* 36(1–2): 17–35.

Moore, R. Laurence. 1997. *Selling God: American Religion in the Marketplace of Culture.* Oxford: Oxford University Press.

Moran, Mary, Javier Guzman, Anne-Laure Ropars, Alina McDonald, Nicole Jameson, Brenda Omune, Sam Ryan, and Lindsey Wu. 2009. "Neglected Disease Research and Development: How Much Are We Really Spending?" *PLOS Medicine* 6(2): e1000030.

Morgan, Stephen G. 2007. "Direct-to-Consumer Advertising and Expenditures on Prescription Drugs: A Comparison of Experiences in the United States and Canada." *Open Medicine* 1(1): e37–e45.

Morozov, Evgeny. 2011. *The Net Delusion: The Dark Side of Internet Freedom.* New York: PublicAffairs.

Morris, Aldon. 1984. *The Origins of the Civil Rights Movement: Black Communities Organizing for Change.* New York: Free Press.

Morris, Aldon. 2007. "Civil Rights Movement." Pp. 507–512 in *The Blackwell Encyclopedia of Sociology,* edited by G. Ritzer. Malden, MA: Blackwell.

Morris, Betsy. 2013. "More Consumers Prefer Online Shopping." *Wall Street Journal,* June 3.

Morris, J. Glenn, Lynn M. Grattan, Brian M. Mayer, and Jason K. Blackburn. 2013. "Psychological Responses and Resilience of People and Communities Impacted by the Deepwater Horizon Oil Spill." *Transactions of the American Clinical and Climatological Association* 124: 191–201.

Morrow, Virginia and Kirilly Pells. 2012. "Integrating Children's Human Rights and Child Poverty Debates: Examples from *Young Lives* in Ethiopia and India." *Sociology* 46: 906–920.

Moses, Jonathon W. 2006. *International Migration: Globalization's Last Frontier.* London: Zed Books.

Mosley, Philip E. 2009. "Bigorexia: Bodybuilding and Muscle Dysmorphia." *European Eating Disorders Review* 17: 191–198.

Moss, Dana M. 2013. "Arab Spring." Pp. 118–125 in *The Wiley-Blackwell Encyclopedia of Social and Political Movements,* 3 vols., edited by

D. A. Snow, D. Della Porta, B. Klandermans, and D. McAdam. Malden, MA: Wiley-Blackwell.

Mucherah, Winnie and Andrea Dawn Frazier. 2013. "How Deep Is Skin-Deep? The Relationship between Skin Color Satisfaction, Estimation of Body Image, and Self-Esteem among Women of African Descent." *Journal of Applied Social Psychology* 43: 1177–1184.

Mundy, Liza. 2012. *The Richer Sex: How the New Majority of Female Breadwinners Is Transforming Our Culture.* New York: Free Press.

Muniz, Albert M., Jr. 2007. "Brands and Branding." Pp. 357–360 in *The Blackwell Encyclopedia of Sociology,* edited by G. Ritzer. Malden, MA: Blackwell.

Muniz, Albert M., Jr. and Thomas C. O'Guinn. 2001. "Brand Community." *Journal of Consumer Research* 27: 412–432.

Muniz, Ana. 2014. "Maintaining Racial Boundaries: Criminalization, Neighborhood Context, and the Origins of Gang Injunctions." *Social Problems* 61(2): 216–236.

Munro, Ealasaid. 2013. "Feminism: A Fourth Wave?" *Political Insight* 4: 22–25.

Murphy, Susan and Patrick Paul Walsh. 2014. "Social Protection beyond the Bottom Billion." *Economic and Social Review* 45(2): 261–284.

Murphy, Wendy Wiedenhoft. Forthcoming. *Consumer Culture and Society: An Introduction.* Thousand Oaks, CA: Sage.

Musick, Kelly. 2007. "Fertility: Nonmarital." Pp. 1734–1737 in *The Blackwell Encyclopedia of Sociology,* edited by G. Ritzer. Malden, MA: Blackwell.

Myers, Daniel J. 2007. "Riots." Pp. 3921–3926 in *The Blackwell Encyclopedia of Sociology,* edited by G. Ritzer. Malden, MA: Blackwell.

Myers, Daniel J. 2013. "Riots." Pp. 1124–1129 in *The Wiley-Blackwell Encyclopedia of Social and Political Movements,* 3 vols., edited by D. A. Snow, D. Della Porta, B. Klandermans, and D. McAdam. Malden, MA: Wiley-Blackwell.

Nagourney, Adam. 2013. "Unfinished Luxury Tower Is Stark Reminder of Las Vegas's Economic Reversal." *New York Times,* January 22.

Nagourney, Adam. 2015. "The Debate over California's Drought Crisis." *New York Times,* April 15.

Naples, Nancy A. 2009. "Presidential Address: Crossing Borders: Community Activism, Globalization, and Social Justice." *Social Problems* 56: 2–20.

Naples, Nancy A. and Manisha Desai. 2002. "Women's Local and Transnational Responses: An Introduction to the Volume." In *Women's Activism and Globalization: Linking Local Struggles and Transnational Politics,* edited by N. A. Naples and M. Desai. New York: Routledge.

Naples, Nancy A. and Barbara Gurr. 2012. "Genders and Sexualities in Global Context: An Intersectional Assessment of Contemporary Scholarship." Pp. 304–332 in *The Wiley-Blackwell Companion to Sociology,* edited by G. Ritzer. Malden, MA: Wiley-Blackwell.

Napoli, Lisa. 1999. "Dispensing of Drugs on Internet Stirs Debate." *New York Times,* April 6. Retrieved March 31, 2012 (http://query.nytimes.com/gst/fullpage.html?res=9B02E1D61139F935A35757C0A96F958260&scp=8&sq=pharmaceutical%20purchase%20over%20internet&st=cse).

Naquin, Charles E., Terri R. Kurtzberg, and Liuba Y. Belkin. 2008. "E-mail Communication and Group Cooperation in Mixed Motive Contexts." *Social Justice Research* 21: 470–489.

Nardi, Peter M., David Sanders, and Judd Marmor. 1994. *Growing Up before Stonewall: Life Stories of Some Gay Men.* London: Routledge.

Nash, Catherine J. and Andrew Gorman-Murray. 2014. "LGBT Neighbourhoods and 'New Mobilities': Towards Understanding Transformations in Sexual and Gendered Urban Landscapes." *International Journal of Urban & Regional Research* 38(3): 756–772.

National Coalition of Anti-Violence Programs. 2014. "National Report on Hate Violence against Lesbian, Gay, Bisexual, Transgender, Queer and HIV-Affected Communities Released Today." Press release, May 29. Retrieved April 17, 2015 (http://www.avp.org/storage/documents/2013_mr_ncavp_hvreport.pdf).

National Poverty Center. 2015. "Poverty in the United States: Frequently Asked Questions." Retrieved May 8, 2015 (http://www.npc.umich.edu/poverty).

National Safety Council. 2014. "NSC Releases Latest Injury and Fatality Statistics and Trends." Press release, March 25. Retrieved April 27, 2015 (http://www.nsc.org/NewsDocuments/2014-Press-Release-Archive/3-25-2014-Injury-Facts-release.pdf).

Nederveen Pieterse, Jan. 2009. *Globalization and Culture: Global Melange.* 2nd ed. Lanham, MD: Rowman & Littlefield.

Neuendorf, Kimberly A., Thomas D. Gore, Amy Dalessandro, Patricie Janstova, and Sharon Snyder-Suh. 2009. "Shaken and Stirred: A Content Analysis of Women's Portrayals in James Bond Films." *Sex Roles* 62: 747–776.

Neuman, William. 2015. "Americans May See Appeal of Medical Tourism in Cuba." *New York Times,* February 17.

Newport, Frank. 2011. "Americans Prefer Boys to Girls, Just as They Did in 1941." Gallup, June 23. Retrieved April 20, 2015 (http://www.gallup.com/poll/148187/americans-prefer-boys-girls-1941.aspx).

Newton, David E. 2009. *Gay and Lesbian Rights: A Reference Handbook.* Santa Barbara, CA: ABC-CLIO.

Newton, Michael. 2002. *Savage Girls and Wild Boys: A History of Feral Children.* London: Faber and Faber.

Nguyen, Tomson H. and Henry N. Pontell. 2011. "Fraud and Inequality in the Subprime Mortgage Crisis." Pp. 3–24 in *Economic Crisis and Crime,* edited by M. Deflem. Bingley, England: Emerald.

Nichols, Brian J. 2012. "Buddhism." Pp. 142–145 in *The Wiley-Blackwell Encyclopedia of Globalization,* edited by G. Ritzer. Malden, MA: Wiley-Blackwell.

Nicholson, Linda. 2008. *Identity before Identity Politics.* Cambridge: Cambridge University Press.

Niebuhr, Gustav. 1995. "Where Shopping-Mall Culture Gets a Big Dose of Religion." *New York Times,* April 16.

Noble, David F. 2011. *Forces of Production: A Social History of Industrial Automation.* New Brunswick, NJ: Transaction.

Nobles, Jenna. 2011. "Parenting from Abroad: Migration, Nonresident Father Involvement, and Children's Education in Mexico." *Journal of Marriage and Family* 73: 729–746.

Noller, Patricia and Gery C. Karantzas. 2012. "Conflict in Family Relationships." Pp. 129–143 in *The Wiley-Blackwell Handbook of Couples and Family Relationships,* edited by P. Noller and G. C. Karantzas. Malden, MA: Wiley-Blackwell.

Nordberg, Jenny. 2014. *The Underground Girls of Kabul: In Search of a Hidden Resistance in Afghanistan.* New York: Crown Group.

Nordenmark, Mikael. 2007. "Unemployment." Pp. 5090–5091 in *The Blackwell Encyclopedia of Sociology,* edited by G. Ritzer. Malden, MA: Blackwell.

Nordgren, Johan. 2013. "The Moral Entrepreneurship of Anti-khat Campaigners in Sweden: A Critical Discourse Analysis." *Drugs and Alcohol Today* 13(1): 20–27.

Norris, Dawn. 2011. "Interactions That Trigger Self-Labeling: The Case of Older Undergraduates." *Symbolic Interaction* 34: 173–197.

Norris, Trevor. 2011a. *Consuming Schools: Commercialism and the End of Politics.* Toronto: University of Toronto Press.

Norris, Trevor. 2011b. "Response to David Waddington's Review of *Consuming Schools: Commercialization and the End of Politics.*" *Studies in the Philosophy of Education* 30: 93–96.

"North Korea Country Profile—Overview." 2015. BBC News, April 30. Retrieved May 18, 2015 (http://www.bbc.com/news/world-asia-pacific-15256929).

Norton, Michael I. and Dan Ariely. 2011. "Building a Better America—One Wealth Quintile at a Time." *Perspectives on Psychological Science* 6(1): 9–12.

Noueihed, Lin and Alex Warren. 2012. *The Battle for the Arab Spring: Revolution, Counter-revolution and the Making of a New Era.* New Haven, CT: Yale University Press.

"Number of Megacities Has Nearly Tripled since 1990, UN Report Says." 2014. *Yale Environment 360,* October 6. Retrieved April 17, 2015 (http://e360.yale.edu/digest/number_of_megacities_has_nearly_tripled_since_1990_un_report_says/4267).

Nunn, Samuel. 2007. "Cybercrime." Pp. 960–961 in *The Blackwell Encyclopedia of Sociology,* edited by G. Ritzer. Malden, MA: Blackwell.

Nuru-Jeter, Amani, Tyan Parker Dominguez, Wizdom Powell Hammond, Janxin Leu, Marilyn Skaff, Susan Egerter, Camara P. Jones, and Paula Braveman. 2009. "'It's the Skin You're In': African-American Women Talk about Their Experiences of Racism. An Exploratory Study to Develop Measures of Racism for Birth Outcome Studies." *Maternal Child Health Journal* 13(1): 29–39.

Nwachukwu, Saviour L. and Rajiv P. Dant. 2014. "Consumer Culture in Developing Economies: Is It Really So Different?" *Proceedings of the Academy of Marketing Science 2015,* November 25, 35–40.

Nyden, Philip W., Leslie H. Hossfeld, and Gwendolyn E. Nyden. 2011. *Public Sociology: Research, Action, and Change.* Thousand Oaks, CA: Sage.

Obara-Minnitt, Mika. 2014. "Alternative Globalizations: An Integrative Approach to Studying Dissident Knowledge in the Global Justice Movement." *Journal of Contemporary European Studies* 22: 222–223.

Oberschall, Anthony. 2012. "Ethnic Cleansing." Pp. 547–551 in *The Wiley-Blackwell Encyclopedia of Globalization,* edited by G. Ritzer. Malden, MA: Wiley-Blackwell.

Ochiai, Emiko. 2014. "The Meaning of the Second Demographic Transition and the Establishment of a Mature Society." *European Societies* 16: 343–346.

Ocloo, Josephine Enyonam. 2010. "Harmed Patients Gaining Voice: Challenging Dominant Perspectives in the Construction of Medical Harm and Patient Safety Reforms." *Social Science & Medicine* 71: 510–516.

O'Connor, Brendan and Martin Griffiths. 2005. *The Rise of Anti-Americanism.* London: Routledge.

Ogas, Ogi and Sai Gaddam. 2012. *A Billion Wicked Thoughts: What the Internet Tells Us about Sexual Relationships.* New York: Plume.

Ogburn, William F. 1922. *Social Change.* New York: Viking Press.

O'Grady, Siobhán. 2014. "Colonial Lines Drawn Again for Ebola Aid." *Foreign Policy,* September 22.

O'Guinn, Thomas C. and Russell W. Belk. 1989. "Heaven on Earth: Consumption at Heritage Village, USA." *Journal of Consumer Research* 16: 227–238.

Ohlsson-Wijk, Sofi. 2011. "Sweden's Marriage Revival: An Analysis of the New-Millennium Switch from Long-Term Decline to Increasing Popularity." *Population Studies* 65: 183–200.

Oliver, Pamela. 2013. "Collective Action (Collective Behavior)." Pp. 210–215 in *The Wiley-Blackwell Encyclopedia of Social and Political Movements,* 3 vols., edited by D. A. Snow, D. Della Porta, B. Klandermans, and D. McAdam. Malden, MA: Wiley-Blackwell.

Olivier, Jos G. J., Greet Janssens-Maenhout, and Jeroen A. H. W. Peters. 2012. *Trends in Global CO_2 Emissions: 2012 Report.* The Hague: PBL Netherlands Environmental Assessment Agency. Retrieved April 17, 2015 (http://www.pbl.nl/en/publications/2012/trends-in-global-co2-emissions-2012-report).

Olshansky, S. Jay, Toni Antonucci, Lisa Berkman, Robert H. Binstock, Axel Boersch-Supan, John T. Cacioppo, Bruce A. Carnes, Laura L. Carstensen, Linda P. Fried, Dana P. Goldman, James Jackson, Martin Kohli, John Rother, Yuhui Zheng, and John Rowe. 2012. "Differences in Life Expectancy Due to Race and Educational Differences Are Widening, and Many May Not Catch Up." *Health Affairs* 31: 1803–1813.

Olson, Lynn. 2002. *Freedom's Daughters: The Unsung Heroines of the Civil Rights Movements from 1830 to 1970.* New York: Scribner.

Omi, Michael and Howard Winant. 1994. *Racial Formation in the United States: From the 1960s to the 1990s.* New York: Routledge.

Ong, Paul. 2007. "Bovine Spongiform Encephalopathy." Pp. 102–106 in *Encyclopedia of Globalization,* edited by J. A. Scholte and R. Robertson. New York: MTM.

Opsal, Tara D. 2011. "Women Disrupting a Marginalized Identity: Subverting the Parolee Identity through Narrative." *Journal of Contemporary Ethnography* 40(2): 135–167.

Orfield, Gary. 2001. *Schools More Separate: Consequences of a Decade of Resegregation.* Cambridge, MA: Harvard University, Civil Rights Project. Retrieved July 8, 2013 (http://www.civilrightsproject.harvard.edu/research/deseg/Schools_More_Separate.pdf).

Organisation for Economic Co-operation and Development. 2014. "Statistics." Retrieved November 12, 2014 (http://www.oecd.org/statistics).

Orlikowski, Wanda J. 2010. "Technology and Organization: Contingency All the Way Down." Pp. 239–246 in *Technology and Organization: Essays in Honour of Joan Woodward,* edited by N. Phillips, G. Sewell, and D. Griffiths. Bingley, England: Emerald.

Orloff, Ann S. 1993. *The Politics of Pensions: A Comparative Analysis of Britain, Canada, and the United States, 1880s–1940.* Madison: University of Wisconsin Press.

Orr, Martin. 2012. "Great Recession." Pp. 890–891 in *The Encyclopedia of Globalization,* edited by G. Ritzer. Malden, MA: Wiley-Blackwell.

Ortiz, Susan Y. and Vincent J. Roscigno. 2009. "Discrimination, Women, and Work: Processes and Variations by Race and Class." *Sociological Quarterly* 50(2): 336–359.

Ortmeyer, David L. and Michael A. Quinn. 2012. "Coyotes, Migration Duration, and Remittances." *Journal of Developing Areas* 46: 185–203.

Orum, Anthony M. 2007. "Urbanization." Pp. 5151–5154 in *Blackwell Encyclopedia of Sociology,* edited by G. Ritzer. Malden, MA: Blackwell.

Orwell, George. 1949. *Nineteen Eighty-Four.* London: Secker and Warburg.

Osman, Suleiman. 2011. *The Invention of Brownstone Brooklyn: Gentrification and the Search for Authenticity in Postwar New York.* New York: Oxford University Press.

Ostergaard, Per, James Fitchett, and Christian Jantzen. 2013. "A Critique of the Ontology of Consumer Enchantment." *Journal of Consumer Behaviour* 12: 337–344.

Otnes, Cele C. and Linda Tuncay Zayre, eds. 2012. *Gender, Culture, and Consumer Behavior.* New York: Routledge.

Outlaw, Lucius T. 2010. "Toward a Critical Theory of 'Race.'" Pp. 140–159 in *Arguing about Science,* edited by A. Bird and J. Ladyman. New York: Routledge.

"Over 70% of Chinese Have Had Pre-marital Sex: Survey." 2012. Want China Times, April 10. Retrieved May 13, 2015 (http://www.wantchinatimes.com/news-subclass-cnt.aspx?id=20120410000035andcid=1103).

Pace, Julie. 2010. "Obama Takes on Election-Year Fears over Big Debt." CBS News, September 19. Retrieved March 31, 2012 (http://www.cbsnews.com/stories/2010/09/19/national/main6881308.shtml).

Padilla, Mark. 2007. *Caribbean Pleasure Industry: Tourism, Sexuality, and AIDS in the Dominican Republic.* Chicago: University of Chicago Press.

Pager, Devah. 2009. *Marked: Race, Crime, and Finding Work in an Era of Mass Incarceration.* Chicago: University of Chicago.

Pager, Devah and Hana Shepherd. 2008. "The Sociology of Discrimination: Racial Discrimination in Employment, Housing, Credit, and Consumer Markets." *Annual Review of Sociology* 34: 181–209.

Pager, Devah and Bruce Western. 2012. "Identifying Discrimination at Work: The Use of Field Experiments." *Journal of Social Issues* 68: 221–237.

Pager, Devah, Bruce Western, and Bart Bonikowski. 2009. "Discrimination in a Low-Wage Labor Market: A Field Experiment." *American Sociological Review* 74(5): 777–799.

Pakulski, Jan. 2014. "Confusions about Multiculturalism." *Journal of Sociology* 50: 23–36.

Pantzar, Mike and Elizabeth Shove. 2010. "Understanding Innovation in Practice: A Discussion of the Production and Re-production of Nordic Walking." *Technology Analysis and Strategic Management* 22: 447–461.

Park, Julie and Dowell Myers. 2010. "Intergenerational Mobility in the Post-1965 Immigration Era: Estimates by an Immigrant Generation Cohort Method." *Demography* 47: 369–392.

Park, Robert E. [1927] 1973. "Life History." *American Journal of Sociology* 79: 251–260.

Parker, Richard, Jonathan Garcia, and Robert M. Buffington. 2014. "Sexuality and the Contemporary World: Globalization and Sexual Rights." Pp. 221–260 in *A Global History of Sexuality: The Modern Era*, edited by R. M. Buffington, E. Luibhéid, and D. J. Guy. Chichester, England: Wiley.

Parkinson, Cyril Northcote. 1955. "Parkinson's Law." *Economist*, November 19.

Parlapiano, Alicia, Robert Gebeloff, and Shan Carter. 2015. "The Shrinking American Middle Class." *New York Times*, January 26.

Parreñas, Rhacel Salazar. 2001. *Servants of Globalization: Women, Migration, and Domestic Work*. Stanford, CA: Stanford University Press.

Parrillo, Vincent N. 2007. "Urban." Pp. 5101–5104 in *The Blackwell Encyclopedia of Sociology*, edited by G. Ritzer. Malden, MA: Blackwell.

Parsons, Talcott. 1966. *Societies*. Englewood Cliffs, NJ: Prentice Hall.

Passel, Jeffrey. 2010. "Race and the Census: The 'Negro' Controversy." Pew Research Center, January 21. Retrieved January 16, 2012 (http://www.pewsocialtrends.org/2010/ 01/21/race-and-the-census-the-%E2%80%9 Cnegro%E2%80%9D-controversy).

Patch, Jason and Neil Brenner. 2007. "Gentrification." Pp. 1917–1920 in *The Blackwell Encyclopedia of Sociology*, edited by G. Ritzer. Malden, MA: Blackwell.

Patchin, Justin W. and Sameer Hinduja. 2010. "Trends in Online Social Networking: Adolescent Use of MySpace over Time." *New Media and Society* 12: 197–216.

Paternoster, Ray. 2007. "Capital Punishment." Pp. 385–388 in *The Blackwell Encyclopedia of Sociology*, edited by G. Ritzer. Malden, MA: Blackwell.

Paternoster, Raymond, Robert Brame, and Sarah Bacon. 2007. *The Death Penalty: America's Experience with Capital Punishment*. Oxford: Oxford University Press.

Patterson, Maurice and Jonathan Schroeder. 2010. "Borderlines: Skin, Tattoos and Consumer Culture Theory." *Marketing Theory* 10: 253–267.

Patterson, Orlando and Ethan Fosse, eds. 2015. *The Cultural Matrix: Understanding Black Youth*. Cambridge, MA: Harvard University Press.

Patton, Elizabeth and Mimi Choi, eds. 2014. *Home Sweat Home: Perspectives on Housework and Modern Relationships*. Lanham, MD: Rowman & Littlefield.

Patton, Peter L. 1998. "The Gangstas in Our Midst." *Urban Review* 30: 49–76.

Paulson, Michael. 2014. "Latin America Losing Bond to Catholicism, Study Says." *New York Times*, November 15.

Payne, Elizabeth and Melissa Smith. 2014. "The Big Freak Out: Educator Fear in Response to the Presence of Transgender Elementary School Students." *Journal of Homosexuality* 61(3): 399–418.

Payton, Andrew and Peggy A. Thoits. 2011. "Medicalization, Direct-to-Consumer Advertising, and Mental Illness Stigma." *Society and Mental Health* 1: 55–70.

PBS. 2010. *Frontline: Digital Nation*. Retrieved May 25, 2011 (http://www.pbs.org/wgbh/pages/frontline/digitalnation/view).

Pearce, Diane. 1978. "The Feminization of Poverty: Women, Work, and Welfare." *Urban and Social Change Review* 11: 28–36.

Pearlin, Leonard I. 1989. "The Sociological Study of Stress." *Journal of Health and Social Behavior* 30: 241–256.

Pearson, Ruth. 2000. "Moving the Goalposts: Gender and Globalization in the Twenty-First Century." *Gender and Development* 8(1): 10–19.

Peçanha, Sergio and Tim Wallace. 2015. "The Flight of Refugees around the Globe." *New York Times*, June 20. Retrieved August 24, 2015 (http://www.nytimes.com/interactive/2015/06/21/world/map-flow-desperate-migration-refugee-crisis.html?smid=tw-share&_r=0).

Penn, Roger. Forthcoming. "Marital Endogamy, Friendship Homogamy, and Ethnic/Nationality Group." *Journal of Marriage and Family*.

Pennington, Bill. 2015. "Brady Receives a 4-Game Ban." *New York Times*, May 12.

Pennington, Jon C. 2003. "It's Not a Revolution but It Sure Looks Like One: A Statistical Accounting of the Post-sixties Sexual Revolution." *Radical Statistics* 83: 104–116.

Peoples, Clayton D. 2012. "Welfare State." Pp. 2218–2221 in *The Encyclopedia of Globalization*, edited by G. Ritzer. Malden, MA: Wiley-Blackwell.

Perelli-Harris, Brienna and Nora Sanchez Gassen. 2012. "How Similar Are Cohabitation and Marriage? Legal Approaches to Cohabitation across Western Europe." *Population and Development Review* 38: 435–467.

Perez-Agote, Alfonso. 2014. "The Notion of Secularization: Drawing the Boundaries of Its Contemporary Scientific Validity." *Current Sociology*, published online May 30. doi: 10.1177/0011392114533333.

Perez-Felkner, Lara. 2013. "Socialization in Childhood and Adolescence." Pp. 119–149 in *Handbook of Social Psychology*, 2nd ed., edited by J. DeLamater and A. Ward. Dordrecht, Netherlands: Springer.

Perloff, Richard M., Bette Bonder, George B. Ray, Eileen Berlin Ray, and Laura A Siminoff. 2006. "Doctor–Patient Communication, Cultural Competence, and Minority Health: Theoretical and Empirical Perspectives." *American Behavioral Scientist* 49(6): 835–852.

Perlroth, Nicole. 2014. "Reporting from the Debt's Underbelly." *New York Times*, February 16.

Perrin, Robin D. 2007. "Deviant Beliefs/Cognitive Deviance." Pp. 1140–1142 in *The Blackwell Encyclopedia of Sociology*, edited by G. Ritzer. Malden, MA: Blackwell.

Perrow, Charles. 1999. *Normal Accidents*. Princeton, NJ: Princeton University Press.

Peter, Lawrence J. and Raymond Hull. 1969. *The Peter Principle: Why Things Always Go Wrong*. New York: Morrow.

Peters, Jeremy W. 2014. "After Immigration Action, a Blast of Energy for the Tea Party." *New York Times*, November 25.

Pew Research Center. 2013. "A Survey of LGBT Americans: Attitudes, Experiences and Values in Changing Times." June 13. Retrieved April 17, 2015 (http://www.pewsocialtrends.org/2013/06/13/a-survey-of-lgbt-americans).

Pfeffer, Max J. and Pilar A. Parra. 2009. "Strong Ties, Weak Ties, and Human Capital: Latino Immigrant Employment outside the Enclave." *Rural Sociology* 74(2): 241–269.

Pfeffer, Naomi. 2011. "Eggs-ploiting Women: A Critical Feminist Analysis of the Different Principles in Transplant and Fertility Tourism." *Reproductive Biomedicine Online* 23: 634–641. doi: 10.1016/j.rbmo.2011.08.005

Phelan, Jo C., Bruce G. Link, Ana Diez-Roux, Ichiro Kawachi, and Bruce Levin. 2004. "'Fundamental Causes' of Social Inequalities in Mortality: A Test of the Theory." *Journal of Health and Social Behavior* 45: 265–285.

Phelan, Jo C., Bruce G. Link, and Parisa Tehranifar. 2010. "Social Conditions as Fundamental Causes of Health Inequalities: Theory, Evidence, and Policy Implications." *Journal of Health and Social Behavior* 51: S28–S40.

Phelps, Michelle S. 2011. "Rehabilitation in the Punitive Era: The Gap between Rhetoric and Reality in U.S. Prison Programs." *Law and Society Review* 45: 33–68.

Phelps, Nicholas A. and Andrew M. Wood. 2011. "The New Post-suburban Politics?" *Urban Studies* 48: 2591–2610.

Phillips, Leigh, Kate Connolly, and Lizzy Davies. 2010. "EU Turning Blind Eye to Discrimination against Roma, Say Human Rights Groups." *The Guardian*, July 30. Retrieved November 29, 2011 (http://www.guardian.co.uk/world/2010/jul/30/european-union-roma-human-rights).

Picca, Leslie Houts and Joe R. Feagin. 2007. *Two-Faced Racism: Whites in the Backstage and Frontstage*. New York: Routledge.

Pickering, Mary. 2011. "Auguste Comte." Pp. 30–60 in *The Wiley-Blackwell Companion to Major Social Theorists*, Vol. 1, *Classical Theorists*, edited by G. Ritzer and J. Stepnisky. Malden, MA: Wiley-Blackwell.

Piketty, Thomas. 2014. *Capital in the Twenty-First Century*. Cambridge, MA: Belknap Press.

Pilcher, Jane. 2013. "'Small but Very Determined': A Novel Theorization of Children's Consumption of Culture." *Cultural Sociology* 7: 86–100.

Piquero, Alex R., Raymond Paternoster, Greg Pogarsky, and Thomas Loughran. 2011. "Elaborating the Individual Difference Component in Deterrence Theory." *Annual Review of Law and Social Science* 7: 335–360.

Pitts, Victoria. 2003. *In the Flesh: The Cultural Politics of Body Modification*. New York: Palgrave Macmillan.

Plante, Rebecca F. 2014. "Sexuality." Pp. 108–133 in *Investigating Social Problems*, edited by A. J. Treviño. Thousand Oaks, CA: Sage.

Plante, Rebecca F. 2015. *Sexualities in Context: A Social Perspective.* 2nd ed. New York: Routledge.

Plante, Rebecca F. and Andrew P. Smiler. 2014. "Time for a Sexual-Climate Change." *Chronicle of Higher Education,* November 26. Retrieved April 17, 2015 (http://chronicle.com/blogs/conversation/2014/11/26/time-for-a-sexual-climate-change).

Pleyers, Geoffrey. 2010. *Alter-Globalization: Becoming Actors in the Global Age.* Cambridge: Polity Press.

Plummer, Ken. 1975. *Sexual Stigma: An Interactionist Account.* London: Routledge.

Plummer, Ken. 2007a. "Sexual Identities." Pp. 4238–4242 in *The Blackwell Encyclopedia of Sociology,* edited by G. Ritzer. Malden, MA: Blackwell.

Plummer, Ken. 2007b. "Sexual Markets, Commodification, and Consumption." Pp. 4242–4244 in *The Blackwell Encyclopedia of Sociology,* edited by G. Ritzer. Malden, MA: Blackwell.

Plummer, Ken. 2012. "Critical Sexuality Studies." Pp. 243–268 in *The Wiley-Blackwell Companion to Sociology,* edited by G. Ritzer. Malden, MA: Wiley-Blackwell.

Pogue, David. 2014. "Smart Sharing." *Scientific American,* June.

"Police Discover Five Children 'Hidden from Society in Squalid Home and Raised without Schooling or Healthcare.'" 2010. *Daily Mail,* November 30. Retrieved May 25, 2015 (http://www.dailymail.co.uk/news/article-1334132/Police-discover-5-children-hidden-society-squalid-home.html).

Polonko, Karen. 2007. "Child Abuse." Pp. 448–451 in *The Blackwell Encyclopedia of Sociology,* edited by G. Ritzer. Malden, MA: Blackwell.

Pontell, Henry N. 2007. "Deviance, Reactivist Definitions of." Pp. 1123–1126 in *The Blackwell Encyclopedia of Sociology,* edited by G. Ritzer. Malden, MA: Blackwell.

Popenoe, David. 1987. "Beyond the Nuclear Family: A Statistical Portrait of the Changing Family in Sweden." *Journal of Marriage and the Family* 49: 173–183.

Popenoe, David. 2009. "Cohabitation, Marriage, and Child Wellbeing: A Cross-National Perspective." *Society* 46: 429–436.

Popham, James and Sirotnik, Kenneth. 1973. *Educational Statistics: Use and Interpretation.* New York: Harper & Row.

Population Reference Bureau. 2010. "World Population Data Sheet." Retrieved October 28, 2010 (http://www.prb.org/Publications/Datasheets/2010/2010wpds.aspx).

Postmes, Tom and Russell Spears. 1998. "Deindividuation and Antinormative Behavior: A Meta-analysis." *Psychological Bulletin* 123(3): 238–259.

Powell, Brian, Catherine Bolzendahl, Claudia Geist, and Lala Carr Steelman. 2010. *Counted Out: Same-Sex Relations and Americans' Definitions of Family.* New York: Russell Sage Foundation.

Powell, Jason L. 2012. "Internet." Pp. 1188–1190 in *The Wiley-Blackwell Encyclopedia of Globalization,* edited by G. Ritzer. Malden, MA: Wiley-Blackwell.

Powell, Joe and Karen Branden. 2007. "Family, Sociology of." Pp. 1614–1618 in *The Blackwell Encyclopedia of Sociology,* edited by G. Ritzer. Malden, MA: Blackwell.

Prechel, Harlan. 2007. "Taylorism." Pp. 4939–4940 in *The Blackwell Encyclopedia of Sociology,* edited by G. Ritzer. Malden, MA: Blackwell.

Preibisch, Kerry L. and Evelyn Encalada Grez. 2010. "The Other Side of el Otro Lado: Mexican Migrant Women and Labor Flexibility in Canadian Agriculture." *Signs* 35(2): 289–316.

Preisendorfer, Peter and Andreas Diekmann. 2007. "Ecological Problems." Pp. 1281–1286 in *The Blackwell Encyclopedia of Sociology,* edited by G. Ritzer. Malden, MA: Blackwell.

Presser, Harriet B. 2005. *Working in a 24/7 Economy.* New York: Russell Sage Foundation.

Preston, Julia. 2006. "Low-Wage Workers from Mexico Dominate Latest Great Wave of Immigrants." *New York Times,* December 19.

Preves, Sharon E. and Jeylan T. Mortimer. 2013. "Socialization for Primary, Intimate and Work Relationships in the Adult Life Course." Pp. 151–187 in *Handbook of Social Psychology,* 2nd ed., edited by J. DeLamater and A. Ward. Dordrecht, Netherlands: Springer.

Prior, Nick. 2011. "Critique and Renewal in the Sociology of Music: Bourdieu and Beyond." *Cultural Sociology* 5: 121–138.

Pritchard, Mary and Brooke Cramblitt. 2014. "Media Influence on Drive for Thinness and Drive for Muscularity." *Sex Roles* 71: 208–218.

Provost, Claire. 2014. "Foreign Aid Reaches Record High." *The Guardian,* April 8.

Pudrovska, Tetyana and Amelia Karraker. 2014. "Gender, Job Authority, and Depression." *Journal of Health and Social Behavior* 55: 424–441.

Pugh, Allison. 2009. *Longing and Belonging: Parents, Children, and Consumer Culture.* Berkeley: University of California Press.

Pugh, Derek S., David Hickson, C. R. Hinings, and C. Turner. 1968. "The Context of Organizational Structures." *Administrative Science Quarterly* 14: 91–114.

Pullum, Amanda. 2013. "Tea Party Movement (United States)." Pp. 1327–1328 in *The Wiley-Blackwell Encyclopedia of Social and Political Movements,* 3 vols., edited by D. A. Snow, D. Della Porta, B. Klandermans, and D. McAdam. Malden, MA: Wiley-Blackwell.

Qian, Zhenchao and Daniel T. Lichter. 2011. "Changing Patterns of Interracial Marriage in a Multiracial Society." *Journal of Marriage and Family* 73: 1065–1084.

Qin, Amy. 2014. "Smoking Prevalence Steady in China, but Numbers Rise." *New York Times,* Sinosphere blog, January 9. Retrieved April 28, 2015 (http://sinosphere.blogs.nytimes.com/2014/01/09/smoking-prevalence-steady-in-china-but-numbers-rise).

Quach, Thu et al. 2012. "Experiences and Perceptions of Medical Discrimination among a Multiethnic Sample of Breast Cancer Patients in the Greater San Francisco Bay Area, California." *American Journal of Public Health* 102: 1027–1034.

Quadagno, Jill and Deana Rohlinger. 2009. "Religious Conservatives in U.S. Welfare State Politics." Pp. 236–266 in *The Western Welfare State and Its Religious Roots,* edited by K. van Kersbergen and P. Manow. New York: Cambridge University Press.

Radesky, Jenny S. et al. 2014. "Patterns of Mobile Device Use by Caregivers and Children during Meals in Fast Food Restaurants." *Pediatrics,*

published online March 10. doi: 10.1542/peds.2013-3703.

Rafferty, Rebecca and Thomas Vander Ven. 2014. "'I Hate Everything About You': A Qualitative Examination of Cyberbullying and Online Aggression in a College Sample." *Deviant Behavior* 35: 364–377.

Ragin, Charles. 2014. *The Comparative Method: Moving beyond Qualitative and Quantitative Strategies.* Rev. ed. Berkeley: University of California Press.

Ram, Uri. 2007. *The Globalization of Israel: McWorld in Tel Aviv, Jihad in Jerusalem.* London: Routledge.

Ramirez, Francisco O., Yasemin Soysal, and Suzanne Shanahan. 1997. "The Changing Logic of Political Citizenship: Cross-National Acquisition of Women's Suffrage Rights, 1890–1990." *American Sociological Review* 62: 735–745.

Rao, Smriti and Christina Presenti. 2012. "Understanding Human Trafficking Origin: A Cross-Country Empirical Analysis." *Feminist Economics* 18: 231–263.

Rape, Abuse, and Incest National Network. 2014. "Who Are the Victims?" Retrieved May 13, 2015 (http://www.rainn.org/get-information/statistics/sexual-assault-victims).

Ratha, Dilip and Sanket Mohapatra. 2012. "Remittances and Development." Pp. 1782–1792 in *The Wiley-Blackwell Encyclopedia of Globalization,* edited by G. Ritzer. Malden, MA: Wiley-Blackwell.

Rauer, Amy J., Gregory S. Pettit, Jennifer E. Lansford, John E. Bates, and Kenneth A. Dodge. 2013. "Romantic Relationship Patterns in Young Adulthood and Their Developmental Antecedents." *Developmental Psychology* 49: 2159–2171.

Ravitch, Diane. 2012. "Schools We Can Envy." *New York Review of Books,* March 8, 19–20.

Rawls, Anne. 2011. "Harold Garfinkel." Pp. 89–124 in *The Wiley-Blackwell Companion to Major Social Theorists,* Vol. 2, *Contemporary Sociological Theorists,* edited by G. Ritzer and J. Stepnisky. Malden, MA: Wiley-Blackwell.

Ray, Larry. 2007. "Civil Society." Pp. 512–513 in *The Blackwell Encyclopedia of Sociology,* edited by G. Ritzer. Malden, MA: Blackwell.

Reay, Barry. 2014. "Promiscuous Intimacies: Rethinking the History of American Casual Sex." *Journal of Historical Sociology* 27: 1–24.

Recording Industry Association of America. 2012. "Piracy Online Facts." Retrieved March 31, 2012 (http://www.riaa.com/physicalpiracy.php?content_selector=piracy-online-scope-of-the-problem).

Reed College. 2015. "Sexual Assault Prevention and Response at Reed." Retrieved March 28, 2015 (http://www.reed.edu/sexual_assault/definitions/consent.html).

Rees, Karen L. 2013. "The Role of Reflective Practices in Enabling Final Year Nursing Students to Respond to the Distressing Emotional Challenges of Nursing Work." *Nurse Education in Practice* 13: 48–52.

Reger, Jo. 2007. "Feminism, First, Second, and Third Waves." Pp. 1672–1681 in *The Blackwell Encyclopedia of Sociology,* edited by G. Ritzer. Malden, MA: Blackwell.

Regnerus, Mark and Jeremy Uecker. 2011. *Premarital Sex in America: How Young Americans Meet,*

Mate, and Think about Marrying. Oxford: Oxford University Press.

Reid, Charles J. 2014. "The Journey to Seneca Falls: Mary Wollstonecraft, Elizabeth Cady Stanton and the Legal Emancipation of Women." *University of St. Thomas Law Journal* 10(4), art. 9.

Reid, Julie A., Sinikka Elliott, and Gretchen R. Webber. 2011. "Casual Hookups to Formal Dates: Refining the Boundaries of the Sexual Double Standard." *Gender & Society* 25(5): 545–568.

Reiman, Jeffrey H. and Paul Leighton. 2012. *The Rich Get Richer and the Poor Get Prison: Ideology, Class, and Criminal Justice.* 10th ed. Boston: Prentice Hall.

Restivo, Emily and Mark M. Lanier. 2015. "Measuring the Contextual Effects and Mitigating Factors of Labeling Theory." *Justice Quarterly* 32(1): 116–141.

"Return Visit to Communist Cuba Finds New Hope Amid Change." 2015. *New York Times,* February 18.

Reuveny, Rafael and William R. Thompson. 2001. "Leading Sectors, Lead Economies and Economic Growth." *Review of International Political Economy* 8(4): 689–719.

Reverby, Susan. 2009. *Examining Tuskegee: The Infamous Syphilis Study and Its Legacy.* Chapel Hill: University of North Carolina Press.

Rich, Motoko. 2015. "Homeschooling: More Pupils, Less Regulation." *New York Times,* January 4.

Richtel, Matt. 2010. "Attached to Technology and Paying a Price." *New York Times,* June 6.

Richtel, Matt. 2011. "Egypt Cuts Off Most Internet and Cell Service." *New York Times,* January 28. Retrieved May 6, 2015 (http://www.nytimes.com/2011/01/29/technology/internet/29cutoff.html?_r=0).

Rideout, Victoria J., Ulla G. Foehr, and Donald F. Roberts. 2010. *Generation M2: Media in the Lives of 8- to 18-Year-Olds.* Menlo Park, CA: Kaiser Family Foundation.

Ridgeway, Cecilia L. and Shelley L. Correll. 2004. "Unpacking the Gender System: A Theoretical Perspective on Gender Beliefs and Social Relations." *Gender & Society* 18(4): 510–553.

Rieger, Jon H. 2007. "Key Informant." Pp. 2457–2458 in *The Blackwell Encyclopedia of Sociology,* edited by G. Ritzer. Malden, MA: Blackwell.

Rieker, Patricia R. and Chloe E. Bird. 2000. "Sociological Explanations of Gender Differences in Mental and Physical Health." In *Handbook of Medical Sociology,* edited by C. E. Bird, P. Conrad, and A. Freemont. New York: Prentice Hall.

Riera-Crichton, Daniel. 2012. "Euro Crisis." Pp. 566–570 in *The Encyclopedia of Globalization,* edited by G. Ritzer. Malden, MA: Wiley-Blackwell.

Riffkin, Rebecca. 2014. "New Record Highs in Moral Acceptability." Gallup, May 30. Retrieved April 17, 2015 (http://www.gallup.com/poll/170789/new-record-highs-moral-acceptability.aspx).

Riis, Ole. 2012. "Combining Quantitative and Qualitative Methods in the Sociology of Religion." Pp. 91–116 in *Annual Review of the Sociology of Religion: New Methods in Sociology of Religion* , edited by L. Berzano and O. Riis. Leiden, Netherlands: Brill.

Rinaldo, Lindsay and Kenneth Ferraro. 2012. "Inequality, Health." Pp. 1034–1037 in *The*

Wiley-Blackwell Encyclopedia of Globalization, edited by G. Ritzer. Malden, MA: Wiley-Blackwell.

Rindermann, Heiner and Antonia E. E. Baumeister. 2015. "Parents' SES vs. Parental Educational Behavior and Children's Development: A Reanalysis of the Hart and Risley Study." *Learning and Individual Differences* 37: 133–138.

Rippeyoug, Phyllis L. F. and Mary C. Noonan. 2012. "Is Breastfeeding Truly Cost Free? Income Consequences of Breastfeeding for Women." *American Sociological Review* 77: 244–267.

Riska, Elianne. 2007. "Health Professions and Occupations." Pp. 2075–2078 in *The Blackwell Encyclopedia of Sociology,* edited by G. Ritzer. Malden, MA: Blackwell.

Ritzer, George. 1993. *The McDonaldization of Society.* Newbury Park, CA: Sage.

Ritzer, George. 1995. *Expressing America: A Critique of the Global Credit Card Society.* Thousand Oaks, CA: Pine Forge Press.

Ritzer, George. 2001. *Explorations in the Sociology of Consumption: Fast Food, Credit Cards, and Casinos.* London: Sage.

Ritzer, George. 2006. "Who's a Public Intellectual?" *British Journal of Sociology* 57: 209–213.

Ritzer, George, ed. 2007a. *The Blackwell Encyclopedia of Sociology.* Malden, MA: Blackwell.

Ritzer, George. 2007b. *The Globalization of Nothing.* Thousand Oaks, CA: Pine Forge Press.

Ritzer, George. 2010a. "Cathedrals of Consumption: Rationalization, Enchantment, and Disenchantment." Pp. 234–239 in *McDonaldization: The Reader,* 3rd ed., edited by G. Ritzer. Thousands Oaks, CA: Pine Forge Press.

Ritzer, George. 2010b. *Enchanting a Disenchanted World: Continuity and Change in the Cathedrals of Consumption.* Thousand Oaks, CA: Sage.

Ritzer, George, ed. 2010c. *The McDonaldization of Society: The Reader.* 3rd ed. Thousand Oaks, CA: Pine Forge Press.

Ritzer, George. 2012a. "'Hyperconsumption' and 'Hyperdebt': A 'Hypercritical' Analysis." Pp. 60–80 in *A Debtor World: Interdisciplinary Perspective on Debt,* edited by R. Brubaker, R. W. Lawless, and C. J. Tabb. New York: Oxford University Press.

Ritzer, George, ed. 2012b. *The Wiley-Blackwell Encyclopedia of Globalization.* Malden, MA: Wiley-Blackwell.

Ritzer, George. 2013. "The 'New' Prosumer: Collaboration on the Digital and Material 'New Means of Prosumption.'" Paper presented at the annual meeting of the Eastern Sociological Society, Boston, March.

Ritzer, G. 2014. Automating prosumption: The decline of the prosumer and the rise of the pro-suming machines. *Journal of Consumer Culture,* 1469540514553717.

Ritzer, George. 2015. *The McDonaldization of Society.* 8th ed. Thousand Oaks, CA: Sage.

Ritzer, George, ed. Forthcoming. *The Wiley-Blackwell Encyclopedia of Sociology.* 2nd ed. Malden, MA: Wiley-Blackwell.

Ritzer, George and Paul Dean. 2015. *Globalization: A Basic Text.* 2nd ed. Malden, MA: Wiley-Blackwell.

Ritzer, George, Paul Dean, and Nathan Jurgenson, eds. 2012. "The Coming of Age of Prosumption and the Prosumer." Special issue, *American Behavioral Scientist* 56: 379–640.

Ritzer, George, Douglas Goodman, and Wendy Wiedenhoft. 2001. "Theories of Consumption." Pp. 410–427 in *Handbook of Social Theory,* edited by G. Ritzer and B. Smart. London: Sage.

Ritzer, George and Nathan Jurgenson. 2010. "Production, Consumption, Prosumption: The Nature of Capitalism in the Age of the Digital 'Prosumer.'" *Journal of Consumer Culture* 10(1): 13–36.

Ritzer, George and Craig Lair. 2007. "Outsourcing: Globalization and Beyond." Pp. 307–329 in *The Blackwell Companion to Globalization,* edited by G. Ritzer. Malden, MA: Blackwell.

Ritzer, George and Jeffrey Stepnisky, eds. 2014. *Sociological Theory.* 9th ed. New York: McGraw-Hill.

Rizvi, Fazal. 2012. "Bollywood." Pp. 120–121 in *The Wiley-Blackwell Encyclopedia of Globalization,* edited by G. Ritzer. Malden, MA: Wiley-Blackwell.

Roberts, Sam. 2008. "Study Foresees the Fall of an Immigration Record That Has Lasted a Century." *New York Times,* February 12.

Roberts, Sam. 2009. "In 2025, India to Pass China in Population, U.S. Estimates." *New York Times,* December 16.

Roberts, Sam. 2010. "More Men Marrying Wealthy Women." *New York Times,* January 19.

Robertson, Craig. 2010. *The Passport in America: The History of a Document.* New York: Oxford University Press.

Rochon, T. R. 1990. "The West European Peace Movements and the Theory of Social Movements." In *Challenging the Political Order,* edited by R. Dalton and M. Kuchler. Cambridge: Polity Press.

Roda, Allison, and Amy Stuart Wells. 2013. "School Choice Policies and Racial Segregation: Where White Parents' Good Intentions, Anxiety, and Privilege Collide." *American Journal of Education* 119: 261–293.

Roehling, Patricia, Loma Hernandez Jarvis, and Heather Swope. 2005. "Variations in Negative Work–Family Spillover among White, Black, and Hispanic American Men and Women." *Journal of Family Issues* 26(6): 840–865.

Rohlinger, Deana A. 2007. "Socialization, Gender." Pp. 4571–4574 in *The Blackwell Encyclopedia of Sociology,* edited by G. Ritzer. Malden, MA: Blackwell.

Rojas, Rene and Jeff Goodwin. 2013. "Revolutions." Pp. 1102–1110 in *The Wiley-Blackwell Encyclopedia of Social and Political Movements,* 3 vols., edited by D. A. Snow, D. Della Porta, B. Klandermans, and D. McAdam. Malden, MA: Wiley-Blackwell.

Rojek, Chris. 2007. "George Ritzer and the Crisis of the Public Intellectual." *Review of Education, Pedagogy and Cultural Studies* 29: 3–21.

Roof, Wade Clark. 2001. *Spiritual Marketplace: Baby Boomers and the Remaking of American Religion.* Princeton, NJ: Princeton University Press.

Roscoe, Will. 1998. *Changing Ones: Third and Fourth Genders in Native North America.* New York: Palgrave/St. Martin's Press.

Rose, Arnold. 1967. *The Power Structure.* New York: Oxford University Press.

Rose, Claire. 2010. *Making, Selling, and Wearing Boys' Clothes in Late-Victorian England.* Burlington, VT: Ashgate.

Rosenberg, Morris. 1979. *Conceiving the Self*. New York: Basic Books.

Rosenfield, Richard. 2011. "The Big Picture: 2010 Presidential Address to the American Society of Criminology." *Criminology* 49: 1–26.

Rosenthal, Elisabeth. 2007. "W.H.O. Urges Effort to Fight Fast-Spreading Disease." *New York Times*, August 27.

Rostow, Walt. 1960. *The Stages of Economic Growth: A Non-Communist Manifesto*. Cambridge: Cambridge University Press.

Rostow, Walt. 1978. *The World Economy: History and Prospect*. Austin: University of Texas Press.

Roszak, Theodore. [1968] 1995. *The Making of a Counter Culture: Reflections on the Technocratic Society and Its Youthful Opposition*. Berkeley: University of California Press.

Roth, Benita. 2004. *Separate Roads to Feminism: Black, Chicana and White Feminist Movements in America's Second Wave*. Cambridge: Cambridge University Press.

Roth, Silke. 2007. "Social Movements, Biographical Consequences of." Pp. 4451–4453 in *The Blackwell Encyclopedia of Sociology*, edited by G. Ritzer. Malden, MA: Blackwell.

Roudometof, Victor. 2012. "Imagined Communities." Pp. 996–998 in *The Wiley-Blackwell Encyclopedia of Globalization*, edited by G. Ritzer. Malden, MA: Wiley-Blackwell.

Rousseau, Nicole. 2011. *Black Women's Burden: Commodifying Black Reproduction*. New York: Palgrave Macmillan.

Rozdeba, Suzanne. 2011. "Firefighters Recall Spirit of 9/11 Hero." *New York Times*, East Village Local, January 10. Retrieved March 31, 2012 (http://eastvillage.thelocal.nytimes.com/2011/01/10/firefighters-recall-spirit-of-911-hero/?scp=3&sq=9/11%20heroism&rst=cse).

Rudrappa, Sharmila. 2012. "Rape." Pp. 1748–1751 in *The Wiley-Blackwell Encyclopedia of Globalization*, edited by G. Ritzer. Malden, MA: Wiley-Blackwell.

Rueschemeyer, Dietrich, Evelyne Huber Stephens, and John D. Stephens. 1992. *Capitalist Development and Democracy*. Chicago: University of Chicago Press.

Ruiz, Ariel G., Jie Zong, and Jeanne Batalova. 2015. "Immigrant Women in the United States." Migration Policy Institute, March 20. Retrieved May 11, 2015 (http://www.migrationpolicy.org/article/immigrant-women-united-states).

Runyon, Anne Sisson. 2012. "Gender." Pp. 725–734 in *The Wiley-Blackwell Encyclopedia of Globalization*, edited by G. Ritzer. Malden, MA: Wiley-Blackwell.

Rupp, Leila J. 1997. *Worlds of Women: The Making of an International Women's Movement*. Princeton, NJ: Princeton University Press.

Rupp, Leila and Verta Taylor. 1999. "Forging Feminist Identity in an International Movement: A Collective Identity Approach to Twentieth-Century Feminism." *Signs* 24(2): 363–386.

Rutherford, Paul. 2007. *The World Made Sexy: Freud to Madonna*. Toronto: University of Toronto Press.

Rutledge, Leigh W. 1992. *The Gay Decades: From Stonewall to the Present*. New York: Plume.

Ryan, Barbara. 2007. "Sex and Gender." Pp. 4196–4198 in *The Blackwell Encyclopedia of Sociology*, edited by G. Ritzer. Malden, MA: Blackwell.

Ryan, Camille. 2013. "Language Use in the United States: 2011." American Community Survey Reports ACS-22. U.S. Census Bureau, August. Retrieved April 24, 2015 (http://www.census.gov/prod/2013pubs/acs-22.pdf).

Ryan, Kevin. 1994. "Technicians and Interpreters in Moral Crusades: The Case of the Drug Courier Profile." *Deviant Behavior* 15: 217–240.

Ryan, M. K. and S. A. Haslam. 2005. "The Glass Cliff: Evidence That Women Are Over-represented in Precarious Leadership Positions." *British Journal of Management* 16: 81–90.

Ryan, William. 1976. *Blaming the Victim*. New York: Pantheon.

Ryave, A. Lincoln and James N. Schenkein. 1974. "Notes on the Art of Walking." Pp. 265–275 in *Ethnomethodology: Selected Readings*, edited by R. Turner. Harmondsworth, England: Penguin.

Rysst, Mari. 2008. *"I Want to Be Me. I Want to Be Kul": An Anthropological Study of Norwegian Preteen Girls in the Light of a Presumed "Disappearance" of Childhood*. PhD dissertation, University of Oslo.

Sabo, Don. 1998. "Masculinities and Men's Health: Moving Towards Post-Superman Era Prevention." In *Men's Lives*, edited by M. Kimmel and M. Messner. Needham Heights: Allyn & Bacon.

Sacchi, Agnese and Simone Salotti. 2014. "The Effects of Fiscal Decentralization on Household Income Inequality: Some Empirical Evidence." *Spatial Economic Analysis* 9: 202–222.

Sadker, Myra and David Sadker. 1994. *Failing at Fairness: How Our Schools Cheat Girls*. New York: Simon & Schuster.

Saez, Emmanuel and Gabriel Zucman. 2014. "The Explosion in U.S. Wealth Inequality Has Been Fuelled by Stagnant Wages, Increasing Debt, and a Collapse in Asset Values for the Middle Classes." London School of Economics and Political Science. Retrieved April 20, 2015 (http://bit.ly/1pXQ3Or).

Sahlberg, Pasi. 2011. *Finnish Lessons: What Can the World Learn from Educational Change in Finland?* New York: Teachers College Press.

Said, Edward W. [1979] 1994. *Orientalism*. New York: Knopf.

Salkind, Neil. 2004. *Statistics for People Who (Think They) Hate Statistics*. Thousand Oaks, CA: Sage.

Sallaz, Jeffrey. 2010. "Talking Race, Marketing Culture: The Racial Habitus in and out of Apartheid." *Social Problems* 57(2): 294–314.

Saltmarsh, Matthew. 2010. "Sarkozy Toughens on Illegal Roma." *New York Times*, July 29.

Sanders, George. 2014. "Religious Non-places: Corporate Megachurches and Their Contributions to Consumer Capitalism." *Critical Sociology*, published online July 7. doi: 10.1177/0896920514531605.

Sanders, Teela. 2013. *Sex Work*. London: Routledge.

Sanger, David E. 2013. "In Cyberspace, New Cold War." *New York Times*, February 24.

Sanneh, Kelefa. 2015. "Don't Be Like That: Does Black Culture Need to Be Reformed?" *New Yorker*, February 9, 62–69.

Santos, Fernanda and Motoko Rich. 2013. "With Vouchers, States Shift Aid for Schools to Families." *New York Times*, March 27.

Santos, Xuan. 2009. "The Chicana Canvas: Doing Class, Gender, Race, and Sexuality through Tattooing in East Los Angeles." *NWSA Journal* 21: 91–120.

Sarwal, Amit. 2012. "A Journey through Places: Politics of Spatial Location in the Stories of South Asian Diaspora in Australia." *South Asian Diaspora* 4: 195–213.

Sassatelli, Roberta. 2007. *Consumer Culture: History, Theory and Politics*. London: Sage.

Sassen, Saskia. 1991. *The Global City: New York, London, Tokyo*. Princeton, NJ: Princeton University Press.

Sassen, Saskia. 2004. "Local Actors in Global Politics." *Current Sociology* 52(4): 649–670.

Sassen, Saskia. 2012. "Cities." Pp. 187–202 in *The Wiley-Blackwell Encyclopedia of Globalization*, edited by G. Ritzer. Malden, MA: Wiley-Blackwell.

Sassler, Sharon. 2010. "Partnering across the Life Course: Sex, Relationships, and Mate Selection." *Journal of Marriage and Family* 72: 557–575.

Sassler, Sharon and Amanda J. Miller. 2011. "Class Differences in Cohabitation Processes." *Family Relations* 60: 163–177.

Sauter, Mike, Thomas C. Frohlich, and Alexander E. M. Hess. 2013. "Fast-Food Chains Costing Taxpayers the Most Money." Yahoo! Finance, October 23. Retrieved April 21, 2015 (http://finance.yahoo.com/news/fast-food-chains-costing-taxpayers-173510741.html).

Saxon, Wolfgang. 2003. "Adm. Richard E. Bennis, a Hero of 9/11, Dies at 52." *New York Times*, August 9. Retrieved March 31, 2012 (http://www.nytimes.com/2003/08/09/nyregion/adm-richard-e-bennis-a-hero-of-9-11-dies-at-52.html).

Sayyid, Salman. 2012. "Political Islam." Pp. 1202–1204 in *The Wiley-Blackwell Encyclopedia of Globalization*, edited by G. Ritzer. Malden, MA: Wiley-Blackwell.

Scaff, Lawrence A. 2011. "Georg Simmel." Pp. 205–235 in *The Wiley-Blackwell Companion to Major Social Theorists*, Vol. 1, *Classical Theorists*, edited by G. Ritzer and J. Stepnisky. Malden, MA: Wiley-Blackwell.

Scambler, Graham and Frederique Paoli. 2008. "Health Work, Female Sex Workers and HIV/AIDS: Global and Local Dimensions of Stigma and Deviance as Barriers to Effective Interventions." *Social Science & Medicine* 66: 1848–1862.

Scelfo, Julie. 2015. "A University Recognizes a Third Gender: Neutral." *New York Times*, February 3.

Schaefer, David R. 2012. "Homophily through Nonreciprocity: Results of an Experiment." *Social Forces* 90: 1271–1295.

Scheffer, David. 2008. "Rape as Genocide in Darfur." *Los Angeles Times*, November 13.

Schemo, Diana Jean. 2003. "Rate of Rape at Academy Is Put at 12% in Survey." *New York Times*, August 23. Retrieved December 3, 2011 (http://www.nytimes.com/2003/08/29/national/29ACAD.html?th).

Scheper-Hughes, Nancy. 2001. "Commodity Fetishism in Organs Trafficking." *Body and Society* 7: 31–62.

Scherschel, Karin. 2007. "Migration, Ethnic Conflicts, and Racism." Pp. 3011–3014 in *The Blackwell Encyclopedia of Sociology*, edited by G. Ritzer. Malden, MA: Blackwell.

Schilt, Kristen. 2010. *Just One of the Guys? Transgender Men and the Persistence of Inequality*. Chicago: University of Chicago Press.

Schlanger, Zoë. 2014. "'When We Rape, We Feel Free': Congolese Soldiers Open Up in Harrowing New Documentary." *Newsweek,* June 10. Retrieved April 21, 2015 (http://www.newsweek.com/when-we-rape-we-feel-free-congolese-soldiers-open-harrowing-new-documentary-254405).

Schlosser, Eric. 2002. *Fast Food Nation.* New York: Harper Perennial.

Schmidt, John, Kris Warner, and Sarika Gupta. 2010. *The High Budgetary Cost of Incarceration.* Washington, DC: Center for Economic and Policy Research.

Schmidt, Susanne, Ulrike Roesler, Talin Kusserow, and Renate Rau. 2014. "Uncertainty in the Workplace: Examining Role Ambiguity and Role Conflict, and Their Link to Depression—A Meta-analysis." *European Journal of Work and Organizational Psychology* 23(1): 91–106.

Schoch, Deborah and Rong-Gong Lin II. 2007. "15 Years after L.A. Riots, Tension Still High." *Los Angeles Times,* April 29. Retrieved March 31, 2012 (http://articles.latimes.com/2007/apr/29/local/me-riots29).

Scholz, Trebor, ed. 2013. *Digital Labor: The Internet as Playground and Factory.* New York: Routledge.

Schor, Juliet. 1993. *The Overworked American: The Unexpected Decline of Leisure.* New York: Basic Books.

Schor, Juliet. 1998. *The Overspent American: Why We Want What We Don't Need.* New York: Basic Books.

Schor, Juliet. 2005. *Born to Buy: The Commercialized Child and the New Consumer Culture.* New York: Scribner.

Schorzman, Cindy M., Melanie A. Gold, Julie S. Downs, and Pamela J. Murray. 2007. "Body Art: Attitudes and Practices regarding Body Piercing among Urban Undergraduates." *Journal of the American Osteopathic Association* 107: 432–438.

Schroeder, Jonathan E. 2007. "Brand Culture." Pp. 351–353 in *The Blackwell Encyclopedia of Sociology,* edited by G. Ritzer. Malden, MA: Blackwell.

Schudson, Michael. 1987. *Advertising, the Uneasy Persuasion: Its Dubious Impact on American Society.* New York: Basic Books.

Schuster, Liza. 2012. "Asylum-Seekers." Pp. 89–92 in *The Wiley-Blackwell Encyclopedia of Globalization,* edited by G. Ritzer. Malden, MA: Wiley-Blackwell.

Schutt, Russell K. 2007. "Secondary Data Analysis." Pp. 4127–4129 in *The Blackwell Encyclopedia of Sociology,* edited by G. Ritzer. Malden. MA: Blackwell.

Schwalbe, Michael, Sandra Godwin, Daphne Holden, Douglas Schrock, Shealy Thompson, and Michele Wolkomir. 2000. "Generic Processes in the Reproduction of Inequality: An Interactionist Analysis." *Social Forces* 79: 419–452.

Schweinhart, Lawrence J. W., Steven Barnett, and Clive R. Belfield. 2005. *Lifetime Effects: The High/Scope Perry Preschool Study through Age 40.* Ypsilanti, MI: High/Scope Press.

Scott, Amy. 2011. "Pumping Up the Pomp: An Exploration of Femininity and Female Bodybuilding." *Explorations in Anthropology* 11: 70–88.

Scott, Barbara Marliene and Mary Ann A. Schwartz. 2008. *Sociology: Making Sense of the Social World.* New York: Allyn & Bacon.

Scott, W. Richard. 2008. *Institutions and Organizations: Ideas and Interests.* 3rd ed. Thousand Oaks, CA: Sage.

Searcy, Dionne and Robert Gebeloff. 2015. "Middle Class Shrinks Further as More Fall Out Instead of Climbing Up." *New York Times,* January 25.

Seidman, Steven. 2003. *The Social Construction of Sexuality.* New York: Norton.

Sekulic, Dusko. 2007a. "Ethic Cleansing." Pp. 1450–1452 in *The Blackwell Encyclopedia of Sociology,* edited by G. Ritzer. Malden, MA: Blackwell.

Sekulic, Dusko. 2007b. "Social Change." Pp. 4360–4364 in *The Blackwell Encyclopedia of Sociology,* edited by G. Ritzer. Malden, MA: Blackwell.

Sekulic, Dusko. 2007c. "Values, Global." Pp. 5172–5176 in *The Blackwell Encyclopedia of Sociology,* edited by G. Ritzer. Malden, MA: Blackwell.

Seligson, Hannah. 2014. "Facebook's Last Taboo: The Unhappy Marriage." *New York Times,* December 26.

Selingo, Jeffrey. J. 2014. "Demystifying the MOOC." *New York Times,* October 29.

Sen, Jai, Anita Anand, Arturo Escobar, and Peter Waterman, eds. 2004. *World Social Forum: Challenging Empires.* New Delhi: Viveka Foundation.

Serra-Majem, Luis and Joy Ngo. 2012. "Undernutrition." Pp. 2055–2058 in *The Wiley-Blackwell Encyclopedia of Globalization,* edited by G. Ritzer. Malden, MA: Wiley-Blackwell.

Settle, Jaime E., Christopher T. Dawes, Nicholas A. Christakis, and James H. Fowler. 2010. "Friendships Moderate an Association between a Dopamine Gene Variant and Political Ideology." *Journal of Politics* 72: 1189–1198.

Shalin, Dmitri. 2014. "Interfacing Biography, Theory and History: The Case of Erving Goffman." *Symbolic Interaction* 37: 2–40.

Shamir, Ronen. 2005. "Without Borders? Notes on Globalization as a Mobility Regime." *Sociological Theory* 23(2): 197–217.

Shane, Scott and Ben Hubbard. 2014. "ISIS Displaying a Deft Command of Varied Media." *New York Times,* August 14.

Shanker, Thom. 2011. "U.S. Accuses China and Russia of Internet Espionage." *New York Times,* November 4. Retrieved November 6, 2011 (http://www.nytimes.com/2011/11/04/world/us-report-accuses-china-and-russia-of-internet-spying.html?scp=2&sq=china%20russia&st=cse).

Sharp, Gwen. 2012. "Gender in the Hidden Curriculum (Update)." Society Pages, November 16. Retrieved April 11, 2013 (http://www.thesocietypages.org/socimages/2012/11/16/gender-in-the-hidden-curriculum).

Shattuck, Roger. 1980. *The Forbidden Experiment: The Story of the Wild Boy.* New York: Kodansha Globe.

Shaw, Susan M. and Janet Lee. 2009. *Women's Voices, Feminist Visions.* New York: McGraw-Hill.

Shear, Michael D. 2013. "Obama Calls for 'Moral Courage' at Naval Academy Graduation." *New York Times,* May 24.

Shehan, Constance and Susan Cody. 2007. "Inequalities in Marriage." Pp. 2301–2304 in *The Blackwell Encyclopedia of Sociology,* edited by G. Ritzer. Malden, MA: Blackwell.

Sheldon, Jane P. 2004. "Gender Stereotypes in Educational Software for Young Children." *Sex Roles* 51(7/8): 433–444.

Shelley, Louise, John Picarelli, and Chris Corpora. 2011. "Global Crime Inc." Pp. 141–169 in *Beyond Sovereignty: Issues for a Global Agenda,* 4th ed., edited by M. C. Love. Boston: Wadsworth, Cengage Learning.

Sherif, Muzafer, O. J. Harvey, William R. Hood, Carolyn W. Sherif, and Jack White. [1954] 1961. *Intergroup Conflict and Cooperation: The Robbers Cave Experiment.* Norman: University of Oklahoma Book Exchange.

Shevchenko, Olga. 2012. "Socialism." Pp. 1882–1886 in *The Wiley-Blackwell Encyclopedia of Globalization,* edited by G. Ritzer. Malden, MA: Wiley-Blackwell.

Shildrick, Tracy and Robert MacDonald. 2013. "Poverty Talk: How People Experiencing Poverty Deny Their Poverty and Why They Blame the Poor." *Sociological Review* 61: 285–303.

Shinberg, Diane S. 2007. "Women's Health." Pp. 5275–5279 in *The Blackwell Encyclopedia of Sociology,* edited by G. Ritzer. Malden, MA: Blackwell.

Shroedel, Jean Reith and Pamela Fiber. 2000. "Lesbian and Gay Policy Priorities: Commonality and Difference." Pp. 97–118 in *The Politics of Gay Rights,* edited by C. A. Rimmerman, K. D. Wald, and C. Wilcox. Chicago: University of Chicago Press.

Shull, Kristina Karin. 2005. "Is the Magic Gone? Weber's 'Disenchantment of the World' and Its Implications for Art in Today's World." *Anamesa* 3(2): 61–73.

Shullenberger, Geoff. 2014. "The Rise of the Voluntariat." *Jacobin,* May 15. Retrieved April 23, 2015 (https://www.jacobinmag.com/2014/05/the-rise-of-the-voluntariat).

Siegel, Larry J. 2014. *Criminology: The Core.* Stamford, CT: Cengage.

Silva, Eric Orion. 2014. "Neutralizing Problematic Frames in the Culture Wars: Anti-evolutionists Grapple with Religion." *Symbolic Interaction* 37: 226–245.

Silver, Hilary. 2007. "Disasters." Pp. 1174–1176 in *The Blackwell Encyclopedia of Sociology,* edited by G. Ritzer. Malden, MA: Blackwell.

Silvernail, David L. and Amy F. Johnson. 2014. "The Impacts of Public Charter Schools on Students and Traditional Public Schools: What Does the Empirical Evidence Tell Us?" Maine Education Policy Research Institute, University of Southern Maine, January. Retrieved April 17, 2015 (https://usm.maine.edu/sites/default/files/cepare/PublicCharterSchoolsWeb.pdf).

Simmel, Georg. [1904] 1971. "Fashion." Pp. 294–323 in *Georg Simmel: On Individuality and Social Forms,* edited by D. Levine. Chicago: University of Chicago Press.

Simmel, Georg. [1906] 1950. "The Secret and the Secret Society." Pp. 307–376 in *The Sociology of Georg Simmel,* edited and translated by K. H. Wolff. New York: Free Press.

Simmel, Georg. [1907] 1978. *The Philosophy of Money,* edited and translated by T. Bottomore and D. Frisby. London: Routledge & Kegan Paul.

Simmel, Georg. [1908] 1971. "The Stranger." Pp. 143–149 in *Georg Simmel: On Individuality and Social Forms,* edited by D. Levine. Chicago: University of Chicago Press.

Simmel, Georg. 1950. *The Sociology of Georg Simmel,* edited and translated by K. H. Wolff. New York: Free Press.

Simon, Bryant. 2009. *Everything but the Coffee: Learning about America from Starbucks.* Berkeley: University of California Press.

Simon, David R. 2012. *Elite Deviance.* 10th ed. Boston: Pearson/Allyn & Bacon.

Simon, Herbert A. [1945] 1976. *Administrative Behavior.* New York: Macmillan.

Simone, Alina. 2015. "How My Mom Got Hacked." New York Times, January 2. Retrieved April 27, 2015 (http://www.nytimes.com/2015/01/04/opinion/sunday/how-my-mom-got-hacked.html?_r=0).

Simons, Marlise. 2010a. "France: Roma Policy Challenged." *New York Times,* August 28.

Simons, Marlise. 2010b. "International Court Adds Genocide to Charges against Sudan Leader." *New York Times,* July 13. Retrieved November 5, 2013 (http://www.nytimes.com/2010/07/13/world/africa/13hague.html).

Simons, Marlise. 2010c. "Rights Panel Criticizes France over Roma Policy." *New York Times,* August 27.

Simpson, Colton. 2006. *Inside the Crips: Life inside L.A.'s Most Notorious Gang.* New York: St. Martin's Griffin.

Simpson, George Eaton and J. Milton Yinger. 1985. *Racial and Cultural Minorities: An Analysis of Prejudice and Discrimination.* 5th ed. New York: Plenum Press.

Simpson, Sally S. 2002. *Corporate Crime, Law, and Social Control.* New York: Cambridge University Press.

Simpson, Sally S. 2013. "White-Collar Crime: A Review of Recent Developments and Promising Directions for Future Research." *Annual Review of Sociology* 39: 309–331.

Simpson, Sally S. and David Weisburd, eds. 2009. *The Criminology of White-Collar Crime.* New York: Springer.

Singer, Natasha. 2009. "Lawmakers Seek to Curb Drug Commercials." *New York Times,* July 27.

Singer, Natasha. 2010. "The Financial Time Bomb of Longer Lives." *New York Times,* October 16.

Singer, Natasha. 2011. "On Campus, It's One Big Commercial." *New York Times,* September 10, 2011.

Singh, Devendra and Dorian Singh. 2011. "Shape and Significance of Feminine Beauty: An Evolutionary Perspective." *Sex Roles* 64: 723–731.

Singh, Gopal K. and Mohammad Siahpush. 2014. "Widening Rural–Urban Disparities in Life Expectancy, U.S., 1969–2009." *American Journal of Preventive Medicine* 46: e19–e29.

Sisario, Ben. 2011. "Master of the Media Marketplace, and Its Demanding Gatekeeper." *New York Times,* October 7. Retrieved November 5, 2011 (http://www.nytimes.com/2011/10/07/business/media/master-of-the-media-marketplace-and-its-demanding-gatekeeper.html?scp=5&sq=music%20industry&st=cse).

Sklair, Leslie. 2002. *Globalization: Capitalism and Its Alternatives.* Oxford: Oxford University Press.

Slater, Don. 1997. *Consumer Culture and Modernity.* Cambridge: Polity Press.

Slatton, Brittany Chevon and Joe R. Feagin. 2012. "Racial and Ethnic Issues: Critical Race Approaches in the United States." Pp. 287–303 in *The Wiley-Blackwell Companion to Sociology,* edited by G. Ritzer. Malden, MA: Wiley-Blackwell.

Smart, Barry, ed. 2011. *Post-industrial Society.* London: Sage.

Smelser, Neil. 1994. *Sociology.* Cambridge, MA: Blackwell.

Smith, David Norman, Brock Ternes, James P. Ordner, Russell Schloemer, Gabriela Moran, Chris Goode, Joshua Homan, Anna Kern, Lucas Keefer, Nathan Moser, Kevin McCannon, Kaela Byers, Daniel Sullivan, and Rachel Craft. 2011. "Mapping the Great Recession: A Reader's Guide to the First Crisis of 21st Century Capitalism." *New Political Science* 33(4): 577–601.

Smith, Jackie. 2008. *Social Movements for Global Democracy.* Baltimore: Johns Hopkins University Press.

Smith, Jessi L. and Meghan Huntoon. 2014. "Women's Bragging Rights: Overcoming Modesty Norms to Facilitate Women's Self-Promotion." *Psychology of Women Quarterly* 38: 447–459.

Smith, Paula. 2007. "Recidivism." Pp. 3818–3819 in *The Blackwell Encyclopedia of Sociology,* edited by G. Ritzer. Malden, MA: Blackwell.

Smith, William C., Emily Anderson, Daniel Salinas, Renata Horvatek, and David P. Baker. 2015. "A Meta-analysis of Education Effects on Chronic Disease: The Causal Dynamics of the Population Education Transition Curve." *Social Science & Medicine* 127: 29–40.

Smock, Pamela J. and Wendy Manning. 2004. "Living Together Unmarried in the United States: Demographic Perspectives and Implications for Family Policy." *Law and Policy* 26(1): 87–117.

Smyth, Bruce. 2007. "Non-resident Parents." Pp. 3223–3227 in *The Blackwell Encyclopedia of Sociology,* edited by G. Ritzer. Malden, MA: Blackwell.

Snow, David A. 2013a "Grievances, Individual and Mobilizing." Pp. 540–542 in *The Wiley-Blackwell Encyclopedia of Social and Political Movements,* 3 vols., edited by D. A. Snow, D. Della Porta, B. Klandermans, and D. McAdam. Malden, MA: Wiley-Blackwell.

Snow, David A. 2013b. "Social Movements." Pp. 1200–1204 in *The Wiley-Blackwell Encyclopedia of Social and Political Movements,* 3 vols., edited by D. A. Snow, D. Della Porta, B. Klandermans, and D. McAdam. Malden, MA: Wiley-Blackwell.

Snow, David A., D. Della Porta, B. Klandermans, and D. McAdam, eds. 2013. *The Wiley-Blackwell Encyclopedia of Social and Political Movements.* 3 vols. Malden, MA: Wiley-Blackwell.

Snow, David A. and Peter B. Owens. 2013. "Crowds (Gatherings) and Collective Behavior (Action)." Pp. 289–296 in *The Wiley-Blackwell Encyclopedia of Social and Political Movements,* 3 vols., edited by D. A. Snow, D. Della Porta, B. Klandermans, and D. McAdam. Malden, MA: Wiley-Blackwell.

Snow, David A., Sarah A. Soule, and Daniel M. Cress. 2005. "Identifying the Precipitants of Homeless Protest across 17 U.S. Cities, 1980 to 1990." *Social Forces* 83: 1183–1210.

Snyder, Kieran. 2014. "The Abrasiveness Trap: High-Achieving Men and Women Are Described Differently in Reviews." *Fortune,* August 26. Retrieved May 12, 2015 (http://fortune.com/2014/08/26/performance-review-gender-bias).

Snyder, Patricia. 2007. "Survey Research." Pp. 4898–4900 in *The Blackwell Encyclopedia of Sociology,* edited by G. Ritzer. Malden, MA: Blackwell.

Snyder, R. Claire. 2008. "What Is Third-Wave Feminism? A New Directions Essay." *Signs* 34(1): 175–196.

Song, Miri. 2007. "Racial Hierarchy." Pp. 3360–3364 in *The Blackwell Encyclopedia of Sociology,* edited by G. Ritzer. Malden, MA: Blackwell.

Sontag, Deborah. 2012. "Rebuilding in Haiti Lags after Billions in Post-quake Aid." *New York Times,* December 23.

Sontag, Deborah. 2015. "'Every Day I Struggle': Transgender Inmate Cites Attacks and Abuse in Men's Prison." *New York Times,* April 6.

Southern Poverty Law Center. 2013. "Hate Map." Retrieved March 31, 2014 (http://www.splcenter.org/get-informed/hate-map).

Soysal, Yasemin Nuhoglu. 2012. "Citizenship, Immigration, and the European Social Project: Rights and Obligations of Individuality." *British Journal of Sociology* 63: 1–21.

Spada, Marcantonio M. 2014. "An Overview of Problematic Internet Use." *Addictive Behaviors* 39: 3–6.

Spade, Joan Z. and Catherine G. Valentine. 2011. *The Kaleidoscope of Gender: Prisms, Patterns, and Possibilities.* Thousand Oaks, CA: Pine Forge Press.

Specter, Michael. 2015. "Extreme City." *New Yorker,* June 1, 32–37.

Spencer, Herbert. 1851. *Social Statics.* London: Chapman.

Spencer, James H. 2004. "Los Angeles since 1992: How Did the Economic Base of Riot-Torn Neighborhoods Fare after the Unrest?" *Race, Gender and Class* 11(1): 94–115.

Spotts, Greg and Robert Greenwald. 2005. *Wal-Mart: The High Cost of Low Price.* New York: Disinformation Press.

Spröber, Nina, et al. 2014. "Child Sexual Abuse in Religiously Affiliated and Secular Institutions: A Retrospective Descriptive Analysis of Data Provided by Victims in a Government-Sponsored Reappraisal Program in Germany." *BMC Public Health* 14, published online. doi: 10.1186/1471-2458-14-282.

Stacey, Clare L. and Lindsey L. Ayers. 2012. "Caught between Love and Money: The Experiences of Paid Family Caregivers." *Qualitative Sociology* 35: 47–64.

Standing, Guy. 1989. "Global Feminization through Flexible Labor: A Theme Revisited." *World Development* 27(3): 583–602.

Staples, Brent. 1986. "Black Men and Public Space." *Harper's Magazine,* December, 19.

Stark, Rodney and William Sims Bainbridge. 1979. "Of Churches, Sects, and Cults: Preliminary Concepts for a Theory of Religious Movements." *Journal for the Scientific Study of Religion* 18(2): 117–131.

Statista. 2015. "Statistics and Facts about the Pharmaceutical Industry Worldwide." Retrieved May 19, 2015 (www.statista.com/topics/1764/global-pharmaceutical-industry).

Stearns, Cindy A. 2009. "The Work of Breastfeeding." *Women's Studies Quarterly* 37: 63–80.

Stearns, Cindy A. 2011. "Cautionary Tale about Extended Breastfeeding and Weaning." *Health Care for Women International* 32: 538–554.

Stein, Joel. 2015. "Baby, You Can Drive My Car, and Do My Errands, and Rent My Stuff . . ." *Time,* February 9, 34–40.

Steinberg, L. and K. C. Monahan. 2007. "Age Differences in Resistance to Peer Influence." *Developmental Psychology* 43: 1531–1543.

Steinhauer, Jennifer and Jonathan Weisman. 2015. "U.S. Surveillance in Place since 9/11 Is Sharply Limited." *New York Times,* June 2. Retrieved August 20, 2015 (http://www.nytimes.com/2015/06/03/us/politics/senate-surveillance-bill-passes-hurdle-but-showdown-looms.html?_r=0).

Steinmetz, George. 2012. "Geopolitics." Pp. 800–823 in *The Wiley-Blackwell Encyclopedia of Globalization,* edited by G. Ritzer. Malden, MA: Wiley-Blackwell.

Steinmetz, Katy. 2014. "The Transgender Tipping Point." *Time,* May 29. Retrieved April 21, 2015 (http://time.com/135480/transgender-tipping-point).

Steinmetz, Suzanne K. 1987. "Family Violence." In *Handbook of Marriage and the Family,* edited by M. B. Sussman and S. K. Steinmetz. New York: Plenum Press.

Steketee, Gail and Randy Frost. 2011. *Stuff: Compulsive Hoarding and the Meaning of Things.* Boston: Mariner Books.

Stepan-Norris, Judith and Caleb Southworth. 2007. "Churches as Organizational Resources: A Case Study in the Geography of Religion and Political Voting in Postwar Detroit." *Social Science History* 31(3): 343–380.

Stermer, S. Paul and Melissa Burkley. 2015. "SeX-Box: Exposure to Sexist Video Games Predicts Benevolent Sexism." *Psychology of Popular Media Culture* 4(1): 47–55.

Stevens, Mitchell L. 2001. *Kingdom of Children: Culture and Controversy in the Home Schooling Movement.* Princeton, NJ: Princeton University Press.

Stevens, Mitchell L. 2007. "Schooling, Home." Pp. 4032–4034 in *The Blackwell Encyclopedia of Sociology,* edited by G. Ritzer. Malden, MA: Blackwell.

Stevis, Dimitris. 2005. "The Globalization of Environment." *Globalizations* 2(3): 323–333.

Stewart, Heather. 2013. "Eurozone Bailouts: Which Countries Remain?" *The Guardian,* December 13.

Stockdill, Brett C. 2013. "ACT UP (AIDS Coalition to Unleash Power)." Pp. 5–9 in *The Wiley-Blackwell Encyclopedia of Social and Political Movements,* 3 vols., edited by D. A. Snow, D. Della Porta, B. Klandermans, and D. McAdam. Malden, MA: Wiley-Blackwell.

Stokoe, Elizabeth. 2006. "On Ethnomethodology, Feminism, and the Analysis of Categorical Reference to Gender in Talk-in-Interaction." *Sociological Review* 54(3): 467–494.

Stolow, Jeremy. 2004. "Transnationalism and the New Religio-politics: Reflections on a Jewish Orthodox Case." *Theory, Culture and Society* 21(2): 109–137.

Stone, Amy and Jill Weinberg. 2015. "Sexualities and Social Movements: Three Decades of Sex and Social Change." In *Handbook of the Sociology of Sexualities,* edited by J. DeLamater and R. F. Plante. Dordrecht, Netherlands: Springer.

Stoolmiller, Michael. 1999. "Implications of the Restricted Range of Family Environments for Estimates of Heritability and Nonshared Environments in Behavior-Genetic Adoption Studies." *Psychological Bulletin* 125: 392–409.

Story, Louise and Stephanie Saul. 2015. "Stream of Foreign Wealth Flows to Elite New York Real Estate." *New York Times,* February 7.

Stouffer, S. A., E. A. Suchman, L. C. DeVinney, S. A. Star, and R. M. Williams. 1949. *The American Soldier: Adjustment during Army Life.* Vol. 1. Princeton, NJ: Princeton University Press.

Strandbu, Ase and Ingela Lundin Kvalem. 2014. "Body Talk and Body Ideals among Adolescent Boys and Girls: A Mixed-Gender Focus Group Study." *Youth & Society* 46(5): 623–641.

Stratton, Greg and Jeremy Northcote. 2014. "When Totems Beget Clans: The Brand Symbol as the Defining Marker of Brand Communities." *Journal of Consumer Culture,* published online April 4. doi: 10.1177/1469540514528194.

Straus, Murray A. 1980. "Victims and Aggressors in Marital Violence." *American Behavioral Scientist* 23: 681–704.

Streitfeld, David. 2014. "Airbnb Listings Mostly Illegal, State Contends." *New York Times,* October 16.

Struck, Doug. 2007. "Warming Will Exacerbate Global Water Conflicts." *Washington Post,* October 22.

Stryker, Sheldon. 1959. "Symbolic Interaction as an Approach to Family Research." *Marriage and Family Living* 21(2): 111–119.

Subramaniam, Mangala, David Whitlock, and Beth Williford. 2012. "Water Crisis." Pp. 2210–2212 in *The Wiley-Blackwell Encyclopedia of Globalization,* edited by G. Ritzer. Malden, MA: Wiley-Blackwell.

Subramanian, Ramesh. 2012. "Computer Viruses." Pp. 220–274 in *The Wiley-Blackwell Encyclopedia of Globalization,* edited by G. Ritzer. Malden, MA: Wiley-Blackwell.

Subramanian, Ramesh and Eddan Katz, eds. 2011. *The Global Flow of Information: Legal, Social, and Cultural Perspectives.* New York: New York University Press.

Sullivan, Gail. 2014. "United Kingdom's First 'Poo Bus' Runs on Human Waste." *Washington Post,* November 21. Retrieved April 21, 2015 (http://www.washingtonpost.com/news/morning-mix/wp/2014/11/21/united-kingdoms-first-poo-bus-runs-on-human-waste).

Sumner, William Graham. [1906] 1940. *Folkways: A Study of the Sociological Implications of Usages, Manners, Customs, Mores and Morals.* Boston: Ginn.

Surtees, Nicola. 2008. "Teachers Following Children? Heteronormative Responses within a Discourse of Child-Centredness and the Emergent Curriculum." *Australian Journal of Early Childhood* 33(3): 10–17.

Sutherland, Edwin H. 1924. *Criminology.* Chicago: University of Chicago Press.

Sutton, Susan Buck. 2014. "On the Ground Overseas: How the International Engagement of US Institutions of Higher Learning Prepares Students for a Global Future." Retrieved April 21, 2015 (http://www.wm.edu/offices/reves-center/internationalization/papers%20and%20presentations/bucksutton.pdf).

Swami, Viren, Amy Henry, Nicola Peacock, Ahkin Roberts-Dunn, and Alan Porter. 2013. "'Mirror, Mirror . . .': A Preliminary Investigation of Skin Tone Dissatisfaction and Its Impact among British Adults." *Cultural Diversity and Ethnic Minority Psychology* 19(4): 468–476.

Sykes, Gresham. [1958] 2007. *The Society of Captives: A Study of a Maximum Security Prison.* Princeton, NJ: Princeton University Press.

Sylvia Rivera Law Project. 2015. "Who Was Sylvia Rivera?" Retrieved March 17, 2015 (http://srlp.org/about/who-was-sylvia-rivera).

Sztompka, Piotr. 1993. *The Sociology of Social Change.* West Sussex, England: Wiley-Blackwell.

Tabuchi, Hiroko. 2010. "Beef Bowl Economics: In Japan, a Price War at Popular Restaurants Is the Face of Deflation." *New York Times,* January 30, B1, B6.

Tam, Pui-Wing and Michael J. de la Merced. 2015. "Uber Fund-Raising Points to $50 Billion Valuation." *New York Times,* May 9.

Tatangelo, Gemma L. and Lina A. Ricciardelli. 2013. "A Qualitative Study of Preadolescent Boys' and Girls' Body Image: Gendered Ideals and Sociocultural Influences." *Body Image* 10: 591–598.

Taylor, Charles. 2007. *A Secular Age.* Cambridge, MA: Belknap Press.

Taylor, J. L. 2007. "Buddhism." Pp. 108–113 in *Encyclopedia of Globalization,* edited by J. A. Scholte and R. Robertson. New York: MTM.

Taylor, Paul, Cary Funk, and April Clark. 2007. "From 1997 to 2007, Fewer Mothers Prefer Full-Time Work." Pew Research Center, July 12. Retrieved April 21, 2015 (http://www.pewsocialtrends.org/files/2010/10/WomenWorking.pdf).

Taylor, Paul C. 2011. "William Edward Burghardt Du Bois." Pp. 426–447 in *The Wiley-Blackwell Companion to Major Social Theorists,* Vol. 1, *Classical Theorists,* edited by G. Ritzer and J. Stepnisky. Malden, MA: Wiley-Blackwell.

Taylor, Yvette. 2007. "Sexualities and Consumption." Pp. 4256–4260 in *The Blackwell Encyclopedia of Sociology,* edited by G. Ritzer. Malden, MA: Blackwell.

Teivainen, Teivo. 2007. "World Social Forum." Pp. 1302–1304 in *Encyclopedia of Globalization,* edited by J. A. Scholte and R. Robertson. New York: MTM.

Terranova, Tiziana. 2013. "Free Labor." Pp. 33–57 in *Digital Labor: The Internet as Playground and Factory,* edited by T. Scholz. New York: Routledge.

Tescione, Sara. 2013. "Civil Disobedience." Pp. 191–193 in *The Wiley-Blackwell Encyclopedia of Social and Political Movements,* 3 vols., edited by D. A. Snow, D. Della Porta, B. Klandermans, and D. McAdam. Malden, MA: Wiley-Blackwell.

Tetrault, Lisa. 2014. *The Myth of Seneca Falls: Memory and the Women's Suffrage Movement, 1848–1898.* Chapel Hill: University of North Carolina Press.

Thoits, Peggy A. 1985. "Self-Labeling Processes in Mental Illness: The Role of Emotional Deviance." *American Journal of Sociology* 91(2): 221–249.

Thoits, Peggy A. 2011. "Perceived Social Support and the Voluntary, Mixed, or Pressured Use of Mental Health Services." *Society and Mental Health* 1: 4–19.

Thomas, George. 2012. "Christianity." Pp. 179–187 in *The Wiley-Blackwell Encyclopedia of Globalization,* edited by G. Ritzer. Malden, MA: Wiley-Blackwell.

Thomas, Landon, Jr. 2011. "Pondering a Day: Leaving the Euro." *New York Times*, December 13.

Thomas, William I. and Dorothy S. Thomas. 1928. *The Child in America: Behavior Problems and Programs*. New York: Knopf.

Thompson, Ginger and Marc Lacey. 2010. "U.S. and Mexico Revise Joint Antidrug Strategy." *New York Times*, March 23. Retrieved March 31, 2012 (http://www.nytimes.com/2010/03/24/world/americas/24mexico.html).

Thorn, Elizabeth. 2007. "Gender, Work, and Family." Pp. 1880–1885 in *The Blackwell Encyclopedia of Sociology*, edited by G. Ritzer. Malden, MA: Blackwell.

Thorne, Barrie. 1993. *Gender Play: Girls and Boys in School*. New Brunswick, NJ: Rutgers University Press.

Thornton, Arland, William Axinn, and Y. Xie. 2007. *Marriage and Cohabitation*. Chicago: University of Chicago Press.

Timasheff, Nicholas S. 1965. *War and Revolution*. New York: Sheed and Ward.

Timberlake, Michael and Xiulian Ma. 2007. "Cities and Globalization." Pp. 254–271 in *The Blackwell Companion to Globalization*, edited by G. Ritzer. Malden, MA: Blackwell.

Timmermans, Stefan and Hyeyoung Oh. 2010. "The Continued Social Transformation of the Medical Profession." *Journal of Health and Social Behavior* 51: S94–S106.

Timms, Jill. 2012. "Labor Movements." Pp. 1259–1261 in *The Encyclopedia of Globalization*, edited by G. Ritzer. Malden, MA: Wiley-Blackwell.

Tiryakian, Edward. 1991. "Modernization: Exhumateur in Pace (Rethinking Macrosociology in the 1990s)." *International Sociology* 6(2): 165–180.

Tocqueville, Alexis de. [1835–1840] 1969. *Democracy in America*. Garden City, NY: Doubleday.

Toennies, Ferdinand. [1887] 1957. *Community and Society*. New York: Harper Torchbooks.

Tolbert, Pamela. 2013. "The Iron Law of Oligarchy." Pp. 637–639 in *The Wiley-Blackwell Encyclopedia of Social and Political Movements,* 3 vols., edited by D. A. Snow, D. Della Porta, B. Klandermans, and D. McAdam. Malden, MA: Wiley-Blackwell.

Tomlinson, John. 1999. *Globalization and Culture*. Chicago: University of Chicago Press.

Tomlinson, John. 2000. "Globalization and Cultural Identity." Pp. 269–277 in *The Global Transformations Reader,* edited by D. Held and A. McGrew. Cambridge: Polity Press.

Tomlinson, John. 2012. "Cultural Imperialism." Pp. 371–374 in *The Wiley-Blackwell Encyclopedia of Globalization*, edited by G. Ritzer. Malden, MA: Wiley-Blackwell.

Tong, Rosemarie. 2009. *Feminist Thought: A More Comprehensive Introduction*. 3rd ed. Boulder, CO: Westview Press.

Torpey, John C. 2000. *The Invention of the Passport: Citizenship, Surveillance, and the State*. New York: Cambridge University Press.

Torpey, John C. 2012. "Passports." Pp. 1644–1647 in *The Wiley-Blackwell Encyclopedia of Globalization*, edited by G. Ritzer. Malden, MA: Wiley-Blackwell.

Transgender Europe. 2014. "Transgender Europe's Trans Murder Monitoring Project Reveals 226 Killings of Trans People in the Last 12 Months." Press release, October 30. Retrieved April 21, 2015 (http://www.transrespect-transphobia.org/uploads/downloads/2014/TDOR2014/TvT-TDOR2014PR-en.pdf).

Trask, Bahira Sherif. 2010. *Globalization and Families: Accelerated Systemic Social Change*. New York: Springer.

Treas, Judith, Jonathan Lui, and Zoya Gubernskaya. 2014. "Attitudes on Marriage and New Relationships: Cross-National Evidence on the Deinstitutionalization of Marriage." *Demographic Research* 30: 1495–1526.

Trebay, Guy. 2008. "Tattoos Gain Even More Visibility." *New York Times,* September 24. Retrieved December 20, 2011 (http://www.nytimes.com/2008/09/25/fashion/25tattoo.html?scp=1&sq=September%2025,%202008%20tattoo&st=cse).

Tremblay, Manon, David Paternotte, and Carol Johnson, eds. 2013. *The Lesbian and Gay Movement and the State: Comparative Insights into a Transformed Relationship*. Farnham, England: Ashgate.

Trepagnier, Barbara. 2010. *Silent Racism: How Well-Meaning People Perpetuate the Racial Divide*. Boulder, CO: Paradigm.

Tsuda, Takeyuki, Maria Tapias, and Xavier Escandell. 2014. "Locating the Global in Transnational Ethnography." *Journal of Contemporary Ethnography* 43: 123–147.

Tsutsui, Kiyoteru and Christine Min Wotipka. 2004. "Global Civil Society and the International Human Rights Movement: Citizen Participation in Human Rights International Nongovernmental Organizations." *Social Forces* 83(2): 587–620.

Tufekci, Zeynep. 2010. "Internet Use and Social Ties of Americans: An Analysis of General Social Survey Data." Paper presented at the annual meeting of the American Sociological Association, Atlanta, GA.

Tumin, Melvin E. 1953. "Some Principles of Stratification: A Critical Analysis." *American Sociological Review* 18: 387–394.

Tunnell, Kenneth D. 2007. "Crime, Political." Pp. 835–836 in *The Blackwell Encyclopedia of Sociology*, edited by G. Ritzer. Malden, MA: Blackwell.

Turkle, Sherry. 1995. *Life on Screen: Identity in the Age of the Internet*. New York: Simon & Schuster.

Turkle, Sherry. 2011. *Alone Together: Why We Expect More from Technology and Less from Each Other.* New York: Basic Books.

Turner, Bryan S. 2007a. "Body and Cultural Sociology." Pp. 324–328 in *The Blackwell Encyclopedia of Sociology*, edited by G. Ritzer. Malden, MA: Blackwell.

Turner, Bryan S. 2007b. "Body and Society." Pp. 335–38 in *The Blackwell Encyclopedia of Sociology*, edited by G. Ritzer. Malden, MA: Blackwell.

Turner, Bryan S. 2008. *The Body and Society: Explorations in Social Theory*. 3rd ed. London: Sage.

Turner, Bryan S. 2011. *Religion and Modern Society: Citizenship, Secularisation and the State*. Cambridge: Cambridge University Press.

Turner, Bryan S. 2014. "Religion and Contemporary Sociological Theories." *Current Sociology* 62: 771–788.

Turner, Fred. 2008. *From Counterculture to Cyberculture: Stewart Brand, the Whole Earth Network, and the Rise of Digital Utopianism.* Chicago: University of Chicago Press.

Turner, Jonathan. 2005. "A New Approach for Theoretically Integrating Micro and Macro Analysis." Pp. 403–422 in *The Sage Handbook of Sociology,* edited by C. Calhoun, C. Rojek, and B. Turner. London: Sage.

Turner, Leigh. 2007. "'First World Health Care at Third World Prices': Globalization, Bioethics and Medical Tourism." *BioSocieties* 2: 303–325.

Turner, Ralph H. 1978. "The Role and the Person." *American Journal of Sociology* 84: 1–23.

Turner, Ralph H. and Lewis M. Killian. 1987. *Collective Behavior*. 3rd ed. Englewood Cliffs, NJ: Prentice Hall.

Turner, Victor. 1967. *The Forest of Symbols: Aspects of Ndembu Ritual*. Ithaca, NY: Cornell University Press.

Tyrell, Hartmann. 2010. "History and Sociology—the First Century: From Ranke to Weber." *InterDisciplines: Journal of History and Sociology* 1(1): 94–111.

Uchitelle, Louis. 2010. "Another Shifting Industry." *New York Times,* January 19.

Ultee, Wout. 2007a. "Mobility, Horizontal and Vertical." Pp. 3060–3061 in *The Blackwell Encyclopedia of Sociology*, edited by G. Ritzer. Malden, MA: Blackwell.

Ultee, Wout. 2007b. "Mobility, Intergenerational and Intragenerational." Pp. 3061–3062 in *The Blackwell Encyclopedia of Sociology*, edited by G. Ritzer. Malden, MA: Blackwell.

UNAIDS. 2008. *Report on the Global AIDS Epidemic.* Geneva: Author.

United Nations. 2006. "Ending Violence against Women: From Words to Action Study of the Secretary-General, Fact Sheet." Retrieved March 31, 2012 (http://www.un.org/womenwatch/daw/vaw/launch/english/v.a.w-exeE-use.pdf).

United Nations. 2014. "World's Population Increasingly Urban with More than Half Living in Urban Areas." July 10. Retrieved April 21, 2015 (http://www.un.org/en/development/desa/news/population/world-urbanization-prospects-2014.html).

United Nations Department of Economic and Social Affairs. 2015. "Probabilistic Population Projections Based on the *World Population Prospects: The 2012 Revision*." Retrieved March 19, 2015 (http://esa.un.org/unpd/ppp/Data-Output/UN_PPP2012_output-data.htm).

United Nations Development Programme. 2014. "Gender and Poverty Reduction." Retrieved April 21, 2015 (http://www.undp.org/content/undp/en/home/ourwork/povertyreduction/focus_areas/focus_gender_and_poverty).

United Nations General Assembly. 2006. *In-Depth Study on All Forms of Violence against Women: Report of the Secretary-General.* A/61/122/Add.1. New York: Author.

United Nations Global Initiative to Fight Human Trafficking. 2007. "Human Trafficking: The Facts." Retrieved March 31, 2012 (http://www.unglobalcompact.org/docs/issues_doc/labour/Forced_labour/HUMAN_TRAFFICKING_-_THE_FACTS_-_final.pdf).

United Nations Office on Drugs and Crime. 2012. *World Drug Report 2012.* UN pub., Sales No. E.12.XI.1. New York: United Nations. Retrieved September 5, 2013 (http://www.unodc.org/

documents/data-and-analysis/WDR2012/ WDR_2012_web_small.pdf).

United Nations Population Fund. 2015. "Migration." Retrieved March 19, 2015 (http://www.unfpa. org/migration).

UN Women. 2014. "Facts and Figures: Ending Violence against Women." October. Retrieved April 18, 2015 (http://www.unwomen.org/en/ what-we-do/ending-violence-against-women/ facts-and-figures#sthash.5L0ZPGBH.dpuf).

Uriely, Natan and Yaniv Belhassen. 2005. "Drugs and Tourists' Experiences." *Journal of Travel Research* 43(3): 238–246.

Urry, John. 2007. *Mobilities*. Cambridge: Polity Press.

U.S. Census Bureau. 2011a. "Poverty." Current Population Survey: Annual Social and Economic Supplement. Retrieved March 31, 2012 (http:// www.census.gov/hhes/www/cpstables/032011/ pov/new01_100_01.htm).

U.S. Census Bureau. 2011b. "Statistical Abstract of the United States 2011" (Tables 225 and 226). Retrieved March 31, 2012 (http://www.census .gov/compendia/statab/2011/tables/11s0225 .pdf).

U.S. Census Bureau. 2011c. "2010 Census Shows America's Diversity." Press release, March 24. Retrieved May 7, 2015 (https://www.census. gov/newsroom/releases/archives/2010_census/ cb11-cn125.html).

U.S. Census Bureau. 2012a. "International Programs." Retrieved October 27, 2013 (http://www .census.gov.iii-server.ualr.edu/population/ international).

U.S. Census Bureau. 2012b. "Population." 2011 Statistical Abstract. Retrieved March 31, 2012 (http://www.census.gov/compendia/statab/cats/ population.html).

U.S. Census Bureau. 2013. "Trade in Goods with China." Retrieved February 14, 2013 (http:// www.census.gov/foreign-trade/balance/c5700. html).

U.S. Census Bureau. 2014a. Current Population Survey, 2014 Annual Social and Economic (ASEC) Supplement (machine-readable data file). Retrieved April 23, 2015 (ftp://ftp2 .census.gov/programs-surveys/cps/techdocs/ cpsmar14.pdf).

U.S. Census Bureau. 2014b. "Income, Poverty and Health Insurance Coverage in the United States, 2013." Press release CB14-169, September 16. Retrieved April 29, 2015 (http://www.census.gov/newsroom/press- releases/2014/cb14-169.html).

U.S. Census Bureau. 2015. "Income: Frequently Asked Questions." Retrieved February 19, 2015 (https://www.census.gov/hhes/www/income/ about/faqs.html).

U.S. Department of Commerce, Economics and Statistics Administration; Executive Office of the President, Office of Management and Budget; and White House Council on Women and Girls. 2011. "Women in America: Indicators of Economic and Social Well-Being." Retrieved May 25, 2011 (http://www.whitehouse.gov/ sites/default/files/rss_viewer/Women_in_ America.pdf).

U.S. Department of Defense, Sexual Assault Prevention and Response. 2014. *Department of Defense Annual Report on Sexual Assault in the Military: Fiscal Year 2013*. Washington, DC: Author.

Retrieved April 27, 2015 (http://www.sapr. mil/public/docs/reports/FY13_DoD_SAPRO_ Annual_Report_on_Sexual_Assault.pdf).

U.S. Department of Education, National Center for Education Statistics. 2014. "Fast Facts: Homeschooling." Retrieved May 14, 2015 (http://nces.ed.gov/fastfacts/display.asp?id=91).

U.S. Department of Health and Human Services. 2014. "HHS Disparities Action Plan." Retrieved April 21, 2015 (http://minorityhealth.hhs.gov/ omh/browse.aspx?lvl=2&lvlid=10).

U.S. Department of Health and Human Services, Assistant Secretary for Planning and Evaluation. 2014. "2014 Poverty Guidelines." Retrieved April 29, 2015 (http://aspe.hhs.gov/ poverty/14poverty.cfm).

U.S. Department of Health and Human Services, National Institutes of Health. 2011. "Human Genome Project." Retrieved April 15, 2011 (http://report.nih.gov/NIHfactsheets/ ViewFactSheet.aspx?csid=45&key=H#H).

U.S. Department of Justice, Bureau of Justice Statistics. 2008. "Identity Theft." Retrieved November 6, 2011 (http://www.bjs.gov/index. cfm?ty=tp&tid=42).

U.S. Department of Justice, Bureau of Justice Statistics. 2011. "Sourcebook of Criminal Justice Statistics" (Section 6: Persons Under Criminal Supervision). Retrieved April 21, 2015 (http:// www.albany.edu/sourcebook/tost_6.html#6_e).

U.S. Department of Labor, Bureau of Labor Statistics. 2009. "Ranks of Discouraged Workers and Others Marginally Attached to the Labor Force Rise during Recession." *Issues in Labor Statistics*, April.

U.S. Department of Labor, Bureau of Labor Statistics. 2013. "Earnings and Unemployment Rates by Educational Attainment." Retrieved June 26, 2013 (http://www.bls.gov/emp/ep_chart_001.htm).

U.S. Department of State. 2007. *Trafficking in Persons Report 2007*. Washington, DC: Author. Retrieved May 15, 2015 (http://www.state.gov/j/tip/rls/ tiprpt/2007/index.htm).

U.S. Department of State. 2011. *Trafficking in Persons Report 2011*. Washington, DC: Author. Retrieved May 15, 2015 (http://www.state.gov/j/tip/rls/ tiprpt/2011/index.htm).

Useem, Elizabeth L. 1992. "Middle Schools and Math Groups: Parents' Involvement in Children's Placement." *Sociology of Education* 65: 263–279.

Vail, D. Angus. 1999. "Tattoos Are Like Potato Chips . . . You Can't Have Just One: The Process of Becoming and Being a Collector." *Deviant Behavior* 20: 253–273.

Vail, D. Angus. 2007. "Body Modification." Pp. 328– 330 in *The Blackwell Encyclopedia of Sociology*, edited by G. Ritzer. Malden. MA: Blackwell.

Valenzuela, Sebastián. 2013. "Unpacking the Use of Social Media for Protest Behavior: The Roles of Information, Opinion Expression, and Activism." *American Behavioral Scientist* 57: 920–942.

Valocchi, Stephen. 2007. "Gay and Lesbian Movement." Pp. 1833–1838 in *The Blackwell Encyclopedia of Sociology*, edited by G. Ritzer. Malden, MA: Blackwell.

Valocchi, Stephen. 2013. "Gay and Lesbian Movement." Pp. 498–503 in *The Wiley-Blackwell Encyclopedia of Social and Political Movements*, 3 vols., edited by D. A. Snow, D. Della Porta, B.

Klandermans, and D. McAdam. Malden, MA: Wiley-Blackwell.

Van de Poel, Ellen, Ahmad Reza Hosseinpoor, Niko Speybroeck, Tom Van Ourti, and Jeanette Vega. 2008. "Socioeconomic Inequality in Malnutrition in Developing Countries." *Bulletin of the World Health Organization* 86(4): 241–320.

van der Lippe, Tanja, Vincent Frey, and Milena Tsvetkova. 2012. "Outsourcing of Domestic Tasks: A Matter of Preferences?" *Journal of Family Issues* 34(12): 1574–1597.

Van de Werfhorst, Herman G. and Jonathan J. B. Mij. 2010. "Achievement Inequality and the Institutional Structure of Educational Systems: A Comparative Perspective." *Annual Review of Sociology* 36: 407–428.

Van Dijk, Jan A. G. M. 2012. *The Network Society*. 3rd ed. Thousand Oaks, CA: Sage.

van Dyke, Nella and David S. Meyer, eds. 2014. *Understanding the Tea Party Movement*. Farnham, England: Ashgate.

Vanek, Joann, Martha Chen, Ralf Hussmanns, and Francoise Carre. 2014. *Women and Men in the Informal Economy: A Statistical Picture*. 2nd ed. Geneva: International Labour Organization.

van Gennep, Arnold. 1961. *The Rites of Passage*. Chicago: University of Chicago Press.

Van Kessel, Ineke. 2013. "Antiapartheid Movements (South Africa)." Pp. 60–66 in *The Wiley-Blackwell Encyclopedia of Social and Political Movements*, 3 vols., edited by D. A. Snow, D. Della Porta, B. Klandermans, and D. McAdam. Malden, MA: Wiley-Blackwell.

van Leeuwen, Marco H. D. and Ineke Maas. 2010. "Historical Studies of Social Mobility and Stratification." *Annual Review of Sociology* 36: 429–451.

Van Maanen, John. 1983. "The Moral Fix: On the Ethics of Field Work." In *Contemporary Field Research: Perspectives and Formulations*, edited by R. M. Emerson. Longrove, IL: Waveland Press.

Varcoe, Ian. 2007. "Historical and Comparative Methods." Pp. 2133–2136 in *The Blackwell Encyclopedia of Sociology*, edited by G. Ritzer. Malden, MA: Blackwell.

Vaughan, Diane. 1996. *The Challenger Launch Decision: Risky Technology, Culture, and Deviance at NASA*. Chicago: University of Chicago Press.

Veblen, Thorstein. [1899] 1994. *The Theory of the Leisure Class*. New York: Penguin.

Veldkamp, Ted I. E. et al. 2014. "Impact of Socio- economic Trends and Climate Variability on the Occurrence and Severity of Blue Water Shortage and Stress Events at the Global Scale." *EGU General Assembly Conference Abstracts* 16. Retrieved April 21, 2015 (http://meetingor- ganizer.copernicus.org/EGU2014/EGU2014- 2146.pdf).

Venkatesh, Alladi. 2007. "Postmodern Consumption." Pp. 3552–3556 in *The Blackwell Encyclopedia of Sociology*, edited by G. Ritzer. Malden, MA: Blackwell.

Venkatesh, Sudhir. 2008. *Gang Leader for a Day: A Rogue Sociologist Takes to the Streets*. New York: Penguin.

Venkatesh, Sudhir. 2013. *Floating City: A Rogue Sociologist Lost and Found in New York's Underground Economy*. New York: Penguin.

Verde Group. 2007. "He Buys, She Shops: A Study of Gender Differences in the Retail Experience." Executive summary. Retrieved April 18, 2015 (http://www.wharton.upenn.edu/bakerretail/files/He_Buys_She_Shops_fall_2007_exec_summary.pdf).

Verkaik, Robert. 2006. "Sex Harassment in Armed Forces Is Rife, Say Women." *Independent*, May 26. Retrieved December 3, 2011 (http://www.independent.co.uk/news/uk/crime/sex-harassment-in-armed-forces-is-rife-say-women-479769.html).

Vertigans, Stephen. 2011. *The Sociology of Terrorism: People, Place and Processes*. New York: Routledge.

Vieraitis, Lynne M., Heith Copes, Zachary A. Powell, and Ashley Pike. 2015. "A Little Information Goes a Long Way: Expertise and Identity Theft." *Aggression and Violent Behavior* 20: 10–18.

Viladrich, Anahi and Rita Baron-Faust. 2014. "Medical Tourism in Tango Paradise: The Internet Branding of Cosmetic Surgery in Argentina." *Annals of Tourism Research* 45: 116–131.

Villareal, Andres and Wei-hsin Yu. 2007. "Economic Globalization and Women's Employment: The Case of Manufacturing in Mexico." *American Sociological Review* 72(3): 365–389.

Vlase, Ionela and Mălina Voicu. 2014. "Romanian Roma Migration: The Interplay between Structures and Agency." *Ethnic and Racial Studies* 37(13): 2418–2437.

Vlasic, Bill. 2013. "Lawyer Outlines Challenges in New Job Fixing Detroit." *New York Times*, March 25.

Voas, David and Fenella Fleischmann. 2012. "Islam Moves West: Religious Change in the First and Second Generations." *Annual Review of Sociology* 38: 525–545.

Vogel, Ezra F. 2011. *Deng Xiaoping and the Transformation of China*. Cambridge, MA: Belknap Press.

Vogli, Roberto De, Anne Kouvonen, Marko Elovainio, and Michael Marmot. 2014. "Economic Globalization, Inequality and Body Mass Index: A Cross-National Analysis of 127 Countries." *Critical Public Health* 24(1): 7–21.

Vohs, Kathleen D., Jaideep Sengupta, and Darren W. Dahl. 2014. "The Price Had Better Be Right: Women's Reactions to Sexual Stimuli Vary with Market Factors." *Psychological Science* 25(1): 278–283.

vom Lehn, Dirk. 2007. "Interaction." Pp. 2361–2365 in *The Blackwell Encyclopedia of Sociology*, edited by G. Ritzer. Malden, MA: Blackwell.

von Grebmer, Klaus et al. 2013. *2013 Global Hunger Index*. Washington, DC: International Food Policy Research Institute.

von Sivers, Isabella, Anne Templeton, Gerta Köster, John Drury, and Andrew Philippides. 2014. "Humans Do Not Always Act Selfishly: Social Identity and Helping in Emergency Evacuation Simulation." *Transportation Research Procedia* 2: 585–593.

Waddington, Ivan. 2007. "Health and Sport." Pp. 2091–2095 in *The Blackwell Encyclopedia of Sociology*, edited by G. Ritzer. Malden, MA: Blackwell.

Wajcman, Judy. 2010. "Feminist Theories of Technology." *Cambridge Journal of Economics* 34: 143–152.

Wakefield, Kelly. 2013. "Global Digital Divide: Inequality and Internet Access." *Geography Review* 26: 10–13.

Walder, Andrew. 2009. "Political Sociology and Social Movements." *Annual Review of Sociology* 35: 393–412.

Waldmeir, Patti. [1997] 2001. *Anatomy of a Miracle: The End of Apartheid and the Birth of a New South Africa*. New Brunswick, NJ: Rutgers University Press.

Walker, Henry A. and David Willer. 2007. "Experimental Methods." Pp. 1537–1541 in *The Blackwell Encyclopedia of Sociology*, edited by G. Ritzer. Malden. MA: Blackwell.

Wallerstein, Immanuel. 1974. *The Modern World-System*. New York: Academic Press.

Wallerstein, James S. and Clement J. Wyle. 1947. "Our Law-Abiding Law-Breakers." *Federal Probation* 25: 107–112.

Walsh, Anthony. 1990. "Twice Labeled: The Effect of Psychiatric Labeling on the Sentencing of Sex Offenders." *Social Problems* 37: 375–389.

Walsh, Declan. 2015. "Fake Diplomas, Real Cash: A Net of Made-Up Schools." *New York Times*, May 18.

Walters, G. D. 2003. "Changes in Criminal Thinking and Identity in Novice and Experienced Inmates: Prisonization Revisited." *Criminal Justice and Behavior* 30(4): 399–421.

Wang, Wendy, Kim Parker, and Paul Taylor. 2013. "Breadwinner Moms." Pew Research Center, Pew Social and Demographic Trends, May 29. Retrieved April 29, 2015 (http://www.pewsocialtrends.org/2013/05/29/chapter-3-married-mothers-who-out-earn-their-husbands).

Ward, Kathryn. 1990. "Introduction and Overview." Pp. 1–24 in *Women Workers and Global Restructuring*, edited by K. Ward. Ithaca, NY: ILR Press.

Warren, Cortney S. 2014. "Body Area Dissatisfaction in White, Black and Latina Female College Students in the USA: An Examination of Racially Salient Appearance Areas and Ethnic Identity." *Ethnic and Racial Studies* 37: 537–556.

Warren, John Robert and Elaine M. Hernandez. 2007. "Did Socioeconomic Inequalities in Morbidity and Mortality Change in the United States over the Course of the Twentieth Century?" *Journal of Health and Social Behavior* 48: 335–351.

Wasserman, J., M. A. Flannery, and J. M. Clair. 2007. "Raising the Ivory Tower: The Production of Knowledge and Distrust of Medicine among African Americans." *Journal of Medical Ethics* 33(3): 177–180.

Wasson, Leslie. 2007. "Identity Politics/Relational Politics." Pp. 2214–2215 in *The Blackwell Encyclopedia of Sociology*, edited by G. Ritzer. Malden, MA: Blackwell.

Watkins, S. Craig. 2009. *The Young and the Digital: What the Migration to Social Network Sites, Games, and Anytime, Anywhere Media Means for Our Future*. Boston: Beacon Press.

Watson, Matthew and Elizabeth Shove. 2008. "Product, Competence, Project and Practice: DIY and the Dynamics of Craft Consumption." *Journal of Consumer Culture* 8: 69–89.

Webb, Haley J., Melanie J. Zimmer-Gembeck, and Caroline L. Donovan. 2014. "The Appearance Culture between Friends and Adolescent Appearance-Based Rejection Sensitivity." *Journal of Adolescence* 37: 347–358.

Weber, Harry R. 2010. "Gulf Oil Spill Declared 'Effectively Dead.'" CBS News, September 20. Retrieved March 29, 2012 (http://www.cbsnews.com/stories/2010/09/19/national/main6881308.shtml).

Weber, Max. [1903–1917] 1949. *The Methodology of the Social Sciences*. New York: Free Press.

Weber, Max. [1904–1905] 1958. *The Protestant Ethic and the Spirit of Capitalism*. New York: Scribner.

Weber, Max. [1919] 1958. "Politics as a Vocation." In *From Max Weber: Essays in Sociology*, edited by H. Gerth and C. Wright Mills. New York: Oxford University Press.

Weber, Max. [1921] 1968. *Economy and Society: An Outline of Interpretive Sociology*, edited by G. Roth and C. Wittich. Totowa, NJ: Bedminster Press.

Webster, Murray and Jane Sell. 2012. "Groups and Institutions, Structures and Processes." Pp. 139–163 in *The Wiley-Blackwell Companion to Sociology*, edited by G. Ritzer. Malden, MA: Wiley-Blackwell.

Weeks, John R. 2007. "Demographic Transition Theory." Pp. 1033–1038 in *The Blackwell Encyclopedia of Sociology*, edited by G. Ritzer. Malden, MA: Blackwell.

Weeks, John R. 2011. *Population: An Introduction to Concepts and Issues*. 11th ed. Belmont, CA: Wadsworth.

Wegener, B. 1991. "Job Mobility and Social Ties: Social Resources, Prior Job, and Status Attainment." *American Sociological Review* 56: 60–71.

Weiler, Bernd. 2007. "Cultural Relativism." Pp. 908–910 in *The Blackwell Encyclopedia of Sociology*, edited by G. Ritzer. Malden, MA: Blackwell.

Weinstein, Jay. 2010. *Social Change*. 3rd ed. Lanham, MD: Rowman & Littlefield.

Weinstein, Mary. 2013. "How Many People Shop Online?" Ecommerce, August 9. Retrieved April 27, 2015 (http://www.cpcstrategy.com/blog/2013/08/ecommerce-infographic).

Weisenthal, Joe. 2013. "Here's the New Ranking of Top Countries in Reading, Science, and Math." Business Insider, December 3. Retrieved May 17, 2015 (http://www.businessinsider.com/pisa-rankings-2013-12#ixzz3SokWhusf).

Weitz, Rose. 2010. *The Sociology of Health, Illness, and Health Care: A Critical Approach*. 5th ed. Boston: Wadsworth Cengage.

Weitz, Rose. 2013. *The Sociology of Health, Illness, and Health Care: A Critical Approach*. 6th ed. Belmont, CA: Thompson Wadsworth.

Weitzer, Ronald. 2012. *Legalizing Prostitution: From Illicit Vice to Lawful Business*. New York: New York University Press.

Weitzer, Ronald. 2014. "New Directions in Research on Human Trafficking." *Annals of the American Academy of Political and Social Science* 653(1): 6–24.

"Welcome to Our Shrinking Jungle." 2008. *Economist*, June 5. Retrieved March 9, 2012 (http://www.economist.com/node/11496950).

Wellard, Ian. 2012. "Body-Reflexive Pleasures: Exploring Bodily Experiences within the Context of Sport and Physical Activity." *Sport, Education and Society* 17: 21–33.

Wellford, Charles. 2012. "Criminology." Pp. 229–242 in *The Wiley-Blackwell Companion to*

Sociology, edited by G. Ritzer. Malden, MA: Wiley-Blackwell.

Wellings, Kaye, Martine Collumbien, Emma Slaymaker, Susheela Singh, Zoe Hodges, Dhavai Patel, and Nathalie Bajos. 2009. "Sexual Behavior in Context: A Global Perspective." *The Lancet* 368: 349–358.

Wellman, Elizabeth. 2004. *The Road to Seneca Falls: Elizabeth Cady Stanton and the First Woman's Rights Convention.* Champaign: University of Illinois Press.

Welzel, Christian and Ronald Inglehart. 2009. "Mass Beliefs and Democratization." In *Democratization,* edited by C. W. Haerpfer, P. Bernhagen, R. F. Inglehart, and C. Welzel. New York: Oxford University Press.

Wessel, Anika and Erich Kasten. 2014. "Body Piercing and Self-Mutilation: A Multifaceted Relationship." *American Journal of Applied Psychology* 3(4): 104–109.

West, Candace and Don Zimmerman. 1987. "Doing Gender." *Gender & Society* 1: 125–151.

Westergaard, Ryan P., Mary Catherine Beach, Somnath Saha, and Elizabeth A. Jacobs. 2014. "Racial/Ethnic Differences in Trust in Health Care: HIV Conspiracy Beliefs and Vaccine Research Participation." *Journal of General Internal Medicine* 29(1): 140–146.

Western, Bruce and Jake Rosenfeld. 2012. "Workers of the World Divide: The Decline of Labor and the Future of the Middle Class." *Foreign Affairs,* May/June.

Wharton, Amy S. and Mary Blair-Loy. 2006. "Long Work Hours and Family Life: A Cross-National Study of Employees' Concerns." *Journal of Family Issues* 27(3): 415–436.

White, James M. 2013. "The Current Status of Theorizing about Families." Pp. 11–38 in *Handbook of Marriage and the Family,* 3rd ed., edited by G. W. Peterson and K. R. Bush. New York: Springer.

Whitehead, John T. 2007. "Crime." Pp. 818–822 in *The Blackwell Encyclopedia of Sociology,* edited by G. Ritzer. Malden, MA: Blackwell.

Whiteside, Alan. 2008. *A Very Short Introduction to HIV/AIDS.* Oxford: Oxford University Press.

Whiteside, Alan. 2012. "AIDS." Pp. 45–49 in *The Wiley-Blackwell Encyclopedia of Globalization,* edited by G. Ritzer. Malden, MA: Wiley-Blackwell.

Whyte, William Foote. 1943. *Street Corner Society: The Social Structure of an Italian Slum.* Chicago: University of Chicago.

Wieringa, Saskia and Horacio Sívora. 2013. "Sexual Politics in the Global South: Framing the Discourse." Pp. 1–21 in *The Sexual History of the Global South,* edited by S. Wieringa and H. Sívora. New York: Zed Books.

Wight, Vanessa R. 2007. "Demography." Pp. 1038–1045 in *The Blackwell Encyclopedia of Sociology,* edited by G. Ritzer. Malden, MA: Blackwell.

Wiklund, Maria, Carita Bengs, Eva-Britt Malmgren-Olsson, and Ann Öhman. 2010. "Young Women Facing Multiple and Intersecting Stressors of Modernity, Gender Orders and Youth." *Social Science Medicine* 71(9): 1567–1575.

Wilk, Kenneth Aarskaug, Eva Bernhardt, and Turid Noack. 2010. "Love or Money? Marriage Intentions among Young Cohabitors in Norway and Sweden." *Acta Sociologica* 53: 269–287.

Williams, Christine L. 1995. *Still a Man's World.* Berkeley: University of California Press.

Williams, Christine L. 2006. *Inside Toyland: Working, Shopping, and Social Inequality.* Berkeley: University of California Press.

Williams, Christine L., Chandra Muller, and Kristine Kilanski. 2012. "Gendered Organizations in the New Economy." *Gender & Society* 26: 549–573.

Williams, Christine L. and Laura Sauceda. 2007. "Gender, Consumption and." Pp. 1848–1852 in *The Blackwell Encyclopedia of Sociology,* edited by G. Ritzer. Malden, MA: Blackwell.

Williams, David R. 1999. "Race, Socioeconomic Status, and Health: The Added Effects of Racism and Discrimination." *Annals of the New York Academy of Sciences* 896: 173–188.

Williams, Glyn, Paula Meth, and Katie Willis. 2014. *Geographies of Developing Areas: The Global South in a Changing World.* 2nd ed. New York: Routledge.

Williams, Joan. 2001. *Unbending Gender: Why Family and Work Conflict and What to Do about It.* New York: Oxford University Press.

Williams, Rosalind. [1982] 1991. *Dream Worlds: Mass Consumption in Late Nineteenth-Century France.* Berkeley: University of California Press.

Williams, Simon J. 2012. "Health and Medicine in the Information Age: Castells, Informationism and the Network Society." Pp. 167–192 in *Contemporary Theorists for Medical Sociology,* edited by G. Scambler. London: Routledge.

Williams, Stacy J., Laura Pecenco, and Mary Blair-Loy. 2013. "Medical Professions: The Status of Women and Men." Center for Research on Gender in the Professions, University of California, San Diego. Retrieved April 21, 2015 (http://crgp.ucsd.edu/documents/GenderinMedicalProfessionsCaseStudy.pdf).

Williams, Victoria. 2014. "Foreign Aid." In *Encyclopedia Britannica.* Retrieved April 21, 2015 (http://www.britannica.com/EBchecked/topic/213344/foreign-aid).

Williamson, Oliver E. 1975. *Markets and Hierarchies: Analysis and Antitrust Implications.* New York: Free Press.

Williamson, Oliver E. 1985. *The Economic Institutions of Capitalism.* New York: Free Press.

Williamson, Vanessa, Theda Skocpol, and John Coggin. 2011. "The Tea Party and the Remaking of Republican Conservatism." *Perspectives on Politics* 9: 25–43.

Willyard, Cassandra. 2014. "Malaria Vaccine, Destined for Africa, Seeks OK from Europe." *Nature Medicine* 20: 968–969.

Wilper, Andrew P., Steffie Woolhandler, Karen E. Lasser, Danny McCormick, David H. Bor, and David U. Himmelstein. 2009. "Health Insurance and Mortality in US Adults." *American Journal of Public Health* 99(12): 2289–2295.

Wilson, Bryan R. 1966. *Religion and Secular Society.* London: Watts.

Wilson, George, Vincent J. Roscigno, and Matt L. Huffman. 2013. "Public Sector Transformation, Racial Inequality, and Downward Occupational Mobility." *Social Forces* 91: 975–1006.

Wilson, Midge and Kathy Russell. 1996. *Divided Sisters: Bridging the Gap between Black and White Women.* New York: Anchor Books.

Wilson, Stephen R. 1984. "Becoming a Yogi: Resocialization and Deconditioning as Conversion Processes." *Sociological Analysis* 45(4): 301–314.

Wilson, William Julius. 1997. *When Work Disappears: The World of the New Urban Poor.* New York: Vintage.

Wilterdink, Nico. 2007. "Inequality, Wealth." Pp. 2310–2313 in *The Blackwell Encyclopedia of Sociology,* edited by G. Ritzer. Malden, MA: Blackwell.

Wimmer, Andreas. 2013. *Ethnic Boundary Making: Institutions, Power, Networks.* New York: Oxford University Press.

Winant, Howard. 2001. *The World Is a Ghetto: Race and Democracy since World War II.* New York: Basic Books.

Wines, Michael. 2011. "Picking Brand Names in China Is a Business Itself." *New York Times,* November 11. Retrieved April 1, 2012 (http://www.nytimes.com/2011/11/12/world/asia/picking-brand-names-in-china-is-a-business-itself.html).

Wingfield, Nick. 2014a. "Feminist Critics of Video Games Facing Threats in 'Gamergate.'" *New York Times,* October 15.

Wingfield, Nick. 2014b. "In Games Like Minecraft, Tech Giants See More than Fun." *New York Times,* September 11.

Wingfield, Nick. 2014c. "Virtual Games Draw Real Crowds and Big Money." *New York Times,* August 31.

Wise, Tim. 2010. *Colorblind: The Rise of Post-racial Politics and the Retreat from Racial Equity.* San Francisco: City Lights.

Wisman, Jon D. 2013. "Wage Stagnation, Rising Inequality, and the Financial Crisis of 2008." *Cambridge Journal of Economics* 37: 921–945.

Wolf, Naomi. [1991] 2002. *The Beauty Myth: How Images of Beauty Are Used against Women.* New York: Harper & Row.

Wolfers, Justin. 2015. "We Can't Blame a Few Rich People for Global Poverty." *New York Times,* January 28.

Wolfsfeld, Gadi, Elad Segev, and Tamir Sheafer. 2013. "Social Media and the Arab Spring: Politics Comes First." *International Journal of Press/Politics* 18(2): 115–137.

Wong, Edward. 2010. "18 Orgies Later, China Swinger Gets Prison Bed." *New York Times,* May 21.

Wong, William C. W., Eleanor Holroyd, and Amie Bingham. 2011. "Stigma and Sex Work from the Perspective of Female Sex Workers in Hong Kong." *Sociology of Health and Illness* 33: 50–65.

Wood, Robert T. 2006. *Straightedge Youth: Complexity and Contradictions of a Subculture.* Syracuse, NY: Syracuse University Press.

Woods, Andrew. 2011. "These Revolutions Are Not All Twitter." *New York Times,* February 1.

Woolf, Steven H. and Laudan Y. Aron. 2013. "The US Health Disadvantage Relative to Other High-Income Countries: Findings from a National Research Council/Institute of Medicine Report." *Journal of the American Medical Association* 309(8): 771–772.

World Bank. 2014a. "Country and Lending Groups." Retrieved November 10, 2014 (http://data.worldbank.org/about/country-and-lending-groups).

World Bank. 2014b. "Fertility Rate, Total (Births per Woman), 2010–2014." Retrieved April 21,

2015 (http://data.worldbank.org/indicator/SP.DYN.TFRT.IN).

World Bank. 2014c. "Health Expenditure, Total (% of GDP), 2010–2014." Retrieved April 21, 2015 (http://data.worldbank.org/indicator/SH.XPD.TOTL.ZS).

World Bank. 2014d. "Urban Population (% of Total), 2010–2014." Retrieved March 19, 2015 (http://data.worldbank.org/indicator/SP.URB.TOTL.IN.ZS).

World Bank. 2015. "Data: Fertility Rate, Total (Births per Woman)." Retrieved May 21, 2015 (http://data.worldbank.org/indicator/SP.DYN.TFRT.IN).

World Economic Forum. 2014. *The Global Gender Gap Report 2014*. Geneva: Author. Retrieved May 15, 2015 (http://www3.weforum.org/docs/GGGR14/GGGR_CompleteReport_2014.pdf).

World Health Organization. 2010a. "Tobacco Free Initiative: China Releases Its Global Adult Tobacco Survey Data." Retrieved April 1, 2012 (http://www.who.int/tobacco/surveillance/gats_china/en/index.html).

World Health Organization. 2010b. "World Health Report: Health Systems Financing: The Path to Universal Coverage." Retrieved April 1, 2012 (http://whqlibdoc.who.int/whr/2010/9789241564021_eng.pdf).

World Health Organization. 2013. "Tobacco." Retrieved October 2013 (http://www.who.int/mediacentre/factsheets/fs339/en/index.html).

World Health Organization. 2015. "Water Sanitation and Health." Retrieved March 19, 2015 (http://www.who.int/water_sanitation_health/mdg1/en).

Worldometers. 2015. "Current World Population." Retrieved March 19, 2015 (http://www.worldometers.info/world-population).

World Values Survey. N.d. "Values Change the World." Retrieved April 1, 2012 (http://www.worldvaluessurvey.org/wvs/articles/folder_published/article_base_110/files/WVSbrochure5-2008_11.pdf).

Wortham, Jenna. 2013. "A Growing App Lets You See It, Then You Don't." *New York Times*, February 9.

Wortmann, Susan L. 2007. "Sex Tourism." Pp. 4200–4203 in *The Blackwell Encyclopedia of Sociology*, edited by G. Ritzer. Malden, MA: Blackwell.

Wren, Anne. 2013. *The Political Economy of the Service Transition*. New York: Oxford University Press.

Wu, Caiwei, Yongping Wei, and Mark Y. Wang. 2014. "Planned Gated Communities in Urban China." Pp. 189-201 in *Transforming Chinese Cities*, edited by M. Y. Wang, P. Kee, and J. Gao. New York: Routledge.

Wunder, Delores F. 2007. "Agents, Socialization of." Pp. 4566–4568 in *The Blackwell Encyclopedia of Sociology*, edited by G. Ritzer. Malden, MA: Blackwell.

Wyatt, Edward. 2014. "Obama Asks F.C.C. to Adopt Tough Net Neutrality Laws." *New York Times*, November 10.

Yamamoto, Ryoko. 2012. "Undocumented Immigrants." Pp. 1005–1008 in *The Wiley-Blackwell Encyclopedia of Globalization*, edited by G. Ritzer. Malden, MA: Wiley-Blackwell.

Yamane, David. 2007. "Civil Religion." Pp. 506–507 in *The Blackwell Encyclopedia of Sociology*, edited by G. Ritzer. Malden, MA: Blackwell.

Yancy, George. 2008. *Black Bodies, White Gazes: The Continuing Significance of Race*. Lanham, MD: Rowman & Littlefield.

Yardley, Jim. 2010. "Soaring above India's Poverty, a 27-Story Single-Family Home." *New York Times*, October 29.

Yearley, Steve. 2007. "Globalization and the Environment." Pp. 239–253 in *The Blackwell Companion to Globalization*, edited by G. Ritzer. Malden, MA: Blackwell.

Yeates, Nicola. 2009. *Globalizing Care Economies and Migrant Workers: Explorations in Global Care Chains*. New York: Palgrave Macmillan.

Yeates, Nicola. 2012. "Global Care Chains: A State-of-the-Art Review and Future Directions in Care Transnational Research." *Global Networks* 12(2): 135–154.

Yetman, Norman R., ed. 1991. *Majority and Minority: The Dynamics of Race and Ethnicity in American Life*. 5th ed. Boston: Allyn & Bacon.

York, Richard and Riley E. Dunlap. 2012. "Environmental Sociology." Pp. 504–521 in *The Wiley-Blackwell Companion to Sociology*, edited by G. Ritzer. Malden, MA: Wiley-Blackwell.

Yoshihara, Susan and Douglas A. Sylva, eds. 2011. *Population Decline and the Remaking of Great Power Politics*. Washington, DC: Potomac Books.

Young, Michael and Johan Muller, eds. 2014. *Knowledge Expertise and the Professions*. New York: Routledge.

Yuval-Davis, Nira. 2006. "Human/Women's Rights and Feminist Transversal Politics." In *Global Feminism: Transnational Women's Activism, Organizing, and Human Rights*, edited by M. M. Ferree and A. M. Tripp. New York: New York University Press.

Zafirovski, Milan. 2013. "Beneath Rational Choice: Elements of 'Irrational Choice Theory.'" *Current Sociology* 61: 3–21.

Zammuel, Elnat, Orna Sasson-Levy, and Guy Ben-Porat. 2014. "Voluntary Simplifiers as Political Consumers: Individuals Practicing Politics through Reduced Consumption." *Journal of Consumer Culture* 14: 199–217.

Zeiler, Kristin and Annette Wickstrom. 2009. "Why Do 'We' Perform Surgery on Newborn Intersexed Children? The Phenomenology of the Parental Experience of Having a Child with Intersex Anatomies." *Feminist Theory* 10: 359–377.

Zellner, William W. 1995. *Counterculture: A Sociological Analysis*. New York: St. Martin's Press.

Zeni, Jane. 2007. "Ethics, Fieldwork." Pp. 1442–1447 in *The Blackwell Encyclopedia of Sociology*, edited by G. Ritzer. Malden. MA: Blackwell.

Zerelli, Sal. 2007. "Socialization." Pp. 4558–4563 in *The Blackwell Encyclopedia of Sociology*, edited by G. Ritzer. Malden, MA: Blackwell.

Zhang, Yang and Michael John Hitchcock. 2014. "The Chinese Female Tourist Gaze: A Netnography of Young Women's Blogs on Macao." *Current Issues in Tourism*, published online June 9. doi: 10.1080/13683500.2014.904845.

Zhuge, Ying, Joyce Kaufman, Diane M. Simeone, Herbert Chen, and Omaida C. Velazquez. 2011. "Is There Still a Glass Ceiling for Women in Academic Surgery?" *Annals of Surgery* 253: 637–643.

Zilberfarb, Ben-Zion. 2005. "From Socialism to Free Market: The Israeli Economy, 1948–2003." *Israel Affairs* 11: 12–22.

Zimbardo, Philip. 1973. "On the Ethics of Intervention in Human Psychological Research: With Special Reference to the Stanford Prison Experiment." *Cognition* 2: 243–256.

Zimmer, Ron and Richard Buddin. 2009. "Is Charter School Competition in California Improving the Performance of Traditional Public Schools?" *Public Administration Review* 69(5): 831–845.

Zinn, Maxine Baca. 2012. "Patricia Hill Collins: Past and Future Innovations." *Gender & Society* 26: 28–32.

Zippel, Kathrin. 2007. "Sexual Harassment." Pp. 4233–4234 in *The Blackwell Encyclopedia of Sociology*, edited by G. Ritzer. Malden, MA: Blackwell.

Zukin, Sharon. 1982. *Loft Living: Culture and Capital in Urban Change*. Baltimore: Johns Hopkins University Press.

Zukin, Sharon. 2004. *Point of Purchase: How Shopping Changed American Culture*. New York: Routledge.

Zureik, Elia. 2011. "Colonialism, Surveillance, and Population Control: Israel/Palestine." Pp. 3–46 in *Surveillance and Control in Israel/Palestine: Population, Territory, and Power*, edited by E. Zureik, D. Lyon, and Y. Abu-Laban. New York: Routledge.

INDEX

Bosnia and Herzegovina, 195, 196, 196 (figure)
Bossler, Adam M., 141
Boston, Massachusetts, 258 (figure)
Bostwick, J. Michael, 384
Boswell, A. Ayres, 215
Botswana, 267 (figure)
Botz-Bornstein, Thorsten, 312
Bouazizi, Mohamed, 1, 2
Bouchard, Genevieve, 209
Boukus, Ellyn R., 319
Bounded rationality, 102
Bourdain, Anthony, 37
Bourdieu, Pierre, 37, 92, 163, 262
Boushey, Heather, 161, 209 (figure)
Boustan, Leah P., 343
Bovine spongiform encephalopathy (BSE), 324
Bowen, Ted Smalley, 165
Bowler, Kate, 269
Bowling, Ben, 144
Bowman, John R., 212
Boykoff, Jules, 359
Bradley, Karen, 14, 207
Bradsher, Keith, 294
Brady, Tom, 106
Braga, Anthony A., 138
Braithwaite, John, 126
Brame, Robert, 139
Branch Davidians, 271
Brand communities, 60
Branden, Karen, 228
Branding/brand names, 58, 377, 378
Brandle, Gaspar, 377
Bratton, William J., 136
Braun, Virginia, 310
Braveman, Paula
    see Nuru-Jeter, Amani
Braverman, Samantha, 312 (figure)
Bravve, Elina, 296 (figure)
Braw, Elisabeth, 205
Brazil
    beauty standards, 310
    cultural gender stereotypes, 201
    deforestation, 348–349
    Fordlandia, 292
    foreign aid, 171
    global stratification, 172
    life expectancy, 322, 323 (figure)
    megacities, 344 (figure)
    minimum wage rates, 170 (figure)
    offshore outsourcing, 108 (table)
    racial categories, 181
    religiosity, 267 (figure)
    Roma people, 180
    women's suffrage, 362 (figure)
    World Social Forum (WSF), 375
Brazil (film), 26
Breadwinner wives, 151, 151 (figure), 208, 209 (figure)
Breast augmentation, 310, 310 (table)
Breast-feeding percentages, 60
Breeden, Aurelien, 180
Brennan, Bridget, 212
Brennan, Denise, 219
Brennan, John, 254
Brenner, Neil, 343
Brewster, Zachary W., 184
Bribery, 140
Brick-and-mortar cathedrals of consumption, 298
Briggs, Laura, 248
Brimeyer, T. M., 86
Britannica, 271
British Empire, 179, 183, 192
British Petroleum (BP), 373
Bronfenbrenner, Kate, 119
Bronner, Ethan, 118
Brooklyn, New York, 343
Brooks, Robert A., 315
Brouwer, Steve, 276
Brown Berets, 190
Brown, David, 350, 351
Brownmiller, Susan, 223
Brown, Stephen E., 66, 135, 186

Brown, Timothy C., 39
Brown v. Board of Education (1954), 186
Brubaker, Ralph, 9
Bruce, Steve, 267
Brulle, Robert J., 347, 351
Brumberg, Joan Jacobs, 309
Brummund, Peter, 210
Brundage, Sarah, 296 (figure)
Bryant, Melanie, 133
Bryk, Anthony, 256
Bryman, A., 35
Buchmann, Claudia, 207, 254
Buck, Brad, 348
Buckingham, Christopher D.
    see Adams, Ann
Buckingham, David, 87
Buddhism, 271, 273 (figure), 274
Buddin, Richard, 261
Budig, Michelle J., 161
Buffett, Warren, 150, 165
Buffington, Robert M., 217
Bühlmann, Felix, 158
Bui, Bonnie, 338
Buie, Lisa, 55
Bulgaria, 118, 180, 210 (figure), 267 (figure), 333
Bulletproof vests, 142
Buraku, 192
Burawoy, Michael, 4, 12, 37
Burdack, Joachim, 342
Burden of disease, 166
Bureaucracies
    authority structures, 101–102
    basic concepts, 100
    democratic states, 282
    ideal type model, 100–101, 102
    informal organization, 103–104
    McDonaldization, 9, 10, 35, 108–109, 110
    organizational structure, 100–101, 101 (figure)
    rationality versus irrationality, 102–103
Bureaucratic personality, 103
Bureau of Alcohol, Tobacco, and Firearms, 271
Bureau of Justice Statistics, 137, 141, 244 (figure)
Bureau of Labor Statistics, 209 (figure), 210, 211 (figure), 220 (figure), 254, 255 (figure), 297 (figure), 314 (figure)
Burger King, 149, 150
Burgess, Ernest W., 232
Burglary rates, 139 (figure), 140
Burkina Faso, 58
Burkley, Melissa, 363
Burning Man, 72
Burns, Thomas J., 349
Burroughs Wellcome, 366
Burton, Michael, 285
Burundi, 195, 196 (figure)
Bush, George H. W., 154
Bush, George W., 154, 276
Bush, Jeb, 154, 359, 361
Bush, Prescott, 154
Butler, Judith, 31, 204
Buzinde, Christine N., 318
Byers, Kaela
    see Smith, David Norman
Byrd, Scott, 375

Cable, Sherry, 314
Cabrera, Nolan L., 83
Cacioppo, John T.
    see Olshansky, S. Jay
Cagatay, Nilufer, 167, 220
Cahill, Spencer E., 83
Caird, Jeff K., 313
Cai, Tianji, 179
Calasanti, Toni, 185
Calculability, 9
Caldwell, Christopher, 5, 335
Calhoun, Craig, 267

Caliphates, 2
Callimachi, Rukmini, 383
Camacho, Danica May, 331, 332
Cambodia, 8, 8 (figure), 165, 196 (figure), 274, 286
Cameroon, 267 (figure)
Campbell, Colin, 68, 274
Campbell, Jacquelyn, 220
Campbell, James Quick, 107
Campbell, Nnenia M., 182
Campbell, Oona M. R.
    see Fillipi, Veronique
Canada
    border security and controls, 144
    cohabiting households, 236 (figure)
    glass-ceiling index, 105 (figure)
    government-supported parental leave, 210, 210 (figure)
    health care expenditures, 317 (figure)
    life expectancy, 323 (figure)
    minimum wage rates, 170 (figure)
    natural catastrophes, 351 (figure)
    religiosity, 267 (figure)
    same-sex marriage, 238
    Starbucks stores, 67 (figure)
    student learning outcomes, 263 (figure)
Cancer, 336
Caniglia, Beth, 352
Cannato, Vincent J., 182
Cannon, Lou, 372
Cape Verde, 58
Capitalism/capitalists
    background and characteristics, 291–293
    conflict/critical theories, 347
    consumption, 6–7
    deviant behaviors, 131
    gender inequalities, 161
    global sex industry, 218–219
    global women's movement, 223
    Marxist theory, 25, 35, 289
    micro-macro continuum, 14–15
    occupy movements, 357–358
    poverty levels, 156
    social reforms, 17
    structuralist theory, 29
    voluntarians, 32
    Weber's theory, 25–26, 42
    World Social Forum (WSF), 374–375
Capital punishment, 138 (figure), 139–140
Caprile, Maria, 109
Carbonaro, William, 207, 256, 259
Carbon dioxide emissions, 350, 350 (figure), 352
Career pathways, 14, 14 (figure)
Care labor, 168–169
Carey, Stephen, 35
Caribbean region
    body satisfaction, 310
    colonial regimes, 179
    HIV/AIDS, 325, 326 (table)
    Internet access, 11 (figure)
    labor force participation, 168 (figure)
    low-income economies, 165
    natural catastrophes, 351 (figure), 372
    racial categories, 181
Carlson, Stephanie M., 258
Carmichael, Stokely, 188
Carmody, Dianne Cyr, 241, 242
Carnegie Mellon University, 264
Carne, Glenda
    see Harmon, Corinne
Carnes, Bruce A.
    see Olshansky, S. Jay
Caron, Marcia L.
    see Flack, William F., Jr.
Carrefour, 347
Carre, Francoise
    see Vanek, Joann

Carrere, Sybil
    see Gottman, John M.
Carr, Ian, 383
Carrier, Neil, 378
Carrillo, Héctor, 218
Carstensen, Laura L.
    see Olshansky, S. Jay
Carter, Bill, 54
Carter, Bob, 178
Carter, Shan, 154
Carty, Victoria, 363, 370
Casinos, 89, 298
Cassil, Alwyn, 319
Castellani, Brian, 315
Castells, Manuel, 2, 110, 370
Castles, Stephen, 249
Castle, Stephen, 181, 383
Castro, Fidel, 130, 247
Casual sexual relationships, 212
Catch-22 (Heller), 103
Cathedrals of consumption, 269, 297–298, 347
Catholic Church, 106, 271, 272, 273 (figure), 275
Catton, William R., Jr., 347
Cave, Damien, 142
Cell phones, 11, 54–56, 55 (figure), 313
    see also Smartphones
Cenogamy, 229
Censorship, 100, 113–114, 283
Center for Research on Education Outcomes, 261, 261 (table)
Centers for Disease Control and Prevention (CDC), 242, 319, 334, 334 (figure), 335 (figure), 366
Centers for Medicare and Medicaid Services, 316
Central African Republic (CAR), 283, 286, 287 (figure), 323 (figure)
Central America, 338, 338 (figure)
Central Asia, 326 (table)
Central Intelligence Agency (CIA), 316, 323 (figure)
Cerkez, Aida, 196
Cerny, Phillip G., 113
Chad, 206, 206 (figure), 267 (figure), 322, 323 (figure)
Chakravarti, Arjun, 42
Challenger disaster, 107, 373
Chambers, Erve, 7
Chambliss, William J., 130
Chanda, Nayan, 377
Chang, C. H.
    see Gehlert, S.
Chan, Priscilla, 310
Chan, Sewell, 384
Chapman, John, 182
Charismatic authority, 102
Charismatic leadership, 270, 271
Charles, Maria, 14, 207
Charlie Hebdo, 77, 133, 275, 277
Charter schools, 261, 261 (table)
Cha, Youngjoo, 158, 161
Cheal, David, 238
Chen, Chung-shiuan
    see Gu, Dongfeng
Chen, Herbert
    see Zhuge, Ying
Chen, James K. C., 314
Chen, Ji-chun
    see Gu, Dongfeng
Chen, Jing
    see Gu, Dongfeng
Chen, Katherine, 72
Chen, Martha
    see Vanek, Joann
Chen, Zihong, 220
Cherlin, Andrew J., 151, 231, 232, 233, 243
Chernilo, Daniel, 286
Chernobyl nuclear accident, 112–113, 113 (figure)
Chia, Robert, 285

Hausmann, Ricardo, 161
Hawkesworth, Mary, 220
Hayes, Dennis, 35
Hay, Harry, 365
Haynie, L., 86
Hays, Sharon, 59
"Head Injuries in Football," 311
Health care
    Alzheimer's disease,
        306, 307 (figure), 308
    consumerism, 320–322, 327
    globalization impact, 306–307,
        322–328
    health inequalities, 166–167, 306,
        317–320, 322–323, 327–328
    health-protective behaviors,
        306, 335
    insurance companies, 316, 320, 321
    Internet resources, 321–322, 327
    medicalization, 320
    medical marijuana, 305–306
    medical professionals, 315–316, 320
    mortality rates, 335
    total expenditures/gross domestic
        product percentages,
        316, 317 (figure)
    United States, 316–320
Healthcare Bluebook, 321
Health inequality, 166–167
Health in Reach, 321
Heaphy, Brian, 238
Heart disease, 319, 336
Heat waves, 350
Hechter, Michael, 34
Heckman, James J., 258
Hegedus, Gabor, 341
Hegemonic masculinity, 203–204
Hegemony, 188
Heggeness, Misty L., 157
Hein, Michelle M., 212
Heintz, James, 167, 220
He, Jiang
    see Gu, Dongfeng
Heller, Joseph, 103
Heller, Nathan, 13, 256 (table)
Helliwell, Christine, 202, 383
Hendershott, Anne, 127
Henningsen, David Dryden, 79
Henry, Amy
    see Swami, Viren
Hepburn, Stephanie, 219
Heritage, John, 90
Hermaphrodite, 202
Hernandez, Aaron, 131–132
Hernandez, Elaine M., 317
Hernandez Jarvis, Loma, 91
Hernandez, Melba A.
    see Acierno, Ron
Herod, Andrew, 17
Heroin, 143
Herper, Matthew, 327
Herrington, Carolyn D., 260
Herrnstein, Richard J., 179, 257
Hershkovitz, Shay, 286
Hess, Alexander E. M., 294
Hesse-Biber, Sharlene, 212
Hester, Rita, 204–205
Heterosexism, 31, 213
Heterosexual double standard, 214
Hetherington, E. M., 246
Hickson, David J., 100
    see also Pugh, Derek S.
Hidalgo, Danielle Antoinette, 364
Hidden curriculum, 206
Hidden structures, 29–30
Hier, Sean P., 112, 133
Higgins, Vaughan, 133
Higher education, 70
High-income economies, 164, 164
    (figure), 167, 169, 322
High-performing students, 259
High/Scope Perry Preschool, 258
High-track classes, 259
Higley, John, 285
Hildebrandt, Achim, 364

Hill, Jessica, 134
Hillyard, Daniel, 126, 127
Himanen, Pekka, 73
Himmelstein, David U.
    see Wilper, Andrew P.
Hindin, Michelle J., 90
Hinduism, 271, 273 (figure), 274, 277
Hinduja, Sameer, 11
Hinings, C. R.
    see Pugh, Derek S.
Hinze, Susan W., 157
Hipsman, Faye, 338
Hirsch, Barry T., 295 (figure)
Hispanic Americans
    body satisfaction, 309
    educational attainment, 257 (figure)
    ethnic identities, 190
    institutional racism, 188
    poverty rates, 157, 187, 187 (figure)
    social stratification, 187
    unemployment, 297 (figure)
    United States, 181, 182 (table)
    see also Minority groups
Historical-comparative research, 42
Hitchcock, Michael John, 38
HIV/AIDS, 9, 212, 306, 321, 324–326,
    326 (table), 366
Hoang, Kimberly Kay, 37–38
Hobsbawm, E. J., 288
Hochschild, Adam, 222
Hochschild, Arlie Russell,
    168, 208, 219
Hodge, David, 8
Hodges, Zoe
    see Wellings, Kaye
Hodson, Randy, 106
Hoecker-Drysdale, Susan, 24
Hoefer, Michael, 339
Hoekstra, Arjen J., 349
Hoffmann, Diane E., 384
Hoffnung, Michele, 233
Hogg, Michael A., 54
Hokayem, Charles, 157
Holden, Daphne
    see Schwalbe, Michael
Holdstock, Nick, 192
Holland, Arianne M., 310
Holland, Peter, 256
Hollifield, James E., 338
Hollister, Geoff, 378
Holloway, Sarah
    see Laurie, Nina
Holocaust, 178, 186, 196, 273
Holroyd, Eleanor, 134
Holstein, James A.
    see Gubrium, Jaber F.
Holt, Douglas B., 163, 378
Holton, Robert J., 5
Holt, Thomas J., 141
Holy Land Experience, 269
Homan, Joshua
    see Smith, David Norman
Homans, George, 33
Home Depot, 61
Home mortgage crisis, 126
Homeschooling, 260 (table), 260–261
Homophile movements, 365
Homophobia, 213, 214 (figure), 218
Homosexuality, 31, 46, 127, 128,
    128 (figure), 186, 213, 364–365
    see also Lesbian, gay, bisexual,
        and transgender (LGBT)
        community
Honda, 292
Hondagneu-Sotelo, Pierrette, 220, 339
Honduras, 142, 338, 338 (figure)
"Honduras, Guatemala Establish Joint
    Anti-drug Force," 142
Hong Kong
    beauty standards, 310
    consumerism, 68
    fantasy cities, 347
    global organizations, 108
    government protests, 100
    Internet censorship, 283

minimum wage rates, 170 (figure)
    sex tourism, 217
    student learning outcomes,
        263 (figure)
Honor killings, 245
Hood, William R.
    see Sherif, Muzafer
Hooking up, 212, 214
hooks, bell, 31, 363
Horizontal mobility, 159
Horovitz, Bruce, 9
Horrey, William J., 55
Horrigan, John, 7
Horton, Richard, 328
Horvatek, Renata
    see Smith, William C.
Hosseinpoor, Ahmad Reza
    see Van de Poel, Ellen
Hossfeld, Leslie H., 4
Hotchkiss, H. Lawrence
    see Aguirre, B. E.
Houck, Davis W., 362
Houseal, Richard, 272 (figure)
Households
    categories, 231 (figure)
    cohabiting households, 127, 128,
        232, 235–237, 236 (figure)
    income, 26 (figure), 208 (figure)
    nonfamily households,
        234 (figure), 234–235
    power and decision-making,
        244–245
    tasks, 208, 209 (figure), 244,
        245 (figure)
House Un-American Activities
    Committee (HUAC), 370
Housing crisis, 359
Hout, Michael
    see Fischer, Claude S.
Hou, Yubo, 310
HSBC, 108
Huaco, George, 161
Huang, Jian-feng
    see Gu, Dongfeng
Huang, Penelope M., 235, 236
Hubbard, Ben, 166, 275
Huber, Franz, 80
Huesemann, Joyce, 352
Huesemann, Michael, 352
Huffington Post, 71
Huffman, Matt L., 159
Hughes, Michael, 91
Hull, Kathleen E., 233
Hull, Raymond, 103
Humane treatments, 307
Human Genome Project, 179
Human interaction, 78–79
Human-made disasters, 373
Human-nonhuman distinctions, 79, 80
Human resources, 368
Human trafficking, 8 (figure), 8–9, 144,
    169, 249, 338
Humphreys, Laud, 45–46
Hungary
    border security and controls, 6
    gated communities, 341
    glass-ceiling index, 105 (figure)
    government-supported parental
        leave, 210 (figure)
    health care expenditures,
        317 (figure)
    refugees, 119
    religiosity, 267 (figure)
    student learning outcomes,
        263 (figure)
Hunger, 165, 166
Hunger Games (film), 26
Hunter, James Davison, 61
Huntington, Samuel P., 67
Huntoon, Meghan, 161
Hunt, Stephen, 92
Hurdle, Jon, 11
Hurricanes, 351 (figure)
Hurwitz, Heather McKee, 361, 364
Husain, Ed, 275

Hussmanns, Ralf
    see Vanek, Joann
Hutchison, Ray, 341
Hutson, Brittany, 161
Hutterites, 270
Hutus, 195, 196, 196 (figure)
Hwang, Jinyoung, 337
Hyperconsumption, 33, 299
Hyperdebt, 299
Hypersexualization, 212, 219
Hypotheses, 35, 35 (table)
Hyundai, 107, 292

IBM, 119
Ibn Khaldun, Abdel Rahman, 2
Icahn, Carl, 165
Iceland
    gender stratification,
        205, 206 (figure)
    government-supported parental
        leave, 210 (figure)
    health care expenditures,
        317 (figure)
    nonmarital fertility, 334
    student learning outcomes,
        263 (figure)
    urban areas, 341
Iceland, John, 156
Ideal culture, 59–60
Ideal type bureaucracy model,
    100–101, 102
Identity politics, 66
Identity-related crime, 61, 140, 141
Ideologies, 60
Ideoscapes, 115–116
IKEA, 108, 109, 293, 347
Illegal acts, 45
Illegal flows, 140, 143–144, 194, 344
Illicit drugs, 142, 143–144, 188, 313,
    317, 344
    see also Drug cartels
I Love Lucy (1951–1957), 227
Imagined communities, 286
"I"–"Me" connections, 82
Immigrant populations
    assimilation, 63–64, 182
    birthrates, 335
    borderless diseases, 324–326
    child migrants, 338, 338 (figure)
    crime control, 144
    female migration,
        219 (figure), 219–220
    global families, 249
    global flow, 376
    illegal immigrant deaths, 7 (figure)
    institutional religion, 272, 274, 277
    language and cultural differences,
        64–65
    mobility, 5–6, 338
    moral panics, 133–134
    occupations, 219 (figure)
    percentage of U.S. population,
        5 (figure)
    reference groups, 94
    region of origin, 64 (figure)
    social mobility, 159
    urban areas, 340
    world's great cities, 345
    see also Undocumented immigrants
Impression management, 83
Incarceration rates, 136 (figure),
    136–138
Income
    basic concepts, 151
    breadwinner wives, 151,
        151 (figure), 208, 209 (figure)
    college enrollment rates,
        261–262, 262 (figure)
    economic inequality, 151–152
    educational attainment-earnings
        relationship, 254, 255 (figure)
    female-to-male earnings ratio,
        158 (figure), 211 (figure)
    household income, 26 (figure),
        208 (figure)

Musisi, Seggane
 see Liebling-Kalifani, Helen
Muslim fundamentalist movements,
 275, 276
Muslim immigrants, 65, 277, 376
 see also Immigrant populations;
 Islam
Muzzy, Wendy
 see Acierno, Ron
Myanmar, 274, 338
Myers, Daniel J., 372
Myers, Dowell, 159

Nadelmann, Ethan, 140, 143, 144
Nagin, Daniel, 136, 138, 139
 see also Cohen-Cole, Ethan; Cullen,
 Francis T.
Nagourney, Adam, 11, 349
Napier, Nancy C., 105
Naples, Nancy A., 118, 214, 223
Napoli, Lisa, 322
Naquin, Charles E., 89
Nardi, Peter M., 365
Nash, Catherine J., 218
National Aeronautics and Space
 Administration (NASA),
 107, 373
National Association for the
 Advancement of Colored People
 (NAACP), 191, 367
National Baptist Convention,
 USA, Inc., 272 (figure)
National borders, 6
 see also Border security and
 controls
National Center for Education Statistics,
 207 (figure), 208 (figure),
 260, 260 (table)
National Coalition of Anti-Violence
 Programs, 205
National Crime Victimization Survey,
 244 (figure)
National Football League (NFL), 106
National Institutes of Health, 179, 319
National Oceanic and Atmospheric
 Administration (NOAA),
 350 (figure), 373 (figure)
National Opinion Research Center, 40
National Organization for Women
 (NOW), 362–363
National Poverty Center, 181
National Safety Council, 55
National University of Singapore, 264
Nations, 113, 286
Nation-states
 basic concepts, 113
 environmental challenges, 351–352
 ethnic conflicts, 195–196
 ethnic identities, 190, 192
 genocide, 196, 196 (figure)
 global flow control, 113–117,
 286, 344
 global stratification, 172–173
 ideoscapes, 115–116
 illegal flows, 143
 money and finance, 299
 organizational barriers, 119
 social stratification, 163–164
Native Americans, 182 (table),
 186, 205, 216
Native Hawaiians, 182 (table)
Natural catastrophes, 351, 351 (figure),
 372–374, 373 (figure)
Natural experiments, 42
Natural habitat destruction, 348–349
Natural resources, 347–348
Nature-nurture argument, 78
Nazi Germany, 43, 105, 178, 186, 195,
 196, 196 (figure), 273
Ncayiyana, Dan
 see Godlee, Fiona
Near poor population, 157
Nederveen Pieterse, Jan, 67
Negative flow, 194, 196
Negative stereotypes, 184–185

Negro press, 191
Nelson, Donna, 207
Nelson, Michelle R., 88
Neoliberal economics, 192
Neomodernization, 172
Neo-Nazis, 189
Nepal, 165, 169, 372
Netflix, 107, 376
Netherlands
 cohabiting households, 236 (figure)
 government-supported parental
 leave, 210 (figure)
 health care expenditures,
 317 (figure)
 immigrant populations, 65
 marijuana use, 127, 129
 multiculturalism, 64
 same-sex marriage, 238
 student learning outcomes,
 263 (figure)
 women's suffrage, 362 (figure)
Net neutrality, 63
Netnography, 38
Network organizations, 109–111
Networks, 93
 see also Social networks
Neuendorf, Kimberly A., 87
Neuman, William, 318, 383
Neuman, W. Russell
 see DiMaggio, Paul J.
Never-married adults, 231, 231
 (figure), 232 (figure)
Newcomb, Alyssa, 384
New England Patriots, 106, 131
New media, 87–88
Newport, Frank, 203, 203 (table)
New religious movements, 271
New Songdo, South Korea, 6
Newton, David E., 364
Newton, Michael, 78
New words, 58
New York Globe, 191
New York, New York, 6, 342, 343,
 344 (figure), 345, 346, 357
New York Times, 71, 270, 384
New York University, 264
New Zealand
 glass ceilings, 105, 105 (figure)
 government-supported parental
 leave, 210 (figure)
 health care expenditures,
 317 (figure)
 looks-related stress, 310
 minimum wage rates, 170 (figure)
 stability rankings, 287 (figure)
 student learning outcomes,
 263 (figure)
Nexium, 321, 327
Ngo, Joy, 166, 322
Nguyen, Tomson H., 126
Nicaragua, 165
Nichols, Brian J., 274
Nicholson, Linda, 66
Nichol, Theo, 289
Niebrugge-Brantley, Gillian, 31
Niebuhr, Gustav, 269
Niger, 58
Nigeria
 ebola epidemic, 324, 325 (figure)
 life expectancy, 323 (figure)
 megacities, 344 (figure)
 natural catastrophes, 351 (figure)
 personal freedoms, 56
 religiosity, 267 (figure)
 terrorist attacks, 287, 288 (figure)
Nike, 377, 378
9/11 terrorist attacks, 276, 373, 374
Nineteen Eight-Four (Orwell), 26
Nineteenth Amendment (U.S.
 Constitution), 362
Nir, Sarah Maslin, 384
Nissan, 292
Nixon, Richard, 131
Noack, Turid, 236
Noble, David F., 294

Nobles, Jenna, 246
No-fault divorce, 246
Noller, Patricia, 239
Nonbinary genders, 204
Nonfamily households,
 234 (figure), 234–235
Nongovernmental organizations
 (NGOs), 5
Nonhuman-human distinctions, 79, 80
Nonmarital fertility, 334
Nonmedical marijuana
 see Marijuana use
Nonnegligent manslaughter,
 139 (figure), 140
Nonparticipant observation, 37
Nonrandom samples, 41
Nonrenewable resources, 347–348
Nonresident parents, 237
Nontraditional consumer settings,
 70–71
Nontraditional families,
 235–238, 236 (figure)
Nonviolence, 370
Noonan, Mary C., 60
Nordberg, Jenny, 205
Nordenmark, Mikael, 295
Nordgren, Johan, 133
Norms, 57, 57 (table), 89, 129, 206,
 218, 246, 371
Norris, Dawn, 133
North Africa, 165, 167, 168 (figure),
 220, 282, 326 (table), 337
North America
 HIV/AIDS, 326 (table)
 Internet access, 11, 11 (figure)
 Jewish population, 273
 legal migration, 64 (figure)
 natural catastrophes, 351 (figure)
 occupy movements, 357
Northcote, Jeremy, 60
North Korea
 capital punishment, 139
 cybercrime, 141
 freedom ratings, 283
 Internet restrictions, 283
 life expectancy, 323 (figure)
 low-income economies, 165
 military threats, 30
 political system, 284, 290
"North Korea Country Profile—
 Overview," 290
Norton, Michael I., 18
Norway
 cohabiting households, 235,
 236 (figure)
 foreign aid, 171
 glass-ceiling index, 105 (figure)
 global stratification, 206 (figure)
 government-supported parental
 leave, 210 (figure)
 health care expenditures,
 317 (figure)
 immigrant populations, 65
 McDonaldization, 68
 same-sex marriage, 238
 stability rankings, 287 (figure)
 student learning outcomes,
 263 (figure)
 women's suffrage, 362 (figure)
Nose reshaping, 310, 310 (table)
Noueihed, Lin, 2
Nuccitelli, Dana
 see Cook, John
Nuclear family, 85, 231, 232, 238
Null, Crystal, 140
Nunn, Samuel, 140
Nurses, 316
Nuru-Jeter, Amani, 319
Nussbaum, A. David, 158
Nutrition, 166
Nwachukwu, Saviour L., 68
Nyden, Gwendolyn E., 4
Nyden, Philip W, 4
Nystrand, Martin
 see Gamoran, Adam

Obama, Barack, 101, 104, 181, 187,
 247, 290, 359
Obamacare
 see Affordable Care Act (2010)
Obara-Minnitt, Mika, 61
Oberschall, Anthony, 195
Obesity, 166, 313, 317, 322, 336
Objectifying gaze, 310
Objectivity, 46
Observation, 36
Observational research, 36–38
Occupational segregation, 207
Occupations
 see Employment/employment
 opportunities
Occupy movements, 357–358
Occupy Wall Street, 357
Oceania, 11 (figure), 64 (figure),
 287 (figure), 325, 326 (table)
Ochiai, Emiko, 337
Ocloo, Josephine Enyonam, 316
Ocobock, Abigail, 228
O'Connor, Brendan, 67
O'Driscoll, Sean, 264
Official development assistance
 (ODA), 171
Offshore outsourcing, 108, 108 (table)
Ogas, Ogi, 217
Ogburn, William F., 216
O'Grady, Siobhán, 167
O'Guinn, Thomas C., 60, 269
Oh, Hyeyoung, 315
Ohlsson-Wijk, Sofi, 237
Öhman, Ann
 see Wiklund, Maria
Oil rig disaster, 373
Ojiambo-Ochieng, Ruth
 see Liebling-Kalifani, Helen
Oligarchy, 104
Oliver, Pamela, 371
Olivier, Jos G. J., 348
Ollila, Eeva, 306
Olshansky, S. Jay, 319
Olson, Brad
 see McAdams, Dan P.
Olson, Linda, 159
Olson, Lynn, 367
O'Malley, Ann S., 319
O'Malley, Patrick, 40 (figure)
Omi, Michael, 178
Omune, Brenda
 see Moran, Mary
On Crimes and Punishments
 (Beccaria), 136
One-directional socialization, 85
One-person households,
 234 (figure), 235
Ong, Paul, 324
Online cathedrals of consumption, 298
Online courses, 12
Online shopping, 7, 9, 70–71, 88, 347
Online video games, 363
Open-ended questions, 39
Open-source software, 63, 72–73
Opinion polls, 40
Opsal, Tara D., 37
Ordner, James P.
 see Smith, David Norman
O'Reilly, Bill, 63
Oreskes, Naomi, 383
Orfield, Gary, 257
Organ donations, 8
Organisation for Economic
 Co-operation and Development
 (OECD), 171, 236 (figure), 262,
 263 (figure), 316, 317 (figure)
Organization of the Petroleum
 Exporting Countries (OPEC), 5
Organizations
 barriers, 119
 basic concepts, 100
 bureaucracies, 100–104,
 101 (figure)
 contemporary perspectives,
 104–111

immigrant populations, 68, 187
influencing factors, 156
landscapes, 115
megacities, 344
poorest people, 165, 167, 192, 350
racism, 181, 187, 187 (figure)
sex tourism, 219
United States, 156–157, 157 (figure)
water-related problems, 350
Poverty line, 156–157
Powell, Brian, 127, 230
Powell, Jason L., 376
Powell, Joe, 228
Powell, Walter W., 218
Powell, Zachary A.
 see Vieraitis, Lynne M.
Power, 151, 154, 222, 239–240,
 244–245, 315
Power elite theory, 285
Powers, Charles H., 295
Prague, Czech Republic, 374
Prause, JoAnn, 297
Prechel, Harlan, 289
Predictability, 9
Preibisch, Kerry L., 167
Preisendorfer, Peter, 347
Prejudice, 184–185, 188–189,
 192, 218
Premarital sexual relationships,
 56, 127, 128, 215, 216, 218
Premenstrual dysphoric disorder
 (PMDD), 320
Premenstrual syndrome (PMS), 320
Presbyterian, 271
Preschool programs, 258
Presenti, Christina, 8
Presser, Harriet B., 158
Prestigious occupations, 90, 91 (figure),
 150–151
Preston, Julia, 339
Prestructured interviews, 39
Prevacid, 327
Preves, Sharon E., 86
Priestly Sins, The (Greeley), 270
Primary deviance, 133
Primary groups, 94
Primary socialization, 85
Prior, Beatrice, 87
Prior, Nick, 163
Prison population, 88–89, 136 (figure),
 136–138
Prison system, 88–89, 136–139, 307
Pritchard, Mary, 310
Private schools, 259–260
Private troubles versus public issues,
 13–14
Probation, 137
Problematic organizations,
 14, 105–107
Proctor, Bernadette D., 25, 158
Product movement, 6
Product placement, 311
Profane, 266
Professional degrees, 254, 255 (figure)
Professional families, 258
Professions, 315
Program for International Student
 Assessment (PISA), 262,
 263 (figure)
Proletariat, 25, 32, 131, 289
Promundo, 201
Promundo Global, 383
Propaganda, 283
Property crimes, 139 (figure), 140
Prostitution, 8, 134, 217, 220, 249
Prosumers, 71, 107
Protective flows, 193–195
Protective tariffs, 119
Protestant Christian groups,
 271, 272 (figure), 273 (figure)
*Protestant Ethic and the Spirit of
 Capitalism, The* (Weber), 25
Protestant work ethic, 298
Psychological harm, 44, 44 (figure)
Psychology, 17–18

Public school alternatives, 259–261,
 260 (table), 261 (table)
Public sociology
 Andrew M. Greeley, 270
 basic concepts, 4
 branding, 377
 criminology research, 137
 culture wars, 62
 flat world theory, 117
 globalization impact, 117
 low-paying jobs, 296
 McDonaldization, 10
 modern romance, 229
 Negro press, 191
 theatrical presentations, 308
 underground economies, 155
Pudrovska, Tetyana, 211
Pugh, Allison, 39
Pugh, Derek S., 102
Pullum, Amanda, 359
Punishment, 307
Puranam, Phanish, 103
Pure relationships, 234, 245–246
Purpel, David E., 206

Al-Qaeda, 14, 105, 133
Qat, 378
Qatar, 264, 323 (figure)
Qian, Zhenchao, 229, 249
Qin, Amy, 127
Quach, Thu, 319
 see also Perloff, Richard M.
Quadagno, Jill, 369
Qualitative research, 36
Quantitative research, 36
Queergender, 31
Queer Nation, 366
Queer theory, 31
Questionnaires, 40
Quinn, Michael A., 5

Race/racism
 barriers, 194–195
 basic concepts, 178, 186
 beauty standards, 310
 capital punishment, 140
 civil rights movement, 189–190,
 362, 366–367
 critical theories, 31
 cultural explanations, 179, 181
 discrimination, 104–105, 184–190,
 187 (figure)
 Du Bois's theory, 28
 educational system composition,
 258 (figure)
 feminism, 363
 front stage/back stage actions,
 83, 186
 global flow, 192–196, 194 (figure)
 hate groups/hate crimes, 140, 189,
 190 (figure), 205
 health inequalities, 317, 319
 historical perspective, 178–179,
 181–182
 institutional racism, 188–189
 intelligence levels, 257–258
 majority–minority relations,
 182–183, 192–196
 mortality rates, 335
 online video games, 363
 police brutality, 371
 poverty rates, 181, 187, 187 (figure)
 power movements, 190
 racial categories, 181
 racial identities, 181–182
 riots, 372, 375
 "scientific" justifications, 179
 social structures, 187
 stereotypes, 87, 184–185, 187–188
 tattoos, 312, 312 (figure)
 United States, 181, 182 (table)
 white racial frame, 187–188
 women of color, 31, 204–205
Race to the bottom, 170–171
Rademacher, Mark A., 88

Radesky, Jenny S., 12
Radiation exposure, 313–314
Radiation releases, 112–113,
 113 (figure)
Radical Islam, 2, 5, 14, 77, 287,
 288 (figure)
 see also Islamic State (IS)
Rafferty, Rebecca, 141
Ragin, Charles, 36, 42
Raj, Suhasini, 345
Ramirez, F., 5
Ramirez, Francisco O., 223
Ramsay, Clay, 316
Ram, Uri, 35, 290
Random samples, 40–41, 41 (figure)
Rao, Smriti, 8
Rape
 basic concepts, 215
 consequences, 216
 crime rates, 139 (figure), 140
 ethnic cleansing, 195–196
 global flow, 218
 homophobia, 213
 migrant women, 220
 sex trafficking, 9
 social constraints, 215–216
 transgender individuals, 205
 as weapon of war, 222, 223
Rape, Abuse, and Incest National
 Network (RAINN), 216
Rapson, Richard L., 230
Rastafari, 271
Ratha, Dilip, 299
Rational choice theory, 34
Rationalization, 26
Rationalized bureaucracies, 35, 100
Rational-legal authority, 101–102
Rational systems, 9, 102–103
Rauer, Amy J., 234
Rau, Renate
 see Schmidt, Susanne
Ravitch, Diane, 263
Rawls, Anne, 17
Ray, Eileen Berlin
 see Perloff, Richard M.
Ray, George B.
 see Perloff, Richard M.
Ray, Larry, 111
Reagan, Wen, 269
Real culture, 59–60
Reay, Barry, 127
Rebels, 130
Recessions, 299–300
Recidivism, 138
Reciprocity, 89
Recording Industry Association of
 America, 141
Recreational marijuana
 see Marijuana use
Redbox, 107
Red Bull, 313
Red Cross, 327
Red tape, 102–103
Reed College, 215
Rees, Karen L., 316
Reference groups, 94
Refined taste, 162–163
Reflexivity, 307–308, 311, 312
Refugees, 118, 119, 338, 339
 see also Immigrant populations
Reger, Jo, 361
Regnerus, Mark, 127
Rehabilitated prisoners, 138
Reicher, Stephen, 223
Reid, Charles J., 361
Reid, Julie A., 214
Reiman, Jeffrey H., 131
Reiner, Robert, 135
Reisenauer, Eveline, 192, 220, 334
Relevant literature, 35, 35 (table)
Reliability, 43
Religion
 Baha'i faith, 271, 273 (figure)
 basic concepts, 265–266
 beliefs, 266

Buddhism, 271, 273 (figure), 274
Christianity, 271, 273 (figure),
 275–276, 277
 churches, 269, 270–271
 components, 266–267
 consumerism, 269
 cults, 271
 declining significance, 267–268
 denominations, 271, 272 (figure)
 experiences, 267
 fundamentalism, 275, 276
 genocide, 338
 globalization impact, 271–272,
 273 (figure), 276–277
 Hinduism, 271, 273 (figure),
 274, 277
 importance, 266–267, 267 (figure)
 Islam, 271, 273 (figure), 274–275,
 277
 Judaism, 271, 273 (figure),
 273–274, 277
 Mormonism, 273 (figure), 276, 336
 new religious movements, 271
 religious affiliation, 267, 268 (figure)
 rituals/rites of passage, 266–267
 sects, 270
 separation of church and state,
 253–254, 260
 Sikhism, 271, 273 (figure)
 transnational migration, 272
Religious bias, 190 (figure)
Renewable resources, 347–348
Rennison, Callie Marie, 341
Representative democracies, 282
Repressiveness, 30
Research methodologies
 ethics, 43–46
 experiments, 41–42
 interviews, 38–40
 objectivity, 46
 observational research, 36–38
 qualitative and quantitative
 research, 36
 reliability and validity, 43
 scientific method, 35, 35 (table)
 secondary data analysis, 42
 survey research, 40 (figure), 40–41,
 41 (figure), 43
Resnick, Heidi S.
 see Acierno, Ron
Resocialization, 88–89
Resource mobilization theory, 368
Restivo, Emily, 132
Retreatists, 130
"Return Visit to Communist Cuba Finds
 New Hope Amid Change," 247
Reuveny, Rafael, 119
Reverby, Susan, 43
Reverse socialization, 85
Revolutionary movements, 368
Rey, P. J., 4, 141
Ricciardelli, Lina A., 309
Rice, Ray, 106
Richardson, Mark
 see Cook, John
Richest people, 165, 192
Rich, Motoko, 260
Richtel, Matt, 114, 240
Ridgeway, Cecilia L., 14
Rieger, Jon H., 39
Rieker, Patricia R., 335
Riera-Crichton, Daniel, 299
Riffkin, Rebecca, 215
Rinaldo, Lindsay, 166
Rindermann, Heiner, 258
Rio de Janeiro, Brazil, 201
Riots, 185, 204, 365, 372, 373, 375
Rippeyoug, Phyllis L. F., 60
Riska, Elianne, 316
Risk societies, 112
Risman, Barbara J., 214
Rites of passage, 266
Ritualists, 130
Rituals, 266